A Treatise
on the
Measure of Damages

A Treatise

on the

Measure of Damages

OR

**AN INQUIRY INTO THE PRINCIPLES WHICH GOVERN
THE AMOUNT OF PECUNIARY COMPENSATION
AWARDED BY COURTS OF JUSTICE**

BY

THEODORE SEDGWICK

AUTHOR OF " A TREATISE ON STATUTORY AND CONSTITUTIONAL LAW "

CUM PRO *EO QUOD INTEREST* DUBITATIONES ANTIQUAE IN INFINITUM PRODUCTAE SINT,
MELIUS NOBIS VISUM EST, HUJUSMODI PROLIXITATEM, PROUT POSSIBLE EST, IN ANGUSTUM COARCTARE.
Cod. De sent. quœ pro eo quod int. prof. lib. vii, tit. xlvii

NINTH EDITION

REVISED, REARRANGED, AND ENLARGED
BY
ARTHUR G. SEDGWICK
AND
JOSEPH H. BEALE

Volume III

BeardBooks

Washington, D.C.

CHAPTER XXXI

CONTRACTS OF SERVICE

§ 664. Compensation for services performed.

664a. Evidence of value of services.

665. Damages for wrongful discharge.

666. Prospective damages recoverable.

667. General rule — Duty to seek employment.

668. Employment terminable on notice—Domestic service.

669. Compensation by share or percentage of an uncertain amount.

670. Compensation payable on a contingency.

671. Services rendered in expectation of compensation.

672. Interruption of service by unavoidable cause.

§ 673. Services rendered on a contract rescinded by mutual consent

673a. Services rendered by an infant.

673b. Services rendered under an agreement within the statute of frauds.

673c. Services rendered under a void agreement.

673d. Services voluntarily rendered.

673e. Services outside the scope of employment.

673f. Recovery by party in default.

674. Remedy of master for improper service.

675. Consequential damages.

675a. The English workmen's compensation act.

§ 664. Compensation for services performed.

If a servant fully performs his contract, but the contract allows him no definite compensation, he is allowed to recover on a *quantum meruit* the value of the services performed,[1] without regard to the amount of benefit which the principal or master received from them.[2] If the contract fixes the compensation, that amount is the sole measure of damages,[3] so that the recovery cannot exceed the agreed amount,[4] nor on the

---

[1] *Ante,* § 650.

[2] *Massachusetts:* Stowe *v.* Buttrick, 125 Mass. 449.

Ohio: Bagley *v.* Bates, Wright, 705.

[3] *United States:* Perkins *v.* Hart, 11 Wheat. 237, 6 L. ed. 463.

Missouri: Crump *v.* Rebstock, 20 Mo. App. 37; Pim *v.* Greer, 64 Mo. App. 175 (agreement on amount after work done was binding, and superseded the *quantum meruit*).

New York: Fells *v.* Vestvali, 2 Keyes, 152.

[4] Sherman *v.* Mayor, 1 N. Y. 316. Staderman *v.* Heins, 78 App. Div. 563, 79 N. Y. Supp. 674, was an action on a contract by which plaintiff agreed to serve the intestate as nurse. The

other hand can the defendant reduce the agreed amount by showing that the services were worth less.[5] Where the payment for the services was by the agreement to be made by the delivery of commodities, the plaintiff is entitled to recover no more than the value of the commodity to be delivered at the time fixed by the contract for the delivery;[6] but where the wages are fixed in money, with an option to pay in commodities, the master who has not exercised the option must upon suit pay in money.[7]

In a case in Minnesota, where by the contract the defendant was to fix the amount of compensation, the court refused to give more than the amount fixed by the defendant;[8] but in Illinois such a contract was held to be equivalent to a contract to pay a reasonable compensation, and the plaintiff was allowed to recover on a *quantum meruit*,[9] and in Ohio the court, without deciding this point, held that if the employer did not fix the value of the services at the termination of the employment he could not do so later, at the trial of the case, but the jury should find the reasonable value of the services.[10]

Where the plaintiff began to perform the services under an express contract, and continued after the period named in the

agreement was for a dollar a day. After services had been rendered for some time the deceased signed papers stating her desire that plaintiff should receive 250 dollars. Held, that since a stipulated price of one dollar a day was proved, that alone could be recovered.

[5] Ludlow v. Dole, 62 N. Y. 617.

[6] *Indiana:* State v. Beard, 1 Ind. 460 (canal scrip).

Kentucky: Owens v. Durham, 5 Dana, 536 (share of crop; cannot recover enhanced value at time of subsequent demand).

Missouri: Gibson v. Whip Pub. Co., 28 Mo. App. 450 (shares of stock: if corporation unsuccessful, damages are nominal).

[7] *Nebraska:* Culbertson I. & W. P. Co. v. Wildman, 45 Neb. 663, 63 N. W. 947, 56 Am. St. Rep. 565 (wages $100 per month, $60 in cash and $40 in water rights. The servant, not being paid, could recover $100, since the option to pay him in water rights had not been exercised).

Pennsylvania: McDonald v. Liggett, 146 Pa. 460, 23 Atl. 338. (Contract by which plaintiff performed services in procuring an oil lease and was to be paid by an interest in the lease or $200. The lease was procured, but defendant did nothing under it. Since he had not exercised his option the plaintiff was entitled to compensation for his services at the value fixed by the defendant himself.)

[8] Butler v. Winona M. Co., 28 Minn. 205, 41 Am. Rep. 277.

[9] Van Arman v. Byington, 38 Ill. 443.

[10] *Ohio:* Toledo, A. A. & N. M. Ry. v. Lott, 10 Ohio C. Ct. 249.

contract, he was held entitled to compensation at the contract rate;[11] and the other terms, such as the duration of the employment, are presumed to continue as in the contract.[12] If, however, there is any change in the relation of the parties, there is no presumption that the rate of compensation continues. Thus the old rate of wages does not continue when the character of the service is changed,[13] or if an interval elapses between the terms of employment,[14] or if the servant continues in the employment after receiving a notice of a change in the rate of wages.[15]

Where it is claimed that services were rendered under an express contract the burden of proving such a contract is upon the defendant, since the plaintiff who claims to recover the value of the services on the *quantum meruit* proves a *prima facie* case by proving that the services were rendered at request.[16] When there is a dispute as to the price agreed to be paid in the

---

[11] *Arkansas:* Ewing *v.* Janson, 57 Ark. 237, 21 S. W. 430.

California: Nicholson *v.* Patchin, 5 Cal. 474.

Illinois: Grover & B. S. M. Co. *v.* Bulkley, 48 Ill. 189; Ingalls *v.* Allen, 132 Ill. 170, 23 N. E. 1026, 22 Am. St. Rep. 515; Crane Bros. Manuf. Co. *v.* Adams, 142 Ill. 125, 30 N. E. 1030; Glucose Sugar Refining Co. *v.* Flinn, 184 Ill. 123, 56 N. E. 400.

Maryland: Travelers' Ins. Co. *v.* Parker, 92 Md. 22, 37 Atl. 1042.

New Hampshire: New Hampshire Iron Factory Co. *v.* Richardson, 5 N. H. 294.

New York: Huntingdon *v.* Claffin, 38 N. Y. 182; Vail *v.* Jersey Little Falls Manuf. Co., 32 Barb. 564; Adams *v.* Fitzpatrick, 56 N. Y. Super Ct. 580.

Ohio: Kelly *v.* Carthage Wheel Co., 62 Oh. St. 598, 57 N. E. 984.

Pennsylvania: Wallace *v.* Floyd, 29 Pa. 184, 72 Am. Dec. 620; Ranck *v.* Albright, 36 Pa. 367.

Wisconsin: Kellogg *v.* Citizens' Ins. Co., 94 Wis. 554, 69 N. W. 362; Dickinson *v.* Norwegian Plow Co., 101 Wis. 157, 76 N. W. 1108.

It has been held in Minnesota that there is no presumption of the renewal of a contract void by the statute of frauds. Lally *v.* Crookston Lumber Co., 85 Minn. 257, 88 N. W. 846.

[12] *Michigan:* Sines *v.* Superintendents of the Poor, 58 Mich. 503, 25 N. W. 485.

Ohio: Kelly *v.* Carthage Wheel Co., 62 Oh. St. 598, 57 N. E. 984.

Wisconsin: Dickinson *v.* Norwegian Plow Co., 101 Wis. 157, 76 N. W. 1108.

England: Beeston *v.* Collyer, 4 Bing. 309.

Contra, Tucker *v.* Philadelphia & R. C. & I. Co., 53 Hun, 139, 6 N. Y. Supp. 134 (new hiring is at will).

[13] *Arkansas:* Ewing *v.* Janson, 57 Ark. 237, 21 S. W. 430.

Illinois: Ingalls *v.* Allen, 132 Ill. 170, 23 N. E. 1026, 22 Am. St. Rep. 515.

[14] Ingalls *v.* Allen, 132 Ill. 170, 23 N. E. 1026, 22 Am. St. Rep. 515.

[15] Crane Bros. Manuf. Co. *v.* Adams, 142 Ill. 125, 30 N. E. 1030.

[16] *California:* Pendleton *v.* Cline, 85 Cal. 142, 24 Pac. 659.

Illinois: Howard *v.* Gobel, 62 Ill. App. 497.

express contract, evidence of the value of the work or of the reasonable or customary compensation may be offered as bearing on the issue.[17]

§ 664a. Evidence of value of services.

In order to determine the value of services the plaintiff is entitled to introduce such evidence as is admissible for the purpose under the rules of evidence. The nature and circumstances of the employment may be shown in order to indicate their value.[18] Thus, facts which make the circumstances peculiarly difficult may be shown,[19] and on the other hand evidence may be introduced that the work was improperly and inefficiently done.[20] Expert evidence of the value may be introduced.[21] It is usually held that such evidence is introduced subject to the judgment of the jury, and that the jury may if it choose find a value for the services different from the value stated in the opinion of the witness or even when there has been no opinion evidence as to the value.[22]

[17] *Nebraska:* Spurck v. Dean, 49 Neb. 66, 68 N. W. 375.
New Hampshire: Swain v. Cheney, 41 N. H. 232.
See Crump v. Rebstock, 20 Mo. App. 37.
[18] Peters v. Craig, 6 Dana (Ky.), 307, 32 Am. Dec. 92 (services of artist known not to be skilful; plaintiff held entitled to such compensation as is reasonable considering his lack of skill); Chiles v. Craig, 4 Dana (Ky.), 544 (services for nursing deceased, who had expressed the desire that they should be liberally compensated; this must be considered in determining reasonable remuneration which, however, cannot go beyond compensation).
[19] *Missouri:* Crowe v. Gallenkamp, 58 Mo. App. 396 (nursing cancer patient in plaintiff's house; plaintiff cannot show effect of stench on value of house, though it would affect value of services).
New York: Reynolds v. Robinson, 64 N. Y. 589 (nursing cancer patient;

plaintiff may show stench and its effect on his health, not in order to recover for loss of health, but to prove nature of services).
Ohio: Berry v. Collins, 9 Ohio C. Ct. 656 (services as housekeeper; plaintiff may show bad condition of house).
[20] Farnsworth v. Garrard, 1 Camp. 38.
[21] McCollum v. Seward, 62 N. Y. 316; Reynolds v. Robinson, 64 N. Y. 589 (physician may testify as to value of services as nurse); Mercer v. Vose, 67 N. Y. 56; Seymour v. Fellows, 77 N. Y. 178; Keenan v. Getsinger, 1 App. Div. 172, 37 N. Y. Supp. 826 (physician may testify as to value of services as nurse); Gall v. Gall, 27 App. Div. 173, 50 N. Y. Supp. 563 (services of unusual kind).
[22] *Kentucky:* Craig v. Durrett, 1 J. J. Marsh. 365.
Ohio: Hossler v. Trump, 62 Oh. St. 139, 56 N. E. 656.
But in Wood v. Barker, 49 Mich. 295, 13 N. W. 597, the court held that

When the plaintiff presents an account charging a certain amount for his services, and the account is not accepted or paid, he is not thereby precluded from recovering a larger amount if the jury find that his services were worth more than the amount of his charge.[23]

Evidence of the charges of other persons for similar services (at least where they are not customary charges) cannot be shown; [24] as for instance the amount paid to one employed in the plaintiff's place.[25]

§ 665. Damages for wrongful discharge.

The general rule in cases of wrongful discharge of a servant by the master is that the plaintiff has a right to recover the stipulated wages for the full time, subject to the defendant's right to recoup whatever the plaintiff might during the period have reasonably earned.[26]

The agent or servant who has been wrongfully discharged may in fact choose one of three courses.[27] First, he may con-

---

the jury could not disregard the expert evidence, that being the only evidence of value offered.

[23] *New York:* Williams v. Glenny, 16 N. Y. 389; Stryker v. Cassidy, 76 N. Y. 50, 32 Am. Rep. 262; Sherwood v. Hauser, 94 N. Y. 626.

Wisconsin: Brauns v. Green Bay, 78 Wis. 81, 46 N. W. 889.

But see *contra,* Daniels v. Wilber, 60 Ill. 526.

[24] *Iowa:* Forey v. Western Stage Co., 19 Iowa, 535.

New York: Lyon v. Valentine, 33 Barb. 271.

In Cullen v. Gallagher, 15 N. Y. Misc. 146, 36 N. Y. Supp. 468, a suit in which a contractor sued to recover on a *quantum meruit* for work done in cutting stone, no direct evidence of value of the work having been offered the plaintiff was allowed to show what amount he paid his workmen for doing the work.

[25] Scott v. Wight, 138 Ill. App. 105 (deputy county treasurer).

[26] See the cases collected and examined in the next two sections.

In a few early English cases the court took a different view, and asserted the right of the jury to fix the amount of compensation due the plaintiff. Smith v. Thompson, 8 C. B. 44; Richardson v. Mellish, 2 Bing. 229. But these cases are illustrations of an obsolete view. Actions of this sort are for breach of contract, and the damages are fixed by rules of law.

[27] *Georgia:* Rogers v. Parham, 8 Ga. 190; Beck v. Thompson, 108 Ga. 242, 33 S. E. 894.

New York: Colburn v. Woodworth, 31 Barb. 381; Banta v. Banta, 84 App. Div. 138, 82 N. Y. Supp. 113.

Tennessee: Jones v. Jones, 2 Swan, 605.

If he elects to sue at once he must recover compensation once for all. If he is allowed only partial compensation and accepts it without appeal, he is barred from subsequent suit. Colburn v. Woodworth, 31 Barb. (N. Y.) 381.

sider the contract as rescinded, and recover on a *quantum meruit* what his services were worth, deducting what he had received for the time during which he had worked.[28] Second, he may wait until the end of the term, and then sue for the full amount, less any sum which the defendant may have a right to recoup.[29] Third, he may sue at once for breach of

[28] *Alabama:* Fowler *v.* Armour, 24 Ala. 194, 60 Am. Dec. 459.

Hawaii: Hanuu *v.* Williams, 2 Hawaii, 233.

Maryland: Bull *v.* Schuberth, 2 Md. 57.

New Hampshire: Clark *v.* Manchester, 51 N. H. 594.

North Carolina: Brinkley *v.* Swicegood, 65 N. C. 626.

South Carolina: Watts *v.* Todd, 1 McMull. 26.

Tennessee: Glasgow *v.* Hood, 57 S. W. 162 (limited to *pro rata* share of contract price).

Vermont: Green *v.* Hulett, 22 Vt. 188; Chamberlin *v.* Scott, 33 Vt. 80 (not limited to *pro rata* share of contract price).

England: Planche *v.* Colburn, 8 Bing. 14.

When a portion of the compensation is to be paid in some other way than in money, and the employer wrongly discharges the servant before such other compensation is earned, the latter may sue for the value of his services over and above the money paid him.

In Woodberry *v.* Warner, 53 Ark. 488, 14 S. W. 671, the defendant contracted to employ plaintiff as pilot of a river-boat for a certain amount, and also agreed to convey half the boat as soon as its earnings amounted to $8,000. Defendant sold the boat before she earned $8,000. It was held that if the amount named in money was less than a reasonable salary, plaintiff could recover the reasonable salary during the time he worked.

In Adams *v.* Pugh, 7 Cal. 150, 68 Am. Dec. 233, the plaintiff was employed by partners with the agreement that he was to draw only part of the salary agreed on and that the remainder should remain in the hands of the firm until a certain amount should be accumulated, when plaintiff was to be received as partner. The partnership was dissolved before the balance accumulated reached the given amount. It was held that since defendant had prevented the performance of this contract the plaintiff could recover the remainder of the salary on account for work and labor.

[29] *Alabama:* Strauss *v.* Meertief, 64 Ala. 299, 38 Am. Rep. 8; Holloway *v.* Talbot, 70 Ala. 389.

California: Webster *v.* Wade, 19 Cal. 291, 79 Am. Dec. 218.

Delaware: Hitchens *v.* Sussex School Dist., 5 Pennew. 325, 62 Atl. 897.

Massachusetts: Murdock *v.* Phillips Academy, 12 Pick. 244.

Pennsylvania: Schnuth *v.* Aber, 13 Pa. Super. Ct. 174.

Wyoming: Dunn *v.* Hereford, 1 Wyo. 206.

England: Callo *v.* Brouncker, 4 C. & P. 518.

If the wages are payable in instalments, he may sue at the end of each instalment period, and recover the wages then due. McMullan *v.* Dickinson Co., 60 Minn. 156, 62 N. W. 120, 51 Am. St. Rep. 511, 27 L. R. A. 409.

And he may then sue again for subsequent instalments.

Georgia: Blun *v.* Holitzer, 53 Ga. 82.

Missouri: Higgins *v.* Breen, 9 Mo. 493.

Where he sued for the first instalment only after two were due, he could

the contract of employment. This is the course ordinarily pursued.[30] Not all these courses, however, are open to the plaintiff in every jurisdiction. In many States he is not allowed to treat the contract as rescinded.[31] And in some States he cannot wait until the end of the term and then recover the contract price, upon showing readiness to perform, but must bring suit upon the breach created by the discharge, and recover such damages only as are consequent upon that; in other words, he is restricted to the third course.[32] Where, at the time of the wrongful discharge, no services have been performed under the contract that have not been paid for, it has been held in several cases by the Court of Common Pleas for

<hr/>

sue thereafter for a subsequent instalment, but not for the second, which was due when he sued. Smith *v.* Cashie & C. R. & L. Co., 142 N. C. 26, 54 S. E. 788, 5 L. R. A. (N. S.) 439. He can recover such instalments only as are due at the date of the writ, not those also which fall due before the time of trial. Hamlin *v.* Race, 78 Ill. 422.

And he cannot recover for any period during which he had employment elsewhere. Culbertson Irr. & W. P. Co. *v.* Wildman, 45 Neb. 663, 63 N. W. 947, 50 Am. St. Rep. 565.

It is not necessary that he should present himself to defendant and offer to perform services. If he was ready and willing to perform the services, and made reasonable efforts to obtain other employment, that is enough. McMullan *v.* Dickinson Co., 63 Minn. 405, 65 N. W. 661, 663.

[30] *Alabama:* Davis *v.* Ayres, 9 Ala. 292; Martin *v.* Everett, 11 Ala. 375.

Colorado: Manger *v.* Grodnick, 3 Colo. App. 534, 34 Pac. 688.

Illinois: Chiles *v.* Belleville Nail Mill Co., 68 Ill. 123.

Massachusetts: Jewett *v.* Brooks, 134 Mass. 505; Paige *v.* Barrett, 151 Mass. 67, 23 N. E. 725.

Mississippi: Pritchard *v.* Martin, 27 Miss. 305.

New York: Howard *v.* Daly, 61 N. Y.

362, 19 Am. Rep. 285; Davis *v.* Dodge, 126 App. Div. 469, 110 N. Y. Supp. 787.

Texas: Nations *v.* Cudd, 22 Tex. 550; G. A. Kelly Plow Co. *v.* London, (Tex. Civ. App.), 125 S. W. 974.

In Park *v.* Independent School Dist., 65 Iowa, 209, 21 N. W. 567, a teacher discharged by school board appealed to state superintendent and eventually the state superintendent reversed the discharge, and declared him legally teacher. He then wrote to the school board offering to teach the remainder of the term and received no answer. He did not go in person and offer to teach. The court held that he was not entitled to recover compensation for the unexpired portion of the term after this time. This seems doubtful, since the action was brought to recover damages for the discharge.

[31] Such is the tendency of modern decisions. The question is, however, one rather of the right of action than of damages, and will not be further discussed here.

[32] *Maryland:* Olmstead *v.* Bach, 78 Md. 132, 22 L. R. A. 74, 27 Atl. 501, 44 Am. St. Rep. 273.

Ohio: James *v.* Allen Co., 44 Oh. St. 226, 6 N. E. 246, 58 Am. Rep. 821.

Texas: Litchenstein *v.* Brooks, 75 Tex. 196, 12 S. W. 975.

the city of New York, that no action can be maintained for *wages* under the contract, and that the servant's only remedy is an action for damages for breach of the contract, in which he recovers full and final satisfaction.[33]

The servant cannot recover compensation for injured feelings in having been discharged prematurely.[34]

§ 666. Prospective damages recoverable.

In an action to recover damages for breach of the contract of employment, brought by the servant at once upon his discharge, the plaintiff must recover in one action his entire damage; and the measure of damages is, therefore, the amount of wages due at the time of trial, together with compensation for the future benefit the plaintiff would probably have realized under the contract, with the proper deductions.[35] Thus in a case where the plaintiff had been injured while in the defendant's employ, and the defendant contracted to continue to employ him while his disability continued, it was held that upon his discharge without cause the plaintiff might sue for the entire damage he had suffered by the discharge, not merely for the wages that were due at the time of trial.[36]

If, as often happens, the trial takes place before the end of the agreed term of employment, the damages accruing after the trial must of course be estimated; this, according to the view which is usually adopted, can be done with sufficient certainty, and the jury bases its verdict upon the probable duration of the employment and the probability of the plaintiff securing other employment after the time of the trial.[37]

[33] Moody *v.* Leverich, 4 Daly, 401; Polk *v.* Daly, 4 Daly, 411.

[34] Addis *v.* Gramophone Co. [1909], A. C. 488.

[35] *Indiana:* Ricks *v.* Yates, 5 Ind. 115; Richardson *v.* Eagle M. Works, 78 Ind. 422, 41 Am. Rep. 584, 95 N. E. 271; Ætna L. I. Co. *v.* Nexsen, 84 Ind. 347, 43 Am. Rep. 91; Inland Steel Co. *v.* Harris (Ind. App.), 95 E. N. 271.

Maine: Sutherland *v.* Wyer, 67 Me. 64.

New York: Everson *v.* Powers, 89 N. Y. 527, 42 Am. Rep. 319.

Ohio: James *v.* Allen County, 44 Oh. St. 226, 58 Am. Rep. 821.

Tennessee: East Tennessee, V. & G. R. R. *v.* Staub, 7 Lea, 397.

Texas: Litchenstein *v.* Brooks, 75 Tex. 196, 12 S. W. 975.

England: Hartland *v.* General Exch. Bank, 14 L. T. Rep. 863.

[36] East Tenn., V. & G. R. R. *v.* Staub, 7 Lea, 397.

[37] *United States:* Pierce *v.* Tennessee,

So where the servant was employed for life, the probable length of the term of employment is determined by annuity tables and compensation is given for loss of the employment during such a term.[38]

C. I. & R. R., 173 U. S. 1, 19 Sup. Ct. 335, 43 L. ed. 591; American C. D. Co. v. Boyd, 148 Fed. 258.

California: Seymour v. Oelrichs, 156 Cal. 782, 106 Pac. 88.

Colorado: Saxonia Mining & Reduction Co. v. Cook, 7 Colo. 569, 4 Pac. 1111.

Indiana: Hamilton v. Love, 152 Ind. 641, 53 N. E. 181, 54 N. E. 437, 71 Am. St. Rep. 384; Inland Steel Co. v. Harris (Ind. App.), 95 N. E. 271.

Kentucky: Forked Deer Pants Co. v. Shipley, 80 S. W. 476, 25 Ky. Law Rep. 2299; Bridgeford v. Meagher, 139 S. W. 750.

Louisiana: De Camp v. Hewitt, 11 Rob. 290, 43 Am. Dec. 204.

Maine: Sutherland v. Wyer, 67 Me. 64.

Maryland: Dugan v. Anderson, 36 Md. 567, 11 Am. Rep. 509; Olmstead v. Bach, 78 Md. 132, 27 Atl. 501, 22 L. R. A. 74, 44 Am. St. Rep. 273.

Massachusetts: Cutter v. Gillette, 163 Mass. 95, 39 N. E. 1010; Daniell v. Boston & M. R. R., 184 Mass. 337, 68 N. E. 337, 339.

Michigan: Webb v. Depew, 152 Mich. 698, 116 N. W. 560, 16 L. R. A. (N. S.) 813.

Mississippi: Prichard v. Martin, 27 Miss. 305.

Missouri: Boland v. Glendale Quarry Co., 127 Mo. 520, 30 S. W. 151; Miller v. Boot & Shoe Co., 26 Mo. App. 57; Lally v. Cantwell, 40 Mo. App. 50.

Nebraska: School District v. McDonald, 68 Neb. 610, 94 N. W. 829, 97 N. W. 584.

New Jersey: Larkin v. Hecksher, 51 N. J. L. 133, 16 Atl. 703, 3 L. R. A. 137; Moore v. Central Foundry Co., 68 N. J. L. 14, 52 Atl. 292.

New York: Davis v. Dodge, 126 App. Div. 469, 110 N. Y. Supp. 787; Cottone v. Murray's, 138 App. Div. 874, 123 N. Y. Supp. 420.

Ohio: Kelly v. Wheel Co., 62 Oh. St. 598, 57 N. E. 984; Lake Erie & W. Ry. v. Tierney, 75 Oh. St. 565, 80 N. E. 1128, affirming 29 Ohio Cir. Ct. 83.

Pennsylvania: Wilke v. Harrison, 166 Pa. 202, 30 Atl. 1125.

Texas: G. A. Kelly Plow Co. v. London, (Tex. Civ. App.), 125 S. W. 974.

Vermont: Remelee v. Hall, 31 Vt. 582, 76 Am. Dec. 140.

Washington: Howay v. Going Northrup Co., 24 Wash. 88, 64 Pac. 135, 6 L. R. A. (N. S.) 49 (*semble*).

West Virginia: Rhoades v. Chesapeake & O. Ry., 49 W. Va. 500, 39 S. E. 209, 55 L. R. A. 170, 87 Am. St. Rep. 826.

Wisconsin: Winkler v. Racine W. & C. Co., 99 Wis. 184, 74 N. W. 793.

England: Yelland's Case, L. R. 4 Eq. 350.

In Kennedy v. South Shore Lumber Co., 102 Wis. 284, 78 N. W. 567, a person employed to scale logs was wrongly discharged. It was held that the limit of damages was his wages for the amount of time it would probably have taken him to scale the logs.

If the trial does not take place until after the expiration of the term, although suit was brought during the term, the damages will of course be the same as if the plaintiff had not sued until the term expired. Howay v. Going-Northrup Co., 24 Wash. 88, 64 Pac. 135, 6 L. R. A. (N. S.) 49.

[38] *United States:* Pierce v. East Tenn., C. I. & R. R., 173 U. S. 1, 19 Sup. Ct. 335, 43 L. ed. 591.

Indiana: Pennsylvania Co. v. Dolan, 6 Ind. App. 109, 32 N. E. 802, 51 Am. St. Rep. 289.

In a few cases, however, it has been held that prospective damages for loss of service after the time of the trial are too uncertain for recovery. Thus in an early case in the Supreme Court of Wisconsin, where a clerk engaged at a salary of $2,000 a year for five years was discharged without cause at the end of the first year, and brought his action without waiting for the end of the term, it was held that he could recover damages measured by the contract down to the day of the trial only, with such deductions as were proper on the principles already stated.[39] This case has occasionally been followed; [40] but the decision seems to lose sight of the fact that the burden of proving the possibility of other employment (the seriously uncertain element in the case) is on the defendant, and the uncertainty should therefore not prejudice the plaintiff's recovery.

§ 667. General rule—Duty to seek employment.

In an action brought by a servant for breach of the contract of employment by his wrongful discharge, the measure of damages is the actual loss inflicted by the discharge.[41] It

Michigan: Brighton v. Lake Shore & M. S. Ry., 103 Mich. 420, 61 N. W. 550, 112 Mich. 217, 70 N. W. 432; Stearns v. Lake Shore & M. S. Ry., 112 Mich. 651, 71 N. W. 148.

New York: Schell v. Plumb, 55 N. Y. 592; Banta v. Banta, 84 App. Div. 138, 82 N. Y. Supp. 113.

West Virginia: Rhoades v. Chesapeake & O. Ry., 49 W. Va. 494, 39 S. E. 209, 89 Am. St. Rep. 826, 55 L. R. A. 170.

[39] Gordon v. Brewster, 7 Wis. 355 (overruled in Wisconsin by a subsequent decision: *supra*, note 37).

[40] *Minnesota:* McMullan v. Dickinson Co., 60 Minn. 156, 62 N. W. 120, 51 Am. St. Rep. 511, 27 L. R. A. 409 (*semble*).

Two similar decisions in the Federal courts to the same effect: (Darst v. Mathieson Alkali Works, 81 Fed. 284; Schroeder v. California-Yukon T. Co. 95 Fed. 296) seem to be overruled by

Pierce v. East Tenn., C. I. & R. R., 173 U. S. 1, 19 Sup. Ct. 335, 43 L. ed. 591, *supra*. A few cases in the lower courts· of New York [Maguire v. Woodside, 2 Hilt. (N. Y.).59; Bassett v. French, 10 Misc. 672, 31 N. Y. Supp. 667; Zender v. Seliger-Toothill Co., 17 Misc. 126, 39 N. Y. Supp. 346] appear to be inconsistent with the cases in the Court of Appeals cited *supra*.

[41] *United States:* Emerson v. Howland, 1 Mason, 45.

Kentucky: Whitaker v. Sandifer, 1 Duv. 261; William Tarr Co. v. Kimbrough, 17 Ky. L. Rep. 1284, 34 S. W. 528.

Pennsylvania: Nixon v. Myers, 141 Pa. 477, 21 Atl. 670.

Texas: Meade v. Rutledge, 11 Tex. 44.

Virginia: Willoughby v. Thomas, 24 Gratt. 521.

England: Goodman v. Pocock, 15 Q. B. 576.

is the plaintiff's duty to use reasonable efforts to avoid loss by securing employment elsewhere.[42] The measure of damages is, therefore, *prima facie* the amount of wages he would have earned under the contract,[43] deducting, however, such

In Kelly *v.* Carthage Wheel Co., 62 Oh. St. 598, 57 N. E. 984, the plaintiff was to be paid by a percentage of the value of the work done under his supervision; with a guarantee, however, of a certain amount. If it had not been for the guarantee, plaintiff's damages would have been nominal, as there was no obligation on the defendant to manufacture any of the goods. In view of the guarantee the measure of damages is the proper proportion of the guarantee.

[42] *Alabama:* Wright *v.* Falkner, 37 Ala. 274.

Arkansas: Van Winkle *v.* Satterfield, 58 Ark. 617, 25 S. W. 1113, 23 L. R. A. 853.

Missouri: Ream *v.* Watkins, 27 Mo. 516, 72 Am. Dec. 283.

New Jersey: Goebel *v.* Pomeroy Bros. Co., 69 N. J. L. 610, 55 Atl. 690.

New York: Howard *v.* Daly, 61 N. Y. 362, 19 Am. Rep. 285; Polk *v.* Daly, 4 Daly, 411.

Vermont: Sherman *v.* Champlain Tr. Co., 31 Vt. 162.

Contra, Stewart *v.* Walker, 14 Pa. 293 (*semble*), is not to be supported.

The servant, however, is not obliged to accept employment of a different nature.

United States: Leatherberry *v.* Odell, 7 Fed. 641.

Illinois: McKinley *v.* Goodman, 67 Ill. App. 374.

Michigan: Farrell *v.* School Dist., 98 Mich. 43, 56 N. W. 1053 (teacher employed in graded school need not teach in district school).

Missouri: Barney *v.* Spangler, 131 Mo. App. 58, 109 S. W. 855.

New York: Costigan *v.* Mohawk & H. R. R., 2 Denio, 609, 43 Am. Dec.

758; Fuchs *v.* Koerner, 107 N. Y. 529, 14 N. E. 445.

Pennsylvania: Harger *v.* Jenkins, 17 Pa. Super. Ct. 615 (inferior position).

Nor in a different region. Costigan *v.* Mohawk & H. R. R., 2 Denio (N. Y.), 609.

In Tarrell *v.* School Dist., 98 Mich. 43, 56 N. W. 1053, it was held that a school teacher could not be expected to go to work during her vacation, which was given her for rest, to find other employment.

In *Texas* the servant is allowed a reasonable time to find other employment of the same sort; but if after a reasonable time he cannot do so, he must accept different employment: Simon *v.* Allen, 76 Tex. 398, 13 S. W. 296; Kramer *v.* Wolf Cigar Stores Co., 91 S. W. 775.

In *Louisiana* a discharged servant is by statute entitled to recover the entire amount of his wages, without seeking other employment: Lartigue *v.* Peet, 5 Rob. 91, 43 Am. Dec. 204; DeCamp *v.* Hewitt, 11 Rob. 290, 43 Am. Dec. 204; Sherburne *v.* Orleans Cotton Press Co., 15 La. 360; De-Puilly *v.* St. Louis Church, 7 La. Ann. 443; Lambert *v.* King, 12 La. Ann. 662; Trefethen *v.* Locke, 16 La. Ann. 19; Jones *v.* Jackson, 22 La. Ann. 112; Bormann *v.* Thiele, 23 La. Ann. 495; Leche *v.* Claverie, 25 La. Ann. 308; Taylor *v.* Kehlor, 26 La. Ann. 369; Tete *v.* Lanaux, 45 La. Ann. 1343, 14 So. 241.

[43] *United States:* Leatherberry *v.* Odell, 7 Fed. 641.

Alabama: Hartsell *v.* Masterson, 132 Ala. 275, 331 So. 616.

Arkansas: Gates *v.* School District, 57 Ark. 770, 21 S. W. 1060, 38 Am. St. Rep. 249.

sums as he earned or by reasonable diligence might have earned elsewhere,[44] and making allowance for the expenses of

Illinois: School Directors *v.* Kimmel, 31 Ill. App. 537.

Iowa: Worthington *v.* Oak & H. P. I. Co., 100 Iowa, 39, 69 N. W. 202.

Missouri: Nearns *v.* Harbert, 25 Mo. 352; Koenigkraemer *v.* Missouri Glass Co., 24 Mo. App. 124; Hansard *v.* Menderson Clothing Co., 73 Mo. App. 584; Rose *v.* Williamsville, G. & S. L. Ry., 146 Mo. App. 215, 123 S. W. 946; Simpson *v.* Ball, 145 Mo. App. 268, 129 S. W. 1017.

Nebraska: Omaha School Dist. *v.* McDonald, 68 Neb. 610, 94 N. W. 829.

New York: Costigan *v.* Mohawk & H. R. R., 2 Denio, 609; Milage *v.* Woodward, 186 N. Y. 252, 78 N. E. 873; Decker *v.* Hassell, 26 How. Pr. 528; Dearing *v.* Pearson, 8 Misc. 269, 28 N. Y. Supp. 715; Graff *v.* Blumberg, 53 Misc. 296, 103 N. Y. Supp. 184; Schleiff *v.* Berglas, 110 N. Y. Supp. 266.

Pennsylvania: King *v.* Steiren, 44 Pa. 99, 84 Am. Dec. 419.

South Carolina: Latimer *v.* New York Cotton Mills, 66 S. C. 135, 44 S. E. 559.

Where the amount of wages was not fixed by the contract the basis of recovery is reasonable wages during the term. McDaniel *v.* Parks, 19 Ark. 671.

[44] *United States:* Foye *v.* Dabney, 1 Sprague, 212.

Colorado: Saxonia M. Co. *v.* Cook, 7 Colo. 569.

Connecticut: Perry *v.* Simpson Waterproof Mfg. Co., 37 Conn. 520.

Delaware: Spahn *v.* Willman, 1 Pennew. 125, 39 Atl. 787.

Georgia: Ansley *v.* Jordan, 61 Ga. 482; Roberts *v.* Crowley, 81 Ga. 429.

Illinois: Brown *v.* Board of Education, 29 Ill. App. 572; School Directors *v.* Kimmel, 31 Ill. App. 537; School Directors *v.* Birch, 93 Ill. App. 499.

Indiana: Hinchcliffe *v.* Koontz, 121 Ind. 422, 16 Am. St. Rep. 403; Pape *v.* Lathrop, 18 Ind. App. 633, 46 N. E. 154; Elkhart Rubber Works *v.* Neff (Ind. App.), 92 N. E. 553.

Iowa: Beymer *v.* McBride, 37 Ia. 114; Byrne *v.* Independent School Dist., 139 Ia. 618, 117 N. W. 983.

Kentucky: Whitaker *v.* Sandifer, 1 Duv. 261; Hayworth *v.* Haldeman, 14 Ky. L. Rep. 202; Mortonville Coal Co. *v.* Sisk, 139 L. W. 1086.

Maine: Sutherland *v.* Wyer, 67 Me. 64.

Maryland: Cumberland & P. R. R. *v.* Slack, 45 Md. 161; Baltimore Base Ball Club Co. *v.* Pickett, 78 Md. 375, 28 Atl. 279, 44 Am. St. Rep. 304, 22 L. R. A. 690.

Massachusetts: Dickinson *v.* Talmage, 138 Mass. 249; Maynard *v.* Royal W. C. Co., 200 Mass. 1, 85 N. E. 877.

Michigan: Harrington *v.* Gies, 45 Mich. 374; Champlain *v.* Detroit Stamping Co., 68 Mich. 238.

Mississippi: Prichard *v.* Martin, 27 Miss. 305.

Missouri: Estes *v.* Desnoyers Shoe Co., 155 Mo. 577, 56 S. W. 316; Squire *v.* Wright, 1 Mo. App. 172.

New York: Everson *v.* Powers, 89 N. Y. 527, 42 Am. Rep. 319; Gillis *v.* Space, 63 Barb. 177; DeLeon *v.* Echeverria, 45 N. Y. Super. Ct. 610; Heim *v.* Wolf, 1 E. D. Smith, 70; Thompson *v.* Wood, 1 Hilt. 93; Huntington *v.* Ogdensburgh & L. C. R. R., 33 How. Pr. 416; Davis *v.* Dodge, 126 App. Div. 469, 110 N. Y. Supp. 787; King *v.* Will J. Block Amusement Co., 115 N. Y. Supp. 243; Goldberg *v.* Weinberger, 115 N. Y. Supp. 1098.

North Carolina: Hendrickson *v.* Anderson, 50 N. C. (5 Jones L.) 246, 72 Am. Dec. 549; Currier *v.* W. M. Ritter Lumber Co., 150 N. C. 694, 64 S. E. 763.

Ohio: St. Bernard *v.* Reig, 13 Ohio Cir. Ct. 540, 7 Ohio Cir. Dec. 539.

Pennsylvania: King *v.* Steiren, 44

obtaining employment.[45]   The burden of proof is on the defendant to show that the plaintiff might have obtained other employment,[46] for the failure of the plaintiff to obtain other

Pa. 99, 84 Am. Dec. 419; Kirk v. Hartman, 63 Pa. 97.

South Carolina: Latimer v. New York Cotton Mills, 66 S. C. 135, 44 S. E. 559.

Tennessee: Congregation of Children of Israel v. Peres, 2 Cold. 620.

Texas: Fowler v. Waller, 25 Tex. 695; Bluefields Banana Co. v. Wollfe (Civ. App.), 22 S. W. 269; Gulf, C. & S. F. Ry. v. Jackson, 29 Tex. Civ. App. 342, 69 S. W. 89; G. A. Kelly Plow Co. v. London (Tex. Civ. App.), 125 S. W. 974.

Virginia: Willoughby v. Thomas, 24 Gratt. 521.

Wisconsin: Barker v. Knickerbocker Ins. Co., 24 Wis. 630, 1 Am. Rep. 187; Winkler v. Racine Wagon & C. Co., 99 Wis. 184, 74 N. W. 793.

England: Yelland's Case, L. R. 4 Eq. 350.

In Allen v. Maronne (Tenn.), 23 S. W. 113, the plaintiff employed for a year was wrongfully discharged after a month by reason of defendant's insolvency. He then got employment with another for an indefinite term and was discharged for his alleged misconduct after a month; this employer went out of business in three months. Plaintiff meanwhile got other employment during the remainder of the three months at higher wages but the third employment then ceased. It was held that whether or not he could be charged with the wages which he would have earned on the second employment but for his misconduct, since the employment would have lasted only till the second employer went out of business, and as in fact he earned more in this case than he would have done if he had retained his second employment, the cause of his discharge from that employment was immaterial.

In Gates v. School Dist., 57 Ark. 370, 21 S. W. 1060, 38 Am. St. Rep. 249, it was held that damages are not reduced by the fact that, having moved out to a farm, plaintiff's expenses of living were less than in the city where he was employed. That is not part of the expense of performing the contract.

[45] *United States:* Development Co. of America v. King, 170 Fed. 923, 96 C. C. A. 139.

Massachusetts: Dickinson v. Talmage, 138 Mass. 249.

In Tufts v. Plymouth Gold Min. Co., 14 Allen (Mass.), 407, a workman was improperly discharged, at a distance from his home. It was held that he could not recover the cost of getting home; but in determining how much he might have realized elsewhere the cost of getting where he could receive employment might be considered. But in Tickler v. Andrae Mfg. Co., 95 Wis. 352, 70 N. W. 292, one discharged before the end of his term of service was held not entitled to deduct from the amount of wages that he earned elsewhere the expenses of moving himself and his family back where he came from in order to get the new employment.

[46] *United States:* Leatherberry v. Odell, 7 Fed. 641; Schroeder v. California Y. T. Co., 95 Fed. 296; Mathesius v. Brooklyn Heights R. R., 96 Fed. 792.

Arkansas: Van Winkle v. Satterfield, 58 Ark. 617, 25 S. W. 1113, 23 L. R. A. 853.

California: Rosenberger v. Pacific Coast Ry., 111 Cal. 313, 43 Pac. 963.

Illinois: Fish v. Glass, 54 Ill. App. 655.

Massachusetts: Maynard v. Royal Worcester Corset Co., 200 Mass. 1, 85 N. E. 877.

employment does not affect the right of action, but only goes in reduction of damages, and if nothing else is shown, the plaintiff is entitled to recover the contract price upon proving the defendant's violation of the contract, and his own willingness to perform.[47]   The fact that the plaintiff obtained new em-

Michigan: Allen v. Whitlark, 99 Mich. 492, 58 N. W. 470.

Minnesota: Bennett v. Morton, 46 Minn. 113, 48 N. W. 678.

Mississippi: Hunt v. Crane, 33 Miss. 669, 69 Am. Dec. 381.

Missouri: Nearns v. Harbert, 25 Mo. 352; Koenigkraemer v. Missouri Glass Co., 24 Mo. App. 124; Simpson v. Ball, 145 Mo. App. 268, 129 S. W. 1017.

Nebraska: Wirth v. Calhoun, 64 Neb. 316, 89 N. W. 785.

New York: Costigan v. Mohawk & H. P. R. R., 2 Denio, 609, 43 Am. Dec. 758; Howard v. Daly, 61 N. Y. 362, 19 Am. Rep. 285; Milage v. Woodward, 186 N. Y. 252, 78 N. E. 873; Dearing v. Pearson, 8 Misc. 269, 28 N. Y. Supp. 715; Graff v. Blumberg, 53 Misc. 296, 103 N. Y. Supp. 184; Schleiff v. Berglas, 110 N. Y. Supp. 266.

Pennsylvania: Kirk v. Hartman, 36 Pa. 97; Heyer v. Cunningham Piano Co., 6 Pa. Super. Ct. 504.

South Carolina: Latimer v. York Cotton Mills, 66 S. C. 135, 44 S. E. 559.

Texas: Allgeyer v. Rutherford (Civ. App.), 45 S. W. 628; Weber Gas & G. E. Co. v. Bradford, 34 Tex. Civ. App. 543, 79 S. W. 46; Pacific Exp. Co. v. Walters (Tex. Civ. App.), 93 S. W. 496; Peacock v. Coltrane, 44 Tex. Civ. App. 530, 99 S. W. 107.

Wisconsin: Babcock v. Appleton Manuf. Co., 93 Wis. 124, 67 N. W. 33.

Plaintiff need not allege in the declaration that he could not have obtained other employment. Wirth v. Calhoun, 64 Neb. 316, 89 N. W. 785.

In John C. Lewis Co. v. Scott, 14 Ky. L. Rep. 713, it was held that a

servant wrongfully discharged must allege in his declaration that he could get no other employment, or else he is entitled to only nominal damages; but this case is clearly wrong.

Where it is shown that other employment was or could have been had, it would seem that the burden remains on the defendant to show what wages could have been obtained.

United States: Schroeder v. California Yukon Trading Co., 95 Fed. 296.

California: Rosenberger v. Pacific Coast Ry., 111 Cal. 313, 43 Pac. 963.

Contra, Ruland v. Waukesha Water Co., 52 App. Div. 280, 65 N. Y. Supp. 87.

In Hunt v. Crane, 33 Miss. 669, 69 Am. Dec. 381, it was held that the burden of showing that the wages obtained in other employment were lower than they should have been was on the employer.

[47] *Alabama:* Strauss v. Meertief, 64 Ala. 299, 38 Am. Rep. 8.

Colorado: Saxonia M. Co. v. Cook, 7 Colo. 569.

Georgia: Ansley v. Jordan, 61 Ga. 482; Roberts v. Crowley, 81 Ga. 429.

Illinois: Brown v. Board of Education, 29 Ill. App. 572.

Indiana: Gazette P. Co. v. Morss, 60 Ind. 153, Hinchcliffe v. Koontz, 121 Ind. 422; 23 N. E. 271, 16 Am. St. Rep. 403.

Minnesota: Horn v. Western Land Assoc., 22 Minn. 233.

Missouri: Pond v. Wyman, 15 Mo. 175.

Pennsylvania: King v. Steiren, 44 Pa. 99, 84 Am. Dec. 419.

Wisconsin: Barker v. Knickerbocker Ins. Co. 24 Wis. 630.

ployment does not constitute a defense. It is one of the facts for the jury to consider in estimating the plaintiff's loss; [48] and to entitle the defendant to reduce the recovery on the ground that the plaintiff had earned money in another employment, it must be shown that if he had not been discharged, he could not have earned it without violating his duty under his contract. [49] Of course, if the plaintiff, at request of the defendant, held himself in readiness to go to work again after his discharge, he may recover the full amount of wages. [50]

Where the plaintiff immediately after his wrongful discharge obtained another employment at a higher salary, it was held that he could recover only nominal damages. [51] And an offer by the defendant to take the plaintiff back into his employ may be shown in reduction of damages, if there was nothing that should have prevented the plaintiff from accepting the offer. [52]

---

[48] *Alabama:* Morris Mining Co. *v.* Knox, 96 Ala. 320, 11 So. 207; Troy Fertilizer Co. *v.* Logan, 96 Ala. 619, 12 So. 712.

Illinois: Williams *v.* Chicago Coal Co., 60 Ill. 149.

[49] *Arkansas:* Van Winkel *v.* Satterfield, 58 Ark. 617, 25 S. W. 1113, 23 L. R. A. 853.

California: Nuckolls *v.* College of Physicians and Surgeons, 7 Cal. App. 233, 94 Pac. 81.

Maryland: Jaffray *v.* King, 34 Md. 217.

Therefore if the servant has before discharge performed all the work he was to do, he can recover the whole contract without deduction. In Adams *v.* Cox, 1 Nott & McC. (S. C.) 284, an overseer was turned off before the end of the year but after a crop had been made. *Held,* that he was entitled to recover his salary for the whole year. In Seed *v.* Johnston, 63 App. Div. 340, 71 N. Y. Supp. 579, plaintiff was to give defendant his advice during his life, so far as it should be required, and he was to receive 50 dollars a month. It was held that if plaintiff was discharged from the employment, since

there was nothing for him to do under the contract if he was not called upon, he could sue from month to month and recover each month the instalment due for that month.

[50] Bromley *v.* School Dist. No. 5, 47 Vt. 381.

[51] Williams *v.* Anderson, 9 Minn. 50.

[52] *Illinois:* Trawick *v.* Peoria & F. C. St. Ry., 68 Ill. App. 156.

Mississippi: Birdsong *v.* Ellis, 62 Miss. 418.

Missouri: Squire *v.* Wright, 1 Mo. App. 172.

New York: Bigelow *v.* American F. P. Mfg. Co., 39 Hun, 599.

South Carolina: Mitchell *v.* Toale, 25 S. C. 238, 60 Am. Rep. 502.

England: Brace *v.* Calder, [1895] 2 Q. B. 253.

New Zealand: Wilson *v.* Kisri, 18 N. Z. (Sup. Ct.) 807.

Where the acceptance of employment offered by the employer at a lower rate would be taken as a modification of the original agreement, the servant is of course not called upon to accept it.

Alabama: People's Co-operative Assoc. *v.* Lloyd, 77 Ala. 387.

Thus in Beymer v. McBride,[53] the defendant had agreed to make the plaintiff agent for the sale of certain machines for which he was agent, and to turn over to him all the orders already given and the machines required to fulfil the orders. On his failure to keep the agreement, it was held proper to show that two days after the breach the owners of the machines offered to turn the orders and machines over to the plaintiff, and that the plaintiff had refused to accept; for the plaintiff was bound to use ordinary efforts to make the damages as light as possible.

Where the plaintiff, after seeking other employment without success, does work for himself, it has been held in Michigan that the value of such work need not be deducted;[54] but in New York where he went to work on his own account, the value of his work was deducted from the amount he recovered.[55] In all such cases the question would seem to be: was his work on his own account incompatible with the performance of the original service?[56] If he engaged in business on his own account, the profits of the business should be deducted from the agreed wages;[57] and if the business had acquired a value, although no profits were realized, it has been held that such value should be deducted.[58]

§ 668. Employment terminable on notice—Domestic service.

A servant is often employed on a contract terminable by notice within a certain time, or at once by paying wages for

Iowa: Jackson v. Steamboat Rock Independent School District, 110 Iowa, 313, 77 N. W. 860.

Michigan: Chisholm v. Preferred Bankers' L. Assur. Co., 112 Mich. 50, 70 N. W. 415.

Missouri: Howard v. Vaughan-Monnig Shoe Co., 82 Mo. App. 405.

New York: Whitmarsh v. Littlefield, 46 Hun, 418.

For the same reason the servant need not accept the tender of employment of a different sort.

Iowa: Jackson v. Steamboat Rock Independent School Dist., 110 Ia. 313, 77 N. W. 860.

New York: Hecht v. Brandus, 4 Misc. 58, 23 N. Y. Supp. 1004.

[53] 37 Ia. 114.

[54] Harrington v. Gies, 45 Mich. 374.

[55] Huntington v. Ogdensburgh & L. C. R. R., 33 How Pr. 416; *acc.,* Gates v. School Dist., 57 Ark. 370, 21 S. W. 1060, 38 Am. St. Rep. 249.

[56] Van Winkle v. Satterfield, 58 Ark. 617, 25 S. W. 1113, 23 L. R. A. 853.

[57] Richardson v. Hartman, 68 Hun (N. Y.) 9, 22 N. Y. Supp. 645.

[58] Kramer v. Wolf Cigar Stores Co., 99 Tex. 597, 91 S. W. 775, 777.

that time. Such are the contracts of domestic servants, terminable by a month's warning or a month's wages. In such a case the month's wages is in the nature of stipulated damages; [59] it may be recovered upon discharge without warning.[60] If the servant employed on such a contract leaves without notice, the employer is entitled to the actual damages he suffers from the breach of contract.[61]

When the contract is terminable at any time on notice, and the servant is discharged without formal notice, the discharge is to be regarded as notice, and he may recover wages up to the time of discharge,[62] but only nominal damages for the discharge.[63] Where the servant left without giving notice it was held in an early case that he thereby forfeited wages earned before that time.[64]

[59] Fewings v. Tisdal, 1 Ex. 295.

[60] *Delaware:* Shea v. Kerr, 1 Pennewill, 530, 40 Atl. 241.

Michigan: Derry v. East Saginaw Bd. of Education, 102 Mich. 631, 61 N. W. 61.

England: East Anglian Ry. v. Lythgoe, 10 C. B. 726; Robinson v. Hindman, 3 Esp. 235; Gordon v. Potter, 1 F. & F. 644.

In Maw v. Jones, 25 Q. B. D. 107, the plaintiff was an apprentice under a contract which gave defendant a right to discharge on a week's notice. Plaintiff was wrongfully discharged without notice. It was held that the jury could consider that he might be discharged on a week's notice in arriving at the amount of damages but was not necessarily confined to a week's wages.

In Stowell v. Greenwich Ins. Co., 20 App. Div. 188, 46 N. Y. Supp. 802, where the time of notice was 90 days the court appears to have thought that the jury should consider the chance of other employment. But in Briscoe v. Litt, 19 N. Y. Misc. 5, 42 N. Y. Supp. 908, where the time was 2 weeks, the court ruled that the plaintiff was not bound to seek other employment.

[61] *Connecticut:* Satchwell v. Williams, 40 Conn. 371.

Massachusetts: Hunt v. Otis Co., 4 Met. 464.

In Hughes v. Wamsutta Mills, 11 Allen (Mass.), 201, the plaintiff was arrested and imprisoned for crime. It was held that this being outside his own volition, he was excused from giving two weeks' notice and might recover. The fact that his crime was the cause of it is immaterial because it was a remote cause.

[62] *New York:* Gates v. Davenport, 29 Barb. 160.

North Carolina: Steed v. McRae, 1 Dev. & Bat. 435.

[63] *Minnesota:* Bolles v. Sachs, 37 Minn. 315.

New York: Davis v. Barr, 12 N. Y. St. 111 (one day's wages); Frank v. Manhattan M. & Dispensary, 107 N. Y. Supp. 404.

Wisconsin: Cronemillar v. Duluth-Superior Milling Co., 134 Wis. 248, 114 N. W. 432.

[64] Monell v. Burns, 4 Denio (N. Y.), 121; Quære whether this case would be followed to-day. The contrary was held in Evans v. Bennett, 7 Wis. 404.

§ 669. Compensation by share or percentage of an uncertain amount.

When a person is employed on an agreement by which he is to be compensated by the whole or a part of an amount to be fixed in the future, and he is discharged before the amount can be fixed, recovery according to the contract may be difficult, or impossible.[65] Thus where a superintendent was to be paid a commission on goods manufactured under his supervision, and he was discharged before the end of his term of service, only nominal damages could be recovered, since there was no way of fixing the amount of goods that would have been manufactured.[66] But if the enterprise continued after the plaintiff's discharge, so that the amount can be fixed, he is entitled to compensation based on the percentage of the actual amount thus fixed. So where a fisherman is to be paid according to the catch of fish, and he is discharged wrongfully before the termination of the voyage, he is entitled to compensation based on the actual catch.[67] And where the plaintiff was hired for a year as overseer of the defendant, and was to receive a proportion of the crop, he was allowed, upon being wrongfully discharged just before harvest, to recover the agreed proportion of the matured crop.[68] In a case where the plaintiff was employed to measure lumber for a logger at a certain price per thousand feet, and was wrongfully discharged, he was held entitled to his commission on the amount of lumber cut during the year.[69] And where the compensation of the overseer of a manufacturer was to be a percentage on the actual sales, and during the employment certain goods were manufactured which were sold after the employment ceased, it was held that plaintiff was entitled to his percentage on them.[70] On this principle, where the plaintiff served defendant as minister,

[65] For a consideration of this subject in the case of agency, see *infra*, § 834c.

[66] Kelly *v.* Carthage Wheel Co., 62 Oh. St. 598, 57 N. E. 984 (*semble*).

[67] *United States:* Fee *v.* Orient Fertilizing Co., 36 Fed. 509.
Massachusetts: Dennis *v.* Maxfield, 10 Allen, 138.

[68] Clancey *v.* Robertson, 2 Mills (S. C.), 404, 12 Am. Dec. 682. But when the discharge was at an earlier stage of the crop, an allowance of the agreed proportion of a *probable average crop* is questionable. Such an allowance was made in Hassell *v.* Nutt, 14 Tex. 260.

[69] Pinet *v.* Montague, 103 Mich. 516, 61 N. W. 876.

[70] Byrnes *v.* Baldwin, 17 N. Y. Misc. 280, 40 N. Y. Supp. 386.

agreeing to receive in compensation the amount of subscriptions, which the defendant agreed to collect, and the defendant did not collect the subscriptions, it was held that plaintiff might recover the amount of the uncollected subscriptions which could have been collected by reasonable diligence, but was not entitled to recover on a *quantum meruit*.[71]

§ 670. Compensation payable on a contingency.

The compensation of a servant or agent often depends upon a contingency. In such a case, where a breach of the contract by the employer prevents the happening of the contingency he will not be allowed by taking advantage of his own breach of contract to prevent the plaintiff from recovering compensation altogether.[72] If in such a case the amount of compensation can be determined, the plaintiff will be allowed to recover it, though, through the defendant's default, the contingency upon which it was payable has not happened. Thus, where the plaintiff was to receive £20 at Lady Day, if he stayed till then, and the defendant wrongfully discharged him before Lady Day, he was allowed to recover the £20.[73]

Where the amount of compensation, which would be due under the contract, cannot be determined, the plaintiff may recover the value of his services. Thus, where the plaintiff was engaged by the defendant to train, enter in races and ride the

[71] Myers v. Baptist Society, 38 Vt. 614.

[72] In Schreiber v. Klingerstein, 95 N. Y. Supp. 549, plaintiff was to receive for his services $10 a week while traveling and $20 while at home and was to travel whenever directed to do so by the defendant. Being wrongly discharged, the court held that his compensation was to be reckoned at $20 a week. While at home he would have to board himself, and therefore it was proper to give him that except when he was sent on the road; and the defendant could reduce the amount to $10, only by giving him orders to travel.

In Rightmire v. Hirner, 188 Pa. 325, 41 Atl. 538, plaintiff was to sell machines for defendant. Defendant discharged plaintiff before the end of term. Under the contract the defendant was not bound to continue the manufacture of the machines. *Held*, that the measure of damages was the value of the contract at the time of the breach, and in considering the value the jury were to bear in mind that the defendants were not obliged to continue the manufacture of the machines, that the plaintiff's rights were subject to the contingencies of business, which might tend to reduce the sales; and they were also to take into consideration what the plaintiff could probably have earned in some other employment during the period of the contract.

[3] Lake v. Campbell, 5 L. T. Rep. 582.

defendant's horse in races for a year, his compensation to be two-thirds of the net profits, and the defendant broke the contract, the defendant claimed that the measure of damages was two-thirds of the value of the use of the horse for a year. The court, however, allowed the plaintiff to recover the value of his services, on the ground that the defendant had put it entirely out of the plaintiff's power to secure remuneration at the contract rate.[74]

§ 671. Services rendered in expectation of compensation.

Where services are rendered upon request of the defendant, or are voluntarily accepted by him,[75] or are rendered in the mutual expectation of compensation but without any express agreement as to the terms of service, the plaintiff is entitled to recover as compensation what the services were worth.[76] Thus where the plaintiff took the defendant's horse to train with the understanding that a formal agreement should be made later,

[74] Barr v. Van Duyn, 45 Ia. 228. In Ellsler v. Brooks, 54 N. Y. Super. Ct. 73, the plaintiff was employed as an actress, to receive 50% of the net profits. After a season lasting several weeks carried on at a loss the defendant refused to fulfil his contract any longer. It was held that since the measure of damages was the amount of profits to which she would have been entitled, and as on the evidence it was impossible to show any profits that would have been earned, she was entitled to nominal damages only. This must be distinguished on the ground that the defendant was able to prove with reasonable certainty that there would have been no profits.

[75] *Alabama:* McFarland v. Dawson, 125 Ala. 428, 29 So. 327.

Illinois: Moline W. P. & M. Co. v. Nichols, 26 Ill. 90.

[76] *Illinois:* Heffron v. Brown, 155 Ill. 322, 40 N. E. 583.

Maryland: Gambrill v. Schooley, 89 Md. 546, 43 Atl. 918.

Missouri: Crole v. Thomas, 19 Mo. 70; Sprague v. Lea, 152 Mo. 327, 53 S. W. 1074; Ryans v. Hospes, 167 Mo. 342, 67 S. W. 285.

New Jersey: Cooke v. Independent T. & T. C. Co., 77 N. J. L. 454, 68 Atl. 790.

So where plaintiff acted as secretary of a corporation, not being a director or officer of the corporation, he was entitled to compensation like any other employee on a *quantum meruit.* Smith v. Long Island R. R., 102 N. Y. 190, 6 N. E. 397.

In Boardman v. Ward, 40 Minn. 399, 42 N. W. 202, 12 Am. St. Rep. 749, the plaintiff lived in her guardian's family, performing services, under the assumption that she was getting her board and clothing as compensation for such services, and that nothing would be charged for them. The guardian knew that that was her understanding, but nevertheless in his guardian's account charged for her board and clothes. It was held that she was entitled to recover compensation for services rendered by her in spite of the fact that she did not expect to be paid for them when she rendered them.

and after the plaintiff had rendered services the defendant took the horse away, it was held that the plaintiff might recover the value of his services.[77] And on the same principle, where services are rendered and there is a misunderstanding as to the amount of compensation, the plaintiff may recover the value of the services;[78] and so where they are rendered under an express agreement, but the agreement is silent as to the price.[79] So where a person performs services with the understanding between him and his employer that compensation for the services is to be made by will, the person so serving is entitled if he does not receive full compensation by will to recover the value of the services;[80] but if the servant rendered the services merely in the hope of obtaining a legacy but without any understanding to that effect with the employer, he is entitled to no compensation.[81]

§ 672. Interruption of service by unavoidable cause.

Where the performance of the service is interrupted before its conclusion by some cause which absolves the parties from continuing the performance of the contract, the servant should

[77] Wright v. Broome, 67 Mo. App. 32.

[78] *California:* Hartman v. Rogers, 69 Cal. 643, 11 Pac. 581.

Kansas: Turner v. Webster, 24 Kan. 38.

New York: Constable v. Lefever, 66 Hun, 628, 21 N. Y. Supp. 38.

Vermont: Tucker v. Preston, 60 Vt. 473.

[79] *Arkansas:* McDaniel v. Parks, 19 Ark. 671.

Illinois: Lockwood v. Onion, 56 Ill. 506.

Massachusetts: Stowe v. Buttrick, 125 Mass. 449.

New York: Erben v. Lorillard, 2 Keyes, 567.

[80] *United States:* Little v. Dawson, 4 Dall. 111, 1 L. ed. 763.

New Jersey: Updike v. Ten Broeck, 32 N. J. L. 105 (adult son).

New York: Jacobson v. Le Grange, 3 Johns. 199 (nephew); Robinson v. Raynor, 28 N. Y. 494; Reynolds v. Robinson, 64 N. Y. 589; Collier v. Rut-

ledge, 136 N. Y. 621, 32 N. E. 626; Stokes v. Pease, 79 Hun, 304, 29 N. Y. Supp. 430; Miller v. Richardson, 88 Hun, 49, 34 N. Y. Supp. 506; Hopkins v. Clark, 90 Hun, 4, 34 N. Y. Supp. 506.

Pennsylvania: Kauss v. Rohner, 172 Pa. 481, 33 Atl. 1016, 51 Am. St. Rep. 762 (adopted child).

In Hudson v. Hudson, 90 Ga. 581, 16 S. E. 349, a son agreed to take care of his father during life, and the father agreed to leave plaintiff his property. The father became insane and could not do so. Plaintiff was entitled to recover on a *quantum meruit* the value of his services, less what he received from the property during his father's lifetime over and above the cost of taking care of his father.

[81] *United States:* Little v. Dawson, 4 Dall. 111, 1 L. ed. 763.

New Jersey: Grandin v. Reading, 10 N. J. Eq. (2 Stockt.) 370.

England: Osborn v. Guy's Hospital, 2 Str. 728.

be allowed to recover compensation for the service which he performed. Thus, where the performance of service is interrupted by illness on the part of the workman he is entitled to recover compensation for that portion of the whole work which he has done.[82] So where a person engaged to serve dies before completing the service his representatives are entitled to recover compensation for his services up to the time of his death;[83] and where the employer dies and the service is personal the servant can recover wages to the date of the death only.[84] So where an epidemic disease prevents the complete performance of the service the servant is entitled to recover for what he has done before the outbreak of the disease.[85]

[82] *Connecticut:* Ryan *v.* Dayton, 25 Conn. 188, 65 Am. Dec. 560.

Missouri: Hughes *v.* Toledo S. & C. R. R., 112 Mo. App. 91, 86 S. W. 895.

New York: Wolfe *v.* Howes, 20 N. Y. 197, 75 Am. Dec. 388; Clark *v.* Gilbert, 26 N. Y. 279, 84 Am. Dec. 189.

South Dakota: McClellan *v.* Harris, 7 S. D. 447, 64 N. W. 522.

Vermont: Hubbard *v.* Belden, 27 Vt. 645.

Washington: MacFarlane *v.* Allan-Pfeiffer Chemical Co., 59 Wash. 154, 109 Pac. 604.

Wisconsin: Green *v.* Gilbert, 21 Wis. 395.

See also *ante,* § 655c.

In a few cases it has been intimated that there should be a deduction of the amount of loss caused to the employer. *Alabama:* Hunter *v.* Waldron, 7 Ala. 753; Jones *v.* Deyer, 16 Ala. 221, 50 Am. Dec. 177.

Connecticut: Ryan *v.* Dayton, 25 Conn. 188, 65 Am. Dec. 560.

Vermont: Patrick *v.* Putnam, 27 Vt. 759.

Washington: Mendenhall *v.* Davis, 52 Wash. 169, 100 Pac. 336; MacFarlane *v.* Allan-Pfeiffer C. Co., 59 Wash. 154, 109 Pac. 604.

Wisconsin: Walsh *v.* Fisher, 102 Wis. 172, 78 N. W. 437, 72 Am. St. Rep. 865.

Of course entire performance of the contract may expressly be made a condition of any recovery of wages whatever; in such a case, failure completely to perform, even though caused by illness, is a complete bar to recovery.

Alabama: Givhan *v.* Dailey, 4 Ala. 336 (as explained in Hunter *v.* Waldron, 7 Ala. 753).

Massachusetts: Noon *v.* Salisbury Mills, 3 Allen, 340.

In Greene *v.* Linton, 7 Port. (Ala.) 133, 31 Am. Dec. 707, recovery was refused on the form of the pleadings.

In Jennings *v.* Lyons, 39 Wis. 553, 20 Am. Rep. 57, it was held that if the illness was one which the husband should have foreseen (pregnancy), he cannot recover for services of his wife which were interrupted before full performance by the illness.

[83] *Alabama:* Hunter *v.* Waldron, 7 Ala. 753.

Rhode Island: Parker *v.* Macomber, 17 R. I. 674, 24 Atl. 464, 16 L. R. A. 858.

South Carolina: Clendinen *v.* Black, 2 Bailey, 488, 23 Am. Dec. 149.

Washington: Mendenhall *v.* Davis, 52 Wash. 169, 100 Pac. 336.

[84] Lacy *v.* Getman, 119 N. Y. 109, 23 N. E. 452, 16 Am. St. Rep. 806, 6 L. R. A. 728.

[85] Lakeman *v.* Pollard, 43 Me. 463, 69 Am. Dec. 77.

In some cases it is said that the plaintiff is entitled to complete compensation in spite of absence for illness. So where a person was engaged to teach school for a term and the school was closed for a portion of the term on account of an epidemic disease, the teacher was held to be entitled to her entire salary.[86] Such also was held to be the rule of the admiralty law in case of an injury to a seaman in the course of the voyage;[87] and in a Colorado case it was held that a stenographer employed by the week, who was absent for some time by reason of illness, in accordance with the business custom should receive entire wages in spite of time lost.[88]   In Gray v. Murray[89] the plaintiff's intestate went out as supercargo for defendant under an agreement for a commission and percentage of profits. After the voyage was partly completed he was prevented by illness from going further, and substituted another in his place, to be paid by himself. This substitution was approved by the defendant. It was held that, whatever might be the rule of law, in equity at least the administrator was entitled to recover the entire amount of commissions and percentages of profits, paying the substitute as agreed. And this would seem to be the true rule of damages at law.

The rule appears to be the same if performance of the service is interrupted by the law,[90] or by other unavoidable cause for which the plaintiff is not responsible.[91]

§ 673. Services rendered on a contract rescinded by mutual consent.

Where a contract of service is cancelled by mutual consent of the parties the servant is entitled to recover the value of the

---

[86] McKay v. Barnett, 21 Utah, 239, 247, 60 Pac. 1100, 50 L. R. A. 371.

[87] Chandler v. Grieves, 2 H. Bl. 606.

[88] Mott v. Baxter, 13 Colo. App. 63, 56 Pac. 192.

[89] 3 Johns. Ch. (N. Y.) 167.

[90] Ante, § 655c. In Jewell v. Thompson, 2 Litt. (Ky.) 52, however, where the plaintiff agreed to act as defendant's substitute in the army for six months for an agreed compensation and he was discharged from the army at the end of a few weeks on account of peace, it was held that he could recover nothing.

[91] In Walsh v. Fisher, 102 Wis. 172, 78 N. W. 437, 72 Am. St. Rep. 865, the plaintiff left the employment before the end of the term because of the threats of strikers. It was held that if he was justified in leaving for such a cause he was entitled to the same compensation as if his service had been interrupted by illness.

services rendered by him up to the time of rescission at the contract rate.[92] This doctrine must be the explanation of a series of cases in South Carolina which would otherwise seem opposed to sound principle.[93]

§ 673a. Services rendered by an infant.

If an infant agrees to serve upon certain terms he is not bound by the contract but may at the proper time repudiate it; and in that case since he has the right to repudiate the contract he can be held bound by no term of it whatever. He is therefore not bound by the rate of compensation named in the contract, and is entitled to recover the value of the services without regard to the contract rate.[94] Similarly, if a minor

[92] *Texas:* Ratcliff v. Baird, 14 Tex. 43.
Vermont: Patnote v. Sanders, 41 Vt. 66, 98 Am. Dec. 564; Boyle v. Parker, 46 Vt. 343.
See *ante,* § 655e.
[93] Byrd v. Bord, 4 McCord, 246, 17 Am. Dec. 740; Eaken v. Harrison, 4 McCord, 249, 17 Am. Dec. 740; McClure v. Pyatt, 4 McCord, 26; Suber v. Vanlew, 2 Speer, 126; Saunders v. Anderson, 2 Hill (S. C.), 486.
[94] *Illinois:* Ray v. Haines, 52 Ill. 485.
Indiana: Dallas v. Hollingsworth, 3 Ind. 537; Wheatly v. Miscal, 5 Ind. 142; Van Pelt v. Corwine, 6 Ind. 363; Garner v. Noard, 27 Ind. 323.
Maine: Judkins v. Walker, 17 Me. 38, 35 Am. Dec. 229; Derocher v. Continental Mills, 58 Me. 217, 4 Am. Rep. 286.
Massachusetts: Moses v. Stevens, 2 Pick. 332; Nickerson v. Easton, 12 Pick. 110; Vent v. Osgood, 19 Pick. 572; Gaffney v. Hayden, 110 Mass. 137, 14 Am. Rep. 580.
New Hampshire: Lufkin v. Mayall, 25 N. H. 82 (overruling Weeks v. Leighton, 5 N. H. 343); Hagerty v. Nashua Lock Co., 62 N. H. 576.
New York: Medbury v. Watrous, 7 Hill, 110 (overruling McCoy v. Huffman, 8 Cow. 84); Whitemarsh v. Hall, 3 Denio, 375.

Wisconsin: Mountain v. Fisher, 22 Wis. 93.
An infant who contracted to perform services in payment for a house left the service on coming of age. It was held that he was entitled on a *quantum meruit* to get the value of the services performed, without reference to the value of the house. Medbury v. Watrous, 7 Hill (N. Y.), 110. In Dunton v. Brown, 31 Mich. 182, however, an infant made a contract of partnership and rendered services. He afterwards repudiated the contract before he came of age. It was held that infants could not repudiate contracts before age, and so could not substitute a *quantum meruit*. The court was uncertain whether he could do it after age if the contract had meanwhile been executed.
Allowance must of course be made for any money or property received by the infant under the contract and retained by him.
Missouri: Sherlock v. Kimmell, 75 Mo. 77 (infant had part of his time allowed him to earn money for himself).
Vermont: Taft v. Pike, 14 Vt. 405, 39 Am. Dec. 228.
In Burroughs v. Morse, 48 Mich. 520, 12 N. W. 684, a minor was em-

enter the service of the defendant without permission of his father, the father may recover the reasonable value of his services, less the amount of compensation which the minor has received.[95] In so far, however, as the contract has been completely performed on both sides it is usually held that the servant cannot repudiate it, but is bound by its terms as to compensation, provided it was a beneficial contract.[96] If the minor continues to serve after he comes of age he thereby ratifies the agreement and he is then bound by it in all its parts.[97]

In a few cases it has been intimated that the infant who repudiates his contract must allow in reduction such damages as his premature leaving the service caused to his master.[98] This doctrine appears to be unsound since the infant repudiating his agreement should be protected from every portion of it; and it is usually held that no allowance can be made for the employer's loss.[99] In certain cases the infant may be legally

ployed to work, and was to receive board and clothes and schooling in winter. He was kept at work during winter and not sent to school. *Held*, since this work was outside the contract he was entitled to recover compensation for it. In Roundy v. Thatcher, 49 N. H. 526, the father of a minor made an agreement that the minor should serve for a certain time for his board and clothes. Having served part of the time and received board and clothes, the minor left. *Held*, that plaintiff could recover nothing since the contract had been broken. Even under the doctrine of Britton v. Turner, the plaintiff would be entitled to recover no further compensation, since the compensation provided for in the contract had been paid exactly as called for. But note, that this is a case of breach of valid contract made by the father, not a case of repudiation of his own contract by an infant.

[95] *Missouri:* Sherlock v. Kimmell, 75 Mo. 77.

New Hampshire: Huntoon v. Hazelton, 20 N. H. 388.

[96] *Massachusetts:* Stone v. Dennison, 13 Pick. 1, 23 Am. Dec. 654.

Wisconsin: Mountain v. Fisher, 22 Wis. 93.

[97] *Ohio:* Fordyce v. Easthope, 10 Ohio Dec. 610.

Vermont: Forsyth v. Hastings, 27 Vt. 646.

In Henderhen v. Cook, 66 Barb. (N. Y.) 21, a minor agreed to serve for a certain time at a certain rate. His father sued on the contract, the minor having left the employment before the expiration of the term. *Held*, by suing on the contract the father adopted it, and could not make any claim except in accordance with the terms of it; and as the minor had failed to serve out the term, no compensation was due on the contract.

[98] *Missouri:* Lowe v. Sinklear, 27 Mo. 308, 72 Am. Dec. 266.

Vermont: Thomas v. Dike, 11 Vt. 273, 34 Am. Dec. 690; Hoxie v. Lincoln, 25 Vt. 206 (but see Meeker v. Hurd, 31 Vt. 639).

[99] *Maine:* Derocher v. Continental Mills, 58 Me. 217, 4 Am. Rep. 286.

bound by the contract for service, as for instance, in States where he is allowed to make a binding contract of apprenticeship or in any State where the contract is made for him by his parent or guardian. In such a case the recovery by or against the infant is as in ordinary cases.[100]

§ 673b. Services rendered under an agreement within the statute of frauds.

Where services are rendered under a contract for compensation which is void by the statute of frauds, the plaintiff is entitled to recover compensation.[101] If the contract, being void, is repudiated by the employer, who discharges the plaintiff, the latter is entitled to recover the entire value of his services up to the time of his discharge without regard to the contract price.[102] But if the contract has been fully carried out by the

New York: Whitemarsh v. Hall, 3 Denio, 375.

[100] Services rendered under valid contract of apprenticeship; no compensation can be recovered on a *quantum meruit:* Olney v. Myers, 3 Ill. 311, 35 Am. Dec. 110.

Services rendered under contract with parent:

Delaware: Rodman v. Woolman, 2 Houst. 581 (rescission by mutual consent; recovery for services before rescission at contract rate).

Iowa: Lowen v. Crossman, 8 Iowa, 325 (contract broken by son; reduce compensation for services performed by damages for breach).

Ohio: Abbott v. Inskip, 29 Ohio St. 59 (contract legally made with mother of an infant for his services during minority, but void under statute of frauds. By terms of the contract the infant was to get his board, clothes, etc., and on reaching majority was to have a horse. He left during minority, and sued for value of services. *Held,* he could not recover, since the terms of the original contract bound him as to compensation).

In Potter v. Greene, 39 Hun (N. Y.), 72, it appeared that an infant might make a valid contract of apprenticeship. Here he was illegally indentured by others and claimed to have been compelled by force to stay with the defendant. *Held,* if he remained voluntarily, although the indenture itself was not legal, he would be bound by the agreement as one he had voluntarily accepted; but if he was compelled by force to remain and perform the agreement, then he was not bound by it and might recover compensation for the services.

[101] *Florida:* Bucki v. McKinnon, 37 Fla. 391, 20 So. 540.

Kansas: Wonsettler v. Lee, 40 Kan. 367, 19 Pac. 862.

Maryland: Hamilton v. Thirston, 93 Md. 213, 48 Atl. 709.

Massachusetts: Hill v. Hooper, 1 Gray, 131.

Michigan: Cadman v. Markle, 76 Mich. 448.

Nevada: Lapham v. Osborne, 20 Nev. 168, 18 Pac. 881.

New York: Hartwell v. Young, 67 Hun, 472, 22 N. Y. Supp. 486.

See on this subject in general *ante,* § 651.

[102] *Florida:* Mills v. Joiner, 20 Fla. 479.

plaintiff and nothing is left to be done but payment by the defendant, it is sometimes held that the amount of recovery for value of the services would be limited by the price fixed in the contract.[103] In other jurisdictions, however, it is held that, the contract being entirely void, the contract price is immaterial and the plaintiff may recover the actual value of his services on a *quantum meruit*.[104] In a few cases it has been held or intimated that if the plaintiff in breach of the terms of the oral agreement left the employment before the performance was completed, he would be entitled to no compensation;[105] but this view is questionable, since the contract is in no respect binding on the plaintiff.

§ 673c. Services rendered under a void agreement.

Where the servant serves under a contract or other obliga-

[Illinois:] William Butcher Steel Works *v.* Atkinson, 68 Ill. 421, 18 Am. Rep. 560; Schanzenbach *v.* Brough, 58 Ill. App. 526.

Vermont: Stone *v.* Stone, 43 Vt. 180.

In *Minnesota* a different doctrine prevails. It is held that even if the plaintiff was wrongfully discharged he could recover at no greater than the contract rate, such being settled doctrine of the court although in the actual case the doctrine was stated by the court to be unsatisfactory. Spinney *v.* Hill, 81 Minn. 316, 84 N. W. 116.

[103] *Connecticut:* Clark *v.* Terry, 25 Conn. 395.

Illinois: Swanzey *v.* Moore, 22 Ill. 63, 74 Am. Dec. 134 (*semble*).

Minnesota: Lally *v.* Crookston Lumber Co., 85 Minn. 257, 88 N. W. 846.

New York: King *v.* Brown, 2 Hill, 485; Nones *v.* Homer, 2 Hilt. 116; Porter *v.* Dunn, 61 Hun, 310, 16 N. Y. Supp. 77. But see Gall *v.* Gall, 27 App. Div. 173, 50 N. Y. Supp. 563.

In La Du-King Manuf. Co. *v.* La Du, 36 Minn. 473, 31 N. W. 938, the plaintiff was treasurer of a corporation for five years, to be paid by a share of the profits. The contract was void by the statute of frauds. He served for three years, and then left on account of illness. It was held that he could recover, but it must be on the terms of the contract so far as that had been carried out by both parties. As no profits had been realized, he could recover no compensation as yet, but it was intimated that if profits were afterwards realized during the five years he might sue for them.

[104] *Indiana:* Wallace *v.* Long, 105 Ind. 522, 55 Am. Rep. 222, 5 N. E. 666.

Kentucky: Thomas *v.* McManus, 23 Ky. L. Rep. 837, 64 S. W. 446.

Massachusetts: Seemore *v.* Bennet, 14 Mass. 266, 7 Am. Dec. 213.

Michigan: Leslie *v.* Smith, 32 Mich. 64.

New Hampshire: Emery *v.* Smith, 46 N. H. 151.

Wisconsin: Koch *v.* Williams, 82 Wis. 186, 52 N. W. 257.

[105] *Illinois:* Swanzey *v.* Moore, 22 Ill. 63, 74 Am. Dec. 134.

Minnesota: Kriger *v.* Leppel, 42 Minn. 6, 43 N. W. 484.

See Clark *v.* Terry, 25 Conn. 395.

tion which proves to be void, he is entitled to recover the value of his service on a *quantum meruit* ; [106] and so where the performance of the service by the servant is obtained by fraud of the master, who by his fraud induces the servant to serve gratuitously, the servant on discovering the fraud is entitled to recover the value of his services.[107] Where, however, the contract is not merely void but is illegal as regards both parties, there can be no recovery.[108]

§ 673d. Services voluntarily rendered.

Where a person voluntarily renders services for another without request and with no expectation of being paid, he cannot recover compensation for the value of his services.[109] A common example occurs when a child after he becomes of age, or a stranger voluntarily received into a family, renders ordinary domestic services for the family. In the absence of some special circumstances showing that such services were rendered with the expectation of compensation on both sides, these are regarded as voluntary services not entitled to compensation.[110]

[106] *New York:* Lewis v. Trickey, 20 Barb. 387 (service under void contract of apprenticeship).

Tennessee: Guadelupo y Calvo Mining Co. v. Beatty, 3 Tenn. Cas. 271 (service under contract with corporation not binding on the corporation).

Wisconsin: Martin v. Estate of Martin, 108 Wis. 284, 84 N. W. 439, 81 Am. St. Rep. 895 (service as adopted child; the adoption proving invalid).

[107] *Mississippi:* Williams v. Luckett, 77 Miss. 394, 26 So. 967 (woman fraudulently induced to enter into invalid marriage).

Missouri: Hickam v. Hickam, 46 Mo. App. 496 (slave kept at service in ignorance of emancipation).

[108] *Massachusetts:* Stewart v. Thayer, 170 Mass. 560, 49 N. E. 1020 (service on Sunday).

Missouri: Barney v. Spangler, 131 Mo. App. 58, 109 S. W. 855 (service on Sunday).

Nebraska: Richardson v. Scott's Bluff County, 59 Neb. 400, 81 N. W. 309, 80 Am. St. Rep. 682 (lobbying).

[109] *Missouri:* Lynch v. Bogy, 19 Mo. 170; Kerr v. Cusenbary, 60 Mo. App. 558.

New York: Bartholomew v. Jackson, 20 Johns. 28, 11 Am. Dec. 237.

South Carolina: Hort v. Norton, 1 McCord, 22.

[110] In the case of a child it is very clear that if after coming of age he continues to perform the same services he had performed as minor, there is no claim for compensation in the absence of affirmative evidence of an agreement to that effect:

Iowa: Scully v. Scully, 28 Iowa, 548.

New York: Ulrich v. Ulrich, 60 N. Y. Super. Ct. 237, 17 N. Y. Supp. 721.

And where a young person is received into the house of a relative and treated as a child he can recover no compensation.

Another example of services which are presumably gratuitous is afforded by the case of extra work done outside the regular or statutory hours by a workman. Where a workman is employed on a day's work which is limited to a certain number of hours, and without an express agreement for compensation he performs service in excess of the proper number of hours, it is held that he is entitled to no extra compensation.[111] And if a workman is entitled to a vacation with full pay and he does not take a vacation, he is not entitled to extra compensation.[112] Another example is the case of a director of a corporation who performs special services for the corporation. So long as there is no special vote passed before his performance of the services by virtue of which he is to be compensated and the services are not of such a nature as would ordinarily be outside the scope

Missouri: Sloan v. Dale, 90 Mo. App. 87 (niece).

North Carolina: Dodson v. McAdams, 96 N. C. 149, 60 Am. Rep. 408 (grandchild).

Pennsylvania: Defrance v. Austin, 9 Pa. 309 (nephew).

The same thing is true where a minor resides in the house of a stranger as a member of his family and is treated in all respects as a child.

Indiana: Waechter v. Walters, 41 Ind. App. 408, 84 N. E. 22.

Iowa: Smith v. Johnson, 45 Iowa, 308.

Pennsylvania: Zimmerman v. Zimmerman, 129 Pa. 229, 18 Atl. 129, 15 Am. St. Rep. 720.

Rhode Island: Newell v. Lawton, 20 R. I. 307, 38 Atl. 946.

If, on the other hand, an adult stranger is serving in a family as a member of the household, he is presumptively entitled to compensation for it. Gill v. Staylor, 93 Md. 453, 49 Atl. 650.

And in one case where a person was taken as a child into the family of a stranger and remained until she was twenty-four years old, performing domestic services, and was then turned off, it was held that presumptively

these services were entitled to compensation. Coleman v. Simpson, 2 Dana (Ky.), 166.

[111] *United States:* U. S. v. Martin, 94 U. S. 400, 24 L. ed. 128.

Connecticut: Luske v. Hotchkiss, 37 Conn. 219, 9 Am. Rep. 314.

Illinois: Christian County v. Merrigan, 191 Ill. 484, 61 N. E. 479; Sanitary Dist. v. Burke, 88 Ill. App. 196.

Indiana: Grisell v. Noel Brothers Flour Feed Co., 9 Ind. App. 251, 36 N. E. 452.

Michigan: Schurr v. Savigny, 85 Mich. 144, 48 N. W. 547.

Missouri: Barney v. Spangler, 131 Mo. App. 58, 109 S. W. 855.

New Hampshire: Brooks v. Cotton, 48 N. H. 50.

New York: McCarthy v. Mayor, 96 N. Y. 1, 48 Am. Rep. 601; McGraw v. Gloversville, 32 App. Div. 176, 52 N. Y. Supp. 916.

An express statute may of course make it the duty of a municipal corporation to pay at a certain rate for an eight hour day and in that case the town must pay extra for a longer time of service. Gilligan v. Waterford, 91 Hun, 21, 36 N. Y. Supp. 88.

[112] Schurr v. Savigny, 85 Mich. 144, 48 N. W. 547.

of a director's activities, they are presumably voluntary services and he is entitled to no compensation for them.[113] On this principle where a slave went with his master into free territory and there continued to serve his master in the free territory it was held that he was entitled to no compensation since the services were rendered without the expectation of compensation.[114]

§ 673e. Services outside the scope of employment.

Where a person employed for a certain service renders services entirely outside the scope of his employment, which are received by the employer, these are presumptively rendered for compensation and the person who renders them is entitled to recover extra compensation.[115] So where a director of a corporation performs extraordinary services entirely outside the scope of his duties as director, he may recover compensation for such extraordinary services; [116] as, for instance, where a director performs services as attorney or land commissioner.[117]

[113] *Illinois:* Brown v. De Young, 167 Ill. 549, 47 N. E. 863; Jones v. Vance Shoe Co., 92 Ill. App. 158.
Massachusetts: Pew v. First Nat. Bank, 130 Mass. 391.
Missouri: Besch v. Western C. M. Co., 36 Mo. App. 333; Pfeiffer v. Lansberg Brake Co., 44 Mo. App. 59; Rose v. Eclipse Carbonating Co., 60 Mo. App. 28; Remmers v. Seky, 70 Mo. App. 364; Beach v. Stouffer, 84 Mo. App. 395.
Pennsylvania: Loan Assoc. v. Stonemetz, 29 Pa. 534; Martindale v. Wilson-Cass Co., 134 Pa. 348, 19 Atl. 680, 19 Am. St. Rep. 706.
[114] Alfred v. Fitzjames, 3 Esp. 3.
[115] *Indiana:* Martin v. Prince, 12 Ind. App. 213, 40 N. E. 33 (plaintiff employed as farm hand at $1.00 per day; at request of defendant he rendered services as nurse at night. *Held*, not necessary to assume that they were rendered as part of the original service).
New York: Merzbach v. Mayor, 10 Misc. 131, 30 N. Y. Supp. 908.
In Ranck v. Albright, 36 Pa. 367, it

was held that the fact that the employer increased the size of his family by having hired men live with him did not entitle a domestic servant to recover for extra work.
[116] *United States:* National L. & I. Co v. Rockland Co., 36 C. C. A. 370, 94 Fed. 335.
California: Bassett v. Fairchild, 132 Cal. 637, 64 Pac. 1082, 52 L. R. A. 611.
Colorado: Brown v. Republican Mountain Silver Mines, 17 Colo. 421, 30 Pac. 66, 16 L. R. A. 426.
Connecticut: New York v. N. H. R. R. v. Ketchum, 27 Conn. 181.
Illinois: Rockford, R. I. & S. L. R. R. v. Sage, 65 Ill. 328, 16 Am. Rep. 587.
Maryland: Santa Clara Mining Assoc. v. Meredith, 49 Md. 389, 33 Am. Rep. 247.
New Jersey: Evans v. Trenton, 21 N. J. L. (11 Zab.) 769.
Vermont: Henry v. Rutland & B. R. R., 27 Vt. 455.
[117] *Minnesota:* Rogers v. Hastings & D. Ry., 22 Minn. 25.

And so where one employed as housekeeper renders services as nurse she is entitled to compensation.[118] So where a person holding government office is detailed to perform the duties of an entirely different office in addition to his own, he is entitled to compensation for the extra services.[119] And when the Mayor of a city was employed as attorney in matters in which the city was interested, he was entitled to extra compensation.[120]

§ 673f. Recovery by party in default.

In case a servant who is employed on an entire contract to complete a certain piece of work or to serve during a certain time, voluntarily leaves the service before completing the work or serving during the entire term, he can recover nothing for that portion of the work he has done or the time he has served.[121]

Missouri: Taussig v. St. Louis & K. R. R., 166 Mo. 28, 65 S. W. 969, 89 Am. St. Rep. 674.

[118] *Kansas:* Houghton v. Kittleman, 7 Kan. App. 207, 52 Pac. 898.

See, however, *Pennsylvania:* Rosencrance v. Johnson, 191 Pa. 520, 43 Atl. 360.

[119] United States v. Brindle, 110 U. S. 688, 4 Sup. Ct. 180, 28 L. ed. 286; Converse v. U. S., 21 How. 463, 16 L. ed. 192.

[120] Mayor v. Muzzy, 33 Mich. 61, 20 Am. Rep. 670.

[121] Plaintiff left before the expiration of the term of service:

Alabama: Whitley v. Murray, 34 Ala. 155.

Colorado: Cody v. Raynaud, 1 Colo. 272.

District of Columbia: Lewis v. Esther, 2 Cranch C. C. 423.

Hawaii: Hanuu v. Williams, 2 Hawaii, 233.

Illinois: Dunn v. Moore, 16 Ill. 151; Angle v. Hanna, 22 Ill. 429, 74 Am. Dec. 161; Hansell v. Erickson, 28 Ill. 257.

Indiana: DeCamp v. Stevens, 4 Blackf. 24.

Massachusetts: Stark v. Parker, 2 Pick. 267, 13 Am. Dec. 425; Thayer v. Wadsworth, 19 Pick. 349; Davis v. Maxwell, 12 Met. 286.

Missouri: Aaron v. Moore, 34 Mo. 79.

New Jersey: Ewing v. Ingram, 24 N. J. L. (4 Zab.) 520.

New York: Reab v. Moor, 19 Johns. 337; Marsh v. Rulesson, 1 Wend. 514; Lantry v. Parks, 8 Cow. 63.

Ohio: Snyder v. Walker, 13 Ohio C. Ct. 93.

Tennessee: Hughes v. Cannon, 1 Sneed, 622; Halloway v. Lacy, 4 Humph. 468; Abernathy v. Black, 2 Cold. 314, 88 Am. Dec. 598.

Vermont: St. Albans Steam Boat Co. v. Wilkins, 8 Vt. 54; Brown v. Kimball, 12 Vt. 617.

Wisconsin: Jennings v. Lyons, 39 Wis. 553, 20 Am. Rep. 57; Walsh v. Fisher, 102 Wis. 172, 78 N. W. 437, 72 Am. St. Rep. 865.

Plaintiff ceased to work before doing all the work:

Missouri: Hinson v. Hampton, 32 Mo. 408 (to serve during voyage; left before end of voyage).

England: Bates v. Hudson, 6 Dowl. & R. 3 (to cure all sheep of a flock; succeeded in curing part only).

So in a strong case where a seaman was employed upon a certain voyage and was to assist in discharging the cargo at the end of the voyage and he voluntarily left at the end of the voyage without excuse before the cargo was discharged, it was held that he was entitled to no wages for the voyage.[122] If, however, wages are payable in instalments the servant may recover the instalments which were due at the time of leaving;[123] and so where the parties had entered into a settlement and had agreed upon the amount due and the employer had given a note for the amount and the servant afterwards left without excuse, it was held that he would not forfeit the amount due him on the note.[124]

If the master waives the breach by agreeing to pay wages due, notwithstanding the voluntary breach of the plaintiff, the servant may recover, and it is said that slight evidence of such an agreement will be accepted by the court as such a waiver.[125]

In jurisdictions following the case of Britton v. Turner,[126] the servant who leaves prematurely is entitled to recover the amount of the benefit he has conferred upon his employer which will be measured by the value of his work less the damage caused by his breach of the contract.[127]

§ 674. Remedy of master for improper service.

Improper service, contrary to the terms of the employment,

[122] Webb v. Duckingfield, 13 Johns. (N. Y.) 390, 7 Am. Dec. 388.

[123] Vermont: Winn v. Southgate, 17 Vt. 355, 98 Am. Dec. 564 (could keep payments already made).

England: Taylor v. Laird, 1 H. & N. 266 (could recover payments due).

But see McMillan v. Vanderlip, 12 Johns. (N. Y.) 165, 7 Am. Dec. 299 (agreement to serve for a certain time to be paid by the piece; plaintiff left before end of time. Held, he could not recover for what he had done according to the price set by the piece. The court pointed out that labor might be worth a good deal more at one time in the year than in another).

[124] Thorpe v. White, 13 Johns. (N. Y.) 53.

[125] California: Hogan v. Titlow, 14 Cal. 255.

Vermont: Cahill v. Patterson, 30 Vt. 592.

[126] Ante, § 660.

[127] Iowa: Pixler v. Nichols, 8 Iowa, 106, 74 Am. Dec. 298; Tait v. Sherman, 10 Iowa, 60; Powers v. Wilson, 47 Iowa, 666.

Louisiana: Taylor v. Peterson, 9 La. Ann. 251; Kessee v. Mayfield, 14 La. Ann. 90.

Tennessee: Congregation of Children of Israel v. Peres, 2 Cold. 620.

Texas: Riggs v. Horde, 25 Tex. Supp. 456, 78 Am. Dec. 584.

Wisconsin: Hildebrand v. American Fine Art Co., 109 Wis. 171, 180, 85 N. W. 268.

may be cause for dismissal and if the master discharges the servant for good cause the servant can recover nothing for his services.[128] If, however, wages were payable by instalments the servant forfeits only such wages as have accrued since the last pay day.[129] In jurisdictions following the doctrine of Britton v. Turner,[130] however, the servant who is discharged for cause may recover on a *quantum meruit* the value of his services,[131] and indeed this is allowed in some jurisdictions which do not allow a recovery of wages in case the servant voluntarily leaves the employment, the ground for distinction as given being that in the latter case it is the servant's fault and no injustice is done him in requiring him to forfeit his wages.[132]

If the master chooses not to discharge the servant but to continue him in the employment in spite of his breach of agreement, damages for improper service may be recouped against the servant's claim for wages.[133]

Breach of obligation on the part of the servant may also be

[128] *California:* Hartman v. Rogers, 69 Cal. 643, 11 Pac. 581.

Georgia: Henderson v. Stiles, 14 Ga. 135.

Pennsylvania: Libhart v. Wood, 1 W. & S. 265, 37 Am. Dec. 461; Williams v. Eldridge, 9 Kulp, 566.

England: Spain v. Arnot, 2 Stark. 256; Atkin v. Acton, 4 C. & P. 208; Turner v. Robinson, 6 C. & P. 15

[129] *New Jersey:* Beach v. Mullin, 34 N. J. L. 343.

Ohio: Voelckel v. Banner Brewing Co., 9 Ohio C. Ct. 318.

England: Ridgway v. Hungerford Market Co., 3 A. & E. 171.

[130] *Ante,* §§ 658–662.

[131] *Indiana:* Fulton v. Heffelfinger, 23 Ind. App. 104, 54 N. E. 1079.

Maryland: Mallonee v. Duff, 72 Md. 283, 19 Atl. 708.

Mississippi: Hariston v. Sale, 6 Sm. & M. 634; Robinson v. Sanders, 24 Miss. 391.

Missouri: Lamb v. Brolaski, 38 Mo. 51.

So where the employer accepts the performance as the best he can get.

Ewing v. Janson, 57 Ark. 237, 21 S. W. 430.

[132] *Maine:* Lawrence v. Gullifer, 38 Me. 532.

Tennessee: Massey v. Taylor, 5 Cold. 447, 98 Am. Dec. 429.

[133] *California:* Kalkman v. Baylis, 17 Cal. 291; E. E. Thomas Fruit Co. v. Start, 107 Cal. 206, 40 Pac. 336 (recoupment though master sold the product of the labor without deduction for the defect).

Connecticut: Bixby v. Parsons, 49 Conn. 483, 44 Am. Rep. 246 (seduction of employer's daughter).

Georgia: Lee v. Clements, 48 Ga. 128.

Illinois: Ward v. Salisbury, 12 Ill. 369.

Michigan: Alberts v. Stearns, 50 Mich. 349, 5 N. W. 505.

Mississippi: Dunlap v. Hand, 26 Miss. 460; Harper v. Ray, 27 Miss. 622 (burden on employer to prove amount).

New York: Still v. Hall, 20 Wend. 51; Allaire Works v. Guion, 10 Barb. 55 (malicious destruction of property).

North Carolina: Branch v. Chappell, 119 N. C. 81, 25 S. E. 783 (by plain-

an independent cause for the recovery of damages by the master. Thus, a servant may be sued by his master for improperly performing his work,[134] or for failure to complete the term of service agreed upon in the contract.[135] In the latter case the measure of damages is the difference between the contract price and the amount which the employer has to pay to procure the work done elsewhere.[136] So where the servant's breach consisted in a temporary unexcused absence from service instead of service which was bad in quality, the master may bring suit and recover damages.[137]

§ 675. Consequential damages.

Where the mate of a vessel was unlawfully wounded by the

tiff's negligence fires were set and defendant's timber destroyed).

Vermont: Morris v. Redfield, 23 Vt. 295.

In Duncan v. Blundell, 3 Stark. 6, it was held that one who undertakes work and because of lack of skill fails to do it properly cannot recover compensation.

Damages so recouped must be sufficiently certain; no speculative damages may be recovered. Weymer v. Belle Plaine Broom Co. (Ia.), 132 N. W. 27.

[134] *United States:* Forman v. Miller, 5 McLean, 218 (measure of damages, difference in value of the product as it should have been and as it was).

Massachusetts: Corey v. Eastman, 166 Mass. 279, 44 N. E. 217, 55 Am. St. Rep. 401.

[135] *Iowa:* Riech v. Bolch, 68 Iowa, 526, 27 N. W. 507.

Kentucky: Fuqua v. Massie, 95 Ky. 387, 393, 25 S. W. 875.

Mississipii: Pritchard v. Martin, 27 Miss. 305.

[136] *Colorado:* Cannon Coal Co. v. Taggart, 1 Colo. App. 60, 27 Pac. 238.

New York: Peters v. Whitney, 23 Barb. 24.

Where the place of the servant is not or cannot be supplied, the value of his services to the master may be re-

covered. Myers R. S. Co. v. Griswold, 77 Neb. 487, 109 N. W. 736.

In Riech v. Bolch, 68 Iowa, 526, 27 N. W. 507, plaintiff, employed by defendant as a farm hand, left in the middle of the haying season. *Held,* the loss of the hay by reason of his leaving was too remote to be charged to him. *Quære* as to the correctness of this decision.

[137] Ayling v. London & India Docks Committee, 9 T. L. Rep. 409 (plaintiff left the employment without notice on a strike. The strike having been settled he came back to work. *Held,* that the employer might obtain damages for the wrongful interruption in the service); Bowes v. Press, 10 T. L. Rep. 55 (defendant, employed as a miner, refused to go down into the mine and work with a non-union man, and this refusal continued for several days. *Held,* a breach of the contract for which the employer could get damages).

In Prentiss v. Ledyard, 28 Wis. 131, the plaintiff was to receive a certain amount for services if he continued temperate. He occasionally became drunk, but was retained in the service. *Held,* if he was retained in the service that was a waiver of the condition and he could recover.

master in a foreign port during a voyage for which he had shipped, and was in consequence taken on shore, detained there, and subjected to medical treatment, it was held in an action against the owners for the breach of the shipping articles that his compensation for lost time was not restricted to the period of the contract. He was entitled to damages equivalent to the injury, which included wages for such reasonable time as was lost by his detention, and till he could return home, besides the medical and other expenses necessitated by the wound.[138]

In an English case, the plaintiff shipped as a seaman at a certain monthly rate of wages for a commercial voyage, not to exceed twelve months, to Rio and elsewhere, and to end by his being brought back to some port in the United Kingdom, or on the continent of Europe between Elbe and Brest. On arriving at Rio the defendant proceeded to employ his vessel as a ship of war in the service of the Peruvian government. The plaintiff thereupon refused to proceed any further with the voyage, on the ground that it was illegal, and exposed him to risks not contemplated by his contract, left the ship and went on shore. There he was arrested as a Peruvian deserter and committed to prison, where he remained some days. On coming out he found that the ship had sailed, taking his clothes and other articles which he had left on board. In an action for damages for the breach of contract the jury found a verdict for the plaintiff, and assessed the damages for the breach under three heads, namely: First, £12 10s. for loss of wages under the contract; second, £20 for loss of clothes; third, £30 for general damages for the imprisonment and otherwise by reason of the defendant's breach. It was held that the damages under the second and third heads were too remote.[139]

It was held in Missouri, in a case not very fully reported,[140] where a hand employed on board a steamboat at a stipulated

[138] Croucher v. Oakman, 3 All. (Mass.) 185.

[139] Burton v. Pinkerton, L. R. 2 Ex. 340. But see Hunt v. Colburn, 1 Sprague, 215. In that case, where the facts were similar, it was held that the plaintiff might recover for the loss of clothes carried off in the vessel; and being detained by sickness in the foreign port, he was also allowed wages during the time of his detention and passage-money home.

[140] Cunningham v. Steamboat Low Water, 28 Mo. 338.

rate of wages for a trip, was discharged and put off the boat without cause before the end of the trip, and the boat, owing to an accident to her machinery, was detained for some days beyond the regular period of her trips, that he could recover wages only for the time usually consumed in a trip, and not for that of the additional detention. This decision seems to admit of question, and not to be fully borne out by the case of the Elizabeth,[141] which is referred to as authority for it. That case decided that when a ship bound to St. Petersburg from Portsmouth and back had met with an accident, the repairs necessitated by which detained her in a northern port where she would have been blocked up by the ice and detained all the winter, the master had a right to discharge his crew, on condition of paying their passage back to England and wages up to the time of such return. This was a reasonable and justifiable course, and furnished the crew with a full and fair indemnity, which in the other case the boat hand failed to receive. To bring the latter case within the authority or analogy of the former, the hand should have been brought or sent back to the place where he was shipped, or indemnified for the expense of getting there, and have received wages for the time required for his return.

In an action by a domestic servant for wages, evidence was given tending to show that the plaintiff had been dismissed from the defendant's residence in the country between eleven and twelve o'clock at night, and was left all night in the space between the hall door and the outer gate. The plaint contained a count for wrongful dismissal, with an averment of special damages. The jury, under this count, found for the plaintiff, with £20 damages, ten shillings of which only were for wages due, and £19 10s. were for the injury suffered by the plaintiff from the circumstances of the dismissal. The defendant having moved to reduce the verdict to ten shillings, the court granted the motion, holding that under the pleadings the plaintiff was entitled only to the wages due her by the contract of hire, and "could not recover as special damage in respect of any matters save such as would not have happened to her had the contract been fulfilled by payment of those moneys at the

[141] 2 Dods. Adm. 403.

time of her dismissal." Mr. Baron Deasy, however, inquired of the plaintiff's counsel whether they could not frame a count upon the implied duty of a master to his servant that would meet such a case.[142] And in a Texas case such damages were allowed in an action for breach of contract. Plaintiff was employed to work for defendant at a distant point. He went there and was then refused employment and was left without food or lodging and suffered from hunger and cold. It was held that the plaintiff was entitled to secure as direct damages the wages he would have earned under the contract, provided he showed that he used due diligence in obtaining other employment and failed to do so, or if he did obtain other employment, deducting the amount thereby realized; and that he could also recover damages for his sufferings from cold and hunger.[143] Where a servant is wrongfully discharged, he may recover the expense of obtaining a new employment.[144]

No damages can be recovered because of loss of earnings or gratuities from others which plaintiff would have received if he had continued in the employment,[145] or because the fact of his having been dismissed made it more difficult to obtain other employment.[146]

No special damages can be recovered unless they are claimed in the declaration.[147]

§ 675a. The English workmen's compensation act.

Under the Workmen's Compensation Act (6 Edw. 7, c. 58), which went into effect July 1, 1907, an employer is made to bear a large part of the burden of unavoidable accidents or of diseases peculiar to the employment, resulting in the temporary or permanent incapacity of his workmen or in death, and even of injuries founded on their serious and wilful misconduct, if causing death. Elaborate provision is made for the determination by judges, arbitrators, committees of employers and employed, and the parties themselves of questions of law and fact arising under the act.

---

[142] Breen v. Cooper, Ir. R. 3 C. L. 621.

[143] Gulf, C. & S. F. Ry. v. Jackson, 29 Tex. Civ. App. 342, 69 S. W. 89.

[144] Ante, § 667.

[145] Tucker v. Horn, 31 Ky. L. Rep. 805, 103 S. W. 717.

[146] Addis v. Gramophone Co. [1909], A. C. 488.

[147] Lufkin v. Patterson, 38 Me. 282.

The measure of recovery for incapacity and death are fixed with reference to the earnings of the workman affected and the extent of others' dependence upon him. Where incapacity for work results from the injury, the employer is called upon to make weekly payments not exceeding in amount 50% of the workman's average weekly earnings during the twelve months preceding the injury. No weekly payment is to equal more than £1. If the workman at the time of the injury be less than 21 years of age and his weekly earnings be less than 20 shillings, recovery may be had in a sum equal to 100% of their amount, with the proviso that no payment for injuries to a minor shall equal more than 10 shillings weekly. In estimating the amount of weekly payments to which a workman is entitled, suitable deduction is made on account of allowances and benefits received from the employer during the period of incapacity apart from the Act and for earnings, if the incapacity be partial only and there is provision for the redemption of long-continued weekly payments by the discharge of the whole obligation in one lump sum.

If the injury be fatal and the workman leave persons wholly dependent upon himself, his employer is obligated to pay a sum equal to the workman's earnings during the preceding three years, but no more than £300, or £150 if such sum be less than £150. Where the deceased leaves persons partially dependent upon himself, the employer is called upon to pay a sum reasonable and proportionate to the loss sustained by them, such sum to be in no case greater than what would have been the extent of his liability in case the beneficiaries had been wholly dependent. If a workman die without dependents, the employer is made liable to pay the reasonable expenses of medical attendance and burial, in a sum not exceeding £10.

Weekly earnings and earnings, within the contemplation of the act, may have, as the basis for the estimation of the amounts due in weekly payments or of a lump sum at death, a wider meaning than wages merely; for example, the terms have been held to include the fees of a waiter,[148] and a seaman's board and lodging.[149] A complete discussion of the elaborate processes of

[148] Renn v. Spiers [1908], 1 K. B. 766.

[149] Rosenquist v. Bowring, 24 T. L. R. 504.

estimating earnings in cases where the employee has been within the periods named in the act, only casually employed or employed in different grades of work, or employed by several masters, will be found in the important decision of Perry v. Wright,[150] and of the several cases decided with it.

Where the defendant was ordered to make weekly payments to the workman, these payments will be continued, even though the physical injury is entirely cured if mental and nervous suffering continues.[151]

[150] [1908] 1 K. B. 441. The consideration of this Act, and of the similar American acts, as well as of the Employers' Liability Acts (e. g., the English Act of 1880; 43 and 44 Vict., c. 42) fall entirely outside the scope of the present edition of this work.

[151] Eaves v. Blaenclydach Colliery Co., [1909] 2 K. B. 73.

CHAPTER XXXII

ACTIONS UPON BONDS

A.—Bonds in General

§ 675b. Debt on bond.
675c. Damages less than the penalty.
675d. Assignment of breaches.
675e. Only the plaintiff's actual loss now recoverable.
676. Penalty and liquidated damages.
677. Damages in excess of penalty.
678. Interest on penalty.

§ 679. Bonds containing express covenants.
679a. Compensation for breach of condition.
679b. Contractors' bonds.
680. Statutory bonds and undertakings.
681. Reduction of damages.
681a. Actions against sureties.

B.—Bonds Given in Judicial Proceedings

§ 682. Attachment bonds.
682a. Counsel fees and expenses in procuring dissolution of attachment.
683. Exemplary damages.
684. Forthcoming bonds—Bonds to dissolve attachment — Receiptors.
684a. Bonds to indemnify attaching sheriff.
685. Injunction bonds — General principles.
685a. Injunctions preventing use of land.
685b. Injunctions against taking a profit from land.
685c. Other injunctions concerning land.
685d. Injunctions against doing work.
685e. Injunctions against carrying on business.
685f. Injunctions against constructing a building or other work.
685g. Injunctions against collecting a judgment or other debt.
685h. Injunctions against a sale.
685i. Injunctions against other acts.

§ 685j. Counsel fees incurred on account of the injunction.
685k. Counsel fees in the entire litigation.
685l. Counsel fees not chargeable to defendant.
685m. Amount of counsel fees recoverable — Exorbitant charges.
685n. Other expenses of litigation.
685o. Bonds for vacating injunction.
686. Bail bonds.
686a. Bonds for arrest.
687. Arbitration bonds.
688. Appeal and supersedeas bonds.
688a. Recovery of damages from the appeal.
689. Replevin bonds.
689a. Measure of recovery.
690. Value of property when to be estimated.
691. Destruction of property before payment.
691a. Reduction of damages.
691b. Limitations of plaintiff's title.
691c. Detinue bonds.
691d. Other judicial bonds.

1378

C.—Official Bonds

§ 692. Official bonds in general.

692a. Acts outside official duty.

692b. Liability for acts before or after regular term of bond.

692c. Liability on cumulative bonds.

692d. Successive bonds to cover successive terms of office.

692e. Default in payment of money at end of last term.

692f. Bonds of financial officers.

692g. Bonds of judicial officers.

§ 692h. Bonds of clerks of courts.

692i. Bonds of sheriffs and constables.

692j. Bonds of executors and administrators.

692k. Bonds of guardians.

693. Bonds of county and town officers.

694. Bonds of officers of corporations.

A.—Bonds in General

§ 675b. Debt on bond.

*Of all forms of debt, that of debt on bond was the most frequent. In the early periods of our jurisprudence debt was the common action for goods sold and delivered, and for work and labor done; but it was subsequently to a great extent superseded by the proceeding in assumpsit.[1]

It is true, as a general rule, that in the action of debt, which was brought for the recovery of a sum certain, no damages could be claimed on account of the debt itself, this being recoverable *in numero;* but damages were given on account of the detention of the debt. In an action of debt on bond, therefore, only nominal damages were assessed, nor was it in general necessary to have them assessed to the amount even of what was due for interest, because, as under the verdict, the plaintiff was entitled to the whole penalty; this, which is double the sum mentioned in the condition, was usually sufficient to cover what was due for interest.

The form of the *obligation* or *bond* of the English law is technical and peculiar. The obligor *binds*, or *obliges* himself to pay a certain sum of money, at a certain time, to the obligee; This, if under seal, would be a single bond, or *simplex obligatio,* and would only differ from a note, in being under seal, and not negotiable. But in the bond we find a clause appended, declaring that the previous obligation shall be void on the payment of some lesser sum of money, or the performance of some particular act. The latter part, or *condition,* of the bond, is that which

---

[1] Rudder *v.* Price, 1 H. Bl. 547.

discloses the real nature of the contract, and contains its essence; the former part is the *penalty*.[2] *Penal obligations* are well known to other systems of law besides our own;[3] but the precise form of contract by which an absolute obligation is at first declared, and this converted into a mere penalty by the addition of a subsequent condition, is entirely peculiar to the English law.

From this form of obligation or contract, various results, flowing from the technical rules of the common law, were deduced by the founders of our jurisprudence. If the condition was not strictly complied with, as in regard to the payment of money on a day certain, the moment the day was passed the penalty became the debt, and was at law recoverable; and neither payment nor tender after the day would avail, because a condition once broken was gone forever. If the condition were to do anything other than pay money, and were not fulfilled, the penalty again became the debt, and was recoverable without any reference whatever to the actual damages incurred. Hence many difficulties arose. Lord Kaimes says,[4] that the bond was introduced originally to evade the common law of England, which prohibited the taking interest for money. Whatever reason led to its introduction, certain it is, that its peculiar form has occasioned infinite doubt and contradiction.**

§ 675c. Damages less than the penalty.

* The action of debt, as has been said, was the usual remedy provided by the common law for the recovery of a sum certain. And in an action of debt for condition broken, the amount of the plaintiff's recovery was originally, as has also been said, the penalty; nor could the action be relieved against, either by payment or tender: no defense would avail but a release under seal. And this severe rule of the common law was only mitigated by the practice of the courts of chancery, which interposed, and would not allow a man to take more than in conscience he ought.[5] It became early settled in equity, that the

---

[2] Black. Com. ii, ch. 20, p. 340.

[3] Pothier, Traité des Obligations, part ii, ch. v, des Obligations Penales.

[4] Prin. of Equity, book iii, ch. ii, p. 279.

[5] Black. Com., book ii, ch. 20, p. 341.

condition of the bond was the agreement of the parties, and as such the obligor was relieved from the penalty.[6] Lord Somers said,[7] "that where the party might be put in as good a plight as where the condition itself was literally performed, there the Court of Chancery would relieve, though the letter of it were not strictly performed, as payment of money, etc. But where the condition was collateral and in recompense, and no value could be put on the breach of it, then no relief could be had for the breach of it." This practice was followed by the common-law tribunals, which ordered the proceedings to be stayed upon bringing into court the principal debt, interest, and costs.[8] Finally, this discretionary power was confirmed by a statutory regulation, which provided that in actions on bonds with penalties, the defendant might bring in the principal debt, interest, and costs, and be discharged.[9]

This legislation was followed in this country. In New York,[10] it was declared that, in actions on penalty bonds, the plaintiff might plead payment of the debt made before suit brought, though not according to the condition; and that after suit brought, the defendant might bring debt, principal, and costs into court, and that thereupon the action should be discontinued. Speaking of the English original of this statute, Lord Mansfield said:[11]

"That it was made to remove the absurdity which Sir Thomas More unsuccessfully attempted to persuade the judges to remedy in the reign of Hen. VII.; for he summoned them to a conference concerning the granting relief at law, after the

For cases of this description in chancery see Hale v. Thomas, 1 Vern. 349, and Stewart v. Rumball, 2 Vern. 509; also, Duvall v. Price, Show. Par. Cas. 15; Bond and Penalty, Abr. Eq. 91, 92.

[6] Acton v. Pierce, 2 Vern. 480; Cannel v. Buckle, 2 P. Wms. 243; Watkyns v. Watkyns, 2 Atk. 96; Bishop v. Church, 3 Atk. 691; Parks v. Wilson, 10 Mod. 515; Hobson v. Trevor, 2 P. Wms. 191; Chilliner v. Chilliner, 2 Ves. 528; Collins v. Collins, 2 Burr. 820. See Pothier, by Evans, on Penal Obligations, Appendix, and Fonblanque's Treatise on Equity.

[7] Prec. in Ch. 487.
[8] Gregg's Case, 2 Salk. 596; Anon., 6 Mod. 11; Butler v. Rolfe, Ibid. 25; Anon. Ibid. 29; Burridge v. Fortescue, Ibid. 60, and Ireland's Case, Ibid. 101. In Burridge v. Fortescue, the court said: "It is an equitable motion, to be relieved against the penalty."
[9] 4 and 5 Anne, ch. 16, §§ 12 and 13.
[10] Rev. Stat., vol. ii, p. 353, §§ 12 and 13, superseded by the provisions of the Code Civ. Proc., § 1915.
[11] Wyllie v. Wilkes, 2 Doug. 519.

forfeiture of bonds, upon payment of principal, interest, and costs, and when they said they could not relieve against the penalty, he swore by the body of God he would grant an injunction."

And in another case,[12] he said:

"It was extraordinary that after it was settled in *equity* that the forfeiture might be saved by the performing the intent, and that this was the nature of a bond, the courts of law did not follow equity, but still continued to do *injustice as of course*, and put the parties to the delay and expense of setting it right *elsewhere as of course*." [13]

§ 675d. Assignment of breaches.

Notwithstanding this statute, however, it is apparent that great injustice might be committed, because the plaintiff was entitled to judgment for the whole amount of the penalty, and the defendant could only be discharged by addressing himself to the equitable consideration of the court. Hence was imposed the obligation to *assign breaches*. By a statute enacted at nearly the same time,[14] it was declared "that in all actions, etc., upon any bond or bonds, or on any penal sum for nonperformance of any covenants or agreements in any indenture, deed, or writing certain, the plaintiff or plaintiffs *may* assign as many breaches as he or they shall think fit; and the jury, upon trial of such action or actions, shall and may assess, not only such damages and costs of suit as have heretofore been usually done in such cases, but also damages for such of said breaches so to be assigned as the plaintiff on the trial of the same shall prove to have been broken." The language here is, that the plaintiff *may* assign breaches; but it was settled that the statute was compulsory,[15] and that a judgment obtained under the former practice of the common law was bad in error. In the case last cited, Lord Kenyon and Mr. J. Buller said:

"It is apparent to us that the law was made in favor of defendants, and is highly remedial, calculated to give plaintiffs

[12] Bonafous *v.* Rybot, 3 Burr. 1370, 1374.

[13] In this last case it was held that bonds conditioned for payment of money by instalments were within the act of 4 Anne.

[14] 8 and 9 Will. III, ch. xi, § 8.

[15] Roles *v.* Rosewell, 5 T. R. 538, and Hardy *v.* Bern, Ibid. 636.

relief up to the extent of the damage sustained, and to protect defendants against the payment of further sums than what is in conscience due; and also to take away the necessity of proceedings in equity to obtain relief against an unconscientious demand of the whole penalty in cases where small damages only had accrued."

And it was accordingly held, that the plaintiff *must* assign breaches, and that the jury *must* assess the damages.

The principles of this act were engrafted upon the legislation of this country. In New York it was provided:[16]

"When an action shall be prosecuted in any court of law, upon any bond, for the breach of any condition other than for the payment of money, or shall be prosecuted for any penal sum for the non-performance of any covenant or written agreement, the plaintiff *in his declaration* shall assign the specific breaches for which the action is brought.

"Upon the trial of such action if the jury find that any assignment of such breaches is true, and that the plaintiff should recover damages therefor, they shall assess such damages, and shall specify the amount thereof in their verdict, in addition to their finding upon any other question of fact submitted to them.

"In every such action, if the plaintiff recover, the verdict of the jury assessing the plaintiff's damages shall be entered on the record, and judgment shall be rendered for the penalty of the bond, or for the penal sum forfeited as in other actions of debt, together with costs of suit; and with a further judgment that the plaintiff have execution to collect the amount of the damages so assessed by the jury, which damages shall be specified in such judgment."

§ 675e. Only the plaintiff's actual loss now recoverable.

These two statutes together produced this reasonable and equitable result, that in the case of an agreement to do or refrain from doing any particular act secured by a penalty, the amount of the penalty was in no sense the measure of compensation; and the plaintiff must show the particular injury of

[16] Revision of 1813 (R. Laws, vol. i, p. 518), and Revised Statutes, vol. ii, p. 300, 2d ed.; 378, 1st ed. Now super- seded in New York by the provisions of the Code Civ. Proc., § 1915.

which he complains, and have his damages assessed by the jury. It, therefore, became a settled rule that no other sum can be recovered under a penalty, than that which shall compensate the plaintiff for his actual loss.[17] **

§ 676. Penalty and liquidated damages.

As has already been said [18] the sum named in a bond as the amount of the debt (commonly called the "penal sum" of the bond) is *prima facie* named as a penalty, and not as liquidated damages for breach of the condition, and the plaintiff is not entitled to recover the amount in an action for the breach.[19] It is possible, however, to show in any particular case that the penal sum was really intended to be recovered as liquidated damages,[20] as for instance in the case of a bond conditioned on paying an amount of money exactly equal to the penal sum named.[21]

[17] Consequently where a judgment has been recovered in one State for the amount of the penalty of a bond, a plaintiff suing on such judgment in another State can recover the amount of damages only for which execution was awarded in the original suit. Battey *v.* Holbrook, 11 Gray (Mass.), 212. In an action of debt on bond, conditioned for the support of the plaintiff and her husband during their lives, it was held that damages must be assessed so as to cover not only present but prospective loss; the decision being based on the ground that as the bond contained no covenant and there could be but one breach, the plaintiff was entitled to have all her damages assessed on the trial. Philbrook *v.* Burgess, 52 Me. 271.

[18] §§ 389 *et seq.*

[19] *Colorado:* Twick *v.* Marshall S. M. Co., 8 Colo. 113, 5 Pac. 838.
Georgia: Swift *v.* Crow, 17 Ga. 609; Dart *v.* Southwestern B. & L. Assoc., 99 Ga. 794, 27 S. E. 171; Ripley *v.* Eady, 106 Ga. 422, 32 S. E. 343.
Montana: O'Keefe *v.* Dyer, 20 Mont. 477, 52 Pac. 196.

North Carolina: Disoway *v.* Edwards, 134 N. C. 254, 46 S. E. 501.
Oklahoma: Kelley *v.* Seay, 3 Okla. 527, 41 Pac. 615.
Pennsylvania: Curry *v.* Larer, 7 Pa. 470, 49 Am. Dec. 486.
Utah: McIntosh *v.* Johnson, 8 Utah, 359, 31 Pac. 450.
Vermont: Smith *v.* Wainwright, 24 Vt. 97.
Washington: Aberdeen *v.* Honey, 8 Wash. 251, 35 Pac. 1097.

[20] *United States:* Blewett *v.* Front St. C. R. R., 51 Fed. 625, 7 U. S. App. 285, 2 C. C. A. 415.
New York: Gerard *v.* Cowperthwait, 2 Misc. 371, 21 N. Y. Supp. 1092, 50 N. Y. St. R. 492.
North Carolina: Bazemore *v.* Bynum, 127 N. C. 11, 37 S. E. 67.

[21] Fleming *v.* Tolee, 7 Gratt. 310. This is usually held to be the case in bonds given to the government or to a city to perform some obligation, the value of which is uncertain. The sum named is to be recovered. *Ante*, § 416a.
United States: United States *v.* Hatch, 1 Paine, 336; U. S. *v.* Alcorn, 145 Fed. 995.

But though the penal sum named is to be treated as a penalty, yet the amount to be recovered in the old action of debt was measured by it; and if the plaintiff proceeds as at common law for debt on the bond as is still the case in some States the judgment should be for the entire penal sum.[22] And this is true although the condition is for the performance of several things, such as a payment of instalments, or the payment of interest from time to time and finally of the principal; the whole bond is forfeited by the first breach, and in such jurisdictions judgment must be entered for the entire penal sum,[23] and stands as security for the future acts of performance.[24] The recovery of this penal sum is in form like the recovery of any debt; and the amount of it must be found by the jury.[25]

But while the penal sum may be in form the amount due and to be recovered, the real finding upon which execution issues is universally the actual damage caused by breach of the condition.[26] This amount must be proved by the plain-

Kentucky: American Book Co. *v.* Wells, 83 S. W. 622, 26 Ky. L. Rep. 1159 (to sell school books at lowest rates).

New Jersey: Camden *v.* Greenwald, 65 N. J. L. 458, 47 Atl. 458 (street paving contract). But the penal sum in a bond for the return of merchandise imported being twice the estimated value of the merchandise, is a penalty. Dieckerhoff *v.* United States, 136 Fed. 545, 69 C. C. A. 255. See *ante,* § 416a. If the condition of the bond is without meaning it becomes a bond single and the defendant is responsible for the whole amount. Swain *v.* Graves, 8 Cal. 549.

[22] *United States:* Hagood *v.* Blythe, 37 Fed. 249.

Alabama: Moore *v.* Harton, 1 Port. 15.

Illinois: Toles *v.* Cole, 11 Ill. 562.

Maine: Gardner *v.* Niles, 16 Me. 279.

Massachusetts: Leighton *v.* Brown, 98 Mass. 515.

New York: Western Bank *v.* Sherwood, 29 Barb. 383 (but see Howard *v.* Farley, 18 Abb. Pr. 260, 3 Robert. 308).

On a bond to two jointly the recovery must be joint.

Illinois: Burns *v.* Follansbee, 20 Ill. App. 41.

Kentucky: Sims *v.* Harris, 8 B. Mon. 55.

[23] *District of Columbia:* Davidson *v.* Brown, 1 Cranch C. C. 250; Nailor *v.* Kearney, 1 Cranch C. C. 112.

Georgia: Stephens *v.* Crawford, 3 Ga. 499.

Minnesota: Allan *v.* Everoth, 111 Minn. 395, 127 N. W. 426.

New Jersey: Rosenkrantz *v.* Durling, 5 Dutch. 191.

[24] *United States:* Whitmore *v.* Rice, 1 Biss. 237.

Massachusetts: Battey *v.* Holbrook, 11 Gray (Mass.), 212, 71 Am. Dec. 707.

New Jersey: Rosenkrantz *v.* Durling, 5 Dutch. 191.

New York: Brown *v.* Hallett, 1 Caines, 517.

[25] Hinckley *v.* West, 9 Ill. 136.

[26] *United States:* Whitmore *v.* Rice, 1 Biss. 237; Adler *v.* Newcomb, 2 Dill. 45; Hagood *v.* Blythe, 37 Fed. 249;

tiff [27] and found by the jury; [28] and if no actual damages are proved, only a nominal recovery is allowed. [29] If further breaches occur, damages will be allowed and execution will issue for those also. [30] This actual damage for which execution issues is the real judgment, on which action may be brought in another State, and not the nominal judgment for the penal sum. [31]

§ 677. Damages in excess of penalty.

* The question has been much agitated as to damages in gross, and also as to interest, and both as against a principal and against a surety.** It is fully settled, however, that in an action on a bond no damages in gross can be recovered, against either principal or surety, beyond the penalty. [32] Thus where a

Union G. & T. Co. v. Robinson, 79 Fed. 420, 24 C. C. A. 650.

Illinois: Wales v. Bogue, 31 Ill. 464.

Maine: Gardner v. Niles, 16 Me. 279.

Massachusetts: Leighton v. Brown, 98 Mass. 515.

New York: Van Wyck v. Montrose, 12 Johns. 350.

Ohio: Cairnes v. Knight, 17 Oh. St. 68.

South Carolina: Miller v. Nichols, 1 Bail. 226.

Tennessee: Williams v. Patterson, 2 Overt. 229.

All the damage suffered to the time of trial will be included. Gardner v. Niles, 16 Me. 279. And all damages caused by all breaches up to that time must be recovered in the original action. State v. Scoggin, 10 Ark. 326.

[27] Caverly v. Nichols, 4 Johns. (N. Y.) 189.

[28] *New Jersey:* Richman v. Richman, 10 N. J. L. 114.

New York: Van Benthuyson v. De Witt, 4 Johns. 213, 4 Am. Dec. 262.

Or a court of equity may assess the damages, where it has control of the action. Russell v. Farley, 105 U. S. 103, 26 L. ed. 1060.

[29] *Iowa:* Linder v. Lake, 6 Ia. 164.

Missouri: Middleton v. Moore, 36 Mo. App. 627.

North Carolina: Creech v. Creech, 98 N. C. 155, 3 S. E. 814.

South Carolina: Alderman v. Roesel, 52 S. C. 162, 29 S. E. 385.

[30] *Illinois:* People v. Compher, 14 Ill. 447.

Maryland: Young v. Reynolds, 4 Md. 375; Ahl v. Ahl, 60 Md. 207.

Massachusetts: Waldo v. Fobes, 1 Mass. 10.

New York: Munroe v. Allaire, 2 Cai. 320; Rogers v. Coleman, 3 Cow. 62.

[31] Merrill v. McIntyre, 13 Gray (Mass.), 157.

[32] *United States:* Leggett v. Humphreys, 21 How. 66, 16 L. ed. 50; Bank of U. S. v. Magill, 1 Paine, 661; Lawrence v. U. S., 2 M'Lean, 581; Terry v. Robbins, 122 Fed. 725; U. S. v. Walker, 128 Fed. 1012; U. S. v. Lewis Pub. Co., 160 Fed. 989.

Illinois: Freeman v. The People, 54 Ill. 153.

Indiana: King v. Brewer, 19 Ind. 267; Graeter v. De Wolf, 112 Ind. 1, 13 N. E. 111.

Iowa: Sweem v. Steele, 10 Ia. 374; Sweem v. Steele, 5 Ia. 352.

Michigan: Spencer v. Perry, 18 Mich.

railroad company executed a bond to nine persons, according to their relative and respective several interests, in the penal sum of $3,000, as follows: "On this express condition that the said railroad company shall, on the assessment of damages to be made to secure right of way for said railroad, pay the obligees relatively and respectively, damages which may be assessed as aforesaid, then this bond to be void," which was a several instrument, on which each obligee might sue, it was held that no one could recover more than his *pro rata* share of the penalty. If the damages assessed in favor of all exceeded the penalty, each obligee could recover only his share of it.[33]

The rule, it should be observed, does not apply to costs; the full judgment, including costs, may, therefore, be in excess of the penalty.[34]

§ 678. Interest on penalty.

But there has been more doubt on the question of recovery of interest on the penalty. At one time the American rule to be deduced from all the cases seemed to be, that against a surety in *debt on bond*, nothing could be recovered beyond the penalty;[35] that against the principal in that form of action, in-

394; Fraser v. Little, 13 Mich. 195, 87 Am. Dec. 741.

Missouri: Farrar v. Christy, 24 Mo. 453; State v. Sandusky, 46 Mo. 377.

New York: Culver v. Green, 4 Hill (N. Y.), 570.

North Carolina: New Home S. M. Co. v. Seago, 128 N. C. 158, 38 S. E. 805; Hughes v. Pritchard, 129 N. C. 42, 39 S. E. 632.

Pennsylvania: New Holland T. Co. v. Lancaster County, 71 Pa. 442.

South Carolina: Hale v. Hall, 2 Brev. 316.

Texas: Grand Lodge A. O. U. W. v. Cleghorn, 20 Tex. Civ. App. 134, 48 S. W. 750.

Wisconsin: Chase v. Dearborn, 23 Wis. 143 (triple damages not recoverable on bond).

Canada: Black v. Queen, 29 Can. 693.

[33] St. Louis, A. & R. I. R. R. v. Coultas, 33 Ill. 188.

[34] Dwyer v. United States, 93 Fed. 616.

[35] *United States:* United States v. Arnold, 1 Gall. 348, 360; s. c. 9 Cranch, 194; Bank of United States v. Magill, Paine, 661.

Kansas: Simmons v. Garrett, McC. 82.

Massachusetts: Harris v. Clap, 1 Mass. 308, 2 Am. Dec. 21; Perkins v. Lyman, 11 Mass. 76, 6 Am. Dec. 75.

New Jersey: Tunison v. Cramer, 5 N. J. L. 498.

New York: Smedes v. Hooghtaling, 3 Caines, 48, 2 Am. Dec. 247; Fairlie v. Lawson, 5 Cowen, 424; Clark v. Bush, 3 Cowen, 151; Cook v. Tousey, 3 Wend. 444; Rayner v. Clark, 7 Barb. 581.

Pennsylvania: Graham v. Bickham, 4 Dall. 149, s. c. 2 Yeates, 32; Balsley v. Hoffman, 13 Pa. 203.

South Carolina: Stroble v. Large, 3

terest might perhaps be recovered beyond the penalty; while in England the penalty in all cases, except perhaps in equity, was the absolute limit.[36]

The later authorities, however, take an entirely different view; the better opinion now is, that interest may be recovered, in addition to the penalty, in an action whether against the principal [37]

McCord, 112 (see, however, Roulain v. McDowall, 1 Bay, 490); Smith v. Macon, 1 Hill Eq. 339; Bonsall v. Taylor, 1 McC. 503; Smith v. Vanderhorst, 1 McC. 328, 10 Am. Dec. 674; Winslow v. Ancrum, 1 McC. Eq. 100; Richardson v. Richardson, McMull Eq. 103.

Virginia: Payne v. Ellzey, 2 Wash. 143.

In United States v. Arnold, 1 Gall. 348, 360, Story, J., said: "Notwithstanding some contrariety in the books, I think the true principle, supported by the better authorities, is that the court cannot go beyond the penalty and interest thereon, from the time it becomes due by the breach."

[36] Lowe v. Peers, 4 Burr. 2225, which was covenant on a sealed contract not to marry; Winter v. Trimmer, 1 W. Bl. 395; Bird v. Randall, 1 W. Bl. 373, 387; 3 Burr. 1345; Brangwin v. Perrot, 2 W. Bl. 1190, on an indemnity bond against the maintenance of a bastard; Knight v. Maclean, 3 Br. Ch. 496; Tew v. Earl of Winterton, 3 Br. Ch. 490; White v. Sealy, Doug. 49, on a bond conditioned for the payment of rent; Londsale v. Church, 2 T. R. 388, overruled by Wilde v. Clarkson, 6 T. R. 303; and M'Clure v. Dunkin, 1 East, 436; Harrison v. Wright, 13 East, 343; Hefford v. Alger, 1 Taunt. 218; Evans v. Brander, 2 H. B. 547; Paul v. Goodluck, 2 Bing. N. C. 220; Hellen v. Ardley, 3 C. & P. 12; Grosvernor v. Cook, 1 Dick. 208; Macworth v. Thomas, 5 Ves. 329; Clarke v. Sexton, 6 Ves. 411.

In a case in the Queen's Bench it was said, that a replevin bond is no exception to the general rule, that on a bond

the plaintiff cannot recover beyond the penalty and costs of suit. Branscombe v. Scarborough, 6 Q. B. 13. For the present English law see Heynes v. Dixon [1900], 2 Ch. 561.

[37] *United States:* Ives v. Merchants' Bank, 12 How. 159, 13 L. ed. 936; U. S. v. Arnold, 1 Gall. 348.

Alabama: Tyson v. Sanderson, 45 Ala. 364; Borden v. Bradshaw, 68 Ala. 362.

Colorado: Crane v. Andrews, 10 Colo. 265.

Connecticut: Carter v. Carter, 4 Day, 30, 4 Am. Dec. 177; Lewis v. Dwight, 10 Conn. 95; Washington County Ins. Co. v. Colton, 26 Conn. 42.

Georgia: Moss v. Wood, R. M. Charlt. 42; Frink v. Southern Exp. Co., 82 Ga. 33.

Illinois: Holmes v. Standard Oil Co., 183 Ill. 70, 55 N. E. 647, 82 Ill. App. 476.

Iowa: Getchell & M. L. & M. Co. v. Peterson, 124 Ia. 599, 100 N. W. 550.

Kansas: Bunchfield v. Haffey, 34 Kan. 42, 7 Pac. 548.

Kentucky: Carter v. Thorn, 18 B. Mon. 613; Highes v. Wickcliffe, 11 B. Mon. 202.

Massachusetts: Pitts v. Tilden, 2 Mass. 118; Warner v. Thurlo, 15 Mass. 154; Bank of Brighton v. Smith, 12 All. 243, 90 Am. Dec. 144; Rowe v. Peabody, 207 Mass. 226, 93 N. E. 604.

New Jersey: Robbins v. Long, 16 N. J. Eq. 59; Gloucester v. Eschbach, 54 N. J. L. 150, 23 Atl. 360.

New York: Brainard v. Jones, 18 N. Y. 35; Ringle v. O'Matthiessen, 39 N. Y. Supp. 92.

or the surety.[38] In Lyon v. Clark,[39] it is pointed out, in the very clear opinion of Comstock, J., that there is a distinction between the question whether, at the time of the default, the liability can exceed the penalty, and the question whether, after default, interest can be allowed in excess of the penalty. The first is a question of the effect of the contract; the second is one of compensation for a breach of the contract. This distinction appears to be perfectly sound, and upon the whole there seems no reason why interest on the penalty should not be allowed. In a few States, however, the recovery is still limited to the penalty without interest.[40] In New York, by

Pennsylvania: Perit v. Wallis, 2 Dall. 252; Boyd v. Boyd, 1 Watts, 365.

Rhode Island: Walcott v. Harris, 1 R. I. 404.

Texas: Austin v. Townes, 10 Tex. 24.

Virginia: Tennant v. Gray, 5 Munf. 494; Baker v. Morris, 10 Leigh, 284; Bailey v. James, 11 Gratt. 468, 62 Am. Dec. 659; Tazewell v. Saunders, 13 Gratt. 354.

Washington: Spokane & Idaho Lumber Co. v. Loy, 21 Wash. 501, 58 Pac. 672 (where the recovery in excess of the penal sum is due to including interest in the actual damages).

West Virginia: Perry v. Horn, 22 W. Va. 381.

Wisconsin: Clark v. Wilkinson, 59 Wis. 543, 18 N. W. 481; Whereatt v. Ellis, 103 Wis. 348, 79 N. W. 416, 74 Am. St. Rep. 865.

Canada: Beam v. Beatty, 3 Ont. L. R. 345.

The rate of interest is fixed by the law of the place where the bond is payable. Kavanaugh v. Day, 10 R. I. 393, 14 Am. Rep. 691.

[38] *Arkansas:* James v. State, 65 Ark. 415, 46 S. W. 937 (from time of breach).

Colorado: Crane v. Andrews, 10 Colo. 265.

Kansas: Burchfield v. Haffey, 34 Kan. 42.

Maine: Wyman v. Robinson, 73 Me. 384, 40 Am. Rep. 560.

Maryland: State v. Wayman, 2 G. & J. 254.

Mississippi: Maryland v. Winter, 43 Miss. 666 (from time of breach).

New York: Lyon v. Clark, 8 N. Y. 148; Brainard v. Jones, 18 N. Y. 35; Hood v. Hayward, 124 N. Y. 12, 26 N. E. 331; Furber v. McCarthy, 12 N. Y. Supp. 794; Steinbock v. Evans, 122 N. Y. 551, 25 N. E. 929, 34 N. Y. St. R. 138 (from time of breach).

Oregon: Carlon v. Dixon, 14 Ore. 293, 12 Pac. 394 (from time of breach).

Pennsylvania: Pennsylvania Co. v. Swain, 189 Pa. 626, 42 Atl. 297, 69 Am. St. Rep. 830 (from time of demand); Folz v. Tradesmen's T. & S. F. Co., 201 Pa. 583, 51 Atl. 379 (from time of demand); New York L. Ins. Co. v. Seckel, 8 Phila. 92 (from time of breach).

[39] 8 N. Y. 148.

[40] *Michigan:* Fraser v. Little, 13 Mich. 195; White S. M. Co. v. Dakin, 86 Mich. 581, 49 N. W. 583, 13 L. R. A. 313; People's Savings Bank v. Campau, 124 Mich. 106, 82 N. W. 803.

Mississippi: Rubon v. Stephan, 25 Miss. 253.

Missouri: State v. Sandusky, 46 Mo. 377; Showles v. Freeman, 81 Mo. 540; Turner v. Lord, 92 Mo. 113.

North Carolina: State v. Estes, 101 N. C. 541.

South Carolina: Murray v. Aiken

statute, interest may be recovered on a bond for the payment of money, but not on a bond for the performance of an act.[41]

§ 679. Bonds containing express covenants.

In certain bonds, the party affirmatively stipulating to do or to refrain from doing some particular act, proceeds to secure his agreement by a penalty, and in such cases the plaintiff at common law had his election whether to sue in debt or in covenant. There is a clear distinction between such a bond and the common bond, which merely stipulates for the payment of a sum of money, and makes its payment depend on a condition; for the performance of that condition there is no promise, unless one can be implied from the joint effect of the condition and penalty.

Where a common-law action of covenant could be brought upon a bond, the measure of damages would be compensation, irrespective of the penalty, and even beyond it.[42] "There is a difference between covenants in general and covenants *secured* by a penalty or forfeiture. In the latter case, the obligee has his election; he may either bring an action of debt and recover the penalty, after which recovery of the penalty he cannot resort to the covenant; or, if he does not choose to go for the penalty, he can proceed upon the covenant, and recover more or less than the penalty, *toties quoties*."[43] The same principle was laid down in Pennsylvania,[44] where the defendant had agreed to pay $22,318.49 for certain stock, and bound himself for the performance of the agreement in the sum of $1,000; here it was held that this was not stipulated damages, but a penalty merely: and the plaintiff recovered damages beyond

---

Min. etc. Co., 39 S. C. 457, 18 S. E. 5 (*semble*).

Tennessee: Cherry v. Mann, Cooke 268; State v. Blakemore, 7 Heisk. 638.

[41] Brainard v. Jones, 18 N. Y. 35; Polhemus Printing Co. v. Hallenbeck, 46 App. Div. 563, 61 N. Y. Supp. 1056; Sachs v. America Surety Co., 72 App. Div. 60, 76 N. Y. Supp. 335, affirmed 177 N. Y. 551, 69 N. E. 1130.

[42] Martin v. Taylor, 1 Wash. C. C. 1. So L. C. J. Tenterden, in his trea-

tise on Shipping, assumes that as to charter-parties, damages may be recovered beyond the amount of the penalty and costs. Abbott on Shipping, part iv, ch. ii, of the shipowner's lien for profits, etc.

[43] Lord Mansfield in Lowe v. Peers, 4 Burr. 2225. See, also, Bird v. Randall, 1 W. Bl. 373, 387; Winter v. Trimmer, 1 W. Bl. 395; Harrison v. Wright, 13 East, 343.

[44] Graham v. Bickham, 4 Dall. 149.

the penalty. "The plaintiff," said the court, "is entitled, notwithstanding the penalty, to recover damages commensurate with the injury suffered by a non-performance." So again in New York, in a case on a building agreement,[45] it was said: "As the articles contained a penalty and an express covenant by the defendant to pay the instalment for which the action was brought, the plaintiffs could, at their election, sue for either."[46]

But the question still remains: * does an ordinary bond imply an agreement to do the thing, on condition of the performance of which the penalty is to become void; and can an action of covenant be brought on it? This is an embarrassing and vexed question. Mr. Chitty says:[47] "It seems that covenant lies on a bond, for it proves an agreement." It is doubtful what is the purport of this language. A bond undoubtedly proves an agreement; but is the agreement proved, the one stated in the penalty—to pay the money for which the obligee declares himself bound—or in the condition?[48] The matter is of importance, and it seems impossible, on any just construction of the instrument, to imply from the condition an absolute agreement. This is not the proper place for a more elaborate discussion of the matter, but it could not with propriety be altogether overlooked.** In New York the Supreme Court has clearly intimated an opinion that an action of covenant will lie on a bond to enforce the condition;[49] and in Beale v. Hayes[50] Duer, J., used the following language:

[45] Haggart v. Morgan, 5 N. Y. 422, 55 Am. Dec. 350.

[46] Acc., Noyes v. Phillips, 60 N. Y. 408; Richards v. Edick, 17 Barb. 260.

[47] Chitty on Pleading, vol. i, p. 132.

[48] Mr. Chitty cites several cases: Hill v. Carr, 1 Ch. Cas. 294; Holles v. Carr, 3 Swanst. 649, which is in fact the same; Norrice's Case, Hardr. 178, and Com. Dig. Covenant, A. 2. The two first cases (in fact one) contain the *obiter dictum*, that "*covenant lies upon a bond.*" The third was covenant on a covenant proper, the word *oblige* only being used instead of the usual phrase;

and Lord C. B. Comyns, with his usual precision, says: "Covenant lies, *if an agreement appear*, in an obligation." This is unquestionably true—"*if the agreement appear.*" But in the condition of a bond to do or refrain from doing any particular act secured by a given penalty, does any agreement appear, absolutely to do the act or to respond in indefinite damages? Practically, we well know that it is not so understood; the obligor always considers the penalty as limiting the extent of his obligation.

[49] Clark v. Bush, 3 Cowen, 151. In

[50] 5 Sandf. 640.

"As all distinctions resulting merely from the form of the action, are now abolished, it appears to be a necessary consequence that, as a general rule, every action for the breach of an executory contract, whether the agreement contains a penalty or not, must be considered as an action for damages, in which the amount of the recovery will be limited only by the proof, and by the sum for which judgment is demanded in the complaint. The only exception will be, when, from the nature of the contract and the terms in which it is expressed, damages, as liquidated by the parties, may be justly treated, not as a penalty, but as a contingent debt, for this is a distinction in law which the Code has not abolished nor affected. It is true, that upon this construction, the insertion of a penalty in an agreement is a useless form, but this is no alteration of the law, since, for more than a century past, such has been its real character."

Notwithstanding these remarks, the practice of recovering damages beyond the penalty of a money bond is unknown, a condition of things which could hardly exist if covenant would lie on such an agreement.

§ 679a. Compensation for breach of condition.

For breach of condition of a bond the plaintiff must prove that he suffered loss; and if no actual damages are proved, nominal damages only can be recovered.[51] On a bond to secure

Martin v. Taylor (1 Wash. C. C. 1), in an action of covenant on an agreement secured by a penalty, Washington, J., said, that, "where there is a penalty in an agreement under seal, the party injured may at common law sue for the whole penalty, and must be satisfied with it; or he may bring covenant, and recover in damages more or less than the penalty." It is to be remarked here that the agreement contained an express covenant to do the act for the non-performance of which the action was brought. The case, therefore, decides nothing as to the main point, whether covenant can be brought on a bond upon an agreement contained in the condition, and whether

in such suit damages can be assessed beyond the penalty.

[51] *Illinois:* Dent v. Davison, 52 Ill. 109 (to pay firm debts); Karr v. Peter, 60 Ill. App. 209 (to pay all bills contracted by defendant in building house). *Massachusetts:* Pollard v. Porter, 3 Gray, 312, 63 Am. Dec. 741 (to foreclose mortgage and pay balance to mortgagor; instead of foreclosing defendant assigned mortgage, assignee foreclosed and sold, no balance realized). *Minnesota:* Sprague v. Wells, 47 Minn. 504, 50 N. W. 535 (to erect house on defendant's own premises). *Missouri:* Fidelity & D.Co.v. Colvin, 83 Mo. App. 204 (to erect building).

the payment of money or the delivery of property, the measure of damages is the value of the money or property at the time of performance; [52] to buy, the difference between the contract price and the market rate; [53] to give a good title, the value of the land; [54] to erect a building on land, the additional value it would give to the land, [55] or if the bond is given to a mortgagee of the land, the enhancement of the security; [56] and, in general, in any case, the loss caused to the plaintiff by failure to perform the condition. [57]

§ 679b. Contractors' bonds.

For breach of a bond given by a contractor for the perform-

[52] *Arizona:* Finley *v.* Tucson, 7 Ariz. 108, 60 Pac. 872 (to refund salary if held not entitled to office).

Connecticut: Babbet *v.* Belding, 1 Root, 445 (to return public securities on demand).

Mississippi: Lanier *v.* Trigg, 6 Sm. & M. 641, 45 Am. Dec. 293 (to pay in notes of particular bank).

North Carolina: Lackey *v.* Miller, 61 N. C. 26 (to pay in current bank bills).

South Carolina: McKeegan *v.* McSwiney, 2 S. C. 191 (to pay in Confederate money). In North Carolina the measure of recovery on an obligation payable in Confederate money was the value of the consideration. McRae *v.* McNair, 69 N. C. 12. See *ante,* § 278.

[53] *Georgia:* Ripley *v.* Eady, 106 Ga. 422, 32 S. E. 343.

Ontario: Beam *v.* Beatty, 3 Ont. L. R. 345.

Where the goods were to be manufactured (labels to be printed) the cost of a specially constructed machine (special plate) is recoverable in a case where loss of profits is not shown. Crocker *v.* Field's B. & C. Co., 93 Cal. 532, 29 Pac. 225.

[54] Bryant *v.* Hambrick, 9 Ga. 133. In States where the consideration only is recoverable for breach of covenant

of title, that limits recovery here. Stewart *v.* Noble, 1 G. Greene (Ia.), 26. See *post,* § 959 *et seq.*

[55] *Missouri:* United R. E. Co. *v.* McDonald, 140 Mo. 605, 41 S. W. 913.

Pennsylvania: German-American Title & Trust Co. *v.* Citizens' Trust & Surety Co., 190 Pa. 247, 42 Atl. 682.

[56] *Minnesota:* Longfellow *v.* McGregor, 61 Minn. 494, 63 N. W. 1032.

New York: Sachs *v.* American Surety Co., 72 App. Div. 60, 76 N. Y. Supp. 335.

[57] *Arkansas:* Sullivant *v.* Reardon, 5 Ark. 140, 39 Am. Dec. 368 (to clear land: cost of clearing).

Massachusetts: Brookfield *v.* Reed, 152 Mass. 568, 26 N. E. 138 (to repair a highway: cost of completing repairs, and evidence of expenses incurred after action commenced could be received).

Michigan: Wheeler *v.* Meyer, 95 Mich. 36, 54 N. W. 689 (to sell goods for plaintiff's benefit; amount realized from goods actually sold, and value at time of demand of goods unsold); Bell *v.* Paul, 35 Neb. 240, 52 N. W. 1110 (to turn over buildings free from liens: amount of unpaid liens, not of unpaid debts on which liens might be filed); Scott *v.* Phillips, 140 Pa. 51, 21 Atl. 241 (to pay premiums on insurance policy; amount of the premiums).

ance of the work called for in the contract, the measure of damages is the same as in an action for breach of the contract itself,[58] including all damages that have accrued even after bringing the suit.[59] There is no liability on the bond for defaults of a sub-contractor.[60]

Materialmen are entitled to recover on bonds given for their benefit.[61]

§ 680. Statutory bonds and undertakings.

In suits on statutory undertakings and bonds given to secure a defendant against damages and costs resulting from an attachment, injunction, or other provisional remedy wrongfully issued or applied, the measure of damages is substantially indicated by the terms of the instrument as authorized by the statute. The cases turn chiefly on the interpretation of particular words, and the construction of particular statutes; and the ordinary rules for measuring damages yield to the construction of the statute under which the bond is given.[62] Usually exemplary damages are not allowed;[63] and in all actions upon statutory bonds remote or uncertain damages are excluded,[64] and the penalty fixed in the bond is the absolute limit of the damages, except that, as shown above, the plaintiff might, in a proper case recover interest.[65] These considerations, of course,

[58] *United States:* Mercantile Trust Co. v. Hensey, 205 U. S. 298, 51 L. ed. 811, 27 Sup. Ct. 535, affirming 27 App. D. C. 210; Clark v. Barnard, 108 U. S. 436, 27 L. ed. 780, 2 Sup. Ct. 878.

Indiana: Donaldson v. State (Ind. App.), 90 N. E. 132.

Minnesota: Allen v. Eneroth, 111 Minn. 395, 127 N. W. 426.

Vermont: Spear v. Stacy, 26 Vt. 61.

In Chambers v. Ft. Bend County, 14 Tex. 34, the actual damages were not allowed, on the ground that they were unconscionable. *Ante,* § 606c.

[59] *Minnesota:* Allen v. Eneroth, 111 Minn. 395, 127 N. W. 426.

Vermont: Spear v. Stacy, 26 Vt. 91.

[60] State v. Hinsdale-Doyle Granite Co., 117 Ind. 476, 20 N. E. 437.

[61] *District of Columbia:* U. S. v. Burgdorf, 13 D. C. App. 506.

Indiana: United States F. & G. Co. v. American Blower Co., 41 Ind. App. 620, 84 N. E. 555.

[62] *Minnesota:* Grams v. Murphy, 103 Minn. 219, 114 N. W. 753.

South Dakota: Palmer v. Schurz, 22 S. D. 283, 117 N. W. 150.

[63] Cobb v. People, 84 Ill. 511 (liquor dealer's bond).

[64] *Alabama:* Higgins v. Mansfield, 62 Ala. 267; Drake v. Webb, 63 Ala. 596.

Illinois: Silsbe v. Lucas, 53 Ill. 479.

New York: Bennett v. Brown, 20 N. Y. 99.

Vermont: Campbell v. Tarbell, 55 Vt. 455.

[65] *Alabama:* Windham v. Coats, 8 Ala. 285; Seamans v. White, 8 Ala. 656.

relate to actions on the bond; the measure of damages in actions of which the gist is the misuse of legal process, or trespass to the person, actions to which resort may often be had in addition to the remedy by debt on bond, is determined by wholly different considerations.[66] A bond given under a statute must conform strictly to the statutory requirements; but if by reason of failing to do so it is void as a statutory bond, it may nevertheless be valid as a common-law bond. In that case the measure of damages upon it will be regulated by the principles of the common law.[67]

§ 681. Reduction of damages.

In conformity with the general principle of indemnity, the rules of reduction applicable to trover and other classes of action, are recognized here. Thus where a plaintiff in the original action in which he had obtained an attachment, had been nonsuited, he was permitted to show in reduction of damages in the action on the attachment bond, that the property thus attached had been reattached in a subsequent action by him, which had been prosecuted to a judgment, under which the property was sold.[68] Had the original taking been *mala fide*, however, without color of legal right, it may be inferred, from the opinion of the court, that this would not have been allowed. But in Oregon the same decision has been reached where the first attachment was not made in good faith.[69] So, again, where the statute provided that in actions to determine claims to real property, the plaintiff must recover on the strength of his own title, it was held in an action on a bond given upon the granting of an injunction to restrain a plaintiff from cutting timber on a

Iowa: Perry v. Denson, 1 Gr. 467.
Maryland: Levy v. Taylor, 24 Md. 282.
Mississippi: Rubon v. Stephan, 25 Miss. 253.
New York: Roberts v. White, 73 N. Y. 375.
Vermont: Sturges v. Knapp, 36 Vt. 439.
[66] *Kentucky:* Pettit v. Mercer, 8 B. Mon. 51.

Missouri: State v. Thomas, 19 Mo. 613, 61 Am. Dec. 580.
[67] *United States:* Dixon v. U. S., 1 Brock. 177.
Illinois: Moulding v. Wilhartz, 169 Ill. 422, 48 N. E. 189, 67 Ill. App. 659.
New Hampshire: Claggett v. Richards, 45 N. H. 360.
[68] Earl v. Spooner, 3 Den. (N. Y.) 246.
[69] Morrison v. Crawford, 7 Ore. 472.

tract of land, that the defendant might show in reduction that the plaintiff had no title to the land and no right to cut timber on it.[70] In short, in a proper case the defendant, in order to reduce the damages, may show any admissible facts to prove the damages less than they would at first seem,[71] as that the consequences should have been avoided.[72] A set-off may be allowed in a proper case.[73]

§ 681a. Actions against sureties.

The liability of the sureties on a bond is to be construed strictly, and is limited by the actual language of the bond,[74] though the natural meaning of the language will be followed.[75] Therefore, in the absence of provisions in the bond which would lead to an opposite result, the sureties are not liable for defaults preceding the execution and delivery of the bond; [76] nor can they be called upon to contribute to losses for which the liability lies primarily on the parties to other bonds.[77] If the parties on two bonds are jointly liable, the sureties on both

[70] Jenkins v. Parkhill, 25 Ind. 473; but see Waterman v. Frank, 21 Mo. 108 (suit on delivery bond; defendant cannot show title in himself).

[71] *Maryland:* Rawlings v. Adams, 7 Md. 26 (bond for deed; title had come to heir of plaintiff and plaintiff's equitable title would defeat ejectment).
Massachusetts: Merrill v. McIntire, 13 Gray, 157 (bond to pay money; may show payment, though not set up in the answer).
Missouri: Wagner v. Dette, 2 Mo. App. 254 (to keep property clear of liens; payment by plaintiff to discharge lien reduced amount he must pay for building house).

[72] Niagara F. P. Co. v. Lee, 20 App. Div. 217, 47 N. Y. Supp. 1.

[73] Van Etten v. Kosters, 48 Neb. 152, 66 N. W. 1106.

[74] *California:* Ogden v. Davis, 116 Cal. 32, 47 Pac. 772.
Illinois: People v. Moon, 4 Ill. 123.
Maryland: Fullerton v. Miller, 22 Md. 1.
New York: Sutorius v. Dunstan, 59

N. Y. Super. Ct. 166, 13 N. Y. Supp. 601.
Ohio: Smith v. Huesman, 30 Oh. St. 662.
Therefore they are not liable for any act of the principal not covered by the bond.
United States: Johnston v. Sexton, 159 Fed. 70, 86 C. C. A. 260.
California: Gomez v. Scanlan, 155 Cal. 528, 102 Pac. 12.

[75] Shreffler v. Nadelhoffer, 133 Ill. 536, 25 N. E. 630.

[76] *United States:* Meyers v. U. S., 1 McLean, 493.
Illinois: Bartlett v. Wheeler, 195 Ill. 445, 63 N. E. 169.
New Jersey: Jeffers v. Johnson, 18 N. J. L. 382.
Texas: Wandelohr v. Grayson County Nat. Bank (Tex. Civ. App.), 106 S. W. 413.

[77] *New York:* Barnes v. Cushing, 43 App. Div. 158, 59 N. Y. Supp. 345.
Tennessee: Moore v. Lassiter, 16 Lea, 630.

bonds contribute to the loss.[78] Sureties cannot be held liable
in exemplary damages, even when such damages may be re-
covered against the principal.[79] The sureties being privies to an action against their principal, they are bound by a judgment against him with regard
both to the fact of liability and to the amount of damages;[80]
and they are also bound, as to amount of damages, by his ad-
missions,[81] and by the recitals of the bond.[82]

[78] *Iowa:* State *v.* McGlothlin, 61
Iowa, 312, 16 N. W. 137.
North Carolina: Liles *v.* Rogers, 113
N. C. 197, 18 S. E. 104, 37 Am. St. Rep.
627.
Ohio: Swisher *v.* McWhinney, 64
Oh. St. 343, 60 N. E. 565.
Oregon: Thompson *v.* Dekum, 32
Ore. 506, 52 Pac. 517, 755.

[79] *Kentucky:* Johnson *v.* Williams, 111
Ky. 289, 63 S. W. 759; Growbarger *v.*
United States F. & G. Co., 126 Ky.
118, 102 S. W. 873, 31 Ky. L. R. 555,
11 L. R. A. (N. S.) 758.
Minnesota: North *v.* Johnson, 58
Minn. 242, 59 N. W. 1012.
Oklahoma: Hixon *v.* Cupp, 5 Okla.
545, 49 Pac. 927.

[80] *Illinois:* McAllister *v.* Clark, 86
Ill. 236.
Iowa: Mason *v.* Richards, 12 Ia. 73;
Krepper *v.* Glenn, 73 Ia. 730, 36 N. W.
763.
Kansas: Kennedy *v.* Brown, 21 Kan.
171; First State Bank *v.* Martin, 81
Kan. 794, 106 Pac. 1056; O'Loughlin
v. Carr, 9 Kan. App. 818, 60 Pac.
478.
Kentucky: Hobbs *v.* Middleton, 1 J.
J. Marsh. 176.

Massachusetts: McKim *v.* Haley, 173
Mass. 112, 53 N. E. 152.
Michigan: People *v.* Laning, 73 Mich.
284, 41 N. W. 424.
Minnesota: Jacobson *v.* Anderson,
72 Minn. 426, 75 N. W. 607.
Missouri: State *v.* Berning, 74 Mo.
87, 41 Am. Rep. 305; Wolff *v.* Schaefer,
74 Mo. 154.
Montana: Botkin *v.* Kleinschmidt,
21 Mont. 1, 52 Pac. 563, 69 Am. St.
Rep. 641.
New York: Methodist Church *v.*
Barker, 18 N. Y. 363; Douglass *v.*
Ferris, 138 N. Y. 192, 34 Am. St. Rep.
435, 33 N. E. 1041; Poillon *v.* Volken-
ning, 11 Hun, 385 (finding of referee
and judgment on it).
Ohio: Braiden *v.* Mercer, 44 Oh. St.
339, 7 N. E. 155; Slagle *v.* Entrekin,
44 Oh. St. 637, 10 N. E. 675.
Oregon: Drake *v.* Sworts, 24 Ore. 198,
33 Pac. 563; Thompson *v.* Dekum, 32
Ore. 506, 52 Pac. 517, 755.
Contra:
Maryland: Inglehart *v.* State, 2 Gill
& J. 235 (only *prima facie* evidence
against surety).
Massachusetts: Dawes *v.* Shed, 15
Mass. 6, 8 Am. Dec. 80 (sureties may

[81] *Massachusetts:* Singer Mfg. Co. *v.*
Reynolds, 168 Mass. 588, 47 N. E. 438,
60 Am. St. Rep. 417.
Tennessee: Young *v.* Hare, 11
Humph. 303.
So on a mechanic's lien bond the
price fixed in the contract between the
contractor (the principal) and a sub-

contractor will ordinarily measure the
liability of the sureties. St. Paul
Foundry Co. *v.* Wegmann, 40 Minn.
419, 42 N. W. 288.
[82] Capital Lumbering Co. *v.* Learned,
36 Ore. 544, 59 Pac. 454, 7 Am. St. Rep.
792.

Questions of the discharge of sureties from liability because of particular circumstances, not presenting questions of the measure of damages, do not fall within the scope of this work and cannot be discussed at length.[83]

B.—BONDS GIVEN IN JUDICIAL PROCEEDINGS

§ 682. Attachment bonds.

Where a party gives a bond before suing out an attachment on personal property, the direct loss of the owner is the loss of use of the property pending attachment proceedings; and the value of the use of the property may therefore be recovered in an action on the bond.[84] The owner may also recover compen-

set up statute of limitations though principal did not).

North Carolina: McKellar *v.* Powell, 4 Hawks, 34.

Tennessee: Atkins *v.* Baily, 9 Yerg. 111 (judgment confessed by principal on an official bond after he retired from office).

West Virginia: State *v.* Nutter, 44

[83] Sureties have been held discharged in the following cases:

Arkansas: Haden *v.* Swepston, 64 Ark. 477, 43 S. W. 393 (order of removal of principal afterward rescinded).

Louisiana: McMillen *v.* Gibson, 10 La. 517 (increase of obligation on the bond).

New York: People *v.* Jansen, 7 Johns. 332, 5 Am. Dec. 275 (laches).

Tennessee: Johnson *v.* Hacker, 8 Heisk. 388 (extension of time).

They have been held not discharged in the following cases:

Mississippi: Denio *v.* State, 60 Miss. 949 (change of principal's duties).

New York: People *v.* Russell, 4 Wend. 570 (laches); Horner *v.* Lyman, 2 Abb. App. 399, 4 Keyes, 237 (change of statute as to costs); Atlantic & P. T. Co. *v.* Barnes, 64 N. Y. 385, 21 Am. Rep. 621 (failure to give notice of principal's default).

W. Va. 385, 30 S. E. 67 (only evidence: *semble.* In this case the condition of the bond was to pay a judgment against the principal).

They are of course equally entitled to the benefit of a prior judgment in favor of their principal against the same plaintiff. Renkert *v.* Elliott, 11 Lea (Tenn.), 235.

Ohio: Hanna *v.* International Petroleum Co., 23 Oh. St. 622 (immaterial change in process); Dawson *v.* State, 38 Oh. St. 1 (change of principal's duties); McGaughey *v.* Jacoby, 54 Oh. St. 487, 44 N. E. 231 (fraud of principal in procuring signatures).

[84] *Arkansas:* Boatwright *v.* Stewart, 37 Ark. 614.

Iowa: Porter *v.* Knight, 63 Ia. 365, 19 N. W. 282.

Kentucky: Blakely *v.* Bogard, 136 S. W. 616.

Missouri: State *v.* McKeon, 25 Mo. App. 667.

Ohio: Bruce *v.* Coleman, 1 Handy, 515.

Texas: Munnerlyn *v.* Alexander, 38 Tex. 125.

So where money is garnished interest on the money during the period of detention may be recovered on the bond.

Alabama: Alabama S. L. Co. *v.* Reed, 99 Ala. 19, 13 So. 43.

sation for a depreciation in the value of the property, measured by the difference in the value of the property at the time of suing out the attachment and at the dissolution of it.[85] Where the property was sold, the measure of damages is the value of the property, not necessarily the amount for which it sold;[86] diminished, however, by the fact that the proceeds were paid over to the owner,[87] or went to discharge a debt legally due from him.[88] The value taken is the value of the property at the time of the attachment, not at the time of sale, together with

Georgia: Fourth Nat. Bank *v.* Mayer, 96 Ga. 728, 24 S. E. 453.

Illinois: Strong *v.* Hasterlik, 146 Ill. App. 346.

Kentucky: Vanatta *v.* Vanatta, 21 Ky. L. Rep. 1464, 55 S. W. 685.

Missouri: State *v.* Flarsheim, 13 Mo. App. 1, 119 S. W. 17.

New York: Northampton Nat. Bank *v.* Wylie, 52 Hun, 148, 4 N. Y. Supp. 907.

Where the goods did not belong to the plaintiff he could not recover damages for loss of use of the goods. Tebo *v.* Betancourt, 73 Miss. 868, 19 So. 833, 55 Am. St. Rep. 573.

Where the goods attached were a portion of a stock in trade, plaintiff could not recover for loss of use of the entire shop. Charles City Plow & M. Co. *v.* Jones, 71 Ia. 234, 32 N. W. 280.

[85] *Arkansas:* Boatwright *v.* Stewart, 37 Ark. 614.

California: Frankel *v.* Stern, 44 Cal. 168.

Ohio: Bruce *v.* Coleman, 1 Handy, 515.

Tennessee: Doll *v.* Cooper, 9 Lea, 576.

At least where the depreciation in value was caused by negligent keeping of the goods by the sheriff:

Alabama: Crofford *v.* Vassar, 95 Ala. 548, 10 So. 350; Vandiver *v.* Waller, 143 Ala. 411, 39 So. 136.

California: Witherspoon *v.* Cross, 135 Cal. 96, 67 Pac. 18.

Iowa: Blaul *v.* Tharp, 83 Ia. 665, 94 N. W. 1044; Ruthven *v.* Beckwith,

84 Ia. 715, 45 N. W. 1073, 51 N. W. 153.

But when the market price of stock fell while it was under attachment the court held that since it was not due to the attachment it was not recoverable on the bond. Miller *v.* Ferry, 50 Hun, 256, 2 N. Y. Supp. 863.

[86] *Alabama:* Hundley *v.* Chadwick, 109 Ala. 575, 19 So. 845.

Arkansas: Norman *v.* Fife, 61 Ark. 33, 31 S. W. 740.

Indiana: Trentman *v.* Wiley, 85 Ind. 33.

Iowa: Porter *v.* Knight, 63 Ia. 365, 19 N. W. 282.

Mississippi: Woolner *v.* Spalding, 65 Miss. 204.

Missouri: State *v.* Gage, 52 Mo. App. 464; State *v.* Ryley, 76 Mo. App. 412.

North Carolina: Stein *v.* Cozart, 122 N. C. 280, 30 S. E. 340.

[87] *Arkansas:* Boatwright *v.* Stewart, 37 Ark. 614.

Indiana: Trentman *v.* Wiley, 85 Ind. 33.

[88] *Alabama:* Hamilton *v.* Maxwell, 119 Ala. 23, 34 So. 455 (applied on debt sued on by consent of debtor).

Arkansas: Norman *v.* Fife, 61 Ark. 33, 31 S. W. 740 (debt on which attachment suit was brought).

Iowa: Ruthven *v.* Beckwith, 84 Ia. 715, 45 N. W. 1073 (debt on which attachment is brought); Schwarts *v.* Davis, 90 Ia. 324, 330, 57 N. W. 849, 48 Am. St. Rep. 446 (mortgage debt).

interest on the value.[89] Damages cannot be obtained, according to the prevailing doctrine, for loss of credit caused by the attachment of a stock of goods used in business;[90] but on the other hand the weight of authority allows the recovery of compensation for loss of business caused by such attachment.[91] Consequential damages may be recovered in a proper case. So where by the attachment a party is prevented from performing a contract, and material or property prepared or procured to enable him to do so is thus depreciated in its value to him,

In some jurisdictions as has been seen (*ante,* § 60), the amount applied in the suit in which the wrongful attachment was made, without consent of the debtor, cannot be deducted. Hundley *v.* Chadwick, 109 Ala. 575, 19 So. 845.

[89] *Missouri:* State *v.* Ryley, 76 Mo. App. 412.

Pennsylvania: Keeler *v.* Ricker, 3 Northampton Co. Rep. 48.

[90] *United States:* L. Bucki & Son L. Co. *v.* Fidelity & D. Co., 109 Fed. 393, 48 C. C. A. 436.

Arkansas: Holliday *v.* Cohen, 34 Ark. 707.

California: Heath *v.* Lent, 1 Cal. 410.

Illinois: Oberne *v.* Gaylord, 13 Ill. App. 30 (see MacVeagh *v.* Bailey, 29 Ill. App. 606).

Iowa: Campbell *v.* Chamberlain, 10 Ia. 337; Plumb *v.* Woodmansee, 34 Ia. 116; Lowenstein *v.* Monroe, 55 Ia. 82, 7 N. W. 406.

Kentucky: Mocerf *v.* Stirman, 16 Ky. L. Rep. 587, 29 S. W. 324; Pettit *v.* Mercer, 8 B. Mon. 51.

Mississippi: Marqueze *v.* Sontheimer, 59 Miss. 430.

Missouri: State *v.* Stark, 75 Mo. 566; State *v.* McHale, 16 Mo. App. 478; State *v.* Coombs, 67 Mo. App. 199.

Ohio: Alexander *v.* Jacoby, 23 Oh. St. 358.

Oregon: Drake *v.* Sworts, 24 Ore. 198, 33 Pac. 563, 41 Am. St. Rep. 854.

Texas: Kirbs *v.* Provine, 78 Tex. 353, 14 S. W. 849.

Vermont: Weeks *v.* Prescott, 53 Vt. 57.

Washington: Seattle Crockery Co. *v.* Haley, 6 Wash. 302, 33 Pac. 650.

Wisconsin: Braunsdorf *v.* Fellner, 76 Wis. 1, 45 N. W. 97.

In some jurisdictions, however, damages may be recovered for loss of credit.

Alabama: Pollock *v.* Gantt, 69 Ala. 373, 44 Am. Rep. 519; Flournoy *v.* Lyon, 70 Ala. 308; Marx *v.* Leinkauff, 93 Ala. 453, 9 So. 318; Birmingham D. G. Co. *v.* Finley, 122 Ala. 534, 26 So. 138.

Nebraska: Meyer *v.* Fagan, 34 Neb. 184, 51 N. W. 753.

Where money is attached, loss of credit is of course disallowed as remote. Alabama State Land Co. *v.* Reed, 99 Ala. 19, 13 So. 43.

[91] *Alabama:* Pollock *v.* Gantt, 69 Ala. 373, 44 Am. Rep. 519; Marx *v.* Leinkauff, 93 Ala. 453, 460, 9 So. 318; Birmingham Dry Goods Co. *v.* Finley, 122 Ala. 534, 26 So. 138.

Illinois: Oberne *v.* Gaylord, 13 Ill. App. 30.

Kentucky: Mocerf *v.* Stirman, 16 Ky. L. Rep. 587, 29 S. W. 324.

Nebraska: Meyer *v.* Fagan, 34 Neb. 184, 51 N. W. 753.

Ohio: Alexander *v.* Jacoby, 23 Oh. St. 358.

See Com. *v.* Magnolia V. L. & I. Co., 163 Pa. 99, 29 Atl. 793.

Contra, L. Bucki & Son L. Co. *v.* Fidelity & D. Co., 109 Fed. 393, 48 C. C A. 436.

such damage has been held to be embraced in the attachment bond,[92] and he may also recover the loss of the profit of the contract.[93] If he is able by other means to perform the contract, the expense of the employment of such means may be shown.[94] So in an action on an attachment bond, where the property attached—cattle—was removed from a good range to a bad one, plaintiff was allowed to recover the increased value they would have acquired by being fattened on a good range.[95] But on the other hand no remote or merely speculative loss is a subject of compensation;[96] thus no damages can be recovered for an illegal act of the sheriff, not directed by the defendant, since it is not a proximate result of the attachment;[97] and where after dissolution of the attachment an appeal is taken, no damages can be recovered on the bond because of the appeal.[98] Where property is tied up by a wrongful attachment the owner cannot recover the amount of taxes assessed and paid pending the attachment.[99] Where real estate is attached, the owner's possession not being disturbed, the damages will usually be nominal. No recovery can be had for depreciation in the value of the property,[100] or for loss of credit by reason of the attachment.[101]

Damages may in a proper case be reduced, as by showing that the plaintiff got back his goods without expense or injury by

[92] Carpenter v. Stevenson, 6 Bush (Ky.), 259.

[93] State v. Andrews, 39 W. Va. 35, 19 S. E. 385.

[94] State v. McKeon, 25 Mo. App. 667 (expense of hire of teams to perform contract, for which the teams attached had been provided, may be shown, as establishing the value of the use of the teams attached).

[95] Hoge v. Norton, 22 Kan. 374.

[96] *Pennsylvania:* Com. v. Magnolia V. L. & I. Co., 163 Pa. 99, 29 Atl. 793.

Texas: Moore v. United States F. & G. Co., 52 Tex. Civ. App. 286, 113 S. W. 947.

[97] *Alabama:* Watts v. Rice, 75 Ala. 289; Jefferson County Bank v. Eborn, 84 Ala. 529, 4 So. 386; Crofford v. Vassar, 95 Ala. 548, 10 So. 350.

Illinois: Crow v. National Bank, 62 Ill. App. 24.

[98] Gerard v. Gateau, 15 Ill. App. 520.

[99] So where property in the hands of a receiver was taxed, it could not be assumed that the receiver would have disposed of the funds so as to escape taxation. Nor are the ordinary expenses of managing the fund chargeable on the bonds since they are incidental to the existence of the fund. Stringfield v. Hirsch, 94 Tenn. 425, 29 S. W. 609, 45 Am. St. Rep. 733.

[100] *California:* Heath v. Lent, 1 Cal. 410.

Iowa: Tisdale v. Major, 106 Iowa, 1, 75 N. W. 663, 68 Am. St. Rep. 263; Ames v. Chirurg, 132 N. W. 427.

[101] Elder v. Kutner, 97 Cal. 490, 32 Pac. 563.

replevin,[102] by filing a forthcoming or restitution bond,[103] or by default of appearance of the creditor in the attachment suit.[104] It has however been held that the existence of a chattel mortgage on the property would not diminish the plaintiff's recovery.[105]

§ 682a. Counsel fees and expenses in procuring dissolution of attachment.

On the attachment bond the plaintiff may recover his counsel fees and other legal expenses in procuring a dissolution of the attachment,[106] but not expenses incurred in defending the

[102] Painter v. Munn, 117 Ala. 322, 23 So. 83, 67 Am. St. Rep. 170.

[103] Bick v. Lang, 15 Ind. App. 503, 14 N. E. 555.

[104] Groat v. Gillespie, 25 Wend. (N. Y.) 383.

[105] Hartmann v. Hoffman, 65 App. Div. 443, 72 N. Y. Supp. 982.

[106] *United States:* L. Bucki & Son L. Co. v. Fidelity & D. Co., 109 Fed. 393, 48 C. C. A. 436.

Alabama: Dothard v. Sheid, 69 Ala. 135; Troy v. Rogers, 113 Ala. 131, 20 So. 999; Vandiver v. Waller, 143 Ala. 411, 39 So. 136.

Arkansas: Boatwright v. Stewart, 37 Ark. 614.

Florida: Gonzales v. De Funiak H. T. Co., 41 Fla. 471, 26 So. 1012.

Georgia: Fourth Nat. Bank v. Mayer, 96 Ga. 728, 24 S. E. 453.

Illinois: Damron v. Sweetser, 16 Ill. App. 339.

Indiana: Trentman v. Wiley, 85 Ind. 33.

Iowa: Porter v. Knight, 63 Ia. 365, 19 N. W. 282; Peters v. Snavely-Ashton, 144 Ia. 147, 122 N. W. 836.

Kentucky: United States F. & G. Co. v. Hows, 109 S. W. 343, 33 Ky. L. Rep. 131; Blakely v. Bogard, 136 S. W. 616.

Louisiana: Littlejohn v. Wilcox, 2 La. Ann. 620; Accessory T. Co. v. McCerren, 13 La. Ann. 214.

Michigan: Swift v. Plessner, 39 Mich. 178.

Mississippi: Buckley v. Van Diver, 70 Miss. 622, 12 So. 905.

Missouri: State v. O'Neill, 4 Mo. App. 221 (including fees in proceedings for dissolution after attachment dissolved by giving bond); State v. Allen, 124 Mo. App. 465, 103 S. W. 1090; State v. Flarsheim, 13 Mo. App. 1, 119 S. W. 17.

Nebraska: Raymond v. Green, 12 Neb. 215, 10 N. W. 709, 41 Am. Rep. 763.

New York: Hartmann v. Burtis, 65 App. Div. 481, 72 N. Y. Supp. 914; Epstein v. United States F. Co., 29 Misc. 295, 60 N. Y. Supp. 527; Marks v. Massachusetts B. & I. Co., 117 N. Y. Supp. 1019.

Ohio: Alexander v. Jacoby, 23 Oh. St. 358.

Oregon: Drake v. Sworts, 24 Ore. 198, 33 Pac. 563.

Pennsylvania: Com. v. Magnolia V. L. & I. Co., 163 Pa. 99, 29 Atl. 793; Berwald v. Ray, 165 Pa. 192, 30 Atl. 727.

Washington: Helfrich v. Meyer, 11 Wash. 186, 39 Pac. 455.

No counsel fees can be recovered if the suit was not defended. Baldwin v. Walker, 94 Ala. 514, 10 So. 391. Or if no attachment was in fact made, since no defense was necessary. State v. Binney, 127 Mo. App. 710, 106 S. W. 1114. But fees may be recovered even if the attempt to vacate the attach-

principal suit; [107] and if there were no expenses caused solely by the attachment proceedings, there can be no recovery on this account.[108] Recovery of legal expenses includes necessary travelling fees in attending court.[109] In a few States no recovery can be had for counsel fees unless they have actually been paid.[110] No recovery can be had on the bond for the legal expenses of a third person who intervened to claim the goods.[111]

In a few States the statute under which the bond is given is interpreted as allowing a recovery on the bond of the legal expenses in the entire suit.[112]

§ 683. Exemplary damages.

Under the statutes of some States, if the wrongful attach-

ment failed, if the motion was not denied on the merits, and the attaching party ultimately failed on the main issue. Tyng v. American Surety Co., 69 App. Div. 137, 74 N. Y. Supp. 502.

[107] *Florida:* Gonzales v. De Funiak H. T. Co., 41 Fla. 471, 26 So. 1012.

Illinois: Danron v. Sweetser, 16 Ill. App. 339.

Iowa: Porter v. Knight, 63 Ia. 365, 19 N. W. 282; Ames v. Chirurg, 132 N. W. 427.

Kentucky: Vannatta v. Vannatta, 21 Ky. L. Rep. 1464, 55 S. W. 685.

Louisiana: Adam v. Gomila, 37 La. Ann. 479.

Minnesota: Frost v. Jordan, 37 Minn. 544, 36 N. W. 713 (though the attachment was necessary to give jurisdiction).

New York: Northampton Nat. Bank v. Wylie, 52 Hun, 146, 4 N. Y. Supp. 907, 26 N. Y. St. Rep. 286, 16 N. Y. Civ. Proc. 326.

Ohio: Alexander v. Jacoby, 23 Oh. St. 358.

Washington: Helfrich v. Meyer, 11 Wash. 186, 39 Pac. 455.

If one sum is paid for the entire defence, such part of it as is reasonably to be charged to the attachment may be recovered. McClure v. Renaker, 21 Ky. L. Rep. 360, 51 S. W. 317.

In New York if the attachment is necessary to found jurisdiction it has been held that where the suit is dismissed on the merits counsel fees on the whole suit may be recovered. Fixel v. Tallman, 116 N. Y. Supp. 639.

[108] Northampton Nat. Bank v. Wylie, 52 Hun, 148, 4 N. Y. Supp. 907, 26 N. Y. St. Rep. 286, 16 N. Y. Civ. Proc. 326.

[109] State v. Shobe, 23 Mo. App. 474.

[110] *California:* Elder v. Kutner, 97 Cal. 490, 32 Pac. 563.

Kentucky: Shulz v. Morrison, 3 Met. 98.

Contra, Missouri: Holthaus v. Hart, 9 Mo. App. 1; State v. Gage, 52 Mo. App. 464.

New York: Epstein v. U. S. Fidelity Co., 29 Misc. 295, 60 N. Y. Supp. 527; Marks v. Massachusetts B. & I. Co., 117 N. Y. Supp. 1019. See *post,* § 685, n.

[111] *Alabama:* Thompson v. Gates, 18 Ala. 32 (by claim of title); Flournoy v. Lyon, 70 Ala. 308 (by claim as garnishee).

North Carolina: Stein v. Cozart, 122 N. C. 280, 30 S. E. 340 (by claim of title).

[112] Greaves v. Newport, 41 Minn. 240, 42 N. W. 1059.

ment be malicious, exemplary damages may be recovered in an action on the bond.[113] This is the same measure of damages which is adopted in an action of tort for malicious attachment.[114] The allowance of exemplary damages is based, in Alabama at least, on the peculiar wording of the statute, which expressly provides for damages for "the wrongful or the vexatious" suing out of the writ.[115] As a consequence of this right to recover exemplary damages, probable cause may be shown in mitigation.[116]

In most jurisdictions exemplary damages cannot be recovered in an action on the bond, since the action is for breach of a contract, in which exemplary damages cannot be had.[117]

§ 684. Forthcoming bonds—Bonds to dissolve attachment—Receiptors.

Bonds to dissolve attachment (also called forthcoming bonds)

[113] *Alabama:* Kirksey v. Jones, 7 Ala. 622; McCullough v. Walton, 11 Ala. 492; Sharpe v. Hunter, 16 Ala. 765; Forrest v. Collier, 20 Ala. 175; Seay v. Greenwood, 21 Ala. 491; Dothard v. Sheid, 69 Ala. 135; City Nat. Bank v. Jeffries, 73 Ala. 183; Watts v. Rice, 75 Ala. 289; Schloss v. Rovelsky, 107 Ala. 596, 18 So. 71; Mobile F. C. Co. v. Little, 108 Ala. 399, 19 So. 443; Van Diver v. Waller, 143 Ala. 411, 39 So. 136.

Iowa: Gaddis v. Lord, 10 Ia. 141; Nordhaus v. Peterson, 54 Ia. 68, 6 N. W. 77; International H. Co. v. Iowa H. Co., 122 N. W. 951.

Tennessee: Doll v. Cooper, 9 Lea, 576; Renkert v. Elliott, 11 Lea, 235.

Washington: Sloane v. Langert, 6 Wash. 26, 32 Pac. 1015; Levy v. Fleischner, 12 Wash. 15, 40 Pac. 384.

No damages can be recovered by the plaintiff, it has been held, where the malice was directed against a third person only. Wood v. Barker, 37 Ala. 60. Nor where there is no actual damage. Helfrich v. Meyer, 11 Wash. 186, 39 Pac. 455.

Exemplary damages cannot be re-covered against a principal for the act of his agent. Jackson v. Smith, 75 Ala. 97. Unless it was ratified by the principal with full knowledge. Baldwin v. Walker, 94 Ala. 514, 10 So. 391. A corporation may be subjected to exemplary damages for the act of its agent. Jefferson County Bank v. Eborn, 84 Ala. 529, 4 So. 386.

In Washington "exemplary damages" does not mean damages by way of punishment but indeterminable actual damages such as damages to reputation, pride, and feeling. Levy v. Fleischner, 12 Wash. 15, 40 Pac. 384.

[114] *Ante,* § 467.

[115] On a *ne exeat* bond, under a statute providing only for damages caused by the "wrongful" suing out of the writ, it was held that the plaintiff could recover his actual damages; but that if he would recover damages as for a malicious act, he must sue in case. Spivey v. McGehee, 21 Ala. 417.

[116] Metcalf v. Young, 43 Ala. 643. As, advice of counsel. Raver v. Webster, 3 Ia. 502.

[117] *Arkansas:* Goodbar v. Lindsley,

are conditioned sometimes to produce the property, sometimes to pay the judgment, sometimes in the alternative to do one or the other. If the bond binds the party to pay the judgment, the measure of damages for a breach of it is the amount of the judgment.[118] If, however, the bond is in the alternative, or is merely to produce the property, the limit of recovery, if the property is not produced, is the value of the property at the time it was given,[119] limited, however, by the amount of the judgment, with interest and costs.[120]

If the property is returned there is of course no breach of the bond; and if a portion of it is returned, the recovery is for the balance only.[121] If the property is returned in a damaged condition, the measure of damages is the amount of the deterioration.[122] If the property is not returned, but an excuse is offered which is sufficient, there can be no recovery; as where live-stock

51 Ark. 380, 11 S. W. 577, 14 Am. St. Rep. 54. .

California: Elder *v.* Kutner, 97 Cal. 490, 32 Pac. 563.

Georgia: Fourth Nat. Bank *v.* Mayer, 96 Ga. 728, 24 S. E. 453.

South Carolina: McClendon *v.* Wells, 20 S. C. 514.

[118] *Florida:* Collins *v.* Mitchell, 3 Fla. 4 (*semble*).

Kentucky: Keel *v.* Ogden, 3 Dana, 103.

Massachusetts: Berry *v.* Wasserman, 179 Mass. 537, 61 N. E. 228.

Michigan: Phansteihl *v.* Vanderhoof, 22 Mich. 296.

New York: Morange *v.* Edwards, 1 E. D. Smith, 414.

[119] *California:* Hammond *v.* Starr, 79 Cal. 556; Curtin *v.* Harvey, 120 Cal. 620, 52 Pac. 1077.

Florida: Collins *v.* Mitchell, 3 Fla. 4.

Georgia: Jolley *v.* Rutherford, 112 Ga. 342, 37 S. E. 358.

Kentucky: Moon *v.* Story, 2 B. Mon. 354 (*semble*).

Mississippi: Irion *v.* Hume, 50 Miss. 419.

Missouri: Lee *v.* Moore, 12 Mo. 458;

McDonald *v.* Loewen (Mo. App.), 130 S. W. 52.

New York: Bruck *v.* Feiner, 26 Misc. 724, 56 N. Y. Supp. 1025.

Rhode Island: Pearce *v.* Maguire, 17 R. I. 55, 20 Atl. 98.

Texas: Jones *v.* Hays, 27 Tex. 1.

[120] *Alabama:* McElrath *v.* Whetstone, 89 Ala. 623, 8 So. 7.

California: Mullally *v.* Townsend, 119 Cal. 47, 50 Pac. 1066.

Georgia: Whelchel *v.* Duckett, 91 Ga. 132, 16 S. E. 643; Jolley *v.* Rutherford, 112 Ga. 342, 37 S. E. 358.

Indiana: Mitchell *v.* Denbo, 3 Blackf. 259.

Louisiana: Canfield *v.* McLaughlin, 10 Martin, 48.

Missouri: Lee *v.* Moore, 12 Mo. 458.

Texas: Wallace *v.* Terry (Tex. Civ. App.), 15 S. W. 35.

Interest cannot be added where the defendant was obliged by legal process to hold the amount as garnishee. Huntress *v.* Burbank, 111 Mass. 213.

[121] Lee *v.* Moore, 12 Mo. 458.

[122] *Colorado:* Creswell *v.* Woodside, 8 Colo. App. 514, 46 Pac. 842.

Louisiana: Lallande *v.* Trezevant, 39 La. Ann. 830, 2 So. 573.

was taken and died without the fault of the defendant,[123] or a slave was taken and died [124] or was emancipated.[125] It is no excuse to show that the property did not belong to the debtor [126] unless indeed it was taken by the true owner.[127] If the goods were subject to a prior mortgage, which subjected the property to the satisfaction of the debt, the defendant is not excused, since he might have kept and produced the property by paying the mortgage; but the damages are nominal only.[128]

The liability of a receiptor is much the same. He is responsible for the value of the goods, as valued in the receipt; [129] and if goods are taken from him on a prior mortgage the value of the goods so taken is deducted from the value in the receipt.[130] So if goods are taken away by a paramount owner, the value of them is deducted.[131]

No recovery can be had on the bond for counsel fees incurred after the dissolution of the attachment.[132]

§ 684a. Bonds to indemnify attaching sheriff.

Where a bond is given to an attaching sheriff to indemnify him, he is entitled to recover all damages suffered by him, but not damages suffered by the creditor.[133] He may recover the amount of a judgment recovered against him because of the attachment, even though he has not paid it and is not solvent,[134]

[123] Carr v. Houston G. & W. Co., 105 Ga. 268, 31 S. E. 178 (the burden is on the defendant to show that he was without fault).

[124] Haralson v. Walker, 23 Ark. 415.

[125] Irion v. Hume, 50 Miss. 419.

[126] *Illinois:* Gray v. McLean, 17 Ill. 404.
Michigan: Dorr v. Clark, 7 Mich. 310.

[127] Gray v. McLean, 17 Ill. 404 (*semble*).

[128] Dehler v. Held, 50 Ill. 491.

[129] *Massachusetts:* Wakefield v. Stedman, 12 Pick. 562.
New Hampshire: Healy v. Hutchinson, 66 N. H. 316, 20 Atl. 332; Cross v. Brown, 41 N. H. 283.

[130] Healy v. Hutchinson, 66 N. H. 316, 20 Atl. 332.

[131] Haynes v. Tenney, 45 N. H. 183; Spear v. Hill, 52 N. H. 323; Stone v. Sleeper, 59 N. H. 205.

[132] State v. Fargo, 151 Mo. 280, 52 S. W. 199.

[133] *Delaware:* Staats v. Herbert, 4 Del. Ch. 508.
Iowa: Constantine v. Rowland, 124 N. W. 189.
Mississippi: Moore v. Lowrey, 74 Miss. 413, 21 So. 237.
Pennsylvania: Clement v. Courtright, 9 Pa. Super. Ct. 45.

[134] *Kansas:* Gardner v. Cooper, 9 Kan. App. 587, 58 Pac. 230.
Massachusetts: Briggs v. McDonald, 166 Mass. 37, 43 N. E. 1003.
Nevada: Jones v. Child, 8 Nev. 121.
New York: Wheeler v. Sweet, 137 N. Y. 435, 33 N. E. 483 (*semble*).

together with his costs,[135] not exceeding the amount of the penalty with interest.[136]   No damages can be recovered which were not the result of the particular attachment for which the bond was given,[137] and therefore (since they could be allowed only for some personal malice or other wrong of the sheriff itself) no exemplary damages can be allowed.[138]

In some jurisdictions the bond enures to the benefit of the attachment or execution defendant, who may therefore recover his damages; which would be the value of the property, if it has been sold,[139] and all such damages as he could recover on an attachment bond.[140]

§ 685. Injunction bonds—General principles.

An injunction bond is a statutory bond, and its form is governed by the statute, which therefore determines what will amount to a breach,[141] and what damages are covered by the

Ohio: Miller *v.* Rhoades, 20 Oh. St. 494.

Oklahoma: Armour Packing Co. *v.* Orrick, 4 Okla. 661, 46 Pac. 573.

Contra, California: Oaks *v.* Scheiferly, 74 Cal. 478, 16 Pac. 252 (but see White *v.* Fratt, 13 Cal. 521).

In Wheeler *v.* Sweet, 137 N. Y. 435, 33 N. E. 483, binding force was refused to the judgment because the sheriff by collusion prevented the present defendants from presenting their defence in the earlier suit.

[135] *California:* Stark *v.* Raney, 18 Cal. 622.

New York: Dyett *v.* Hyman, 129 N. Y. 351, 29 N. E. 261, 26 Am. St. Rep. 533.

Washington: Brotton *v.* Lunkley, 11 Wash. 581, 40 Pac. 140.

[136] *Massachusetts:* White *v.* French, 15 Gray, 339.

New York: Casani *v.* Dunn, 44 App. Div. 248, 60 N. Y. Supp. 756.

Texas: Stevens *v.* Wolf, 77 Tex. 215, 14 S. W. 29.

[137] *Idaho:* Fury *v.* White, 2 Ida. 639, 23 Pac. 535.

Massachusetts: Briggs *v.* McDonald, 166 Mass. 37, 43 N. E. 1003.

[138] *Iowa:* Constantine *v.* Rowland, 147 Ia. 142, 124 N. W. 189.

Virginia: Crump *v.* Ficklin, 1 P. & H. 201.

[139] *Kentucky:* Winstead *v.* Hicks, 121 S. W. 1018.

Michigan: Lee *v.* Maxwell, 98 Mich. 496, 57 N. W. 581.

Virginia: Crump *v.* Ficklin, 1 P. & H. 201.

[140] Manning *v.* Grinstead, 90 S. W. 553, 28 Ky. L. R. 787.

[141] Dismissal of the suit is *prima facie* evidence that injunction was wrongfully issued. Findlay *v.* Carson, 97 Ia. 537, 66 N. W. 759. Final dismissal on the merits is conclusive. Bemis *v.* Gannett, 8 Neb. 236; Manufacturers' Bank *v.* Dare, 67 Hun (N. Y.), 44, 21 N. Y. Supp. 806. Vacation of temporary injunction not conclusive when court on final hearing found plaintiff entitled to injunction. New York S. & T. Co. *v.* Lipman, 83 Hun (N. Y.), 569, 32 N. Y. Supp. 65. Dissolution of injunction by plaintiff under order of court as penalty for contempt not a determination that it was wrongfully issued. Apollinaris Co. *v.* Venable, 136 N. Y. 46, 32 N. E. 555. Agree-

bond.[142] Where the obligee of the bond is an official, or other nominal party, the real party in interest should bring suit on the bond.[143] The recovery cannot exceed the amount of the penalty, with interest; [144] actual damages must be proved,[145] and remote damages cannot be allowed.[146]

ment to submit dispute to arbitration and finding by arbitrators against plaintiff not a judgment as to injunction. Columbus, etc., Ry. v. Burke, 54 Oh. St. 98, 34 N. E. 282. Discontinuance by plaintiff is not a decision as to issuance of injunction. Palmer v. Foley, 71 N. Y. 106; Johnson v. Elwood, 82 N. Y. 362; De Berard v. Priale, 34 App. Div. 502, 54 N. Y. Supp. 534; Taylor Worsted Co. v. Beolchi, 37 N. Y. Misc. 691, 76 N. Y. Supp. 379. But see N. Y. Cent. & H. R. R. R. v. Hastings-on-Hudson, 9 App. Div. 256, 41 N. Y. Supp. 492. Injunction against several acts dissolved as to all but one act; damages sustained by the injunction recoverable except those sustained by that part of the injunction which was continued. Pierson v. Ells, 46 Hun (N. Y.), 336.

[142] *Mississippi:* Martin v. Kelly, 59 Miss. 652; Williams v. Bank of Commerce, 71 Miss. 858, 16 So. 238.

New Hampshire: Towle v. Towle, 46 N. H. 431.

Special damages must be alleged: *United States:* Sullivan v. Cartier, 147 Fed. 222, 77 C. C. A. 448.

Montana: Parker v. Bond, 5 Mont. 1, 1 Pac. 209.

And in the absence of proof of damage, nominal damages may be recovered on breach: Stone v. Cason, 1 Ore. 100. But see Foster v. Stafford Nat. Bank, 58 Vt. 658, 5 Atl. 890.

[143] *California:* Lally v. Wise, 28 Cal. 539.

Colorado: Wason v. Frank, 7 Colo. App. 541, 44 Pac. 378.

Montana: Helena v. Brulo, 15 Mont. 429, 39 Pac. 456.

But see *New York:* Andrews v. Glenville Woolen Co., 50 N. Y. 282.

In Montana Mining Co. v. St. Louis M. & M. Co., 19 Mont. 313, 48 Pac. 305, where the obligation ran to several parties it was held that they must sue jointly, though their interests were different.

Where a bond runs to a corporation no recovery can be had on it for damages to the stockholders. Eaton v. Larimer & W. R. Co., 3 Colo. App. 366, 33 Pac. 278.

[144] *Alabama:* Ehrman v. Stanfield, 80 Ala. 118.

Kentucky: Hughes v. Wickcliffe, 11 B. Mon. 202.

New York: Hovey v. Rubber Tip Pencil Co., 38 N. Y. Super. Ct. 428.

Vermont: Glover v. McGaffey, 56 Vt. 294.

West Virginia: Peerce v. Athey, 4 W. Va. 22; State v. Purcell, 31 W. Va. 44, 5 S. E. 301.

But see *Louisiana:* Jackson v. Larche, 11 Mart. 284.

Damages allowed in the original suit upon dissolution may exceed the penalty named in the bond: Kohlsaat v. Crate, 144 Ill. 14, 32 N. E. 481; but in that case only the penalty, with interest and costs, may be recovered in an action on the bond. Lawton v. Green, 64 N. Y. 326.

[145] *Louisiana:* Meaux v. Pittman, 35 La. Ann. 360.

Tennessee: Boyd v. Knox, 53 S. W. 972.

Washington: White v. Brooke, 11 Wash. 99, 39 Pac. 237.

[146] *United States:* Lehman v. McQuown, 31 Fed. 138.

Whether damages shall be assessed in the original suit or in an action on the bond depends upon the law of the jurisdiction, or the terms of the bond.[147] If they are legally assessed in the original suit, the amount so found is conclusive.[148] If they are not so assessed, they may be found in an action on the bond.[149]

Where the injunction is immediately vacated, no damages can be recovered, since none were suffered, though the suit itself goes on; [150] and if the plaintiff disobeys the injunction from the first, though he is not thereby barred from action on the bond,[151] still as he suffered no damages he can recover none.[152] If a preliminary injunction was made perpetual on the hearing, but upon appeal it was dissolved, recovery can be had on the bond only to the time when the injunction was made perpetual; [153] but if at the hearing a dissolution is decreed, and an appeal taken, and the decree affirmed, recovery can be had on the bond for all damages, including those accrued while the appeal was pending.[154]

If the injunction was against doing an illegal act the plaintiff,

England: Smith *v.* Day, 21 Ch. D. 421, 31 Wkly. Rep. 187.

[147] *United States:* Meyers *v.* Block, 120 U. S. 206, 30 L. ed. 642, 7 Sup. Ct. 525 (damages on the bond by its terms to be recovered in action on bond); West *v.* East Coast Cedar Co., 113 Fed. 742, 51 C. C. A. 416 (damages may be recovered in original suit).

Arkansas: Blakeney *v.* Ferguson, 18 Ark. 347 (damages must be so assessed).

Contra, Alabama: Bogacki *v.* Welch, 94 Ala. 429, 10 So. 330.

[148] Lothrop *v.* Southworth, 5 Mich. 436.

[149] *Illinois:* Hibbard *v.* McKindley, 28 Ill. 240; Brown *v.* Gorton, 31 Ill. 416; Edwards *v.* Edwards, 31 Ill. 474; Keith *v.* Henkleman, 173 Ill. 137, 50 N. E. 692.

New Hampshire: Jackman *v.* Eastman, 62 N. H. 273.

New Jersey: Easton *v.* New York, etc., Ry., 26 N. J. Eq. 359.

[150] Hyde *v.* Teal, 46 La. Ann. 645, 15 So. 416.

[151] *Illinois:* Colcord *v.* Sylvester, 66 Ill. 540.

Maryland: Phœnix Pad Co. *v.* U. S., 111 Md. 549, 75 Atl. 394.

Missouri: Van Hoozer *v.* Van Hoozer, 18 Mo. App. 19.

[152] *Maryland:* Phœnix Pad Co. *v.* U. S., 111 Md. 549, 75 Atl. 394.

Missouri: Van Hoozer *v.* Van Hoozer, 18 Mo. App. 19.

[153] *California:* Webber *v.* Wilcox, 45 Cal. 301; Lambert *v.* Haskell, 80 Cal. 611, 22 Pac. 327.

Illinois: Milligan *v.* Nelson, 188 Ill. 139, 58 N. E. 938.

So where an injunction is modified so as to permit the act restrained, damages can be recovered only up to the time of modification. Tyler Mining Co. *v.* Last Chance Mining Co., 90 Fed. 15, 32 C. C. A. 498.

[154] *Maryland:* Hamilton *v.* State, 32 Md. 348.

But see *Missouri:* C. H. Albers C. Co. *v.* Spencer, 139 S. W. 321.

though entitled to recover, cannot get damages for not being allowed to do the illegal act.[155] When the injunction was ambiguous, the person enjoined is entitled to such damages as he may have sustained by obeying it as he reasonably understood it.[156]

Upon an undertaking or bond entered into as a condition of granting a temporary restraining order damages cannot be allowed after the order is superseded by an injunction.[157]

§ 685a. Injunction preventing use of land.

Where the injunction prevented the use of land, the owner may recover on the bond the value of the use of land, which in the ordinary case would be its rental value, for the time during which he was deprived of the use.[158] If a crop was made from the land, or other mesne profits were realized by the defendant on the bond, the owner is entitled to recover the value.[159] If the land is under lease, the plaintiff may recover the rent reserved during the period.[160]

If the defendant committed waste while the injunction was in force, the amount of the waste may be recovered on the bond;[161] and so if personal property prepared for use in connection with the land and on the land is lost or depreciates in

---

[155] Turnpike Co. v. Kelley, 41 Oh. St. 144.

If the question of the legality of the acts was passed upon in the original action in favor of the present plaintiff, their illegality cannot be set up in an action on the bond. Omaha Lith. Co. v. Simpson, 29 Neb. 96, 45 N. W. 261.

[156] Webb v. Laird, 62 Vt. 448, 20 Atl. 599, 22 Am. St. Rep. 121.

[157] Houghton v. Cortelyou, 208 U. S. 149, 28 Sup. Ct. 234, 52 L. ed. 432.

[158] Wadsworth v. O'Donnell, 7 Ky. L. Rep. 837 (i. e., rental value for any purpose; but in Alexander v. Colcord, 85 Ill. 323, the court appears to have confined the plaintiff to its value for the use he intended to make of it).

[159] *California:* Rice v. Cook, 92 Cal. 144, 38 Pac. 219.

Georgia: Richardson v. Allen, 74 Ga. 719.

Illinois: Edwards v. Edwards, 31 Ill. 474; Hosmer v. Campbell, 98 Ill. 572.

Indiana: Rutherford v. Moore, 24 Ind. 311.

New York: Roberts v. White, 73 N. Y. 375.

[160] *New York:* Bray v. Poillon, 4 Thomps. & C. 663.

Vermont: Sturges v. Knapp, 36 Vt. 439 (railroad).

[161] *Georgia:* Richardson v. Allen, 74 Ga. 719.

Illinois: Alexander v. Colcord, 85 Ill. 323 (cutting timber).

Indiana: Winship v. Clendenning, 24 Ind. 439 (cutting timber).

North Carolina: Nansemond Timber Co. v. Rountree, 122 N. C. 45, 29 S. E. 61 (cutting timber).

value, recovery may be had for the damage.[162] So where trees had been girdled preparatory to being cut for timber before the injunction, and during the injunction they greatly deteriorated in value, the amount of the deterioration could be recovered.[163] But where the land at the time of the injunction had a purely speculative value, due to the belief that it contained oil, and before the injunction was dissolved it had been found that there was no oil in the land and its value fell, this depreciation in value (in the absence of evidence that a specific offer to pay the high price was lost because of the injunction) is too remote.[164]

§ 685b. Injunction against taking a profit from land.

Where the injunction is against taking some profit from the land, without restraining its use for other purposes, the plaintiff may recover the loss caused by failure to get the profit at the time. So where the injunction prevented the harvesting of an annual crop,[165] the cutting of ice,[166] mining,[167] getting crude petroleum,[168] or cutting timber,[169] the measure of damages is the profit that might have been realized from the operation.

Consequential damages may be recovered in a proper case; as for the expense of moving a saw-mill and machinery to another tract of land, in order not to lose the use of it, and then moving it back again.[170] But merely speculative damages cannot be recovered,[171] nor damages which should have been

[162] *Illinois:* Alexander v. Colcord, 85 Ill. 323 (materials for fencing).
Tennessee: South Penn Oil Co. v. Stone (Tenn. Ch.), 57 S. W. 374 (machinery for oil wells).
[163] Drews v. Williams, 50 La. Ann. 579, 2 So. 897.
[164] South Penn Oil Co. v. Stone (Tenn. Ch.), 57 S. W. 374.
[165] Collins v. Sinclair, 51 Ill. 328.
[166] Brown v. Cunningham, 82 Iowa, 512, 48 N. W. 1042, 12 L. R. A. 583.
[167] *United States:* Corsair M. Co. v. Carolina M. Co., 75 Fed. 860.
Colorado: Quinn v. Baldwin Star Coal Co., 19 Colo. App. 497, 76 Pac. 552.
Iowa: Findlay v. Carson, 97 Iowa, 537, 66 N. W. 759.

So of removing sand: Chicago T. & T. Co. v. Chicago, 209 Ill. 172, 70 N. E. 572.
[168] Livingston v. Exum, 19 S. E. 223.
[169] *South Carolina:* Moorer v. Andrews, 36 S. C. 427, 17 S. E. 948.
Texas: French v. McCready (Tex. Civ. App), 57 S. W. 894.
Vermont: Lillie v. Lillie, 55 Vt. 470.
[170] French v. McCready (Tex. Civ. App.), 57 S. W. 894.
[171] *United States:* Coosaw Min. Co. v. Carolina Mfg. Co., 75 Fed. 860 (phosphate rock of fluctuating value).
Illinois: Chicago T. & T. Co. v. Chicago, 209 Ill. 172, 70 N. E. 572 (uncertain fluctuating deposits of sand and gravel).

avoided by the plaintiff;[172] and where the injunction restrained the plaintiff from cutting timber on certain land, the defendant, in an action on the bond, may show that the plaintiff had no title to the land and no right to cut timber on it.[173] Where pending the injunction loss was caused by act of God, as by flood or wind, damages cannot be recovered on the bond, since they were not caused by the injunction.[174]

§ 685c. Other injunctions concerning land.

Where the use of an irrigation ditch is enjoined, and plaintiff could not have obtained water elsewhere, he may recover for the resulting loss of crops.[175] If water can be procured elsewhere, the expense and trouble of so procuring it may be recovered.[176] If an irrigation company is enjoined from cutting off a water supply, it cannot recover on the bond for the water furnished during the pendency of the injunction, where the defendant is solvent,[177] but must enforce payment for the water by an ordinary action.

Where one is enjoined from interfering with a tenant or collecting rents the plaintiff on the bond may recover the amount of the rent he has lost,[178] which would ordinarily be nothing unless the tenant had become insolvent or had vacated the premises because of the injunction, or the defendant had collected rent.[179] If the person enjoined was mortgagee he cannot recover so long as the security is ample.[180]

In case of an injunction against moving a house the party

Kentucky: Epenbaugh *v.* Gooch, 15 Ky. L. Rep. 576 (profits of cutting timber).

[172] *Iowa:* Behrens *v.* McKenzie, 23 Ia. 333, 92 Am. Dec. 428 (loss of moulded brick by rain).

Kentucky: United States F. & G. Co. *v.* Jones, 33 Ky. L. Rep. 737, 111 S. W. 298 (loss of use of teams); Citizens' T. & G. Co. *v.* Ohio Valley Tie Co., 128 S. W. 317.

North Carolina: Nansemond Timber Co. *v.* Rountree, 122 N. C. 45, 29 S. E. 61 (loss of use of teams).

[173] Jenkins *v.* Parkhill, 25 Ind. 473.

[174] *Illinois:* Chicago T. & T. Co. *v.* Chicago, 209 Ill. 172, 70 N. E. 572.

Kentucky: Citizens' T. & G. Co. *v.* Ohio Valley Tie Co., 128 S. W. 317.

[175] Mack *v.* Jackson, 9 Colo. 536, 13 Pac. 542.

[176] Rohwer *v.* Chadwick, 7 Utah, 385, 26 Pac. 1116.

[177] Edmison *v.* Sioux Falls Water Co., 14 S. D. 486, 85 N. W. 1016.

[178] Sturgis *v.* Knapp, 33 Vt. 486 (a railroad lease).

[179] McDonald *v.* James, 38 N. Y. Super. Ct. 76, 47 How. Pr. 474.

[180] Schening *v.* Cofer, 97 Ala. 726, 12 So. 414.

enjoined cannot recover for loss of use of tools and machinery used to support the house, since the injunction did not prevent him from removing such tools and machinery from the house.[181] And where the injunction was to prevent the removal of certain buildings which could not be removed as structures, but would have to be torn down, and the material removed, it was held that the amount of damages was the loss in the value of the buildings and material between the time when the injunction was issued and the time when it was dissolved, with interest during that time.[182]

§ 685d. Injunctions against doing work.

Where one is prevented by an injunction from doing work, he may recover for injury by the delay to materials collected for the work,[183] but not, it has been held, for loss of workmen [184] or for the increased cost of doing the work after the injunction was dissolved.[185] For mere delay in performance, without evidence of special damage by waste of materials or labor, only nominal damages can be recovered.[186]

In a case where a street railway was enjoined from repairing a break in their line, and after the break passengers walked round the obstruction, and in consequence of the injunction the company ceased running cars beyond the break and reduced fares because of the shorter distance run, it was held that the company could recover the decrease in tolls arising from the decrease in travel caused by the break in the line, but could not recover the decrease in tolls arising from stopping the cars beyond the break and reducing fares.[187]

In a case where the plaintiff was enjoined from doing certain work on a railroad, it was held that he could recover interest on money detained from him on his contract during the pendency of the injunction, from the time when the contract would have been completed until the dissolution of the injunction;

[181] Hermann v. Allen (Tex.), 128 S. W. 115.

[182] Ridpath v. Merriam, 22 Wash. 311, 60 Pac. 1120.

[183] Dougherty v. Dore, 63 Cal. 170 (materials for grading washed away).

[184] Moorer v. Andrews, 39 S. C. 427, 17 S. E. 948.

[185] Morgan v. Negley, 53 Pa. 153.

[186] Cooper v. Hames, 93 Ala. 280, 9 So. 341.

[187] Hawthorne v. McArthur, 8 Ky. L. Rep. 526.

and the cost of putting the work in the same condition it was in when the injunction was served.[188]

§ 685e. Injunctions against carrying on business.

Where the injunction prevents the carrying on of a business, the plaintiff on the bond can recover the profits he was prevented from realizing, provided the business was an established one so that the amount of profits can be shown with sufficient certainty.[189] The profits expected from a new business are of course too uncertain and conjectural for recovery.[190]

The plaintiff may recover the value of the use of the premises, and wages paid for guarding the property and to the employees under contract of service.[191] Where the plaintiff was enjoined from working a mine, it was held he could recover the value of the time while he was necessarily idle;[192] and for necessary expense of keeping the mine clear of water.[193] He may recover for a loss of property on account of the injunction.[194] If in spite of the injunction it appears that the plaintiff persisted in carrying on his business and he cannot show the loss of any sales on account of the injunction, he can recover nothing for loss of business.[195]

[188] St. Louis, I. M. & S. Ry. v. Schneider, 30 Mo. App. 620.

[189] *California:* Lambert v. Haskell, 80 Cal. 611, 22 Pac. 327.

Illinois: Landis v. Wolf, 206 Ill. 392, 69 N. E. 103.

Virginia: Whitehead v. Cape Henry Syndicate, 111 Va. 193, 68 S. E. 263 (*semble*).

Washington: Steel v. Gordon, 14 Wash. 521, 45 Pac. 151.

Wisconsin: Gear v. Shaw, 1 Pin. 608. In Schlesiger v. Bedford, [1893] W. N. 57, 9 T. L. Rep. 370, where the injunction was against producing a play, the lost profits from this particular play were allowed, deducting, however, the earnings from another play produced instead of it.

[190] *Illinois:* Chicago C. Ry. v. Howison, 86 Ill. 215 (extension of railroad).

New York: Manufacturers' & Traders' Bank v. C. W. F. Dare Co., 67 Hun, 44, 21 N. Y. Supp. 806 (manufacture).

Virginia: Whitehead v. Cape Henry Syndicate, 111 Va. 193, 68 S. E. 263 (fishery).

[191] Wood v. State, 66 Md. 61 (injunction against working a saw-mill).

[192] Muller v. Fern, 35 Ia. 420. The burden is here upon the plaintiff to show due diligence in seeking other employment, for he must show that he was damaged; the case differs from an action on a contract of service, where it is for the defendant to show why he should not pay the amount named in the contract.

[193] Tyler Mining Co. v. Last Chance Mining Co., 90 Fed. 15, 32 C. C. A. 498.

[194] Hotchkiss v. Platt, 8 Hun (N. Y.), 46.

[195] Steel v. Gordon, 14 Wash. 521, 45 Pac. 151.

§ 685f. Injunctions against constructing a building or other work.

In case of injunction against constructing a building, the owner may recover the value of the use during the period of delay.[196] Where the plaintiff was enjoined from building a stable he was allowed to recover for injury to his cattle by being without shelter, and for the decreased supply of milk.[197] And where the injunction is against repairing and rebuilding a dam, he may recover for the consequent loss of use of his mill.[198] He may also recover any increase in the cost of construction due to the injunction,[199] and any loss of labor or materials caused by the interruption of the work.[200]

§ 685g. Injunctions against collecting a judgment or other debt.

When the collection of a judgment or other debt is enjoined, the bond is sometimes conditioned on paying the amount of the debt if the injunction is dissolved; and upon such a bond of course the entire amount of the debt may be collected,[201] including such costs, damages and interest as may have been included in the judgment.[202] But on the ordinary form of bond the amount of the debt cannot be recovered unless for some reason it has ceased to be collectible.[203] If the statute of limitations has run and the debt has thus become barred pending the

[196] Hutchins v. Munn, 209 U. S. 246, 28 Sup. Ct. 504, 52 L. ed. 776.

[197] Lange v. Wagner, 52 Md. 310, 36 Am. Rep. 380. One not himself a party to the injunction cannot recover. Marengo County v. Matkin, 144 Ala. 574, 42 So. 33.

[198] Webb v. Laird, 62 Vt. 448, 20 Atl. 599, 22 Am. St. Rep. 121.

[199] Morgan v. Negley, 53 Pa. 153 (railroad; but not where the premises are sold pending the injunction).

[200] Creek v. McManus, 17 Mont. 445, 43 Pac. 497.

[201] *United States:* Allen v. Jones, 79 Fed. 698.
Arkansas: Hunt v. Burton, 18 Ark. 188.
Illinois: Roberts v. Fahs, 36 Ill. 268. In Ryan v. Anderson, 25 Ill. 372, re-

covery was not allowed because the bond did not run to the person entitled to payment.

[202] *Alabama:* Moore v. Harton, 1 Port. 15.
Virginia: Fox v. Mountjoy, 6 Munf. 36.

[203] *Arkansas:* Neal v. Taylor, 56 Ark. 521, 20 S. W. 352 (form of bond changed since decision in Hunt v. Burton, *supra*).
Illinois: Rosenthal v. Boass, 27 Ill. App. 430.
Iowa: Grove v. Bush, 86 Iowa, 94, 53 N. W. 88.
Louisiana: Hefner v. Hesse, 29 La. Ann. 149.
Texas: Dillard v. Stringfellow, 50 Tex. Civ. App. 410, 111 S. W. 769 (injunction against levy of execution).

injunction, the loss of the debt thereby caused must be compensated.[204] If the debtor has become insolvent, pending the injunction, and a part or the whole of the debt has thereby been lost, the amount so lost may be recovered;[205] but this involves proof that the debt could have been recovered before the injunction,[206] and also that at least a portion of it cannot be recovered after the dissolution.[207] So where the enforcement of an execution was enjoined, and the property which had been levied on was put in the hands of a receiver who sold it, the amount recoverable on the bond after the dissolution of the injunction was the difference between the amount actually obtained by the receiver and what would have been realized on a sale by the officer.[208]

It is usually held that interest on the amount of money tied up by the injunction may be recovered in an action on the bond;[209] though in a few cases it is held that interest on the amount of the debt cannot be recovered unless for some reason no interest can be recovered from the debtor upon the debt, as for instance through his insolvency,[210] or because he has paid the money into court pending the injunction.[211]

[204] Terrell v. Ingersoll, 10 Lea (Tenn.), 77.

[205] United States: Jones v. Allen, 85 Fed. 523, 29 C. C. A. 318, 56 U. S. App. 529.

Tennessee: Terrell v. Ingersoll, 10 Lea, 77.

[206] Alabama: Ansley v. Mock, 8 Ala. 444.

Tennessee: Terrell v. Ingersoll, 10 Lea, 77.

[207] Illinois: Walker v. Pritchard, 135 Ill. 103, 35 N. E. 573, 11 L. R. A. 577.

Nebraska: Stull v. Beddeo, 78 Neb. 119, 112 N. W. 315, 14 L. R. A. (N. S.) 507.

[208] Dodge v. Cohen, 14 D. C. App. 582.

[209] California: Heyman v. Landers, 12 Cal. 107.

District of Columbia: Dodge v. Cohen, 14 D. C. App. 582. In Grundy v. Young, 11 Fed. Cas. No. 5,851, 2 Cranch C. C. 114, it was held that

interest could not be recovered as damages in an action on the bond after the principal had been paid.

Illinois: Boynton Strong Co. v. Williams, 57 Ill. App. 434.

Maryland: Gist v. M'Guire, 4 Har. & J. 9; Wallis v. Dilley, 7 Md. 237.

Mississippi: Weatherby v. Shackleford, 37 Miss. 559.

Tennessee: Staples v. White, 88 Tenn. 30.

Texas: Attoway v. Still, 2 Tex. Unrep. 697.

Virginia: Washington v. Park, 6 Leigh, 581.

In Richards v. Green, 3 Ariz. 227, 32 Pac. 266, recovery of interest was refused, but the decision turned on the form of the pleadings.

[210] New Hampshire: Derry Bank v. Heath, 45 N. H. 524.

South Carolina: Gadsden v. Georgetown Bank, 5 Rich. 336.

[211] Bullock v. Ferguson, 30 Ala. 227.

When during the pendency of the injunction the value in gold of legal tender notes depreciated, it was held that the amount of the depreciation could not be recovered in an action on the bond, since the amount legally due, that is, the amount of the debt in legal tender, had not been changed.[212]

§ 685h. Injunctions against a sale.

Where the injunction prevented the sale of property, the plaintiff may recover in an action on the bond, the depreciation in the value of the property between the time of obtaining the injunction and the time of its dissolution.[213] If the property was lost or destroyed pending the injunction, its value may be recovered;[214] and if it was sold at a loss as perishable the amount of such loss may be recovered.[215]

Where the sale enjoined was an execution sale or a foreclosure sale, no damages may be recovered for loss of use of the property, since the seller was not entitled to the beneficial use of the property unless he bid it in at the sale, and it cannot be proved that he would have bid it in;[216] nor upon depreciation in value, if the security is still sufficient.[217] Interest may, however, be recovered on the money which the plaintiff would

[212] Riddlesbarger v. McDaniel, 38 Mo. 138.

[213] *Colorado:* Slack v. Stephens, 19 Colo. App. 538, 76 Pac. 741 (shares of stock).

Illinois: Sturges v. Hart, 45 Ill. 103 (law); Brandamour v. Trant, 45 Ill. 372.

Iowa: Langworthy v. McKelvey, 25 Ia. 48 (security).

Louisiana: Lallande v. Trezevant, 39 La. Ann. 830, 2 So. 573 (animals injured by bad treatment).

Maryland: Levy v. Taylor, 24 Md. 282.

Mississippi: Rubon v. Stephan, 25 Miss. 253.

Missouri: Meysenburg v. Schlieper, 48 Mo. 426.

The difference in the value of paper money reckoned in gold coin, cannot be recovered since the amount in legal tender is the same. Riddlesbarger v. McDaniel, 38 Mo. 138.

[214] *New York:* Aldrich v. Reynolds, 1 Barb. Ch. 613 (crops removed).

Washington: White v. Brooke, 11 Wash. 99, 39 Pac. 237 (chattels sold on foreclosure of subsequent mortgage and removed).

[215] Rhodes v. Auld, 5 Kan. App. 225, 47 Pac. 170.

[216] Execution sale: Johnson v. Moser, 72 Ia. 654, 34 N. W. 459; Colby v. Meservey, 85 Ia. 555, 52 N. W. 499.

Foreclosure sale: Schening v. Cofer, 97 Ala. 726, 12 So. 414 (in absence of evidence that on sale there would have been a deficiency which rent might have been taken to make up); Curry v. American F. L. M. Co., 124 Ala. 614, 27 So. 454, 82 Am. St. Rep. 311.

[217] Fidelity & Deposit Co. v. Walker, 158 Ala. 129, 48 So. 600.

have received from the sale, since he has been kept out of the money.[218]

Consequential damages may be recovered in a proper case. Loss of an advantageous sale may be recovered if it can be proved with reasonable certainty that the sale would have taken place;[219] but not where the sale was not prevented by the injunction itself,[220] but by the cloud which the suit threw upon the title.[221] The plaintiff may recover the amount spent for advertising the sale,[222] and the cost of storing and insuring the goods by the sheriff pending the injunction against an execution sale.[223] Profits which the plaintiff expected to realize from the use of the purchase-money are too speculative,[224] and the plaintiff cannot be called upon to enter into a speculation to reduce damages.[225]

The amount of the plaintiff's claim cannot be recovered,[226] but only the loss actually proved.[227]

§ 685i. Injunctions against other acts.

Where the injunction restrained the taking possession of

---

[218] *Iowa:* Johnson v. Moser, 72 Iowa, 654, 34 N. W. 459 (execution sale).

Maryland: Wood v. Fulton, 2 H. & G. 71 (foreclosure sale).

New York: Aldrich v. Reynolds, 1 Barb. Ch. 613 (foreclosure sale).

South Carolina: Hill v. Thomas, 19 S. C. 230.

Where the mortgage debt was payable in instalments, the recovery is confined to interest on the instalments due at the time of the injunction. Cannon v. Labarre, 13 La. 399.

[219] *District of Columbia:* Kerngood v. Gusdorf, 5 Mack. 161 (expected average sale of stock of goods).

Illinois: Sturges v. Hart, 45 Ill. 103 (*bona fide* offer had been made).

Contra, Washington: Donahue v. Johnson, 9 Wash. 187, 37 Pac. 322 (*bona fide* offer).

[220] Steel v. Gordon, 14 Wash. 521, 45 Pac. 151.

[221] Sweet v. Mowry, 71 Hun, 381, 25 N. Y. Supp. 32.

[222] *Illinois:* Edwards v. Pope, 4 Ill. 465.

Missouri: Alliance Trust Co. v. Stewart, 115 Mo. 236, 21 S. W. 793.

New York: Willet v. Scovill, 4 Abb. Pr. 405.

[223] Fox v. Oriel Cabinet Co., 70 Ill. App. 322.

[224] Elms v. Wright-Blodgett Co., 106 La. 19, 30 So. 315.

[225] O'Connor v. New York, etc., Land Imp. Co., 8 Misc. 243, 28 N. Y. Supp. 544.

[226] Alliance Trust Co. v. Stewart, 115 Mo. 236, 21 S. W. 793; unless as in Lockwood v. Saffold, 1 Ga. 72, the bond called for the payment of the debt.

[227] *Colorado:* Belmont Mining & Milling Co. v. Costigan, 21 Colo. 465, 42 Pac. 650, 52 Am. St. Rep. 254.

Kentucky: Hord v. Trimble, 1 Litt. 413.

property, which was destroyed by the possessor pending the injunction, it has been held that the value of the property may be recovered in an action on the bond.[228] On an injunction against removing negroes, the hire of the negroes may be recovered in an action on the bond together with compensation for any injury done them by taking them away; but loss of expected crops for lack of their services is not recoverable, unless the crops were then ready for harvest.[229] On a bond given in connection with an injunction against the use of a machine in manufacturing it seems that the plaintiff may recover the increased cost of manufacture due to his not having the machine.[230] Where the injunction restrained the city from issuing or disposing of its municipal bonds for the purpose of erecting an electric lighting plant, damages were allowed for the depreciation in the price at which its bonds could be sold during the delay, but not for the increased price which it was obliged to pay for machinery.[231] In case of an injunction against paying money, the party entitled to receive it can recover interest on the amount while payment was delayed.[232]

§ 685j. Counsel fees incurred on account of the injunction.

All counsel fees which resulted from the granting of the preliminary injunction may be recovered, and these include at least the fees incurred for a successful motion to dissolve the injunction, before a hearing on the merits.[233]

[228] Barton v. Fisk, 30 N. Y. 166; contra, Cummings v. Mugge, 94 Ill. 186.
[229] McDaniel v. Crabtree, 21 Ark. 431.
[230] San Jose Fruit Packing Co. v. Cutting, 133 Cal. 237, 65 Pac. 565.
[231] Clay Center v. Williamson, 79 Kan. 485, 100 Pac. 59.
[232] Missouri: C. H. Albers C. Co. v. Spencer, 139 S. W. 321 (against paying out money deposited).
Tennessee: Heck v. Bulkley, 1 S. W. 612 (against paying a dividend).
[233] Alabama: Holmes v. Weaver, 52 Ala. 516; Bolling v. Tate, 65 Ala. 417, 39 Am. Rep. 5, (including fees in the Supreme Court made necessary by the injunction).

Georgia: Richardson v. Allen, 74 Ga. 719.
Illinois: Elder v. Sabin, 66 Ill. 126; Keith v. Henkleman, 173 Ill. 137, 50 N. E. 692, 68 Ill. App. 623; Marks v. Chicago Yacht Club, 121 Ill. App. 308; Kerz v. Wold, 131 Ill. App. 387; Fordham v. Thompson, 144 Ill. App. 342.
Indiana: Binford v. Grimes, 26 Ind. App. 481, 59 N. E. 1085.
Kentucky: Fidelity & D. Co. v. Tinsley, 100 S. W. 272, 30 Ky. L. R. 1095.
Louisiana: Pargoud v. Morgan, 2 La. 99; Gamard v. Hart, 4 La. Ann. 503.
Minnesota: Neilson v. Albert Lea, 87 Minn. 285, 91 N. W. 1113.
Mississippi: Allen v. Leflore County, 80 Miss. 298, 31 So. 815.

In the Federal courts, according to the doctrine there prevailing, counsel fees cannot be recovered in an action on the bond, even if they are fees for securing a dissolution of the injunction; and this doctrine is applied to all actions on bonds given in the Federal courts, even though action on the bond is originally brought in the State court.[234] And in a few States it is held that no counsel fees can in any case be recovered in an action on the bond.[235]

Where an appeal is taken from the order on the motion for dissolution, and the temporary injunction is finally dissolved

Missouri: Wabash R. R. *v.* McCabe, 118 Mo. 640, 24 S. W. 217 (distinguishing earlier cases as based on a different and unusual statute); Helmkampf *v.* Wood, 85 Mo. App. 227.

Montana: Helena *v.* Brule, 15 Mont. 429, 39 Pac. 456, 852; Montgomery *v.* Gilbert, 24 Mont. 121, 60 Pac. 1038.

Nebraska: Carnes *v.* Heimrod, 45 Neb. 364, 63 N. W. 809 (a distinction was made in this respect between an undertaking given on a temporary restraining order and a bond on an injunction); Gyger *v.* Courtney, 59 Neb. 555, 81 N. W. 437; Jameson *v.* Bartlett, 63 Neb. 638, 88 N. W. 860.

New Jersey: Cook *v.* Chapman, 41 N. J. Eq. 152.

New York: Rose *v.* Post, 56 N. Y. 603; Sargent *v.* St. Mary's O. B. Asylum, 190 N. Y. 394, 83 N. E. 38; Fitzpatrick *v.* Flagg, 12 Abb. Pr. 189; Aldrich *v.* Reynolds, 1 Barb. Ch. 613; Coates *v.* Coates, 1 Duer, 664; London & B. Bank *v.* Walker, 74 Hun, 395, 26 N. Y. Supp. 844; Ten Eyck *v.* Sayers, 76 Hun, 37, 27 N. Y. Supp. 588; Edwards *v.* Bodine, 11 Paige, 223.

Ohio: Noble *v.* Arnold, 23 Oh. St. 264.

Washington: Steel *v.* Gordon, 14 Wash. 521, 45 Pac. 151.

West Virginia: State *v.* Medford, 34 W. Va. 633, 12 S. E. 864; State *v.* Corwin, 51 W. Va. 19, 41 S. E. 211.

Wisconsin: Wisconsin M. & F. I. Co.

Bank *v.* Durner, 114 Wis. 369, 90 N. W. 435.

Such fees may be recovered even though the court which granted the injunction was without jurisdiction. Littleton *v.* Burgess, 16 Wyo. 58, 91 Pac. 832, 16 L. R. A. (N. S.) 49.

[234] *United States:* Tullock *v.* Mulvane, 184 U. S. 497, 22 Sup. 372, 46 L. ed. 657 (reversing Mulvane *v.* Tullock, 58 Kan. 622, 50 Pac. 897); Missouri, K. & T. Ry. *v.* Elliott, 184 U. S. 530, 22 Sup. Ct. 447, 46 L. ed. 673 (reversing Elliott *v.* Missouri, K. & T. Ry., 77 Mo. App. 652); Browning *v.* Porter, 12 Fed. 460, 2 McCrary, 581; Lindeberg *v.* Howard, 146 Fed. 467, 77 C. C. A. 23; Sullivan *v.* Cartier, 147 Fed. 222, 77 C. C. A. 448.

Arizona: Richards *v.* Green, 3 Ariz. 227, 32 Pac. 266.

New York: National Society of U. S. Daughters of 1812 *v.* American Surety Co., 107 N. Y. Supp. 820, 56 Misc. 627.

[235] *Mississippi:* Canadian & A. M. & T. Co. *v.* Fitzpatrick, 71 Miss. 347, 16 So. 877 (statutory).

Oklahoma: Revell *v.* Smith, 25 Okla. 508, 106 Pac. 863 (bond given in Indian Territory, where Arkansas law prevailed, which did not allow counsel fees).

Tennessee: Stringfield *v.* Hirsch, 94 Tenn. 425, 29 S. W. 609, 45 Am. St. Rep. 733.

on appeal, counsel fees on the appeal as well as on the original motion may be recovered.[236]

Where the injunction is the final relief asked in the suit, it is held in several jurisdictions that counsel fees incurred on the hearing may be recovered, on the ground that the question whether the temporary injunction shall be dissolved involves a trial of the whole case.[237] But in other jurisdictions it is held that in such a case no counsel fees can be recovered, since the legal services necessary to secure a final decree for the defendant were not in any way increased by the granting of the temporary injunction.[238]

§ 685k. Counsel fees in the entire litigation.

Since the bond secures the payment of the damages caused by the issuance of the injunction only, and not those caused by the entire litigation in the course of which the injunction is issued, the counsel fees incurred in the general course of the litigation cannot be recovered in an action on the bond, at least where the injunction is not the principal relief sought, but merely ancillary to the principal relief,[239] since in such a case

[236] *Alabama:* Cooper *v.* Hames, 93 Ala. 280, 9 So. 341; Jesse French Piano & Organ Co. *v.* Porter, 134 Ala. 302, 32 So. 67, 92 Am. St. Rep. 31.

Missouri: Lewis *v.* Leahey, 14 Mo. App. 564.

Contra, New York: Guilford *v.* Cornell, 4 Abb. Pr. 220.

[237] *Iowa:* Colby *v.* Meservey, 85 Ia. 555, 52 N. W. 499; Williams *v.* Ballinger, 125 Ia. 410, 101 N. W. 139.

In *Louisiana:* Elms *v.* Wright-Blodgett Co., 106 La. 19, 30 So. 315, it is said that the recovery of counsel fees in such case depends upon the particular facts of the case.

Mississippi: Jameson *v.* Dulaney, 74 Miss. 890, 21 So. 972.

Missouri: Holloway *v.* Holloway, 103 Mo. 274, 15 S. W. 536.

Ohio: Dwelle *v.* Wilson, 14 Ohio Cir. Ct. 551, 7 Ohio Cir. Dec. 611.

[238] *Alabama:* Bush *v.* Kirkbride, 131 Ala. 405, 30 So. 780.

California: San Diego Water Co *v.* Pacific Coast Steamship Co., 101 Cal. 216, 35 Pac. 651.

Kentucky: New National Turnpike Co. *v.* Dulaney, 86 Ky. 516, 6 S. W. 590, 9 Ky. L. Rep. 697; Chicago S. L. & N. O. R. R. *v.* Sullivan, 26 Ky. L. Rep. 46, 80 S. W. 791; Shepherd *v.* Gambill, 96 S. W. 1104, 29 Ky. L. Rep. 1163.

Oregon: Olds *v.* Cary, 13 Ore. 362, 10 Pac. 786.

[239] *Alabama:* Robertson *v.* Robertson, 58 Ala. 68.

California: Porter *v.* Hopkins, 63 Cal. 324; San Diego Water Co. *v.* Pacific C. S. S. Co., 101 Cal. 216, 35 Pac. 651.

Colorado: Tabor *v.* Clark, 15 Colo. 434, 25 Pac. 181; Baldwin S. C. Co. *v.* Quinn, 46 Colo. 590, 105 Pac. 1101.

Illinois: Landis *v.* Wolf, 206 Ill. 392, 69 N. E. 103; McQuown *v.* Law, 18 Ill. App. 34; Dunning *v.* Young, 67 Ill. App. 668.

all such fees would have been paid if the temporary injunction had never issued.[240] On this ground counsel fees paid for resisting the motion for a temporary injunction are not recoverable in an action on the bond, since they were not caused by the issuance of the injunction, but would have been the same even though it had been refused.[241] If it is impossible to show what portion of an entire fee for the services of counsel was paid on account of the motion to dissolve and what portion is ascribed to the defence of the whole action, nothing can be

Iowa: Bullard v. Harkness, 83 Ia. 373, 49 N. W. 855; Ady v. Freeman, 90 Ia. 402, 57 N. W. 879; Leonard v. Capital Ins. Co., 101 Ia. 482, 70 N. W. 629.

Kentucky: Thapnell v. McAfee, 3 Met. 34, 77 Am. Dec. 152; Green v. Quisenberry, 118 S. W. 361.

Louisiana: Lemeunier v. McClearley, 41 La. Ann. 411, 6 So. 338.

Maine: Thurston v. Haskell, 81 Me. 303, 17 Atl. 73; Barrett v. Bowers, 87 Me. 185, 32 Atl. 871.

Missouri: Brown v. Baldwin, 121 Mo. 126, 25 S. W. 863; Louisville Banking Co. v. M. V. Monarch Co., 68 Mo. App. 603.

Nebraska: Trester v. Pike, 60 Neb. 510, 83 N. W. 676; Darling v. McBride, 86 Neb. 481, 125 N. W. 1088.

New York: Newton v. Russell, 87 N. Y. 527; Strong v. De Forest, 15 Abb. Pr. 427; Allen v. Brown, 5 Lans. 511; McDonald v. James, 38 N. Y. Super. Ct. 76, 47 How. Pr. 474; Whiteside v. Cottage Assoc., 64 Hun, 557, 32 N. Y. Supp. 725; Phœnix B. Co. v. Keystone B. Co., 10 App. Div. 176, 41 N. Y. Supp. 891.

Ohio: Riddle v. Cheadle, 25 Oh. St. 278; Tarbell v. Ennis, 10 Ohio S. & C. Pl. Dec. 346, 7 Ohio N. P. 416.

South Carolina: Gadsden v. Georgetown Bank, 5 Rich. 336; Darlington v. Copeland, 43 S. C. 389, 21 S. E. 317.

Texas: Brown v. Tyler, 34 Tex. 168.

Virginia: Wisecarver v. Wisecarver, 97 Va. 452, 34 S. E. 56.

Washington: Donahue v. Johnson, 9 Wash. 187, 37 Pac. 322; Anderson v. Philadelphia P. L. Co., 26 Wash. 192, 66 Pac. 415; Collins v. Huffman, 48 Wash. 184, 93 Pac. 220.

West Virginia: State v. Taylor, 68 S. E. 379.

In *Montana,* Miles v. Edwards, 6 Mont. 180, 9 Pac. 814, it was held that plaintiff could recover the attorney's fees for dissolving the temporary order and also fees for resisting a final injunction even though the attorney's services were rendered after the time when the temporary injunction expired.

On an injunction bond given in an action to restrain a suit at law, counsel fees incurred in the action restrained cannot be recovered. Allport v. Kelby, 2 Mont. 343.

[240] *Minnesota:* Lamb v. Shaw, 43 Minn. 507, 45 N. W. 1134.

Ohio: Riddle v. Cheadle, 25 Oh. St. 278.

[241] *California:* Alaska Imp. Co. v. Hirsch, 119 Cal. 251, 47 Pac. 124.

Colorado: Quinn v. Silka, 19 Colo. App. 507, 76 Pac. 555.

New York: Youngs v. McDonald, 56 App. Div. 14, 67 N. Y. Supp. 375 (affirmed, 166 N. Y. 639, 60 N. E. 1123); Whiteside v. Assoc., 84 Hun, 555, 32 N. Y. Supp. 724.

Vermont: Sturges v. Knapp, 33 Vt. 486.

Contra, Indiana: Swan v. Timmons, 81 Ind. 243; Robertson v. Smith, 129 Ind. 422, 28 N. E. 587, 15 L. R. A. 273.

recovered on the bond.[242] So where a gross fee was agreed upon for the whole litigation nothing can be recovered on the bond,[243] and where the plaintiff on the bond was a city and the services were performed by the city attorney, who was paid an annual salary, nothing can be recovered on account of attorney's fees;[244] but if he reasonably employed assistant counsel for the purpose of securing an injunction, the cost may be recovered.[245]

§ 6851. Counsel fees not chargeable to defendant.

Counsel fees which are recoverable on the bond do not include the expense of an unsuccessful attempt to secure a dissolution of the injunction, even though on the final hearing it was dissolved; apparently because it is regarded as the fault of the party or his counsel that the dissolution was not obtained.[246] If, however, the court itself continues the injunction not because it so decides upon the merits as the motion presents them, but because it deems it desirable not to consider the merits of the preliminary injunction until hearing, the costs of the motion may be recovered.[247] But when the injunction is not dissolved by the court, but is superseded or modified by

[242] *Colorado:* Church *v.* Baker, 18 Colo. App. 369, 71 Pac. 888.

Illinois: Lambert *v.* Alcorn, 144 Ill. 313, 33 N. E. 53, 21 L. R. A. 611.

Kentucky: Boyd *v.* Chambers, 9 Ky. L. R. 56.

Montana: Campbell *v.* Metcalf, 1 Mont. 378; Creek *v.* McManus, 17 Mont. 445, 43 Pac. 497.

South Carolina: Hill *v.* Thomas, 19 S. C. 230; Darlington *v.* Copeland, 43 S. C. 389, 21 S. E. 317.

But in Jesse French P. & O. Co. *v.* Porter, 134 Ala. 302, 32 So. 67, it seems to have been held that such portion of the whole fee as is reasonable for the services in securing dissolution could be recovered. And see Hyatt *v.* Washington, 20 Ind. App. 148, 50 N. E. 402, 67 Am. St. Rep. 248.

[243] Bustamente *v.* Stewart, 55 Cal.

115; Mitchell *v.* Hawley, 79 Cal. 301, 21 Pac. 833.

[244] *Illinois:* Kerz *v.* Wold, 131 Ill. App. 387; Fordham *v.* Thompson, 144 Ill. 342.

Mississippi: Nixon *v.* Biloxi, 76 Miss. 810, 25 So. 664.

[245] Fordham *v.* Thompson, 144 Ill. App. 342.

[246] *California:* Curtiss *v.* Bachman, 110 Cal. 433, 42 Pac. 910, 52 Am. St. Rep. 111.

Minnesota: Lamb *v.* Shaw, 43 Minn. 507, 45 N. W. 1134.

Nebraska: Pollock *v.* Whipple, 57 Neb. 82, 77 N. W. 355; Cunningham *v.* Finch, 63 Neb. 189, 88 N. W. 168.

New York: Randall *v.* Carpenter, 88 N. Y. 293; Langdon *v.* Gray, 22 Hun, 511; Childs *v.* Lyons, 3 Rob. 704.

[247] Andrews *v.* Glenville Woolen Co., 50 N. Y. 282.

agreement of the parties, no counsel fees can be recovered.[248] And if the injunction is not dissolved but modified the whole fee at least cannot be recovered.[249] Where the injunction did no harm so that a motion for a dissolution was needless, it would seem that the expense of such an unnecessary motion could not be recovered on the bond.[250] And no counsel fees can be recovered which were incurred in defending plaintiff from an attachment for contempt for violating the injunction, since it was the fault of the plaintiff himself.[251]

§ 685m. Amount of counsel fees recoverable—Exorbitant charges.

The amount recovered cannot exceed a reasonable amount,[252] and must not be swelled by unnecessarily employing several counsel.[253] Exorbitant charges cannot be allowed; and it seems that where the defendant is himself a lawyer and acts as counsel for himself, he can recover nothing on this ground, as it costs him nothing.[254] If there was no agreement upon the amount of the fee, a reasonable amount may be recovered;[255] but if there was an agreement upon the amount, no more can be recovered.[256] Where counsel fees were paid in the original suit, as where after dissolution of an injunction against a fore-

---

[248] *Iowa:* Ady v. Freeman, 90 Ia. 402, 57 N. W. 879.

Vermont: Barre Water Co. v. Carnes, 68 Vt. 23, 33 Atl. 898.

Contra, Alabama: Jackson v. Mills-paugh, 100 Ala. 285, 14 So. 44, where it was continued by agreement.

[249] Ford v. Loomis, 62 Ia. 586, 16 N. W. 193, 17 N. W. 910. The court intimated that part of the fee might perhaps be recovered.

[250] *Colorado:* Grove v. Wallace, 11 Colo. App. 160, 52 Pac. 639.

Mississippi: Wynne v. Mason, 72 Miss. 424, 18 So. 422.

Contra, Alabama: Rosser v. Timber-lake, 78 Ala. 162, on the ground that it does not lie in the mouth of the defendant to say that the injunction obtained by him was of no detriment to the other party.

[251] Bennett v. Lambert, 100 Ky. 737, 39 S. W. 419, 18 Ky. L. Rep. 1057, 66 Am. St. Rep. 370.

[252] *Alabama:* Jesse French P. & O. Co. v. Porter, 134 Ala. 302, 32 So. 67, 92 Am. St. Rep. 31.

Florida: Wittich v. O'Neal, 22 Fla. 592.

[253] Collins v. Sinclair, 51 Ill. 328.

[254] Jevne v. Osgood, 57 Ill. 340, 347; Stinnett v. Wilson, 19 Ill. App. 38.

[255] *Florida:* Wittich v. O'Neal, 22 Fla. 592.

Kansas: Nimocks v. Welles, 42 Kan. 39, 21 Pac. 787.

Montana: Cook v. Greenough, 14 Mont. 352, 36 Pac. 35.

West Virginia: State v. Medford, 34 W. Va. 633, 12 S. E. 864.

[256] Steele v. Thatcher, 56 Ill. 257; Lomax v. Ragor, 85 Ill. App. 679.

closure sale the sale took place and counsel fees were paid out of the proceeds as part of the costs, they could not again be recovered on the bond.[257] In California it is held that liability to pay the fees is not sufficient to justify recovery; no compensation being allowed on that ground unless the fees have actually been paid.[258] But in other jurisdictions a different view is taken, and it is held that if the liability has been incurred there may be a recovery of the amount of it, though it is as yet unpaid.[259] A party personally liable for the fees may recover though he was acting in a representative capacity,[260] or was only one of several parties.[261]

§ 685n. Other expenses of litigation.

Other necessary expenses of the motion to dissolve the injunction may be recovered; such as the value of the party's time lost in consulting counsel or attending the hearing;[262] and his personal expenses,[263] including his travelling expenses.[264]

[257] Curry v. American Freehold Land Mortg. Co., 124 Ala. 614, 27 So. 454, 82 Am. St. Rep. 211.

[258] Wilson v. McEvoy, 25 Cal. 170; Prader v. Grimm, 28 Cal. 11; Roussin v. Stewart, 33 Cal. 208; Bustamente v. Stewart, 55 Cal. 115; Hooper v. Patterson (Cal.), 32 Pac. 514.

In Corder v. Martin, 17 Mo. 41, the same doctrine was asserted.

[259] Alabama: Miller v. Garrett, 35 Ala. 96.

Florida: Wittich v. O'Neal, 22 Fla. 592.

Illinois: Steele v. Thatcher, 56 Ill. 257; Rees v. Peltzer, 1 Ill. App. 315; Patterson v. Rinard, 81 Ill. App. 80.

Kansas: Underhill v. Spencer, 25 Kan. 71.

Kentucky: Shultz v. Morrison, 3 Met. 98.

Louisiana: McRae v. Brown, 12 La. Ann. 181; Meaux v. Pittman, 35 La. Ann. 360.

Nevada: Brown v. Jones, 5 Nev. 374.

Ohio: Noble v. Arnold, 23 Oh. St. 264.

[260] Baylis v. Scudder, 6 Hun (N. Y.), 300.

[261] Babcock v. Reeves, 149 Ala. 665, 43 So. 21.

[262] Missouri: Skrainka v. Oertel, 14 Mo. App. 474; Helmkampf v. Wood, 85 Mo. App. 227.

Montana: Campbell v. Metcalf, 1 Mont. 378.

New York: Edwards v. Bodine, 11 Paige, 223.

Contra, Illinois: Densch v. Scott, 58 Ill. App. 33 (time at court and procuring witnesses).

New Jersey: Cook v. Chapman, 41 N. J. Eq. 152.

[263] Illinois: Tamatroa v. Southern Ill. Normal University, 54 Ill. 334.

Missouri: Wabash R. R. v. McCabe, 118 Mo. 640, 24 S. W. 217.

New York: Lyon v. Hersey, 32 Hun, 253.

[264] Alabama: Bolling v. Tate, 65 Ala. 417, 39 Am. Rep. 5.

New York: Crounse v. Syracuse & R. R. R., 32 Hun, 497 (special train).

§ 685o. Bonds for vacating injunction.

When a temporary injunction is vacated or modified upon a bond being given by the defendant, the plaintiff in an action on the bond recovers the loss to him caused by the defendant doing the act enjoined after the injunction was so modified or vacated as to allow it.[265] So where the defendant, the owner of a controlling interest in the stock of a corporation, was enjoined at suit of a stockholder from removing property of the corporation from the State, and after the injunction was vacated he removed the property the measure of damages was not the value of the property, removed, but the diminution in value of the plaintiff's stock caused by the removal.[266]

§ 686. Bail bonds.

In an action upon a bail bond in a civil suit given to the sheriff to secure the release of a debtor, the measure of damages is the amount of the judgment upon the debt,[267] but the defendant may show that at the time of the breach the debtor was insolvent.[268] In a suit upon a poor debtor's bond, the damages will be the amount of the judgment and the costs of the action in which it was given, with the interest thereon.[269] The same is the measure on a prison-bounds' bond,[270] and a voluntary return by the prisoner will not mitigate the damages.[271] In an

[265] De Camp v. Burns, 33 App. Div. 517, 53 N. Y. Supp. 1035.

[266] Moulton v. Richardson, 49 N. H. 76.

[267] *Arkansas:* Leach v. Pirani, 5 Ark. 118.

Connecticut: New Haven Bank v. Miles, 5 Conn. 587.

Illinois: Murphy v. Sommerville, 7 Ill. 360, 43 Am. Dec. 58.

[268] *Maine:* Sargent v. Pomroy, 33 Me. 388.

New York: Kellogg v. Manro, 9 Johns. 300.

Canada: Brown v. Paxton, 19 Up. Can. Q. B. 426.

Contra, Connecticut: Hall v. White, 27 Conn. 488.

Indiana: Rooksby v. State, 92 Ind. 71.

Canada: Kerr v. Fullarton, 10 Up. Can. C. P. 250; M'Kenzie v. Marsh, 2 Kerr (N. B.), 629.

[269] *Maine:* Richards v. Morse, 36 Me. 240; Houghton v. Lyford, 39 Me. 267; Call v. Foster, 52 Me. 257.

Ohio: Laines v. Philips, 4 Ohio, 172.

Insolvency of the debtor cannot be shown in mitigation of damages. Kiersted v. State, 1 Gill & J. (Md.) 231.

[270] *New York:* Smith v. Jansen, 8 Johns. 111; Sprague v. Seymour, 15 Johns. 474.

Virginia: McGuire v. Pierce, 9 Gratt. 167.

[271] *Connecticut:* Seymour v. Harvey, 8 Conn. 63.

Indiana: Spader v. Frost, 4 Blackf. 190.

New York: Flynn v. Union S. & G.

action upon a bail bond in a criminal proceeding the penalty may be recovered,[272] but without interest.[273]

§ 686a. Bonds for arrest.

When a bond is given to secure the arrest of a person he may recover on the bond only such special damages as he can prove; which do not include any damages which would have been suffered if the action had been begun without an arrest.[274] Compensation may be recovered for counsel fees and other expenses incurred in securing discharge from the arrest, and for loss of time, but not for the personal injury and false imprisonment.[275]

§ 687. Arbitration bonds.

In an action upon a bond to abide the award of arbitrators, the measure of damages is the amount of the award, if a pecuniary award was made,[276] even though the authority of the arbitrators was revoked by the defendant, one of two debtors, after the testimony was in and pending the decision.[277] Where the award required security to be given at once, and the money paid in instalments, the plaintiff upon a failure to give security, may at once recover the whole amount of the award.[278] When the bond was to abide an award as to a disputed boundary line, it was held that the plaintiff could recover the expenses incurred in defending a suit in equity brought by the defendant to set aside the award.[279] In such a case, the damages recoverable for violation of the award are such only as are personal to the party.[280]

Co., 61 App. Div. 170, 70 N. Y. Supp. 403.

[272] Steinbock v. Evans, 122 N. Y. 551, 25 N. E. 929.

[273] United States v. Broadhead, 127 U. S. 212, 8 Sup. Ct. 1191, 32 L. ed. 147; contra, Steinbock v. Evans, 122 N. Y. 551, 25 N. E. 929.

[274] Wallis v. Keeney, 88 Ill. 370.

[275] Bamberger v. Kahn, 43 Hun (N. Y.), 411; Krause v. Rutherford, 45 App. Div. 132, 60 N. Y. Supp. 1047. But in Vanderberg v. Connoly, 18 Utah, 112, 54 Pac. 1097, the plaintiff was allowed in an action on the bond to recover damages for mental and physical suffering caused by the arrest and imprisonment, and attorneys' fees in procuring the discharge.

[276] Delaware: Stewart v. Grier, 7 Houst. 378, 32 Atl. 328.

Indiana: Shroyer v. Bash, 57 Ind. 349, 26 Am. Rep. 57.

[277] Hatheway v. Cliff, 2 All. (N. B.) 267.

[278] Bond v. Bond, 16 Up. Can. C. P. 327.

[279] Henry v. Davis, 123 Mass. 345.

[280] Webb v. Fish, 4 N. J. L. 371.

In New York, when there is a revocation of the submission, damages are limited by statute to costs and expenses, and all damages incurred in preparing for the arbitration, and in conducting the proceedings to the time of revocation.[281]

§ 688. Appeal and supersedeas bonds.

The appeal or supersedeas bond in the United States courts and in several of the states binds the obligors to pay the amount of the judgment, up to the penalty of the bond;[282] while in other States the amount of the judgment itself cannot be recovered in an action on the bond.[283] If the amount of the judgment is ordinarily recoverable, nominal damages only can be recovered when the judgment has in fact been paid, even though there has been a technical breach of the bond;[284] and so where for any other reason the appellant has nothing to pay on the

---

[281] Code Civ. Pro., § 2384; Allen v. Watson, 16 John. 204; Union Ins. Co. v. Central Trust Co., 157 N. Y. 633, 52 N. E. 671.

[282] *United States:* Sessions v. Pintard, 18 How. 106, 15 L. ed. 298; Tarr v. Rosenstein, 53 Fed. 112, 3 C. C. A. 466; Wood v. Brown, 104 Fed. 203, 43 C. C. A. 474.

Colorado: Dye v. Dye, 12 Colo. App. 206, 55 Pac. 205.

Florida: Raney v. Baron, 1 Fla. 327, 46 Am. Dec. 346.

Illinois: Stelle v. Lovejoy, 125 Ill. 352.

Indiana: Opp v. Ten Eyck, 99 Ind. 345.

Michigan: Healy v. Newton, 96 Mich. 228, 55 N. W. 666.

New York: Donovan v. Clark, 76 Hun, 339, 27 N. Y. Supp. 686.

Virginia: McClung v. Beirne, 10 Leigh, 410, 34 Am. Dec. 739.

Of course this is true only in case of a money judgment; in case of a non-pecuniary judgment there is no amount to recover. So on appeal from a decree of foreclosure of a mortgage of land the amount of the mortgage debt cannot be recovered on the bond.

United States: Supervisors v. Kennicott, 103 U. S. 554, 26 L. ed. 486.

Kentucky: Graham v. Swigert, 12 B. Mon. 522.

If the judgment is partly for the payment of money recovery may be had on the bond for that portion of the judgment. Rice v. Rice, 13 Ind. 562.

The recovery is limited to the penalty of the bond, though by mistake that is too small. Sears v. Seattle Consolidated St. R. R., 7 Wash. 286, 34 Pac. 918.

[283] *Maryland:* Keen v. Whittington, 40 Md. 489.

Tennessee: Smith v. Erwin, 5 Yerg. 296.

In New York the bond is conditioned on paying the damages of appeal, which means the sum awarded as damages in the appellate court. Post v. Doremus, 60 N. Y. 371; Onderdonk v. Emmons, 9 Abb. Pr. 187.

[284] *Illinois:* George v. Bischoff, 68 Ill. 236.

Massachusetts: Brennan v. Quinn, 148 Mass. 562, 20 N. E. 184.

Minnesota: First Nat. Bank v. Rogers, 13 Minn. 407, 97 Am. Dec. 239.

judgment.[285]   Costs on the appeal are recoverable on the bond,[286] though not usually costs in the original action; [287] so are counsel fees on appeal.[288]

Where an appeal is taken to an intermediate court and a bond given, and a second appeal is then taken to a higher court and a second bond given, the execution of the second bond does not, by the better opinion, release the parties to the first bond from liability on it for the entire loss caused by both appeals.[289]   In New York, however, this is not always true.   If the judgment is reversed in the intermediate court, and on a second appeal the original judgment is restored, the parties to the first bond are bound for the loss caused by both appeals; [290] but if the judgment is affirmed successively in both courts, the execution of the second bond relieves the parties to the first bond from liability to further damages, to the extent to which compensation is recoverable on the second bond.[291]

§ 688a. Recovery of damages from the appeal.

Besides the judgment and costs, recovery may be had on the

[285] *Alabama:* Lunsford *v.* Baskins, 6 Ala. 512 (judgment against executor; estate insolvent).

New York: Markoe *v.* American Surety Co., 44 App. Div. 285, 60 N. Y. Supp. 674 (decree payable only out of a trust fund). But in Yates *v.* Burch, 87 N. Y. 409, the sureties on the bond were held liable for the amount of the judgment, though it was against an executor, and the assets of the estate were insufficient.

[286] *Alabama:* Shows *v.* Pendry, 93 Ala. 248, 9 So. 462.

Massachusetts: Swan *v.* Picquet, 4 Pick. 465.

Michigan: Dunn *v.* Sutliff, 1 Mich. 24; Kennedy *v.* Nims, 52 Mich. 153, 17 N. W. 735.

New York: Burdett *v.* Lowe, 85 N. Y. 241.

[287] *New York:* Burdett *v.* Lowe, 85 N. Y. 241.

Tennessee: Denton *v.* Wood's Adm'r,

11 Lea, 505. See Dawson *v.* Holt, 12 Lea, 27.

Contra, Michigan: Day *v.* Litchfield, 11 Mich. 497; Prosser *v.* Whitney, 46 Mich. 405, 9 N. W. 449.

[288] Drake *v.* Webb, 63 Ala. 596; but see Swan *v.* Picquet, 4 Pick. (Mass.) 465.

[289] *Colorado:* Shannon *v.* Dodge, 18 Colo. 164, 32 Pac. 61.

Illinois: Becker *v.* People, 164 Ill. 267, 45 N. E. 500.

Kentucky: Ashby *v.* Sharp, 1 Litt. 156.

Michigan: Marquette County *v.* Ward, 50 Mich. 174, 45 Am. Rep. 30.

North Carolina: State *v.* Bradshaw, 10 Ired. L. 229.

[290] Robinson *v.* Plimpton, 25 N. Y. 484; Smith *v.* Crouse, 24 Barb. 433.

[291] Hinckley *v.* Kreitz, 58 N. Y. 583; Chester *v.* Broderick, 131 N. Y. 549, 30 N. E. 507. But see Mackellar *v.* Farrell, 57 N. Y. Super. Ct. 398, 8 N. Y. Supp. 307.

appeal bond for damages suffered by the appeal.[292] Of course damages suffered prior to the appeal cannot be recovered,[293] nor damages suffered from failing to take advantage of the judgment, if the appeal did not suspend its operation.[294]

When the payment of money is delayed by the appeal, interest on the money pending the appeal may be recovered.[295] And so where a judgment for the sale of property was appealed from, the plaintiff in an action on the bond may recover interest on the amount that would have been realized.[296] And where the debtor has become insolvent, pending the appeal, the plaintiff may recover compensation for damage to his chance of collecting the debt, to be determined by proof of amount of the appellant's property from the time of the appeal to final judgment.[297]

When the judgment is for the recovery of property, the damage suffered from the temporary or permanent loss of the property may be recovered. So where a judgment for the recovery of land is appealed from, the measure of damages in an action upon the appeal bond includes the value of the use of the premises pending the appeal.[298]

[292] *United States:* Supervisors v. Kennicott, 103 U. S. 554, 26 L. ed. 486.

Illinois: Shreffler v. Nadelhoffer, 133 Ill. 536, 25 N. E. 630, 23 Am. St. Rep. 626.

[293] *Illinois:* Mix v. Singleton, 86 Ill. 194.

New York: Rosenquest v. Noble, 21 App. Div. 583, 48 N. Y. Supp. 398.

[294] Shows v. Pendry, 93 Ala. 248, 9 So. 462.

[295] *Alabama:* Drake v. Webb, 63 Ala. 596.

Illinois: Nat. Bank of Ill. v. Baker, 58 Ill. App. 343.

Kansas: Kansas B. P. Co. v. United States F. & G. Co., 106 Pac. 45.

Kentucky: Bingham v. Vanbuskirk, 6 B. Mon. 197.

Tennessee: Gholson v. Brown, 4 Yerg. 198.

Contra, Vermont: Roberts v. Warner, 17 Vt. 46.

Where, however, the judgment superseded does not bear interest, none can be recovered on the bond. Louisville & N. R. R. v. Com., 89 Ky. 531, 12 S. W. 1064.

[296] *Kentucky:* Hargis v. Mayes, 20 Ky. L. Rep. 1965, 50 S. W. 844.

Maryland: Jenkins v. Hay, 28 Md. 547.

[297] *Indiana:* Roberts v. Lovitt, 13 Ind. App. 281, 41 N. E. 554, 55 Am. St. Rep. 224.

Kentucky: Mahlman v. Williams, 89 Ky. 282, 12 S. W. 335.

Minnesota: Vent v. Duluth Trust Co., 77 Minn. 523, 80 N. W. 640.

Texas: Trent v. Rhomberg, 66 Tex. 249, 18 S. W. 510.

Vermont: McGregor v. Balch, 17 Vt. 562.

[298] *United States:* Kountze v. Omaha Hotel Co., 107 U. S. 378, 27 L. ed. 609, 2 Sup. Ct. 911; Woodworth v. Northwestern M. L. I. Co., 185 U. S. 354, 46 L. ed. 945, 22 Sup. Ct. 676.

Where personal property has deteriorated during the appeal, the amount of the deterioration may be recovered; [299] and if real estate affected by the judgment has suffered physical deterioration or waste, though without fault on the part of the appellant, the amount of the waste may be recovered, [300] but not a decrease in value for other reasons than physical deterioration. [301] Where an order appointing a receiver of property was appealed from, and the owner sold the property pending the appeal, the value of the property at the time of the appeal is the measure of damages. [302] The plaintiff brought an action of *quo warranto* against the defendant, who had usurped an office to which the plaintiff was elected. Judgment having been

Alabama: Cahall v. Citizens' M. B. Assoc., 74 Ala. 539.

Illinois: Shunick v. Thompson, 25 Ill. App. 619.

Indiana: Opp v. Ten Eyck, 99 Ind. 345; Hays v. Wilstach, 101 Ind. 100.

Massachusetts: Braman v. Perry, 12 Pick. 118; Davis v. Alden, 2 Gray, 309.

New York: Shankland v. Hamilton, 1 T. & C. 239.

Ohio: Curry v. Homer, 62 Oh. St. 233, 56 N. E. 870.

Pennsylvania: Johnson v. Hessel, 134 Pa. 315, 19 Atl. 700, 19 Am. St. Rep. 700.

Utah: Tarpey v. Sharp, 12 Utah, 383, 43 Pac. 104.

Where it appeared that the defendant was entitled to reimbursement for valuable improvements, the recovery on the bond was limited to the value of the use of the land without the improvements. Hentig v. Collins, 1 Kan. App. 173, 41 Pac. 1057.

When a lease of the premises was renewed during appeal, recovery on the bond would include rent on the renewed lease as well as on the original. Pray v. Wasdell, 146 Mass. 324, 16 N. E. 266.

The value of the use cannot be recovered on a bond given in the form required in the United States courts, if not recovered in the original action. Burgess v. Doble, 149 Mass. 256, 21 N. E. 438. And on any bond the peculiar form of the condition may preclude the recovery of rent. McWilliams v. Morgan, 70 Ill. 62.

Where the appeal stayed the sale of mortgaged premises, the rents can be recovered only if the amount finally realized on the sale is insufficient to satisfy the debt. Utica Bank v. Finch, 3 Barb. Ch. 293, 49 Am. Dec. 175.

[299] *United States:* Kountze v. Omaha Hotel Co., 107 U. S. 378, 27 L. ed. 609, 2 Sup. Ct. 911.

District of Columbia: Fulton v. Fletcher, 12 D. C. App. Cas. 1.

Illinois: Cook v. Marsh, 44 Ill. 178.

Indiana: Hinkle v. Holmes, 85 Ind. 405.

Kansas: Kansas B. P. Co. v. United States F. & G. Co., 106 Pac. 45.

Kentucky: Welch v. Welch, 20 Ky. L. Rep. 1990, 50 S. W. 697, 22 Ky. L. Rep. 1259, 60 S. W. 409.

[300] *Kansas:* Hughan v. Grimes, 62 Kan. 258, 62 Pac. 326.

Massachusetts: Davis v. Alden, 2 Gray, 309 (burning of building).

[301] *Kansas:* Hughan v. Grimes, 62 Kan. 258, 62 Pac. 326.

Kentucky: Buckner v. Terrell, 8 Ky. L. Rep. 701.

[302] Everett v. State, 28 Md. 190.

given for the plaintiff, the defendant appealed and gave bond. In an action upon the bond, after the appeal had been dismissed, it was held that the plaintiff in an action upon the bond could recover the amount of salary received by the defendant pending the appeal.[303] When the appeal delayed the crossing of the defendant's railroad by the plaintiff's railroad, the plaintiff was allowed to recover on the bond the loss of profits suffered by not being allowed to make the crossing.[304]

§ 689. Replevin bonds.

A replevin bond, given by the plaintiff in the replevin suit, is conditioned on a return of the property if the plaintiff does not maintain his claim. If his claim is abandoned for any reason and the suit discontinued without going to judgment, and the property is not returned, the condition is broken and action will lie on the bond.[305] If the case proceeds to judgment, and a judgment is rendered in favor of the defendant for a return, this judgment is conclusive in an action on the bond, against all parties to the bond, including the sureties.[306] In such a case the jury should find and the court award damages;[307] but if the jury fails to assess damages in the replevin suit, damages may nevertheless be recovered for the unlawful taking in an action on the bond.[308]

[303] *United States:* U. S. *v.* Addison, 6 Wall. 291, 18 L. ed. 919.
New York: Nichols *v.* MacLean, 101 N. Y. 526; People *v.* Nolan, 101 N. Y. 539.
[304] Waycross Air Line R. R. *v.* Offerman & W. R. R., 114 Ga. 727, 40 S. E. 738.
[305] *Kansas:* McKey *v.* Lauflin, 48 Kan. 581, 30 Pac. 16; Little *v.* Bliss, 55 Kan. 94, 39 Pac. 1025.
Maine: Pettygrove *v.* Hoyt, 11 Me. 66.
But see *Massachusetts:* Whitwell *v.* Wells, 24 Pick. 34.
If the property is redelivered, the condition is not broken and there can be no recovery on the bond. Larabee *v.* Cook, 8 Kan. App. 776, 61 Pac. 815.
Sureties are liable only when there is

a judgment for a return. Vinyard *v.* Barnes, 124 Ill. 346, 16 N. E. 254; New England Furniture & Carpet Co. *v.* Bryant, 64 Minn. 256, 66 N. W. 974.
[306] *Indiana:* Smith *v.* Mosby, 98 Ind. 445.
Ohio: Richardson *v.* People's Nat. Bank, 57 Oh. St. 299.
Texas: Wandelohr *v.* Grayson County Nat. Bank, 102 Tex. 20, 108 S. W. 1154 (unless fraud is shown).
Vermont: Miltimore *v.* Bottom, 66 Vt. 168, 28 Atl. 872.
[307] In Vermont damages are not assessed where the plaintiff's action fails for any other reason than the merits of the case. Collamer *v.* Page, 35 Vt. 387.
[308] *United States:* Boley *v.* Griswold, 20 Wall. 486, 22 L. ed. 375.

§ 689a. Measure of recovery.

In debt on a replevin bond conditioned to pay all such damages as the defendants in the action should recover, the measure of damages is the judgment in the replevin suit.[309] But a commoner form of replevin bond is conditioned to pay the value of the property replevied. The measure of damages in a suit upon such a bond is the value of the property,[310] with interest.[311]

Colorado: Cox v. Sargent, 10 Colo. App. 1, 50 Pac. 201.

Connecticut: Persse v. Watrous, 30 Conn. 139.

Iowa: Hall v. Smith, 10 Ia. 45, 74 Am. Dec. 370.

Kansas: Little v. Bliss, 55 Kan. 94.

Maine: Washington Ice Co. v. Webster, 62 Me. 341.

Massachusetts: Smith v. Whiting, 100 Mass. 122.

Missouri: Woodburn v. Cogdal, 39 Mo. 222.

New Jersey: Lutes v. Alpaugh, 23 N. J. L. 165.

Pennsylvania: Pittsburgh Nat. Bank v. Hall, 107 Pa. 583.

Rhode Island: Gardiner v. McDermott, 12 R. I. 206.

Contra, however, in *California,* where the sureties at least are not liable on the bond for the value of the property unless it is found by the jury in the replevin suit. Clary v. Rolland, 24 Cal. 147.

[309] *Arkansas:* Morrill v. Daniel, 47 Ark. 316, 1 S. W. 702.

Indiana: M'Coy v. Elder, 2 Blackf. 183.

Kentucky: Kenley v. Commonwealth, 6 B. Mon. 583.

Maryland: Karthaus v. Owings, 6 H. & J. 134, 14 Am. Dec. 261.

New Hampshire: Claggett v. Richards, 45 N. H. 360.

Pennsylvania: Hicks v. McBride, 3 Phila. 377; Ingram v. Cox, 5 Pa. Dist. Rep. 617.

[310] *Alabama:* Ward v. Hood, 124 Ala. 570, 27 So. 245, 82 Am. St. Rep. 205.

Connecticut: Ormsbee v. Davis, 18 Conn. 555.

Delaware: Harmon v. Collins, 2 Pennew. 36, 45 Atl. 541.

Illinois: Pace v. Neal, 92 Ill. App. 416.

Indiana: Peffley v. Kenrick, 4 Ind. App. 510, 31 N. E. 40.

Indian Territory: McAlester v. Suchy, 1 Ind. Ty. 666, 43 S. W. 952.

Kansas: Citizens' State Bank v. Morse, 60 Kan. 526, 57 Pac. 115.

Kentucky: Kentucky L. & I. Co. v. Crabtree, 118 Ky. 395, 80 S. W. 1161.

Massachusetts: Kafer v. Harlow, 5 All. 348; Leighton v. Brown, 98 Mass. 515; Maguire v. Pan American Amusement Co., 205 Mass. 64, 91 N. E. 135.

New Mexico: Butts v. Woods, 4 N. M. 187, 16 Pac. 617 (plaintiff bound by value stated in his affidavit).

New York: Pettit v. Allen, 64 App. Div. 579, 72 N. Y. Supp. 287.

Pennsylvania: Gibbs v. Bartlett, 2 W. & S. 29.

Texas: Jacobs v. Daugherty, 78 Tex. 682, 15 S. W. 160.

See Plano Manuf. Co. v. Downey, 100 Ill. App. 36 (the actual value, and not the value to the plaintiff, which was affected by contracts made by him). Schrader v. Wolflin, 21 Ind. 238 (the actual value, and not the amount for which defendant may have sold).

[311] *Alabama:* Ward v. Hood, 124 Ala. 570, 27 So. 245, 82 Am. St. Rep. 205.

Connecticut: Ormsbee v. Davis, 18 Conn. 555.

Illinois: Hopkins v. Ladd, 35 Ill. 178; Walls v. Johnson, 16 Ind. 374.

The plaintiff may also recover his costs in the replevin suit,[312] and his counsel fees in that suit.[313] Consequential damages may also be recovered; as for damage to the goods,[314] or depreciation in value,[315] or for loss of a special use.[316]

§ 690. Value of property when to be estimated.

Under the judgment for a return the same question arises, which we have already examined, as to the time when the value should be computed: whether at the time of the original wrongful taking, the time of the replevin, or the time the return should be made.[317] In some cases the time of replevin is to furnish the rule;[318] in other cases the actual value of the property at the time of the demand made under the writ of restitution is to be recovered,[319] provided that if the goods have been used or destroyed, or have deteriorated in value, the value at

Kansas: Swartz *v.* English, 4 Kan. App. 509, 44 Pac. 1004.
Kentucky: Kentucky L. & I. Co. *v.* Crabtree, 118 Ky. 395, 80 S. W. 1161.
New York: Emerson *v.* Booth, 51 Barb. 40.
See *Maine:* Howe *v.* Handley, 28 Me. 241 (right of plaintiff ceased during the pendency of the proceedings by reason of a fiat in bankruptcy: he is entitled to interest up to that time).
[312] *Delaware:* Harmon *v.* Collins, 2 Pennew. 36, 45 Atl. 541.
Indiana: Kellar *v.* Carr, 119 Ind. 127, 21 N. E. 463.
Kansas: Swartz *v.* English, 4 Kan. App. 509, 44 Pac. 1004.
Maine: Hovey *v.* Coy, 17 Me. 266.
New York: Tibbles *v.* O'Connor, 28 Barb. 538.
Oregon: Carlon *v.* Dixon, 14 Ore. 293, 12 Pac. 394; Jordan *v.* La Vine, 15 Ore. 329, 15 Pac. 281.
Pennsylvania: Tibbal *v.* Cahoom, 10 Watts, 232.
South Carolina: Rhodes *v.* Burkart, 28 S. C. 155, 5 S. E. 347.
Contra, Brock *v.* Bolton, 37 S. C. 40, 16 S. E. 370 (by statute and form of the bond)).
And see *Massachusetts:* Maguire *v.*

Pan-American Amusement Co., 205 Mass. 64, 91 N. E. 135.
[313] Harts *v.* Wendell, 26 Ill. App. 274; Pace *v.* Neal, 92 Ill. App. 416.
Contra, Davis *v.* Crow, 7 Blackf. (Ind.) 129.
[314] Newton *v.* Round, 109 Iowa, 286, 80 N. W. 391.
[315] *Connecticut:* Bradley *v.* Reynolds, 61 Conn. 271, 23 Atl. 928.
New York: Rowley *v.* Gibbs, 14 Johns. 385.
[316] Miltimore *v.* Bottom, 66 Vt. 168, 28 Atl. 872.
[317] *Ante,* § 533.
[318] *United States:* Washington Ice Co. *v.* Webster, 125 U. S. 426, 31 L. ed. 799, 8 Sup. Ct. 947.
Kansas: Union Stove & Machine Works *v.* Breidenstein, 50 Kan. 53, 31 Pac. 703.
New York: Brizsee *v.* Maybee, 21 Wend. 144.
[319] *Indiana:* Lindsey *v.* Hewitt, 42 Ind. App. 573, 86 N. E. 446.
Maine: Washington Ice Co. *v.* Webster, 62 Me. 341, 16 Am. Rep. 462.
Massachusetts: Leighton *v.* Brown, 98 Mass. 515; Swift *v.* Barnes, 16 Pick. 194.

the time of replevin, with interest, should be allowed.[320] Where the property replevied was grain it appeared that the plaintiff in the replevin suit had threshed and marketed the grain. In an action on the bond it was said that ordinarily the measure of damages was the value of the property at the time the return was ordered, but in this case the cost of threshing and marketing would be deducted in the absence of evidence that the plaintiff did not act in good faith.[321]

§ 691. Destruction of property before payment.

In a case in New York, it was decided in a suit on the replevin bond, that the non-return of the property was excused by its inevitable destruction before judgment.[322] This decision was based on the old rule that if the condition of a bond becomes impossible by the act of God, the penalty is saved.[323] The case has been expressly disapproved.[324] But in Walker v. Osgood [325] it appeared that the property, a horse, had been replevied by one who claimed to be owner from a sheriff who seized it as the property of another. In an action upon the replevin bond by the sheriff, who had succeeded in the replevin suit, the claimant was held excused by showing that the horse had died without his fault; for, the court said, he had as good right to litigate his claim as the attaching creditor. And in a similar case on a forthcoming bond to deliver a slave, the death of the slave before forfeiture was held a defence.[326] Where under a statute a license was replevied, which was in force at the time the judgment for a return was issued, but had expired before a demand was made, it was held that the value of the license at the time of the judgment could be recovered on the bond.[327]

Where the property accidentally becomes worthless, as by the death of an animal, without the fault of anyone, the conclusion would seem to be either (1) that the old view that the

---

[320] *Indiana:* Lindsey v. Hewitt, 42 Ind. App. 573, 86 N. E. 446.

   Massachusetts: Parker v. Simonds, 8 Met. 205, 41 Am. Dec. 497.

[321] Clement v. Duffy, 54 Iowa, 632, 7 N. W. 85.

[322] Carpenter v. Stevens, 12 Wend. (N. Y.) 589.

[323] 2 Black. Com. 341.

[324] Suydam v. Jenkins, 3 Sandf. (N. Y.) 614. See Hinkson v. Morrison, 47 Iowa, 167.

[325] 53 Me. 422.

[326] Philipi v. Capell, 38 Ala. 575.

[327] Quinnipiac Brewing Co. v. Hackbarth, 74 Conn. 392, 50 Atl. 1023.

condition has become impossible through an act of God, settles the matter, or (2) that for this purpose, the loss of the property is to be considered as one of the necessary perils which existed in the fact that questions of possessory right cannot be litigated and decided without *delay*, and that this is an exposure to risk to be imputed to the law itself, or (3) that the loss should fall upon the person who turns out to have been wrong in the original assertion of title. Were the question a new one, we should be inclined to think the third view the correct one. While it is true, as Kent, J., in Walker v. Osgood [328] points out, that one side has as much right as the other to litigate the first, the very object of the bond is to compel the person in possession to give security for the benefit of the party out of possession, and he should therefore be held responsible for the consequences of the delay caused by his mistake, however honest. Of course, if it can be proved that the property was actually worthless at the time of the replevin through some inherent defect, the case is different, for the property then never had anything but a nominal value.

§ 691a. Reduction of damages.

Though the suit was not entered in court, the defendant, in an action upon the bond, may show that the title to the property replevied was in himself; and in that case only nominal damages can be recovered. [329] So it may be shown that the action of replevin failed merely because it was prematurely brought. [330] Even if judgment was given for a return, that does not necessarily bar the defendant in an action on the bond from showing his title. Replevin is a possessory action, and the issue may have been found in favor of a return without the title having been litigated. In that case the defendant is not concluded by the judgment, and may show in reduction of dam-

[328] 53 Me. 422.

[329] *Illinois:* Schweer v. Schwabacher, 17 Ill. App. 78.
Indiana: Wallace v. Clark, 7 Blackf. 298.
Kansas: Little v. Bliss, 55 Kan. 94, 39 Pac. 1025.
Maine: Jones v. Smith, 79 Me. 452.

Massachusetts: Easter v. Foster, 173 Mass. 39, 53 N. E. 132, 73 Am. St. Rep. 257.
Michigan: Pearl v. Garlock, 61 Mich. 419, 28 N. W. 155, 1 Am. St. Rep. 603.

[330] Davis v. Harding, 3 All. (Mass.) 302.

ages that he owned the property [331] or an interest in it.[332] If, however, title was put in issue in the replevin suit, the question cannot again be raised in an action on the bond.[333]

So if the property itself, or a part of it, or its proceeds have come to the plaintiff in the action on the bond, his recovery will be reduced by the property or value that has come to him.[334] And any other matter which may properly be shown in reduction will have the same effect.[335]

§ 691b. Limitations of plaintiff's title.

The fact that the plaintiff has a limited or partial title only cannot be set up by the defendant to defeat a full recovery,

[331] *Connecticut:* Fielding v. Silverstein, 70 Conn. 605, 40 Atl. 454.

Illinois: Hanchett v. Gardner, 138 Ill. 571, 28 N. E. 788; O'Donnell v. Colby, 153 Ill. 324, 38 N. E. 1067; Farson v. Gilbert, 85 Ill. App. 364; Magerstadt v. Harder, 95 Ill. App. 303.

Indiana: Stockwell v. Byrne, 22 Ind. 6.

Iowa: Buck v. Rhodes, 11 Ia. 348.

Kansas: Little v. Bliss, 55 Kan. 94, 39 Pac. 1025.

Maryland: Crabbs v. Koontz, 69 Md. 59, 13 Atl. 591.

[332] *Illinois:* King v. Ramsey, 13 Ill. 619 (general title subject to attachment).

Indiana: McFadden v. Ross, 108 Ind. 512, 8 N. E. 161 (lien); Ringgenberg v. Hartman, 124 Ind. 186, 24 N. E. 987 (mortgage); Consolidated T. L. Co. v. Bronson, 2 Ind. App. 1, 28 N. E. 155 (mortgage).

Maryland: Walter v. Warfield, 2 Gill, 216 (agent of owner).

Massachusetts: Leonard v. Whitney, 109 Mass. 265 (part owner).

North Carolina: Hall v. Tillman, 115 N. C. 500, 20 S. E. 726 (contract of purchase).

[333] *Indiana:* Denny v. Reynolds, 24 Ind. 248.

Iowa: Hawley v. Warner, 12 Iowa, 42.

[334] *Connecticut:* Vinton v. Mansfield, 48 Conn. 474 (property sold and proceeds paid to plaintiff).

Indiana: Story v. O'Dea, 23 Ind. 326

(plaintiff had forcibly taken the property from defendant).

Iowa: Harrow v. Ryan, 31 Ia. 156 (plaintiff obtained property by legal proceedings); Stuart v. Trotter, 75 Ia. 96, 39 N. W. 212 (judgment for value paid to plaintiff).

Kansas: Boyd v. Huffaker, 39 Kan. 525, 18 Pac. 508 (property sold pending proceedings and proceeds delivered to present plaintiff).

Kentucky: Board v. Moore, 12 Ky. L. Rep. 682 (part of property returned; recovery for value of remainder only).

Nebraska: Barton v. Shull, 62 Neb. 570, 87 N. W. 322 (plaintiff obtained property by levy on execution); Rinker v. Lee, 29 Neb. 783, 46 N. W. 211 (property replevied from present defendant pending proceedings and returned to present plaintiff).

Pennsylvania: Pure Oil Co. v. Terry, 209 Pa. 403, 58 Atl. 814 (property bought by present plaintiff at sale).

See *Massachusetts:* Flagg v. Tyler, 6 Mass. 33, 4 Am. Dec. 76 (owner became bankrupt; goods given to his assignee).

[335] *Connecticut:* Bradley v. Reynolds, 61 Conn. 271, 23 Atl. 928 (tender after breach).

Illinois: Harts v. Wendell, 26 Ill. App. 274 (tender after breach).

Pennsylvania: Snyder v. Frankfield, 4 Pa. Dist. Rep. 767 (set-off).

when the defendant does not himself own a part interest in it.[336]
But if the defendant can show not only that the plaintiff owns
a part interest only, but also that he himself owns the remaining interest, the plaintiff's recovery is limited to the value of his
interest.[337]

§ 691c. Detinue bonds.

A detinue bond is similar to a replevin bond, and damages
are assessed on the same principles. Damages may be recovered
though not assessed in the detinue action,[338] and include damages actually sustained by the seizure, but not for loss of time
and hotel bills paid in procuring sureties on the bond, and in
attending the trial of the case.[339] Counsel fees paid by the
plaintiff may be recovered.[340] The defendant may show in reduction of damages that he was the owner of the property sued
for.[341] Where part of the property was burned after the bond
was given, the measure of recovery in an action on the bond
was the value of the property destroyed as found by the jury
and the amount of damage to the other property; for *prima
facie*, the injury is the result of the detention.[342]

[336] *Illinois:* Atkins v. Moore, 82 Ill.
240, 25 Am. Rep. 313.
Maine: Farnham v. Moor, 21 Me.
508 (attaching sheriff).
Michigan: Williams v. Vail, 9 Mich.
162, 80 Am. Dec. 76; Ryan v. Akeley,
42 Mich. 516, 4 N. W. 207 (attaching
sheriff).
Missouri: Fallon v. Manning, 35 Mo.
271 (part owner); Frei v. Vogel, 40 Mo.
149 (attaching sheriff).
[337] *Colorado:* Imel v. Van Deren, 8
Colo. 90, 5 Pac. 803 (attaching sheriff
and owner).
Connecticut: Hannon v. O'Dell, 71
Conn. 698, 43 Atl. 147 (partners).
Georgia: Holmes v. Langston, 110 Ga.
861, 36 S. E. 251 (pledgee and pledgor).
Illinois: King v. Ramsey, 13 Ill. 619
(attaching sheriff and owner); Warner
v. Matthews, 18 Ill. 83; Jackson v. Bry,
3 Ill. App. 586 (mortgagor and mortgagee); Tanton v. Slyder, 93 Ill. App.
455 (owner and sheriff levying by virtue
of executions)

Iowa: Hawley v. Warner, 12 Ia. 42;
Hayden v. Anderson, 17 Ia. 158 (at-
taching sheriff and owner).
Maine: Hacker v. Johnson, 66 Me.
21, 22 Am. Rep. 547 (partner).
Maryland: Mason v. Sumner, 22 Md.
312 (landlord and tenant).
Michigan: Henry v. Ferguson, 55
Mich. 399, 21 N. W. 381 (attaching
sheriff and owner of judgment).
Missouri: Dilworth v. McKelvy, 30
Mo. 149.
New York: Russell v. Butterfield, 21
Wend. 300 (mortgagor and mortgagee).
[338] Hudson v. Young, 25 Ala. 376.
[339] Foster v. Napier, 74 Ala. 393.
[340] Ferguson v. Baker, 24 Ala. 402;
Miller v. Garrett, 35 Ala. 96; Foster v.
Napier, 74 Ala. 393.
[341] Savage v. Gunter, 32 Ala. 467;
Ernst v. Hogue, 86 Ala. 502, 5 So.
738.
[342] Heard v. Hicks, 101 Ala. 102, 13
So. 256.

§ 691d. Other judicial bonds.

A sequestration bond is security for damages caused by the seizure of the property and does not cover counsel fees incident to the defense of the suit.[343] The plaintiff in an action on the bond may recover loss of rents and compensation for the expense and inconvenience of removal.[344]

In an action on a bond to contest a "claim of exemptions," the plaintiff may recover the legal and other expenses incurred in meeting the contest.[345]

In an action on a bond given to secure the appointment of a receiver for plaintiff's business, she may recover the value of the property sold by the receiver, and damages for injury to the business.[346]

C.—OFFICIAL BONDS

§ 692. Official bonds in general.

The questions examined in the chapter upon the measure of damages in suits against public officers may arise, as in the instances which we have considered, in suits brought by the aggrieved party against the officer directly; or otherwise, on the bond, given by him for the faithful discharge of his duty; or again, they may be brought against the sureties of the officer. In the case of the suit being brought on the bond, much depends on the form of the instrument and the statute under which it is given. The statute must be substantially complied with.[347] If, however, the penalty is larger than the statute permits, the bond is valid up to the legal amount, and judgment may be given for the penalty, execution being limited to the legal amount;[348] and if the bond does not comply with the statute it may be good as a common-law bond.[349]

[343] Stauffer v. Garrison, 61 Miss. 67.

[344] Blum v. Gaines, 57 Tex. 135.

[345] Kirby v. Forbes, 141 Ala. 294, 37 So. 411.

[346] Haverly v. Elliott, 39 Neb. 201, 57 N. W. 1010.

[347] *Mississippi:* Brown v. Phipps, 6 Sm. & M. 51 (cannot be extended to cover other cases than those intended by the act).

North Carolina: State Bank v. Locke, 4 Dev. 529.

Ohio: Creswell v. Nesbitt, 16 Oh. St. 35.

[348] *Pennsylvania:* McCaraher v. Commonwealth, 5 W. & S. 21, 39 Am. Dec. 106.

South Dakota: State v. Taylor, 10 S. D. 182, 72 N. W. 407, 65 Am. St. Rep. 707.

[349] *Maine:* Scarborough v. Parker, 53 Me. 252.

New York: Allegany County v. Van Campen, 3 Wend. 49.

The bond is usually given to the State, but is for the benefit of any person injured by the official misfeasance.[350] The commonest practice is to give judgment for the amount of the penalty, and issue execution for the damages found by the jury, as in the case of an ordinary bond,[351] and the judgment then remains as security for further recovery by other persons injured.[352] When the penalty has been exhausted, either by one recovery or by successive proceedings, no further recovery may be had on the bond;[353] and all suits pending at one time

North Carolina: State *v.* Perkins, 10 Ired. L. 333.

Ohio: Davisson *v.* Burgess, 31 Oh. St. 78, 27 Am. Rep. 496.

Pennsylvania: Forsyth *v.* Dickson, 1 Grant, 26.

Tennessee: Goodrum *v.* Carroll, 2 Humph. 490, 37 Am. Dec. 564.

[350] *Massachusetts:* Skinner *v.* Phillips, 4 Mass. 68.

New York: People *v.* Holmes, 2 Wend. 281.

South Carolina: Mitchell *v.* Laurens, 7 Rich. 109.

Tennessee: Governor *v.* Allen, 8 Humph. 176, 47 Am. Dec. 601 (to the governor).

No individual can recover for an injury to another individual. Wilson *v.* Cantrel, 19 Ala. 642.

[351] *Arkansas:* Byrd *v.* State, 15 Ark. 175.

Iowa: Nelson *v.* Gray, 2 Greene, 397; Cameron *v.* Boyle, 2 Greene, 154.

Kentucky: Wells *v.* Commonwealth, 8 B. Mon. 459, 48 Am. Dec. 401.

Pennsylvania: Scarborough *v.* Thornton, 9 Pa. 451; Com. *v.* Sayres, 1 Miles, 235.

There can be no recovery beyond the penalty, with interest.

Connecticut: Olmstead *v.* Olmstead, 38 Conn. 309.

Kentucky: Woods *v.* Com., 8 B. Mon. 112.

But see *Pennsylvania:* Hughes *v.* Hughes, 54 Pa. 240.

In Georgia and Pennsylvania by statute judgment is entered only for the amount of the damages proved, and further judgments may be given in subsequent actions.

Georgia: Taylor *v.* Johnson, 17 Ga. 521.

Pennsylvania: Wolverton *v.* Commonwealth, 7 S. & R. 273; Campbell *v.* Commonwealth, 8 S. & R. 414; Withrow *v.* Commonwealth, 10 S. & R. 231.

In *New York,* under the old practice, debt on the bond must be brought in the name of the State, for the penalty; but an individual might sue in covenant and get judgment for the injury to him. Lawton *v.* Erwin, 9 Wend. 233; O'Connor *v.* Such, 9 Bosw. 318.

In *Illinois,* in the case of executor's bond only, successive suits might be brought on the bond and separate judgments had. People *v.* Randolph, 24 Ill. 324.

In Maine and Pennsylvania damages are to be assessed by the court and not by the jury, at the actual damage sustained by the breach.

Maine: Clifford *v.* Kimball, 39 Me. 413.

Pennsylvania: Com. *v.* Allen, 30 Pa. 49, 72 Am. Dec. 685.

[352] *Colorado:* Taylor *v.* Blyth, 9 Colo. App. 81, 47 Pac. 662.

New York: Fellows *v.* Gilman, 4 Wend. 414.

North Carolina: State *v.* McAlpin, 6 Ired. 347.

[353] *Illinois:* People *v.* Summers, 16 Ill. 173.

should be consolidated, and if the aggregate of the damages exceeds the amount of the penalty (or the amount still due on the bond) all the plaintiffs should recover ratably.[354]

The amount recovered is the actual damage; and therefore if a statute gives a penalty for official misfeasance the amount of the penalty cannot be recovered on the bond, but only the actual loss.[355] Nor can exemplary damages be recovered on the bond.[356] But where interest at a high rate is fixed by statute as recoverable for failure by a public officer to pay over money, this is not regarded as penalty, and interest at the statutory rate may be recovered on the bond.[357]

Actual compensation for the injury is the measure of recovery on the bond. Thus, where a commissioner to construct a drain filed a bond, and collected the assessment for building it, but failed to complete the drain, in an action on the bond it was held that the measure of damages was the amount required to complete the drain.[358] But where a receiver of public moneys neglected the duties of the office, it was held that the government could not pay an extravagant sum for the performance of the labor neglected by the receiver, and charge his sureties with such sum; it could only recover what would be a reasonable compensation for the labor performed.[359]

§ 692a. Acts outside official duty.

Parties on an official bond are liable only for such acts as are violations of official duty; and their liability therefore does not extend to any act not within the scope of such duty.[360] So, for

Indiana: State *v.* Ford, 5 Blackf. 392.

[354] *Indiana:* Moody *v.* State, 84 Ind. 433.

Iowa: Edmonds *v.* Edmonds, 73 Ia. 427, 53 N. W. 505; Hooks *v.* Evans, 68 Ia. 52, 25 N. W. 925.

Missouri: State *v.* Ruggles, 20 Mo. 99.

South Carolina: Mitchell *v.* Laurens, 7 Rich. 109.

[355] *Mississippi:* Foote *v.* Van Zandt, 34 Miss. 40.

South Carolina: Treasurers *v.* Buckner, 2 McMull. 323.

[356] *Indiana:* Peelle *v.* State, 118 Ind. 512, 21 N. E. 288.

Kentucky: Johnson *v.* Williams, 23 Ky. L. Rep. 658, 63 S. W. 759, 54 L. R. A. 220; United States F. & G. Co. *v.* Milstead, 33 Ky. L. Rep. 186, 109 S. W. 875.

Oklahoma: Hixon *v.* Cupp, 5 Okla. 545, 49 Pac. 927.

[357] *Georgia:* Wyche *v.* Myrick, 14 Ga. 584.

Kentucky: Sanders *v.* Bank of Kentucky, 2 Met. 327.

[358] Smith *v.* State, 117 Ind. 167.

[359] United States *v.* Wann, 3 McLean, 179.

[360] *District of Columbia:* United States *v.* West, 8 D. C. App. 59, 67.

instance, if it is not the duty of an officer to collect money, his bondsmen are not liable for money collected and embezzled by him.[361] And if after the bond is executed new duties of a different sort are put upon the officer, such as the duty of collecting money on a mere clerical officer, the bond, while it continues to cover the original duties,[362] does not cover acts done in pursuance of the newly assumed duties.[363] And so if a county treasurer has placed upon him also the duty of collector of school funds he nevertheless does not collect them in his capacity as treasurer; and the parties to his treasurer's bond are

Illinois: Burlington Ins. Co. v. Johnson, 120 Ill. 622, 12 N. E. 205; People v. Foster, 133 Ill. 496, 23 N. E. 615.

So where one employed to sell machines bought one himself and failed to pay for it the sureties on his bond were not liable for the price, since the purchase was not within the scope of his employment. Weed Sewing Machine Co. v. Winchel, 107 Ind. 260, 7 N. E. 881.

[361] *Alabama:* Dean v. Governor, 13 Ala. 526 (sheriff embezzling money collected after return day).

California: Heidt v. Minor, 89 Cal. 115, 26 Pac. 627 (notary public borrowing money on forged deed).

Georgia: Mason v. Com., 104 Ga. 35, 48, 30 S. E. 513 (county treasurer embezzling money received on a void loan).

Illinois: People v. Moon, 4 Ill. 123 (county treasurer embezzling money deposited by State, with county).

Indiana: Jenkins v. Lemonds, 29 Ind. 294 (clerk of court embezzling money received from counsel); Salem v. McClintock, 16 Ind. App. 656, 46 N. E. 39, 59 Am. St. Rep. 330 (superintendent of waterworks embezzling rents collected by him).

Kentucky: Commonwealth v. Cole, 7 B. Mon. 250 (constable embezzling money voluntarily paid him by debtors); Hardin v. Carrico, 3 Met. 289, 77 Am. Dec. 174 (clerk of court embezzling money paid into court).

Massachusetts: Boston v. Moore, 3 Allen, 126 (constable embezzling money voluntarily paid him by debtors).

Mississippi: Matthews v. Montgomery, 25 Miss. 150 (clerk of court embezzling fees paid to other officers).

Nebraska: State v. Moore, 56 Neb. 82, 76 N. W. 474 (auditor embezzling fees collected from insurance companies); Stephens v. Hendee, 80 Neb. 754, 115 N. W. 283 (county judge takes estate prior to appointment of administrator).

New York: People v. Pennock, 60 N. Y. 426 (town supervisor).

North Carolina: Mills v. Allen, 7 Jones, 564, 78 Am. Dec. 265 (sheriff embezzling money collected without process).

A justice of the peace collects a note in his official capacity; his bondsmen are holden if he embezzles the money collected. Widener v. State, 45 Ind. 244; *acc.,* Bosley v. Smith, 3 Humph. (Tenn.) 406 (money collected by constable without process).

[362] Mayor v. Kelly, 98 N. Y. 467, 50 Am. Rep. 699.

[363] *New Jersey:* Kellogg v. Scott, 58 N. J. Eq. 344, 44 Atl. 190.

New York: Mayor v. Kelly, 98 N. Y. 467, 50 Am. Rep. 699.

Pennsylvania: Shackamaxon Bank v. Yard, 150 Pa. 351, 24 Atl. 635, 30 Am. St. Rep. 807; Harrisburg S. & L. Assoc. v. United States F. & G. Co., 197 Pa. 177, 46 Atl. 910.

not liable if he embezzles money so collected.[364] So where a chief of police made an arrest under color of office, but quite beyond his official duties, the sureties on his bond were not liable.[365] And where a sheriff was not given the duty of collecting taxes in arrear, due to his predecessor, his bondsmen were not liable for his embezzlement of taxes so collected.[366]

The duties for the performance of which the sureties are liable are such as may be defined by law; and for all duties so defined at the time the bond is executed the sureties must answer.[367] The duties may be defined after the execution of the bond; but in that case they cannot be extended beyond the ordinary duties of such an office.[368]

If the official is transferred to a different office, his old bond does not cover the duties of the new office; [369] and it has been held that where an official held two offices and gave a single bond to cover both, and the offices were afterward divided and he continued to hold one of them, the bond did not cover his acts thereafter, because the radical alteration in his duties discharged his sureties.[370]

§ 692b. Liability for acts before or after regular term of bond.

Since the term of a public officer ordinarily extends until his successor is elected and qualified, it is not uncommon for a term to be prolonged by reason of the failure of the successor to qualify promptly. The official bond sometimes expressly

---

[364] *Minnesota:* State *v.* Young, 23 Minn. 551.

North Carolina: County Board of Education *v.* Bateman, 102 N. C. 52, 8 S. E. 862, 11 Am. St. Rep. 708.

And see to the same effect:

California: People *v.* Gardner, 55 Cal. 304 (same person being Surveyor General and Registrar of Land Office).

Kentucky: Anderson *v.* Thompson, 10 Bush, 132 (sheriff also acting as collector of taxes).

Ohio: State *v.* Corey, 16 Oh. St. 17 (township treasurer acting also as school treasurer).

[365] State *v.* McDonough, 9 Mo. App.

63; *acc.,* Governor *v.* Pearce, 31 Ala. 465.

[366] Middleton *v.* Caldwell, 4 Bush (Ky.), 392.

[367] Richland County *v.* Owen, 68 S. E. 753.

[368] Lafayette *v.* James, 92 Ind. 240, 47 Am. Rep. 140.

[369] *Maryland:* First Nat. Bank *v.* Gerke, 68 Md. 449, 13 Atl. 358.

New York: National M. B. Assoc. *v.* Conkling, 90 N. Y. 116, 43 Am. Rep. 146.

North Carolina: Sun L. I. Co. *v.* United States F. & G. Co., 130 N. C. 129, 40 S. E. 975.

[370] King *v.* Herron, [1903] 2 Ire. 474.

covers defaults during this period; [371] and even when there is no express provision the bond is sometimes held to cover such defaults.[372] But by the prevailing view the bond does not cover defaults after the expiration of the term for which it was given.[373] In Iowa the bond covers defaults while the officer is holding over pending the qualification of a successor, but not where he holds office for several terms without newly qualifying.[374]

The liability on the bond ceases at the end of the original term though during the term the legislature increases the length of it; [375] and on the other hand it continues throughout the original term though the legislature by an unconstitutional act attempts to shorten the term.[376] And if the term of office lasts for more than a year the original bond continues in force during the term, though a statute requires a new bond to be given annually, and this was not done.[377]

The bondsmen are not generally responsible for defaults be-

[371] *Indiana:* State v. Berry, 50 Ind. 496.
New Jersey: Camden v. Ward, 67 N. J. L. 558, 52 Atl. 392.
New York: Ulster County Savings Institution v. Young, 161 N. Y. 23, 55 N. E. 483.
[372] *California:* Placer Co. v. Dickerson, 45 Cal. 12.
Illinois: People v. Beach, 77 Ill. 52.
Iowa: Plymouth Co. v. Kerseborm, 108 Ia. 304, 79 N. W. 67, 65 Am. St. Rep. 257.
Kentucky: Rodes v. Commonwealth, 6 B. Mon. 359 (statutory).
Mississippi: Thompson v. State, 37 Miss. 518.
Missouri: State v. Kurtzeborn, 78 Mo. 98.
North Carolina: State v. Daniels, 6 Jones, 444.
See Tuley v. State, 1 Ind. 500 (no provision for officer holding over till successor qualified: sureties not liable for defaults after expiration of term).
[373] *Indiana:* Rany v. Governor, 4 Blackf. 2; Steinback v. State, 38 Ind. 483.

Kansas: Riddel v. School District, 15 Kan. 168.
Massachusetts: Bigelow v. Bridge, 8 Mass. 274, 5 Am. Dec. 105.
New Hampshire: Dover v. Twombly, 42 N. H. 59.
New Jersey: Rahway v. Crowell, 40 N. J. L. 207, 29 Am. Rep. 224.
North Carolina: Thomas v. Summey, 1 Jones, 554.
South Carolina: South Carolina Society v. Johnson, 1 McCord, 41, 10 Am. Dec. 644; Commissioners v. Greenwood, 1 Desaus. 450.
[374] Wapello v. Bigham, 10 Ia. 39, 72 Am. Dec. 370, explained in Plymouth Co. v. Kerseborm, 108 Ia. 304, 79 N. W. 67, 65 Am. St. Rep. 257.
[375] *California:* Brown v. Lattimore, 17 Cal. 93.
Indiana: Mulliken v. State, 7 Blackf. 77.
Washington: King County v. Ferry, 5 Wash. 536, 32 Pac. 538, 34 Am. St. Rep. 880, 19 L. R. A. 500.
[376] People v. Foote, 19 Johns. (N. Y.) 58.
[377] Kelly v. Moody, 12 Ky. L. Rep. 389.

fore the execution of the bond.[378] But if a default is discovered during the term the bondsmen are responsible unless they prove that the default occurred before the execution of the bond.[379] And where an executor's bond was conditioned on obeying all orders of the court touching the administration of the estate, the sureties were liable for money lost before the bond was executed, but brought into the account and ordered to be paid over while the bond was in force.[380]

§ 692c. Liability on cumulative bonds.

It sometimes happens that officers are ordered to file additional bonds; and the question may then arise as to the liability on the successive bonds. It is usually held that the second bond covers defaults before it is given as well as after, since the liability to account exists after the giving of the second bond.[381] If the first bond is discharged upon the approval of the second, recovery may still be had upon it for all defaults prior to the discharge.[382]

The sureties on the two bonds are entitled to have their respective rights adjusted in equity. In the ordinary case they will contribute equally.[383] But where the sureties on a subsequent bond become liable for a default which really occurred

[378] Farrar *v.* United States, 5 Pet. 373, 8 L. ed. 373; United States *v.* Spencer, 2 McLean, 405.

[379] United States *v.* Dudley, 21 D. C. 337.

[380] Scofield *v.* Churchill, 72 N. Y. 565.

[381] *Arkansas:* Dugger *v.* Wright, 51 Ark. 232, 11 S. W. 213, 14 Am. St. Rep. 48.

Illinois: Ammons *v.* People, 11 Ill. 6 (additional surety on same bond); Pinkstaff *v.* People, 59 Ill. 148; Moulding *v.* Wilhartz, 169 Ill. 422, 48 N. E. 189.

Iowa: Douglass *v.* Kessler, 57 Ia. 63, 10 N. W. 313 (but see Bessinger *v.* Dickerson, 20 Ia. 260; Thompson *v.* Dickerson, 22 Ia. 360); Knox *v.* Kearns, 73 Ia. 286, 34 N. W. 861.

Kansas: Brown *v.* State, 23 Kan. 235.

Massachusetts: Choate *v.* Arrington, 116 Mass. 552; Loring *v.* Baker, 3 Cush. 465.

Missouri: State *v.* Finn, 23 Mo. App. 290.

Oregon: Thompson *v.* Dekum, 32 Ore. 506, 56 Pac. 517, 755.

Tennessee: Miller *v.* Moore, 3 Humph. 189.

[382] *Massachusetts:* McKim *v.* Bartlett, 129 Mass. 226.

Missouri: Wolff *v.* Schaefer, 74 Mo. 154; State *v.* Berning, 74 Mo. 87, 41 Am. Rep. 305.

[383] *Massachusetts:* Choate *v.* Arrington, 116 Mass. 552.

North Carolina: Bright *v.* Lennon, 83 N. C. 183.

Oregon: Thompson *v.* Dekum, 32 Ore. 506, 56 Pac. 517, 755.

before their bond was executed, they are entitled to reimbursement from the sureties on the earlier bond, who are primarily liable.[384]

Where separate bonds are given to cover different things, as for instance to cover the management of separate funds, or where a general bond is given and also a separate bond for a special duty, the liabilities of the bondsmen are distinct, each being liable only for defaults covered by his own bond.[385]

§ 692d. Successive bonds to cover successive terms of office.

Where a bond is given in each of several successive terms, each bond covers the defaults of that term only for which it is given; and the bondsmen are not liable either for defaults before their term began [386] or for defaults after their term was completed.[387] It is often the case, however, that an officer is called upon during his term to perform an act which cannot be completed before the expiration of the term, and the law provides that his authority and duty shall continue until full per-

---

[384] Corrigan v. Foster, 51 Oh. St. 225, 37 N. E. 263.

[385] Milwaukee County v. Ehlers, 45 Wis. 281. And where a bond is given for the management of one of two separate funds held by the officer, and he embezzles from both funds in an unknown proportion, the bondsmen will be liable for a *pro rata* proportion of the entire amount embezzled. Britton v. Fort Worth, 78 Tex. 227, 14 S. W. 585.

[386] *United States:* Meyers v. United States, 1 McLean, 493.

Illinois: Coons v. People, 76 Ill. 383; Schoenemann v. Martyn, 68 Ill. App. 412.

Iowa: Mahaska County v. Ingalls, 16 Ia. 81; Warren County v. Ward, 21 Ia. 85.

Massachusetts: Rochester v. Randall, 105 Mass. 295, 7 Am. Rep. 519.

Michigan: Grand Haven v. United States F. & G. Co., 128 Mich. 106, 87 N. W. 104, 92 Am. St. Rep. 446.

Missouri: State v. Elliott, 157 Mo. 609, 57 S. W. 1087, 80 Am. St. Rep. 643.

North Carolina: State v. Lackey, 3 Ire. L. 25.

[387] *United States:* United States v. Kirkpatrick, 9 Wheat. 720, 6 L. ed. 199; United States v. Eckford, 1 How. 250, 11 L. ed. 120.

Connecticut: Williams v. Miller, Kirby, 189.

New Hampshire: Dover v. Twombly, 42 N. H. 59.

North Carolina: Governor v. Cobb, 2 Dev. 489.

South Carolina: State v. Bird, 2 Rich. 99.

Vermont: First Nat. Bank v. Briggs, 69 Vt. 12, 37 Atl. 231, 60 Am. St. Rep. 922, 37 L. R. A. 845.

Virginia: Commonwealth v. Fairfax, 4 Hen. & M. 208; Munford v. Rice, 6 Munf. 81.

England: Lord Arlington v. Merricke, 2 Saund. 411; Liverpool Water Works v. Atkinson, 6 East, 507; Hassell v. Long, 2 M. & S. 363; Peppin v. Cooper, 2 B. & Ald. 431.

Canada: Waterford School Trustees v. Clarkson, 23 Ont. App. 213.

formance. In such a case the liability on the bond given for the term during which the act was begun will continue until it is completed.[388] And a bond may by its express provisions continue beyond the term.[389] Where a default continues through two terms (as where it is a failure to collect money which the officer was at all times under a duty to collect) both sets of bondsmen are liable.[390]

§ 692e. Default in payment of money at end of last term.

Where a default occurs in the payment of money, those bondsmen alone are accountable within whose term the money was received and not paid over. So where it appears that all moneys received during the first term were either properly expended or actually on hand at the beginning of the second term, the bondsmen during the first term will not be liable for a subsequent defalcation: [391] and on the other hand, the bondsmen on the second bond are not liable for money misapplied during the first term, and never actually coming to their

[388] *Colorado:* People v. Kendall, 14 Colo. App. 175, 59 Pac. 409 (attachment during first term, judgment later).

Illinois: Elkin v. People, 4 Ill. 207, 36 Am. Dec. 541 (sheriff sells land during term, receives money to redeem later); McCormick v. Moss, 41 Ill. 352 (execution received during first term, levied later).

Massachusetts: Larned v. Allen, 13 Mass. 295 (warrant for collection given during term, collection completed later).

Missouri: Marney v. State, 13 Mo. 7 (sheriff sells on execution during first term, collects later).

New York: People v. McHenry, 18 Wend. 482 (execution levied during first term; proceeds embezzled later, *semble*).

Virginia: Tyre v. Wilson, 9 Gratt. 59, 58 Am. Dec. 21 (sheriff levies during term, sells later).

In a few such cases, however, the bondsmen during the first term were

held not liable for a default after the expiration of the term.

California: Wood v. Lowden, 117 Cal. 232, 49 Pac. 132 (attachment during first term, property injured by neglect later).

Maryland: Robey v. Turner, 8 Gill & J. 125 (execution received during first term, failure to levy later).

Tennessee: Sherrell v. Goodrum, 3 Humph. 419.

[389] Fink v. Farmers' Bank, 178 Pa. 154, 35 Atl. 636, 56 Am. St. Rep. 746.

[390] *Mississippi:* McWilliams v. Norfleet, 63 Miss. 183.

Missouri: Ingram v. McComb, 17 Mo. 558.

North Carolina: State v. Wall, 9 Ired. L. 20.

[391] *Missouri:* State v. Paul, 21 Mo. 51.

Nebraska: Paxton v. State, 59 Neb. 460, 476, 81 N. W. 383, 80 Am. St. Rep. 689.

New York: Overacre v. Garrett, 5 Lans. 156.

hands.[392] And though the account at the end of the first year
shows the correct balance carried over, the bondsmen for the
second year are not concluded by the recitals of the account,
but may show that no balance was in fact carried over;[393] nor
does the account, though showing a correct balance, operate to
discharge the first bond.[394] The presumption is nevertheless
against the last bondsmen; and they will be held liable for a
default discovered during their term unless they can prove
that the default took place in a previous term.[395]

When income received during the second year is to be applied either to a deficiency of the first year or to one in the
second year, a difficult question is presented as to the legal
rules for application of payments; and there is some difference
in the authorities. If the officer himself applies the payment to
the deficit of the first year, the application is either legal, or, if
illegal, is itself a default for which his bondsmen of the second
year are liable.[396] If no application is directed by the defaulting officer, the money will by the weight of authority be applied on the earliest debt, and the second bondsmen will
therefore be held for the default.[397] It would seem that the

[392] *Iowa:* Independent School Dist. v.
McDonald, 39 Ia. 564.
Kentucky: Newman v. Metcalf, 4
Bush, 67; Paducah v. Cully, 9 Bush,
323, 15 Am. Rep. 711.
Wisconsin: Vivian v. Otis, 24 Wis.
518, 1 Am. Rep. 199.
[393] *Indiana:* Goodwine v. State, 81
Ind. 109.
Mississippi: Mann v. Yazoo, 31
Miss. 574.
New Jersey: Frost v. Mixsell, 38 N.
J. Eq. 586.
[394] Miller v. Macoupin County, 7 Ill.
50.
[395] *United States:* Bruce v. United
States, 17 How. 437, 443, 15 L. ed.
129; Alvord v. United States, 13
Blatchf. 279.
California: Heppe v. Johnson, 33
Cal. 265.
Illinois: Moulding v. Wilhartz, 169
Ill. 422, 48 N. E. 189, 61 Am. St. Rep.
185.

Maine: Readfield v. Shaver, 50 Me.
36, 79 Am. Dec. 592.
Minnesota: Board of Education v.
Robinson, 81 Minn. 305, 84 N. W. 105,
83 Am. St. Rep. 374.
Ohio: Kelley v. State, 25 Ohio St.
567.
Tennessee: Anderson County v. Hays,
99 Tenn. 542, 42 S. W. 266.
[396] *Indiana:* Cook v. State, 13 Ind.
154.
Iowa: Independent School Dist. v.
McDonald, 39 Ia. 564.
Massachusetts: Colerain v. Bell, 9
Met. 499.
Minnesota: Pine County v. Willard,
39 Minn. 125, 39 N. W. 71, 12 Am. St.
Rep. 622.
Vermont: Lyndon v. Miller, 36 Vt.
329.
Virginia: Chapman v. Common-
wealth, 25 Gratt. 721.
[397] *Connecticut:* Hartford v. Franey,
47 Conn. 76, 36 Am. Rep. 51.

creditor cannot determine the application so as to exonerate the sureties on one of the bonds.[398] If the income can be traced and shown to be the proceeds of a defalcation in either term, it will be applied in discharge of it.[399]

§ 692f. Bonds of financial officers.

Treasurers are usually held to be debtors for the money received by them, and not mere bailees, and are therefore liable on their bond for a loss of the money even though it was deposited in an apparently solvent bank and lost by failure of the bank,[400] or in a bank or other safe place and lost by robbery,[401]

Indiana: Goodwine v. State, 81 Ind. 109; Rogers v. State, 99 Ind. 218.

Maine: Readfield v. Shaver, 50 Me. 36, 79 Am. Dec. 592.

Massachusetts: Sandwich v. Fish, 2 Gray, 298.

New Jersey: Frost v. Mixsell, 38 N. J. Eq. 586.

New York: Seymour v. Van Slyck, 8 Wend. 403.

In *Missouri* there appears to be no presumption, though if it can be shown that the payment was made on account of charges for one year it will be applied to that year. Draffen v. Boonville, 8 Mo. 395; State v. Smith, 26 Mo. 226, 72 Am. Dec. 204; St. Joseph v. Merlatt, 26 Mo. 233, 72 Am. Dec. 207.

[398] Porter v. Stanley, 47 Me. 515, 74 Am. Dec. 501.

There is an intimation to the contrary in State v. Smith, 26 Mo. 226, 72 Am. Dec. 204. And see United States v. January, 7 Cranch, 572, 3 L. ed. 443.

[399] Rogers v. State, 99 Ind. 218.

[400] *Georgia:* Lamb v. Dart, 108 Ga. 602, 34 S. E. 160.

Illinois: Oeltjen v. People, 160 Ill. 409, 43 N. E. 610, 56 Ill. App. 138; Ramsay v. People, 197 Ill. 572, 64 N. E. 549, 90 Am. St. Rep. 177.

Kansas: Rose v. Douglass Township, 52 Kan. 451, 34 Pac. 1046, 39 Am. St. Rep. 354.

Mississippi: Griffin v. Levee Com., 71 Miss. 767, 15 So. 107.

Missouri: State v. Moore, 74 Mo. 413, 41 Am. Rep. 322.

Nebraska: Thomssen v. Hall County, 63 Neb. 777, 89 N. W. 393, 57 L. R. A. 303.

New York: Tillinghast v. Merrill, 151 N. Y. 135, 45 N. E. 375, 56 Am. St. Rep. 612, 34 L. R. A. 678.

North Carolina: Havens v. Lathene, 75 N. C. 505.

Texas: Wilson v. Wichita County, 67 Tex. 647.

[401] *United States:* United States v. Prescott, 3 How. 578, 11 L. ed. 734; Boyden v. United States, 13 Wall. 17, 20 L. ed. 527.

Indiana: Halbert v. State, 22 Ind. 125; Morbeck v. State, 28 Ind. 86.

Iowa: Taylor v. Morton, 37 Ia. 550.

Massachusetts: Hancock v. Hazzard, 12 Cush. 112, 59 Am. Dec. 171.

Minnesota: Board of Education v. Jewell, 44 Minn. 427, 46 N. W. 914, 20 Am. St. Rep. 586.

Missouri: State v. Gatzweiler, 49 Mo. 17 (taken by military force).

Montana: Com. v. Lineberger, 3 Mont. 231, 35 Am. Rep. 462.

Nevada: State v. Nevin, 19 Nev. 162, 7 Pac. 650, 3 Am. St. Rep. 873.

New Jersey: New Providence v. McEachron, 33 N. J. L. 339, aff'd 35 N. J. L. 528.

New Mexico: United States v. Watts, 1 New Mex. 553.

even if it was lost from a safe provided for the purpose by the county.[402] In a few jurisdictions, however, the treasurer and his bondsmen are relieved from responsibility if without negligence or other breach of duty he deposits the money in a bank which fails,[403] or if he is robbed [404] or loses the money otherwise without fault.[405] The more stringent liability has been held to rest on treasurers only, and not on other officials who have other principal duties but receive money incidentally.[406]

Since the officer must account for all money in his hands, the sureties are liable for all money received before the bond was executed, if there was a liability to account for it after the execution of the bond.[407]

Where the default does not consist in loss of the money, but in some other failure of duty, the measure of damages is such sum as will be compensation for the wrong. For delay in paying over money interest is recoverable.[408] For failure to turn

New York: Muzzy *v.* Shattick, 1 Denio, 233.

Ohio: State *v.* Harper, 6 Oh. St. 607.

Pennsylvania: Commonwealth *v.* Comly, 3 Pa. 372.

[402] *Minnesota:* Hennepin County *v.* Jones, 18 Minn. 199.

Mississippi: Arnold *v.* State, 77 Miss. 463, 27 So. 596, 78 Am. St. Rep. 533.

It seems, however, that where the *bank of deposit* is selected by law the treasurer is not responsible for its failure without his fault. State *v.* Bobleter, 83 Minn. 479, 86 N. W. 461.

[403] State *v.* Copeland, 96 Tenn. 296, 34 S. W. 427, 31 L. R. A. 844, 54 Am. Rep. 59.

[404] *Alabama:* State *v.* Houston, 78 Ala. 576.

California: Healdsburg *v.* Mulligan, 113 Cal. 205, 33 L. R. A. 461, 45 Pac. 337.

[405] Wilson *v.* People, 19 Colo. 199, 34 Pac. 944, 22 L. R. A. 449, 41 Am. St. Rep. 243.

[406] People *v.* Lucas, 93 N. Y. 585.

[407] *Arkansas:* State *v.* Buck, 63 Ark. 218, 27 S. W. 881.

Massachusetts: McIntire *v.* Lineham, 178 Mass. 263, 59 N. E. 767.

In Bockenstedt *v.* Perkins, 73 Ia. 23, 34 N. W. 488, 5 Am. St. Rep. 652, a suit on a guardian's bond, it appeared that the guardian received the money six days before the bond was executed. It was held that the sureties were not liable for any defalcation before the bond was executed, but they were liable for all money which was in his hands at the time of the execution of the bond; and evidence of the time that elapsed between his receipt of the money and of the execution of the bond would justify a finding that the money was in his hands at the time of execution of it.

[408] *Maryland:* Richardson *v.* State, 2 Gill, 439.

New Jersey: Board of Justices *v.* Fennimore, 1 N. J. L. 242.

See United States *v.* Curtis, 100 U. S. 119, 25 L. ed. 571.

over a tax warrant the bondsmen are liable for the amount of taxes thereby lost.[409] For failure to cancel a paid warrant, whereby it got into circulation again and had to be paid a second time, the damages are the amount of the warrant.[410] For failure to render accounts [411] or to make annual reports [412] only so much may be recovered as the plaintiff can prove to have been lost by reason of the failure. For receiving securities in payment instead of cash, the bondsmen are holden for the amount of the cash.[413]

The approval of the officer's accounts does not release his bondsmen from liability,[414] nor does negligence of the official board which examined and passed the accounts.[415] But the accounting may be so acted on as to amount to a full discharge. So in an action on a state treasurer's bond, it appeared that in turning over his account to his successor the treasurer turned over a large balance evidenced only by certificates of deposit of certain banks. The total amount of the certificates of deposit was the amount for which the treasurer was accountable, less a small amount paid in cash. The treasurer's successor accepted these certificates as cash and opened a running account with the banks in question to the same amount. It was held that this was such a settlement with the preceding treasurer as would discharge him and charge his successor, even though such successor was unable to realize money on these accounts owing to subsequent failure of the banks.[416] Payment of the claim by the officer, in whole or in part, after default will reduce the amount of recovery on the bond.[417] But no re-

[409] Olean v. King, 116 N. Y. 355, 22 N. E. 559.

[410] Johnson v. Hughes, 12 Ia. 360.

[411] Bocard v. State, 79 Ind. 270.

[412] Jemison v. Governor, 47 Ala. 390.

[413] Board of Justices v. Fennimore, 1 N. J. L. 242.

[414] *Nebraska:* Bush v. Johnson County, 48 Neb. 1, 66 N. W. 1023, 5 Am. St. Rep. 373.

New York: Richmond County v. Wandel, 6 Lans. 33.

[415] *Nebraska:* Bush v. Johnson County, 48 Neb. 1, 66 N. W. 1023, 5 Am. St. Rep. 373.

New York: Supervisors v. Otis, 62 N. Y. 88.

[416] State v. Hill, 47 Neb. 456, 66 N. W. 541.

[417] Morris Bldg. Assoc. No. 2 v. Altmaier, 10 Pa. Co. Ct. 645. But where money was retained by a public officer on false vouchers, application of it to the benefit of the government but in an unauthorized way would not diminish the amount recovered. Ewing v. United States, 11 Ariz. 1, 89 Pac. 593.

duction will be made because of failure to prove the claim against the estate of the bankrupt officer and receive a dividend, since there is a right to rely upon the bond for the entire claim.[418] The amount of the compensation due the officer may be withheld, and will then be deducted from recovery on the bond;[419] but not if the officer has made up and rendered his accounts without making any claim for compensation.[420]

§ 692g. Bonds of judicial officers.

A judge is liable on his bond for malfeasance in any ministerial duty.[421] Thus he is liable for refusal to issue a license[422] or an execution,[423] or for the embezzlement of money paid to him by an executor in discharge of an account.[424] A commissioner in equity who accepts an irregular injunction bond is liable on his official bond for the amount of damages suffered by the parties restrained in the injunction suit.[425] Where a notary public takes an acknowledgment of a forged deed, his bondsmen are liable for the value of the property which was supposed to pass by the deed.[426] If the deed was a mortgage deed, it is commonly said that the amount of the loan may be recovered on the bond;[427] but it is more correct to say that the amount recoverable is the value of the property, unless that exceeds the amount of the loan.[428]

Where a probate judge was also the officer to register conveyances, and he neglected to index a deed properly, it was held

---

[418] Board of County Com'rs v. Security Bank, 75 Minn. 174, 77 N. W. 815, 74 Am. St. Rep. 447.

[419] Brunswick v. Snow, 73 Me. 177.

[420] Independent School Dist. v. McDonald, 39 Ia. 564.

[421] *United States:* Branch v. Davis, 29 Fed. 888 (failure to issue proper process for levy of tax to pay plaintiff's claim; plaintiff gets not entire amount of judgment, but damages for delay unless it has become impossible to secure payment).
North Carolina: State v. Windley, 99 N. C. 4, 5 S. E. 14 (failure to require sufficient bond from guardian; plaintiff, the ward, recovers amount received and embezzled by guardian with interest).

[422] Grider v. Tally, 77 Ala. 422, 54 Am. Rep. 65.

[423] Noel v. State, 6 Blackf. (Ind.) 523. The insolvency of the execution defendant may be shown in mitigation.

[424] Wright v. Harris, 31 Iowa, 272.

[425] Treasurers v. Clowney, 2 McMull. (S. C.) 510.

[426] Joost v. Craig, 131 Cal. 504, 63 Pac. 840, 82 Am. St. Rep. 734.

[427] *Michigan:* Doran v. Butler, 74 Mich. 643, 42 N. W. 273.
Missouri: State v. Ryland, 163 Mo. 280, 63 S. W. 819.

[428] Heidt v. Minor, 89 Cal. 115, 26 Pac. 627.

that a purchaser of the land who was injured thereby could recover on the bond the amount of his loss.[429]

§ 692h. Bonds of clerks of courts.

Where a clerk of court has the duty of acknowledging or recording deeds or of indexing the records, his bondsmen are liable for damage caused by a mistake.[430] So where he took an acknowledgment of a forged mortgage the mortgagee may hold the bondsmen for his loss; [431] when he enters a forged cancellation of mortgage, the purchaser may recover on the bond the amount paid to discharge the mortgage; [432] and where he made a mistaken reference to a mortgage, a grantee could recover his loss from the bondsmen.[433] Where it is the duty of a clerk to receive money his bondsmen are liable for the embezzlement of it.[434] As in other cases, no recovery can be had for consequences which are not proximate results of the wrong. So where a clerk failed to record plaintiff's mortgage on land, but plaintiff was at the time he lent the money chargeable with notice that the title was not in the mortgagor, no damages can be recovered on the bond.[435]

§ 692i. Bonds of sheriffs and constables.

In an action on the bond of a sheriff only the actual damages may be recovered. If a statute provides a penalty or treble damages against a sheriff for misconduct in office, the penalty cannot be recovered in an action on the bond; [436] and the bond covers only breaches of official duty. A breach of an obligation undertaken by the sheriff outside his official duty is not cov-

---

[429] Norton v. Kumpe, 121 Ala. 446, 25 So. 841.

[430] Strain v. Babb, 30 S. C. 342, 9 S. E. 271, 14 Am. St. Rep. 905 (failure to enroll lien; plaintiff recovers value of lien).

[431] People v. Bartels, 138 Ill. 322, 27 N. E. 1091.

[432] Appleby v. State, 45 N. J. L. 161.

[433] Howe v. Taylor, 9 Ore. 288.

[434] State v. Boone, 108 N. C. 78, 12 S. E. 897.

[435] Terrell v. McLean, 130 Ga. 633, 61 S. E. 485.

[436] United States: Gwin v. Barton, 6 How. 7, 12 L. ed. 321.

California: Glascock v. Ashman, 52 Cal. 493.

Colorado: State Bank v. Brennan, 7 Colo. App. 427, 43 Pac. 1050.

Kentucky: Commonwealth v. Bradley, 1 Litt. 48, 13 Am. Dec. 214.

South Carolina: Treasurers v. Hilliard, 8 Rich. 412.

Texas: De la Garza v. Booth, 28 Tex. 478.

ered by the bond, as failure to pay compensation to a custodian of attached property,[437] or failure to return to a debtor securities which the creditor refused to receive;[438] and so where a sheriff who had no writ of execution pretended to seize and sell land on execution, there was no liability on the bond.[439]

For a wrongful arrest, or for illegal force used in making arrest, the bondsmen are liable, though it was in excess of official duty, since the act was done under color of office.[440] But where the arrest is not apparently legal, the act is not done under color of office, and the bondsmen are not liable; as where the arrest was made outside the State,[441] or on a warrant obviously illegal.[442] Where imprisonment is resorted to as a means of enforcing liability, in an action upon the officer's bond for an escape, the measure of damages is *prima facie* the amount of the judgment; and the insolvency of the prisoner cannot be shown to mitigate the damages; perhaps, as has been suggested, because to allow it would nullify the coercive nature of imprisonment for debt.[443] A later rearrest of the prisoner may be shown in mitigation.[444]

For failure to levy an execution on property the limit of recovery is the value of the property, though that may be less

[437] Wilson v. State, 13 Ind. 341.

[438] Brown v. Mosely, 11 Sm. & M. (Miss.) 354.

[439] Eaton v. Kelly, 72 N. C. 110.

[440] *Indiana:* State v. Druly, 3 Ind. 431.

Iowa: Clancy v. Kenworthy, 74 Ia. 740, 35 N. W. 427, 7 Am. St. Rep. 508 (ill-treatment after arrest).

Kentucky: Johnson v. Williams, 111 Ky. 289, 23 Ky. L. Rep. 658, 63 S. W. 759, 98 Am. St. Rep. 416, 54 L. R. A. 220 (wrong person shot); Growbarger v. United States F. & G. Co., 126 Ky. 118, 102 S. W. 873 (arrested person killed after arrest by sheriff).

Mississippi: Brown v. Weaver, 76 Miss. 7, 23 So. 388, 71 Am. St. Rep. 512, 42 L. R. A. 423 (escaping misdemeanant shot).

Nebraska: Kendall v. Aleshire, 28

Neb. 707, 45 N. W. 167, 26 Am. St. Rep. 367 (illegal imprisonment).

The damages include damages for mental suffering. Young v. Carney, 91 Ia. 559, 60 N. W. 114.

[441] Kendall v. Aleshire, 28 Neb. 707, 45 N. W. 167, 26 Am. St. Rep. 367.

[442] Allison v. People, 6 Colo. App. 80, 39 Pac. 903.

[443] *Indiana:* Lines v. State, 6 Blackf. 464; Lakin v. State, 89 Ind. 68 (but see State v. Johnson, 1 Ind. 158).

Maryland: State v. Lawson, 2 Gill, 62.

Pennsylvania: Karch v. Commonwealth, 3 Pa. 269.

Contra, Virginia: Perkins v. Giles, 9 Leigh, 397.

See ante, § 554.

[444] State v. Newcomer, 109 Ind. 243, 8 N. E. 920.

than the amount of the execution.[445] It may be shown in mitigation that the property in question was not subject to levy,[446] or that the same or other property of the debtor is still subject to execution, so that the debt is not lost.[447] In an action for failure to return an execution the plaintiff may recover the entire value of the property sold, where the failure to return the execution has invalidated the sale; [448] otherwise interest on the debt, the payment of which was delayed,[449] or if the failure resulted in the loss of the judgment, the amount of it.[450] When the sheriff took a forthcoming bond which after litigation was adjudged void, the expense of the litigation was held recoverable on the sheriff's bond.[451] For taking an insufficient bond the measure of damages is the amount that would have been recoverable on a good bond.[452] And for other defaults the actual damage only may be recovered.[453] For failure to collect

[445] *Kentucky:* Johnson v. Gwathney, 2 Bibb, 186, 4 Am. Dec. 694.

Ohio: State v. Myers, 14 Ohio, 538.

But see *Georgia:* Crawford v. Word, 7 Ga. 445, where it was held that it could not be shown that the property was incumbered to its full value.

In Harris v. Murfree, 54 Ala. 161, it was pointed out that the property would not realize its full value on an execution sale, and that the recovery should be limited to what would be realized at such sale.

[446] Snoddy v. Foster, 1 Met. (Ky.) 160.

[447] *Indiana:* State v. Dixon, 80 Ind. 150.

Kentucky: Arnold v. Commonwealth, 8 B. Mon. 109.

[448] Dunphy v. Whipple, 25 Mich. 10.

[449] Norris v. State, 22 Ark. 524. See *ante,* § 692.

[450] In Robertson v. County Com'rs, 10 Ill. 559, the amount of the judgment was held recoverable although the defendant was wholly insolvent from the time of its issue; but this appears to be based on the form of the statute. It is usually held that the insolvency of

the judgment creditor may be shown, with other circumstances bearing on the amount of damages; but the defendant must show the non-collectibility at the time of execution or its collectibility later, the burden being upon him.

South Carolina: Treasurers v. Hilliard, 8 Rich. 412.

Texas: Griswold v. Chandler, 22 Tex. 637.

[451] Burns v. George, 119 Ala. 504, 24 So. 718.

[452] Magnus v. Woolery, 14 Wash. 43, 44 Pac. 130. So no recovery can be had for taking a void replevin bond where the plaintiff's claim was proved of no value. Shull v. Barton, 67 Neb. 311, 93 N. W. 132.

[453] *United States:* Gwin v. Barton, 6 How. 7, 12 L. ed. 321 (failure to levy execution); United States v. Moore, 2 Brock. 317 (failure to serve process).

Connecticut: Swan v. Bridgeport, 70 Conn. 143, 30 Atl. 110 (failure to return process).

Missouri: State ex rel. Polster v. Miles, 149 Mo. App. 638, 129 S. W. 731 (false return; at least nominal damages).

a debt when collection is within the duty of the officer, the recovery is *prima facie* the amount of the debt, subject, however, to reduction.[454]

The bondsmen are liable for a wrongful attachment of personal property of a third party as property of the debtor,[455] but the sheriff may show in reduction delivery to the owner or to a mortgagee.[456] So where property belonging to the judgment debtor himself is wrongfully sold, he may recover on the bond the value of the property,[457] or if he has bought it back the amount he had to pay for it.[458] If the writ was void, or was not legally executed, the act was nevertheless done under color of office, and the bondsmen are liable,[459] unless it is apparently void on its face.[460]

For failure to pay over money collected by the officer within the scope of his office, the bondsmen are liable for the amount collected, with interest.[461] If securities are taken instead of currency, the value of the securities may be recovered.[462] If, however, the money was collected outside his official duty, it cannot be recovered on the bond.[463]

[454] State v. Eskridge, 5 Ire. (N. C.) 411; State v. Mangum, 9 Ire. (N. C.) 210.

[455] *Alabama:* Ellis v. Allen, 80 Ala. 515, 2 So. 676.
Massachusetts: Turner v. Sisson, 137 Mass. 191.
Virginia: Sangster v. Commonwealth, 17 Gratt. 124.

[456] *Illinois:* People v. Crowe, 130 Ill. App. 349.
Indiana: McDaniel v. State, 118 Ind. 239, 20 N. E. 739 (mortgaged property sold; may show in mitigation that mortgage still binds the property).
Massachusetts: Lowell v. Parker, 10 Met. 309, 43 Am. Dec. 436 (settlement with mortgagee).

[457] *Indiana:* Butler v. State, 20 Ind. 169 (constable sells note pledged to him).
Missouri: State v. Finn, 13 Mo. App. 285 (sheriff makes false return, resulting in judgment).

[458] *California:* Blewett v. Miller, 131

Cal. 149, 62 Pac. 157, 82 Am. St. Rep. 338 (property exempt from execution).
Missouri: State ex rel. Schreiber v. Dickmann, 124 Mo. App. 653, 102 S. W. 44 (exempt land sold; recovers cost of suit to set aside sheriff's deed).

[459] *Massachusetts:* Turner v. Sisson, 137 Mass. 191.
Missouri: Rollins v. State, 13 Mo. 437, 53 Am. Dec. 151.

[460] State v. Timmons, 90 Md. 10, 44 Atl. 1003.

[461] *Arkansas:* Faulkner v. State, 9 Ark. 14.
Georgia: Governor v. Raley, 34 Ga. 173.
Missouri: State v. Cayce, 85 Mo. 456.
North Carolina: State v. Pool, 5 Ired. 105.
Ohio: King v. Nichols, 16 Oh. St. 80.

[462] *Kentucky:* Fowler v. Com., 3 Dana, 135 (bank notes).
Ohio: Griffin v. Underwood, 16 Oh. St. 389.

[463] *Illinois:* Henckler v. County

§ 692j. Bonds of executors and administrators.

Recovery may be had on an administration bond for the amount of assets of the estate embezzled, wasted, or lost by the executor or administrator.[464] Since a debt owed to the testator by an executor or administrator is regarded by the law as paid to the estate at the moment of appointment, the bondsmen are responsible for the amount of such a debt as well as for the other assets of the estate,[465] even though at the time of his appointment the executor or administrator was in fact insolvent.[466] In an action upon the bond of an administrator *de bonis non* it appeared that he was himself one of the sureties on a bond of a previous administrator. As surety on the bond of the previous administrator he was liable at the moment of his appointment for default of the previous administrator, and although that had not been settled by a decree, it became assets of the estate upon his appointment and his sureties were liable for it. It was his duty as administrator to ascertain the amount and to charge himself with it, and the sureties on his bond were held liable for the amount.[467] In a few States, however, the harshness of the common-law rule is modified, and the bondsmen are liable only for the appraised value of the debt, in view of the insolvency of the debtor.[468] In California the

Court, 27 Ill. 39, 79 Am. Dec. 393 (collection without process).

North Carolina: Governor v. Barr, 1 Dev. 65 (collection of taxes).

Ohio: Webb v. Anspack, 3 Oh. St. 522 (sale of property by agreement of parties, not on execution).

In *New York:* People v. Faulkner, 107 N. Y. 477, 14 N. E. 415, 1 Am. St. Rep. 851, recovery was refused because the default did not come within the language of the bond.

[464] *Alabama:* Thomson v. Searcy, 6 Port. 393.

New York: Gottsberger v. Smith, 5 Duer, 566.

Ohio: Slagle v. Entrekin, 44 Oh. St. 637, 10 N. E. 675.

Tennessee: Horton v. Cope, 6 Lea, 155.

In *Mississippi* recovery may be had

for the entire value of property removed from the State. Bridges v. Maxwell, 34 Miss. 309.

No prior judgment against the administrator is necessary. Chairman v. Moore, 2 Murph. (N. C.) 22.

[465] *Alabama:* Wright v. Lang, 66 Ala. 389.

Connecticut: Davenport v. Richards, 16 Conn. 310.

Ohio: Foster v. Wise, 46 Oh. St. 20, 16 N. E. 687, 15 Am. St. Rep. 542.

[466] Treweek v. Howard, 105 Cal. 434, 39 Pac. 20.

[467] Choate v. Thorndike, 138 Mass. 371.

[468] *Indiana:* State v. Gregory, 119 Ind. 503, 22 N. E. 1.

Missouri: McCarty v. Frazer, 62 Mo. 263 (statutory).

common-law rule applies to executors, but not to administrators, who are chargeable only with the appraised value of their debts to the estate.[469]

The estate for which the executor or administrator must account in any State includes money received as ancillary administrator in another State and ordered transmitted to the first State,[470] or otherwise brought into the domestic account;[471] but it does not include a balance left from the sale of land in another State after paying the debts there, since such balance belongs to the heirs there, and does not form part of the general personal estate.[472]

The executor or administrator remains liable as such for a portion of the estate set apart by order of court for a special purpose, as the payment of an annuity or of a deferred legacy.[473] And where he is ordered to sell land to pay debts he is responsible as such, and his bondsmen are therefore held for the proper disposition of the proceeds, since it is a part of his official duty.[474] But when money comes to the executor not as assets of the estate, but in some other way, his bondsmen are not liable for the misuse of it. So if the will gives him power to sell land to pay debts or legacies, he sells the land and receives the proceeds as devisee in trust, and his bondsmen are not held,[475] but he should give a bond as trustee if the administration of the devise is to be secured;[476] and so generally if money is given to him by the will in trust for any purpose.[477] So his bondsmen are not liable for money received upon a policy of

Tennessee: Rader v. Yeargin, 85 Tenn. 486, 3 S. W. 178.

[469] In Sanchez v. Forster, 133 Cal. 614, 65 Pac. 1077, an administrator with the will annexed was entitled to a legacy under the will; the debt being collectible to that extent, at least, his sureties were chargeable for the debt he owed to the amount of the legacy.

[470] Probate Judge v. Heydock, 8 N. H. 491.

[471] Strong v. White, 19 Conn. 238, 48 Am. Dec. 158.

[472] Snodgrass v. Snodgrass, 1 Baxter (Tenn.), 157.

[473] *Iowa:* Ellyson v. Lord, 124 Ia. 125, 99 N. W. 582.

Massachusetts: Hall v. Cushing, 9 Pick. 395.

[474] Even though an additional bond be given:
Alabama: Clarke v. West, 5 Ala. 117.
Indiana: Salyers v. Ross, 15 Ind. 130.
Ohio: Wade v. Graham, 4 Ohio, 126.

[475] *Illinois:* People v. Huffman, 182 Ill. 390, 398, 55 N. E. 981.
Kentucky: Shields v. Smith, 8 Bush, 601; Clay v. Hart, 7 Dana, 1.

[476] State v. Thresher, 77 Conn. 70, 58 Atl. 460.

[477] Hinds v. Hinds, 85 Ind. 312.

insurance payable to the estate,[478] or for income of the real estate collected by him,[479] or for any other money collected by him which does not legally form part of the estate.[480]

For other defaults of the executor or administrator the bondsmen are liable for the actual damage only. Thus for failure to file an inventory the damages are nominal, unless actual damage is shown; [481] but if the omitted assets were converted to the use of the administrator, their value may be recovered on the bond.[482] The rule is the same where the breach alleged was failure to render an account.[483] For failure to pay debts the amount of any particular debt may be recovered, as fixed by a judgment in favor of the creditor,[484] or if the estate is insolvent the percentage of the debt which was paid to other creditors.[485] For failure to distribute the bondsmen are responsible for the amount ordered by the court to be paid over; [486] or if no order of court has been obtained, then an amount based on the balance left in the estate,[487] estimating this amount either by taking the appraised value of the estate with interest or the actual value at the time for distribution, at the election of the distributee.[488]

If a special bond is given the general principles are the same. When upon judgment being given against an administrator he gave a special bond to comply with the order of court, and the court ordered the payment of the judgment out of assets, and there were no assets found, the sureties were liable for costs only, the amount of the judgment not coming within the order

---

[478] People v. Petrie, 191 Ill. 497, 61 N. E. 499, 85 Am. St. Rep. 268 (affirming 94 Ill. App. 652).

[479] Denton v. Crouch, 101 Ky. 386, 41 S. W. 277.

[480] Pace v. Pace, 19 Fla. 438.

[481] *Connecticut:* Edwards v. White, 12 Conn. 28.

Delaware: State v. Bloxom, 1 Houst. 446.

Indiana: State v. Gregory, 119 Ind. 503, 22 N. E. 1.

[482] *Connecticut:* Minor v. Mead, 3 Conn. 289.

Ohio: Dawson v. Dawson, 25 Oh. St. 443.

[483] *Arkansas:* Scarborough v. State, 24 Ark. 20.

Massachusetts: Choate v. Arrington, 116 Mass. 552.

[484] *Connecticut:* Willey v. Paulk, 6 Conn. 74.

North Carolina: Washington v. Hunt, 1 Dev. 475.

[485] Warren v. Powers, 5 Conn. 373.

[486] Scofield v. Churchill, 72 N. Y. 565.

[487] Rowland v. Isaacs, 15 Conn. 115.

[488] Burch v. State, 4 Gill & J. (Md.) 444.

of the court.[489] In an action on a bond given by an administrator upon obtaining a license to sell real estate, the measure of damages is the amount of the proceeds of the sale not accounted for by the administrator, and the costs of proceedings to compel him to account, but not counsel fees paid in such proceedings.[490]

Where there are two executors and they give a joint bond, both principals are liable for the default of either.[491]

§ 692k. Bonds of guardians.

In a suit on a guardian's bond, the actual loss suffered by the plaintiffs furnishes the measure of damages. By suit on the bond the guardian may be called upon to pay over any balance found due from him, with interest.[492] Such a suit is in several jurisdictions not allowed until the court of probate or of chancery has called upon the guardian to render an account, and has found a balance due from him.[493] Into this account must be brought all property received by the guardian in another State on account of the appointment for which the bond was given.[494] So where a guardian in Massachusetts was appointed ancillary guardian in Missouri and collected money there, which she included in her account in Massachusetts, but had not yet secured a discharge in Missouri, and upon her resignation as guardian she was ordered to hand over the balance, but claimed that she could not safely hand it over until her accounts in Missouri were approved by the Missouri court, it was held that since she had voluntarily brought the Missouri money into the Massachusetts court of probate and had not appealed from its decree she was bound, and her refusal to hand over the money was a breach of her bond for which she was liable.[495] Such charges as the guardian is entitled to make may be deducted

[489] Banks v. McDowel, 1 Cold. (Tenn.) 84.

[490] Mann v. Everts, 64 Wis. 372, 25 N. W. 209.

[491] Overton v. Woodson, 17 Mo. 453.

[492] Georgia: Ray v. The Justices, 6 Ga. 303.

Indiana: Peelle v. State, 118 Ind. 512, 21 N. E. 288.

Kentucky: Carter v. Thorn, 18 B. Mon. 613.

[493] Indiana: Hunt v. White, 1 Ind. 105. (See State v. Strange, 1 Ind. 538.)

New York: Stilwell v. Mills, 19 Johns. 304.

[494] McDonald v. Meadows, 1 Met. (Ky.) 507.

[495] Brooks v. Tobin, 135 Mass. 69.

from the recovery on the bond; but not expenses of maintaining the ward where they could not form the subject of a suit.[496] For other breaches of the guardian's duty such damages may be recovered on the bond as the breach caused. For a mere failure to render an account, the damages are nominal only;[497] and the same is true for a mere failure to file an inventory,[498] unless it has resulted in a loss of the property, in which case the value of the property may be recovered.[499] For improper investments the bondsmen are liable for the amount invested and lost, with interest;[500] for failure to collect a claim of the ward's estate they are liable for the value of the claim lost by the failure;[501] and for wrongfully incumbering the ward's estate, for the amount of the incumbrance.[502]

Where a guardian obtains authority to sell real estate of the ward, this is not part of his regular official duty; a special bond is given to account for the proceeds, and the sureties on his general bond are not liable.[503] A fortiori the bondsmen are not liable for real estate sold wrongfully without proper authority from the court.[504] Where, however, the real estate is not sold by the guardian, but in the course of proceedings for partition, the guardian receives the proceeds as part of the estate

---

[496] Otis v. Hall, 117 N. Y. 131, 22 N. E. 563, 15 Am. St. Rep. 497.

[497] Probate Court v. Slason, 23 Vt. 306.

[498] *Indiana:* Buchanan v. State, 106 Ind. 251, 6 N. E. 614.

Maine: Fuller v. Wing, 17 Me. 222.

[499] Blakeman v. Sherwood, 32 Conn. 324.

[500] State v. Washburn, 67 Conn. 187, 34 Atl. 1034.

[501] Ames v. Williams, 74 Miss. 404, 20 So. 877.

[502] State v. Tittmann, 134 Mo. 162, 35 S. W. 579.

[503] *Indiana:* Lowry v. State, 64 Ind. 421.

Iowa: Madison County v. Johnston, 51 Ia. 152, 50 N. W. 492; Bunce v. Bunce, 65 Ia. 106, 21 N. W. 205.

Kansas: Morris v. Cooper, 35 Kan. 156, 10 Pac. 588.

Maine: Williams v. Morton, 38 Me. 47, 61 Am. Dec. 229.

Massachusetts: Lyman v. Conkey, 1 Met. 317, 35 Am. Dec. 374.

Missouri: State v. Peterman, 66 Mo. App. 257.

Nevada: Henderson v. Coover, 4 Nev. 429.

New York: Allen v. Kelley, 55 App. Div. 454, 67 N. Y. Supp. 97.

Contra, Montana: Hughes v. Goodale, 26 Mont. 93, 66 Pac. 702, 91 Am. St. Rep. 410 (*semble*).

And if a special bond is given to secure the management of a particular fund, even if it comes within the scope of the guardians' general bond, the sureties on the special bond are primarily liable. Findley v. Findley, 42 W. Va. 372, 26 S. E. 433.

[504] Johnson v. Chamberlain, 18 App. Div. 495, 46 N. Y. Supp. 132.

for which he is accountable, and his bondsmen are liable for
misapplication of the proceeds.[505]

§ 693.[a] Bonds of county and town officers.

The general principle of compensation applies to bonds of
county and town officers. So where the mayor under color of
his office caused a person to be illegally arrested, his bondsmen
were liable for damages for the false imprisonment.[506] Where an
auditor drew a warrant for payment of an illegal claim, his
sureties claimed that the treasurer should not have paid it; but
it was held that the treasurer was justified in paying a regularly
audited claim and the amount of it could be recovered on the
bond.[507] Where a recording officer by an error recorded a $500
mortgage as $200, he was held liable on his bond for the dif-
ference.[508] And where a school commissioner sold land at
auction, and upon the purchaser refusing to take it sold it again
for a smaller sum, he was held liable for failure to compel the
first purchaser to take the land; and the measure of damages
on the bond was the difference between the purchase price at
the two sales, with interest from the time he should have collected the amount from the first purchaser.[509]

In an action on the bond of a city clerk to recover a balance
due from him, where it appeared he was entitled to salary, but
he also owed the city for a claim not covered by the bond, the
city was held entitled to set the salary off against the unsecured
claim, and the bondsmen could not demand that the claim on
the bond be reduced by the amount of the unpaid salary.[510]

§ 694. Bonds of officers of corporations.

The same general principles apply to the measure of damages
on bonds of officers of corporations which we have found to

---

[a] For § 693 of the eighth ed., see § 681a.

[505] Hooks v. Evans, 68 Iowa, 52, 25 N. W. 925.

[506] State v. MacDaniel, 78 Miss. 1, 27 So. 994, 50 L. R. A. 118, 84 Am. St. Rep. 618.

[507] Graham v. State, 66 Ind. 386.

[508] State v. Davis, 96 Ind. 539. So

where a registrar of deeds failed to index a mortgage, he is responsible for
the amount lost by a person who lent
money subsequently on a mortgage.
Title G. & S. Co. v. Commonwealth,
141 Ky. 570, 133 S. W. 577.

[509] Frazier v. Laughlin, 6 Ill. 347.

[510] Lowe v. Guthrie, 4 Okla. 287, 44
Pac. 198.

exist on bonds of public officers. The limit of recovery is the penalty of the bond,[511] with interest.[512] The measure of recovery is the actual loss. Where the default is an embezzlement of money, the amounts embezzled, with interest on each amount from the time of embezzlement, may be recovered.[513] If the corporation still owes salary to the officer, the amount of it may be set off, and the balance, with interest, recovered; [514] but the sureties cannot claim to have the amount reduced by salary or other credits of the officer which might have been applied to the reduction of the deficit, but were not so applied.[515] Where the officer wrongfully changed the security held for a debt due to the corporation the measure of damages is not the amount of such debt, but the actual loss caused by the difference in value of the securities.[516] Where the officer failed to protest a note the face of the note is *prima facie* the measure of damages, but the damages may be reduced by showing the insolvency of the parties on the note.[517] Where an assistant cashier failed to prevent or connived at a misappropriation of money by the cashier, his sureties are liable for the amount of the defalcation with interest.[518]

Defaults before the bond was given are not usually covered by it.[519] Where the officer took money before the bond was executed, but falsified his accounts after the bond was in force, it was held that the bondsmen were liable only for the loss caused by the falsification of accounts, which was nominal.[520] Where there is a regular term of office, and the incumbent is elected for successive years, his bond may be indefinite in duration, and thus cover his conduct during his successive terms; [521] but it is ordinarily limited to cover a single term only, in which

[511] State Bank v. Johnson, 1 Mill. Const. (S. C.) 404, 12 Am. Dec. 645.

[512] Bank of Brighton v. Smith, 12 Allen (Mass.), 243, 90 Am. Dec. 144.

[513] McShane v. Howard Bank, 73 Md. 135, 20 Atl. 776.

[514] Murray v. Aiken Mining Co., 39 S. C. 457, 18 S. E. 5.

[515] McShane v. Howard Bank, 73 Md. 135, 20 Atl. 776.

[516] Barrington v. Washington Bank, 14 Serg. & R. (Pa.) 405.

[517] Union Bank v. Thompson, 8 Rob. (La.) 227.

[518] Fiala v. Ainsworth, 63 Neb. 1, 88 N. W. 135, 94 N. W. 153, 93 Am. St. Rep. 420.

[519] State Treasurer v. Mann, 34 Vt. 371, 80 Am. Dec. 688.

[520] State v. Atherton, 40 Mo. 209.

[521] Amherst Bank v. Root, 2 Met. (Mass.) 522.

case the bondsmen are liable for such defaults only as occur during the term,[522] or at most for a reasonable time thereafter for the qualification of a successor.[523] If when a defalcation is discovered it is impossible to determine in which term it occurred, the presumption is that it occurred during the current term, and the sureties on the last bond are therefore liable unless they can show that the defalcation happened before that term.[524]

[522] *Connecticut:* Welch v. Seymour, 28 Conn. 387.

New York: Ulster County Savings Institution v. Ostrander, 163 N. Y. 430, 57 N. E. 627.

Ante, § 692b.

[523] Chelmsford Co. v. Demerest, 7 Gray (Mass.), 1.

[524] McMullen v. Winfield Building & Loan Assoc., 64 Kan. 298, 67 Pac. 892, 91 Am. St. Rep. 236; *ante*, § 692e.

CHAPTER XXXIII

ACTIONS UPON NEGOTIABLE INSTRUMENTS

§ 695. The face value recoverable.
695a. Partial payment.
695b. Application of payments.
695c. Attorney's fees.
696. Interest.
697. Interest by the civil law.
698. Interest not formerly allowed.
699. Now universally allowed.
700. Foreign bills—Cost of protest and re-exchange.
700a. Re-exchange on promissory notes and inland bills.

§ 701. Costs of protest and re-exchange, when not allowed.
702. Accommodation paper.
703. Pledged paper.
704. Measure of liability of an indorser.
705. Costs of prior suits.
706. Indorser's damages.
707. Damages for failure to accept or pay.
708. Damages in cases of fraud and estoppel.

§ 695. The face value recoverable.

* The subject of negotiable paper is so amply discussed in the various treatises devoted to this particular branch of the law, that it will only be necessary for us in this place to take a brief view of the general principles regulating the compensation awarded for the breach of contracts of this class.**

When recovery can be had upon a negotiable instrument, the amount of recovery is the face value of the instrument, without regard to the amount actually paid for it by the *bona fide* holder.[1] This is usually and correctly held to be true even

---

[1] *Illinois:* Dickinson *v.* Bull, 72 Ill. App. 75 (legal holder not beneficial owner).

Indiana: Murphy *v.* Lucas, 58 Ind. 360; Harvey *v.* Baldwin, 124 Ind. 59, 24 N. E. 347, 19 Am. St. Rep. 73; Farber *v.* National Forge & Iron Co., 140 Ind. 54, 39 N. E. 249.

Iowa: Nat. Bank *v.* Green, 33 Ia. 140.

Kansas: St. Louis, F. S. & W. R. R. *v.* Chenault, 36 Kan. 51, 12 Pac. 303 (holder is treasurer of company that made the note).

Michigan: Vinton *v.* Peck, 14 Mich. 287.

New Jersey: Durant *v.* Banta, 27 N. J. L. 624.

New York: Murray *v.* Judah, 6 Cow. 484; Deas *v.* Harvie, 2 Barb. Ch. 448.

Wisconsin: Croft *v.* Bunster, 9 Wis. 503.

A purchaser who has paid only part of the amount agreed upon, and then receives notice of fraud or lack of consideration, can recover only the amount he advanced before notice. Dresser *v.*

though the maker might have a complete defence against the original payee;[2] but in several jurisdictions the holder is limited, in such a case, to the amount he paid for it.[3] The case of a pledgee presents an exception to this general rule, which will be considered later.[4]

In Massachusetts the anomalous doctrine prevails that in a suit between the original parties, if the consideration of a note is inadequate, or fails in part, the amount equitably due may be recovered in an action upon the note.[5] So where a note was given for the purchase of a horse, which proved to be unsound, the court deducted from the amount of the note the difference in value of the horse if he had been sound and as he actually was.[6] This peculiar doctrine is to be distinguished from the well-established principle allowing, in the proper case, recoup-

Missouri & I. R. R., 93 U. S. 92, 23 L. ed. 815.

In California, in accordance with the provisions of the Code, the measure of damages for failure to pay a certificate of deposit is the value of the certificate (which, as has been seen (*ante*, § 256) is taken as against the maker to be the face of the certificate, with due allowance, of course, for exchange). Dollar *v.* International Banking Corp., 10 Cal. App. 791, 109 Pac. 499.

[2] *United States:* Cromwell *v.* County of Sac, 96 U. S. 51, 24 L. ed. 681.

Connecticut: Bissell *v.* Dickerson, 64 Conn. 61, 73, 29 Atl. 226.

Iowa: Sully *v.* Goldsmith, 32 Ia. 397.

Maine: Hobart *v.* Penny, 70 Me. 248.

Maryland: Williams *v.* Huntington, 68 Md. 590, 13 Atl. 336, 6 Am. St. Rep. 477.

Massachusetts: Woodruff *v.* Hill, 116 Mass. 310.

Ohio: Heller *v.* Meis, 2 Cin. 287; Tod *v.* Wick, 36 Oh. St. 370.

Oregon: Lassas *v.* McCarty, 47 Ore. 474, 84 Pac. 76.

Pennsylvania: Moore *v.* Baird, 30 Pa. 138.

Texas: Denton Lumber Co. *v.* First Nat. Bank, 18 S. W. 962; Petri *v.* First

Nat. Bank, 83 Tex. 424, 18 S. W. 752, 29 Am. St. Rep. 657, 84 Tex. 212, 20 S. W. 777; First Nat. Bank *v.* Oliver, 16 Tex. Civ. App. 428, 41 S. W. 414.

Washington: McNamara *v.* Jose, 28 Wash. 461, 68 Pac. 903.

Wisconsin: Bange *v.* Flint, 25 Wis. 544.

[3] *Connecticut:* Roe *v.* Jerome, 18 Conn. 138 (New York law).

Nebraska: Faulkner *v.* White, 33 Neb. 199, 50 N. W. 328.

New Jersey: Holcomb *v.* Wyckoff, 35 N. J. L. 35, 10 Am. Rep. 219; De Kay *v.* Hackensack Water Co., 38 N. J. Eq. 158.

New York: Moore *v.* Ryder, 65 N. Y. 438; First Nat. Bank *v.* Haulenbeek, 65 Hun, 54, 19 N. Y. Supp. 567; Perry *v.* Council Bluffs City Waterworks Co., 67 Hun, 456, 22 N. Y. Supp. 151, 51 N. Y. St. 326; Hyman *v.* American Electric Forge Co., 18 Misc. 381, 41 N. Y. Supp. 655.

Tennessee: Oppenheimer *v.* Bank, 97 Tenn. 19, 56 Am. St. Rep. 778, 33 L. R. A. 767, 36 S. W. 705.

[4] *Post,* § 703.

[5] Sanger *v.* Cleveland, 10 Mass. 415; Daggett *v.* Daggett, 8 Cush. 520.

[6] Davis *v.* Elliott, 15 Gray (Mass.), 90.

ment of damages arising out of the transaction in which the note was given.[7]

§ 695a. Partial payment.

Where a payment has been made on the note, the amount of the payment is to be deducted from the face of the note to arrive at the damages.[8] Where the payment was made in goods, the value of the goods at the time and place of payment is deducted, if the parties did not agree on a price.[9] If the note was secured by a mortgage and the mortgage was foreclosed, the price realized at the foreclosure sale, and not the real value of the mortgaged property, is to be deducted, even if it was bought in by the holder of the note.[10] Where the maker of a note had made payments on it, but was entitled to recover them back on the ground of usury, it was held that a surety on the note could not avail himself of the payments.[11]

§ 695b. Application of payments.

The general rule for the application of payments on a note is that a payment will first be applied to the payment of interest,

[7] *California:* Reese v. Gordon, 19 Cal. 147.

Illinois: Carpenter v. First Nat. Bank, 119 Ill. 352, 10 N. E. 18.

Pennsylvania: Fessler v. Love, 43 Pa. 313.

Vermont: Richardson v. Sanborn, 33 Vt. 75.

See § 1050.

[8] *Indiana:* Henderson v. Reeves, 6 Blackf. 102.

Missouri: Bush v. Brandecker, 123 Mo. App. 470, 100 S. W. 48.

Texas: Houston v. Morrison, 10 Tex. 1.

Contra, Kentucky, where promissory notes are not negotiable. Phelps v. Taylor, 4 J. J. Mon. 170.

[9] Phillips v. Commercial Bank, 1 Sm. & M. (Miss.) 636.

[10] West v. St. Paul Nat. Bank, 54 Minn. 466, 56 N. W. 54.

Where mortgaged cattle had been taken in replevin by the mortgagee, but the mortgagor had secured them by giving a bond, and the replevin suit was still undecided, in an action on the note against an indorsee it was held that the amount of recovery would not be reduced on account of the *cattle,* but if finally the plaintiff defaulted and got the cattle or the proceeds of them, the defendant would have a claim on him for that amount. Trower Bros. Co. v. Hanson, 110 Fed. 611.

Where a note was transferred to plaintiff in fraud of defendant (the maker), and security was given by the transferor, and after learning of the fraud plaintiff surrendered the security, it was held that he should have kept it, until after notice of the fraud, to protect the defendant, and he was entitled to recover only the amount actually paid by him less the value of the security surrendered. Campbell v. Brown, 100 Tenn. 245, 48 S. W. 970.

[11] Savage v. Fox, 60 N. H. 17.

and the balance will be applied on the principal.[12]   Where several claims exist, it is usually said that a payment, in the absence of directions by the debtor, should be applied to the earliest claim,[13] unless there is an agreement, understanding, or custom to the contrary,[14] which a court is prone to find in favor of the sureties on a preferred claim.[15]   There are authorities, however, which in such a case hold that in the absence of directions to the contrary the creditor may apply the payment where he pleases, as to an unsecured as against a secured claim.[16]

§ 695c. Attorney's fees.

Promissory notes often include provisions for an attorney's fee in case of collection by suit.   In some States this is held invalid; and in a jurisdiction so holding no such fees can be collected, though the stipulation was valid where made, since the allowance is regarded as contrary to public policy.[17]   If the stipulation is allowed, it is not allowed where the fee is unreasonable; but it is usually held that the stipulated fee will be regarded as reasonable in the absence of evidence to the contrary.[18]   The fees are to be reckoned upon the entire amount of

---

[12] *Alabama:* McQueen v. Whetstone, 127 Ala. 417, 30 So. 548 (statutory).

Missouri: Riney v. Hill, 14 Mo. 500, 55 Am. Dec. 119; Call v. Moll, 89 Mo. App. 386.

[13] *Alabama:* Stickney v. Moore, 108 Ala. 590, 19 So. 76 (*semble*).

Michigan: Grasser & Brand B. Co. v. Rogers, 112 Mich. 112, 70 N. W. 445, 67 Am. St. Rep. 389 (where the creditor has not himself made the application).

[14] *Alabama:* Stickney v. Moore, 108 Ala. 590, 19 So. 76.

Illinois: Drake v. Sherman, 179 Ill. 362, 53 N. E. 628.

[15] Drake v. Sherman, 179 Ill. 362, 53 N. E. 628.

[16] *Michigan:* Grasser & Brand Brewing Co. v. Rogers, 112 Mich. 112, 70 N. W. 445, 67 Am. St. Rep. 389 (*semble*).

Rhode Island: Burt v. Butterworth, 19 R. I. 127.

[17] Exchange Bank v. Appalachian Land & Lumber Co., 128 N. C. 193, 38 S. E. 813.

[18] *Alabama:* Stephenson v. Allison, 123 Ala. 439, 26 So. 290.

Indiana: Starnes v. Schofield, 5 Ind. App. 4, 31 N. E. 480; Rouyer v. Miller, 16 Ind. App. 519, 44 N. E. 51, 45 N. E. 674.

New Mexico: Dallas Exch. v. Tuttle, 5 N. M. 427, 23 Pac. 241, 7 L. R. A. 445 (unless the stipulated fee is so large as to seem unreasonable on its face).

Texas: Carver v. J. S. Mayfield Lumber Co. (Tex. Civ. App.), 68 S. W. 711. [explaining Land, etc., Co. v. Robertson (Tex. Civ. App.), 85 S. W. 1020]; Dashiell v. Moody (Tex. Civ. App.), 97 S. W. 843.

Contra, that the plaintiff must prove the reasonable fee and can recover only that.

the damages, interest as well as principal.[19]   The fee is not due unless the litigation was reasonable; [20] and can be collected only for services in the trial court, not on appeal.[21]

§ 696. Interest.

* In actions brought on promises to pay a liquidated sum of money, as on promissory notes or bills, where no question arises as to the currency or rate of exchange, the rule of damages is a fixed and arbitrary one.   It is identical with the rate of legal interest.   The actual damages may be much greater; the non-performance of the obligation may have occasioned the greatest distress, nay, even extreme positive loss; it may have produced actual insolvency.   These remote results the law, however, does not investigate.[22]   It takes the rate of interest as the measure of damages; and so, says Pothier, "as the different damages which may result from the failure to perform this kind of obligation vary infinitely, and as it is as difficult to foresee as to excuse them, it has been found necessary to regulate them as by a species of penalty, and fix them at a precise sum." [23] **

§ 697. Interest by the civil law.

* With this, the general language of the modern civil law accords.   The damages resulting from the non-performance of contracts to pay money are limited to the infliction of interest. "Interest," says Domat,[24] "is the name applied to the compen-

Alabama: Camp v. Randle, 81 Ala. 240, 2 So. 287 (of Georgia law).

Minnesota: Campbell v. Worman, 58 Minn. 561, 60 N. W. 668.

Where the provision is for attorney's fees "up to 10%" it must be proved what the services were and what they were worth.   Patillo v. Alexander, 96 Ga. 60, 22 S. E. 646, 29 L. R. A. 616.

[19] *Georgia:* Morgan v. Kiser, 105 Ga. 104, 31 S. E. 45.

Texas: Hopkins v. Halliburton, 6 Tex. Civ. App. 451, 25 S. W. 1005; Carver v. J. S. Mayfield Lumber Co., 29 Tex. Civ. App. 434, 68 S. W. 711.

[20] *Tennessee:* Tyler v. Walker, 101 Tenn. 306, 47 S. W. 424 (suit for usurious interest).

If the maker is garnished but does not pay the amount of it into court, he will be liable for the attorney's fee if necessary to collect.   Brahan v. Clarksville First Nat. Bank, 72 Miss. 266, 16 So. 203.

[21] McCormick v. Falls City Bank, 57 Fed. 107.

[22] Lewis v. Lee, 15 Ind. 499.   See § 622b.

[23] Traité des Oblig., part i, ch. ii, art. 3, 170.   See Heyman v. Landers, 12 Cal. 107.

[24] Liv. iii, tit. v, § 1.

sation which the law gives to the creditor who is entitled to recover a sum of money from his debtor in default." So, too, the Roman law: *In bonæ fidei contractibus usuræ ex morâ debentur.*[25]

These principles, equally recognized by our system, are embodied in the French Code by a positive provision,[26] the correctness of which is thus supported and expounded by one of the ablest commentators on that law:

"It is certain that the non-payment of money when due may cause, and often actually causes, the creditor loss much beyond the legal interest on the sum. For want of the funds on the receipt of which his calculations are made, he may have been compelled to borrow, himself, and to submit to the exactions of the usurer. He may have been prosecuted, in a manner calculated to destroy his credit. He may have been ejected from his property; have become bankrupt; his house may have gone to ruin for want of repair. He may have lost highly advantageous bargains.

"But how are we to distribute these losses according to their real cause, and fix on those which should be imputed to the party in default? How is any equitable valuation to be made of them? Add to this, that the non-payment of money is the most common of all cases which give rise to damages, and we shall perceive that the peace of society would be harassed by this infinite multitude of settlements, and the litigation that would result from them.

"The law prevents this, by declaring that the damages shall never exceed legal interest from the day that payment becomes due; and this, which is a species of forfeiture, may often be advantageous to the creditor.

"Whatever may be the damage that he has suffered by the delay in receiving his funds, whether the debtor was animated by malicious or even fraudulent motives, the creditor cannot, it

---

[25] L. 32, § 2, Ff. Deusur.; *propter moram.* L. 17, § 3, *in fine eodem.*

[26] *Dans les obligations qui se bornent au paiement d'une certaine somme, les dommages et intérêts résultants du retard dans l'exécution ne consistent jamais que dans la condamnation aux intérêts fixés par la loi, sauf les règles particulières au commerce et au cautionnement.*

Ces dommages et intérêts sont dus, sans que le créancier soit tenu de justifier d'aucune perte.

Ils ne sont dus que du jour de la demande, excepté dans les cas où la loi les fait courir de plein droit. Code C., Art. 1153.

is true, demand any other compensation than legal interest on his demand. But, on the other hand, he is not required to prove the damages that the delay may have caused. And this provision, which fixes the measure of damages for non-payment of money at legal interest, is founded on a principle of equity.

"In cases of the non-performance of other contracts, the party in default, as the lessee who violates his contract of letting, or the architect who, by his negligence, causes the destruction of a house, must be fully apprised of the nature of the loss that may result from the non-performance of his duty; whereas with money it is different.

"On the contrary, the engagement to pay a sum of money has no precise relation to any particular damage; it is impossible to know what will result from its non-payment; it is impossible to see what the creditor will lose, or how much he will lose; whether he will be compelled to borrow—whether he will be driven from his house and reduced to bankruptcy—whether his business or his credit will suffer; it is impossible to predict any one event among the thousand which are possible, and which depend upon the situation of the creditor's affairs.

"Money being the common measure of all things, has not, like other things, any peculiar function. It takes the place of all other things. The loss experienced, then, by those who are not paid at maturity is as diversified as the use that they might make of the money, and as unforeseen as the wants from which the injury might arise. They are, in regard to the debtors, like fortuitous cases, impossible to foresee, and which for this reason their obligation does not embrace." [27]

And it should be borne in mind, as Pothier also well remarks, that if, on the one hand, the creditor cannot recover anything beyond the legal interest, so, on the other hand, he is not put to any proof of damage whatever.[28] It is an arbitrary assessment of damages, in the nature of the *Lex Aquilia* of the Roman system. He can, it is true, recover but the legal rate of interest; but then, on the other hand, he might, in fact, not have been

[27] Touillier, vol. vi, liv. 3, tit. 3, ch. iii. *De l'Effet des Obligations*, 230 *et seq.*

[28] So says the civil code of Louisiana, "The damages due for delay in the performance of an obligation to pay money, are called interest. The creditor is entitled to these damages without proving any loss, and whatever loss he may have suffered, he can recover no more." Art. 1935.

able to gain any interest whatever during the time he has been deprived of his funds.**

§ 698. Interest not formerly allowed.

* "It is a dictate of natural justice and the law of every civilized country, that a man is bound in equity not only to perform his engagements, but also to repair all the damages that accrue naturally from their breach. Hence, every nation, whether governed by the civil or the common law, has established a certain common measure of reparation for the detention of money not paid according to contract, which is usually calculated at a certain and legal rate of interest." [29] Such is the language of the Supreme Court of the United States; but is to be taken with much allowance. The thunders of the early church [30] were levelled against interest and usury indiscriminately: and up to the time of Henry VIII., as we are told by Lord Mansfield,[31] "all interest on money lent was prohibited by the common law, as it is now in Roman Catholic countries."[32] This statute simply provided that none should take for any loan or commodity above the rate of ten pounds for one hundred pounds for one whole year, which rate was reduced to five per cent by a subsequent statute, passed in the reign of Queen Anne.[33] ** The tendency of enlightened modern opinion is in favor of leaving the whole matter to be regulated by contract, and this has led in England, Massachusetts, and elsewhere to the repeal of the old statutes against usury; the law merely providing a rate to be applied in the absence of express contracts.

§ 699. Now universally allowed.

Interest is now everywhere regarded as the proper measure of damages for the non-payment of bills and notes. In the United States it seems that a jury should be instructed to give

[29] Curtis v. Innerarity, 6 How. 146, 154, 12 L. ed. 380.

[30] See Voltaire's article, *Intérêt*, in the Dictionnaire Philosophique, where he represents a Jansenist Abbé remonstrating with a Dutch merchant against taking interest: *Prenez garde; vous vous damnez; l'argent ne peut produire de l'argent—ne peut produire de l'ar-* *gent: nummus nummum non parit.* The hostility of the church was founded on the prohibition in the Old Testament, "Thou shalt not lend upon usury to thy brother." Deut. xxii, 19, 20.

[31] Lowe v. Waller, Doug. 736, 740.

[32] See also Robinson v. Bland, 2 Burr. 1077, 1086.

[33] 12 Anne, Stat. 2, c. xvi.

interest, on the same principle on which they are instructed to give the market value of goods or the market price of the hire of an article, for interest is the market price of the hire of the use of money;[34] and that is in fact the rule universally adopted.[35]

§ 700. Foreign bills—Cost of protest and re-exchange.

*In regard to foreign bills of exchange, the general rule is, that the holder of a bill protested for non-payment is entitled to the amount of the bill, re-exchange, and charges.[36]

"Re-exchange," says Mr. Chitty,[37] "is the exchange incurred by the bill being dishonored in a foreign country in which it is payable and returned to the country in which it is made or indorsed, and there taken up. The amount of it depends on the course of the exchange between the countries through which the bill has been negotiated. It is not necessary for the plaintiff to show that he has paid the re-exchange; it suffices if he be liable to pay it; but if the jury find that there was not at the time any course of re-exchange between the two foreign places, then no re-exchange is recoverable." [38]

"By re-exchange," says Mr. Justice Story, "is meant the amount for which a bill can be purchased in the country where the acceptance is made, drawn upon the drawer or indorser, in the country where he resides, which will give the holder of the original bill a sum exactly equal to the amount of that bill at the time when it ought to be paid, or when he is able to draw the re-exchange bill, together with his necessary expenses and interest, for that is precisely the sum which the holder is entitled to receive, and which will indemnify him for its non-payment." [39]

The question of re-exchange usually arises in regard to the drawers and indorsers; for the acceptor is not, upon non-

---

[34] See, per Spencer, Senator, Rensselaer Glass Factory v. Reid, 5 Cow. 587, 610.

[35] See ante, § 301.

[36] In re Gillespie, 16 Q. B. D. 702. Acc., Pavenstedt v. New York L. I. Co. (N. Y.), 96 N. E. 104.

When necessary, notice of protest may be sent by a special messenger, and the cost recovered. Pearson v. Crallan, 2 Smith, 404.

[37] Bills, 684.

[38] See, also, De Tastet v. Baring, 11 East, 265, where the origin and principle of the right to redraw is gone into at large. Mellish v. Simeon, 2 H. Black. 378, 379; Pollard v. Herries, 3 B. & P. 335.

[39] Story on Bills, § 400.

payment of the bill, ordinarily liable to the holder for anything more than the principal sum, and the expenses of the protest, with interest.[40] But if he has expressly or impliedly agreed with the drawer, or with any indorser, for a valuable consideration, to pay the bill at its maturity, and has failed to do so, and the drawer or indorser has been compelled to take up the bill, and pay damages and other expenses necessarily incurred thereby, he may, perhaps, be compellable fully to indemnify the drawer or indorser for all the damage and expense so paid by him, on account of the breach of his contract.[41]

The subject of re-exchange is very differently treated in England and in the United States. The rate which the holder is entitled to recover depends in the former country on the actual course of exchange, as proved at the trial; while in this country, with that leaning to a fixed rule, which we shall have occasion again to notice, when speaking of the subject of insurance, the amount of re-exchange is generally regulated by positive statutory provision.

To obtain a correct appreciation of this branch of our law, it is necessary to consult those treatises which are specially devoted to it; it will be enough here to make a brief examination of a few of the cases which have been decided in this country, and a reference to the statutory provisions of the various States; in making which it should be borne in mind that these statutes have no extra-territorial operation. Thus it has been held in Massachusetts, that the statute of Maine, which enacts, that in an action on a bill of exchange drawn or indorsed in that State, but payable out of it, and protested for non-payment, the holder shall recover three per cent damages in addition to the contents of the bill and interest—does not entitle the holder to recover those damages in a suit against the acceptor in the courts of Massachusetts.[42]

---

[40] Bowen v. Stoddard, 10 Met. 375, 43 Am. Dec. 442; Newman v. Goza, 2 La. Ann. 642.

[41] Story on Bills, § 398; Chitty on Bills, part 2, ch. vi, 684 to 687; Woolsey v. Crawford, 2 Camp. 445; Napier v. Schneider, 12 East, 420; Bayley on Bills, ch. ix, 353; Riggs v. Lindsay, 7

Cranch, 500; Bowen v. Stoddard, 10 Met. 375; Pothier de Change, 115, 117.

It has been decided in Pennsylvania that the acceptor is not liable for re-exchange. Watt v. Riddle, 8 Watts, 545.

[42] Fiske v. Foster, 10 Met. 507, 43 Am. Dec. 450.

The desire to establish a fixed rule in the matter of re-exchange manifested itself in this country at an early period of our colonial history. In Pennsylvania, as far back as the year 1700, the legislature enacted, that if any person within that province should draw or indorse any bill of exchange upon any person in England, or other parts of Europe, and the same should be returned unpaid, with a legal protest, the drawer and all concerned should pay the contents of the bill, with *twenty per cent advance for the damage* thereof, in the same specie as the bill was drawn, or current money of that province, equivalent to that which was first paid to the drawer or indorser.[43] So in Massachusetts, the old rule, founded on usage (since modified by the statute), was to allow on all foreign bills drawn on England, and probably also upon any part of Europe, ten per cent as damages in lieu of re-exchange.[44]

In New York, the original usage was to allow twenty per cent damages, in lieu of re-exchange, on all bills drawn on England or any part of Europe. In an action brought in New York, on a bill drawn by the defendant on a Liverpool house, indorsed to the plaintiff, and protested for non-payment, the plaintiff claimed twenty per cent damages and interest, together with two per cent for the difference of exchange, it being two per cent above par when the defendant was notified of the non-payment of the bill. But the claim for this difference was refused, notwithstanding reliance was placed on a usage of the Chamber of Commerce. Spencer, J., said:

"The right to recover damages on the protest of a foreign bill of exchange rests with us on immemorial commercial usage, sanctioned by a long course of judicial decision. . . . It is presumed that our rule to allow twenty per cent on the protest of a foreign bill, was originally co-extensive with the rule established in Pennsylvania, and that the same reasons induced both

---

[43] See Francis *v.* Rucker, Ambler, 672, and Hendricks *v.* Franklin, 4 Johns. 119. In Rhode Island, as early as 1743, an act of similar purport was passed, fixing the damages at *ten per cent*. Brown *v.* Van Braam, 3 Dall. 344, 346, 1 L. ed. 629.

[44] Grimshaw *v.* Bender, 6 Mass. 157, 161, 162. In Maine, the mercantile usage is the same. Wood *v.* Watson, 53 Me. 300. Such a rule of damages established by long usage has the force of law. It must be taken as part of the contract of indorsement, and cannot be changed by the court, whatever monetary crisis may occur.

rules. The twenty per cent was in lieu of damages, in case of re-exchange, and because there was no course of exchange from London to New York, and to avoid the constant fluctuation and uncertainty of exchange."

After saying that the usage of the Chamber of Commerce was too recent to alter the rule of law, he closed by stating:

"In my opinion, the twenty per cent is in lieu of all claims for damages in such cases; and the claim for the difference in the price of the bills cannot be supported, and therefore it must be deducted in this case." [45]

In a subsequent case, however, in the Court of Errors,[46] though the twenty per cent was allowed, the rule in regard to the sum on which it was assessed was altered. The court decided that the holder of a bill of exchange, drawn here on England, and protested there, was entitled to recover the contents of the bill at *the rate of exchange* on England *at the time of the return* of the dishonored bill and notice given to the drawer, and that the twenty per cent damages and interest were to be calculated on this amount, as the principal sum, and not upon the fixed par of exchange. The judgment of the Supreme Court was reversed, but no reasons were assigned.[47]

---

[45] Hendricks *v.* Franklin, 4 Johns. 119.

[46] Graves *v.* Dash, 12 Johns. 17.

[47] *Acc.,* Denston *v.* Henderson, 13 Johns. 322. But the holder of a bill of exchange remitted to pay an antecedent debt is not entitled to recover the twenty per cent. Kenworthy *v.* Hopkins, 1 Johns. Cas. 108; Thompson *v.* Robertson, 4 Johns. 27. The American Jurist for July, 1829, vol. ii, p. 79, contains an interesting article on the subject of Damages on Bills of Exchange. It states the difference between the system of re-exchange in force in Great Britain and France, and that of arbitrary damages adopted in the United States, and discusses various questions,—whether the European or American system is the best; whether the want of a uniform law on the subject in the different States is an evil; and if so, in what manner it should be redressed. An able report was made on the subject by Mr. Verplanck to the House of Representatives of the United States, in March, 1826, maintaining the right of Congress to control the subject, urging the importance of establishing a uniform rule, and strongly contending for the rule of actual re-exchange as opposed to that of arbitrary damages. "In fact," says the report, "this principle is the only one which can perfectly and under all circumstances and fluctuations of exchange, secure anything like a fair compensation of the loss sustained by the holder of a dishonored bill, without the hazard of one party being sometimes but partially paid or the other oppressed with the payment of unequal and ruinous damages. . . . If this principle be adopted, no valid reason

We have thus far considered the damages and re-exchange on bills protested for non-payment. The same general principles govern the case of bills protested for non-acceptance. "On failure of the performance of the engagement that the drawee will accept," says Mr. Chitty,[48] "the drawer of a bill will immediately, and before the time specified in the bill for payment, be liable to an action, not only for the principal sum, but also in certain cases for interest, re-exchange, and costs, as a consequence of the bill not being honored." This was decided as early as the year 1765,[49] and again by Lord Mansfield,[50] on the ground that what the drawer had undertaken has not been performed, the drawer not having given the credit which was the ground of the contract; and the same point was held in an action by the indorsee against the indorser,[51] each indorser being considered as a new drawer. It had been decided in bankruptcy to the same effect at an earlier day;[52] and the rule in this country is the same.[53] ** In New York, the damages in cases of protest for *non-acceptance* are by statute fixed at the same rate as for non-payment. This was the rule before the statute.[54] In Maine, in the absence of a statutory provision,

appears why arbitrary damages should be added. If provision be made for the substantial fulfilment of the engagement of the seller of the bill, and if he acted in good faith, the requiring any additional sum as a mulct or penalty for the failure of some other person is useless and unjust, and as recent examples in some of our cities have proved, may be of the most dangerous consequences, and overturn the credit of many a fair trader who had made the amplest arrangements to meet all his engagements."

[48] Bills, 194.

[49] Bright *v.* Purrier, Bull. Nisi Prius, 269.

[50] Milford *v.* Mayor, 1 Doug. 54.

[51] Ballingalls *v.* Gloster, 3 East, 481.

[52] Macarty *v.* Barrow, 2 Strange, 949, of which a fuller report is given in Chilton *v.* Whiffin, 3 Wils. 13, 16.

[53] Mason *v.* Franklin, 3 Johns. 202; and again in Weldon *v.* Buck, 4 Johns.

144. In France the rule appears to be different. On the protest for non-acceptance, the obligation of the parties indebted, says Pardessus, Cours de Droit Commercial, part ii, tit. iv, ch. iv, sec. 7, vol. 2, p. 424, is either to pay, to deposit the amount, or to give security. And there are traces of some similar or analogous custom in England. In Bright *v.* Purrier, Bull. N. P. 269, the defendant offered to prove a commercial usage not to pay till protest for *payment;* and in Buller's Nisi Prius, p. 271, it is said: "When the bill is returned protested, the party that draws the bill is obliged to answer the money and damages, or to *give security to answer the same beyond sea,* within double the time the first bill ran for."

[54] See reviser's notes to the 22d section, 1 R. S. 771. The point was expressly decided in Weldon *v.* Buck, 4 Johns. 144; and the same is the rule in England.

damages for protest are not allowed in a suit on a promissory note, though brought by an indorsee against an indorser, and payable in another State.[55] In Kansas, where the general statutes provide that "drawers, indorsers, makers, and obligors" shall be liable for protest charges, it is held that guarantors are not included.[56]

§ 700a. Re-exchange on promissory notes and inland bills.

No allowance for re-exchange is usually made in the case of promissory notes or inland bills in the absence of statute; such allowance is, however, very commonly authorized by statute.[57] Such a statute covers bank checks.[58]

§ 701. Costs of protest and re-exchange, when not allowed.

Costs of protest are not allowable unless protest is necessary to fix the liability of the indorsers.[59] They are not allowed when there are no indorsers,[60] nor unless notice is given to the indorsers.[61] Where a bill of exchange is only nominally a foreign bill, and is sent abroad, not that funds may there be used, but that they may be there obtained and remitted, there can be no recovery of re-exchange.[62]

§ 702. Accommodation paper.

* "In general," says Mr. Chitty, "between the original parties, or a holder who has not given full value, the defendant is at liberty to show that he drew, accepted, indorsed, or made the bill or note for the accommodation of the plaintiff, or of one of them, or of a person for whom he is a trustee, who either expressly or impliedly engaged to provide for the bill; or the defendant may show that he received no consideration, or none that was in point of law adequate, and thus may entirely defeat the action or reduce the claim."[63] Therefore, where the

[55] Loud v. Merrill, 47 Me. 351.
[56] Woolley v. Van Volkenburgh, 16 Kan. 20.
[57] *Mississippi:* Buck v. Little, 24 Miss. 463.
Pennsylvania: Wood v. Kelso, 27 Pa. 241.
[58] German Nat. Bank v. Beatrice Nat. Bank, 63 Neb. 246, 88 N. W. 480.
[59] Woolley v. Van Volkenburgh, 16 Kan. 20.
[60] Cramer v. Eagle M. Co., 23 Kan. 399.
[61] Curtis v. Buckley, 14 Kan. 449.
[62] Willans v. Ayers, 3 App. Cas. 133.
[63] Chitty on Bills, 70.

defendant accepted the bill for the accommodation of the plaintiff, except as to a part; and where the plaintiff, as indorsee, had only advanced a part of the money made payable by the bill accepted for the indorser's accommodation, neither was allowed to recover more than he had advanced. [64] But as against any other party the accommodation maker is of course obliged to pay the full amount, even if the real principal has been discharged in whole or in part.[65] But the consideration of this subject, in truth, appertains more properly to the right of recovery than to the measure of damages.**

§ 703. Pledged paper.

The pledgee of negotiable paper generally recovers the whole amount at maturity.[66] But if the defendant had a valid defence against the pledgor, recovery can be only for the amount of the plaintiff's interest.[67] So where the note was given originally to secure the defendant's debt, the measure of recovery in an action by the maker is the amount of the debt secured; [68] and the same is true where the plaintiff is an indorsee with notice.[69] So an insurance company can recover upon a premium note only the premiums already earned.[70] And the *bona fide* holder of fraudulently issued warehouse receipts (if the issuer is es-

---

[64] Darnell *v.* Williams, 2 Stark. 166; Wiffen *v.* Roberts, 1 Esp. 261.

But where the defendant made a note to the plaintiff's order and the plaintiff indorsed it for the defendant's accommodation, who negotiated it, the plaintiff, having taken up the note at its maturity by paying half its face value, was allowed to recover the whole face value. Fowler *v.* Strickland, 107 Mass. 552. The plaintiff in other words was treated as an ordinary purchaser of the note.

[65] Chafoin *v.* Rich, 92 Cal. 471, 28 Pac. 488.

[66] Reid *v.* Furnival, 1 C. & M. 538.

[67] *United States:* Cromwell *v.* County of Sac, 96 U. S. 60, 24 L. ed. 681.

Illinois: Steere *v.* Benson, 2 Bradw. 560.

Massachusetts: Fisher *v.* Fisher, 98 Mass. 303.

Minnesota: St. Paul Nat. Bank *v.* Cannon, 46 Minn. 95, 48 N. W. 526, 24 Am. St. Rep. 189.

New Jersey: Allaire *v.* Hartshorne, 21 N. J. L. 665, 47 Am. Dec. 175.

[68] *California:* Vogan *v.* Caminetti, 65 Cal. 438.

New York: Williams *v.* Smith, 2 Hill, 301; Rogers *v.* Smith, 47 N. Y. 324, 7 Am. Rep. 450.

Pennsylvania: Davis *v.* Funk, 39 Pa. 243, 80 Am. Dec. 519.

Wisconsin: Union Nat. Bank *v.* Roberts, 45 Wis. 373.

[69] Atlas Bank *v.* Doyle, 9 R. I. 76, 98 Am. Dec. 368.

[70] Maine M. M. Ins. Co. *v.* Farrar, 66 Me. 133; Maine M. M. Ins. Co. *v.* Stockwell, 67 Me. 382.

topped to deny their validity) recovers the amount of the loan they were issued to secure and not their face value.[71]

§ 704. Measure of liability of an indorser.

In an action by the indorsee against the indorser of a promissory note, the measure of damages is the amount paid by the indorsee, with interest, subject to the limitation that the recovery must not exceed the sum due on the face of the note.[72] So also where the law permits the assignment of a non-negotiable promissory note, and owing to the insolvency of the maker, or other sufficient cause, the assignee has failed to recover the amount from him; in an action against the assignor, the measure of the assignee's damages is the amount of the consideration paid by him and interest.[73] So where a claim on the government had been assigned for a valuable consideration, but was not paid in consequence of its having been paid before under an authority previously given by the assignor, the assignee was held entitled to recover only the consideration paid with interest from the time of presenting the claim to the government.[74] The amount paid by the indorsee or assignee is, however, presumably the face value of the note.[75]

This rule rests upon the ground that the consideration for the payment of the purchase-money by the indorsee or assignee

[71] Corn Exchange Bank v. American D. & T. Co., 163 N. Y. 332, 57 N. E. 477.

[72] United States: In re Many, 17 N. B. R. 514.
Alabama: Cook v. Cockrill, 1 Stew. 475, 18 Am. Dec. 67; Hutchins v. McCann, 7 Port. 94; Noble v. Walker, 32 Ala. 456.
Georgia: Bethune v. McCrary, 8 Ga. 114.
Illinois: Hawkinson v. Olson, 48 Ill. 277; Shaeffer v. Hodges, 54 Ill. 337; Short v. Coffeen, 76 Ill. 245, 20 Am. Rep. 243.
Maine: French v. Grindle, 15 Me. 163.
New York: Braman v. Hess, 13 Johns. 52; Munn v. Commission Co., 15 Johns. 43. But contra, Watson v. Hahn, 1

Colo. 385; Cook v. Clark, 4 E. D. Smith, 213.
[73] Arkansas: Jones v. State, 40 Ark. 344 (semble).
Colorado: Jones v. Hayden, 3 Colo. App. 305, 33 Pac. 76 (county warrant).
Indiana: Foust v. Gregg, 68 Ind. 399; Schmied v. Frank, 86 Ind. 250.
Kentucky: Davis v. Harrison, 2 J. J. Marsh. 189.
Missouri: Muldrow v. Agnew, 11 Mo. 616; Whisler v. Bragg, 31 Mo. 124.
West Virginia: Goff v. Miller, 41 W. Va. 683, 24 S. E. 643, 56 Am. St. Rep. 886.
[74] Eaton v. Mellus, 7 Gray, 566.
[75] Foust v. Gregg, 68 Ind. 399; Felton v. Smith, 88 Ind. 149, 45 Am. Rep. 454.

has failed, and the amount of it is therefore the measure of recovery. The reasoning does not apply to the case of an accommodation indorser, and the whole face value of the instrument may therefore be recovered from him.[76]

§ 705. Costs of prior suits.

* Some other decisions have been made upon the subject of the amount of recovery, which it may be proper to notice. An indorser who is sued on his indorsement, and subjected to costs, cannot recover those costs against the maker. He can only have the amount of the note and interest;[77] because, says the Supreme Court of New York, "if the indorser of a note be duly fixed, he ought to pay it without being sued; but if he finds it more convenient to delay taking up the note until he is prosecuted to judgment and execution, the drawer ought not to pay for that convenience. . . . The mere fact of drawing the note does not imply a promise to save the payee harmless from all costs and charges that he may be subjected to as indorser. There must be a special promise to save harmless before the payee can call upon the drawer for costs accrued by the default of the payee (indorser) himself." In a suit against the indorser, the fees of protest are a proper charge.[78] And an indorser who has paid the note can, it seems, recover the costs of protest against the maker.[79]

On the same principle, it has been held, in England, where an accommodation acceptor was sued by a *bona fide* holder, that as he ought to have paid it when demanded, he could not recover the costs against the party who had improperly indorsed it to the holder.[80] So, also, the acceptor of a bill with funds who has failed to pay, is not liable for the costs of a suit against the drawer.[81] And the indorser of a bill is not liable for the costs of a suit by the holder against the acceptor, nor for commissions

---

[76] Ingalls v. Lee, 9 Barb. 647.

[77] *Missouri:* Fenn v. Dugdale, 31 Mo. 580.

New York: Simpson v. Griffin, 9 Johns. 131.

South Carolina: Steele v. Sawyer, 2 McCord, 459; Richardson v. Presnall, 1 McCord, 192.

[78] Merritt v. Benton, 10 Wend. 116.

[79] Morgan v. Reintzel, 7 Cranch, 273.

[80] Bleaden v. Charles, 7 Bing. 246. See this case commented on in Asprey v. Levy, 16 M. & W. 851; Roach v. Thompson, M. & M. 487.

[81] Barnwell v. Mitchell, 3 Conn. 101.

paid on the collection of the money.[82]   In like manner the indorser of a regular bill who has been sued by an indorsee, is not entitled to recover from the acceptor his costs in such action.[83] But a party who makes or indorses or accepts an accommodation bill or note is regarded as a surety, and can charge the party for whose benefit his signature is given with the costs of a suit for the collection of such note or bill if he be compelled to pay it.   So the accommodation acceptor of a bill who is sued, can recover his costs of the drawer.[84]   And so it has been held between the accommodation indorser of a note and the maker.[85]**

Where an indorsee of a promissory note sues the maker, who defends on account of failure of consideration, and after notice the indorser does not take up the case, and the indorsee continues it, it is held that he may recover of the indorser the costs and expenses of the suit.[86]

§ 706.[a] Indorser's damages.

An indorser being a surety for the maker, his position cannot be altered by the holder, without the latter's making himself liable.   Thus when the holder of an indorsed note exchanged collateral security held to secure the note without the indorser's consent, the measure of the latter's damages was held to be the difference in value between the original and the substituted security.[87]

§ 707. Damages for failure to accept or pay.

We have seen that for breach of a *promise to pay* money, the face of the paper furnishes the measure of damages.   But the rule is otherwise if the contract is a contract to accept or pay in the future.   Here the plaintiff can recover substantial damages.[88]   In Boyd v. Fitt,[89] the defendant failed to meet a draft

---

[a] For § 706 of the eighth ed., see chap. lix.

[82] Bangor Bank v. Hook, 5 Me. 174. [disapproved in Hargous v. Lahens, 3 Sandf. (N. Y.) 213].

[83] Dawson v. Morgan, 9 B. & C. 618.

[84] Jones v. Brooke, 4 Taunt. 464.

[85] Hubbly v. Brown, 16 Johns. 70; Baker v. Martin, 3 Barb. 634; and see

post, chap. xxxvi, Of Contracts of Indemnity.

[86] Daskam v. Ullman, 74 Wis. 474, 43 N. W. 321.

[87] Nelson v. First Nat. Bank, 69 Fed. 798, 32 U. S. App. 554, 16 C. C. A. 425.

[88] Marzetti v. Wiliams, 1 B. & A. 415; Rolin v. Steward, 14 C. B. 595.

[89] 14 Ir. C. L. 43.

of the plaintiffs, whereby the plaintiffs' business in Glasgow was suspended, their business in Dublin much injured, and they lost the agency of an Australian firm. The jury having given damages on each of these three heads, the verdict was sustained, the court holding that the suspension of the Glasgow trade was within both branches of the rule in Hadley v. Baxendale, and that the damages sustained under the other two heads of loss were within the rule in Rolin v. Steward,[90] the natural result of the defendant's breach of contract. The extent of these damages it was for the jury to determine. In Prehn v. Royal Bank of Liverpool[91] the defendants, bankers at Liverpool, had agreed to accept the drafts of bankers at Alexandria. The defendants notified the plaintiffs that they could not meet their engagements. The latter were allowed to recover the commission they were obliged to pay another house to take up their bills, and also the expense of protesting the bills at Liverpool and Alexandria, and the expense of telegrams which they had despatched. In Larios v. Bonany y Gurety,[92] a case appealed from the Supreme Court of Gibraltar, the plaintiffs had been allowed in that court to recover for the defendant's failure to accept a draft: 1. The expense of protest; 2. Loss on some pork which he had been obliged to sell to get money; 3. Expenses of journeys to the place of trial, and expenses while at the trial; 4. General damages for injury to his personal credit, and for other loss. On appeal it was held that the plaintiff could not recover item 2, because that was too remote, such loss not being a natural consequence of the breach of contract. He was not allowed to recover item 3, for costs are a full indemnity. He was, however, allowed to recover items 1 and 4.[93] In Isley v. Jones,[94] an action for failure to accept a draft for the plaintiff's accommodation, it was held that the measure of damages was the inconvenience and loss which the plaintiff sustained from the defendant's offer to accept, and failure to do so.

§ 708. Damages in cases of fraud and estoppel.

In an action by the maker of a negotiable promissory note,

[90] 14 C. B. 595.
[91] L. R. 5 Ex. 92.
[92] L. R. 5 P. C. 346.

[93] *Acc.*, Urquhart v. McIver, 4 Johns. (N. Y.) 103.
[94] 12 Gray (Mass.), 260.

against one who has wrongfully negotiated it, so as to render the maker liable upon it, the measure of damages is the amount of the note, and proof that the plaintiff has already paid the note is unnecessary.[95] So where defendant, as plaintiff's agent, wrongfully issued bonds of the plaintiff, the market value of the securities could not be shown. The defendant was, however, allowed to show the plaintiff's inability to pay the bonds.[96] In an action to recover the damages sustained by the plaintiff by the act of the defendant in fraudulently transferring to him a promissory note, as a valid and subsisting demand, when it had been in fact previously paid and cancelled, the measure of damages is, *prima facie*, the amount of the note and interest. The ability of the maker to pay the note will be presumed, until the contrary is proved.[97] Where one is estopped from denying his signature to a note, as where he has adopted the signature knowing it to be a forgery, the general rule will apply, and the measure of the damages will be the whole amount of the note.[98]

---

[95] Decker *v.* Mathews, 12 N. Y. 313.

[96] Western R. R. *v.* Bayne, 75 N. Y. 1.

[97] *Indiana:* Foust *v.* Gregg, 68 Ind. 399.

New York: Neff *v.* Clute, 12 Barb. 466.

[98] Casco Bank *v.* Keene, 53 Me. 103; so in case of the signature of an indorser. Fall River Nat. Bank *v.* Buffinton, 97 Mass. 498.

CHAPTER XXXIV

CONTRACTS OF INSURANCE

I.—Marine Insurance

§ 709. Marine insurance a contract of indemnity.
710. Total loss.
711. Constructive total loss.
712. Measure of loss on open policy.
712a. Recovery by owner of a limited interest.
713. Valued policy.

§ 714. Partial loss.
715. One-third new for old.
716. Exceptions to rule of indemnity.
717. General average.
718. Proximate cause and consequential loss.
719. Reduction of damage.

II.—Fire Insurance

§ 720. Fire insurance a contract of indemnity.
721. Measure of loss.
722. Actual value of the property lost.
722a. Valued policies.
723. Election of insurer to rebuild: —Alternative contract.

§ 723a. Proximate cause.
724. Consequential loss.
725. Recovery by owner of a limited interest.
726. Clauses limiting liability.
727. Breach of contract to issue policy.
728. Re-insurance.

III.—Life Insurance

§ 729. Life insurance not a contract of indemnity.
730. Refusal to issue or continue a policy.

§ 731. Accident insurance.
732. Assessment policies.

I.—Marine Insurance

§ 709.—Marine insurance a contract of indemnity.

* Marine insurance is defined to be a "contract of indemnity in which the insurer, in consideration of the payment of a certain premium, agrees to make good to the assured all losses, not exceeding a certain amount, that may happen to the subject insured, from the risks enumerated or implied in the policy, during a certain voyage or period of time."[1] ** The more com-

---

[1] Duer on Marine Insurance, vol. i, p. 58; Hamilton *v.* Mendes, 2 Burr, 1198, 1210.

mon subjects of such policies are the vessel outfits, the cargo, freight, and profits.

* In England this contract retains more nearly its original and proper character as a contract of indemnity measured by the actual loss; but in the United States it has been very materially modified by the introduction of various arbitrary rules, among which the most prominent are the deduction of "one-third new for old," [2] the doctrine of abandonment for constructive total loss, and the principles adopted in the settlement of general averages. There is no branch of the law in which the rule of compensation has been made so much to yield to that of arbitrary remuneration, if it may be so called—in other words, the principle analogous to that of the *Lex Aquilia* of the Roman law, by which, instead of an inquiry into the exact circumstances of the particular case, a fixed rate or proportion is determined by which the recovery in all instances is governed.

The losses for which the insurer becomes liable fall under one of these three heads: partial loss; total loss; or general average.**

§ 710. Total loss.

* A total loss occurs where the thing insured is physically destroyed or rendered valueless; [3] or where, under the doctrine of constructive losses, the deterioration is so great as to authorize the insured to abandon to the underwriters and demand payment as for an actual physical total loss.**

In some of the early cases *actual destruction* was said to be necessary to enable the insured to recover for a total loss; [4] but the rule now is as just stated. Hence where a vessel is so damaged by perils insured against that its sale by the master is justifiable there is a total loss without abandonment. [5] So, if goods are by perils of the sea reduced to such a condition that they cannot be restored to the assured in their original char-

---

[2] This is, however, common to the English system.

[3] *United States:* Insurance Co. *v.* Fogarty, 19 Wall. 640, 22 L. ed. 216.

New York: Wallerstein *v.* Columbian Ins. Co., 44 N. Y. 204, 4 Am. Rep. 664.

[4] *New York:* Depeyster *v.* Sun M. I. Co., 17 Barb. 306.

England: Navone *v.* Haddon, 9 C. B. 30.

[5] *Maine:* Stephenson *v.* Piscataqua F. & M. Ins. Co., 54 Me. 55.

Maryland: Mutual Safety Ins. Co. *v.* Cohen, 3 Gill 459, 43 Am. Dec. 341.

New York: McCall *v.* Sun Mut. Ins. Co., 66 N. Y. 505.

acter, at the original place of their destination, this is a total loss of cargo.[6] So too, where, though the goods arrive in specie, they are so damaged as to be unmerchantable in their original character, there is a total loss.[7] It would seem to follow that if the cargo cannot be carried to its destination in merchantable condition there is a total loss of freight.[8] But it is generally held that if the goods can be carried in specie there can be no recovery for a total loss of freight though the goods when so carried would be valueless.[9] The rule applies though the goods are surrendered to the shipper or abandoned by him as a total loss.[10] Where the vessel is a total loss and no freight *pro rata itineris* has been earned and expense of forwarding cargo on another vessel equals or exceeds the whole amount agreed upon there can be recovery for total loss of freight without abandonment.[11]

Where there is an entire loss of any separate part of the cargo there is a total loss of that portion of the cargo; so where a number of mules were insured, and some of them were lost, the recovery was for a total loss of that portion of the property insured, and the case being that of a valued policy the recovery was of a proportionate amount of the whole valuation.[12]

§ 711. Constructive total loss.

Where there is not an actual total loss it has been settled that in many cases the assured may abandon to the underwriters

[6] Navone v. Haddon, 9 C. B. 30; Roux v. Salvador, 3 Bing. N. Cas. 266, 2 Hodges, 219, 7 L. J. Exch. 328, 4 Scott, 1, 32 E. C. L. 130.

[7] Asfar v. Blumdell, 8 Aspin. 106, 65 L. J. Q. B. 138, 73 L. T. Rep. (N. S.) 648, 44 Wkly. Rep. 130; Parry v. Aberdeen, 9 B. & C. 411, 7 L. J. K. B. O. S. 260, 4 M. & R. 343, 17 E. C. L. 189. But see Williams v. Kennebec Mut. Ins. Co., 31 Me. 455.

[8] See Asfar v. Blumdell, *supra*.

[9] *United States:* Jordan v. Warren Ins. Co., 1 Story, 342, 13 Fed. Cas. No. 7,524.

Massachusetts: Lord v. Neptune Ins. Co., 10 Gray 109.

[10] *Maryland:* Merchants' M. I. Co. v. Butler, 20 Md. 41.

New York: Griswold v. New York I. Co., 3 Johns. 321, 3 Am. Dec. 490.

[11] *New York:* Robertson v. Atlantic M. I. Co., 68 N. Y. 192.

England: Trinder v. Thames M. I. Co., 8 Aspin. 373, 67 L. J. Q. B. 666, 78 L. T. Rep. (N. S.) 485, 46 Wkly. Rep. 561.

[12] *Louisiana:* Brooke v. Louisiana S. I. Co., 16 Mart. 640, 681.

New York: Harris v. Eagle Fire Co., 5 Johns. 368.

England: Wilkinson v. Hyde, 3 C. B. (N. S.) 30, 4 Jur. (N. S.) 482, 27 L. J. C. P. 116, 91 E. C. L. 30.

and claim payment of the sum insured. A constructive total loss is one which as a matter of physical fact is but partial, but which as a matter of law gives the assured an option to treat it as total. The doctrine was not introduced into the law of insurance until long after the contract was familiarly known to commerce and is very differently applied in different countries.

Capture is everywhere treated as constructive total loss necessitating abandonment. By the American authorities the fact that the vessel is released after the abandonment will not defeat the recovery for a technical total loss.[13] The English rule seems otherwise.[14] If the vessel was in fact released or recaptured at the time of abandonment, there can be recovery for partial loss only, although the assured was ignorant of the rescue.[15]

In the United States wherever the thing insured is damaged by a peril insured against, more than half its value, the assured can abandon to the underwriters and claim a total loss. Instead of compensation for the actual damage sustained he may recover the whole value of his interest at risk. Thus, when perils of the sea have caused a deterioration of cargo exceeding half its value or when the expense of salvage would exceed that amount, there is a constructive total loss,[16] but a total loss of a distinct portion of the cargo amounting to more than half is not a constructive total loss of the whole.[17] In determining whether or not the cost of repairing a vessel amounts to half its value, the actual value of the vessel at the port of repairs and

[13] *United States:* Rhinelander v. Pennsylvania Ins. Co., 4 Cranch, 29, 2 L. ed. 540.
New York: Bordes v. Hallet, 1 Cai. 444.
Pennsylvania: Dutilh v. Gatliff, 4 Dall. 446, 1 L. ed. 903.
[14] Brotherston v. Barber, 5 M. & S. 418, 17 Rev. Rep. 378. But *cf.* Ruys v. Royal Exch. Assur. Corp., 8 Aspin. 294, 66 L. J. Q. B. 534, 77 L. T. Rep. (N. S.) 23; Bainbridge v. Nielson, 1 Camp. 237, 10 East, 329, 10 Rev. Rep. 316.
[15] *United States:* Marshall v. Delaware Ins. Co., 4 Cranch, 202, 2 L. ed.

596 (but *contra*, Rumford v. Church, 1 Johns. Cas. 147).
New York: Church v. Bedient, 1 Cai. Cas. 21.
[16] *Michigan:* Harvey v. Detroit F. & M. I. Co., 120 Mich. 501, 79 N. W. 898.
New York: Devitt v. Providence Washington Ins. Co., 61 App. Div. 390, 70 N. Y. Supp. 654.
South Carolina: Mordecai v. Fireman's Ins. Co., 12 Rich. 512.
[17] *United States:* Seton v. Delaware Ins. Co., 21 Fed. Cas. No. 12,675.
Massachusetts: Forbes v. Manf. Ins. Co., 1 Gray, 371.

not its value at destination or the valuation in the policy is the basis of calculation.[18] But the policy may make the agreed valuation the criterion.[19] The cost to be estimated is what it would take to repair the vessel completely, not merely what it would take to make her seaworthy.[20] The cost of getting a stranded vessel off a beach and to a place of safety [21] and the cost of temporary repairs at the port of necessity are to be added to the probable expense of additional repairs at the port where the vessel would be repaired in full.[22] Items of general average cannot be included in estimating the amount of loss, nor expenses of ascertaining the extent of loss, nor wages and provisions of crew while the ship is undergoing repairs.[23] The amount due the shipowner in contribution for general average from owners of freight and cargo must be deducted from the cost of repairs.[24] By weight of authority the rule of a deduction of one-third new for old is not applied.[25] That the unfitness of a vessel to be repaired is partly due to previous defective condition is no ground of deduction in computing the degree of injury.[26] If at the time the abandonment was made it reasonably seemed that the vessel could not be saved for less than half its value, the fact that it was subsequently saved and repaired for a less sum will not reduce the amount of recovery to that for partial loss.[27]

[18] *United States:* Bradlie v. Maryland Ins. Co., 12 Pet. 378, 9 L. ed. 1123; Peabody Ins. Co. v. Memphis Packet Co., 5 Am. L. Rec. 499 (*contra,* Howell v. Phila. M. I. Co., 12 Fed. Cas. No. 6,781).

New York: American Ins. Co. v. Ogden, 20 Wend. 287.

[19] Orrok v. Commonwealth Ins. Co., 21 Pick. (Mass.) 456, 32 Am. Dec. 271.

[20] Lincoln v. Hope Ins. Co., 8 Gray (Mass.), 22.

[21] Young v. Union Ins. Co., 24 Fed. 279.

[22] American Ins. Co. v. Center, 4 Wend. (N. Y.) 45.

[23] Hall v. Ocean Ins. Co., 21 Pick. 472, 32 Am. Dec. 271.

[24] Pezant v. National Ins. Co., 15 Wend. (N. Y.) 453.

[25] *United States:* Bradlie v. Maryland Ins. Co., 12 Pet. 378, 9 L. ed. 1123; Wallace v. Thames, etc., Ins. Co., 22 Fed. 66; Memphis Packet Co. v. Peabody Ins. Co., 1 Cinc. L. Bul. 42.

Contra, Massachusetts: Orrok v. Commonwealth Ins. Co., 21 Pick. 456, 32 Am. Dec. 271; Deblois v. Ocean Ins. Co., 16 Pick. 303, 28 Am. Dec. 245.

New York: Center v. American Ins. Co., 7 Cow. 564; Murray v. Great Western Co., 75 Hun, 282, 25 N. Y. Supp. 414.

[26] Taber v. China M. I. Co., 131 Mass. 239.

[27] *United States:* Orient M. I. Co. v. Adams, 123 U. S. 67, 8 Sup. Ct. 68, 31 L. ed. 63.

Illinois: Norton v. Lexington F. I. Co., 16 Ill. 235.

There is a constructive total loss of profits when more than half in value of the subject has been lost.[28]

The American rule in modified form prevails in France and generally on the continent, but the English rule firmly maintains the more salutary doctrine that no abandonment can be sustained unless the thing is injured to its full value.

Abandonment must be made within a reasonable time after notice of loss and must state the true cause thereof. If the underwriter does not seasonably reject the abandonment, he will be taken to have accepted. If abandonment is accepted it is immaterial that the loss does not exceed fifty per cent of the value and recovery is not thereby reduced to that for partial loss.[29] If abandonment is justifiably rejected, but the underwriter takes the vessel to repair her and fails to return her in a reasonable time properly repaired, there can be recovery for constructive total loss;[30] but where the vessel is so repaired and returned, acceptance by assured does not bar recovery for subsequently discovered deficiencies in her repairs as a partial loss.[31]

After abandonment is accepted the property is that of the underwriter who is liable for all expenses connected therewith and entitled to all proceeds arising therefrom.

§ 712. Measure of loss on open policy.

The measure of loss on an open marine policy is the actual value of the property lost. Thus where an insured vessel is lost, the value and not the cost of the vessel is recoverable; [32] and where the market value was depressed through temporary causes it was held that the jury was not restricted to such market value, but might find a higher actual value.[33] But where the owner of the vessel is also the owner of the cargo any amount due from the cargo as general average must be

Kentucky: Louisville Underwriters v. Pence, 93 Ky. 96, 19 S. W. 10, 14 Ky. L. Rep. 21, 40 Am. St. Rep. 176.

[28] Abbott v. Sebor, 3 Johns. Cas. (N. Y.) 39, 2 Am. Dec. 139.

[29] Northwestern Transp. Co. v. Thames, etc., Ins. Co., 59 Mich. 214, 26 N. W. 336.

[30] Copelin v. Phœnix Ins. Co., 46 Mo. 211, 2 Am. Rep. 504.

[31] Reynolds v. Ocean Ins. Co., 22 Pick. (Mass.) 191, 33 Am. Dec. 727.

[32] Snell v. Delaware Ins. Co., 4 Dall. 430, 1 L. ed. 896.

[33] McCuaig v. Quaker City Ins. Co., 18 Up. Can. Q. B. 130.

deducted from the loss on the ship.[34]   In arriving at the value of a cargo, the insurance premium, commissions and charges are to be added to the invoice price at the loading port.[35]   The value at the place of destination is not the criterion.[36]   Under an open policy on freight the measure of recovery is the gross amount to be received on the bill of lading without deducting expenses,[37] and where the owner of the vessel himself supplies the cargo the recovery in a policy on freight is the amount he might have obtained under the usual rate of freight on the voyage at the port of departure.[38]

The recovery upon an open policy is not restricted to the actual value of the property lost; the owner may also recover the necessary expenses of laboring for the safety and recovery of the vessel.[39]   Where a vessel meets with a partial loss, is repaired, proceeds on her voyage, and meets with a total loss, not only the value of the vessel, but also the expense of the repairs may be recovered, even though the amount of both losses will exceed the amount named in the policy.[40]   A general custom to pay the gross and not the net amount of freight on an open policy has been held good, though it affords more than complete indemnity.[41]   A statement of the amount of loss in the proofs of loss does not estop the assured from claiming a larger amount.[42]

[34] Potter v. Providence Washington Ins. Co., 19 Fed. Cas. No. 11,336, 4 Mason, 298.

[35] *Kentucky:* Louisville M. & F. I. Co. v. Bland, 9 Dana, 143, 157.

New York: Minturn v. Columbian Ins. Co., 10 Johns. 75.

England: Usher v. Noble, 12 East 639.

Contra, Massachusetts: Warren v. Franklin Ins. Co., 104 Mass. 518, 6 Am. Rep. 261 (market value at inception of risk).

[36] Wolf v. National M. & F. I. Co., 20 La. Ann. 583.

[37] Lockwood v. Atlantic M. I. Co., 47 Mo. 50.

[38] Paradise v. Sun M. I. Co., 6 La. Ann. 596.

[39] McBride v. Marine Ins. Co., 7 Johns. 431; as, in case of a captured vessel, legal expenses in the prize courts, Lawrence v. Van Horne, 1 Cai. 276, or expenses of travel to obtain release of property, Watson v. Marine Ins. Co., 7 Johns. 57.

[40] *United States:* Christie v. Buckeye Ins. Co., 5 Fed. Cas. No. 2,700.

Massachusetts: Matheson v. Equitable Mar. Ins. Co., 118 Mass. 209, 19 Am. Rep. 441.

England: Le Cheminant v. Pearson, 4 Taunt. 367.

[41] Palmer v. Blackburn, 1 Bing. 61.

[42] American Ins. Co. v. Griswold, 14 Wend. (N. Y.) 399.

§ 712a. Recovery by owner of a limited interest.

Where the pecuniary value of a limited interest cannot be precisely determined, the owner of such an interest may recover the full value of the property under a marine policy thereon. Thus an unpaid vendor may recover the value of the vessel, not being limited to the price at which he contracted to sell,[43] and a mortgagor's interest is not restricted to such proportion of the value of the vessel as the surplus after paying the debt bears to the whole.[44] But when the value of the interest can be accurately measured, the rule is otherwise. The recovery of a mortgagee is limited to the amount of the debt,[45] and that of a part owner to the value of his interest,[46] or where the policy is valued such proportion of the valuation as his interest bears to the whole actual value.[47]

§ 713. Valued policy.

The open marine policy has been almost superseded by the valued policy, in which the amount to be paid upon total loss is liquidated.[48] The agreed valuation is recovered upon a total loss, notwithstanding the market value has risen or fallen between the valuation and the loss,[49] or that after the issuance of the policy but before total loss the insured vessel was greatly damaged by a peril not insured against.[50] Where a carrier insures its liability on cargo under a valued policy, the measure of the insurer's liability is the face of the policy irrespective of the amount paid by the shipowners to the owners of the cargo.[51] But if the overvaluation is fraudulent the policy is voidable.[52]

---

[43] Stuart v. Columbia Ins. Co., 2 Cranch C. C. 442.

[44] Lazarus v. Com. Ins. Co., 19 Pick. (Mass.) 81.

[45] Irving v. Richardson, 1 M. & R. 153.

[46] Hebner v. Sun Ins. Co., 157 Ill. 144, 41 N. E. 627.

[47] *Massachusetts:* Finney v. Warren Ins. Co., 1 Met. 16, 35 Am. Dec. 343.

Ohio: Knight v. Eureka Ins. Co., 26 Oh. St. 664, 20 Am. Rep. 778.

[48] "A 'valued policy' is not understood to be one which estimates the value of the property insured merely, but which values the loss, and is equivalent to an assessment of damages in the event of a loss." Agnew, J., in Lycoming Ins. Co. v. Mitchell, 48 Pa. 367, 372.

[49] Portsmouth Ins. Co. v. Brazee, 16 Oh. 81.

[50] Woodside v. Globe M. I. Co., 8 Aspin. 118, 65 L. J. Q. B. 117, 73 L. T. Rep. (N. S.) 626, 44 Wkly. Rep. 187.

[51] Ursula I. Co. v. Amsinck, 115 Fed. 242.

[52] *New York:* Voisin v. Commercial Mut. Ins. Co., 62 Hun, 4, 16 N. Y. Supp. 419.

Where there is a valued policy on profits, loss of the cargo entitles the assured to the amount of the policy without proof that some profits would have arisen.[53] A valued policy on freight at and from A to B and at and from B back to A covers freight to the full amount of the valuation on both outward and homeward voyages, and where the cargo is a total loss on the homeward voyage the full valuation is recoverable without deduction for freight earned on the outward voyage.[54] Nor are the expenses of completing the voyage to be deducted.[55] In case of a valued policy upon cargo or freight, there is sometimes a total loss before the cargo has been entirely loaded, or after part has been discharged. Where a valued policy is issued on cargo it has finally been decided to mean that cargo which the vessel is intended to carry, not such goods as may form the whole load at a particular moment; consequently when a total loss happens after part of the cargo has been taken on or discharged the valuation is not recoverable, but only such proportion thereof as the value of the cargo loaded bears to that intended to be covered by the valuation.[56] So where there is a valued insurance on freight, and only part of the cargo has been taken on at the time of loss, there will be a *pro rata* recovery though it be proved that a full return cargo would have been secured.[57] The same rule applies to insurance upon profits.[58]

England: Haigh *v.* De la Cour, 3 Campb. 319, 13 Rev. Rep. 813.

[53] Patapsco Ins. Co. *v.* Coulter, 3 Pet. 222, 7 L. ed. 659.

[54] Davy *v.* Hallett, 3 Cai. 16, 2 Am. Dec. 241; Insurance Co. *v.* Mordecai, 22 How. 111, 16 L. ed. 329.

[55] Lockwood *v.* Atlantic M. I. Co., 47 Mo. 50.

[56] Tobin *v.* Harford, 13 C. B. (N. S.) 791, 17 C. B. N. S. 528, overruling Shawe *v.* Felton, 2 East, 109. *Cf.* Wolcott *v.* Eagle Ins. Co., 4 Pick. (Mass.) 429 (valuation excluded goods not covered by policy).

In Voisin *v.* Providence Washington Ins. Co., 51 App. Div. 553, 65 N. Y. Supp. 333, the master of the vessel and the consignor conspired to issue bills of lading for an amount of goods greater than was shipped. A purchaser of the bill of lading insured the goods under a valued policy. *Held*, that recovery is limited to that proportion of the valuation which the amount of goods actually shipped bore to that represented to have been shipped and forming the basis of valuation).

[57] Williams *v.* North China Ins. Co., 1 C. P. D. 757, 3 Aspin. 342, 35 L. T. Rep. (N. S.) 884; Forbes *v.* Aspinall, 13 East, 323. But the court added that the valuation could have been recovered if the whole cargo had been shipped, though the voyage had not yet begun.

[58] Alsop *v.* Commercial Ins. Co., 1 Fed. Cas. No. 262, 1 Sumn. 451.

§ 714. Partial loss.

Partial loss is, as its name implies, a partial destruction of the thing insured. In adjusting a partial loss on goods, the ratio of deterioration is estimated by the relative value of sound and damaged goods at the port of delivery. This ratio, in case of an open policy, is then applied to the invoice price of the goods at the port of lading without reference to the rise and fall of the market.[59] A proportionate amount of the premium is also to be included.[60] Under a valued policy the recovery should be that fraction of the agreed valuation proportionate to the depreciation,[61] but there are decisions that a valued policy is opened where the loss is partial.[62] Return duties received by the owners of the goods from the customhouse should not be deducted from the amount to which the insurers are to contribute.[63]

Where the insured vessel is so strained that repairs do not put her in her original condition, the insurer is liable for the diminution in value as well as for expenses of repairs.[64] But where a total loss occurs by an excepted peril, there can be no recovery for repairs necessitated by a previous partial loss within the policy if such repairs have not yet been made.[65] There can be no recovery for expenses of the crew during delay of the vessel for repairs, nor for commissions paid to secure an advance for repairs.[66]

It is a rule peculiar to marine insurance that where the

[59] *New York:* Lawrence v. New York Ins. Co., 3 Johns. Cas. 217.

England: Usher v. Noble, 12 East, 639.

[60] Louisville M. & F. I. Co. v. Bland, 9 Dana (Ky.), 143.

[61] *United States:* Griswold v. Union Mut. Ins. Co., 11 Fed. Cas. No. 5,840, 3 Blatchf. 231.

England: Pitman v. Universal Mar. Ins. Co., 9 Q. B. D. 192, 4 Aspin. 544, 51 L. J. Q. B. 561, 46 L. T. Rep. (N. S.) 863, 30 Wkly. Rep. 906; Lewis v. Rucker, 2 Burr. 1167.

[62] *United States:* Watson v. Insurance Co. of N. Am., 29 Fed. Cas. No. 17,286, 3 Wash. 1.

Massachusetts: Clark v. United M. & F. Co., 7 Mass. 365, 5 Am. Dec. 50. [But *cf.* Fay v. Alliance Ins. Co., 16 Gray, 455, 77 Am. Dec. 419, valued policy on freight].

[63] Cory v. Boylston Ins. Co., 107 Mass. 140, 9 Am. Rep. 14.

[64] *Maine:* Hagar v. Eng. M. M. I. Co., 59 Me. 460, 8 Am. Rep. 428.

Massachusetts: Giles v. Eagle Ins. Co., 2 Met. 140.

[65] Livie v. Janson, 12 East, 648, 11 Rev. Rep. 513.

[66] *Ohio:* Webb v. Protection Ins. Co., 6 Ohio, 456.

England: Shelbourne v. Law Investment & Ins. Corp., [1898] 2 Q. B. 626.

actual or agreed value of the subject-matter of the policy exceeds the total amount of insurance, the assured is a coinsurer as to such uninsured part. Hence any underwriter is liable only for such proportion of the loss as the amount subscribed bears to the value of the interest covered.[67] But upon an open policy the whole amount of the risk may be recovered upon a partial loss, if the actual loss reaches that amount.[68]

§ 715. One-third new for old.

* In regard to partial losses, the allowance of *one-third new for old* is the most important arbitrary limitation of the amount of relief which usage has engrafted on the policy. In case of a partial loss on the ship, the underwriters are nominally liable on the face of their contract to pay for the actual damage sustained. But it is considered that where old timbers or other materials are replaced by new, the vessel, when repaired, is better than she was before the damage was sustained. And, accordingly, it is held that the assured must himself bear a part of the expense of the repairs.[69] Mr. Justice Story has said that if the difference between the value of the vessel before the damage and after the repairs, "were to be ascertained in every particular case by actual inspection and estimates, there would be no end to controversies; and, therefore, general usage, which the law follows as founded on public convenience, has applied a certain rule to all cases." [70] This rule is "that the assured shall pay one-third part of the expense of labor and materials requisite to make the repairs, and shall recover only two-thirds of the underwriters, it being considered that in general the ship

[67] *United States:* Western Assur. Co. v. Southwestern Transp. Co., 68 Fed. 923, 16 C. C. A. 65; Chicago Ins. Co. v. Graham, etc., Co., 108 Fed. 271.

Illinois: Egan v. British M. I. Co., 193 Ill. 295, 61 N. E. 1081, 86 Am. St. Rep. 342.

Maine: Thomas v. Rockland Ins. Co., 45 Me. 116.

Maryland: Phillips v. St. Louis Perpetual Ins. Co., 15 Md. 297.

Massachusetts: Brewer v. American Ins. Co., 123 Mass. 78, 25 Am. Rep. 24.

England: Etches v. Aldan, 1 M. & R. 165.

But see Mason v. Marine Ins. Co., 110 Fed. 452, 49 C. C. A. 106, 54 L. R. A. 700.

[68] Am. Ins. Co. v. Griswold, 14 Wend. 399, 458.

[69] Phillips on Insurance, 2d ed., vol. ii, p. 197.

[70] Peele v. Merchants' Ins. Co., 3 Mason, 27, 73.

is better by the amount of one-third of the expense of the repairs. This allowance is called the deduction of *one-third new for old*." [71]

The Supreme Court of Massachusetts, speaking of this rule, have said that it "is arbitrary, and operates in some cases unjustly, giving to the insured more or less than a full indemnity, to which he is entitled by the policy, and to no more. The rule originated from the usages among merchants and underwriters, probably from the great difficulty of ascertaining the actual loss without first repairing the damage done or estimating the cost of repairs." [72] ** The rule applies though the advantage of the new materials over the old is much more than a third of the expenditure,[73] but in England it does not apply to a first voyage.[74] This distinction is not taken in the United States.[75] The rule applies only to those expenses from which the assured derives an enhanced value beyond the loss, and not to such items as towage.[76] The deduction is made from the balance of the cost of repairs after first deducting therefrom the value of old materials saved and not from the gross cost.[77]

§ 716. Exceptions to rule of indemnity.

The American policies on vessels frequently contain a declaration, that "no partial loss, or particular average, shall in any case be paid unless amounting to five per cent" or some similar clause, often limiting liability to cases of total loss; and the cargo policies have an analogous provision, defining the extent of the underwriters' liability. By these clauses it will be seen that in a large class of cases no partial loss whatever is to be paid, and in others, none unless amounting to a certain por-

[71] Phillips on Insurance, 2d ed., vol. ii, p. 197; Poingdestre v. Royal Exchange, Ry. & M. 378.

[72] Brinley v. National Ins. Co., 11 Met. (Mass.) 195.

[73] Aitchison v. Lohre, 4 App. Cas. 755, 4 Aspin. 168, 49 L. J. Q. B. 123, 41 L. T. Rep. (N. S.) 323, 28 Wkly. Rep. 1.

[74] Fenwick v. Robinson, 3 C. & P. 323; Pirie v. Steele, 8 C. & P. 200, 2 M. & Rob. 49, 34 E. C. L. 689.

[75] *Massachusetts:* Nickels v. Maine F. & L. Ins. Co., 11 Mass. 253.
New York: Dunham v. Commercial Ins. Co., 11 Johns. 315, 6 Am. Dec. 374.

[76] Potter v. Ocean Ins. Co., 9 Fed. Cas. No. 11,335, 3 Sumn. 27. See also, De Costa v. Newnham, 2 T. R. 407.

[77] *Massachusetts:* Eager v. Atlas Ins. Co., 14 Pick. 141, 25 Am. Dec. 363.
New York: Byrnes v. National Ins. Co., 1 Cow. 265.

tion of the whole value insured. In the former case, to found a claim for recovery, the subject at risk must be totally lost. And as to what constitutes a total loss, many very interesting cases have been decided. But this inquiry is foreign to our present subject. Unless the injury comes up to the limit fixed by the policy, the insured can claim no damages; he can have no remuneration or compensation for any loss less than that required by the contract.[78] The valuation in the policy is to be taken as the basis of determining the percentage of loss [79] and there must be a deduction of one-third new for old.[80] A particular average cannot be combined with a general average to make up the required percentage.[81] The expense of salvage may be added to the actual depreciation of the property.[82] In the United States distinct losses during the same voyage can-\ not be added together.[83] The rule is otherwise in England, but losses occurring in more than one voyage cannot be taken together under a time policy.[84]

In an English case, a time policy contained a warranty "free from average under three per cent." During the voyage the vessel sustained damage which was not discovered until the end of the voyage. The voyage having been completed, and the vessel put into dock for repairs other than those covered by the policy, the injury was for the first time discovered. The ship was in port eight days. Had it not been for the injury covered by the policy she would have been there but three days. The repairs of that injury alone would have taken the whole eight days. If the dock charges for the last five days only where added to the cost of repairs, there was not a loss

[78] The Irish Court of Admiralty has applied this rule to the claims of seamen for clothing lost by a marine collision. The Cumberland, 5 L. T. R. 496.

[79] Riley v. Ocean Ins. Co., 11 Rob. (N. Y.) 255.

[80] *District of Columbia:* Sanderson v. Columbian Ins. Co., 21 Fed. Cas. No. 12,298, 2 Cranch C. C. 218.
Missouri: Kerr v. Quaker City Ins. Co., 33 Mo. 158.

[81] Price v. Ships Small Damage Ins. Assoc., 22 Q. B. D. 580, 6 Aspin. 435,

58 L. J. Q. B. 269, 61 L. T. Rep. (N. S.) 278, 27 Wkly. Rep. 566.

[82] Hall v. Rising Sun Ins. Co., 1 Disn. (Ohio) 308, 12 Ohio Dec. 639.

[83] Hagar v. England M. M. I. Co., 59 Me. 460, 8 Am. Rep. 428. But see Donnell v. Columbian Ins. Co., 7 Fed. Cas. No. 3,987, 2 Sumn. 366.

[84] Blackett v. Royal Exch. Assur. Co., 2 Cromp. & J. 244, 1 L. J. Exch. 101, 2 Tyrw. 266; Stewart v. Merchants' M. I. Co., 16 Q. B. D. 619, 5 Aspin. 506, 55 L. J. Q. B. 81, 53 L. T. Rep. (N. S.) 892, 34 Wkly. Rep. 208.

of three per cent. But it was held that the dock charges for
the first three days ought to be attributed partly to the injury
insured against, and partly to the ordinary repairs; and one-
half the charges should be attributed to the injury.[85]

§ 717. General average.

* General average or contribution in general average, is that
sum which on any voluntary sacrifice of a part of the interests
at risk for the joint benefit of all, becomes due from the other
parties to the adventure to make up for the sacrifice.** Casual
and inevitable loss is not a subject of general average,[86] nor
can there be recovery on a marine policy as for general average
when part of a cargo is thrown over to take on board the crew
of another sinking vessel.[87] In the United States wages and
provisions of the crew during detention in an intermediate port
for repairs necessitated by a sacrifice for the common benefit
are recoverable as general average.[88] The English rule is otherwise.[89] Unless a custom in a particular trade is otherwise, there
can be no recovery for the jettison of goods carried on deck.[90]

* The interests generally in jeopardy in these cases are the
vessel, freight, and cargo; and when the sacrifice is to be made
good in general average, the values of these subjects are to be
arrived at as forming the basis of contribution. Although there
has until recently been some want of precision in the rule on
the subject of contribution by the cargo, owing chiefly to the
false assumption that "prime cost," "invoice price," and "market value" were synonymous and convertible terms,[91] it is now

[85] Marine Ins. Co. v. China Trans-
pacific Steamship Co., 11 App. Cas.
573, 6 Aspin. 68, 57 L. J. Q. B. 100, 55
L. T. Rep. (N. S.) 491, 35 Wkly. Rep.
169.
[86] Shiff v. Louisiana S. I. Co., 6 Mart.
(La.), N. S. 629.
[87] Dabney v. New England M. M. I.
Co., 14 Allen, 300.
[88] *United States:* Hobson v. Lord, 92
U. S. 397, 23 L. ed. 613.
Louisiana: Hanse v. New Orleans M.
& F. I. Co., 10 La. 1, 29 Am. Dec. 456.
Massachusetts: Padelford v. Boardman, 4 Mass. 548.

But see *South Carolina:* Wightman
v. Macadam, 2 Brev. 230.
[89] Power v. Whitmore, 4 M. & S. 141.
But see De Costa v. Newnham, 2
T. R. 407.
[90] *United States:* Wood v. Phœnix Ins.
Co., 1 Fed. 235.
England: Miller v. Letherington, 6
H. & N. 278, 7 C. B. (N. S.) 954.
In Gould v. Oliver, 4 Bing. N. C. 134,
custom of the trade entitled the owner
of goods shipped on deck to contribution for their jettison.
[91] Gahn v. Broome, 1 Johns. Cas. 120;
Marshall on Ins., 5th ed., pp. 502, 503·

practically settled in the United States, that in estimating a loss under an open policy, the rule of damages or insurable interest is the *market value* of the vessel or goods at the beginning of the risk, ascertained according to the rate of exchange at that time, together with the premium of insurance, and in the case of goods, the expenses necessarily incurred upon them at the time of shipment.[92] ** Where a cargo jettisoned had no market value at the port of departure the valuation in the bill of lading was taken, and the court said that in the absence of such valuation the cost price including shipping charges would be the valuation.[93] In England the insurable interest under open policies is now said to be its worth *to the assured* at the outset of the risk, with the expenses of insurance.[94] * The vessel and freight are of more fluctuating and uncertain value. The actual worth of the vessel diminishes during the voyage with each day's wear and tear; and the value of the freight is also diminishing by reason of the wages, provisions, and expenses, which are in a constant state of disbursement to earn it. In New York, to arrive at the value of the vessel, one-fifth of its value at the time of sailing is deducted; and the freight contributes on one-half, and is contributed for on the whole.[95] And this principle of arbitrary valuation, though the rate or proportion may differ, prevails, we believe, universally throughout the United States.[96] ** Where there is a total loss of part of the freight, as in the case of a ship being too damaged on the voyage to return, the loss must be estimated on the value of the ship and freight, and not that of the freight only.[97]

Goods contribute on their actual net value; that is, on their

Coffin *v.* Newburyport Mar. Ins. Co., 9 Mass. 436.

[92] 2 Phil. on Ins., §§ 1221, 1222, 1229, 1231; Carson *v.* The Marine Ins. Co., 2 Wash. C. C. 468; Warren *v.* Franklin Ins. Co., 104 Mass. 518, 6 Am. Rep. 261; Cox *v.* Charleston Fire & Mar. Ins. Co., 3 Rich. 331, 45 Am. Dec. 771.

[93] Tudor *v.* Macomber, 14 Pick. (Mass.) 34.

[94] 1 Arnould on Mar. Ins. (6th ed.), p. 318.

[95] This was the rule laid down in the case of Leavenworth *v.* Delafield, 1 Cai.

573, and has been acted on ever since. The principle has been somewhat shaken by Judge Betts in the District Court of the United States. The Mutual Safety Ins. Co. *v.* The George, Olcott, 157, to which here, however, it is only necessary to call attention thus briefly.

[96] So it is held that the contributory value of freight in general average is to be ascertained by a deduction of one-third of the gross freight. Humphreys *v.* Union Ins. Co., 3 Mason, 429.

[97] Moss *v.* Smith, 9 C. B. 94.

market price at the port of adjustment, free of all charges for freight, duty, and expenses of landing. But in a case where the goods brought at the intermediate port more than they would have done at the port of destination, the court, per Abbott, C. J., refused to set aside the valuation which had been adopted, which was the price actually obtained.[98] Where the insured has been forced to make contribution in respect of an average loss, the insurers are held for that proportion of the contribution which the value of his interest as assured bears to its value as estimated for the purposes of contribution. There may be recovery by the owner of jettisoned goods to their full value without first collecting the contribution to which he is entitled from the owners of the ship and cargo.[99] But where ship, freight, and cargo belong to the same person, the owner cannot recover of the insurers on the vessel the whole general average but can recover only the portion chargeable to the vessel.[100] An insurer is liable to pay the amount of general average as adjusted in a foreign port though greater than if it had been adjusted in the domestic port.[101]

* It may be proper to add, that the American rule of arbitrary remuneration has been greatly extended by the general adoption in this country of the practice of valuation. It has become habitual to value the thing assured in the policy; and these valuations fix the basis of recovery, and forbid inquiry into the actual damage sustained, unless the overestimate is so great as to induce a belief of fraud.[102] **

[98] Richardson v. Nourse, 3 B. & Ald. 237.

[99] Dickenson v. Jardine, L. R. 3 C. P. 639, 37 L. J. C. P. 321, 18 L. T. Rep. (N. S.) 17, 16 Wkly. Rep. 1169.

See, also, *United States:* International Nav. Co. v. Atlantic M. I. Co., 100 Fed. 304 (ship).

Massachusetts: Lord v. Neptune Ins. Co., 10 Gray, 109 (freight).

[100] Jumel v. Mar. Ins. Co., 7 Johns. 412, 5 Am. Dec. 283.

[101] *United States:* Croshaw v. Ins. Co. of N. Am., 66 Fed. 604.

Massachusetts: Loring v. Neptune Ins. Co., 20 Pick. 411.

New York: Strong v. N. Y. Firemen's Ins. Co., 11 Johns. 323.

England: Dent v. Smith, L. R. 4 Q. B. 414, 38 L. J. Q. B. 144, 20 L. T. Rep. (N. S.) 868, 17 Wkly. Rep. 646.

Canada: Avon M. I. Co. v. Bateaux, 2 Nova Scotia Dec. 195.

But see *Maine:* Thornton v. U. S. Ins. Co., 12 Me. 150.

New York: Lenox v. United Ins. Co., 3 Johns. Cas. 178.

[102] Irving v. Manning, 6 C. B. 391; Lamar Ins. Co. v. McGlashen, 54 Ill. 513, 5 Am. Rep. 162. See as to adjustment of general average in various

§ 718. Proximate cause and consequential loss.

The law of Marine Insurance, which in the plan of this book is touched on but lightly, is full of nice questions both as to consequential damages and proximate cause, the latter generally involving the right of action, the former the limits of recovery. Where a vessel is injured by a peril of the sea, and further injury occurs from the master's neglect to have her repaired; where, in the case of an insurance on cargo, the ship is lost and the goods are saved, but are afterwards partially lost in consequence of the master's neglect to tranship them; and generally, where the master's neglect is the immediate cause by which the injury, although arising from a peril insured against, produces the damage, the insurers are not liable.[103] So where the vessel was wrecked in time of war, and the cargo would have been saved but for the interference of hostile troops, the loss was held to be due to war, and not to a peril insured against.[104] But if the loss was a remote consequence only of the negligence of the master or crew, but a direct one of a peril insured against, the underwriters are not discharged.[105] So a collision is a peril within a policy insuring against the perils of the sea, and the insured may recover the damage which was the immediate consequence of it, although the vessel was brought within the peril by the fault of the master or crew.[106] But the underwriters in such a case are not liable to pay the owners of the insured vessel the damages which the latter have been compelled to pay the owners of the other vessel to avoid

cases, Meeker v. Klemm, 11 La. Ann. 104; Greely v. The Tremont Insurance Company, 9 Cush. (Mass.) 415; Nelson v. Belmont, 5 Duer (N. Y.), 310; Lee v. Grinnell, Ibid. 400; Nimick v. Holmes, 25 Pa. 366, 64 Am. Dec. 710.

[103] *United States:* Hazard v. New England M. I. Co., 1 Sumn. 218.

Massachusetts: Cleveland v. Union Ins. Co., 8 Mass. 308; Copeland v. New England M. I. Co., 2 Met. 432.

New York: Schieffelin v. New York Ins. Co., 9 Johns. 21.

[104] Ionides v. Universal M. I. Co., 14 C. B. (N. S.) 259, 32 L. J. C. P. 170, 8 L. T. Rep. (N. S.) 705.

[105] American Ins. Co. v. Bryan, 26 Wend. 563, 583.

[106] *United States:* General M. I. Co. v. Sherwood, 14 How. 351, 14 L. ed. 352.

New York: Mathews v. Howard Ins. Co., 11 N. Y. 9.

South Carolina: Street v. Augusta Ins. Co., 12 Rich. 13.

These cases establish the present rule on the point, and those of Peters v. Warren Ins. Co., 14 Peters, 99, 10 L. ed. 99; Hale v. The Washington Ins. Co., 2 Story, 176; Nelson v. The Suffolk Ins. Co., 8 Cush. 477, which are in conflict with it, can no longer be regarded as of general authority.

being sold.[107]   And where a policy on a boat excepts from the
perils insured against, perils and misfortunes arising from a
want of ordinary care and skill in lading or navigating her,
the fact that the master placed her in a dangerous position for
being towed, is material in determining the insurer's liability.[108]
A boat insured struck a rock and sank. The insurers were
sued. The wages and provisions of the crew, during the detention, were not allowed to be estimated as a part of the damages.[109]   In Massachusetts, the plaintiff is allowed to recover
on his insurance policy the damages paid to another vessel for
injury by the collision. The plaintiff's vessel having been held
liable in a foreign court of admiralty for the injury, the plaintiff
and the owner settled the damages between themselves. Although the insurers had no notice of the suit, they were held
liable for this amount, but not for interest for time previous to
filing the writ.[110]   The obligation of the insurer, in cases of
partial loss, is simply to pay such loss. It does not extend to
consequential losses, nor to loans obtained in a foreign port for
repairs, though the expense of raising the money on bottomry
is part of the partial loss which he must pay.[111]

§ 719. Reduction of damage.

* We have already had occasion to notice, that though the
plaintiff's loss had been made good by charitable contributions,
his claim for legal relief is not thereby prejudiced; and there are
other cases where he has been allowed remuneration beyond his
positive loss. So, it is no defence to an action for a partial
loss on a policy of marine insurance, that the expense of the
repairs for the amount of which the loss is claimed was covered
by a loan made by the correspondent of the owner on a bottomry of the vessel, and that the bottomry loan was realized
by such correspondent, after the subsequent total loss of the
vessel, out of an insurance effected by him on his bottomry interest, and that no part of the loan was ever paid by the

[107] Mathews v. Howard Ins. Co., 11
N. Y. 9.
[108] Savage v. Corn Exchange Ins. Co.,
4 Bosw. 1.
[109] May v. Delaware Ins. Co., 19 Pa.
312.

[110] *Massachusetts:* Thwing v. Great
Western Ins. Co., 111 Mass. 93.
Contra, New York: Mathews v. How-
ard Ins. Co., 11 N. Y. 9.
[111] Bradlie v. Maryland Ins. Co., 12
Pet. 378, 9 L. ed. 1123.

owner.[112] ** But where a loss occurs under a valued policy, the plaintiff can only recover the difference between the amount he has received from other insurances and the agreed value.[113] And where upon an actual total loss the sale of the hulk produced a certain sum, that sum is to be deducted from the valuation.[114] So too, where the owner of a ship furnishes the cargo and on damage to the ship abandons the same to the underwriter, the latter may deduct from the valuation of the vessel the freight from the point where the ship was abandoned to the port of destination.[115]

II.—FIRE INSURANCE

§ 720. Fire insurance a contract of indemnity.

* When we turn to the subject of fire insurance, we find that the policy retains much more nearly its original character as a contract of indemnity. In this branch of the great business of insurance, the practice of valuation is less common than in other branches of insurance; the doctrine of abandonment has never been introduced; and the right to recover depends, in all cases, on the actual loss sustained,[116] to be proved in the particular instance.[117] **

Any evidence conducing to show the loss less than that claimed, is admissible. The doctrine relative to reduction of damages has no application to such a case.[118] A fire insurance company which insured goods, and the government tax on the same, has been held liable for the amount of that tax, although not paid, where the government had entered judgment and the insured had given bonds for payment. These bonds were given in Kentucky, where they operate under the statutes as satisfaction of the judgment. It was held not to be an

[112] Read v. Mutual Safety Ins. Co., 3 Sandf. (N. Y.) 54.

[113] Bruce v. Jones, 1 H. & C. 769.

[114] Smith v. Manufacturers' Ins. Co., 7 Met. (Mass.) 448.

[115] Miller v. Woodfall, 8 E. & B. 493, 4 Jur. (N. S.) 302, 27 L. J. C. B. 120, 92 E. C. L. 493.

[116] An interesting discussion of some important points on the measure of damages in cases of insurance against

fire, will be found in the opinion of Jones, C. J., in Laurent v. Chatham F. I. Co., 1 Hall (N. Y.), 41.

[117] *Illinois:* Illinois M. F. I. Co. v. Andes Ins. Co., 67 Ill. 362, 16 Am. Rep. 620.

Pennsylvania: Ellmaker v. Franklin F. I. Co., 5 Pa. 183.

[118] Franklin F. I. Co. v. Hamill, 6 Gill (Md.), 87.

answer to say that the government could not have collected the tax if the insurers had refused to defend the suit.[119]

On a fire insurance policy the whole amount of the loss is recovered, up to the amount of the risk, though the loss is only partial.[120] Nor is it material that the value of the goods insured exceeds the total amount of insurance, for the doctrine of coinsurance by the owner as applied to marine policies is not applicable to fire policies.[121] Where several buildings, or goods in several buildings, are insured in one policy, the whole loss incurred by the destruction of one building may be recovered up to the amount of the risk.[122]

§ 721. Measure of loss.

* In Ireland, the general rule in cases of fire insurance has been thus laid down in a case where a mill and machinery were injured by fire. The court directed the jury to say, "what state of repairs the machinery was in, what it would cost to replace it by new machinery, and how much better, if at all, the mill in which the machinery was placed would be with the new machinery than it was at the time of the fire; the difference to be deducted from the entire expense of placing there such new machinery."[123] This rule has been adopted in this country in cases where the property is injured and repaired so as to replace it substantially as it was before the accident.[124] But in cases of total destruction much confusion once existed.

Mr. Greenleaf has said,[125] that the actual loss is to be as-

[119] Insurance Co. v. Thompson, 95 U. S. 547, 24 L. ed. 487.

[120] *Massachusetts:* Liscom v. Boston M. F. I. Co., 9 Met. 205; Underhill v. Agawam M. F. I. Co., 6 Cush. 440.

Mississippi: Mississippi M. I. Co. v. Ingram, 34 Miss. 215.

Pennsylvania: Phœnix F. I. Co. v. Cochran, 51 Pa. 143, 88 Am. Dec. 569.

[121] *Louisiana:* Nicolet v. Insurance Co., 3 La. 366, 23 Am. Dec. 458.

Canada: Peddie v. Quebec F. Assur. Co., Stuart, 174.

But the policy may provide that the owner shall be deemed a coinsurer if insurance is not carried to a specified amount. Cheseborough v. Home Ins. Co., 61 Mich. 333, 28 N. W. 110.

[122] *Louisiana:* Nicolet v. Insurance Co., 3 La. 366, 23 Am. Dec. 458; Wallace v. Insurance Co., 4 La. 289.

Massachusetts: Commonwealth v. Hide & L. I. Co., 112 Mass. 136, 17 Am. Rep. 72.

New Hampshire: Rix v. Mutual Ins. Co., 20 N. H. 198.

[123] Vance v. Forster, 1 Irish Circ. Cas. 47, 3 Stephens' N. P. 2084.

[124] Brinley v. National Ins. Co., 11 Met. (Mass.) 195.

[125] 2 Greenleaf on Ev., § 407.

certained by the expense of restoring the property, without
any deduction for the difference of value between the old and
new materials; and, on the other hand, an effort was made in
Massachusetts, in a suit on a fire policy, to introduce the analogies of marine insurance; the defendants insisting on deducting from the estimated cost of a new building, the difference
in value between the old and such new building. The property
had been totally destroyed, and a different building had been
erected on the premises. In this case both these rules were rejected; the court saying as to the latter, with great justice,
that it was not supported by any authority or principle. They
also refused to sanction the principle laid down by Mr. Greenleaf, saying that, if it were followed, the assured, in some cases
would recover more than an indemnity, and much more when
the building is dilapidated and out of repairs; that the underwriters are liable only to pay a fair indemnity for the loss; and
that, whatever the rule might be when the building insured is
partially injured by the peril assured against, it has no application to cases like the present, where the building is totally destroyed and to be replaced by a new one; and they proceeded
to say: "If the rule laid down in Vance v. Forster were applied,
the jury must ascertain by the estimates and opinions of witnesses the amount of the expenses of a new building, and they
must estimate the value of the old building, in order to ascertain the difference, if any there be, between the new and the
old. We can perceive no use in requiring this double estimate;
for when the plaintiff is only entitled to recover the amount of
the value of the building destroyed, the estimate of the cost of
a new building is useless. We are, therefore, of opinion that
there is no rule of damages applicable to the present case; and
that, in all cases where no rule of damages is established by law,
the jury are to decide upon the question, and that to their decision there can be no legal exception." And a new trial was
ordered.[126] **

§ 722. Actual value of the property lost.

But this case is not any longer to be considered as expressing
the law, even in Massachusetts. The measure of damages is

[126] Brinley v. National Ins. Co., 11 Met. (Mass.) 195.

now recognized as a question for the court. The general rule is the value of the property at the time of the fire.[127] The amount of the risk is not even *prima facie* evidence of the extent of loss.[128] Where a house is destroyed, the measure of damages is not its cost originally or to rebuild,[129] nor its value if removed, nor the difference in value of the land with and without it, but is the value of the house itself, as it stood on the land just before its destruction. This is to be arrived at by comparing its value with that of a new house of the same size and kind.[130] Evidence of the original cost of the building [131] or of the cost of erecting a similar building at the time [132] of the fire is admissible only as showing its present value, and the income from rentals at the time of the building's destruction may be shown for the same purpose.[133] Where an insured building was destroyed by fire at the order of a board of health on the ground that it was infected, it was held that the loss was recoverable under a fire policy and that the buildings were not valueless because condemned.[134] Where the assured has contracted for the erection of a building upon his land and has secured the same before its completion, recovery is not affected by the fact that the contractor may be compelled to replace the building without expense to the assured.[135] Nor is the measure of damages affected by the fact that, in accordance with a contract between the plaintiff and a third party, the building was soon to be removed, and its value for removal was less.[136] Upon partial loss of a building the measure of damages

[127] Fowler *v.* Old North State Ins. Co., 74 N. C. 89.

[128] Lion F. I. Co. *v.* Starr, 71 Tex. 733.

[129] *Iowa:* Guinn *v.* Phœnix Ins. Co., 80 Ia. 346, 45 N. W. 880.

Pennsylvania: Waynesboro Mut. F. Ins. Co. *v.* Creaton, 98 Pa. 451.

[130] *Colorado:* State Ins. Co. *v.* Taylor, 14 Colo. 499, 24 Pac. 333, 20 Am. St. Rep. 281.

Kentucky: Ætna Ins. Co. *v.* Johnson, 11 Bush, 587, 21 Am. Rep. 223.

[131] Scott *v.* Security F. I. Co., 98 Ia. 67, 66 N. W. 1054.

[132] Holter Lumber Co. *v.* Fireman's F. I. Co., 18 Mont. 282, 45 Pac. 207.

[133] *Colorado:* Atlanta Ins. Co. *v.* Manning, 3 Colo. 224.

Pennsylvania: Cumberland Valley M. P. Co. *v.* Schell, 29 Pa. 31.

[134] Lee Ahlo *v.* Ins. Co., 16 Hawaii, 737.

[135] *New York:* Foley *v.* Manufacturers' & B. I. Co., 152 N. Y. 131, 46 N. E. 318, 43 L. R. A. 664.

Wisconsin: St. Clara Female Academy *v.* Northwestern N. I. Co., 98 Wis. 257, 73 N. W. 767, 67 Am. St. Rep. 805.

[136] Washington M. E. M. Co. *v.* Weymouth & B. M. F. I. Co., 135 Mass. 503.

is the difference between the value of the property whole and damaged.[137] That after the fire the assured sold the premises for the same price at which he had contracted to sell them before the fire does not prevent recovery of the actual amount of damage to the property insured.[138]

The amount of recovery for a total loss of personalty is the value of the property at the time and place of the loss. If the assured is a manufacturer the damages are not limited to the cost of production but are the amount for which he could sell the goods in the market.[139] So where a policy on lumber provides that the liability of the insurer shall not exceed "what it would then cost the insured to replace" the property, an owner of milled lumber can recover the market value of the same and is not restricted to the cost of cutting an equal amount of his own standing timber;[140] an underwriter may always show that the property is worth less than the cost of manufacture.[141] A retail dealer may recover the amount necessary to replace the goods in the wholesale market,[142] and that he obtained them at a considerable discount is immaterial.[143] Nothing can be added to the wholesale value on account of estimated profits.[144] Where a stock of goods was replaced

[137] *Louisiana:* Hoffman *v.* Western M. & F. I. Co., 1 La. Ann. 216.

Tennessee: Burkett *v.* Georgia Home Ins. Co., 105 Tenn. 548, 58 S. W. 848.

Texas: German Ins. Co. *v.* Everett, 18 Tex. Civ. App. 514, 46 S. W. 95.

[138] Tiemann *v.* Citizens' Ins. Co., 76 App. Div. 5, 78 N. Y. Supp. 620.

[139] *Illinois:* Birmingham F. Ins. Co. *v.* Pulver, 126 Ill. 329, 18 N. E. 804, 9 Am. St. Rep. 598.

New York: Hoffman *v.* Ætna Ins. Co., 1 Rob. 489, 501.

North Carolina: Boyd *v.* Royal Ins. Co., 111 N. C. 372, 16 S. E. 289.

Texas: Hartford F. I. Co. *v.* Cannon, 19 Tex. Civ. App. 305, 46 S. W. 851.

Canada: Equitable F. Ins. Co. *v.* Quinn, 11 L. C. Rep. 170.

Contra, Pennsylvania: Standard S.

M. Co. *v.* Royal Ins. Co., 201 Pa. 645, 51 Atl. 354.

[140] Mitchell *v.* St. Paul G. F. I. Co., 92 Mich. 594, 52 N. W. 1017.

But the rule is otherwise where the policy stipulates that the measure of damages "shall in no case exceed the actual cost of producing the lumber destroyed." Chippewa Lumber Co. *v.* Phœnix Ins. Co., 80 Mich. 116, 44 N. W. 1055.

[141] Commonwealth Ins. Co. *v.* Sennett, 37 Pa. 205, 77 Am. Dec. 418 (defective machinery).

[142] Hoffman *v.* Ætna Ins. Co., 1 Rob. (N. Y.) 489.

[143] Chapman *v.* Rockford Ins. Co., 89 Wis. 572, 62 N. W. 422, 28 L. R. A. 405.

[144] Niagara F. I. Co. *v.* Heflin, 60 S. W. 393, 22 Ky. L. Rep. 1212.

within thirty days after the loss, the cost of replacing them was held to fix the amount of recovery.[145] The price at which the owner of personalty offered to sell it shortly before the fire is evidence of its value,[146] but a contract by the assured for the future delivery of like property is irrelevant.[147] If there is no market at the place of the loss, the value of the property at the nearest market with proper addition or deduction for freight is to be taken.[148] The owner of household furniture or clothing recovers its usable value to himself and not merely its value to a secondhand dealer, though no sentimental value can be taken into account.[149] What the property brought at auction after the loss is evidence of its then value.[150] Where, by the terms of a policy of insurance upon goods contained in the public stores, the underwriters agreed to make good to the assured, all such loss as should happen to the goods by fire, "to be estimated according to the true and actual cash value of the property at the time the loss should happen," the measure of damages was such value, notwithstanding the duties upon the goods had not been paid or secured.[151] So where a distiller is liable for the tax on whiskey destroyed in bond, the measure of damages is the value including the tax.[152]

The measure of damages is not, however, always or necessarily equal to the market value of the property. "The contract of the insurer is not that, if the property is burned, he will pay its market value; but that he will indemnify the assured, that is, save him harmless, or put him in as good a condition, so far as practicable, as he would have been in if no fire had oc-

---

[145] Plow Co. v. Ins. Co. (Tex. Civ. App.), 87 S. W. 192.

[146] Joy v. Security Ins. Co., 83 Ia. 12, 48 N. W. 1049.

But cf. De Groat v. Fulton, etc., Ins. Co., 4 Rob. 504.

[147] Western Assur. Co. v. Studebaker Bros. Manuf. Co., 124 Ind. 176, 23 N. E. 1138.

[148] Grubbs v. N. S. Home Ins. Co., 108 N. C. 472, 13 S. E. 236.

[149] Sun Fire Office v. Ayerst, 37 Neb. 184, 55 N. W. 635.

[150] Massachusetts: Clement v. British Assur. Co., 141 Mass. 298, 5 N. E. 847.

New York: Henderson v. Western M. & F. Ins. Co., 10 Rob. 164, 43 Am, Dec. 176.

But see United States: Reading Ins. Co. v. Egelhoff, 115 Fed. 393.

Iowa: Lewis v. Burlington Ins. Co., 80 Ia. 259, 45 N. W. 749.

[151] Kentucky: Queen Ins. Co. v. McCoin, 105 Ky. 806, 49 S. W. 800.

New York: Wolfe v. Howard Ins. Co., 7 N. Y. 583.

[152] Hedger v. Union Ins. Co., 17 Fed. 498.

curred."[153]   If the policy provides for an appraisement of the loss by arbitrators or the parties agree to arbitration, the award is binding upon both parties in the absence of fraud.[154]

A statement in the proofs of loss does not prevent recovery of a greater sum than there claimed.[155]   After a partial loss has been paid recovery for a total loss occurring thereafter is limited to the amount of the policy less the amount paid on the prior loss.[156]

§ 722a. Valued policies.

Though the practice of valuation is not common in fire policies, whenever the subject-matter of the insurance is valued the analogies of marine policies would seem applicable.   The agreed valuation is binding in the absence of fraud [157] and partial losses should be adjusted on that basis.   The words "valued at" or "worth" or some equivalent expression are necessary to constitute a valuation: the mere insurance of specified sums on specified property is not such.[158]

In several jurisdictions statutes have been enacted whereby the sum insured is taken as conclusive of the value of the property at the time of the loss and the measure of recovery for a total loss thereof.[159]   Such statutes are usually confined to in-

[153] Morton, C. J., in Washington M. E. M. Co. *v.* Weymouth & B. M. F. I. Co., 135 Mass. 503, 506.

[154] *Pennsylvania:* Snowden *v.* Kittanning Ins. Co., 122 Pa. 502, 16 Atl. 22, 9 Am. St. Rep. 124.

Canada: Heron *v.* Hartford Ins. Co., 4 Montreal Super. Ct. 388.

[155] *Iowa:* Crittenden *v.* Springfield F. & M. Ins. Co., 85 Ia. 652, 62 N. W. 548, 39 Am. St. Rep. 321.

Michigan: Sibley *v.* Prescott Ins. Co., 57 Mich. 14, 23 N. W. 473.

[156] Mechanics' Ins. Co. *v.* Hodge, 46 Ill. App. 479.

[157] *Maine:* Cushman *v.* Northwestern Ins. Co., 34 Me. 487.

New York: Buffalo Elevating Co. *v.* Prussian Nat. Ins. Co., 64 App. Div. 182, 71 N. Y. Supp. 918.

[158] Wallace *v.* Insurance Co., 4 La. 289.

[159] *Arkansas:* Rev. St., § 4375.

Delaware: Laws of Del., chap. 695, Vol. 18.

Florida: Gen. St. (1906), § 2776.

Kansas: Gen. St. (1905), § 3538.

Kentucky: Ky. St., § 700.

Louisiana: Rev. St., Act 135 (1900), §§ 1-2.

Minnesota: Rev. Laws (1905), § 1642.

Mississippi: Code of 1906, § 2592.

Missouri: Rev. St., § 7969.

Nebraska: Comp. St. (1907), chap. 43, § 43.

New Hampshire: Pub. St., chap. 170, § 5.

Ohio: Rev. St., § 3643.

Oklahoma: Gen. St. (1908), § 3356.

South Carolina: Civil Code, § 1815.

South Dakota: Civil Code (1903), § 1953.

Texas: Civil St., Art. 3089.

West Virginia: Code (1906), § 1108.

surance upon realty [160] and are not applicable save in case of total loss. Clauses in a policy limiting liability to a fraction of the cash value of the property, or to such proportion of the value as the sum insured bears to the total insurance, provisions for arbitration of the amount of loss, or giving the underwriter an election to rebuild are generally held invalid as inconsistent with these statutes. A building is a total loss within the meaning of such acts when it has lost its identity as such, though there are portions of the walls remaining and capable of being used in rebuilding.[161] Where there are several concurrent policies with the consent of the underwriters the aggregate of all the policies is taken as the value of the property and the several amounts named are recoverable.[162]

§ 723. Election of insurer to rebuild—Alternative contract.

It is a frequent provision in fire policies, that in case of loss the insurers, instead of paying it in money, may rebuild or repair the premises, on giving notice to the insured of their election to do so. The policy is in this respect an alternative contract, and the exercise of the election, by giving the notice, converts the contract of insurance into a building contract; and in case the rebuilding is thereupon begun and discontinued by the insurance company, the rule of damages is no longer the amount insured, but that necessary to complete the rebuilding. And where several companies have given the notice, and the contract thus substituted is broken by all, the insured can recover

---

Wisconsin: Rev. St., § 1943.

See, also, *Iowa:* Code of 1897, § 1742.

[160] A house built on a leased lot with privilege of removal was held to be realty within the meaning of the statute. Orient Ins. Co. *v.* Parlin Orendorff Co., 14 Tex. Civ. App. 512, 38 S. W. 60.

[161] *California:* Williams *v.* Hartford Ins. Co., 54 Cal. 442, 450, 35 Am. Rep. 77.

Kentucky: Palatine Ins. Co. *v.* Weiss, 59 S. W. 509, 22 Ky. L. Rep. 994.

Missouri: Stevens *v.* Ins. Co., 120 Mo. App. 88. 96 S. W. 684.

Texas: Murphy *v.* American C. I. Co., 25 Tex. Civ. App. 241, 54 S. W. 407.

Wisconsin: Linder *v.* St. Paul F. & M. I. Co., 93 Wis. 526, 67 N. W. 1125.

Contra, Minnesota: Northwestern M. L. I. Co. *v.* Rochester G. I. Co., 85 Minn. 48, 88 N. W. 265, 56 L. R. A. 108, 89 Am. St. Rep. 534.

[162] *Iowa:* Wensel *v.* Ins. Assoc., 129 Ia. 295, 105 N. W. 522.

Missouri: Barnard *v.* National F. I. Co., 38 Mo. App. 107, 117.

Wisconsin: Oshkosh Gas Light Co. *v.* Germania F. I. Co., 71 Wis. 454, 5 Am. St. Rep. 233.

against any one of them the whole cost of completing the restoration of the building, leaving the company against whom the judgment is recovered to obtain contribution from the others.[163] Where the company elects to rebuild, and after waiting some time refuses to do so, the insured may recover under the policy what it would have cost the company to rebuild at the date of refusal, together with damages for injury to the property through the exposure.[164] But it has been held that if he so desires the assured may in such a case treat the election of the underwriter as no longer binding and may sue on the original contract for money indemnity.[165] Rent of the land during the period of the delay was also allowed in an Illinois case.[166] This rule seems questionable in that it loses sight of the fact that the contract, by the election of the company, has become a contract to rebuild. If the repairs are made in good faith, but do not make the building equal in value to the original structure, the difference in value between the building before loss and as repaired is the measure of damages.[167] Upon a partial loss the insurer elected to reinstate; but the public authorities condemned the building for causes apart from those insured against and removed it. The insurer, notwithstanding the action of the authorities, was held bound to reinstate, which in this case practically compelled them to pay for a total loss.[168] Where building inspectors refused to allow the erection of a frame building the underwriter was held bound to rebuild with brick.[169] If during the running of the policy and before complete reinstatement of a partial loss, a second fire destroys the

[163] Morrell v. Irving F. I. Co., 33 N. Y. 429, 88 Am. Dec. 396.

[164] American C. I. Co. v. McLanathan, 11 Kan. 533.

[165] Langan v. Ætna Ins. Co., 99 Fed. 374.

[166] Home M. F. I. Co. v. Garfield, 60 Ill. 124, 14 Am. Rep. 27.

[167] United States: Hartford F. I. Co. v. Peebles Hotel Co., 82 Fed. 546. *Massachusetts:* Parker v. Eagle F. I. Co., 9 Gray, 152.

Where the building collapsed owing to defective rebuilding and the tenant of the insured was obliged to discontinue occupancy, the assured was allowed to recover the value of the lost term. Henderson v. Sun M. I. Co., 48 La. Ann. 1031, 20 So. 164, 55 Am. St. Rep. 292.

[168] Brown v. Royal Ins. Co., 1 E. & E. 853. It would seem that the company would be called upon to pay the whole value of the building, even if it were greater than the risk; for having elected to reinstate, the owner became entitled to a building equal in value to the one destroyed.

[169] Fire Assoc. v. Rosenthal, 108 Pa. 474, 1 Atl. 303.

entire property, the insurer is not entitled to credit for the amount already expended but must make good the whole of the second loss up to the amount insured.[170] Where there is no clause in the policy giving the insurer the right to rebuild, no such right exists.[171]

§ 723a. Proximate cause.

A policy against fire covers only such damage as is caused by a hostile or unintended fire.[172] Where such a fire causes the loss there may be recovery for all ensuing damage irrespective of intervening acts of human agents. Thus where a wooden building is injured by fire and a city ordinance prevents its repair it is deemed a total loss,[173] or if the cost of repairs is increased by reason of such an ordinance the increased cost is recoverable.[174] So too where a building is blown up to prevent the spread of a conflagration there may be recovery whether the act was legal or illegal.[175] The insurer is liable for all losses arising out of *bona fide* efforts to extinguish the fire or save the insured property therefrom, such as damage by water,[176] expense of packing goods preparatory to removal from a threatened building,[177] or damage sustained during such

[170] Smith v. Colonial Mut. F. Ins. Co., 6 Vict. L. R. 200.

[171] Wallace v. Insurance Co., 4 La. 289.

[172] *Massachusetts:* Way v. Abington Mut. F. Ins. Co., 166 Mass. 67, 43 N. E. 1032, 32 L. R. A. 608, 55 Am. St. Rep. 379.

England: Austin v. Drewe, 6 Taunt. 436.

[173] *Louisiana:* Monteleone v. Royal Ins. Co., 47 La. Ann. 1563, 18 So. 472.

Michigan: Brady v. North Western Ins. Co., 11 Mich. 425.

Minnesota: Larkin v. Glen Falls Ins. Co., 80 Minn. 527, 83 N. W. 409.

Missouri: O'Keefe v. Liverpool, etc., Ins. Co., 140 Mo. 558, 41 S. W. 922, 39 L. R. A. 819, 62 Am. St. Rep. 742.

[174] *Massachusetts:* Hewins v. London Assur. Co., 184 Mass. 177, 68 N. E. 62.

Pennsylvania: Pennsylvania L. Co. v. Phila. Contributionship, 201 Pa. 497, 51 Atl. 351.

[175] *New York:* City F. Ins. Co. v. Corlies, 21 Wend. 367, 34 Am. Dec. 258.

Pennsylvania: Greenwald v. Ins. Co., 3 Phila. 323, 7 Am. L. Reg. 282.

[176] *Louisiana:* Geisek v. Crescent M. I. Co., 19 La. Ann. 297.

Massachusetts: Lewis v. Springfield F. & M. I. Co., 10 Gray, 159.

Michigan: John Davis & Co. v. Insurance Co. of N. America, 115 Mich. 382, 73 N. W. 393.

Missouri: Cohn v. National F. I. Co., 96 Mo. App. 315, 70 S. W. 259.

North Carolina: Whitehurst v. Fayetteville M. I. Co., 51 N. C. (6 Jones) 352.

[177] Ins. Co. v. Leader, 121 Ga. 260, 48 S. E. 972.

removal [178] including loss by theft.[179] Where a fire caused a short circuit of an electric current, the damage to machinery of which the electricity was the immediate cause was held recoverable.[180] Damage from falling walls which had been weakened by fire but did not fall for several days thereafter has been held to be covered by a fire policy.[181]

§ 724. Consequential loss.

The damages for delay in payment are confined to interest on the amount from the time payment is due under the policy. Thus where there is a provision for payment within a stipulated time after proof of loss, interest is recoverable from the date set.[182] If the policy does not fix the date of payment, interest is recoverable from the date of demand and refusal.[183] Where it does not appear that there was a demand and wrongful refusal before action brought, interest should be allowed only from the filing of the writ,[184] but where the insurer waives proofs of loss and repudiates all liability interest is computed from the time of the loss.[185] When the delay in payment is due to fault

---

[178] *District of Columbia:* Holtzman v. Franklin Ins. Co., 12 Fed. Cas. No. 6,649, 4 Cranch C. C. 295.

Georgia: Case v. Hartford Fire Ins. Co., 13 Ill. 676.

Maine: White v. Republic F. I. Co., 57 Me. 91, 2 Am. Rep. 22.

Oklahoma: Farmers' & M. I. Co. v. Cuff, 116 Pac. 435.

[179] *Kentucky:* Leiber v. Liverpool Ins. Co., 6 Bush, 639, 99 Am. Dec. 695.

Louisiana: Talamon v. Home M. I. Co., 16 La. Ann. 426.

New York: Tilton v. Hamilton F. I. Co., 14 How. Pr. 363.

Oklahoma: Farmers' & M. I. Co. v. Cuff, 116 Pac. 435.

Pennsylvania: Independent M. I. Co. v. Agnew, 34 Pa. 96, 75 Am. Dec. 638.

[180] Lynn G. & E. Co. v. Meriden F. I. Co., 158 Mass. 570, 33 N. E. 690, 20 L. R. A. 297, 35 Am. St. Rep. 540.

[181] Russell v. Ins. Co., 100 Minn. 528, 111 N. W. 400.

But see Cuesta v. Royal Ins. Co., 98 Ga. 720, 27 S. E. 172.

[182] *Florida:* Hanover F. I. Co. v. Lewis, 27 Fla. 219, 10 So. 297.

Illinois: Knickerbocker Ins. Co. v. Gould, 80 Ill. 388.

Iowa: Wensel v. Ins. Assoc., 129 Ia. 295, 105 N. W. 522.

Kentucky: Home Ins. Co. v. Patterson, 12 Ky. L. Rep. 941.

Montana: Randall v. American F. I. Co., 10 Mont. 340, 25 Pac. 953, 24 Am. St. Rep. 50.

New York: Schmitt v. Boston Ins. Co., 82 App. Div. 234, 81 N. Y. Supp. 767.

[183] Baltimore F. I. Co. v. Loney, 20 Md. 20.

[184] Thwing v. Great Western Ins. Co., 111 Mass. 93.

[185] *Nebraska:* Hartford F. I. Co. v. Landfare, 63 Neb. 559, 88 N. W. 779.

Washington: Glover v. Rochester G. I. Co., 11 Wash. 143, 39 Pac. 38.

of the assured, these rules do not apply,[186] nor is the insurer liable for interest when the proceeds of the policy have been subjected to trustee process.[187]

The contract of insurance does not permit recovery for loss suffered by interruption of business, loss of possible profits or of rents during the period of rebuilding unless especially stipulated for in the policy.[188] In a peculiar case in New York the defendant insured from loss by fire the plaintiff's royalties, accruing under an exclusive license to use the plaintiff's patent for refining oil. The manufactory of the licensee was destroyed by fire. The measure of recovery was held to be the loss of royalties caused by loss of use of the works during rebuilding, not merely the loss of royalties on the oil destroyed.[189]

§ 725. Recovery by owner of a limited interest.

Any person having any legal interest in property may insure it for the benefit of all concerned and recover the whole loss up to the amount of insurance, holding the balance (if any) above his own interest for the benefit of the equitable or legal owner of it. A bailee—for instance, a consignee or commission agent— may insure and recover the whole value, holding the balance over his own interest for the owner.[190] A fire policy on goods described generally as "the property of the insured or held by him in trust," covers cloth of other parties left with him to be made into clothing, and extends to the whole value of such goods. It is not limited to the bailees' interest or lien for

---

[186] *Louisiana:* Gettwerth v. Teutonia Ins. Co., 29 La. Ann. 30.

Minnesota: Schrepfer v. Rockford Ins. Co., 77 Minn. 291, 79 N. W. 1005.

Oregon: Stemmer v. Scottish Ins. Co., 33 Ore. 65, 49 Pac. 588.

[187] *New Hampshire:* Swamscot Mach. Co. v. Partridge, 25 N. H. 369.

Vermont: Platt v. Continental Ins. Co., 62 Vt. 166, 19 Atl. 637.

[188] *Louisiana:* Pontalba v. Phœnix Ass. Co., 2 Rob. 131, 38 Am. Dec. 205.

Massachusetts: Hewins v. London Assur. Corp., 184 Mass. 177, 68 N. E. 62.

Pennsylvania: Farmers' Mut. Ins. Co. v. New Holland Turnpike Co., 122 Pa. 37.

England: In the Matter of Wright and Pole, 1 A. & E. 621.

[189] Natural F. O. Co. v. Citizens' Ins. Co., 106 N. Y. 535, 60 Am. Rep. 473.

[190] *United States:* Home Ins. Co. v. Baltimore Warehouse Co., 93 U. S. 527, 23 L. ed. 868.

Maryland: Hough v. People's F. I. Co., 36 Md. 398.

New York: De Forest v. Fulton F. I. Co., 1 Hall, 84.

charges.[191] Warehousemen and wharfingers with whom goods are deposited have an insurable interest in such goods, although no previous authority to insure has been given by the real owners, nor any notice given to them of such insurance, and the insured are entitled in such a case to recover from the insurance office the full value of the goods destroyed by fire. They are, of course, liable to account to the true owners for the excess of the money received beyond the amount of their own charges in respect of such goods.[192]

A mortgagor who insures recovers the whole amount of loss,[193] and so does the mortgagee who insures in connection with the mortgagor.[194] But where the mortgagee insures without the privity of the mortgagor, he is by the better opinion restricted to the amount of the loan unpaid at the time of loss;[195] though in some jurisdictions he is allowed to recover the whole value of the property.[196] He is generally required to surrender his mortgage to the insurer.[197] If, after the destruction of the property, the mortgagee has foreclosed the mortgage, it has been said that he can recover only such an amount, besides what he got on the foreclosure sale, as would indemnify

[191] Stillwell v. Staples, 19 N. Y. 401. Contra, Parks v. General Interest Assur. Co., 5 Pick. (Mass.) 34.

[192] Waters v. Monarch Ins. Co., 5 E. & B. 870.

[193] United States: Carpenter v. Providence W. I. Co., 16 Pet. 495, 10 L. ed. 1044 (semble).
Massachusetts: Strong v. Manufacturers' Ins. Co., 10 Pick. 40, 20 Am. Dec. 507.

[194] Kernochan v. New York B. F. I. Co., 17 N. Y. 428.

[195] United States: Carpenter v. Providence W. I. Co., 16 Pet. 495, 10 L. ed. 1044.
Maryland: Hanover F. I. Co. v. Brown, 77 Md. 64, 25 Atl. 989, 27 Atl. 314, 39 Am. St. Rep. 386.
Massachusetts: Haley v. Mfg. F. & M. I. Co., 120 Mass. 292.
Missouri: Convis v. Citizens' M. F. I. Co., 18 Mo. 262, 59 Am. Dec. 299.

New Jersey: Sussex Ins. Co. v. Woodruff, 26 N. J. L. 541.
Washington: Herzog v. Ins. Co., 36 Wash. 611, 79 Pac. 287.

[196] Illinois: Honore v. Lamar F. I. Co., 51 Ill. 409.
Maine: Concord U. M. F. I. Co. v. Woodbury, 45 Me. 447; Biddeford Savings Bank v. Dwelling House Ins. Co., 81 Me. 566, 18 Atl. 298.
Massachusetts: King v. State M. F. I. Co., 7 Cush. 1, 54 Am. Dec. 683.

[197] United States: Carpenter v. Providence W. I. Co., 16 Pet. 495, 10 L. ed. 495.
Illinois: Honore v. Lamar F. I. Co., 51 Ill. 409.
New Jersey: Sussex Ins. Co. v. Woodruff, 26 N. J. L. 541.
Contra, Massachusetts: King v. State M. F. I. Co., 7 Cush. 1, 54 Am. Dec. 683.

him.[198] So too a deduction was made where the property was sold after the fire and the proceeds applied to the mortgage debt.[199] Where a mortgagee insures property, his recovery is not affected by the fact that the mortgagor has repaired the premises,[200] or that there still remains adequate security for the debt.[201] The assignee of a mortgagee may recover the full damage to the property not exceeding the mortgage debt or the amount of the policy irrespective of the amount paid for the assignment.[202]

Levy of execution does not prevent recovery by the execution debtor for the full damage to the property insured so long as he retains an equity of redemption therein.[203]

Inasmuch as the interest of an unpaid vendor of realty is precisely measurable, recovery on a fire policy covering such an interest should be limited to the amount of the unpaid purchase money,[204] but in many instances the full value of the property not exceeding the amount of the policy has been awarded, the vendor holding the surplus above his own interest for the vendee.[205] The conditional vendor of personalty has also been allowed to recover the full amount of the policy not exceeding the value of the property though in excess of the unpaid purchase money.[206] Where the vendee is still liable for the price such a holding seems erroneous. An assured vendor of realty who has conveyed the premises but is seeking to set aside the deed for fraud cannot recover the value of the building or of possession in the absence of a writ for possession.[207] A vendee

[198] Hadley v. Insurance Co., 55 N. H. 110.

[199] Harris v. Gaspee F. & M. Co., 9 R. I. 207.

[200] Foster v. Equitable Ins. Co., 2 Gray (Mass.), 216.

[201] *New York:* Kent v. Ætna Ins. Co., 84 App. Div. 428, 82 N. Y. Supp. 817; Uhfelder v. Ins. Co., 44 Misc. 153, 89 N. Y. Supp. 792.

Pennsylvania: Rex v. Merchants' Ins. Co., 2 Phila. 357.

[202] Excelsior F. I. Co. v. Royal Ins. Co., 55 N. Y. 343, 14 Am. Rep. 271.

[203] Clark v. New England M. F. I. Co., 6 Cush. (Mass.) 342, 53 Am. Dec. 441.

[204] Shotwell v. Jefferson Ins. Co., 5 Bosw. (N. Y.) 247.

[205] *Maine:* Grant v. Elliot M. F. I. Co., 76 Me. 514.

Pennsylvania: Insurance Co. v. Updegraff, 21 Pa. 51, 59 Am. Dec. 749.

England: Collingridge v. Royal Exchange Assur. Corp., 3 Q. B. D. 173.

[206] *Massachusetts:* Boston, etc., Ice Co. v. Royal Ins. Co., 12 Allen, 381, 90 Am. Dec. 151.

Pennsylvania: Burson v. Fire Assoc., 136 Pa. 267, 20 Atl. 401, 20 Am. St. Rep. 919.

[207] Monroe v. Southern M. I. Co., 63 Ga. 669.

who has entered into possession but has not yet received a conveyance or paid the whole of the purchase price may recover the full value of the building to the extent of the sum insured.[208] A reversioner who has given to the lessee an option to purchase is entitled to the full value of the property at the time of the fire.[209] Where a lessee is bound to restore the premises in their original condition at the expiration of the term,[210] or where the lessee has erected buildings upon the demised premises with privilege of removal, the amount of recovery is the actual cash value of the property as it stood before the fire, but not merely the value of the buildings for purposes of removal.[211] Otherwise, however, the insurable interest of a lessee for years is the value of his lease, and that is the measure of his recovery[212] unless the policy is so issued as to cover the interests of both lessor and lessee.[213] As to the measure of damages upon a policy issued to a life tenant the authorities are in conflict. The true rule seems to be the full amount of the damage to the premises not exceeding the amount of the policy,[214] for the interest of a life tenant is not accurately measurable and those cases which award damages upon the basis of the assured's expectancy of life[215] do not guarantee complete indemnity.

Recovery by a part owner or tenant in common should be

[208] Ætna Ins. Co. v. Tyler, 16 Wend. (N. Y.) 385, 30 Am. Dec. 90.

[209] Planters' M. I. Co. v. Rowland, 66 Md. 236.

[210] Imperial F. I. Co. v. Murray, 73 Pa. 13.

[211] New York: Laurent v. Chatham Ins. Co., 1 Hall, 41.

Ohio: Merchants' Ins. Co. v. Frick, 2 Am. L. Rec. 336.

See United States: Washington Mills M. Co. v. Commercial F. I. Co., 13 Fed. 646.

Massachusetts: Washington Mills E. M. Co. v. Weymouth & B. I. Co., 135 Mass. 503.

[212] Niblo v. North American F. I. Co., 1 Sandf. (N. Y.) 551.

[213] Home Ins. Co. v. Gibson, 72 Miss. 58, 17 So. 13, 48 Am. St. Rep. 535.

[214] Illinois: Andes Ins. Co. v. Fish, 71 Ill. 620.

Iowa: Merrett v. Farmers' Ins. Co., 42 Ia. 11.

Pennsylvania: Welsh v. London Assur. Corp., 151 Pa. 607, 25 Atl. 142, 31 Am. St. Rep. 786.

Canada: Caldwell v. Stadacona F. & L. I. Co., 11 Can. 212.

[215] Kentucky: Agricultural Ins. Co. v. Yates, 10 Ky. L. Rep. 984; Hartford Ins. Co. v. Haas, 87 Ky. 531, 9 S. W. 720, 10 Ky. L. Rep. 573, 2 L. R. A. 64.

New York: Beekman v. Fulton Counties Farmers' Mut. F. Ins. Assoc., 66 App. Div. 72, 73 N. Y. Supp. 110.

See also Massachusetts: Doyle v. American F. Ins. Co., 181 Mass. 139, 145, 63 N. E. 394 (recovery by tenant by courtesy initiate estimated accord-

limited by the value of his interest unless the policy is for the benefit of all concerned.[216] A carrier who is liable to the owner may recover the full value of the property insured.[217]

§ 726. Clauses limiting liability.

Unless the policy contains provisions to the contrary the insured under a fire policy may recover from any underwriter the full amount of damage to the property up to the amount of the insurance.[218] Frequently, however, recovery is expressly limited to a definite fraction of the cash value of the property, or to such proportion of the loss as the sum underwritten bears to the whole amount of insurance upon the property. Apart from statutes these conditions are valid. Where by law or by the terms of the policy only a certain proportion of the total value of property is to be insured, that proportion is to be determined by the value at the time of the loss, and not by the value stated in the policy.[219] Clauses providing for a pro-rating of the loss among the various insurers apply only to insurance in force at the time of the loss [220] and covering the same interest in the same property.[221] Thus policies taken out by mortgagee and mortgagor do not constitute double insurance,[222] but where a policy is taken by a warehouseman upon goods "his own or held in trust" and the owner also insures, the loss must be apportioned between the two companies.[223] Occasionally a policy

ing to the life expectancies of both the assured and his wife).

[216] Curry v. Commonwealth Ins. Co., 10 Pick. 535, 20 Am. Dec. 547; Clement v. British-America Assur. Co., 141 Mass. 298, 5 N. E. 847.

[217] Western, etc., Pipe Lines v. Home Ins. Co., 145 Pa. 346, 22 Atl. 665, 27 Am. Rep. 703.

[218] *Kentucky:* London, etc., F. Ins. Co. v. Turnbull, 86 Ky. 230, 5 S. W. 542, 9 Ky. L. Rep. 544.
Missouri: Clem v. German Ins. Co., 36 Mo. App. 560.

[219] *Massachusetts:* Post v. Hampshire M. F. I. Co., 12 Met. 555, 46 Am. Dec. 702. (But see Ellis v. Albany City Ins. Co., 4 Met. 206; Phillips v. Merrimack Mut. F. Ins. Co., 10 Cush. 350.)

New Hampshire: Atwood v. Union M. F. I. Co., 28 N. H. 234; Huckins v. People's M. F. I. Co., 31 N. H. 238.

[220] Hoffman v. Insurance Co., 88 Tenn. 735, 14 S. W. 72.

[221] Traders' Ins. Co. v. Pacaud, 150 Ill. 245, 37 N. E. 460, 41 Am. St. Rep. 355.

[222] *Illinois:* Niagara F. I. Co. v. Scammon, 144 Ill. 490, 28 N. E. 919.
Kentucky: Home Ins. Co. v. Koob, 113 Ky. 360, 68 S. W. 453, 24 Ky. L. Rep. 223, 101 Am. St. Rep. 354, 58 L. R. A. 58.
New Hampshire: Tuck v. Hartford F. Ins. Co., 56 N. H. 326.

[223] Home Ins. Co. v. Baltimore Warehouse Co., 93 U. S. 527, 23 L. ed. 868; Robbins v. Firemen's Fund Ins. Co., 20

may contain a clause of double limitation. Thus under a policy of fire insurance for $2,000, on property insured elsewhere for $3,000, which contained the following provisions: "When property is insured by this company solely, three-fourths only of the value will be taken; and in cases of loss this company will be liable to pay three-fourths only of the value at the time of the loss, but in no case more than is insured by this company. In case of loss or damage of property on which authorized double insurance subsists, this company shall be liable to pay only such proportion thereof as the sum insured by this company bears to the whole amount insured thereon, such amount not to exceed three-fourths of the actual value of the property at the time of the loss," the plaintiff was held, by the Supreme Court of Massachusetts, entitled to recover only two-fifths of three-fourths of the loss.[224] Many interesting cases have arisen as to the apportionment of losses on property covered by both specific and blanket policies, the latter also including other property, but an analysis of these authorities is beyond the scope of the present work.[225]

Where a single policy insures several different classes of property for separate amounts indemnity for any class is limited to the fund assigned to it and an excessive loss on one class cannot be made up out of another.[226]

§ 727. Breach of contract to issue policy.

A contract to execute a fire policy is a proper subject for

Fed. Cas. No. 11,881, 16 Blatchf. 122.

[224] Haley v. Dorchester M. & F. I. Co., 12 Gray (Mass.), 545.

[225] See the following cases:

United States: Page v. Sun Ins. Office, 74 Fed. 203, 20 C. C. A. 397, 33 L. R. A. 249.

Connecticut: Schmaelzle v. London, etc., F. Ins. Co., 75 Conn. 397, 53 Atl. 763, 96 Am. St. Rep. 233, 60 L. R. A. 536.

Iowa: Erb v. Fidelity Ins. Co., 99 Ia. 727, 69 N. W. 261; Lesure Lumber Co. v. Mutual F, I. Co., 101 Ia. 514, 70 N. W. 761.

New York: Mayer v. American Ins. Co., 2 N. Y. Supp. 227; Ogden v. East River Ins. Co., 50 N. Y. 388, 10 Am. Rep. 492.

Canada: Toronto First Unitarian Congregation v. Western Assur. Co., 26 U. C. Q. B. 175.

[226] *United States:* Carlwitz v. Germania F. Ins. Co., 5 Fed. Cas. No. 2,415a.

Alabama: Home Ins. Co. v. Adler, 71 Ala. 516.

Kentucky: Ætna Ins. Co. v. Glasgow E. L. Co., 107 Ky. 77, 52 S. W. 975, 21 Ky. L. Rep. 726.

specific performance and when a loss has occurred before the filing of the bill, equity, in order to avoid multiplicity of suits, will decree the payment of the same damages as would be recoverable at law.[227] It has also been held that in a suit at law for refusal to issue a policy, the measure of damages after a fire is the same amount as would have been recovered had the policy been issued.[228]

§ 728. Reinsurance.

An insurer frequently finds it advisable to secure protection from loss by reinsuring in another insurance company. The insurer still remains liable upon the original contract, but is indemnified against loss by the reinsurer. Upon a loss happening, the original insurer, upon a principle that will be discussed in a later chapter, may at once sue the reinsurer and recover the amount of the loss, without first having paid it.[229] It has been held that this may be done even if the insurer is insolvent and unable to pay the claim [230] or has paid but a small portion of the amount of the judgment.[231] But if the insurer has adjusted the loss without suit, he can recover no more than the amount he has paid.[232] Upon claim being brought against the insurer, notice may be given to the reinsurer, whose duty it then becomes either to contest the claim or to adjust it.[233] In a case of this sort [234] Story, J., said:

"If notice of a suit, threatened or pending, upon the original

[227] *United States:* Tayloe *v.* Merchants' Ins. Co., 9 How. 390, 13 L. ed. 187.

Kentucky: Security Ins. Co. *v.* Kentucky Ins. Co., 7 Bush, 81, 3 Am. Rep. 301.

Maryland: Phœnix Ins. Co. *v.* Ryland, 69 Md. 437, 16 Atl. 109.

[228] *New York:* Post *v.* Ætna Ins. Co., 43 Barb. 357; Angell *v.* Hartford F. I. Co., 59 N. Y. 171, 17 Am. Rep. 322.

Wisconsin: Campbell *v.* American F. I. Co., 73 Wis. 100, 40 N. W. 661.

See *ante*, § 623.

[229] *Indiana:* Eagle Insurance Co. *v.* Lafayette Insurance Co., 9 Ind. 443.

Missouri: Gantt *v.* American Central Ins. Co., 68 Mo. 503, 30 Am. Rep. 802.

New York: Blackstone *v.* Alemannia F. I. Co., 56 N. Y. 104. See chap. xxxvi.

[230] *Missouri:* Strong *v.* American Cent. Ins. Co., 4 Mo. App. 7.

New York: Hone *v.* Mutual Safety Ins. Co., 1 Sandf. 137.

[231] Consolidated Ins. Co. *v.* Cashow, 41 Md. 59.

[232] Illinois Mut. F. I. Co. *v.* Andes Insurance Co., 67 Ill. 362, 16 Am. Rep. 620.

[233] New York C. I. Co. *v.* National Protection I. Co., 20 Barb. (N. Y.) 468.

[234] N. Y. State Marine Ins. Co. *v.* Protection Ins. Co., 1 Story, 458, 462.

policy, be given to the reassurers, they have a fair opportunity
to exercise an election whether to contest or admit the claim.
It is their duty to act upon such notice, when given, within a
reasonable time. If they do not disapprove of the contestation
of the suit, or authorize the party reassured to compromise or
settle it, they must be deemed to require that it should be carried on; and then, by just implication, they are held to indemnify the party reassured against the costs and expenses necessarily and reasonably incurred in defending the suit.

"If they decline to interfere at all, or are silent, they have no
right afterwards to insist that the costs and expenses of the
suit ought not to be borne by them, as they are exclusively
under such circumstances incurred for the benefit of the reassurers, and are indispensable for the protection of the party
reassured."

The Supreme Court of Missouri, after quoting this language
with approval, added: [235]

"Such defence when made in good faith, for the protection of
the reinsurers, will render any judgment obtained by the original assured in such suit, binding upon the reinsurers, as to all
matters which could have been litigated therein, and make
them liable also for the costs and expenses of the litigation. It
necessarily follows that in all cases where the reinsurers fail,
after notice, to participate in the defence, the original insurer,
by operation of law, becomes *sub modo* their agent for the management of such defence, and in the conduct thereof is bound
to exercise the utmost good faith: and any judgment against
him, collusively obtained, would not support a recovery over
against the reinsurers."

If the original insurer fails to notify the reinsuring company
of an action by the assured it cannot recover the expenses of
successfully defending the same.[236]

III.—LIFE INSURANCE

§ 729. Life insurance not a contract of indemnity.

* Contracts of assurance on lives form another very impor-

[235] Gantt *v.* American Central Ins.
Co., 68 Mo. 503, 535, 30 Am. Rep. 802,
per Hough, J.

[236] Faneuil Hall Ins. Co. *v.* Liverpool
Ins. Co., 153 Mass. 63, 26 N. E. 244, 10
L. R. A. 423, 25 Am. St. Rep. 611.

96

tant division of this branch of our subject. Where the policy was taken out on the life of a third person, it was originally said that, like marine and fire policies, it was a mere contract of indemnity; [237] that if not damnified, the plaintiff could not recover; and so, where the creditors of Mr. Pitt had effected an insurance on his life, and their debts had been subsequently paid, it was held that they could not recover. [238] But this case has been overruled; and it has been decided that a contract of life assurance is a mere contract to pay a certain sum of money upon the death of a person, in consideration of the payment of certain premiums; that it is not a contract of indemnity; [239] and that the termination of a creditor's interest before the death does not defeat the recovery. [240] ** So too where husband and wife took a policy on their joint lives payable to the survivor, the wife was allowed to recover though the death of the husband occurred after a divorce. [241] It must be remembered, however, that the modern doctrine is anomalous and that life insurance still so retains its character as a contract of indemnity as to require an insurable interest at the time of the issuance of the policy.

Since the value of a life is not calculable in terms of money, a policy on life is deemed valued and the sum insured is the measure of damages. [242] But as the interest of a creditor in the life of his debtor is accurately measurable it would seem that his recovery should be limited to the amount of the debt with interest and cost of maintaining insurance. However, the law is otherwise and the face of the policy is recoverable though exceeding the debt. [243] Policies frequently stipulate that the bal-

---

[237] Bevin v. Connecticut M. L. I. Co., 23 Conn. 244.

[238] Godsall v. Boldero, 9 East, 72, cited, with approbation, in Tyler v. Ætna Fire Ins. Co., 12 Wend. 507.

[239] Acc., Trenton M. L. & F. I. Co. v. Johnson, 24 N. J. L. 576, 585.

[240] United States: Manhattan L. Ins. Co. v. Hennessy, 99 Fed. 64.

New York: Rawls v. American M. L. I. Co., 27 N. Y. 282, 84 Am. Dec. 280.

Rhode Island: Mowry v. Home L. Ins. Co., 9 R. I. 346, 354.

England: Law v. London I. L. P. Co., 1 K. & J. 223; Dalby v. India & London Life Assurance Co., 15 C. B. 365.

[241] Connecticut M. L. I. Co. v. Schaefer, 94 U. S. 457, 24 L. ed. 251.

[242] Loomis v. Eagle Ins. Co., 6 Gray (Mass.), 396.

[243] Massachusetts: Forbes v. American Mut. L. Ins. Co., 15 Gray, 249, 254, 77 Am. Dec. 360.

Mississippi: Natchez Ins. Co. v. Buckner, 4 How. 63.

ance after payment of the debt to the named creditor shall inure to the benefit of the debtor's estate.[244] Where a partnership consisting of A and B took a policy on the life of B and was subsequently dissolved, all the assets being assigned to A, it was held that A's beneficial interest in the policy was limited to the amount of B's indebtedness to the partnership with interest and the amount expended to preserve the policy, the balance going to B's estate.[245]

§ 730. Refusal to issue or continue a policy.

Where an insurance company breaks a contract to issue a paid-up policy, the measure of damages is the cost of reinsuring in a first-rate company, or if the plaintiff is not insurable at the time, the value of the policy.[246] So where a company agrees, on the payment of the third annual premium due on a life insurance policy, to issue a paid-up policy and fails to do so, the measure of damages is the difference in value between a paid-up policy and the life policy held by the plaintiff.[247] It has been held in some cases that if the company breaks the conditions of its policy or repudiates it the measure of damages is not what it would cost the plaintiff to reinsure, but the whole amount of the premiums paid by him with interest;[248] which amounts to a

---

New York: Hoyt v. New York L. I. Co., 3 Bosw. 440.

[244] *Maryland:* Rittler v. Smith, 70 Md. 261, 16 Atl. 890, 2 L. R. A. 844.

New York: Goodwin v. Mass. M. L. I. Co., 73 N. Y. 480, 497.

Pennsylvania: American L. & H. I. Co. v. Robertshaw, 26 Pa. 189.

[245] Cheeves v. Anders, 87 Tex. 287, 22 S. W. 274, 47 Am. St. Rep. 107.

[246] *Illinois:* Phœnix M. L. I. Co. v. Baker, 85 Ill. 410.

Kansas: Missouri V. L. I. Co. v. Kelso, 16 Kan. 481.

Missouri: Rumbold v. Penn M. L. I. Co., 7 Mo. App. 71.

Nebraska: Union C. L. I. Co. v. McHugh, 7 Neb. 66.

New York: Speer v. Phœnix M. L. I. Co., 36 Hun, 322; Farley v. Union M. L. I. Co., 41 Hun, 303. So in an action

for conversion of a policy. Barney v. Dudley, 42 Kan. 212, 16 Am. St. Rep. 476.

[247] American L. I. & T. Co. v. Shultz, 82 Pa. 46.

[248] *Georgia:* Alabama G. L. I. Co. v. Garmany, 74 Ga. 51.

Illinois: Ætna L. I. Co. v. Paul, 10 Ill. App. 431.

Iowa: Van Werden v. Equitable L. Ass. Society, 99 Ia. 621, 68 N. W. 892.

Michigan: Frain v. Metropolitan L. I. Co., 67 Mich. 527, 35 N. W. 108.

Missouri: McKee v. Phœnix Ins. Co., 28 Mo. 383, 75 Am. Dec. 129; Suess v. Imperial L. I. Co., 64 Mo. App. 1.

New York: Fischer v. Hope M. L. I. Co., 69 N. Y. 161, 25 Am. Rep. 162; Meade v. St. Louis M. L. I. Co., 51 How. Pr. 1.

North Carolina: Braswell v. American

rescission of the contract and a recovery by the assured of the entire consideration paid by him, without allowance for the risk taken by the company. The better measure would seem to be the increased cost of reinsuring, if the assured is still insurable, during the life of the policy; if, however, the assured has become uninsurable, then his measure of damages will be the present value of his policy as of the date of death, less the estimated cost of carrying the same, from the date of cancellation, at his then age.[249] But if the repudiated policy was a tontine or investment policy or where the assured is entitled to accumulations and profits, the plaintiff is further entitled to all such profits or accumulations.[250]

Upon breach of the policy by the insurer transferring its business to another company and going out of business, the assured may recover the value of the policy.[251] The same rule is applicable when the insurer becomes insolvent.[252] In determining the value, the health of the assured, if it is a life policy, and all other facts tending to show what it would cost him to replace himself, should be taken into account.[253] The items

L. I. Co., 75 N. C. 8; Burrus v. Life Ins. Co., 124 N. C. 9, 32 S. E. 323.

Ohio: Union Central L. I. Co. v. Bernard, 33 Ohio St. 459, 31 Am. Rep. 555.

Oregon: Thompson v. New York L. I. Co., 21 Ore. 466, 28 Pac. 628.

Pennsylvania: American L. I. Co. v. McAden, 109 Pa. 399, 1 Atl. 256.

West Virginia: McCall v. Phœnix M. L. I. Co., 9 W. Va. 237, 27 Am. Rep. 558.

[249] *United States:* New York L. I. Co. v. Statham, 93 U. S. 24, 23 L. ed. 789; Lovell v. St. Louis M. L. I. Co., 111 U. S. 264, 4 Sup. Ct. 390, 28 L. ed. 423; Mutual R. F. L. Assoc. v. Ferrenbach, 144 Fed. 342, 75 C. C. A. 304, 7 L. R. A. (N. S.) 1163.

Connecticut: Day v. Conn. G. L. I. Co., 45 Conn. 480, 29 Am. Rep. 693.

Illinois: Brooklyn L. I. Co. v. Weck, 9 Ill. App. 358.

Indiana: Continental L. I. Co. v. Houser, 89 Ind. 258.

Minnesota: Ebert v. Mutual R. F. L. Assoc., 81 Minn. 116, 83 N. W. 506, 84 N. W. 457.

Missouri: Smith v. Charter Oak L. I. Co., 64 Mo. 330.

New York: Speer v. Phœnix M. L. I. Co., 36 Hun, 322.

Pennsylvania: Marshall v. Franklin L. I. Co., 176 Pa. 628, 35 Atl. 204, 34 L. R. A. 159.

Texas: Piedmont L. I. Co. v. Fitzgerald, 1 Tex. Civil Cas. 784, 788.

Virginia: Universal L. Ins. Co. v. Binford, 76 Va. 103.

[250] *United States:* Krebs v. Security T. & L. I. Co., 156 Fed. 294.

West Virginia: Abell v. Penn M. L. I. Co., 18 W. Va. 400.

[251] Union C. L. I. Co. v. Poettker, 4 Am. Law Rec. 109.

[252] People v. Security L. I. & A. Co., 78 N. Y. 114, 34 Am. Rep. 522.

[253] Universal L. I. Co. v. Binford, 76 Va. 103.

See, also, Attorney-General v. Guard-

which go to make up the value of a policy were considered in New York Life Insurance Co. v. Statham.[254] The assured had, in that case, been prevented by the war of the rebellion from paying the premiums. It would seem that if the war did not excuse the non-payment, the policy should, according to its terms, have lapsed; if the war excused the non-payment, then it would seem that the policy must have been in force at the time of the death of the assured. But the Supreme Court took a different view, holding that the plaintiff could recover the equitable value of the policy at the time of the first default, with interest from the close of the war, and that there should be no deduction as in the case of surrendered policies. As to the method of determining the value, the court said: "In each case the rates of mortality and interest used in the tables of the company will form the basis of the calculation." In case of a mutual insurance company the reserve fund for the policy under consideration must be considered in determining its value.[255] Where the defendant refused to receive the premium for a policy on account of the breaking out of the war, the plaintiff residing in Virginia (the offer to pay the premium being made before the proclamation of non-intercourse with that State), it was held that the subsequent enlistment of the plaintiff in the confederate army did not annul the contract, and that the measure of his damages was the value of the policy at the time of refusal, with interest.[256]

§ 731. Accident insurance.

The same principle which prevents recovery for loss of rents in case of fire insurance prevents recovery for loss of time or of profits in an action on an accident insurance policy. The risk insured against is physical accident, compensation for which is the expense of curing the injury and the pain of it. So where in a suit on a policy of insurance, by which £1,000 was to be paid to the representatives of the assured, in case of his death by railway accident, and a proportionate part of that sum to him in case of his injury by such accident, the injury had fallen short

ian M. L. I. Co., 82 N. Y. 336; Clemmitt v. New York L. I. Co., 76 Va. 355 (life terminated before judgment).

[254] 93 U. S. 24, 23 L. ed. 789.

[255] Nashville L. I. Co. v. Mathews, 8 Lea (Tenn.), 499.

[256] Smith v. Charter Oak L. I. Co., 64 Mo. 330.

of death, it was held not to be a true measure of damages to assume the sum insured as the value of the life, and to estimate a proportionate sum for the injury. In such a case, the measure of damages is the amount of injury the plaintiff has sustained as a *direct consequence* of the accident, *i. e.*, compensation for the pain and medical expense; but loss of time or profits in such a case are not regarded.[257] Pollock, C. B., said:

"We think that, in considering the damage done to the traveller, the consequential mischief of losing some profit is not to be taken into consideration; otherwise, a passenger whose time or business is more valuable than that of another would for precisely the same personal injury receive a greater remuneration than that other. What the insurance company calculate on indemnifying the party against is the expense and pain and loss immediately connected with the accident, and not remote consequences that may follow according to the business or profession of the passenger."

It is to be noted, however, that accident policies usually expressly insure against loss of time and stipulate a liquidated periodic indemnity.[258] In such a case the fact that the employer of the assured allows him wages during the time he is incapacitated does not prevent recovery of the agreed indemnity.[259]

§ 732. Assessment policies.

Where an assessment insurance company, which pays, in case of loss, the whole or part of an amount levied upon its members by assessment, refuses to levy an assessment to pay the plaintiff's claim, the plaintiff may maintain an action at law against the company, and recover the amount assessable on policy-holders up to the amount of his claim, unless the company alleges and proves that a less amount would have been paid in by the policy-holders.[260]

[257] Theobald *v.* Railway Passenger Assurance Co., 10 Ex. 45, 57.

[258] Bean *v.* Travelers' Ins. Co., 94 Cal. 581, 29 Pac. 1113.

[259] Globe Acc. Ins. Co. *v.* Helwig, 13 Ind. App. 539, 41 N. E. 976, 55 Am. St. Rep. 247.

[260] *United States:* United States M. A. Assoc. *v.* Barry, 131 U. S. 100, 9 Sup. Ct. 755, 33 L. ed. 60; Lueders *v.* Hartford L. I. Co., 4 McCr. 149.

Arkansas: Masons' Fraternal Assoc. *v.* Riley, 65 Ark. 261, 45 S. W. 684.

In O'Brien v. Home Benefit Society,[261] Earl, J., said: "The plaintiff was entitled to recover something, and what was the measure of his damages? Just what he lost by the defendant's breach of its contract. He was entitled to have an assessment made and collected, and the proceeds thereof paid to him. What was the contract worth to him, and what would the assessment have produced for him? It was incumbent upon the plaintiff to give evidence which would enable the jury to answer these questions. As the assessment was not made, it was impossible for the plaintiff to show accurately or precisely what such an assessment would have produced. He was bound to give such evidence as the nature of the case permitted bearing upon the matter of damages, and legitimately tending to prove their amount."

The reason for allowing the plaintiff to recover substantial damages is that, although it is not in his power to establish what would have been paid in, the presumption is, nothing appearing to the contrary, that the money would have been collected.

Connecticut: Lawler v. Murphy, 58 Conn. 294.

Illinois: Covenant M. B. Assoc. v. Hoffman, 110 Ill. 603.

Indiana: Elkhart M. A. Assoc. v. Houghton, 103 Ind. 286, 53 Am. Rep. 514.

Iowa: Newman v. Covenant M. I. Co., 76 Ia. 56, 40 N. W. 87, 14 Am. St. Rep. 196, 1 L. R. A. 56 (overruling Newman v. Covenant Mutual Benefit Association, 72 Ia. 242, which allowed only nominal damages); Hart v. National M. A. Assoc., 105 Ia. 717, 75 N. W. 508.

Kansas: Kansas Protective Union v. Whitt, 36 Kan. 760, 59 Am. Rep. 607.

Michigan: Burland v. Mutual Benefit Assoc., 47 Mich. 424.

Minnesota: Kerr v. Minnesota M. B. Assoc., 39 Minn. 174, 39 N. W. 312, 12 Am. St. Rep. 631; Bentz v. Northwestern Aid Assoc., 40 Minn. 202.

Missouri: Taylor v. National T. R. Union, 94 Mo. 35; McFarland v. United States M. A. Assoc., 124 Mo. 204, 27 S. W. 436.

Nebraska: Modern Woodman Acc. Assoc. v. Shryock, 54 Neb. 250; 74 N. W. 607, 39 L. R. A. 826.

New York: O'Brien v. Home Benefit Society, 117 N. Y. 310; Freeman v. National Benefit Society, 42 Hun, 252.

[261] 117 N. Y. 310, 319, 22 N. E. 954.

CHAPTER XXXV

ACTIONS UPON CONTRACTS OF SALE OF PERSONAL PROPERTY

I.—BREACH BY VENDOR

§ 733. Introductory.
733a. Rescission.
734. General rule.
735. Reason generally given for it doubtful.
735a. Actual value and cost of replacement.
735b. Market value and price at resale.
735c. Delay in delivery.
736. Failure to deliver stock.
737. Time when market value is to be taken.
738. Place where market value is to be taken.
739. Nearest market.
740. Price receivable on a subcontract.

§ 741. Avoidable loss.
742. Consequential loss.
742a. Profits.
743. Waiver.
744. Payment in advance.
745. The rule of higher intermediate value followed in some jurisdictions.
746. The rule disapproved in other jurisdictions.
747. Distinction between stock and merchandise.
748. No just distinction.
749. Same reason for rule where property has fallen.
749a. Collateral agreement broken by vendor.

II.—BREACH BY VENDEE

§ 750. Rule where title has passed.
751. Instances.
752. Manufacturing contracts.
752a. Property to be severed from the realty.
753. Rule where title has not passed.

§ 754. Rescission.
755. Resale after default.
756. Promise to give a bill or note.
757. Consequential damages—Avoidable consequences.

III.—COUNTERMAND BEFORE TIME FOR PERFORMANCE

§ 758. Effect of notice of countermand.

IV.—BREACH OF WARRANTY AND FRAUD

§ 759. Warranties.
760. Cases allowing difference between price and actual value.
761. Between value as warranted and actual value.
761a. Discussion of principles.
762. Difference in values the general rule.

§ 762a. Recoupment.
763. Warranty of quantity or value.
764. Avoidable consequences.
765. Consequential damages.
766. Upon warranty of fitness for a purpose.
767. Upon warranty of machines.
768. Of seeds.

1528

§ 769. By communication of disease.
770. Upon a sub-contract.
771. Purchase for sale at a distance.
772. Expenses.
773. Litigation expenses.
774. Warranty of title.
775. Warranty of indorsements.

§ 776. That a certain sum is due.
777. Fraud in sale of chattels.
778. Smith v. Bolles.
779. English rule.
780. General discussion.
781. Considerations of practical justice.

V.—FOREIGN LAW

§ 782. Justinian's laws.   § 783. Civil law authorities.

I.—BREACH BY VENDOR

§ 733. Introductory.

* We now approach the consideration of a large class of cases falling under the head of the common-law action of assumpsit,—that of contracts for the sale of chattels or personal property. These contracts may be broken, either completely, by the vendor's neglect to deliver the article, or by the vendee refusing to pay the price; or partially, by the article proving different from some warranty made in regard to it at the time of sale. Generally, it may be said that these agreements furnish their own measure of damages; in other words, that courts of justice, without desiring to fix any arbitrary rate of remuneration, endeavor solely to carry into effect the contract of the parties; and to this rule the only exception that can be said to exist is that in regard to agreements of an unconscionable and oppressive character, which we have already considered.[1] **

§ 733a. Rescission.

When the vendor himself makes performance of the contract impossible, as by converting to his own use the property which he has agreed to deliver, or tendering inferior goods, the vendee has a choice of remedies. He may treat the contract as rescinded and sue to recover back the consideration, or he may sue for damages for breach of the agreement.[2] If he elects to

[1] § 612.

[2] *United States:* Nash v. Towne, 5 Wall. 689, 701, 18 L. ed. 527; Reynolds v. Manhattan Trust Co., 83 Fed. 593, 27 C. C. A. 620, 55 U. S. App. 96, 109; Smiley v. Barker, 83 Fed. 684, 28 C. C. A. 9, 55 U. S. App. 125, 133.

Pennsylvania: Byrne v. Elfreth, 41 Pa. Sup. Ct. 572.

England: Anon., 1 Strange, 407.

This is said to be derived from a universal principle, applicable to all contracts not under seal. Ankeny v. Clark, 148 U. S. 345, 37 L. ed.

rescind, his recovery is limited to the consideration paid, together with any expense he may have been caused, such as payment of freight; but since he has chosen to put an end to the obligation from the beginning he cannot complain of any result of the failure to furnish the goods, such as loss of use of them.[3]

§ 734. General rule.

* We have first to consider the cases arising from the failure of the seller to perform his agreement. When contracts for the sale of chattels are broken by the vendor failing to deliver the property according to the terms of the bargain, it seems to be well settled, as a general rule, both in England and the United States, that the measure of damages is the difference between the contract price and the market value of the article at the time when ** and the place where it should have been delivered, with interest.[4] Where the parties agreed to exchange

475, 13 Sup. Ct. 617. See *supra*, § 654.

[3] Houser & H. M. Co. v. McKay, 53 Wash. 337, 101 Pac. 894, 27 L. R. A. (N. S.) 925, and cases cited.

[4] *United States:* Marsh v. McPherson, 105 U. S. 709, 26 L. ed. 1139; Blydenburgh v. Welsh, Baldwin, 331; Barnard v. Conger, 6 McLean, 497; Halsey v Hurd, 6 McLean, 102; Gilpin v. Consequa, Pet. C. C. 85; Missouri Furnace Co. v. Cochran, 8 Fed. 463; Haff v. Pilling, 134 Fed. 294.

Alabama: McGhee v. Posey, 42 Ala. 330; Neel v. Clay, 48 Ala. 252; Harralson v. Stein, 50 Ala. 347; Bozeman v. Rose, 51 Ala. 321; Bell v. Reynolds, 78 Ala. 511, 56 Am. Rep. 52; Haas v. Hudmon, 83 Ala. 174; Clements v. Beatty, 87 Ala. 238, 6 So. 151; Young v. Cureton, 87 Ala. 727, 6 So. 352; Ala. Chemical Co. v. Geiss, 143 Ala. 591, 39 So. 255.

Arkansas: Leach v. Smith, 25 Ark. 246; Bunch v. Potts, 57 Ark. 257, 21 S. W. 437; Border City Ice & Coal Co. v. Adams, 69 Ark. 219, 62 S. W. 591; Walnut R. M. Co. v. Cohn, 79 Ark.

338, 96 S. W. 413 (anticipatory breach accepted by plaintiff, damages are difference between contract and market price on day of such acceptance); L. N. Lanier & Co. v. Little Rock Cooperage Co., 88 Ark. 557, 115 S. W. 401.

California: Tobin v. Post, 3 Cal. 373; Crosby v. Watkins, 12 Cal. 85, 73 Am. Dec. 518; Bullard v. Stone, 67 Cal. 477; Rayner v. Jones, 90 Cal. 78, 27 Pac. 24; Russ v. Tuttle, 158 Cal. 224, 110 Pac. 813; Fairchild-Gilmore-Wilton Co. v. Southern Refining Co., 158 Cal. 264, 110 Pac. 951; Connell v. Harron, 7 Cal. App. 745, 95 Pac. 916; Cal. Code, §§ 3308, 3354.

Colorado: Cole v. Cheovenda, 4 Colo. 17; Staab v. Borax Soap Co., 12 Colo. App. 286, 55 Pac. 618.

Connecticut: Crug v. Gorham, 74 Conn. 541, 51 Atl. 519.

Delaware: Love v. Barnseville Mfg. Co., 3 Pennew. 152, 50 Atl. 526.

District of Columbia: McAllister v. Douglas, 1 D. C. (1 Cr. C. C.) 241.

Florida: Robinson v. Hyer, 35 Fla. 544, 577, 17 So. 745.

Georgia: Southwestern R. R. v.

property, and the defendant refused to carry out the agreement, the measure of damages is the difference between the

Rowan, 43 Ga. 411; Erwin *v.* Harris, 87 Ga. 333, 13 S. E. 513; Wappoo Mills *v.* Commercial Guano Co., 91 Ga. 396, 18 S. E. 308; Pitcher *v.* Lowe, 95 Ga. 423, 429, 22 S. E. 678; Piedmont Wagon Co. *v.* Hudgens, 4 Ga. App. 393, 61 S. E. 835; Trigg Candy Co. *v.* Emmett Shaw Co. (Ga. App.), 71 S. E. 679; Wright *v.* Vaughan, 72 S. E. 412.

Illinois: Sleuter *v.* Wallbaum, 45 Ill. 43; Smith *v.* Dunlap, 12 Ill. 184; Deere *v.* Lewis, 51 Ill. 254; Richard *v.* Shaw, 67 Ill. 222; Kitzinger *v.* Sanborn, 70 Ill. 146; Driggers *v.* Bell, 94 Ill. 223; Trunkey *v.* Hedstrom, 131 Ill. 204, 23 N. E. 587; Loescher *v.* Deisterberg, 26 Ill. App. 520; Delaware & Hudson Canal Co. *v.* Mitchell, 92 Ill. App. 577; Whitsell *v.* Rising, 109 Ill. App. 91.

Indiana: Parks *v.* Marshall, 10 Ind. 20; Gatling *v.* Newell, 12 Ind. 118, 125 (*semble*); Zehner *v.* Dale, 25 Ind. 433; Frink *v.* Tatman, 36 Ind. 259, 10 Am. Rep. 19; McCollum *v.* Huntington, 51 Ind. 229; Fell *v.* Muller, 78 Ind. 507; Vickery *v.* McCormick, 117 Ind. 594, 20 N. E. 495; Rahm *v.* Deig, 121 Ind. 283, 23 N. E. 141.

Iowa: Cannon *v.* Folsom, 2 Ia. 101; Boies *v.* Vincent, 24 Ia. 387; Jemmison *v.* Gray, 29 Ia. 537; Osgood *v.* Bauder, 75 Ia. 550, 39 N. W. 887; Black *v.* De Camp, 78 Ia. 718, 43 N. W. 625; Faulkner *v.* Closter, 79 Ia. 15, 44 N. W. 208; Laporte Improvement Co. *v.* Brock, 99 Ia. 485, 68 N. W. 810; Welch *v.* Urvany, 112 Ia. 531, 84 N. W. 497; Chesmore *v.* Barker, 101 Ia. 576, 70 N. W. 701; H. D. Wetmore & Co. *v.* Henry, 124 N. W. 791.

Kansas: Gray *v.* Hall, 29 Kan. 704; York D. M. Co. *v.* Lusk, 45 Kan. 182, 25 Pac. 646; Halstead Lumber Co. *v.* Sutton, 46 Kan. 192, 26 Pac. 444; York-Draper Co. *v.* Lusk, 6 Kan. App. 629, 49 Pac. 788.

Kentucky: Mudd *v.* Phillips, Litt. Sel.

Cas. 50; Dills *v.* Dougherty, 6 Dana, 253; Koch *v.* Godshaw, 12 Bush, 318; Miles *v.* Miller, 12 Bush, 134; Guenther *v.* Taylor, 63 S. W. 439, 23 Ky. L. Rep. 536; Parry Mfg. Co. *v.* Lyon, 111 Ky. 613, 64 S. W. 436.

Louisiana: Marchesseau *v.* Chaffee, 4 La. Ann. 24; Thompson *v.* Howes, 14 La. Ann. 45; Hafner Mfg. Co. *v.* Lieber L. & S. Co., 127 La. 348, 53 So. 646.

Maine: Smith *v.* Berry, 18 Me. 122; Bush *v.* Holmes, 53 Me. 417; Bell *v.* Jordan, 112 Me. 67, 65 Atl. 759.

Maryland: Kribs *v.* Jones, 44 Md. 396; Pinckney *v.* Dambmann, 72 Md. 173, 19 Atl. 450; McGrath *v.* Gegner, 77 Md. 331, 26 Atl. 502, 39 Am. St. Rep. 415.

Massachusetts: Shaw *v.* Nudd, 8 Pick. 9; Bartlett *v.* Blanchard, 13 Gray, 429; Essex M. Co. *v.* Pacific Mills, 14 All. 380, 92 Am. Dec. 777; Meserve *v.* Ammidon, 109 Mass. 415.

Michigan: Clark *v.* Moore, 3 Mich. 55; Haskell *v.* Hunter, 23 Mich. 305; McKercher *v.* Curtis, 35 Mich. 478; Chadwick *v.* Butler, 28 Mich. 349; Austrian *v.* Springer, 94 Mich. 343, 54 N. W. 50, 34 Am. St. Rep. 359; Aulls *v.* Young, 98 Mich. 231, 57 N. W. 119; Trotter *v.* Tousey, 131 Mich. 624, 92 N. W. 544; Pittsburgh Coal Co. *v.* Northy, 158 Mich. 530, 123 N. W. 47.

Minnesota: Olson *v.* Sharpless, 53 Minn. 91, 55 N. W. 125; Hewson-Herzog Supply Co. *v.* Minnesota Brick Co., 55 Minn. 530, 57 N. W. 129; Reeves *v.* Cress, 80 Minn. 466, 83 N. W. 443; Coxe Bros. & Co. *v.* Anoka Water Works, 91 Minn. 50, 97 N. W. 459.

Missouri: Northrup *v.* Cook, 39 Mo. 208; Harrison Wire Co. *v.* Hall & W. H. Co., 97 Mo. 289; Warren *v.* A. B. Mayer Manuf. Co., 161 Mo. 112, 61 S. W. 644, 84 Am. St. Rep. 669, *n.;* Murphy *v.* St. Louis, 8 Mo. App. 483; Shouse *v.* Neiswaanger, 18 Mo. App. 236, 244; Smith

value of the defendant's property and that of the plaintiff.[5]

It follows from this rule, that if, at the time fixed for the

v. Keith & P. Coal Co., 36 Mo. App. 567; Wilson v. Russler, 91 Mo. App. 275; Howard v. Haas, 131 Mo. App. 499, 109 S. W. 1076; Barnett v. Elwood Grain Co. (Mo. App.), 133 S. W. 856.

Nebraska: Denver & R. G. R. R. v. Hutchins, 31 Neb. 572, 48 N. W. 398; Boyer v. Cox, 34 Neb. 813, 52 N. W. 715; Russell v. Horn, 41 Neb. 567, 59 N. W. 901; Graham v. Frazier, 49 Neb. 90, 68 N. W. 367; Carter v. Roberts, 85 Neb. 480, 124 N. W. 94.

New Hampshire: Stevens v. Lyford, 7 N. H. 360; Trask v. Hamburger, 70 N. H. 453, 48 Atl. 1087.

New York: Davis v. Shields, 24 Wend. 322; McKnight v. Dunlop, 5 N. Y. 537, 55 Am. Dec. 370; Dana v. Fiedler, 12 N. Y. 40, 62 Am. Dec. 130; Parsons v. Sutton, 66 N. Y. 92; Windmuller v. Pope, 107 N. Y. 674; Taylor v. Saxe, 134 N. Y. 67, 31 N. E. 258; Todd v. Gamble, 148 N. Y. 382, 42 N. E. 982, 52 L. R. A. 225; Saxe v. Penokee Lumber Co., 159 N. Y. 371, 54 N. E. 14; Haddane Gr. Co. v. Brooklyn H. R. R., 186 N. Y. 247, 78 N. E. 858; Billings v. Vanderbeck, 23 Barb. 546; Williams v. Sherman, 48 Barb. 402; Leavenworth v. Packer, 52 Barb. 132; Townshend v. Shepard, 64 Barb. 41; Yorke v. Ver Planck, 65 Barb. 316; Brock v. Knower, 37 Hun, 609; Taylor v. Reed, 4 Paige, 561; Norton v. Wales, 1 Robt. 561; Beals v. Terry, 2 Sandf. 127; Wamsley v. Wamsley, 48 App. Div. 330, 62 N. Y. Supp. 954; Rosenthal v. Empire B. & S. Co., 123 App. Div. 503, 108 N. Y. Supp. 347; Thedford v. Herbert, 119 N. Y. Supp. 1025, 135 App. Div. 174; Brody v. Birnbaum, 108 N. Y. Supp. 581; Albert Gas Fixture Co. v. Kabat, 109 N. Y. Supp. 737; Barton-Child Co. v. Scarborough, 61 Misc. 334, 114 N.

Y. Supp. 1043; Dunlevie v. Spangenberg, 121 N.Y. Supp. 299, 66 Misc. 354.

North Carolina: Whitsett v. Forehand, 79 N. C. 230; Crawford v. Geiser Manuf. Co., 88 N. C. 554; Indian M. J. C. Co. v. Ashville I. & C. Co., 134 N. C. 574, 47 S. E. 115; Tillinghast, Styles Co. v. Providence Cotton Mills, 143 N. C. 268, 55 S. E. 621.

North Dakota: Talbott v. Boyd, 11 N. Dak. 81, 88 N. W. 1026.

Ohio: Smith v. Sloss M. L. Co., 57 Oh. St. 518, 49 N. E. 695; Lloyd Lumber Co. v. Solon, 17 Ohio C. Ct. 194.

Oregon: Livesley v. Johnson, 48 Ore. 40, 84 Pac. 1044.

Pennsylvania: Fessler v. Love, 43 Pa. 313; White v. Tompkins, 52 Pa. 363, 91 Am. Dec. 163; Billmeyer v. Wagner, 91 Pa. 92, 36 Am. Rep. 659; Culin v. Woodbury Glass Works, 108 Pa. 220; Arnold v. Blabon, 147 Pa. 372, 23 Atl. 575; Canovan v. Neeld, 189 Pa. 208, 42 Atl. 115; Kimports v. Breton, 193 Pa. 309, 44 Atl. 436; Bradley v. McHale, 19 Pa. Super. Ct. 300; Homesdale Ice Co. v. Lake L. I. Co., 81 Atl. 306.

South Carolina: Price v. Justrobe, Harper, 111; Davis v. Richardson, 1 Bay, 105.

Tennessee: Doak v. Snapp, 1 Coldw. 180; Harris v. Rodgers, 6 Heisk. 626.

Texas: Randon v. Barton, 4 Tex. 289; Duncan v. McMahan, 18 Tex. 597 (*semble*); Day v. Cross, 59 Tex. 595; Guice v. Crenshaw, 60 Tex. 344; Ullman v. Babcock, 63 Tex. 68.

Utah: California P. B. & L. Co. v. Wasatch Orchard Co., 117 Pac. 35.

Vermont: Worthen v. Wilmot, 30 Vt. 555; Hill v. Smith, 34 Vt. 535; Humphreysville Co. v. Vermont Copper Mining Co., 33 Vt. 92.

[5] *Colorado:* Montelius v. Atherton, 6 Colo. 224.

New York: Woodworth v. Curtis, 7 Wend. 112.

delivery, the article has not risen in value, the vendee having lost nothing can recover only nominal damages.[6] Accordingly, where goods are sold, and it is agreed that the market price shall be paid for them, damages for non-delivery are only nominal;[7] and the same is true where the price of the goods is by the contract to be fixed by appraisers at the time of delivery.[8] The plaintiff sold the defendant a slave, with an agreement that if the defendant wished to sell the slave, the plaintiff should have the privilege of repurchasing at the price paid by the defendant. The defendant sold the slave to a third party. The measure of damages was the difference between the market value of the slave at the time of the sale to the third party and the agreed price.[9]

The reason of the rule is usually said to be that this is the plaintiff's real loss, because with this sum he can go into the market and supply himself with the same article from another vendor.[10] Accordingly in an action brought by a retail coal dealer against a wholesaler for non-delivery of coal the measure of damages is the difference between the contract price and the

Virginia: Smith *v.* Snyder, 77 Va. 432; Smith *v.* Snyder, 82 Va. 614 (*semble*).

Washington: Sweeney *v.* Jamieson, 2 Wash. 254; Carney *v.* Vogel, 52 Wash. 571, 100 Pac. 1027; R. J. Menz Lumber Co. *v.* McNeeley, 58 Wash. 223, 108 Pac. 621, 28 L. R. A. (N. S.) 1007.

Wisconsin: Noonan *v.* Ilsley, 17 Wis. 314, 84 Am. Dec. 742; Starr *v.* Light, 22 Wis. 433; Hill *v.* Chipman, 59 Wis. 211; Seefeld *v.* Thacker, 93 Wis. 518, 67 N. W. 1142; Vogt *v.* Schienebeck, 122 Wis. 491, 100 N. W. 820; Southern F. & G. Co. *v.* McGeehan, 144 Wis. 130, 128 N. W. 879.

England: Peterson *v.* Ayre, 13 C. B. 353; Tyers *v.* Rosedale, etc., Co., L. R. 8 Ex. 305.

Ireland: O'Neill *v.* Rush, 12 Ir. L. 34.

Canada: Feehan *v.* Hallman, 13 Up. Can. Q. B. 440.

New Zealand: Fleming *v.* Grigg, 14 N. Z. 499.

[6] *Iowa:* Faulkner *v.* Closter, 79 Ia. 15, 44 N. W. 208.

New York: Currie *v.* White, 6 Abb. (N. S.) 352, 386.

Wisconsin: Merriman *v.* McCormick Harvesting Machine Co., 96 Wis. 600, 71 N. W. 1050, 65 Am. St. Rep. 83.

[7] Wire *v.* Foster, 62 Ia. 114.

[8] Koch *v.* Godshaw, 12 Bush (Ky.), 318.

[9] Brent *v.* Richards, 2 Gratt. (Va.) 539.

[10] *Iowa:* Laporte Improvement Co. *v.* Brock, 99 Ia. 485, 68 N. W. 810, 61 Am. St. Rep. 485.

Maine: Furlong *v.* Polleys, 30 Me. 491, 50 Am. Dec. 635.

New York: Dey *v.* Dox, 9 Wend. 129; Davis *v.* Shields, 24 Wend. 322; Beals *v.* Terry, 2 Sandf. 127; McKnight *v.* Dunlop, 5 N. Y. 537; Clark *v.* Dales, 20 Barb. 42; Belden *v.* Nicolay, 4 E. D. S. 14.

England: Owen *v.* Routh, 14 C. B. 327; Josling *v.* Irvine, 6 H. & N. 512.

wholesale market price, not the retail price.[11] When the article contracted for is not readily obtainable on the market at the place for delivery under the contract it has been held that the purchaser may recover the difference between the agreed price and the actual cost of procuring similar articles by due diligence.[12] So where in order to get the articles it becomes necessary for the buyer to manufacture them himself the cost of manufacture less the contract price is the measure of recovery,[13] and no allowance is to be made for manufacturer's profits.[14] It may be impossible to procure an article exactly like that contracted for; in that case the cost of the best available substitute will furnish the measure of damages, in addition to any consequential damages resulting from the substitution which were within the contemplation of the parties.[15] In an English case [16] the defendant had agreed to manufacture and sell to the plaintiff 2,000 pieces of gray shirtings. Upon a breach the plaintiffs in order to fill a sub-contract procured at an advanced price 2,000 pieces of shirting of a somewhat superior quality, after vainly endeavoring to find an exact equivalent of that due under the contract. The sub-vendees accepted this substitute but paid no extra price. The plaintiff recovered the difference between the contract price and

[11] *Connecticut:* Righter v. Clark, 60 Atl. 741.

New York: Kilpatrick v. William Whitmer & Sons, 118 App. Div. 98, 103 N. Y. Supp. 75.

[12] *United States:* Vulcan Iron Works Co. v. Roquemore, 175 Fed. 11, 99 C. C. A. 77.

Alabama: McFadden v. Henderson, 128 Ala. 221, 29 So. 640.

Georgia: Hardwood Lumber Co. v. Adams, 134 Ga. 821, 68 S. E. 725, 32 L. R. A. (N. S.) 192.

Michigan: Den Bleyker v. Gaston, 97 Mich. 354, 56 N. W. 763.

New Jersey: Rhind v. Freedley, 74 N. J. L. 138, 64 Atl. 963.

New York: Miller v. Stern, 25 Misc. 690, 55 N. Y. Supp. 765; Lande v. A. G. Hyde & Sons, 66 Misc. 259, 121 N. Y. Supp. 258.

North Carolina: Hassard-Shord v. Hardison, 117 N. C. 60, 19 S. E. 728, 23 S. E. 96.

[13] *United States:* Dolph v. Troy Laundry Mach. Co., 28 Fed. 553.

Minnesota: Paine v. Sherwood, 21 Minn. 225, 19 Am. Rep. 215.

New York: Gallagher v. Baird, 54 App. Div. 398, 66 N. Y. Supp. 759.

Vermont: Forsyth v. Mann, 68 Vt. 116, 34 Atl. 481, 32 L. R. A. 788.

[14] Pittsburg Sheet Manuf. Co. v. West Penn. Sheet Steel Co., 201 Pa. 150, 50 Atl. 935.

[15] Crowley v. Burns B. & M. Co., 100 Minn. 178, 110 N. W. 969.

[16] Hinde v. Liddell, L. R. 10 Q. B. 265. *Cf.* Hamilton v. Kirby, 199 Pa. 466, 49 Atl. 214.

the price he had paid for the substituted shirtings. In no case is it necessary that the vendee should actually purchase other goods to take the place of those which the vendor failed to deliver, in order to invoke the general rule as to damages.[17] The rule applies where there is a delivery of part only of the goods contracted for.[18] Where the vendor puts it out of his power to fulfil his contract of sale by selling a portion of the goods to a third party before the time stipulated for the delivery, the vendee in an action for the breach of the contract is entitled to the difference between the market value and the contract price, on all the goods contracted to be sold, and not merely those which the vendor had thus put it out of his power to deliver;[19] for the entire contract was broken by the vendor's act. The vendee could not be required to accept part only of the goods. Where the defendant contracted to deliver his crop of corn growing on about 30 acres of ground in merchantable order at a stipulated time and price, and one-fourth of the crop only turned out sound, and he refused to deliver that portion only, but insisted on delivering the whole, if any, it was held a breach of the contract, and the vendees were held entitled to recover the difference between the contract price and the market value of the merchantable corn on the ground.[20]

If the defendant not only failed to deliver the goods to the plaintiff, but sold and delivered the same goods to another, he cannot complain if for the purpose of estimating damages the price he received on the latter sale is taken as the market value at the time for delivery.[21]

§ 735. Reason generally given for it doubtful.

It has been so often said that the reason for the rule is as just stated—that the plaintiff's loss is measured by the market value of the article, because for this sum he can *replace himself*,—that it is with great hesitation that we venture to make even a suggestion to the contrary; but the sounder explanation of the rule as ordinarily stated appears to be that it represents

[17] Bliss *v.* Buffalo Tin Can Co., 131 Fed. 51.

[18] Valpy *v.* Oakeley, 16 Q. B. 941.

[19] Crist *v.* Armour, 34 Barb. (N. Y.) 378.

[20] Hamilton *v.* Ganyard, 34 Barb. (N. Y.) 204.

[21] Moers *v.* Dietz, 52 Misc. 173, 101 N. Y. Supp. 590.

the difference in value between the property right which the buyer actually had and that which he would have had if the seller had performed his contract. The notion of a general practice of replacement is objectionable for a variety of reasons. In the first place, it does not correspond to the facts. A person failing to receive an article bought can be under no absolute duty to society or his vendor to replace himself, nor can it be said that it is so universally done that it is an expected act from one in such a position.[22] But in the second place, if it were, and the doctrine of replacement were supposed to be an invariable rule of law, how are we to explain the rule that the law measures the damages at the very instant of breach? Is it to be supposed that at the very instant of breach every one who has made a contract is in the market ready to replace himself? If not, the rule, if founded on the reason given, ought to be the difference between the contract and the market price within a reasonable time after notice for replacement. But outside of a few jurisdictions which have established such a rule in contracts of a peculiar character,[23] we know of no authority for it.

The doctrine of replacement has undoubtedly a peculiar fitness in one class of sales or agreements for the future delivery of articles—where the defendant has notice of a subcontract which makes it necessary that the plaintiff should replace himself. But we think that the repeated assertion that the reason of the rule of damages in sales is that the purchaser can go into the market and replace himself has a tendency to breed confusion in the whole subject.

§ 735a. Actual value and cost of replacement.

Where the cost of replacement greatly exceeds the actual value it cannot be the basis of damages, even where there is no market value. Upon breach of a contract to deliver full-paid stock it appeared that the stock could not be procured in the market, and the only way by which the buyer could replace

---

[22] The market value fixes the measure of damages and the law does not require the vendee to go into the market and buy. Saxe v. Penokee Lumber Co., 159 N. Y. 376, 54 N. E. 14.

[23] Shreve v. Brereton, 51 Pa. 175; and see chapter on Higher Intermediate Value and Replacement.

himself was by subscribing for other shares and paying in $200,000, the full par value. In the New York Supreme Court it was held that this was the measure of the buyer's recovery, but in the Court of Appeals, it appearing that the stock was in fact intrinsically worthless and would have remained so even if the full payment had been made, the court limited the recovery to nominal damages.[24] The court said:

"The claim that because the creation or issue of this worthless stock would cost its par value, the plaintiff is entitled to recover that sum does not seem to have the support of any well-defined principle of law. . . . While the performance of their agreement may have required them to pay to the company two hundred thousand dollars, the entire value of its performance to the plaintiff was in the stock which they undertook to deliver to him, and this was the only benefit he was entitled to take under the contract. The value of the stock, or its pecuniary equivalent, was the measure of his injury by the default."

On the other hand, if the plaintiff was in a position to buy the goods at less than the market price, it has been held that he can recover no more than the difference between the market price and the cost to him of replacement.[25] This decision, however, seems questionable. If the plaintiff can make a good bargain with a third party he, and not the defendant, should be entitled to the benefit of the bargain; furthermore, if the defendant had performed his agreement the plaintiff would have received the profit of that bargain, and might in addition have made the same advantageous bargain with the third party and have realized the profit of that also.

§ 735b. Market value and price at resale.

In Startup v. Cortazzi [26] it was intimated that the reason of the rule is that the market value represents what the plaintiff *would have got on a resale*, that is, the true value of his bargain. This does not mean that he buys necessarily for a resale; but that what the article would bring in anyone's hands on a

[24] Barnes v. Seligman, 55 Hun, 339, 346; Barnes v. Brown, 130 N. Y. 372, 385, 29 N. E. 760.

[25] Harrison Wire Co. v. Hall & W. H. Co., 97 Mo. 289.

[26] 2 C. M. & R. 165.

resale, is the value to which he is entitled. Yet in a few cases the view seems to be accepted that the price at which the plaintiff has contracted to resell the goods is the limit of recovery, and that the measure of damages is the difference between that amount and the contract price; so that if the plaintiff had contracted to resell the goods at less than the contract price his recovery would be diminished by the difference.[27] This decision, however, appears to lose sight of the fact that the plaintiff must purchase other goods in the market to perform his contract of resale, and is therefore in fact a loser of the entire market value of the goods; and if the goods had been delivered to him, without being in a worse position as to his contract of resale, he might have sold the goods for the market price. Therefore by the better view damages should be recovered according to the general rule.[28]

In a recent English case the goods were finally delivered after a delay. During the delay the market value of the goods fell. Before the time for delivery the plaintiff resold the goods at a price higher than the market price at the time of actual delivery, but lower than that at the time for delivery fixed by the contract. It was held that the damages were the difference between the market value at the time for delivery and the price of resale.[29] This case seems to be open to a similar criticism to that already made.

§ 735c. Delay in delivery.

When the goods are not delivered on the day fixed by the contract, even though time is of the essence, the buyer is not bound to accept this failure to deliver as a total breach of the contract. If he refrains from doing so and the seller later tenders the goods, which are accepted by the purchaser, the latter is entitled to recover the difference in the market value of the goods at the time when they should have been delivered and when they were delivered.[30] If the article sold was a

[27] Foss v. Heineman, 144 Wis. 881, 128 N. W. 881.

[28] Floyd v. Mann, 146 Mich. 356, 109 N. W. 679.

[29] Wertheim v. Chicoutimi Pulp Co., [1911] A. C. 301.

[30] *California:* Ramish v. Kirschbraun, 98 Cal. 676, 33 Pac. 780, 107 Cal. 659, 40 Pac. 1045 (eggs).

Massachusetts: Clement & H. Manuf. Co. v. Meserole, 107 Mass. 362 (hoes).

machine intended for use and the injury consisted in the deprivation of such use, the measure of damages is the fair rental value during the delay;[31] though if in fact it appear that the machine would not have been used during the period of delay it has been held that no damages can be recovered for loss of use.[32] Special damages may of course be added in a proper case.[33]

§ 736. Failure to deliver stock.

In case of a refusal to deliver stock which is to be paid for, the measure of damages is governed by the same principles.[34]

Minnesota: Whalon v. Aldrich, 8 Minn. 346.

New York: Boomer v. Flagler, 51 N. Y. Super. Ct. 211; Davis Provision Co. v. Fowler Bros., 47 N. Y. Supp. 206 (meat).

North Carolina: Spiers v. Halsted, 74 N. C. 620.

Texas: Tyler Car & Lumber Co. v. Wettermark, 12 Tex. Civ. App. 399, 34 S. W. 807.

If there is no market at the place of delivery, the value is taken at the nearest mrket. Shepherd, Croan & Co. v. Templeman, 136 S. W. 648 (Ky).

[31] *Indiana:* Singer v. Farnsworth, 2 Ind. 597.

Maryland: Cent. Trust Co. v. Arctic Ice Mach. Mfg. Co., 77 Md. 202, 26 Atl. 493; Maryland Ice Co. v. Arctic Ice Mach. Mfg. Co., 79 Md. 103, 29 Atl. 69.

North Carolina: Tompkins Co. v. Dallas Cotton Mills, 130 N. C. 347, 41 S. E. 938.

South Carolina: Standard Supply Co. v. Carter, 81 S. C. 181, 62 S. E. 150, 19 L. R. A. (N. S.) 155.

See *post*, § 742.

[32] *California:* Hendry v. Irvine, 9 Cal. App. 376, 99 Pac. 408.

Washington: Eichbaum v. Caldwell Bros. Co., 58 Wash. 163, 108 Pac. 434.

[33] Iowa Mfg. Co. v. B. F. Sturtevant Co., 162 Fed. 460, 89 C. C. A. 346.

[34] *Connecticut:* Shelton v. French, 33 Conn. 489.

Illinois: Plumb v. Campbell, 129 Ill. 101, 18 N. E. 790.

Indiana: Coffin v. State, 144 Ind. 578, 43 N. E. 654, 55 Am. St. Rep. 188.

Maryland: Baltimore City P. R. R. v. Sewell, 35 Md. 238, 6 Am. Rep. 402.

Massachusetts: Eastern R. R. v. Benedict, 10 Gray, 212; Hussey v. Manufacturers' & M. Bank, 10 Pick. 415; Murray v. Stanton, 99 Mass. 345; Allen v. South Boston R. R., 150 Mass. 200, 22 N. E. 917.

New York: Wintermute v. Cooke, 73 N. Y. 107; Van Allen v. Illinois C. R. R., 7 Bosw. 515; Chapman v. Fowler, 32 App. Div. 250, 116 N. Y. Supp. 962.

North Dakota: Patterson v. Plummer, 10 N. Dak. 95, 86 N. W. 111.

South Carolina: Davis v. Richardson, 1 Bay, 105.

Tennessee: Memphis, etc., R. R. v. Walker, 2 Head, 467; Feder v. Gass, 59 S. W. 175.

Virginia: Orange & A. R. R. v. Fulvey, 17 Gratt. 366.

Washington: Saunders v. U. S. Marble Co., 25 Wash. 475, 485, 65 Pac. 782, 87 Am. St. Rep. 782; Delden v. Krom, 34 Wash. 184, 75 Pac. 636.

Wyoming: Kuhn v. McKay, 7 Wyo. 42, 65, 49 Pac. 473, 51 Mo. 205.

So where a stockholder has a right to

So in an action for the non-delivery of railway shares on a given day, pursuant to contract, the property not having been paid for, the measure of damages is the difference between the contract price and the market price on the day when the contract was broken.[35] So the vendee of shares in a projected railway, under a contract to be completed at a future day, may recover as damages for the non-delivery the difference between the price agreed on and the market price on the day on which the defendant refused to complete the sale, and that only. He is not entitled to damages in respect to an advance of price taking place afterwards at the time of the actual issue of the scrip. In other words, the time when the defendant refused to comply with his contract is the determining point.[36]

§ 737. Time when market value is to be taken.

The plaintiff recovers the value at the time the contract should have been performed.[37] Where the defendant agreed to deliver wood *as needed* and subsequently repudiated the contract, the plaintiff was allowed to recover the value of the wood at the different times it was needed, and was not confined to the price at the time of the repudiation.[38] * A doubt may arise as to what is the time stipulated for delivery. Where oats were to be delivered "on or about" a certain day, it was held that the plaintiff was not limited to the difference between the contract price and the market value on the precise day named, but might recover the difference between the contract price and the market value within a reasonable time after that day.[39] ** Where delivery was to be on demand, the

subscribe for his proportion of new stock at par, but is deprived of this right by the company, he may recover the difference between par and the market price at the time he had the right to subscribe. Stokes v. Continental Trust Co., 186 N. Y. 285, 78 N. E. 1090, 12 L. R. A. (N. S.) 969.

[35] *District of Columbia:* Tayloe v. Turner, 2 D. C. (2 Cr. C. C.) 203.

Louisiana: Vance v. Tourné, 13 La. 225.

New Hampshire: Rand v. White M. R. R., 40 N. H. 79.

Vermont: Jones v. Chamberlain, 30 Vt. 196.

England: Shaw v. Holland, 15 M. & W. 136.

[36] Tempest v. Kilner, 3 C. B. 249.

[37] Taylor v. McFatter (Tex. Civ. App.), 109 S. W. 395.

[38] *Illinois:* Long v. Conklin, 75 Ill. 32; Delaware & H. C. Co. v. Mitchell, 31 N. E. 1026.

New York: Reeve v. Gallivan, 89 Hun, 59, 34 N. Y. Supp. 1000.

[39] Kipp v. Wiles, 3 Sand. (N. Y.) 585.

market value is to be taken at the time of demand.[40] In a case in Massachusetts, the contract was, that George should deliver to Quarles 1,000 barrels of flour at $6 per barrel, at any time within six months—George to give Quarles six days' notice prior to delivery; Quarles to pay the price aforesaid, and either party to be released, if desiring it, within three months, on paying $500 to the other. This last provision was not taken advantage of. On the 13th of February, Quarles demanded it; it was not delivered; and the question was, on what day the damages were to be computed, it being agreed that such damages were the difference between the price mentioned in the contract and the actual value. The court held that the defendant had to do the first act, *i. e.*, give notice; that he had still six days before the 14th of February to give notice; and as, if he had then given notice, he would have had till the last day to deliver the flour, the actual breach by the non-delivery of the flour must be taken to have occurred on that day, and damages were computed accordingly.[41] If no time is fixed for the delivery, it has been said in Maryland that damages will be calculated from the period at which the defendant refuses to perform.[42] But the general rule is that, if no time is fixed for delivery, the article is deliverable in a reasonable time. What such time is must depend on the circumstances of each case; and the difference between the stipulated price and the price at the time proper for the delivery is the measure of damages.[43] If growing crops are sold, the value is to be calculated at the time when they are mature and ready for delivery.[44] Where the vendor is to ship goods from a distance on a specified day, and there is a breach, it has been held that the proper basis for calculating the damages is the market value on the day when the vendee receives notice of the breach, that

[40] Smith *v.* Berry, 18 Me. 122.

[41] Quarles *v.* George, 23 Pick. (Mass.) 400.

[42] *Maryland:* Williams *v.* Woods, 16 Md. 220; United R. & E. Co. *v.* Wehr, 103 Md. 323, 63 Atl. 475.

And see *Kentucky:* Booth *v.* Booth, 1 A. K. Marsh. 355.

Texas: Palestine C. S. O. Co. *v.* Cotton Oil Co., 61 S. W. 433.

[43] Thompson *v.* Woodruff, 7 Cold. (Tenn.) 401; Paragon Refining Co. *v.* Lee, 98 Tenn. 643, 41 S. W. 362.

[44] *Missouri:* Smock *v.* Smock, 37 Mo. App. 56.

Tennessee: Harris *v.* Rodgers, 6 Heisk. 626.

being the earliest time when he could reasonably be expected to go into the market and replace himself.[45] If the seller is given a certain time within which to deliver, the damages are measured by the market value in the last day for delivery.[46] If the delivery is postponed by an agreement between the parties, the measure of damages is the difference between the contract and market price at the time the article is deliverable by the subsequent agreement.[47] When the time of delivery is postponed without definitely fixing the new time for delivery, the measure of damages would seem to be the difference between the contract price and the market value at a reasonable time after demanding performance.[48] The fact that the vendor gives the vendee notice of repudiation of the contract before the time set for delivery does not obligate the vendee to go at once into the market and repurchase, and the rule of damages is not altered.[49] Where delivery is required to be made by instalments, the measure of damages will be estimated by the value at the time each delivery should have been made.[50] So where a contract is for the delivery of goods in equal proportions in a given number of months, and the action for non-delivery is brought after the period stipulated for the last

[45] *New York:* Boyd v. Quinn Co., 41 N. Y. Supp. 391.

England: Ashmore v. Cox, [1899] 1 Q. B. 436.

[46] *Kentucky:* Stahr v. Hickman Grain Co., 132 Ky. 496, 116 S. W. 785.

Missouri: Gill v. Johnson-Brinkman Com. Co., 84 Mo. App. 456.

[47] *United States:* Roberts v. Benjamin, 124 U. S. 64, 8 Sup. Ct. 393, 31 L. ed. 334.

Illinois: Houston v. Wendnagel, 135 Ill. App. 95; Pope Metal Co. v. Sandoval Zinc Co., 148 Ill. App. 444.

Michigan: McDermid v. Redpath, 39 Mich. 372.

Virginia: Smith v. Snyder, 77 Va. 432.

England: Ogle v. Vane, L. R. 2 Q. B. 275, L. R. 3 Q. B. 272; Tyers v. Rosedale & F. I. Co., L. R. 8 Ex. 305, per Martin, B.; L. R. 10 Ex. 195.

In Glenn v. Schaffer, 17 W. L. Rep. 273 (Can., 1911), the facts were not regarded as showing an agreement to postpone, and the value was taken at the time originally fixed.

[48] *United States:* Ralli v. Rockmore, 111 Fed. 874.

England: Hickman v. Haynes, L. R. 10 C. P. 598; Tyers v. Rosedale & F. I. Co., L. R. 10 Ex. 195.

[49] *Massachusetts:* P. P. Emory Manuf. Co. v. Salomon, 178 Mass. 582, 60 N. E. 377.

Michigan: Austrian v. Springer, 94 Mich. 343, 54 N. W. 50.

England: Brown v. Muller, L. R. 7 Ex. 319.

[50] *United States:* Youghiogheny & O. C. Co. v. Verstine, Hibbard & Co., 176 Fed. 972.

Illinois: Sagola L. Co. v. Chicago T. & T. Co., 121 Ill. App. 292.

delivery, the proper measure of damages is the sum of the differences between the contract and market prices on the last day of each month respectively.[51] And where in such a case the contract was repudiated by the defendant, and the action was brought and tried before the expiration of the stipulated number of months, it was held (in the absence of evidence on the part of the defendant that the plaintiffs could have obtained a new contract to reduce their loss), that the true measure of damages was the sum of the differences between the contract price and the market price, at the several periods fixed for delivery; the breach being treated by the court as final.[52]

§ 738. Place where market value is to be taken.

The difference in value is to be taken at the *place* as well as time of delivery, when it can be there ascertained.[53] This is the invariable rule if there is a market price at that place. So, even where the defendant had a monopoly of the coal market at the place where he had agreed to make the delivery, the market price at that place fixed the measure of damages, and it was held by the Supreme Court of the United States error to charge that the measure of damages was the cash value of the

[51] *United States:* Missouri Furnace Co. *v.* Cochrane, 8 Fed. 463; Haff *v.* Pilling, 134 Fed. 294.

Colorado: Cole *v.* Cheovenda, 4 Colo. 17.

New York: Brock *v.* Knower, 37 Hun, 609.

But where it was left optional with the vendee how much to take each month but he was to take the whole by December 31, that date was held to be the time of the breach. Duluth Furnace Co. *v.* Iron Belt Mining Co., 117 Fed. 138, 55 C. C. A. 154.

[52] *Massachusetts:* Barrie *v.* Quimby, 206 Mass. 259, 92 N. E. 451.

England: Ex parte Llansamlet T. P. Co., L. R. 16 Eq. 155; Roper *v.* Johnson, L. R. 8 C. P. 167; Tyers *v.* Rosedale & F. I. Co., L. R. 8 Ex. 305, L. R. 10 Ex. 195.

[53] *Illinois:* Phelps *v.* McGee, 18 Ill. 155.

Iowa: Osgood *v.* Bauder, 75 Ia. 550, 39 N. W. 887, 1 L. R. A. 655.

Kansas: Field *v.* Kinnear, 4 Kan. 476.

Missouri: White *v.* Salisbury, 33 Mo. 150.

Pennsylvania: Schmertz *v.* Dwyer, 53 Pa. 335.

Texas: Specialty Furniture Co. *v.* Kingsbury, 60 S. W. 1030.

Vermont: Worthen *v.* Wilmot, 30 Vt. 555.

West Virginia: Boyd *v.* Gunnison, 14 W. Va. 1.

In the case of San Francisco securities the value taken was that at the San Francisco Stock Exchange, not a (fictitious) New York quotation, though New York was the place of delivery. Zimmermann *v.* Timmermann, 193 N. Y. 486, 86 N. E. 540.

kind of coal mentioned at other towns near the place of delivery, "after deducting the contract price of the coal and the cost and expenses of transporting thither." Bradley, J., said, that although the plaintiff would probably have received those prices, the rule was firmly established that the value at the place of delivery fixed the measure of damages.[54] So in New York, where assumpsit was brought for breach of a contract to deliver 100,000 shingles at a landing-place called Bailey Town, on Seneca Lake, on the 1st of June, 1828, for which the plaintiff was to pay $125, or $1.25 per thousand, the plaintiff proved the value of the shingles at the place of delivery on the day (1st of June) to have been $1.87 or $2.00 per thousand. The defendant was allowed to prove the value of shingles at Geneva *and other places*, and from an *average of prices* to find the value; but, the plaintiff moving for a new trial, this was held wrong, and that the true rule of damages was the difference between the price as fixed by the parties on the day and *at the place* of delivery and the market value at the same time and place; and a new trial was ordered.[55] Where cheese sold to the plaintiff had been warranted to be worth nineteen cents a pound in the New York market, and was proved to be worth there only twelve, proof that it was shipped to London and netted to the plaintiff, over all expenses, by sales made in the ordinary course of business, sixteen and a half cents a pound, was held inadmissible to reduce the damages.[56] For a breach of a contract by the vendor to deliver goods to a carrier at A, to be shipped to the vendee at B, a few cases hold the measure of damages to be the difference between the contract price and the market value at B, at the time the goods should have arrived, deducting the cost of transportation,[57] on the ground

[54] Grand Tower Co. *v.* Phillips, 23 Wall. 471, 23 L. ed. 71.

[55] Gregory *v.* McDowel, 8 Wend. 435. In a case in Arkansas, in an action on an agreement by which Hanna sold Harter ten hogs, where the defendant below refused to deliver, it was held that the measure of damages was the difference between the price agreed on between the parties and the market price of the pork at the time of the delivery at the place fixed on by the agreement. Hanna *v.* Harter, 2 Ark. 397.

[56] Durst *v.* Burton, 47 N. Y. 167, 7 Am. Rep. 428.

[57] *Alabama:* Buist *v.* Guice, 96 Ala. 255, 11 So. 280; Cawthon *v.* Lusk, 97 Ala. 674, 11 So. 731.

Nebraska: McCormick Harvesting Co. *v.* Jensen, 29 Neb. 102, 45 N. W. 160.

that the contract contemplates a beneficial delivery to the vendee and therefore he is entitled to full compensation for the failure to receive it; but by the better view the ordinary rule is followed, and the market price at the place of delivery to the carrier, if there is there a market value, is taken.[58]

§ 739. Nearest market.

On the principles stated in an earlier chapter,[59] if there is no market value at the place of delivery, the true value of the goods at the time fixed for delivery is to be shown by the best evidence possible. If there is a neighboring market, the price at such market is competent evidence after making due allowance for the cost of transportation between points. Whether such cost should be added to or subtracted from the price in the nearest market depends on circumstances. If the goods were bought to be used at the place of delivery the buyer can be compensated only by adding such cost to the price. This would represent the cost of replacement. On the other hand, if the goods are intended for resale full compensation is awarded if the cost of transportation to the neighboring market be subtracted from the price there. The measure of damages, however, should not depend on the undisclosed purposes of the vendee, and, at least in the absence of knowledge by the vendor of such purposes, there should be but one rule applicable to both cases. The correct rule seems to be this: if the place of delivery is one where the consumption normally exceeds the production the cost of transportation thither should be added to the price in the nearest market; otherwise if the production normally exceeds the consumption.[60]

New York: Boyd v. L. H. Quinn Co.. 17 Misc. 278, 40 N. Y. Supp. 370.

[58] *Iowa:* Tuttle-Chapman Coal Co. v. Coaldale Fuel Co., 136 Ia. 382, 113 N. W. 827.

[59] Chap. v.

[60] In the following cases the cost of transportation was added to the price in the nearest market.

United States: Grand Tower Co. v. Phillips, 23 Wall. 471, 23 L. ed. 71, (coal intended for use, as the vendor knew).

Colorado: Sellar v. Clelland, 2 Colo. 532.

Connecticut: Righter v. Clark (Conn.), 60 Atl. 741 (coal sold at wholesale prices; there was no wholesale market at the place for delivery).

Illinois: Capen v. De Steiger G. Co., 105 Ill. 185 (fruit jars).

Indiana: Vickery v. McCormack, 117 Ind. 594, 20 N. E. 495 (lumber to be used for building).

Maine: Furlong v. Polleys, 30 Me.

If the goods were purchased for resale at another place, and there is no market at which others can be procured to send to that place, the difference between the market price at the place of resale and the contract price, plus the cost of transportation, may be recovered.[61] It would seem that if the place of resale is not the nearest market, knowledge of the destination of the goods on the part of the seller should be proved,[62] as otherwise the loss of the price at the place of resale would not be a natural consequence. Such knowledge is often shown by the fact that the goods were to be delivered to a carrier, to be forwarded to that place.[63]

§ 740. Price receivable on a sub-contract.

The rule in Hadley v. Baxendale, as generally understood, requires a notice of special damages to be given, or circumstances amounting to such notice to be within the contemplation of the parties, in order to enable a plaintiff to recover

491, 50 Am. Dec. 635 (hay intended for use in a lumber camp).

New Hampshire: Stevens v. Lyford, 7 N. H. 360 (lumber).

Virginia: Nottingham Ice Co. v. Preas, 102 Va. 820, 47 S. E. 823 (ice).

Cf. Yellow Poplar Lumber Co. v. Chapman, 20 C. C. A. 503, 74 Fed. 444.

In these cases the cost was deducted: *California:* Hill v. McKay, 94 Cal. 5, 29 Pac. 406 (logs).

Indiana: Pape v. Ferguson, 28 Ind. App. 298, 62 N. E. 712 (lumber purchased for resale).

Maine: Berry v. Dwinel, 44 Me. 255 (logs).

Missouri: Vanstone v. Hopkins, 49 Mo. App. 386 (wheat); Cobb v. Whitsett, 51 Mo. App. 146 (corn); National W. & S. Co. v. Toomy, 144 Mo. App. 516, 129 S. W. 423 (hay).

New York: Wemple v. Stewart, 22 Barb. 154 (lumber); Rice v. Manley, 66 N. Y. 82, 23 Am. Rep. 30 (cheese).

Canada: Hendrie v. Neelon, 12 Ont. App. 41, 3 Ont. 603 (lumber).

In McCleskey & Whitman v. Howell Cotton Co., 147 Ala. 573, 42 So. 67, no allowance for transportation was suggested.

In Houston I. & B. Co. v. Tiemer (Tex. Civ. App.), 139 S. W. 992, where the goods were bought for export, and freight to the export point was cheaper from the nearest market than from the point of delivery, the cost of transportation was not added.

See § 246.

[61] *Alabama:* Johnson v. Allen, 78 Ala. 387, 56 Am. Rep. 34.

Iowa: Louis Cook Mfg. Co. v. Randall, 62 Ia. 244.

Kentucky: Campbellsville Lumber Co. v. Bradley, 96 Ky. 494, 29 S. W. 313.

Nebraska: McCormick H. Co. v. Jensen, 29 Neb. 102, 45 N. W. 160.

Oregon: Hocker-Smith v. Hanley, 29 Ore. 27, 44 Pac. 497.

Tennessee: McDonald v. Unaka T. Co., 88 Tenn. 38.

Wisconsin: Cockburn v. Ashland Lumber Co., 54 Wis. 619.

[62] Cockburn v. Ashland Lumber Co., 54 Wis. 619.

[63] McCormick H. Co. v. Jensen, 29 Neb. 102, 45 N. W. 160.

any other damages than the difference between the contract and the market price.   Where a vendee, therefore, has, between the time of making the original contract and that limited for its performance, made a sub-contract for the resale of the goods at a higher price than the market rate at the time fixed for delivery under the original contract, he cannot recover for his loss of the profits he would have made by carrying out the resale.[64]   It has, however, been held that if there is no market price, the plaintiff can recover what he was to obtain on a sub-contract, if a usual one, less the contract price.[65]   The rule has been put on the ground that the sub-contract shows the value.   Where the defendant had notice of a sub-contract or any special damages which a plaintiff would suffer, such damages are undoubtedly recoverable.[66]   The notice must

[64] *Alabama:* Ala. Chemical Co. *v.* Geiss, 143 Ala. 591, 39 So. 255.

Georgia: Orr *v.* Farmers' Alliance Warehouse & Com. Co., 97 Ga. 241, 22 S. E. 937; Huggins *v.* South Eastern L. & C. Co., 121 Ga. 311, 48 S. E. 933.

Texas: Anderson Electric Co. *v.* Cleburne Water Co., 27 S. W. 504.

England: Williams *v.* Reynolds, 6 B. & S. 495.

[65] *California:* McKay *v.* Riley, 65 Cal. 623.

Illinois: Van Arsdale *v.* Rundel, 82 Ill. 63; Loescher *v.* Deisterberg, 26 Ill. App. 520.

Pennsylvania: McHose *v.* Fulmer, 73 Pa. 365.

Virginia: Trigg *v.* Clay, 88 Va. 330, 13 S. E. 434, 29 Am. St. Rep. 723.

England: Borries *v.* Hutchinson, 18 C. B. (N. S.) 445.

This rule was applied in Carroll-Porter B. & T. Co. *v.* Columbus Machine Co., 55 Fed. 451, 5 C. C. A. 190, in which, however, the damages were claimed for a breach of warranty. See *post,* §§ 759 *et seq.*

[66] *United States:* Wilmoth *v.* Hamilton, 127 Fed. 48.

Florida: Robinson *v.* Ayer, 35 Fla. 544, 17 So. 745.

Georgia: Fontaine *v.* Baxley, 90 Ga. 416, 17 S. E. 835.

Illinois: Benton *v.* Fay, 64 Ill. 417; Carpenter *v.* First Nat. Bank, 119 Ill. 352, 10 N. E. 18; Lapp *v.* Illinois Watch Co., 104 Ill. App. 255.

Kansas: Stewart *v.* Powers, 12 Kan. 596.

Louisiana: Gauthin *v.* Green, 14 La. Ann. 788.

New York: Messmore *v.* New York S. & L. Co., 40 N. Y. 422; Heinemann *v.* Heard, 50 N. Y. 27; Laird *v.* Townsend, 5 Hun, 107; Baxter *v.* Gilson Collins Co., 57 N. Y. Supp. 815.

Virginia: Trigg *v.* Clay, 88 Va. 330, 13 S. E. 434, 29 Am. St. Rep. 723; Perry T. & L. Co. *v.* Reynolds, 100 Va. 264, 40 S. E. 919.

Wisconsin: Hammer *v.* Schoenfelder, 47 Wis. 455.

England: Smeed *v.* Foord, 1 E. & E. 602; Elbinger Actien-Gesellschaft *v.* Armstrong, L. R. 9 Q. B. 473; Borries *v.* Hutchinson, 18 C. B. (N. S.) 445; Grebert-Borgnis *v.* Nugent, 15 Q. B. Div. 85.

Canada: Watrous *v.* Bates, 5 Up. Can. C. P. 366.

be given at the time of entering into the contract.[67] There need be no notice of *the terms* of a sub-contract, unless the terms are exceptional.[68] But there must be a notice of exceptional terms.[69] If there is no notice the plaintiff can still recover an amount not to exceed what would usually result from the breach of contract.[70]

§ 741. Avoidable loss.

In accordance with the principle that the plaintiff should do the best he can to reduce the damages, he will not be allowed to recover damages which could have been avoided by the acceptance of a tender made by the defendant subsequently to the proper time of performance.[71] So if it be readily in the power of the vendee to procure the article elsewhere, he should do so, and his damages in such case are limited to compensation for the delay and expense thereby sustained.[72] It has been held that if he acquires the article for less than the prevailing market value, the damages are the difference between the price paid and the contract price.[73] The vendee is under no duty to go into the market and replace himself before the day for delivery even though the vendor has given notice of his repudiation, and if he does repurchase on the market, he does so at his own risk that the market price on the day for delivery will be less than the price he paid.[74] Nor can

[67] Gee *v.* Lancashire & Y. Ry., 6 H. & N. 211; Hydraulic Engineering Co. *v.* McHaffie, 4 Q. B. Div. 670.

[68] *New York:* Booth *v.* Spuyten Duyvil R. M. Co., 60 N. Y. 487, 19 Am. Rep. 204.

Wisconsin: Guetzkow *v.* Andrews, 92 Wis. 214, 66 N. W. 119, 53 Am. St. Rep. 909.

[69] Horne *v.* Midland Ry., L. R. 7 C. P. 583, L. R. 8 C. P. 131.

[70] Cory *v.* Thames I. W. & S. B. Co., L. R. 3 Q. B. 181.

[71] *Missouri:* Barnett *v.* Elwood Grain Co. (Mo. App.), 133 S. W. 856.

New York: Parsons *v.* Sutton, 66 N. Y. 92.

[72] *Alabama:* Watson *v.* Kirby, 112 Ala. 436, 20 So. 624.

Arkansas: Bench *v.* Potts, 57 Ark. 257.

Kentucky: Barker *v.* Mann, 5 Bush, 672, 96 Am. Dec. 373.

Missouri: Shose *v.* Neiswaanger, 18 Mo. App. 236, 244.

New York: Taylor *v.* Read, 4 Paige, 561; Aronson *v.* H. B. Claflin Co., 115 N. Y. Supp. 97; Joseph *v.* Sulzberger, 136 App. Div. 499, 121 N. Y. Supp. 73; Diamond M. P. Co. *v.* Independent P. P. Co., 121 N. Y. Supp. 1108.

[73] Theiss *v.* Weiss, 166 Pa. 9, 31 Atl. 63, 45 Am. St. Rep. 638.

[74] *United States:* Missouri Furnace Co. *v.* Cochrane, 8 Fed. 463.

Kansas: York-Draper Co. *v.* Lusk (Kan.), 49 Pac. 788.

the vendee recover for any damages which are the result of his own carelessness. So where, on the defendant's failure, he purchased an inferior article and had it manufactured so as to perform a sub-contract he had entered into, he was not allowed to recover the expenses of sending the manufactured article to his vendee, who refused them, for he was not warranted in such a proceeding.[75] It has been held that the defendant cannot reduce the damages by an offer to sell to the plaintiffs at a price below the market value on the day of delivery;[76] but on this point the authorities are in conflict.[77] In a Federal case where the defendant had agreed to sell lumber to the plaintiff on credit but on the day for delivery refused to extend credit and offered the goods for cash at a reduced price, which offer was refused, the buyer being unable to obtain the goods elsewhere, the court held that the buyer could not recover special damages because he should have accepted the seller's offer and thus minimized his loss.[78] And where the goods could not be procured in the market, but the defendant, though he did not deliver the goods sold, offered similar goods which would have answered as a substitute, the plaintiff should have accepted the offer and avoided further loss.[79]

§ 742. Consequential loss.

Allowances for consequential loss in addition to, or differing from the usual measure of damages, will be made or refused in accordance with the rule in Hadley v. Baxendale, the rule of avoidable consequences, and the other general principles affecting contracts.[80] Where it is known to the seller that the goods

---

Massachusetts: Emory Mfg. Co. v. Salomon, 178 Mass. 582, 60 N. E. 377.

Michigan: Austrian v. Springer, 94 Mich. 343, 54 N. W. 50.

Pennsylvania: Morris v. Supplee, 208 Pa. 253, 57 Atl. 566.

And see *Illinois:* Follansbee v. Adams, 86 Ill. 13.

Nebraska: Carter v. Roberts, 85 Neb. 480, 124 N. W. 94.

[75] McHose v. Fulmer, 73 Pa. 365.

[76] *United States:* Campfield v. Sauer, 189 Fed. 576.

New York: Havemeyer v. Cunningham, 35 Barb. 515.

[77] *Ante,* § 222.

[78] Lawrence v. Porter, 63 Fed. 62, 11 C. C. A. 27, 26 L. R. A. 167. *Cf.* American Cotton Co. v. Herring, 84 Miss. 693, 37 So. 117.

[79] Lande v. A. G. Hyde & Sons, 66 Misc. 259, 121 N. Y. Supp. 258.

[80] *Colorado:* Richner v. Plateau L. S. Co., 44 Colo. 302, 98 Pac. 178 (sale of hay to feed cattle; plaintiff recovers expense of securing other hay and of

were ordered by the buyer for a particular occasion, and were to be delivered in time for that occasion, and the contract is broken by the seller, and no time remains to the buyer after the breach to purchase similar goods elsewhere, the seller may be held for such damage as directly and naturally arises from the breach, although "beyond, to this extent, the difference between the contract and the market price."[81]   In Benton v. Fay,[82] a purchaser who gave notice of the object of his purchase was allowed to recover, for failure to send him a planing machine, a fair rent for the use of his buildings and other machinery, they being otherwise in running order, during the time they lay idle in consequence of the defendant's refusal to deliver the machine, but only for so long a time as was reasonably necessary to supply himself with another machine of similar character, after being advised of the defendant's refusal to send the machine sold to him.   The profits that might have been made were held not recoverable where the vendor knew that a mill sold was to be used in grinding corn for cattle; the measure of damages was the difference between the cost of corn meal as ground in the contemplated mill and the price which the vendee necessarily paid for a reasonable substitute for the meal.[83]   Where the defendant contracted to supply

removing cattle to another place to feed, and shrinkage of cattle).

Kentucky: Enterprise Mfg. Co. v. Campbell, — Ky. L. Rep. —, 121 S. W. 1040 (sale of sawmill and fixtures; plaintiff recovers expense of looking up the mill, and value of use while delayed, but not for loss of use of the lumber intended to be sawed, nor, in absence of notice, loss of particular profits from sawing).

New York: Nicholls v. American S. & W. Co., 117 App. Div. 21, 102 N. Y. Supp. 227 (sale of material for manufacture; plaintiff recovers loss of rent of factory and return on capital invested).

South Carolina: Gadsden v. Howe F. & C. Co., 72 S. E. 15 (failure to deliver fertilizer; in absence of notice plaintiff cannot recover for delay in planting).

Texas: Kirby Lumber Co. v. C. R.

Cummings & Co. (Tex. Civ. App.), 122 S. W. 273 (purchase for resale in foreign market; plaintiff recovers ordinary profits of resale in such market).

[81] *Kansas:* Halsted Lumber Co. v. Sutton, 46 Kan. 192, 26 Pac. 444.

Massachusetts: Abbott v. Hapgood, 150 Mass. 248, 22 N. E. 907, 15 Am. St. Rep. 193.

West Virginia: Davis v. Grand Rapids Furn. Co., 41 W. Va. 717, 24 S. E. 630.

Wisconsin: Richardson v. Chynoweth, 26 Wis. 656.

[82] 64 Ill. 417.   *Cf.* Pallett v. Murphy, 131 Cal. 192, 63 Pac. 366, 82 Am. St. Rep. 341 (water for irrigation; rental value of land awarded); Berkey & G. Furniture Co. v. Hascall, 123 Ind. 502, 24 N. E. 336, 9 L. R. A. 65 (furniture for hotel).

[83] Chalice v. Witte, 81 Mo. App. 84.

ornamental bricks for the front of a building and failed to do so, and no other bricks of the sort could be procured, damages were allowed for the lessened value of the building from the front being built with inferior bricks.[84] A water company agreed to furnish water sufficient to extinguish fires. The measure of damages for a breach was the value of the property destroyed by fire, this loss being clearly in the contemplation of the parties.[85] Where the vendor broke its contract to deliver iron ore and the vendee was unable to procure ore of the same quality in the market, the vendee recovered the increased expense of using ore of an inferior grade, it appearing that the defendant was cognizant of all the facts.[86] Under a contract by the defendant to sell and deliver a large quantity of coal at a fixed price during a certain time, to be transported at the plaintiff's expense to their factory, it was held in an action to recover for a breach of the contract by delivering inferior coal, and in not delivering it till after the contract time, that the measure of damages for the inferior quality was the difference between the value at the factory of the coal called for by the contract, and that of the coal delivered; and the measure of damages for the failure to deliver in time was not the difference in market value, but the difference between the actual charge for freight and insurance, and the average rates during the time covered by the contract, especially in the absence of evidence that the average rates were higher than the rates at the end of the contract period.[87] Where the plaintiff upon a breach by the defendant of a contract of sale was unable to procure a substitute to fill a sub-contract of which the defendant had notice and the sub-vendee recovered damages for the breach, the plaintiff in this action was allowed to recover the amount of damages awarded the sub-vendee.[88] Expenses rea-

Cf. Carroll-Porter B. & T. Co. *v.* Columbus Mach. Co., 55 Fed. 451, 5 C. C. A. 190.

[84] Sweeney *v.* Jamieson, 2 Wash. 254.

[85] Harris *v.* Columbia & L. Co., 114 Tenn. 328, 85 S. W. 897.

[86] Thomas Iron Co. *v.* Jackson Iron Co., 131 Mich. 130, 91 N. W. 137.

[87] Merrimack Manuf. Co. *v.* Quintard, 107 Mass. 127, 9 Am. Rep. 13.

[88] *United States:* Iowa Mfg. Co. *v.* Sturtevant Mfg. Co., 162 Fed. 460, 89 C. C. A. 346, 18 L. R. A. (N. S.) 575.

New York: Czarnikow, MacDougall & Co. *v.* Baxter, 130 N. Y. Supp. 617.

England: Grebert-Borgnis *v.* Nugent, 15 Q. B. Div. 85.

And see *Iowa:* Black *v.* De Camp, 78 Ia. 718.

sonably incurred in preparation to receive the articles sold are recoverable.[89] If the plaintiff has incurred reasonable expenses, so as to prevent injurious consequences, he can recover them.[90] The expenses of delay, caused by reliance on the defendant's intention to perform, were held recoverable in Grand Tower Co. v. Phillips.[91]

In case the breach by the vendor is only by a delay in delivery, consequential damages are awarded in accordance with the principles applicable in case of non-delivery. Unavoidable loss of time of the vendee's workmen [92] and injuries to property [93] which are in the contemplation of the parties are elements of damages. So too expenses incurred in preparation to receive [94] are recoverable, as are also demurrage charges on a vessel detained until the goods arrive.[95] And where the delay results in loss of use of property, the value of such use, usually the rental value, is recoverable.[96]

[89] *California:* Cole v. Swanston, 1 Cal. 51, 52 Am. Dec. 288.

Colorado: Farrer v. Caster, 17 Colo. App. 41, 67 Pac. 171.

Iowa: Mann v. Taylor, 78 Ia. 355, 43 N. W. 220.

Michigan: Cuddy v. Major, 12 Mich. 368 (demurrage charges).

Missouri: Warren v. A. B. Mayer Mfg. Co., 161 Mo. 112, 61 S. W. 644, 84 Am. St. Rep. 869.

Virginia: Perry v. Reynolds, 100 Va. 264, 40 S. E. 919 (demurrage charges). *Cf.* Harrow Spring Co. v. Whipple Harrow Co., 90 Mich. 147, 51 N. W. 197, 30 Am. St. Rep. 421 (expenses of a resale recovered).

[90] Borries v. Hutchinson, 18 C. B. (N. S.) 445; Lalor v. Burrows, 18 Up. Can. C. P. 321. But incidental expenses cannot be considered in the absence of special circumstances known to the seller. Moffit-West Drug Co. v. Byrd, 34 C. C. A. 351, 92 Fed. 290.

[91] 23 Wall. 471, 23 L. ed. 71.

[92] *Kentucky:* Clark v. Bailey, 22 Ky. L. Rep. 1668, 61 S. W. 30.

New York: Raymore Realty Co. v. Pfotenhauer-Nesbit Co., 129 N. Y. Supp. 1002.

Washington: Interstate Engineering Co. v. Archer, 117 Pac. 470.

[93] *Massachusetts:* Lonergan v. Waldo, 179 Mass. 135, 60 N. E. 479, 88 Am. St. Rep. 365.

North Carolina: Neal v. Pender-Hyman Hardware Co., 122 N. C. 104, 29 S. E. 96, 65 Am. St. Rep. 697.

Washington: Interstate Engineering Co. v. Archer, 117 Pac. 470.

[94] Chatham v. Jones, 69 Tex. 744, 7 S. W. 600.

[95] *New York:* Miner v. Blume, 64 App. Div. 511, 72 N. Y. Supp. 320.

England: Agius v. Great Western Colliery Co., [1899] 1 Q. B. 413.

[96] *United States:* Dustin Co. v. St. Petersburg Ins. Co., 126 Fed. 816 (machinery).

Iowa: Brownell v. Chapman, 84 Ia. 504, 51 N. W. 249, 35 Am. St. Rep. 326 (machinery).

New York: Jones v. National Printing Co., 13 Daly, 192 (materials).

Texas: Dilley v. Ratcliss, 69 S. W. 237 (machinery).

But in an action for delay in furnish-

§ 742a. Profits.

It follows from what has already been said that in general in this class of cases lost profits cannot be recovered. To make a recovery of them possible it must appear that they were within the contemplation of the parties, and that they were not too conjectural.[97] The ordinary case is that of failure to supply goods bought for resale [98] or failure to supply machinery [99] or materials to be used by the purchaser in building or manufacturing.[100] So where the defendant failed to deliver bottles for essences manufactured by the plaintiff, the plaintiff's loss in business through inability to bottle his essences is recoverable.[101] Where the defendant agreed to supply logs for the plaintiff's mill, the net profits to be divided be-

ing machinery for a mill the rental value of the entire mill cannot be recovered without evidence of special circumstances. Munson v. James Smith W. M. Co., 118 App. Div. 398, 103 N. Y. Supp. 502.

See ante, § 195.

[97] *Alabama:* Young v. Cureton, 87 Ala. 727, 6 So. 352.

Kentucky: Hay v. Williams, 8 Ky. L. Rep. 434.

New York: Vuccino & Co. v. Brown, 92 N. Y. Supp. 319.

[98] *United States:* Howard Supply Co. v. Wells, 176 Fed. 513, 100 C. C. A. 70.

Kentucky: Roberts, Wicks & Co. v. Lee, 102 S. W. 300, 31 Ky. L. Rep. 266.

Michigan: Duvall v. Ferwerda, 146 Mich. 13, 108 N. W. 1115.

Rhode Island: Eddy v. Fay Fruit Co. (R. I.), 67 Atl. 586.

Texas: Weatherford M. & F. Co. v. Tate, 49 Tex. Civ. App. 392, 109 S. W. 406.

[99] *United States:* Howard v. Stillwell B. Mfg. Co., 139 U. S. 199, 35 L. ed. 147, 11 Sup. Ct. 500.

Kentucky: Bates Mach. Co. v. Norton Iron Works, 113 Ky. 372, 68 S. W. 423.

Massachusetts: Abbott v. Hapgood,

150 Mass. 248, 25 N. E. 311, 5 L. R. A. 586, 15 Am. St. Rep. 193.

Michigan: Industrial Works v. Mitchell, 114 Mich. 29, 72 N. W. 25.

North Carolina: Bender Lumber Co. v. Wilmington Iron Works, 130 N. C. 584, 41 S. E. 797.

Texas: Alamo Mills Co. v. Hercules Iron Works, 1 Tex. Civ. App. 683, 22 S. W. 1097; Fred W. Wolf Co. v. Galbraith, 35 Tex. Civ. App. 505, 80 S. W. 648; Reagan R. B. Co. v. Dickson C. W. Co., 121 S. W. 526.

[100] *California:* Friend & T. Lumber Co. v. Miller, 67 Cal. 464, 8 Pac. 40.

Kentucky: Guenther v. Taylor, 23 Ky. L. Rep. 536, 63 S. W. 439.

Maryland: Equitable G. L. Co. v. Baltimore, C. T. & M. Co., 65 Md. 73.

Michigan: Axle Co. v. Michigan Buggy Co., 106 Mich. 445, 64 N. W. 466; Thorn v. Morgan, 135 Mich. 51, 97 N. W. 43.

Pennsylvania: Imperial C. & C. Co. v. Port Royal C. & C. Co. (Pa.), 20 Atl. 937.

Tennessee: Chisholm & M. Mfg. Co. v. U. S. Canopy Co., 111 Tenn. 202, 77 S. W. 1062.

[101] Culin v. Woodbury Glass Works, 108 Pa. 220.

tween them, the plaintiff upon breach is entitled to recover the profits he would have realized.[102]

If, however, the goods which the defendant contracted to deliver can be procured in the market the plaintiff must get them elsewhere, and cannot charge the defendant with loss of profits from their use or resale.[103]

§ 743. Waiver.

Where a vendor has partly failed to comply with his part of the contract, yet if the vendee have received and made use of part of the property purchased, and is benefited by it, he must still pay for the property so received and used within the limit of the contract price, provided its value exceed the damage he has sustained from the failure to complete the contract.[104] But the right to delivery of the full amount is not necessarily waived by accepting a partial delivery.[105] Neither is the right to damages for delay in delivery waived by acceptance of the goods at a later date.[106]

§ 744. Payment in advance.

* But a different case is presented where the purchaser has paid the price in advance, or has otherwise, as by the transfer of stock, been deprived of the use of his property; and here it has been insisted that the purchaser is not to be limited to the value of the article at the time of delivery, but shall have the advantage of any rise in the market value of the article which may have taken place up to the time of the trial; and on this point different and conflicting decisions have been made.**

---

[102] Robinson v. Bullock, 66 Ala. 548; see § 193.

For other instances where profits were recoverable see the following:

Kansas: Brown v. Hadley, 43 Kan. 267, 23 Pac. 492.

Kentucky: New Market Co. v. Embry, 20 Ky. L. Rep. 1130, 48 S. W. 980.

Australia: Australian Smelting Co. v. British Broken Hill Proprietary Co., 22 Vict. L. R. 190.

[103] Atlas P. C. Co. v. Hopper, 116 App. Div. 445, 101 N. Y. Supp. 948; Stecker v. Weaver C. & C. Co., 116 App. Div. 772, 102 N. Y. Supp. 89; McManus v. American Woolen Co., 126 App. Div. 68, 110 N. Y. Supp. 680.

[104] Koeltz v. Bleckman, 46 Mo. 320.

[105] Creighton v. Comstock, 27 Oh. St. 548.

[106] Digman v. Spurr, 3 Wash. 309, 28 Pac. 529.

The ground of the latter rule has not been clearly defined. The courts seem to have been influenced by the fact that, whereas, in the ordinary case of breach by the vendor, the vendee may take the money he was to have given the vendor, and go into the market and replace himself; when the vendor has received the price, the vendee may be unable to purchase other goods, and hence, having been deprived of the use of his property, he is entitled to the best price he could have obtained for the article purchased up to the time of the settlement of the question. The general question of the allowance of a higher intermediate value has already been discussed.[107] It is only necessary here to examine the application of that rule in this particular case.

The application of this principle in the case now under consideration was first made in some early English and New York cases.[108] A case in New York frequently cited upon this point,[109] was an action of assumpsit on a note, promising, for value received, to pay one hundred and fifty dollars in good salt, at one dollar and a half per barrel, to be delivered on the 15th of April then next. This the court held to be a contract to deliver salt, and decided that, as the goods had been paid for, the measure of damages was the difference between the contract price and the highest value at any time between the period for delivery and the day of trial.

* In Connecticut, it has been held that where the price is paid in advance, the advance at all events can be recovered without any investigation into the state of the market. In a case in that State, suit was brought on an agreement to deliver flour. The plaintiff paid part of the price in advance. At the time fixed for the performance, flour had fallen in price, and it was held that he was entitled to recover his advance with interest. It was admitted that where one contracts to deliver any article other than money, and fails to do it, the rule of damages is the value of the article at the time and place of delivery, with interest for the delay, because it is supposed that the party will have supplied himself else-

---

[107] See chap. xxii.
[108] Shepherd v. Johnson, 2 East, 211; Gainsford v. Carroll, 2 B. & C. 624;

Cortelyou v. Lansing, 2 Caines Cas. 200; West v. Wentworth, 3 Cow. 82.
[109] Clark v. Pinney, 7 Cow. 681, 695.

where with the article at that price; but it was held that this reasoning did not apply to a case where the defendant had violated his contract and retained the plaintiff's money without consideration.[110] In a case in the same State, on an agreement by the defendant to give a deed of certain land in consideration of the transfer to him of a farm worth $2,000, the defendant insisted that the plaintiff could only recover the value of the farm conveyed by him; and it was so held at the trial. But the rule that the value of the article at the time and place of delivery, and interest for delay, furnished the measure of damages, was again declared by the court. It was said "that the *consideration of a contract* is never the rule of estimating the damages for the breach of an express agreement;" and a new trial was granted.[111] ** The whole subject was, however, afterwards reviewed in that State, and the rule of allowing the *value of the goods at the time of trial* adopted,[112] the court saying "that it was founded upon principles of natural justice."

§ 745. The rule of higher intermediate value followed in some jurisdictions.

In England, in the Nisi Prius case of Elliot *v.* Hughes,[113] the rule is approved by which the measure of damages for the non-delivery of goods paid for in advance is the difference between the price paid and the highest price up to the trial; but the case of Startup *v.* Cortazzi [114] seems opposed to this,

---

[110] Bush *v.* Canfield, 2 Conn. 485. See an able dissenting opinion by Hosmer, J. This case presents, in fact, the question whether the loss by the depreciation of the article should fall on the vendor or purchaser; the court, in awarding to the plaintiff his advance and interest, really extricated him from a losing bargain.

[111] Wells *v.* Abernethy, 5 Conn. 222, 227. "The reason of the rule," said Hosmer, C. J., "is so simple and obvious, that it has been universally embraced, except in cases of stock contracts; and the anomaly in such cases

has arisen from the specific relief which chancery has been in the habit of giving, and which courts of law, not universally, but in most instances, have in substance thought proper to pursue. Whenever a case on this subject occurs, I shall be desirous of putting an end to this exception without cause, by the establishment of perfect uniformity, as no just reason can be assigned for any discrimination."

[112] West *v.* Pritchard, 19 Conn. 212.

[113] 3 F. & F. 387.

[114] 2 C. M. & R. 165.

and the law of England is said to be unsettled, except in the case of sales of stock, where the value at the time of trial is allowed.[115]

The modification of the general rule in case of payment in advance is sanctioned in Indiana in regard to commercial transactions. In the case of Kent v. Ginter,[116] the court, after stating that the ordinary rule for measuring damages in suits by the vendee against the vendor is the value of the property at the time and place of delivery, declares that one exception is well established in the case of stocks, and approves also those authorities which make a second exception in the case of the payment in advance for an article which is one of a class or quantity. In this case the vendee has two remedies: one to treat the contract as rescinded, and sue to recover the money paid, with interest; the other, to sue for damages which include, besides the value of the article at the time of the purchase, the benefit of its rise; whether this second exception extends to the case of a specific article, the title to which passed by the purchase, so that trover or replevin could be maintained for it, by the vendee, the court leaves undecided. In Pennsylvania it is held that where bank stock has been wrongfully withheld from a party entitled to it, the measure of damages, if the consideration for the stock has been paid, is "the highest market value between the breach and the trial, together with the bonus and dividends which have been received in the meantime;" but if the consideration "has not been paid, the plaintiff should be allowed the difference between it and the value of the stock, together with the difference between the interest on the consideration and the dividends on the stock." [117] Such also is the rule in California,[118] where in one case the court sustained an alternative instruction to the jury that they might find the amount of the purchase money and interest, or the highest market price of the property to the time of trial,[119]

---

[115] Mayne on Damages, 4th ed., p. 179; Harrison v. Harrison, 1 C. & P. 412.

[116] 23 Ind. 1.

[117] Bank of Montgomery v. Reese, 26 Pa. 143; acc., Musgrave v. Beckendorff, 53 Pa. 310; Kountz v. Kirkpatrick, 72 Pa. 376, 13 Am. Rep. 687.

[118] Dabovich v. Emeric, 12 Cal. 171, 73 Am. Dec. 529.

[119] Maher v. Riley, 17 Cal. 415.

and in Oregon.[120] In Texas, also, upon much consideration, the rule has been declared that, on breach of a contract to deliver chattels, where the purchase money has been paid, the highest price at any time between the time appointed for delivery and the day of trial, and interest from the time appointed for delivery, is the true measure of damages.[121]

In the Supreme Court of the United States Chief-Justice Marshall intimated that this was the correct rule;[122] but he spoke only for himself. The rule of higher intermediate value, as now modified in New York, has been recently adopted by that court in the case of breach of a broker's contract to carry stocks on a margin;[123] but it is doubtful whether the rule would be extended by that court to the case of non-delivery of goods sold.

In Iowa the plaintiff has been allowed to recover the price of the goods when they were demanded, that being the highest price previous to the trial. When delivery should have been made, the price was much lower. The court in that case stated the Iowa rule to be that the plaintiff could recover the highest price previous to the day of bringing suit, where not unnecessarily delayed.[124]

Where at the time of making a contract for the purchase of personal property *in futuro* a small sum was paid as earnest money, but was returned before the vendor's breach of the contract, or any tender of the rest of the purchase money, this was held in Vermont not such a payment in advance as to come within the rule.[125] In England, actions for the non-delivery of railway shares pursuant to a contract of sale are distinguished from actions for not replacing borrowed stock,

---

[120] Livesley v. Krebs Hop Co. (Ore.), 107 Pac. 460.

[121] Brasher v. Davidson, 31 Tex. 190, 98 Am. Dec. 525; Gregg v. Fitzhugh, 36 Tex. 127. So where payment is to be made in goods at a stipulated price. Ranger v. Hearne, 37 Tex. 30.

In a later case, on the question of interest the court held that that should be awarded not from the date of breach but from the date on which the high-

est intermediate value was determined. Masterton v. Goodlett, 46 Tex. 402; Randon v. Barton, 4 Tex. 289; Calvit v. M'Fadden, 13 Tex. 324.

[122] Shepherd v. Hampton, 3 Wheat. 200, 4 L. ed. 369.

[123] Galigher v. Jones, 129 U. S. 193, 32 L. ed. 658, 9 Sup. Ct. 335.

[124] Stapleton v. King, 40 Ia. 278.

[125] Worthen v. Wilmot, 30 Vt. 555.

and in the former class of cases the market price on the day
when the contract of sale is to be formed, instead of that on the
day of trial, is fixed as the standard for the computation of
the damages.[126]

§ 746. The rule disapproved in other jurisdictions.

But, as has been seen, the rule of higher intermediate value
has been disapproved in many jurisdictions; and in them the
measure of damages is held to be the same, whether the consideration was or was not paid in advance.[127]   The rule in
Vermont was thus stated by Redfield, C. J., in delivering the
opinion of the court in Humphreysville Copper Co. v. Copper
Mining Co.: [128]   "The only general damages which the vendee
of personal property is entitled to recover for failure to deliver the articles according to the contract, whether the price be
paid or not, is the difference between the contract price and the
market price of the article at the stipulated time and place of
delivery, when the price has advanced, together with the
money paid towards the price."   And in Hill v. Smith,[129] the
same learned court, after adverting to the conflict of authority
on this question, said: "It has not been adjudged in this State,
that payment in advance in such a case varies the rule of damages, and so far as any indication can be gathered from the
cases, . . . it seems to be in the direction of not permitting
that fact to affect the rule. Upon principle, as well as in view
of practical consequences, we prefer the result at which Mr.
Sedgwick has arrived, upon a most elaborate and able examination of the subject, that the market value or price on the
day of the breach of the contract controls the measure of damages."   This is so, also, as we shall presently see, in actions
against the vendee.   In Rider v. Kelley,[130] a case of this kind
in the same State, the court said: "It stands upon this reason-

---

[126] Tempest v. Kilner, 2 C. B. 300, 3
C. B. 249; Shaw v. Holland, 15 M. & W.
136; Barned v. Hamilton, 2 Railw. &
Can. Cas. 624.

[127] *Alabama:* Neel v. Clay, 48 Ala. 252;
Vann v. Lunsford, 91 Ala. 576, 8 So. 719.

Illinois: Cushman v. Hayes, 46 Ill.
145.

Maine: McKenney v. Haines, 63 Me.
74 (*semble*).

Tennessee: Coffman v. Williams, 4
Heisk. 233, 240.

[128] 33 Vt. 92, 99.

[129] 32 Vt. 433.

[130] 32 Vt. 268, 273.

able ground, that as the title to the property remains in the seller, he can, upon non-acceptance by the vendee, sell the property at once for its market price, and therefore that the difference between such market price and the contract price will indemnify him against loss." [131] In Rose v. Bozeman,[132] it was held that the measure of damages for the breach of a contract to deliver cotton at a specified time and place was its value at the time of the breach, and that the payment of the price in advance did not affect the rule. In Kentucky, where one Yoder covenanted to furnish Allen, by a given day, two slaves, in consideration of $450 then paid, and $210 to be paid on their delivery, it was said by the Court of Appeals, that for a failure to furnish the slaves according to contract, the obligors were liable for damages to Allen. "The measure of those damages was the value of the negroes described at the time and place of performance. This was the province of the jury to ascertain. It has done so, and the amount of consideration did not form a subject of material inquiry." [133]

In Gray v. Portland Bank,[134] an action for refusal to accept a subscription for stock, Sedgwick, J., said: "The price of the stock at the time it should be transferred or delivered (and the same rule applies to other personal property) shall be that by which the damages shall be assessed. If the plaintiff intends to *retain* the stock, the then price is what he must pay for an equal amount,' and if he intends it for *sale*, that price is what he would obtain for it." And so it was held in Massachusetts,[135] that where the defendant had agreed to deliver a certificate of ten shares of the corporate stock of a certain manufacturing company, whose capital was to be one hundred thousand dollars, divided into not more than two hundred shares, and instead thereof made a tender of a certificate of ten shares of the stock of the company, of which thirty-four thousand dollars only were paid, divided into seventy shares; that the measure of damages was the value of ten shares in the full capital stock, if it had been made up at the time stipulated,

---

[131] *Acc.*, Cofield v. Clark, 2 Colo. 101; Smith v. Dunlap, 12 Ill. 184.

[132] 41 Ala. 678; s. c. 40 Ala. 212.

[133] Yoder v. Allen, 2 Bibb (Ky.), 338.

[134] 3 Mass. 364, 390, 3 Am. Dec. 151.

[135] Dyer v. Rich, 1 Met. 180.

and the company had then been ready in good faith to operate upon the capital, pursuant to their charter.[136]

§ 747. Distinction between stock and merchandise.

In some jurisdictions, though a higher intermediate value is allowed in the case of non-delivery of stock, it is not allowed in the case of other personal property, though the price has been paid in advance. So in Pennsylvania, though, as we have seen, the rule prevails in stock transactions, it is not approved with regard to chattels generally. In an early case [137] it appeared that Woolston bought of Bosler 13,000 *morus multicaulis*, and paid the price; the trees were not delivered. Smethurst, the defendant, gave a guaranty for the performance by Bosler of his contract to deliver the trees on five days' notice. Smethurst being proved liable, it was insisted that the measure of damages was the value of *morus multicaulis* at the time of the breach of contract, or about that time. But the judge who tried the cause said that the sum paid by Woolston, the plaintiff, to Bosler, furnished the rule. On writ of error, the Supreme Court of Pennsylvania held the charge wrong. After noting the case of Shepherd *v.* Hampton, above cited, the court said, it is evident that C. J. Marshall "failed to advert to the difference between a suit on the contract itself, and a suit grounded on the rescision of the contract." In the latter case, the court said, the money paid could be recovered; but in the former, the value must be always the measure of damages.

In other jurisdictions it is said that there should be no distinction.[138] So in New York, while the rule giving the vendee the advantage of the rise in value where the price is paid in advance is recognized,[139] no distinction is made between the case of the sale of stocks and other personal property where the price is not paid in advance, and in the former case as well as the latter, the plaintiff is restricted to the difference in mar-

---

[136] *Acc.*, Struthers *v.* Clark, 30 Pa. 210.

[137] Smethurst *v.* Woolston, 5 W. & S. 106.

[138] *Texas:* Cartwright *v.* McCook, 33 Tex. 612; Gregg *v.* Fitzhugh, 36 Tex. 127.

Virginia: Enders *v.* Board of Public Works, 1 Gratt. 364.

[139] Arnold *v.* Suffolk Bank, 27 Barb. 424.

ket value on the day when the property should have been delivered.[140]

§ 748. No just distinction.

* There appears no solid reason for making any difference between stock and any other vendible commodity. Where stock is loaned, or the price of the article paid for, in either case the party entitled to the delivery parts with his property on the faith of the contract, and in either case is prevented from using it, up to the time of trial. The question is, whether, in either case, the law should act on the assumption that the plaintiff would have retained the property if the contract had been complied with, till the period of the highest value, and have realized that price, and thus give damages which are purely conjectural. It will be noticed that in the case of Clark v. Pinney it was intimated by the Supreme Court of New York, that the rule ought to be limited to the case of articles intended for sale; and that in Startup v. Cortazzi, it was suggested that the plaintiffs had given no proof of the purpose for which the article was intended; the niceness of the first distinction, the difficulty of furnishing satisfactory proof under the second head, and the general policy of the law which denies conjectural relief, seem strongly to point to the period of breach as the true time, in all cases, of estimating the damages, unless it be shown that the article was to be delivered for some specific object known to both parties at the time, and that thus a loss, within the contemplation of both parties, has been sustained. The fact of payment in advance throws no light on the injury sustained by the purchaser; nor does it at all increase the probability that he would have retained the article till the rise of price. The value of the article at the time of breach, with interest for delay, and subject to the above exception, seems as near an approach to the actual loss sustained as can be effected, without embarking upon a vague search after facts impossible, in most cases, to be proved with any degree of satisfaction.

§ 749. Same reason for rule where property has fallen.

And if this rule be sound, it applies as well to cases where

[140] Belden v. Nicolay, 4 E. D. Smith, 14.

the property has fallen as to those where it has risen. The purchaser claims his advance; but if he gets the value of the article at the time of the breach, the contract is performed; and if this sum be less than his advance, his loss is ascribable purely to his own bargain. It may undoubtedly be urged, and with force, that the contract being violated by the defendant, the retention of any part of the plaintiff's money is against conscience. It has already, however, been said that in actions of contract the only object of the tribunal must be to carry into effect the agreement of the parties as far as possible, and that the motives of the defaulter are not to be taken into view. If this be correct, then certainly it removes the last objection to the adoption of the general rule, that the value at the time of the breach, with interest for the delay, is, with the exception of the defendant's liability to make remuneration for loss resulting from facts within the knowledge and in the contemplation of both parties at the time of the contract, to furnish the measure of damages.**

§ 749a. Collateral agreement broken by vendor.

Where the vendor's breach consists not in a failure to deliver the goods sold but in failure to perform some collateral agreement, the ordinary measure of damages for breach of contract applies. So where bicycles were sold by the manufacturer with an agreement to keep the price at a certain figure, and the price was reduced within the time limited, it was held that vendor could recover the difference between the stipulated price and that to which it was reduced, not as profits lost which the vendee would have made, but because by the reduction of the price the vendor had in effect delivered an article of less market value than he had contracted to deliver.[141]

II.—Breach by Vendee

§ 750. Rule where title has passed.

In some cases of sale of personal property the title to the property passes to the purchaser at or before delivery or time for delivery. In these cases the contract fixes the price or it does not. If this point be left doubtful, the value of the article

[141] Lozier *v.* Hannan (Colo.), 54 Pac. 399.

in the market is the rule.[142] * If the vendee resell the article, he can be made liable for the price received, deducting usual charges and commissions. He is treated as a trustee or agent of the plaintiff, selling on his account and for his benefit; and it is both equitable and legal that, having received the money, he should pay it over to the owner, after retaining a due compensation for his services.[143] But this is a very unusual case, and the contract generally fixes the price.

Where a vendee is sued for non-performance of the contract on his part, in not paying the contract price, if the goods have been delivered, the measure of damages is of course the price named in the agreement;[144] but if their possession has not been changed, it has been doubted whether the rule of damages is the price itself, or only the difference between the contract price and the value of the article at the time fixed for its delivery. It seems to be well settled in cases where the title to the goods has passed before delivery and the purchaser refuses to accept that the vendor may resell the goods if he see fit, and charge the vendee with the difference between the contract price and that realized at the sale.[145] Though perhaps more prudent, it is not necessary that the sale should be at auction. It is only requisite to show that the property was sold for a fair

[142] *United States:* Henckley v. Hendrickson, 5 McLean, 170.
Arkansas: Burr v. Williams, 23 Ark. 244.
Connecticut: Abbott v. Wyse, 15 Conn. 254.
Georgia: McCarthy v. Nixon Grocery Co., 126 Ga. 762, 56 S. E. 72.
Massachusetts: Taft v. Travis, 136 Mass. 95; Deutsch v. Pratt, 149 Mass. 415, 14 Am. St. Rep. 430, 21 N. E. 1072.
Michigan: Lovejoy v. Michels, 88 Mich. 15, 49 N. W. 901, 13 L. R. A. 770.
Missouri: Deck v. Feld, 38 Mo. App. 674.
New York: Booth v. Bierce, 38 N. Y. 463, 98 Am. Dec. 73.
Wisconsin: Althouse v. Alvord, 28 Wis. 577.

[143] Greene v. Bateman, 2 W. & M. 359.
[144] *Arkansas:* Jackson v. Jones, 22 Ark. 158.
Missouri: Fairbanks, Morse & Co. v. Midvale Co., 105 Mo. App. 644, 80 S. W. 13.
South Carolina: Suber v. Pullin, 1 S. C. 273.
Vermont: Smith v. Coolidge, 68 Vt. 516, 35 Atl. 432, 54 Am. St. Rep. 902.
Canada: Phillips v. Merritt, 2 Up. Can. C. P. 513.
[145] *New York:* Sands v. Taylor, 5 Johns. 395.
England: Langford v. Tyler's Adm'r, 1 Salk. 113; s. c. 6 Mod. 162; Cuddee v. Rutter, 5 Vin. Abr. 538; s. c. Cud v. Rutter, 1 P. Wms. 570.

price.[146] ** But if the vendor does not pursue this course, and without reselling the goods sues the vendee for his breach of contract, the rule appears to be, that where the title to the goods has passed to the vendee, the vendor can recover the contract price in full.[147] And the fact that the goods were destroyed without fault of the vendor before possession was taken does not affect the amount of the recovery.[148]

§ 751. Instances.

* In a suit brought by vendor against vendee, the plaintiff had contracted to sell the defendant three hundred tons of Campeachy logwood; "such as may be determined to be otherwise by impartial judges to be rejected;" the defendant refused to accept the wood offered, because it was not all Campeachy logwood; it was insisted on his behalf that he was not bound by the contract price, as a part only of the stipulated quantity had been furnished; and that the measure of damages was the difference between the contract price and what the article would have sold for at the time when the true quantity of Campeachy logwood was ascertained. But the Court of King's Bench held that the defendant was bound to take the part which was Campeachy, and that, he having repudiated the whole contract, the measure of the damages was the contract price on that quantity, i. e., the Campeachy wood.[149]

[146] *Louisiana:* White v. Kearney, 2 La. Ann. 639.

New York: Crooks v. Moore, 1 Sandf. 297.

[147] *United States:* Pittsburgh H. & H. S. Co. v. Bown, 174 Fed. 981, 98 C. C. A. 593.

Georgia: McCarthy v. Nixon Grocery Co., 126 Ga. 762, 56 S. E. 72.

Indiana: Vickery v. Evans, 16 Ind. 331; Burke v. Keystone Mfg. Co., 19 Ind. App. 556, 48 N. E. 382.

Maine: Merrill v. Parker, 24 Me. 89, 41 Am. Dec. 374.

Massachusetts: Morse v. Sherman, 106 Mass. 430; Pearson v. Mason, 120 Mass. 53.

Missouri: Stresovich v. Kesting, 63 Mo. App. 57.

New Hampshire: Woolsey v. Bailey, 27 N. H. 217.

New York: Hunter v. Wetsell, 84 N. Y. 549, 38 Am. Rep. 544.

Pennsylvania: Henderson v. Jennings, 228 Pa. 188, 77 Atl. 453, 30 L. R. A. (N. S.) 27.

Wisconsin: Crawford v. Earl, 38 Wis. 312.

[148] *Kentucky:* Sweeney v. Owsley, 14 B. Mon. 413.

Minnesota: Rail v. Little Falls Lumber Co., 47 Minn. 422, 50 N. W. 471.

New York: Texter v. Norton, 55 Barb. 272.

England: Brown v. Hare, 3 H. & N. 484; Tarling v. Baxter, 6 B. & C. 369.

[149] Graham v. Jackson, 14 East, 498.

The question has been considered in New York, and decided in the same way.[150] The plaintiff, a carriage-maker, was employed to build a sulky for the defendant. A due tender having been made of the carriage, and it being deposited with a third person, the defendant having refused payment, and suit brought, it was insisted that the measure of damages was not the value of the sulky, but only the expense of taking it to the residence of the defendant, delay, loss of sale, etc.; but the court held otherwise.[151]

It has been held in Pennsylvania, where goods are sold at auction on credit, and the vendee refuses to take them, the owner may, before the expiration of the credit, sue the vendee for his breach of contract; and in such case, the measure of damages is the difference between the price agreed to be paid for the goods and their value at the time that the vendee refused to take them. This is clearly so, because no action can be brought *for the price* of the goods until the time of credit is expired. But in this case, Gibson, J., proceeded to say: "Properly speaking, the seller cannot *recover the price where he has retained the goods* in consequence of the buyer's refusing to comply with any part of the contract."[152] So in Massachusetts, where a contract had been made for the purchase of railway shares, and a part of the price paid, and the vendor caused them to be transferred on the books of the company, but the defendant refused to accept them after such transfer, it was held that the measure of damages was the contract price.[153]

---

[150] Bement v. Smith, 15 Wend. 493, 496.

[151] See to the same effect the following cases:

Iowa: McCormick Harvesting Mach. Co. v. Markert, 107 Iowa, 340, 78 N. W. 33.

Massachusetts: Goddard v. Binney, 115 Mass. 450, 15 Am. Rep. 112.

Missouri: Crown Vinegar & Spice Co. v. Wehrs, 59 Mo. App. 493; Black River L. Co. v. Warner, 93 Mo. 374, 6 S. W. 210, 3 Am. St. Rep. 544.

Nebraska: Lincoln Shoe Manuf. Co.

v. Sheldon, 44 Neb. 279, 62 N. W. 480, 69 Am. St. Rep. 716 (but see Finke v. Allen, 54 Neb. 407, 69 Am. St. Rep. 716, 74 N. W. 832).

New York: Reed v. Hayt, 109 N. Y. 659; 17 N. E. 418.

Oregon: Smith v. Wheeler, 7 Ore. 49, 33 Am. Rep. 698.

Pennsylvania: Ballentine v. Robinson, 46 Pa. 179; Reynolds v. Callender, 19 Pa. Super. Ct. 610.

[152] Girard v. Taggart, 5 S. & R. 19, 34.

[153] Thompson v. Alger, 12 Met. 428.

§ 752. Manufacturing contracts.

A contract for the manufacture of a certain article is in some jurisdictions regarded as a contract for work and labor; in others, as a contract of sale. In the former case the title to the finished article is in the party who orders the article; in the latter case it may be in one party or the other, according to circumstances. In either case, however, if the title is regarded by the court as being in the defendant, the manufacturer should be allowed the full contract price.[154] If the title is still in the manufacturer, however, the measure of damages is not so clear. It is often said that the usual rule in case of a breach by the vendee does not apply to contracts for manufacture, and that the amount of recovery should be the difference between the cost of manufacture and the contract price even though the vendor has completed the articles and tendered them before the vendee has repudiated.[155] Clearly, however, to lay this down as a general rule would be too sweeping. The manufacturer has the goods on hand, and may probably dispose of them to advantage elsewhere. To be sure if the goods are made expressly for the defendant, and will be of value to him alone, the plaintiff should recover the entire contract price less the amount saved him by the defendant's breach,[156] deducting any amount which the plaintiff has obtained by sale to others,[157]

---

[154] *United States:* Bookwalter *v.* Clark, 11 Biss. 126.

New Hampshire: Gordon *v.* Norris, 49 N. H. 376.

Ohio: Shawhan *v.* Van Nest, 25 Oh. St. 490, 18 Am. Rep. 313.

Pennsylvania: Ballentine *v.* Robinson, 46 Pa. 177.

[155] *United States:* Olyphant *v.* St. Louis Ore & Steel Co., 28 Fed. 729; Lincoln *v.* Levi Cotton Mill Co., 128 Fed. 865.

California: Hale *v.* Trout, 35 Cal. 230.

Illinois: Kingman & Co. *v.* Hanna Wagon Co., 176 Ill. 545, 52 N. E. 328.

Missouri: Chapman *v.* Kansas City, etc., Co., 146 Mo. 481, 48 S. W. 646.

Nebraska: Diels *v.* Kennedy, 88 Neb. 777, 130 N. W. 740.

New York: Dryfoos *v.* Uhl, 69 App.

Div. 118, 74 N. Y. Supp. 532; Oswego F. P. & P. Co. *v.* Stecher Lithographic Co., 130 N. Y. Supp. 897.

Pennsylvania: Mitchell *v.* Baker, 208 Pa. 377, 57 Atl. 760.

Virginia: Duke *v.* Norfolk & W. Ry., 106 Va. 152, 55 S. E. 548.

[156] *New York:* Isaacs *v.* Terry & Tench Co., 132 App. Div. 657, 117 N. Y. Supp. 369, 113 N. Y. Supp. 731, 125 App. Div. 532, 109 N. Y. Supp. 792, 56 Misc. 586, 107 N. Y. Supp. 136.

Pennsylvania: Ridgeway D. & E. Co. *v.* Pennsylvania Cement Co., 221 Pa. 160, 70 Atl. 557, 18 L. R. A. (N. S.) 613.

[157] *Kentucky:* Louisville & N. R. R. *v.* Coyle, 30 Ky. L. Rep. 201, 97 S. W. 772, 8 L. R. A. (N. S.) 433.

or, obviously, anything which it can be proved with reasonable
certainty that he might obtain. Even though the goods are not
especially adapted to the purpose for which they are manufactured, still if there is no market for them it is impossible
to show what the manufacturer could sell them for; and the
cost of manufacture is therefore the criterion.[158] If, however,
the goods have been manufactured and are on hand, and they
have a market value, the plaintiff may realize that value by
selling them; and his measure of loss in the ordinary case should
therefore be restricted to the difference between the contract
and the market price.[159]

Where the defendant repudiated the contract before the
manufacture was completed, the rule just considered cannot
apply, because the breach does not leave the manufactured
product on the plaintiff's hands; hence we have to fall back
on the general rule that the measure of damages is the net
profits of the contract: i. e., the difference between the contract price and the cost of manufacture, after making due
allowance for the value of materials on hand, etc.[160]

New York: Isaacs v. Terry & Tench
Co., 132 App. Div. 657, 117 N. Y. Supp.
369.

[158] Willis v. Jarrett Const. Co., 152
N. C. 100, 67 S. E. 265.

[159] *United States:* Knowlton v. Oliver,
28 Fed. 516; Malcomson v. Reeves Pulley Co., 167 Fed. 939, 93 C. C. A.
339.

Alabama: Gate City Cotton Mills v.
Rosenau Hosiery Mills, 159 Ala. 414,
49 So. 228.

Delaware: Speakman v. Price, 80 Atl.
627 (crop of tomatoes).

Kansas: Geiss v. Hardware Co., 37
Kan. 130.

Kentucky: Louisville & N. R. R. v.
Coyle, 30 Ky. L. Rep. 201, 97 S. W.
772, 8 L. R. A. (N. S.) 433.

Maine: Tufts v. Grewer, 83 Me. 407,
22 Atl. 382.

North Carolina: Marshall v. Macon
County Savings Bank, 108 N. C. 639,
13 S. E. 182; Cleveland-Canton Springs
Co. v. Goldsboro Buggy Co., 148 N. C.

533, 62 S. E. 637; Pool v. Walker, 72
S. E. 70 (output of shingle mill).

Pennsylvania: Puritan Coke Co. v.
Clark, 204 Pa. 556, 54 Atl. 350.

Wisconsin: Lincoln v. Charles Als-
huler Mfg. Co., 142 Wis. 475, 125 N. W.
908, 28 L. R. A. (N. S.) 780.

See also a learned note, 4 L. R. A.
(N. S.) 740.

[160] *United States:* United States v.
Behan, 110 U. S. 338, 28 L. ed. 168, 4
Sup. Ct. 81; Hinckley v. Pittsburg B.
S. Co., 121 U. S. 264, 30 L. ed. 967, 7
Sup. Ct. 875; Kingman v. Western
Mfg. Co., 92 Fed. 486, 34 C. C. A. 489;
Portland Co. v. Searle, 169 Fed. 968.

Delaware: Taylor v. Trustees of
Poor, 63 Atl. 613.

Indiana: W. J. Holliday & Co. v.
Highland I. & S. Co., 43 Ind. App. 342,
87 N. E. 249.

Iowa: Kimball v. Deere, 108 Ia. 676,
684, 77 N. W. 1041; Thistle Coal Co.
v. Rex C. & M. Co., 132 Ia. 592, 109
N. W. 1094.

In a carefully considered case in the Circuit Court of Appeals for the eighth circuit,[161] the following rules were laid down: 1. For breach of a contract to purchase, the ordinary rule is the difference between the contract and market price, if the latter be less than the former. 2. The same rule applies in the case of a contract to purchase goods to be manufactured, if they are ready for delivery at the time of the breach, otherwise not. 3. Where, before notice of the breach, materials have been purchased and labor expended, the vendor's damages are the difference between the amount it would cost him to make and deliver them, and their contract price, if greater, plus the difference between the value of the partly manufactured articles and the cost of the labor and materials, if the cost be greater than the value. 4. If materials have been purchased, but no labor expended, the measure of damages is the difference between what it would cost to make and deliver, including the cost of the materials, and their contract price, if greater, plus the difference between the cost, and the market value of the materials purchased at the time of the breach, if the latter be less than the former. 5. If no materials have been bought, or labor expended, the measure of damages is the difference between the amount it would cost the manufacturer to make and deliver them and their contract price, if that is greater than their cost.

As a general rule when the vendee gives notice of repudiation

Kentucky: Gaither v. Bland, 7 Ky. L. Rep. 518.

Missouri: Black River L. Co. v. Warner, 93 Mo. 374, 6 S. W. 210, 3 Am. St. Rep. 544; American Publishing & Engraving Co. v. Walker, 87 Mo. App. 503.

New York: Todd v. Gamble, 148 N. Y. 382, 42 N. E. 982; Masterton v. the Mayor, 7 Hill, 61; Bishop v. Autographic Register Co., 19 App. Div. 268, 46 N. Y. Supp. 97; Kelso v. Marshall, 24 App. Div. 128, 49 N. Y. Supp. 728; H. D. Taylor Co. v. Niagara Bedstead Co., 52 Misc. 356, 102 N. Y. Supp. 173; Lehmaier v. Standard S. & T. Co., 123 App. Div. 431, 108 N. Y.

Supp. 402; Thomas v. Cauldwell, 58 N. Y. 142.

Pennsylvania: Puritan Coke Co. v. Clark, 204 Pa. 556, 54 Atl. 350; Winslow Bros. Co. v. Du-Puy, 208 Pa. 98, 57 Atl. 189; Imperial R. S. Co. v. Steinfeld Bros., 81 Atl. 413.

Tennessee: Gardner v. Deeds, 116 Tenn. 128, 92 S. W. 518, 4 L. R. A. (N. S.) 740, and case note at p. 740, collecting many cases.

Wisconsin: Cameron v. White, 74 Wis. 425, 43 N. W. 155, 5 L. R. A. 493; Walsh v. Myers, 92 Wis. 297, 66 N. W. 250.

[161] Kingman v. Western Mfg. Co., 92 Fed. 486, 34 C. C. A. 489.

before the vendor has manufactured the goods the vendor cannot increase the damages by going on with the contract and completing the goods. If, however, he does complete them, and thereby his damages are lessened, the amount of his recovery is measured by the market value and not the cost of manufacture.[162]   Whenever the circumstances do justify the completion by the vendor he may invoke, to his own advantage, the usual rule of damages for breach by the vendee and recover the difference between the contract price and the market value of the articles.   Thus when the plaintiff was manufacturing out of cotton seed, by the same process, a variety of products and sold a year's output of two of these products in advance to the defendant, who gave notice that he would not receive the product; it was held that plaintiff was not obliged to stop and sue but might execute the contract on his side and claim damages as in the case of an ordinary sale.[163]

§ 752a. Property to be severed from the realty.

The rule allowing the difference between the contract price and the cost of production has been applied to contracts for the sale of minerals,[164] gravel [165] and of standing timber, to be cut by the seller.[166]

§ 753. Rule where title has not passed.

Where the title has not passed, the measure of damages is the difference between the contract and the market price of

[162] *United States:* Hemmingway Manuf. Co. *v.* Council Bluffs Canning Co., 62 Fed. 897.

Wisconsin: Tufts *v.* Weinfeld, 88 Wis. 647, 60 N. W. 992.

See, however, Southern Cotton Oil Co. *v.* Hefflin, 99 Fed. 339, 39 C. C. A. 546.

[163] Southern Cotton Oil Co. *v.* Heflin, 99 Fed. 339, 39 C. C. A. 546.

[164] *United States:* Engineering Co. *v.* Broadman, 136 Fed. 351 (granite).

Pennsylvania: Scott *v.* Kittanning Coal Co., 89 Pa. 231, 33 Am. Rep. 753; C. P. Mayer Brick Co. *v.* D. J. Ken-

nedy Co., 230 Pa. 98, 79 Atl. 246 (brick).

Virginia: Allegheny Iron Co. *v.* Teaford, 96 Va. 372, 31 S. E. 525.

[165] *California:* Coburn *v.* Cal. Cement Co., 144 Cal. 81, 77 Pac. 771.

West Virginia: Hare *v.* Parkersburg, 24 W. Va. 554.

So of cracked stone: Viernow *v.* Carthage, 139 Mo. App. 276, 123 S. W. 67.

[166] Williams *v.* Crosby Lumber Co., 118 N. C. 928, 24 S. E. 800; Willis *v.* Jarrett Const. Co., 152 N. C. 100, 67 S. E. 265.

the article at the time when and the place where it should have been accepted.[167] "The vendor of personal property in a suit

[167] *United States:* Friedenstein v. United States, 35 Ct. Cl. 1; Rhodes v. Cleveland Rolling Mill Co., 17 Fed. 426; Knowlton v. Oliver, 28 Fed. 516; Fisher v. Newark City Ice Co., 62 Fed. 569, 10 C. C. A. 546, 76 Fed. 427, 22 C. C. A. 261; Cherry Valley Iron Works v. Florence Iron River Co., 64 Fed. 569, 12 C. C. A. 306; Yellow Poplar Lumber Co. v. Chapman, 74 Fed. 444, 20 C. C. A. 503; Salem Iron Co. v. Lake Superior Consolidated Iron Mines, 112 Fed. 239, 50 C. C. A. 213; Denver E. W. Co. v. Elkins, 179 Fed. 922.

Alabama: Cassels' Mills v. Strater Bros. Grain Co., 166 Ala. 224, 51 So. 969; Scruggs v. Riddle, 54 So. 641.

Arkansas: Morris v. Cohn, 55 Ark. 401, 17 S. W. 342; Nelson v. Hirschberg, 70 Ark. 39, 66 S. W. 347.

California: Haskell v. McHenry, 4 Cal. 411; Hewes v. Germain Fruit Co., 106 Cal. 441, 39 Pac. 853; Tahoe Ice Co. v. Union Ice Co., 109 Cal. 242, 41 Pac. 1020; Scribner v. Schenkel, 128 Cal. 250, 60 Pac. 860; Central Oil Co. v. Southern Refining Co., 154 Cal. 165, 97 Pac. 177; Levis v. Royal Packing Co., 1 Cal. App. 241, 81 Pac. 1086.

Colorado: Kincaid v. Price, 18 Colo. App. 73, 70 Pac. 153.

Delaware: Barr v. Logan, 5 Harr. 52.

Georgia: Groover v. Warfield, 50 Ga. 644; Camp v. Hamlin, 55 Ga. 259; Barrett v. Verdery, 93 Ga. 526, 21 S. E. 64; Georgia R. R. v. Augusta O. Co., 74 Ga. 497.

Illinois: Thrasher v. Pime County R. R., 25 Ill. 393; McNaught v. Dodson, 49 Ill. 446; Ullmann v. Kent, 60 Ill. 271; Burnham v. Roberts, 70 Ill. 19; Sanborn v. Benedict, 78 Ill. 309; Kadish v. Young, 108 Ill. 170, 48 Am. Rep. 548; Thurman v. Wilson, 7 Ill. App. 312; Murray v. Doud, 167 Ill. 368, 47 N. E. 717; Great W. C. & C. Co. v. St. Louis

& B. M. C. C. Co., 140 Ill. App. 368; Finch v. Zenith F. Co., 146 Ill. App. 257.

Indiana: Pittsburgh, C. & St. L. Ry. v. Heck, 50 Ind. 303, 19 Am. Rep. 713; Dwiggins v. Clark, 94 Ind. 49, 48 Am. Rep. 140; McComas v. Haas, 107 Ind. 512, 57 Am. Rep. 128; Ridgley v. Mooney, 16 Ind. App. 362, 45 N. E. 348; Browning v. Simons (Ind.), 46 N. E. 86; Dill v. Mumford, 49 N. E. 861 (Ind.).

Iowa: Harris Manuf. Co. v. Marsh, 49 Ia. 11; Hamilton v. Finnegan, 117 Ia. 623, 91 N. W. 1039.

Kansas: Lawrence Tanning Co. v. Lee Mercantile Co., 5 Kan. App. 77, 48 Pac. 749.

Kentucky: Williams v. Jones, 1 Bush. 621; Bell v. Hatfield, 121 Ky. 560, 89 S. W. 544, 2 L. R. A. (N. S.) 529; J. Zinsmeister & Bro. v. Rock Island Canning Co., 139 S. W. 1068.

Louisiana· Jochams v. Ong, 45 La. Ann. 1289, 1294, 14 So. 247.

Maine: Tufts v. Grewer, 83 Me. 407, 22 Atl. 382; Bonney v. Blaisdell, 105 Me. 121, 73 Atl. 811.

Massachusetts: Collins v. Delaporte, 115 Mass. 159; Whitney v. Thacher, 117 Mass. 523; Tufts v. Bennett, 163 Mass. 398, 40 N. E. 172; Moffatt v. Davitt, 200 Mass. 452, 86 N. E. 929.

Michigan: Brownlee v. Bolton, 44 Mich. 218; Simons v. Ypsilanti Paper Co., 77 Mich. 185, 43 N. W. 864; Peters v. Cooper, 95 Mich. 191, 54 N. W. 694, 35 Am. St. Rep. 554; Mohr Hardware Co. v. Dubey, 136 Mich. 677, 100 N. W. 127; Kellogg v. Frohlich, 139 Mich. 612, 102 N. W. 1057.

Missouri: Whitmore v. Coats, 14 Mo. 9; Lee v. Sickles Saddlery Co., 38 Mo. App. 201; Northrup v. Cook, 39 Mo. 208 (*semble*); Black River L. Co. v. Warner, 93 Mo. 374, 3 Am. St. Rep. 544; Brown v. Trinidad A. M. Co., 210

against the vendee for not taking and paying for the property," said Earl, C., in Dustan *v.* McAndrew,[168] "has the choice

Mo. 260, 109 S. W. 22; Parlin *v.* Boatman, 84 Mo. App. 67.

Nebraska: Dodge *v.* Keine, 28 Neb. 216, 44 N. W. 191; Lincoln Shoe Co. *v.* Sheldon (Neb.), 44 N. W. 279; Funke *v.* Allen, 54 Neb. 407, 74 N. W. 832, 69 Am. St. Rep. 716; Backes *v.* Black, 97 N. W. 321; Trinidad A. M. Co. *v.* Buckstaff Bros. Mfg. Co., 86 Neb. 623, 126 N. W. 293, 136 Am. St. Rep. 710; Tacoma Mill Co. *v.* F. H. Gilcrest Lumber Co., 132 N. W. 926.

New Hampshire: Stevens *v.* Lyford, 7 N. H. 360; Rand *v.* White Mountains Railroad, 40 N. H. 79; Gordon *v.* Norris, 49 N. H. 376; Haines *v.* Tucker, 50 N. H. 307; Tripp *v.* Forsaith Mach. Co., 69 N. H. 23.

New Jersey: Massman *v.* Steiger, 79 N. J. L. 442, 75 Atl. 746.

New York: Pollen *v.* Le Roy, 30 N. Y. 549; Dustan *v.* McAndrew, 44 N. Y. 72; Hayden *v.* Demets, 53 N. Y. 426; Bridgford *v.* Crocker, 60 N. Y. 627; Cahen *v.* Platt, 69 N. Y. 348, 25 Am. Rep. 199; Canda *v.* Wick, 100 N. Y. 127; Billings *v.* Vanderbeck, 23 Barb. 546; Mallory *v.* Lord, 29 Barb. 454; Hewitt *v.* Miller, 61 Barb. 567; Kirschmann *v.* Lediard, 61 Barb. 573; Duryea *v.* Rayner, 46 N. Y. Supp. 437; Deery *v.* Williams, 50 N. Y. Supp. 138; National Cash Register Co. *v.* Schmidt, 48 App. Div. 472, 62 N. Y. Supp. 952;

Schwartzenbes *v.* Hass, 74 N. Y. Supp. 884; Kiley *v.* Lee Canning Co., 93 N. Y. Supp. 986; Lekas *v.* Schwartz, 56 Misc. 954, 107 N. Y. Supp. 145; Netter *v.* Trenton W. B. Works, 140 App. Div. 287, 125 N. Y. Supp. 141.

North Carolina: Clements *v.* State, 77 N. C. 142.

North Dakota: Minneapolis T. M. Co. *v.* McDonald, 10 N. D. 408, 87 N. W. 993.

Ohio: Nixon *v.* Nixon, 21 Oh. St. 114; Cullen *v.* Bimm, 37 Oh. St. 236.

Oregon: Krebs Hop Co. *v.* Livesley, 114 Pac. 944, 118 Pac. 165.

Pennsylvania: Unexcelled Fireworks Co. *v.* Polites, 130 Pa. 536, 18 Atl. 1058, 17 Am. St. Rep. 788; Dorser *v.* Hale, 149 Pa. 274, 24 Atl. 285; Herd *v.* Thompson, 149 Pa. 434, 24 Atl. 282; Jones *v.* Jennings, 168 Pa. 493, 32 Atl. 51; Guillou *v.* Farnshaw, 169 Pa. 463, 32 Atl. 545; Sharpsville Furnace Co. *v.* Snyder, 223 Pa. 372, 72 Atl. 786; Charles J. Webb & Co. *v.* Novelty Hosiery Co., 231 Pa. 297, 80 Atl. 173; Andrews *v.* Hoover, 8 Watts, 239; Keeler Co. *v.* Schott, 1 Pa. Super. Ct. 458; Schnelby *v.* Shirtcliff, 7 Phila. 236.

South Carolina: Huguenot Mills *v.* Jempson, 68 S. C. 363, 47 S. E. 687; Millar *v.* Hilliard, Cheves, 149.

South Dakota: Dowagiack Mfg. Co.

---

[168] 44 N. Y. 72, 78.

See to the same effect the following cases:

United States: Habeler *v.* Rogers, 131 Fed. 43.

Colorado: Magnes *v.* Sioux City Nursery & Seed Co., 14 Colo. App. 219, 59 Pac. 879.

Indiana: Dwiggins *v.* Clark, 94 Ind. 49.

Kentucky: Cook *v.* Brandies, 3 Met. 555.

Missouri: Ozark Lumber Co. *v.* Chicago Lumber Co., 51 Mo. App. 555.

Oregon: Krebs Hop Co. *v.* Livesley, 118 Pac. 165.

Tennessee: Cook *v.* Zucarello, 104 Tenn. 64, 56 S. W. 850.

The rules laid down above apply to all kinds of personal property, *e. g.,* an interest in a partnership. Van Brocklin *v.* Smallie, 140 N. Y. 70, 35 N. E. 415.

ordinarily of either one of three methods to indemnify himself: (1) He may store or retain the property for the vendee and sue him for the entire purchase price; (2) He may sell the property, acting as the agent for this purpose of the vendee, and recover the difference between the contract price and the price obtained on such resale; (3) He may keep the property as his own, and recover the difference between the market price at the time and place of delivery and the contract price." The remedies are, however, mutually exclusive and when the vendor has chosen one, the others are gone forever; [169] and in many jurisdictions he is restricted to the third remedy.[170]   In Fisher v. Newark City Ice Co.,[171] when the vendee refused to receive ice under a contract the court said that from the contract price must be deducted not only the market value but also the expense of loading, etc., saved to the plaintiff by the failure to take it. Where a purchaser extends the time for the delivery of goods, the vendor, suing for a failure to accept, recovers the difference between the contract price and the value at a reasonable time after a final demand for the vendee to take them.[172]   The market price at the place to which the defendant intended to ship the goods cannot be taken.[173]

v. White Rock Lumber Co., 18 S. Dak. 105, 99 N. W. 854.

Tennessee: Cole v. Zucarello, 104 Tenn. 64, 56 S. W. 850; Alpha P. C. Co. v. Oliver, 140 S. W. 595.

Texas: Woldert v. Arledge, 4 Tex. Civ. App. 692, 23 S. W. 1052; Avant v. Watson, 122 S. W. 586.

Virginia: Oriental Lum. Co. v. Blades Lum. Co., 103 Va. 730; Am. Can'g Co. v. Flat Top Grocery Co., 70 S. E. 756.

West Virginia: Weltners v. Riggs, 3 W. Va. 445; Hall v. Pierce, 4 W. Va. 107; James v. Adams, 8 W. Va. 568; s. c. 16 W. Va. 245; Acme Food Co. v.

Older, 64 W. Va. 255, 61 S. E. 235, 17 L. R. A. (N. S.) 807.

Wisconsin: Ganson v. Madigan, 13 Wis. 67; Chapman v. Ingram, 30 Wis. 290; Gehl v. Milwaukee Produce Co., 105 Wis. 573, 81 N. W. 666; Pratt v. S. Freeman & Sons Manuf. Co., 115 Wis. 648, 92 N. W. 368; Carle v. Nelson, 145 Wis. 593, 130 N. W. 467.

England: Hickman v. Haynes, L. R. 10 C. P. 598.

Canada: Chapman v. Larin, 4 Can. 349; Boswell v. Kilborn, 6 Low. Can. Jur. 108; Moore v. Logan, 5 Up. Can. C. P. 294.

[169] Westfall v. Peacock, 63 Barb. 209.

[170] Acme Food Co. v. Older, 64 W. Va. 255, 61 S. E. 235, 17 L. R. A. (N. S.) 807.

[171] 76 Fed. 427, 17 U. S. App. 514, 525, 22 C. C. A. 261.

[172] *Virginia:* Smith v. Snyder, 77 Va. 432.

England: Hickman v. Haynes, L. R. 10 C. P. 598.

[173] Cahen v. Platt, 69 N. Y. 348, 25 Am. Rep. 199.

Where the contract price and the market price are the same, only nominal damages can be recovered; [174] and the same is true where the sale is at such price as should be mutually agreed upon. [175] So where the plaintiff has not the goods that he agrees to sell, but makes a side-contract with another party to furnish them, he will only be allowed to recover the difference between the original contract price and the market price at the time of the offer, with interest. [176] If the property is worthless in the hands of the plaintiff, the whole price agreed should be recovered. [177] Where a quantity of straw was sold, a portion of which only was taken away, and the buyer subsequently refused to take the remainder, and the vendor threw it, the next spring, it having become damaged, into the barn-yard to his cattle, it was held that the measure of damages against the vendee for refusing to complete his contract was the contract price, less its value to the vendor for the use to which it was applied. [178] When there is no market at the place of delivery the price of getting the goods to the nearest market is to be subtracted from (or, as the case may be, added to) the price at that market in order to find the value at the place of delivery. [179] Where there is no open market, the best offer ob-

---

[174] *United States:* Ellithorpe A. B. Co. v. Sire, 41 Fed. 662.

California: Hill v. McKay, 94 Cal. 5, 29 Pac. 406.

Illinois: Foos v. Sabin, 84 Ill. 564.

Iowa: Wire v. Foster, 62 Ia. 114.

[175] Smith v. Loag, 132 Pa. 301, 19 Atl. 137. See Indiana Tie Co. v. Phelps (Ky.), 124 S. W. 833.

[176] *New York:* Stanton v. Small, 3 Sandf. 230.

Vermont: Danforth v. Walker, 37 Vt. 239.

So, too, in *Ohio:* M'Naughter v. Cassally, 4 M'Lean, 530; though in this case it is said a portion of the property was ready to be delivered.

[177] Allen v. Jarvis, 20 Conn. 38. So of an agreement with a corporation to buy a portion of its capital stock; upon breach, the corporation may recover the entire purchase price. Person & Riegel

Co. v. Lipps, 219 Pa. 99, 67 Atl. 1081. And where defendant contracted to buy plaintiff's stock, which was at the time in the hands of a pledgee, but refused to pay for it, and the stock was thereupon sold to satisfy the lien and was bought in and divided by the pledgee and the defendant it was held that defendant had really deprived plaintiff of the stock, and must pay the agreed price. Lydon v. Sullivan, 101 S. W. 940, 31 Ky. Law Rep. 227.

[178] Chamberlain v. Farr, 23 Vt. 265.

[179] *United States:* Grand Tower Co. v. Phillips, 23 Wall. 471, 23 L. ed. 71; Yellow Poplar Lumber Co. v. Chapman, 74 Fed. 444, 20 C. C. A. 503; Salmon v. Helena Box Co., 147 Fed. 408, 77 C. C. A. 586.

Arkansas: Kirchman v. Tuffli Bros. P. I. & C. Co., 92 Ark. 111, 122 S. W. 239.

tainable will constitute competent evidence of the value. In any case it is the actual value which furnishes the standard: [180] the market price is only evidence of this. [181]

§ 754. Rescission.

The question of the rescission of a contract must not be confounded with the question of breach. It is settled that a breach may arise by refusal of one of the parties to go on with performance. [182] This, however, is not recission. Parties can only rescind a contract by annulling it, or withdrawing themselves from it altogether, in which case it is as if it had been voluntarily cancelled by both. In such an event, it would seem that properly speaking damages for a breach should not be allowed; the plaintiff should recover, but not on the basis of the contract. The consequences of rescission depend on the circumstances of the particular case. And so where plaintiff and defendant contracted for the sale of 50,000 bricks, and the plaintiff delivered 20,000, when the defendant wrongfully refused to receive any more and the plaintiff treated the contract as rescinded, it was held that plaintiff was entitled to recover the full market value of those delivered. [183] But where the defendant refused to fulfil his agreement to take back stock he had sold the plaintiff, this was regarded by the court as a rescission of the contract of sale, only so far as to revest the title to the stock in the defendant; and the plaintiff was allowed to recover the full price agreed upon. [184] And where a misunderstanding arose between the parties to a sale, and it was agreed

---

[180] *Delaware:* Pancoast *v.* Vail, 6 Pennew. 512, 65 Atl. 512.

Missouri: St. Louis S. R. Co. *v.* Kline-Drummond M. Co., 120 Mo. App. 438, 96 S. W. 1040.

Montana: Welch *v.* Nichols, 41 Mont. 435, 110 Pac. 89.

So if no value is proved, damages must be nominal. Fisher H. S. & M. Co. *v.* Warner, 188 Fed. 465.

[181] *United States:* Salem Iron Co. *v.* Lake Superior Iron Mines, 112 Fed. 239, 50 C. C. A. 213.

Massachusetts: Barry *v.* Cavanagh, 127 Mass. 394.

[182] Hochster *v.* De La Tour, 2 E. & B. 678. For a discussion of Rescission generally, see *ante*, Ch. xxx.

[183] *New York:* Terwilliger *v.* Knapp, 2 E. D. Smith, 86.

Washington: Houser & H. M. Co. *v.* McKay, 53 Wash. 337, 101 Pac. 894, 27 L. R. A. (N. S.) 925.

[184] *Massachusetts:* Thorndike *v.* Locke, 98 Mass. 340.

Minnesota: Browne *v.* St. Paul Plow Works, 62 Minn. 90, 64 N. W. 66.

Pennsylvania: Laubach *v.* Laubach, 73 Pa. 387.

that the sale should be cancelled and the buyer should return the goods, and he failed to do so, it was held that the seller might recover at his option the actual value of the goods.[185] In the ordinary case of a contract procured by fraud the party defrauded is said to be entitled to rescind it and recover back what he has parted with. There obviously the contract is treated as a nullity, the fraud being the cause of action.[186]

§ 755. Resale after default.

It is often said that where the vendor resells the property, the difference between the price obtained at the resale and the contract price is absolutely the measure of damages;[187] or,

[185] American F. & F. Co. v. Settergren, 130 Wis. 338, 110 N. W. 238.
[186] Whitney v. Albani, 1 N. Y. 305; Pryor v. Foster, 130 N. Y. 171, 29 N. E. 123.
[187] *United States:* Pope v. Filby, 3 McCr. 190.
Alabama: Penn v. Smith, 93 Ala. 476, 9 So. 609, 98 Ala. 560, 12 So. 818.
California: Habenocht v. Lisak, 77 Cal. 139, 19 Pac. 260; Hewes v. Germain Fruit Co., 106 Cal. 441, 39 Pac. 853; Gibbs v. Ranard, 86 Cal. 531, 25 Pac. 63; Scribner v. Schenkel, 128 Cal. 250, 60 Pac. 860.
Colorado: Colorado Springs Livestock Co. v. Godding, 2 Colo. App. 1, 29 Pac. 529; Magnes v. Sioux City Seed Co., 14 Colo. App. 219, 59 Pac. 879.
Delaware: Barr v. Logan, 5 Harr. 52.
Illinois: Saladin v. Mitchell, 45 Ill. 79; Morris v. Wilbaux, 159 Ill. 627, 43 N. E. 837.
Iowa: Ingram v. Wackernagel, 83 Ia. 82, 48 N. W. 998.
Kentucky: Marshall v. Piles, 3 Bush, 249; Applegate v. Hogan, 9 B. Mon. 69; Clore v. Robinson, 100 Ky. 402, 38 S. W. 687; Sanders v. Bond, 23 Ky. L. Rep. 2084, 66 S. W. 635.
Maine: Atwood v. Lucas, 53 Me. 508, 89 Am. Dec. 713.
Massachusetts: McLean v. Richardson, 127 Mass. 339.
Michigan: Madden v. Lemke, 86 Mich. 139, 48 N. W. 785.
Missouri: Van Horn v. Rucker, 33 Mo. 391, 84 Am. Dec. 52; Black River L. Co. v. Warner, 93 Mo. 374, 6 S. W. 210, 3 Am. St. Rep. 544.
New Jersey: Townsend v. Simon, 38 N. J. L. 239.
New York: Van Brocklen v. Smeallie, 140 N. Y. 70, 35 N. E. 415; Crooke v. Moore, 1 Sandf. 297; Schwartzenbes v. Hass, 74 N. Y. Supp. 884.
North Carolina: Clifton v. Newsom, 1 Jones, 108.
Oklahoma: Mansur v. Willard, 10 Okla. 383, 61 Pac. 1066.
Pennsylvania: Tompkins v. Haas, 2 Pa. 74; Tindle's Appeal, 77 Pa. 201.
South Carolina: Blackwood v. Brennan, 1 Harp. 219.
Tennessee: Williams v. Godwin, 4 Sneed, 558.
Virginia: Rosenbaums v. Weeden, 18 Gratt. 785, 98 Am. Dec. 737; American Canning Co. v. Flat Top Grocery Co., 70 S. E. 756.
West Virginia: James v. Adams, 8 W. Va. 568.
Wisconsin: Pickering v. Bardwell, 21 Wis. 562, 94 Am. Dec. 564; T. B. Scott Lumber Co. v. Hafner-Lothman Manuf. Co., 91 Wis. 667, 65 N. W. 513.
England: Anderson v. Beard, [1900] 2 Q. B. 260.

more exactly, the difference between the net proceeds of the resale (the price obtained less the expense) and the contract price.[188] The vendor, in such a case, is said to be the agent of the vendee to make the resale. This is not, however, strictly accurate. He is not an actual agent and the obligation under which he rests to make a fair sale arises from the fact that the proceeds of the sale are to measure the damages: to call him the agent of the vendee is to indulge in a "mere fiction of law." This is well brought out in a New York case,[189] where the vendee company, after refusing to accept goods purchased, went into the hands of a receiver. The vendor re-sold the goods and sought to recover the difference between the proceeds and the contract price. It was objected that to recover that amount the vendor had to rely on the doctrine of agency and that as the agent of one who was in the hands of a receiver he had no right to resell without first securing an order from the court. The vendor, however, was awarded the sum which he claimed, the court distinctly repudiating the agency theory, and holding that the title remained in the vendor.

The price obtained on a resale is therefore not a conclusive measure of damages and it is more properly held that it is only evidence of the market value.[190] Since, however, the sale

Canada: Brunskill *v.* Mair, 15 Up. Can. Q. B. 213.

[188] *Arizona:* Slaughter *v.* Marlow, 3 Ariz. 429, 31 Pac. 547.

Georgia: Barnes *v.* Bluthenthal, 101 Ga. 598, 28 S. E. 1017, 65 Am. St. Rep. 598.

Illinois: Bagley *v.* Findlay, 82 Ill. 524.

Kentucky: Mattingly *v.* Mathews, 14 Ky. L. Rep. 300.

Massachusetts: Whitney *v.* Boardman, 118 Mass. 242.

Missouri: Whitmore *v.* Coats, 14 Mo. 9; Strauss *v.* Labsap, 59 Mo. App. 260.

New York: Sawyer *v.* Dean, 114 N. Y. 469, 21 N. E. 1012.

South Carolina: Woods *v.* Cramer, 34 S. C. 508, 13 S. E. 660, 27 Am. St. Rep. 839.

Texas: White *v.* Matador Land & C. Co., 75 Tex. 465, 12 S. W. 866.

Wisconsin: Chapman *v.* Cochran, 30 Wis. 295.

[189] Moore *v.* Potter, 155 N. Y. 481, 50 N. E. 271, 63 Am. St. Rep. 692. *Cf.* Pollen *v.* Le Roy, 30 N. Y. 549.

[190] *California:* Frisbie *v.* Rosenberg Bros. & Co., 9 Cal. App. 583, 105 Pac. 943.

Georgia: Camp *v.* Hamlin, 55 Ga. 259; Atkins *v.* Cobb, 56 Ga. 86; Davis Sulphur Ore Co. *v.* Atlanta Guano Co., 109 Ga. 607, 34 S. E. 1011.

Illinois: Ullmann *v.* Kent, 60 Ill. 271.

Kentucky: Sanders *v.* Bond, 23 Ky. L. Rep. 2084, 66 S. W. 635.

Massachusetts: Croak *v.* Owens, 121 Mass. 28.

Michigan: Williams *v.* Robb, 104 Mich. 242, 62 N. W. 352, 53 Am. St. Rep. 457.

must be conducted with due diligence so as to obtain the best price, the price realized is, perhaps, the best evidence of market value. It is sometimes said that the price obtained or a resale will be binding on the defendant only if he had notice of the resale.[191] The importance of the notice, however, seems to be only in negativing any possible presumption that the vendor intended a rescission of the contract or in tending to show good faith on the part of the vendor.

Where the sale is made by one acting in an official capacity, as an administrator, the difference between the prices of the two sales is, it would seem, the absolute measure of damages.[192] A resale will not furnish the measure of damages, if it does not take place within a reasonable time after the failure to accept. In Smith v. Pettee,[193] it was held that four months was not a reasonable time. Nor is it necessary for the vendor to resell at the place of delivery fixed by the contract. If the property cannot readily be sold there, or if a more advantageous sale can be made elsewhere, it is the duty of the vendor to make the resale at such other place.[194]

New Hampshire: Tripp v. Forsaith Mach. Co., 69 N. H. 233, 45 Atl. 746.

New York: Ackerman v. Rubens, 167 N. Y. 405, 60 N. E. 750, 82 Am. St. Rep. 728; Fancher v. Goodman, 29 Barb. 315; Almy v. Simonson, 52 Hun, 535.

Pennsylvania: Freyman v. Knecht, 78 Pa. 141; Guillou v. Farnshaw, 169 Pa. 463, 32 Atl. 545; Firard v. Taggard, 5 S. & R. 19, 9 Am. Dec. 327; Andrews v. Hoover, 8 Watts, 239; Baltimore Smelting Co. v. Ammonia Co., 2 Pa. Super. Ct. 555; Hooper v. Bromley Brothers Carpet Co., 11 Pa. Super. Ct. 634.

Texas: Leonard v. Portier, 15 S. W. 414.

Wisconsin: Gehl v. Milwaukee Produce Co., 105 Wis. 573, 81 N. W. 666, 116 Wis. 263, 93 N. W. 26.

[191] *Illinois:* Bagley v. Findlay, 82 Ill. 524.

Missouri: Rickey v. Tenbroeck, 63 Mo. 563.

New York: Pollen v. Le Roy, 30 N. Y. 549; Van Brocklen v. Smeallie, 140 N. Y. 70, 35 N. E. 415; McEachron v. Randles, 34 Barb. 301.

[192] *Alabama:* Lamkin v. Crawford, 8 Ala. 153 (sheriff).

Georgia: Alexander v. Herring, 54 Ga. 200.

Pennsylvania: Gaskell v. Morris, 7 W. & S. 33.

So where the sale was necessary because the property was perishable. Ziegler v. Gerlach (Tex. Civ. App.), 125 S. W. 80.

[193] 7 Hun, 334. *Cf.* Lawrence Canning Co. v. Lee Mercantile Co., 5 Kan. App. 77, 48 Pac. 749 (one month too long). In Zinsmeister & Bro. v. Rock Island Canning Co. (Ky.), 139 S. W. 1068, it was held to be a question for the jury whether about four months was reasonable.

[194] *New York:* Lewis v. Greider, 49 Barb. 606.

Texas: Waples v. Overaker, 77 Tex.

The question must be determined by all the circumstances. In a case of the sort under discussion, where, after notice, the seller resold the goods at auction, the Court of Appeals of New York said:[195] "The price obtained after such default, upon a resale, within a reasonable time, although at auction, is evidence of the market value of an article and to be allowed such weight as the circumstances of the sale entitled it to." And, on the other hand, a resale at private sale, without reasonable notice or efforts to secure the best price possible, and no evidence being offered that the price obtained was a fair one, does not fix the legal measure of damages.[196]

In Cherry Valley Iron Works v. Florence River Iron Co.,[197] the contract was for the sale of ore to be delivered in seven monthly instalments, and contained a clause giving the vendor the right to "cancel" the contract in case of default. Plaintiff, the vendee, made three payments but did not call for the full amount of ore deliverable against them. For failure to continue the payments, defendants cancelled the contract. It was held that this did not amount to an absolute rescission restoring both parties to their original position, but gave the defendant the right to treat the contract as broken. The title of the undelivered ore remaining in the vendor, his measure of damages was the difference between the contract and market price taken at the average value during the months in which delivery was due. The measure of damages could not be fixed by a resale because the title had not passed and a sale of a quantity of ore equal to the amount undelivered could not be proved to fix the market value because it was made several months after the period fixed for delivery. This case seems to confirm the general view of rescission taken above.[198]

§ 756. Promise to give a bill or note.

* Where goods are sold to be paid for by note or bill payable at a future day, and the note or bill is not given, it is well settled in England and in this country, that the vendor cannot main-

---

7, 19 Am. St. Rep. 727, 13 S. W. 527; Texas & L. L. Co. v. Rose, 103 S. W. 444.

[195] Bigelow v. Legg, 102 N. Y. 652.

[196] Case v. Simonds, 7 N. Y. Supp. 253.

[197] 22 U. S. App. 655, 12 C. C. A. 306, 64 Fed. 569.

[198] Acc., Hubbardston Lumber Co. v. Bates, 31 Mich. 573.

tain assumpsit on the general count for goods sold and delivered, until the credit has expired; but he can sue immediately for a breach of the special agreement.[199] And in New York it has been held, that in such action he will be entitled to recover as damages the whole price of the goods, with the suggestion that there should be a rebate of interest during the stipulated period of credit; [200] the court, Bronson, J., saying: "The right of action is as perfect on a neglect or refusal to give the note or bill as it can be after the credit has expired. The only difference between suing at one time or the other relates to the *form of the remedy*. In the one case, the plaintiff must declare specially, in the other he may declare generally. The remedy itself is the same in both cases. The damages are the price of the goods. The party cannot have two actions for one breach of a single contract, and the contract is no more broken after the credit expires than it was the moment that the note or bill was wrongfully withheld."

So in a case in Pennsylvania,[201] it was charged at the trial, that where goods are sold on credit, the vendee to give his note, which he refuses to do after the goods are delivered, suit may be brought for a breach of the contract before the expiration of the credit, in which case the measure of damages is the price of the goods. And the direction was held right.** But while the rule is usually stated in this form,[202] since the action is for

[199] Mussen v. Price, 4 East, 147; Dutton v. Solomonson, 3 Bos. & Pull. 582; Hoskins v. Duperoy, 9 East, 498; Hutchinson v. Reid, 3 Camp. 329; Loring v. Gurney, 5 Pick. 15; Hunneman v. Inhabitants of Grafton, 10 Met. 454.

[200] Hanna v. Mills, 21 Wend. 90, 34 Am. Dec. 216. In the English cases nothing is said as to the amount which the plaintiff is entitled to recover. In the case of Hutchinson v. Reid, the plaintiff, though without discussion, was permitted to take a verdict for the price of the goods.

[201] Rinehart v. Olwine, 5 W. & S. 157.

[202] *Indiana:* Carnahan v. Hughes, 108 Ind. 225, 9 N. E. 79.

Maine: Thomas Mfg. Co. v. Watson, 85 Me. 300, 27 Atl. 176.

Massachusetts: Worthy v. Jones, 11 Gray, 168, 71 Am. Dec. 696.

North Dakota: Kelly v. Peirce, 16 N. D. 234, 112 N. W. 995, 12 L. R. A. (N. S.) 180.

Ohio: Stephenson v. Repp, 47 Oh. St. 551, 25 N. E. 803, 10 L. R. A. 620.

Pennsylvania: Girard v. Taggart, 5 S. & R. 19, 9 Am. Dec. 327.

Texas: Parks v. O'Connor, 70 Tex. 377, 8 S. W. 104; Young v. Dalton, 83 Tex. 497, 18 S. W. 819.

Vermont: Foster v. Adams, 60 Vt. 392, 15 Atl. 169, 6 Am. St. Rep. 120.

The value of the property sold is of course immaterial: Bicknell v. Buck, 58 Ind. 354.

failure to give the note, a more accurate statement of the measure of damages is, that it is the face of the note with interest.[203] This rule does not apply, of course, where the note to be given in payment for goods is that of a third party. So where the defendant agreed to pay for goods by the transfer of the note of a third party, secured by a second mortgage on certain property, and the third party was insolvent and the security worthless, only nominal damages were allowed upon breach.[204] This is on the same principle which restricts recovery for the value of a note to its actual value.[205]

§ 757. Consequential damages—Avoidable consequences.

In McCracken v. Webb [206] the plaintiff was allowed to recover the difference between the contract and market price of some hogs he had sold the defendant, *plus* the expense of keeping them from the time of defendant's refusal to accept to the date of resale.

The question of avoiding further loss by accepting an offer of the vendee to take the goods below the contract price, but above the market price, is one on which the authorities are not clear.[207] It has been held that the vendor need not accept such an offer.[208]

III.—COUNTERMAND BEFORE TIME FOR PERFORMANCE

§ 758. Effect of notice of countermand.

* An effort has been made in many cases by the purchaser to relieve himself from the contract of sale before the time fixed for performance, by giving notice that he would not be ready to complete the agreement; and in these cases it has been insisted that the damages should be estimated as at the time of giving notice.** It has been held in some cases [209] that if upon

---

[203] *Connecticut:* Stoddard v. Mix, 14 Conn. 12, 24

Minnesota: Geiser Mfg. Co. v. Holzer, 110 Minn. 138, 124 N. W. 827.

Missouri: Aultman v. Daggs, 50 Mo. App. 280.

[204] Derleth v. Degraaf, 51 N. Y. Super. Ct. 369.

[205] Thompson v. Halbert, 40 Hun, 536; see § 256.

[206] 36 Ia. 551.

[207] See *supra,* § 741.

[208] Krebs Hop Co. v. Livesley (Ore.), 114 Pac. 944.

[209] *United States:* Roehm v. Horst, 178 U. S. 1, 44 L. ed. 953, 20 Sup. Ct.

a contract for the future delivery of goods the purchaser, before the time for delivery, gives notice that he will not accept the goods, this may be treated by the seller as a breach of contract and he may bring an action forthwith. In Massachusetts,[210] however, this doctrine of anticipatory breach was rejected, after careful consideration. Even when it is adopted the seller is not obliged to treat the notice as an immediate breach. He may wait until the time for delivery, and then, upon a tender of the goods and a refusal to accept them, bring suit. When in such a case the value of the goods has fallen between the notice and the time for delivery, the purchaser has in some cases claimed that damages should have been assessed as of the time of the notice, because the plaintiff should then have sold the goods in the market. A sufficient answer to this contention, however, is that the plaintiff had a right to regard the contract as still in force until the time fixed for performance, and on a familiar principle, that the plaintiff is not required to anticipate wrong, he could not be called upon to take any steps to avoid loss before breach by the defendant.[211]

The point was elaborately discussed by the Supreme Court of Illinois in the case of Kadish v. Young.[212] In that case appellees sold barley to appellants, to be delivered in January. The purchasers gave notice in December that they did not consider themselves bound by the contract, and would not comply with its terms. The sellers tendered the barley in January. It was held that the measure of damages was the diffence between the contract price and the market price at the time of tender. Scholfield, J., said: [213]

"Nothing would seem to be plainer than that while the contract is still subsisting and unbroken, the parties can only be compelled to do that which its terms require. This contract im-

780; Horst v. Roehm, 84 Fed. 565; Roehm v. Horst, 62 U. S. App. 520, 91 Fed. 345, 33 C. C. A. 550.

   Illinois: Chamber of Commerce v. Sollitt, 43 Ill. 519.

   Iowa: Barron v. Mullin, 46 Iowa, 235.

   See Smoot's Case, 15 Wall. 36, 21 L. ed. 107; Dingley v. Oler, 117 U. S. 490, 29 L. ed. 984, 6 Sup. Ct. 850.

   Ante, § 636c.

[210] Daniels v. Newton, 114 Mass. 530, 19 Am. Rep. 384.

[211] § 224.

[212] 108 Ill. 170, 48 Am. Rep. 548.

[213] p. 183.

posed no duty upon appellees to make other contracts for January delivery, or to sell barley in December to protect appellants from loss. It did not even contemplate that appellees should have the barley ready for delivery until such time in January as they should elect. If appellees had then the barley on hand, and had acted upon appellants' notice, and accepted and treated the contract as then broken, it would, doubtless, then have been their duty to have resold the barley upon the market, precisely as they did in January, and have given appellants credit for the proceeds of the sale; but it is obviously absurd to assume that it could have been appellees' duty to have sold barley in December to other parties which it was their duty to deliver to appellants, and which appellants had a legal right to accept in January."

The appellants cited the dictum of Keating, J., in the analogous case of Roper v. Johnson.[214] "If there had been any fall in the market, or any other circumstance calculated to diminish the loss, it would be for the defendant to show it;" and the words of Cockburn, C. J., in Frost v. Knight,[215] to the effect that the damages are subject to abatement in respect of any circumstances which would entitle him to a reduction. On this point the court said: [216]

"It is enough to observe in answer to this, that in both Frost v. Knight and Roper v. Johnson the notice that defendant would not comply with the contract was accepted and acted upon by the plaintiff as a breach of the contract; and so what was said in respect of the duty of the plaintiff to mitigate damages was said with reference to a case wherein he recognized the contract as having been broken by the notice of the adverse party, and with reference to what was to be done by him upon and after the recognition of that breach, and hence can have no application here. If a party is not compelled to accept the declaration of the other party to a contract that he will not perform it, as a breach, it must logically follow that he is under no obligation to regard that declaration for any purpose, for the theory in such case, as laid down by Cockburn, C. J., in Frost v. Knight, is: 'He keeps the contract alive for the benefit of the other party as

[214] L. R. 8 C. P. 167, 178.   [216] p. 182.
[215] L. R. 7 Ex. 111, 113.

well as his own. He remains subject to all his own obligations and liabilities under it, and enables the other party not only to complete the contract, if so advised, notwithstanding his previous repudiation of it, but also to take advantage of any supervening circumstance which would justify him in declining to complete it.'"

* In an action of assumpsit [217] by plaintiff against defendant for not accepting a quantity of wheat which the plaintiff, early in January, 1839, contracted to sell to the defendant, to be delivered at Birmingham, as soon as vessels could be obtained for the carriage thereof, the defendant gave notice, on the 26th of January, that he would not accept the wheat if delivered—wheat having then fallen in price. It was at that time on its way to Birmingham, and on its arrival was offered to the defendant; but he refused to take it. On the trial, it was contended that the measure of damages was the difference between the contract price and the price on the 26th of January, when notice was given. But on argument, the Exchequer held that the true rule was the difference between the contract price and that on the day when it was offered at Birmingham; and they relied on the case of Leigh v. Patterson.[218]

So in another case,[219] which was an action of assumpsit for not accepting certain railway shares, the contract of sale was made on the 26th of August, 1840; on the 7th of September, the defendant refused to take them. On the 15th, the plaintiff resold the shares at a loss of £161 from the price agreed on; and the jury, under the charge of the judge, found a verdict for this amount. The defendant, on a motion for a new trial, insisted that the damages should have been calculated only to the 7th of September, when the defendant declared off. But Alderson, B., said: "The damages are to be calculated at the difference between the contract price and the price to be obtained within a reasonable time after the breach of contract; and it was for the jury to say what was such reasonable time."

So where a person had contracted for a certain quantity of oil, it was held that in an action for not accepting and paying for the oil, the proper measure of damages was the difference

---

[217] Phillpotts v. Evans, 5 M. & W. 475.   [218] 8 Taunt. 540.

[219] Stewart v. Cauty, 8 M. & W. 160.

between the price he had contracted to pay for the oil, and the market price at the time when the contract was broken.[220]** And where, by the terms of the contract, the goods were to be delivered at stated periods, but were not all delivered at the respective times, the purchaser not countermanding them, but requesting from time to time that the supply might be delayed, and finally refusing to accept any more; it was held, that damages might be given for the whole quantity remaining on hand, though consisting in part of quantities which, without being actually countermanded, had, by desire of the purchasers, been kept back at the time appointed for delivery; and that it was a proper direction to the jury to give such damages as would leave the plaintiffs in the same situation as if the defendants had fulfilled their contract.[221] Where, however, the contract calls for the manufacture and delivery of goods, the plaintiff, after notice that the defendant will not fulfil his contract, cannot go on manufacturing and upon tender recover the whole contract price.[222]

The same question may arise where the countermand is by the vendor. Thus in England,[223] in an action to recover damages for the breach of a contract by which the defendant had engaged to furnish the plaintiff a certain quantity of tallow in *all December*, at 65s. per cwt., the defendant had apprised the plaintiff, on the 1st of October, that he could not execute the contract, and he insisted that the difference between the contract price (65s.) and that of the 1st of October (71s.) was the rule of damages, on the ground that the plaintiff could, as soon as apprised that the contract would not be executed, have gone into the market and supplied himself at the then rates. The plaintiff, however, insisted that he was entitled to the difference between the contract price (65s.) and the price on the 31st December (81s.) that being the last day for the performance of the contract; and of that opinion was the court.

[220] Boorman v. Nash, 9 B. & C. 145.
[221] Cort v. Ambergate, N. & B. & E. J. Ry., 17 Q. B. 127.
[222] *Missouri:* Frederick v. Willoughby, 136 Mo. App. 244, 116 S. W. 1109.
North Carolina: Heiser v. Mears, 120 N. C. 443, 27 S. E. 117.

Texas: Tufts v. Lawrence, 77 Tex. 526, 19 Am. St. Rep. 772.
The general rule was laid down in Clark v. Marsiglia, 1 Den. 317, *ante,* § 636.
[223] Leigh v. Paterson, 8 Taunt. 540.

Park, J., said: "For anything that appears, the plaintiff never assented to rescind the contract, and the defendant might have delivered the tallow at any moment up to the 31st of December; and the price on that day should have regulated the verdict of the jury."

The result of these cases seems to be that a countermand by either party does not change the time at which damages are to be estimated, nor affect the general rule of damages. If the countermand is treated as a breach, the person so treating it acts thereafter under the rule of avoidable consequences; but if it is not treated as a breach, the rule of avoidable consequences can have no application before the time fixed for performance.

IV.—BREACH OF WARRANTY AND FRAUD

§ 759. Warranties.

* We come next to the subject of warranties. The contract of sale may be complied with on the part of the vendor, so far that delivery may have been made, but the article may still not satisfy the warranties, either express or implied, that have been made at the time of sale; and in this case the rule of damages is now to be investigated. We, for the present, assume that no fraud enters into the transaction, inasmuch as, in that case, we shall presently see different rules apply; and, moreover, it transfers the subject of compensation in a great degree to the discretion of the jury. It will be noticed that, in one branch of the question which we now proceed to examine, the rights and liabilities of the parties concerned are often identical with those of principal and surety; but reserving for separate inquiry that subject in its more extended form, we shall confine ourselves at present to the examination of warranties as contained in sales.

In cases of executory contracts, or contracts to deliver a specific article, if on delivery they prove not to satisfy the agreement, the plaintiff, as we have seen, is not bound to retain the articles, but he may return them within a reasonable time. So it was originally held in regard to chattels sold with warranty, that if they did not answer the agreement, the plaintiff had his election of two remedies: he might either return the article and recover the price paid; or he might sell the article and recover damages in an action on the warranty.[224]** To-day, however, the question of the buyer's right to rescind is one upon which there exists an irreconcilable conflict in the authorities.[225] Whatever the rule it can have no effect upon the measures of damages when the vendee sues for a breach of the warranty.

The uncertainty in which the whole law of warranties is involved has produced a variety of decisions as to the measure of relief. *It seems originally to have been held that the measure of damages in these cases was the difference between the price paid and the actual value; but it is now well settled that the rule is the difference between the actual value and the value that the article would have possessed if it had conformed to the warranty, the price paid being mere evidence of that value.** The conflict has doubtless been caused, in part, by the origin of the action of warranty. Originally based on tort, and differing from the ordinary action of deceit only in that there was no requirement of *scienter*, the nature of the action has changed, until it has now become customary to sue in assumpsit. If the action sounds in tort, as an original question at least, the damages would be estimated from the price; but if contract is the gist of the action, then the value of the article as represented should control.[226]

§ 760. Cases allowing difference between price and actual value.

*In an early case,[227] Mr. J. Buller, discussing the question whether an action for money had and received would lie on an executed contract, said: "In a late case before me, on a warranty of a pair of horses to Dr. Compton, that they were five years old, when in fact they turned out to be only four, I held that, *as the plaintiff had not rescinded the contract*, he could only recover damages; and then the question was, what was the difference *of the value* of horses of four or five years old."

---

[224] So held in the Special Court of Appeals of Virginia. Graham *v.* Bardin, 1 Patt. & H. 206.

[225] See Williston on Sales, § 608.

[226] See Williston on Sales, §§ 195 *et seq.*

[227] Towers *v.* Barrett, 1 T. R. 133.

In a subsequent case,[228] it was insisted that the plaintff should have returned the animal which had been warranted sound. But it was held by all the judges that neither such return nor notice of the unsoundness was necessary to enable the plaintiff to maintain his action for the damages sustained. In another case,[229] an action being brought on the warranty of a horse sold by the defendant to the plaintiff for £20; the warranty and the unsoundness being proved, the jury was directed that if the horse was kept, the verdict *ought to be for the difference between the value and the price paid.* The jury, however, contrary to this direction, found for the plaintiff £30 10s.; £20 for the horse, and 10 guineas for its keep. The defendant moved for a new trial; and the verdict was reduced to £20, the plaintiff undertaking to deliver back the horse, *free of any expense for its keep.***

In a few cases this rule, making the difference between the price paid and the value of the thing with the defect, has been laid down; [230] but in every jurisdiction the rule actually adopted is probably otherwise,[231] and these cases merely stand for a mistaken method of stating the sound rule.

[228] Fielder v. Starkin, 1 H. Bl. 17.

[229] Caswell v. Coare, 1 Taunt. 566.

[230] *Colorado:* Canon City Electric Light & Power Co. v. Medart Patent Pulley Co., 11 Colo. App. 300, 52 Pac. 1030; Tilley v. Montelius Piano Co., 15 Colo. App. 204, 61 Pac. 483.
Georgia: Badget v. Broughton, 1 Kelly, 591; Oxford Knitting Mills v. Wooldridge, 6 Ga. App. 301, 64 S. E. 1008.
Illinois: Morgan v. Ryerson, 20 Ill. 343; Crabtree v. Kile, 21 Ill. 180; Callendar I. & W. Co. v. Badger, 30 Ill. App. 314.
Maryland: Rice v. Forsyth, 41 Md. 389.
Michigan: Sinker v. Diggins, 76 Mich. 557, 43 N. W. 674.
Mississippi: Hambrick v. Wilkins, 65 Miss. 631, 3 So. 67.
Missouri: Courtney v. Boswell, 65 Mo. 196; Anslyn v. Frank, 8 Mo. App. 242.

New York: Bedford v. Hol-Tan Co. 140 App. Div. 282, 128 N. Y. Supp. 78.
North Carolina: Kester v. Miller, 119 N. C. 475, 26 S. E. 115; Huyett-Smith Manuf. Co. v. Gray, 129 N. C. 438, 57 L. R. A. 198, 40 S. E. 178.
Oregon: Schumann v. Wager, 36 Ore. 65, 58 Pac. 770.
Pennsylvania: West Republic Mining Co. v. Jones, 108 Pa. 55, 65.
Texas: Anderson v. Duffield, 8 Tex. 237; Browne v. Allen, 53 Tex. Civ. App. 458, 116 S. W. 133.
Wisconsin: Park v. Richardson, 81 Wis. 399, 51 N. W. 572; Duecker v. Goeres, 104 Wis. 29, 80 N. W. 91.
England: Dingle v. Hare, 7 C. B. (N. S.) 145.
Canada: Mooers v. Gooderham, 14 Ont. 451.

[231] *Infra,* § 762.

§ 761. Between value as warranted and actual value.

The rule laid down in the preceding cases is not the law in most jurisdictions. In another English case,[232] in an action of assumpsit on a warranty of soundness in a horse, Lord Eldon spoke of the difference between the value of the article warranted and its actual value when sold, as the measure of damages; but the case did not turn on this point. Later, however, the precise subject was considered, and this rule finally adopted in another action brought for the breach of a warranty.[233] The plaintiff had bought a horse of the defendant for £45, warranted sound. The plaintiff has sold the horse with warranty to one Collins for £55; Collins returned the horse as unsound; and the plaintiff was obliged to repay the £55, and the animal was sold for £17 15s. The plaintiff claimed the difference between that sum and £45, the price paid; the expense of bringing the horse to London; his keep from the time of purchase to the sale as unsound; the £10 paid to Collins; £1 15s. for an examination at the veterinary college; and £1 15s. for opinion of counsel. Lord Denman, C. J., at the trial of the cause, said: "As the warranty and the unsoundness are admitted on the record, the only question is the amount of the damages. I am of opinion that the amount of damages is what the horse would *be worth if sound*, deducting the price it sold for after the discovery of the unsoundness; and I think the price at which it was sold to the plaintiff *is not conclusive as to its value*, though I think it very strong evidence. The fair value of the horse, if sound, is the measure of the damages; and the sum the plaintiff gave is only the evidence of the value." He refused to allow the £10 paid Collins, because there was no evidence that the horse was worth more than the plaintiff gave for it. The expense of bringing the horse to London, and of keeping him there also, was allowed. The court was moved for a new trial as to the £10 paid Collins; but they refused to disturb the verdict, saying that this claim in substance amounted to a claim of compensation for the loss of a good bargain, which could not be allowed as damages in such an action.[234]

[232] Curtis *v.* Hannay, 3 Esp. 82.
[233] Clare *v.* Maynard, 7 C. & P. 741.
[234] From the report of this case in the King's Bench, 6 A. & E. 519, it appears that a question arose as to the sufficiency of the declaration. The plain-

In a case in New York,[235] assumpsit was brought on a warranty that 120 barrels of flour were superfine flour, of good quality. The price paid was $9.50 per barrel; 60 barrels were defective. The defendant's counsel insisted that the measure of damages was the difference in value between the 60 barrels when sold and the value of superfine flour; but Willard, C. J., held at the trial that the plaintiffs were entitled to recover back the balance of the whole purchase money paid for the 60 barrels, with interest, crediting the amount realized by them from their sale at auction. On a motion for a new trial, Cowen, J., said: "Regarding this case as one of simple warranty without fraud, the measure of damages adopted at the trial was wrong. It should have been the difference between the *value of the sixty barrels* at the time of the sale considered as good superfine flour, and *the value of the inferior article sold*. The purchaser is entitled to have the article made equal in quality to what the warranty assured it to be." A new trial was granted.

The question has been still more distinctly decided by the same court in another case.[236] Gruman sued Cary on a warranty of soundness in a horse; the price paid was $90, and the breach was a disease of the eyes. The defendant insisted that the proper measure of damages was the difference between the real value of the horse, if sound, and his value with the defect complained of. The court below, however, decided that the measure of damages was the difference between the price paid and the value with the defect. A verdict being found in conformity to this charge, on exception and writ of error, it was said by the Supreme Court:

"The court below erred in laying down the rule of damages. The warranty cannot be satisfied, except by paying to the vendee such sum as, together with the cash value of the defective article, shall amount to what it would have *been worth* if the defect had not existed. . . . The rule, undoubtedly, is,

tiff insisted that the £10 should be allowed as expenses, if not as profit. But to cover this, the court said there was no adequate allegation. See also Cox *v.* Walker, in notes to this case.

See to the same effect:

Delaware: Burton *v.* Young, 5 Harr. 233.

New York: Muller *v.* Eno, 14 N. Y. 597.

[235] Voorhees *v.* Earl, 2 Hill, 288, 291.

[236] Cary *v.* Gruman, 4 Hill, 625, per Cowen, J.

that the agreed price is strong evidence of the actual value; and this should never be departed from unless it be clear that such value was more or less than the sum at which the parties fixed it. . . . It is impossible to say, nor have we the right to inquire, whether the real value of the horse in question, supposing him to have been sound, would have turned out to be more or less than the $90 paid. Suppose the jury thought, with one witness whom the court allowed to state such value for another purpose, that it was not more than $80, the plaintiff then recovered ten dollars, not on account of the defect, but because he had been deficient in care or sound judgment as a purchaser. On the other hand, had the horse been actually worth $100, the defendant would have been relieved from the payment of the ten dollars, because he had made a mistake of value against himself. The cause might thus have turned on a question entirely collateral to the truth of the warranty."

And a new trial was granted. Mr. Chancellor Kent [237] seems to prefer the rule as laid down in Curtis v. Hannay, cited above, on the ground of its being in harmony with the measure of damages on the covenant of warranty in the sale of land. But it is proper to notice that the doctrine settled is in analogy to the principle in another class of cases. It has been laid down as a general rule,[238] in regard to actions for nonperformance of contracts (other than conveyances of lands), that the party ready to perform may recover damages to the extent of his injury, and that the price agreed to be paid on actual performance is not the measure of damages. This also seems the rule in other States where in the case of sale by sample, in an action on the implied representation or warranty, the measure is held to be the difference between the value of the articles delivered and the commodity sold.[239]

§ 761a. Discussion of principles.

These conflicting views may be satisfactorily explained if not reconciled by reference to the historical development of

[237] 2 Com. 480, in notes.
[238] Shannon v. Comstock, 21 Wend. 457.
[239] *Arkansas:* Murry v. Meredith, 25 Ark. 164.

New York: Roberts v. Carter, 28 Barb. 462.
Pennsylvania: Borrekins v. Bevan, 3 Rawle, 23.

the action for breach of warranty. It appears that this originated in the tort action of deceit, wherein it resembles the action of *assumpsit* itself. But though the action of *assumpsit* early assumed a distinct form, the action for breach of warranty retained its tort characteristics and only gradually were the strict requirements for an action of deceit dispensed with. At length, however, it became unnecessary to allege fraud, or that the seller knew his affirmations to be untrue. And it is the law to-day that though the action may be framed in tort no *scienter* need be alleged.[240] The remedy is, therefore, rather an action in the nature of deceit than a given action of deceit.

These changes in the tort action were doubtless affected by the invention of a new form of relief for breach of warranty,— an action framed in *assumpsit*. Here too time has wrought important modifications: the original requirement of an express promise [241] has been abolished and an affirmation which was in fact untrue will now sustain an action of *assumpsit*.[242] Thus though the plaintiff has these two alternative forms of relief the requirements for both are identical. As a question of logic one would expect the rule of damages to vary according to the form of action. Yet, when as here there is no substantial difference between the two actions it is natural that the distinction should be entirely obliterated if a good reason for so doing presents itself. Whatever the origin of the remedy for breach of warranty, it is certain that to most persons the term "warranty" imports a promise. A modification of legal technicalities to conform to ordinary business usage and understanding is by no means unusual in our law. Therefore it is not altogether surprising that the courts should ignore the form of the action for breach of warranty and in either case award the measure of damage regularly applied for breach of contract; that is, the difference between the value if as warranted and the actual value. This result is all the more acceptable if it be remembered that the action of *assumpsit* itself was founded partly, if not wholly, in tort, and only by a slow process assumed the nature of an action of covenant.[243]

---

[240] See Williston on Sales, §§ 195–197.
[241] Chandelor *v.* Lopus, Cro. Jac. 4.
[242] Williston on Sales, § 196.

[243] Ames, History of Assumpsit, 2 Harv. L. Rev. 1.

§ 762. Difference in values the general rule.

From these considerations it follows that whatever the rule may be when such actual fraud exists as would support an action of deceit, yet when this element is lacking or the action is for simple breach of an express or implied warranty, whether framed in tort or in contract, the better rule for measuring damages is the difference between the value which the thing sold would have had at the time of the sale, if it had been sound or corresponding to the warranty, and its actual value with the defect. And such is now the almost universally recognized rule.[244] The rule is the same whether the suit is brought by

[244] *United States:* Mack v. Sloteman, 21 Fed. 109; Newberry v. Bennett, 38 Fed. 308; Hudmon v. Cuyas, 57 Fed. 355; English v. Spokane Com. Co., 6 C. C. A. 416, 57 Fed. 451, 48 Fed. 196, 15 U. S. App. 218; Crane Co. v. Columbus Const. Co., 73 Fed. 984, 20 C. C. A. 233; Nashua Iron & Steel Co. v. Brush, 91 Fed. 213, 33 C. C. A. 456; Florence Oil & Refining Co. v. Farrar, 119 Fed. 150, 55 C. C. A. 656; McDonald v. Kansas City Bolt Co., 149 Fed. 360, 365, 79 C. C. A. 298; Meyer, Wilson & Co. v. Everett P. & P. Co., 184 Fed. 945.

Alabama: Willis v. Dudley, 10 Ala. 933; Marshall v. Wood, 16 Ala. 806; Worthy v. Patterson, 20 Ala. 172; Gingles v. Caldwell, 21 Ala. 444, 56 Am. Dec. 252; Davis v. Dickey, 23 Ala. 848; Foster v. Rodgers, 27 Ala. 602; Stoudenmeier v. Williamson, 29 Ala. 558; Herring v. Skaggs, 62 Ala. 180, 73 Ala. 446, 34 Am. Rep. 4.

Arkansas: Tatum v. Mohr, 21 Ark. 349; Murry v. Meredith, 25 Ark. 164; B. A. Stevens Co. v. Whalen, 95 Ark. 488, 129 S. W. 1081.

California: Hughes v. Bray, 60 Cal. 284; McLennan v. Ohmen, 75 Cal. 558; Woody v. Bennett, 88 Cal. 241, 26 Pac. 117; Silberhorn Co. v. Wheaton (Cal.), 51 Pac. 689; Erie City Iron Works v. Tatum, 82 Pac. 92, 1 Cal. App. 202; Germain Fruit Co. v. J. K. Armsby

Co., 153 Cal. 585, 96 Pac. 319; Tibbals Oakum Co. v. Meigs (Cal. App.), 104 Pac. 844; Cal. Civ. Code, § 3313.

Colorado: Smith v. Mayer, 3 Colo. 207.

Connecticut: Murray v. Jennings, 42 Conn. 9, 19 Am. Rep. 527.

Delaware: Burton v. Young, 5 Harr. 233; Ellison v. Simons, 65 Atl. 591; Collins v. Tigner, 5 Pennew. 345, 60 Atl. 978.

Florida: Merritt v. Wittich, 20 Fla. 27.

Georgia: Clark v. Neufville, 46 Ga. 261; Atkins v. Cobb, 56 Ga. 86; Van Winkle v. Wilkins, 81 Ga. 93, 7 S. E. 644, 12 Am. St. Rep. 299; Seaboard Lumber Co. v. Cornelia Planing Mill Co., 122 Ga. 370, 50 S. E. 121.

Illinois: Woodworth v. Woodburn, 20 Ill. 184; Strawn v. Cogswell, 28 Ill. 457; Wallace v. Wren, 32 Ill. 146; McClure v. Williams, 65 Ill. 390; Wilson v. King, 83 Ill. 232; Carpenter v. First Nat. Bank, 119 Ill. 352; Wheelock v. Berkely, 138 Ill. 153, 27 N. E. 942; Moore Furniture Co. v. Sloane, 166 Ill. 457, 46 N. E. 1108; C. W. Dooley & Co. v. Hasenwinkle Grain Co., 120 Ill. App. 43; Swartz v. Atchison, 120 Ill. App. 119; Miller v. Aldrich, 123 Ill. App. 464; Nave v. Gross, 146 Ill. App. 104.

Indiana: Overbay v. Lighty, 27 Ind. 27; Street v. Chapman, 29 Ind. 142, 92 Am. Dec. 345; Ferguson v. Hosier, 58

the vendee, or an assignee holding his right of action.[245] So the damages for breach of warranty that cows are with calf,

Ind. 438; Means v. Means, 88 Ind. 196; Hege v. Newsom, 96 Ind. 426; Blacker v. Slown, 114 Ind. 322; Johnson v. Culver, 116 Ind. 278; Crist v. Jacobi, 10 Ind. App. 688, 38 N. E. 543; Williamson v. Brandenburg, 133 Ind. 594, 32 N. E. 834; Bushman v. Taylor, 2 Ind. App. 12, 28 N. E. 97; Green v. Witte, 5 Ind. App. 343, 32 N. E. 214; Elwood Planing Mill Co. v. Harting, 21 Ind. App. 408, 52 N. E. 621.

Iowa: Likes v. Baer, 8 Ia. 368; Lacey v. Straughan, 11 Ia. 258; Boies v. Vincent, 24 Ia. 387; McCormick v. Vanatta, 43 Ia. 389; Jackson v. Mott, 76 Ia. 263; Short v. Mattesin, 81 Ia. 638, 47 N. W. 874; Douglass v. Moses, 89 Ia. 40, 56 N. W. 271, 48 Am. St. Rep. 353; Love v. Ross, 89 Ia. 400, 56 N. W. 528; Aultman v. Shelton, 90 Ia. 288, 57 N. W. 857; Eagle Iron Works v. Des Moines S. R. Co., 101 Ia. 289, 70 N. W. 193; Alpha Checkrower Co. v. Bradley, 105 Ia. 537, 75 N. W. 369; Davidson Bros. Co. v. Smith, 143 Ia. 124, 121 N. W. 503; Loxtercamp v. Lininger Implement Co., 147 Ia. 29, 125 N. W. 830.

Kansas: Weybrich v. Harris, 31 Kan. 92; Wheeler & W. M. Co. v. Thompson, 33 Kan. 491; Tufts v. Mabie, 7 Kan. App. 129, 53 Pac. 84; Loomis Milling Co. v. Vawter, 8 Kan. App. 437, 57 Pac. 43.

Kentucky: Wood v. Wood, 1 Met. 512; Sharpe v. Bettis, 17 Ky. L. Rep. 673, 32 S. W. 395; Mosby v. Larue, 143 Ky. 433, 136 S. W. 887; Leavell v. Coleman, 139 S. W. 1079.

Louisiana: Foster v. Baer, 7 La. Ann. 613; Slaughter v. M'Rae, 3 La. Ann. 455.

Maine: Moulton v. Scruton, 39 Me. 287; Ponce v. Smith, 84 Me. 266, 24

Atl. 854; Thoms v. Dingley, 70 Me. 100, 35 Am. Rep. 310.

Maryland: Williamson v. Dillon, 1 H. & G. 444; Lane v. Lantz, 27 Md. 211; Horn v. Buck, 48 Md. 358; Central Trust Co. v. Arctic Ice Mach. Co., 77 Md. 202, 238, 26 Atl. 493; Sloan v. Alleghany Co., 91 Md. 501, 46 Atl. 1003.

Massachusetts: Bradford v. Manly, 13 Mass. 139, 7 Am. Dec. 122; Door v. Fisher, 1 Cush. 271; Reggio v. Braggiotti, 7 Cush. 166; Tuttle v. Brown, 4 Gray, 457, 64 Am. Dec. 80; Whitmore v. South Boston Iron Co., 2 All. 52; Lothrop v. Otis, 7 All. 435; Grose v. Hennessey, 13 All. 389; Morse v. Brackett, 98 Mass. 205; Miller v. Smith, 112 Mass. 475; Case v. Stevens, 137 Mass. 551; Deutsch v. Pratt, 149 Mass. 415, 14 Am. St. Rep. 430, 21 N. E. 1072; Noble v. Fagnant, 162 Mass. 275, 38 N. E. 507.

Michigan: White v. Brockway, 40 Mich. 209; Maxted v. Fowler, 94 Mich. 106, 53 N. W. 921; Henry v. Hobbs, 165 Mich. 183, 130 N. W. 616.

Minnesota: Converse v. Burrows, 2 Minn. 229; Minnesota H. W. v. Bonnallie, 29 Minn. 373; Merrick v. Wiltse, 37 Minn. 41, 33 N. W. 3; Fitzgerald v. Evans, 49 Minn. 541, 52 N. W. 143; St. Anthony Lumber Co. v. Bardwell-Robinson Co., 60 Minn. 199, 62 N. W. 274; Hansen v. Gaar, 63 Minn. 94, 65 N. W. 254; Miamisburg Twine & Cordage Co. v. Wohlhuter, 71 Minn. 484, 74 N. W. 175; Benson v. Port Huron Co., 83 Minn. 321, 86 N. W. 327; Piano Manuf. Co. v. Richards, 86 Minn. 94, 90 N. W. 120.

Mississippi: Stillwell v. Biloxi Canning Co., 78 Miss. 779, 29 So. 513.

Missouri: Smith v. Steinkamper, 16

[245] Sweet v. Bradley, 24 Barb. 549. Of course if the contract is rescinded by agreement and the property taken back the rule no longer applies. What

the purchaser loses in such a case is the purchase price and this he is entitled to recover from the vendor. Lewis v. Doyle, 43 N. Y. Supp. 201.

are measured by the difference between their value in that
condition and in the condition they in fact are in.[246]   In the

Mo. 150; Stearns v. McCullough, 18
Mo. 411; St. Louis Brewing Assoc. v.
McEnroe, 80 Mo. App. 429; Thummel
v. Dukes, 82 Mo. App. 53; June v.
Falkinburg, 89 Mo. App. 563.

Montana: Hogan v. Shuart, 11 Mont.
498, 28 Pac. 969.

Nebraska: Holmes v. Boydston, 1
Neb. 346; Birdsall v. Carter, 11 Neb.
143; Aultman v. Stout, 15 Neb. 586, 19
N. W. 464; Young v. Filley, 19 Neb.
543, 26 N. W. 256; Clark v. Deering, 29
Neb. 293, 45 N. W. 456; Burr v. Redhead, 52 Neb. 617, 72 N. W. 1058; Mc-
Clatchey v. Anderson, 84 Neb. 783,
122 N. W. 67.

New Hampshire: Union Bank v.
Blanchard, 65 N. H. 21, 18 Atl. 90.

New Jersey: Rutan v. Ludlam, 5
Dutch. 398; Perrine v. Serrell, 30 N. J.
L. 454.

New York: Muller v. Eno, 14 N. Y.
597; Rust v. Eckler, 41 N. Y. 488;
Leonard v. Fowler, 44 N. Y. 289, 4 Am.
Rep. 675; Conor v. Dempsey, 49 N. Y.
665; Brigg v. Hilton, 99 N. Y. 517, 3
N. E. 51, 52 Am. Rep. 63; Hooper v.
Story, 155 N. Y. 171, 49 N. E. 773;
Isaacs v. Wannamaker, 189 N. Y. 122,
81 N. E. 763; Mathes v. McCarthy, 195
N. Y. 40, 87 N. E. 768; Comstock v.
Hutchinson, 10 Barb. 211; Sharon v.
Mosher, 17 Barb. 518; Brower v. Lewis,
19 Barb. 574; Roberts v. Carter, 28
Barb. 462; Richardson v. Mason, 53
Barb. 601; Wells v. Selwood, 61 Barb.
238; Kiernan v. Rocheleau, 6 Bosw.
148; Voorhees v. Earl, 2 Hill, 288, 38
Am. Dec. 588; Cary v. Gruman, 4 Hill,
625, 40 Am. Dec. 299; Rich v. Smith, 34
Hun, 136; Hunt v. Van Deusen, 42 Hun,
392; Sprout v. Newton, 48 Hun, 209;
Fales v. McKeon, 2 Hilt. 53; Hoe v.
Sanborne, 35 How. Pr. 197; Carman v.
Trude, 25 How. Pr. 440; Messenger v.
Pratt, 3 Lans. 234; Edwards v. Collson,

5 Lans. 324; Van Valkenburgh v. Evert-
son, 13 Wend. 76; Blanchard v. Ely, 21
Wend. 342, 34 Am. Dec. 250; Ahein
v. O'Brien, 18 N. Y. Supp. 821; Bank of
North Collins v. Cary Safe Co., 42 App.
Div. 233, 59 N. Y. Supp. 643; Russell
v. Corning Manf. Co., 49 App. Div.
610, 63 N. Y. Supp. 640; Steinhardt v.
Phelps, 32 Misc. 730, 66 N. Y. Supp.
311; Ideal Wrench Co. v. Gavin Mach.
Co., 72 N. Y. Supp. 662, 65 App. Div.
235; McQuade v. Newman, 88 N. Y.
Supp. 363; Hano v. Simons, 92 N. Y.
Supp. 337; McCarthy v. Ellers, 94 N.
Y. Supp. 1109; Westinghouse C. K. &
Co. v. Remington Salt Co., 116 App.
Div. 123, 101 N. Y. Supp. 303; Ames
v. Norwich Light Co., 122 App. Div.
319, 106 N. Y. Supp. 952; Sears v.
Bailey, 58 Misc. 145, 110 N. Y. Supp.
467; Bodger v. Hills, 113 N. Y. Supp.
879; Mitchell v. Rowley, 63 Misc. 643,
118 N. Y. Supp. 751; Stratton v. Spaeth,
131 N. Y. Supp. 333.

North Carolina: Pritchard v. Fox, 4
Jones, 140; Hobbs v. Bland, 124 N. C.
284, 32 S. E. 683; Critcher v. Porter-
McNeal Co., 135 N. C. 542, 47 S. E.
604; Parker v. Fenwick, 138 N. C. 209,
50 S. E. 627; Wrenn v. Morgan, 148
N. C. 101, 61 S. E. 641; Hardie-Tynes
Mfg. Co. v. Eastern C. O. Co., 150 N.
C. 150, 63 S. E. 676.

North Dakota: Aultman & Co. v.
Ginn, 1 N. Dak. 402, 48 N. W. 336.

Ohio: Beresford v. McCune, 1 Cin.
Sup. Ct. 50.

Oregon: Bump v. Cooper, 19 Ore. 81,
23 Pac. 806.

Pennsylvania: Cothers v. Keever, 4
Barr, 168; Seigworth v. Leffel, 76 Pa.
476; Freyman v. Knecht, 78 Pa. 141;
Heines v. Kiehl, 154 Pa. 190, 25 Atl.
632; Joseph v. Richardson, 2 Pa. Super.
Ct. 208; Shoe v. Maerky, 35 Pa. Super.
Ct. 270.

---

[246] Richardson v. Mason, 53 Barb. 601.

English Common Pleas it was held that payment in advance did not affect the rule in such a case. The measure is the difference at the time of the delivery between the value of goods of the quality contracted for and that of those delivered, provided the goods can then be resold. Where there is a necessary or reasonable delay in the resale, the difference is to be computed on the day of the resale.[247] The law of Louisiana imposes on the seller the obligation of warranting the thing sold against its hidden defects, which are those which could not be discovered by simple inspection; and the purchaser may retain the thing sold, and have an action for the reduction of the price by reason of the difference in value between the thing as warranted and as it was in fact. But such a part of the price only as will indemnify the vendee for the difference between the value of the thing as warranted and the thing actually sold, together with the expenses incurred on the thing after deducting its fruits, can be recovered.[248]

Where the goods were to be shipped abroad, which fact was known to the vendor, and the defect could not be dis-

South Carolina: Garrett v. Stuart, 1 McCord, 514; Rose v. Beatie, 2 N. & McC. 538; Verdier v. Trowell, 6 Rich. L. 166; Parker v. Pringle, 2 Strobh. 249.

South Dakota: Western Twine Co. v. Wright, 11 S. D. 521, 78 N. W. 942, 44 L. R. A. 438; Cavanagh v. A. W. Stevens Co., 24 S. D. 349, 123 N. W. 681.

Tennessee: McGavock v. Wood, 1 Sneed, 181; Smith v. Cozart, 2 Head, 526; Allen v. Anderson, 3 Humph. 581, 39 Am. Dec. 197; Reese v. Miles, 99 Tenn. 398, 41 S. W. 1065.

Texas: Wright v. Davenport, 44 Tex. 164; Stark v. Alford, 49 Tex. 260; Routh v. Caron, 64 Tex. 289; Ford v. Oliphant (Tex. Civ. App.), 32 S. W. 437; Florida Athletic Club v. Hope Lumber Co., 18 Tex. Civ. App. 161, 44 S. W. 10; Danner v. Fort Worth Implement Co., 18 Tex. Civ. App. 621, 45 S. W. 856; Ash v. Beck (Tex. Civ. App.), 68 S. W. 53.

Vermont: Woodward v. Thacher, 21 Vt. 580, 52 Am. Dec. 73; Mayer v. Dwinell, 29 Vt. 298; Penny v. Andrus, 41 Vt. 631.

Virginia: Thornton v. Thompson, 4 Gratt. 121; Eastern Ice Co. v. King, 86 Va. 97.

Washington: Abrahamson v. Cummings, 117 Pac. 709.

Wisconsin: Merrill v. Nightingale, 39 Wis. 247; Aultman & T. Co. v. Hetherington, 42 Wis. 622; Osborne v. McQueen, 67 Wis. 392; J. I. Case Plow Works v. Niles & Scott Co., 90 Wis. 590, 603, 63 N. W. 1013.

England: Jones v. Just, L. R. 3 Q. B. 197, 202; Clare v. Maynard, 7 C. & P. 743.

Canada: La Roche v. O'Hagan, 1 Ont. 300; Copeland v. Hamilton, 9 Manitoba, 143.

Australia: Spence v. Duffield, 1 Vict. 49.

---

[247] Loder v. Kekule, 3 C. B. (N. S.) 128.

[248] Bulkley v. Honold, 19 How. 390, 15 L. ed. 663.

covered till they reached their destination, it was held that the measure of damages was the difference between the marketable value of the article contracted for on the day of arrival and the actual value there,[249] which might be the price realized by a sale of the article received, together with expenses of sale.[250] And where the goods were sold abroad before the breach of warranty was discovered, and the plaintiff was compelled to take them back on account of the defect, and sold them again at a lower price, he was allowed to recover the difference between the prices realized at the two sales.[251]

Upon breach of contract of warranty of quality of tobacco sold, the purchaser gave notice to the seller that he would not accept it; the seller not receiving it back, the purchaser on notice sold it at auction. It was held that the price received at auction could be shown.[252] Danforth, J., said: "It was for the plaintiffs to show the market value of the tobacco delivered by the defendants. For that purpose a sale at auction was properly resorted to, and its result was some evidence of the fact in question, not conclusive, but quite satisfactory in the absence of explanation or testimony from the defendants."

It results from the general rule, that it is erroneous in an action on a note given for the price of a chattel for the court to charge the jury that, although they should find the covenant to have been broken, if at the time of the sale the chattel in its unsound state was worth the price for which it was sold, the defendant had sustained no damage.[253] Nor is the rule affected by proof that the purchaser afterwards sold the prop-

[249] Krasilnikoff v. Dundon, 8 Cal. App. 406, 97 Pac. 172.

[250] Camden C. O. Co. v. Schlens, 59 Md. 31, 43 Am. Rep. 537.

In Hudmon v. Cuyas, 57 Fed. 355, 6 C. C. A. 381, 13 U. S. App. 443, cotton was sold, under a warranty, to be delivered at Savannah, f. o. b. The case was decided on other grounds but the court said that in such a case delivery of an inferior quality having been made and the goods resold by the vendee and he having replaced himself in the market the cost of reselling and replacing might be a necessary and natural ele-ment of damages as much to be considered as difference in price. (Toulmin, J., diss.) Cf. Barker v. Marn, 5 Bush. 672, 96 Am. Dec. 373; Penn v. Smith, 93 Ala. 476, 9 So. 609.

[251] Rose v. Beatie, 2 N. & McC. 538.

[252] New York: Bach v. Levy, 101 N. Y. 511, 515.

England: Powell v. Horton, 2 Bing. N. C. 668.

[253] Georgia: Hook v. Stovall, 26 Ga. 704.

New York: Shields v. Pettie, 4 N. Y. 122.

erty for as much as and more than he paid for it.[254] Where the property at the time of the sale had no market value, and it is impossible to get at its real value at that time if it had been as warranted, the price paid may be taken to represent that value.[255] And it is sometimes said generally that the price at which the property was sold is evidence of its value at that time if as warranted.[256] Where, in an action for damages for a breach of warranty, the consideration given for the warranted article consisted in another article which was exchanged for it, evidence of the value of the exchanged property will be allowed, as tending to show what the value of the other would have

[254] *United States:* Union Selling Co. v. Jones, 128 Fed. 672, 63 C. C. A. 224.

Georgia: Atkins v. Cobb, 56 Ga. 86; Americus Grocery Co. v. Brackett, 119 Ga. 489, 46 S. E. 657.

Illinois: Wheelock v. Berkely, 138 Ill. 153, 27 N. E. 942.

Massachusetts: Brown v. Bigelow, 10 All. 242.

Missouri: Missouri & I. C. Co. v. Consolidated C. Co., 127 Mo. App. 320, 105 S. W. 682.

Minnesota: Miamisburg Twine Co. v. Wohlhuter, 71 Minn. 484, 74 N. W. 175.

New York: Hunt v. Van Deusen, 42 Hun, 392.

South Carolina: Ellison v. Johnson, 74 S. C. 202, 54 S. E. 202, 5 L. R. A. (N. S.) 1151.

South Dakota: Western Twine Co. v. Wright, 11 S. D. 521, 78 N. W. 942, 44 L. R. A. 438.

Wisconsin: J. I. Case Plow Works v. Niles & S. Co., 90 Wis. 590, 63 N. W. 1013.

The price received on resale may be taken as evidence of value.

Georgia: Berry v. Shannon, 98 Ga. 459, 25 S. E. 514, 58 Am. St. Rep. 314.

New York: Muller v. Eno, 14 N. Y. 597.

Vermont: Brock v. Clark, 60 Vt. 551, 15 Atl. 175.

See also *Missouri:* Joplin Water Co. v. Bathe, 41 Mo. App. 285.

New York: Wait v. Borne, 123 N. Y. 592, 25 N. E. 1053; Sherman v. Billings, 90 Hun, 544.

[255] South C. & C. S. Ry. v. Gest, 34 Fed. 628; Meyer, Wilson & Co. v. Everett P. & P. Co., 184 Fed. 945.

[256] *Alabama:* Marshall v. Wood, 16 Ala. 812.

Georgia: Feagin v. Beaseley, 23 Ga. 17.

Minnesota: Minneapolis Harvester Works v. Bonnallie, 29 Minn. 373, 13 N. W. 149.

Massachusetts: Day v. Mapes-Reeve Construction Co., 174 Mass. 412, 54 N. E. 878.

Minnesota: Miamisburg Twine Co. v. Wohlhuter, 71 Minn. 484, 74 N. W. 175.

North Carolina: Williamson v. Conday, 3 Ired. 349.

Tennessee: Garr, Scott & Co. v. Young (Tenn.), 62 S. W. 631.

Texas: Ash v. Beck (Tex.), 68 S. W. 53; Gutta Percha & R. M. Co. v. Cleburne (Tex. Civ. App.), 107 S. W. 157.

Vermont: Houghton v. Carpenter, 40 Vt. 588.

Virginia: Thornton v. Thompson, 4 Gratt. 121.

Wisconsin: Case Plow Works v. Niles & Scott Co., 90 Wis. 590, 63 N. W. 1013.

been if it had corresponded with the warranty.[257]   The price realized on a second sale is admissible as one mode of determining the value.[258]

* Where fraud intervenes, as we shall presently see, the contract can be rescinded, the thing returned, and the price paid recovered back, or the party defrauded may stand to the bargain and recover damages for the fraud.[259] **

§ 762a. Recoupment.

When a breach of warranty has occurred and the buyer is sued for the price he may either counterclaim or recoup his damages. If he chooses the former remedy he may set off against the price the sum which under the law of the jurisdiction represents the measure of damages for a breach of warranty, *i. e.*, usually the difference in values. But the remedy of recoupment results quite differently. There the vendor's claim is in effect reduced to a quasi-contractual claim and the buyer need pay only the actual value of the article delivered.[260] This is of course equivalent to holding the measure of damages for a breach of warranty to be the difference between the price and the actual value. The terms counterclaim and recoupment are frequently, though erroneously, used interchangeably and the real distinction often unrecognized.

§ 763. Warranty of quantity or value.

* There is sometimes a warranty of quantity, either expressed or implied; and in that case the purchaser is entitled to have the article made equal in quantity to what the warranty de-

[257] Chaplin *v.* Warner, 23 Wis. 448. So in the analogous action for deceit. Fisk *v.* Hicks, 31 N. H. 535.

[258] *Alabama:* Milton *v.* Rowland, 11 Ala. 732; Foster *v.* Rodgers, 27 Ala. 602.

Massachusetts: Reggio *v.* Braggiotti, 7 Cush. 166.

North Carolina: Houston *v.* Starnes, 12 Ired. 313.

[259] *New York:* Voorhees *v.* Earl, 2 Hill, 288; Putman *v.* Wise, 1 Hill, 234, where the doctrine is considered at length in a learned note; Sharon *v.* Mosher, 17 Barb. 518.

England: Campbell *v.* Fleming, 1 A. & E. 40.

[260] *United States:* Lyon *v.* Bertram, 20 How. 149, 15 L. ed. 847.

California: Polhemus *v.* Heiman, 45 Cal. 573.

Connecticut: McAlpin *v.* Lee, 12 Conn. 129, 30 Am. Dec. 609.

District of Columbia: Fenton *v.* Braden, 2 Cr. C. C. 550.

Georgia: Watkins *v.* Paine, 57 Ga. 50; Berry *v.* Shannon, 98 Ga. 459, 25 S. E. 514.

Maryland: Birdsall Co. *v.* Palmer, 74 Md. 201, 21 Atl. 705.

clared it to be.[261] ** So, again, there may be a warranty that the thing sold shall, without reference to its intrinsic quality or value, be worth a certain price or have a certain value in the market within a specified time; and in that case the measure of damages is the difference between the warranted amount and the actual value.[262] So in a case in Massachusetts the defendant had sold the plaintiff twenty shares of the stock of an express company, with a warranty that it should be "worth $700 market value, within one year." The highest price reached by the stock during the year was $500. At the end of the year its market value was $330. The plaintiff insisted that the measure of damages was the difference between $330 and $700. But the defendant contended he was only liable to pay the difference between $500 and $700, and the court so held.[263] So where the defendant guaranteed to sell bonds for the plaintiff at a certain price and time, the measure of damages is the difference between the price received and that guaranteed.[264] In Vance v. McBurnett [265] where as part payment on an exchange of properties notes of a third party had been given under circumstances which amounted to a warranty of the notes and the makers were insolvent it was held that the measure of damages was the value placed upon the notes in the exchange.

§ 764. Avoidable consequences.

The rule of avoidable consequences applies here as elsewhere, and if the defect can be remedied, the cost of so doing is

Massachusetts: Bradley v. Rea, 14 Allen, 20; Perley v. Balch, 23 Pick. 283, 34 Am. Dec. 56.

New York: Judd v. Dennison, 10 Wend. 512.

Vermont: Brown v. Sayles, 27 Vt. 227; Mayer v. Dwinell, 29 Vt. 298.

Washington: Huntington v. Lombard, 22 Wash. 202, 60 Pac. 414.

England: Mandel v. Steel, 8 M. & W. 858.

[261] *Georgia:* Parker v. Barlow, 93 Ga. 700, 21 S. E. 313.

New York: Voorhees v. Earl, 2 Hill, 288; Hargous v. Ablon, 3 Denio, 406.

Pennsylvania: Kinports v. Breon, 193 Pa. 309, 44 Atl. 436.

[262] *Georgia:* Florence v. Pattillo, 105 Ga. 577, 32 S. E. 642.

Massachusetts: Woodward v. Powers, 105 Mass. 108, 7 Am. Rep. 503.

New York: Titus v. Poole, 145 N. Y. 426, 40 N. E. 228.

Pennsylvania: Struthers v. Clark, 30 Pa. 210.

[263] Woodward v. Powers, 105 Mass. 108, 7 Am. Rep. 503.

[264] Plumb v. Campbell, 129 Ill. 101, 16 Am. St. Rep. 242, 18 N. E. 790.

[265] 21 S. E. 520.

the measure of damages.[266]   One had sold another for the price of good pork, well packed in good barrels, a quantity of pork in barrels with a warranty that the barrels would not leak. After the barrels had been properly stowed by the vendee, he found that a part of them were leaky, and the brine had in consequence escaped. He, thereupon, under the advice of some experts, filled up the barrels with new brine, in good faith, intending and expecting thereby to preserve the pork; but the barrels continuing to leak, a portion of them were either wholly spoiled or deteriorated to an extent exceeding the balance due for the pork. The vendee did not notify the vendor of the leaking of the barrels, nor offer to return the imperilled pork, nor did he repack the pork in new barrels, which it appeared it was customary and necessary to do under such circumstances. Whether the vendee, in fact, knew of this custom or necessity did not appear. Both parties were free from fraud. In an action by the vendor for the unpaid balance of the purchase money, it was held that the vendee was entitled to no deduction on account of the loss of the pork, but only to what it would have cost to procure new barrels in lieu of the old ones and repack the pork therein.[267]   Even where a plaintiff gives notice of a special object in purchasing an article, he cannot recover damages suffered by continuing to use it when he discovers its defects.[268]   So the plaintiff is not allowed to recover the rental value of a distillery where he is prevented

---

[266] *United States:* Benjamin v. Hillard, 23 How. 149, 16 L. ed. 518; Marsh v. McPherson, 105 U. S. 709, 26 L. ed. 1139; Vulcan Iron Works Co. v. Roquemore, 175 Fed. 11, 99 C. C. A. 77.

Alabama: Snow v. Schomacker Mfg. Co., 69 Ala. 111, 44 Am. Rep. 509.

Arkansas: B. A. Stevens Co. v. Whalen, 95 Ark. 488, 129 S. W. 1081.

Illinois: Strawn v. Cogswell, 28 Ill. 457.

Kansas: Frick Co. v. Falk, 50 Kan. 644, 32 Pac. 360.

Louisiana: Leathers v. Sweeney, 41 La. Ann. 287.

Massachusetts: Whitehead & A. M. Co. v. Ryder, 139 Mass. 366.

Michigan: Kimball & A. M. Co. v. Vroman, 35 Mich. 310, 24 Am. Rep. 558.

Minnesota: Wyckoff v. Horan, 39 Minn. 429.

New York: Bates v. Fisk Brothers' Wagon Co., 50 App. Div. 38, 63 N. Y. Supp. 649.

Canada: M'Mullen v. Williams, 5 Ont. App. 518.

Only reasonable expenditures can be undertaken, having regard to the value of the warranted article. Tennis v. Gifford, 133 Ia. 372, 110 N. W. 586.

[267] Hitchcock v. Hunt, 28 Conn. 343.
[268] Draper v. Sweet, 66 Barb. 145.

from using it by a defect in a pump which he knew to be defective when he placed it in the well; he is confined to the difference in value per day between what the pump would have been worth had it been as warranted, and what it was actually worth.[269] The plaintiff should have protected himself from loss. On an action for breach of warranty of seeds which failed to grow, the court deducted from the amount of recovery the sum which the vendee might have made by renting the land or planting another crop, after he discovered that the seeds planted were worthless.[270]

§ 765. Consequential damages.

* The rights of the parties in a case of warranty are not, however, always presented in the simple form that we have just been considering. The vendee, in some instances, confiding in the warranty, is subjected to indirect or consequential loss. And the recovery of such consequential loss will depend on the general principles which we have heretofore examined.[271] So where a slave was sold with warranty of soundness, and two months afterwards received a gunshot wound and died, and it was proved that he had labored under a chronic affection of the lungs at the time of the sale, and but for that disease the wound would not have proved mortal; it was held, notwithstanding, that the vendor was liable only for the diminution of his value at the time of the sale in consequence of the disease, and not for the combined consequence of the wound and the disease.[272] ** In Randall v. Newson,[273] the plaintiff had bought of the defendant a pole for his carriage. In driving, the horses swerved and the pole broke short off at the carriage. The horses became restive and were injured. The court below had refused to allow damages for this injury. In Banc this was held to be error, the court saying: "We think that a ques-

[269] Nye v. Iowa C. A. Works, 51 Ia. 129, 33 Am. Rep. 121.

[270] Reiger v. Worth, 127 N. C. 230, 37 S. E. 217, 52 L. R. A. 362, 80 Am. St. Rep. 798.

[271] *Indiana:* Williamson v. Brandenburg, 133 Ind. 594, 32 N. E. 834.

Missouri: Neil v. Cunningham Store Co., 149 Mo. App. 53, 130 S. W. 503.

Texas: Ford v. Oliphant (Tex. Civ. App.), 32 S. W. 437.

[272] Marshall v. Gantt, 15 Ala. 682.

[273] 2 Q. B. D. 102, 111. *Cf.* Woodward v. Miller, 119 Ga. 618, 46 S. E. 847.

tion should have been left to the jury similar to that which was left in Smith *v.* Green,[274] namely, whether the injury to the horses was or was not a natural consequence of the defect in the pole." In Zuller *v.* Rogers [275] it was held that for breach of warranty of the soundness of a canal-boat, the plaintiff was liable not only for the difference in value, but also for special damages sustained by reason of delay, loss of time, and other injury suffered unavoidably on the first trip before the defects were discovered.

In Leavitt *v.* Fiberloid Co.[276] the defendant sold material to be used by the plaintiff in a process which developed heat, and warranted that the material would not start a fire; but it did catch fire during the process. It was held that plaintiff could recover compensation for the damage caused by the fire. Where defendant sold fruit trees of a certain variety but delivered trees of an inferior variety, which could not be discovered until after several years' cultivation, the plaintiff was allowed the diminished value of the land by reason of the inferiority of the trees.[277] Where plaintiff was to take care of sheep for half the wool and half the lambs, defendant falsely representing that they were in good condition, and many died from disease, the measure of damages was held to be the cost of taking care of them and the value of the time spent, less the profits made under the contract.[278] Where a boiler, warranted sound, exploded and injured the plaintiff's mill, it was held that the rental value of the mill during the necessary repairs might be recovered.[279] Where white-lead had been spilled on the defendant's hay, and he had partially separated the poisoned hay from the rest, and wrongly supposed he had done so completely, and under this impression sold some of the remaining hay to the plaintiff, and the plaintiff's cow died from eating the hay, it was held that the defendant was liable, and that the rule of damages was the value of the cow.[280]

[274] 1 C. P. D. 92; cited *infra,* § 769.

[275] 7 Hun, 540.

[276] 196 Mass. 440, 82 N. E. 682, 15 L. R. A. (N. S.) 855.

[277] Long *v.* Pruyn, 128 Mich. 57, 87 N. W. 88.

[278] Parker *v.* Marquis, 64 Mo. 38.

[279] Sinker *v.* Kidder, 123 Ind. 528.

[280] French *v.* Vining, 102 Mass. 132, 3 Am. Rep. 440.

See to the same effect:

Oklahoma: Coyle *v.* Baum, 3 Okla. 695, 41 Pac. 389.

Texas: Houston Cotton Oil Co. *v.*

On the other hand, when the plaintiff, a retail grocer, purchased from the defendant a quantity of milk, and in ignorance of the fact that it was skimmed milk resold it to customers, and was arrested and fined ten dollars, it was held that he could recover only the difference between the value of skimmed milk and unskimmed milk.[281]

We proceed to consider some of the more common instances of the allowance of consequential damages.

§ 766. Upon warranty of fitness for a purpose.

Where an article is warranted fit for a particular purpose, the purchaser can recover the damages caused by an attempt to use it for that purpose.[282] This sometimes gives a larger measure of recovery than would be allowed under the ordinary rule. Where the chattel sold has different values, according to the use for which it is intended, the value which measures the damage is that which the vendor represented it to have with reference to the purpose to which he knew it was to be applied by the vendee. So where oxen purchased for work, and represented sound, proved unsound, and by reason of the unsoundness were worth ten dollars less for beef and twenty-five dollars for work, the larger sum was held to be the measure.[283] The plaintiff purchased from a druggist an article supposed to be Paris green for the known purpose of killing cotton worms. It was worthless and consequently the crop of cotton was destroyed by the worms. The measure of damages was held to be the value of the crop destroyed.[284] Where barrels were purchased for use in storing cider, as the seller

---

Trammell, 96 Tex. 598, 72 S. W. 244.

Ireland: Wilson v. Dunville, 6 L. R. Ir. 210.

[281] Sloggy v. Crescent Creamery Co., 72 Minn. 316, 75 N. W. 225.

[282] *California:* McLennan v. Ohmen, 75 Cal. 558; Fox v. Stockton C. H. & A. Works, 83 Cal. 333, 17 Am. Rep. 252.

Georgia: Cochran v. Jones, 85 Ga. 678, 11 S. E. 811.

Iowa: Swift & Co. v. Redhead, 147 Ia. 94, 122 N. W. 140.

In Leifer Mfg. Co. v. Gross, 93 Ark. 277, 124 S. W. 1039, the fact of consequential damage was not proved.

This rule has been held not to authorize a recovery of the value of goods stolen from a safe warranted burglar-proof. Herring v. Skaggs, 62 Ala. 180, 34 Am. Rep. 4. *Contra,* Deane v. Michigan Stove Co., 69 Ill. App. 106.

See *ante,* § 164a.

[283] Ladd v. Lord, 36 Vt. 194.

[284] Jones v. George, 61 Tex. 345, 48 Am. Rep. 280.

knew, and in consequence of defects the cider was lost, the vendor was held liable for the value of the cider,[285] and where oxen sold were warranted easily yoked by an old man, and were not, the measure of damages is the difference between the value of oxen as warranted and the value of the oxen sold.[286] So where a refrigerator was warranted to keep chickens frozen for market, the measure of damages was the diminished value of the refrigerator, and the value of chickens lost, reckoned at their value in the market at the time to which the refrigerator was warranted to keep them, less the expense of reaching market and selling.[287] Where coloring matter purchased for the purpose of coloring ice-cream by a manufacturer of that article proved to be poisonous, the purchaser was allowed to recover the value of the ice-cream lost through the use of the poisonous coloring matter, and also compensation for injury to business.[288]

Where a horse was warranted kind and gentle, and it was not so in fact, but ran away, the plaintiff recovered damages for personal injuries sustained thereby.[289]

In Dushane v. Benedict [290] the plaintiff sold to the defendant rags, which he represented to be clean rags though, as he knew, they had been infected with smallpox. The vendee's workmen caught the disease and he suffered damages, including sums paid by him to support disabled workmen, a loss resulting from running his mill short-handed, and a loss of trade. In an action for the price the vendee was held entitled to counterclaim and recover for all those items of damage.

Where steel sold proved to be of an inferior description to what it was warranted to be, the purchaser, having used the

[285] *Indiana:* Poland v. Miller, 95 Ind. 387, 48 Am. Rep. 730.
Michigan: Tatro v. Brower, 118 Mich. 615, 77 N. W. 274.

[286] Wing v. Chapman, 49 Vt. 33.

[287] Beeman v. Banta, 118 N. Y. 538, 16 Am. St. Rep. 779, 23 N. E. 887.

[288] Swain v. Schieffelin, 134 N. Y. 471, 18 L. R. A. 385, 31 N. E. 1025. Red umbrella covers were sold with a warranty that the color would not come off; the color did come off and stained the umbrellas; *held* that the damage to the umbrellas could be recovered. Jones v. Mayer, 38 N. Y. Supp. 801. *Cf.* Borradaile v. Bruntor, 8 Taunt. 535; *ante,* § 134.

[289] Bruce v. Fiss, 26 Misc. 472, 56 N. Y. Supp. 234, 47 App. Div. 273, 62 N. Y. Supp. 96.
See, however, Jones v. Ross, 98 Ala. 448, 13 So. 319.

[290] Dushane v. Benedict, 120 U. S. 630, 7 Sup. Ct. 696, 30 L. ed. 810.

steel in the manufacture of axes, was allowed to recover the difference between the value of these axes and that of axes made of the quality of steel this was described to be. The court stated that the reason of these decisions was that the plaintiff could not have discovered the defect before the axes were manufactured, and therefore could not replace himself till then.[291]

Where the heating apparatus installed by the defendant proved wholly inadequate to heat a greenhouse and the stock contained therein was damaged by the cold, the defendant was held liable for the diminution in value.[292] Where varnish was warranted fit to varnish wood mouldings, and upon being used for that purpose proved to be of an inferior sort, the measure of damages was held to be the difference in value of the mouldings varnished as they should have been and as they were.[293] In any case actual loss may be recovered. On breach of warranty of steel furnished for manufacturing into vises, the measure of damages is the cost of the labor and material wasted, with interest.[294] In case of warranty of steel springs sold to manufacture carriages, the purchaser may recover the expense of taking defective springs out of carriages manufactured and replacing them by new ones.[295]

Where worthless cement is sold to be used in plastering a house and in consequence thereof it becomes necessary to replaster, the cost of such work is recoverable from the vendor.[296] And if the plaster has fallen the injury resulting is an element of damages, to which may be added the rental value

[291] Parks v. Morris A. & T. Co., 54 N. Y. 586; acc., Milburn v. Belloni, 39 N. Y. 53, 100 Am. Dec. 403.

[292] Laufer v. Boynton Furnace Co., 84 Hun, 311, 32 N. Y. Supp. 362. Cf. Fowler v. Pauly, 67 Mo. App. 632; Russell v. Corning Manuf. Co., 49 App. Div. 610, 63 N. Y. Supp. 640. In the latter case a physician's office became unfit for use because of improper heating: the measure of damages was held to be the rental value of the office.

[293] Moore v. King, 57 Hun, 224.

Cf. Dommerich v. Garfunkel, 28 Misc. 433, 58 N. Y. Supp. 1006 (cloth made into garments); Stranahan Co. v. Coit, 55 Oh. St. 398, 45 N. E. 634 (impure milk used in manufacturing certain products).

[294] Bagley v. Cleveland R. M. Co., 22 Blatch. 342.

[295] Thoms v. Dingley, 70 Me. 100, 35 Am. Rep. 310.

[296] Indiana: Zimmerman v. Druecker, 15 Ind. App. 512, 44 N. E. 557.

Massachusetts: Noble v. Fagnant, 162 Mass. 275, 38 N. E. 507.

Nebraska: Omaha, etc., Co. v. Fay, 37 Neb. 68, 55 N. W. 211; Nye v. Snyder, 56 Neb. 754, 77 N. W. 118.

of the premises pending the repairing.[297] Where an animal is sold for breeding purposes, and warranted fit, damages for keeping it until its unfitness is discovered may be recovered.[298]

§ 767. Upon warranty of machines.

Under the foregoing head would properly come cases of warranty of machines. Where a machine turned out not to be what it was warranted, it was held that the plaintiffs could not recover for profits lost during the time which was required to put it in the condition it was warranted to be, since the more certain compensation is its rental value.[299] In an action for breach of a contract to construct and set up, within a specified time, engines on a steamboat of a stipulated quality and power; where it proved that the engines were not delivered within the time fixed by the contract, and did not conform to it, the measure of the plaintiff's damages was held to be the difference between the machinery furnished and that called for by the contract, together with expenses actually incurred by the plaintiff as a consequence of the breach, which would include the wages of the officers and crew while they remained idle during the delay in furnishing the machinery, and such reasonable further time as was consumed in testing and repairing it, or procuring other machinery instead, to which might be added interest.[300] Damages may also be recovered for materials consumed or injured by an attempted use of the

---

[297] Riss v. Messmore, 58 N. Y. Super. Ct. 23, 9 N. Y. Supp. 320.

[298] *California:* Hodgkins v. Dunham, 10 Cal. App. 690, 103 Pac. 351.

Indiana: Williamson v. Brandenburg, 133 Ind. 594, 32 N. E. 834.

Iowa: Steele v. M. E. Andrews & Sons, 144 Ia. 360, 121 N. W. 17.

[299] Booher v. Goldsborough, 44 Ind. 490.

[300] Fisk v. Tank et al., 12 Wis. 276, 78 Am. Dec. 737.

See to the same effect:

California: Fox v. Stockton Harvester, etc., Works, 83 Cal. 333, 23 Pac. 295, 17 Am. St. Rep. 252.

Delaware: Wilmington Candy Co.

v. Remington Mach. Co., 5 Pennew. 543, 65 Atl. 74.

Georgia: Aultman v. Mason, 83 Ga. 212, 9 S. E. 536.

Massachusetts: Whitehead v. Ryder, 139 Mass. 366, 31 N. E. 736.

Nebraska: Burr v. Redhead, 52 Neb. 617, 72 N. W. 1058.

Wisconsin: Optenberg v. Skelton, 109 Wis. 241, 85 N. W. 356.

So in the case of expenses incurred by a street car company in constructing devices necessary for the installation of a storage battery system which proved to be useless. Accumulator Co. v. Dubuque St. R. R., 64 Fed. 70, 12 C. C. A. 37, 27 U. S. App. 364, 379;

machine before its inadequacy is known.[301] Where the plaintiff
has ascertained that the materials are being injured, he must,
of course, desist from attempting to use.[302] Where a steam
boiler exploded while being properly used for the purpose
for which it was intended, the seller is liable for injuries thus
caused to adjacent property[303] and to employes.[304] Mc-
Cormick v. Vanatta[305] was an action for breach of a warranty
that a reaping and mowing machine would reap and rake small
grain or flax, in all conditions, as well as it could be done by
hand. The vendee claimed to recover for loss of part of his
crop by a delay which was due to defects in the machine sold.
The court refused to give such damages, holding that such a
consequence was too remote, and saying that the true measure
of damages was the difference in the value of the machine as it
was and as it should have been. But if it had been within the
contemplation of the parties at the time of the contract that
it would be impracticable to procure another machine to do
the work and save the crop, it has been intimated that the
loss would be recoverable.[306] Where the warranted machine
was bought for the manufacture of cotton-seed oil, the plaintiff
may recover the deterioration in value of cotton seed bought
to run in the machine.[307] For breach of warranty of a varnish-
ing machine, the measure of damages is the difference between
the value of the machine, had it corresponded with the warranty, and its actual value. This may be recouped in an action
for the price.[308]

In all such cases when the losses on sub-contracts were

acc., O. H. Jewell Filter Co. v. Kirk,
102 Ill. App. 246.

[301] Wilmington Candy Co. v. Remington Mach. Co., 5 Pennew. 543, 65
Atl. 74.

[302] Kansas: Gale S. H. M. Co., v.
Moore, 46 Kan. 324, 26 Pac. 703
(seeder).

Texas: Ellis v. Fips, 16 Tex. Civ.
App. 82, 40 S. W. 524 (cotton gin).

[303] Indiana: Page v. Ford, 12 Ind. 46.

Pennsylvania: Erie City Iron Works
v. Barber, 106 Pa. 125, 51 Am. Rep.
508.

[304] Boston W. H. & R. Co. v. Ken-

dall, 178 Mass. 232, 59 N. E. 657, 86
Am. St. Rep. 478, 51 L. R. A. 781.
Acc. Tyler v. Moody, 111 Ky. 191,
63 S. W. 433.

[305] 43 Ia. 389; acc., Frohreich v. Gam-
mon, 28 Minn. 476; Wilson v. Reedy,
32 Minn. 256; Smoots v. Foster, 16
Ohio C. Ct. 612.

[306] Minnesota: Frohreich v. Gam-
mon, 28 Minn. 476.

Wisconsin: Aultman v. Case, 68 Wis.
612, 32 N. W. 772.

[307] Van Winkle v. Wilkins, 81 Ga.
93, 7 S. E. 644, 12 Am. St. Rep. 299.

[308] Hooper v. Story, 155 N. Y. 171,
49 N. E. 773.

within the contemplation of the parties and capable of proof they may be recovered. Thus in Carroll-Porter Boiler Co. v. Columbus Machine Co.,[309] in which damages were claimed for breach of warranty of capacity of a machine, it was held error to reject proof of what it would have cost to do the work required by a dependant contract had the machine conformed to the warranty and what was the actual cost. Expenditures for advertising and losses incurred in the general business of the party injured were treated as too remote and uncertain.

The plaintiff may recover for freight paid on the machine,[310] and for the expense of setting up and testing it in the attempt to make it work.[311] In a strong enough case, recovery may be had for the loss of income from its use.[312]

§ 768. Of seeds.

We have already discussed the cases turning upon warranty of seeds, and shown how they illustrate the principles of consequential damages.[313] It is not necessary to do more than summarize the results here. Where seed is warranted to be of a certain quality and turns out to be of an inferior quality, the purchaser is not, *where the seed grows, and produces a crop*, confined to the difference between the price of seed of one quality and that of the other. He has been allowed to recover the difference between the value of a crop produced by the seed delivered and the value a crop produced by other seed would have had.[314] In the case of Randall v. Raper [315] the defendant

[309] 55 Fed. 451, 3 U. S. App. 631, 5 C. C. A. 190.

[310] *Arkansas:* W. T. Adams Mach. Co. v. Castleberry, 92 Ark. 310, 122 S. W. 998.

California: Luitweiler P. E. Co. v. Ukiah W. & I. Co. (Cal. App.), 116 Pac. 707.

Kentucky: Pennebaker Bros. v. Bell City Mfg. Co., 130 Ky. 592, 113 S. W. 829.

[311] *Arkansas:* W. T. Adams Mach. Co. v. Castleberry, 92 Ark. 310, 122 S. W. 998.

North Carolina: Waynesville Wood Mfg. Co. v. Berlin Mach. Works, 57 S. E. 455, 144 N. C. 689.

In Sturtevant Mill Co. v. Kingsland Brick Co. (N. J. L.), 70 Atl. 732, the expense for which the plaintiff claimed to recover was not one which he had a right to incur at the defendant's risk.

[312] Murray Co. v. Putman, 130 S. W. 631 (Tex. Civ. App.).

[313] § 191.

[314] *Illinois:* Phillips v. Vermillion, 91 Ill. App. 133.

Kentucky: Haycroft v. Walden, 14 Ky. L. Rep. 892.

England: Wagstaff v. Short Horn Dairy Co., Cab. & E. 324.

[315] E. B. & E. 84.

had sold the plaintiff some barley, warranting it to be "Chevalier seed barley." The plaintiff on the faith of that warranty had resold it with a similar one. The barley proved to be not "Chevalier seed barley," but of an inferior quality, in consequence of which the plaintiff's vendee obtained a poor crop. It was held that the plaintiff was entitled to recover the amount to which he had become liable to the vendee, although it was unliquidated as between him and his vendee. In Passinger v. Thorburn,[316] the last cited case was approved by the New York Court of Appeals, in a judgment affirming that of the court below.[317] The defendant sold cabbage seed, warranting that it would produce Bristol cabbages, and the plaintiff having sowed it in the anticipation of producing that crop, the warranty proved untrue. The damages were held to be the value of a crop such as should have been produced by the seed that year, had it conformed to the warranty, *deducting the expense of raising the crop*, and the value or product of the one in fact raised. The strong cases of Borradaile v. Brunton,[318] and Brown v. Edgington,[319] with other English cases to the same purport, are cited and approved; and the doctrine of Hadley v. Baxendale is applied to its full extent to the case of a breach of warranty. The rule in Passinger v. Thorburn, by which the expenses of raising the crop are deducted, has been followed in a Nebraska case.[320] But it is difficult to explain on principle. Such an expense is surely in the contemplation of the parties, if the seeds are sold for planting; and the same expense was actually incurred in raising the inferior crop. The true measure of damages is, therefore, to deduct from the value of the crop which should have been raised, only the value of the actual crop. Indeed, this is all that Passinger v. Thorburn squarely decided, for as was pointed out in a later New York decision,[321]

---

[316] 34 N. Y. 634, 90 Am. Dec. 753, See to the same effect:
Massachusetts: Edgar v. Joseph Breck & Sons Co., 172 Mass. 581, 52 N. E. 1083.
New Jersey: Wolcott v. Mount, 36 N. J. L. 262, 13 Am. Rep. 438.
New York: White v. Miller, 71 N. Y. 118, 27 Am. Rep. 13.

Contra, in *Tennessee:* Hurley v. Buchi, 10 Lea, 346.
[317] 35 Barb. 17.
[318] 8 Taunt. 535.
[319] 2 M. & G. 279.
[320] Dunn v. Bushnell, 63 Neb. 568, 88 N. W. 693, 93 Am. St. Rep. 474.
[321] Van Wyck v. Allen, 69 N. Y. 61,

that case came upon an exception by the defendant to the court's charge. The deduction of the cost of raising the crop not being prejudicial to the defendant was not ground for reversal and the judgment was therefore rightly affirmed.

In the case of Flick v. Wetherbee,[322] the lessor of farming land having covenanted to supply seed, was held bound to supply good seed, and the above measure was applied to the lessee's damages by reason of a partial failure of the crop in consequence of the inferiority of the seed furnished. But, on the other hand, a more restricted rule has been adopted in the case of seeds *which do not in fact grow.* There the value of a possible crop is too conjectural. In such cases the damages should be the cost of the seed, the value of the labor in preparing the ground for it (less the general benefit to the land from such labor), the value of the labor in planting it, with interest on the several amounts.[323] *Where the seed grows, but does not produce a crop,* the rule is that the loss of crop is not too conjectural.[324] Where seed was sold as prime clover seed, but contained plantain, it was held that the purchaser could recover the difference in the value of the farm before the weed was sowed and after. The expense of uprooting and killing out the plantain is evidence to show the damage to the land.[325]

Another instance where the breach of warranty has a more permanent effect upon the value of the land is in the sale of fruit trees. Where trees of an inferior kind are delivered and planted by the buyer in ignorance of the facts, the measure of damages is the difference in the value of the premises with the inferior trees and the value if the trees had been as or-

25 Am. Rep. 136. But see Landreth v. Wycoff, 67 App. Div. 145, 73 N. Y. Supp. 388.

[322] 20 Wis. 392.

[323] *Connecticut:* Ferris v. Comstock, 33 Conn. 513.

Georgia: Butler v. Moore, 68 Ga. 780, 45 Am. Rep. 508.

Kansas: Shaw v. Smith, 45 Kan. 334, 25 Pac. 886, 11 L. R. A. 681.

North Carolina: Reiger v. Worth, 127 N. C. 230, 37 S. E. 217, 52 L. R. A. 362, 80 Am. St. Rep. 798.

But see Page v. Pavey, 8 C. & P. 769.

[324] *Kentucky:* Crutcher v. Elliott, 13 Ky. L. Rep. 592.

New York: Schutt v. Baker, 9 Hun, 556.

Washington: Fuhrman v. Interior Warehouse Co. (Wash.), 116 Pac. 666.

[325] *New York:* Fox v. Everson, 27 Hun, 355; Bell v. Mills, 68 App. Div. 531, 74 N. Y. Supp. 224.

Canada: McMullan v. Free, 13 Ont. 57.

dered.[326] This difference is to be estimated at the time the trees first began to bear fruit, or whenever the breach of warranty was first discovered.[327]

§ 769. By communication of disease.

Where animals sold are warranted free from disease, loss through communication of disease to other animals of the purchaser may be recovered.[328] It is not necessary to the recovery of such damages to show that the vendor knew that the diseased animal was to be placed with others belonging to the plaintiff.[329] The defendant is presumed to anticipate that the animals he sells will be placed with others as a natural consequence of his act.[330] The expenses of nursing and curing other animals, which contract disease from those sold, may be recovered.[331]

§ 770. Upon a sub-contract.

No recovery can be had for delay in executing existing con-

[326] Heilmen v. Pruyn, 122 Mich. 301, 81 N. W. 97, 81 Am. St. Rep. 570; Angell v. Pruyn, 126 Mich. 16, 85 N. W. 258.

[327] Shearer v. Park Nursery Co., 103 Cal. 415, 37 Pac. 412, 42 Am. St. Rep. 125.

That the statute of limitations runs from the day of the sale, see Allen v. Todd, 6 Lans. 222 (N. Y.). But compare Ashworth v. Wells, 14 T. L. Rep. 227 (orchid).

[328] *Delaware:* Cummins v. Ennis, 4 Pennew. 424, 56 Atl. 377.

Georgia: Snowden v. Waterman, 105 Ga. 384, 31 S. E. 110.

Illinois: Wheeler v. Randall, 48 Ill. 182.

Iowa: Sherrod v. Langdon, 21 Ia. 518; Joy v. Bitzer, 77 Ia. 73; Mitchell v. Pinckney, 127 Ia. 696, 104 N. W. 286.

Kansas: Broquet v. Tripp, 36 Kan. 700.

Kentucky: Faris v. Lewis, 2 B. Mon. 375; Greenley v. Brooks, 13 Ky. L. Rep. 298.

Massachusetts: Bradley v. Rea, 14 All. 20.

Minnesota: Marsh v. Webber, 16 Minn. 418.

Mississippi: McKee v. Jones, 67 Miss. 405, 7 So. 348.

Nebraska: Long v. Clapp, 15 Neb. 417.

New York: Jeffrey v. Bigelow, 13 Wend. 518, 28 Am. Dec. 476.

Texas: Wintz v. Morrison, 17 Tex. 372, 67 Am. Dec. 658; Routh v. Caron, 64 Tex. 289.

Vermont: Packard v. Slack, 32 Vt. 9, 76 Am. Dec. 148.

Wisconsin: McCann v. Ullman, 109 Wis. 574, 579, 85 N. W. 493.

England: Mullett v. Mason, L. R. 1 C. P. 559; Smith v. Green, 1 C. P. D. 92; Knowles v. Nunns, 14 L. T. R. 592.

See § 131.

[329] Packard v. Slack, 32 Vt. 9, 76 Am. Dec. 148.

[330] Sherrod v. Langdon, 21 Ia. 518.

[331] *Delaware:* Cummins v. Ennis, 4 Pennew. 424, 56 Atl. 377.

Georgia: Snowden v. Waterman, 105 Ga. 384, 31 S. E. 110.

Nebraska: Long v. Clapp, 15 Neb. 417.

tracts on account of the breach of warranty where the fact of such contract was not made known to vendor.[332]   Where pianos turned out to be defective, it was held that the plaintiff could not include transportation to and from sub-purchasers and hire of other pianos during time of repair.[333]   But where it is known to the defendant that the property was bought to fill a contract, the plaintiff may recover the profits of the sub-contract.[334]   But if the profits expected would have been extraordinarily large, the vendor is, in the absence of knowledge of this fact, liable only for ordinary profits.[335]

In a case in the Irish Exchequer [336] the plaintiff sued for breach of warranty on a sale of scrap iron.   The defendant had notice at the time of purchase that the contract was made in order to enable the plaintiff to accept an offer for such iron from one Wright, in Philadelphia; after making the contract with the defendant, the plaintiff accepted Wright's offer, which was for a price found by the jury to be not an unusual advance over the purchasing price.   It was held that the plaintiff could recover the difference between the actual value of the iron delivered by the defendant and the price he would have received on the sub-contract.

§ 771. Purchase for sale at a distance.

In a case [337] where the defendant had sold the plaintiff certain merchandise, called in the bill of parcels scarlet cuttings, intended for the China market, which turned out not to be so, Lord Ellenborough held that such a description implied a warranty that they were the article named, and charged that the plaintiff was entitled to recover such a sum as he would have received had the warranty been true with reference to the China market; the value to be recovered being the value which the plaintiff would have received had the defendant faithfully performed his contract.   So where a quantity of

[332] Weybrick v. Harris, 31 Kan. 92.
[333] Snow v. Schomacker Mfg. Co., 69 Ala. 211.
[334] Carpenter v. First Nat. Bank, 119 Ill. 352; see § 162.   But if goods to fill the sub-contract can be obtained elsewhere, such damages cannot be recovered.   National Coke Co. v. Cin-

cinnati G. C. C. & M. Co. (Mich.), 132 N. W. 88.
[335] Guetzkow v. Andrews, 92 Wis. 214, 66 N. W. 119.
[336] Hamilton v. Magill, 12 L. R. Ir. 186, 202.
[337] Bridge v. Wain, 1 Stark. 504.

pork, although contracted for delivery at one place, was known to the vendor to be intended for use by the vendee at another place, and when it had reached the latter proved to be damaged, the difference in value at the ultimate point was held to furnish the measure; [338] and in an action for breach of warranty, where the seller knew the articles were bought for a customer of the purchaser at Salt Lake City, it was said that the purchaser should recover the difference between the value of the articles at the place where the contract was made and the worth when delivered, *plus* the cost of transportation and the profits the plaintiff would have made by a resale.[339] But this rule was not followed in New York. The defendant sold plaintiff a quantity of apples, to be delivered at Barre, in New York. At the time of the sale it was agreed that the apples were to be "good ingrafted winter fruit," and it was understood that they were intended to be put up for the Canada market. They were accordingly delivered to the plaintiff at Barre, and he took them to Toronto, Canada, where the barrels were opened, and some of the apples found to be damaged. It was held, in an action for breach of warranty, that the true measure of damages was not the difference between the real value of the apples, as they proved to be, and the price of good merchantable fruit *in the Canada market*, deducting the price of transportation to that place, but the difference in value between a sound and the unsound article *at the place of delivery;* and that the plaintiff was not entitled to recover anything on the ground of a loss of profits. If the apples had been wholly lost in consequence of the fault of the vendor, the vendee might recover the expenses of transportation to the contemplated market, in addition to the price paid for the fruit. But he could in no event go beyond that, and recover anything on the ground of a loss of profits.[340] Under the general view now taken of the rule in Hadley v. Baxendale, this last case would hardly be followed.

§ 772. Expenses.

In a suit on the warranty of a slave, reasonable medical and

[338] Converse v. Prettyman, 2 Minn. 229.

[339] Thorne v. McVeagh, 75 Ill. 81.

[340] Lattin v. Davis, Hill & Denio Supp. 9.

other expenses, sustained by reason of the unsoundness warranted against, have been included in the damages,[341] with interest from the time of payment.[342] Nor is the right of recovery made to depend on the fact of payment. It is enough that they have been fairly incurred.[343] In Arkansas, on breach of warranty as to the soundness of a slave, the plaintiff was allowed to recover the expenses necessarily incurred in consequence of the unsoundness, but not interest on the value.[344] In cases of breach of warranty of soundness in the sale of animals, where the rule of compensation cannot be enlarged so as to include consequential damages, the jury should be instructed as to what evidence tends to show the difference in value between the animals sound and unsound, and what recoverable expenses have been seasonably, properly, and reasonably incurred in taking care of them and trying to cure them.[345] And in an action for breach of warranty of soundness of a slave who had died, the measure of damages was held to be the price paid and interest, and if the vendee offered to return the slave, and the offer was refused, the subsequent expenses of his keeping.[346] And on the same principle the plaintiff is entitled to recover the expenses of keeping an animal for such a reasonable time as may be necessary to sell him to the best advantage.[347] Where the vendor of machines knew they were purchased for resale and the vendee, before discovering the breach of warranty, sold them to customers who refused to

---

[341] *Alabama:* Hogan v. Thorington, 8 Port. 428; Kornegay v. White, 10 Ala. 255; Buford v. Gould, 35 Ala. 265; Stone v. Watson, 37 Ala. 279.

Georgia: Feagin v. Beasley, 23 Ga. 17.

New Jersey: Perrine v. Serrell, 30 N. J. L. 454.

[342] Roberts v. Fleming, 31 Ala. 683.

[343] Kelly v. Cunningham, 36 Ala. 78, 76 Am. Dec. 318.

[344] Tatum v. Mohr, 21 Ark. 349.

[345] *Arkansas:* Murry v. Meredith, 25 Ark. 164.

Iowa: Raeside v. Hamm, 87 Ia. 720, 54 N. W. 1079.

Vermont: Pinney v. Andrus, 41 Vt. 631.

Contra, Merrick v. Wiltse, 37 Minn. 41.

[346] Scranton v. Tilley, 16 Tex. 183.

In Williamson v. Brandenburg, 133 Ind. 594, 32 N. E. 834 (Ind.), the vendee of a horse recovered the cost of keeping until he had had a reasonable time in which to ascertain that the horse was defective.

[347] *Kentucky:* Leavell v. Coleman, 139 S. W. 1079.

England: McKenzie v. Hancock, Ryan & Moody, 436; Chesterman v. Lamb, 2 A. & E. 129; Ellis v. Chinnock, 7 C. & P. 169; Clare v. Maynard, 7 C. & P. 741.

accept because of the defects, the vendee recovered the reasonable expense incurred in making such resale.[348]

§ 773. Litigation expenses.

* The vendor may be liable for the expenses of litigation incurred in consequence of his warranty. It seems when the chattel has been sold a second time by the vendee, relying on the original warranty, and he is prosecuted by the second vendee, and recovery had, the first vendor, if duly notified of the claim, and it is not unnecessarily resisted, is liable for the whole amount of the damages and costs recovered against the first vendee by the second vendee, as well as his costs of defence.[349] ** So in an action on the warranty of a horse, the defendant had sold the horse to the plaintiff with warranty, and the plaintiff had resold with warranty to one Dowling. Dowling sued the plaintiff, and recovered the price of the horse, with £88 costs. The plaintiff had given the defendant notice of Dowling's action. This action was brought for the price of the horse and the costs, and the plaintiff had a verdict for the whole amount. On a motion for a new trial, and to set aside the verdict as to the costs of Dowling's action, it was urged that, if the horse was unsound, the plaintiff had incurred this expense needlessly, and in his own wrong. But the rule was refused, the court saying that as the plaintiff received no directions from the defendant to give up the cause, the costs were a part of the damages which the plaintiff had sustained.[350]

[348] Punteney-Mitchell Manuf. Co. v. T. G. Northwall Co., 66 Neb. 5, 91 N. W. 863.

[349] *Arkansas:* Marlett v. Clary, 20 Ark. 251.

California: Erie City Iron Works v. Tatum, 1 Cal. App. 286, 82 Pac. 92.

New York: Carleton v. Lombard, 46 N. Y. Supp. 120.

England: Battley v. Faulkner, 3 B. & Ald. 288; Hammond v. Bussey, 20 Q. B. Div. 79.

But see Joseph v. Richardson, 2 Pa. Sup. Ct. 208.

Costs, but not counsel fees: Reggio v. Braggiotti, 7 Cush. 166; Jeter v. Glenn, 9 Rich. L. 374.

[350] Lewis v. Peake, 7 Taunt. 153; but it has been since held that notice is not conclusive. The same question was presented in Wrightup v. Chamberlain, 7 Scott, 598, and it being found that the plaintiff, before he defended the action brought against him, might have ascertained, by a reasonable examination of the horse, that it was not sound, the court said that the defence was a rash one, and the plaintiff not entitled to charge the defendant "with the costs of such improvident defence." And in Penley v. Watts, 7 M. & W. 601, 609, this case is spoken of as reconsidering that of Lewis v. Peake.

We shall see when we come to examine the subject of principal and surety in its more extended aspect, that it has been frequently held that the party, though holding a warranty, defends the suit at his peril, and that if it appear to have been unnecessarily defended, the expense will be charged on him. The only effect of notice is to shift the burden of proof. If no notice be given, the warrantee will be held to proof of the propriety of the litigation. If such notice has been given, the original warrantor will be obliged to prove that the expense was unnecessarily incurred.

Where the defendants had sold the plaintiff a picture, warranted to be painted by Claude, but in fact not painted by him; and the plaintiff sold it to a third party with like warranty; and the second vendee sued the plaintiff on the warranty, and recovered damages and costs,—it was held that if the sale was a *bona fide* sale, the plaintiff could recover the costs paid the sub-vendee, and all the costs of his own defence; nothing is said in the case of notice or the propriety of the litigation.[351]

§ 774. Warranty of title.

* The same questions which we are now considering are sometimes presented where the warranty, instead of referring to the quality of the article, is one of title. The result of the older English authorities is, that by the law of England there is no warranty of title in the actual contract of sale, any more than there is of quality; and so it was held in a case in the Court of Exchequer.[352] But according to the Roman law,[353] and in France,[354] and Scotland, and generally in the United States, there is always an implied contract that the vendor has a right to dispose of the subject which he sells. In an action (on the case),[355] on the warranty of title implied in the sale of a horse, Blasdale bought the horse of Babcock, but was afterwards sued by Snow in trover for the animal; he gave notice to the defendant of the suit; and judgment was obtained against him for the value of the horse, with costs. It was held at the

---

[351] Pennell *v.* Woodburn, 7 C. & P. 117.

[352] Morley *v.* Attenborough, 3 Ex. 500, where the English cases are examined.

[353] Domat, book i, tit. 2, § 2, art. 3.

[354] Code Civil, ch. 4, § 1, art. 1603.

[355] Blasdale *v.* Babcock, 1 Johns. 517.

trial that the judgment was strong but not conclusive evidence
of Snow's title; and that, if not rebutted, the measure of damages was the amount of the recovery against Blasdale in the
other action (verdict and costs). And this was held right by
the Supreme Court of New York.

In an action (of assumpsit) under somewhat different circumstances,[356] the plaintiff bought a horse of the defendant for
$55 cash, and another horse valued at $85, in all $140; the
plaintiff sold the horse to one Milligan, and shortly after, one
Gordon replevied the horse of Milligan, and recovered judgment, $72.32 for damages, and $33.95 costs, which were paid
by Milligan; Milligan also paid the costs of his own defence.
The plaintiff then settled with Milligan amicably, and claimed
of the defendant the original amount paid by him, and also
the damages and costs paid by Milligan and repaid by the
plaintiff to him. The cause was referred; and the defendant
insisted that the measure of damages was the price of the horse,
with the interest thereof, deducting his services since the sale
to the plaintiff, and that the plaintiff was not entitled to recover
the costs and expenses in the replevin suit of Gordon. On a
motion to set aside the report, the court held that the referees
should have allowed the plaintiff the price paid by the defendant for the horse, and interest, together with the costs which he
became liable to pay Gordon, in the suit brought to establish
his title; and the expenses paid by Milligan in his own defence
were disallowed.[357] It may be proper to observe that the court
here appears to have lost sight of the principle laid down in
the cases already cited, that the recovery should be estimated,
not by the price paid, but by the real value. If this rule is
true in regard to a warranty of soundness, there seems no reason
why it should not apply to a warranty of title.**

The warranty of title is often construed by courts as equivalent to a warranty of quiet enjoyment, usually given in sales
of realty. Under such a view no cause of action accrues, until

[356] Armstrong v. Percy, 5 Wend.
535.
[357] Defendant sold to plaintiff a
patent right for two counties, but the
title failed as to one; the measure of
damages was held to be that proportion of the purchase price which the
value of that part of the right to which
the title failed bore to the whole value.
Moorehead v. Davis, 92 Ind. 303.

the vendee has been dispossessed by the true owner.[358] And it would seem that the damages would be measured by the value of the chattel at that time.

The general rule is that the measure of damages for breach of a warranty of title to a chattel is the value of the chattel [359] at the time of the purchase, with interest, and the necessary costs of defending a suit brought against a vendee to test the title, with interest from the time of payment.[360] Many cases, however, lay down the rule that the measure of damages is not the value but the price paid for the goods.[361] Such cases

[358] *California:* Gross v. Kierski, 41 Cal. 111.

Kentucky: Patrick v. Swinney, 5 Bush, 421, 96 Am. Dec. 360.

Massachusetts: Bennett v. Bartlett, 6 Cush. 225 (but see Grose v. Hennessee, 13 All. 389).

New York: Burt v. Dewey, 40 N. Y. 283, 100 Am. Dec. 482; McGiffin v. Baird, 62 N. Y. 329, 331.

North Carolina: Hodges v. Wilkinson, 111 N. C. 56, 15 S. E. 941, 17 L. R. A. 545, 32 Am. St. Rep. 782.

See Wanser v. Messler, 29 N. J. L. 256; Lines v. Smith, 4 Fla. 47.

Where there was actual fraud the vendee may successfully resist an action for the price though he is still in undisturbed possession. Sweetman v. Prince, 62 Barb. 256. And see Sumner v. Gray, 4 Ark. 467; Brown v. Smith, 5 How. (Miss.) 387; Richardson v. McFadden, 13 Tex. 278.

See Williston on Sales, § 221.

[359] *Alabama:* Rowland v. Shelton, 25 Ala. 217.

Illinois: Linton v. Porter, 31 Ill. 107.

Maryland: Myers v. Smith, 27 Md. 91.

Massachusetts: Brown v. Pierce, 97 Mass. 46, 93 Am. Dec. 57.

Minnesota: Close v. Crossland, 47 Minn. 500, 50 N. W. 694.

Missouri: Johnson v. Blanks, 34 Mo. 255.

Canada: Confederation Life Assoc. v. Labatt, 27 Ont. App. 321.

[360] *Illinois:* Scaling v. Knollin, 94 Ill. App. 443.

Maine: Eldridge v. Wadleigh, 12 Me. 371; Pierce v. Banton, 98 Me. 553, 57 Atl. 889.

New York: Armstrong v. Percy, 5 Wend. 535; Schmumacher v. Kennedy, 88 N. Y. Supp. 943.

South Carolina: Davis v. Wilborne, 1 Hill, 27, 26 Am. Dec. 154 (costs in defending suit brought by sub-vendee).

Tennessee: Brown v. Woods, 3 Cold. 182.

Cf. Noel v. Wheatly, 30 Miss. 181.

[361] *California:* Jeffers v. Easton, 113 Cal. 345, 45 Pac. 680.

Illinois: Scaling v. Knollin, 94 Ill. App. 443.

Kentucky: Ellis v. Gosney, 7 J. J. Marsh. 109.

Mississippi: Noel v. Wheatly, 30 Miss. 180.

New York: Atkins v. Hosley, 3 Thomp. & C. 322; Armstrong v. Percy, 5 Wend. 535.

Oregon: Arthur v. Moss, 1 Ore. 193.

South Carolina: Glover v. Hutson, 2 M'Mullan, 109; Ware v. Weathnall, 2 McCord, 413.

Tennessee: Crittenden v. Posey, 1 Head. 311.

Texas: Goss v. Dysant, 31 Tex. 186.

England: Eicholz v. Bannister, 17 C. B. (N. S.) 708; Raphel v. Burt, Cab. & Ell. 325.

Canada: Peuchen v. Imperial Bank, 20 Ont. 325.

may be explained on a variety of grounds. The rule is quite consistent with the tort-origin of the action for breach of warranty [362] and this is perhaps the only theoretical justification. On the other hand, even when the measure of damages usually applied in actions of assumpsit is followed, the price paid is very good evidence of the actual value of the chattel. It may even be treated as *prima facie* evidence. Finally, the courts may have confused the right to sue for breach of warranty with his right to rescind. For the vendee may disaffirm the contract and recover the consideration paid, though that is greater than the value of the property.[363] Where a steamboat sold was warranted free from liens, but was subsequently seized under a lien, and while in custody was burned, the purchaser has been allowed to recover only the amount of the lien and the cost of disputing it, the destruction of the boat being considered too remote a consequence.[364] Where there is not a total failure of title, but only an incumbrance, the measure of damages is the amount the vendee was compelled to pay to protect his possession.[365]

§ 775. Warranty of indorsements.

It has been held in Massachusetts,[366] that where a warranty is given that the indorsements on a note are genuine, and they prove to be forged, the measure of damages will be the difference between the amount of the note and its actual value, whatever that may be.[367]

It has been decided in the same State, in an action of assumpsit, brought on a warranty of an indorsement as genuine, that the plaintiff was entitled to recover, as part of his damages, the

[362] See § 761a.

In Tennessee the courts have applied to actions on covenants for the failure of title to chattels the same measure as in the case of land, which in that State is the price paid and interest. Crittenden v. Posey, 1 Head, 311; and see Ware v. Weathnall, 2 McCord, 413.

[363] Wilkinson v. Ferree, 24 Pa. 190.
See Williston on Sales, § 615.

[364] Harper v. Dotson, 43 Ia. 232, 22 Am. Rep. 245.

[365] Sargent v. Currier, 49 N. H. 310, 6 Am. Rep. 524.

So where the goods were subject to a patent, plaintiff could recover the amount necessarily paid the patentee for the right to use them. National M. E. B. Co. v. Gotham, 125 App. Div. 101, 109 N. Y. Supp. 450.

[366] Coolidge v. Brigham, 1 Met. 547.

[367] Thrall v. Newell, 19 Vt. 202, 47 Am. Dec. 682. But see Aldrich v. Jackson, 5 R. I. 218.

costs incurred by him in an unsuccessful suit against the supposed indorser, if the plaintiff commenced the suit in good faith, not knowing that the signature was forged, and gave the warrantor seasonable notice of the pendency of the suit, and requested him to furnish evidence of the genuineness of the signature; and the court held that the rule established in actions for a breach of the covenant of warranty in the conveyance of real estate, must govern the case.[368]

In Wisconsin, the measure of damages on breach of an implied warranty of an indorsement has been held to be the difference between the values of the note with and without the indorsement, and the costs and reasonable expenses of suing the other indorsers, the question of notice not being raised. The defendant was allowed to show the insolvency of the indorser.[369]

§ 776. That a certain sum is due.

In an action for breach of such a warranty, the warrantee can recover what the note of such a maker would be worth, *e. g.,* what a judgment against him would be worth. *Prima facie,* the amount recoverable would be the whole amount due on the note at the time the suit was brought.[370] So where the assignor of a judgment covenanted that there was due a certain sum, and that he would not discharge the judgment, it being proved that he had previously discharged one judgment debtor, the plaintiff was allowed to recover the difference between the actual value of the judgment and the value it would have had if the debtor had not been discharged, and this although the

[368] Coolidge *v.* Brigham, 5 Met. 68; Swett *v.* Patrick, 12 Me. 9. In Alabama, it is held that, in an action by the vendee of personal property against the vendor, upon a warranty of title, a judgment against the vendee, at the instance of a third person, claiming to be the rightful owner, of which suit the vendor had no notice, is not evidence to prove that the title of the latter was defective. But it seems that such judgment is admissible to prove the amount of damages recovered, and is conclusive of the validity of the vend-

or's title, if it was obtained without fraud or collusion, upon notice given to him of the pendency of the action. And the measure of damages in an action for a breach of a warranty of title on the sale of personal property, cannot exceed the damages sustained by the vendee. Salle *v.* Light, 4 Ala. 700.

[369] Giffert *v.* West, 33 Wis. 617.

[370] *United States:* Head *v.* Green, 5 Biss. 311.

Minnesota: Book Co. *v.* Maybell, 86 Minn. 241, 90 N. W. 392.

price paid was only ten per cent of the amount of the judgment.[371] Where at the defendant's request suit had been brought without success by the plaintiff, he may recover the costs of that suit.[372]

§ 777. Fraud in sale of chattels.

In a case in New York,[373] the Court of Appeals said: "The measure of damages in an action upon a warranty, and for fraud in the sale of personal property, are the same. In either case they are determined by the difference in value between the article sold, and what it should be according to the warranty or representation," and this has usually been stated as a general rule.[374] So where the defendant sold to the plaintiff

---

[371] Bennett v. Buchan, 61 N. Y. 222, 19 Am. Rep. 272.

[372] Smith v. Corege, 53 Ark. 295, 14 S. W. 93.

[373] Whitney v. Allaire, 1 N. Y. 305, 312.

[374] *Arkansas:* Morton v. Scull, 23 Ark. 289; Thompson v. Bertrand, 23 Ark. 730; May v. Dyer, 57 Ark. 441, 21 S. W. 1064.

California: Spreckels v. Gorrill, 152 Cal. 383, 92 Pac. 1011; Neher v. Hansen, 12 Cal. App. 370, 107 Pac. 565.

Colorado: Herfort v. Cramer, 7 Colo. 483.

Florida: Williams v. McFadden, 23 Fla. 143, 1 So. 618, 11 Am. St. Rep. 345.

Georgia: Millirons v. Dillon, 100 Ga. 565, 28 S. E. 385.

Illinois: Winslow v. Newlan, 45 Ill. 145; Cox v. Gerkin, 38 Ill. App. 340; Chrystal v. Leval, 144 Ill. App. 533.

Indiana: McAvoy v. Wright, 25 Ind. 22, 87 Am. Dec. 346; Bowman v. Clemmer, 50 Ind. 10; Nysewander v. Lowman, 124 Ind. 584, 24 N. E. 355; Brier v. Mankey (Ind. App.), 93 N. E. 672.

Iowa: Likes v. Baer, 8 Ia. 368; Boddy v. Henry, 113 Ia. 462, 85 N. W. 771, 53 L. R. A. 769; Warfield v. Clark, 118 Ia. 69, 91 N. W. 833.

Kentucky: Exchange Bank v. Gaits- kill, 37 S. W. 160, 18 Ky. L. Rep. 532; Drake v. Holbrook, 92 S. W. 297, 28 Ky. L. R. 1319; Long v. Douthitt, 134 S. W. 453 (but see Crews v. Dabney, 1 Litt. 278; Singleton v. Kennedy, 9 B. Mon. 222; Ligon v. Minton, 125 S. W. 304).

Massachusetts: Morse v. Hutchins, 102 Mass. 439; Whiting v. Price, 172 Mass. 240, 51 N. E. 1084; Honsucle v. Ruffin, 172 Mass. 420, 52 N. E. 538.

Michigan: Page v. Mills, 37 Mich. 415; Jackson v. Collins, 39 Mich. 557; Totten v. Burhams, 91 Mich. 495, 51 N. W. 1119, 30 Am. St. Rep. 492; Maxted v. Fowler, 94 Mich. 106, 53 N. W. 921, 34 Am. St. Rep. 324; Smith v. Werkheiser, 152 Mich. 177, 115 N. W. 964, 15 L. R. A. (N. S.) 1092. (See Woolenslagle v. Runals, 76 Mich. 545, 43 N. W. 454.)

Missouri: Atchison County Bank v. Byers, 139 Mo. 627, 41 S. W. 325; Ryan v. Miller (Mo. App.), 139 S. W. 128.

Nebraska: Young v. Filley, 19 Neb. 543; Woolman v. Wirtebaugh, 22 Neb. 490, 35 N. W. 216.

New Hampshire: Fisk v. Hicks, 31 N. H. 535; Page v. Parker, 40 N. H. 47, 80 Am. Dec. 172, 43 N. H. 363; Carr v. Moore, 41 N. H. 131; Noyes v. Blodgett, 58 N. H. 502.

a bond and mortgage, which afterwards proved voidable, at less than the face value, and the plaintiff's recovery on the bond was restricted to the amount he had paid, he was allowed to recover of the defendant the difference between the face of the bond and the amount he had recovered upon the bond.[375] In Grissler v. Powers [376] the court said:

"The estoppel created by a false representation acted upon is commensurate with the thing represented, and operates to put the party entitled to the benefit of the estoppel in the same position as if the thing represented was true, and when the representation is made on the sale of a chattel or security, the remedy of the purchaser is not limited to a recovery simply of the money advanced, if the purchaser would receive a benefit beyond that if the facts had been as represented."

Where the defendant sold to the plaintiff slaves in which, as it proved, the vendor had only a life estate, the same general rule was followed, but it was held that what occurred between the sale and the trial should be considered, such as the death

New York: Hubbell v. Meigs, 50 N. Y. 480; Miller v. Barber, 66 N. Y. 558; Krumm v. Brach, 96 N. Y. 398; Vail v. Reynolds, 118 N. Y. 297, 23 N. E. 301; Yeomans v. Bell, 151 N. Y. 230, 45 N. E. 552; Graves v. Spier, 58 Barb. 349; Mason v. Raplee, 66 Barb. 180; Wyeth v. Morris, 13 Hun, 338; Benedict v. Guardian Trust Co., 91 App. Div. 103, 86 N. Y. Supp. 370; Davidge v. Guardian Trust Co., 136 App. Div. 78, 120 N. Y. Supp. 628; Spotten v. De Freest, 140 App. Div. 792, 125 N. Y. Supp. 497.

North Carolina: Small v. Pool, 30 N. C. 47; Lunn v. Shermer, 93 N. C. 164; Robertson v. Halton, 72 S. E. 316.

North Dakota: Fargo Gas & Coke Co. v. Fargo Gas & Electric Co., 4 N. D. 219, 59 N. W. 1066, 37 L. R. A. 593; Beare v. Wright, 14 N. D. 26, 103 N. W. 632.

Ohio: Norton v. Parker, 17 Ohio Cir. Ct. 714, 8 Ohio Cir. Dec. 572.

Pennsylvania: Stetson v. Crocksey, 52 Pa. 230.

South Dakota: McCabe v. Desnoyers, 20 S. Dak. 581, 108 N. W. 341.

Tennessee: Hogg v. Cardwell, 4 Sneed, 151.

Texas: Davenport v. Anderson, 28 S. W. 922 (Tex. Civ. App.); Ford v. Oliphant, 32 S. W. 437 (Tex. Civ. App.); Carson v. Houssels, 51 S. W. 290 (Tex. Civ. App.); Pitman v. Self, 127 S. W. 907 (Tex. Civ. App.); Reed v. Holloway, 127 S. W. 1189 (Tex. Civ. App.). See, however, Wimple v. Patterson (Tex. Civ. App.), 117 S. W. 1034; George v. Hesse, 100 Tex. 44, 93 S. W. 107, 8 L. R. A. (N. S.) 804, 123 Am. St. Rep. 772.

Vermont: Woodward v. Thacher, 21 Vt. 580, 52 Am. Dec. 73.

Wisconsin: Warner v. Benjamin, 89 Wis. 290, 62 N. W. 179, 46 Am. St. Rep. 834.

[375] Grissler v. Powers, 81 N. Y. 57; Miller v. Zeimer, 12 Daly, 126.

[376] 81 N. Y. 57, 61, 37 Am. Rep. 475.

of a slave, and an improvement in the health and probable length of life of the defendant.[377]

* So, where case was brought for fraud and deceit in the sale of a vessel, which was represented to be British, whereas in fact she was Spanish, Story, J., before whom the cause was tried, held the rule of damages to be the difference between the value of the vessel if she had been what she was represented to be, and her actual value, together with such part of the costs of repairs laid out on her, on faith of the false representations, as the jury should see fit to allow.[378]

So, again, where fraud has been practiced in a sale, as of a horse, the measure of damages was held to be, as in an action for the breach of warranty, the difference between the value of the article sold and the value of such an article as it was represented to be, even if, at the time of the sale, the property was fairly worth the price paid.[379] **

The contract price is frequently taken as the value of the property represented,[380] and in the absence of other evidence of value, it is properly so taken. If the plaintiff rescinds the contract on account of the fraud, upon returning the consideration he may recover the purchase money and interest.[381]

§ 778. Smith v. Bolles.

The Supreme Court of the United States, however, has refused to follow this well-established rule. In an action of tort for fraud in the sale of stock, it was held that the measure of damages was not the same as upon breach of warranty, but was compensation for the injury done by the fraud, that is, the purchase money less the actual value of the stock.[382] Fuller, C. J., said:

"The measure of damages was not the difference between the contract price and the reasonable market value if the property had been as represented to be, even if the stock had been

[377] Campbell v. Hillman, 15 B. Mon. 508, 61 Am. Dec. 195.

[378] Sherwood v. Sutton, 5 Mason, 1, 9.

[379] Stiles v. White, 11 Met. (Mass.), 356.

[380] Estell v. Myers, 56 Miss. 800;

Carr v. Moore, 41 N. H. 131; Lunn v. Shermer, 93 N. C. 164; McCabe v. Desnoyers, 20 S. Dak. 581, 108 N. W. 341.

[381] Hauk v. Brownell, 120 Ill. 161.

[382] Smith v. Bolles, 132 U. S. 125, 129, 33 L. ed. 279, 10 Sup. Ct. 39.

worth the price paid for it; nor if the stock were worthless could the plaintiff have recovered the value it would have had if the property had been equal to the representations. What the plaintiff might have gained is not the question, but what he had lost by being deceived into the purchase. The suit was not brought for breach of contract. The gist of the action was that the plaintiff was fraudulently induced by the defendant to purchase stock upon the faith of certain false and fraudulent representations, and so as to the other persons on whose claims the plaintiff sought to recover. If the jury believed from the evidence that the defendant was guilty of the fraudulent and false representations alleged, and that the purchase of stock had been made in reliance thereon, then the defendant was liable to respond in such damages as naturally and proximately resulted from the fraud. He was bound to make good the loss sustained, such as the moneys the plaintiff had paid out and interest, and any other outlay legitimately attributable to defendant's fraudulent conduct, but this liability did not include the expected fruits of an unrealized speculation. The reasonable market value, if the property had been as represented, afforded, therefore, no proper element of recovery.

"Nor had the contract price the bearing given to it by the court. What the plaintiff paid for the stock was properly put in evidence, not as the basis of the application of the rule in relation to the difference between the contract price and the market or actual value, but as establishing the loss he had sustained in that particular. If the stock had a value in fact that would necessarily be applied in reduction of the damages, 'The damage to be recovered must always be the *natural* and *proximate consequence* of the act complained of,' says Mr. Greenleaf; [383] and 'the test is,' adds Chief-Justice Beasley in Crater *v.* Binninger,[384] 'that those results are proximate which the wrongdoer from his position must have contemplated as the probable consequence of his fraud or breach of contract.'"

The doctrine of this case, which is the law of the Federal Courts, is accepted in several jurisdictions.[385]

[383] Vol. 2, § 256.

[384] 33 N. J. L. 513.

[385] *United States:* Sigafus *v.* Porter,

179 U. S. 116, 21 Sup. Ct. 34, 45 L. ed. 113; McHose *v.* Earnshaw, 55 Fed. 584, 5 C. C. A. 210; The Normannia, 62

The *ratio decidendi* of this case would seem to be that the action was brought, not upon the contract of warranty, but for a tort. Compensation is asked for loss caused by the defendant's *false statements;* and to determine its amount, the question should be, what greater amount of property would the plaintiff have if the defendant's statements had not been made? The plaintiff's loss is not the value of his bargain; for it is necessary to the very maintenance of the action to show that the bargain would not have been made if the defendant had not made the false statements complained of. If these had not been made, therefore, the plaintiff would have the consideration he paid, but nothing more; and the difference between that consideration and the actual value of the property represents all the loss that was caused by the defendant's tort. It is usually said that if the statements had not been false the plaintiff would have property of the quality represented, which he loses by the defendant's wrong, and, therefore, that his loss is measured by the rule as ordinarily stated. To this the answer seems to be that the defendant's tort did not consist in the *falseness* of the statement, but in the *making* of the statement fraudulently; the result of the tort being not to change the value of a bargain, but to cause the plaintiff to part with his property against his will. The whole value of the consideration would be the amount to be recovered, if the rule of reduction of damages did not re-

Fed. 469, 481; Wilson v. New U. S. Cattle Ranch Co., 73 Fed. 994, 20 C. C. A. 244; Rockefeller v. Merritt, 76 Fed. 909, 22 C. C. A. 608, 35 L. R. A. 633; Hindman v. First Nat. Bank, 112 Fed. 931, 50 C. C. A. 623, 57 L. R. A. 108; Pittsburg L. Ins. Co. v. Northern C. L. Ins. Co., 140 Fed. 888; Kell v. Trenchard, 142 Fed. 16, 73 C. C. A. 202.

Maryland: Pendergast v. Reed, 29 Md. 398, 96 Am. Dec. 539; Buschman v. Codd, 52 Md. 202, 209.

Minnesota: Reynolds v. Franklin, 44 Minn. 30, 46 N. W. 139, 20 Am. St. Rep. 540; Redding v. Godwin, 44 Minn. 355, 46 N. W. 563; Wallace v. Hallowell, 56 Minn. 501, 58 N. W. 292, 45 Am.

St. Rep. 491; Freeman v. F. P. Harbaugh Co., 130 N. W. 1111.

New Jersey: Crater v. Binninger, 33 N. J. L. 513, 97 Am. Dec. 737.

Oregon: Cawston v. Sturgis, 29 Ore. 331, 43 Pac. 656.

Pennsylvania: High v. Berret, 148 Pa. 261, 23 Atl. 1004.

Washington: Tacoma v. Tacoma Light, etc., Co., 17 Wash. 458, 50 Pac. 55; Klieb v. McInturff, 114 Pac. 184.

The same rule applies to sales of land induced by fraud of the vendor. Atwater v. Whiteman, 41 Fed. 427; Glasful v. Northern Pac. Ry., 43 Fed. 900; Sigafus v. Porter, 179 U. S. 116, 21 S. C. 34, 45 L. ed. 113; *post,* § 1029.

quire the value of property obtained by the defendant's act to be subtracted.

Under this doctrine lost profits cannot be allowed, but any fact bearing on the actual value of the property received is admissible, *e. g.*, the cost of repairs needed to put it in condition for use.[386] If notwithstanding the misrepresentation the property was actually worth what was paid for it, there can be no recovery in an action for deceit.[387] But the vendee is not remediless; there is nothing in the doctrine of Smith *v.* Bolles which excludes the vendee from suing for breach of warranty.[388] In that case he is entitled to have the representation made good.

§ 779. English rule.

The rule in England accords with the doctrine of Smith *v.* Bolles. In Peek *v.* Derry,[389] an action for false representations in the sale of shares, Cotton, L. J., delivering the opinion of the Court of Appeal on the question of damages, said: "The damage to be recovered by the plaintiff is the loss which he sustained by acting on the representations of the defendants. That action was taking the shares. Before he was induced to buy the shares, he had the £4,000 in his pocket. The day when the shares were allotted to him, which was the consequence of his action, he paid over the £4,000 and he got the shares; and the loss sustained by him in consequence of his acting on the representations of the defendants was having the shares, instead of having in his pocket the £4,000. The loss, therefore, must be the difference between his £4,000 and the then value of the shares." And Sir James Hannen added: "The question is, how much worse off is the plaintiff than if he had not bought the shares? If he had not bought the shares he would have had

---

[386] Nashua Sav. Bank *v.* Burlington Electric Lighting Co., 100 Fed. 673.

[387] *United States:* Kell *v.* Trenchard, 142 Fed. 16, 73 C. C. A. 202.

Minnesota: Alden *v.* Wright, 47 Minn. 225, 49 N. W. 767.

That the value of the property is to be estimated not at the time of the sale but at the time the fraud was discovered, see Smith *v.* Duffy, 57 N. J. L.

679; Goodwin *v.* Wilbur, 104 Ill. App. 45.

[388] Wilson *v.* New U. S. Cattle Ranch Co., 73 Fed. 994, 36 U. S. App. 634, 20 C. C. A. 244.

[389] 37 Ch. Div. 541, 591, 594; *acc.*, Twycross *v.* Grant, 2 C. P. Div. 469, 544; McConnell *v.* Wright, [1903] 1 Ch. 546.

his £4,000 in his pocket. To ascertain his loss we must deduct from that amount the real value of the thing he got."

§ 780. General discussion.

Since the action sounds in tort the natural rule for damages is that adopted by the Supreme Court. If the fraud had been perpetrated by some third person inducing the vendee to purchase there can be no doubt as to the measure of damages: the plaintiff would then be entitled only to the difference between what he paid and what he received. Logically it should make no difference that the fraud was perpetrated by the vendor, instead of by the third person. And to have a different rule might lead to peculiar results. Thus, suppose a fraud were jointly perpetrated by the seller and a third person. It is a strange rule of law which would give a different measure of damages in an action against one joint tort feasor from that given in an action against the other, yet that would seem to be the consequence of the old rule.

At any rate if a different rule is to be applied against the vendor some affirmative reason for so doing must be shown. Let us examine some of the reasons advanced. It is usually urged that the misrepresentation gives rise to an action for breach of warranty as well as an action for deceit, and that it is absurd to apply a different rule of compensation according to the form of the action. First of all it is to be noted that this reason proceeds upon the assumption that the same facts give rise either to an action for breach of warranty or for deceit; in other words, that these actions are merely alternative forms of relief for the same wrong. If this were so the argument would have weight. But it is an erroneous assumption arising from a confusion by the courts of three different actions: (1) the action of *assumpsit* for breach of warranty; (2) the action of tort, *in the nature of deceit*, for breach of warranty; (3) the strict action of deceit. As we have seen [390] all three forms of action sprang from a common origin—the old action of deceit. But the requisites for an action on the warranty gradually lapsed. No *scienter* was required; [391] and in time a mere representation, which in fact was untrue, gave rise

[390] *Supra*, § 761a.   [391] Williston on Sales, §§ 195 *et seq.*

to an action for breach of warranty; and the action might be brought either in assumpsit, or in tort. The requisites for both were identically the same, and hence in this instance the strict logic of the law has readily yielded to common commercial understanding and the same measure of damages is now applied to either form of action. But the reasons which justify ignoring the distinctions between the action of assumpsit and the action of tort in the nature of deceit do not apply when we are considering the strict action of deceit. For, just as the action of assumpsit itself originated in the action of deceit,[392] and developed into a separate action, to redress a distinct wrong, so the actions for breach of warranty have become distinct, from the old action of deceit. The requisites of the three actions are not the same. The very gist of the action of deceit is fraud,—an element unnecessary to an action on the warranty. It is true that the fraudulent representation also gives rise to an action on the warranty. But the converse is not true; an action of warranty may be brought when deceit does not lie. Hence it follows that the additional element of fraud creates a wholly distinct wrong, with a remedy peculiar to itself. The fact that under some circumstances this remedy does not give the vendee so much as the remedy for another wrong incidentally done, is simply a reason for seeking that other remedy.

§ 781. Considerations of practical justice.

Are there any reasons of practical justice that require the courts to treat the action of deceit as equivalent to an action for breach of warranty? Let us consider this question, *first* from the point of view of the vendee; *second* from the point of view of the vendor.

Adherence to logical principles can by no possibility work a hardship to the vendee. If his damages in an action of deceit, under the Smith *v.* Bolles rule, are less than under the other rule, he has simply made a blunder in suing for the fraud. He has the right to sue in *assumpsit* for breach of warranty.[393] This circumstance also disposes of the objection that under

[392] *Supra,* § 761.
[393] Wilson *v.* New U. S. Cattle Ranch   Co., 73 Fed. 994, 36 U. S. App. 634, 639, 20 C. C. A. 244.

the Smith *v.* Bolles doctrine a vendor can with impunity misrepresent the goods since he is certain, ultimately, to realize the actual value of the goods and thus can lose nothing by his fraud.

On behalf of the vendor it is urged that even though he did misrepresent the goods yet he should not lose the benefit of his bargain. Suppose for example that the vendee was induced to pay $11,000 for goods actually worth $9,000, but which would have been worth $10,000 if the representations were true. Under the rule in Smith *v.* Bolles the vendee's recovery would be $2,000. Under the other rule, $1,000. It is contended that if the vendee was willing to give $11,000 for $10,000 worth of goods he should have no redress to that extent. But this is not an argument against the Smith *v.* Bolles doctrine; it is, rather, an argument against the measure of damages generally adopted in actions of deceit, whether against vendors or third parties. It has frequently been rejected by the courts, when urged by a fraudulent third party, on this ground; there is no basis for assuming that the vendee would have given $10,000 for the goods if there had been no misrepresentation. Indeed, the qualities which the goods were represented to have had may have been the very thing that induced the vendee to purchase at an excessive valuation. Where such a doubt exists it does not lie in the mouth of the fraudulent person to ask to have the doubt resolved in his favor. The same reasoning applies when the vendor is the defendant.

Moreover, the old rule is really inconsistent with allowing a defrauded vendee the well-recognized alternative remedy of rescission. The fact that he has this remedy shows conclusively that the vendor has no such "right to the benefit of his bargain" as is claimed. And if this benefit can be taken away from him where rescission is possible, it is difficult to see why the vendee's right should be less where rescission is impracticable or where he elects to pursue the alternative remedy and sue for the tort. The amount of the damages to be recovered in tort should therefore be as nearly as possible equivalent to rescission. And this result is just what the Smith *v.* Bolles rule accomplishes.

Instead of finding positive reasons for departing from the logical measure of damages in an action of tort, therefore, the reasons both theoretical and practical seem to support the Smith *v.* Bolles doctrine. The defrauded vendee has, accordingly, three alternative remedies: [394] *first*, rescission and recovery of the consideration; *second*, an action for deceit and recovery for his actual loss, *i. e.*, the difference between the value of what he parts with and of what he receives; *third*, an action for breach of any warranty contained in the contract of purchase and recovery of the difference in values between the property as received and the value as warranted.

V.—FOREIGN LAW

§ 782. Justinian's laws.

* The general language of the Roman law is, that in case of the breach of contract of sale by non-delivery, the measure of damages is all that the buyer loses or fails to gain in relation to the thing itself, over and above the price paid; *id quod interest propter rem ipsam non habitam.* And, embarrassed by no form of action, the civil law inquires in each case into the motives of the defendant, and apportions the damages according to his delay, fault, or fraud.

The language of the Digest on the subject of damages for non-delivery is as follows: *Si res vendita non tradatur, in id quod interest agitur; hoc est quod rem habere interest emptoris.*[395] *Si traditio rei venditæ, juxta emptoris contractum, procacia venditoris non fiat, quanti interesse compleri emptionem fuerit arbitratus præses provinciæ, tantum in condemnationis taxationem deducere curabit. Hoc autem pretium egreditur, si pluris interest quam res valet, vel empta est.* And so, again, *Quum per venditorem steterit quominus rem tradat, omnis utilitas emptoris in æstima-*

---

[394] Wilson *v.* New U. S. Cattle Ranch Co., 73 Fed. 994, 20 C. C. A. 244, 36 U. S. App. 634, 639. The court in a second statement of these principles makes the rule in the second case "the difference between the value of what he had before he made the contract and the value of what he would have had after the contract was made if it had been duly performed by both parties," *i. e.*, the difference between the consideration and the value as represented. This, however, is obviously an error in restatement.

[395] Pandects by Pothier, vol. 7, pp. 120, 121, lib. xix, tit. i, de Actionibus Emti et Venditi.

tionem venit, quæ modo circa ipsam rem consistit. Neque enim si potuit ex vino (puta) negotiari et lucrum facere, id æstimandum est: non magis quam si triticum emerit, et ob eam rem quod non sit traditum, familia ejus fame laboraverit. Nam pretium tritici, non servorum fame necatorum, consequitur. Nec major fit obligatio quod tardius agitur, quamvis æstimatio crescat, si vinum hodie pluris sit: merito; quia, sive datum esset, haberet emptor, sive non; quoniam saltem hodie dandum est quod jam olim dare oportuit.

The form of action prescribed against the seller of any merchantable commodity, who was in fault for not delivering, was the *Condictio triticiaria;* [396] and when treating of this subject, the Digest says: *Si merx aliqua, quæ certo die dari debebat, petita sit; veluti vinum, oleum, frumentum, tanti litem æstimandum Cassius ait, quanti fuisset eo die quo dari debuit; si de die nihil convenit, quanti tunc judicium acciperetur.*[397]

But these and other texts of the Justinian law on this subject, as on many treated of in that wonderful repository of acute and profound but ill-arranged decisions, are contradictory and perplexing. And their general terms throw little light on the complex relations of modern commerce.**

§ 783. Civil law authorities.

* The modern writers of the civil law furnish us with but little assistance on the questions which we have considered in this chapter. Even the masterly treatises of Pothier, and the profound commentary by his favorite author, Molinæus or

---

[396] *Condictio triticiaria a tritico, tanquam nobilissimo mercium genere, vel a primis edicti verbis dicta, est actio personalis arbitraria ad rem quamlibet, præter pecuniam numeratam spectans, et ex quâcumque causâ debitam, vel etiam nostram, ex causis quibus condici potest, veluti ex causâ furtivâ vel re mobili vi abrepta.* Vicat Vocabularium Utruisque Juris, in voc. Conf. Hevelke, Juristisches Wörterbuch.

The original Roman proceeding, *per condictionem,* one of the earliest of their curious and complex forms of action, and the true character of which had become dubious even in the time of Gaius,

took its name from the act peculiar to it, namely, the *condictio,* or notice given by the plaintiff to the defendant, to be present on the thirtieth day to select a judge, *ut ad judicem capiendum, die tricesimo adesset.* Das Römische Privat Recht, von Wilhelm Rein, book 5. The *condictio* of the Digest, in the time of Justinian, was a more modern form. It seems to have been analogous to our action of debt, in that it demanded some certain thing, or a sum certain of money, the price of it.

[397] Dig. De Con. Trit. lib. xiii, tit. 3, § 4.

Dumoulin, on this subject, are rather to be referred to for the purpose of philosophical speculation than as authorities for our guidance.[398] The total diversity of our forms of action, together with the far greater arbitrary discretion exercised in the matter of damages by the civil law and those systems which adhere to its teaching, render its authors on this subject of comparatively little value to us.

The following is one of many instances put by Molinæus: *Venditor fundi vel domus, recepto pretio, fuit primum in morâ tradendi: unde damnatus ad fructus vel mercedes moræ, et in id quod extrinsecus emptoris ob eam moram interfuit, quod probatum fuit ascendere ad ducenta, quæ solvitâ, re traditâ, sed posteâ evincitur, et emptor multo magis extrinsecus damnificatur: utrum in æstimatione, et interesse evictionis debeant in duplo computari illa ducenta ob præteritam moram non tradendi soluta?* § 90. Here, beyond the direct loss sustained by the delay, *extrinsic damage* is allowed.

The arbitrary discretion of the tribunal which has cognizance of the cause, is clearly stated by him in the following language: *Ut si inter mercatores et negotiatores frumentum certo die et loco: puta, tali portu promissum sit, quo tempore et loco prævidebant contrahentes creditoris interesse, et eum alioquin damna passurum, et tamen debitor per moram vel culpam etiam circa dolum malum fefellit. Ipsa enim æquitas et communis commerciorum utilitas, et fides hoc casu exigit, non solum æstimationem quanti plurimi si qua sit, sed etiam extrinsecum interesse (verumtamen propinquum et efficax prestari) quod etiam jura apertè volunt, dum hoc casu faciunt actionem arbitrariam, ut videlicet detur judici judicaturo arbitriam et potestas, non solum super principali et æstimatione quanti plurimi, quæ videtur pars rei, sed etiam super adjudicatione et taxatione hujus interesse.* § 97.

A large portion of this treatise is occupied with the subject of eviction. The phrase is also used by the civil law where the title to personal property fails; and here we shall see that the

[398] Pothier, Contract de Vente, part ii, ch. i, art. 5, §§ 79 *et seq.* and sect. 2, art. viii, §§ 150 *et seq.* Pothier's "Contract of Sale," translated by L. S. Cushing. Pothier allows the buyer the expense of the contract, the fees paid to the head landlord, expense of journeys to see the property, wagoners sent to fetch it, §§ 69 and 70; and the rise in price of the article, even where there has been a subsequent fall, is expressly given by § 86.

limit of recovery is not, as in regard to land, the price paid, but the value of the article at the time of sale. Molinæus thus discusses the case of eviction of a slave, who, after being long serviceable to the purchaser, is finally taken from him in advanced age, by title paramount; and he well holds that the price would not be the just measure of damage against the seller in such a case. *Tum cum non venderetur res soli nec perpetuo durabilis, sed quæ ultra certum tempus vivere et usui esse non posset, certum est non esse actum, nec cogitatum, ut frui, te habere liceret perpetuo, sed solum ad tempus vitæ, quod verisimiliter prævisum et æstimatum fuit, et ad verisimilem durationem majus vel minus definitum pretium. Igitur hoc casu pretium conventum non est pretium perpetuæ durationis, et fruitionis vitæ verisimiliter expensæ, et appreciatæ. Cum ergo toto ferè tempore vitæ prævisæ fruitus sit emptor nec per evictionem absit nisi modicum et ferè inutile tempus non potest totum pretium repetere, cum intus habeat totum ferè commodum et fructum prævisæ fruitionis et usus.* § 127.[399]

HUBERUS, another very eminent master of the modern civil

[399] Dumoulin's Treatise, De eo quod Interest (Caroli Molinæi Opera Omnia, Parisiis, 1681, vol. 3, p. 423), is a commentary on the code, De Sententiis quæ pro eo quod interest proferuntur. Cod. lib. vii, tit. xlvii; the leading clause in which is, *Sancimus itaque in omnibus casibus qui certam habent quantitatem vel naturam, velut in venditionibus et locationibus et omnibus contractibus, hoc quod interest dupli quantitatem minime excedere.*

A great portion of this treatise is now entirely valueless. Thus, no small part of it is occupied with laborious discussions of the true definition of the term *interest*—*interesse extrinsecum, interesse communis, interesse conventum et non conventum,* § 16; and a variety of questions growing out of the terms of the law commented on, as *quid sit illud simplum ad quod interesse singulare refertur et duplatur; qui sint casus certi et qui incerti.* § 20.

No small portion of it is devoted to

refuting other glossators and discutants of similar questions, thus: *Ex quibus apparet Curt. aliorum scripta neglectim, et prefunctorie transcurrisse, et novam hanc opinionem ex capite proprio fabricasse,* § 28; and again, *Jacobus autem Renal. in suo confusaneo de his tractatib. jactat se novam opinionem affere sed inani prolixæ ineptæ verbositatis fumo nihil enim prorsus novi adfert, sed post multam inanem elocutionem in Bart. et communem opinionem sese revolvit, et nihil addit nisi quod confusionem auget.* § 29.

It contains, also, much discussion on the subject of evictions, of the *stipulatio duplæ,* and the remote damages due in case of negligence. It is curious throughout, replete with the learning of that age, and with a vigor and subtlety which would do credit to any age, but of little practical utility to us.

No one can fail, in turning to the treatises of the great masters of the civil law, to perceive how much they

law, after defining damages according to the civil law to be, nothing other than the profit lost, or the injury sustained, *æstimatio damni illati et lucri cessantis*, declares the subject to be controlled by these three rules: *first*, that taken from the code, which we have elsewhere considered, that in regard to things certain the compensation shall not exceed the *double*. *Second*, that the direct and not the remote results are to be accounted for, subject, however, to the provision that, in cases of fraud, all damage sustained is to be made good; and *third*, that in estimating injury, the general opinion, or, in regard to things vendible, the market value, and not the particular estimate of the injured party, is to govern. But it is doing injustice to the clear brevity of the original to attempt a translation: I. *In casibus certis, ubi de speciebus vel quantitatibus definitis agitur, non potest excedere duplum: l. un. C. de Sent. quæ pro eo quod int.* II. *Lucrum oportet circa rem ipsam consistat, in eâque sit radicatum, ut DD. loquuntur, non foris advenians aut fortuitum: l. 21, § 3, de act. empt. Detrimenta tamen omnia præstantur si dolus intervenerit; aliter quanti minoris: l. 13, pr. d. t. de ac. empt., l. 19, § 1, locati.* III. *Lucri et damni ratio ex judicio communi, non affectione peculiari initur; nam hæc in phantasia hominum consistit, cujus æstimatio nulla est: l. 33. ad L. Aquil.*[400]

He then proceeds to illustrate these rules. A party who had let a certain pottery to another was unable to perform his agreement. The hirer proved that he could have made in a year (the term is not stated) a thousand florins, and recovered that amount. But, says the author, he should only have had judg-

are benefited by the superior harmony and logic of their system. Unembarrassed by any conflict of legal and equitable jurisdictions, unperplexed by forms of action, relieved from a great portion of our distinctions between real and personal property, and thus emancipated from a multitude of futile technicalties which have no bearing whatever on the rights of parties, their discussions have a clearness, an order, and a scientific precision, that it is in vain to hope for under our incongruous system.

But, on the other hand, we are not without compensation. We search in vain in the pages of these writers for the accurate practical teaching of our law; and we sadly miss the sharp analysis of actually occurring cases, which gives so much interest and value to the great body of our jurisprudence, making it, instead of a mere repository of theoretical discussions, a faithful portraiture of the actual wants, interests, and passions of mankind.

[400] Huber, Prael. Jur. i, 405, § 17.

ment for 300 florins, because the annual rent of the farm was 150 florins: *Quod erat simplum, et contractus locationis est certus, id est certæ quantitatis; tales autem duplum egredi non possunt: quæ regula*, exclaims Huberus, *incredibile est quam vulgo ignota visa est!* [401]

In illustration of the second rule, he states this case: Hypolytus ab Arssen had purchased certain turf pits, with an agreement that the seller should give him the right of way through a certain ditch, requisite to remove his turf. After the sale, however, the purchaser found that the seller had intentionally (*per dolum*) left a strip of earth between him and the ditch, so that he could not use it. The plaintiff proved that at the time of the obstruction he could daily make forty florins; but that, afterwards, prices had fallen to twenty florins, at which he had been obliged to sell his turf. *Condemnatus est venditor in id quod emptoris interesset. Cum ad taxationem ejus quod interest preventum esset,* the plaintiff claimed this sum, namely, the price at forty florins, which greatly exceeded twice the purchase money of the whole land. But for the defense it was contended, 1. That the alleged price of turf was extraordinary. 2. The injury was not sufficiently direct, for the plaintiff might have gone round through the land of other parties, or he could have thrown a bridge over the obstacle, and thus transported his turf. 3. That the buyer had an offer of thirty-two florins, which he had refused; and that, consequently, the seller was not liable unless, perhaps, for the expense of the bridge that the buyer might have made, and the transportation of the turf over it. Huberus thus answers these arguments: 1. The price was the common one, and, at all events, the objection was inadmissible in a case like this of fraud. *Præterea per dolum hic prætextus excludebatur.* 2. The objection came too late, because the seller was already condemned to respond in damages. As to the bridge, it was not to be required that this idea should have suggested itself to the buyer, nor was he bound to resort to such an expedient in case of fraud. 3. The buyer was not bound to receive thirty-two florins for his turf at a time when he could sell them for forty. But the cause was decided on the basis of the offer of thirty-two florins; and Huberus seems

[401] Vol. iii, p. 88.

to deplore the arbitrary control exercised by the courts over the subject of compensation. *Quanquam juris ignitur rationes, pro triumphante* (the plaintiff) *militaire viderentur, tamen ut est hujus rei praxis valde lubrica et tantum non arbitraria, factum est ut venditor vix ultra quam obtulerat sit condemnatus.*[402] It might be curious, if our space permitted, to compare the decision here made with what it would be in a similar case—say, a conveyance with a covenant of right of way—according to our jurisprudence.

Among the more recent writers on the modern civil law, we find the same absence of any definite rule, of which I have already complained. Domat says,[403] the seller who fails to deliver must pay the damages caused by his default, according to the circumstances of the case. Thus, he who contracts to deliver any article of merchandise, the price of which rises at the time and place fixed for delivery, must pay the actual value at such time and place, as well on account of the profit that the purchaser would have made by reselling them there, as on account of the loss that he sustains by being obliged to purchase other articles at a price exceeding that of his bargain. So, he says that the purchaser would be entitled to his expenses actually incurred on coming to receive the article which was to have been delivered, but that remote and unforeseen consequences are not to be taken into consideration. Thus, for instance, if the seller failing to deliver the commodity at the time and place fixed on, the purchaser has been made unable to transport them to another place, where he could sell them at an advance; or if, by reason of the non-delivery of the article, he has been obliged to send off his workmen, and to stop some work of which the cessation causes him considerable injury, the seller will be considered liable, neither for the profit lost nor the injury sustained; for these consequences are not to be imputed to the default of delivery, but result from the arrangements of a higher power, and accidental circumstances which no one can control.[404] **

---

[402] Huberus, Prael. Juris., vol. iii, pp. 88, 89, §§ 30 to 35.

[403] Contrat de Vente, Loix Civiles, liv. 1, tit. 2, sec. 2, § 27. Troplong, in his masterly treatise *De la Vente*, complains of the looseness of Domat on the subject of the measure of damages; but the difficulty appears to be rather in the system than in the author.

[404] Cont. de Vente, liv. i, tit. 2, sec. 2, § 18.

CHAPTER XXXVI

ACTIONS UPON CONTRACTS OF INDEMNITY

§ 784. Contract of principal and surety.
785. Implied contract of indemnity.
786. Express contract of indemnity.
787. Interpretation of the contract.
788. Measure of damages on contracts of indemnity.
789. Contracts to pay or discharge a debt.
790. The rule not to be approved on principle.
791. Contracts to indemnify or save harmless.
792. Early cases erroneous.
793. Later cases follow the true rule.
793a. No recovery without actual loss.
794. Actual loss always recoverable.
795. Contracts to save from liability, etc.
796. Payment.
797. Payment by note.

§ 798. Note must be accepted as payment.
799. Payment by bond or nonnegotiable note.
800. Payment in land or goods.
801. Compensation for actual loss only.
802. Judgment against surety often conclusive on principal.
803. Litigation expenses.
804. None where suit was unnecessary.
805. Notice of suit.
806. Consequential loss.
807. Co-sureties.
807a. Amount of contribution.
807b. Insolvency or discharge of a surety.
807c. Interest and attorney's fees.
808. Costs and legal expenses.
808a. Reduction of surety's claim.

§ 784. Contract of principal and surety.

* The contract of suretyship is one of very frequent occurrence, arising in some cases by implication of law, as between the parties to negotiable paper, or debtors and their bail; in others it is created by express agreements of guarantee. These, again, sometimes take the form of indemnities and contracts to save harmless, and at others assume the more binding shape of express contracts to do the particular thing in question; in which last case, indeed, the peculiar relation of principal and surety often ceases to exist.[1]

[1] "In ancient times," said Buller, J., in Toussaint v. Martinnant, 2 T. R. 100, "no action could be maintained *at law*, where a surety had paid the debt of his principal. Now, why does the law raise such a promise? Because there is no security given by the party. But if the party choose to take a security, there is no occasion for the law to raise a promise."

1638

The questions that ordinarily present themselves, as between the principal debtor and the party who has assumed for him the obligations of a surety, relate to the circumstances which entitle the latter to call for repayment of any sum he may have been obliged to pay for him; the mode of that payment; and the collateral expenses, legal or otherwise, of which he can demand reimbursement. These questions sometimes arise in actions by sureties against their principals, sometimes in suits against the sureties themselves; and though the law generally tends to favor the surety, still, so far as the construction of the contract is concerned, no difference is made as to the manner in which the case is presented.

There is another class of cases of a mixed character, where actions are brought against sureties for sheriffs, constables, or other public officers. As these cases involve the consideration of the principles of the measure of damages in actions on official bonds, we have already treated them in the chapter on that subject. It is only necessary, therefore, here to consider the liabilities of principal and surety as arising out of private contract.

Let us first bear in mind the clear distinction that exists between two classes of cases, falling under the general head. "It is the distinction between an affirmative covenant for a specific thing, and one of indemnity against damage by reason of the non-performance of the thing specified. The object of both may be to save the covenantee from damages, but their legal consequences are essentially different." [2] **

§ 785. Implied contract of indemnity.

* A surety for the payment of money cannot call on his principal until he has paid the debt.[3] So it was early held by Lord Mansfield, in regard to a surety in a bond; "till damnified," said his lordship, "which he could not be till he had been called upon and had paid, he could not bring an action." [4] And so

---

[2] Gilbert v. Wiman, 1 N. Y. 550, 562, 49 Am. Dec. 359.

[3] *Kansas:* Churchill v. Moore, 15 Kan. 255.

Michigan: Hall v. Nash, 10 Mich. 303; Butler v. Ladue, 12 Mich. 173;

Thompson v. Richards, 14 Mich. 172; Kenyon v. Woodruff, 33 Mich. 310.

New York: Burt v. Dewey, 40 N. Y. 283, 100 Am. Dec. 482.

[4] *United States:* Pigou v. French, 1 Wash. C. C. 278.

it has been held in New York, where the surety had been sued and charged in execution, that not having paid the debt, and having no promise to indemnify him, he could not recover against his principal.[5] For this a technical reason also exists, that the only action that can be maintained in such case is assumpsit for money paid, which, of course, will not lie until money or its equivalent is paid.** There is in this case no express contract of indemnity, and no reason for the law to create a promise until the surety has actually lost property for which the principal should in equity compensate him.

§ 786. Express contract of indemnity.

* Where the plaintiff holds an express promise to indemnify and save him harmless, there he can maintain an action without having paid the debt; and we shall presently examine the extent of compensation allowed for the injury he alleges himself to have sustained.[6] But where the plaintiff holds not merely an agreement to indemnify and save him harmless against the consequences of the default of the other, but an express promise to pay a debt, or to do some particular act, then the position of the parties entirely changes. The relation of principal and surety disappears, and it has been held that the failure to perform the act agreed on gives the plaintiff a right of action even before he has suffered any direct damage himself; and so it has also been decided as a rule of pleading.

Where the defendant agrees to discharge the plaintiff from any bond or other particular thing, there the defendant, having agreed to do a particular act, cannot plead *non damnificatus;* but where the condition is to discharge the plaintiff *from damage* by reason of any particular thing, or to *indemnify and save harmless,* there the damage must be shown, and consequently *non damnificatus* is a good plea.[7] **

New York: Powell *v.* Smith, 8 Johns. 249; Rodman *v.* Hedden, 10 Wend. 498.

England: Taylor *v.* Mills, Cowp. 525; Paul *v.* Jones, 1 T. R. 599.

[5] Powell *v.* Smith, 8 Johns. 249.

[6] Rodman *v.* Hedden, 10 Wend. 498. The bail of a deputy sheriff are not liable unless the sheriff has been damnified or made legally liable in conse-

quence of the dereliction of the deputy. Hughes *v.* Smith, 5 Johns. 168; Rowe *v.* Richardson, 5 Barb. 385.

[7] *New York:* Port *v.* Jackson, 17 Johns. 239; s. c. aff'd in Error, *Id.* 479; Thomas *v.* Allen, 1 Hill, 145. These two last cases overrule that of Douglass *v.* Clarke, 14 Johns. 177.

England: Cutler *v.* Southern, 1

§ 787. Interpretation of the contract.

In all covenants of indemnity, therefore, a preliminary question of interpretation arises; and it becomes necessary to decide whether the contract is to pay a sum of money or discharge one from a debt or liability, or whether it is merely to save harmless or to protect from damage. If the former is the case, the contract is broken, and damages are to be recovered upon the defendant's failure to pay the money or discharge the debt; if the latter, the contract is broken only when the plaintiff suffers damage by reason of the liability covenanted against.

§ 788. Measure of damages on contracts of indemnity.

The general rules are as follows: If the defendant contracted to pay or discharge a debt, the measure of damages is the amount of the debt.[8] If the defendant contracted to save the defendant harmless from a *liability*, it has been held that the amount of the liability is the measure of damages, though the plaintiff has not paid it.[9] But if the contract was merely to indemnify or save the plaintiff harmless from a debt, the measure of damages is the amount the plaintiff has already paid on the debt.[10]

§ 789. Contracts to pay or discharge a debt.

Upon breach of a contract to pay or to discharge another's debt, an action lies at once, upon default, to recover the amount of the debt, without proof by the plaintiff that he has paid it; [11]

Saund. 116, note 1; Holmes *v.* Rhodes, 1 B. & P. 638; Hodgson *v.* Bell, 7 T. R. 97.

[8] Cases cited in § 789.

[9] Cases cited in § 795.

[10] Cases cited in § 793.

[11] *Connecticut:* Lathrop *v.* Atwood, 21 Conn. 117.

Illinois: Gage *v.* Lewis, 68 Ill. 604; Pierce *v.* Plumb, 74 Ill. 326; (but see Israel *v.* Reynolds, 11 Ill. 218).

Indiana: Smith *v.* Rogers, 14 Ind. 224, 227, 77 Am. Dec. 67 (*semble*).

Iowa: Stout *v.* Folger, 34 Ia. 71, 11 Am. Rep. 138.

Maryland: Dorsey *v.* Dashiell, 1 Md. 198, 54 Am. Dec. 649.

Massachusetts: Farnsworth *v.* Boardman, 131 Mass. 115; Shattuck *v.* Adams, 136 Mass. 34.

Minnesota: Merriam *v.* Pine City Lumber Co., 23 Minn. 314.

Missouri: Ham *v.* Hill, 29 Mo. 275, 77 Am. Dec. 572.

New Hampshire: Richards *v.* Whittle, 16 N. H. 259.

New York: Belloni *v.* Freeborn, 63 N. Y. 383; Seligman *v.* Dudley, 14 Hun, 186; Fletcher *v.* Derrickson, 3 Bosw. 181.

even though he is not personally liable for it,[12] and without reference to the consideration he has received.[13] Thus where one guarantees the payment of a certain sum, he is responsible at once, on non-payment at the time the payment is due, for the entire amount.[14] And this is true though no action would lie for the amount against the person who was to pay it.[15] So where, upon the conveyance of mortgaged land, one of the parties to the conveyance agrees to pay the mortgage debt when it becomes due, action can be brought on the agreement and the whole amount recovered upon the debt falling due and not being paid, though there has been no demand of payment.[16] So where one of a firm, having, on its dissolution, undertaken to collect its outstanding claims, gave his bond to pay all demands against it, and save the other partner and his sureties and indorsers, on account of said firm, harmless, it was held that the obligee could recover on the bond the amount of the partnership debts existing due and unpaid.[17] In Gage v. Lewis,[18]

Ohio: Porter v. State, 23 Oh. St. 320.

Pennsylvania: Dayton v. Gunnison, 9 Pa. 347.

England: Carr v. Roberts, 5 B. & A. 78.

Canada: Raymond v. Cooper, 8 Up. Can. C. P. 388.

But *contra* (that nominal damages only can be recovered unless the plaintiff has paid the debt), Dye v. Mann, 10 Mich. 291.

[12] Hodgson v. Wood, 2 H. & C. 649.

[13] Cooper v. Page, 24 Me. 73, 41 Am. Dec. 371; Oakley v. Boorman, 21 Wend. (N. Y.) 588.

[14] *United States:* Marbury v. Kentucky Union Land Co., 62 Fed. 335, 10 C. C. A. 393.

Iowa: Adams & F. Harvester Co. v. Tomlinson, 58 Ia. 129, 12 N. W. 13.

Nebraska: Flentham v. Steward, 45 Neb. 640, 63 N. W. 924.

[15] *Illinois:* Holm v. Jamieson, 173 Ill. 295, 50 N. E. 702 (guaranteed note void).

North Carolina: James v. Long, 68

N. C. 218 (principal debtor entitled to legislative scale).

[16] Promise by the grantee:

Connecticut: Redfield v. Haight, 27 Conn. 31.

Illinois: Gage v. Lewis, 68 Ill. 604.

Massachusetts: Locke v. Homer, 131 Mass. 93, 109, 41 Am. Rep. 199.

New York: In re Negus, 7 Wend. 499. Promise by the grantor: Stearns v. Stearns, 129 Mich. 451, 89 N. W. 41.

[17] *Illinois:* Miller v. Kingsbury, 128 Ill. 45.

Indiana: Devol v. McIntosh, 23 Ind. 529.

Michigan: Lee v. Burrell, 51 Mich. 132.

Missouri: Ham v. Hill, 29 Mo. 275.

Nebraska: Ley v. Miller, 28 Neb. 822, 45 N. W. 174.

New York: Ralph v. Eldridge, 137 N. Y. 525, 33 N. E. 559; Sinsheimer v. Tobias, 53 N. Y. Super. Ct. 508.

Ohio: Wilson v. Stilwell, 9 Oh. St. 467.

See, however, Duran v. Ayer, 67

[18] 68 Ill. 604, 617.

a case of this nature, Scholfield, J., said: "It has ever been held that where a bond is given, intended as a bond of indemnity, but containing a covenant that the obligor will pay certain debts, for the payment of which the obligee is liable, and the obligor fails to perform, an action lies for the breach, and the obligee is entitled to recover the sums agreed to be paid, although it is not shown that he has been damnified, unless, from the whole instrument, it manifestly appears that its sole object was a covenant of indemnity." In a case before the Supreme Court of the United States,[19] it appeared that the defendant agreed that if the plaintiff would prosecute a claim against a third party and obtain judgment and levy on the property, he, the defendant, "would bid it off for whatever the judgment and costs might be." This he did not do, and the property was knocked down to the plaintiff for a nominal sum. Suit was then brought for the breach of the agreement, and the court held the defendant liable for the full amount of the judgment, with interest and costs. This ruling the Supreme Court affirmed, after a full consideration, notwithstanding the fact that the plaintiff would apparently by this decision be able to make use of the two judgments, and thus might recover more than the amount of his claim. * So in New York, where the plaintiff, as lessee for a term of years, had assigned it to the defendant, who executed a covenant

Me. 145, where the plaintiff recovered only what he had paid, but he did not except to the decision. The point decided was, that the plaintiff could recover, on a contract to pay the debts of a third party and to hold the plaintiff harmless, the full amount of the loss sustained, not to exceed the amount of the notes and interest. See also, Smith v. Riddell, 87 Ill. 165. The contract in Walker v. Broadhurst, 8 Ex. 889, was of a slightly different nature. The plaintiff entered into partnership with A. and B., on condition that they should furnish security as to the state of the firm. The defendant covenanted with the plaintiff that the amount due the old firm should not be less than a sum specified, and that the debts of the firm should not exceed a certain sum. It appearing that the debts exceeded the amount specified, but also that less than that amount had been paid on account of the liabilities of the old firm, it was held that the defendant's covenant was a contract of indemnity only, but that the plaintiff was entitled to recover as damages the actual loss which he had sustained by reason of the defendant's breach of covenant; and that the amount of such damage was purely a question for the jury.

[19] Wicker v. Hoppock, 6 Wall. 94, 18 L. ed. 752. See argument of plaintiff in error, p. 95.

to pay the rent to the head landlord, it was insisted on the part of the defendant, that the plaintiff could only recover nominal damages unless he showed that he paid the rent; but the court said: "The covenant is express and positive that the defendant will pay the rent; and it would be against all reason and justice to say that the plaintiff shall himself first pay and advance the money before his right of action against the defendant to recover it arises"; and the rent was held to be the measure of damages.[20] ** The same rule has been applied by the New York Commission of Appeals to the breach by a lessee of an absolute covenant to pay taxes or assessments on the demised premises.[21] So where the defendant had agreed to pay certain notes and mortgages made by the plaintiff, to third parties, the plaintiff was allowed to recover the full amount, though unpaid.[22] And on an agreement by the purchaser of an equity of redemption that if the mortgage were foreclosed no personal judgment should be taken against the plaintiff the measure of damages is the amount of a judgment so recovered, though it has not been paid.[23]

* So again, if one, by bond, guarantees that a third party shall pay a certain sum of money by a given day, on demand, the plaintiff must assign the non-payment of the money by the third party as a breach of the condition of the bond sued on, but he is not bound to give any further evidence of the extent of his damages, the instrument itself fixing the amount he is entitled to recover; and it was so held against the defendant, who insisted that, in the absence of such evidence, the plaintiff could only recover nominal damages.[24]

---

[20] *New York:* Port v. Jackson, 17 Johns. 239, 245; s. c. in error, *Id.* 479.
  England: See Toussaint v. Martinnant, 2 T. R. 100; Martin v. Court, 2 T. R. 640; Hodgson v. Bell, 7 T. R. 97; Atkinson v. Coatsworth, 8 Mod. 33.
  [21] Trinity Church v. Higgins, 48 N. Y. 532.
  [22] Furnas v. Durgin, 119 Mass. 500, 20 Am. Rep. 341.
  [23] Banfield v. Marks, 56 Cal. 185. Upon the analogy of these decisions the case is probably to be upheld else-

where cited, where it was decided that in an action brought on a covenant to discharge an existing incumbrance, the plaintiff was entitled to recover the full amount of the incumbrance, though nothing had been paid. Lethbridge v. Mytton, 2 B. & A. 772.
  [24] Mann v. Eckford, 15 Wend. 502; *In re* Negus, 7 Wend. 499. So where the defendant, having guaranteed to keep the plaintiff clear of back interest, failed to do so, it was held that the plaintiff was damnified from the mo-

And a similar decision was made in the English Exchequer.[25] The defendant was indebted to H. D. and G. B. in the sum of £400, secured by a promissory note made by the defendant, and by the plaintiff as the defendant's surety; and thereupon the defendant covenanted that he *would pay H. D. and G. B.* the sum of £400, on or before the thirteenth of August then next; breach, non-payment by the day. On the trial it appeared that the plaintiff had been notified that he would be held liable on the note; but the note was not paid, and the defendant insisted that the plaintiff was only entitled to nominal damages. The Lord Chief Baron Abinger overruled the objection; and the plaintiff had a verdict for the note and interest. On showing cause why there should not be a new trial, this was held right. Alderson, B., said: "To what extent has the plaintiff been injured by the defendant's default? Certainly to the amount of the money that the defendant ought to have paid according to his covenant;" [26] and he likened it to an action of trover for title deeds.**

The following case carries out this doctrine to its fullest extent: One Jennings had bequeathed to the children of his granddaughter, a Mrs. Button, on her death, a legacy of £400, to be paid at the age of twenty-one to the survivors who reached that age, and the testator devised part of his estate charged with the legacy, in moieties to his two daughters; the plaintiff, as heir at law to one of the daughters, who had then died, effected a partition of the estate with the other daughter, each covenanting with the other to pay half the legacy. The plaintiff subsequently sold his part to the defendant, subject to the payment, by the defendant, of one moiety of the legacy to W. H. Parker, the only surviving child of Mrs. Button, who was dead, on his attaining the age of twenty-one, or to his personal representatives in case of his death under age, and *the defendant covenanted with the plaintiff to pay such moiety, and*

ment judgment was obtained against him, and might sue on the agreement. Gardner *v.* Grove, 10 S. & R. 137. In another case, however, the court told the jury they were at liberty to find for the whole amount of the plaintiff's liability, but *recommended* them to find only for the amount actually paid. Bauer *v.* Roth, 4 Rawle, 83.

[25] Loosemore *v.* Radford, 9 M. & W. 657.

[26] See Gunel *v.* Cue, 72 Ind. 34; Malott *v.* Goff, 96 Ind. 496.

indemnify the plaintiff against all liability on account of it.
Parker died under twenty-one, and his administrator claimed
a moiety of the legacy, which the plaintiff, claiming it himself,
notified the defendant not to pay. A bill having been filed by
Parker's administrator to compel the payment of the legacy
to him by the plaintiff, it was, on the ground that the legacy
was no longer a charge on his estate, dismissed with costs,
though the plaintiff had to pay some costs as between attorney
and client. The plaintiff having brought an action on the
covenant alleging as breaches the non-payment of the moiety to
Parker's personal representatives and the non-indemnity of
the plaintiff, whereby the plaintiff incurred costs, it was held
by all the judges that the plaintiff was entitled not merely to
nominal damages, but to the full indemnity, including the £200
and the costs paid by the plaintiff.[27]

One English case seems to be opposed to the rule above
stated. In that case it appeared that the plaintiffs lent the
defendant £600 on the security of an indenture by which two
policies on the defendant's life were charged with the loan.
In the indenture the defendant covenanted to pay the premiums
on the policies, which would become void unless these should
be annually paid. The defendant paid the first premium only,
and the plaintiffs sued him on his covenant for non-payment
of three years' premiums. It was held that, as it did not appear
the plaintiffs had sustained any loss, they were entitled to
nominal damages only.[28]

§ 790. The rule not to be approved on principle.

* These decisions appear somewhat to conflict with the important and fundamental rule which has already been stated,
that actual compensation will not be given for merely probable
loss. Nor is the argument that the party, having bound himself to do a particular act, must therefore be held liable in the
full amount, of greater weight.[29] There is a multitude of con-

[27] Hodgson v. Wood, 2 H. & C. 649.
[28] National A. & I. Assoc. v. Best, 2 H. & N. 605.
[29] This and the preceding remark are disapproved by Leonard, C., in Trinity Church v. Higgins, 48 N. Y. 532, 538.

He observed that "parties have the just right to make all lawful contracts guarding their rights and securing per-formance of their intentions, including that of contravening the rule of actual compensation for actual loss; and when

tracts of the same character, to which no such doctrine is applied. If, instead of a contract to pay a certain sum of money, the agreement be to do any other particular act, an inquiry is indispensable to ascertain how far the party plaintiff has been damnified by the non-feasance. It is, perhaps, no great stretch of reasoning to say that the damages arising from the non-payment of money should be measured by the sum itself. Still, a doubt may often arise whether the *party who holds the agreement* has been injured to that extent; and this is well pointed out by a very accurate judge, in Loosemore *v.* Radford.[30]   Parke, B., said: "The defendant may, perhaps, have an *equity*, that the money he may pay to the plaintiff shall be applied in discharge of his debt; but, *at law*, the plaintiff is entitled to be placed in the same situation, under this agreement, as if he had paid the money to the payees of the bill." This remark of a very acute judge states the evil, but suggests no remedy. The law is thus carried into execution unattended by the equity which should temper it. It is one of many instances illustrating the inconvenience and serious hardships that often flow from the separation of the jurisdictions. Either the plaintiff should only be allowed to recover for actual loss; or, if the court proceed upon the idea of compelling the defendant specifically to perform his promise, it should carry the engagement into full execution, by applying the proceeds of the judgment where they belong. This a court of law possesses no power to do; and as it is incompetent to do complete justice, it should confine its remedies exclusively to those cases where actual injury appeals for redress.**

§ 791. Contracts to indemnify or save harmless.

* It appears, upon the whole, settled that if the engagement be collateral, or, more properly speaking, indirect, whether only implied in law, or whether it be an undertaking to indemnify and save harmless against the consequences of the default, there damage to be recovered must be proved. And

expressed in apt and suitable language, it would be flagrant wrong if courts of justice should assume to disregard it, in favor of some technical rule framed for other and wholly different circumstances."
[30] 9 M. & W. 657.

so it is held whether the action be by the surety against the principal, or by the creditor against the surety.**

§ 792. Early cases erroneous.

In a case at Nisi Prius, before Lord Ellenborough, on a bond conditioned to indemnify the plaintiff against a bond given by him to a third party, though it did not appear that he had paid it, his lordship said that he did not see any measure of damages except the penalty of the bond; and the jury so found.[31] *In a case in New York, this erroneous view of the subject was carried to a great length; and it is desirable carefully to notice the decision, and those by which it has been since overruled; for unless we adhere strictly to the principle that actual compensation shall only be awarded for actual loss, we are without any guide whatever in this branch of the law. Suit was brought [32] by the overseers of the poor against the sureties in a bond given by the father of an illegitimate child, before its birth, to save harmless and indemnify the town against all expenses by reason of the child. After the birth, an order was made by two justices, according to the statute, fixing the amount of the defendant's liability. It was insisted that this order was competent evidence against the defendant, and that the town was not bound to show the actual expenditure of the sum claimed; and it was so held by the Court of Errors.

It will be observed that here the covenant was merely to indemnify and save harmless, and did not reach to the extent of a promise to do the thing in the first place. It is to be noticed, also, that the whole scope of this reasoning is opposed to the general rule that actual compensation will only be given for actual loss, and cannot be supported but on the idea that a court of law is to assume the powers of a court of equity, and compel an imperfect kind of specific performance. If this

---

[31] Wood v. Wade, 2 Starkie, 167.

[32] Rockfeller v. Donnelly, 8 Cowen, 623, 639, 647, reversing Donely v. Rockfeller, 4 Cow. 253. The same point was again decided in People v. Corbett, 8 Wend. 520. But in Churchill v. Hunt, 3 Denio, 321, these decisions are said to rest entirely on the spirit and intent of the statute, "giving these bonds an effect which they would not have at common law;" and it is there said to be for the same reason that in a claim against the sheriff on bonds for the jail liberties, it is unnecessary to prove damage. Kip v. Brigham, 7 Johns. 168.

doctrine were maintained, covenantors against incumbrances would be compelled to pay before the incumbrance was discharged; covenantors for quiet enjoyment would be obliged to pay before eviction; and all parties agreeing to do a specific thing would be mulcted in the sum equivalent to performance without any proof whatever that the other party had been injured, or that his position was such that he could be.**

§ 793. Later cases follow the true rule.

* But this is not the result of the more recent authorities of the courts in this country. In an early case, the question "whether on an escape the bail to the liberties became liable for the whole penalty, or for the damages sustained by the sheriff by reason of the escape?" was raised in New York, but not decided.[33] But it was soon after said that neither the sheriff nor his assignee could recover without showing injury sustained, and that, consequently, recapture after the escape, or voluntary return, was an answer to a suit against the sureties for the liberties.[34] ** In another case, on an agreement to indemnify and save harmless against a certain demand, a judgment having been recovered on the claim in question against the plaintiff, but nothing having been paid thereon, the case of Rockfeller v. Donnelly was pronounced "a very questionable" one, and judgment was given for the defendant, the court saying: "This is not an agreement to indemnify against liability, but it is the common case of an agreement to indemnify against the claim or demand of a third person; and before the plaintiff can recover, he must show that he has been damnified; the mere fact that the demand has changed its form by having passed into a judgment is not enough." [35] Again, on a bond "to save harmless," it was said, "Here is no absolute agreement to pay, and no agreement to keep the party clear from liability, but merely to indemnify"; and it was held, that, in order to recover, damage, and that involuntarily sustained, must be shown. It was intimated, however, that "perhaps after a suit commenced, and notice given to the obligor, and neglect by him to defend, the obligee would be warranted in

---

[33] Jansen v. Hilton, 10 Johns. 549.
[34] Barry v. Mandell, 10 Johns. 563.

[35] Aberdeen v. Blackmar, 6 Hill, 324.

putting a stop to the costs." [36]   In a later case in New York, the whole subject was considered in the Court of Appeals. The covenant was, that the plaintiff should not sustain any damage or molestation by reason of any liability incurred by his deputy. Judgment has been recovered against the plaintiff, but not paid; and it was held that he was not entitled to recover.[37]

In Valentine v. Wheeler,[38] where the contract (condition of bond) was to pay all demands, acceptances for which the plaintiff should be in any way responsible on account of the obligee, and to hold the plaintiff harmless and free from loss or inconvenience on account of any debts and claims of the obligee, the court construed this to be merely a contract of indemnity, and allowed the plaintiff to recover only what he had actually paid.[39]   So in an action on a promissory note or other instrument given as an indemnity by a principal to his surety the measure of damages is the amount paid by the surety at any time before trial, and unless he has made an actual payment he can recover nominal damages only.[40]   So in Truckie Lodge v. Wood,[41] where the defendant had put up a building for the plaintiff and had allowed liens to attach contrary to his agreements that it should not be "accountable" for any of the materials of construction, it was held that evidence of their amount was properly excluded, as the plaintiff had not paid them, although they were then in process of foreclosure.

§ 793a. No recovery without actual loss.

According to these authorities, the later American decisions establish the rule that if the contract is one of indemnity merely there can be no recovery without actual loss.[42]   So where a

[36] Crippen v. Thompson, 6 Barb. 532, 536.

[37] Gilbert v. Wiman, 1 N. Y. 550, 49 Am. Dec. 359; acc., Jeffers v. Johnson, 21 N. J. L. 73. In Ohio, see Ohio Life Ins. and Trust Co. v. Reeder, 18 Ohio, 35.

[38] 122 Mass. 566, 23 Am. Rep. 404.

[39] Acc., Martindale v. Brock, 41 Md. 571; Kraft v. Fancher, 44 Md. 204.

[40] Massachusetts: Cushing v. Gore, 15 Mass. 69; Little v. Little, 13 Pick. 426.

New Hampshire: Osgood v. Osgood, 39 N. H. 209; Child v. Eureka Powder Works, 44 N. H. 354.

[41] 14 Nev. 293.

[42] United States: Baetjer v. Bors, 7 Ben. 280.

California: Lott v. Mitchell, 32 Cal. 23.

Connecticut: Redfield v. Haight, 27 Conn. 31.

Maine: Hussey v. Collins, 30 Me. 190.

water company, before being permitted to dig up a highway gave a bond to save the village harmless from damage arising from its negligence, and a person injured by the excavation had brought suit against the village, it was held that there could be no recovery until the claim had been paid.[43] It follows that if a portion of the loss has been paid, the plaintiff can recover the balance of his loss, but that only;[44] and if a payment is made even after suit brought it is to be deducted from the amount recovered.[45] These decisions replace this branch of the law on its proper basis, and declare the salutary principle, that actual compensation can only be given for positive loss unless it is evident that the parties have stipulated for a more extensive remuneration.**

§ 794. Actual loss always recoverable.

But the actual loss is always recoverable upon a contract of indemnity.[46] So where the defendant guaranteed the payment of a note which provided for interest after maturity at the rate of 20 per cent. per annum, he must pay interest at that rate.[47] Upon a contract of indemnity given to a mort-

---

Maryland: Gillespie v. Creswell, 12 G. & J. 36.

Massachusetts: Spencer Savings Bank v. Cooley, 177 Mass. 49, 58 N. E. 276.

Missouri: Citizens' State Bank v. Pettit, 85 Mo. App. 499.

New Hampshire: Osgood v. Osgood, 39 N. H. 209; Conner v. Bean, 43 N. H. 202.

New York: Scott v. Tyler, 14 Barb. 202; Selover v. Harpending, 54 N. Y. Super. Ct. 251; Selover v. Harpending, 18 Abb. New Cas. 252.

Texas: Clayton v. Franco-Texan Land Co., 15 Tex. Civ. App. 365, 39 S. W. 645.

In Boyle v. Boyle, 106 N. Y. 654, 12 N. E. 709, it was held that one who had received an indemnity against liability as surety on a bond cannot recover for litigation expenses not reasonable, but caused by his vain fears.

[43] Eldridge v. Crow, 7 N. Y. Misc. 150, 27 N. Y. Supp. 362.

But in Gamble v. Cuneo, 21 App. Div. 413, 47 N. Y. Supp. 548, an agreement to save plaintiff harmless from any damages he might sustain by reason of his continuance as one of the sureties on an appeal undertaking, it was held that the defendant must pay the entire amount of a judgment obtained against plaintiff on the appeal undertaking.

[44] Buffalo G. Ins. Co. v. Title & T. Co., 51 Misc. 267, 99 N. Y. Supp. 883.

[45] Shattuck v. Adams, 136 Mass. 34.

[46] *District of Columbia:* McKenzie v. Underwood, 21 D. C. 126.

New York: De Camp v. Bullard, 159 N. Y. 450, 54 N. E. 26.

Pennsylvania: Union Trust Co. v. Citizens' Trust Co., 185 Pa. 217, 39 Atl. 886.

[47] Gridley v. Capen, 72 Ill. 11. He

gagee upon selling timber from the mortgaged land, the measure of damages is the amount the land was depreciated in value by the removal of the timber. Where the land itself was not injured, and the sale was a fair one, the measure of damages is the amount realized from the sale.[48]

Action was brought on a bond of indemnity against damage to a vessel by reason of existing contracts. The vessel was libelled on an alleged contract and detained twenty-three days, when the libel was discharged upon the giving of a bond. It was held that the validity of the contract on which she was libelled need not be established, since the detention on the contract was indemnified against.[49] So a contract of indemnity against claims of a certain person on certain insurance moneys was held not to include merely valid claims, but any claims that might subject the party indemnified to costs or expense.[50] And on an agreement by a lessor, surrendering his lease and representing that the sub-tenants were yearly tenants, to indemnify the owner against claims of longer leases, the measure of damages where a longer lease was established was the difference between the rent reserved in such a lease and the actual rental value.[51]

§ 795. Contracts to save from liability, etc.

* Liability is a very different thing from damage; and the literal object of the covenant is not attained unless the plaintiff may rest on showing mere proof of *liability*, and is relieved from the obligation of proving *damage*. The only way to relieve the plaintiff from being liable to be made to pay the debt, is for the law to see to its extinguishment.[52] ** Thus, on a bond "to save harmless and indemnify against all damages, costs and charges to which the plaintiff's intestate might be sub-

cannot charge the principal with interest at that rate on the amount actually paid out by him. Waldrip v. Black, 74 Cal. 409, 16 Pac. 226.

[48] Curtis v. Baugh, 79 Ill. 242.

[49] Niagara Falls Paper Co. v. Lee, 20 N. Y. App. Div. 217, 47 N. Y. Supp. 1.

[50] Home Ins. Co. v. Watson, 59 N. Y. 390.

[51] Rosenberg v. Frankel, 123 App. Div. 700, 108 N. Y. Supp. 353.

[52] See, in Virginia, a suit by a sheriff on an indemnity bond against damages on levying an execution upon certain specified property. Dabney v. Catlett, 12 Leigh, 383. See, in the same State, a suit on an indemnity against injury to a mill-dam. Chapman v. Ross, 12 Leigh (Va.), 565.

jected, or *become liable for*," it was said by the Supreme Court of New York:

"There is no doubt as to the general proposition that, in order to recover upon a *mere bond of indemnity*, actual damage must be shown; if the indemnity be against the payment of money, the plaintiff must, in general, prove actual payment, or that which the law considers equivalent to actual payment; but if the indemnity be not only against actual damage or expense, but also against *any liability* for damages or expenses, then the party need not wait until he has actually paid such damages, but his right of action is complete when he becomes legally liable for them."

And on the ground that the bond before the court was against *liability*, the plaintiff was allowed to recover.[53] In the case of Spark *v.* Heslop,[54] the defendant, in a letter to the plaintiff requesting him to pay to a banking company for his account a bill of exchange for £400, drawn by one Henderson on and accepted by one Hutchinson, and indorsed by the defendant, and also requesting him to bring an action against Hutchinson for the recovery of the amount and interest, added the following engagement:

"And I hereby agree to be answerable to you for the due payment of the amount of the said bill and interest which you may pay to the said banking company, and for all costs, damages, and expenses which you may *sustain* by reason of such payment and the trying of the said action against the said John Hutchinson, and in any manner relating or incidental thereto, you giving me credit for all money you may receive from the said John Hutchinson in such action."

The plaintiff having brought the action against Hutchinson unsuccessfully, the court distinguished this undertaking from the case of an indemnity, and between "sustaining" costs, damages, and expenses, and paying them. They held that the plaintiff sustained damage when the liability was incurred, and that he could recover the costs he was liable for to his own attorney, although he had not paid them, as well as those of

[53] Chace *v.* Hinman, 8 Wend. (N. Y.) 452, 456, 24 Am. Dec. 39; *In re* Negus, 7 Wend. 499; Webb *v.* Pond, 19 Wend. 423; McGee *v.* Roen, 4 Abb. Pr. 8; Martin *v.* Bolenbaugh, 42 Oh. St. 508.   [54] 1 E. & E. 563.

the defendant in the other suit which he had paid. Accordingly, the plaintiff has recovered the whole amount of a judgment obtained against him, though he has paid nothing on it, when the defendant agreed to indemnify him against liability,[55] against actions, suits, or claims,[56] judgments,[57] debt,[58] or trouble.[59] And where the defendant gave the plaintiff a bond to pay all taxable costs which the plaintiff should "incur and become bound to pay" in a certain suit, it was held that the plaintiff could recover the amount of costs for which judgment had been rendered against him, though he had not paid the judgment.[60]

In an early New York case, where a bond was given "to save harmless and indemnify the plaintiffs *against their liability* as makers of a certain note, and *to pay or cause to be paid* the said note," it was held that the plaintiffs, though they had not paid the note, and were insolvent, were entitled to recover its amount, under the absolute terms of the covenant; but that the plaintiffs could not recover the costs of a suit against them on the note. As to these costs the bond was declared to be purely an agreement to indemnify; and the learned judge (Beardsley) proceeded to say: "Notwithstanding what is said in the case of Chace *v.* Hinman, I must say that I am not aware of any distinction at common law between an indemnity

[55] *Alabama:* Kirksey *v.* Friend, 48 Ala. 276.

Nevada: Jones *v.* Childs, 8 Nev. 121.

New York: Merchants' & Manufs. Nat. Bank *v.* Cumings, 149 N. Y. 360, 44 N. E. 173; Wright *v.* Chapin, 87 Hun, 144; Miller *v.* Miller Knitting Co., 23 Misc. 404, 52 N. Y. Supp. 184.

The plaintiff indemnified against a liability on a steamboat, was one of several co-owners; he paid the entire debts. It was held that he could recover only his share of the debts unless the other owners were insolvent. Ewing *v.* Reilly, 34 Mo. 113.

[56] *Massachusetts:* Cook *v.* Merrifield, 139 Mass. 139.

New York: Conkey *v.* Hopkins, 17 Johns. (N. Y.) 113.

England: Warwick *v.* Richardson, 10 M. & W. 284.

Canada: Smith *v.* Teer, 21 Up. Can. Q. B. 412.

In Kansas City, M. & B. R. R. *v.* Southern Ry. News Co., 151 Mo. 373, 390, 52 S. W. 205, 74 Am. St. Rep. 545, 45 L. R. A. 380, where judgment by consent was suffered on the claim, it was held that the plaintiff had the burden of proving the judgment reasonable in amount. If the judgment had not been by consent, the amount of it would have been conclusive.

[57] *New York:* Conner *v.* Reeves, 103 N. Y. 527.

Ohio: Martin *v.* Bolenbaugh, 42 Oh. St. 508.

[58] Carman *v.* Noble, 9 Pa. 366.

[59] Fish *v.* Dana, 10 Mass. 46.

[60] Jarvis *v.* Sewall, 40 Barb. (N. Y.), 449.

against damage and one against liability, which warrants a recovery on the latter on simply showing the fact of liability. In both, as I think, there must be evidence of actual damage, by the payment of money or otherwise."[61] But the rule laid down here seems to be overruled by the later decisions.

§ 796. Payment.

As we have seen, * the general rule is that the surety cannot proceed against his principal debtor until he has paid the debt; it still remains to be seen what in judgment of law is considered as payment. The suit of the surety against the principal is at common law an action of assumpsit, sometimes special, but frequently on the common counts for money paid for the defendant's use; and we now proceed to determine what proofs will satisfy the allegation of payment.[62]

It will be perceived at once that this inquiry involves various questions, some of a technical character, and springing from the form of the action, others relating to the substantial rights of the parties. Is the payment of *money* in all cases necessary? Can the surety, by giving his bond or note in payment of the original debt, raise a claim against the principal? Will the transfer of land, whether by mortgage or deed, be treated as payment? and if so, at what value shall it be computed? These, and similar inquiries, are often complicated and perplexing.

The rule appears to be well settled in this country, though far from being clear in England, that the giving by the surety of his negotiable promissory note, which is received not collat-

[61] Churchill v. Hunt, 3 Denio (N. Y.), 321.

[62] "It is an equitable principle of every general application," says Mr. Chancellor Walworth, in Hunt v. Amidon, 4 Hill, 345, 348, "that where one person is in the situation of a mere surety for another, whether he became so by actual contract or by operation of law, if he is compelled to pay the debt which the other in equity and justice ought to have paid, he is entitled to relief against the other, who was in fact the principal debtor. And when courts of law, a long time since, fell in love with a part of the jurisdiction of the Court of Chancery, and substituted the equitable remedy of an action of assumpsit on the common money counts for the more dilatory and expensive proceeding by a bill in equity in certain cases, they permitted the person thus standing in the situation of surety, who had been compelled to pay money for the principal debtor, to recover it back again from the person who ought to have paid it, in this equitable action of assumpsit as for money paid, laid out, and expended for his use and benefit."

erally, but as actual payment of the original debt, will be held to be payment as against the principal debtor, and that the surety may at once proceed against him for the amount of his note; in other words, the note is treated as money. While on the other hand, it is also held that the giving a bond will not have the like effect, and that, until the payment of the bond, the surety has no claim against his principal.

It is also well settled, that an absolute conveyance of the land by the surety will be sufficient to raise a claim on his behalf against the principal to its full value, and that it will be treated as money paid for the use of the original debtor. An examination of the decisions will best elucidate these rules.

In an early case in the King's Bench,[63] an application was made to discharge the defendant from custody on filing common bail; and it appeared that the defendant being indebted to one Creswell, the plaintiff Taylor had given Creswell *a bond* and warrant of attorney, and paid him £7 or £8 of costs; that this security was accepted as payment and satisfaction of the debt; and it was contended that this was the same as if the debt had been paid in money. But Lord Ellenborough said: "There is no pretence for considering the giving of this new security as so much *money paid* for the defendant's use;" and the rule to discharge the defendant from custody was made absolute.[64]

On the authority of this case the same point has been decided in New York.[65] The plaintiffs being accommodation indorsers for the defendant, had, on being sued, executed to the holders of the accommodation paper, on the 15th April, 1807, two bonds, one payable in eighteen months and the other in two years, which bonds had not been paid. The plaintiffs, subsequently, were discharged under the insolvent act. The judge charged that the two bonds amounted in law to the payment of the notes, but the jury found a verdict for the defendants. On the motion for a new trial, the court said: "The question is whether giving a bond, in discharge of the

---

[63] Taylor *v.* Higgins, 3 East, 160.

[64] No attenton appears to have been paid to the payment of the costs. This case was sustained in Maxwell *v.* Jame-

son, 2 B. & Ald. 51, noticed more fully hereafter.

[65] Cumming *v.* Hackley, 8 Johns. 202.

liability of the plaintiffs, is to be considered as a payment of money. . . . . An obligation to pay is not the same thing as the actual payment. A bond has no analogy to cash. . . . . The technical rule operates with perfect justice in this case; for the bond has not, and never will be paid, as the plaintiffs have since been discharged under the insolvent act; and if the money now demanded was to be recovered, their estate would receive it without ever having given an equivalent."

The motion for a new trial was denied.

The rule laid down in this case appears to be the same where a mortgage is given. So where an accommodation indorser gave a mortgage to secure his debt, and subsequently released the equity of redemption, and made a conveyance of the land, the case of Cumming v. Hackley was cited with approbation; and it was held that though the conveyance gave a right of action, the mortgage furnished no basis of claim.[66] ** Where a surety on administrator's bond himself became administrator on the resignation of the defendant, and included the balance due from the defendant in his inventory, it was held that this was a payment of the debt and he might recover from the principal.[67]

§ 797. Payment by note.

* A different rule has been adopted, where the payment, if such it can be called, is made by giving a note. Where the plaintiff became security for the defendant's subscription to a brewers' benefit club, the club called on the plaintiff, and he gave his note for the amount of the subscription.[68] On the trial of the cause, it being an action of assumpsit for money paid, and the objection being taken that the giving a note was no payment, Lord Kenyon held: "That the club having consented to take the note from the plaintiffs, it was as payment to them of the money due by the defendant; and so the action

---

[66] Ainslie v. Wilson, 7 Cow. 662.
[67] Hazelton v. Valentine, 113 Mass. 472.
[68] Barclay v. Gooch, 2 Esp. 571. This case was referred to by the court, in Taylor v. Higgins, 3 East, 169; but Lord Ellenborough did not commit

himself to the correctness of the decision. "*Supposing*, even," he says, "the case of the note of hand or bill of exchange, as the current representative of money, to have been rightly decided, still," etc.

was maintainable." It is added, that at the next term a new trial was moved for; but the court agreeing with his lordship, the rule was refused.

This authority was much shaken by a subsequent case.[69] It was an action for contribution. The plaintiffs and defendants united in a promissory note to Batson & Co.; Maxwell took up the note, by giving his own bond to Batson & Co. for the amount. No money was paid. On this state of facts Maxwell sued Jameson in *assumpsit for money paid.*** The court held that since there had been no discharge of the note, and no money had yet come out of the plaintiff's pocket, the action could not be maintained.

These cases leave the rule in England in a very unsettled state.[70]

* In this country, however, the original decision of Barclay *v.* Gooch has been followed, both in New York and Massachusetts. In a case already cited,[71] the case of Barclay *v.* Gooch was referred to by the Supreme Court of New York, with a qualified approbation. "There are some cases," they say, "in which the giving negotiable paper has been held equivalent to the payment of money; and there may be some reason for this distinction (*i. e.*, between bonds and notes), for otherwise a party may be obliged to pay a debt twice, if the paper should pass into the hands of an innocent indorsee."

The precise point came up subsequently for adjudication in an action of assumpsit for money paid.[72] The plaintiff became surety for the defendants in a promissory note to one Vanderlyn, on which judgment was recovered. The plaintiff thereupon gave his negotiable note for the amount of the judgment. This had been accepted by Vanderlyn in full satisfaction, but it remained unpaid. The judge having charged in favor of the plaintiff's right to recover, and a verdict being obtained, a motion was made for a new trial; but this was refused by the court.

[69] Maxwell *v.* Jameson, 2 B. & Ald. 51.

[70] In McVicar *v.* Royce, 17 Up. Can. Q. B. 529, it was attempted to reconcile these cases upon the ground that in the two latter it did not appear that the obligation of the surety was taken in payment.

[71] Cumming *v.* Hackley, 8 Johns. 202.

[72] Witherby *v.* Mann, 11 Johns. 518. See also Beardsley *v.* Root, 11 Johns. 464, 6 Am. Dec. 386.

In another case [73] which came up on error from the New York Common Pleas, Hedden, the plaintiff below, by way of accommodation for Rodman indorsed a note on the 30th of August, 1819, for $118, payable in sixty days. In July, 1820, a judgment was obtained against Hedden, as indorser, by one Jacot; in October, 1820, Hedden paid $20 on account of this judgment; on the 26th of May, 1821, $100 more, and gave his note for $28.10, which was accepted by Jacot in full payment and satisfaction of the judgment. The note for $28.10 was paid by Hedden on the 28th of July, 1821, previous to which (on the 25th of July, 1821), Rodman had left the State of New York, and did not return till 1830, when the suit was brought. The note for $28.10 was thus given and accepted in satisfaction *before* the defendant, Rodman, left the State, but not paid till *after* his departure. The defendant set up the statute of limitations, insisting that the plaintiff's cause of action accrued when the original notes made by Rodman with Hedden's indorsement came to maturity, and that, as the defendant was then in the State, the statute had attached, and the claim was consequently barred. This defence was unsuccessful in the Common Pleas, and the plaintiff had a verdict and judgment; to reverse which, error was brought, and the judgment was reversed.[74] So where agreements had been given by the defendants as principals, to pay or save harmless, and the plaintiffs as sureties, after verdict, had given their negotiable note for the debts and costs, it was held that the verdict was evidence against the principals, though without notice, and that the negotiable note, given and accepted in full satisfaction and discharge, was equivalent to the payment of cash; the court adding: "So it would now probably be holden of a note not negotiable." [75] And the rule appears to be the same in Massachusetts.[76] **

[73] Rodman v. Hedden, 10 Wend. 498.
[74] This is a hard case, and evinces a determination to carry the rule to its greatest extent. And it is to be noticed that the judgment was reversed on a ground that by the report does not appear to have been taken at all at the trial. The defendant there insisted that the plaintiff's cause of action accrued when the original notes set forth in the declaration came to maturity— *i. e.*, Nov., 1819, and April, 1820. The court, however, disregarding this line of defence, decided that the cause of action accrued on the acceptance of the note by Jacot—*i. e.*, 28th of May, 1821 —which point does not appear to have been raised below.

[75] Lee v. Clark, 1 Hill, 56.
[76] Cornwall v. Gould, 4 Pick. 444;

The rule thus established is almost universally followed in this country,[77] and it is held that where a surety pays the debt

Doolittle *v.* Dwight, 2 Met. 561. So in England: Drake *v.* Mitchell, 3 East, 251.

[77] It is proper to notice that the American rule, as applicable to negotiable paper—*i. e.*, that when given by a surety or secondary debtor, and accepted by the creditor in full satisfaction of his demand, it gives at once a right of action against the principal debtor—is also the rule of the civil law. *La caution,* says Pothier, in his *Traité des Obligations,* part ii, ch. 6, section 7, art. 1, §§ 1 & 2, ed. of 1781, vol. 1, 212, *a recours contre le débiteur principal après qu'elle a payé.*—*Il y a même des cas auxquels la caution a action contre le débiteur principal, même avant qu'-elle ait payé;* and again, *Il n'importe que le paiement ait été une paiment réel, ou une compensation, ou une novation* This term, *novation,* is defined by Crivelli: *de novatio, convention nouvelle. On appelle de ce nom, en termes de droit, le changement d'un contrat en une autre, et par lequel il est derogué au premier. Dictionnaire du Droit Civil, in voc.* All the cases which we have just examined in the text, where bonds or notes were given to extinguish prior obligations, would, according to the civil or French law, be novations. *En tous ces cas,* continues Pothier, *la caution a droit de demander que le débiteur principal la rembourse, soit de la somme qu'-elle a payée, soit de celle qu'elle a compensée, soit de celle qu'elle s'est obligée de payer pour éteindre l'obligation du principal débiteur.*

The French Code also recognizes the right of the surety to proceed against the debtor before payment, and carefully defines the cases in which it is to be exercised. The provisions are as follows:

Art. 2028. *La caution qui a payé a son recours contre le débiteur principal,* *soit que le cautionnement ait été donné au su ou à l'insu débiteur.* Art. 2032. *La caution même avant d'avoir payé put agir contre le débiteur pour être par lui indemnisée.*

1. *Lorsqu'elle est poursuivie en justice pour le paiement.*

2. *Lorsque le débiteur a fait faillite, ou est en déconfituse.*

3. *Lorsque le débiteur s'est obligé de lui rapporter sa décharge dans un certain temps.*

4. *Lorsque la dette est devenue exigible par l'échéance du terme sous lequel elle avait été contractée.*

5. *Au bout de dix années, lorsque l'obligation principale n'a point de terme fixe d'échéance, à moins que l'obligation principale, telle qu'une tutelle, ne soit de nature à pouvoir être éteinte avant un temps détermine.*

It is to be borne in mind, however, that the courts of France follow the course of the civil law, and that there is no division of jurisdictions.

The enumeration of *cautions* under the French Code is not confined to the mere money paid. 2028. *La caution a aussi recours pour les dommages et intérêts, s'il a lieu.*

L'engagement des débiteurs envers leurs cautions n'est pas compris, says Toullier, *sous la règle* (1153); *car ce n'est pas de l'argent que les débiteurs doivent à leurs cautions: ils doivent les indemniser des dommages qu'elles pourront suffrir de la part du créancier qui n'est pas payé, comme s'il fait saisir leurs biens. Ainsi, l'indemnité que le débiteur doit à sa caution l'oblige, sans qu'il soit besoin de stipulation aux dommages et intérêts qui resulteraient de la saisse et vente des biens de la caution.* Toullier, vol. 6, 280, *des Contrats.*

This would not be so with us, as has already been said, unless the surety held a contract to indemnify and save

of his principal with his own negotiable note, *which is received in satisfaction of the debt,* he may sue at once and recover the amount of his note of the principal,[78] or contribution from a co-surety.[79]

§ 798. Note must be accepted as payment.

* It is to be borne in mind, however, in all these cases, that it is essential that the note should be given and accepted by the creditor as full payment and in complete satisfaction.[80] This has been repeatedly decided. So where an action of covenant was brought [81] by plaintiffs, who had sold the defendants certain coal mines, for which they covenanted to pay a sum certain in instalments, the defendants pleaded payment of part, and a bill of exchange given for *payment and in satisfaction* of the residue on which judgment had been recovered, and to this plea the plaintiff demurred; it was held bad, because it was not averred that *the bill was accepted in satisfaction, nor that it had produced it;* that, not having been accepted as satisfaction for the debt, the bill could only operate as a collateral security; and that, therefore, the plaintiff might resort to his original

him harmless. In the case of a suretyship arising by implication, or without a contract to indemnify, the recovery is limited strictly to the money paid for the use of the principal.

[78] *Arkansas:* Bone *v.* Torry, 16 Ark. 83.

Georgia: Mims *v.* McDowell, 4 Ga. 182, 48 Am. Dec. 221.

Indiana: White *v.* Miller, 47 Ind. 385; (but see Romine *v.* Romine, 59 Ind. 351).

Kansas: Rizer *v.* Callen, 27 Kan. 339.

New Hampshire: Pearson *v.* Parker, 3 N. H. 366.

New York: Elwood *v.* Deifendorf, 5 Barb. 398, 410.

South Carolina: Peters *v.* Barnhill, 1 Hill, 234.

Contra, North Carolina: Brisendine *v.* Martin, 1 Ired. L. 286.

[79] *Alabama:* Pinkston *v.* Taliaferro, 9 Ala. 547.

Arkansas: Anthony *v.* Percifull, 8 Ark. 494.

California: Stone *v.* Hammell, 83 Cal. 547, 23 Pac. 703, 17 Am. St. Rep. 272, 8 L. R. A. 425 (*semble*).

Illinois: Ralston *v.* Wood, 15 Ill. 159, 58 Am. Dec. 604.

Indiana: Keller *v.* Boatman, 49 Ind. 104; White *v.* Carlton, 52 Ind. 371.

Kentucky: Robertson *v.* Maxcey, 6 Dana, 101; Stubbins *v.* Mitchell, 82 Ky. 535.

Missouri: Ryan *v.* Krusor, 76 Mo. App. 496.

Contra, North Carolina: Brisendine *v.* Martin, 1 Ired. L. 286; Nowland *v.* Martin, 1 Ired. L. 307.

In Bell *v.* Boyd, 76 Tex. 133, 13 S. W. 232, contribution was refused where the new note was that of the principal and surety; but the general rule was recognized.

[80] White *v.* Miller, 47 Ind. 385.

[81] Drake *v.* Mitchell, 3 East, 251.

remedy on the covenant; and, said Le Blanc, J.: "The giving of another security, which in itself would not operate as an extinguishment of the original one, cannot operate as such by being pursued to judgment, unless it produce the fruit of a judgment." The principle of this case has been repeatedly recognized in New York,[82] where it is held that a note is not payment of a precedent debt, unless there is an express agreement to receive it as payment.[83]

In another case, in New York,[84] the doctrine that negotiable notes are to be considered as money, has been restricted to cases where the notes have been parted with to *bona fide* holders for value. The plaintiff, Reed, bought of the defendants a threshing-machine, and gave three negotiable notes of $200 each for the purchase-money. The machine proving worthless, the plaintiff brought an action for *money paid* against the defendants. A verdict was obtained, but it was set aside and a new trial granted, the court, by Savage, C. J., saying: "Had the notes in question been given to a third person in payment and discharge of a debt due by the defendants to such third person, then the case would have come within previous decisions. But I cannot find that the giving a note ever has been considered, as between maker and payee, the payment of money by the former to the latter. In my judgment, the mere giving a note cannot be considered payment of the very money for

---

[82] Witherby *v.* Mann, 11 Johns. 518; Tobey *v.* Barber, 5 Johns. 68, 4 Am. Dec. 326; Johnson *v.* Weed, 9 Johns. 310, 6 Am. Dec. 279.

[83] In Massachusetts it would seem that, in some cases, this express agreement is inferred from the mere fact of giving a negotiable note.

The giving a negotiable note for a debt on a simple contract raises a legal presumption that the note was received in payment, and will operate as a discharge of the simple contract, unless the presumption be controlled by evidence of a contrary intent. Thacher *v.* Dinsmore, 5 Mass. 299, 4 Am. Dec. 61; Maneely *v.* M'Gee, 6 Mass. 143, 4 Am. Dec. 105; Huse *v.* Alexander, 2 Met.

157. So, also, in that State it is held, in an action by the indorsee against the maker of a negotiable note, indorsed when overdue, that a negotiable note made to the defendant by the payee, intended as a payment of the note, may be shown in defence as a set-off. Holland *v.* Makepeace, 8 Mass. 418, 5 Am. Dec. 107; Sargent *v.* Southgate, 5 Pick. 312, 16 Am. Dec. 409. "A negotiable promissory note, by the common law of this State, is holden to be a discharge of a simple contract on which it is founded." Emerson *v.* Prov. H. M. Co., 12 Mass. 237.

[84] Van Ostrand *v.* Reed, 1 Wend. 424, 430.

which such note is given as security, so as to justify a recovery of it by the maker against the payee."

In a more recent action, in the same State, where the facts hypothetically put by the court in the case last cited, were actually presented, the notes having been transferred to a *bona fide* holder for value, the plaintiff was held entitled to recover as for money paid and received.[85] **

§ 799. Payment by bond or non-negotiable note.

It is held in some jurisdictions that payment by any obligation of the surety other than a negotiable promissory note, though accepted in satisfaction of the debt, will not give an immediate right of action to the surety; [86] and the attempt is made to reconcile the English cases upon this distinction. Most of the cases recognize no such distinction; and in some cases it is expressly denied.[87] There seems no foundation for it, and it indeed appears to have arisen from the form of action brought by the surety. The action was usually brought on a count for money paid, and the courts making the distinction were averse to allowing that count to lie when neither money nor a negotiable note had been given. It is needless to say that a distinction founded entirely upon the form of action should not be supported at the present time. The cases allowing an action where payment has been made by the property of the surety, now to be considered, seem opposed to it.

§ 800. Payment in land or goods.

* It remains to be seen how far the conveyance or transfer of land or other property in discharge of a pecuniary liability furnishes the surety an action against his principal.

In an action of assumpsit for money paid,[88] the defendant, on the 12th of April, 1817, obtained from the plaintiffs their indorsement on two notes, each for $2,059.35. The notes were

[85] Colville *v.* Besly, 2 Denio, 139.

[86] *Indiana:* Bennett *v.* Buchanan, 3 Ind. 47.

Pennsylvania: Morrison *v.* Berkey, 7 S. & R. 238.

South Carolina: Peters *v.* Barnhill, 1 Hill, 237.

Texas: Boulware *v.* Robinson, 8 Tex. 327, 58 Am. Dec. 117.

[87] *Kentucky:* Robertson *v.* Maxcey, 6 Dana, 101.

Canada: McVicar *v.* Royce, 17 Up. Can. Q. B. 529.

[88] Ainslie *v.* Wilson, 7 Cow. 662, 668.

indorsed to John B. Murray & Son, then again indorsed over, and paid by the subsequent indorser. The plaintiffs executed to the Murrays a mortgage on four lots (subject to a previous mortgage for $1,770), as a security for the indorsements, and subsequently released the equity of redemption to the Murrays, who received the release as payment of $1,200 on the plaintiffs' indorsement, and discharged them from all further liability as indorsers. Evidence was taken as to the value of the lots, and the jury found for the plaintiffs $804.45. On a motion for a new trial, it was contended that the conveyance of land would not sustain an action for money paid; but the court, after deciding that under Cumming v. Hackley,[89] and Taylor v. Higgins,[90] the mortgage was no payment, used this language, as to the release of the equity of redemption: "We have no doubt that, as the conveyance of the land was received in discharge of a money debt due from the plaintiff, it is in judgment of law to be considered the same thing as if the plaintiff had actually paid money. The Murrays received it as money, or an equivalent for money. They had the right of electing. To the defendant it was immaterial whether the payment was made in one way or the other." And a new trial was denied. This case, however, leaves the question open as to the rate at which land under such circumstances is to be taken. The court say: "There is some question whether the equity of redemption, taken subject to the previous mortgage, was equal in value to the $1,200. The jury found $804.45 only; and, from the evidence, we think they were warranted in finding that amount." This would seem to imply that the actual and not the agreed value of the land is to be the guide. Nor does the question appear to have been raised how far the maker and principal debtor, Wilson, the defendant, was benefited by this transaction. The court say, that on the conveyance of the land at the agreed valuation of $1,200, and the release of the plaintiff, Ainslie, "the remainder due on the notes constituted a valid claim in favor of the Murrays, against Wilson, the maker." But is it clear that the claim of the Murrays as against Wilson was good for *only* the remainder? If the Murrays had sued Wilson on the note, what, as between them, would have been

---

[89] 8 Johns. 202.   [90] 3 East, 169.

the measure of damages? Could, in such an action, Wilson have had the benefit of the valuation of the land at $1,200 to which he was not privy? As between the Murrays and Wilson, was the land satisfaction for anything more than it was actually worth? What if it had been foreclosed under the first mortgage, and no surplus realized, would Wilson have still had the benefit of the $1,200 agreement?

In a subsequent case,[91] where the plaintiff, an accommodation maker, had paid the defendant's debt, after judgment recovered for $401.61, by a conveyance of land for a consideration expressed in the deed of $548.31, it was held, after affirming the main point decided in the last case, that the defendant was at liberty to reduce the amount of the recovery by showing that the land conveyed in satisfaction of the judgment was not of value equal to the amount of the note and interest; and, this evidence having been excluded at the circuit, a new trial· was ordered.** So where the land of the surety was sold on execution by the creditor, he may maintain an action; [92] and the same was held where a mortgage of the surety's land was accepted as payment.[93]

The same doctrine has been declared in Massachusetts. So under a plea of payment in an action of debt on judgment, the defendant is not confined to evidence of payment in money, but he may show that a chattel or deed of land was given and received in satisfaction of the judgment. He must, however, prove that the thing received was of the full value of the debt, or that it was agreed to be received as such.[94] So where the promissory note of a third party was indorsed by the surety and received by the creditor in payment of the debt, the surety may at once maintain an action,[95] and the same is true where a note and mortgage of a third party is transferred by the surety to the creditor in payment.[96] But taking possession of a mortgaged estate for the purpose of foreclosure, does not operate

---

[91] Bonney v. Seely, 2 Wend. 481.
[92] Lord v. Staples, 23 N. H. 448.
[93] McVicar v. Royce, 17 Up. Can. Q. B. 529.
[94] Howe v. Mackay, 5 Pick. 44; and the same rule was laid down in Presi-

dent of Newburyport Bank v. Stone, 13 Pick. 420.
[95] Hommell v. Gamewell, 5 Blackf. (Ind.) 5.
[96] Fahey v. Frawley, 26 L. R. Ir. 78.

as a payment of the mortgage money; for the land still remains only a security for the money.[97]

§ 801. Compensation for actual loss only.

In contracts of indemnity as elsewhere the ordinary rule is that actual compensation can only be given for actual loss,[98] and that a surety who pays the debt of his principal for less than its face can recover only the amount he paid.[99] And where the plaintiffs had sold the defendants three-sixteenths of a steamboat, the rest of which was owned by third parties, taking from the defendants an agreement to indemnify them against "all liability of loss" on account of the debts of the boat, it was held, in an action brought by the plaintiffs to recover the amount of a judgment against them for a debt of the boat, that they could not recover more than three-sixteenths of it until they had shown that they could not compel the other part owners, because of insolvency or for some other good cause, to contribute their proportion.[100] So in an action by a sheriff against a surety in an indemnity bond given on an attachment, he is entitled to recover the whole amount of costs paid by him in the successful defense of an action brought against him by a claimant of the goods attached, and not merely a proportionate share, though other creditors who did not indemnify received the surplus proceeds of the goods attached after satisfying the indemnifying creditors.[101] And

[97] West v. Chamberlin, 8 Pick. (Mass.) 336.

[98] See Willson v. McEvoy, 25 Cal. 169, where the cases are reviewed, and the principle above stated approved.

[99] *Illinois:* Coggeshall v. Ruggles, 62 Ill. 401 (*semble*).

Indiana: Gieseke v. Johnson, 115 Ind. 308, 17 N. E. 573; Goodwin v. Davis, 15 Ind. App. 120, 43 N. E. 881.

Louisiana: Pickett v. Bates, 3 La. Ann. 627.

Maryland: Martindale v. Brock, 41 Md. 571.

Nebraska: Eaton v. Lambert, 1 Neb. 339.

New Jersey: Delaware, L. & W. R. R. v. Oxford Iron Co., 38 N. J. Eq. 151.

New York: Cobb v. Titus, 10 N. Y. 198.

Virginia: Blow v. Maynard, 2 Leigh, 29.

England: Ex parte Rushforth, 10 Ves. 409; Butcher v. Churchill, 14 Ves. 567; Reed v. Norris, 2 My. & Cr. 361.

But see *contra*, Fowler v. Strickland, 107 Mass. 552, where an accommodation indorser having taken up a note for half its value was allowed to recover the face value from the maker. The attention of the court does not seem to have been called to the fact that the indorser was a surety.

[100] Ewing v. Reilly, 34 Mo. 113.

[101] Chamberlain v. Bellar, 18 N. Y. 115, 72 Am. Dec. 498.

upon the same principle it is held that a surety who has paid
the principal's debt in depreciated currency can only recover
the value at the time of the payment, with interest.[102]   And
a surety to a bond indemnifying a sheriff from damage can
show that he received a certain sum as proceeds of the sale.[103]
Where both principal and surety were sued, and judgment
recovered, which the surety paid, the principal cannot claim
a reduction in the amount to be repaid to the surety on the
ground that usurious interest was included in the judgment.[104]
But if the surety knew, or should have known, that the claim
was usurious, or that the principal was not bound to pay so
much, his recovery will be reduced by the amount he ought
not to have paid.[105]

§ 802.   Judgment against surety often conclusive on principal.

* It has been sometimes held that the record of judgment
against the surety is conclusive evidence against his principal,
and fixes the amount of recovery.   So in an action by the sheriff
against the sureties in a bond to the jail liberties, it was held
that the sheriff, having given notice to the defendants of the
escape suit against himself, and they having thereupon assisted
in its defense, the record of the recovery in that suit was conclusive evidence that the plaintiff had been damnified to the

---

[102] *Arkansas:* Jordan *v.* Adams, 7
Ark. 348.

Kentucky: Miles *v.* Bacon, 4 J. J.
Marsh, 457; Crozier *v.* Grayson, 4 J. J.
Marsh, 514.

Maryland: Gillespie *v.* Creswell, 12
G. & J. 36.

Virginia: Kendrick *v.* Forney, 22
Gratt. 748.

West Virginia: Butler *v.* Butler, 8
W. Va. 674; Feamster *v.* Withrow, 9
W. Va. 296.

In Southall *v.* Farish, 85 Va. 403, 7
S. E. 534, 1 L. R. A. 641, the surety
paid a claim of the principal with
certificates of deposit in a bank which
were worth less than par, under an
agreement with the principal that he
would pay the face of the deposits. It

was held that, while usually a surety
can recover no more than the value he
paid, yet where there is an express
agreement by the principal, as here, he
may recover the greater amount.

[103] O'Brien *v.* McCann, 58 N. Y.
373.

[104] *Michigan:* Thurston *v.* Prentiss,
1 Mich. 193.

Tennessee: Wade *v.* Green, 3 Humph.
547.

[105] *Georgia:* Jones *v.* Joyner, 8 Ga.
562 (*semble*).

Kentucky: Lucking *v.* Gegg, 12 Bush.
298.

South Carolina: Sloan *v.* Gibbes, 56
S. C. 480, 35 S. E. 408, 76 Am. St. Rep.
559.

extent of the judgment.[106] So again, in an action by overseers of the poor on an order of bastardy to recover against the putative father the weekly sum directed to be paid for the maintenance of the child, the order was held to be *prima facie* evidence of the demand, and that it rested with the defendant to show himself exonerated from the payment in order to avoid the recovery.[107]

On this subject a few observations may be permitted. A judgment against the surety may, upon the ground of privity, be proper evidence against the principal, and *vice versa;* but it is manifest that the record can only be evidence of the facts which it declares and that payment is not one of these. The judgment, though perhaps conclusive evidence of the debt being incurred, is no proof whatever that that debt has been paid, or that it ever will be.[108] **

The principle that it is conclusive evidence of the amount of the debt is illustrated by the following cases: In Hare *v.* Grant,[109] the judgment procured against a surety was held conclusive where the surety notified the principal of the action. Where the defendant had failed to carry out, as he had agreed to do, the plaintiff's contracts with a third party, it was held

---

[106] Kip *v.* Brigham, 7 Johns. 168.

[107] Wallsworth *v.* Mead, 9 Johns. 367. "A judgment against the person to be indemnified, if fairly obtained, especially if obtained on notice to the warrantor, is admissible in a suit against him on his contract of indemnity." Clark *v.* Carrington, 7 Cranch, 308, 322, 3 L. ed. 354. "When one is responsible by force of law, or by contract, for the faithful performance of the duty of another, a judgment against that other for a failure in the performance of such duty, if not collusive, is *prima facie* evidence in a suit against the party so responsible for that other." Lowell *v.* Parker, 10 Met. 309, 43 Am. Dec. 436. See also Heard *v.* Lodge, 20 Pick. 53, 32 Am. Dec. 197; Train *v.* Gold, 5 Pick. 380; Foxcroft *v.* Nevens, 4 Me. 72; Hayes *v.* Seaver, 7 Me. 237. In Ver-

mont, if one promise to indemnify another for all damage, etc., which he shall incur in giving up to the promisor a certain horse, and in bringing a suit against the vendor thereof, for fraudulently selling a horse belonging to another, if he fail therein,—if the suit is brought, and the plaintiff defeated, the record of the judgment is competent evidence in a suit against the promisor founded on the promise, so far as to show the bringing and failure of the action; and this, though notice of the bringing of the suit was given to the defendant. But the amount of damages depends on the title to the horse; and as to this the judgment is not evidence. Lincoln *v.* Blanchard, 17 Vt. 464.

[108] Lyon *v.* Northup, 17 Iowa, 314.

[109] 77 N. C. 203.

that the plaintiff could recover the amount recovered by the third party against him.[110] Where a contractor to lay pipes for a town had agreed to be liable for any damages occurring through his neglect, it was held, in Campbell v. Somerville,[111] that the amount of his liability for a personal injury suffered by a third party, was conclusively determined by the judgment recovered against the town by that third party, where the plaintiff himself had defended the action with the town. Where defendant insured goods, making itself liable for the government tax, as well as for the value of the goods, the judgment of the government recovered against the assured was held to determine the amount of the defendant's liability.[112] Where a sheriff levied wrongfully on property, owing to misrepresentations of the defendants, the defendants were held liable for the amount of the judgment recovered against the sheriff by the owner.[113] In this case it appeared that the defendants had taken part in the defence of the action by the owner against the sheriff. Norfolk v. American Steam Gas Co.[114] was a bill in equity brought against the officers of a company, that company having failed to pay a judgment obtained against it as trustee in trustee process. It was held that the plaintiff could recover the amount of the judgment obtained against the company. Where a defendant had made excavations in a sidewalk, by which a person was injured, and the plaintiff (a city) was held liable, the plaintiff was allowed to recover the amount of the judgment obtained against it.[115] Where a sheriff sued for the act of his deputy, who had notice of the suit, the judgment fixes the measure of damages in an action by the sheriff on the deputy's bond.[116]

§ 803. Litigation expenses.

* Having thus examined the rules requiring the surety to pay before he proceeds against his principal, and also discussed the questions that present themselves as to the mode of payment, we have now to examine those cases where the surety

---

[110] Dubois v. Hermance, 56 N. Y. 673.

[111] 114 Mass. 334.

[112] Insurance Companies v. Thompson, 95 U. S. 547, 24 L. ed. 487.

[113] Kenyon v. Woodruff, 33 Mich. 310.

[114] 108 Mass. 404.

[115] Ottumwa v. Parks, 43 Ia. 119.

[116] Kettle v. Lipe, 6 Barb. 467.

is obliged to pay under compulsion of law, or where, by reason of his engagement, he is put to indirect or consequential loss. Where the surety is compelled by suit to pay the debt for which his principal is previously liable, or where a party holding an indemnity against a claim is obliged by legal proceedings to pay the demand in the first instance, the general rule is that he can recover against the principal or indemnitor, not only the amount which he has been obliged to pay, but also his costs incurred in defending the action; [117] ** and also his counsel fees and expenses, at least where he has an express contract of indemnity.[118] * A party who makes, accepts, or indorses an accommodation note or bill for the accommodation of a party thereto, is regarded as a surety, and can charge such party with the costs of a suit for the collection of the note which he may have been compelled to pay.[119] So it has been held, as between the accommodation acceptor of a bill and the drawer; [120] the accommodation indorser of a promissory note, and the maker; [121] as between the indorser of a note com-

---

[117] *Colorado:* Watson *v.* Hahn, 1 Col. 385.

Indiana: Keesling *v.* Frazier, 119 Ind. 185.

Maine: Nutt *v.* Merrill, 40 Me. 237; Ripley *v.* Mosely, 57 Me. 76.

Massachusetts: Lindsey *v.* Parker, 142 Mass. 582, 56 Am. Rep. 709.

Michigan: Knickerbocker *v.* Wilcox, 83 Mich. 200, 47 N. W. 123.

Mississippi: Whitworth *v.* Tilman, 40 Miss. 76.

New Jersey: Apgar *v.* Hiler, 24 N. J. L. 812.

New York: Thompson *v.* Taylor, 11 Hun, 274.

North Carolina: Atlantic & N. C. R. R. *v.* Atlantic & N. C. Co., 147 N. C. 368, 61 S. E. 185, 23 L. R. A. (N. S.) 223.

Ohio: Finckh *v.* Evers, 25 Oh. St. 82.

Texas: Bennett *v.* Dowling, 22 Tex. 660.

Vermont: Downer *v.* Baxter, 30 Vt. 467.

England: Smith *v.* Howell, 6 Ex.

730; Howard *v.* Lovegrove, L. R. 6 Ex. 43.

Canada: Spence *v.* Hector, 24 Up. Can. Q. B. 277.

But see *Kentucky:* Gaines *v.* Poor, 3 Met. 503, 79 Am. Dec. 559.

[118] *Maine:* Ripley *v.* Mosely, 57 Me. 76.

Massachusetts: Lindsey *v.* Parker, 142 Mass. 582, 56 Am. Rep. 709.

Ohio: Finckh *v.* Evers, 25 Oh. St. 82.

England: Howard *v.* Lovegrove, L. R. 6 Ex. 43.

[119] Baker *v.* Martin, 3 Barb. 634.

[120] Jones *v.* Brooke, 4 Taunt. 464.

[121] Hubbly *v.* Brown, 16 Johns. 70. But an indorser of a regular bill of exchange who has been sued by the indorsee, is not entitled to recover from the acceptor the costs incurred in such action. There is no privity between them. Dawson *v.* Morgan, 9 B. & C. 618; King *v.* Phillips, Peters C. C. 350. Nor is the maker liable to pay the indorser his costs if he is sued. "The mere fact of drawing the note does not

pelled to pay, and a party who had agreed to indemnify him on his indorsements.[122] **

A surety is not liable for the costs of a suit against the principal.[123] But where a defendant guarantees the *collection* of a note, he is liable for the costs of an action against the maker.[124] On a bond to indemnify the plaintiff against all costs and claims on account of doing some act, the plaintiff may recover the expense of an unfounded suit brought against him.[125]

§ 804. None where suit was unnecessary.

* We have already had occasion to consider this question in regard to warranties; and it would seem that the liability for costs should depend on the grounds of the original litigation, and the notice given to the party sought to be charged with the costs. It would certainly be inequitable that a party should be obliged to defray the expense of a controversy, either unnecessary in itself, or which he might not have chosen to incur.[126] "No person," says Lord Chief-Justice Denman,[127] "has a right to inflame his own account against another by incurring additional expense in the unrighteous resistance to an action which he cannot defend." In this case, the defendant, as lessee of a certain house, had covenanted with his lessor to put and keep the premises in repair, under penalty of forfeiture, and in his assignment to the plaintiff had covenanted that all the cove-

imply a promise to save the payee harmless from all costs and charges that he may be subjected to as indorser." Simpson v. Griffin, 9 Johns. 131.

[122] Mott v. Hicks, 1 Cowen, 513.

[123] Woodstock Bank v. Downer, 27 Vt. 539.

[124] Mosher v. Hotchkiss, 3 Abb. App. 326; Tuton v. Thayer, 47 How. Pr. 180.

[125] *Louisiana:* Kern v. Creditors, 49 La. Ann. 886, 22 So. 40 (indemnity against attachment on property sold). *New York:* Newburgh v. Galatian, 4 Cow. 340; Beekman v. Van Dolsen, 70 Hun, 288, 24 N. Y. Suppl. 414 (indemnity against former lease); Grant v. Lawrence, 79 Hun, 565, 22 N. Y. Supp. 901 (using patented article).

Oregon: Henry v. Hand, 36 Ore. 492, 501, 59 Pac. 330 (indemnity against liens.)

Vermont: Chilson v. Downer, 27 Vt. 536.

Contra, District of Columbia: Donovan v. Johnson, 13 D. C. App. Cas. 356.

And see *Massachusetts:* Whiting v. Aldrich, 117 Mass. 582.

[126] *California:* March v. Barnet, 114 Cal. 375, 46 Pac. 152 (expense resulting from failure to pay judgment). *Connecticut:* Redfield v. Haight, 27 Conn. 31. *Mississippi:* Whitworth v. Tilman, 40 Miss. 76. *New York:* Holmes v. Weed, 24 Barb. 546; Hallock v. Belcher, 42 Barb. 199.

[127] Short v. Kalloway, 11 A. & E. 28.

nants had been performed. The covenants had not been performed; the lease had become voidable; and the plaintiff having sub-assigned the lease to one Clark, with a covenant similar
to that which he had received from the defendant, was sued
by him (Clark), and obliged to pay £120 to settle the demand,
together with £119 costs incurred in the defence; and it was
held, for the above reason, that these costs could not be recovered over against the defendant. The principle of this decision has been repeatedly affirmed in cases where it has been
held that it is not necessary for the surety to stand suit, in
order to charge his principal. So in New York, where the defendant gave the plaintiff a promise to indemnify him against
an act which proved to be trespass, and the plaintiff being
sued for the trespass gave a cognovit, it was held that, it satisfactorily appearing that the cognovit was not for too much,
he was entitled to recover the amount of the judgment.[128]

So, in Pennsylvania, it has been held that a surety is not
bound to subject himself to costs by waiting till the creditor
brings suit; but he may consult his own safety, provided it
does not involve a wanton sacrifice of the interests of his principal.[129] So, again, in the same State, it is held that a surety
cannot claim reimbursement for expenses unnecessarily incurred.[130] This is in analogy also with the sound rule hereafter to be noticed in regard to real estate—that the vendor
who holds a warranty may surrender to a paramount title,
thereby only assuming the burden of proof that he did not
surrender without just cause.[131] And a very similar decision
has been had in England:[132] it was an action on the case for
running down a ship, in consequence of which the plaintiffs were
obliged to accept the aid of salvors, and were compelled to pay
a large sum of money, and certain costs in addition thereto.

---

[128] Stone v. Hooker, 9 Cow. 154.
[129] Craig v. Craig, 5 Rawle, 91.
[130] Wynn v. Brooke, 5 Rawle, 106.
[131] So in Massachusetts, it has been
said on the subject of eviction, "There
is no necessity for the party holding a
covenant of warranty to involve himself in a lawsuit to defend himself
against a title which he is satisfied must

ultimately prevail. But he consents at
his own peril. If the title to which he
has yielded be not good, he must abide
the loss; and in a suit against his
warrantor, the burden of proof will be
on the plaintiff." Parsons, C. J., in
Hamilton v. Cutts, 4 Mass. 349, 352,
3 Am. Dec. 223.
[132] Tindall v. Bell, 11 M. & W. 228.

It appeared that the plaintiffs, after a negotiation with the salvors, who demanded £150, had tendered £20, and by a decision of the Admiralty were finally obliged to pay £45 damages, and £124 costs. The plaintiffs had a verdict for £45, with liberty to move to increase it by the amount of costs. It was held that it should have been left with the jury to say what a reasonable man would do under similar circumstances; and if the litigation were found to be prudently incurred, then the costs should be allowed; and Parke, B., said: "The parties were in the same situation as if the defendants had entered into a contract with the plaintiffs not to do the wrong complained of. That is not a contract of indemnity." ** Where the sureties on a forthcoming bond refused to pay the amount of the original judgment, and defended an action on the bond, it was held that they could not recover from their principal the costs of the action on the bond.[133]

§ 805. Notice of suit.

* But if the suit be brought against the surety, and there appear good reason to resist the claim, then the further question arises as to notice. Its effect has been thus stated: "The purpose of giving notice is, not in order to give a ground of action; but if a demand be made, which the person indemnifying is bound to pay, and notice be given to him, and he refuse to defend the action, in consequence of which the person to be indemnified is obliged to pay the demand, that is equivalent to a judgment, and estops the other party from saying that the defendant in the first action was not bound to pay the money." And in this case it was held that notice was not essential, and that the plaintiff could recover his costs though no notice had been given.[134]

Its operation has been still more clearly defined by Lord Chief-Justice Tenterden, in an action on a breach of the covenant of title: "The only effect of want of notice in such a case as this is to let in the party who is called upon for an indemnity to show that the plaintiff has no claim in respect of the alleged loss, or not to the amount alleged; that he made an improvident

---

[133] Robinson v. Sherman, 2 Gratt. (Va.) 178, 44 Am. Dec. 381.

[134] Per Buller, J., in Duffield v. Scott, 3 T. R. 374.

bargain, and that the defendant might have obtained better terms, if the opportunity had been given him." This was said in a case where the plaintiff had been obliged after suit to settle with a party claiming under title paramount; and the court said: "As to the costs," incurred by the plaintiff in defending the action, "the plaintiff here had a right to claim an indemnity; and he is not indemnified unless he receives the amount of the costs paid by him to his own attorney." [135] It may, therefore, be said that notice in these cases is not necessary; if given, however, and the defendant neither endeavors to arrest the litigation, nor undertakes to direct it, he will be made responsible for its result; [136] while, on the other hand, the only effect of not giving it, is to throw on the plaintiff the burden of showing that the first suit, the costs of which he claims, was not improperly contested.[137]

This view of the matter has been very fully stated by Mr. Justice Story, on the Massachusetts Circuit, and applied to the subject of reinsurance; [138] and the Supreme Court of the United States has declared, that a judgment against the person to be indemnified, if fairly obtained, especially if obtained on notice to the warrantor, is admissible in a suit against him on his contract of indemnity; [139] and the law has been similarly declared in New Hampshire, on a suit upon an execution bond.[140]

To these general rules an exception was taken by Lord Chancellor Hardwicke as to extents. In an early case, where extent was taken out against a surety to the crown, and after contesting it some time, he paid the claim, and prosecuted his

---

[135] Smith v. Compton, 3 B. & A. 407. Dumoulin considers the question of notice at length, and its effect on the expenses, both in the case when notice is given, and when not given; and when given pending the suit; and as to the motives for not giving: §§ 150–153.

[136] *Vermont:* Brown v. Haven, 37 Vt. 439.

Canada: Spence v. Hector, 24 Up. Can. Q. B. 277.

[137] Mr. Chitty says: "In cases of guarantee, a notice of the claim and action of the creditor against the surety should always be given to the principal, with an intimation (if there be clearly no defence) that the action will be settled unless the party forthwith desire that it be defended; and that he will be looked to for indemnity." Chitty on Contracts, 400; on Guaranties and Indemnities, *in notis.*

[138] N. Y. State Marine Ins. Co. v. Protection Insurance Co., 1 Story, 458.

[139] Clark v. Carrington, 7 Cranch, 308, 322, 3 L. ed. 354.

[140] French v. Parish, 14 N. H. 496.

principal for the amount paid by him, including his expenses, it was insisted that, the debt being a just one, and improperly disputed, the principal should not be charged with the expense of the litigation; but Lord Hardwicke said: "I know of no such distinction"; and then taking notice that an extent is both an action and an execution, and that the surety could not be supposed prepared to pay the claim immediately, he allowed the demand.[141] But the general rule seems well and clearly established, that the principal shall not be subjected to the expense of unnecessary litigation; how the fact is to be arrived at, and on whom the burden of proof lies, will, as has been said, frequently turn on the question of notice. Where bail employed a third party to find the principal debtor, and then, refusing to pay the expenses of the person so employed, was sued and compelled to pay his bill with costs, it was held in a suit against the principal debtor that the bail could recover the sum paid, but not the costs; Lord Ellenborough, at Nisi Prius, saying: "As for the costs of the action which the plaintiff took defence to unadvisedly, he should have either defended that action if the demand was unfounded, or paid the money if it could be legally claimed from him; but having defended that action without foundation, he cannot charge the defendant with the costs incurred in such an improvident defence." [142]

In a case at Nisi Prius, where the plaintiff, an auctioneer, was employed by the defendant to sell an estate, and the title proved defective, the purchaser brought suit against the auctioneer for his deposit; the auctioneer gave notice to the defendant, who refused to defend the suit. The auctioneer then paid the deposit, with the purchaser's costs and his own, and brought suit against the defendant, claiming these costs and the excise duty on the sale. The action was assumpsit for money paid, with the usual money counts, but Lord Ellenborough held that, as to the costs, "there should have been a special count, inasmuch as the right to these costs by the plaintiff was not

---

[141] *Ex parte* Marshall, 1 Atk. 262.

[142] Fisher *v.* Fallows, 5 Esp. 171. No action will lie by bail for his trouble or loss of time in taking a journey to become bail, because he does not undertake the journey as such, or labor as a person employed by the defendant, but he does it as a friend, and to do him kindness. Reason *v.* Wirdnam, 1 C. & P. 434.

so apparent. The plaintiff might have defended the action of his own wrong, and without any authority from the defendant. If he had done so, he would not be entitled to call upon his principal to pay the costs, as they were incurred without his consent;" and, on the ground that the declaration should have been special, the costs were refused.[143] **

* In a case on a guaranty to indemnify the plaintiff against the expense of a commission of bankruptcy, the messenger had sued the plaintiff for his bill of six pounds. The plaintiff defended the suit, and claimed sixty pounds costs paid to the messenger in his suit, and also his own costs; but the claim was denied, Lord Tenterden saying: "I think the defendant is not liable for the costs beyond the writ; a man has no right, merely because he has an indemnity, to defend an action, and to put the person guaranteeing to useless expense." [144] But, on the other hand, where debt was brought by the plaintiff, as sheriff, against the defendants, on a bond given to the plaintiff as surety to the jail liberties for a debtor in execution, it appeared that the sheriff had given notice to the defendants, and that they assisted in the defence of the suit; it was held in New York that the costs of the suit against the plaintiff were properly recoverable against the defendants.[145] ** Where a surety allowed a suit to go by default without notice, he was only allowed to recover the costs incident on the service of the summons, as he should have notified his principal and allowed him to settle without further costs.[146]

* The French law peremptorily requires notice, if the surety desires to charge the debtor with his expenses. Its language is clear: "The surety who has paid has recourse against the principal debtor, whether he entered into the contract of suretyship with or without the knowledge of the debtor. And he shall recover the principal, interest, and expenses; but the surety shall recover only such expenses as are incurred after the princi-

[143] Spurrier v. Elderton, 5 Esp. 1.

[144] Gillett v. Rippon, 1 Moo. & Mal. 406. It is suggested in this case, by Gurney, of counsel for plaintiff, that "notice was given to the defendant, and he might have paid or stopped the action;" but nothing is said of any notice in the statement of the case, which was at Nisi Prius. See Freeman's Bank v. Rollins, 13 Me. 202.

[145] Kip v. Brigham, 7 Johns. 168.

[146] Steinhart v. Doellner, 34 N. Y. Super. Ct. 218.

pal debtor is notified of the suit against the surety; and the surety shall also recover damages in a proper case." [147] **

* The same principles which we have been considering are applied to claims made against sureties; so it has been said, that if one becomes surety for a debtor, the creditor cannot recover from the surety the costs of a fruitless suit against the debtor unless he give notice of his intention to sue.[148] ** In New Hampshire, in a suit by a sheriff on a bond given by sureties of his deputy, conditioned to indemnify him against all loss, damages, and costs, on account of the acts and neglects of the deputy, he is entitled to receive, as damages, in addition to the sums paid by him or his sureties on his official bond to the county to satisfy judgments recovered against him for the default of the deputy, and interest thereon, all such reasonable expenses as were incurred by him in and about the defence of the suits in which the judgments were rendered, including counsel fees and a reasonable compensation for his personal services; and in the suit on the bond the same expenses and compensation for services, beyond the taxable costs, but not the costs or expenses incurred in a suit upon his official bond, brought to enforce payment of such judgment; and upon a judgment in favor of the sheriff for the penalty of the bond, execution will be awarded as well for the damages that may have accrued subsequently to the commencement of the suit upon the bond, as for those prior thereto.[149] So in New York, in an action by a sheriff against the sureties of his deputy to recover damages for the neglect of the deputy to levy on execution, in consequence of which the execution creditor has recovered a judgment against the sheriff, the reasonable expenses of the sheriff in defending the suit against himself are recoverable as a part of his damages.[150]

§ 806. Consequential loss.

On a covenant to indemnify against all damages, costs, and expenses, by reason of a demand, the surety is not liable for a

---

[147] Code Civil, Art. 2028.

[148] Baker v. Garratt, 3 Bing. 56, per Best, C. J. This was an action against the sheriff for taking insufficient sureties on a replevin bond.

[149] Hoitt v. Holcombe, 32 N. H. 185.

[150] Westervelt v. Smith, 2 Duer, 449; acc., Robertson v. Morgan, 3 B. Mon. 307.

premium or bonus which the party is compelled to pay to raise the amount necessary to meet the demand,[151] or for a loss through selling his property at a sacrifice to pay the debt.[152] In an action on an indemnity bond, if the plaintiff states no special damage in his complaint, he is confined in his recovery to such only as arise from the breach, and then such only as are proximate and the fair, legal, and natural result of the act complained of.[153] In a bond of indemnity from loss by reason of suits for infringement of a patent on goods sold by the defendant to the plaintiff, to be retailed by the latter, the plaintiff can recover the deterioration of his goods by attachment in the patent suit, but not for loss of credit by the attachment, or for the expense of a bond for dissolution of the attachment.[154] Where the defendant guaranteed a debt which was secured by a second mortgage on property of the debtor, he was not liable for the cost of foreclosing the mortgage when it appeared that the prior mortgage had already been foreclosed.[155] Where a surety on a stay bond, whose property has been sold in satisfaction of the judgment, moves for judgment against his principal, the measure of his damages is the amount of the judgment paid by the sale of his property, not the value of the property.[156] But in Indiana it was held that where the defendant had engaged "to pay and satisfy the mortgage, together with all interest and costs thereon accrued, accruing, and to accrue, and in every respect" save the plaintiff harmless, the value of the land sold in consequence of the breach of this engagement was held the measure of the plaintiff's damages.[157] In a similar case, the plaintiff was allowed to recover his attorney's fees, expenses, and costs on account of the sale and in proceedings to redeem.[158] Upon a bond to indemnify the plaintiff, a trustee, for loss in paying the defendant's debts, the plaintiff can recover the difference between the market price of bonds sold to pay the debts and the price actually obtained, plus the broker's commissions; but no damages can

[151] Low v. Archer, 12 N. Y. 277.
[152] Vance v. Lancaster, 3 Hayw. 130.
[153] Hallock v. Belcher, 42 Barb. 199.
[154] Ripley v. Mosely, 57 Me. 76.
[155] Peck v. Cohen, 40 N. Y. Super. Ct. 142.
[156] Coleman v. Riggs, 61 Ia. 543.
[157] Atherton v. Williams, 19 Ind. 105.
[158] Kansas City Hotel Co. v. Sauer 65 Mo. 279.

be obtained for a subsequent rise in the value of the bonds.[159]
Upon a bond given to pay all damages of whatsoever nature
and kind, that might be suffered by the construction of a pipe
line, where the construction of the line made it necessary for
plaintiff to remove his business, it was held that the bond by
its terms covered consequential damages for loss of business
suffered by reason of the necessity of removal.[160]   And where
sureties on a bail bond were obliged to pursue and rearrest the
principal, they were allowed to recover the expense of so doing.[161]

§ 807. Co-sureties.

* We have now to consider the relative rights and liabilities
of co-sureties.   The right of action of the surety against the
co-surety or his representatives arises when the surety pays
more than his share of the obligation, and not before.[162]   The
obligation arises out of the relation between the parties, and
does not exist where the suretyship is not joint.   Thus where
the plaintiff signed a bond as surety for another, and defendant
signed as surety for plaintiff, the defendant cannot be called
upon to contribute, but the plaintiff must exonerate him.[163]
Since the recovery rests upon the relationship of the parties,
and suit is not brought upon the debt itself the fact that the
defendant was not liable upon the debt would not relieve him
from the obligation to contribute, if the plaintiff was obliged
to pay.   So if the statute of limitations had run in favor of the
defendant, but the plaintiff was compelled to pay, he may call
on the defendant to contribute.[164]   If however the surety was
not compelled to pay he cannot recover.[165]

[159] Beckley v. Munson, 22 Conn. 299.

[160] Pennsylvania Nat. Gas Co. v.
Cook, 123 Pa. 170, 16 Atl. 762.

[161] Milk v. Waite, 18 Abb. New Cas.
236.

[162] *Massachusetts:* Wood v. Leland, 1
Met. 387.

Tennessee: Gross v. Davis, 87 Tenn.
226, 11 S. W. 92, 10 Am. St. Rep. 635.

Wisconsin: Bushnell v. Bushnell, 77
Wis. 435, 46 N. W. 442, 9 L. R. A. 411.

[163] Cutter v. Emery, 37 N. H. 567.

[164] *Alabama:* Preslar v. Stallworth, 37
Ala. 402.

Maine: Crosby v. Wyatt, 23 Me. 156.

Massachusetts: Wood v. Leland, 1
Met. 388.

New Hampshire: Boardman v. Paige,
11 N. H. 431.

Ohio: Camp v. Bostwick, 20 Oh. St.
337, 5 Am. Rep. 669.

Tennessee: Reeves v. Pulliam, 7 Baxt.
119.

Texas: Faires v. Cockerell, 88 Tex.
428, 437, 31 S. W. 190, 28 L. R. A. 528.

Vermont: Aldrich v. Aldrich, 56 Vt.
324, 48 Am. Rep. 791.

[165] In Russell v. Failor, 1 Oh. St.

§ 807a. Amount of contribution.

The surety is entitled to recover against the co-surety, or, if more than one, against any of them, his aliquot portion of the sum paid, if they are sureties in equal degree. It is possible for sureties to agree in advance as to the share of the debt for which each is to be responsible; and in that case no surety is entitled to contribution except for such amount as he has paid beyond his agreed proportion.[166] If several sureties are bound in different amounts, the contribution is to be determined in proportion to the amount for which each is bound.[167]

The surety's claim for contribution must be based on what he actually paid. So if he discharged the debt for less than its face value, he can recover no more than the proper proportion of what he paid;[168] and if he discharged the debt in a debased currency or by a conveyance of land, his recovery must be based on the actual value of what he gave.[169] So if he paid the

327, 59 Am. Dec. 631, a surety paid a note which was void for usury. It was held that he could not get contribution from his co-surety. But in Ford v. Keith, 1 Mass. 139, 2 Am. Dec. 4, it was held that the surety was not obliged to take advantage of the technical law imposing a penalty for usury, but having paid the debt might recover.

In Harley v. Stapleton, 24 Mo. 248, a surety on a note given for a bet, invalid when given, was compelled by a Mexican judgment to pay. It was held that the surety could not recover contribution, since he was the party to an illegal transaction.

[166] Gourdin v. Trenholm, 25 S. C. 362, 377.

In an action for refusal to contribute to loss suffered in carrying stock, an agreement to *pro rata* the loss or gain was held to mean that the defendants were to share equally with the plaintiff the loss and gain, and not to mean that the defendants were to share among themselves the loss or gain and to indemnify the plaintiff for all loss suffered by him. Penniman v. Stanley, 122 Mass. 310.

[167] Ellesmere Brewery Co. v. Cooper, [1896] 1 Q. B. 75.

[168] *Indiana:* Hall v. Hall, 42 Ind. 585.

Missouri: Hearne v. Keath, 63 Mo. 84.

Wisconsin: Boutin v. Etsell, 110 Wis. 276, 85 N. W. 964.

[169] Edmonds v. Shehan, 47 Tex. 443.

Where the value of the property was agreed on by the surety and the creditor, it would seem that this should be taken as the actual value in the absence of evidence of bad faith. In Jones v. Bradford, 25 Ind. 305, 308, an action by sureties against the co-surety for contribution, where the debt was paid by a transfer of land the Supreme Court of Indiana said:

"The price at which the lands were received in payment would, we think, ordinarily constitute the proper rule in such cases. If they were taken on a compromise of a doubtful claim, or from parties of doubtful solvency, at a price greatly above their value, perhaps the amount on which contribution by a co-surety would be estimated would be the actual value of the lands.

debt without suit, he cannot recover, in addition to the proper
proportion of the debt, any portion of an attorney's fee allowed
in the obligation in case of suit.[170]

§ 807b. Insolvency or discharge of a surety.

If one of the sureties is insolvent, or for any other reason
cannot be made to pay his proportion of the debt, he is left
out of the calculation, and the amount recovered is based upon
the number of solvent sureties.[171] The considerations bearing
on the distribution of the burden between the sureties are well
illustrated by the case of Currier v. Baker.[172] There were several
sureties on a claim. Part payments had been made by A,
one of the sureties, but he had left the state. Other sureties
had died insolvent or left the state. Three were left, plaintiff,
defendant and X. Plaintiff had paid $1,800, X had paid $1,200,
and defendant had paid nothing. Plaintiff had obtained $450
from one of the sureties out of the state and given him a full
discharge from his claim. It was held that this would count
as if the surety out of the state had paid plaintiff his entire
share. A, not having claimed contribution, would be left entirely out of the present settlement. The three thousand dollars paid by plaintiff and X would be shared between plaintiff, defendant, X and the out of state contributory, counting
him as having paid his share of it; i, e., the defendant would
pay a quarter of the whole amount to the plaintiff and X as
their interest might appear. The insolvent estates of the deceased were not to be taken into account since it was as much
the duty of one remaining surety as another to proceed against

---

The lands were the plaintiffs', and
without regard to their cost they were
clearly entitled to the increase in their
value, or the legitimate profits made
by their purchase, not, however, exceeding the amount paid by them on
the debt for which the defendant was
liable."

[170] Acers v. Curtis, 68 Tex. 432, 4
S. W. 551.

[171] Insolvency of a surety:
Nebraska: Smith v. Mason, 44 Neb.
610, 63 N. W. 41.

South Carolina: Sloan v. Gibbes, 56
S. C. 480, 486, 35 S. E. 408, 76 Am. St.
Rep. 559.

Tennessee: Gross v. Davis, 87 Tenn.
226, 11 S. W. 92, 10 Am. St. Rep.
635.

Wisconsin: Faurot v. Gates, 86 Wis.
569, 57 N. W. 294.

Contra, England: Cowell v. Edwards,
2 B. & P. 268.

Absence of a surety: Faurot v. Gates,
86 Wis. 569, 57 N. W. 294.

[172] 51 N. H. 613.

them, and no one having proceeded, they would be left out of the account.

'§ 807c. Interest and attorney's fees.

Since the recovery for contribution is not based upon the original claim, the surety cannot call upon his co-sureties to pay interest at the rate provided in the contract,[173] nor is he entitled to recover attorney's fees allowed in the contract.[174] He is however entitled to interest at the legal rate upon the amount he actually paid out.[175]

§ 808. Costs and legal expenses.

* The question has been examined as to the right of the co-surety to be reimbursed for a proportion of any costs paid by him. In a case at Nisi Prius between co-sureties for a tax collector it appeared the plaintiff had been sued on the principal's default, and judgment had been recovered, and the plaintiff claimed, besides half the verdict against him, half the costs of both parties in the original suit. But Lord Chief-Justice Tenterden held, at Nisi Prius, that the defendant was only liable for half the verdict.[176] No question was made either as to notice or the necessity of the suit, nor, would it seem, could any such question properly arise between co-sureties.

But in a more recent case, in the Exchequer, where the plaintiff and defendant had executed, as co-sureties, a warrant of attorney given as a collateral security for a sum of money advanced on mortgage to the principal, and on default being made by the principal, judgment was entered upon the warrant of attorney, and execution issued against the plaintiff, it was held that he was entitled to recover from the defendant, as his co-surety, a moiety of the costs of such execution, Parke, B., saying: "They were costs incurred in a proceeding to recover

---

[173] *California:* Waldrip *v.* Black, 74 Cal. 409, 16 Pac. 226.

Texas: Scott *v.* Rowland, 14 Tex. Civ. App. 370, 37 S. W. 380.

Wisconsin: Bushnell *v.* Bushnell, 77 Wis. 435, 46 N. W. 442, 9 L. R. A. 411.

[174] Scott *v.* Rowland, 14 Tex. Civ. App. 370, 37 S. W. 380.

[175] *California:* Waldrip *v.* Black, 74 Cal. 409, 16 Pac. 226.

Texas: Scott *v.* Rowland, 14 Tex. Civ. App. 370, 37 S. W. 380.

[176] Knight *v.* Hughes, 3 C. & P. 467; s. c. M. & M. 247.

a debt for which, on default of the principals, both the sureties were jointly liable; and the plaintiff having paid the whole costs, I see no reason why the defendant should not pay his proportion." [177] ** And it is now well settled that the costs and expenses of a reasonable defence of the suit may be included in the settlement, [178] though not the costs of a frivolous defence. [179]

§ 808a. Reduction of surety's claim.

Any fact which goes to show that the plaintiff surety is not equitably entitled to contribution will to that extent defeat his claim. So where he has received a security or indemnity, the amount of it must be deducted and contribution sought for the balance only; security given to one surety inures to the benefit of all. [180] So it may be shown, in order to defeat the claim for contribution, that the surety suing for contribution was indebted to the principal in a larger amount than he was compelled as surety to pay for the principal, and thus

[177] Kemp v. Finden, 12 M. & W. 421. A distinction may, perhaps, be taken between costs incurred in a suit and upon entering up judgment on a warrant of attorney; otherwise these decisions are inconsistent, and if so, the former would seem the more correct in principle; for, as between the indorser and maker of a note, there is no contract to save harmless, and each surety should stand ready to pay the debt.

[178] *Alabama:* Carter v. Fidelity & Deposit Co., 134 Ala. 369, 32 So. 632, 92 Am. St. Rep. 41.

Illinois: Wagenseller v. Prettyman, 7 Ill. App. 192.

Kentucky: Bosley v. Taylor, 5 Dana, 157, 30 Am. Dec. 677.

Maine: Davis v. Emerson, 17 Me. 64.

Massachusetts: Newcomb v. Gibson, 127 Mass. 396.

Michigan: Backus v. Cayne, 45 Mich. 584.

North Carolina: Bright v. Lennon, 83 N. C. 183.

Oregon: Van Winkle v. Johnson, 11 Ore. 469, 50 Am. Rep. 495.

Rhode Island: Conolly v. Dolan, 22 R. I. 60, 46 Atl. 36, 84 Am. St. Rep. 810.

Tennessee: Gross v. Davis, 87 Tenn. 226, 11 S. W. 92, 10 Am. St. Rep. 635.

Vermont: Marsh v. Harrington, 18 Vt. 150; Fletcher v. Jackson, 23 Vt. 581, 56 Am. Dec. 98; Briggs v. Boyd, 37 Vt. 534.

[179] Jones v. Jones, 16 Ala. 545.

So where one of the sureties desired to settle the claim rather than defend the suit, and did in fact pay his share, he could not be held to contribute toward the expenses of litigation. Van Winkle v. Johnson, 11 Ore. 469, 50 Am. Rep. 495.

[180] *District of Columbia:* Gibson v. Shehan, 5 D. C. App. Cas. 391, 28 L. R. A. 400.

Iowa: Hoover v. Mowrer, 84 Ia. 43, 50 N. W. 62, 35 Am. St. Rep. 293.

North Carolina: Carr v. Smith, 129 N. C. 232, 39 S. E. 831.

This is however not the case where the indemnity is received from a third party. So where the principal's wife

defeat the claim for contribution.[181]   And the same principle applies where the judgment against the principal was the result of the wrongful act of the surety.[182]   So where the surety of a corporation was also a director and got hold of money of the corporation which could have been applied to the payment of the debt and misapplied it, and was then forced to pay one of the debts of the corporation, it was held that he could not call on his co-surety for contribution.[183]

indemnified one surety from property not liable for the debt, it was held that the other sureties had no right to share the indemnity. Leggett v. McClelland, 39 Oh. St. 624.

[181] Bezzell v. White, 13 Ala. 422.

[182] *Missouri:* Block v. Estes, 92 Mo. 318, 4 S. W. 731 (as deputy of the principal acted illegally).

Pennsylvania: Eshleman v. Bolenius, 144 Pa. 269, 22 Atl. 758 (negligently advised bad investment).

[183] Simmons v. Camp, 71 Ga. 54.

CHAPTER XXXVII

THE MEASURE OF DAMAGES IN ACTIONS INVOLVING AGENCY

I.—PRINCIPAL AGAINST AGENT

§ 809. General principles.
810. Damages not controlled by form of action.
811. The law fixes the measure.
812. Nominal damages.
813. Actual loss the criterion.
814. Burden of proof.
815. Avoidable consequences.
816. Proximate cause.
817. Agents to insure.
818. Liable only if insurer would have been.
818a. Agents of insurer.
818b. Agents to obtain security.
819. Agents to deal with obligations.
820. Agent makes the debt his own.
821. Agents to sell goods—Unauthorized sale.

§ 822. Sale below price fixed by principal.
823. Sale on wrong terms.
824. Neglect to sell.
824a. Sale at a greater price than that fixed.
825. Agents to purchase—Neglect to purchase.
826. Purchase of wrong goods.
827. Purchase at excessive price.
828. Agents to deal in stocks.
829. Real estate agents.
830. Negligence of directors of a corporation.
831. Attorneys.
831a. Title companies.
832. Auctioneers.
832a. Customhouse brokers.
833. Liability of sub-agents to agents.

II.—AGENT AGAINST PRINCIPAL

§ 834. Indemnity for loss or expense.
834a. Compensation for services.
834b. Damages for failure to employ.
834c. Damages for wrongful discharge—Compensation by a commission.

§ 834d. Compensation by percentage of an amount that can be fixed.
834e. Commissions on insurance renewals.
834f. Commission from both parties.
834g. Discharge of an attorney.

III.—THIRD PARTY AGAINST PRETENDED AGENT

§ 835. Liability for acting without authority.
836. Loss of bargain.

§ 837. Expense of litigation.
838. Incidental expenses.
839. Unauthorized suits.

I.—PRINCIPAL AGAINST AGENT

§ 809. General principles.

Controversies involving questions of agency may arise between a principal and agent, or they may arise between the

1685

principal or agent and a third party. Controversies between principal and agent often involve peculiar questions of the measure of damages. Controversies by principal or agent with a third party, however, seldom involve peculiar questions of the measure of damages. An action, whether by principal or by agent, against a third party is brought either on a contract entered into or a tort committed by the defendant, whose liability to the plaintiff, if it exists, is measured by a general rule of damages. So if a third party sues either principal or agent for the act of the agent, the measure of damages involves no peculiar question, but is determined by general rules. The question of agency involved in such an action is one of substantive law; namely, whether an action lies by or against the principal or agent. Where, however, one party sues the other for falsely representing that he had authority to act as agent, a peculiar rule of damages is involved; and though the defendant is not strictly an agent, the case will be conveniently considered along with cases of agency.

§ 810. Damages not controlled by form of action.

* The class of cases which we now proceed to consider presents some difficulty in regard to the arrangement of the subject, inasmuch as it is impossible, in considering it, to adhere closely to any line of division drawn from the forms of action. Demands made by principals against their agents may be said to arise either from the breach of the agent's contract or from the violation of his duty, and the actions of assumpsit or case under the common-law practice can be indifferently used; in the one instance the proceeding being *ex contractu*, and in the other *ex delicto*. But inasmuch as the amount of damages, in the absence of any circumstance of fraud or other species of aggravation, is in either form of action a question of law under the control of the court,[1] this branch of our subject, as well as that springing from the liability of common carriers, will be considered under the general head of contracts.

In regard to the contract of agency, there is a very interesting class of cases growing out of the liability of the principal for the act of the agent. The maxim of the civil law, *Qui facit*

---

[1] Ashley *v.* Root, 4 Allen (Mass.), 504.

per alium facit per se, and the rule resulting therefrom of *Respondeat superior*, have been adopted in our law to an extent making the principal in many cases responsible for the negligence or want of skill of the party employed by him. There is also a large class of exceptions, where the person, though employed by another, still carries on a separate and independent calling, recognized by common usage; [2] but these cases rather regard the right of action than the measure of compensation; and so we turn to the rule of damages as between principal and agent where a clear cause of action exists.

It will also be observed that the questions embraced under the head which we are now considering, are very closely connected with another very large class of cases growing out of the relation of master and servant.** But questions arising out of this relation have been already considered.

§ 811. The law fixes the measure.

* In some of the early cases growing out of the contract of agency it seems to have been held, with that disregard of any fixed rule which we have had occasion elsewhere to notice, that the jury had an unlimited control over the amount of compensation; [3] thus, in an action against an attorney for negligence, "the jury were told they might find what damages they pleased." [4] But, according to the more precise and much safer view of the subject now uniformly taken in all cases of tort, where no aggravation is proved, the law fixes the measure of damages; and more especially is this true in those cases which we are now considering, where the action, though it may be shaped so as to be technically, and in form, an action of tort, is in reality in all cases, founded on a contract either express or implied. [5] **

* The law is perfectly clear, that wherever an agent violates his obligation to his principal, whether by exceeding his au-

---

[2] Laugher *v.* Pointer, 5 B. & C. 547; Quarman *v.* Burnett, 6 M. & W. 499; Rapson *v.* Cubitt, 9 M. & W. 710; Milligan *v.* Wedge, 12 A. & E. 737; Martin *v.* Temperley, 4 Q. B. 298. In North Carolina, Wiswall *v.* Brinson, 10 Ired. 554. See the subject well dis-

cussed by Mullett, J., in Blake *v.* Ferris, 5 N. Y. 48, 59.

[3] Pope *v.* Barrett, 1 Mason, 117; Courcier *v.* Ritter, 4 Wash. C. C. 549.

[4] Russel *v.* Palmer, 2 Wils. 325.

[5] Bank of Orange *v.* Brown, 3 Wend. 158.

thority, by misconduct or omission, and any damage results to
his principal, he is responsible for such injurious consequence,
and bound to make indemnity.[6] ** In the language of Mr.
Chief-Justice Marshall, "a person acting on commission, who
by his misconduct has brought loss upon his principal, is responsible to the precise extent of the loss produced by that misconduct."[7]

* In a case in the King's Bench,[8] the plaintiffs, who had
shipped certain goods on board the *Mary Stevens*, to be carried
from Liverpool to Trieste, brought their action against the
owners of the ship, on the ground that the vessel had deviated,
and having subsequently been captured, the plaintiffs had thus
lost the benefit of a policy of insurance. The cost price of the
goods, with the shipping charges, amounted to £4,411 13s. 9d.
The plaintiffs had paid for premium of insurance, £720 16s. 6d.
The defendants had paid the plaintiffs the sum of £4,411 13s.
9d., but refused to pay the £720 16s. 6d. And Lord Ellenborough said that the premiums were not recoverable.**

§ 812. Nominal damages.

* We have already seen, that wherever an engagement is
broken, or an obligation violated, the law, in the absence of
the proof of actual injury, infers nominal damage to have resulted from it. In regard to agents, however, language has
been used from which it might be supposed that this class of
cases formed an exception to the general rule, and that unless
positive loss were shown to have resulted from the agent's
illegal act, no recovery whatever could be had. Thus says
Mr. Justice Story, "There must be a real loss or actual damage, and not merely a probable or possible one." And again:
"It is a good defense, or rather excuse, that the misconduct of
the agent has been followed by no loss or damage whatever to
the principal; for then the rule applies, that though it is a
wrong it is without any damage; and to maintain an action,
both must concur, for *damnum absque injuria* and *injuria absque damno*, are equally objections to any recovery.[9] " ** In

---

[6] Laverty *v.* Snethen, 68 N. Y. 522,
23 Am. Rep. 184; Wilts *v.* Morrell, 66
Barb. 511; Story on Agency, ch. viii.

[7] Hamilton *v.* Cunningham, 2 Brock.
350, 366.

[8] Parker *v.* James, 4 Camp. 112.

[9] Story on Agency, §§ 222 and 236.

one jurisdiction it seems to be the present law that in the absence of substantial damage a principal is without remedy against an agent.[10] Story's language was, however, probably used with reference rather to the compensation than the right of action. * No distinction can be taken in this respect between the breach of an agent's engagements and that of any other contract; and if the inference of nominal damage from any illegal act is correct and logical, it should apply uniformly to all transactions embraced within the wide domains of the law.** And it has accordingly been held that, though the principal shows no actual loss he may recover damages;[11] even if the action is in form an action of tort, for it is really an action arising out of the contract.[12] There is, however, a class of cases where, the agency being entirely gratuitous, there is no contract relation between the principal and the agent.[13] If in such case the agent acts negligently it is questionable whether he would be liable to his principal except in case of actual loss.

§ 813. Actual loss the criterion.

* Assuming, then, that in the absence of proof of positive loss, nominal damage will be inferred, we have to consider those cases where actual injury results, and where, as we have said, the agent is bound to make it good. In applying this rule we shall find the distinction taken, to which we have already frequently alluded, between proximate and remote damage. The loss for which remuneration is sought need not be directly caused by the act done or omitted. It will be sufficient if it is

See this passage cited in Blot v. Boiceau, 3 N. Y. 78.

[10] Lancaster Mills v. Merchants' Cotton-Press Co., 89 Tenn. 1, 14 S. W. 317; Deming v. Merchants' Cotton-Press, etc., Co., 90 Tenn. 306, 17 S. W. 89, 13 L. R. A. 518.

[11] Alabama: Bank of Mobile v. Huggins, 3 Ala. 206.

Arkansas: Pennington v. Yell, 11 Ark. 212, 52 Am. Dec. 262.

New Hampshire: Frothingham v. Everton, 12 N. H. 239.

New York: Blot v. Boiceau, 3 N. Y. 78, 51 Am. Dec. 345; First Nat. Bank v. Fourth Nat. Bank, 77 N. Y. 320, 33 Am. Rep. 618.

Tennessee: Collier v. Pulliam, 13 Lea, 114.

England: Van Wart v. Woolley, 3 B. & C. 439.

[12] McLeod v. Boulton, 3 Up. Can. Q. B. 84.

[13] Wilkinson v. Coverdale, 1 Esp. 75.

a natural or a necessary consequence; but remote or merely possible consequences are excluded from consideration.

This principle will be best illustrated by the cases which have been decided; but it may be stated as a general rule, that in all cases of agency, whether the agent be one of private selection or *virtute officii,* whether factor or sheriff, the omission or misconduct of the agent in regard to the matter with which he is charged or intrusted renders him liable to the principal in damages; and where he has been appointed to obtain or receive any given sum of money, or security therefor, and it appears that he was guilty of misconduct, and that the money or security was not obtained, these two facts will, in the absence of other proof, be treated as cause and effect. The negligence will be held to be the cause of the loss, and the sum of money in question or the security therefor will be *prima facie* the measure of damages sustained by the principal. Evidence, however, that such is not the case, that the negligence was not and could not have been the cause of the loss, or that the real damage is less, will throw the burden of proof back upon the plaintiff, and compel him to show the damage he has actually sustained by the neglect of the agent.**

This doctrine was not at first sanctioned in New York,[14] where it was held that if the misconduct of the agent was such as to involve the whole of the property intrusted to him, he should be held to answer for the value of the whole of the property; and the defendant would not be allowed to show that the actual damage resulting from his misconduct was less. The contrary was, however, soon adjudged in an English case,[15] and that case was at once followed in New York.[16]

In a case in New York, the plaintiff, a Pennsylvania bank, sent a draft on a New York firm to the defendant, a New York bank, for collection. The defendant delivered the draft to the drawees, on receipt of their check for the amount; but, through delay in presenting the check, payment was refused, the drawees having failed before its presentation. The defendant thereupon returned the check, received back the draft, and

[14] Le Guen *v.* Gouverneur, 1 Johns. Cas. 437, *n.* (a).

[15] Van Wart *v.* Woolley, 3 B. & C. 439.

[16] Allen *v.* Suydam, 20 Wend. 321, 32 Am. Dec. 555.

protested it. The plaintiff claimed that the defendant was liable for the whole amount of the draft. The court, however, held that an agent "may show in reduction of the damages, that if he had used the greatest diligence the bill would not have been accepted or paid, or that his principal holds collaterals, or has an effectual remedy against the prior parties to the bill:" and here, since it did not appear that the remedy against the drawer was lost, the plaintiff should have been allowed only nominal damages.[17] At a second trial it was proved to have been adjudged, in a suit in Pennsylvania, that the drawer was discharged from liability on the draft; and the New York court thereupon awarded damages against the defendant to the full amount of the draft.[18]

§ 814. Burden of proof.

When the principal shows that through the agent's negligence he has been obliged to pay money, or that his property has been injured or destroyed, it is clear that, unless the agent proves facts that would reduce the apparent damage, the principal can recover the whole amount of his payment, or the whole value of his property. The burden is on the agent to reduce the damages. Thus where an attorney is employed to defend a claim, and negligently fails to do so, the burden is upon him to prove that the defence he was employed to make could not have succeeded.[19] In an action for the price of goods sold by a factor, a verdict for the highest market price is proper, in the absence of proof of the price actually obtained.[20]

But if the principal claims that through the agent's negligence he has failed to secure an expected gain, it seems clear that he should be obliged to prove the actual amount of his loss, and that in the absence of explicit proof of such loss, he should recover only nominal damages. And it is well established that in actions against agents for failure to collect claims, the plaintiff must show what loss, if any, has resulted from the agent's negligence.[21] As Goldthwaite, J., said in Bank of

[17] First National Bank v. Fourth National Bank, 77 N. Y. 320, 33 Am. Rep. 618.

[18] First National Bank v. Fourth National Bank, 89 N. Y. 412.

[19] Grayson v. Wilkinson, 5 Sm. & M. 268, 289.

[20] Clark v. Miller, 4 Wend. 628.

[21] *Alabama:* Bank of Mobile v. Huggins, 3 Ala. 206.

Mobile v. Huggins, a case of suit against an agent for failure to collect a note,[22] "the mere production of a paper, with a name signed to it, promising to pay a sum of money, does not import, necessarily, that the paper has any actual value. Its value depends entirely upon the ability of the parties to comply with what they have promised." [23]

§ 815. Avoidable consequences.

On the principle of avoidable consequences where an agent wrongfully sells stock, the principal can recover only the amount that the stock has advanced within a reasonable time after he learns of the agent's act, and is able to replace it, not the amount it may finally advance.[24]

§ 816. Proximate cause.

* The damage, as we have heretofore had occasion to say, must be proximately caused by the act or omission of the agent, but it need not be the direct result of it. Thus, says Mr. J. Story, "If an agent knowingly deposit goods in an improper place, and a fire accidentally ensue, by which they are de-

Arkansas: Pennington v. Yell, 11 Ark. 212, 52 Am. Dec. 262.

Indiana: Slauter v. Favorite, 107 Ind. 291, 57 Am. Rep. 106.

Iowa: Fox v. Davenport Nat. Bank, 73 Ia. 649.

Kentucky: Eccles v. Stephenson, 3 Bibb, 517.

Minnesota: Borup v. Nininger, 5 Minn. 523; Joy v. Morgan, 35 Minn. 184.

New Hampshire: Frothingham v. Everton, 12 N. H. 239.

New York: First National Bank v. Fourth National Bank, 77 N. Y. 320, 33 Am. Rep. 618; In re Cornell, 110 N. Y. 351 (but see Allen v. Suydam, 20 Wend. 321, 32 Am. Dec. 555; Hoard v. Garner, 3 Sandf. 179).

North Carolina: Stowe v. Bank of Cape Fear, 3 Dev. 408.

Tennessee: Bruce v. Baxter, 7 Lea, 477, 481; Collier v. Pulliam, 13 Lea, 114.

England: Van Wart v. Woolley, 3 B. & C. 439.

Contra, Brown v. Arrott, 6 W. & S. 404; s. c. 6 Whart. 9.

[22] 3 Ala. 206, 219.

[23] The phrase *burden of proof* is constantly used in two different senses. The burden, in every action at law, is upon the plaintiff throughout to establish his case by a preponderance of evidence. In this sense the burden of proof never shifts. But the burden is also said to shift from one side to the other, when what is meant is that evidence as to a particular issue in a given state of the case, must come from one side or the other.

[24] Colt v. Owens, 90 N. Y. 368; Wright v. Bank of the Metropolis, 110 N. Y. 237, 6 Am. St. Rep. 555. But see ante, § 520.

stroyed, he would be responsible for the loss;" and so the Master of the Rolls said, speaking of trustees, "If the loss had happened by fire, lightning, or any other accident, that would not be an excuse for them if guilty of previous negligence."[25]   In these cases, though the loss is not the immediate consequence of the negligence, but of the fire, still it may be truly said that it would not have occurred except from such negligence.[26]   So, if an agent, in procuring a policy of insurance, should so negligently execute his duty as that the risk (for example, a peril of the seas by which a loss was caused) should not be included, although the loss was directly owing to the peril of the seas, still it was proximately owing to the negligence of the agent, and the principal may accordingly recover.** Agents instructed to place the proceeds of a sale in a certain bank deposited them in another, which failed two days later. The principal was allowed to recover all his loss to the value of the deposit.[27]   Where the defendant, entrusted with goods for delivery to a certain carrier, turned them over to another in whose hands they were destroyed, he was held liable for the value of the goods less the insurance money.[28]   Similarly, an agent for sale at a certain place who shipped goods to another locality was, on their destruction by earthquake in transit, made to account for their value.[29]

In a Canadian case [30] the plaintiffs gave orders from Southampton, England, that certain goods purchased by them in Montreal be forwarded to Kingston, to the care of the schooner "Regina." The captain of the "Regina" was unable to wait for the arrival of the property at Kingston, and directed the defendants, forwarding agents, to send it on by mail-steamer and rail to a point where he would pick them up. The goods were shipped by propeller, which was burned with its contents. The plaintiffs' insurance on the property covered only shipment by the "Regina;" because of the change it was cancelled. The defendants were held liable for the value of the goods.

[25] Story on Agency, § 218; Caffrey v. Darby, 6 Ves. 488, 496; Davis v. Garrett, 6 Bing. 716; Wallace v. Swift, 31 Up. Can. Q. B. 523.
[26] Williams v. Littlefield, 12 Wend. 362.

[27] Ernest v. Stoller, 5 Dill. 438.
[28] Goodrich v. Thompson, 4 Robert, 75.
[29] Catlin v. Bell, 4 Camp. 183.
[30] Wallace v. Swift, 31 Up. Can. Q. B. 523.

The court declared an agent's liability for his wrongdoing to be without the ordinary limitation of the rule of proximate cause, but this was clearly a mistaken *obiter dictum.*

§ 817. Agents to insure.

* These questions very frequently arise between merchants and insurance brokers or factors. So in a case [31] where the defendants, in taking out a policy for the plaintiffs, had omitted "a liberty to touch at the Canary Islands," and the vessel having touched there, and been captured, the underwriters refused to pay on the ground of deviation, Lord Ellenborough held that the plaintiffs were entitled to recover a verdict for the sum insured, deducting the premiums. Again, in a case [32] where the defendant, in effecting a policy, had departed from his instructions, and the vessel being lost, the underwriters, in consequence of the agent's neglect were not liable; two of the underwriters for £200 having paid the loss, and a third for the same sum having become bankrupt, Gibbs, C. J., held that the plaintiff was entitled to recover the amount directed to be insured, less the £400 paid, and the £200 subscribed by the bankrupt underwriter; and the plaintiff accordingly took a verdict for the balance.[33]

In a case in New York, where premiums had been paid at Savannah to an agent of underwriters doing business in New York, and a bill was filed against the company to compel the execution of a policy, Mr. Senator Golden said: "Suppose an action had been brought against the Savannah agent for not sending the premium to New York in due time, can there be a doubt but that the appellant would have recovered in a court of law, and that the measure of damages would have been the amount which was to have been insured, and for which the premium was paid?" [34]

Again, if an agent who is bound to procure insurance for his principal neglects to procure any, and a loss occurs to his principal from a peril ordinarily insured against, the agent will be

---

[31] Mallough *v.* Barber, 4 Camp. 150.
[32] Park *v.* Hamond, 4 Camp. 344.
[33] See this case, 6 Taunt. 495, where a new trial was refused, but nothing was said as to the measure of damages.
[34] Perkins *v.* Washington Ins. Co., 4 Cow. 645, 664.

bound to pay the principal the full amount of the loss occasioned by his negligence.**

The English Common Bench seems at one time to have held that the measure of the principal's damages in such a case is a question of fact for the jury, and not a question of law. The consignor sued for loss of freight, and the defendant pleaded, as a plea of circuity of action, that it was the duty of the consignor to insure. The plaintiff demurred; and the question was, whether the damages for failure to insure were measured exactly by the amount of the loss. It was held that they were not so measured, and the demurrer was sustained. Jervis, C. J., and Maule, J., delivered elaborate opinions, the reasoning of which is not clear. The ground of the decision appears to be, that since the amount of loss at the time of the breach of duty could not certainly be said to equal the value of the property, the law can never say that the measure of damages is fixed at that amount. Thus Maule, J., said: "The question is, what damage has the party sustained at the time the cause of action vested in him? If nothing had happened, and a policy might then have been effected, the jury would consider what was probable; if the loss had then happened, they perhaps might have given the full amount, but they were not bound to do so; there were a variety of circumstances which they might properly take into their consideration." [35]

This case has never been overruled, or apparently even noticed, by an English court since it was decided. But, in a later case, the Court of Chancery held the opposite opinion. [36] In that case a bankrupt had failed to insure property of the petitioner, as he should have done, and the property was burned. The petitioner presented a claim for the value of the property, as a liquidated claim provable in bankruptcy, and the claim was allowed. Turner, L. J., said: "I apprehend that the value of the timber would be the measure of damages in an action for breach of the contract." The court of Common Bench, in an opinion delivered by Erle, C. J., noticed this decision, calling it "the sound judgment of Lord Justice Turner," and said of the case: "The amount due for not insuring was precisely the

[35] Charles v. Altin, 15 C. B. 46, 66.　　[36] Ex parte Bateman, 8 De G. M. & G. 263, 268.

same as would have been due for the same quantity of timber sold and delivered. It was held, therefore, to be equivalent to a debt, though technically a right to damages." [37]

This seems to establish the law in England on the true basis. In America it has never been doubted that the measure of damages was the exact amount of the loss. The leading case was on the Pennsylvania circuit,[38] where the learned Mr. Justice Washington charged: "That if one merchant is in the habit of effecting insurances for his correspondent, and is directed to make an insurance, and neglects to do so, he is himself answerable for the losses as insurer, and is entitled to a premium as such. That the amount of loss for which an underwriter who had subscribed the policy would have been answerable is the only measure of damages against him. If he can excuse himself for not having effected the insurance, he is answerable for nothing; if he cannot excuse himself, he is then answerable for the whole." And it appears that, on exception to the charge, this judgment was affirmed in the Supreme Court of the United States.[39] The same point was laid down in another case, by the same able judge,[40] still more broadly: "The law is clear, that if a foreign merchant, who is in the habit of insuring for his correspondent here, receives an order for making an insurance, and neglects to do so, or does so differently from his orders, or in an insufficient manner, he is answerable not for damages merely, but as if he were himself the underwriter; and he is, of course, entitled to the premium." The language of the court above quoted is not to be taken as

[37] Betteley v. Stainsby, 12 C. B. (N. S.) 477, 499; acc., Callender v. Oelrichs, 5 Bing. N. C. 58; Smith v. Price, 2 F. & F. 748.
[38] Morris v. Summerl, 2 Wash. C. C. 203.
[39] See to the same effect the following cases:
Illinois: Chicago Building Society v. Crowell, 65 Ill. 453; Schoenfeld v. Fleisher, 73 Ill. 404.
Indiana: Crissell v. Riley, 5 Ind. App. 496, 503, 30 N. E. 1101.
Louisiana: Area v. Milliken, 35 La. Ann. 1150.

Maine: Storer v. Eaton, 50 Me. 219 (semble).
Minnesota: Everett v. O'Leary, 90 Minn. 154, 95 N. W. 901.
New Hampshire: Ela v. French, 11 N. H. 356.
New York: Gray v. Murray, 3 Johns. Ch. 167; Beardsley v. Davis, 52 Barb. 159.
Canada: Douglass v. Murphy, 16 Up. Can. Q. B. 113; Wallace v. Swift, 31 Up. Can. Q. B. 523.
[40] De Tastett v. Crousillat, 2 Wash. C. C. 132, 136.

meaning that the agent could be sued on the contract of insurance, but that the measure of damages is the amount that could have been recovered on the policy, less the premiums. So where a defendant had agreed to procure insurance for the plaintiff, but before the insurance was effected, the property was destroyed in the Chicago fire of 1872, it was held that the defendant was not liable for the face value of the policy, but only for the amount of dividends which the insurance company contemplated rendered insolvent by that fire, would have declared on a policy of that face value.[41] And the negligent agent cannot claim the premium as an insurer if the ship comes safe to port.[42]

In an action against a broker for negligence or unskilfulness in effecting an insurance, "the plaintiff," says Mr. Sergeant Marshall,[43] "is entitled to recover the same amount as he might have recovered against the underwriters had the policy been properly effected." And so, says Mr. Phillips,[44] the agent "puts himself in the place of an underwriter, and must pay the loss, or the part of it for which the underwriter is not liable, but for which he would have been liable had the policy been made according to the instructions, or in such manner as the principal had a right to expect and require." [45]

The same principle was applied in an action of assumpsit,[46] where the defendants had been employed as factors to settle with underwriters as for a total loss. The defendants adjusted the loss at 20 per cent., and cancelled the policy; and the court said: "If the defendants, as agents or factors of the plaintiffs, have, through mistake or design, disobeyed their instructions, they are undoubtedly responsible, and are to be considered as substituted for the insurers. This was a point conceded on the argument;" and a motion for a new trial on the ground of

[41] Chicago Building Society v. Crowell, 65 Ill. 453.

[42] Storer v. Eaton, 50 Me. 219.

[43] Marshall on Insurance, 4th ed., p. 244.

[44] 2 Phillips' Insurance, 2d ed., p. 566.

[45] *United States:* De Tastett v. Crousillat, 2 Wash. C. C. 132.

New York: Thorne v. Deas, 4 Johns. 84.

Pennsylvania: Miner v. Tagert, 3 Binn. 204.

England: Delaney v. Stoddart, 1 T. R. 22; Wilkinson v. Coverdale, 1 Esp. 75; Wallace v. Telfair, 1 Esp. 76 (cited); Harding v. Carter, 1 Park, Insur., 7th ed., 4.

[46] Rundle v. Moore, 3 Johns. Cas. 36.

excessive damages was denied. Where a life insurance policy
lapsed through the negligence of an agent, the plaintiff recovered its net value at the time.[47]

§ 818. Liable only if insurer would have been.

* But the plaintiff can only have judgment for the same sum
which in point of law he might have recovered on the policy,
and not for any amount which the indulgence or liberality
of the underwriters might possibly have induced them to pay.
So,[48] where the plaintiff had requested insurance to be effected
at Liverpool on certain slaves, and the defendant had neglected
it, it was contended that though the plaintiff could not have
recovered the value of the slaves in an action against the underwriters, yet that in point of the fact slaves were frequently the
subject of insurance at Liverpool, where the loss was always
paid by the underwriters without disputing the question; and
that consequently the plaintiff might recover the value of them
in this action, because by means of the defendant's negligence
the plaintiff had sustained the loss. "But the court were clearly
of opinion that the slaves were not the subject of insurance,
and that the plaintiff could not recover in this action more than
he could have recovered *in an action* against the underwriters." [49] And so, says Mr. Justice Story; [50] "there must be a
real loss or actual damage, and not merely a probable or possible one." So, if the ship deviate, or the voyage or insurance
be illegal, or the principal had no interest, or the voyage as
described in the order would not have covered the risk,—in all
such cases the agent will not be responsible.

Nor will the plaintiff in such an action be allowed the costs
of an unsuccessful suit against the underwriters, unless such
action was necessary, or brought by the direction of the agent.
So,[51] where the plaintiff had been nonsuited in an action against
the underwriters, on the ground of concealment of material
information, and in the suit against his agent, claimed to include the costs of the action on the policy, Lord Eldon said,

[47] Grindle v. Eastern Express Co., 67
Me. 317.
[48] Webster v. De Tastet, 7 T. R. 157.
[49] Fomin v. Oswell, 3 Camp. 357.

[50] Agency, § 222.
[51] Seller v. Work, Marsh. Insur., 4th
Eng. ed., 243.

that there was no necessity to bring that action to entitle the plaintiff to recover in the aforesaid case, and as it did not appear that the action on the policy was brought by the desire or with the concurrence of the present defendant, he ought not to be charged with the costs of it; and this is in analogy to the rule, as we have seen it laid down between principal and surety.**

§ 818a. Agents of insurer.

An agent of an insurance company placing insurance in violation of orders upon a building, which is afterwards destroyed, is liable for damages measured by the amount recovered by the insured from the company with interest and costs, but no allowance is made for the plaintiff's counsel fees in the defense of the action brought by the insured, nor, where the agent has not prompted it, for the expenses of a useless appeal.[52] Damages for failing to cancel a risk are computed on the same principle, as those for wrongfully placing it.[53] The defendant is entitled to his commission on the insurance obtained,[54] but, it has been held,[55] not to deduction for the return premium that the company would have been obligated, on the cancellation of the policy, to pay the insured. For failure to inform the company of facts that rendered void a policy which he should himself have cancelled, an agent has been held liable to his principal to the amount at which settlement was made.[56]

§ 818b. Agents to obtain security.

One employed to obtain security is liable for all loss sustained through failure to obtain proper security.[57] Normally this can be measured by the difference in value between the

[52] Sun F. Office v. Ermentrout, 2 Pa. Dist. Rep. 77.

[53] *United States:* Franklin Ins. Co. v. Sears, 21 Fed. 290.

Iowa: State Ins. Co. v. Jamison, 79 Ia. 245, 44 N. W. 371, 18 Am. St. Rep. 366.

Minnesota: Royal Ins. Co. v. Clark, 61 Minn. 476, 63 N. W. 1029.

Pennsylvania: Kraber v. Union Ins. Co., 129 Pa. 8, 18 Atl. 491; London Assur. Corp. v. Russell, 1 Pa. Super. Ct.

320; American Central Ins. Co. v. Burkert, 11 Pa. Super. Ct. 427.

[54] Franklin Ins. Co. v. Sears, 21 Fed. 290.

[55] London Assur. Corp. v. Russell, 1 Pa. Super. Ct. 320.

[56] American Central Ins. Co. v. Burkert, 11 Pa. Super. Ct. 427.

[57] *Massachusetts:* Coffing v. Dodge, 167 Mass. 231, 45 N. E. 928.

Missouri: Marshall v. Ferguson, 94 Mo. App. 175.

security called for and that obtained.[58] Sometimes, however, it equals the full value of the interest to be secured.[59] An agent to invest money in a mortgage who fails to find a prior incumbrance which is on the land is liable for the loss that results. If the principal discovers and removes the prior incumbrance, the measure of damages is the amount paid to remove the incumbrance,[60] even though part of the land covered by the mortgage was not subject to the prior incumbrance.[61] But if the principal does not discover the existence of the prior incumbrance until the land is sold to satisfy it and lost to him, the measure of his damages is the amount of his loan.[62] Where an agent takes a mortgage signed by a husband alone, without release of dower, he is liable for the actual loss; which would be the amount by which the loan exceeded the value of the husband's interest, but no more in any case than the value of the wife's interest in the land.[63]

§ 819. Agents to deal with obligations.

An agent to collect a claim who fails to do so is accountable in the exact measure of his principal's loss proximately caused thereby.[64] Thus where agents for sale neglected to obtain the cotton in which payment was to be made they were held liable for its value at the time of their breach of duty with interest;[65] similarly a factor receiving and failing to collect notes for the sale of another's property was made to account for principal and interest.[66] In an Alabama case[67] one holding

[58] *Indiana:* Welsh v. Brown, 8 Ind. App. 421, 35 N. E. 921.

Iowa: Lunn v. Guthrie, 115 Ia. 501, 88 N. W. 1060, 91 Am. St. Rep. 175.

Kentucky: Bank of Owensboro v. Western Bank, 13 Bush, 526, 26 Am. Rep. 211.

Massachusetts: Coffing v. Dodge, 167 Mass. 231, 45 N. E. 928.

[59] First Nat. Bank v. First Nat. Bank, 116 Ala. 520, 22 So. 976.

Illinois: Shepherd v. Field, 70 Ill. 438.

Missouri: Marshall v. Ferguson, 94 Mo. App. 175. *Cf.* Lowenburg v. Walley, 25 Can. 51.

[60] *Pennsylvania:* McFarland v. Mc-Clees, 17 W. N. C. 547.

Canada: Harrison v. Brega, 20 Up. Can. Q. B. 324.

[61] Whiteman v. Hawkins, 4 C. P. D. 13.

[62] Shepherd v. Field, 70 Ill. 438.

[63] Slanter v. Favorite, 107 Ind. 291, 57 Am. Rep. 106.

[64] Chapman v. McCrea, 63 Ind. 360.

[65] Dickson v. Screven, 23 S. C. 212.

[66] Bastable v. Denegal, 22 La. Ann. 124.

[67] First Nat. Bank v. First Nat. Bank, 116 Ala. 520, 538, 22 So. 976.

transfers of land certificates as collateral security for a debt deposited them with a bank for collection; the bank lost them. The damages recoverable were held to equal the expenses of making substitution for the documents to no greater amount than the value of the documents as security. Included in these expenses were the cost of legal advice and the investigation of land office records, the amount laid out in a trip to obtain some of the transfer documents from a holder and the costs, expenses, and attorneys' fees involved in litigation to establish the plaintiff's interest in the remainder.

These principles seem best developed in cases concerning the collection of money due on mercantile instruments. If a bank receive a note for collection in another State, and neither collects nor gives the owner notice of non-payment, nor returns it till barred by the statute of limitations, and there be no evidence of the insolvency of the maker, the measure of damages is the amount of the note less the charges for collection.[68]   Where one with whom commercial paper is deposited for collection fails to present it on time he is liable for the difference between the amount due upon the instrument with interest and the amount realized from it.[69]   If owing to the maker's insolvency, nothing

[68] Wingate v. Mechanics' Bank, 10 Pa. St. 104.

[69] *United States:* Hamilton v. Cunningham, 2 Brock. 350, 366.

Alabama: Bank of Mobile v. Huggins, 3 Ala. 206.

Indiana: Tyson v. State Bank, 6 Blackf. 225, 38 Am. Dec. 139; American Express Co. v. Dunlevy, 3 Amer. L. Reg. N. S. 266; Chapman v. McCrea, 63 Ind. 360.

Massachusetts: Whitney v. Merchants' Exp. Co., 104 Mass. 152, 6 Am. Rep. 207.

Michigan: Mitchell v. Shuert, 16 Mich. 444.

Minnesota: Borup v. Nininger, 5 Minn. 523; West v. St. Paul Nat. Bank, 54 Minn. 466, 56 N. W. 54.

Nebraska: Dern v. Kellogg, 54 Neb. 560, 74 N. W. 844.

New Hampshire: Grafton Bank v. Flanders, 4 N. H. 239; Knapp v. U. S. & Canada Express Co., 55 N. H. 348.

New York: Smedes v. Bank, 20 Johns. 372; Hitchcock v. Bank, 57 App. Div. 458, 68 N. Y. Supp. 234; Walker v. Bank, 9 N. Y. 582; First National Bank v. Fourth National Bank, 89 N. Y. 412.

North Carolina: Stowe v. Bank of Cape Fear, 3 Dev. 408.

North Dakota: Commercial Bank v. Red River Valley Nat. Bank, 8 N. D. 382, 79 N. W. 859.

Wisconsin: Merchants' Bank v. State Bank of Phillips, 94 Wis. 444, 69 N. W. 170.

England: Van Wart v. Woolley, 3 B. & C. 439.

In Gray's Harbor Commercial Co. v. Continental Nat. Bank, 74 Mo. App. 633, 638, where the defendant bank's wrongdoing was negligent merely, it

is collected, the measure of the agent's liability is then presumptively the face value with interest, the burden being upon him to show that even had he displayed due diligence, and thereby kept alive the holder's rights against endorsers, the realizable would have proved less than the face value of the papers.[70]

If an agent to collect a bill gives a defective notice of protest, and in a suit against the indorsers they are held discharged, the holder of the bill cannot, it seems, in an action against the agent on his contract, recover the costs of his suit against the indorsers; for, as one court said, the suit was not brought on account of the defective notice.[71] If the agent is to be charged with the costs of the suit, it must be in an action of tort, on the ground that he has falsely represented to his principal that he had given a proper notice.[72] But this distinction seems hardly sound; for it is the duty of the agent, under his contract, to keep his principal informed of his acts.

A collecting agent who by mistake receives less than the amount of an obligation is accountable for the difference between the amount due and that obtained.[73] An agent instructed to make collection in one form of property who receives payment in another is subject to an action for the full value of the claim in the medium of discharge intended[74] and the principal may elect to take instead the property in fact received.[75]

An agent who has made collection is in general to hold the receipts for his principal; for unauthorized dealings with them

was held that the plaintiff was not entitled to interest on the note.

[70] *Nebraska:* Dern v. Kellogg, 54 Neb. 560, 74 N. W. 844.

New Hampshire: Grafton Bank v. Flanders, 4 N. H. 239.

New York: Smedes v. Bank, 20 Johns. 372; Hitchcock v. Bank, 57 App. Div. 458, 68 N. Y. Supp. 234; Walker v. Bank, 9 N. Y. 582.

Wisconsin: Merchants' Bank v. State Bank of Phillips, 94 Wis. 444, 69 N. W. 170.

[71] Downer v. Madison County Bank,

6 Hill, 648; Hitchcock v. Bank, 57 App. Div. 458, 68 N. Y. Supp. 234; *contra,* Smedes v. Bank, 20 Johns. 372 (*semble*).

[72] Downer v. Madison County Bank, 6 Hill, 648.

[73] Kempker v. Roblyer, 29 Ia. 274.

[74] *Illinois:* Rush v. Rush, 170 Ill. 623, 48 N. E. 990.

Mississippi: Mangum v. Ball, 43 Miss. 288, 5 Am. Rep. 488.

[75] Griffin v. Gorman, 13 Ky. L. Rep. 879.

by way of gratuitous disbursement,[76] sale [77] or conversion into
other forms of property [78] the measure of damages is the value
of the interest disposed of. Where a bank collects the amount
due on notes for a depositor, and fails to pay over the amount of
the notes on demand, the measure of damages is the value of the
notes at the time of collection.[79]   In a New York case, the Bank
of Wilmington was the owner of a bill of exchange payable at
sight, at Troy, and indorsed and transmitted it to the Commercial Bank of Pennsylvania, under an arrangement by which
the latter collected and retained the proceeds of paper thus remitted to it, and with the same redeemed the circulating notes
of, and paid drafts drawn by, the Bank of Wilmington. The
Commercial Bank indorsed and transmitted the bill to the
Union Bank of New York, its correspondent in New York,
for collection, and the same was by the latter sent to the Troy
City Bank for the same purpose. *Held*, that the Commercial
Bank of Pennsylvania could recover of the Union Bank of
New York the amount of the bill, if collected by the Troy City
Bank, or if the same were lost by the omission of the latter to
charge the drawer and indorser.[80]   The extent of an agent's
liability to his principal for the wrong-doing of one employed
by himself is a problem in the substantive law of agency. It
has been settled in New York, that on a deposit of the bill of
exchange with a banker for collection in another State where
it was payable, the banker was liable to the holder for any
neglect or omission of duty, in respect of such collection on the
part of his agent or the notary employed by him in the foreign
State; [81] and, on the authority of this case, it has also been decided that where a person undertakes the collection of a bond
and mortgage, and covenants in express terms "*to take proper
means* to collect the mortgage," he is responsible for the default of the solicitor employed by him,[82] and it is probably the

[76] Hancock v. Gomez, 50 N. Y. 668.
[77] Allen v. Brown, 51 Barb. 68.
[78] *Kentucky:* Byrne v. Schwing, 6
B. Mon. 199.
New York: Nunnemaker v. Lanier,
48 Barb. 234.
[79] Planters' Bank v. Union Bank, 16
Wall. 483, 21 L. ed. 473.

[80] Commercial Bank of Pennsylvania v. Union Bank of New York, 11
N. Y. 203.
[81] Allen v. Merchants' Bank, 22
Wend. 215, 34 Am. Dec. 289.
[82] Hoard v. Garner, 3 Sandf. 179;
acc., Butts v. Phelps, 79 Mo. 302.

law that an express company receiving a note for collection at a point beyond the end of its own line is liable for the negligence of its connecting carrier.[83] In all these cases the measure of damages is the actual loss proved to have been sustained, which presumptively equals, where nothing is collected, the face value of the obligation with interest.[84]

An agent to make remittances has a position much like that of one whose duty it is to collect a claim. It was held by Story that in assumpsit against a factor for breach of his promise to render an account damages may not be recovered for failure to remit when the exchange was favorable; there was added a strong intimation that a different form of pleading might have enlarged the recovery.[85] Factors directed to remit bills at sight on "some good house" who did not take reasonable precautions to ascertain the state of the drawee's credit were held liable for loss sustained by their principals to the amount of the bill.[86] Where an agent entrusted with the duty of remitting by one method as by express, substitutes another, and the money is not received, his liability equals the entire sum involved.[87]

The rule that the principal recovery is measured by the loss ultimately caused by the agent's wrong-doing has been applied to other dealings with obligations. An agent to procure acceptance of a draft by a corporation took, with knowledge of its valuelessness, an acceptance from the secretary treasurer alone; the principal recovered the amount of the draft.[88] Agents for the sale at discount of a promissory note by false statements procured an endorsement from the principals; the latter were declared in general terms entitled to damages for the loss sustained through liability on the endorsement,[89] bankers for the plaintiff who agreed, being provided with funds for the purpose, to honor the plaintiff's drafts and who failed to do so

[83] *New Hampshire:* Knapp v. U. S. & Canada Express Co., 55 N. H. 348.

New York: Palmer v. Holland, 51 N. Y. 416.

[84] Hoard v. Garner, 3 Sandf. 179; Palmer v. Holland, 51 N. Y. 416, 10 Am. Rep. 616.

[85] Pope v. Barrett, 1 Mason, 117.

[86] Leverick v. Meigs, 1 Cow. 645.

[87] *New York:* Foster v. Preston, 8 Cow. 198.

Tennessee: Walker v. Walker, 5 Heisk. 425.

[88] Kirkeys v. Crandall, 90 Tenn. 532, 13 S. W. 246.

[89] Bruce v. Davenport, 36 Barb. 349.

were held liable in damages that included the injury to the plaintiff's credit.[90]

§ 820. Agent makes the debt his own.

Where an agent to collect becomes himself the creditor of the debtor, as, for instance, by taking in payment of the original instrument a note in his own name, with the intention of becoming principal creditor thereon, the principal may recover the whole amount of the original instrument from the agent, notwithstanding the subsequent insolvency of the debtor.[91] In a similar case it was said that a bank, acting as collecting agent for another, is liable, in case payment is lost through its negligence, for the full amount of the draft, though the drawee had failed, the defendant bank having become legal owner of the draft.[92]

* In a case in Pennsylvania, where the principal sued the agent for neglect, the neglect complained of was in regard to the liability of the defendant for a debt of one Young, which he had failed to collect and secure. The plaintiff insisted that the defendant had, by his neglect, made himself liable for the whole amount of the debt. The defendant, on the other hand, contended that the plaintiff was bound to prove his actual loss, and that he could recover no more. But the Supreme Court of Pennsylvania held that the burden lay on the defendant, as to the actual loss; and, no such proof being given, that the defendant had made himself liable to the plaintiff for the full value of the goods placed in the hands of Young, or at least for the amount of money produced by the sales made of them. In this decision the court recognized as a general rule, however, that for an agent's omission to keep the principal regularly informed of the agent's transactions and the state of the interests intrusted to him, the measure of damages is to be proportioned to the actual loss sustained; with the exception, where the information transmitted is such as to induce the principal,

[90] Larios v. Bonany y Gurety, L. R. 5 P. C. 346.

[91] *United States:* Jackson v. Baker, 1 Wash. C. C. 394.

Massachusetts: Amory v. Hamilton, 17 Mass. 103.

North Carolina: Symington v. McSin, 1 Dev. & Bat. 291.

Cf. Byrne v. Schwing, 6 B. Mon. 199.

[92] Trinidad National Bank v. Denver National Bank, 4 Dill. 290.

in the adaptation of his operations to his means, to rely on an outstanding debt as a fund on which he may confidently draw, that in such case the agent makes the debt his own.[93] **

§ 821. Agents to sell goods—Unauthorized sale.

Where goods are consigned to an agent with instructions not to sell for a certain time, and the agent sells before that time, he is liable for the difference between the price at the time when the goods were sold and the price at the time when they should have been sold;[94] or the wrongful sale may be treated as a conversion of the goods, and the principal may elect to recover the value at the time of sale. Thus in an action[95] brought by principal against factor, for selling cotton contrary to orders, it appeared that it was sold on the third day of June, and the plaintiff insisted it should not have been sold before the twenty-third of August. The Supreme Court of the United States said: "Supposing the sale made by the defendants on the third of June to have been tortious and in violation of orders, the plaintiff had his election, either to claim damages for the value of the cotton on that day, as a case of tortious conversion, or for the value of the cotton the twenty-third of August following, when the letter of the plaintiff of the twenty-third of July was received, which authorized a sale. If the price of cotton was higher on that day than at any intermediate period, he was entitled to the benefit thereof. If, on the other hand, the price was lower, he could not justly be said to be damnified to any extent beyond what he would lose by the difference of the price of cotton on the third of June and the price on the twenty-third of August."

When a factor intrusted with goods for sale on commission, pledges them for advances made to him, and gives the pledgee authority to sell them to reimburse himself, this is a conversion and the rule of damages to which the principal is entitled is the difference between the value of the goods at the time of the con-

[93] Brown v. Arrott, 6 W. & S. 402; s. c. 6 Whart. 9; Harvey v. Turner, 4 Rawle, 223; Amory v. Hamilton, 17 Mass. 103.
[94] *United States:* Fordyce v. Peper, 16 Fed. 516.

Georgia: Gray v. Bass, 42 Ga. 270.
Mississippi: Thompson v. Gwyn, 46 Miss. 522.
[95] Brown v. M'Gran, 14 Pet. 479, 496, 10 L. ed. 550; acc., Marfield v. Douglass, 1 Sandf. 360 (semble).

version and their proceeds when sold by the pledgee.[96] But in Canada where stock was deposited as collateral, and the pledgee was authorized to sell on default of payment, it was held, when the pledgee sold before default, that the measure of damages was the highest market price of the stock between the time of sale and the time when default was actually made; the rule of highest intermediate value being adopted.[97]

It has been held that where an agent fails to use due care in ascertaining the financial standing of one to whom he makes a sale on credit and who before payment fails, the principal may recover the difference between the price promised by the insolvent and that later obtained from another purchaser.[98] And an agent who in direct violation of orders sold goods to a certain purchaser, on whose insolvency the price was lost, was declared accountable to the principal for their value.[99] In a New Jersey case agents to sell brown goods without authority from the principal had them printed and sold them as print goods. The owners were allowed to claim the proceeds of sales at a profit; as to goods sold at a loss the measure of recovery was declared to be the value of the articles in their brown state.[100]

Where agents in violation of orders to forward merchandise, sold it at their own place of business, the principal was allowed to recover the price that would have been received by a sale at the locality directed.[101] Conversely, an agent who without authority sends goods away for sale, is accountable for their value at the place of shipment.[102]

§ 822. Sale below price fixed by principal.

Authorities are in conflict as to the measure of damages in

[96] Kelly v. Smith, 1 Blatch. 290. Any indebtedness to the factor for which he has a lien on the goods should be deducted. Halsey v. Bird, 99 Fed. 525, 39 C. C. A. 638; but see Osborne v. Synnot, 3 Vict. L. R. 148.

[97] Carnegie v. Federal Bank of Canada, 5 Ont. 418; acc., Thompson v. Gwyn, 46 Miss. 522. More accurately, the measure of damages is the price attained by the stock within a reasonable time after notice of the con-

version. Barber v. Ellingwood, 135 App. Div. 549, 122 N. Y. Supp. 369.

[98] Howe v. Sutherland, 39 Ia. 4, 84.

[99] Howell v. Morlan, 78 Ill. 162.

[100] Vandyke v. Brown, 8 N. J. Eq. 657, 671.

[101] Ryder v. Thayer, 3 La. Ann. 149.

[102] *Illinois:* Phy v. Clark, 35 Ill. 377.

Maine: Marr v. Barrett, 41 Me. 403.

North Carolina: Bessent v. Harris, 63 N. C. 542.

case the agent sells at a price below that fixed by the principal. It was once held that in such case the agents having wilfully deprived the principal of the benefit of an expected rise in the market, should be held to pay the price set by the principal,[103] and it was urged that any other rule would allow the agent to defraud his principal with impunity. But it soon became apparent that the principal by this rule was generally more than compensated, and the rule that he could recover only the actual value of the property, and not necessarily the value he had put upon it, prevailed.[104] So where the plaintiff had instructed the defendant not to sell a horse for less than $500, and the orders were disobeyed, it was nevertheless held that, notwithstanding the instructions, the plaintiff could only recover the actual value of the animal.[105]

The question, however, remained, at what time the value of the property was to be estimated. If the principal were allowed to recover only the market value of the property at the time of the sale, he would lose all the benefit of his foresight, if the value afterwards rose. The cases accordingly have allowed him the benefit of a rise in value. In some jurisdictions he is allowed to recover the highest market price until suit brought,[106] or even until trial.[107]

So in the State of Alabama, where an agent was instructed not to sell cotton for less than fourteen cents a pound, it was held that a disregard of these orders did not authorize the principal to recover up to the limit he had set, but that the criterion was the price at which other cotton of that quality had been sold during the season.[108]

---

[103] *Missouri:* Switzer v. Connell, 11 Mo. 88.

New York: Guy v. Cahley, 13 Johns. 332.

[104] *Illinois:* Rollins v. Duffy, 18 Ill. App. 398.

Massachusetts: Patterson v. Cussier, 106 Mass. 410; Dalby v. Stearns, 132 Mass. 230.

New York: Blot v. Boiceau, 3 N. Y. 78.

Ohio: Woodward v. Suydam, 11 Ohio, 360.

Vermont: Bigelow v. Walker, 24 Vt. 149, 58 Am. Dec. 156.

[105] Ainsworth v. Partillo, 13 Ala. 460.

[106] Nelson v. Morgan, 2 Martin (La.), 256.

[107] *Illinois:* Rollins v. Duffy, 18 Ill. App. 398.

New York: Taylor v. Ketchum, 5 Robt. 507.

This is of course limited by the price at which sale was directed. Goesling v. Gross (N. Mex.), 113 Pac. 608.

[108] Austill v. Crawford, 7 Ala. 335.

In Nelson *v.* Morgan,[109] where wine was consigned by a New York house to the defendant, a New Orleans agent, to sell at a limited price, the defendant, after keeping it a long time on hand, reshipped it, without further directions, to the plaintiffs at New York; who received it, but under protest, and wrote to the defendant that they abandoned the property, and held it merely as belonging to the defendant, and subject to his order. It was afterwards sold by them at auction in New York, but at a price below the first limit, and they then sued the defendant for the damages resulting from the disobedience of their orders, insisting that they were entitled to recover the full value of the wine. But the Supreme Court of Louisiana held that the measure of damages ought to be the value of the wine at the highest market price in New Orleans, at any time before the suit brought, adding thereto the freight to New York, and deducting therefrom the value of the wine at New York where the plaintiffs resold it. Where a consignee was instructed, unless he could obtain 22s. a barrel for a cargo of flour on its arrival, to hold it until a newly enacted tariff should "have produced its results," but sold it prematurely and in violation of the instructions, as was found by the jury to whom the question of violation was submitted at the trial, it was held by the Superior Court of the city of New York that in computing the damages to be recovered, if any, by the consignor, the jury were to determine the time when the flour might reasonably and prudently have been sold, and having done so, the consignee was to be charged with the amount. His advances and expenses were to be credited him with interest, and the balance with interest from the time the sale might have properly been made, the plaintiff was entitled to recover.[110] The judgment was reversed by the Court of Appeals [111] on the ground that the factors had been vested with a discretion which they had rightfully exercised, and did not violate their instructions. The rule of damages was therefore not considered on the appeal.

The true rule, however, seems to be that the highest mar-

[109] 2 Martin (La.), 256.

[110] Milbank *v.* Dennistoun, 1 Bosw. (N. Y.), 246.

[111] 121 N. Y. 386, 24 N. E. 841.

ket value for a reasonable time after notice of the sale can be recovered,[112] for in these cases the act of the defendant results in depriving the plaintiff of his property for a time, during which he is entitled to the benefit of any value it may have had, even the highest. In a case in Massachusetts, where the action was against factors for the breach of an agreement not to sell tobacco at less than forty cents a pound, but to hold it subject to the plaintiff's orders till they should sell it at that price, the plaintiff was allowed to recover for the loss sustained, by a failure to obey his orders, an amount not exceeding forty cents a pound, or the market value at the time when the return of the tobacco was demanded. The increase of market value up to forty cents a pound before the demand, was an item of damage. This ruling was sustained.[113] In delivering the opinion of the court, Mr. Justice Foster uses the following language: "We do not find it necessary to decide what rule of damages is absolutely correct. It has sometimes been said that the highest market price before action brought is the standard; at others, that the highest value before the trial may be awarded. It is safe to say that the factor is at least liable for the highest market value of the goods within a reasonable time after the sale in violation of instructions."

Unless, however, it appears that the market value of the property rose after the sale, the agent, upon proving that he sold the goods at the market price, will be liable for only nominal damages.[114] In Frothingham v. Everton,[115] it was held that where goods are consigned to a commission merchant or factor for sale, and the factor sells at a price below the limit without notice, the consignor may recover damages, or may have the amount of the damages allowed in a suit brought by the factor to recover his advances. The measure of damages in such a case is the amount of injury sustained by the sale contrary to the orders of the principal. If no actual loss appeared to have

---

[112] Loraine v. Cartwright, 3 Wash. C. C. 151, and cases cited below. See this whole subject discussed in chap. xxxv.

[113] Maynard v. Pease, 99 Mass. 555.

[114] *Massachusetts:* Dalby v. Stearns, 132 Mass. 230.

New Hampshire: Frothingham v. Everton, 12 N. H. 239.

New York: Blot v. Boiceau, 3 N. Y. 78; Hinde v. Smith, 6 Lans. 464.

[115] 12 N. H. 239.

been sustained in consequence of the wrongful act, the principal will be entitled only to nominal damages. And in accordance with this case it was held in Blot *v.* Boiceau,[116] where a factor sold contrary to his principal's orders, and below his limits, that he could discharge himself from liability by showing that the articles in question could not be made to bring more than the sum which they produced, or, in other words, that the goods were never worth more than they actually sold for.[117] It is, however, of course true that if a factor guarantees that goods consigned to him will yield not less than a certain sum, he is liable for that sum.[118]

In Bancroft *v.* Scribner,[119] the defendant below, a book-seller, in return for the exclusive agency for the sale of Stanley's "Darkest Africa," agreed with the publishers to remit the subscription price within a year for 10,000 copies. On the agent's breach the court allowed the publishers to recover the subscription price of the volumes less the cost to the publisher of their production and the amount of commissions upon them.

§ 823. Sale on wrong terms.

In Pennsylvania, where a party in London consigned goods to a correspondent in Philadelphia, to be delivered to a third party, only in case of his paying the amount or giving satisfactory security, and the agent delivered the goods without requiring either payment or security, it was held that the agent had thereby made himself liable for the full amount of the original debt, with a reasonable compensation for the delay of payment.[120] Such, too, is the language of all the most eminent authors of

[116] 3 N. Y. 78, 51 Am. Dec. 345.

[117] Bronson, J., intimated (p. 87) that where the property consists of articles which have no market value, such, for example, as antique paintings, statues, or vases, the rule will not apply, and the principal may recover the price he set upon the property. It would seem, however, that the true principle in such a case would be to make such proof of the real value as may be pos-sible. There is no principle of compensation which should allow the plaintiff to fix his own measure of damages.

[118] *California:* Pugh *v.* Porter Bros. Co., 118 Cal. 628, 50 Pac. 772.

Illinois: Rollins *v.* Duffy, 18 Ill. App. 398.

[119] Bancroft *v.* Scribner, 72 Fed. 988, 21 C. C. A. 352.

[120] Walker *v.* Smith, 4 Dall. 389.

1712

our law. "In this," to use the clear language of Mr. Sergeant Marshall,[121] "as in all other cases where a man, either by an express or implied undertaking, engages to do an act for another, and he either wholly neglects to do it, or does it improperly or unskilfully, an action on the case will lie against him for the loss or damage resulting from his negligence, carelessness, or want of skill." And it has been held that an agent for a cash sale who transfers for credit becomes liable for the purchase price.[122] In most such cases, however, the plaintiff's recovery has been measured by the market value, which might or might not equal the rate of exchange in the particular transaction.[123]

So in a case in the English Common Pleas, where agents, notwithstanding what the jury found were instructions not to part with certain goods consigned to them until they had received their price, caused the goods on their arrival in London to be transhipped on board a vessel named by them, taking the mate's receipt in their own names, and the vessel sailed to Melbourne with the goods on board without the vendee paying for them, the agents were held liable, and the value of the goods was the measure of the plaintiff's damages.[124] In Crawford v. Cockran,[125] the defendant was the plaintiff's agent to sell logs. Instead of having the official "scaler" measure the logs he negligently allowed the purchaser to do so, and the measurement was too small. The measure of damages was held to be the difference between the true value of the logs and the price obtained for them. In Howe v. Sutherland,[126] the defendant sold oats for future delivery on account of the plaintiff, but negligently failed to require a deposit from the vendee. The price of oats having fallen, and the vendee having become insolvent, it was held that the plaintiff could recover the difference between the amount for which the oats were first sold and that obtained on resale.

[121] On Insurance, 4th ed., p. 242.

[122] Harlan v. Ely, 68 Cal. 522, 9 Pac. 947.

[123] *Michigan:* Sheffield v. Linn, 62 Mich. 151, 28 N. W. 761; Birdsell Manufacturing Co. v. Brown, 96 Mich. 213, 55 N. W. 801.

Vermont: Catlin v. Smith, 24 Vt. 85. *Wisconsin:* Hall v. Storrs, 7 Wis. 253.

[124] Stearine Kaarsen Fabrick Gonda Co. v. Heintzmann, 17 C. B. (N. S.) 56.

[125] 2 Wash. 117.

[126] 39 Ia. 484.

§ 824. Neglect to sell.

Where a principal consigns property to his factor with instructions to sell it *upon its arrival*, the latter is bound to follow the instructions, and sell for the price it will command; and if he do not, he will become liable for the damage his principal may sustain in case of a fall in the market.[127] The damages in such a case are the difference between the amount finally realized, and that which would have been realized at once had the principal's instructions been obeyed.[128] But as in the case of sale at wrong price, the principal cannot recover more than the market price at the time when the goods should have been sold . So where a factor neglected to sell bales of wool consigned to him by the plaintiff, it was held error to charge the jury that the plaintiff could recover the highest price between the time when the order to sell was received and the time of the trial, Miller, J., saying that he could recover the value within a reasonable time after the order was received.[129] A principal, who directed a sale within a reasonable time, and whose order was disobeyed, was in a New York case [130] declared entitled to recover its value during such time, the computation to be made by averaging the range of the market during the period.

One rescinding without valid excuse his contract to act as selling agent is liable to his former principal for all loss sustained through the employment of a substitute at a higher salary or through the increase in expenses involved in making sales without an agent.[131]

§ 824a. Sale at a greater price than that fixed.

If the agent sells at a greater price than that fixed by the

[127] Evans *v.* Root, 7 N. Y. 186, 57 Am. Dec. 512. So if the agent is to sell at a fixed price, he is liable if he fails to do so when he could, for a fall in the market. Allen *v.* McCoushe, 12 N. Y. Supp. 232.

[128] *Illinois:* Cothran *v.* Ellis, 107 Ill. 413.

Iowa: Butterfield *v.* Stephens, 59 Ia. 596, 13 N. W. 751.

Kentucky: Atkinson *v.* Burton, 4 Bush, 299.

Michigan: Howland *v.* Davis, 40 Mich. 545.

[129] Whelan *v.* Lynch, 60 N. Y. 469, 19 Am. Rep. 202.

[130] Graham *v.* Maitland, 37 How. Pr. (N. Y.) 307.

[131] *Colorado:* Cannon Coal Co. *v.* Taggart, 1 Colo. App. 60, 27 Pac. 238.

Massachusetts: John Hetherington & Sons *v.* William Firth Co., 95 N. E. 961.

principal he cannot discharge himself by paying over the amount fixed. The agent, being in a fiduciary position, cannot profit at the expense of his principal; and he must account for the entire amount for which he sold the land.[132]

§ 825. Agents to purchase—Neglect to purchase.

A case in the Supreme Court of the United States,[133] exhibits another species of injury inflicted by an agent on a principal. Cunningham & Co., of Boston, owners of the *Halcyon*, sent her from Havana to the defendants below, Bell, De Yongh & Co., with directions to invest of the freight (which was about 4,600 pesos), 2,200 pesos in marble tiles, and the balance in wrapping paper, to be shipped by the same vessel to Havana. The defendants disobeyed the directions, and invested the whole in wrapping paper. The tiles would have made a considerable profit; the paper made a heavy loss. Trial and verdict for the plaintiff; exception and writ of error. The plaintiffs in error (the defendants below) insisted that Cunningham & Co. were entitled to no more than the value of the money at Leghorn, which ought to have been invested in tiles, and not its value in Havana; or, in other words, that the value of 2,200 pesos at Leghorn, with interest, and not the value of the tiles at Havana, ought to be given. But the court overruled this, saying, that it would be tantamount to a declaration that the breach of contract consisted in the *non-payment* of two thousand two hundred pesos, not in the *failure to invest that sum* in tiles. Speculative damages dependent on possible successive schemes, ought never to be given; but positive and direct loss, resulting plainly and immediately from the breach of orders, may be taken into the estimate. Thus, in this case, an estimate of possible profit to be derived from investments at Havana of the money arising from the sale of the tiles, taking into view a distinct operation, would have been to transcend the proper limits which a jury ought to respect; but the actual value of

---

[132] *Colorado:* Collins v. McClurg, 1 Colo. App. 348, 29 Pac. 299.

Illinois: Helberg v. Nichol, 149 Ill. 249, 37 N. E. 63.

Iowa: Borst v. Lynch, 133 Ia. 567, 110 N. W. 1031.

Massachusetts: Bassett v. Rogers, 165 Mass. 377, 43 N. E. 180.

New Mexico: Duncan v. Holder, 107 Pac. 685.

[133] Bell v. Cunningham, 3 Pet. 69, 7 L. ed. 606.

the tiles themselves at Havana affords a reasonable standard for the estimate of damages.[134] For similar reasons in an action [135] against an agent for refusing to deliver wheat bought for a principal, which immediately after purchase rose twenty cents per bushel, it was held that the plaintiff's damages should include recovery for the twenty cent profit of which the agent deprived him. It is proper to notice that in these cases the courts are making an allowance of profits, on the principles which we have heretofore had occasion to consider, but when it can be proved with reasonable certainty, as in such cases, what profits would have been earned, and such profits were within the contemplation of the parties when the agent was ordered to buy the goods, the plaintiff is entitled to recover them.[136]

§ 826. Purchase of wrong goods.

In an English case an agent at Hong Kong, instructed to purchase a certain grade of opium and ship it to England, bought and shipped an inferior grade. No opium of the grade ordered could have been purchased in Hong Kong at the time. It was held that the agent was liable for the actual loss of his principal—that is for the cost of the opium and the expense of importation and sale, less the amount obtained by sale of it; but that he was not liable for the value of the better grade of opium at the port of destination—that is, for expected profits.[137]

It is to be observed that in this case it was not possible for the agent to buy the opium ordered, and consequently the case differs from Bell v. Cunningham. The court noticed the latter case, but declined to give any opinion of its correctness.

§ 827. Purchase at excessive price.

An agent to buy paid too high a price, in fraud of his prin-

---

[134] This case will be found reported at Nisi Prius, 5 Mason, 161, where Story, J., told the jury in very general terms, that they were at liberty to compensate the plaintiffs for the actual loss sustained in consequence of the defendant's default, but were not at liberty to give vindictive damages.

[135] Nading v. Howe, 23 Ind. App. 690, 55 N. E. 1032.

[136] *Missouri:* Farwell v. Price, 30 Mo. 587.

New York: Heinemann v. Heard, 50 N. Y. 27.

[137] Cassaboglou v. Gibb, 9 Q. B. D. 220; 11 Q. B. D. 797.

cipal. It was held that the principal could recover only the difference between the price paid by the agent and the market price of the goods at the time of purchase.[138]

§ 828. Agents to deal in stocks.

Where a stock-broker, in the course of his dealing for his principal, fails to use skill and good judgment in buying or selling, he is liable for the actual loss. When the transaction is on a "margin," it may be the broker's duty to close it at a favorable time; and in that case if he negligently closes it without waiting a reasonable time, he is liable for the difference between the amount realized and what would have been obtained by waiting till a proper time. In Harris v. Tumbridge,[139] the defendant, a stock-broker, bought for the plaintiff a "straddle," that is, an option to buy or sell a certain stock at a certain price within the time limited. Instead of waiting for a proper time to exercise the option, the defendant sold the stock "short" for the plaintiff next day. The court said: "She is entitled to recover what she has lost by his neglect; and the price of the stock from day to day during the remainder of the option having been shown, it was for the jury to determine the amount." This does not mean that the measure of damages is in the hands of the jury. They are to determine the time when the defendant should have closed the transaction, and the variations in the price of stock are evidence from which they may determine when the option should have been exercised; that determined, the damages, as a matter of law, are measured by the price of stock at that time.

In transactions in which the broker is to buy, and then at a profit to sell, stock for a principal, if he neglects to buy or sell, or buys or sells too soon, the damages are measured by the value of the stock within a reasonable time after notice of that fact has been received by the customer.[140] But if the principal directs the broker, who is both agent and pledgee (and in New

---

[138] McMillan v. Arthur, 98 N. Y. 167.

[139] 83 N. Y. 92, 99, 38 Am. Rep. 398.

[140] *Connecticut:* Sing v. Malcolm, 77 Conn. 517, 59 Atl. 698.

District of Columbia: Gurley v. Mac-Lennan, 17 D. C. App. Cas. 170.

New York: Baker v. Drake, 53 N. Y. 211, 13 Am. Rep. 507; Colt v. Owens, 90 N. Y. 368; Gruman v. Smith, 81 N. Y. 25, 37 Am. Rep. 468; Minor v. Beveridge, 141 N. Y. 399, 36 N. E. 404, 38 Am. St. Rep. 804.

York has the legal title) to sell at a certain price, which can be obtained, and the broker neglects to do so, and subsequently sells at a lower price, the difference between the two prices is the measure of damages. The principal has neither possession nor control, and the stock, after the broker's refusal to execute the order, is carried at his own risk.[141] Where the facts show no intent on the part of the principal to sell the stock, failure to execute an order to purchase does not subject the agent to a liability for a rise in value of the stock subsequent to the breach of duty.[142]

In White v. Smith,[143] the defendant, a broker, sold for the plaintiff 100 shares "short" at 186. He afterwards bought 100 shares to cover the sale without notifying the plaintiff and without the plaintiff's authority. Subsequently the plaintiff sent an order to buy when the stock was at 180. The plaintiff was allowed to recover the difference between the price at which the stock was sold short and the market price upon the day when the order was received to purchase, with interest, deducting, however, commissions.

In a Massachusetts case the defendant was agent of the plaintiff to sell certain rights in stock at a minimum price. The defendant, without the plaintiff's knowledge, took the rights himself at the limited price, which was less than the market price. In an action by the principal, the agent was held liable for the difference between the price at which he took the rights and the market price at the time with interest; but not for dividends since paid on the stock.[144] If a broker illegally transfers the stock to his own name, the principal has a right to demand the price of the stock on that day, or to disaffirm the broker's act and recover for any rise in the market within a reasonable time.[145] And so a principal whose stock has been unlawfully retained by the broker can recover for the highest

[141] Allen v. McConihe, 12 N. Y. Supp. 232, 58 Hun, 605, 124 N. Y. 342, 26 N. E. 812.
[142] Gurley v. MacLennan, 17 D. C. App. Cas. 170.
[143] 54 N. Y. 522; acc. Rogers v. Wiley, 14 N. Y. Supp. 622; Campbell v. Wright, 118 N. Y. 594, 23 N. E. 914.
[144] Greenfield Savings Bank v. Simons, 133 Mass. 415.
[145] Massachusetts: Parsons v. Martin, 11 Gray, 111.
New York: Taussig v. Hart, 49 N. Y. 301.

intermediate value between the conversion and such time after his notice of it as affords reasonably sufficient opportunity for him to replace the shares.[146] In Kountz v. Gates [147] it was laid down that if the agent after being adjudged guilty of conversion could not deliver the shares he would be liable for the highest market value between the times of demand and of trial.

§ 829. Real estate agents.

In Tuers v. Tuers,[148] the defendant was an agent to collect the rents from the plaintiff's real estate, and to pay out of the rents the taxes and water-rents. He collected the rents, and retained enough to pay the taxes, but did not pay them. The plaintiff was required to pay an increased rate of interest on the overdue taxes, and a mortgagee commenced foreclosure proceedings on account of the non-payment of taxes. It was held that the plaintiff was entitled to recover something on account of these facts; but just what amount could be recovered, not being before the court, could not be decided. In Blood v. Wilkins [149] the court said: "Where one person furnishes money to another to discharge an incumbrance from the land of the person furnishing the money, and the person undertaking to discharge the incumbrance neglects to do it, and the land is lost to the owner by reason of the incumbrance, the measure of damages may be the money furnished with interest, or the value of the land lost, according to circumstances. If the land owner has knowledge of his agent's failure in time to redeem the land himself, his damages will be the money furnished with interest. But if the land owner justly relies upon his agent to whom he has furnished money to discharge the incumbrance, and the land is lost without his knowledge, and solely through the fault of the agent, then the agent will be liable for the value of the land at the time it is lost." The plaintiff's title having been lost by tax sales, it was held that the measure of damages was the value of the land at the time when the redemption from tax sales expired.

The agent of a town to keep its roads in repair negligently

---

[146] McKinley v. Williams, 74 Fed. 94, 20 C. C. A. 312; In re Swift, 114 Fed. 947.

[147] 78 Wis. 415, 47 N. W. 729.

[148] 100 N. Y. 196.

[149] 43 Ia. 565, 567; acc., Lowe v. Turpie, 147 Ind. 652, 44 N. E. 25.

allowed the roads to fall into disrepair. It was held that the agent was liable to the town for damages paid to a person injured through the bad state of the roads, and for the costs and incidental expenses of the suit brought by the injured person, as well as for the expense of properly repairing the roads.[150] An agent without reasonable care recommending a tenant who becomes insolvent is liable for all damage sustained by reason of the insolvency;[151] and one instructed to receive a payment of rent in cash, taking a check to his own order is accountable for the whole sum involved.[152] In Triggs v. Jones[153] the plaintiff delivered a deed to the defendant to be transferred to a third party on the happening of certain conditions; the defendant turned the document over without waiting for the event, and the third party then executed a conveyance to a *bona fide* purchaser. The plaintiff was allowed to recover the value of the land with interest.

An agent for sale of real property at a certain price conveying for a less price is accountable for the difference between the market value and the receipts.[154] In Dunn v. Mackey,[155] the measure of liability of one contracting to sell a piece of land within a year for a specified amount and failing to do so was held to be the difference between the amount contracted to be realized from the property and its value at the end of the period. A principal whose agent surrenders a contract made in his behalf for the conveyance of a valuable piece of property may recover the difference between the actual value of the property and the price agreed to be paid for it.[156]

An agent to buy real property making false representations in regard to its value is liable in an action upon them for all injury proximately caused by them.[157] In Richardson v. Dunn,[158] the defendant, agent of the plaintiff in the purchase of a public house, reported that the owner's manager declared

---

[150] Wilson v. Greensboro, 54 Vt. 533.

[151] Heys v. Tindall, 1 B. & S. 296.

[152] Pape v. Westacott [1894], 1 Q. B. 272; acc., Paul v. Grimm, 165 Pa. 139, 30 Atl. 721, 44 Am. St. Rep. 648.

[153] 46 Minn. 277, 48 N. W. 1113.

[154] *Indiana:* Storms v. Storms, 21 Ind. App. 191, 51 N. E. 955.

New Zealand: Logie v. Gillies, 4 N. Z. L. R. Sup. Ct. 65.

[155] 80 Cal. 104, 22 Pac. 64.

[156] Kountz v. Gates, 78 Wis. 415, 47 N. W. 729.

[157] Palmer v. Pirson, 4 N. Y. Misc. 455, 24 N. Y. Supp. 333.

[158] 8 C. B. (N. S.) 655.

the receipts to average a certain sum daily. On the strength
of this estimate the plaintiff bought the property. The estimate proved grossly exaggerated and the plaintiff, basing his
action on the manager's reported misstatement sued the former
owner. The jury, satisfied that the manager made no such
statement, found against the plaintiff. It was held, in an action
by him against his agent, that he could recover the difference
between the price paid for the house and that received on a
sale of it and damages for his loss of time, but not the costs
of the abortive action against the vendor. If without fraud the
agent reported negligently as to the value of the land, and his
principal bought the land as a consequence of the report, the
principal may recover the difference between the fair value
of the land as represented and as it actually was.[159]

§ 830. Negligence of directors of a corporation.

Directors of a corporation stand to the company in a fiduciary
relation, and are responsible to it for losses caused by their
breaches of trust, negligence, etc. When simple negligence is
involved, although equity may be resorted to, an action at law
will also lie; the rules as to the measure of damages must be
nearly if not altogether, identical with such one as would
govern in an action at law by principal against agent. In
such cases the corporation is usually the plaintiff, but if it
will not act (for instance, when it is under the control of the
directors at fault themselves), the action may be maintained
e. g., by a receiver for its benefit. The damages recoverable
are governed by the ordinary rules in other actions, of which
the gist is negligence in the performance of duty. Nothing can
be recovered beyond what the corporation could have recovered
if it had sued, and the liability cannot go beyond the natural
and proximate results of the acts or omissions involved. In
such an action the directors cannot be held liable for ordinary
corporate disbursements, nor for the contingent statutory
liability of the stock-holders for debts which they may never
be called on to pay.[160]

[159] Durward v. Hubbell, 149 Ia. 722, 128 N. W. 953.
[160] Bloom v. National U. B. Savings & Loan Co., 152 N. Y. 114, 46 N. E. 166, 57 Am. St. Rep. 500.

§ 831. Attorneys.

The liability of an attorney who is negligent in the prosecution of a claim is for the actual loss, not necessarily for the amount of the claim.[161] If the debtor continues solvent or was insolvent at the time the attorney took the claim, or if there is valid security, the measure of damages will be less than the amount of the claim.[162] If an attorney is negligent in the defence of a suit, the measure of damages is not necessarily the amount that is recovered in that suit from the client. The attorney may show, for instance, that the defence he was employed to make was not a good one.[163] An attorney, who had been employed to complete a purchase of leasehold property which had been bought at auction by his client, on conditions requiring that the purchaser should take an under lease and not demand an abstract of the vendor's title, nor inquire into that of the lessor, made no inquiries, but simply got what purported to be a lease executed by the pretended seller, but which recited no title, the pretended seller having none. The purchaser was evicted by the real owner. It was held that the attorney had been guilty of negligence for which his estate was liable in damages, the proper measure of which was the sum which the plaintiff (who had bought back the property) had been obliged to pay to get the title, with interest, and without deduction for rent, as he was liable over for mesne profits during the time he had occupied the premises rent free.[164] In an action against an attorney for failure to perform services agreed upon, the plaintiff recovers the value of the services.[165] In an action against a conveyancer to recover damages for negligence in looking up a title, in failing to discover the existence of an obligation to fence, the measure of damages is what it would cost the plaintiff to build the fence together with an amount of

[161] Cox v. Sullivan, 7 Ga. 144, 58 Am. Dec. 386.

[162] *Arkansas:* Pennington v. Yell, 11 Ark. 212, 52 Am. Dec. 262.

Connecticut: Huntington v. Rumnill, 3 Day, 390.

Georgia: Cox v. Sullivan, 7 Ga. 144, 50 Am. Dec. 386.

Illinois: Stevens v. Walker, 55 Ill. 151.

Kentucky: Eccles v. Stephenson, 3 Bibb, 517.

Vermont: Crooker v. Hutchinson, 2 D. Chip. 117.

England: Russel v. Palmer, 2 Wils. 325.

[163] Grayson v. Wilkinson, 5 Sm. & M. (Miss.), 268, 289.

[164] Allen v. Clark, 7 L. T. Rep. 781, 11 W. R. 304.

[165] Quinn v. Van Pelt, 56 N. Y. 417.

money which would produce annually what it would cost to maintain the fence in good repair.[166]

§ 831a. Title companies.

Conveyancing companies employed to conduct the purchase of real estate, assume the duties and responsibilities of attorneys; in case of negligence, they are responsible in damages in the same way. Such a company, undertaking to arrange for the conveyance of a house without a mortgage of $9,000, conducted the transaction negligently, so that the plaintiff received property encumbered additionally by a second mortgage of $5,000, and on foreclosure proceedings under this mortgage, was assisted. It was held that he could recover the money paid for the property from the Title Company.[167]

§ 832. Auctioneers.

Where an auctioneer failed to demand a deposit, according to the terms of sale, and the vendee did not take the property, it was held that the owner might recover of the auctioneer the difference between the price bid and that which could be obtained on a resale.[168] Where an auctioneer, selling land for the plaintiff, so misdescribed it that the purchaser refused to take the title, the plaintiff could, it seems, recover from the auctioneer an amount which he had been forced to pay to the purchaser on account of examination of title; but he could not recover on account of a tenant moving out or for deterioration of the premises during vacancy, these not being proximate consequences of the misrepresentation.[169]

§ 832a. Customhouse brokers.

Customhouse brokers act as agents to pay duties for importers. If such a broker negligently fails to enter goods as soon as he might have done and in consequence, while they are in the customhouse, a new tariff law goes into effect raising the duties, he is liable to his principal for the amount of the enhancement in the duties.[170]

[166] Bodine v. Wayne Title & Trust Co., 33 Pa. Super. Ct. 68.
[167] Ehmer v. Title Guarantee & T. Co., 165 N. Y. 10, 50 N. E. 420.
[168] Hibbert v. Bayley, 2 F. & F. 48.
[169] Dranow v. MacDonald, 76 N. J. L. 259, 69 Atl. 1009.
[170] Vernier v. Knauth, 39 N. Y. Supp. 784.

§ 833. Liability of sub-agents to agents.

* It has been held, that where a factor employs a sub-agent for the purpose of carrying out the instructions of the principal, if the sub-agent, by neglecting the directions of the factor, commit a breach of duty for which the factor is compelled to answer the principal in damages, the factor will be entitled to recover over from the sub-agent the damages which he has so sustained. This is the measure of his damages.[171]   Thus,[172] where the plaintiff had been commissioned by Gevers & Co. to ship a quantity of *best* Porto Rico tobacco for them to Holland, the defendants were employed by the plaintiff to execute the order, but bought Porto Rico tobacco not of the best quality, and which was proved at the trial to be very bad. Gevers & Co. refused to receive it, and sued the present plaintiff. He notified the defendants to furnish a defence to the action. Gevers & Co. recovered, and it was contended, in the action against the sub-agent, that the measure of damages was the amount recovered by Gevers & Co. in the former suit, with the costs thereof. The defendants insisted that the true measure of damages was either the difference between the relative prices of the article in the London market, or between the relative values in the market in Holland; but the court held that the measure of relief should be the damages and costs recovered in the first action against the plaintiff—the plaintiff undertaking to assign the tobacco to the defendants, or to sell it and account to the defendants for the proceeds; and this having been so held at the sittings, a rule for a new trial was refused.[173] And on the analogous cases of warranties and sureties, it seems very rightly decided.**

II.—AGENT AGAINST PRINCIPAL

§ 834. Indemnity for loss or expense.

* If an agent, without default, incurs losses or damages in the course of transacting the business of his agency, or in following the instructions of his principal, he will be entitled to

[171] *Minnesota:* Bidwell *v.* Madison, 10 Minn. 135.

Texas: Talkin *v.* Anderson, 19 S. W. 852.

[172] Mainwaring *v.* Brandon, 8 Taunt. 202.

[173] *Vide* Russell on Factors and Brokers, 257.

full compensation therefor.[174]   So an agent has been allowed to recover the damages paid by him on a protested bill drawn for his principal's benefit; [175] ** and an auctioneer has been allowed reimbursement for advertising and for his tax,[176] and the expense of cataloguing the goods,[177] if his commission is revoked before the sale.   Similarly an agent, who was indemnified against the commission of an act which was not known at the time to be a trespass or commission, but which proved to be such, was allowed to recover against his principal the amount of the judgment recovered against himself,[178] with costs and counsel fees.[179]   And it is quite immaterial in these cases, whether the agent have a promise to indemnify him or not; the law implies an agreement on the part of the principal to save him harmless.[180]

Where merchants here gave a written engagement to their agent at Havana, to save them harmless from all costs, damages, and expenses which might arise in consequence of any lawsuit which then was or might be brought against them for the recovery of freight or average on the cargo of a certain ship, it was held that the agents were entitled to recover for money which they were obliged to pay in consequence of legal proceed-

[174] *United States:* Bibb v. Allen, 149 U. S. 481, 498, 13 Sup. Ct. 950, 37 L. ed. 819.
Maine: Greely v. Bartlett, 1 Me. 172, 10 Am. Dec. 54.
Massachusetts: Packard v. Leinow, 12 Mass. 11.
Missouri: Yeatman v. Corder, 38 Mo. 337.
New York: Feeter v. Heath, 11 Wend. 477; Howe v. Buffalo, N. Y. & Erie R. R., 37 N. Y. 297; Robinson v. Crawford, 31 App. Div. 228, 52 N. Y. Supp. 560.
Pennsylvania: Elliott v. Walker, 1 Rawle, 126.
[175] Riggs v. Lindsay, 7 Cr. 500, 2 L. ed. 500.
New York: Ramsay v. Gardner, 11 Johns. 439.
[176] Russell v. Miner, 25 Hun (N. Y.), 114.

[177] Carpenter v. Le Count, 22 Hun (N. Y.), 106.
[178] *Kentucky:* Pool v. Adkisson, 1 Dana, 110, 115.
Maine: Drummond v. Humphreys, 39 Me. 347.
New York: Allaire v. Ouland, 2 Johns. Cas. 52; Coventry v. Barton, 17 Johns. 142, 8 Am. Dec. 376.
England: Betts v. Gibbins, 2 A. & E. 57.
[179] Adamson v. Jarvis, 4 Bing. 66.
[180] *Connecticut:* Stocking v. Sage, 1 Conn. 519.
New York: Powell v. Trustees of Newburgh, 19 Johns. 284; Castle v. Noyes, 14 N. Y. 329, 332.
Pennsylvania: D'Arcy v. Lyle, 5 Binn. 441.
England: Warlow v. Harrison, 1 E. & E. 309.

ings on an award made previous to obtaining the written engagement.[181] Where the plaintiffs, who were brokers, having been ordered to buy stock, did so, paid for it, taking the certificate in their own name, offered to transfer it, and demanded of their principal payment, which he did not make, and the stock declined in value, it was held that they could recover the price paid by them, and not merely the difference between that price and the market value on the day of their demand.[182] A principal failing to deliver stock sold in accordance with instructions by a broker is liable to him for loss sustained through the purchase of other stock to meet the contract.[183] Agents by direction carrying stock on the exchange may recover from their principal for differences paid upon it, but not for sums paid by them on their being declared defaulters, although the default was induced by the failure of the defendant and other customers to make remittances for the purchasers of the shares, for there is no implied obligation resting upon a principal to indemnify an agent for loss caused by the latter's insolvency.[184]

An attorney to collect a claim who has paid out money for the costs and expenses of bringing suit on the claim is entitled to be reimbursed.[185] A principal doing business in the name of his agent must indemnify him for attorney's fees paid in defence of the principal's property.[186] Where an agent is expressly authorized to employ counsel for the case the principal must reimburse him for expenditures in counsel fees, although the cause of action be an unauthorized undervaluation of the principal's goods.[187]

Where an agent contracted in his own name within his authority for the principal's benefit, and the principal failed to carry out the contract, the agent having paid damages for the breach

[181] Hill v. Packard, 5 Wend. (N. Y.), 375.

[182] Giddings v. Sears, 103 Mass. 311; acc., Ellis v. Pond, [1898] 1 Q. B. 426.

[183] *Arizona:* Bank of Bisbee v. Graf, 100 Pac. 452.

Colorado: Baily v. Carnduff, 14 Colo. App. 169, 59 Pac. 407.

[184] Duncan v. Hill, L. R. 8 Ex. 242.

[185] *United States:* Howe v. Wade, 4 McLean, 319.

Tennessee: Bruce v. Baxter, 7 Lea, 477, 487.

[186] Whitehead v. Darling, 86 Ky. 110, 5 S. W. 356.

[187] Monnet v. Merz, 127 N. Y. 151, 27 N. E. 827.

was allowed to recover against his principal only the actual amount of the third party's damage and not the amount paid, as he should have given the principal opportunity to defend.[188] So, on the other hand, where the principal refuses to defend a suit brought against his agent, if the agent's course in defending it is a prudent and reasonable one, the principal will be liable to him for the costs thus sustained.[189]   In D'Arcy v. Lyle,[190] one who, after the termination of his employment, but in consequence of it, was forced by a Haytian tyrant under threat of possible death to confess judgment for a large sum, was allowed to recover it from his principal.

* It has been said that if an agent abroad, as for example, a foreign factor, should, at his own risk and peril, evade the payment of foreign customs and duties, he would still be entitled to charge them against his principal, as if they had been actually paid. But the lively moral sense of Mr. Justice Story is shocked at this idea; and he justly says, that it may well be doubted whether this doctrine is sound or maintainable.[191] ** And it has been held that where an agent was instructed to insure and did not do so, he could not recover the amount of the premiums of his principal although he had subjected himself to the risk of loss.[192]

§ 834a. Compensation for services.

An agent's claims to compensation for his services and to damages for failure to employ or for wrongful discharge rest upon principles substantially identical with those laid down in an earlier chapter as to contracts of service. Where a broker secures a proper purchaser for his principal, he is entitled to his commission, though the principal refuses to sell,[193] or

[188] Saveland v. Green, 36 Wis. 612. In Clark v. Jones, 16 Lea, 351, though there was no evidence that the principal had been notified to defend the suit, the agent was held to be entitled to recover his attorney's fees.

[189] Illinois: First Nat. Bank v. Tenney, 43 Ill. App. 544.
Missouri: Yeatman v. Corder, 38 Mo. 337.

England: Brom v. Hall, 7 C. B. (N. S.) 503.
[190] 5 Binn. 441.
[191] Story on Agency, § 343, and authorities there cited.
[192] Storer v. Eaton, 50 Me. 219, 79 Am. Dec. 611.
[193] Georgia: McMillan v. Quincey, 72 S. E. 506.
Kansas: Durkee v. Gunn, 41 Kan. 496, 21 Pac. 637, 13 Am. St. Rep. 300.

through defect of title cannot convey.[194] And where the broker was to have all he could get for land over $200, it was held that he could recover what a proper purchaser, secured by him, was willing to pay over $200, though the owner refused to sell.[195] In Fairchild v. Rogers [196] it was held that the agreed commission could be recovered upon breach by the owner on proof that the price named would certainly have been obtained, though the broker did not actually secure a customer.

In Wilson v. Dame,[197] the plaintiff assumed, without authority, to act as agent for the defendant, and his acts were ratified by the defendant; he became entitled to the same compensation as if he had originally acted with authority. Where an attorney was engaged in Iowa to perform services in another State, it was held that his compensation should be at the rate paid in Iowa rather than that paid in the other State.[198] The amount of compensation, where it is not fixed by agreement, may be fixed by custom.[199]

§ 834b. Damages for failure to employ.

The defendant, while negotiating for a license to carry on an insurance business, made a contract to employ plaintiff as its general agent, as soon as it should obtain its license. The contract was terminable by either party on thirty days' notice. There being some delay in securing the license, plaintiff sued the company, alleging a breach through its failure to procure a license, and claimed damages as for breach of an entire contract. It was held that in any view of the case plaintiff was

Mississippi: Stevenson v. Morris Machine Works, 69 Miss. 232, 13 So. 834.

New York: Stone v. Argersinger, 32 App. Div. 208, 53 N. Y. Supp. 63; Moses v. Bierling, 31 N. Y. 462.

England: Prickett v. Badger, 1 C. B. (N. S.) 296. If an agent is employed to sell goods and makes a sale, and the principal refuses to supply the goods, but the agent gets the goods elsewhere to fill the order, he must deduct from the commission which his principal should pay his profit on the goods actually supplied, since he could have filled the order only once. Packers' F.

Assoc. v. Harris, 42 Ind. App. 240, 85 N. E. 375.

[194] Doty v. Miller, 43 Barb. (N. Y.), 529.

[195] Heyn v. Philips, 37 Cal. 529.

[196] 32 Minn. 269.

[197] 58 N. H. 392.

[198] Stanberry v. Dickerson, 35 Ia. 493.

[199] *Kentucky:* Morehead v. Anderson, 125 Ky. 77, 100 S. W. 340, 30 Ky. L. Rep. 1137 (attorney).

West Virginia: Anderson v. Lewis, 64 W. Va. 297, 61 S. E. 160 (broker).

not entitled to damages beyond the commencement of his suit.[200]

§ 834c. Damages for wrongful discharge—Compensation by a commission.

Where an agent wrongfully discharged is to be paid, in part, by a commission, he can in general recover no damages on account of possible future commissions.[201] Thus, where the plaintiff was selling agent for the defendant, and was to receive a salary and a commission on all goods he sold over the amount of $30,000, it was held that, having been wrongfully discharged before his time of service had expired, and before he had sold goods to the value of $30,000, he could recover only the amount of his salary.[202] In Washburn v. Hubbard,[203] the plaintiff sued defendant for breach of a contract making the plaintiff the defendant's general agent for the sale of car springs. It was held that evidence by the plaintiff of the amount of the profits which might have been made during the term of the agreement based on the probable amount of sales, was inadmissible.

In a case often cited,[204] the plaintiff had engaged the defendant to act as agent in the sale of sewing machines. The defendant was to hire a room and team and sell all the machines he could within a certain time. The plaintiff was to supply machines at 25 per cent. below the retail price. For eight months the defendant made almost constant application for machines. Some were supplied, but not enough to meet the demand. The defendant set up these facts as an offset to a claim of the plaintiff. It was held that the defendant could recover the value of the time he was obliged to be idle, and reasonable expenditures, but that the profits were too speculative. The court said:

---

[200] Clark v. National Benefit & Casualty Co., 67 Fed. 222.

[201] *Alabama:* Brigham v. Carlisle, 78 Ala. 243, 56 Am. Rep. 28; Beck v. West, 87 Ala. 213; 6 So. 70; 13 Am. St. Rep. 23.

Kentucky: Louisville Soap Co. v. Vance, 22 Ky. L. Rep. 847, 58 S. W. 985.

Maryland: Hamill v. Foute, 51 Md. 419.

England: Hartland v. General Exchange Bank, 14 L. T. (N. S.) 863.

But see *Georgia:* McMillan v. Quincey, 72 S. E. 506.

[202] Stern v. Rosenheim, 67 Md. 503; acc., Union Refining Co. v. Barton, 77 Ala. 148; Brigham v. Carlisle, 78 Ala. 243, 56 Am. Rep. 28.

[203] 6 Lans. 11.

[204] Howe S. M. Co. v. Bryson, 44 Ia. 159, 163, 24 Am. Rep. 735.

"We would not be understood as holding that where a person is employed to sell goods on commission, and the employer fails to furnish the goods, the person employed may not recover for loss of profits which he might have made if the goods had been furnished. If the quantity to be furnished was a definite amount, and the demand was practically unlimited, possibly he might be allowed to recover for loss of profits. But where a person employs another to sell on commission all the goods he can within a limited territory, especially if the goods are of that kind of which there is no regular consumption or demand, the case is quite different. The number of sewing machines of a particular kind which can be sold within a given county and within a given time is very uncertain. Few cases can be found where profits have been disallowed as speculative, in which the uncertainty is greater."

In Iowa [205] it has been held that where an agent for the sale of real property sues for loss sustained by reason of a wrongful revocation, the damages will be nominal unless he can show that within the period agreed upon he could have obtained a purchaser at his principal's minimum. And in general no recovery can be had for loss of commissions unless it can be proved with reasonable certainty that the commissions would have been earned.[206] In such cases the defendant is, of course, not exempted from making compensation because payment according to the contract was to be by a commission which he has made it impossible for the plaintiff to earn. The true measure of damages in such a case should be the value of the services the plaintiff had performed.[207] In Gifford v. Waters [208] the plaintiff was to receive a proportion of the profits of a business, and was entitled to draw a certain amount each week. It was held that

[205] Milligan v. Owen, 123 Ia. 285, 98 N. W. 792.

But where the land was sold by the principal within the time limited at less than the minimum, it was held that the broker was *prima facie* entitled to his commission, and the burden was on the defendant to show that he could not have effected a sale. Norman v. Vandenberg (Mo. App.), 138 S. W. 47.

[206] *Minnesota:* Emerson v. Pacific C.

& N. P. Co., 92 Minn. 523, 100 N. W. 365.

Texas: Johnson v. Cherokee L. & I. Co., 82 Tex. 338, 18 S. W. 476.

[207] *Missouri:* Glover v. Henderson, 120 Mo. 367, 25 S. W. 175, 41 Am. St. Rep. 695.

Wisconsin: Merriman v. McCormick Harvesting Machine Co., 96 Wis. 600, 71 N. W. 1050, 65 Am. St. Rep. 83.

[208] 67 N. Y. 80.

this sum, being a reasonable compensation, might be recovered.

But such amount as it can be proved with reasonable certainty that plaintiff would have earned may be recovered, even though it was to be paid as a commission.[209] Thus in a case in Maryland [210] the plaintiff was to receive $1,000 a year and 2 per cent commissions on sales above $40,000 a year; and the contract was terminable upon one month's notice. The contract was terminated by the defendant at the end of six months, when the plaintiff had sold goods to the amount of between $30,000 and $40,000. It was held that, in addition to his salary, the plaintiff might recover his commission on all sales above $20,000. The court relied on the fact that the contract was not broken, but was put an end to by its own terms.

§ 834d. Compensation by percentage of an amount that can be fixed.

Where the agent is paid by a percentage of a sum the amount of which did not depend upon his services, and can therefore be fixed notwithstanding his discharge, he is entitled to recover the agreed compensation though he was discharged before completing the work he was to do. Thus where the agent was to receive a commission on all sales made by the principal, whether through his agency or not, it was held that he might recover the amount of his commissions on sales made after his discharge, but during the time for which he was employed.[211] So where an agent is given an exclusive territory for the sale of goods, and goods are sold by others within the territory, he may recover the agreed commission upon such sales; [212] and where the general agent of an insurance company is paid by commission, and his authority is withdrawn, he may recover

[209] *Georgia:* Life Association of America *v.* Ferrill, 60 Ga. 414.

New York: Wakeman *v.* Wheeler & W. Manuf. Co., 101 N. Y. 205, 4 N. E. 264, 54 Am. Rep. 676; Alfaro *v.* Davidson, 40 N. Y. Super. Ct. 87.

Pennsylvania: Pittsburg Gauge Co. *v.* Ashton Valve Co., 184 Pa. 36, 39 Atl. 223.

Wisconsin: Richey *v.* Union C. L. I. Co., 140 Wis. 486, 122 N. W. 1030.

[210] Jenkins *v.* Long, 8 Md. 132.

[211] Blair *v.* Laflin, 127 Mass. 518.

[212] *Kansas:* Sparks *v.* Reliable D. M. C. Co., 116 Pac. 363.

Kentucky: Oberfelder *v.* J. G. Mattingly Co., 120 S. W. 352.

Wisconsin: Dr. Harter Medicine Co. *v.* Hopkins, 83 Wis. 309, 53 N. W. 501.

the agreed commission upon business done within his territory by other agents.[213]   When a broker is employed to sell land, and it is sold by the principal the broker is entitled to his commission on the amount for which it is sold.[214]   Where the agent was to have a certain commission for superintending the repairs on a vessel, and for advancing the expense, and the principal broke the contract, the agent, having been ready to superintend the repairs and to furnish the money required, was allowed to recover commissions at the rate fixed in the contract.[215]

In accordance with this principle, where the plaintiff, an attorney employed to prosecute a claim for a percentage of the amount recovered, was wrongfully discharged, it was held that as the claim proved to be an unfounded one he could recover only nominal damages.[216]

§ 834e. Commissions on insurance renewals.

Commissions of an insurance agent for renewals are held to be capable of accurate measurement, and probable commissions of this nature may therefore be included in the agent's damages.[217]   In Lewis v. Atlas Mutual Life Insurance Co.,[218] the plaintiff was the agent of the defendant under a contract to last five years.   He was to be paid a percentage on first premiums, term insurance, paid-up policies, and renewals. The defendant wound up its business before the five years expired.   It was held that, as the value of the renewals was a sum proximately ascertainable by the calculations of actuaries, this was a proper mode of estimating his damages.[219]   But the average amount of his commissions previously earned monthly on first premiums was, without some other proof of the probable amount of business, of too speculative a character.

---

[213] Wells v. National L. Assoc., 99 Fed. 222, 39 C. C. A. 476, 53 L. R. A. 33.

[214] Arkansas: Blumenthal v. Bridges, 91 Ark. 212, 120 S. W. 974, 24 L. R. A. (N. S.) 279.

California: Justy v. Erro (Cal. App.), 117 Pac. 575.

[215] Mauran v. Warren, 2 Lowell, 53.

[216] Swinnerton v. Monterey Co., 76 Cal. 113, 18 Pac. 135, 9 Am. St. Rep. 173.

[217] Aetna Life Insurance Co. v. Nexsen, 84 Ind. 347; 43 Am. Rep. 91.

[218] 61 Mo. 534.

[219] Acc., Wells v. National L. Assoc., 39 C. C. A. 476, 99 Fed. 222, 53 L. R. A. 33. Stowell v. Greenwich Ins. Co., 20 App. Div. 188, 46 N. Y. Supp. 802.

§ 834f. Commission from both parties.

An agent cannot retain a commission from a party with whom he is employed to deal without the express consent of his principal; and if he receives such a commission, it must be deducted from the amount of the compensation to be paid by his principal.[220] This is an application of the general principle that all gains through breach of fiduciary relation become the property of the beneficiary.

§ 834g. Discharge of an attorney.

Where an attorney is discharged during the time for which he is employed, a peculiar question arises, owing to the nature of the relation existing between an attorney and client. Thus where an attorney is retained by a client, and is wrongfully dicharged from the trust, it is usually held that owing to the confidential relation between the parties, and the impropriety of the attorney accepting other employment in the cause, he may recover the full amount of the compensation agreed upon, less such expenses as would have been incurred by him in carrying out the agreement.[221] No other measure of damages is usually possible, as the Supreme Court of California points out.[222] And when the plaintiff, an attorney, was to have an agreed amount upon obtaining the pardon of a convict, and the pardon was obtained, though after the wrongful discharge of the plaintiff from the employment, he was held entitled to the agreed amount.[223] But circumstances may limit the rule. Thus in the case of Horn v. Western Land Association,[224] it was held that though the contract price could not be reduced by the ordinary earnings of the attorney, yet if the defendant could show affirmatively that the attorney obtained "other employment and compensation inconsistent with his engagement under the contract," such compensation would be deducted from the amount recovered.

[220] Mauran v. Warren, 2 Lowell, 53.

[221] *Alabama:* Hunt v. Test, 8 Ala. 713, 42 Am. Dec. 659.

Arkansas: Brodie v. Watkins, 33 Ark. 545, 34 Am. Rep. 49.

Texas: Myers v. Crockett, 14 Tex. 257.

[222] Baldwin v. Bennett, 4 Cal. 392; Webb v. Trescony, 76 Cal. 621, 18 Pac. 796; Bartlett v. Odd Fellows' S. Bank, 79 Cal. 218, 21 Pac. 743, 12 Am. St. Rep. 139.

[223] Moyer v. Cantieny, 41 Minn. 242.

[224] 22 Minn. 233.

III.—THIRD PARTY AGAINST PRETENDED AGENT

§ 835. Liability for acting without authority.

One who falsely holds himself out to another as an agent is liable for any loss that happens by reason of his lack of authority. In a case in England the defendant falsely represented himself as authorized to sell certain land, and entered into a contract with the plaintiff, on behalf of the owners, to sell the land for a certain sum. The owners repudiated the contract, and conveyed the land at an advanced price to another. The plaintiff filed a bill against the owners for specific performance, but before a hearing the owners and the present defendant swore, in answer to interrogatories, that the defendant was not authorized to make the contract. Having failed in his suit for specific performance, the plaintiff brought action against the defendant. It was held that he could recover, first, the expense of investigating the title; second, the expenses of his suit against the owners, until their testimony made it unreasonable for him to continue the suit; third, damages for the loss of his bargain, that is, the difference between the contract price and the market price of the land. The price for which the land was conveyed would be evidence of the market price.[225] An attorney-at-law executed to a deputy sheriff, in the name of the plaintiffs, in sundry writs, the following agreement: "Know all men by these presents, that we agree to hold harmless A. B., sheriff, for selling stoves and iron on the execution in his hands at this time, to wit, one in Knight *v.* Cheshire Iron Works; the other, Dooley *v.* Same, and from all costs, charges, damages, and expenses whatsoever, that may result or accrue to him for attaching or selling Cheshire Iron Works' property, or property claimed or which belongs or belonged to Cheshire Iron Works." In an action by the deputy sheriff against the attorney for falsely representing that he had authority so to execute it, it was held that the jury might consider on the question of damages a judgment recovered against and paid by the plaintiff for taking and selling the property mentioned in the agreement, deducting therefrom so much as consisted of damages resulting from attach-

---

[225] Godwin *v.* Francis, L. R. 5 C. P. 295.

ments made by the plaintiff after the making of the contract, or, if that amount could not be ascertained, the rule of damages might be the amount of the judgments in favor of the parties whose names had been signed by the defendant to the contract, and which had been satisfied by the application thereon of the avails of the sale of the property so taken by the plaintiff. The plaintiff was, moreover, entitled to recover the costs and expenses of sundry litigations directly necessitated by the fraud, and proper compensation for his own time and services in the matter, besides interest on his expenses up to the verdict.[226]

The plaintiff being in occupation of a house and shop, as assignee of a term which would expire in March, 1867, at a yearly rent of £65, the defendant, who had for several years acted as agent of the freeholder in collecting the rents of the property, agreed, in writing, November 16th, 1863, on behalf of the freeholder, to grant the plaintiff, at the expiration of the existing term, a renewed lease of twenty-one years at a rent of £70, the plaintiff agreeing to put in a new shop front at her expense. The plaintiff put in the new front at an expense of £50, and expended £10 more in permanently improving the premises, and in June, 1865, agreed with one Budd to sell him her interest in the existing and future leases at a premium of £150. The defendant had no authority from the freeholder (his brother) to make the agreement, and the latter refused to ratify it. The plaintiff, who had no notice of the defendant's want of authority, thereupon, in conjunction with Budd, filed a bill against the defendant's brother for a specific performance, and this was dismissed with costs. Budd then sued the plaintiff on her contract with him, and recovered damages to the amount of £280, as follows: £205 assessed by the arbitrator as the value of the lease; £22 10s. for the loss incurred by Budd on the resale of the fixtures, which he had bought upon the premises; £35 for loss of business by removal; £17 for solicitor's charges. These damages, together with the costs of the action and reference, were paid by the plaintiff. It was held, that the plaintiff was entitled to recover against the defendant all the costs paid and incurred by her in the

[226] Jones v. Wolcott, 2 All. 247.

chancery suit, and also the value of the lease which she had lost through the non-performance of the agreement of 16th November, 1863 (assumed to be £205), but not the damages and costs which arose out of the resale of the lease to Budd; these not having necessarily resulted from the defendant's wrongful act were consequently too remote.[227]

§ 836. Loss of bargain.

The plaintiff may, as has been seen, recover what he would have gained by the contract.[228] If the contract was to pay money simply, he may recover the amount to be paid.[229] In an English case, the defendants, warranting themselves as agents of Lloyd & Co., contracted for the sale to the plaintiffs by Lloyd & Co., of certain cargoes of American wool which were soon to arrive. Lloyd & Co. having repudiated the contract, which they had not sanctioned, the plaintiff filed a bill in equity against them for specific performance, which was dismissed with costs. In the action on the warranty, the Court of Queen's Bench held that the damages should include the difference between the contract price of the wool and the value of like wool at the time and place where the cargoes would have been delivered, had the contract been binding, taking into account all the mercantile circumstances affecting the value, and including the taxed costs of the chancery suit and the plaintiff's costs, taxed as between attorney and client.[230] So in a like case in the Court of Queen's Bench, Mr. Justice

[227] Spedding v. Nevell, L. R. 4 C. P. 212.

[228] *Massachusetts:* Jones v. Wolcott, 2 All. 247.

Minnesota: Skaaraas v. Finnegan, 31 Minn. 48.

New York: Taylor v. Nostrand, 134 N. Y. 108, 31 N. E. 246.

Ohio: Trust Co. v. Floyd, 47 Ohio St. 525, 26 N. E. 110, 21 Am. St. Rep. 846.

Pennsylvania: Kroeger v. Pitcairn, 101 Pa. 311, 47 Am. Rep. 718.

Tennessee: Morton v. Hart, 88 Tenn. 427, 12 S. W. 1026.

England: In re National Coffee Palace Co., 24 Ch. D. 367; Firbank v.

Humphreys, 18 Q. B. Div. 54; Godwin v. Francis, L. R. 5 C. P. 295; Weeks v. Profert, L. R. 8 C. P. 427.

Ireland: Maxwell v. Parnell, Ir. Rep. 1 C. L. 234.

Contra, Collen v. Wright, 7 El. & B. 301 (*semble*).

[229] *New York:* Dusenbury v. Ellis, 3 Johns. Cas. 70; Palmer v. Stephens, 1 Den. 471.

Pennsylvania: Hampton v. Speckenagle, 9 S. & R. 212.

England: Meek v. Wendt, 21 Q. B. D. 126.

[230] Hughes v. Graeme, 33 L. J. (N. S.) Q. B. 335.

Crompton remarked: "The damages to be recovered are what was lost to the plaintiff by not having the valid contract, which the agent warranted he had." And a verdict for the difference between the price named in a contract made without authority and repudiated by the alleged principal and that obtained on a resale fairly made, was held right.[231]

§ 837. Expense of litigation.

If the plaintiff brings suit against the supposed principal, having no reason to doubt the authority of the unauthorized agent, he may recover from the latter his costs and expenses in his suit against the principal.[232] But in order to recover the plaintiff must have acted reasonably in bringing or continuing the former suit.[233] So, where one Davis, professing in good faith to have authority to let certain premises, but having no authority in fact, made a parol lease of them for seven years, and the lessee was dispossessed by the owners, in an action of ejectment which he defended, relying on the authority of Davis and on his own attorney's advice, it was, in an action by the lessee against the professed agent, held by the Court of Queen's Bench, that he could recover the expense of certain repairs he had put on the premises, but not of the defence of the ejectment suit, since that could not have been defended, if the agent had possessed authority, the parol lease being void. The attorney's bad advice did not make the defendant liable.[234]

The third party may recover from the agent damages [235] and costs and attorneys' fees [236] sustained in an action by the

[231] Simons v. Patchett, 7 E. & B. 568, 574.

[232] *Massachusetts:* Jones v. Wolcott, 2 All. 247.
Missouri: Wright v. Baldwin, 51 Mo. 269.
New York: White v. Madison, 26 N. Y. 117.
Ohio: Trust Co. v. Floyd, 47 Ohio St. 525, 26 N. E. 110, 21 Am. St. Rep. 846.
Vermont: Clark v. Foster, 8 Vt. 98.
England: Collen v. Wright, 7 El. & B. 301; Polhill v. Walter, 3 B. & A. 114; Randell v. Trimen, 18 C. B. 786; Spedding v. Nevell, L. R. 4 C. P. 212; Godwin v. Francis, L. R. 5 C. P. 295.
Canada: Eckstein v. Whitehead, 10 Up. Can. C. P. 65.
Similarly, the alleged principal who has been subjected to suit may recover his expenses from the pretended agent. Philpot v. Taylor, 75 Ill. 309.

[233] Godwin v. Francis, L. R. 5 C. P. 295.

[234] Pow v. Davis, 1 B. & S. 220.

[235] Starkey v. Bank of England, [1903] App. Cas. 114, [1902] 1 Ch. 610.

[236] Scaling v. Knollin, 94 Ill. App. 443.

principal to recover property unauthorizedly transferred by the agent, where the plaintiff's course in defending the suit was a reasonable one.

§ 838. Incidental expenses.

The plaintiff may recover expenses which flow naturally from the contract. So where the pretended agent let the plaintiff into possession under a lease, he may recover the expense of repairs.[237] If an auctioneer sell real property without sufficient authority, so that the purchaser cannot get a title, the auctioneer will be liable to pay the purchaser's expenses of investigating the title, with interest on the deposit, and also interest on the purchase-moneys if it have been in readiness and unproductive.[238] But it has been held that the plaintiff cannot recover for a loss upon bank shares which he sold to obtain the purchase-money,[239] nor for loss in the purchase of horses to carry on the farm which he had contracted to buy,[240] for these losses are too remote.[241]

§ 839. Unauthorized suits.

Where a party brings an action in the name of another without his direction or consent, he is acting as an unauthorized agent, and is liable to make good to the party sued the damage sustained.[242] The gist of the action is want of authority; but evidence of express malice on the part of the defendant toward the plaintiff is competent.[243] In Bond v. Chapin [244] Hubbard, J., said: "If the defendant suffers injury by reason of the prosecution of the unauthorized suit against him, he may maintain an action for the actual damages sustained by him, in the loss of time, and for money paid to procure the discontinuance of the

[237] Collen v. Wright, 7 El. & B. 301; Pow v. Davis, 1 B. & S. 220; Spedding v. Nevell, L R. 4 C. P. 212.

[238] Bratt v. Ellis, Sugden on Vendors, 812, 14th ed.; Jones v. Dyke, Sugden on Vendors, 813; Godwin v. Francis, L. R. 5 C. P. 295.

[239] Maxwell v. Parnell, Ir. Rep. 1 C. L. 234.

[240] Godwin v. Francis, L. R. 5 C. P. 295.

[241] Wallace v. Bentley, 77 Cal. 19, 18 Pac. 788, 11 Am. St. Rep. 231.

[242] *Maine:* Foster v. Dow, 29 Me. 442.

Massachusetts: Bond v. Chapin, 8 Met. 31.

Texas: Streeper v. Ferris, 64 Tex. 12, 53 Am. Rep. 735.

[243] Smith v. Hyndman, 10 Cush. (Mass.) 554.

[244] 8 Met. (Mass.) 31, 33.

suit, but nothing more. Where, however, in addition to a want of authority, the suit commenced was altogether groundless, and was prosecuted with malicious motives, . . . then, in addition to the actual loss of time and money, the party may recover damages for the injury inflicted on his feelings and reputation."

CHAPTER XXXVIII

ACTIONS BY AND AGAINST CARRIERS

I.—Carriers of Goods

§ 840. The law measures the damages.
841. Compensation of carrier.
842. Refusal to transport.
843. Consequential damages.
843a. Failure to furnish cars.
844. Non-delivery—Value at place of destination, with interest, the general rule.
845. Value, where to be estimated.
846. Connecting lines.
846a. Failure to forward goods.
847. Value, when to be estimated.
848. Reduction of damages—Acceptance of goods.

§ 849. Insurance money.
850. Consequential damages.
851. Limited liability.
852. Injury during transportation.
853. Misdelivery.
854. Delay in delivery.
855. Delay in transportation by sea.
856. Consequential damages.
856a. Notice of special damages.
857. Delay in lading or unlading a vessel.
857a. Discrimination.
858. Agreement to furnish freight.

II.—Carriers of Passengers

§ 859. Form of action.
860. Personal injury.
861. Fright and nervous shock.
862. Failure to carry a passenger.
863. Delay in transporting a passenger.
864. Failure to carry to destination.
864a. Carriage beyond station.
865. Expulsion from train.
865a. Failure to furnish agreed accommodations.

§ 866. Compensation for the risk of injury.
867. Consequences of exposure.
868. American rule.
869. Pullman Palace Car Co. v. Barker.
870. Brown v. Chicago, Milwaukee & St. Paul Railway.
871. General conclusions.
872. Avoidable consequences.
873. Baggage.

III.—Other Similar Agencies

§ 873a. Sleeping or parlor cars.

§ 873b. Inns, theatres, &c.

Carriers of Goods

§ 840. The law measures the damages.

* The class of cases which we now proceed to consider, like those discussed in the last chapter, cannot be made to conform to the broad line that separates contract from tort,

as the actions against common carriers may be framed either *ex contractu* upon the breach of the engagement, or *ex delicto* upon the violation of the public duty. But we shall find that, whether the action be on the contract, or on the violation of duty, the measure of damages is equally a question of law, and as much under the control of the court as if the right rested in agreement merely.**

§ 841. Compensation of carriers.

The carrier is entitled to compensation for transporting the goods. If no rate of freight is fixed by contract, he may recover a reasonable compensation.[1] If the shipper interferes and takes the goods at a point short of destination, the carrier, if he is ready and willing to complete the voyage, may recover full freight.[2] If the owner and the carrier agree that the goods shall be taken by the owner before reaching their destination, the carrier is entitled to compensation *pro rata itineris*.[3] The facts must be such, however, as to raise a fair inference that the further carriage of the goods was intentionally dispensed with. If the goods were accepted from necessity to save their destruction, or because of breach of contract by the carrier, there can be no recovery.[4]

[1] *District of Columbia:* Simmes v. Marine I. Co., 2 D. C. (2 Cr. C. C.) 618.

England: Bastard v. Bastard, 2 Show. 82.

[2] *United States:* Murray v. Ætna Ins. Co., 4 Biss. 417; Jordan v. Warren Ins. Co., 1 Story, 342.

North Dakota: Braithwaite v. Power, 1 N. D. 455, 48 N. W. 354.

[3] *United States:* The Mohawk, 8 Wall. 153, 19 L. ed. 406; Bork v. Nortin, 2 McLean, 422; Marine Insurance Co. v. So. Pac. Co., 55 Fed. 82; Scow No. 190, 88 Fed. 320.

Connecticut: Escopinche v. Stewart, 2 Conn. 262, 391.

Maine: Hunt v. Haskell, 24 Me. 339, 41 Am. Dec. 387.

Maryland: Merchants' Ins. Co. v. Butler, 20 Md. 41.

Michigan: Rossiter v. Chester, 1 Doug. 154.

Mississippi: Bennett v. Byram, 38 Miss. 17, 75 Am. Dec. 90.

New Hampshire: Harris v. Rand, 4 N. H. 259, 261, 17 Am. Dec. 421 (*semble*).

New York: Whitney v. New York F. I. Co., 18 Johns. 208; Parsons v. Hardy, 14 Wend. 215, 28 Am. Dec. 521; Hinsman v. N. Y. Mutual Ins. Co., 5 Bosw. 460.

Pennsylvania: Gray v. Waln, 2 S. & R. 229.

South Carolina: Halwerson v. Cole, 1 Spear, 321, 40 Am. Dec. 603.

Virginia: Hooe v. Mason, 1 Wash. 207.

England: Luke v. Lyde, 2 Burr. 882.

[4] *United States:* Caze v. Baltimore Ins. Co., 7 Cranch, 358, 3 L. ed. 370;

§ 842. Refusal to transport.

If a carrier wrongfully refuses to transport goods, the difference between the value of the goods at the place of shipment and at the place of delivery when they should have arrived furnishes the measure of damages, deducting the freight or price of carriage.[5] * If, however, another conveyance can be found by using ordinary care, the plaintiff is bound to do so; and in such case the measure of damages will be merely the difference between the freight or price of carriage agreed on with the defendant and the sum (if greater) which the plaintiff has been obliged to pay others.[6] ** This

The Ship Nathaniel Hooper, 3 Sumner, 542; Hurtin v. Union Ins. Co., 1 Wash. 530.

Massachusetts: Portland Bank v. Stubbs, 6 Mass. 422.

New York: Marine Ins. Co. v. United Ins. Co., 9 Johns. 186; Western Transportation Co. v. Hoyt, 69 N. Y. 230, 25 Am. Rep. 175; Atlantic Ins. Co. v. Bird, 2 Bosw. 195.

Texas: Adams v. Haught, 14 Tex. 243.

England: Cook v. Jennings, 7 T. R. 381; Liddard v. Lopes, 10 East, 526; Vlierboom v. Chapman, 13 M. & W. 230.

[5] *United States:* Harvey v. Grand Trunk Ry., 2 Hask. 124, 11 Fed. Cas. No. 6,180.

Georgia: Cooper v. Young, 22 Ga. 269, 68 Am. Dec. 502.

Indiana: Chicago, etc., R. R. v. Wolcott, 141 Ind. 267, 39 N. E. 451.

Illinois: Galena & C. U. R. R. v. Rae, 18 Ill. 488, 68 Am. Dec. 574.

Iowa: Bridgman v. The Emily, 18 Ia. 509.

Kentucky: Louisville & N. R. R. v. Queen City Coal Co., 13 Ky. L. Rep. 832.

Massachusetts: Harvey v. Connecticut & P. R. R. R., 124 Mass. 421, 26 Am. Rep. 673.

Michigan: Ward's C. & P. L. Co. v. Elkins, 34 Mich. 439, 22 Am. Rep. 544.

Minnesota: Cowley v. Davidson, 13 Minn. 92.

New York: People v. New York, L. E. & W. R. R., 22 Hun, 533.

Pennsylvania: Fox v. Hayward, 4 Brewster, 32; McGovern v. Lewis, 56 Pa. 231; Pennsylvania R. R. v. Titusville & P. P. R. R., 71 Pa. 350.

Texas: International & G. M. R. R. v. Startz, 33 S. W. 575; Missouri, K. & T. Ry. v. Witherspoon, 38 S. W. 833. If the shipper has contracted to sell the goods below the market price, it has been held that he can recover only the difference between the contract price and the value at the place of shipment. Missouri, K. & T. Ry. v. Witherspoon, 45 S. W. 424. *Sed qu.*

[6] *United States:* Lumberman's Min. Co. v. Gilchrist, 55 Fed. 677, 6 U. S. App. 599, 5 C. C. A. 239.

Indiana: Louisville, N. A. & C. Ry. v. Flanagan, 113 Ind. 488, 14 N. E. 370, 3 Am. St. Rep. 674.

Massachusetts: Colburn v. Phillips, 13 Gray, 64; Metropolitan Coal Co. v. Boutell T. & T. Co., 196 Mass. 72, 81 N. E. 645.

Missouri: Steffen v. Mississippi River etc., R. R., 156 Mo. 322, 56 S. W. 1125.

New York: Grund v. Pendergast, 58 Barb. 216; Briggs v. Davis, 66 Barb. 73.

Wisconsin: Bigelow v. Chicago, B. & N. Ry., 104 Wis. 109, 80 N. W. 95.

second alternative rule is, of course, a deduction from that of avoidable consequences. The substituted cost of transportation must be reasonable. But the shipper need not go further than this and show that the profit on the contract, if executed, would have exceeded or equalled the increase in the freight.[7] If the goods are finally transported by the carrier, the measure of damages is the deterioration in value of the goods caused by the delay,[8] as in the case, hereafter considered, of delay in delivery. Here too, the doctrine of avoidable consequences requires the shipper to use care to preserve the property, but he may recover reasonable expenses incurred therein.[9]

* The plaintiff brought action to recover damages of the defendant for refusing to transport wheat from Pittsburg to Philadelphia, according to contract: the transportation was prevented by the approaching freezing of the canal. The defendant contended that the measure of damages was the difference between the price agreed on for the freight, and that for which their carriage might have been obtained by others; and the court said that this would be the rule, if the plaintiff *could* have obtained other conveyance.[10] "The plaintiff would have no right, by his own negligence or want of care, to incur a voluntary loss for the purpose of imposing it on the defendant as a penalty for the breach of contract. If, as is usually the case here, another conveyance could have been obtained for this wheat before the canal froze up, by a little extra expense and the delay of a day or two, he would have no right to claim greater damages than would have been in-

Canada: McEwan v. McLeod, 9 Ont. App. 239.

Scotland: Connal v. Fisher, 10 Rettie, 824.

[7] The Rossend Castle, 30 Fed. 462; The Oregon, 55 Fed. 666, 5 C. C. A. 229, 6 U. S. App. 581 (in this case the whole subject is fully discussed and the authorities examined); Gilchrist v. Lumberman's Mining Co., 6 U. S. App. 599, 55 Fed. 677, 5 C. C. A. 239.

[8] *Illinois:* Chicago & A. R. R. v. Erickson, 91 Ill. 613, 33 Am. Rep. 70.

Missouri: Shelby v. Missouri Pac. R. R., 77 Mo. App. 205; Hamilton v.

Western N. C. R. R., 96 N. C. 398, 3 S. E. 164.

Texas: Texas P. Ry. v. Nicholson, 61 Tex. 491; Galveston, H. & S. A. Ry. v. Karrer (Tex. Civ. App.), 109 S. W. 440.

Wisconsin: Shores Lumber Co. v. Starke, 100 Wis. 498, 76 N. W. 366.

[9] *Arkansas:* St. Louis A. & T. Ry. v. Neel, 56 Ark. 279, 19 S. W. 963.

Texas: Houston & T. C. R. R. v. Smith, 63 Tex. 322.

[10] O'Conner v. Forster, 10 Watts (Pa.), 418.

curred by such extra expenses and delay." But the defendant offering no such proof the true rule of damages was held to be the difference between the value of the wheat in Pittsburg, with the freight added, and the market price at Philadelphia, at the time it would have arrived there if carried according to the contract.** * So where the contract was to take on board a vessel a cargo of wheat at a certain freight, and it was proved that the defendant refused to receive the wheat, and that the price of freight rose three pence per bushel between the date of the agreement and the sailing of the vessel, it was held that the difference between the price agreed upon for transporting the wheat, and that for which its carriage might have been obtained by others at the time when the ship was to receive it, was the true measure of damages.[11] It was insisted that the shipper was bound to show affirmatively, that he had a cargo of the kind agreed on, ready for shipment at the time fixed by the contract, or that he could only recover nominal damages; but it was decided that this was not necessary.[12] ** So where the carrier failed to have a ship at a foreign port ready to receive goods there, the measure of the damages recoverable against him was held to be the difference between the contract price and the market rate of freight at that port for the voyage, with interest from the time when the freight would have been payable if the contract had been kept.[13]

Where the defendants agreed at a fixed price to convey six vessel loads of lumber from Saginaw to Chicago—one in

[11] *Acc.*, Nelson v. Plimpton F. P. E. Co., 55 N. Y. 480; Grund v. Pendergast, 58 Barb. 216. On the other hand, in Bohn v. Cleaver, 25 La. Ann. 419, the defendants agreed with the plaintiffs to give them a steamer for a full cargo of cotton to Liverpool or Havre, at a stipulated rate, the ship to be ready on the 15th of October. The ship was not ready on the 15th. On that day freights to Liverpool were one penny and one-eighth sterling per pound, an advance on the agreed price. There was no evidence to show that the plaintiff had made any contract to ship cot-

ton. He testified that he did not like to take the risk of making contracts, because he was afraid the vessel could not arrive in time. It was held that the plaintiff could not recover; that the damages were too speculative. Two judges dissented, holding that the measure of damages was the profit which would have arisen on a full cargo from the difference between the contract and the ruling rate.

[12] Odgen v. Marshall, 8 N. Y. 340.

[13] Higginson v. Weld, 14 Gray (Mass.), 165.

August, two in September, two in October, and one in November, and carried five only—one in August, one in September, one in October, and two in November—and freight rose in October and largely in November, and there was no evidence of any agreement of the parties to apply the extra cargo to the default in September or October, it was held that the defendants had a right to have the extra cargo carried in November, and which had been accepted by the plaintiffs, stand as a substituted performance for the cargo they had failed to carry in October, and that the plaintiffs would be entitled to such damages only as they had sustained by the defendants' failure to carry one of the September cargoes.[14]

§ 843. Consequential damages.

The master of a vessel having contracted for the transportation of a cargo, the performance of the contract was interrupted while the lading of the cargo on board was going on, by the death of the master, and afterwards by the freezing up of the vessel. The owner repudiated the contract, and refused either to take on board the residue of the cargo, or to deliver up that already laden. It was held, First: That the shipper could recover damages for the value of the brick laden on board and withheld; for the cost of transporting the residue from his storehouse to the dock; for any injuries received by them while they lay there awaiting acceptance by the owner of the vessel; and for the difference in the shipper's disfavor, if any, between the contract price of transportation, and his actual expenses incurred in obtaining another mode of conveyance. Second: That he could not recover against the vessel for injuries received by the property after notice of the owner's refusal to complete the contract, but that the vessel was chargeable with the cost of transporting the portion of cargo left behind, to its place of destination.[15] Where the defendants, having contracted to be ready with their ship on the river Tyne on a certain day, to receive a cargo of coal to be carried to Havre for the plaintiff, broke their contract, and the plaintiff had, in consequence, not only to charter vessels at an advanced freight, but also to buy coal at a higher price, he was

---

[14] Lord v. Strong, 6 Mich. 61.   [15] The Flash, 1 Abb. Adm. 119.

held entitled, in the absence of proof that there had been an equivalent rise in coal at Havre, to recover for the loss on the coal, as well as on the freight.[16] When the carrier broke its contract to carry tile and arranged with another carrier to do so and the consequent delay caused the detention of the trucks on which the tile was piled and the shipper had to pay for such detention he recovered such expenses from the defaulting carrier.[17]

Where the carrier had notice of a contract of sale for the goods at the place of delivery, the owner may recover the difference between the contract price and the market price at the place of shipment, less freight.[18] Where the carrier had notice that the failure to transport goods would result in a delay in work which was being carried on by the plaintiff, it was held that the latter might recover the expenses caused by stoppage of the work, and the wages lost.[19]

The defendant agreed to transport lumber to Boston, for the plaintiff, at certain rates, for a certain time. The defendant failed to perform the contract and the lumber was not shipped. In the court below the plaintiff was allowed to recover damages for losses on contracts of which the defendant had no notice. On appeal this was held to be error, and that, as the property had not been shipped, the true measure of damages was the difference between the market prices at Boston and at the place of shipment at the time when the defendant should have transported the lumber, less the freight stipulated in the contract of transportation.[20] But in an action for failure to receive and carry corn according to agreement, a shipper can recover for loss of profits which he would have derived out of a sub-contract where he notified the company of the sub-contract on entering into his contract with them.

---

[16] Featherston v. Wilkinson, L. R. 8 Ex. 122.

[17] Welch v. Anderson, 8 T. L. Rep. 119.

[18] *Alabama:* Baxley v. Tallassee & M. R. R., 128 Ala. 183, 29 So. 451 (cross ties).

Iowa: Cobb v. Illinois C. R. R., 38 Ia. 601, 630.

Minnesota: Day v. Gravel, 72 Minn. 159, 75 N. W. 1.

Texas: Gulf C. & S. F. R. R. v. Martin (Tex. Civ. App.), 28 S. W. 576 (cattle).

[19] Pennsylvania R. R. v. Titusville & P. P. R. R., 71 Pa. 350.

[20] Harvey v. Connecticut & P. R. R. R., 124 Mass. 421, 26 Am. Rep. 673.

In such an action the measure of damages is the difference between the market price at the place where the corn was offered for transportation, and the contract price less the cost of transportation.[21]

Where the carrier refused to transport the equipment of a theatrical company, the carrier having notice that it was designed for use in certain theatrical engagements, which by reason of the carrier's default the shipper was compelled to cancel, it was held that the carrier was liable for the loss of profits.[22]

Where a railway company refused to carry, at the ordinary rate, packed parcels for a carrier, whereby he was forced to send them by a circuitous route at a greater expense, he was held not entitled to recover for loss of business alleged to have been sustained in consequence.[23] But where carriers unreasonably made a restriction under which they refused to receive less than 15 loads of coal, and the plaintiffs were thereby prevented from sending a smaller number of loads which they had on hand, it was held that the plaintiff could recover for loss of custom by not being able to send that coal.[24] Where the defendants refused to transport grain, which heated before another carrier could be found, the owner was allowed to recover the loss by the heating of the grain.[25] In an Irish case it appeared that the carrier failed to provide cars to transmit the plaintiff's valuable horses to market. The horses were thereupon sent on foot to market. They had been fed "soft," in consequence of which they arrived at market in a damaged condition; if they had been in ordinary condition little damage would have resulted from the journey. It was held that under the rule in Hadley v. Baxendale, no damages could be recovered for the consequences which ensued from the horses being "soft fed." The measure of damages was the deterioration in value that horses able to make the journey would have suffered, and the time and labor upon the road;[26] from

[21] Cobb v. Illinois C. R. R., 38 Ia. 601.
[22] Leach v. N. Y., N. H. & H. R. R., 35 N. Y. Supp. 305.
[23] Crouch v. Great Northern Ry., 11 Ex. 742.
[24] Lancashire & Y. Ry. v. Gidlow, L. R. 7 H. L. 517.

[25] Pittsburgh, C. & St. L. Ry. v. Morton, 61 Ind. 539, 28 Am. Rep. 682 (semble).
[26] Waller v. Midland G. W. Ry., 4 L. R. Ir. 376.

which, of course, must be subtracted the freight plaintiff must have paid the carrier.

§ 843a. Failure to furnish cars.

For failure to furnish cars, the measure of damages is the difference in value of the goods to be shipped at the time they should have been received by the carrier and at the time they were in fact received at the place of shipment; [27] or if cars are never furnished, or too late for use by the plaintiff, the difference in value at the place of shipment and at the place of destination, less freight.[28] Thus for failure to furnish cars to transport coal from a mine, the measure of damages is the profit on the coal that might have been marketed.[29] But of course no recovery can be had for loss of profits of a specific contract, unless the carrier had notice of it.[30] The cost of taking care of the property during the delay caused by the failure to furnish cars may be recovered in the ordinary case. Thus the ordinary expense of feeding and caring for cattle may be recovered.[31]

§ 844. Non-delivery—Value at place of destination, with interest, the general rule.

As a general rule, where goods are entrusted to a carrier, and they are not delivered according to the contract, the

---

[27] *Georgia:* Thompson v. Chattanooga S. R. R., 133 Ga. 127, 65 S. E. 285.

Minnesota: Richey & Gilbert Co. v. Northern Pac. Ry., 110 Minn. 347, 125 N. W. 897.

Texas: Gulf C. & S. F. Ry. v. Hume, 87 Tex. 211, 27 S. W. 110; Galveston H. & S. A. Ry. v. Thompson (Tex. Civ. App.), 44 S. W. 8.

[28] *Arkansas:* St. Louis Southwestern Ry. v. Leder Bros., 87 Ark. 298, 112 S. W. 744.

Texas: Southern Kan. Ry. v. O'Loughlin L. & C. Co. (Tex. Civ. App.), 127 S. W. 568.

[29] *Arkansas:* Midland V. R. R. v. Hoffman Coal Co., 91 Ark. 180, 120 S. W. 380.

Pennsylvania: Minds v. Pennsylvania R. R., 228 Pa. 575, 77 Atl. 909.

[30] *Alabama:* Baxley v. Tallassee & M. R. R., 128 Ala. 183, 29 So. 451.

Pennsylvania: Clyde Coal Co. v. Pittsburgh & L. E. R. R., 226 Pa. 391, 75 Atl. 596, 26 L. R. A. (N. S.) 1191.

Texas: Gulf C. & S. F. R. R. v. Hodge (Tex. Civ. App.), 39 S. W. 986; but see Houston, E. & W. T. Ry. v. Campbell, 91 Tex. 551, 45 S. W. 2.

[31] *Arkansas:* St. Louis, I. M. & S. Ry. v. Ozier, 86 Ark. 179, 110 S. W. 593, 17 L. R. A. (N. S.) 327.

Texas: Gulf, C. & S. F. Ry. v. Hume, 87 Tex. 211, 27 S. W. 110; Galveston H. & S. A. Ry. v. Thompson (Tex. Civ. App.), 44 S. W. 8.

Not, however, the expense of caring for cattle caused by unprecedented weather. Wallace v. Pecos & N. T. Ry., 50 Tex. Civ. App. 296, 110 S. W. 162.

measure of damages is the value of the goods at the place of destination in the condition in which the carrier undertook to deliver them, at the time when they should have been delivered, together with interest, less the proper charges of transportation and delivery, if these have not been paid; [32]

[32] *United States:* The Patrick Henry, 1 Ben. 292; Woodward *v.* Ill. Cent. R. R., 1 Biss. 403, 30 Fed. Cas. No. 18,006, 1 Biss. 447, 30 Fed. Cas. No. 18,007, 5 Leg. Op. 192; The Gold Hunter, 1 Blatch & H. 300; Burritt *v.* Rench, 4 McLean, 325, 4 Fed. Cas. No. 2,201; Arthur *v.* The Cassius, 2 Story, 81; Bazin *v.* Steamship Co., 3 Wall. Jr. 229; The Nith, 36 Fed. 86; The Arctic Bird, 109 Fed. 167.

Alabama: South & N. A. R. R. *v.* Wood, 72 Ala. 451; Capehart *v.* Granite Mills, 97 Ala. 353, 12 So. 44; Southern Ry. *v.* Jones Cotton Co., 167 Ala. 575, 52 So. 899.

Arkansas: St. Louis, I. M. & S. Ry. *v.* Mudford, 44 Ark. 439 (*semble*).

California: Ringgold *v.* Haven, 1 Cal. 108; Hart *v.* Spalding, 1 Cal. 213.

Colorado: Denver, S. P. & P. R. R. *v.* Frame, 6 Colo. 382.

District of Columbia: Baltimore, etc. R. R. *v.* Dougherty, 7 A. C. D C. 378.

Georgia: Taylor *v.* Collier, 26 Ga. 122; Wilson *v.* Atlanta & C. Ry., 82 Ga. 386; Atlantic & B. Ry. *v.* Howard Supply Co., 125 Ga. 478, 54 S. E. 530.

Hawaii: La Motte *v.* Angel, 1 Hawaii, 136.

Illinois: Sangamon & M. R. R. *v.* Henry, 14 Ill. 156; Chicago & N. W. Ry. *v.* Dickinson, 74 Ill. 249; Plaff *v.* Pacific Exp. Co., 95 N. E. 1089.

Indiana: Wallace *v.* Vigus, 4 Blackf. 260; Michigan S.⁴ & N. I. R. R. *v.* Caster, 13 Ind. 164; Tebbs *v.* Cleveland C. C. & St. L. Ry., 20 Ind. App. 192, 50 N. E. 486.

Iowa: Clements *v.* Burlington, etc., R. R., 74 Iowa, 442, 38 N. W. 144.

Kansas: The Emily *v.* Carney, 5 Kan. 645.

Kentucky: Cincinnati N. O. & T. P. Ry. *v.* Hansford, 125 Ky. 37, 100 S. W. 251, 30 Ky. L. Rep. 1105.

Louisiana: Segura *v.* Reed, 3 La. Ann. 695; Price *v.* The Uriel, 10 La. Ann. 413.

Maine: Nourse *v.* Snow, 6 Me. 208.

Massachusetts: Cushing *v.* Wells, Fargo & Co., 98 Mass. 550; Spring *v.* Haskell, 4 All. 112; Green *v.* B. & L. R. R., 128 Mass. 221, 35 Am. Rep. 370 (*semble*).

Michigan: Marquette, H. & O. R. R. *v.* Langton, 32 Mich. 251.

Missouri: Atkisson *v.* The Castle Garden, 28 Mo. 124; Union R. R. & T. Co. *v.* Traube, 59 Mo. 355; Gray *v.* Missouri R. P. Co., 64 Mo. 47; Dunn *v.* Hannibal & St. J. R. R., 68 Mo. 268; Rice *v.* Indianapolis & St. L. R. R., 3 Mo. App. 27; Ross *v.* Chicago, R. I. & P. R. R., 119 Mo. App. 290, 95 S. W. 977; F. H. Smith Co. *v.* Louisville & N. R. R., 145 Mo. App. 394, 137 S. W. 890.

New Hampshire: Bailey *v.* Shaw, 24 N. H. 297, 55 Am. Dec. 241.

New York: Smith *v.* Richardson, 3 Cai. 219; Watkinson *v.* Laughton, 8 Johns. 213; Elliott *v.* Rossell, 10 Johns. 1; Amory *v.* M'Gregor, 15 Johns. 24; Sturgess *v.* Bissell, 46 N. Y. 462; Sherman *v.* Wells, 28 Barb. 403; Van Winkle *v.* United States M. S. Co., 37 Barb. 122; Krohn *v.* Oechs, 48 Barb. 127.

Nebraska: Atchison T. & S. F. R. R. *v.* Lawler, 40 Neb. 356, 58 N. W. 968.

Ohio: McGregor *v.* Kilgore, 6 Ohio, 358; Louis *v.* The Buckeye, 1 Handy, 150.

Oregon: Prettyman *v.* Oregon Ry. & N. Co., 13 Ore. 341 (*semble*).

Pennsylvania: Hand *v.* Baynes, 4

and where the goods had already been damaged by a cause for which the carrier was not responsible, the measure of damages for their subsequent loss is their value in the damaged condition.[33]

In an action of assumpsit [34] against the defendants, as shipowners, for not delivering a cargo of wheat consigned to the plaintiffs, the cargo reached the port of discharge, but was not delivered, and the price of the cargo at the time it reached its port of destination was held to be the true rule of damages. "As between the parties in this cause," said Parke, J., "the plaintiffs are entitled to be put in the same situation as they would have been if the cargo had been delivered to their order at the time when it was delivered to the wrong party; and the sum it would have fetched at that time is the amount of the loss sustained by non-performance of the defendant's contract." So in another case,[35] where suit was brought on

Whart. 204, 33 Am. Dec. 54; Ludwig v. Meyre, 5 W. & S. 435; Warden v. Greer, 6 Watts, 424; Gillingham v. Dempsey, 12 S. & R. 183.

South Carolina: Shaw v. South Carolina R. R., 5 Rich. L. 462; O'Neall v. South Carolina R. R., 9 Rich. L. 465; Kyle v. Laurens R. R., 10 Rich. 382, 70 Am. Dec. 231; Brown v. Northwestern R. R., 75 S. C. 20, 54 S. E. 829.

Tennessee: Edminson v. Baxter, 4 Hayw. 112, 9 Am. Dec. 751; Dean v. Vaccaro, 2 Head, 488, 75 Am. Dec. 744; Louisville & N. R. R. v. Mason, 11 Lea, 116; Cole v. Rankin (Tenn. Ch.), 42 S. W. 72.

Texas: Wolfe v. Lacy, 30 Tex. 349; International & G. N. Ry. v. Nicholson, 61 Tex. 550; Galveston H. & S. A. Ry. v. Ball, 80 Tex. 602, 16 S. W. 441; Texas & P. Ry. v. Klepper (Tex. Civ. App.), 24 S. W. 567; Texas & P. Ry. v. Sims (Tex. Civ. App.), 26 S. W. 634; Missouri, K. & T. Ry. v. Woods (Tex. Civ. App.), 117 S. W. 196; Texas & P. Ry. v. Hoffecker (Tex. Civ. App.), 123 S. W. 617; Missouri, K. & T. Ry. v. Harriman (Tex. Civ. App.), 128 S. W 932; San Antonio & A. P. Ry. v.

Chittin (Tex. Civ. App.), 135 S. W. 747.

Vermont: Laurent v. Vaughn, 30 Vt. 90; Blumenthal v. Brainerd, 38 Vt. 402, 91 Am. Dec. 349 (*semble*).

Virginia: Norfolk & W. R. R. v. Harman, 91 Va. 601, 22 S. E. 490.

Wisconsin: Chapman v. Chicago & N. W. Ry., 26 Wis. 295, 7 Am. Rep. 81; Whitney v. Chicago & N. W. Ry., 27 Wis. 327.

England: Rice v. Baxendale, 7 H. & N. 96; Sanquer v. London & S. W. Ry., 16 C. B. 163; Rodoconachi v. Milburn, 17 Q. B. D. 316, 18 Q. B. D. 67.

Canada: Worden v. Canadian P. Ry., 13 Ont. 652.

In a few cases where goods on board ship were lost, the measure of damages was held to be the invoice price, with interest. The Vaughan & Telegraph, 14 Wall. 258; Jackson v. The Julia Smith, Newb. Adm. 61; Wheelwright v. Beers, 2 Hall, 391. See §§ 845, 855.

[33] Starr-Hardnett & Edmeiston Co. v. Missouri, K. & T. Ry., 122 Mo. App. 26, 97 S. W. 959.

[34] Brandt v. Bowlby, 2 B. & A. 932.

[35] Bracket v. M'Nair, 14 Johns. 170.

an agreement to carry a quantity of salt from Oswego to Queenston, the difference in value of the article at Oswego and at Queenston at the time, was held the true rule of damages. In a case on the Massachusetts circuit,[36] where a libel was filed in admiralty against vessel and master for not delivering a cargo at Velasco, the vessel arrived out, and the consignee refusing to receive it, the master, contrary to his duty, carried it on to New Orleans. It was held that the libellants were entitled to recover the actual value at Velasco at the time when the cargo should have been landed there, deducting all duties and charges, and the freight for the voyage, as if the cargo had been duly landed.

In Massachusetts, it was agreed by bill of lading, that the net proceeds of the cargo at the port of destination should be paid to the shippers in ninety days after the return of the vessel to her home port; the ship having arrived out, the goods were sold, and the proceeds invested by the owners of the ship on their own account, in return cargo; the ship met with disaster and injured her cargo 50 per cent, but arrived at her home port; and it was held that the shippers were entitled to recover the whole net amount for which the adventure was sold in the foreign port.[37] A carrier who receives goods from a wrong-doer, without the consent of the owner, expressed or implied, can have no right to detain them against the true owner for the payment of his freight. But when the freight is earned in good faith, under a contract of transportation made with an agent of the owner, who, according to the usages of the business, is clothed with apparent authority by his principal, then the charges for freight will constitute a valid lien on the property, although the agent, by an accidental or intentional departure from his instructions, sends the goods by a route not intended, or to the wrong place; and so in an action by the owner of goods against a third person to whom they

---

[36] Arthur v. The Cassius, 2 Story, 81; and Mr. Justice Story said, that the rule adopted in prize cases, of an addition of ten per cent to the price cost of the cargo, did not apply to cases like the present; that rule ordinarily supposing that the vessel has been captured before she arrived at the port of destination, and the court making the presumption of the additional value of ten per cent in odium spoliatoris.

[37] Wallis v. Cook, 10 Mass. 510; Winchester v. Patterson, 17 Mass. 62.

had been sent by mistake, and who had paid the freight on them in good faith, he was held entitled to a deduction of the amount of the freight, as he succeeded to the right of the carrier.[38] Where goods were lost through the negligence of a carrier on the last part of the route, the plaintiff was allowed to recover the value at the place of destination, less the freight. It was held that he could not recover, in addition, the freight paid to another railroad company which carried the goods over the first part of the route.[39] It may, however, be the case that the non-delivery of the goods does not cause a loss to the plaintiff equal to the full value of the goods. This was held to be the case where a carrier allowed the plaintiff's slave to escape; since the plaintiff might recapture the slave, the measure of damages was not necessarily the full value.[40] So where cattle are killed, the value of the hides is to be deducted from the amount recovered.[41] If the goods are shipped to one who has procured them for resale he is not entitled to the profit of resale, or in other words to the retail price.[42] When the lost goods have no market value or when their value in use exceeds the amount they would actually bring in the market and an equivalent is not readily obtainable the measure of damages is this value in use.[43] If the property can be replaced by labor and expense, evidence of the cost of replacing is relevant to prove this value.[44]

[38] Whitney v. Beckford, 105 Mass. 267.

[39] Northern Transportation Co. v. McClary, 66 Ill. 233.

[40] O'Neall v. South Carolina R. R., 9 Rich. L. (S. C.) 465.

[41] Atchison, T. & S. F. Ry. v. Bivins (Tex. Civ. App.), 136 S. W. 1180.

[42] Alabama: Southern Ry. v. T. A. Hatter & Son, 165 Ala. 423, 51 So. 723.
Kentucky: Cincinnati, N. O. & T. P. Ry. v. Hansford, 125 Ky. 37, 100 S. W. 251, 30 Ky. L. Rep. 1105.
Texas: Texas & P. Ry. v. Payne, 15 Tex. Civ. App. 58, 38 S. W. 366.

[43] Illinois: Parmelee v. Raymond, 43 Ill. App. 609 (wearing apparel).
New York: Bennett v. Drew, 3 Bosw. 355 (daguerreotype).

Pennsylvania: Lloyd v. Haugh & K. S. & T. Co., 223 Pa. 148, 72 Atl. 516, 21 L. R. A. (N. S.) 184 (household goods).
Texas: International & G. N. R. R. v. Nicholson, 61 Tex. 550.
England: O'Hanlan v. Great Western Ry., 6 B. & S. 484, 11 Jur. (N. S.) 797, 34 L. J. Q. B. 154, 12 L. T. Rep. (N. S.) 490, 18 Wkly. Rep. 741, 118 E. C. L. 484 (package of clothing).

[44] Kentucky: Adams Exp. Co. v. Hoeing, 9 Ky. L. Rep. 814 (maps for geological survey).
Mississippi: Louisville & N. R. R. v. Stewart, 78 Miss. 600, 29 So. 394 (family portraits).
Texas: Houston & S. C. R. R. v. Burke, 55 Tex. 323, 40 Am. Rep. 808 (family portraits).

Though as a general rule the shipper owes no duty to disclose the nature of the goods shipped, yet when goods of great value are so packed as to indicate to the carrier that they have no extraordinary value, the shipper may be unable to recover the full value. This is, doubtless, because the nondisclosure amounts to fraud, operating both to deceive the carrier as to the amount of care required and to deprive it of the extra compensation to which it would be entitled for assuming the extra risk.[45]

§ 845. Value, where to be estimated.

As we have said, the general rule is that the value at the place of destination governs. A vessel having on board a cargo of flour for transportation, capsized at her wharf before sailing, and the cargo was much damaged. The carriers might easily have communicated with the owners of the cargo, and sought instructions as to the disposal of it; but they neglected to do so, and sold the cargo upon their own authority, at auction; after which the vessel sailed, and in due time arrived at the port of delivery. It was held, 1. That the owners of the cargo were entitled to recover the value of the cargo at the port of delivery, deducting freight and charges, and interest on the balance. 2. That the value of the cargo should be computed by the market price at the port of delivery, at the time of the arrival of the vessel, it appearing that, except for the accident, the cargo would at that time, in the ordinary course of things, have been delivered; with a privilege, however, to the owner to claim the amount realized upon the sale of the goods at auction.[46]

---

[45] *United States:* Kuter v. Michigan Cent. R. R., 1 Biss. 35 (gold coin packed with household goods).

California: Hayes v. Wells, Fargo & Co., 23 Cal. 185, 83 Am. Dec. 89 (letter containing check).

Georgia: Southern Exp. Co. v. Wood, 98 Ga. 268, 25 S. E. 436 (manuscript of opera score).

Maine: Little v. Boston & M. R. R., 66 Me. 239 (*semble*), (box of jewelry).

New York: Magnin v. Dinsmore, 62 N. Y. 35, 20 Am. Rep. 442 (watches).

And see *Massachusetts:* Phillips v. Earle, 8 Pick. 182 (laces).

[46] The Joshua Barker, 1 Abb. Adm. 215. In some jurisdictions in case of a sea voyage a different rule prevails. In such a case in New York, after reviewing the cases, it was held that the measure of damages was their value at that port, not their value at the port of destination, less the cost of transportation. Krohn v. Oechs, 48 Barb. 127; Lakeman v. Grinnell, 5 Bosw. 625. In a case decided by Mr. Justice Story in

A carrier received goods at Oswego to carry to Montreal. They were destroyed *en route*. The measure of damages was held to be the value at Montreal, less freight, computed in Canadian money with no addition or subtraction on account of depreciation in the currency of either country.[47] If there is no market at the point of destination the value is of course the market value at the nearest market, with the proper allowance for cost of transportation.[48]

§ 846. Connecting lines.

It is now generally the law in the United States, although it is not so in England, that the receipt by a carrier of goods destined to a place beyond the terminus of his route, does not in itself imply a contract on his part to carry them beyond such terminus.[49] In such a case the destination of the goods, as regards the carrier on one of the several routes over which they are transported, is the terminus of his particular route; and their value at that point, and not at their ultimate place of consignment, has been held to define his responsibility.[50] But circumstances may modify this rule, and in fixing the amount of damages reference may be had to the ultimate destination intended for the goods. Thus where apples intended for the New York market, which destination was

1844, where a box of gold coin had been shipped from New York to be carried to Mobile, and the ship was wrecked off the coast of Florida, and most of the cargo saved and taken to Key West, where salvage proceedings were instituted, but the coin was lost through the master's gross neglect, the measure of damages was held to be its value at Key West, with interest from the time when the salvage proceedings were taken. King v. Shepherd, 3 Story, 349.

[47] Rice v. Ontario Steamboat Co., 56 Barb. (N. Y.), 384.

[48] Eddy v. Lafayette, 49 Fed. 807, 1 C. C. A. 441.

[49] *United States:* Railroad v. Pratt, 22 Wall. 123, 22 L. ed. 827; Railroad v. Androscoggin Mills, 22 Wall. 594, 22 L. ed. 724.

California: Palmer v. Atchison, T. & S. F. R. R.,101 Cal. 187, 35 Pac. 630.

Connecticut: Elmore v. Naugatuck R. R., 23 Conn. 457, 63 Am. Dec. 143; Naugatuck R. R. v. Waterbury Button Co., 24 Conn. 468.

New York: Hempstead v. New York C. R. R., 28 Barb. 485; Dillon v. New York & E. R. R., 1 Hilt. 231.

[50] *Kentucky:* Cincinnati, N. O. & T. P. R. R. v. Logan, 96 S. W. 910, 29 Ky. L. Rep. 1123.

New York: Harris v. Panama R. R., 5 Bosw. 312.

Ohio: Louis v. The Buckeye, 1 Handy, 150.

Contra in *Texas:* El Paso & N. E. Ry. v. Lumbley (Tex. Civ. App.), 120 S. W. 1050.

known to the carrier, were to be transported by the New York Central Railroad to the intermediate town of Albany, which was the terminus of the railroad, and there delivered to another carrier to be conveyed to New York, Albany was held to be the port of destination as regarded the railroad company, and the value there furnished the rule of damages in an action against it for injury to the apples by freezing while in its charge. But proof of their value in New York was held admissible, the court considering that the value in that city, deducting the freight thither from Albany, would be proper evidence of the value at Albany.[51] Where, however, a carrier enters into a special contract to deliver goods beyond his own route, he will be liable for the value at the ultimate point of destination.[52] In Erie Railway v. Lockwood [53] the defendant had agreed to carry to Jersey City and forward from there to Boston. It was held proper for the judge at *nisi prius* to refuse to charge in such a case that the defendant was only liable for the value of the oil at the terminus of its line where it was to be delivered to the next carrier, the plaintiff being entitled to the benefit of through rates.

§ 846a. Failure to forward goods.

The first carrier instead of forwarding to the next carrier stored the goods in a warehouse subject to the shipper's order. This was held not to be a conversion and the measure of damages was held to be the profits which plaintiff would have made upon contracts into which he had entered in reliance upon the receipt of the goods.[54] When the first carrier wilfully shipped the goods by another route than that mentioned in the contract it is liable for the difference between the special

---

[51] Marshall v. New York C. R. R., 45 Barb. 502.

[52] *Alabama:* East Tenn., V. & G. R. R. v. Johnston, 75 Ala. 596, 51 Am. Rep. 489.

Maine: Perkins v. Portland, S. & P. R. R., 47 Me. 573, 74 Am. Dec. 504.

Pennsylvania: Ruppel v. Allegheny Valley R. R., 167 Pa. 166, 31 Atl. 478, 46 Am. St. Rep. 666.

Texas: Gulf, C. & S. F. R. R. v. Eddins, 7 Tex. Civ. App. 116, 26 S. W. 161.

In *Indiana* the point is left undecided; Michigan, S. & N. I. R. R. v. Caster, 13 Ind. 164.

[53] 28 Oh. St. 358. The report of this case is not very clear.

[54] Buston v. Pennsylvania R. R., 116 Fed. 235.

freight rate agreed upon, and that which the shipper was compelled to pay.[55]

§ 847. Value, when to be estimated.

* In New York,[56] where case was brought against a carrier for delay in forwarding Alpine mulberry-trees, in consequence of which a portion were destroyed, the plaintiff claimed as his damages the market value of the trees—four shillings each. The defendant's counsel offered to prove that, from subsequent experiments, this kind of tree had been ascertained to be of no intrinsic value; that the value put on them when the injury occurred was factitious; and that if as much had been known of them then as at the time of trial, they could have been bought for one cent each. He further offered to prove that Alpine mulberry-trees were not worth cultivating for the purpose of raising silk-worms; that those in question were purchased by the plaintiff with a view of growing seedlings for sale, and that they were of no value for that purpose the next year after they were bought. These offers were overruled, and (notwithstanding the dissenting opinion of Cowen, J.,) the Supreme Court held rightly. Nelson, J., in delivering the opinion of the court, said:

"The damages should afford the plaintiff an adequate indemnity for the loss sustained at the *time the injury happened.* Assuming that there is no defect in the quality of the article, the fair test of its *value,* and consequently of the loss to the owner, is the price at *the time in the market.* The objection to the evidence offered is, that it proposes to take into consideration the fluctuations of the market value long *subsequent to the time* when the injury happened, thereby making the measure of damage to depend on the accidental fall of prices at some future period, which might or might not occur, and if it did, the loss might or might not have fallen on the plaintiff, as for aught the court or jury could know, he may have parted with the property before its depreciation." **

Where it becomes illegal either to deliver or return the goods, on account of the existence of war, the measure of

[55] Pond-Decker Lumber Co. *v.* Spencer, 86 Fed. 846, 30 C. C. A. 430.

[56] Smith *v.* Griffith, 3 Hill (N. Y.),

333; *acc.,* Kent *v.* Hudson R. R. R., 22 Barb. (N. Y.), 278.

damages is the value of the goods at the time of a demand for them at the end of the war.[57]

§ 848. Reduction of damages—Acceptance of goods.

* It is well settled, that in cases of negligence, the subsequent acceptance of the goods is no bar to an action for injuries such as those of which we have been treating. Nothing but a release or satisfaction constitutes such a bar. But acceptance may be given in evidence in reduction of damages, so as to limit the recovery to the actual loss sustained by the owner.[58] **

§ 849. Insurance money.

The carrier in an action against him for injuries to the goods through his negligence, is not entitled to a deduction for so much of the loss as is covered by insurance.[59]

§ 850. Consequential damages.

The reasonable expenses of searching for lost goods may be recovered.[60]   Where the property lost consisted of a set of plans for building a house, damages for delay in building the house are too remote when the defendant had no notice.[61] Loss suffered on account of a sub-contract cannot be recovered[62] unless the carrier had notice of it.[63]   For the non-

---

[57] Caldwell v. Southern Ex. Co., 1 Flip. 85.

[58] *Louisiana:* Lewis v. The Ship Success, 18 La. Ann. 1.

New Hampshire: Hackett v. B. C. & M. R. R., 35 N. H. 390.

New York: Monell v. Northern Cent. R. R., 16 Hun, 585.

[59] *United States:* Mobile & M. Ry. v. Jurey, 111 U. S. 584, 28 L. ed 527, 4 Sup. Ct. 566.

New York: Merrick v. Brainard, 38 Barb. 574; Bowman v. Teall, 23 Wend. 306.

See Story on Bailments, 582a.

[60] *Arkansas:* Evans v. Rudy, 34 Ark. 383.

Kansas: North M. R. R. v. Akers, 4 Kan. 453, 96 Am. Dec. 183.

New York: Farwell v. Davis, 66 Barb. 73.

Ohio: Davis v. Cincinnati, H. & D. R. R., 1 Disney, 23.

Canada: Morrison v. European & N. A. Ry., 2 Pugs. 295.

Contra, Mississippi: Mississippi C. R. R. v. Kennedy, 41 Miss. 671.

[61] Mather v. American Ex. Co., 138 Mass. 55. So also where lumber for building a house was not delivered. Alderson v. Gulf, C. & S. F. Ry. (Tex. Civ. App.), 23 S. W. 617.

[62] Caledonian Ry. v. Colt, 3 Macqueen, 833; Baxendale v. London C. & D. Ry., L. R. 10 Ex. 35.

[63] *Illinois:* Illinois C. R. R. v. Cobb, 64 Ill. 128.

Kansas: Missouri Pac. R. Co. v.

delivery of a piece of machinery, whereby plaintiff's mill was prevented from running until new machinery could be ordered and delivered, the carrier was held not liable for the probable profits plaintiff would have made but for the delay.[64]

§ 851. Limited liability.

Some confusion exists as to what extent a carrier may limit its liability to an amount less than the actual value of the goods, when they are lost by the carrier's negligence. Three situations should be distinguished: (1) Where the carrier limits its liability to a sum arbitrarily fixed with no pretence of approximating the true value. Such a stipulation is generally held bad as against public policy.[65] The same result obtains where there is an attempt to limit the recovery to the value at place of shipment.[66] (2) Where the parties in

Peru-Van Zandt Implement Co., 73 Kan. 295, 85 Pac. 408, 410, 87 Pac. 80, 6 L. R. A. (N. S.) 1058.

England: British Columbia Saw Mill Co. *v.* Nettleship, L. R. 3 C. P. 499.

[64] Sharpe *v.* Southern Ry., 130 N. C. 613, 41 S. E. 799.

[65] *United States:* Eells *v.* St. Louis, K. & N. W. R. R., 52 Fed. 903.

Alabama: Ala. & Great Southern R. R. *v.* Little, 71 Ala. 611.

Colorado: Overland M. & E. Co. *v.* Carroll, 7 Colo. 43, 1 Pac. 682.

Georgia: Central of Ga. Ry. *v.* Murphey, 113 Ga. 514, 38 S. E. 970.

Indiana: Evansville & J. H. R. R. *v.* McKinney, 34 Ind. App. 148, 73 N. E. 148.

Kansas: Kansas City, St. J. & C. B. R. R. *v.* Simpson, 30 Kan. 645, 2 Pac. 821, 46 Am. Rep. 104.

Kentucky: Louisville & N. R. R. *v.* Owen, 93 Ky. 201, 19 S. W. 590.

Louisiana: Kember *v.* Southern Exp. Co., 22 La. Ann. 158, 22 Am. Rep. 719.

Mississippi: Chicago, St. L. & N. O. R. R. *v.* Abels, 60 Miss. 1017.

Nebraska: Chicago, B. & Q. R. R. *v.* Gardiner, 51 Neb. 70, 70 N. W. 508.

New York: Vroman *v.* Exp. Co., 2 Hun, 512, 51 Am. Dec. 319; Marquis *v.* Wood, 29 Misc. 590, 61 N.Y. Supp. 251.

North Carolina: Brown *v.* Postal Tel. Cable Co., 111 N. C. 187, 16 S. E. 179; Gardner *v.* Southern Ry., 127 N. C. 293, 37 S. E. 328.

Tennessee: Louisville & N. R. R. *v.* Wynn, 88 Tenn. 320, 14 S. W. 311.

Wisconsin: Abrams *v.* Milwaukee, L. S. & W. Ry., 87 Wis. 485, 58 N. W. 780, 41 Am. St. Rep. 55; Ullman *v.* Chicago & N. W. R. R., 112 Wis. 150, 88 N. W. 41, 88 Am. St. Rep. 949, 56 L. R. A. 246.

[66] *Indiana:* Baltimore & O. R. R. *v.* Ragesdale, 14 Ind. App. 406, 42 N. E. 1106.

Mississippi: Ill. Central R. R. *v.* Bogard, 78 Miss. 11, 27 So. 879.

North Carolina: McConnell Bros. *v.* Southern R. R., 144 N. C. 87, 56 S. E. 559.

Pennsylvania: Ruppel *v.* Allegheny Valley R. R., 167 Pa. 166, 31 Atl. 478, 46 Am. St. Rep. 666.

Texas: Galveston H. & S. A. R. R. *v.* Ball, 80 Tex. 602, 16 S. W. 441.

Virginia: Chesapeake & O. R. R. *v.* Stock, 104 Va. 97, 51 S. E. 161.

good faith agree as to the actual value. This is simply an agreement as to liquidated damages and is rightly allowed to protect the carrier from exaggerated valuation subsequent to the loss.[67] (3) Where the shipper inaccurately states the value to the carrier or by conduct leads the carrier to believe the goods are of less value than they in fact are, whereby the shipper obtains a freight rate based on the stated valuation and the carrier uses less vigilance in caring for the goods, then the shipper is rightly estopped to set up the true value after loss.[68] But the carrier must be ignorant that the stated value is false.[69] It is on this principle that a stipulation may be sustained limiting recovery "to a certain sum unless the true value be stated;" the silence of the shipper may then be constructive fraud.[70]

Wisconsin: Black v. Goodrich Transportation Co., 55 Wis. 319, 13 N. W. 244, 42 Am. Rep. 713.

[67] *United States:* Hart v. Pennsylvania R. R., 112 U. S. 331, 28 L. ed. 718, 5 Sup. Ct. 151 (citing authorities); Jennings v. Smith, 106 Fed. 139, 45 C. C. A. 249; Metrop. Trust Co. v. Toledo, St. L. & K. C. R. R., 107 Fed. 628.

Alabama: Louisville & N. R. R. v. Sherrod, 84 Ala. 178, 4 So. 29.

Arkansas: St. Louis, I. M. & S. R. R. v. Lesser, 46 Ark. 236.

Georgia: Central of Georgia R. R. v. Glascock, 117 Ga. 938, 43 S. E. 981.

Kentucky: Adams Exp. v. Hoeing, 9 Ky. L. Rep. 814.

Minnesota: Moulton v. St. Paul, M. & M. Ry., 31 Minn. 85, 16 N. W. 497, 47 Am. Rep. 781; Alair v. Northern Pac. R. R., 53 Minn. 160, 54 N. W. 1072, 39 Am. St. Rep. 588.

Missouri: Vaughn v. Wabash R. R., 62 Mo. App. 461, 467.

Rhode Island: Ballou v. Earle, 17 R. I. 441, 22 Atl. 1113, 33 Am. St. Rep. 881, 14 L. R. A. 433.

Texas: Southern Pac. R. R. v. Maddox, 75 Tex. 300, 12 S. W. 815.

Wisconsin: Ullman v. Chicago & N. W. R. R., 112 Wis. 150, 88 N. W. 41, 88 Am. St. Rep. 949.

[68] *United States:* Earnest v. Express Co., 1 Woods, 573; Railroad Co. v. Fraloff, 100 U. S. 24, 25 L. ed. 531; The Lydian Monarch, 23 Fed. 298.

Alabama: Southern Express Co. v. Owens, 149 Ala. 412, 41 So. 752.

Connecticut: Coupland v. Housatonic R. R., 61 Conn. 531, 23 Atl. 870.

Illinois: Chicago, B. & Q. R. R. v. Miller, 79 Ill. App. 473.

Indiana: Rosenfeld v. R. R., 103 Ind. 121, 2 N. E. 344, 53 Am. Rep. 500.

Massachusetts: Hill v. Boston, H. T. & W. R. R., 144 Mass. 284, 10 N. E. 836, 59 Am. Rep. 84.

Missouri: Harvery v. Terre H. & I. R. R., 74 Mo. 538.

Ohio: Railway Co. v. Simon, 15 Oh. Cir. Ct. 123.

Pennsylvania: Relf v. Rapp, 3 W. & S. 21, 37 Am. Dec. 528.

South Carolina: Johnstone v. Richmond & D. R. R., 39 S. C. 55, 17 S. E. 512.

West Virginia: Zouch v. Chesapeake & O. R. R., 36 W. Va. 524, 15 S. E. 185.

England: Tyly v. Morrice, Carth. 485.

[69] United States Exp. Co. v. Backman, 28 Ohio St. 144.

[70] *United States:* Muser v. Holland, 17 Blatch. 412; Calderon v. Atlas Steamship Co., 64 Fed. 874, 69 Fed. 574.

In some jurisdictions a contract is held valid, by which in consideration of reduced freight rates the recovery for loss shall be limited to a stated sum known to be less than the actual value.[71] It is difficult to sustain this view in states where a carrier is not allowed to exempt itself from all liability. In case of partial loss, it has been held that the carrier is liable for all damages up to the amount agreed on as the limit, disregarding the proportion between the actual value and the stipulated limit; [72] measured by the difference between the value of goods at destination and such agreed value.[73] A limitation of liability for loss or damage to the goods does not operate to limit liability for delay in delivery; [74] nor does

California: Michal Itschke *v.* Wells, Fargo & Co., 118 Cal. 683, 50 Pac. 847.

Connecticut: Lawrence *v.* N. Y., N. H. & H. R. R., 36 Conn. 63, 4 Am. Rep. 35.

District of Columbia: Geld *v.* Adams Exp. Co., McA. & M. 124.

Illinois: Oppenheimer *v.* U. S. Exp. Co., 69 Ill. 62, 18 Am. Rep. 596.

Kansas: Pacific Exp. Co. *v.* Foley, 46 Kan. 457, 26 Pac. 665, 26 Am. St. Rep. 107.

Louisiana: Baldwin *v.* Collin, 9 Rob. 468.

Michigan: Smith *v.* Am. Exp. Co., 108 Mich. 572, 66 N. W. 479.

Missouri: Rogan *v.* Wabash R. R., 51 Mo. App. 665, 674.

New Hampshire: Durgin *v.* Exp. Co., 66 N. H. 277, 20 Atl. 328.

New York: Magnin *v.* Dinsmore, 70 N. Y. 410, 26 Am. Rep. 608.

Rhode Island: Ballou *v.* Earle, 17 R. I. 441, 22 Atl. 1113, 33 Am. St. Rep. 881.

Wisconsin: Boorman *v.* Am. Exp. Co., 21 Wis. 152.

England: Harris *v.* Packwood, 3 Taunt. 264; Harris *v.* Great Western Ry., 1 Q. B. Div. 515.

But see, *Alabama:* Southern Exp. Co. *v.* Crook, 44 Ala. 468, 4 Am. Rep. 135.

[71] *Alabama:* Western R. R. *v.* Harwell, 91 Ala. 340, 8 So. 649.

Arkansas: St. Louis, I. M. & S. Ry. *v.* Weakly, 50 Ark. 397, 8 S. W. 134, 7 Am. St. Rep. 104; Little Rock & F. & S. Ry. *v.* Cravens, 57 Ark. 112, 20 S. W. 803, 38 Am. St. Rep. 230.

California: Pierce *v.* Southern Pac. Co., 120 Cal. 156, 47 Pac. 874.

Georgia: Atlantic C. L. R. R. *v.* Goodwin, 1 Ga. App. 351, 57 S. E. 1070.

Minnesota: Douglas *v.* Minnesota Transfer Co., 62 Minn. 288, 64 N. W. 899.

Missouri: Kellerman *v.* Kansas City S. J. & C. B. R. R., 136 Mo. 177, 34 S. W. 41.

New York: Zimmer *v.* New York Cent. R. R., 137 N. Y. 460, 33 N. E. 642.

South Carolina: Johnstone *v.* Richmond & D. R. R., 39 S. C. 55, 17 S. E. 512.

Tennessee: Louisville & N. R. R. *v.* Sowell, 90 Tenn. 17, 15 S. W. 837.

Virginia: Richmond & D. R. R. *v.* Payne, 86 Va. 481, 10 S. E. 749.

[72] Starnes *v.* Railroad, 91 Tenn. 516, 19 S. W. 675.

[73] Pearse *v.* Quebec Steamship Co., 24 Fed. 285.

[74] *Alabama:* Southern R. R. *v.* Webb, 143 Ala. 304, 39 So. 262.

New York: Vroman *v.* American M. U. E. Co., 2 Hun, 512.

it cover a loss happening after an unlawful deviation by the
carrier, even though the deviation was not a cause of the
loss, since the deviation puts the risk of loss absolutely upon
the carrier.[75]

§ 852. Injury during transportation.

Where goods are injured during transportation the measure
of damages is the difference between their value in their damaged state at the place of destination and what it would have
been there if they had been delivered in good order.[76] The

[75] *Massachusetts:* McKahan v. American Express Co. (Mass.), 95 N. E. 785,
and cases cited.
England: Elswick Steamship Co. v.
Montaldi, 76 L. J. K. B. 672, [1907] 1
K. B. 626, 96 L. T. 845, 12 Com. Cas.
240, 10 Asp. M. C. 456, 23 T. L. R.
322 (C. A.).
Ante, § 121a.

[76] *United States:* New York, L. E. &
W. R. R. v. Estill, 147 U. S. 591, 616, 13
Sup. Ct. 444, 37 L. ed. 292; The
Compta, 5 Sawy. 137; The Mangalore,
9 Sawy. 71, 23 Fed. 463; The Colonel
Ledyard, 1 Sprague 530; Strouss v.
Wabash R. R., 17 Fed. 209; Magde-
burg G. I. Co. v. Paulson, 29 Fed. 530;
Western M. Co. v. The Guiding Star,
37 Fed. 641; Estill v. New York, L. E. &
W. R. R., 41 Fed. 849; United S. S. Co.
v. Haskins, 181 Fed. 962.
Arkansas: St. Louis, I. M. & S. R. R.
v. Deshong, 63 Ark. 443, 448, 39 S. W.
260; St. Louis S. W. Ry. v. Phœnix Cot-
ton Oil Co., 88 Ark. 594, 115 S. W. 393.
Georgia: East Tennessee, V. & G. R.
R. v. Herrman, 92 Ga. 384, 17 S. E.
344.
Illinois: Chicago, B. & Q. R. R. v.
Hale, 83 Ill. 360, 25 Am. Rep. 403;
Cleveland O. C. & St. L. R. R. v. Pat-
ton, 104 Ill. App. 550; Michigan Cent.
Ry. v. Osmus, 129 Ill. App. 79.
Iowa: Parsons v. United States Exp.
Co., 144 Ia. 745, 123 N. W. 776, 25 L.
R. A. (N. S.) 842.
Kansas: St. Louis & S. F. Ry. v.
Lieurance, 80 Kan. 424, 102 Pac. 142.

Kentucky: Illinois Cent. R. R. v.
Holt, 92 S. W. 540, 29 Ky. L. Rep.
135.
Louisiana: Lewis v. The Success, 18
La. Ann. 1; Smith Bros. & Co. v. New
Orleans & N. E. R. R., 106 La. 11, 30
So. 265, 87 Am. St. Rep. 285.
Massachusetts: Brown v. Cunard
Steamship Co., 147 Mass. 58, 16 N. E.
717.
Minnesota: Patterson v. Chicago, M.
& S. P. R. R., 95 Minn. 57, 103 N. W.
621.
Missouri: Matney v. Chicago, R. I.
& P. Ry., 75 Mo. App. 233; Blackmer &
P. P. Co. v. Mobile & O. R. R., 137 Mo.
App. 133, 119 S. W. 1.
New York: Schwinger v. Raymond,
83 N. Y. 192, 38 Am. Rep. 415; King v.
Sherwood, 48 N. Y. Supp. 34, 22 App.
Div. 548; D'Olier v. New York Cent. &
H. R. R., 50 Misc. 635, 98 N. Y. Supp.
649.
South Carolina: Davis v. Blue Ridge
Ry., 81 S. C. 466, 62 S. E. 856.
Tennessee: Louisville & N. R. R. v.
Mason, 11 Lea, 116.
Texas: Gulf, C. & S. F. Ry. v. Hume,
87 Tex. 211, 27 S. W. 110; Gulf, C. & S.
F. Ry. v. Stanley, 89 Tex. 42, 33 S. W.
109, 59 Am. St. Rep. 25; Galveston H.
& S. A. Ry. v. Silegman (Tex. Civ.
App.), 23 S. W. 298; International & G.
N. R. R. v. Dimmitt G. P. Co. (Tex.
Civ. App.), 23 S. W. 754; Texas & P.
Ry. v. Klepper (Tex. Civ. App.), 24
S. W. 567; Atchison, T. & S. F. Ry. v.
Grant (Tex. Civ. App.), 26 S. W. 286;

fact that the goods were to be kept for use and not for sale, and that there is no diminution or a less diminution in their value for use is immaterial;[77] the owner is entitled to goods as valuable in every way as they should have been. The cost of the goods to the shipper is also immaterial.[78] If a portion of the injury to the goods was from a cause for which the carrier is not responsible, he will be held for such diminution in value as was due to the cause for which he is responsible.[79] From this amount, however, is to be subtracted the rebate in customs allowed by the customhouse officers on a "damaged appraisement."[80] Such actual value may be ascertained

Texas & P. Ry. v. Avery (Tex. Civ. App.), 33 S. W. 704; International & G. N. R. R. v. Parish (Tex. Civ. App.), 43 S. W. 1066; Gulf, W. T. & P. Ry. v. Staton (Tex. Civ. App.), 49 S. W. 277; St. Louis S. W. Ry. v. Hunt (Tex. Civ. App.), 81 S. W. 322; Missouri, K. & T. Ry. v. Allen (Tex. Civ. App.), 87 S. W. 168; Missouri, K. & T. Ry. v. Kyser (Tex. Civ. App.), 87 S. W. 389; Southern K. Ry. v. Burgess (Tex. Civ. App.), 90 S. W. 189, Missouri, K. & T. Ry. v. Rich (Tex. Civ. App.), 112 S. W. 114; Chicago, R. I. & P. Ry. v. Jones (Tex. Civ. App.), 118 S. W. 759; Scott v. Texas Cent. R. R., 127 S. W. 849; Missouri, K. & T. Ry. v. Harris (Tex. Civ. App.), 138 S. W. 1085 (but see Texas Cent. R. R. v. Watson (Tex. Civ. App.), 118 S. W. 175.

In a few cases where the value of the goods was not fluctuating and the goods were not carried far, the measure of damages was said to be the difference in value when delivered to the company and when received.

Delaware: McHenry v. Philadelphia, W. & B. R. R., 4 Harr. 448.

Iowa: Parsons v. United States Exp. Co., 144 Ia. 745, 123 N. W. 776.

New York: Black v. Camden & A. R. R. & T. Co., 45 Barb. 40.

Contra, Missouri: McHaney v. St. Louis & S. F. R. R., 149 Mo. App. 369, 129 S. W. 1065, where the places were far apart.

In *Kentucky* the measure of damages has been stated to be the difference between the market value before the injury and the market value immediately after the injury; which appears to mean the values at the place of injury rather than at the place of destination. Southern Express Co. v. Fox, 131 Ky. 257, 115 S. W. 184, 131 Ky. L. Rep. 257.

In case of a shipment of household goods the measure of damages is the difference in actual value (not of course in market value, *ante,* § 251) just before and just after the injury. Atchison, T. & S. F. Ry. v. Smythe (Tex. Civ. App.), 119 S. W. 892.

The shipper cannot refuse to receive the goods (if they arrive *in specie*) and recover their entire value, but is limited to a recovery of the amount of damage. Missouri, K. & T. Ry. v. Moore, 47 Tex. Civ. App. 531, 105 S. W. 532.

[77] Gulf, C. & S. F. Ry. v. Gillespie, 118 S. W. 628 (Tex. Civ. App.).

[78] Cleveland, C. C. & S. L. Ry. v. Schaefer (Ind. App.), 90 N. E. 502.

[79] Blackmer & P. P. Co. v. Mobile & O. R. R., 137 Mo. App. 479, 119 S. W. 1 (shipment of sewer pipe, with exemption of liability except for negligence; carrier not liable for breakage from ordinary contingencies of the journey, but liable for all that might have been avoided by due care).

[80] The Mangalore, 9 Sawy. 71, 23

by a public sale to the highest bidder;[81] and the price which is in fact obtained in the open market is evidence of the amount of loss.[82] So where goods were thus damaged during transportation, and were received by consignees upon an understanding that the depreciation was to be made good to them, and they were sold at auction by the consignees, but with the assent of the master: it was held that for the purpose of making adjustment of the amount due from the vessel for the injury, the sum realized at the sale should be regarded as the value of the goods in their damaged state.[83] The law imposes on the carrier by sea the duty of taking such reasonable and ordinary measures as are practicable to preserve the cargo from the serious deterioration which without such measures would result from an accident occurring during the transportation, even although the accident be one for which the ship would not be originally liable. And where a cargo of beans had been to some extent injured by having been wet, and notwithstanding that the ship had stopped for repairs on the voyage at an intermediate port, where the beans might readily have been dried, and thereby saved from further deterioration, the voyage was pursued without this having been done, the owner of the beans was held entitled to recover damages, the measure of which should be the difference between the damage they would probably have sustained if unshipped and dried at the intermediate port, and that which they actually sustained by having been carried thence undried to the port of destination.[84] Similarly where perishable goods arrive damaged, the consignee should take reasonable steps to dispose of them; and he will be held accountable for the amount for which he could have disposed of the goods by the exercise of ordinary care.[85]

Fed. 463; Hamilton v. Bark Kate Irving, 5 Fed. 630; Morrison v. I. & V. Florio S. S. Co., 36 Fed. 569.

[81] *United States:* Pendall v. Rench, 4 McLean, 259, 19 Fed. Cas. No. 10,917; Bancroft-Whitney Co. v. The Queen, 78 Fed. 155, 172.

Louisiana: Henderson v. The Maid of Orleans, 12 La. Ann. 352.

New York: Guiterman v. Liverpool, etc., Steamship Co., 83 N. Y. 358.

[82] Southern Ry. v. Graddy, 109 S. W. 881, 33 Ky. L. Rep. 183.

[83] The Columbus, 1 Abb. Adm. 97.

[84] Notara v. Henderson, L. R. 7 Q. B. 225.

[85] Texarkana & F. S. Ry. v. Shivel (Tex. Civ. App.), 114 S. W. 196.

In an action for injury to goods, the plaintiff may recover the reasonable and necessary expenses of putting the goods in a salable condition, since such expenses are for the defendant's benefit.[86] Similarly where a machine designed for use and not for sale is injured, the cost of repairing is recoverable.[87] Where hops were injured by moisture and delivered to the shipper, and during the time necessary to dry the hops and put them in a salable condition the market value depreciated, the measure of damages awarded was the difference between the market value when the goods became available as marketable goods, and the value at the time when and in the condition in which they should have been delivered.[88]

Where goods were both damaged and delayed in transit, and during the delay the market had risen, so that the increased value through the rise in price was greater than the diminution through the injury, it was nevertheless held that the plaintiff should recover damages for the injury according to the general rule.[89] The court said: "They (the defendants) cannot now be allowed to take advantage of their own wrong, and claim a participation of profits growing out of a rise in the market price. . . . To do this would be to bestow a premium on the misconduct of the respondents." A subsequent rise or fall in price does not affect the measure of damages; they are to be estimated according to the price in the market when the goods were or should have been delivered.[90] Consequently damages may be recovered in a proper case;

[86] *United States:* Kennedy v. Dodge, 1 Ben. 215.
Illinois: Chicago & N. W. Ry. v. Calumet Stock Farm, 194 Ill. 9, 61 N. E. 1095, 88 Am. St. Rep. 68 (horses).
Indiana: Chicago I. & L. R. R. v. Woodward, 164 Ind. 360, 72 N. E. 558 (cattle).
Iowa: Winne v. Illinois C. R. R., 31 Ia. 583 (flour); Wisecarver v. Chicago, R. I. & P. Ry., 141 Ia. 121, 119 N. W. 532 (horses).
Kansas: Kansas City Stock Yard Co. v. Hawkins, 8 Kan. App. 155, 55 Pac. 470 (cattle).
Texas: Houston & T. C. R. R. v. Williamson (Tex. Civ. App.), 31 S. W. 556 (cattle); Galveston H. & S. A. Ry. v. Tuckett (Tex. Civ. App.), 25 S. W. 670 (horses).
[87] *Missouri:* Gray v. St. Louis, I. M. & S. R. R., 54 Mo. App. 666.
New York: Jackson Agricultural Iron Works v. Hurlbut, 158 N. Y. 34, 52 N. E. 665, 70 Am. St. Rep. 432.
[88] Collard v. South Eastern Ry., 7 H. & N. 79, 7 Jur. (N. S.) 950, 30 L. J. Exch. 393, 4 L. T. Rep. (N. S.) 410, 9 Wkly. Rep. 697.
[89] Morrison v. Florio S. S. Co., 36 Fed. 569, 571.
[90] The Compta, 5 Sawy. 137.

thus upon proper notice given the shipper may recover compensation for loss of a resale.[91]

The defendant took hogs to carry through in a car. The hogs were unloaded, and because of a stock quarantine, which prevented their reshipment after once being unloaded, they were obliged to be sold there. It was held, that the measure of damages was the difference between the value of the hogs at their destination when they should have arrived, and the amount actually obtained at the sale.[92] Where the carrier erroneously placarded cars "Southern cattle," whereby the shipper could not get full value for the cattle, he recovered the difference between the value of the cattle as placarded and the value of other cattle of the same kind.[93]

On the other hand, however, damages may be refused in a similar case if they were remote or not within the contemplation of the parties. This was the case in an action against railroad for wrongfully shifting cattle from one car to another. When the cars were unloaded the cattle were seized by the state authorities as cattle imported from Texas, and plaintiff was fined for introducing them, and the cattle were sold. It was held that since defendant was in no way responsible for the act of the state authorities, and there was no notice at the time the cattle were shipped that this would be the result of unloading, and there was nothing to show that it was caused by the unloading, the loss claimed was too remote.[94]

§ 853. Misdelivery.

If the result of a misdelivery is a loss of the goods to the owner, the measure of damages is the same as in case of nondelivery.[95] If the misdelivery destroys the consignor's lien

[91] Gulf, C. & S. F. Ry. v. Coulter (Tex. Civ. App.), 139 S. W. 16.

[92] Wilson v. St. Louis & S. F. R. R., 108 S. W. 612, 129 Mo. App. 347.

[93] Wabash R. R. v. Campbell, 219 Ill. 312, 76 N. E. 346, 3 L. R. A. (N. S.) 1092.

[94] McAlister v. Chicago, R. I. & P. R. R., 74 Mo. 351, 4 Am. & Eng. R. R. Cas. 210. Loss of prize money from exhibition of the injured cattle is too uncertain. Ft. Worth & D. C. Ry. v.

Ikard (Tex. Civ. App.), 140 S. W. 502.

[95] That is, the value at the time and place of delivery less the unpaid freight.

California: Adams v. Blankenstein, 2 Cal. 413, 56 Am. Dec. 350.

Maryland: Baltimore & O. R. R. v. Pumphrey, 59 Md. 390.

Massachusetts: Forbes v. Boston & L. R. R., 133 Mass. 154; Massachusetts L. & T. Co. v. Fitchburg R. R., 143 Mass. 318, 9 N. E. 669.

the measure of recovery is the amount of the lien.[96] If goods are delivered to the owner, but at the wrong place, the cost of removing them to the place where they should have been delivered would be the usual measure of damages.[97]

Where a carrier delivered goods to the wrong person, who accounted for them to the owner, it was held the latter could only recover nominal damages.[98] And when the owner received part of the value of the goods from the person to whom they were delivered, his recovery was reduced by that amount.[99] Where the carrier misdelivered cattle to a stockyard company instead of to the consignee and plaintiff was compelled to pay for the keeping of the stock he was held entitled to reimbursement.[100] Where a carrier, having instructions to deliver cotton at Norfolk to a factor who had been directed to hold it until further orders, delivered it instead to a factor at Petersburg, who, having no instructions about it, sold it immediately, and cotton rose rapidly and steadily after the sale, the court applied the rule of damages that governs the case of factors who sell their principals' goods without authority, and held the carrier liable, at least, for the price at the time the plaintiff got the full advice of the sale.[101]

§ 854. Delay in delivery.

The extent of a carrier's liability for negligent delay in the transportation or delivery of goods has been a subject of much discussion. Where there is no injury to the goods, and they are offered to the owner after the time when, by his express or implied contract, it was the carrier's duty to deliver them,

Minnesota: Foy v. Chicago, M. & St. P. Ry., 63 Minn. 255, 65 N. W. 627.

[96] *California:* Persse v. Cole, 1 Cal. 369.

Kentucky: Louisville & N. R. R. v. Hartwell, 99 Ky. 436, 18 Ky. L. Rep. 745, 36 S.W. 183, 33 S.W. 1041, 59 Am. St. Rep. 467.

Michigan: Hutchings v. Ladd, 16 Mich. 493.

South Dakota: Stone v. Chicago, M. & S. P. Ry., 8 S. D. 1, 65 N. W. 29.

[97] *Illinois:* Chicago & N. W. Ry. v. Stanbro, 87 Ill. 195, 29 Am. Rep. 49.

New York: Richmond v. Union Steamboat Co., 87 N. Y. 240.

Canada: Monteith v. Merchants' Despatch Co., 9 Ont. App. 282.

[98] Rosenfield v. Express Co., 1 Woods, 131.

[99] Jellett v. St. Paul, M. & M. Ry., 30 Minn. 265.

[100] Southern R. R. v. Webb, 143 Ala. 304, 39 So. 262, 111 Am. St. Rep. 45.

[101] Arrington v. Wilmington & W. R. R., 6 Jones (N. C.), 68. For this rule see ch. xxii.

the owner is not entitled to refuse to receive them with the view of holding the carrier for their full value. If he does so, he can recover, in the absence of special circumstances, an indemnity only for his actual loss.[102] The measure of damages in the ordinary case is the difference in the value of the goods at the time and place they ought to have been delivered, and at the time of their actual delivery,[103] less unpaid

[102] *Arkansas:* St. Louis, I. M. & S. Ry. v. Mudford, 44 Ark. 439.

New York: Scovill v. Griffith, 12 N. Y. 509; Briggs v. New York C. R. R., 28 Barb. 515.

South Carolina: Nettles v. South Carolina R. R., 7 Rich. L. 190.

But if the delay is such as to make delivery useless it is conversion. Mitchell v. Weir, 43 N. Y. Supp. 1123; 45 *id.* 1085.

[103] *United States:* Bussey v. M. & L. R. R. R., 4 McCrary, 405; Petersen v. Case, 21 Fed. 885; Goldsmith v. Henderson, 50 Fed. 567.

Alabama: Richmond & D. R. R. v. Trousdale, 99 Ala. 389, 13 So. 23, 42 Am. St. Rep. 69; Pilcher v. Central of Ga. Ry., 155 Ala. 316, 46 So. 765.

Arkansas: Crutcher v. Choctaw, O. & G. R. R., 74 Ark. 358, 85 S. W. 770.

Georgia: (by the Code) Atlanta & W. P. R. R. v. Texas Grate Co., 81 Ga. 602; Wilson v. Atlanta & C. Ry., 82 Ga. 386; East Tennessee, V. & G. Ry. v. Johnson, 11 S. E. 809, 85 Ga. 497; Southern Exp. Co. v. Briggs, 1 Ga. App. 294, 57 S. E. 1066 (goods valueless because of delay).

Illinois: Galena & C. U. R. R. v. Rae, 18 Ill. 488, 68 Am. Dec. 574; Louisville & N. R. R. v. Heilprin, 95 Ill. App. 402; Wabash R. R. v. Foster, 127 Ill. App. 201.

Iowa: Hudson v. Northern Pac. R. R., 92 Ia. 231, 60 N. W. 608, 54 Am. St. Rep. 550.

Kansas: Missouri, K. & T. R. R. v. Fry, 74 Kan. 546, 87 Pac. 754.

Kentucky: Newport News & M. V. R. R. v. Mercer, 96 Ky. 475, 29 S. W. 301.

Louisiana: Lowry v. Young, 1 La. 232.

Maine: Weston v. Grand T. Ry., 54 Me. 376, 92 Am. Dec. 552.

Maryland: Phila., W. & B. R. R. v. Lehman, 56 Md. 209, 40 Am. Rep. 415.

Massachusetts: Ingledew v. Northern R. R., 7 Gray, 86; Cutting v. Grand T. Ry., 13 All. 381; Scott v. Boston & N. O. S. S. Co., 106 Mass. 468; Clement & H. M. Co. v. Meserole, 107 Mass. 362.

Michigan: Houseman v. Merchants' Dispatch Transportation Co., 104 Mich. 300, 62 N. W. 290.

Mississippi: New Orleans, J. & G. N. R. R. v. Tyson, 46 Miss. 729 (semble).

Missouri: Faulkner v. South P. R. R., 51 Mo. 311; Rankin v. Pacific R. R., 55 Mo. 167; Hahn v. St. Louis K. C. & C. R. R., 125 S. W. 1185; Gann v. Chicago Great Western R. R., 72 Mo. App. 34; Parsons v. Louisville & N. R. R., 136 Mo. App. 494, 118 S. W. 101 (limited of course by amount claimed in the pleadings); Dawson v. Quincy, O. & K. C. R. R., 138 Mo. App. 365, 122 S. W. 335.

New York: Ward v. New York C. R. R., 47 N. Y. 29, 7 Am. Rep. 405; Zinn v. New Jersey S. B. Co., 49 N. Y. 442, 10 Am. Rep. 402 (semble); Holden v. New York C. R. R., 54 N. Y. 662; Sherman v. Hudson R. R. R., 64 N. Y. 254; Livingstone v. New York C. & H. R. R. R., 5 Hun, 562.

North Carolina: Van Lindley v. Richmond & D. R. R., 88 N. C. 547.

Ohio: Devereaux v. Buckley, 34 Oh.

freight,[104] with interest.[105] The difference in value is to be determined according to the market value and not according to the contract price, where defendant had no notice of the special contract.[106] But the price at which the goods are reasonably sold after arrival may be shown, as indicating their value then,[107] even though to sell them to the best advantage it was necessary to send them to another market.[108]

So in Vermont, a carrier engaging to transport live stock to market by the following market day, and failing to do so, is liable for the difference between what the stock was necessarily sold for, and what it would have brought on the market

St. 16, 32 Am. Rep. 342; Wyler v. Louisville & N. R. R., 83 Oh. St. 293, 94 N. E. 423.

Oklahoma: Chicago, R. I. & P. R. R. v. Broe, 16 Okla. 25, 86 Pac. 441.

South Carolina: Nettles v. South Carolina R. R., 7 Rich. L. 190; McKerall v. Atlantic C. L. R. R., 76 S. C. 338, 56 S. E. 965.

Tennessee: East Tennessee V. & G. R. R. v. Hale, 85 Tenn. 69.

Texas: Texas P. Ry. v. Nicholson, 61 Tex. 491; Missouri P. Ry. v. Russell, 18 S. W. 594; Gulf, C. & S. F. Ry. v. Gilbert (Tex. Civ. App.), 23 S. W. 320; Gulf, C. & S. F. R. R. v. Butler, 26 Tex. Civ. App. 494, 63 S. W. 650; Chicago, R. I. & P. Ry. v. Young (Tex. Civ. App.), 107 S. W. 127; Pecos & N. T. Ry. v. Bivins (Tex. Civ. App.), 130 S. W. 210.

Vermont: Newell v. Smith, 49 Vt. 255.

Virginia: Norfolk & W. R. R. v. Reeves, 97 Va. 284, 33 S. E. 606.

Wisconsin: Peet v. Chicago & N. W. Ry., 20 Wis. 594, 91 Am. Dec. 446.

England: Collard v. Southeastern Ry. 7 H. & N. 79, 30 L. J. (N. S.) Ex. 393, 4 L. T. Rep. (N. S.) 410.

Canada: Monteith v. Merchants' D. & T. Co., 1 Ont. 47, 9 Ont. App. 282.

If the delay has rendered the goods valueless, the entire value may be recovered. Mitchell v. Weir, 43 N. Y. Supp. 1123, 45 N. Y. Supp. 1085.

[104] *United States:* Page v. Munro, 1 Holmes, 232 (semble).

Arkansas: St. Louis, I. M. & S. Ry. v. Phelps, 46 Ark. 485.

Georgia: Southern Exp. Co. v. Hanaw, 134 Ga. 445, 67 S. E. 944.

North Carolina: Lindley v. Richmond & D. R. R., 88 N. C. 547.

[105] See most of the authorities above cited, and:

United States: Missouri, K. & T. Ry. v. Truskett, 104 Fed. 728, 44 C. C. A. 179, aff'd, 186 U. S. 480, 46 L. ed. 1259, 22 Sup. Ct. 943.

Missouri: Dunn v. Hannibal & S. J. R. R., 68 Mo. 268.

Texas: Houston & T. C. Ry. v. Jackson, 62 Tex. 209.

Vermont: Newell v. Smith, 49 Vt. 255.

[106] Missouri, K. & T. Ry. v. Webb, 20 Tex. Civ. App. 431, 49 S. W. 526.

But in the absence of other evidence, the contract price may be taken as the market value. Norfolk & W. Ry. v. Wilkinson, 106 Va. 775, 56 S. E. 808. So it has been held that the price named in the contract of resale, being shown not to be an unusual price, may be taken as the value. Easton v. Erie R. R., 147 Ill. App. 594.

[107] Fort Worth & D. C. Ry. v. Richards (Tex. Civ. App.), 105 S. W. 236.

[108] Missouri K. & T. Ry. v. Carpenter (Tex. Civ. App.), 114 S. W. 900.

day.[109]   Where cattle shrink in weight through delay in transportation, the loss through the shrinkage may be recovered.[110]
In Sisson v. Cleveland & T. Railroad,[111] the contract of the
carrier was to transport from Toledo to Buffalo cattle whose
ultimate destination, as the carrier was informed at the time,
was the Albany or New York market.   There was no fall in
prices before the cattle had reached Buffalo, but owing to the
defendant's delay, they were not delivered at Albany until
after a decline had occurred.   The court held the loss to be
the direct consequence of the defendant's delay attending the
cattle to their destination, as the effects of a fatal injury
would have followed them to their death, and one therefore
for which the carrier must make compensation.   Where cattle
are delayed in transit so that they reach their destination too
late to be sold in the market on Saturday, the owner may
recover for shrinkage until Monday's market.[112]   So in an
action by a cap manufacturer for damages for the loss sustained by delay in the delivery of cloth, by which the plaintiff had lost the season for making it into caps, it was held
by the English Court of Common Pleas, that although the
loss of profits as such could not be taken into account, within
the rule of Hadley v. Baxendale, yet the loss in the market
value of the goods through their arriving too late for the season
was a proper element of damages.[113]

Where, from the carrier's inexcusable delay, peas shipped

[109] King v. Woodbridge, 34 Vt. 565.

[110] *United States:* The Caledonia, 157 U. S. 124, 39 L. ed. 644, 15 Sup. Ct. 537.

Illinois: Illinois C. R. R. v. Owens, 53 Ill. 391.

Kansas: Kansas P. Ry. v. Reynolds, 8 Kan. 623.

Massachusetts: Smith v. New Haven & N. R. R., 12 All. 531.

Missouri: Sturgeon v. St. Louis, K. C. & N. Ry., 65 Mo. 569; Glascock v. Chicago & A. R. R., 69 Mo. 589; De Lisle v. St. Louis & S. F. R. R., 149 Mo. App. 8, 129 S. W. 252.

Texas: San Antonio & A. P. R. R. v. Timon (Tex. Civ. App.), 99 S. W. 418;

St. Louis & S. F. Ry. v. Wilhehm (Tex. Civ. App.), 108 S. W. 1194.

Wisconsin: Ayres v. Chicago & N. W. Ry., 75 Wis. 215, 43 N. W. 1122.

[111] 14 Mich. 489.

[112] Ayres v. Chicago & N. W. Ry., 75 Wis. 215, 43 N. W. 1122.

Acc., Kansas: Missouri, K. & T. Ry. v. Fry, 79 Kan. 21, 98 Pac. 205.

Texas: Missouri K. & T. Ry. v. Hopkins (Tex. Civ. App.), 113 S. W. 306.

[113] Wilson v. Lancashire & Y. Ry., 9 C. B. (N. S.) 632. *Cf.* Rowe v. The City of Budline, 1 Ben. 46, 20 Fed. Cas. No. 12,094.

from Canada to New York were stopped on the way by the freezing of the lakes, and would have been detained through the season, and on the carrier refusing to carry them to New York by rail, or deliver them to the plaintiff except on payment of freight, the plaintiff replevied them, and sent them to the Boston market, which was a judicious course, he was held entitled to recover the difference between the net proceeds of their sale at Boston and their market value at New York, at the time when they should have been delivered.[114]

If there is no recovery on account of depreciation, the loss of use of the property during the period of delay may be recovered;[115] thus in case of delay in the transportation of money interest may be recovered.[116]

§ 855. Delay in transportation by sea.

In case of transportation by sea, the general rule has been disapproved in England. The Parana [117] was a libel by the assignee of bills of lading (a mortgagee) against a ship-owner for delay in the arrival of his ship. The libellant claimed damages for leakage of some sugar which had been shipped, and for loss on account of a fall in the price of hemp between the time when the ship ought to have arrived and the time when she did arrive. The plaintiff had kept the hemp for some time afterwards, and had then sold it at a considerable loss. It was held proper to allow damages for leakage of the sugar,

[114] Laurent v. Vaughn, 30 Vt. 90, 73 Am. Dec. 288.

[115] *United States:* Port Blakely Mill Co. v. Sharkey, 102 Fed. 259, 42 C. C. A. 329 (horses sent to Alaska to be hired out at high prices); La Conner Co. v. Widmer, 136 Fed. 177 (horses).

Kansas: Atchison, T. & S. F. R. R. v. Bourdett, 74 Kan. 137, 85 Pac. 820 (drill to be used in oil well).

Louisiana: Murrell v. Dixey, 14 La. Ann. 298.

Maine: Lord v. Maine Cent. R. R., 105 Me. 255, 74 Atl. 117.

Minnesota: Conheim v. Chicago & G. W. R. R., 104 Minn. 312, 116 N. W. 581, 17 L. R. A. (N. S.) 1091 (sample trunk).

Missouri: Smith v. Whitman, 13 Mo. 352.

Oregon: Brooks v. Northern Pac. Ry., 114 Pac. 949.

Texas: Texas & P. Ry. v. Hassell, 23 Tex. Civ. App. 681, 58 S. W. 54 (machinery); Gulf, C. & S. F. Ry. v. Gilbert, 4 Tex. Civ. App. 366, 22 S. W. 760, 23 S. W. 320 (machinery); Gulf, C. & S. F. Ry. v. Pettit, 3 Tex. Civ. App. 588, 22 S. W. 761 (merchandise).

England: Schultz v. Great Eastern R. R., 19 Q. B. D. 30, 56 L. J. Q. B. 442, 57 L. T. Rep. (N. S.) 438, 36 Wkly. Rep. 683 (samples).

[116] United States Ex. Co. v. Haines, 67 Ill. 137, 16 Am. Rep. 615.

[117] 1 P. D. 452, 2 P. Div. 118.

but it was held error to allow damages for loss of the market, i. e., the difference in price between the two dates. Such a profit, it was said, was too speculative.

We have already had occasion in the chapter on Sales [118] to criticise the reasons so often given for the rule of market value in that class of cases—that the purchaser can *replace himself* at that price. If what we have said is sound, it is equally objectionable in the class of cases now under consideration to treat the rule of market value as dependent upon the intention of the consignee to sell again. The foundation of the rule is that the consignee is entitled to the *actual value* of the goods at the time agreed upon for delivery. This is what he is deprived of by the breach of contract. There is nothing speculative in this as a measure of damages, and he is equally entitled to it, whether he keeps, sells, gives away, or destroys the goods. Nor can it make any difference whether the transportation is by land or sea.

§ 856. Consequential damages.

Recovery for consequential damages for delay is allowed or refused upon the general principles already discussed.[119] So, generally speaking, the carrier cannot be holden for time, nor for expenses, if they are not the natural and necessary consequences of the delay.[120] Neither is he liable for profits expected on a special contract of which he had no notice or for losses due to special circumstances not communicated by the shipper.[121] So where the plaintiff sent goods to his sales-

[118] § 735.

[119] *Ante*, chaps. vii, viii.

[120] *Colorado:* Denver & R. G. R. R. v. De Witt, 1 Colo. App. 419, 29 Pac. 524.

New York: Benson v. New Jersey R. R. & T. Co., 9 Bosw. 412.

[121] *United States:* Holland v. Seven Hundred, etc., Tons of Coal, 36 Fed. 784.

Georgia: Georgia R. R. v. Hayden, 71 Ga. 518, 51 Am. Rep. 274.

Massachusetts: Swift River Co. v. Fitchburg R. R., 169 Mass. 326, 47 N. E. 1015.

Mississippi: American Exp. Co. v. Jennings, 86 Miss. 329, 38 So. 374.

New York: Katz v. Cleveland, C. C. & St. L. Ry., 46 Misc. 259, 91 N. Y. Supp. 720.

Texas: Pacific Exp. Co. v. Darnell, 62 Tex. 639; Wells, Fargo & Co. v. Battle, 5 Tex. Civ. App. 532, 24 S. W. 353; St. Louis S. W. Ry. v. May (Tex. Civ. App.), 44 S. W. 408.

Wisconsin: Bradley v. Chicago, M. & S. P. Ry., 94 Wis. 44, 68 N. W. 410.

Canada: McGill v. Grand Trunk Ry., 19 Ont. App. 245.

In Yoakum v. Dunn, 1 Tex. Civ.

man and because of a delay the salesman had to leave town
before they arrived and consequently the sales were lost, the
recovery was limited strictly to the depreciation in the market
values, and did not include profits from the prospective sales.[122]
So in Georgia, where a manufacturer's business was suspended
in consequence of delay in the arrival of coal through the
carrier's default, evidence of the amount of profit which
might have been realized but for the delay is held not to be
admissible.[123]   So in an action against a carrier for delay in
delivering machinery, the measure of damages was held to
be the value of the use of the machinery during the period
of improper detention,[124] and not the loss which may have
been suffered by reason of loss of use of the mill in which it
was to be used.[125]

In a case in the Court of Queen's Bench, where some regalia
which were to be used in a procession by the plaintiff, and
which he had hired at an expense of £20, were not delivered
by the carrier in time for the procession, and the plaintiff was
at an expense of £5 in looking for the goods, he was held
entitled to recover the latter item, on account of unreasonable
delay, but not the former, which was too remote, the carrier
having had no notice of the object for which the goods were
to be used.   Lord Cockburn, C. J., said: "It is a reasonable
doctrine not to make the carrier liable for damage sustained
in consequence of goods not arriving in time, unless he had
notice that time was of importance; but the person who sends
his goods is entitled to expect that they shall be sent from
place to place in a reasonable time." [126]   So, also, the hotel
expenses of a traveller waiting for a parcel delayed by a car-

App. 524, 21 S. W. 411, where the carrier failed to transport a collection of
animals in time for an exhibition, the
shipper was allowed the probable net
profits. See *ante*, § 164.

[122] Great Western Ry. *v.* Redmayne,
L. R. 1 C. P. 329.

[123] Cooper *v.* Young, 22 Ga. 269, 68
Am. Dec. 502; *acc.*, Haas *v.* Kansas
City, F. S. & G. R. R., 81 Ga. 792.

[124] Priestly *v.* Northern Indiana & C.
R. R., 26 Ill. 205, 79 Am. Dec. 369; *acc.*,

U. S. Ex. Co. *v.* Haines, 67 Ill. 137, 16
Am. Rep. 615.

[125] *Alabama:* Southern Ry. *v.* Coleman, 153 Ala. 266, 44 So. 837.

Arkansas: Chicago, R. I. & P. Ry. *v.*
Planters' G. & O. Co., 88 Ark. 77, 113
S. W. 352.

Mississippi: Vicksburg & M. R. R. *v.*
Ragsdale, 46 Miss. 458.

[126] Hales *v.* London & N. W. Ry., 4
B. & S. 66, 70.

rier who was not informed of the purpose for which it was intended, were held too remote.[127]   And so the plaintiff cannot recover for consequences which he might reasonably have avoided.[128]

But on the other hand the plaintiff may recover for proximate consequences of the delay. So where in consequence of the delay it became necessary to remove the goods to another place to sell them, it was considered that the expenses of such removal were rightly recoverable; but the question of such necessity is of course for the jury.[129]   Where the delay in transporting goods results in throwing on the shipper the burden of extra care and expense, as for feeding the cattle, or storing the goods, he can recover for such time and expenditures.[130]

§ 856a. Notice of special damages.

If notice is properly given to the carrier of any particular object in view in making the shipment, or of any special damages likely to result from delay, such special damages, if suffered, may be recovered.[131]   When the defendant delayed

[127] Woodger v. Great Western Ry., L. R. 2 C. P. 318. See Briggs v. New York Cent. R. R., 28 Barb. 515.

But in Brooks v. Northern Pac. Ry. (Ore.), 114 Pac. 949, the excess of such expense over the expense of living at home was held recoverable.

[128] Mexican Cent. Ry. v. De Rosear, 109 S. W. 949 (Tex. Civ. App.); Gulf, C. & S. F. Ry. v. Chinski, 114 S. W. 851 (Tex. Civ. App.).

[129] Black v. Baxendale, 1 Ex. 410. Acc., Hahn v. St. Louis, K. C. & C. R. R. (Mo.), 125 S. W. 1185.

[130] *Feeding cattle:*
Illinois: Sangamon & M. R. R. v. Henry, 14 Ill. 156.
Missouri: Ballentine v. N. Mo. R. R., 40 Mo. 491, 93 Am. Dec. 315.
Texas: Gulf, C. & S. F. R. Ry. v. McCarty, 82 Tex. 608, 18 S. W. 716; Galveston, H. & S. A. Ry. v. Thompson (Tex. Civ. App.), 44 S. W. 8.
Storing goods: Norfolk & W. Ry. v. Wilkinson, 106 Va. 775, 56 S. E. 808.

So where a carrier was given medicine for transportation with notice, it was responsible for the increased suffering and medical expenses caused by delay. Pacific Exp. Co. v. Black (Tex. Civ. App.), 27 S. W. 830.

[131] *Alabama:* St. Louis & S. F. R. R. v. Lilly (Ala. App.), 55 So. 937 (samples for traveling salesmen).
Arkansas: Chicago, R. I. & P. Ry. v. Miles, 92 Ark. 573, 123 S. W. 775 (goods shipped for sale at auction); St. Louis I. M. & S. Ry. v. Lamb, 95 Ark. 209, 128 S. W. 1030 (machines to be used for special work).
Georgia: Chappell v. Western Ry., 70 S. E. 208 (theatrical company and properties).
Massachusetts: Weston v. Boston & M. R. R., 190 Mass. 298, 76 N. E. 1050 (theatrical properties to be used in exhibition).
Missouri: Ober v. Indianapolis & St. L. R. R., 13 Mo. App. 81 (factor's commissions on contracted sale lost).

the delivery of a package containing a draft and meanwhile the maker became insolvent, the measure of damages was held to be the face value of the draft.[132]   In Horne v. Midland Railway [133] the defendant knew that the plaintiffs had shipped their goods to meet a contract, but did not know the terms of that contract.   It was held that the notice was not sufficient to charge the defendant with the loss of an exceptional contract, but only of one at the usual market rates.   The plaintiff can recover for the loss of profits he would have made out of a special contract, if he gave notice of that contract.[134]   Where the carrier delayed in delivering church pews designed to fill

---

North Carolina: Lee v. St. Louis, I. M. & S. R. R., 136 N. C. 533, 48 S. E. 809 (freight not delivered to ship whereby plaintiff had to pay for "dead freight").

South Carolina: Strange v. Atlantic C. L. R. R., 77 S. C. 182, 57 S. E. 724 (salesman's samples).

Texas: Pacific Express Co. v. Darnell 62 Tex. 639, 6 S. W. 765 (machinery to be used in mill); Gulf, C. & S. F. R. R. v. Compton (Tex. Civ. App.), 38 S. W. 220 (pop corn wagon intended specially for use on a certain day); Gulf, C. & S. F. Ry. v. Nelson (Tex. Civ. App.), 139 S. W. 81 (material to be used in construction).

England: Jameson v. Midland Ry., 50 L. T. Rep. 426 (cutlery to be exhibited at a show).

In a somewhat early case, where in consequence of the carrier's unreasonable delay in the delivery of an account of the plaintiff against a third party, it was barred by the statute of limitations, he was held liable for the amount. Favor v. Philbrick, 5 N. H. 358. The sum involved in this case was small, and the decision would seem to have gone on the right rather than the measure of recovery. To make it, as regards the latter point, conform to the law as now established, the carrier should have notice beforehand of the particular necessity for punctual de-

livery; and it should have appeared also, if the point were controverted, that the debt would have been collectible but for the statute. On this question there appears to have been no evidence.

[132] Jones v. Wells, 28 Cal. 259.

And see the following cases:

Massachusetts: Whitney v. Merchants' Union Exp. Co., 104 Mass. 152, 6 Am. Rep. 207.

New Hampshire: Knapp v. United States & C. Exp. Co., 55 N. H. 348.

[133] L. R. 7 C. P. 583; L. R. 8 C. P. 131.

[134] *United States:* Schmidt v. The Steamship Pennsylvania, 4 Fed. 548.

Illinois: Illinois Central R. R. v. Cobb, 64 Ill. 128.

New Hampshire: Deming v. Grand Trunk Ry., 48 N. H. 455, 2 Am. Rep. 267.

But not if the jury believe that the sub-contract would not have been carried out. Illinois Cent. R. R. v. Cobb, 64 Ill. 143.   In Central Trust Co. v. Savannah & W. R. R., 69 Fed. 683, fruit trees were received for shipment but were not delivered until after the time when the purchasers from the shippers could be compelled, under their contract, to receive them. Proof of notice was allowed though the bill of lading was silent as to the time of delivery. The court distinguishes such

a "penalty contract" of which the carrier had notice the plaintiff recovered the amount he was compelled to pay as liquidated damages.[135] In New Hampshire, where a large quantity of wool was delivered to the Grand Trunk Railway for transportation to Boston, the agent of the company was informed that it was sold if it could go at once, and agreed that it should go next morning. But the defendant delayed transporting it more than three weeks, and in consequence of the delay the purchaser declined to take it. Meantime the demand and price had declined, and the defendant was held liable for the difference between the contract price and the value of the goods when delivered.[136] So in the case of Wilson v. York, Newcastle and Berwick Railway [137] it was held by Jervis, C. J., at *nisi prius*, that a carrier undertaking to carry fish to a particular market in time for the morning's sale was liable for the profit lost by his failure to get them there in time for that sale. This case, which preceded Hadley v. Baxendale, is also justified by the second head of the rule adopted in that case. In Grindle v. Eastern Express Co.[138] the plaintiff's intestate delivered to the defendant some money to be sent to B. to pay the premium on an endowment policy. The defendant knew the purpose for which the money was sent, but failed to deliver it in time, consequently the policy lapsed. It was held that the plaintiff could recover the net value of the policy when it lapsed. It was also held, however, that the defendant would not be liable for such damages as the plaintiff, by the use of reasonable means, such as by reinstating himself with the company or by reinsuring, might have avoided. It has been held that when goods were addressed

cases of notice operating upon the question of damages from decisions such as Central R. R. v. Hassel, 91 Ga. 382, in which it was held that under an ordinary bill of lading specifying no time for delivery parol evidence is not admissible to show an express agreement to deliver at a specified time. *Sed. qu.*

[135] Railroad Co. v. Cabinet Co., 104 Tenn. 568, 58 S. W. 303, 78 Am. St. Rep. 933.

[136] Deming v. Railroad, 48 N. H. 455; *acc.*, St. Louis, I. M. & S. Ry. v. Mudford, 48 Ark. 502 (*semble*); Chicago & A. R. R. v. Thrapp, 5 Ill. App. 502. In Medbury v. New York & E. R. R., 26 Barb. 564, such damages were allowed, though the report of the case does not show that the carrier had notice of the contract.

[137] 18 Eng. L. & E. 557.

[138] 67 Me. 317.

"To the show ground at N.," there was sufficient notice that they were sent for a special show, and the plaintiff was allowed to recover the loss suffered by missing the show. Damages were allowed for loss of profits and of time.[139] The carrier had notice that a reciprocity treaty was about to expire, and if transportation into the United States was delayed, a heavy duty must be paid. Upon delay it was held that the owner might recover the amount of the duty, though the price at the point of destination had risen more than that amount during the period of delay.[140] Where the defendant had notice that a package contained medicine for a sick person, and the delay in forwarding caused increased illness, the plaintiff recovered for the aggravated suffering and for expenses of additional medical attendance.[141] But where an expressman failed to deliver a trunk in time for a steamer and plaintiff, on learning of this fact, left the steamer at Sandy Hook, hired a tug to return to New York, telegraphed to destination with reference to the other trunk and paid board for sixteen days and then bought a new passage ticket, the recovery was limited to the price of the new ticket, the other items being too remote.[142] Where a railroad delays the transportation of a corpse, it has been held that the carrier is responsible for the expense of delaying the funeral, and the mental anguish so caused.[143]

The general principles as to notice, already discussed, apply in the case of carriage. Thus, notice must be given at the time

Cf. Smith v. Western U. Tel. Co., 150 Pa. 561, 24 Atl. 1049.

[139] Simpson v. London & N. W. Ry., 1 Q. B. D. 274.

[140] Gibbs v. Gildersleeve, 26 Up. Can. Q. B. 471.

[141] Pacific Exp. Co. v. Black, 8 Tex. Civ. App. 363, 27 S. W. 830.

[142] DeLeon v. McKernan, 25 Misc. 182, 54 N. Y. Supp. 167.

[143] Alabama: Alabama C., G. & A. Ry. v. Brady, 160 Ala. 615, 49 So. 351.

Kentucky: Louisville & N. R. R. v. Hull, 113 Ky. 561, 68 S. W. 433, 57 L. R. A. 771.

Not, of course, for the mental anguish of others: Missouri, K. & T. Ry. v. Vandiver, 122 S. W. 955.

Nor where, the corpse having arrived before the hour appointed, the funeral was postponed by the plaintiff's own will: Alabama C. G. & A. Ry. v. Brady, 160 Ala. 615, 49 So. 351.

In Minnesota it was held (Jaggard, J., dissenting) that damages for mental suffering cannot be recovered in such a case; but this was on the ground that such damages cannot be recovered for breach of a contract, not because they were not within the contemplation of the parties. Beaulieu v. Great Northern Ry., 103 Minn. 47, 114 N. W. 353.

of shipment;[144] but it has been held that notice after shipment but before the delay will charge the carrier when the goods arrive safely at destination but delivery is delayed.[145] Notice must be given to an agent or servant whose duty it is to forward the goods, as for instance the person who made out the bill of lading;[146] but notice to a superior traffic officer is enough, though the person actually forwarding the shipment has no notice.[147]

§ 857. Delay in lading or unlading a vessel.

Demurrage, in the strict sense of the term, means a sum of money due by express contract for the detention of a vessel in loading one or more days beyond the time allowed for that purpose in the charter-party. It seems that the *consignee* cannot be made liable *for demurrage* where there is in the charter-party, or bill of lading, no express agreement or stipulation in respect to detention in loading or unloading;[148] but the *freighter* is liable for unnecessary detention, although no express contract is made on the subject; and compensation for such detention may be recovered under the name of demurrage.[149] It was said, however, in a case in the New York Supreme Court, that although there has been no special agreement between a shipper of goods and the master of a vessel for demurrage, yet if the vessel is improperly detained an unreasonable length of time by the freighter or *consignee*, the owner of the vessel may recover damages, in the nature of demurrage, for such detention. That was, however, an action

[144] Pilcher v. Central of Ga. Ry., 155 Ala. 316, 46 So. 765.

[145] Southern Ry. v. Lewis, 165 Ala. 451, 51 So. 863.

See Virginia-Carolina Peanut Co. v. Atlantic C. L. R. R. (N. C.), 71 S. E. 71.

[146] Chicago, R. I. & P. Ry. v. Planters' Gin & Oil Co., 88 Ark. 77, 113 S. W. 352.

[147] Gulf, C. & L. I. Ry. v. Nelson (Tex. Civ. App.), 139 S. W. 81.

[148] *New York:* Dayton v. Parke, 142 N. Y. 391, 37 N. E. 642.

England: Evans v. Forster, 1 B. & Ad. 118, 25 Eng. C. L. 420.

[149] *United States:* Sprague v. West, 1 Abb. Adm. 548; Crawford v. Rittenhouse, 1 Fed. 638; The M. S. Bacon v. Erie & W. Transportation Co., 3 Fed. 344; Keyser v. Jurvelius, 122 Fed. 218, 58 C. C. A. 664.

Massachusetts: Garfield & P. C. Co. v. Pennsylvania C. & C. Co., 199 Mass. 22, 84 N. E. 1020.

New York: Van Etten v. Newton, 134 N. Y. 143, 31 N. E. 334, 30 Am. St. Rep. 630; Jameson v. Sweeney, 29 Misc. 584, 61 N. Y. Supp. 498.

Virginia: Norfolk & W. R. R. v. Adams, 90 Va. 393, 18 S. E. 673, 22 L. R. A. 530.

against the freighter. The damages in these cases should be limited to compensation for the time the vessel was actually detained by the consignee beyond a reasonable time for the discharge of her cargo.[150] Damages are measured by the value of the use of the vessel.[151] The parties may, however, agree in advance as to the demurrage rate, and this if reasonable will be the measure of damages.[152] In an action for delay in discharging the plaintiff's ship, by which the plaintiff lost profits which he would have derived from the passage money of emigrants, it was held that the defendant could not reduce the damages by showing that the plaintiff derived a benefit from this failure, from the fact that the emigrants embarked on other ships in which he was part owner.[153]

§ 857a. Discrimination.

In an action against the carrier for discrimination, either in rates or in facilities, the plaintiff may recover such damages as he suffered from the discrimination. If the discrimination was in rates, he recovers the amount of the excess he was compelled to pay.[154] For discrimination in furnishing cars, the plaintiff is entitled to damages, according to the ordinary rules, for delay in the shipment.[155]

§ 858. Agreement to furnish freight.

* An interesting question is sometimes presented where the

[150] Gabler v. McChesney, 60 App. Div. 583, 70 N. Y. Supp. 191; Clendaniel v. Tuckerman, 17 Barb. 184; acc. Wordin v. Bemis, 32 Conn. 268, 85 Am. Dec. 255; Morse v. Pesant, 2 Keyes, 16.

[151] *United States:* Esseltyne v. Elmore, 7 Biss. 69; The Pietro G., 39 Fed. 366; Huron Barge Co. v. Turney, 79 Fed. 109.

England: In re Trent & Humber Co., L. R. 4 Ch. 112.

[152] *United States:* Creighton v. Dilks, 49 Fed. 107; Randall v. Sprague, 74 Fed. 247, 21 C. C. A. 334.

Georgia: Miller v. Georgia, R. & B. Co., 88 Ga. 563, 15 S. E. 316, 50 Am. & Eng. Ry. Cas. 79.

New York: Crommelin v. New York & H. R. R., 10 Bosw. 77; Baldwin v. Sullivan Timber Co., 20 N. Y. Supp. 496.

[153] Jebson v. East & W. I. D. Co., L. R. 10 C. P. 300.

[154] McGrew v. Mo. Pac. Ry., 230 Mo. 496, 132 S. W. 1076 (long and short haul); Seawell v. Kansas C. F. S. & M. R. R., 119 Mo. 222, 24 S. W. 1002.

For treble damages in case of discrimination, see Union Pac. Ry. v. Goodridge, 149 U. S. 680, 37 L. ed. 896, 13 Sup. Ct. 970; Blair v. Sioux C. & P. Ry., 109 Ia. 369, 73 N. W. 1053, 80 N. W. 673.

[155] *Indiana:* Pittsburgh, C. C. & St. L. Ry. v. Wood, 45 Ind. App. 1, 84 N. E. 1009.

carrier brings suit on the violation of an agreement to furnish him a stipulated quantity of freight. And here the principle applies which we have already had occasion to notice, that the party plaintiff is bound to take reasonable measures to reduce the amount of injury consequent on the defendant's default; and it is held, that the carrier must stand ready to receive any other freight that is offered, and thus, as far as is reasonably practicable, avoid throwing an unnecessary loss on the party in default.[156] Thus in New York it has been decided, where a party contracts to load a ship with a given number of tons at a stipulated price, and fails to deliver the whole quantity, that if goods are offered by a third person to be shipped, to an amount sufficient to make up the deficiency, though at a reduced rate of compensation, but still at current prices, the owner or master is bound to receive such goods, and place to the credit of the original charterer the net earnings of the substituted cargo, after making all reasonable deductions resulting from the circumstances of the case; and such is the English rule.[157]   In Aitkin v. Ernsthausen,[158] the defendant had contracted to ship 15,061 bales of jute; after loading 5,458 bales these were destroyed by fire and the defendant thereby excused from performing as to that portion. Defendant then wrongfully refused to ship the rest and plaintiff procured another full cargo. Defendant claimed a deduction in the amount of damages for the net amount earned by freight which occupied the space that would have been occupied by the 5,458 bales. The court held the measure of damages to be the agreed freight, less a proportional sum as to the bales destroyed, less the amount earned on goods shipped in the space that should have been occupied by the balance of the goods.

Ohio: Toledo & O. C. Ry. *v.* Wren, 78 Oh. St. 137, 84 N. E. 785.

[156] *Alabama:* Murrell *v.* Whiting, 32 Ala. 54.

California: Utter *v.* Chapman, 38 Cal. 659, 99 Am. Dec. 441.

[157] Heckscher *v.* McCrea, 24 Wend. 304; Shannon *v.* Comstock, 21 Wend. 457; Puller *v.* Staniforth, 11 East, 232. See these cases cited and confirmed in

Costigan *v.* Mohawk & Hudson R. R., 2 Denio, 609. See also, the reasoning of these cases adopted in Arkansas, in an able opinion of Scott, J., as to a contract for personal services. Walworth *v.* Pool, 9 Ark. 394; Abbott on Shipping, part iv, ch. 1, of the carriage of goods in merchant ships, and cases there cited.

[158] [1894] 1 Q. B. 773.

In a case that came up in the Supreme Court of the United States, from the Pennsylvania Circuit,[159] the plaintiff's intestate agreed to deliver for the defendant at St. Louis, by a certain time, a quantity of army stores *supposed* to amount to 3,700 barrels, which the defendant on his part agreed to furnish on the Ohio river: the defendant to pay a certain sum per barrel, one-half to be paid at St. Louis and the other half at Cincinnati, with a memorandum "that the payment to be made at Cincinnati was to be made in the paper of the Miami Exporting Company or its equivalent." The defendant did not furnish the whole 3,700 barrels: and the plaintiff brought suit as well for the freight of the portion furnished, as damages for the non-delivery of the remainder. The notes of the Miami Company were not worth more than 66 per cent. The judge who tried the cause held that "the plaintiff could not recover damages according to the *number of tons* the boat was capable of containing. The rule of law in cases where there has been a failure to furnish the stipulated freight, and there exists no charter-party, is for the jury to take all the circumstances into consideration, and to make an allowance for any freight which the master had it in his power to transport in addition to that which was furnished. If the lading should not be complete, without the default of the master, the rule is to estimate the freight by means of an average, so as to take neither the greatest possible freight nor the least; and such average is the proper measure of damages." As to the paper of the Miami Exporting Company, the defendant having failed to tender to the plaintiff's intestate that paper or its equivalent, the plaintiff was entitled to recover the amount in specie with interest. The Supreme Court reversed this judgment on the grounds that the defendant had not stipulated to furnish any precise amount of freight, and that the specie value of the notes at the time they should have been paid

[159] Robinson *v.* Noble, 8 Peters, 181, 184, 8 L. ed. 910. This case, though it raises some important questions, properly decides nothing as to the amount of damages; but it may be noticed, as to the latter point, that it is adverse to the decisions of the courts of New York in regard to notes payable in a specific article, it being there held, that if the specific article is not tendered the party loses his privilege, and must pay in money.

But the general rule is in accordance with the case. See §§ 280, 281.

was the rule by which the damages should have been estimated.**

The measure of damages against a charterer who refuses
to furnish a cargo according to his contract is the freight that
would have been earned less the expense of earning it: or,
under the rule of avoidable consequences, the amount the
vessel would have earned at the rates specified, deducting her
net earnings during the time she would have been occupied
in the charter, including the lay days, or if she remained idle
the amount she should have earned.[160] But where, by the
terms of the charter, different articles of freight are to be
paid for at different rates by weight, and the freighter is at
liberty to supply them in such proportions as he may choose,
the proper measure of damages in an action for not supply-
ing cargo is the average value of freight for the voyage, calculated on the various rates of freight in the proportion of
the different articles usually carried on similar voyages.[161]
But where some of the enumerated articles are limited as to
the amount which may be carried, and that limit has been
reached, the freight of substituted articles can be calculated
only on an average of the remaining goods.[162] Where goods
are wrongfully taken from a vessel by the shipper before the

[160] *United States:* Watts v. Camors,
115 U. S. 353, 362, 29 L. ed. 407, 6 Sup.
Ct. 91; The Gazelle & Cargo, 128 U. S.
474, 487, 32 L. ed. 496, 9 Sup. Ct. 139;
Jordan v. Eaton, 2 Hask. 236; Watts
v. Camors, 10 Fed. 145; Parker v. Tires,
29 Fed. 800; Greenwell v. Ross, 34 Fed.
656; Dolbeattie Steamship Co. v. Card,
59 Fed. 159; Leblond v. McNear, 104
Fed. 826; McNear v. Leblond, 123 Fed.
384; Venus Shipping Co. v. Wilson,
152 Fed. 170, 81 C. C. A. 368; Thebi-
deau v. Cairns, 171 Fed. 233.
California: Utter v. Chapman, 38
Cal. 659, 99 Am. Dec. 441.
Illinois: Bangor Furnace Co. v. Magill, 108 Ill. 656.
Maine: Husten v. Richards, 44 Me.
182.
Maryland: Barker v. Borzone, 48
Md. 474.

Missouri: Dean v. Ritter, 18 Mo.
182.
New York: Heckscher v. McCrea, 24
Wend. 304; Ashburner v. Balchen, 7
N. Y. 272; Stone v. Woodruff, 28 Hun,
534; Mitchell v. Cornell, 44 N. Y.
Super. Ct. 401.
Texas: Heilbroner v. Hancock, 33
Tex. 714.
England: Hunter v. Fry, 2 B. & Ald.
421; Harries v. Edmonds, 1 C. & K.
686; Smith v. McGuire, 3 H. & N.
554.
For delay in loading the measure of
damages is the demurrage during the
period of delay. Creighton v. Dilks, 49
Fed. 107.
[161] Thomas v. Clarke, 2 Starkie, 450.
[162] Cockburn v. Alexander, 6 C. B.
791.

commencement of the voyage, the ship-owner is not entitled to the stipulated freight as such, but only to an indemnity for the breach of contract. All the attendant circumstances should be laid before the jury, to enable them to determine what will be an indemnity. If the carrier has received other goods in place of those withdrawn, or if by diligence he might have done so, or if he could have abandoned the contemplated voyage, and have found other employment for his vessel, these facts may be ground for a deduction from the entire sum stipulated to be paid as freight.[163] On a contract to furnish freight at a distant port to load a vessel which goes to the port, but finds none, and is compelled to return empty, the measure of damages is the contract price.[164]

II.—CARRIERS OF PASSENGERS

§ 859. Form of action.

The liability of a carrier of passengers is a subject which has become of great practical importance since the introduction of railroads, and the subject of the measure of damages for breach of contract of carriage of a passenger has been much discussed. The relation between carrier and passenger is more than a mere contract relation; indeed, it may exist in the absence of contract. It is clear that any person rightfully on the cars of a railway company is entitled to protection by the carrier, though he is a free passenger.[165] Any breach of this duty owed by the carrier to the passenger would seem to be a tort; recovery may be had either in an action of tort or in an action for breach of the contract.[166] The contract made by a common carrier of passengers (and we shall see that the same is true of contracts made by all incorporated telegraph companies) is not a simply voluntary engagement

---

[163] Bailey v. Damon, 3 Gray (Mass.), 92.

[164] Bradley v. Denton, 3 Wis. 557.

[165] *United States:* Philadelphia & R. R. R. v. Derby, 14 How. 468, 485, 14 L. ed. 502, per Grier, J.; New York C. R. R. v. Lockwood, 17 Wall. 357, 21 L. ed. 627.

[166] *North Carolina:* Hansley v. Jamesville & W. R. R., 115 N. C. 602, 20 S. E. 528, 44 Am. St. Rep. 474, 32 L. R. A. 543.

Vermont: Holden v. Rutland R. R., 72 Vt. 156, 47 Atl. 403, 82 Am. St. Rep. 926.

such as an ordinary contract *inter partes*, but an agreement made in pursuance of an obligation towards all the world imposed either by his mere status as common carrier, or under his charter, or both.   In other words, it is a contract which he is under a duty to make, and under a duty to perform, so that a breach is not a mere breach of contract, but also, as we have said, a tort.

In Hobbs *v.* London & Southwestern Railway,[167] Blackburn, J., said (and this explains why this case, in which the pleadings were clearly drawn in tort, was treated as contract): "The action is in reality upon a contract; it is commonly said to be founded upon a duty, *but it is a duty arising out of a contract.*" But surely the duty arising out of a contract is merely another term for the obligation of a contract.   In every carrier's contract, there is of course this contractual or conventional duty; but as just stated, the contract itself is entered into in pursuance of a duty owed to all the world.   Hence it is more true to say that every breach of a carrier's contract is also the breach of an antecedent duty.

§ 860. Personal injury.

Where the passenger is injured physically by the negligence of the carrier, the measure of recovery is usually that adopted in ordinary cases of physical injury,[168] that is, compensation

[167] L. R. 10 Q. B. 111, 119.

[168] *United States:* Kansas City, F. S. & M. R. R. *v.* Stoner, 49 Fed. 209, 1 C. C. A. 231.
California: Lombardi *v.* California St. Ry., 124 Cal. 311, 319, 57 Pac. 66.
Connecticut: Flint *v.* Norwich & W. R. R., 34 Conn. 554.
Indiana: Louisville & N. R. R. *v.* Falvey, 104 Ind. 409, 3 N. E. 389.
Iowa: Muldowney *v.* Illinois Cent. R. R., 36 Ia. 462.
Kansas: Chicago, R. I. & P. Ry. *v.* Posten, 59 Kan. 449, 53 Pac. 465.
Louisiana: De Mahy *v.* Morgan's Louisiana & T. R. R. & Steamship Co., 45 La. Ann. 1329, 14 So. 61.
Maryland: Pittsburg, etc., R. R. *v.*

Andrews, 39 Md. 329, 17 Am. Rep. 568.
Minnesota: Johnson *v.* Northern P. R. R., 47 Minn. 430, 50 N. W. 473; Purcell *v.* St. Paul C. Ry., 48 Minn. 134, 50 N. W. 1034; Kral *v.* Burlington, C. R. & N. Ry., 71 Minn. 422, 74 N. W. 166, 70 Am. St. Rep. 334.
Mississippi: Illinois Cent. R. R. *v.* Minor, 69 Miss. 710, 16 L. R. A. 627, 11 So. 101.
Nevada: Murphy *v.* Southern Pac. Co., 31 Nev. 120, 101 Pac. 322.
New Hampshire: Hopkins *v.* Atlantic & St. L. R. R., 36 N. H. 9, 72 Am. Dec. 287.
New Jersey: Cone *v.* Central R. R., 62 N. J. L. 99, 40 Atl. 780.

for pain and suffering and for loss of time while incapacitated from work, medical expenses, and compensation for any permanent injury or loss of earning power. The fact that services for nursing were rendered gratuitously does not reduce the amount to be recovered on account of reasonable medical expenses.[169] Nor will any deduction be allowed because of a sum recovered on an accident insurance policy.[170] Recovery may be had for physical inconvenience, and in a proper case for mental suffering;[171] but never counsel fees.[172] In order to show the value of his lost time, a professional man may show his past earnings;[173] thus a teacher of French has been allowed to show the number of his scholars and the amount of his earnings in previous years.[174] The general rules as to certainty of proof are to be observed. Thus in a case in Georgia,[175] an action for permanent personal injury,

New York: Matteson v. New York, etc., R. R., 62 Barb. 364.

North Carolina: Ruffin v. Atlantic & N. C. R. R., 142 N. C. 120, 55 S. E. 86.

Oregon: Sullivan v. Oregon R. & N. Co., 12 Ore. 392, 7 Pac. 508, 53 Am. Rep. 364.

Pennsylvania: Pennsylvania R. R. v. Books, 57 Pa. 339, 98 Am. Dec. 229; Smedley v. Hestonville M. & F. P. Ry., 184 Pa. 620, 39 Atl. 544.

Texas: Texas & P. Ry. v. Davidson (Tex. Civ. App.), 21 S. W. 68; Texas & N. O. R. R. v. Clippenger, 47 Tex. Civ. App. 510, 106 S. W. 155; El Paso & N. E. Ry. v. Sawyer (Tex. Civ. App.), 119 S. W. 110.

West Virginia: Ricketts v. Chesapeake & O. R. R., 33 W. Va. 433, 10 S. E. 801, 25 Am. St. Rep. 901, 7 L. R. A. 354.

Wisconsin: Spicer v. Chicago & N. W. Ry., 29 Wis. 580.

And see § 481 et seq.

[169] Pennsylvania R. R. v. Marion, 104 Ind. 239. *Ante,* § 67.

[170] *Missouri:* Ephland v. Mo. Pac. R. R., 57 Mo. App. 147.

England: Bradburn v. Great Western Ry., L. R. 10 Ex. 1.

[171] *Michigan:* Humphrey v. Michigan United Rys., 132 N. W. 447 (shame and humiliation).

Minnesota: Jansen v. Minneapolis & S. L. R. R., 112 Minn. 496, 128 N. W. 826, 32 L. R. A. (N. S.) 1206 (sense of wrong and insult).

Missouri: Dye v. Chicago & A. R. R., 135 Mo. App. 497, 115 S. W. 497 (physical inconvenience).

New Jersey: Cone v. Central R. R., 62 N. J. L. 99, 40 Atl. 780 (indignity).

Texas: Gulf, C. & S. F. Ry. v. Overton, 110 S. W. 736 (physical inconvenience).

[172] United Power Co. v. Matheny, 81 Oh. St. 204, 90 N. E. 154, 28 L. R. A. (N. S.) 761.

[173] See § 180.

[174] Simonin v. New York, L. E. & W. R. R., 36 Hun, 214.

[175] Richmond & D. R. R. v. Allison, 12 S. E. 352 (Va.).

On this ground the Supreme Court of the United States reversed the verdict of the jury after full consideration in Richmond & D. R. R. v. Elliott, 149 U. S. 266, 13 Sup. Ct. 837, 37 L. ed. 728.

it was held erroneous to admit evidence that the plaintiff, a postal clerk, was in the line of promotion, and might have been promoted soon after the accident. Simmons, J., said: "While it is proper in cases of this kind to prove the age, habits, health, occupation, expectation of life, ability to labor and probable increase or diminution of that ability with lapse of time, the rate of wages, etc., and then leave it to the jury to assess the damages, we think it improper to allow proof of a particular possibility, or even probability, of an increase of wages by appointment to a higher public office, especially where, as in this case, the appointment is somewhat controlled by political reasons." The loss of promotion was clearly conjectural, even without considering the political reasons which may influence appointments.

§ 861. Fright and nervous shock.

In Bell v. Great Northern Railway [176] it appeared that while the plaintiff was travelling as a passenger in an excursion train over the defendants' line of railway, the train, which was too heavy to be carried by the engine up an incline, was divided by the defendants' servants, the carriage occupied by the plaintiff remaining attached to the engine. The afterpart of the train having thereupon descended the incline with great velocity, the engine was reversed, and with the remaining carriages (including that in which plaintiff was seated) followed down the incline, also at a high rate of speed, until violently stopped. It was proved that plaintiff was put in great fright by the occurrence, and that she suffered from nervous shock in consequence of such fright. She was incapacitated from performing her ordinary duties, and there was evidence that paralysis might ensue. Upon the trial, the judge charged the jury that if great fright was, in their opinion, a reasonable and natural consequence of the circumstances proved, and if injury to the plaintiff's health was, in their opinion, a reasonable and natural consequence of such great fright, and was actually occasioned thereby, damages for such injury would not be too remote. The defendant requested the judge to charge that if damages or injury were the result of,

[176] 26 L. R. Ir. 428.

or arose from, mere fright, not accompanied by actual physical injury, even though there might be a nervous or mental shock occasioned by the fright, such damages would be too remote. This charge the court declined to give; and the action of the court was upheld on appeal.

The court on appeal referred to the case of Victorian Railway Commissioners *v.* Coultas,[177] in which the Privy Council held that mere mental terror was not a consequence which would ordinarily flow from the negligence proved in that case. This case, however, was not approved; but the court followed an earlier unreported Irish case,[178] where compensation for injury resulting from nervous shock was allowed in a much stronger case than the one at bar. The general considerations involved in this question, and the condition of the authorities upon it, have already been considered in an earlier chapter.[179]

§ 862. Failure to carry a passenger.

Where a carrier fails to transport a passenger, the latter may recover the expense of carriage by another train, and the loss of time and expenses, such as hotel bills, incurred in waiting for the other train.[180] So where a person in a foreign port contracted with the master of a vessel for a passage to this country, and paid a part of the passage-money in advance, but the master failed to fulfil his contract, it was held that the other party was entitled to recover the sum paid in advance, the expenses incurred in awaiting the sailing of another ship, and the sum paid to the second vessel for a passage in her.[181] In these cases it is said that the whole passage-money

[177] 13 App. Cas. 222.

[178] Byrne *v.* Great Southern & W. Ry., in the Court of Appeal.

[179] *Ante*, §§ 43 *et seq.*

[180] *United States:* Morse *v.* Duncan, 14 Fed. 396.

Kentucky: Cincinnati, N. O. & T. P. Ry. *v.* Rose, 115 S. W. 830, 21 L. R. A. (N. S.) 681 (wrong directions resulting in passenger losing train).

Maryland: Baltimore & O. R. R. *v.* Carr, 71 Md. 135, 17 Atl. 1052, 17 Am. St. Rep. 516; Northern Cent. R. R. *v.* O'Conner, 76 Md. 207, 16 L. R. A.

449, 24 Atl. 449, 35 Am. St. Rep. 422.

New York: Rose *v.* King, 76 App. Div. 308; 78 N. Y. Supp. 419.

South Carolina: Millhous *v.* R. R., 72 S. C. 116, 48 S. E. 99.

Texas: Eddy *v.* Harris, 78 Tex. 661,15 S. W. 107; Choctaw O. & G. R. R. *v.* Hill, 75 S. W. 963.

England: Hamlin *v.* Great Northern Ry., 1 H. & N. 408, 2 Jur. (N. S.) 1122, 26 L. J. Exch. 20, 5 Wkly. Rep. 76; Cranston *v.* Marshall, 5 Ex. 395.

[181] The Zenobia, 1 Abb. Adm. 80;

paid for securing other transportation can be recovered; but it would seem that only the excess over what would have been paid the defendant should be recovered.

Damages are also recoverable for time lost by the delay.[182] Where the object of the plaintiff was to go upon an excursion to a certain place, and he took a later train, but was so late as to miss the object of the excursion, it was said that he might have compensation for loss of time until his return.[183] So where the action was for neglect to transport the passenger across the Isthmus of Panama, the latter's expenses during the detention and those of a consequent illness, and the time lost by him both directly from the detention and by the illness afterwards, so far as these were occasioned by the carrier's negligence and breach of duty, were all declared by the New York Court of Appeals legitimate items of damage.[184] In Baltimore & Ohio Railroad v. Carr [185] it is said that compensation in such case may be recovered for mere inconvenience, "if it is such as is capable of being stated in a *tangible form,* and assessed *at a money value.*" In Mississippi the physical condition of a passenger who had suffered great bodily exposure in consequence of the carrier's neglect to stop his vessel and take him on board, according to agreement, was allowed to be shown in aggravation of the damages.[186] But damages for mental suffering cannot be recovered.[187]

A passenger, in order to avoid a delay, can only incur a

Acc., Porter v. The New England, 17 Mo. 290. But not for time lost in waiting for trial of the cause. The Stanley Dollar, 160 Fed. 911, 88 C. C. A. 93.

[182] *Maryland:* Baltimore & O. R. R. v. Carr, 71 Md. 135, 17 Atl. 1052, 17 Am. St. Rep. 516.

[183] Eddy v. Harris, 78 Tex. 661, 15 S. W. 107 *(semble).*

Kentucky: Cincinnati, N. O. & T. P. Ry. v. Rose, 115 S. W. 830, 21 L. R. A. (N. S.) 681.

[184] Williams v. Vanderbilt, 28 N. Y. 217, 84 Am. Dec. 333.

[185] 71 Md. 135, 144, 17 Atl. 1052, 17 Am. St. Rep. 516; *acc.,* International

& G. N. R. R. v. Sammon, 35 Tex. Civ. App. 96, 79 S. W. 854.

[186] Heirn v. McCaughan, 32 Miss. 17, 66 Am. Dec. 588.

But see Berley v. Seaboard A. L. Ry., 83 S. C. 411, 65 S. E. 456.

[187] *Arkansas:* St. Louis, I. M. & S. Ry. v. Groce, 138 S. W. 879.

Maryland: Northern C. Ry. v. O'Conner, 76 Md. 207, 24 Atl. 449.

South Carolina: Berley v. Seaboard A. L. Ry., 83 S. C. 411, 65 S. E. 456.

In *Missouri:* Barnett v. Chicago & A. R. R., 75 Mo. App. 446, mental suffering was considered in exemplary damages.

reasonable expense. He cannot take a special train in order to avoid a slight delay. In Le Blanche *v.* London & North Western Railway [188] it was said that a good test of the reasonableness of taking the special train would be an inquiry whether or not the plaintiff would have taken the special train if he had lost the train through his own fault, and had not the company to look to for compensation.[189]

Plaintiff was a passenger from A to B. There was a break in the line of the defendant at C, the distance between the stations being three-fourths of a mile; an omnibus was provided but plaintiff was asked to pay ten cents. He refused to do so and walked, but the train did not wait. It was held that plaintiff should have paid the ten cents, and the damages were restricted to that sum though by his contract he was entitled to be carried free from station to station.[190]

§ 863. Delay in transporting a passenger.

The rules are much the same where the carrier wrongfully delays transportation. The value of the time lost may be recovered.[191] Evidence of the rate of wages earned by persons of the plaintiff's trade at the place of his destination, during the period of the delay, is admissible to guide the jury in fixing the damages. But that rate is not the measure. The jury are to consider the probabilities that the plaintiff would have obtained employment immediately upon his arrival, and that it would have continued during the entire period of the delay; [192] and the fact that there was no evidence of the

[188] 1 C. P. D. 286.

[189] If the plaintiff takes unreasonable means to avoid the delay, he cannot recover for the consequent damage.

Alabama: Malcomb *v.* Louisville & N. R. R., 155 Ala. 337, 46 So. 768.

Georgia: Williams *v.* Rome R. & L. Co., 4 Ga. App. 372, 61 S. E. 495.

[190] Clarry *v.* Grand Trunk Ry., 29 Ont. 18.

[191] *New York:* Cooley *v.* R. R., 40 Misc. 239, 81 N. Y. Supp. 692.

Virginia: Norfolk & W. R. R. *v.* Lipscomb, 90 Va. 137, 17 S. E. 809.

Where a carrier gave false information to a passenger about his subsequent route, he could recover compensation for his extra time and inconvenience on the longer route on which he was sent, but not for delays or other wrongs on the part of the subsequent carriers. St. Louis S. W. Ry. *v.* White, 99 Tex. 359, 89 S. W. 746, 2 L. R. A. (N. S.) 110.

Mental suffering caused by the delay in seeing friends is too remote. Hot Springs Ry. *v.* Deloney, 65 Ark. 177, 45 S. W. 351.

[192] Yonge *v.* Pacific M. S. S. Co., 1 Cal. 353.

value of the plaintiff's time, does not preclude the jury from giving him such compensation therefor as they think reasonable.[193] In Hamlin v. Great Northern Railway [194] the plaintiff was delayed on the defendant's road so that he could not get from G to H in the evening, as he had intended to do. He therefore remained for the night at G and went to H the next morning. It was held that he could not recover for a failure to keep appointments with customers at H. He could only recover the expense of his night's lodging.[195] Where a passenger was taken suddenly ill and in consequence of a delay was unable to procure medical attendance, the carrier was held liable for the aggravated sickness resulting.[196] In a case in the Texas Court of Appeals it appeared that the plaintiff was forced to wait at the defendant's station for a delayed train. The station was insufficiently warmed, and the plaintiff contracted a severe cold while waiting for the train. It was held that he could recover compensation for the cold.[197]

For delay in transporting members of a theatrical troupe profits lost through inability to give performances at the time arranged for arrival cannot be recovered unless they were within the contemplation of the parties under the contract of carriage.[198] In an action to recover damages against a railroad company for delay in transporting an opera troupe to its destination, the plaintiff claimed damages *first* for loss on account of engagements actually advertised, *second*, for loss of other engagements due to the breaking up of the troupe owing to the loss of the book receipts of engagements missed. The first claim only was allowed, the court saying that while the expected receipts from the advertised performances would have enabled the plaintiff to pay the performers, so would a like amount of money from any other source and the second head of damages could not have been within the contempla-

[193] Ward v. Vanderbilt, 34 How. Pr. (N. Y.), 144.

[194] 1 H. & N. 408.

[195] *Acc.*, Illinois Cent. R. R. v. Pearson, 80 Miss. 26, 31 So. 435.

[196] *New York:* Weed v. Panama R. R., 17 N. Y. 362, 72 Am. Dec. 474.

Texas: Texas & P. Ry. v. Mayes, 15 S. W. 43.

[197] Texas & P. Ry. v. Mayes, 15 S. W. 43.

[198] Southern Ry. v. Myers, 87 Fed. 19, 32 C. C. A. 19.

tion of the parties.[199]   The expenses incurred in waiting at a junction point may be recovered.[200]

§ 864. Failure to carry to destination.

Where the carrier breaks the contract of carriage by failing to carry the passenger to his destination, and set him down there, the measure of damages is in general the same, whether the breach of contract consists in a wrongful expulsion from the train, or in setting the passenger down at the wrong station or carrying him beyond his station.   The passenger may recover all the expenses of delay,[201] such as loss of time,[202] and also the expense of a reasonable conveyance to his destination.[203]   Where a carrier who had contracted to carry plaintiff from Seattle to Dawson City, carried him only as far as Fort Yukon, the plaintiff recovered the price of the ticket from Seattle to Dawson City, and the expense by train back

[199] Foster v. Cleveland, C. C. & St. L. Ry., 56 Fed. 434.

[200] International & G. N. R. R. v. Doolan (Tex. Civ. App.), 120 S. W. 1118.

[201] *United States:* Paddock v. Atchison, T. & S. F. R. R., 37 Fed. 841.

Illinois: Chicago & A. R. R. v. Flagg, 43 Ill. 364, 92 Am. Dec. 133, Pennsylvania R. R. v. Connell, 127 Ill. 419, 20 N. E. 89.

Louisiana: Airey v. Pullman Palace Car Co., 50 La. Ann. 648, 23 So. 512.

Missouri: Trigg v. St. Louis, K. C. & N. Ry., 74 Mo. 147, 41 Am. Rep. 305; Rawlings v. Wabash R. R., 97 Mo. App. 515, 71 S. W. 534.

Pennsylvania: Pennsylvania R. R. v. Spicker, 105 Pa. 142.

Texas: Texas & P. Ry. v. Hartnett (Tex. Civ. App.), 34 S. W. 1057; Texas & P. R. R. v. Armstrong, 93 Tex. 31, 51 S. W. 835.

Washington: Bullock v. White Star Steamship Co., 30 Wash. 448, 70 Pac. 1106.

[202] *Kentucky:* Louisville & N. R. R. v. Gaddie, 102 S. W. 817, 31 Ky. L. Rep. 502.

New York: Hamilton v. Third Ave. R. R., 53 N. Y. 25.

Texas: Jones v. Texas & N. O. R. R., 23 Tex. Civ. App. 65, 55 S. W. 376.

Washington: Ransberry v. North American Transp., etc., R. R., 22 Wash. 476, 61 Pac. 154, 79 Am. St. Rep. 953.

[203] *Illinois:* Indianapolis, B. & W. Ry. v. Birney, 71 Ill. 391 (*semble*); Pennsylvania R. R. v. Connell, 127 Ill. 419, 20 N. E. 89.

Kentucky: Cater v. Illinois Cent. R. R., 17 Ky. L. Rep. 1352, 34 S. W. 907.

Mississippi: Mississippi & T. R. R. v. Gill, 66 Miss. 39, 5 So. 393.

Missouri: Francis v. St. Louis T. Co., 5 Mo. App. 7.

New York: Hamilton v. Third Ave. R. R., 53 N. Y. 25; Miller v. Baltimore & O. R. R., 89 App. Div. 457, 85 N. Y. Supp. 883; Miller v. King, 53 N. Y. Supp. 123.

Texas: Missouri, K. & T. Ry. v. Byas, 9 Tex. Civ. App. 572, 29 S. W. 1122.

In such cases the defendant for the purpose of reducing damages must always be allowed to prove the cost of such conveyance. Miller v. King, 53 N. Y. Supp. 123.

to Seattle but not the profits which plaintiff might have made at Dawson city if he had been duly carried there.[204]

Where the master of one of a line of steamers plying to and from San Francisco, and then bound to that port, having on board a person who had, under pain of death, in case of his return, been expelled thence by the "Vigilance Committee," a revolutionary authority in actual government of the city, stopped his vessel and put the passenger on a return steamer of the same line, to be taken back to the port from which he had embarked, although the act was illegal, the circumstances which induced it were allowed as an important mitigation of the damages, which were therefore reduced by the Supreme Court of the United States, on appeal, from $4,000 to $50. Inconvenience, loss, and delay subsequently sustained by the passenger in getting to San Francisco, in consequence of the generally known power and purpose of the "Vigilance Committee," were not attributable to the master, and could not be compensated in the action.[205] When the passengers were not landed at the port of destination, but carried to a distant port, the measure of damages was held to include their fare, loss of time and expenses of return.[206] The passenger may also recover compensation for physical inconvenience,[207] and for fright and mental suffering.[208]

§ 864a. Carriage beyond station.

The liability of a carrier for carrying a passenger beyond his station is similar; the passenger may recover compensation for the actual loss. He may recover for the inconvenience, loss of time, and expense of returning to his station.[209] If the

---

[204] North Am. Trans. Co. v. Morrison, 178 U. S. 262, 20 Sup. Ct. 869, 44 L. ed. 1061.

[205] Pearson v. Duane, 4 Wall. 605, 18 L. ed. 447.

[206] The President, 92 Fed. 672.

[207] St. Louis S. W. Ry. v. Pearson, 88 Ark. 200, 114 S. W. 211.

[208] *Kentucky:* Dawson v. Louisville & N. R. R., 4 Ky. L. Rep. 801.

Texas: Pullman Co. v. Cox (Tex. Civ. App.), 120 S. W. 1058.

The distinction may not be clear between this case and the case of failure to carry, where as has been seen such damages are not allowed. The distinction seems to lie in the fact that in this case mental suffering is within the contemplation of the carrier, and in the case of failure to carry it is not.

[209] *Alabama:* Central of Ga. Ry. v. Morgan, 161 Ala. 483, 49 So. 865.

Arkansas: St. Louis, I. M. & S. Ry. v. Williams, 140 S. W. 141.

act of the passenger in walking back to the station was unreasonable, he cannot recover for the consequences of such a walk.[210] While loss of time may be recovered, the plaintiff cannot recover special damages for inability to attend to a particular matter of business unless notice of such business was given to the carrier.[211]

§ 865. Expulsion from train.

The plaintiff may recover compensation for the indignity of being ejected from the train.[212] In Michigan, it is held that

Kansas: Dalton *v.* Kansas City, F. S. & M. R. R., 78 Kan. 232, 96 Pac. 475, 17 L. R. A. (N. S.) 1226.

Missouri: Smith *v.* St. Louis & S. F. R. R., 127 Mo. App. 53, 106 S. W. 108. The plaintiff cannot recover for mental anguish because of the fright of the child who was with her. Pullman P. C. Co. *v.* Trimble, 8 Tex. Civ. App. 335, 28 S. W. 96.

[210] *Arkansas:* St. Louis, I. M. & S. Ry. *v.* Williams, 140 S. W. 141.

Mississippi: Natchez C. & M. R. R. *v.* Lambert (Miss.), 54 So. 836.

[211] Martin *v.* Southern Ry. (S. C.) 71 S. E. 236.

[212] *United States:* Zion *v.* Southern Pac. Co., 67 Fed. 500; Northern Pac. R. R. *v.* Pauson, 70 Fed. 585, 17 C. C. A. 287, 30 L. R. A. 730; Pullman P. C. Co. *v.* King, 99 Fed. 380, 39 C. C. A. 573.

Alabama: Louisville & N. R. R. *v.* Whitman, 79 Ala. 328; Kansas City, M. & B. R. R. *v.* Foster, 134 Ala. 244, 32 So. 773, 92 Am. St. Rep. 25.

Arkansas: Hot Springs R. R. *v.* Deloney, 65 Ark. 177, 182, 45 S. W. 351, 61 Am. St. Rep. 913; St. Louis, I. M. & S. Ry. *v.* Brown, 134 S. W. 1194; St. Louis S. W. Ry. *v.* Hammett, 136 S. W. 191.

California: Gorman *v.* Southern Pac. Co., 97 Cal. 1, 31 Pac. 112.

Georgia: Head *v.* Georgia P. Ry., 79 Ga. 358, 11 Am. St. Rep. 434; Georgia R. & E. Co. *v.* Baker, 125 Ga. 562, 54 S. E. 639, 7 L. R. A. (N. S.) 103.

Illinois: Chicago & A. R. R. *v.* Flagg, 43 Ill. 364; Chicago & N. W. Ry. *v.* Williams, 55 Ill. 185, 78 Am. Rep. 641; Chicago & N. W. Ry. *v.* Chisholm, 79 Ill. 584; Pennsylvania R. R. *v.* Connell, 112 Ill. 295; 127 Ill. 419, 20 N. E. 89, 54 Am. Rep. 238.

Indiana: Lake E. & W. Ry. *v.* Fix, 88 Ind. 381, 45 Am. Rep. 464.

Iowa: Shepard *v.* Chicago, R. I. & P. Ry., 77 Ia. 54, 41 N. W. 564, 14 Am. St. Rep. 268; Curtis *v.* Sioux City & H. P. Ry., 87 Ia. 622, 54 N. W. 339; Coine *v.* Chicago & N. W. R. R., 123 Ia. 458, 99 N. W. 134.

Kansas: Kansas City, Ft. S. & M. R. R. *v.* Little, 66 Kan. 378, 71 Pac. 820, 97 Am. St. Rep. 376, 61 L. R. A. 122.

Kentucky: Lexington & E. Ry. *v.* Lyons, 46 S. W. 209, 20 Ky. L. Rep. 516; Schmidt *v.* R. R., 74 S. W. 674, 25 Ky. L. Rep. 11; Louisville & N. R. R. *v.* Fowler, 96 S. W. 568, 29 Ky. L. Rep. 905.

Michigan: Lucas *v.* Michigan Cent. R. R., 98 Mich. 1, 56 N. W. 1039, 39 Am. St. Rep. 517.

Minnesota: Carsten *v.* Northern P. Ry., 44 Minn. 454, 47 N. W. 49, 20 Am. St. Rep. 589; Serwe *v.* Northern P. R. R., 48 Minn. 78, 50 N. W. 1021.

Missouri: Osteryoung *v.* Transit Co., 108 Mo. App. 703, 84 S. W. 179.

New Jersey: Allen *v.* Camden & P. Steamboat Ferry Co., 46 N. J. L. 198.

New York: Hamilton *v.* Third Ave.

if the conductor acted considerately, the plaintiff should have felt no sense of insult, and therefore cannot recover damages for the indignity; [213] but such is not the general rule. Good faith on the part of the conductor may, however, be shown to prevent the allowance of exemplary damages.[214] Damages are also recoverable for humiliation when the plaintiff was compelled to pay a second fare to avoid a threatened expulsion.[215] But if the plaintiff entered the train with the expectation and desire of being put off so as to make a case against the company, he is entitled to no compensation for injury to feelings.[216]

R. R., 53 N. Y. 25; Harrison v. Pennsylvania Co., 118 N. Y. Supp. 1022.

Ohio: Smith v. Pittsburg, F. W. & C. Ry., 23 Oh. St. 10; Pittsburg, C., C. & St. L. R. R. v. Reynolds, 55 Oh. St. 370, 383, 60 Am. St. Rep. 706, 45 N. E. 712.

Pennsylvania: Perry v. Pittsburgh Union Passenger Ry., 153 Pa. 236, 25 Atl. 772.

Tennessee: Choctaw, O. & G. R. R. v. Hill, 110 Tenn. 396, 75 S. W. 963.

Texas: Texas & P. Ry. v. James, 82 Tex. 306, 15 L. R. A. 347, 18 S. W. 589; Galveston H. & S. A. Ry. v. Kinnebrew (Tex. Civ. App.), 27 S. W. 631 (see Houston C. S. Ry. v. Jageman, 23 S. W. 628).

Virginia: Norfolk & W. R. R. v. Neely, 91 Va. 539, 22 S. E. 367.

Washington: Lawshe v. Tacoma R. & P. Co., 29 Wash. 681, 70 Pac. 118.

Wisconsin: Stutz v. Chicago & N. W. Ry., 73 Wis. 147, 40 N. W. 653, 99 Am. St. Rep. 769; Robinson v. Superior R. T. Ry., 94 Wis. 345, 68 N. W. 961.

England: Coppin v. Braithwaite, 8 Jur. 875.

[213] Batterson v. Chicago & G. T. Ry., 49 Mich. 184.

The Iowa cases looking the same way are now superseded by Coine v. R. R., 123 Ia. 458, 99 N. W. 134.

[214] *Iowa:* Fitzgerald v. Chicago, R. I. & P. Ry., 50 Ia. 79.

Maryland: Philadelphia, W. & B. R.

R. v. Hoeflich, 62 Md. 300, 50 Am. Rep. 223.

Missouri: Logan v. Hannibal & S. J. R. R., 77 Mo. 663.

New York: Hamilton v. Third Ave. R. R., 53 N. Y. 25; Yates v. New York C. & H. R. R. R., 67 N. Y. 100, 23 Am. Rep. 90.

North Carolina: Tomlinson v. Wilmington & S. C. R. R., 107 N. C. 327, 12 S. E. 138.

Ohio: United Power Co. v. Matheny, 81 Oh. St. 204, 90 N. E. 154.

[215] *Georgia:* Georgia Ry. & Electric Co. v. Baker, 125 Ga. 562, 54 S. E. 639, 7 L. R. A. (N. S.) 103.

Indiana: Pennsylvania Co. v. Bray, 125 Ind. 229, 25 N. E. 439.

Iowa: Paine v. Chicago, etc., R. R., 45 Ia. 569.

Michigan: Hufford v. Grand Rapids & I. R. R., 53 Mich. 118, 18 N. W. 580.

Minnesota: Hoffman v. Northern Pac. R. R., 45 Minn. 53, 47 N. W. 312.

Ohio: Pittsburg, C., C. & St. L. R. R. v. Ensign, 3 Ohio Dec. 451.

[216] *Arkansas:* St. Louis, I. M. & S. R. R. v. Trimble, 54 Ark. 354, 15 S. W. 899.

Georgia: Southern R. R. v. Barlow, 104 Ga. 213, 30 S. E. 732, 69 Am. St. Rep. 166.

Ohio: Cincinnati, H. & D. R. R. v. Cole, 29 Ohio St. 126, 23 Am. Rep. 729.

Texas: Russell v. Missouri, K. & T. Ry., 12 Tex. Civ. App. 627, 35 S. W.

It has been attempted in some cases to restrict the damages in the case of wrongful expulsion for refusal to pay fare to the amount of fare demanded by the conductor, on the ground that the plaintiff should have paid the fare demanded, and thus avoided expulsion.[217] But this is in other jurisdictions held not to be required of the passenger,[218] and this would seem the more correct view since, as we have seen,[219] a person is not called upon to anticipate a wrong, and need take no steps to avoid the consequences of the defendant's wrongful act before it is committed. A passenger who, through the negligence of one conductor, is not furnished with a stop-over ticket, to which he is entitled, and who, on attempting to resume his journey after a stop, is required by a second conductor to pay additional fare or leave the train, may elect to leave the train, and in that case may recover from the railway company not merely the amount of the additional fare which he is subsequently obliged to pay in order to reach his destination, but all damages sustained by him as the direct and natural consequence of the fault of the first conductor.[220]

724; Missouri, K. & T. Ry. v. Morgan (Tex. Civ. App.), 138 S. W. 216.

[217] *United States:* Gibson v. East Tenn. R. R., 30 Fed. 904.

Arkansas: St. Louis, I. M. & S. Ry. v. Cates, 87 Ark. 162, 112 S. W. 202.

Georgia: Louisville & N. R. R. v. Spinks, 104 Ga. 692, 30 S. E. 968.

Maryland: Western Maryland R. R. v. Stockdale, 83 Md. 245, 34 Atl. 880.

Massachusetts: Bradshaw v. South Boston R. R., 135 Mass. 407, 46 Am. Rep. 481.

Michigan: Van Dusan v. Grand Trunk Ry., 97 Mich. 439, 56 N. W. 848, 37 Am. St. Rep. 354; Zagelmeyer v. Cincinnati, S. & M. R. R., 102 Mich. 214, 60 N. W. 436, 47 Am. St. Rep. 514; Brown v. Rapid Ry., 134 Mich. 591, 96 N. W. 925.

New York: Townsend v. New York C. & H. R. R. R., 56 N. Y. 295, 15 Am. Rep. 419.

Ohio: Shelton v. Railroad Co., 29 Oh. St. 214.

Texas: Gulf, C. & S. F. Ry. v. McCormick, 45 Tex. Civ. App. 425, 100 S. W. 202.

Washington: Sprenger v. Tacoma Traction Co., 15 Wash. 660, 47 Pac. 17, 43 L. R. A. 706.

[218] *California:* Elser v. Southern Pac. Co., 7 Cal. App. 493, 94 Pac. 852.

Mississippi: Ill. Cent. R. R. v. Gortikov, 90 Miss. 787, 45 So. 363.

Missouri: Ferguson v. Missouri Pac. Ry., 128 S. W. 799, 144 Mo. App. 202.

Texas: St. Louis, etc., R. R. v. Mackie, 71 Tex. 491, 10 Am. St. Rep. 766, 9 S. W. 451, 1 L. R. A. 667; Galveston, H. & S. A. Ry. v. Wiseman (Tex. Civ. App.), 136 S. W. 793.

Wisconsin: Yorton v. Milwaukee, L. S. & W. Ry., 62 Wis. 367, 21 N. W. 516. See *ante,* § 222.

[219] *Ante,* § 224.

[220] Yorton v. Milwaukee, L. S. & W. Ry., 62 Wis. 367, 21 N. W. 516. See Missouri, K. & T. Ry. v. Smith, 152 Fed. 608, 81 C. C. A. 598.

In case of a wrongful attempt to expel a passenger, he is entitled to offer a reasonable resistance and if this resistance produces physical injury, or consequential damages, e. g., aggravates a disorder from which he had previously been suffering, it would seem that the defendant is liable.[221]

Compensation will be allowed for loss of time and inconvenience.[222] A child may recover for resulting fright and terror.[223] The amount of fare paid upon demand of the conductor to avoid expulsion may of course be recovered.[224]

§ 865a. Failure to furnish agreed accommodations.

Analogous to cases of expulsion are those in which the carrier refuses the passenger the accommodations to which he is entitled by his ticket. In such a case in admiralty, where there had been annoyance, humiliation and discomfort, but no serious physical injury, $300 was given as damages.[225]

§ 866. Compensation for the risk of injury.

It is a matter of some doubt whether exposure to risk, which

In Leek v. Northern Pac. Ry. (Wash.), 118 Pac. 345, the plaintiff's son, while travelling with her, was shot and killed by a bullet from outside the train; the conductor put off the child's body at the next station, and insisted on the plaintiff and her family leaving the train at the same place, though plaintiff informed him that she had no money. Citizens of the place raised a purse for her, which she used in paying the expenses of her stay, and in purchasing clothes. The court held that the defendant was not entitled to any reduction in damages because of the contributions of citizens; but that neither the expenses of her stop-over, the cost of new clothes, nor her mental anguish was caused by the wrongful expulsion.

[221] *United States:* New York, L. E. & W. R. R. v. Winter, 143 U. S. 60, 73, 36 L. ed. 71, 12 Sup. Ct. 356; Pittsburg, C., C. & St. L. Ry. v. Russ, 67 Fed. 662, 14 C. C. A. 612.

Kentucky: Louisville & N. R. R. v.

Cottengim, 31 Ky. L. Rep. 871, 104 S. W. 280, 13 L. R. A. (N. S.) 624.

New York: English v. Delaware & H. C. Co., 66 N. Y. 454, 23 Am. Rep. 69.

Canada: Dancey v. Grand Trunk Ry., 19 Ont. App. 664.

[222] *Texas:* International & G. N. Ry. v. Campbell, 1 Tex. Civ. App. 509, 20 S. W. 845; Pullman P. C. Co. v. McDonald, 2 Tex. Civ. App. 322, 21 S. W. 945.

Wisconsin: Boehm v. Duluth, S. S. & A. Ry., 91 Wis. 592, 65 N. W. 506.

[223] *Ohio:* Cincinnati N. T. Co. v. Rosnagle, 84 Oh. St. 310, 95 N. E. 884.

Texas: Missouri P. Ry. v. Kaiser, 82 Tex. 144, 18 S. W. 305.

[224] Carr v. Toledo Traction Co., 19 Oh. Cir. Ct. 281. But nothing can be recovered in this action on account of an unused portion of the ticket retained by the conductor: Pierson v. Illinois C. R. R., 159 Mich. 110, 123 N. W. 576.

[225] The Willamette Valley, 71 Fed. 712.

did not result in actual injury, is a matter for compensation. In Chicago & Alton Railroad *v.* Flagg [226] the court said that the plaintiff could recover compensation for "the risk to which he was subjected." But in Trigg *v.* St. Louis, Kansas City & Northern Railway [227] Hough, J., said: "We have not been referred to any case in which a simple exposure to averted danger has been held to be a ground of recovery, and we do not think it should be, unless the exposure were wanton and produced injury." This seems the correct view; for since all circumstances subsequent to the defendant's act are admissible to show the actual injury, the fact that a risk resulted in no actual injury should prevent the allowance of damages for it, since there is no loss to be compensated.

It may, however, appear that the risk caused fright and mental suffering or nervous shock, and in such a case damages may be recovered for the suffering caused by exposure to the risk. [228] So where the plaintiff was suffering from hernia, it was held that the jury in estimating damages for wrongful expulsion from the train might consider his mental suffering caused by the risk of his injury being aggravated, though, in fact, no actual aggravation of the hernia was proved. [229]

§ 867. Consequences of exposure.

The question has been much discussed, in the class of cases now under consideration, whether damages can be recovered for illness caused by exposure to the weather. The leading case upon the subject is Hobbs *v.* London & South Western Railway. [230] In that case, which though in form tort was treated by the court as an action of contract, it appeared that the plaintiff, with his wife and two children, took tickets to H. They were set down at E. It being late at night the plaintiff could not get a wagon or accommodation at an inn. He and his family had to walk four or five miles in a rainy night, and the wife caught cold, was laid up for some time and unable to assist her husband. Expenses were incurred for medical attendance on her. The jury found £8 for the

[226] 43 Ill. 364.
[227] 74 Mo. 147, 154.
[228] See § 861.

[229] Fell *v.* Northern P. R. R., 44 Fed. 248.
[230] L. R. 10 Q. B. 111.

inconvenience suffered by having to walk home, and £20 for the wife's illness and its consequences. It was held that the plaintiff could recover the £8, but not the £20, since the illness was not a natural consequence of putting passengers down at the wrong station. Cockburn, C. J., said: "It is not the necessary consequence, it is not even the probable consequence of a person being put down at an improper place, and having to walk home, that he should sustain either personal injury or catch a cold. That cannot be said to be within the contemplation of the parties so as to entitle the plaintiff to recover, and to make the defendants liable to pay damages for the consequences." And Archibald, J., said: "With regard to what might be the result of the walk home, the wet night, the condition of health, the state of the plaintiff herself, all those things could not have been in the contemplation of the parties when they made the contract." Blackburn and Mellor, JJ., said simply, "they are too remote." This case has been criticised in an earlier chapter.[231]

In McMahon v. Field [232] the Court of Appeal disapproved of this decision. Bramwell, L. J., said: "I must say I do not see why a passenger who, by the default of the railway company, was obliged to walk home in the dark, might not recover in respect of such damage, it being an event which might not unreasonably be expected to occur."

And Brett, L. J., said: "It was said that such damage was too remote to be recovered. Why was it too remote? There was no accommodation or conveyance to be obtained at Esher at that time of night, so that it was not only reasonable that they should walk, but they were obliged to do so. Why was it that which happened was not the natural consequence of the breach of contract? Suppose a man let lodgings to a woman, and then turned her out in the middle of the night with only her night-clothes on, would it not be a natural consequence that she would take a cold? Had Esher station been a large one, and had there been flys which might have been had, or accommodation at an inn, and the passengers had refused such and elected to walk home, I should have thought then that what happened arose from their own fault, but that was not

---

[231] *Ante*, § 150.   [232] 7 Q. B. Div. 591, 594, 596.

so, yet, nevertheless, the judges who decided Hobbs v. London South Western Railway decided, as a matter of fact, that the cold was so improbable a consequence that it was not to be left to the jury whether it was occasioned by the breach of contract. It is not, however, necessary for me to say more than that I am not contented with it, for there is a difference between such a case and the present one."

§ 868. American rule.

In this country the authority of Hobbs v. London & South Western Railway is often acknowledged, at least nominally; and it has been followed to the full extent in a few jurisdictions.[233] But the practical effect of it has been neutralized in most jurisdictions by holding that it is of no authority in cases where the action sounds in tort. Where this is the case any injury directly caused by the *necessary* resulting exposure is a matter for compensation.[234] It is said in these cases that where the breach of contract was caused by an act which was

[233] Pullman P. C. Co. v. Barker, 4 Col. 344, 34 Am. Rep. 89 (an action on the case); Murdock v. Boston & Albany R. R., 133 Mass. 15, 43 Am. Rep. 480 (an action of contract).

[234] *Alabama:* Alabama G. S. R. R. v. Heddleston, 82 Ala. 218.

Arkansas: St. Louis Southwestern R. R. v. Knight, 81 Ark. 429, 99 S. W. 684; Little Rock Traction Co. v. Winn, 75 Ark. 529, 87 S. W. 1025.

California: Delmonte v. Southern Pac. Co., 2 Cal. App. 211, 83 Pac. 269.

Florida: Seaboard A. L. R. R. v. Scarborough, 52 Fla. 425, 42 So. 706.

Georgia: Brown v. Georgia C. & N. R. R., 119 Ga. 88, 46 S. E. 71.

Indiana: Cincinnati, H. & I. R. R. v. Eaton, 94 Ind. 474.

Kentucky: Louisville & N. R. R. v. Sullivan, 81 Ky. 624, 50 Am. Rep. 186.

Maryland: Baltimore C. P. Ry. v. Kemp, 61 Md. 74, 619.

Minnesota: Rosted v. Great N. Ry., 76 Minn. 123, 78 N. W. 971.

Mississippi: Heirn v. M'Caughan, 32 Miss. 17, 66 Am. Dec. 588; Alabama & V. R. R. v. Hanes, 69 Miss. 160, 13 So. 246.

Missouri: Cross v. Kansas City, H. S. & M. Ry., 56 Mo. App. 684.

Nebraska: Chicago, B. & Q. R. R. v. Spirk, 51 Neb. 167, 179, 70 N. W. 926.

New Hampshire: Boothby v. Grand Trunk Ry., 66 N. H. 342, 34 Atl. 157.

New York: Williams v. Vanderbilt, 28 N. Y. 217, 84 Am. Dec. 333.

North Dakota: Hany v. Great N. Ry., 8 N. D. 23, 77 N. W. 97, 73 Am. St. Rep. 727, 42 L. R. A. 664.

Pennsylvania: Tilburg v. Northern Cent. Ry., 217 Pa. 618, 66 Atl. 845.

South Carolina: Pickens v. South Carolina G. R. R., 54 S. C. 498, 32 S. E. 567.

Texas: International & G. N. Ry. v. Terry, 62 Tex. 380, 50 Am. Rep. 529.

Wisconsin: Brown v. Chicago, M. & S. P. Ry., 54 Wis. 342, 41 Am. Rep. 41; Yorton v. Milwaukee, L. S. & W. Ry., 62 Wis. 367, 21 N. W. 516.

not tortious, the rule in Hobbs' case would apply; [235] but in none of these cases has this distinction been applied, for the action has always been treated as sounding in tort.

§ 869. Pullman Palace Car Co. v. Barker.

In Pullman Palace Car Co. *v.* Barker [236] the plaintiff, a woman, who at the time was unwell, was travelling in one of the defendant's cars and was compelled to leave the car at night on account of the burning of the car through the defendant's negligence. She caught a cold, which, owing to the condition of her health at the time, resulted in a serious illness. She brought an action of tort. The court held that the illness was remote. Elbert, J., said: "The exposure to the cold was the direct and necessary result of the appellant's negligence. Her subsequent illness, however, was not the result of the exposure, but the result of the exposure *in her then condition.* Here, then, intervenes an independent cause of her illness, a cause resting in her physical condition, appertaining exclusively to herself, with which the appellant had no concern, and to which it sustained no relations either by contract or by the general duty imposed by law upon carriers of passengers. Where physical weakness or disability is apparent to, or is brought to the attention of the carrier, undoubtedly that high degree of care which the law imposes upon him would, under certain circumstances, involve duties in reference thereto. . . . Persons who are ill have a right to enter the cars of a railroad company and travel therein; as a common carrier of passengers the company has no right to prevent them, but the increased risk arising from conditions affecting their fitness to journey, certainly where they are unknown to the carrier, must rest upon their own shoulders."

The court cited Hobbs *v.* London & South Western Railway in support of its opinion. The case has been severely criticised. [237]

[235] See especially Cincinnati, H. & I. R. R. *v.* Eaton, 94 Ind. 474, 48 Am Rep. 179; Brown *v.* Chicago, M. & S. P. Ry., 54 Wis. 342.

[236] 4 Col. 344, 347, 34 Am. Rep. 89.

[237] Cincinnati, H. & I. R. R. *v.* Eaton, 94 Ind. 474, 48 Am. Rep. 179; Brown *v.* Chicago, M. & S. P. Ry., 54 Wis. 342.

§ 870. Brown v. Chicago, Milwaukee and St. Paul Railway.

The question was again elaborately discussed and the authorities examined in Brown *v.* Chicago, Milwaukee & St. Paul Railway.[238] In that case the plaintiffs were left at night in a place where no houses were to be seen, at a distance from their destination. They walked to their destination, which the jury found a reasonable act. The female plaintiff was pregnant at the time, and the exposure resulted in a miscarriage and illness. The court held that compensation might be recovered for the illness. Taylor, J., said: "Upon the findings of the jury in this case, it appears that the defendant was guilty of a wrong in putting the plaintiffs off the cars at the place they did; that in order to protect themselves from the effects of such wrong they made the walk to Mauston; that in making such walk they were guilty of no negligence, but were compelled to make it on account of the defendant's wrongful act; and that, on account of the peculiar state of health of Mrs. Brown at the time, she was injured by such walk. There was no intervening independent cause of the injury, other than the act of the defendant. All the acts done by the plaintiffs, and from which the injury flowed, were rightful on their part, and compelled by the act of the defendant. We think, therefore, it must be held that the injury to Mrs. Brown was the direct result of the defendant's negligence, and that such negligence was the proximate and not the remote cause of the injury. We can see no reason why the defendant is not equally liable for an injury sustained by a person who is placed in a dangerous position, whether the injury is the immediate result of a wrongful act or results from the act of the party in endeavoring to escape from the immediate danger. . . . . The defendant, by its negligence, placed the plaintiffs in a position where it was necessary for them to act to avoid the consequences of the wrongful act of the defendant, and, acting with ordinary prudence and care to get themselves out of the difficulty in which they had been placed, they sustained injury. Such injury can be, and is, traced directly to the defendant's negligence

[238] 54 Wis. 342.

as its cause; and it is its proximate cause, within the rules of law upon that subject." [239]

§ 871. General conclusions.

The objections to recovery made in Hobbs *v.* London & South Western Railway and the cases following it seem to be two: first, that the consequence is remote; second, that it was not contemplated at the time the contract was entered into. To the first of these objections the reasoning of the court in the case of Brown *v.* Chicago, Milwaukee & St. Paul Railway, just quoted, seems to be a conclusive answer. The defendant has placed the plaintiff in a difficult position, from which he must escape by the best means possible. If the means of escape he adopts are reasonable ones, all loss caused directly by the adoption of such means is the proximate result of the defendant's wrong, and compensation is therefore recoverable for it. To the second objection there appear to be two answers. In the first place, the defendant's act is a tort, and although the relation between the parties probably began in a contract, yet it is not necessary to invoke the contract in order to recover. The rule in Hadley *v.* Baxendale, therefore, even if we assume that that case introduced a distinction between contract and tort, does not apply. But even if the action is upon the contract, as it was in the case of Murdock *v.* Boston & Albany Railroad,[240] the objection would not seem to be sound. This appears plainly upon consideration of the facts of Pullman Palace Co. *v.* Barker, in which the court refused recovery. The plaintiff was actually driven from the car by the defendant's negligence, half-clad, on a cold night; and illness naturally and almost necessarily followed. To say that such a consequence was remote, or to exclude recovery for it because the fact of the plaintiff's physical infirmity was not known to the defendant's agent when she purchased her seat, is indeed, in the language of the Supreme Court of Wiscon-

---

[239] This is an application of the principle so universally acknowledged, that where the plaintiff takes proper means to avoid the consequences of defendant's act (*e. g.*, tries to avoid further injury by getting to her destination as soon as possible), and by doing so, enhances the damages, the defendant is still responsible. See § 226b.

[240] 133 Mass. 15, 43 Am. Rep. 480.

sin,[241] a decision "supported by the principles of neither law nor humanity."

Upon the whole, these cases seem to illustrate very strongly a point upon which too much insistence cannot be laid; that the case of Hadley v. Baxendale introduced no new rule of damages. For proximate and natural consequences of the defendant's act, whether it be a breach of contract or a tort, a recovery can always be had; the only meaning of the rule with regard to the contemplation of the parties is that in contract a particular species of proof as to special consequences is often available which is not so in tort.

§ 872. Avoidable consequences.

An important consideration in such cases is whether the plaintiff might not have avoided the exposure by reasonable efforts. If a journey on foot to the place of destination is not necessary or reasonable, of course any injury contracted by reason of the journey is due to the plaintiff's own folly, and is remote from the defendant's act. So where the plaintiff should have obtained shelter for the night at the place where he was left by the defendant, he cannot recover damages for injury caused by walking to his destination;[242] and so also, where a conveyance can be procured.[243] In an Illinois case [244] the plaintiff, a physician, walked home instead of waiting

[241] In Brown v. Chicago, M. & S. P. Ry., 54 Wis. 342, 360.

[242] *Missouri:* Spry v. Missouri, K. & T. Ry., 73 Mo. App. 203.
New York: Childs v. New York, O. & W. Ry., 28 N. Y. Supp. 894.
Tennessee: Louisville, N. & G. S. R. R. v. Fleming, 14 Lea, 128.
Texas: Galveston, H. & S. A. Ry. v. Turner (Tex. Civ. App.), 23 S. W. 83; Texas & P. Ry. v. Cole, 66 Tex. 562; International & G. N. R. R. v. Flores (Tex. Civ. App.), 26 S. W. 899.
See *Nebraska:* Chicago, B. & Q. R. R. v. Spirk, 51 Neb. 167, 70 N. W. 926.

[243] *Illinois:* Indianapolis, B. & W. Ry. v. Birney, 71 Ill. 391; Ohio & M. Ry. v. Burrow, 32 Ill. App. 161.

Louisiana: Bader v. Southern Pac. R. R., 52 La. Ann. 1060, 27 So. 584.
New York: Childs v. N. Y., O. & W. Ry., 77 Hun, 539, 28 N. Y. Supp. 894, 60 N. Y. St. 276.
So where the plaintiff was offered or might have taken another train or car of the defendant, he cannot recover for the consequences of failure to do so.
Arkansas: St. Louis, I. M. & S. Ry. v. Stroud, 67 Ark. 112, 56 S. W. 870.
Texas: Missouri P. Ry. v. Groesbeck (Tex. Civ. App.), 24 S. W. 702.

[244] Indianapolis, B. & W. Ry. v. Birney, 71 Ill. 391.

for the next train, and contracted an illness from the exposure. Walker, J., said: "Had he procured a carriage and horses to make the trip, the company would no doubt have been liable for reasonable compensation for its use and for a driver, or had he awaited the next train, and gone on it, he would have been entitled to nominal damages at least, and could have recovered for all such actual damages as he could have proved in the way of necessarily increased expenses while awaiting the arrival of the train, and·loss by being unable to visit patients who required his medical advice, or injury or loss he may have actually sustained in his business, caused by the delay; but he had no right to inflict injury upon himself to enhance damages he sought to recover from the road. Having been wrongfully left by the train, if he supposed his business was so urgent as to prevent his awaiting the next train, he should have used all precautions in so making the journey as to produce the least injury to himself that reason would dictate. He had no right to act with recklessness or wantonly, and then claim compensation for the injury thus inflicted. Had he attempted to walk to the next station barefoot, and his feet had been frozen, would any sane man believe he could have recovered for such injury? We presume not, because all would say it was a voluntary wantonness. Then, if two other modes presented themselves, almost perfectly safe from injury, as was the case here, and another, attended with great hazard from the exposure to extreme cold and over-exertion, as all reasonable persons must know, why should he be rewarded for disregarding his safety and the consequent injury? The injury by the journey on foot was unnecessarily incurred —was not the necessary consequence of being left by the train, but was unnecessarily, if not recklessly, induced. It was the improper, voluntary act of the appellee, and for it he has no right to recover."

§ 873. Baggage.

If baggage is lost which the carrier takes charge of without remuneration, the passenger can only recover damages for the loss of what is usually carried as baggage, including such an amount of money as is necessary and proper for the journey under the circumstances of the case.[245] He cannot, for instance, recover for jewelry which was carried in his trunk as merchandise.[246] If the carrier has notice that the trunk contains articles other than baggage and receives extra compensation, it may then be liable as a common carrier for its

[245] *United States:* Hopkins v. Westcott, 6 Blatch. 64 (student's books); Hannibal & S. J. R. R. v. Swift, 12 Wall. 262, 20 L. ed. 422 (surgeon's instruments).

Arkansas: Railway Co. v. Berry, 60 Ark. 433, 30 S. W. 764, 46 Am. St. Rep. 212 (money).

Illinois: Woods v. Devin, 13 Ill. 746 (pistol); Davis v. Michigan Southern & N. I. R. R., 22 Ill. 278, 74 Am. Dec. 151 (revolver); Illinois Cent. R. R. v. Copeland, 24 Ill. 332, 76 Am. Dec. 749 (money); Cincinnati & Chicago A. L. R. R. v. Marcus, 38 Ill. 219 (money).

Kentucky: American Contract Co. v. Cross, 8 Bush, 472, 8 Am. Rep. 471 (gold watch).

New York: Duffy v. Thompson, 4 E. D. Smith, 178 (money); Van Horn v. Kermit, 4 E. D. Smith, 453 (guns for sporting purposes); Davis v. Cayuga & S. R. R., 10 How. Pr. 330 (harness maker's tools); Hawkins v. Hoffman, 6 Hill, 586, 41 Am. Dec. 767 (fishing tackle); Orange County Bank v. Brown, 9 Wend. 85, 24 Am. Dec. 129 (money); Merrill v. Grinnell, 30 N. Y. 594 (money); Adams v. New Jersey Steamboat Co., 151 N. Y. 163, 45 N. E. 369, 56 Am. St. Rep. 616, 34 L. R. A. 652 (money).

Ohio: Jones v. Voorhees, 10 Ohio, 145 (watch).

Pennsylvania: Porter v. Hildebrand, 14 Pa. 129 (carpenter's tools).

Tennessee: Coward v. East Tennessee, V. & G. R. R., 16 Lea, 225, 57 Am. Rep. 226 (watch and chain and diamond ring).

Texas: Bonner v. Blum (Tex. Civ. App.), 25 S. W. 60 (jewelry).

[246] *Illinois:* Michigan C. R. R. v. Carrow, 73 Ill. 348, 24 Am. Rep. 248.

New York: Richards v. Westcott, 2 Bosw. 589.

In the following cases the articles lost were held not baggage.

United States: Humphreys v. Perry, 148 U. S. 627, 13 Sup. Ct. 711, 37 L. ed. 587 (jewelry samples); Wunsch v. Northern Pac. R. R., 62 Fed. 878 (jewelry).

Florida: Brock v. Gale, 14 Fla. 523, 14 Am. Rep. 356 (dentist's instruments).

Indiana: Doyle v. Kiser, 6 Ind. 242 ($4,000).

Kansas: Southern Kansas R. R. v. Clark, 52 Kan. 398, 34 Pac. 1054 (salesman's samples).

Massachusetts: Stimson v. Connecticut R. R. R., 98 Mass. 83, 93 Am. Dec. 140 (salesman's samples); Alling v. Boston & A. R. R., 126 Mass. 121, 30 Am. Rep. 667 (jewelry).

New York: Nevins v. Bay State Steamboat Co., 4 Bosw. 225 (jewelry); Pardee v. Drew, 25 Wend. 459 (merchandise); Steers v. Liverpool & N. Y. & P. S. Co., 57 N. Y. 1, 15 Am. Rep. 453 (jewelry); Simpson v. N. Y., N. H. & H. R. R., 38 N. Y. Supp. 341 (merchandise).

England: Belfast & B. Ry. v. Keys, 9 H. L. Cas. 556 (merchandise); Phelps v. London & N. W. Ry., 19 C. B. (N. S.) 321 (title deed carried by attorney for client); Macrow v. Great Western Ry., L. R. 6 Q. B. 612 (household supplies); Britten v. Great Northern Ry., [1899] 1 Q. B. 243 (bicycle).

loss.[247] Even if the carrier has no notice, and is not held to the degree of liability of a common carrier, yet he is liable as a bailee and may be held in case of loss by active negligence.[248] In Fairfax v. New York Central & Hudson River Railroad,[249] the plaintiff's baggage was delivered to the defendant by a connecting line by mistake for another line. Upon arrival in New York the plaintiff found the defendant had brought the trunk to New York, but on demanding it was unable to find it. In the plaintiff's trunk were thirty-nine sovereigns. The jury were told to allow the value of these if they found the amount was proper, reasonable, and necessary, and in deciding this, to take into consideration the position and circumstances of the plaintiff, the length and character of his journey, the contingencies and accidents that might naturally arise, and the fact that he was in a foreign country, and to give the plaintiff the full value of his clothing for use to him in New York, and not merely what it could be sold for in money. This was held to be correct. "No other rule would give him a compensation for his damages. This rule must be adopted, because such clothing cannot be said

[247] *United States:* Jacobs v. Tutt, 33 Fed. 412.
Arkansas: Kansas City, F. S. & M. R. R. v. McGahey, 63 Ark. 344, 38 S. W. 659, 58 Am. St. Rep. 111, 36 L. R. A. 781.
Georgia: Dibble v. Bron, 12 Ga. 217, 56 Am. Dec. 460.
Massachusetts: Dunlap v. International Steamboat Co., 98 Mass. 371 (*semble*).
Minnesota: McKibbin v. Great Northern R. R., 78 Minn. 232, 80 N. W. 1052.
Mississippi: New Orleans & N. E. R. R. v. Shackelford, 87 Miss. 610, 40 So. 427, 112 Am. St. Rep. 461, 4 L. R. A. (N. S.) 1035.
Missouri: Minter v. Pennsylvania, 41 Mo. 503, 97 Am. Dec. 288; Ross v. Missouri, K. & T. R. R., 4 Mo. App. 582.
New York: Millard v. Missouri, K. & T. R. R., 20 Hun, 191; Glovinsky v.

Cunard Steamship Co., 6 Misc. 388, 26 N. Y. Supp. 751, 56 N. Y. Supp. 407; Trimble v. New York Cent. R. R., 57 N. Y. Supp. 437; Saleeby v. Cent. R. R., 99 App. Div. 163, 90 N. Y. Supp. 1042.
South Carolina: Fleishman v. Southern Ry., 76 S. C. 237, 56 S. E. 974.
England: Cahill v. London & N. W. Ry., 10 C. B. (N. S.) 154 (*semble*); Great Northern Ry. v. Shepherd, 8 Ex. 30.

[248] *Massachusetts:* Blumantle v. Fitchburg R. R., 127 Mass. 322, 34 Am. Rep. 376.
New York: Cole v. Goodwin, 19 Wend. 251, 32 Am. Dec. 470 (*semble*); Gutney v. Grand Trunk Ry., 37 N. Y. St. Rep. 155, 14 N. Y. Supp. 321.
England: Meux v. Eastern Ry., [1895] 2 Q. B. 387.

[249] 73 N. Y. 167, 172, 29 Am. Rep. 119. See § 251.

to have a market price, and it would not sell for what it was really worth." [250]

III.—OTHER SIMILAR AGENCIES

§ 873a. Sleeping or parlor cars.

For refusal to receive a passenger or to provide a berth or seat which has been sold to a passenger, a car company is responsible for all the damages, including personal discomfort; [251] but it has been held that injury to the passenger's health, not being a natural result of the refusal, cannot be charged to the company. [252] When a passenger is wrongfully expelled from the car, he may recover for the discomfort of completing his journey in an ordinary car, [253] and for consequent illness. [254] For personal injury for which the car company is responsible he is entitled to compensation as in ordinary cases of personal injury, [255] including damages for mental suffering, [256] but not to exemplary damages unless there were circumstances of malice or insult. [257]

[250] See to the same effect:
Kentucky: Cincinnati, O. & S. W. R. R. v. Webb, 8 Ky. L. Rep. 44.
Pennsylvania: Douglass v. The Railroad, 1 Phila. 337, 9 Leg. Int. 50.
South Carolina: Turner v. Southern Ry., 75 S. C. 58, 54 S. E. 825, 7 L. R. A. (N. S.) 188.
Texas: Texas & N. O. R. R. v. Russell (Tex. Civ. App.), 97 S. W. 1090.
Wyoming: Lake Shore & M. S. Ry. v. Warren, 3 Wyo. 134, 6 Pac. 724.
[251] *Alabama:* Pullman Co. v. Krauss, 145 Ala. 395, 40 So. 398, 4 L. R. A. (N. S.) 103.
Illinois: Nevin v. Pullman P. C. Co., 106 Ill. 222, 46 Am. Rep. 688.
New York: Buck v. Webb, 58 Hun, 185, 11 N. Y. Supp. 617; Braun v. Webb, 32 Misc. 243, 65 N. Y. Supp. 668.
Texas: Pullman P. C. Co. v. Nelson, 22 Tex. Civ. App. 223, 54 S. W. 624; Pullman P. C. Co. v. Booth (Tex. Civ. App.), 28 S. W. 719.

Australia: Nash v. Copeland, 4 N. S. W. Wkly. N. 41.
[252] Smith v. Pullman Co., 138 Mo. App. 238, 119 S. W. 1072.
[253] *Illinois:* Pullman P. C. Co. v. Reed, 75 Ill. 125, 20 Am. Rep. 232.
Texas: Missouri P. Ry. v. Groesbeck (Tex. Civ. App.), 24 S. W. 702.
[254] Mann B. C. Co. v. Dupré, 54 Fed. 646. *Contra,* Pullman P. C. Co. v. Barker, 4 Colo. 344, 34 Am. Rep. 89, *ante,* § 869.
[255] Hughes v. Pullman P. C. Co., 74 Fed. 499.
[256] *United States:* Campbell v. Pullman P. C. Co., 42 Fed. 484.
Texas: Pullman P. C. Co. v. Booth (Tex. Civ. App.), 28 S. W. 719.
[257] *United States:* Lemon v. Pullman P. C. Co., 52 Fed. 262.
Illinois: Pullman P. C. Co. v. Reed, 75 Ill. 125, 20 Am. Rep. 232.
Texas: Missouri P. Ry. v. Groesbeck (Tex. Civ. App.), 24 S. W. 702.
Virginia: Norfolk & W. R. R. v.

A sleeping car company is not liable for money stolen from a passenger in excess of a reasonable sum for travelling expenses.[258] For failure to put a passenger in the right car as a result of which she lost her train, the company is liable for her hotel bills and her loss of time, but not for personal inconvenience suffered in a hotel to which she went, or for a cold she caught in the hotel.[259] Where the porter of a sleeping car stole a passenger's medicines, it was held that she might recover for physical and mental suffering caused by not having them.[260]

§ 873b. Inns, theatres, etc.

An innkeeper is liable for injuries to a guest by his servant, and the guest may recover for mortification and sense of insult from such injury.[261]

The proprietor of a theatre may be responsible for damages in refusing to admit a ticket-holder, or for expelling him from the theatre after his admission, and the measure of damages is the amount paid for admission, and any incidental expenses to which the plaintiff may have been put;[262] together with compensation in the proper case for the indignity and disgrace of the expulsion,[263] but in the ordinary case exemplary dam-

---

Lipscomb, 90 Va. 137, 17 S. E. 809, 20 L. R. A. 817.

[258] *United States:* Blum v. Southern P. P. C. Co., 1 Flip. 500, Fed. Cas. No. 1,574.

Alabama: Cooney v. Pullman P. C. Co., 121 Ala. 368, 25 So. 712, 53 L. R. A. 690.

Massachusetts: Lewis v. New York S. C. Co., 143 Mass. 267, 9 N. E. 615, 58 Am. Rep. 135.

Mississippi: Illinois Cent. R. R. v. Handy, 63 Miss. 609, 56 Am. Rep. 846.

Missouri: Root v. New York C. S. C. Co., 28 Mo. App. 199.

Nebraska: Pullman P. C. Co. v. Lowe, 28 Neb. 239, 44 N. W. 226, 6 L. R. A. 809, 26 Am. St. Rep. 325.

New York: Williams v. Webb, 49 N. Y. Supp. 1111.

Tennessee: Pullman P. C. Co. v.

Gavin, 93 Tenn. 53, 57, 22 S. W. 70, 42 Am. St. Rep. 902, 21 L. R. A. 298.

Texas: Pullman P. C. Co. v. Matthews, 74 Tex. 654, 12 S. W. 744, 15 Am. St. Rep. 873; Pullman P. C. Co. v. Pollock, 69 Tex. 120, 5 S. W. 814, 5 Am. St. Rep. 31.

See Beale, Innkeepers, § 383.

[259] Cincinnati, N. O. & T. P. Ry. v. Raine, 130 Ky. 454, 113 S. W. 495, 19 L. R. A. (N. S.) 753.

[260] Bacon v. Pullman Co., 159 Fed. 1, 16 L. R. A. (N. S.) 578.

[261] De Wolf v. Ford, 193 N. Y. 397, 86 N. E. 527, 21 L. R. A. (N. S.) 860, 127 Am. St. Rep. 969.

[262] *Massachusetts:* Burton v. Scherpf, 1 All. 133, 79 Am. Dec. 717.

New York: Purcell v. Daly, 19 Abb. N. C. 301.

[263] Smith v. Leo, 92 Hun, 242, 36 N. Y. Supp. 949.

ages are not recoverable.[264] In Buenzle v. Newport Amusement Association [265] the plaintiff, a petty officer in the navy, presented himself at a dance hall in civilian dress and bought a ticket; he then returned to the hall in uniform and was refused admission for that reason. He had evidently appeared in civilian dress, in violation of naval rules, in order to procure a ticket without disclosing the fact that he belonged to the navy. It was held that if he suffered humiliation it was from his own act, and he could not recover compensation for it.

On the other hand, where plaintiff purchased a ticket to defendant's bathing house and was standing in line to get a bathing suit, when she was roughly removed from the line by defendant's servants, without just cause, it was held that she could recover damages for insult and humiliation.[266]

A telegraph company operating a messenger service has been said not to be a common carrier of goods carried by its messengers; but as a bailee for hire it is responsible for loss of the goods. Where a dressmaker gave a messenger a bundle to carry, containing a gown just made to order by her for a particular customer, and the bundle was lost, the owner could recover the value of the gown; and since there was no market value for such a gown the cost of the labor and material might be shown as bearing on the actual value.[267]

[264] McGowan v. Duff, 14 Daly (N. Y.), 315.

[265] 29 R. I. 23, 68 Atl. 721, 14 L. R. A. (N. S.) 1242.

[266] Aaron v. Ward, 136 App. Div. 818, 121 N. Y. Supp. 673.

[267] Murray v. Postal T. C. Co. (Mass.), 96 N. E. 316.

CHAPTER XXXIX

ACTIONS AGAINST TELEGRAPH AND TELEPHONE COMPANIES

§ 874. Nature of contract.
875. Nature of liability—Not common carriers.
876. Reasonable regulations.
877. Action by sender—Contract.
878. Action by receiver—Tort or contract.
879. Compensation only for natural and contemplated consequences.
880. Notice.
881. Consequential loss.
881a. Expenditures caused by failure to deliver or misdelivery.
881b. Consequential physical injury.
882. Loss of intended purchase.
883. Loss of intended sale.
884. Error in transmitting amount of goods.
885. In transmitting price.
886. In transmitting conditions of purchase or sale.
887. Loss of a debt.

§ 888. Speculative loss.
889. Uncertain profits not recoverable.
890. Messages not understood—Cipher messages.
891. Authorities extending liability —Commercial messages.
892. Direct loss.
893. Price of the message—Nominal damages.
894. Mental suffering.
894a. Suggested difference between tort and contract.
894b. Relationship of plaintiff.
894c. Notice of relationship or of other circumstances.
894d. What mental suffering is compensated.
895. Avoidable consequences.
896. Exemplary damages.
897. Causa proxima.
897a. Telephone Companies.

§ 874. Nature of contract.

Suits against telegraph and telephone companies present many peculiar features, both in relation to the question of liability, and of the extent of recovery. Such a company is an agency (usually chartered by the State, and clothed by it with the powers of eminent domain) for conveying intelligence by electricity. A telegraph line might, of course, be operated by an individual, or a partnership, but usually there is a charter. In consequence of its position as a company in public service, the company is obliged to take all messages, for which it is entitled to establish a tariff of charges. It thus stands in a double relation, analogous to that occupied by common

1808

carriers of goods and passengers. It enters into a contract
with the persons employing it, but it does this in pursuance of
a duty imposed upon it by the State. Hence its contract is
different in kind from all ordinary agreements, and a breach
of it is different in its consequences. It is different again from
the contract of a common carrier, because it relates to the
carriage and delivery, not of chattels, but of intelligence, that
is, of something incorporeal and intangible. These peculiar-
ities have led the courts to take somewhat conflicting views
as to the nature of the liability of telegraph companies.[1]

§ 875. Nature of liability—Not common carriers.

Many of the earlier cases in which the question of the
liability of telegraph companies for mistakes and delays in
sending messages arose, inclined to the doctrine that they
were subject to the same liabilities as common carriers of
goods. In the case of Bowen v. Lake Erie Telegraph Co.,[2] the
Court of Common Pleas of Ohio, at nisi prius, on that ground
held the company to the same degree of liability as a common
carrier, although not in terms calling it a common carrier,
considering that as these companies hold themselves out to
transmit dispatches correctly, they are under obligation to
do so, unless prevented by causes over which they have no
control. In this case owing to a mistake of the defendants
in transmitting a dispatch, one hundred shawls, instead of a
single one, were sent from New York to Michigan, and the
damages which the jury found in conformity with the charge
of the court, consisted of a sum equal to the charges for freight

---

[1] It is universally conceded that for
accidents produced by such unforeseen
causes (or acts of God), as electrical
disturbances, a telegraph company is
not responsible.
   Alabama: Daughtery v. Am. Un. Tel.
Co., 75 Ala. 168, 51 Am. Rep. 435.
   Louisiana: Shields v. Washington
Tel. Co., 9 West L. 283.
   Maine: Bartlett v. Western U. T. Co.,
62 Me. 209.
   New York: Leonard v. New York, A.
& B. E. M. T. Co., 41 N. Y. 544.

[2] 1 Am. Law Reg. 685. The same
decision has been arrived at on the
same ground in other cases. Parks v.
Alta C. T. Co., 13 Cal. 422, 73 Am.
Dec. 589; Shearman & Redfield on
Negligence, §§ 545 et seq. See for other
cases Gray on Com. by Tel., § 6. And
see Western U. T. Co. v. Eubanks, 100
Ky. 591, 38 S. W. 1068, 66 Am. St.
Rep. 361; Postal Tel. Cable Co. v.
Schaefer, 23 Ky. L. Rep. 344, 62 S. W.
1119.

and the depreciation in value of the shawls, which had to be reshipped to the plaintiffs, and reached them after the shawl season had closed.

But this theory of the liability of telegraph companies has now been abandoned.[3] It is perfectly well settled that they are not to be classed with common carriers of goods. The question which seems to have caused most difficulty is raised by the nature of the subject of the contract. It is a contract to convey intelligence. The dispatch, however, may as in the case of a cipher dispatch disclose nothing whatever as to the nature of the transaction to which it relates. On the other hand, a message may disclose the general nature of the transaction to which it relates, as in the case of an order to buy something. It may, further, disclose the nature of the thing to be bought. Another message may disclose the quality and quantity ordered, while still another may make it plain that the article is wanted to fill a sub-contract. The telegraph company usually derives its only knowledge of the object to be effected from the message itself, and hence in some cases is in absolute ignorance, in others has complete knowledge, and in still others can only surmise what the object is, or what the loss in consequence of any mistake or negligence in transmission will be. In the case of an ordinary contract, the parties know necessarily the general object of it, and the only question is how far they shall be held bound to have contemplated the consequences of a breach. But in agreements of the sort we are now considering, one party knows in a multitude of cases little or nothing as to the object of the contract or probable consequences of a breach. Some courts have thought that the liability should be treated as that of a bailee for hire; others have suggested an analogy to the liability of

[3] *Illinois:* Tyler v. Western U. T. Co., 60 Ill. 421, 14 Am. Rep. 38.

Maryland: Birney v. New York & W. P. T. Co., 18 Md. 341, 81 Am. Dec. 607.

Massachusetts: Grinnell v. W. U. T. Co., 113 Mass. 299, 18 Am. Rep. 485.

Michigan: Western U. T. Co. v. Carew, 15 Mich. 525.

New York: Leonard v. New York, A. & B. M. T. Co., 41 N. Y. 544, 1 Am. Rep. 446; Breese v. U. S. T. Co., 48 N. Y. 132, 8 Am. Rep. 526; Kiley v. W. U. Tel. Co., 109 N. Y. 231, 16 N. E. 75.

Ohio: W. U. Tel. Co. v. Griswold, 37 Oh. St. 301, 4 Am. Rep. 500.

carriers of passengers. We think, however, that it will be found most safe in the present condition of the authorities not to insist upon a very exact definition of the liability. For our purposes it will be better to examine the extent of recovery allowed by the courts in the various classes of cases that have come before them.

§ 876. Reasonable regulations.

Telegraph companies have the right to make reasonable regulations, and these, if brought home to the party with whom they contract, are binding.[4] One of the most common of these is a rule which has grown out of the character of the business, that unless the sender repeats a message,—that is, has it telegraphed back for comparison, at an increased rate, —the company will not be liable for errors beyond a stipulated amount, usually the price of the message. A repetition is such an obvious safeguard, that the regulation has always commended itself as reasonable and proper; the only question discussed being how far the company can by such a regulation exempt itself from the consequences of its own negligence. It is sometimes held that such regulations will not relieve the company from liability if it was guilty of negligence.[5] And if

[4] *United States:* Primrose v. Western U. T. Co., 154 U. S. 1, 14 Sup. Ct. 1098, 38 L. ed. 883.

Indiana: Bierhaus v. Western U. T. Co., 8 Ind. App. 246, 34 N. E. 581 (free delivery not made after a certain hour, until next day).

Kentucky: Western U. T. Co. v. Steenbergen, 107 Ky. 469, 54 S. W. 829; Western U. T. Co. v. Van Cleave, 107 Ky. 464, 54 S. W. 827, 92 Am. St. Rep. 366 (night message not to be delivered until next morning).

Michigan: Western U. T. Co. v. Carew, 15 Mich. 525.

New York: Schwartz v. Atlantic & P. T. Co., 18 Hun, 157.

Tennessee: Telegraph Co. v. Munford, 87 Tenn. 190, 10 S. W. 318 (not liable for messages sent over lines of other companies).

Texas: Western U. T. Co. v. Neill, 57

Tex. 283, 44 Am. Rep. 589 (liability limited on night messages).

See an interesting note on this subject, 4 L. R. A. 611.

[5] *United States:* Pacific P. T. C. Co. v. Fleischner, 66 Fed. 899, 14 C. C. A. 166.

Alabama: American Tel. Co. v. Daughtery, 89 Ala. 191, 7 So. 660; Western U. T. Co. v. Chamblee, 122 Ala. 428, 25 So. 1068, 82 Am. St. Rep. 89.

Arkansas: Western U. T. Co. v. Short, 53 Ark. 434, 14 S. W. 649.

Kentucky: Western U. T. Co. v. Eubanks, 100 Ky. 591, 38 S. W. 1068, 66 Am. St. Rep. 361.

Tennessee: Pepper v. Telegraph Co., 87 Tenn. 554, 11 S. W. 783, 10 Am. St. Rep. 699.

Texas: Gulf, C. & S. F. R. R. v. Wilson, 69 Tex. 739, 7 S. W. 653.

Utah: Brown v. Western U. T. Co., 6

the regulations are not observed by the company, they are not considered binding on those dealing with it.[6]

The regulation of telegraph companies, that they will not be liable for errors or delays in unrepeated messages beyond a stipulated amount, usually the price of the message, is in most jurisdictions held to be binding on the sender.[7] It has been made a question how far it affects the receiver. In New York & W. P. Telegraph Co. v. Dryburg,[8] Woodward, J., said that if it be granted that the sender, on account of failure to repeat, could not hold the company liable, it did not follow that the receiver could not. Commenting on this in Harris v. Western Union Telegraph Co.,[9] Mitchell, J., said: "It may very well be that the regulation as to repetition of messages will become so universal in the practice of telegraphy, that it will be considered to be known, constructively at least, to all persons sending or receiving messages, and that it will be held negligence in any person to act upon any important telegram without having it repeated; but such custom is not in evidence in this case, and it is not for this court to lead the way in such decision."

Remarks of the same tenor were made by Daly, F. J., in De Rutte v. New York A. & B. Telegraph Co.[10] Until such custom is established, the fact that the message is that of another person, and that the receiver has no opportunity to agree

Utah, 219, 21 Pac. 988; Wertz v. Western U. T. Co., 7 Utah, 446, 27 Pac. 172.

Wisconsin: Thompson v. Western U. T. Co., 64 Wis. 531, 25 N. W. 789, 54 Am. Rep. 644.

[6] *North Carolina:* Hendricks v. Western U. T. Co., 126 N. C. 304, 35 S. E. 543, 78 Am. St. Rep. 658.

Tennessee: Western U. T. Co. v. Robinson, 97 Tenn. 638, 37 S. W. 545.

[7] *California:* Redington v. Pacific P. T. C. Co., 107 Cal. 317, 40 Pac. 432, 48 Am. St. Rep. 132.

Kentucky: Camp v. Western U. T. Co., 1 Met. 164, 71 Am. Dec. 461.

Massachusetts: Grinnell v. Western U. T. Co., 113 Mass. 299, 18 Am. Rep. 485.

Michigan: Western U. T. Co. v. Carew, 15 Mich. 525; Birkett v. Western U. T. Co., 103 Mich. 361, 61 N. W. 645, 50 Am. St. Rep. 374, 33 L. R. A. 404.

New York: Kiley v. Western U. T. Co., 109 N. Y. 231, 16 N. E. 75.

North Carolina: Lassiter v. Western U. T. Co., 89 N. C. 334.

Texas: Western U. T. Co. v. Hearne, 77 Tex. 83, 13 S. W. 970.

England: McAndrew v. Electric Tel. Co., 17 C. B. 3.

Canada: Baxter v. Dominion Tel. Co., 37 Up. Can. Q. B. 470.

[8] 35 Pa. 298, 303.

[9] 9 Phila. 88.

[10] 1 Daly. 547.

to any condition on the subject of repetition before delivery, would seem to be conclusive.[11] This regulation will apply only in cases where the error arose in the course of transmission, for repetition of the message would not prevent loss in cases where a message was either never sent or never delivered.[12] Another common regulation is that the person suffering loss shall make claim on the company within a certain limited time, generally sixty or ninety days. Such regulations are generally held valid,[13] and in some cases are even held binding on the receiver,[14] but sometimes it is held that a claim filed within sixty or ninety days after the default of the company is known to the sender or receiver of the message, will comply with the stipulation,[15] and in a case where the message was sent fifteen thousand miles and no reply expected, it was held that such a stipulation would not be binding.[16]

Messages designed for transmission are now almost uniformly written on printed blanks, defining the conditions upon which the company agrees to send them. So far as these conditions are reasonable, they form part of the contract.[17]

[11] *Louisiana:* De la Grange *v.* Southwestern Tel. Co., 25 La. Ann. 383.

Pennsylvania: Tobin *v.* Western U. T. Co., 146 Pa. 375, 23 Atl. 324, 28 Am. St. Rep. 802.

[12] *Minnesota:* Francis *v.* Western U. T. Co., 58 Minn. 252, 58 N. W. 1078, 49 Am. St. Rep. 507.

New York: Sprague *v.* Western U. T. Co., 6 Daly, 200.

Texas: Western U. T. Co. *v.* Broesche, 72 Tex. 654, 10 S. W. 734, 13 Am. St. Rep. 843; Gulf, Colorado & Santa Fe Ry. *v.* Wilson, 69 Tex. 739, 7 S. W. 653. It was said in this case that the holding would have been different if there had been a mistake in the message, instead of a failure to deliver.

[13] *Georgia:* Western U. T. Co. *v.* James, 90 Ga. 254, 16 S. E. 83; Western U. T. C. *v.* Waxelbaum, 113 Ga. 1017, 39 S. E. 443. This was a case where the message was written on a blank of the Postal company, and sent

by the Western Union, and the court held that the stipulation on the blank would be considered as making a part of the contract.

Pennsylvania: Wolf *v.* Western U. T. Co., 62 Pa. 83, 1 Am. Rep. 387.

South Dakota: Kirby *v.* Western U. T. Co., 7 S. D. 623, 65 N. W. 37.

Texas: Lestern *v.* Western U. T. Co. 84 Tex. 313, 19 S. W. 256.

[14] Maier *v.* Western U. T. Co., 94 Tenn. 442, 29 S. W. 732. *Contra,* Webbe *v.* Western U. T. Co., 169 Ill. 610, 48 N. E. 670, 61 Am. St. Rep. 207.

[15] *North Carolina:* Sherrill *v.* Western U. T. Co., 109 N. C. 527, 14 S. E. 94.

Tennessee: Telegraph Co. *v.* Mellon, 96 Tenn. 66, 33 S. W. 725.

[16] Conrad *v.* Western U. T. Co., 162 Pa. 204, 29 Atl. 888.

[17] *Maryland:* United States T. Co. *v.* Gildersleve, 29 Md. 232, 96 Am. Dec. 519.

And it seems that this is so, even where the statute provides that a telegraph company is liable for all mistakes in transmitting messages.[18] But where under a California statute telegraph companies were required to use great care and diligence, a stipulation that the company would not be liable for unrepeated messages was held not to relieve the company from liability unless it exercised the care and diligence required by the statute.[19] And under the Nebraska law that telegraph companies are not to be exempted from liability for mistakes or non-delivery of messages by reason of any clause or agreement contained in their printed blanks, telegraph companies are practically prohibited from limiting their liability by means of such stipulations.[20] In Bartlett v. Western Union Telegraph Co.,[21] a limitation exempting the defendant from liability for errors to delay, from whatever cause occurring, was held void. The limitation will not excuse gross negligence or fraud.[22] But in Clement v. Western Union Telegraph Co.,[23] where the auditor found that a messenger was guilty of gross negligence, Morton, C. J., said: "The only negligence shown in this case was an unexplained delay in delivering the message on the part of the messenger boy, to whom it was, after its receipt, entrusted for delivery. It may be that the company might be guilty of some fraudulent or gross negligence in transmitting or delivering a message, so that it would not be protected by

Massachusetts: Ellis v. American T. Co., 13 All. 226.

Missouri: Wann v. Western U. T. Co., 37 Mo. 472, 90 Am. Dec. 395.

Pennsylvania: Passmore v. Western U. T. Co., 78 Pa. 238.

Texas: Womack v. Western U. T. Co., 58 Tex. 176.

[18] Sweatland v. Illinois & M. T. Co., 27 Ia. 433, 1 Am. Rep. 285. But where a statute gave $100 damages for sending a telegram out of order, the whole amount was held recoverable without proof of loss, notwithstanding a limitation of liability. Western U. T. Co. v. Buchanan, 35 Ind. 429, 9 Am. Rep. 744.

[19] Western U. T. Co. v. Cook, 61 Fed. 624, 9 C. C. A. 680.

[20] Kemp v. Western U. T. Co., 28 Neb. 661, 44 N. W. 1064, 26 Am. St. Rep. 363; aff'd, 44 Neb. 194, 62 N. W. 451, 48 Am. St. Rep. 723; Western U. T. Co. v. Beals, 56 Neb. 415, 76 N. W. 903, 71 Am. St. Rep. 682.

[21] 62 Me. 209, 16 Am. Rep. 437; acc., True v. International T. Co., 60 Me. 9, 11 Am. Rep. 156.

[22] *Iowa:* Manville v. Western U. T. Co., 37 Ia. 214, 18 Am. Rep. 8.

Massachusetts: Redpath v. Western U. T. Co., 112 Mass. 71.

Texas: Western U. T. Co. v. Weiting, 1 Tex. Civ. App. 801.

[23] 137 Mass. 463, 466.

its regulation from liability for the actual damages, though in excess of the sum stipulated. But the negligence of the messenger boys in delivering messages was plainly contemplated by the parties when they entered into the stipulation; and there are no principles of public policy which should prevent the company from stipulating that it will not be responsible for such negligence beyond a fixed amount, unless it receives a reasonable compensation for assuming further responsibility. Without discussing the question as to what is the difference, if any, between ordinary and gross negligence, we are of opinion that the only negligence proved in this case was such negligence as the parties intended to include in their stipulation; and that such stipulation, as applied to such negligence, is reasonable and valid."

§ 877. Action by sender—Contract.

An action by the sender of a message against a telegraph company for failure to transmit or mistake or delay in transmission is usually an action of contract; and in such an action, in ascertaining the damages caused by a telegraph company's mistake or neglect, the same rules apply as in other cases of breach of contract. If no damages are proved, nominal damages can be recovered, as the law infers some damage from the breach of contract.[24]

§ 878. Action by receiver—Tort or contract.

It is generally held in the United States that an action may be brought by the person to whom the message is addressed.[25] In Elwood v. Western Union Telegraph Co.,[26] the defendant delivered as genuine a message purporting to be from the officer of a bank, addressed to the plaintiff, saying that the

---

[24] First Nat. Bk. of Barnesville v. Western U. T. Co., 30 Oh. St. 555, 27 Am. Rep. 485.

[25] *Iowa:* Wells v. Western U. T. Co., 144 Ia. 605, 123 N. W. 371.

Mississippi: Western U. T. Co. v. Allen, 66 Miss. 549, 6 So. 461.

New York: Wolfskehl v. Western U. T. Co., 46 Hun, 542.

Texas: Railway Co. v. Levy, 59 Tex. 563, 46 Am. Rep. 278.

Canada: Feaver v. Montreal Tel. Co., 23 U. C. C. P. 150.

In *Tennessee:* Western U. T. Co. v. Potts, 120 Tenn. 37, 113 S. W. 789, it was held that one appearing on the face of the telegram to be a beneficiary may sue for delay in delivery.

[26] 45 N. Y. 549, 6 Am. Rep. 140.

bank would pay the checks of a third party to the amount of $20,000. The plaintiff paid $10,000, and the message was then discovered to be a forgery. In an action on the case the company was held liable to the plaintiff for the amount paid. In another case,[27] it was said that when there has been a delay or mistake in the transmission of a message which has been productive of injury or damage to the person by whom or for whom the company was employed, "to that person they are responsible, whether he was the one who sent or the one who was to receive the message." The basis of the right of action is sometimes said to be tort, and sometimes contract. In the former case, the right would rest on the public duty to convey messages assumed by telegraph companies: in the latter upon the interest of the receiver in the contract made by the sender. As in the case of carriers, it will often be found difficult to say that the action sounds exclusively in either.[28] Perhaps the following considerations already adverted to, may throw some light on this point. Every contract made by a telegraph company is made in pursuance of a duty imposed upon it by the State, and any breach of it is not only a breach of contract, but a tort, for the duty assumed involves the performance of this contract, not merely as it affects the sending, but as it affects the delivering of messages. The telegraph company is under a duty to all the world, and a breach of its contract with the sender is a breach of this duty, as it affects the receiver.

In Bank of California v. Western Union Telegraph Co.,[29] a

---

[27] De Rutte v. New York A. & B. Tel. Co., 1 Daly, 547, 555.

[28] *Illinois:* Western U. T. Co. v. Hope, 11 Bradw. 289.

New York: Rose v. U. S. T. Co., 6 Robt. 305.

Pennsylvania: New York & W. P. T. Co. v. Dryburg, 35 Pa. 298, 78 Am. Dec. 338.

South Carolina: Aiken v. W. U. Tel. Co., 5 S. C. 358.

See, for an interesting discussion of the subject, Gray on Com. by Tel., ch. vii.

In England, however, the telegraph company cannot be made liable for loss through neglect to send a message in an action by the sender. Playford v. United Kingdom Tel. Co., L. R. 4 Q. B. 706; Dickson v. Reuter's Tel. Co., 2 C. P. Div. 62, 3 C. P. Div. 1. This is on the ground that the obligation of the company to use due care arises out of contract only, and that the contract is with the sender of such messages only, and not with the receiver.

[29] 52 Cal. 280.

receiver brought an action of tort for loss caused by paying money on a forged telegraphic order. The question was not discussed, but the sender could not have brought any action, as the forgery was committed by him, and he, personating a fictitious person named as payee in the order, collected the money.[30]

§ 879. Compensation only for natural and contemplated consequences.

In determining the telegraph company's liability, the question has usually been taken to be whether the information as to the nature of the dispatch, and of the possible consequences of a failure to deliver it correctly, has been so properly and fully given to the company, as to charge it, in case of its default, under the rules in Hadley v. Baxendale, with the loss sustained. Where the company has no notice of the nature or importance of the transaction, either from the message itself or from information given it at the time of sending the message, the damages have been held to be merely the cost of the message.[31] Thus in Beaupre v. Pacific & Atlantic Telegraph Co.,[32] the plaintiff sent a message, "Will take 200 extra mess," meaning he would take pork of that quantity and quality. The message was delayed. It was held that the plaintiff could not recover for a fall in the market, but only the cost of the message.

In the case of Landsberger v. The Magnetic Telegraph Company,[33] the plaintiff at New Orleans having contracted with a third person to buy goods for him on commission at New

---

[30] Western U. T. Co. v. Fenton, 52 Ind. 1, is a case in which it was held that the receiver could bring an action; but the decision was based on a statute.

[31] *Indiana:* Western U. T. Co. v. Henley, 23 Ind. App. 14, 54 N. W. 775.

Mississippi: Western U. T. Co. v. Clifton, 68 Miss. 307, 8 So. 746; Johnson v. Western U. T. Co., 79 Miss. 58, 29 So. 787, 89 Am. St. Rep. 584.

Missouri: Fitch v. Western U. T. Co., 150 Mo. App. 149, 130 S. W. 44.

Nebraska: Western U. T. Co. v. Mullens, 44 Neb. 732, 62 N. W. 880.

North Carolina: Sparkman v. Western U. T. Co., 130 N. C. 447, 41 S. E. 881.

Texas: Western U. T. Co. v. Shumate, 2 Tex. Civ. App. 429, 21 S. W. 109; Western U. T. Co. v. Parlin (Tex. Civ. App.), 25 S. W. 40; Western U. T. Co. v. Stiles, 89 Tex. 312, 34 S. W. 438; Western U. T. Co. v. Twaddell, 47 Tex. Civ. App. 51, 103 S. W. 1120; Western U. T. Co. v. True, 106 S. W. 315.

[32] 21 Minn. 155.

[33] 32 Barb. 530.

York, and bound himself to fulfil the contract in a specified sum as liquidated damages, remitted funds to New York to be used in the agreed purchase, which he telegraphed his agent in New York to make. The dispatch directed the plaintiff's firm in New York to get from the Pacific Mail Company $10,000, which the plaintiff had remitted thither by that company, but did not indicate the particular purpose to which it was to be applied, in a manner intelligible to the telegraph company. Through the company's default, the message failed to reach New York in time to have the purchase made, so that the plaintiff lost his commissions and the use of his money for the time, and had to pay the stipulated damages. The court, intending to apply the rule in Hadley v. Baxendale and Griffin v. Colver,[34] held that he could recover only the cost of the dispatch and the interest of his money while it lay idle. The loss of the commission and the payment of the liquidated damages were not regarded as having entered into the contemplation of the parties at the time the contract was made. In Lowery v. Western Union Telegraph Co.,[35] A delivered to the defendant a message directed to the plaintiff, asking for $500. By the defendant's negligence this was changed to $5,000. The plaintiff sent A $5,000, who appropriated it and absconded. The plaintiff afterwards recovered part from A. It was held that the plaintiff could not recover his loss from the defendant, as it was not the natural and probable result of the defendant's negligence. In Baldwin v. United States Telegraph Co.,[36] damages for loss of a bargain were refused. The plaintiff had received an offer for his interest in an oil well. He telegraphed by defendant and a connecting company to an agent, inquiring how much the well was producing. At the time of sending the message he informed the operator of the connecting company that unless he received an answer promptly he would sell his interest. The defendant negligently delayed the delivery of the message and the plaintiff accordingly sold his interest. Soon afterwards he received from his agent an offer of $1,200 more than the price for which he had sold it. It was held that this sum

[34] See §§ 144, 145.
[35] 60 N. Y. 198, 19 Am. Rep. 154.
[36] 45 N. Y. 744, 6 Am. Rep. 165.

could not be recovered, as the purpose of the telegram was not known to the defendant, and the damages were not within the contemplation of the parties.

In another case, by a mistake of the telegraph company, the plaintiff was informed that he could be furnished with 8,000 bushels of wheat for transportation from Chatham to Oswego. The dispatch should have stated 3,000 bushels. In consequence of the wrong information, he gave up a contract for a cargo from Detroit, and sent his vessel to Chatham, where he obtained the 3,000 bushels only. It was held that the only damages which would naturally flow from the defendant's default, or which could have been in the contemplation of both parties at the time of the delivery of the dispatch for transmission, was a reasonable compensation for sending the vessel to Chatham and back. The plaintiff was not entitled to freight on the five thousand bushels the vessel did not carry, as it did not appear that he could have obtained this freight if the message had been correctly transmitted. His real damage consisted in giving up his contract; and this he could not recover, because the fact of his having such a contract had not been communicated to the defendant.[37] In a case in Louisiana it appeared that the plaintiff's cane was frosted, and he telegraphed for sulphate of lime, by the use of which damage could be averted; no notice of the use to which it was intended to put the sulphate of lime was given to the company. The message was not delivered, and the crop was lost. The damage was held too remote for compensation.[38]

A dispatch announcing that the plaintiff, as agent for A, had sold pork at a certain price, was not delivered, and when A finally learned the facts he disaffirmed the sale, and the plaintiff was obliged to compensate the purchaser; if the sale had been disaffirmed at once there would have been no loss. It was held that the company had no notice of the importance of the message, since it referred to a past transaction, and the plaintiff was limited to nominal damages.[39]

[37] Lane v. Montreal T. Co., 7 Up. Can. C. P. 23.

[38] Deslottes v. Baltimore & O. T. Co., 40 La. Ann. 183.

[39] Hord v. Western U. T. Co., 6 Amer. Law Rec. 529.

On the other hand, in Hadley *v.* Western Union Telegraph Co.,[40] the message accepted an offer for the sale of cattle and asked the plaintiff to meet the purchaser at a certain place to have the cattle weighed. By a delay in delivery, the cattle were left standing in the street for some time before the plaintiff arrived to superintend the weighing. It was held that he could recover compensation for the shrinkage in weight of the cattle caused thereby. In Western Union Telegraph Co. *v.* Bertram,[41] the plaintiff sent this message: "Cancel order given yesterday." The order was for the purchase of goods. It was held that the measure of damages for failure to transmit was the difference between the price at which the goods had been ordered and that for which the plaintiff could have secured them elsewhere.[42]

In a few cases it is said that where the action sounds in tort the rule in Hadley *v.* Baxendale does not apply and all proximate damages may be recovered, whether or not they were within the contemplation of the parties.[43]

§ 880. Notice.

The question whether the company had notice of the consequences of negligent transmission has, in most cases, been passed upon by the court. Thus in Stevenson *v.* Montreal Telegraph Co.,[44] the message "sell 1500 bbls." was delayed; the court held that there was no notice of the urgency of the message, and therefore that consequential damages could not be recovered for delay in transmission. In Pope *v.* Western Union Telegraph Co.,[45] it was said to be for the jury. The true rule would seem to be that whether the message itself contains enough to notify the company of its importance is a question for the court, since it arises on the interpretation of the contract; but if the plaintiff seeks to prove notice to

[40] 115 Ind. 191, 15 N. E. 845.

[41] 1 Tex. Civ. App. 1152.

[42] See also Daughtery *v.* American Tel. Co., 75 Ala. 168, 51 Am. Rep. 435; American Tel. Co. *v.* Daughtery, 89 Ala. 191, 7 So. 660.

[43] *United States:* Western U. T. Co. *v.* Lawson, 182 Fed. 389.

Iowa: Wells *v.* Western U. T. Co., 144 Ia. 605, 123 N. W. 371.

[44] 16 Up. Can. Q. B. 530; All. Tel. Cas. 71.

[45] 14 Bradw. (Ill.), 531; *acc.,* Garrett *v.* Western U. T. Co., 83 Ia. 257, 49 N. W. 88.

the company outside the message, it is a question for the jury.

Sprague v. The Western Union Telegraph Co.,[46] is a good illustration of the difficulty of applying the rule of damages within the contemplation of the parties to telegraph cases. The suit was contract for non-transmission of a dispatch to an attorney at Buffalo: "Hold my case till Tuesday or Thursday. Please reply." The operator was told that the message was about a cause in Buffalo that was expected to be called, and that it was of great importance to the party sending to get a reply the next day in order that he might know when to go to Buffalo. Not receiving any reply, plaintiff went to Buffalo with his counsel; the journey proved useless, as the cause had been put off. This put the plaintiff to an expense of $60 for travelling expenses and $250 for counsel fee. The court held that with the knowledge possessed by the defendants, they were bound to infer that such might be the consequences of their neglect. But Daly, J., dissented on the ground that such an inference was not natural.[47]

A telegraph company received a message—"Will wire you in the morning about coal," and failed to deliver it. If the addressee had received it, he would have held a steamer, of which he was master, at Buffalo until morning, when a cargo would have been ready. Not receiving it, he proceeded without the cargo. The plaintiff claimed damages for loss of cargo; but it was held, that the message did not indicate to the company the result of breach, and it could not be recovered on under the rule of Hadley v. Baxendale.[48]

[46] 6 Daly (N. Y.), 200.

[47] For two cases where notice was given to the company's agent, see Western U. T. Co. v. Edsall, 74 Tex. 329, 15 Am. St. Rep. 835; Erie T. & T. Co. v. Grimes, 82 Tex. 89, 17 S. W. 831.

The Texas courts have gone very far in finding notice. Where a telegram was sent partly in cipher, but in it were the words, "Kammerer renews orders," the court held that those words were sufficient notice to the company that a commercial transaction was intended, and that plaintiff could recover the profits lost on the cotton which he would have bought had the message been delivered. Western U. T. Co. v. Nagle, 11 Tex. Civ. App. 539, 32 S. W. 707. See also Western U. T. Co. v. Carver, 15 Tex. Civ. App. 547, 39 S. W. 1021; Western U. T. Co. v. Turner, 94 Tex. 304, 60 S. W. 432, 86 Am. St. Rep. 854.

[48] Western U. T. Co. v. Sullivan, 82 Oh. St. 14, 91 N. E. 867.

§ 881. Consequential loss.

Subject to the limitations just stated, the plaintiff may recover compensation for such consequential loss as is the proximate consequence of the company's negligence.[49] Thus upon the non-delivery of a message offering to employ the plaintiff at $2 a day the court at the trial charged that the plaintiff could recover damages at the rate of $2 a day, subject to deduction for employment that the plaintiff found or should have found; and the charge was sustained.[50] The defendant gave the plaintiff a wrong quotation of the price of gold, and the plaintiff, in reliance upon the quotation given him, bought foreign exchange; it was held that he could recover his actual loss on account of the purchase.[51] The plaintiff, a manufacturer, telegraphed an order for iron, but the telegram was not delivered. It was held that he could recover the expense of hire of workmen and the other expenses of delay while waiting for the iron.[52] A telegram was sent to a sheriff directing him to make an attachment for seven hundred dollars. The telegram as delivered read "even hundred." The sender was allowed damages for failure to secure the larger attachment.[53] A telegram was sent from the general agent of an insurance company to a local agent, directing him to cancel a policy. The telegram was not delivered; and after it should have been delivered, but before notice of non-delivery, the prop-

---

[49] *Iowa:* Garrett v. Western U. T. Co., 92 Ia. 449, 58 N. W. 1064; Evans v. Western U. T. Co., 102 Ia. 219, 71 N. W. 219.

Texas: Gulf, C. & S. F. Ry. v. Loonie, 82 Tex. 323, 18 S. W. 221; Western U. T. Co. v. Williford (Tex. Civ. App.), 22 S. W. 244; Western U. T. Co. v. Proctor (Tex. Civ. App.), 25 S. W. 811; Western U. T. Co. v. Bowen, 84 Tex. 476, 19 S. W. 554.

To this an exception must be made where the benefit lost would have been illegal, as where the plaintiff claims the loss of an illegal contract. For this he cannot recover.

Georgia: Moss v. Exchange Bank, 102 Ga. 808, 30 S. E. 267.

Maine: Morris v. Western U. T. Co., 94 Me. 423, 47 Atl. 926.

[50] Western U. T. Co. v. McKibben, 114 Ind. 511.

[51] Bank of New Orleans v. Western U. T. Co., 27 La. Ann. 49.

[52] Reliance L. Co. v. Western U. T. Co., 58 Tex. 394, 44 Am. Rep. 620.

See to the same effect:

Illinois: Western U. T. Co. v. Lycan, 60 Ill. App. 124.

Kansas: Western U. T. Co. v. Collins, 45 Kan. 88, 25 Pac. 187.

Missouri: Lee v. Western U. T. Co., 51 Mo. App. 375.

[53] Western U. T. Co. v. Beals, 56 Neb. 415, 76 N. W. 903.

erty burned, and the company was obliged to pay the loss. The telegraph company was held to pay the entire amount of the loss; its liability was not limited to the value of the increased risk.[54] Plaintiff sent a message to his son, directing him to pay plaintiff's note at the bank. Upon non-delivery of the message the note was unpaid; the company is liable for the resulting protest and injury to credit.[55]

In a Texas case,[56] it has been agreed between plaintiff, a ranchman, and his agent, who was negotiating a sale of cattle, that if the sale was made the agent should send plaintiff a telegram before a certain time. The message was sent but plaintiff never received it, and supposing that the sale had failed, turned loose the cattle which he had collected to fill the expected order. When informed that the sale had been made, he was obliged to re-gather the cattle at considerable expense. The court held that the cost of re-gathering the cattle could be recovered, and also whatever amount the cattle had depreciated owing to being turned loose and re-gathered, measured by the difference between what plaintiff actually received on the sale, and what he could have received before such depreciation, and if any of the cattle had died owing to the re-gathering, without plaintiff's fault, he could also recover their value.

§ 881a. Expenditures caused by failure to deliver or misdelivery.

Where the plaintiff, by reason of failure to receive a telegram or of error in its terms, was led to make an expenditure which would have been avoided if the message had been properly delivered he may recover the amount of the expenditure in an action against the company.[57] So where by

[54] Providence-Washington Ins. Co. v. Western U. T. Co., 247 Ill. 84, 93 N. E. 134, 30 L. R. A. (N. S.) 1170.

[55] Baker v. Western U. T. Co., 87 S. C. 174, 66 S. E. 182.

[56] Pruett v. Western U. T. Co., 6 Tex. Civ. App. 533, 25 S. W. 794. See also, North Packing & Provision Co. v. Western U. T. Co., 70 Ill. App. 275, 89 Ill. App. 301; Marriott v. Western

U. T. Co., 84 Neb. 443, 121 N. W. 241.

[57] *Kentucky:* Cumberland T. & T. Co. v. Quigley, 112 S. W. 897, 19 L. R. A. (N. S.) 575 (on account of failure to deliver message plaintiff made fruitless trips to station to meet corpse; recovers for time and money expended).

Texas: Postal T. C. Co. v. Sunset Const. Co. (Tex. Civ. App.), 109 S.

delay in delivering a telegram, or by mistake in its terms, the receiver is caused to take a fruitless journey, he may recover the expense of the journey; [58] and the same is true where by failure to deliver a message the sender is led to take a fruitless journey.[59] So where the company failed to deliver to plaintiff a message announcing the death of his father, he may recover the expense of a message subsequently sent to inquire about his father's illness.[60]

§ 881b. Consequential physical injury.

Where compensation is claimed for physical injury caused by the non-delivery or misdelivery of a telegram, the main question is one of proximate cause, and the negligence being always distinct from the effect, the damages become conjectural unless the probative force of the evidence is very direct; but in the proper case compensation may be recovered. So in a recent case in Georgia, the allegations of the petition were that the plaintiff, suffering from a disease of the eye, sent a message, as arranged with her physician, to a specialist,

W. 265 (on account of failure to deliver telegram, plaintiff shipped goods to place where they were not needed).

[58] *Kansas:* McInturff *v.* Western U. T. Co., 81 Kan. 476, 106 Pac. 282 (telegram announcing death delivered two days late with date changed; receiver may recover expense of fruitless journey for funeral).

Mississippi: Duncan *v.* Western U. T. Co., 93 Miss. 500, 47 So. 552 (message from boarding school, "son very well," as delivered read "son very ill;" parents may recover expense of unnecessary journey to see son).

South Dakota: Lothian *v.* Western U. T. Co., 25 S. Dak. 319, 126 N. W. 621 (information given to the telegraph company that plaintiff's wife wanted to go to another state to see her sister, if she was still alive; telegram delayed, sister was dead. The expense of a journey to see the sister may be recovered).

Texas: Western U. T. Co. *v.* Shumate, 2 Tex. Civ. App. 429, 21 S. W.

109 (message "close trade, I will come soon," not delivered, trade failed, expense of journey to consummate trade recoverable).

[59] Illinois S. & R. R. *v.* Western U. T. Co., 146 Ill. App. 163 (telegram read, "Take five o'clock train tomorrow morning, meet me at East St. Louis Station." Telegram not sent. Sender can recover for loss of time and money wasted by sender in going to meet sendee).

See, however, Howard *v.* Central of Ga. Ry. (Ga. App.), 71 S. E. 1017 (a father telegraphed money to enable his son to come home; the telegram not being sent, the son did not come, and the father went on a journey to meet him. He was not allowed to recover the expense of the journey. It was obviously too remote).

[60] *South Carolina:* Leppard *v.* Western U. T. Co., 70 S. E. 1004.

Texas: Western U. T. Co. *v.* Jobe (Tex. Civ. App.), 25 S. W. 168.

(well known to the defendant's agent) requesting his attendance; that the message was negligently delayed for a day and a night; that the eye was in consequence lost; that but for the delay, the specialist would have come, and that he would have saved the eye. This complaint, on demurrer, was held good.[61] And in a similar case where an injured person telegraphed for his mother to come to him, and by reason of nondelivery of the message he failed to get her services and care as nurse, it was held that he could recover compensation for the pain resulting from this deprivation.[62]

This principle is often applied where a telegram is sent asking that the sender be met upon arrival at a railroad station, and by reason of failure to deliver the message promptly the sender arrives and finds no friend or conveyance to meet him. In such a case (the company having had due notice of the circumstances) the plaintiff may recover for his physical suffering from the consequent exposure,[63] and for injury resulting from the necessity of carrying children, bundles, etc.[64]

§ 882. Loss of intended purchase.

Where a telegram is sent accepting an offer for the sale of property, but by reason of failure to deliver the message promptly, the sender loses the intended purchase, he may recover the difference between the price named in the offer and the market value of the property at the time he would have secured it if the contract had been completed.[65] And

[61] *Georgia:* Western U. T. Co. *v.* Ford (Ga. App.), 70 S. E. 65. But see Seifert *v.* Western U. T. Co., 129 Ga. 181, 58 S. E. 699, 11 L. R. A. (N. S.) 1149.

Texas: Western U. T. Co. *v.* Stephens, 2 Tex. Civ. App. 129, 21 S. W. 148 (failure to get physician caused death of sick child).

[62] Postal T. C. Co. *v.* Beal, 159 Ala. 249, 48 So. 676.

[63] *South Carolina:* Toale *v.* Western U. T. Co., 76 S. C. 248, 57 S. E. 117.

Texas: Western U. T. Co. *v.* Powell, 54 Tex. Civ. App. 466, 118 S. W. 226.

[64] *Alabama:* Western U. T. Co. *v.* Howle, 156 Ala. 331, 47 So. 341 (discomfort and nausea caused by carrying child and baggage to waiting room).

Oklahoma: Western U. T. Co. *v.* Crawford, 116 Pac. 925 (rupture and premature labor).

In *Florida:* Hildreth *v.* Western U. T. Co., 56 Fla. 387, 47 So. 820, the court held that sufficient notice had not been given to the company.

[65] *United States:* Purdom Naval Stores Co. *v.* Western U. T. Co., 153 Fed. 327.

Arkansas: Brewster *v.* Western U. T. Co., 65 Ark. 537, 47 S. W. 560; Western

115

where an order is sent for goods and not delivered, the measure of damages is the profit he would have made from the purchase.[66] But of course no damages can be allowed unless the message on its face or in connection with information communicated to the company conveys notice of the intended purchase.[67]

Where the telegraph company negligently omitted to deliver to the plaintiff the following message, "Ship oil as soon as possible at the very best rates you can," it was held by the Supreme Court of Colorado, that the profits which the sender might have made upon the oil could not be recovered, but that the measure of damages included, besides the cost of the dispatch, all expenses incurred by the plaintiff by reason of the defendant's failure to fulfil the contract, among which was the increased price of freight he had to pay.[68] It may be observed, in regard to the foregoing case, that while it disallows the recovery of profits, it cites with approval the cases of Squire v. Western Union Telegraph Co.,[69] and Leonard v. New York, A. & B. E. M. T. Co.,[70] in both of which a recovery of the loss in market value was allowed. In these the recovery was necessary to indemnify the plaintiff without giving him a profit. But both cite as authority those decisions, in actions against carriers on the ground of negligent delay,[71] in which a recovery is allowed of the difference in market value of the retarded goods lost at the place of their *destination*. This necessarily includes the shipper's or consignee's profit. We think that, by analogy, the recovery in corresponding cases against the telegraph company, where it has become liable on the ground of negligence, should include the loss in market value, even where the making good of this loss

U. T. Co. v. Askew, 92 Ark. 133, 122 S. W. 107.

Texas: Western U. T. Co. v. Woods (Tex. Civ. App.), 133 S. W. 440; Western U. T. Co. v. Williams (Tex. Civ. App.), 137 S. W. 148.

[66] Postal T. C. Co. v. Talerico (Tex. Civ. App.), 136 S. W. 575.

[67] *North Carolina:* Clark Mfg. Co. v. Western U. T. Co., 67 S. E. 329, 27 L. R. A. (N. S.) 643.

South Carolina: Clio Gin Co. v. Western U. T. Co., 82 S. C. 405, 64 S. E. 426.

[68] Western U. T. Co. v. Graham, 1 Colo. 230, 9 Am. Rep. 130.

[69] 98 Mass. 232, 93 Am. Dec. 157.

[70] 41 N. Y. 544, 1 Am. Rep. 446.

[71] Such as Cutting v. Grand T. Ry., 13 All. 381. See § 854.

imports an actual profit. And by the almost uniform current of authority compensation is allowed for the loss of the proposed purchase.[72] In True v. International Telegraph Co.,[73] the message was as follows: "Ship cargo named at 90 if you can secure freight at 10." The message was one accepting an offer to sell the plaintiff some corn. The defendant failed to send the message. It was held that the plaintiff could recover the difference between the price named and that which he would have been obliged to pay after notice of the failure of the telegram to purchase the like quantity and quality of corn. In Squire v. Western Union Telegraph Co.,[74] the message was: "Will take your hogs at your offer." For a delay in delivering the message the company was held liable for the difference between the contract price and the price the plaintiff was obliged to pay for the same thing at the same time and place. In Manville v. Western Union Telegraph Co.,[75] the plaintiff's agent sent a message: "Ship your hogs at once." Defendant delayed the message. It was held that the measure of damages was the difference between the market price on the day they were delivered and on the day they would have been delivered but for the delay. In Mowry v. Western Union Telegraph Co.,[76] the plaintiff sent a message to complete the purchase of two car-loads of hams. The message was delayed by the defendant, and the price of hams rose before it was delivered. It was held that the plaintiff could recover the difference between the price of the hams when the message was delivered and the price when it should have been delivered. In the case of the United States Telegraph Co. v. Wenger,[77] the message was a direction to buy stock at a limit mentioned in the telegram. The court held that, as the company through gross negligence did not transmit the message, and the stock was, therefore, not purchased till after a delay, and the message disclosed to the company's agents its nature,

---

[72] So in case of the acceptance of an offer of land. Alexander v. Western U. T. Co., 66 Miss. 161, 14 Am. St. Rep. 556, 5 So. 397.

[73] 60 Me. 9, 11 Am. Rep. 156; acc., Pennington v. Western U. T. Co., 67 Ia. 631, 24 N. W. 45, 56 Am. Rep. 367.

[74] 98 Mass. 232, 93 Am. Dec. 157.

[75] 37 Ia. 214, 18 Am. Rep. 8.

[76] 51 Hun (N. Y.), 126.

[77] 55 Pa. 262.

the measure of damages was the rise in the price of the stock between the time when it ought to have arrived and the time when the purchase was made.

In the case of Rittenhouse v. Independent Line of Telegraph,[78] owing to the defendant's mistake in changing the wording of a dispatch transmitted by it from the plaintiffs in Washington to their brokers in New York, the brokers bought at the morning board of brokers in the latter city five hundred shares of Michigan Southern Railroad stock, instead of selling such amount of that stock as the plaintiffs then had on hand, and buying at that board five hundred shares of Hudson River Railroad stock; the plaintiffs, on discovering the defendant's mistake, corrected it by repeating the dispatch, which, in its right form, was not received till after the morning board had adjourned. On receiving it thus corrected, the brokers sold the five hundred shares of Michigan Southern and bought the Hudson River stock "on the street." The former were sold for the best price then obtainable, but less by $475 than they had to pay for them. The brokers also bought on the street five hundred shares of Hudson River stock at a price exceeding by $1,750 the lowest price at which they could have been bought had the message been correctly received in due time, and by $1,375 the average price of the morning board. The case having been tried before the court without a jury, judgment was given for the latter sum, and on appeal to the General Term sustained, the court holding in reference to the loss on the sale of the five hundred shares of Michigan Southern stock, that the shares of that stock first purchased were in legal effect bought for the defendant's account. The company not having been notified beforehand of the intended sale, could not be held for this portion of the loss. From this judgment the defendant appealed to the Commission of Appeals, where the judgment was affirmed.[79]

---

[78] 1 Daly, 474; affirmed 44 N. Y. 263.

[79] See also the following cases:

Arkansas: Western U. T. Co. v. Fellner, 58 Ark. 29, 22 S. W. 917, 41 Am. St. Rep. 81.

New York: Pearsall v. Western U. T. Co., 124 N. Y. 256, 26 N. E. 534, 21 Am. St. Rep. 662.

Texas: Gulf, Colorado & Santa Fe Ry. v. Loonie, 82 Tex. 323, 18 S. W. 221, 27 Am. St. Rep. 891.

§ 883. Loss of intended sale.

A telegram directing a sale of the plaintiff's cotton was not transmitted. Before the failure to send the message was discovered, the price of cotton fell in the market. It was held that the plaintiff could recover the difference between the market value of his cotton at the time the message should have been delivered and at a reasonable time after the omission to transmit had been discovered.[80] In Kinghorne v. Montreal Telegraph Co.,[81] the plaintiff, having received a note saying "we will pay 80c. for rye" sent a message by the defendant to this effect: "Accept: ship to-morrow 1500 or 2000." The message was not sent, and the sale fell through. It was held that there could be no recovery, for the contract as shown was uncertain as to the amount ordered. On the other hand in Wisconsin, for delay in transmitting the following telegram: "Send bay horse to-day. Mock loads to-night;" Mock being a well-known buyer and shipper, whereby a sale was lost, the company was held liable for the loss.[82] Where a telegram accepted an offer to *purchase and sell* certain cotton futures for the plaintiff, and the bargain would have been advantageous in part, and in part not so, the measure of damages for failure to transmit is the *net* profit lost.[83]

In another case plaintiff sent a telegram ordering goods for the sale of which he had already contracted. As the message was not sent, he missed the sale of the goods and lost his commissions. The court held that the loss of these commissions was a sufficiently direct result of the company's negligence to be an element of damage.[84] And where an agent for the sale of land failed to get a telegram transmitting an offer for the land, and thereby lost a sale and the commission he would have realized from it, he was held entitled to recover the amount of this commission from the company and this though after suit brought he had sold the same land to another at a

[80] Daughtery v. American U. T. Co., 75 Ala. 168, 51 Am. Rep. 435; American U. T. Co. v. Daughtery, 89 Ala. 191, 7 So. 660; *acc.*, Hoyt v. Western U. T. Co., 85 Ark. 473, 108 S. W. 1056.

[81] 18 Up. Can. Q. B. 60; Allen Tel. Cas. 98.

[82] Thompson v. Western U. T. Co., 64 Wis. 531.

[83] Western U. T. Co. v. Way, 83 Ala. 542, 3 Am. St. Rep. 768.

[84] Walden v. Western U. T. Co., 105 Ga. 275, 31 S. E. 172.

higher price.[85]   In Williford v. Western Union Telegraph Co.[86] defendant's failure to deliver a telegram caused a sale of cattle to fail. The court held that the measure of damages would be the difference between the value of the cattle in herd, and the prices which plaintiff might have received under the contract which had failed, deducting the cost of transportation to the point where the cattle were to be sold, if the contract required delivery.

In a Utah case [87] a message concerning a sale of horses was not received, and the sale failed. The court said that as it was plain from the face of the message that it referred to a commercial transaction, so that the company was affected with notice of its importance, the measure of damages was the difference between the contract price, and the amount for which the horses had to be sold after due diligence was used to get the best possible price. These cases all concerned commercial dealings in which a sale of goods owned by the injured party or his principal failed through default of the company. A purely speculative transaction is not so treated. A telegram was sent ordering a sale of stock. It appeared that plaintiff did not own any stock at the time when he sent the telegram. The court held that as no transaction went through, and there was no proof that plaintiff bought that amount of stock on the day when the telegram was delivered, there was no proof that he had lost anything, and he could recover only the cost of the message, with interest.[88]

In an unreported case in New York, damages were claimed to have been sustained by the plaintiff from the defendant's failure to transmit a telegram from New York to St. Louis, instructing one D. L. Davison "to sell silver lepines for $10; also others for less." The dispatch was not sent, and owing to the fluctuation in the price of gold, which was at a premium, there was a considerable decline in the market before the ar-

[85] Hise v. Western U. T. Co., 137 Ia. 329, 113 N. W. 819.

[86] 2 Tex. Civ. App. 574, 22 S. W. 244.

[87] Brooks v. Western U. T. Co., 26 Utah, 147, 72 Pac. 499.

[88] Cahn v. Western U. T. Co., 45 Fed. 40. See also, Blackburn v. Ken-

tucky Cent. R. R., 15 Ky. L. Rep. 303; Evans v. Western U. T. Co., 102 Iowa, 219, 71 N. W. 219; Western U. T. Co. v. Wilhelm, 48 Neb. 910, 67 N. W. 870; Wallingford v. Western U. T. Co., 53 S. C. 410, 31 S. E. 275, 69 Am. St. Rep. 870.

rival of a letter from the plaintiff at St. Louis, containing the same instructions with the dispatch. The plaintiff contended that the rule of damages was the difference between the market price of the watches at the time when the dispatch should have been delivered and that when the letter was received. The defendant's counsel insisted that these damages were too remote, and that the company were not informed by the purport of the dispatch or otherwise, that it had a pecuniary value, or what would or might be the nature and extent of a loss from its non-delivery, and that they had entered into no engagement based upon the condition of the gold market, and had not assumed the risk of a fall in gold, nor even been apprised what the consequence of one would be. But the presiding judge (Jones, J.,) denied a motion for a nonsuit on these grounds, and held that the company were bound to exercise due diligence and care in the conduct of their business, without being notified of the specific pecuniary value of any dispatch left with them. They were bound to infer that the dispatch was of importance, and might be of pecuniary value to the persons sending and receiving it; and the damages should be measured by the decline in gold, which made the difference in the market value.[89]

When the message is in form a mere statement of a sale of an article of commerce, it has been treated as disclosing nothing;[90] and so where one telegraphed to his agent, "Buy horses, ship at once, other parties after them," it was held that the message gave no notice either of an option below the market price or of a contract of resale, so that no damages could be recovered for loss of profits.[91] Certainly such a message does not apprise the company of the probable consequence in the same way that an order to buy does, but to say the least such a message is the one usually sent *in reply* to an order to sell, in which case the consequences of error are easily foreseen.

§ 884. Error in transmitting amount of goods.

In the case of the New York & Washington Printing Tele-

[89] Strasburger v. Western U. T. Co., N. Y. Super. Court, April, 1867.

[90] Hord v. Western U. T. Co., 3 Cin. Law Bulletin 147.

[91] Western U. T. Co. v. Barkley (Tex. Civ. App.), 131 S. W. 849.

graph Co. *v.* Dryburg,[92] the agent of the company, who received a message directing the purchase of two hand bouquets, erroneously supposing the word "hand" to be "hund." and to stand for "hundred," delivered it thus altered. The Supreme Court of Pennsylvania, in an action on the case brought by the receiver of the message, held that "though telegraph companies are not like carriers, insurers for the safe delivery of what may be intrusted them, their obligations, as far as they reach, spring from the same sources—namely, the public nature of their employment and the contract under which the particular duty is assumed"; and that one of the plainest of these obligations was to transmit the very message prescribed. And a verdict for the loss and expense sustained by the florist in cutting and procuring a large number of flowers to fulfil the order, was sustained.

Through the carelessness of a telegraphic operator, the following dispatch, transmitted from Chicago to Oswego, "Send five thousand sacks of salt immediately," was transcribed so as to read, "Send five thousand casks of salt immediately." The term "sack" at the time designated a package of fine salt, weighing about 14 pounds, and the term "cask" a package of coarse salt of about 320 pounds. In an action against the telegraph company for damages arising from the mistake, the measure of damages was held to be the difference between the market value at Oswego and that at Chicago (which was less), together with the cost of transportation from Oswego to Chicago.[93] This case was followed in Tyler *v.* Western U. T. Co.[94] In that case the plaintiff sent a message, "sell 100 shares Western Union." The message as delivered read "sell 1,000 shares Western Union." The plaintiff had on hand with the party to whom the message was sent 100 shares, and to replace the others, 900 shares were bought on a rising market. The advance in price was held to be the measure of damages. And so where a message ordering the purchase of 1,000 shares was changed to 100 shares by the negligence of the defendant, the measure of damages was the

[92] 35 Pa. 298, 78 Am. Dec. 338.
[93] Leonard *v.* New York, A. & B. E.
M. T. Co., 41 N. Y. 544, 1 Am. Rep. 446.
[94] 60 Ill. 421, 14 Am. Rep. 38.

increase in value of 900 shares from the time the 100 shares were bought to such reasonable time after notice of the mistake as was necessary for securing the remaining 900 shares.[95]

In the case of Washington & N. O. T. Co. *v.* Hobson [96] the plaintiffs below had delivered to the company a message to be transmitted to the plaintiffs' factors at New Orleans, instructing them to buy five hundred bales of cotton, which number by the company's fault was altered to twenty-five hundred, and the factors, under this misinformation, purchased two thousand and seventy-eight bales before the mistake was discovered. It was held that if the company were liable for the damages arising from the alteration of the message, the measure of these was what was lost on the sale at Mobile of the excess of the cotton above that ordered, or if it were sold elsewhere, what would have been the loss on it if sold at Mobile in the condition and circumstances in which it was when the mistake was discovered, and that the regular commission of the factors in the purchase should be included in the damages.

§ 885. In transmitting price.

If the company transmits the price of goods erroneously and the plaintiff was thereby forced into a contract which he did not intend to make, he may recover the amount of his loss from the company.[97]

[95] Marr *v.* W. U. T. Co., 85 Tenn. 529.

[96] 15 Gratt. (Va.) 122.

[97] Plaintiff sends an offer and the company transmits a lower offer, which is accepted; seller may recover the difference between the price named and the value.

Idaho: Strong *v.* Western U. T. Co., 18 Ida. 409, 109 Pac. 910, 30 L. R. A. (N. S.) 409.

Kentucky: Western U. T. Co. *v.* Fischer, 133 Ky. 768, 119 S. W. 189.

New York: Weld *v.* Postal T. C. Co., 199 N. Y. 88, 92 N. E. 415.

Offer sent to plaintiff from his agent, company lowers price, plaintiff accepts; he may recover the amount paid to secure option which on discovering true price he allows to lapse. Western U. T. Co. *v.* Robertson (Tex. Civ. App.), 126 S. W. 629.

Plaintiff sends his agent price at which to buy; company transmits higher price, agent buys at the higher price, plaintiff may recover the difference in price on the amount he ordered bought, but not on a greater amount actually bought by the agent. Western U. T. Co. *v.* McCants (Miss.), 46 So. 535.

Offer to do work made to government by plaintiff, who later sends message increasing price; message being undelivered the lower price is accepted. Company is liable for the difference.

A telegraph company contracted to furnish the plaintiff with daily reports of the grain market in Chicago. The plaintiff had a contract to deliver grain at $1.32. On one day the defendant reported the price at $1.21½. In fact the price was $1.50; and, under the plaintiff's orders to purchase 5,000 bushels, they were bought at $1.50. Soon after the price dropped to $1.12½. It was held the plaintiff could recover the difference between $1.50 and $1.21½—that the fact that the plaintiff wanted reports of the Chicago market was sufficient to notify the defendant that he dealt in that market, and that fact must be presumed to have been in the contemplation of the parties in making the contract.[98] In the case of De Rutte v. New York A. & B. T. Co.[99] it appeared that in the transmission of a dispatch directing the purchase of wheat at the limit of twenty-two francs the hectolitre, by the defendant's mistake the number 22 was changed to 25, in consequence of which the wheat was purchased at what proved, on a sale of it made by the plaintiff on discovering the error, a loss of more than $2,000. The court held this loss to be the direct and immediate consequence of a breach of the contract of transmission, and to furnish the measure of the plaintiff's damages.

In another case plaintiff wrote to a dealer in apples for a quotation of prices. The message sent quoted apples at $1.75 per barrel, but plaintiff received the message making it $1.55 and ordered a car. The shipper sent a draft on the basis of $1.75 per barrel to plaintiff's bank for collection, attaching the bill of lading so that plaintiff could not get the goods without paying the draft. Being anxious to get the goods plaintiff paid the draft. It was held that he could recover from the company the difference between the price he had

Postal T. C. Co. v. Nichols, 159 Fed. 643, 89 C. C. A. 585, 16 L. R. A. (N. S.) 870.

Offer sent by plaintiff to an intending purchaser, price transmitted below that sent, purchaser accepts and goods are shipped; on learning true price purchaser refuses to complete the purchase. Plaintiff may recover difference

in value at place of delivery and place from which sent, or, if it is less, cost of reshipping. Western U. T. Co. v. Truitt, 5 Ga. App. 809, 63 S. E. 934.

[98] Turner v. Hawkeye T. Co., 41 Ia. 458, 20 Am. Rep. 605; acc., Western U. T. Co. v. Bradford (Tex. Civ. App.), 114 S. W. 686.

[99] 1 Daly 547.

expected to pay and the price which he had to pay, that is 20c. a barrel.[100]

The plaintiff telegraphed to a third party an offer to sell grain at $1.50; the defendant, in transmitting the message, changed the price to $1.05, and the offer in that form was accepted. The plaintiff bought grain at $1.45 to fill his supposed contract; it was held that the loss he suffered thereby must be compensated by the defendant.[101] In a similar case in Georgia [102] the court held that the plaintiff was bound to fulfil the agreement which the company had made in his name, and therefore that the measure of damages was the difference between the price named by the defendant and the market price at the time of delivery, that is, the actual loss of the plaintiff in filling the contract. The case has been disapproved on the ground that the company is not the plaintiff's agent to make an offer, and the plaintiff was properly restricted, as in the former case, to his actual loss by the contract falling through.[103] The plaintiff, having received a telegram offering to sell flour at $5. per barrel, accepted the offer, and resold the flour at an advance over that price. He afterwards learned that the offer as sent was $5.50, and he could not get the flour, and was compelled to buy other flour in the market at $5.50 to fill his contract. He was allowed the difference between

[100] Western U. T. Co. v. DuBois, 128 Ill. 248, 21 N. E. 4, 15 Am. St. Rep. 109.

See also the following cases:

District of Columbia: Ferrerro v. Western U. T. Co., 9 App. D. C. 455, 35 L. R. A. 548.

Georgia: Hollis v. Western U. T. Co., 91 Ga. 801, 18 S. E. 287.

Illinois: Western U. T. Co. v. Hart, 62 Ill. App. 120.

Kansas: Western U. T. Co. v. Collins, 45 Kan. 88, 25 Pac. 187.

New York: Dixon v. Western U. T. Co., 3 App. Div. 60, 38 N. Y. Supp. 1056.

Pennsylvania: Western U. T. Co. v. Richman, 8 Atl. 171; Western U. T. Co. v. Landis, 12 Atl. 467.

[101] Western U. T. Co. v. Griswold, 37 Oh. St. 301, 41 Am. Rep. 500.

[102] Georgia: Western U. T. Co. v. Shotter, 71 Ga. 760; Western U. T. Co. v. Flint River Lumber Co., 114 Ga. 576, 40 S. E. 815, 88 Am. St. Rep. 36.

Maine: Ayer v. Western U. T. Co., 79 Me. 493, 10 Atl. 495.

[103] Pepper v. Telegraph Co., 87 Tenn. 554, 11 S. W. 783, 10 Am. St. Rep. 699.

See also the following cases:

North Carolina: Pegram v. Western U. T. Co., 100 N. C. 28, 6 S. E. 770, 6 Am. St. Rep. 557.

Kentucky: Postal Tel. Cable Co. v. Schaefer, 23 Ky. L. Rep. 344, 62 S. W. 1119.

the price stated to him by the company and the price named by the seller.[104]

§ 886. In transmitting conditions of purchase or sale.

An offer to sell salt to the plaintiff at a certain price, delivered "at our city wharf" was changed by the defendant in transmission to read "at your city wharf." The company was held liable to the plaintiff (who accepted the offer) for the cost of transportation between the seller's and the plaintiff's city wharves.[105] So where by an error in transmitting a dispatch, the goods of the plaintiff were sent to the wrong place, the measure of damages is the difference in value at the two places, or the expense of getting to the right place.[106] The plaintiff telegraphed to his agent "if gold bill is vetoed, buy $100,000." The defendant omitted the word "if" in transmitting the message; the agent bought the gold, and sold it at a loss as soon as the mistake was discovered. It was held that the company was liable for the amount of the loss.[107]

§ 887. Loss of a debt.

In the case of Parks v. Alta C. Telegraph Co.[108] the telegraph company undertook to transmit a message in the following words: "Due 1800. Attach if you can find property. Will send note by tomorrow's stage." Owing, as appeared, to the company's delay in forwarding the dispatch till the following day, the debtor's property was all seized under intervening process, and the plaintiff could attach nothing. It was held that the company was liable for the amount of the debt, the loss of which was considered to be the natural and proximate damage resulting from its breach of contract. The same measure was applied under similar circumstances, in the case

---

[104] T. P. Sims & Sons v. Western U. T. Co. (S. C.), 71 S. E. 783. See Stewart v. Postal T. C. Co., 131 Ga. 31, 61 S. E. 1045, 18 L. Rep. A. (N. S.) 692.

And see Bass v. Postal T. C. Co., 127 Ga. 423, 56 S. E. 465, 12 L. R. A. (N. S.) 489.

[105] Seiler v. Western U. T. Co., 3 Amer. L. Rev. 777.

[106] Western U. T. Co. v. Reid, 83 Ga. 401. The latter rule, presumably, only if less than the difference in value.

[107] Smith v. Independent Line of Telegraph, Scott & J., Tel., 399, n.; Allen Tel. Cas., 662, n.

[108] 13 Cal. 422, 73 Am. Dec. 589.

of Bryant *v.* The American Telegraph Co.[109] In this case, one
of the plaintiffs had learned at a quarter past four o'clock in
the afternoon, that a firm in Providence, Rhode Island, of
which one Bennett was a member, and which owed them
$12,000 was insolvent, and that Bennett, who had been tem-
porarily in New York, had left for Providence by that afternoon's train. They thereupon directed their attorney to send
a dispatch to Providence to have Bennett's house and lot attached for his debt. The attorney accordingly, at half-past
eight o'clock in the evening, left a message to that effect at
the defendant's office in New York, addressed to Mr. Payne,
an attorney in Providence. By the laws of Rhode Island, the
attachment could be made only when Bennett was out of the
State. At the time of leaving the message, the attorney
explained to the defendant's clerk that its object was to get
an attachment on property, and that it would do no good
unless delivered in time for the attachment to be made before
the train on which Bennett was, should enter Rhode Island.
The attorney paid for the dispatch, and offered to pay any
further expense necessary to send it at once. The clerk agreed
to send it promptly, and it was dispatched at ten minutes
past nine and received by the operator in Providence at half-
past nine, with a direction to send it in haste. At the time of
its receipt he was engaged in receiving reports for the press,
which by statute were entitled to precedence over all other
matters, and replied that it could not be sent that night, as
the delivery boy had gone home. The New York operator
rejoined that it must be delivered, to which the other then
signified his assent. The newspaper reports continued uninter-
ruptedly until half-past eleven o'clock, when, an interval
occurring, the Providence operator had the dispatch copied,
and procured a chance messenger to deliver it, which was
done a few minutes after. By the time the attorney was
aroused from his bed and the dispatch delivered to him, it
was too late to effect the attachment before Bennett's arrival
in the State. He went into bankruptcy the next day, and the
plaintiffs obtained but $500 from his estate. The house and
lot were worth over $12,000. Considering that there was gross

[109] 1 Daly (N. Y.), 575.

1838 TELEGRAPH AND TELEPHONE COMPANIES § 887

negligence in the want of promptness in delivering the message at Providence, a majority of the court held that the company was liable, and that the measure of damages was the amount of the debt with interest from the day of delivery of the message, less the $500 collected. Daly, First Judge, dissented in a carefully considered opinion, on grounds of which the following is a summary statement. Notwithstanding the explanation of the message to the defendant's clerk, the defendant having been under no obligation to assume so great a risk, could not, under the circumstances, with this imperfect information, have intended to do so for so trivial a compensation as the price of the dispatch, even assuming the New York clerk to have had the authority necessary to bind the company to this extent. The company was not advised of the exact circumstances making diligence peculiarly necessary. It was not informed that the firm of which the plaintiff's debtor was a member was insolvent, that his house was unincumbered, nor that it was of value enough to pay the debt, nor could it be presumed to know how much time was necessary to make the attachment, nor its precise legal effect. The loss was too remote and contingent a result of the defendant's delay to impose so heavy a liability, and the plaintiffs themselves, with full knowledge of the facts, "had not been especially diligent." The learned judge observed also that the plaintiff's debt had not been extinguished, and that although the debtors were then insolvent, they might become able and be compelled to pay the debt within the period during which it would continue as an obligation against them. Citing with approbation the case of Landsberger v. The Magnetic Telegraph Co.,[110] he held that the measure of the plaintiff's damages should be confined to the expense sustained by them in the transmission of the dispatch. The decision was reversed by the Court of Appeals on technical grounds, without considering the merits. So where the defendant received the message, "you had better come and attend to your claim at once," to be transmitted to the plaintiff, a creditor, and the message was not delivered, and on account of the plaintiff's absence he was able to recover nothing, it

[110] 32 Barb. 530, *supra*.

was held that the plaintiff was entitled to recover the amount of the claim.[111]

§ 888. Speculative loss.

The plaintiff must of course prove that the loss for which he seeks compensation would have happened; compensation will not be given for mere conjectural consequences. So where the plaintiff, a broker, telegraphed the price at which he could sell his principal's goods, and the message was not delivered, it was held that it was entirely conjectural whether the owner would have sold at that price, and therefore that the plaintiff could not recover his expected commissions.[112]

In Hibbard v. Western Union Telegraph Co.[113] a telegram was sent by Hibbard to his agent, directing him to buy goods at a certain price, deliverable in June at the seller's option. The message was not delivered, and the price the next day went up; after that it went down, and continued below the price mentioned in the telegram until after the period fixed for delivery. The agent did not buy the goods. It was held that only nominal damages could be recovered, as the plaintiff could only have made any profit by selling the day after the purchase was made, and it was impossible to say that he would have done this—it depended upon too many contingencies. So where the plaintiff telegraphed to a broker to buy oil on a margin, and the message was not delivered, it was held that the loss of the plaintiff was too uncertain for compensation, though the price of oil afterwards fluctuated.[114] Where the plaintiff, an undertaker, failed to receive a message,

---

[111] Western U. T. Co. v. Sheffield, 71 Tex. 570, 10 Am. St. Rep. 790, 10 S. W. 752. See also Bierhaus v. Western U. T. Co., 8 Ind. App. 246, 34 N. E. 581.

[112] McColl v. Western U. T. Co., 44 N. Y. Super. Ct. 487.

In a few cases the plaintiff's acceptance of the offer, if received, was sufficiently certain for recovery.

Iowa: Herron v. Western U. T. Co., 90 Ia. 129, 57 N. W. 696.

Nebraska: Western U. T. Co. v. Wilhelm, 48 Neb. 910, 67 N. W. 870.

Texas: Western U. T. Co. v. Brown, 84 Tex. 54, 19 S. W. 336.

Where by the fault of the company a veterinary surgeon did not arrive, and plaintiff's sick horse died, the value of the horse cannot be recovered, since the horse's life might not have been saved. Duncan v. Western U. T. Co., 87 Wis. 173, 58 N. W. 75.

[113] 33 Wis. 558, 14 Am. Rep. 775.

[114] Kiley v. Western U. T. Co., 39 Hun, 158.

"Meet me at the depot, prepared to arrange for shipment to I. of my mother-in-law's remains," it was held that since he lost only the possibility of making a profit, he could not recover.[115]   In Western Union Telegraph Co. v. Connelly [116] a message to the plaintiff in these words, "if you want a place, come first train," was delayed; and upon going to the place designated the plaintiff found himself too late.   It was held that he might recover compensation for his time and expenses in going to the place, but that loss from failure to secure employment was too conjectural.[117]   And so where the company failed to transmit an offer for an agreement, since there was no certainty that the offer would have been accepted, the sender of the offer cannot recover for the loss of the agreement.[118]

§ 889. Uncertain profits not recoverable.

In many cases where a telegram is delayed or not delivered, it is impossible to prove that a bargain has been lost; because it does not appear that had the message been duly transmitted, an actual gain would have ensued.[119]   The whole subject has

[115] Clay v. Western U. T. Co., 81 Ga. 285, 6 S. E. 813, 12 Am. St. Rep. 316. See Barker v. Western U. T. Co., 134 Wis. 147, 114 N. W. 439, 14 L. R. A. (N. S.) 533; Johnson v. Western U. T. Co., 79 Miss. 58, 29 So. 787.

[116] 2 Tex. Civ. App. 113.

[117] See to the same effect the following cases:

Colorado: Postal T. C. Co. v. Barwise, 11 Colo. App. 328, 53 Pac. 252.

Georgia: Mondon v. Western U. T. Co., 96 Ga. 499, 23 S. E. 853; Wilson v. Western U. T. Co., 124 Ga. 131, 52 S. E. 153.

Washington: Martin v. Sunset Tel. Co., 18 Wash. 260, 51 Pac. 376.

Wisconsin: Candee v. Western U. T. Co., 34 Wis. 471, 17 Am. Rep. 452.

In *Iowa* a message reading, "Will you accept appointment, $720 per annum," was not delivered. It was held a question for the jury whether plaintiff would have accepted the appointment

and secured it; and if they so found, they might give damages for failure to get it. Larsen v. Postal T. C. Co. (Ia.), 130 N. W. 813. And in *Alabama* a similar decision was reached. Western U. T. Co. v. Bowman, 141 Ala. 175, 37 So. 493.

[118] *Florida:* Hall v. Western U. T. Co., 59 Fla. 275, 51 So. 819.

Mississippi: Western U. T. Co. v. Adams Mach. Co., 92 Miss. 849, 47 So. 412.

[119] *United States:* Cahn v. Western U. T. Co., 48 Fed. 810, 1 C. C. A. 107, affirming 46 Fed. 40.

Arkansas: James v. Western U. T. Co., 86 Ark. 339, 111 S. W. 276; Western U. T. Co. v. Fellner, 58 Ark. 29, 22 S. W. 917.

Kentucky: Rich G. D. Co. v. Western U. T. Co., 13 Ky. L. Rep. 256.

North Carolina: Cannon v. W. U. Tel. Co., 100 N. C. 300, 6 S. E. 731, 6 Am. St. Rep. 590.

been recently reviewed in its bearing on the contracts of telegraph companies by the Supreme Court of the United States.
In Western Union Telegraph Co. *v* Hall,[120] the message was:
"Buy ten thousand if you think it safe. Wire me." The message meant that the person to whom it was addressed should
buy ten thousand barrels of petroleum, if he thought it safe.
Had it been delivered in time, the purchase would have been
made at $1.17 per barrel. On the actual delivery of the dis-
patch the price had risen to $1.35, and no purchase was made.
The court held that the plaintiff could recover only nominal
damages.

So where the plaintiff telegraphed for whiskey for his hands
who were doing rafting for him and informed the company
that without the whiskey his hands might not work, and the
company failed to transmit the message, whereupon the hands
did refuse to work, the plaintiff claimed damages for failure
to get the raft to its destination. The court however refused
to allow damages for the loss of this expected profit, on the
ground that it was too uncertain whether if he got the whiskey
he would have got the raft to its destination and marketed it.
Whiskey, the court said, is very potential at times, but it
cannot be relied upon to produce such beneficial results as
were claimed for it in this case.[121]

§ 890. Messages not understood—Cipher messages.

Where a message cannot be understood by the company's
agents it is usually held that consequential damages cannot
be recovered. Thus in Shields *v.* Washington Telegraph Co.,[122]
Buchanan, J., charged the jury that for negligence in transmitting the message, "oats 56, bran 1-10, corn 73, hay 25,"
no more than the price of the message could be recovered.
And it is, therefore, law in most jurisdictions that for the
wrongful transmission of a *cipher* message consequential damages cannot be recovered.[123] In the leading case in this coun-

[120] 124 U. S. 444, 454, 8 Sup. Ct. 577, 31 L. ed. 479.

[121] Newsome *v.* Western U. T. Co., 153 N. C. 153, 69 S. E. 10.

[122] Allen Tel. Cas. 5, 9 West. L. J. 283.

[123] *United States:* Western U. T. Co. *v.* Hall, 124 U. S. 444, 8 Sup. Ct. 577, 31 L. ed. 479; Primrose *v.* Western U. T. Co., 154 U. S. 1, 14 Sup. Ct. 1098, 38 L. ed. 883; Western U. T. Co. *v.* Coggin, 68 Fed. 137, 15 C. C. A. 231.

try a telegram was sent in cipher by the plaintiff to his agents, directing them to buy a certain amount of stock. The telegram was delayed, and the price rose. It was held that he could only recover nominal damages. The defendant not knowing what was in the telegram, no damages could be said to have been in the contemplation of the parties. To have held the company liable, its agent should have known the contents, and the fact and extent of the plaintiff's liability to loss in case of mistake.[124] In Mackay v. Western Union Telegraph Co.,[125] it was held by the Supreme Court of Nevada that the measure of damages for breach of the contract to deliver a cipher dispatch was the money paid for its transmission. The ground of the decision was that such were the only damages in the contemplation of the parties. In Sanders v. Stuart, where there was error in the transmission of an unintelligible message,[126] Lord Coleridge, C. J., said: "Upon the facts of this case we think that the rule in Had-

Arkansas: Western U. T. Co. v. Aubrey, 61 Ark. 613, 33 S. W. 1063.

Florida: Western U. T. Co. v. Wilson, 32 Fla. 527, 14 So. 1, 37 Am. St. Rep. 125, 22 L. R. A. 434.

Illinois: Western U. T. Co. v. Martin, 9 Bradw. 587.

Maryland: United States Tel. Co. v. Gildersleve, 29 Md. 232, 96 Am. Dec. 519.

Massachusetts: Wheelock v. Postal T. C. Co., 197 Mass. 119, 83 N. E. 313.

North Carolina: Cannon v. Western U. T. Co., 100 N. C. 300, 6 S. E. 731, 6 Am. St. Rep. 590.

Pennsylvania: Fergusson v. Anglo-American Telegraph Co., 178 Pa. 377, 384, 35 Atl. 979, 981, 35 L. R. A. 554, 56 Am. St. Rep. 770.

Texas: Daniel v. Western U. T. Co., 61 Tex. 452, 48 Am. Rep. 305; Houston E. & W. T. R. T. Co. v. Davidson, 15 Tex. Civ. App. 334, 39 S. W. 605.

A message in a foreign language, being the language of the country to which it was to be transmitted, is not to be treated as a cipher message.

Western U. T. Co. v. Olivarri (Tex. Civ. App.), 110 S. W. 930.

[124] Candee v. Western U. T. Co., 34 Wis. 471, 17 Am. Rep. 452.

[125] 16 Nev. 222.

[126] 1 C. P. D. 326. In Western U. T. Co. v. Fontaine, 58 Ga. 433, it was held that plaintiff could recover, for failure to deliver the following message: "Exercise your own discretion as regards covering December contract," damages sustained in sale of his cotton. There was no discussion of the measure of damages, the case turning on the question of liability, and it being held that defendant was not a common carrier, but ordinary bailee for hire. From the very inadequate report of the charge to the jury in the case of Booz v. W. U. Tel. Co., 7 Abb. N. C. 161, it would seem to fall in that class of cases in which relief is denied on account of the unintelligible character of the message. A charge to the same effect was given in Behm v. W. U. Tel. Co., 8 Biss. 131.

ley *v.* Baxendale applies, and that the damages recoverable are nominal only. It is not necessary to decide, and we do not give any opinion how the case might be if the message, instead of being in language utterly unintelligible, had been conveyed in plain and intelligible words. It was conveyed in terms which, as far as the defendant was concerned, were simple nonsense. For this reason, the second portion of Baron Alderson's rule clearly applies. No such damage as above mentioned could be 'reasonably supposed to have been in the contemplation of both parties at the time they made the contract as the probable result of the breach of it,' for the simple reason that the defendant, at least, did not know what his contract was about, nor what, nor whether any, damage would follow from the breach of it. And for the same reason, viz.: the total ignorance of the defendant as to the subject-matter of the contract (an ignorance known to, and, indeed, intentionally procured by the plaintiffs), the first portion of the rule applies also; for there are no damages more than nominal which can 'fairly and reasonably be considered as arising naturally, *i. e.*, according to the usual course of things, from the breach' of such a contract as this."

§ 891. Authorities extending liability—Commercial messages.

There are, however, a good many courts which hold telegraph companies to a stricter accountability for the results of their negligence, whether or not the result was apparent to the company on the face of the message. These courts do not, as suggested in the earlier cases, reach this decision by holding the company to the liability of a common carrier; on the contrary, the difference is insisted upon. The argument generally adopted is that an intelligible portion of the message, or information given independently of the language of the telegram, shows the message to be important, and loss more than likely to result from mistake or delay, and that the company, accepting the message to transmit under such circumstances, has no ground of complaint if it is held liable to compensate for such consequences at least as might have been foreseen if the message had been understood, if not for all consequences which were proximate.[127]   In Western Union Telegraph Co. v. Blanchard [128] the message was "cover 200 Sept. 100 Aug." The message was transmitted "200 Aug." It was held that the consequent loss could be compensated, the court saying, "There was at least enough known to show it was a commercial message of value attached to the message, and that is sufficient." This case stretches the ordinary rule of damages within the contemplation of the parties to its utmost limits. It was shown that the message was intelligible in the cotton trade.

To the telegraph company the difference between such a message and a cipher dispatch must be very slight. The very fact that a message is in cipher would seem to be an indication of its commercial importance. And such is the view which the court now seems to take of the case.[129]   In accordance with this doctrine, it has been held in a number of later cases that substantial damages may be recovered for negligence in transmitting a cipher message.[130]   In Western Union Telegraph Co. v. Hyer [131] McWhorter, C. J., said: "The larger part of all messages sent are of a commercial or business nature which suggest value; the requirements of friendship or pleasure can await other means of less celerity and less expense. If this be true, why

[127] *Florida:* Western U. T. Co. v. Merritt, 55 Fla. 462, 46 So. 1024; Western U. T. Co. v. Milton, 53 Fla. 484, 43 So. 495, 11 L. R. A. (N. S.) 560.

Illinois: Postal Tel. Cable Co. v. Lathrop, 131 Ill. 575, 23 N. E. 583, 7 L. R. A. 474, 19 Am. St. Rep. 55.

Kentucky: Postal T. C. Co. v. Louisville C. O. Co., 136 Ky. 843, 122 S. W. 852.

Nebraska: Smith v. Western U. T. Co., 80 Neb. 395, 114 N. W. 288.

North Carolina: Williamson v. Postal Tel. Co., 151 N. C. 223, 65 S. E. 974.

Pennsylvania: Joshua L. Bailey & Co. v. Western U. T. Co., 227 Pa. 522, 76 Atl. 736.

Tennessee: Pepper v. Western Union Telegraph Co., 87 Tenn. 554, 11 S. W. 783, 4 L. R. A. 660, 10 Am. St. Rep. 699.

[128] 68 Ga. 299, 310.

[129] Western U. T. Co. v. Fatman, 73 Ga. 285, 54 Am. Rep. 877.

[130] *Alabama:* Daughtery v. American U. T. Co., 75 Ala. 168, 51 Am. Rep. 435.

Florida: Western U. T. Co. v. Hyer, 22 Fla. 637, 1 So. 129, 1 Am. St. Rep. 222.

Georgia: Western U. T. Co. v. Fatman, 73 Ga. 285, 54 Am. Rep. 877.

South Carolina: Pinckney v. Western U. T. Co., 19 S. C. 71, 74 (*semble*).

Texas: Western U. T. Co. v. Weiting, 1 Tex. Civ. App. 801.

In *California* it seems to be assumed that such is the law. Hart v. Western U. T. Co., 66 Cal. 579, 56 Am. Rep. 579.

[131] 22 Fla. 637, 645, 1 So. 129, 1 Am. St. Rep. 222.

should the law assume that as a rule all messages sent over it are unimportant, and that an important one is an exception, of which the operator is to be informed? . . . The common carrier charges different rates of freight for different articles according to their bulk and value and their respective risks of transportation, and provides different methods for the transportation of each. It is not shown here that the defendant company had any scale of prices which were higher or lower as the importance of the dispatch was great or small. It cannot be said, then, that for this reason the operator should be informed of its importance, when it made no difference in the charge of transmission. It is not shown that if its importance had been disclosed to the operator that he was required by the rules of the company to send the message out of the order in which it came to the office, with reference to other messages awaiting transmission, that he was to use any extra degree of skill, any different method or agency for sending it, from the time, the skill used, the agencies employed, or the compensation demanded, for sending an unimportant dispatch, or that it would aid the operator in its transmission. For what reason, then, could he demand information that was in no way whatever to affect his manner of action or impose on him any additional obligation? It could only operate on him persuasively to perform a duty for which he had been paid the price he demanded, which in consideration thereof he had agreed to perform, and which the law in consideration of his promise and the reception of the consideration therefor had already enjoined on him."

In Daughtery *v.* American Union Telegraph Co.,[132] an action of assumpsit for non-delivery of a cipher message, it was held by the Supreme Court of Alabama, on a full consideration of the authorities, that the defendant's ignorance of the contents of the dispatch was no excuse, and that the plaintiff was entitled to recover as damages the whole profit he would have made on a sale ordered by it. The principal ground of the decision seems to be that substantial damages were the natural result of such a breach of contract; that the second branch

---

[132] 75 Ala. 168, 51 Am. Rep. 435; approved and followed in Western U. T. Co. *v.* Way, 83 Ala. 542.

of the rule in Hadley *v.* Baxendale, if it was intended to restrict the first, and to mean that such damages are only natural as are in contemplation of the parties, was misleading and erroneous, and that at any rate it could not be applied to transactions in which the same measure of diligence is required, without regard to the quantum of interest to be affected by it.[133] In Virginia the court, partly by interpretation of a statute making it imperative on a telegraph company to transmit promptly any message offered it, and partly, it would appear, on general principles, reached the same conclusion.[134] There was nothing in the statute to affect the rule of damages.[135]

§ 892. Direct loss.

It has been held in some cases that the *direct loss* from failure to transmit a telegraphic dispatch is the sum paid to the company for the transmission. But this cannot be regarded as the true view. The telegraph company makes a contract with the sender to transmit information from one point to another; for this purpose it is chartered, and this it holds itself out to the public as offering to do. The sum paid for transmission is the consideration for this contract, and upon the general principles of damages in actions of contract it is not to be considered in measuring the damages. The direct loss, as in all cases of breach of contract, is the value of the contract. If the contract had been performed, the receiver would have had the information, which he now lacks. The value of the contract, then, is the value of the information transmitted.

This will clearly appear in a simple case. Suppose A employs B as his agent and sends him to a broker to buy 1,000 barrels of oil for delivery the next day. B through mistake orders only 100 barrels. The price of oil rises before the time for delivery. A's loss is not the remuneration paid

---

[133] We cannot too often reaffirm our belief that the result of all the best considered cases under Hadley *v.* Baxendale is that that case introduced no new rule of law.

[134] Western U. T. Co. *v.* Reynolds, 77 Va. 173, 46 Am. Rep. 715. The point was noticed but not decided in Wisconsin, where a similar statute is in force. Cutts *v.* Western U. T. Co., 71 Wis. 46.

[135] See dissenting opinion of Lewis, P. at p. 192.

to the agent, but the value to A of that part of the order which B failed to transmit, that is, the rise in value of 900 barrels of oil between the time of purchase and the time of delivery. This is the direct loss by B's breach of contract. A telegraph company enters into a contract of agency with the sender, very similar to the contract of B with A in the case supposed. The mere fact that the information is transmitted over a wire can make no difference.

In the form in which it is claimed, the loss caused by failure to transmit a dispatch is usually consequential; but the information contained in a dispatch would seem to have an inherent value which in most cases might easily be proved; and this value on principle is the direct loss of the sender, or person who has the right to sue. It is not meant by what is here said that the cases can all be reconciled in accordance with this view; but all those in which the loss caused by cipher dispatches has been allowed, could be rested upon it. It has been already shown that a common carrier is held bound for any direct damages, as for the contents of packages however valuable.[136] It is only in the case of consequential losses that the rule in Hadley v. Baxendale is generally applied. If the cases holding telegraph companies responsible for cipher dispatches are correctly decided, they might be rested on the right to recover direct damages, which would be more satisfactory than vague considerations of public policy, which are more proper for legislative than for judicial consideration. But it must be said that these cases are at present of only local authority, and opposed to the general current of decision. It is to be noted that the rule holding telegraph companies liable for the direct loss caused by cipher dispatches would not make them insurers or common carriers, for that is a question of liability, not of the measure of damages. It makes them liable to precisely the same extent that, according to general rules, they would be liable if the message had been put in intelligible language.

In Strause v. Western Union Telegraph Co.,[137] plaintiffs, who were bankers, had presented to them a bill purporting

[136] Little v. Boston & M. R. R., 66 Me. 239.   [137] 8 Biss. 104.

to be drawn by a bank at Peru. They telegraphed the bank inquiring if the draft was genuine, in answer to which a dispatch was sent saying that it was not. Through the carelessness of defendants' messenger, a forged dispatch was substituted for this one, saying that the bill was correct, and on delivery of this forged message, plaintiff cashed the draft. On these facts it was held by Gresham, J., that the defendant was liable in tort for the whole amount, and that it made no difference that the plaintiffs had another remedy in contract on a genuine indorsement.[138]

A telegram was sent to plaintiff by her agent offering $1300 for certain property. The message was changed in transmission into an offer of $1,900, which plaintiff was willing to accept, though she would not have wished to take $1,300. She ordered the property sold supposing she would get $1,900. The court held that she could recover from the company the difference between $1,300 and the value of the land.[139] In another case plaintiffs sent an order to their buying agent in Chicago not to buy stock on Tuesday. The message was not delivered until the agent had made considerable purchases Tuesday morning. The next day prices on stock went down. And the court held that plaintiffs could recover the difference between the price of the stock on Tuesday and what the same amount of similar stock would have cost on Wednesday.[140]

[138] In such a case, the action being in tort, there is no question of the application of the rule relating to damages contemplated. But if the cause of the loss had been negligence in transmission, according to those authorities which hold the knowledge by the company of the circumstances to be essential, the rule might have been very different. The dispatch was that the bank had drawn "no such bill." Suppose by innocent mistake the word "no" had been omitted, and the inquiry had been in cipher, so that the company could not have understood the purport of the answer, or the act which it was calculated to lead the plaintiffs to do,

according to many courts, the extent of recovery would have been the price of the message. Should such a trivial difference as this alter the measure of damages?

[139] Reed v. Western U. T. Co., 135 Mo. 661, 37 S. W. 904, 58 Am. St. Rep. 609.

[140] North P. & P. Co. v. Western U. T. Co., 70 Ill. App. 275, 89 Ill. App. 300.

See to the same effect the following cases:

Arizona: Stiles v. Western U. T. Co., 15 Pac. 712.

California: Redington v. Postal T. C. Co., 107 Cal. 317, 40 Pac. 432, 48 Am. St. Rep. 132.

§ 893. Price of the message—Nominal damages.

In Logan *v.* Western Union Telegraph Co.,[141] the plaintiff sued for non-delivery of a telegram sent by him to his son, summoning him home to the death-bed of his mother. On demurrer, it was held that plaintiff was entitled to recover at least nominal damages, "including the loss of the price of the telegram." But it should be noticed, in connection with these cipher dispatch cases, that the right to recover nominal damages and the right to recover the price of the message are not the same. If the plaintiff is limited to the price of the message, it is not on the ground that he is entitled to nominal damages; but that the only substantial loss that he can prove is the money paid out.[142] He must always lose at least this, in cases where an action will lie, unless the message has not been prepaid.

§ 894. Mental suffering.

We have already seen [143] that in the majority of jurisdictions no damages for mental suffering may be allowed against a telegraph company.[144] But in other jurisdictions, recovery

Illinois: Western U. T. Co. *v.* Lycan, 60 Ill. App. 124.

Mississippi: Western U. T. Co. *v.* McLaurin, 70 Miss. 26, 13 So. 36; Fairley *v.* Western U. T. Co., 73 Miss. 11, 18 So. 796.

[141] 84 Ill. 468.

[142] For a discussion of this point see the following cases:

Arkansas: Brewster *v.* Western U. T. Co., 65 Ark. 537, 47 S. W. 560.

Georgia: Jenkins *v.* Southern, B. T. & T. Co., 7 Ga. App. 484, 67 S. E. 124.

Tennessee: Jones *v.* Telegraph Co., 101 Tenn. 442, 47 S. W. 699.

[143] § 45a.

[144] *United States:* Chase *v.* Western U. T. Co., 44 Fed. 554, 10 L. R. A. 464; Crawson *v.* Western U. T. Co., 47 Fed. 544; Western U. T. Co. *v.* Wood, 57 Fed. 475; Gahan *v.* Western U. T. Co., 59 Fed. 433; McBride *v.* Sunset Telephone Co., 96 Fed. 81; Stansell *v.* Western U. T. Co., 107 Fed. 668;

Rowan *v.* Western U. T. Co., 449 Fed. 550.

Arkansas: Peay *v.* Western U. T. Co., 64 Ark. 538, 43 S. W. 965, 39 L. R. A. 463 (altered by statute).

Dakota: Russell *v.* Western U. T. Co., 3 Dak. 315.

Florida: International O. T. Co. *v.* Saunders, 32 Fla. 434, 14 So. 148.

Illinois: Western U. T. Co. *v.* Haltom, 71 Ill. App. 63.

Indiana: Western U. T. Co. *v.* Ferguson, 157 Ind. 64, 60 N. E. 674, 1080 (overruling Reese *v.* Western U. T. Co., 123 Ind. 294, 24 N. E. 163); Kazy *v.* Western U. T. Co., 37 Ind. App. 73, 76 N. E. 792.

Kansas: West *v.* Western U. T. Co., 39 Kan. 93, 17 Pac. 807, 7 Am. St. Rep. 530.

Minnesota: Francis *v.* Western U. T. Co., 58 Minn. 252, 58 N. W. 1078, 49 Am. St. Rep. 507.

Mississippi: Western U. T. Co. *v.*

for mental suffering has been allowed in many or in all cases. Thus it has been held in many cases that where a message notifying the plaintiff of the death or severe illness of a near relative is not delivered, the telegraph company is liable to compensate the plaintiff for the mental suffering caused thereby.[145] So in Wadsworth v. Western Union Telegraph Co.,[146] Caldwell, J., said (p. 705):

"To hold that the defendant is not liable in this case for the wrong and injury done to the feelings and affections of Mrs. Wadsworth by its default, would be to disregard the purpose of the telegrams altogether, and to violate that rule

Rogers, 68 Miss. 748, 9 So. 823, 24 Am. St. Rep. 300.

Missouri: Connell v. Western U. T. Co., 116 Mo. 34, 22 S. W. 345, 38 Am. St. Rep. 575, 20 L. R. A. 172.

New York: Curtin v. Western U. T. Co., 13 App. Div. 253, 42 N. Y. Supp. 1109.

Ohio: Morton v. Western U. T. Co., 53 Oh. St. 431, 41 N. E. 689, 53 Am. St. Rep. 648; Kester v. Western U. T. Co., 8 Ohio Cir. Ct. 236.

Oklahoma: Butner v. Western U. T. Co., 2 Okla. 24, 37 Pac. 1087; Thomas v. Western U. T. Co., 118 Pac. 370.

Virginia: Connelly v. Western U. T. Co., 100 Va. 51, 40 S. E. 618, 56 L. R. A. 663.

Wisconsin: Summerfield v. Western U. T. Co., 87 Wis. 1, 57 N. W. 973, 41 Am. St. Rep. 17.

[145] *United States:* Beasley v. Western U. T. Co., 39 Fed. 181 (by statute).

Arkansas: (by statute) Arkansas & L. Ry. v. Stroude, 82 Ark. 117, 100 S. W. 760; Western U. T. Co. v. Hollingsworth, 83 Ark. 39, 102 S. W. 681, 11 L. R. A. (N. S.) 497, 119 Am. St. Rep. 105; Western U. T. Co. v. Arant, 88 Ark. 499, 115 S. W. 136.

Iowa: Mentzer v. Western U. T. Co., 93 Ia. 752, 62 N. W. 1, 57 Am. St. Rep. 294; Cowan v. Western U. T. Co., 122

Ia. 379, 98 N. W. 281, 64 L. R. A. 545, 101 Am. St. Rep. 268; Potter v. Western U. T. Co., 138 Ia. 406, 116 N. W. 130.

Kentucky: Chapman v. Western U. T. Co., 90 Ky. 265, 13 S. W. 880; Western U. T. Co. v. Van Cleave, 107 Ky. 464, 54 S. W. 827, 92 Am. St. Rep. 366; Western U. T. Co. v. Fisher, 107 Ky. 513, 54 S. W. 830; Postal T. C. Co. v. Terrell, 124 Ky. 822, 100 S. W. 292, 14 L. R. A. (N. S.) 927; Western U. T. Co. v. Witt, 33 Ky. L. Rep. 685, 110 S. W. 889; Western U. T. Co. v. Teague, 134 Ky. 601, 121 S. W. 484.

Mississippi: Magouirk v. Western U. T. Co., 79 Miss. 632, 31 So. 206, 89 Am. St. Rep. 663.

Nevada: Barnes v. Western U. T. Co., 27 Nev. 438, 76 Pac. 931, 103 Am. St. Rep. 776, 65 L. R. A. 666.

North Carolina: Young v. Western U. T. Co., 107 N. C. 370, 11 S. E. 1044, 9 L. R. A. 669, 22 Am. St. Rep. 883 (see Thompson v. Western U. T. Co., 107 N. C. 449, 12 S. E. 427); Lyne v. Western U. T. Co., 123 N. C. 129, 31 S. E. 350; Cashion v. Western U. T. Co., 123 N. C. 267, 31 S. E. 493; Wood v. Western U. T. Co., 148 N. C. 1, 61 S. E. 653; Suttle v. Western U. T. Co., 148 N. C. 480, 62 S. E. 593; Cates v. Western U. T. Co., 151 N. C. 497, 66

[146] 86 Tenn. 695, 8 S. W. 574, 6 Am. St. Rep. 86.

of law which authorizes a recovery of damages appropriate to the objects of the contract broken; and, furthermore, such a holding would justify the conclusion that the defendant might, with impunity, have refused to receive and transmit such messages at all; and that it has the right in the future to do as it has done in this case, or, at least, that it cannot be required to respond in damages for doing so. To such a result we think no court should submit. The telegraph company is the servant rather than the master of its patrons. It is their prerogative to determine what messages they will present, and so they are lawful it is bound by law, upon payment of its toll, to transmit and deliver them correctly and promptly. It has no right to say what is important and what is not, what will be profitable to the receiver and what will not, what has a pecuniary value and what has not; but its single and plain duty is to make the transmission and delivery with promptitude and accuracy. When that is done its responsibility is ended; when it is omitted through negligence, the company must answer for all injury resulting, whether to the feelings or to the purse—one or both—subject alone to the proviso that the injury be the natural and direct consequence of the negligent act."

In Western Union Telegraph Co. v. Crocker,[147] the father of a sick child sent a message to his mother asking her to come, and the message was so delayed that she did not arrive until after death of the child. It was held that the father could

S. E. 592, 24 L. R. A. (N. S.) 1286; Battle v. Western U. T. Co., 151 N. C. 629, 66 S. E. 661.

South Carolina (by statute): Simmons v. Western U. T. Co., 63 S. C. 425, 41 S. E. 521; Brown v. Western U. T. Co., 85 S. C. 495, 67 S. E. 146 (this does not extend to an action against the operator in fault, and no damages for mental suffering can be recovered in an action against him. Fail v. Western U. T. Co., 80 S. C. 207, 60 S. E. 697).

Tennessee: Wadsworth v. Western U. T. Co., 86 Tenn. 695, 8 S. W. 574, 6 Am. St. Rep. 86.

Texas: So Relle v. Western U. T. Co.,

55 Tex. 308, 40 Am. Rep. 805; Stuart v. Western U. T. Co., 66 Tex. 580, 18 S. W. 351, 59 Am. Rep. 623 (explaining Gulf, C. & S. F. Ry. v. Levy, 59 Tex. 563, 46 Am. Rep. 278); Western U. T. Co. v. Beringer, 84 Tex. 38, 19 S. W. 336; Western U. T. Co. v. Cooper, 71 Tex. 507, 9 S. W. 598, 10 Am. St. Rep. 772; Western U. T. Co. v. Wingate, 6 Tex. Civ. App. 394, 25 S. W. 439; Western U. T. Co. v. Neel (Tex. Civ. App.), 25 S. W. 661; Western U. T. Co. v. Kendzora (Tex. Civ. App.), 26 S. W. 245; Buchanan v. Western U. T. Co. (Tex. Civ. App.), 100 S. W. 974.

[147] 135 Ala. 492, 33 So. 45.

recover for mental anguish due to absence of the grandmother. In a Tennessee case [148] plaintiff's wife sent him a message that their daughter was very sick, and owing to delay plaintiff did not receive the message in time to be with his wife at the time of their daughter's death and burial. It was held that recovery could be had for the wife's mental anguish owing to her husband's absence. An erroneous message was delivered, "Mother died at 9 tonight." The court held that plaintiff could recover for his mental pain caused by this message.[149]

In a case where a telegram was sent announcing the arrival by train of the sender, a woman, she may recover damages for her mental suffering if on her arrival there is no one to meet her, owing to non-delivery of the telegram; [150] and upon failure to deliver a telegram warning the sendee that a contagious disease is raging in a certain city, by reason of which failure the sendee went to the city and was exposed to the disease, he may recover damages for his apprehension of taking the disease, and for his mental anguish from fear of being kept away from his wife by quarantine.[151]

§ 894a. Suggested difference between tort and contract.

In a few jurisdictions, notably in Alabama and Texas, a distinction is made according as the plaintiff sues in tort or in contract. Holding the view that mental suffering alone cannot be such damage as to give rise to an action of tort in the nature of an action on the case, they yet allow the recovery of such damages when there is an independent cause of action, namely, an action for a breach of contract, although the damage, apart from the mental suffering, is nominal, or is confined to the price of the message. This reasoning is fully expressed by

---

[148] Gray v. Telegraph Co., 108 Tenn. 39, 64 S. W. 1063.

[149] Western U. T. Co. v. Hines, 22 Tex. Civ. App. 315, 54 S. W. 627. For similar cases see Western U. T. Co. v. Odorn, 21 Tex. Civ. App. 537, 52 S. W. 632; Lay v. Postal T. C. Co. (Ala.), 54 So. 529.

[150] *Arkansas:* Western U. T. Co. v. Hanley, 85 Ark. 263, 107 S. W. 1168.

Kentucky: Postal T. C. Co. v. Terrell, 124 Ky. 822, 100 S. W. 292, 30 Ky. L. Rep. 1023; and see Cumberland T. & T. Co. v. Quigley, 112 S. W. 897, 19 L. R. A. (N. S.) 575, where because of the non-delivery of a telegram there was no one at a station to meet a corpse.

[151] Rich v. Western U. T. Co. (Tex. Civ. App.), 110 S. W. 93; Western U. T. Co. v. Rich (Tex.), 126 S. W. 686.

Mr. Justice Holt in Chapman *v.* Western Union Telegraph Co.,[152] as follows: "Many of the text-writers say that a person cannot recover damages for mental anguish alone, and that he can recover such damages only where he is entitled to recover some damages upon some other ground. It will generally be found, however, that they are speaking of cases of personal injury. If a telegraph company undertakes to send a message, and it fails to use ordinary diligence in doing so, it is certainly liable for some damage. It has violated its contract, and, whenever a party does so, he is liable at least to some extent. Every infraction of a legal right causes injury in contemplation of law. The party being entitled, in such a case, to recover something, why should not an injury to the feelings, which is often more injurious than a physical one, enter into the estimate? Why, being entitled to some damage by reason of the other party's wrongful act, should not the complaining party recover all the damage arising from it? . . . Whether the injury be to the feelings or pecuniary, the act of the violator of a right secured by contract has caused it. The source is the same, and the violator should answer for all the proximate damages."

But though on the positive side this reasoning be convincing, it does not prove the negative; and as a practical rule it errs in making the rule of damages depend upon the form of action rather than upon the real injury. A powerful expression of the contrary view may be found in the case of Shaw *v.* Western Union Telegraph Co.[153] The court reasoned thus. It would be reducing the law to an absurdity should it be held that if a party recovers $1 for an injury to his person, or any other invasion of his rights, he may also recover damages for mental anguish caused by the wrong, but if he does not sustain any loss, great or small, apart from that caused by mental anguish resulting from the wrongful act of another, it is *damnum absque injuria*, however much he may have suffered. This would be refining to the last degree, and should not be accepted as a fair and equitable rule of the law. In some cases a person may suffer more—that is, in the sense of an injury to his rights—by mental anguish, than if he had lost many

---

[152] 90 Ky. 265, 13 S. W. 880.   [153] 151 N. C. 638, 66 S. E. 668.

dollars by the negligent act of the defendant in failing to deliver a telegram.

By the prevailing view this reasoning is followed, and recovery for mental suffering is allowed, in a jurisdiction where it is allowed at all, whether the action sounds in tort or in contract.[154] But in a few jurisdictions recovery is confined to actions of contract.[155] The law in Alabama has been settled by a series of decisions. If the action is for a tort, and the only damage alleged is mental suffering, no recovery can be had.[156] If the action is for breach of contract, and the breach is proved, damages for mental suffering may be recovered.[157] And by the latest authorities, even if the action is for a tort recovery for mental anguish will be allowed, provided the plaintiff claims in his declaration a return of the fee for the message, paid in advance, since there is then a cause of action apart from the mental suffering.[158] But it seems that under no circumstances can there be recovery for mental suffering for the non-delivery of a merely social message.[159]

---

[154] *Iowa:* Mentzer v. Western U. T. Co., 93 Iowa, 752, 62 N. W. 1, 57 Am. St. Rep. 294.

Kentucky: Western U. T. Co. v. Fisher, 107 Ky. 513, 54 S. W. 830.

North Carolina: Shaw v. Western U. T. Co., 151 N. C. 638, 66 S. E. 668.

Tennessee: Telegraph Co. v. Frith, 105 Tenn. 167, 58 S. W. 118.

[155] *Alabama:* Blount v. Western U. T. Co., 126 Ala. 105, 27 So. 779; Western U. T. Co. v. Krichbaum, 132 Ala. 535, 31 So. 607.

Texas: Stuart v. Western U. T. Co., 66 Tex. 580, 18 S. W. 351, 59 Am. St. Rep. 623; Western U. T. Co. v. Odom, 21 Tex. Civ. App. 537, 52 S. W. 632; Western U. T. Co. v. Young (Tex. Civ. App.), 133 S. W. 512 (as to law of Alabama).

[156] Blount v. Western U. T. Co., 126 Ala. 105, 27 So. 779; Western U. T. Co. v. Krichbaum, 132 Ala. 535, 31 So. 607; Western U. T. Co. v. Blocker, 138 Ala. 484, 35 So. 468; Western U. T. Co. v. Waters, 139 Ala. 652, 36 So. 773;

Western U. T. Co. v. Jackson, 163 Ala. 9, 50 So. 316; Western U. T. Co. v. Rowell, 153 Ala. 295, 45 So. 73; Western U. T. Co. v. Wright, 169 Ala. 104, 53 So. 95.

[157] Western U. T. Co. v. Wilson, 93 Ala. 32, 9 So. 414, 30 Am. St. Rep. 23; Western U. T. Co. v. Blocker, 138 Ala. 484, 35 So. 468; Western U. T. Co. v. Waters, 139 Ala. 656, 36 So. 773; Western U. T. Co. v. Manker, 145 Ala. 418, 41 So. 850; Western U. T. Co. v. Hill, 163 Ala. 18, 50 So. 248; Western U. T. Co. v. Cleveland, 169 Ala. 131, 53 So. 80; Lay v. Postal T. C. Co. (Ala.), 54 So. 529.

The recovery appears to be allowed on behalf of the sendee, provided the contract was actually made by his agent or for his benefit. Western U. T. Co. v. Rowell, 153 Ala. 295, 45 So. 73.

[158] Western U. T. Co. v. Garthright, 151 Ala. 413, 44 So. 212; Western U. T. Co. v. Burns, 164 Ala. 252, 51 So. 373.

[159] Western U. T. Co. v. Westmoreland, 151 Ala. 319, 44 So. 383; Western

§ 894b. Relationship of plaintiff.

In several states no recovery for mental suffering can be had unless the plaintiff stood toward the sick or dead person in a very close relationship: parent and child, grandparent and grandchild, brother and brother, or husband and wife.[160] The Kentucky court has defended the rule as follows:[161] "This rule may be considered, and indeed it is, arbitrary; but the peculiar and speculative nature of the doctrine upon which the right of recovery rests in cases of this character makes it necessary that there should be limitations placed upon it. It must be conceded that the restrictions we have placed on

U. T. Co. *v.* Sledge, 153 Ala. 291, 45 So. 59, 163 Ala. 4, 50 So. 886.

[160] Recovery in such jurisdictions has been allowed in the following cases:

Parent and child:
Western U. T. Co. *v.* Fisher, 107 Ky. 830, 54 S. W. 830; Thomas *v.* Western U. T. Co., 120 Ky. 194, 85 S. W. 760; Taylor *v.* Western U. T. Co., 101 S. W. 969, 31 Ky. L. Rep. 240.

Grandparent and grandchild:
Western U. T. Co. *v.* Prevatt, 149 Ala. 617, 43 So. 106.

Brother and brother:
Alabama: Western U. T. Co. *v.* Heathcoat, 149 Ala. 623, 43 So. 117; Western U. T. Co. *v.* McMorris, 158 Ala. 563, 48 So. 349.

Kentucky: Western U. T. Co. *v.* Van Cleave, 107 Ky. 464, 54 S. W. 827, 92 Am. St. Rep. 366; Western U. T. Co. *v.* Lacer, 122 Ky. 839, 93 S. W. 34, 5 L. R. A. (N. S.) 751, 121 Am. St. Rep. 502; Western U. T. Co. *v.* Caldwell, 102 S. W. 840, 31 Ky. L. Rep. 497, 12 L. R. A. (N. S.) 748.

Husband and wife:
Western U. T. Co. *v.* Merrill, 148 Ala. 618, 39 So. 121.

In Western U. T. Co. *v.* Ayers, 131 Ala. 391, 31 So. 78, 90 Am. St. Rep. 92, an action against the telegraph company, for the negligent failure to deliver a message sent by the father of a sick child, summoning his brother-in-law to the child's bedside which message the sendee, the uncle of the child, did not receive till too late to reach the child before its death, where the father sought damages for his mental anguish and suffering on account of the absence of his brother-in-law, it was held that the relationship between the sender and sendee was too remote to authorize damages in favor of the former.

In the following cases recovery was disallowed because the relationship was too remote:

Uncle and nephew:
Alabama: Western U. T. Co. *v.* Long, 148 Ala. 202, 41 So. 965 (uncle by marriage: *semble*).

Kentucky: Denham *v.* Western U. T. Co., 87 S. W. 788, 27 Ky. L. Rep. 999; Lee *v.* Western U. T. Co., 130 Ky. 202, 113 S. W. 55.

Father-in-law and son-in-law:
Kentucky: Western U. T. Co. *v.* Steenbergen, 107 Ky. 469, 54 S. W. 829. *Contra, Alabama:* Western U. T. Co. *v.* Crocker, 135 Ala. 496, 33 So. 45, 59 L. R. A. 398; Western U. T. Co. *v.* Saunders, 164 Ala. 234, 51 So. 176.

Affianced man and woman:
Randall *v.* Western U. T. Co., 32 Ky. L. Rep. 859, 107 S. W. 235, 15 L. R. A. (N. S.) 277.

[161] Carroll, J., in Lee *v.* Western U. T. Co., 130 Ky. 202, 113 S. W. 55.

the right of recovery are not satisfactory. Often persons farther removed in kinship and relationship than those we have enumerated would suffer greater mental anguish at being prevented from attending the bedside of a sick or burial of a deceased friend or relative than would a sister or brother. But, as the line must be drawn somewhere, it seems appropriate to put it at the point where the parties are united by close blood relation or marriage ties."

The Supreme Court of Iowa, on the other hand, in refusing to place any arbitrary restriction of this sort on the rule, well said: [162] "We are unable to see any logical ground upon which an arbitrary line or degree of relationship should be established as a matter of law as furnishing the only basis for recovery in cases of this kind. Undoubtedly the burden is upon the plaintiff in all cases to plead and to prove either a close relationship, or such other facts showing such close and affectionate relations as to give rise to the mental pain and suffering upon which the claim for damages is predicated."

In other jurisdictions it is held, with more reason, that while in the case of close relationship mental suffering may be inferred, it must be alleged and proved in the case of more distant relationship; [163] and it has even been suggested that notice of the special circumstances which would cause mental suffering in the particular case must be given to the company.[164]

§ 894c. Notice of relationship or of other circumstances.

In some cases it has been said that the relationship of the parties must be known to the company, either from the message itself or from information given *dehors* the message; [165]

---

[162] Evans, J. in Seddon v. Western U. T. Co. (Ia.), 126 N. W. 969. See also, Foreman v. Western U. T. Co., 141 Ia. 32, 116 N. W. 724, 19 L. R. A. (N. S.) 374.

[163] *Iowa:* Seddon v. Western U. T. Co. (Ia.), 126 N. W. 969 (*semble*).

North Carolina: Cashion v. Western U. T. Co., 123 N. C. 267, 31 S. E. 493, 68 Am. St. Rep. 822; Bennett v. Telegraph Co., 128 N. C. 103, 38 S. E. 294.

South Carolina: Butler v. Western U. T. Co., 77 S. C. 148, 57 S. E. 757;

Little v. Western U. T. Co., 79 S. C. 255, 60 S. E. 663; Johnson v. Western U. T. Co., 81 S. C. 235, 62 S. E. 244.

Texas: Western U. T. Co. v. Wilson, 97 Tex. 22, 75 S. W. 482.

[164] Western U. T. Co. v. McMillan (Tex.), 30 S. W. 298.

Contra, Seddon v. Western U. T. Co. (Ia.), 126 N. W. 969.

[165] McAllen v. Western U. T. Co., 70 Tex. 243; Western U. T. Co. v. Brown, 71 Tex. 723; Western U. T. Co. v. Fitzpatrick, 76 Tex. 217, 13 S. W.

and it has even been held that recovery will be denied unless the company has notice of the exact sort of mental suffering which will result from its default.[166] By the better view, however, any message which on its face shows that someone is seriously ill or dead warns the company that mental suffering is likely to follow in case of non-delivery, and is therefore sufficient notice to justify the allowance of damages for mental suffering.[167] But it is clear that where the message on its

70, 18 Am. St. Rep. 37; Western U. T. Co. v. Lovett, 24 Tex. Civ. App. 84, 58 S. W. 204.

On this ground recovery was refused in the following cases:

Arkansas: Western U. T. Co. v. Weniski, 84 Ark. 457, 106 S. W. 486 ("John is dead").

Kentucky: Western U. T. Co. v. Glover, 138 Ky. 500, 128 S. W. 587 ("wire me if operation successful").

South Carolina: Lewis v. Western U. T. Co., 84 S. C. 54, 65 S. E. 941 ("A's wife is dead").

Recovery was allowed on the ground that sufficient information of the relationship was given in the following cases:

Arkansas: Western U. T. Co. v. Blackmer, 82 Ark. 526, 102 S. W. 366 ("Mother very low").

Kentucky: Thurman v. Western U. T. Co., 127 Ky. 137, 105 S. W. 155, 14 L. R. A. (N. S.) 499 ("Nellie worse. Wife.").

Texas: Western U. T. Co. v. Gilliland (Tex. Civ. App.), 130 S. W. 212 ("Your father is very sick").

So recovery has been refused where the sufferer was not known to the company as a party to the message.

North Carolina: Helms v. Western U. T. Co., 143 N. C. 386, 55 S. E. 831, 8 L. R. A. (N. S.) 249.

Texas: Western U. T. Co. v. Kerr, 4 Tex. Civ. App. 280, 23 S. W. 564; Western U. T. Co. v. Fore, 26 S. W. 783; Maxville v. Western U. T. Co., 140 S. W. 464.

[166] Western U. T. Co. v. Butler, 45 Tex. Civ. App. 28, 99 S. W. 704 (for failure to deliver message saying, "your father is dead, will be buried tomorrow" the sendee cannot recover damages for mental suffering through not being able to be present to comfort his mother, as there was no notice to the telegraph company in the message of such damage).

In Western U. T. Co. v. Landry (Tex. Civ. App.), 108 S. W. 461, the message was "Gus Landry very low, send some one to me." The plaintiff was Landry's wife; the message was sent to his brother. By reason of non-delivery of the message no one came, and she was obliged to bury her husband in Texas instead of having the body taken to Louisiana, which was her purpose in sending the message. The defendant would naturally have expected mental suffering from plaintiff's being alone at the funeral; but, the court said, "if the message had been delivered there would have been no funeral, and the plaintiff did not therefore contemplate such suffering; and as defendant did not contemplate the suffering which actually occurred, nothing could be recovered." See however on this point, *ante*, § 147.

[167] *North Carolina:* Lyne v. Western U. T. Co., 123 N. C. 129, 31 S. E. 350.

Texas: Western U. T. Co. v. Adams, 75 Tex. 531, 12 S. W. 857; Western U. T. Co. v. Feegles, 75 Tex. 537, 12 S. W. 860, 16 Am. St. Rep. 920; Western U. T. Co. v. Moore, 76 Tex. 66, 12 S. W.

face does not import death or serious illness, no recovery can
be had for mental suffering without notice to the company
of the circumstances which make it likely.[168]

§ 894d. What mental suffering is compensated.

The mental suffering for which recovery may be had is actual
anguish, and not mere disappointment and vexation; [169] though

949, 18 Am. St. Rep. 25; Potts v. Western U. T. Co., 82 Tex. 545, 18 S. W. 604; Western U. T. Co. v. Erwin, 19 S. W. 1002; Western U. T. Co. v. McLeod (Tex. Civ. App.), 22 S. W. 988; Western U. T. Co. v. Porter (Tex. Civ. App.), 26 S. W. 866. See Western U. T. Co. v. Waller (Tex. Civ. App.), 47 S. W. 396.

On this ground recovery has been allowed in the following cases:

Arkansas: Western U. T. Co. v. Gullege, 84 Ark. 501, 106 S. W. 957 ("Eugene very sick, wants you," on ground that it suggests close relationship); Western U. T. Co. v. Shofner, 87 Ark. 303, 112 S. W. 751 ("Mother can live but a few hours"); Western U. T. Co. v. Griffin, 92 Ark. 219, 122 S. W. 489 ("Genie died very suddenly. Come at once"); Louisiana & N. W. R. R. v. Reeves, 95 Ark. 214, 128 S. W. 1051 ("Austin very low. Tell Bertie to come at once"); Western U. T. Co. v. Toms, 137 S. W. 559 ("I will come as soon as possible." Operator informed that it was a death message).

North Carolina: Cordell v. Western U. T. Co., 149 N. C. 402, 63 S. E. 71, 22 L. R. A. (N. S.) 540 ("Tell Noah Cordell to come this evening, that his child is just alive").

South Carolina: Lyles v. Western U. T. Co., 77 S. C. 174, 57 S. E. 725, 12 L. R. A. (N. S.) 534 ("Charlie died to-day").

Tennessee: Western U. T. Co. v. Potts, 120 Tenn. 37, 113 S. W. 789, 19 L. R. A. (N. S.) 479 ("Mother died this morning").

Texas: Western U. T. Co. v. Nations, 82 Tex. 539, 18 S. W. 709 ("your step-father died this morning"); Western U. T. Co. v. Linn, 87 Tex. 7, 26 S. W. 490 ("Grace is very low"); Western U. T. Co. v. Carter (Tex. Civ. App.), 20 S. W. 834 ("Gorsuch is dead").

[168] On this ground recovery for mental suffering was refused in the following cases:

Alabama: Western U. T. Co. v. Westmoreland, 151 Ala. 319, 44 So. 382 ("Meet me to-night"); Western U. T. Co. v. Peagler, 163 Ala. 38, 50 So. 913 ("Please let me hear from you at once by wire").

Arkansas: Western U. T. Co. v. Oastler, 90 Ark. 268, 119 S. W. 285 ("will be home on Cannon Ball Sunday").

North Carolina: Darlington v. Western U. T. Co., 127 N. C. 448, 37 S. W. 479 ("leave on this evening's train, be here to-morrow"); Holler v. Western U. T. Co., 149 N. C. 336, 63 S. E. 92, 19 L. R. A. (N. S.) 475 (anguish of person not mentioned in message).

Texas: Western U. T. Co. v. Simpson, 73 Tex. 422 (message transmitting money); Western U. T. Co. v. Kibble, 53 Tex. Civ. App. 222, 115 S. W. 643 ("Come at once").

[169] *Arkansas:* Western U. T. Co. v. Shenep, 83 Ark. 476, 104 S. W. 154, 12 L. R. A. (N. S.) 886.

North Carolina: Gerock v. Western U. T. Co., 147 N. C. 1, 60 S. E. 637.

South Carolina: Johnson v. Western U. T. Co., 81 S. C. 235, 62 S. E. 244.

Texas: Western U. T. Co. v. Carter, 85 Tex. 580, 22 S. W. 961 (mental anguish because relative was buried in unsuitable place); Ricketts v. Western

the anguish may be the result of the subsequent knowledge of events caused by the company's default, the events being unknown at the time of their occurrence.[170] It has been held that a child only ten months old may suffer mentally because of the non-arrival of its father.[171] In Texas it appears to be held that no damages may be recovered for a prolongation of mental suffering not originally caused by the company, as by non-delivery of a telegram announcing that a sick person is better.[172]

In the case of close relationship, damages may be inferred by the jury without proof from the non-delivery of a message announcing death or serious illness,[173] though the court must keep a certain degree of control, and see that the damages were sustained, and that the amount awarded is not excessive.[174] Damages for mental suffering cannot be given, of course, where the suffering would have been as great if the company had performed its whole duty, or generally, where it is not clearly shown that suffering resulted to the plaintiff from the company's default.[175]

U. T. Co., 10 Tex. Civ. App. 226, 30 S. W. 1105.

Recovery has been allowed in the following cases: Western U. T. Co. v. Motley (Tex. Civ. App.), 27 S. W. 51 (inability to attend funeral); Western U. T. Co. v. Proctor, 6 Tex. Civ. App. 300, 25 S. W. 811 (unsuitableness of marriage); Western U. T. Co. v. Carter, 2 Tex. Civ. App. 624, 21 S. W. 688, and Western U. T. Co. v. De Jarles, 8 Tex. Civ. App. 109, 27 S. W. 792 (decomposition of body of relative before plaintiff could see it); Western U. T. Co. v. Steele, 110 S. W. 546 (failure of husband to come home to attend sick child).

[170] Lyles v. Western U. T. Co., 84 S. C. 1, 65 S. E. 832.

[171] Western U. T. Co. v. De Andrea, 45 Tex. Civ. App. 395, 100 S. W. 977.

[172] Rowell v. Western U. T. Co., 75 Tex. 26; Akard v. Western U. T. Co., 44 S. W. 538; Goodhue v. Western U. T. Co. (Tex. Civ. App.), 122 S. W. 41.

But see Womack v. Western U. T. Co. (Tex. Civ. App.), 22 S. W. 417.

Contra, Arkansas: Western U. T. Co. v. Hollingsworth, 83 Ark. 39, 102 S. W. 681, 11 L. R. A. (N. S.) 497.

[173] *Alabama:* Western U. T. Co. v. McMorris, 158 Ala. 563, 48 So. 349; Western U. T. Co. v. Cleveland, 169 Ala. 131, 53 So. 80.

Kentucky: Western U. T. Co. v. Williams, 129 Ky. 515, 112 S. W. 651, 33 Ky. L. Rep. 1062.

North Carolina: Kivett v. Western U. T. Co., 72 S. E. 388.

South Carolina: Johnson v. Western U. T. Co., 82 S. C. 87, 62 S. E. 244; Talbert v. Western U. T. Co., 183 S. C. 68, 64 S. E. 862.

[174] Western U. T. Co. v. Bickerstaff (Ark.), 138 S. W. 998.

[175] *Alabama:* Leland v. Western U. T. Co., 159 Ala. 245, 49 So. 252; Western U. T. Co. v. West, 165 Ala. 399, 51 So. 740.

Arkansas: Tharpe v. Western U. T. Co., 94 Ark. 530, 127 S. W. 730.

§ 895. Avoidable consequences.

The rule that the plaintiff cannot recover for consequential losses which with ordinary care he could avoid applies in cases against telegraph companies as elsewhere.[176] Under ordinary circumstances, the proper course for the sender on learning that his message has not been forwarded, is to repeat it.[177] But the sender may not know that it has not been forwarded. It may be natural for him to act upon the supposition that it has been sent, but has failed to reach its destination. In such a case, if he is put to expense, this expense will be his measure of damages. So where plaintiff telegraphed to his attorney at Buffalo, "Hold my case till Tuesday or Thursday. Please reply," and getting no reply, after waiting a day, went to Buffalo, with counsel, to try the case, at an expense including counsel fee of $310, it was contended that he should have gone to defendant's office a second time; but it was held that defendant was responsible in this amount.[178] In the opinion of Daly, C. J., this question is referred to as one of "contributory negligence." But the rule invoked by defendant was clearly that of avoidable consequences, as it affected, not the right of action, but the extent of recovery.

North Carolina: Kivett v. Western U. T. Co., 72 S. E. 388.
South Carolina: Harrelson v. W. U. T. Co., 72 S. E. 882.
Texas: Western U. T. Co. v. Barrett (Tex. Civ. App.), 118 S. W. 1089; Western U. T. Co. v. Young (Tex. Civ. App.), 130 S. W. 257; Western U. T. Co. v. Murray, 29 Tex. Civ. App. 207, 68 S. W. 549; Western U. T. Co. v. Stone (Tex. Civ. App.), 27 S. W. 144.
[176] *Alabama:* Daughtery v. Am. Tel. Co., 75 Ala. 168, 51 Am. Rep. 435; Dorgan v. The Tel. Co., 1 Am. L. T. R. (N. S.) 406.
Illinois: Western U. T. Co. v. Hart, 62 Ill. App. 120.
Kentucky: Western U. T. Co. v. Taylor, 112 S. W. 844; Western U. T. Co. v. Matthews, 113 Ky. 188, 67 S. W. 849.
Missouri: Miller v. Western U. T. Co. (Mo. App.), 138 S. W. 887 (must

abandon contract void under statute of frauds if such abandonment would prevent loss).
New York: Weld v. Postal T. C. Co., 199 N. Y. 88, 92 N. E. 415.
South Carolina: Mitchiner v. Western U. T. Co., 75 S. C. 182, 55 S. E. 222; Cobb v. Western U. T. Co., 85 S. C. 430, 67 S. E. 549 (must inquire into truth of suspicious message which if true would cause mental pain).
Texas: Gulf, C. & S. F. Ry. v. Loonie, 82 Tex. 323, 18 S. W. 221, 27 Am. St. Rep. 891.
Virginia: Washington & N. O. T. Co. v. Hobson, 15 Grat. 122.
[177] *Alabama:* Daughtery v. American Tel. Co., 75 Ala. 168, 51 Am. Rep. 435.
New York: De Rutte v. New York, A. & B. T. Co., 1 Daly, 547, 560.
[178] Sprague v. Western U. T. Co., 6 Daly (N. Y.), 200.

§ 896. Exemplary damages.

In a proper case exemplary damages may be recovered against a telegraph company.[179] Thus when plaintiff was engaged in Cincinnati as a commercial news agent, furnishing to customers in that city financial and stock reports, which he obtained over defendant's wires from New York, it was held that he might recover exemplary damages for wilful delay in transmission of messages, for the purpose of giving precedence to other business of a rival agency.[180] And in Western Union Telegraph Co. *v.* Lawson,[181] it was held that exemplary damages could be recovered where the company was grossly negligent in failing to deliver a message concerning death of a relative.

§ 897. Causa proxima.

The rule of proximate cause is often of great assistance in defining the liability of telegraph companies. To ascertain whether any damages at all can be recovered,—*i. e.*, whether an action will lie,—the preliminary question must always be asked: whether the loss complained of arises from the act or omission of the telegraph company, or of some intervening agency, or cause. Thus, where B sent a dispatch to plaintiff asking for $500, which the company by mistake changed to $5,000; and B, on obtaining the latter sum, embezzled it and absconded, it was held by the New York Court of Appeals, that the loss was the result, not of the error in the transmission of the dispatch, but of B's independent act.[182] And so in Maier *v.* Western Union Telegraph Co.,[183] delay by the company caused plaintiff's attachment to be postponed to the attachments of other creditors. The goods were later sold at considerably less than their value, pursuant to an agreement

---

[179] *Alabama:* Western U. T. Co. *v.* Seed, 115 Ala. 670, 22 So. 474.

Kansas: Western U. T. Co. *v.* Gilstrap, 77 Kan. 191, 94 Pac. 122; Western U. T. Co. *v.* Bodkin, 79 Kan. 792, 101 Pac. 652; McInturff *v.* Western U. T. Co., 81 Kan. 476, 106 Pac. 282.

South Carolina: Gens *v.* Western U. T. Co., 86 S. C. 242, 68 S. E. 530.

Texas: Gulf, C. & S. F. R. R. *v.* Levy, 59 Tex. 542, 46 Am. Rep. 269.

[180] Davis *v.* Western U. T. Co., 1 Cin. Sup. Ct. 100.

[181] 66 Kan. 660, 72 Pac. 283.

[182] Lowery *v.* Western U. T. Co., 60 N. Y. 198, 19 Am. Rep. 154.

[183] 94 Tenn. 442, 29 S. W. 732.

of the creditors. It appeared that if the goods had been sold at their value plaintiff would have lost nothing. The court held that under the circumstances the delay of the company was not the proximate cause of the loss, so that plaintiff could recover nothing.[184] And on the same principle in an action of contract, where there is no question of a breach, the operation of such an intervening cause would reduce the loss to a nominal sum.[185]

§ 897a. Telephone Companies.

The principles which govern the allowance of damages in actions against telephone companies are similar to those applied in actions against telegraph companies; the chief difference resulting from the fact that the dealing with the company usually consists in hiring telephone service for a season, or at least in asking for connection with another person, rather than in giving a message to the company for transmission. Where the latter is the case, the measure of damages would seem to be the same as in actions against telegraph companies. But where, as usually happens, the telephone company simply undertakes to put one person into communication with another, it is often held that, having no notice of the nature of the desired communication, the company cannot be said to have knowledge of any special damages as likely to result from its breach of obligation, and is therefore not liable for such special damages. So where the operator failed to answer a call, it was held that damages could not be recovered for failure to get a physician to attend a sick person; [186] and for failure to notify a person called of the call damages for loss of a bargain [187] or for annoyance from being unable to get

---

[184] See also Hart v. Direct U. S. C. Co., 86 N. Y. 633; Stafford v. Western U. T. Co., 73 Fed. 273.

[185] First Natl. Bk. of Barnesville v. W. U. T. Co., 30 Oh. St. 555, 27 Am. Rep. 485.

[186] Southwestern T. & T. Co. v. Solomon (Tex. Civ. App.), 117 S. W. 214.

In Volquardsen v. Iowa Teleph. Co., 148 Ia. 77, 126 N. W. 928, where the

plaintiff claimed damages for loss of his factory by fire, the operator having failed to answer his call for help, the damage was held too conjectural, as there was no way of showing that it could have been avoided if the operator had answered quickly.

[187] Southwestern T. & T. Co. v. Flood (Tex. Civ. App.), 111 S. W. 1064.

money [188] cannot be recovered.   It would seem, however, that certain damages may be said to be within the contemplation of the company without notice of any special circumstances. So in Cumberland Telegraph and Telephone Co. *v.* Hobart,[189] where the company having removed a telephone for failure to pay the rent wrongfully refused to reinstate it upon being tendered the rent in arrear, the court held that "the damage sustained by the loss of a telephone in its very nature is largely composed of inconvenience and annoyance," and that compensation might be recovered for such damage; and the case was followed where a failure of the operator to answer a call compelled the plaintiff to go out at night to get a physician.[190] If after wrongful removal of an instrument the company offers to reinstate it, the plaintiff should have avoided further consequences by accepting the offer, and cannot recover for consequential damages suffered after that time.[191]

[188] Southwestern T. & T. Co. *v.* Wilcoxson (Tex. Civ. App.), 129 S. W. 868.

[189] 89 Miss. 252, 42 So. 349, 119 Am. St. Rep. 702. So where the company wrongfully disconnected plaintiff's telephone, knowing that at the time his father-in-law was ill at a hospital, the plaintiff was allowed damages for the general inconvenience and humiliation caused by cutting off the service, and also for the annoyance and anxiety caused by lack of telephone connection under one particular circumstance. Carmichael *v.* Bell Tel. Co. (N. C.), 72 S. E. 619.

[190] Cumberland T. & T. Co. *v.* Jackson, 95 Miss. 49, 48 So. 614.

[191] Ashley *v.* Rocky M. B. T. Co., 25 Mont. 286, 64 Pac. 765.

CHAPTER XL

§ 898. The general principles modified in actions concerning real estate.

899. Actions for possession of real estate.

900. Damages in real actions in the early law.

901. Ejectment.

902. Nominal damages in ejectment suit.

903. Ejectment—Payment for improvements.

904. Improvements under Louisiana Code.

905. Mesne profits and damages.

906. Mesne profits always recoverable.

907. Damages given by the early law.

908. General rule in actions to recover mesne profits.

909. Recovery measured by the net profits.

§ 909a. Use of improvements made by defendant.

910. Waste or injury to the freehold.

911. Period during which compensation may be recovered.

912. Time from which compensation may be recovered.

913. Time to which compensation may be recovered.

914. Statute of limitations.

915. Allowance for improvements.

916. Good faith required.

917. For what improvements allowance is made.

918. Payment of necessary expenses by the defendant.

919. Interest on mesne profits.

920. Costs and counsel fees.

921. Dower.

922. Dower in improvements.

§ 898. The general principles modified in actions concerning real estate.

We have now discussed the principles laid down by the courts with regard to the measure of damages in all ordinary cases of contract and tort (not turning upon the interpretation of statutes), except those relating to land. These we have reserved for consideration here, inasmuch as the rules applicable to them are frequently of a more arbitrary character than those which lie at the foundation of personal actions. This is in a great measure owing to the fact that the courts have here been hampered in applying the general rules of compensation, partly by the peculiar character of the old common-law forms of action, and partly by considerations of public policy or the intent of parties, derived from a condition of society which has passed away. In some jurisdictions these difficulties have been met by a more or less complete assimilation of the law of real to that of personal property. In others they have led to peculiar rules, which cannot be well understood except by considering the special circumstances which have led to their adoption in the light of the general principles, the examination of which has now been completed.

§ 899. Actions for possession of real estate.

* Five of the first chapters of Mr. Sayer's work on Damages are devoted to a consideration of the law of damages in the actions of *Assize of novel disseizin, Entry sur novel disseizin, Assize of mort d'ancestor, Cosinage, Aiel and Besaiel.* Many of the forms of real actions were introduced into America from the mother country,[1] and some still survive; but the particular actions above mentioned have been rarely if ever employed in the Union; and they were in England absolutely abolished by the statutes 3 and 4 Will. IV., ch. 27, § 36, for the "limitations of actions," which swept away, indiscriminately, between fifty and sixty species of proceedings, leaving as the only real or mixed actions, *a writ of dower, dower unde nihil habet, quare impedit, and ejectment.*[2] Repeated statutory changes have also been made in the various States on this same subject, the general result of which has been that the actions of ejectment or trespass to try titles and dower are the only real or mixed actions now in extensive use in the Union.[3] The action of *quare impedit,* relating to a species of property—advowson—which never existed among us, is wholly a stranger to American jurisprudence. There is still another form of action—waste—by which the possession of real estate is sometimes changed, and which may, perhaps, strictly belong to this division of the

[1] As to the extent to which the real actions were adopted by us, see 4 Kent's Commentaries, 70, *in notis;* an article by Judge Jackson in the American Jurist, vol. ii, p. 65; and Stearns on Real Actions, 396, *n.*

[2] Warren's Law Studies, 1st ed., 15 16, *in notis.*

[3] In New England the writ of entry is the form of action for the recovery of land, being in many respects analogous to the action of ejectment, or the statutory action which in most States has taken its place.

subject; but it is more conveniently and appropriately discussed under the head of trespasses, nuisances, and other interferences with the occupation or enjoyment of real property.

The actions above named are the usual modes of procedure with us, by which the possession of real estate is now altered. It is necessary briefly to allude to the general principles regulating damages in real actions as they once existed; but the sweeping changes which have been effected in the original structure of English jurisprudence will make this discussion a very cursory one; and, we shall then examine the law in regard to the substitutes which have now taken their places—ejectment and dower.

§ 900. Damages in real actions in the early law.

In real actions, properly speaking, damages were not originally given at common law,[4] "for it is of the essence of a real action, that only a real thing can be recovered therein; whenever damages, which are a pecuniary recompense, and consequently a personal thing, are recoverable in the same action, the action becomes mixed."[5] By the statutes of Merton, Marlbridge, and Gloucester, however,[6] damages were given in the principal real actions. In those actions where no damages were directly given, and in which, pending the suit, the defendant might impair the value of the property, the ancient writ of *estrepement*[7] gave indirect relief. It lay properly in

---

[4] Sayer, Damages, 5; Stearns, Real Actions, 390.

[5] In the Assize of Novel Disseisin damages were recovered if the tenant was the original disseisor, but not otherwise. 3 Twiss' Bracton 35, 43, 97, 99, 109, 197–205, 341; Symons *v.* Symons, Hetley, 66. So in Pilfold's Case, 10 Co. 115, it is said, "At the common law, before the statute of Gloucester (anno 6 E. I. c. i), a man should not recover damages in any real action, as in dower, before the statute of Merton, c. i, nor in Aiel, Mordancester before the said Statute of Gloucester; but in actions mixed, as in assize, entry in the nature of assize, or in

personal action, as trespass *quare clausum fregit*, of goods taken away, etc. . . . In personal actions they shall declare to damages, because they shall recover damages only for the wrong done before the writ brought, and shall recover no damages for any done pending the writ; but in real actions the demandant shall never count to damages, because he is to recover damages pending the writ." See also I Roscoe on Real Actions, 307.

[6] 20 Hen. III, c. 3; 52 Henry III, c. 16; 6 Edw. I, anno 1278.

[7] Estrepamentum—from the Fr. *estropier—mutilare*.

real actions where the plaintiff could not recover damages by his suit, and, as it were, supplied damages.[8]

In regard to property in advowsons it may be briefly noticed that no damages were recoverable at the common law in an assize of *darrein presentment*, nor an action of *quare impedit.*[9] And the action of *darrein presentment* was abolished in England by the statute of limitation of actions, to which we have already referred. By the statute of 2 West., c. 5, it was provided, in writs of *quare impedit* and *darrein presentment*, if a disturbance of six months took place, that damage should be awarded to two years' value of the church; if six months did not pass, but the presentment were *deraigned* (*i. e.*, proved) within that time, damages should be awarded to half a year's value of the church. If a more particular view of this branch of our subject is desired by the student, he will find it in those English treatises which are devoted to this particular matter. The scope of this work does not allow a further examination of it. We come, then, to consider the law of damages in the actions relating to real property, as in general application in the Union.

§ 901. Ejectment.

While the action of ejectment remained in its original state and the ancient practice prevailed, the measure of damages given by the jury when the plaintiff recovered his term were the profits of the land accruing during the tortious holding of the defendant. But as upon the introduction of the modern system the proceedings became altogether fictitious, and the plaintiff merely nominal, the damages assessed became nominal also; and they have not, since that time, included the injury sustained by the claimant from the loss of his possession,[10] ** in jurisdictions still following the strict common-law

---

[8] Termes de la Ley, *in voc.*, Tomlin's Law Dictionary, *in voc.* In New York, by Co. Civ. Proc., § 1681, the benefit of this writ is given by a provision which, where an action is brought for the recovery of land, or the possession thereof, authorizes the court in which the suit is pending, to make an order restraining the defendant from the commission of waste.

[9] Sayer, 35.

[10] Adams on Ejectment, 333. "Before the time of Henry VII," said Wilmot, C. J., in Goodtitle *v.* Tombs, 3 Wils. 118, "plaintiffs in ejectment did not recover the term, but until about that time the mesne profits were the measure of damages." Reeves Hist. Eng. Law (ed. 1880), 241; Stearns, Real Actions, 401; Davis *v.* Delpit, 25

practice, the action of trespass for mesne profits being used to cover that loss.

In many jurisdictions, however, * the course of proceedings is to recover the mesne profits in the action of ejectment, or in an action of trespass to try the title.[11]   In the latter States the rules that we shall proceed to give, in regard to the action of trespass for mesne profits, will, it is to be supposed, govern in the ejectment suit, or in the action of trespass to try title.

The only case in which actual damages could be recovered in the ejectment suit itself was that where the plaintiff's title expired pending the action.[12]   So in New York,[13] where the plaintiff's life estate had terminated before trial, the Supreme Court said: "The plaintiff has no title to turn the defendant out of possession, but he has a title to the mesne profits and the costs of this suit, and must, therefore, have judgment to enable him to recover them." **   But it is held in North Carolina that, though in ejectment the usual and proper course is to give the plaintiff nominal damages, leaving the real damages to be recovered in the subsequent correlative action of trespass for mesne profits; yet it would not be error to direct

Miss. 445; Emrich v. Ireland, 55 Miss. 390. In Maryland a writ of inquiry of damages for the ouster will lie in ejectment. Joan v. Shiels, 3 H. & McH. 7. But mesne profits cannot be shown on such writ. Gore v. Worthington, 3 H. & McH. 96.

[11] Stearns, Real Actions, 403, n. See White v. St. Guirons, Minor (Ala.) 331, 12 Am. Dec. 56. In such a case if he does not make use of his statutory privilege of claiming mesne profits in the action of ejectment he may bring trespass for mesne profits as at common law. Emrich v. Ireland, 55 Miss. 390.

[12] Runnington on Ejectment, 404; England v. Slade, 4 T. R. 682, 683; Co. Litt., 285a; Doe v. Black, 3 Camp. 447; Thrustout v. Grey, 2 Strange 1056; Adams on Ejectment, 228.

[13] Jackson ex dem. Henderson v. Davenport, 18 Johns. 295, 302; Wilkes v. Lion, 2 Cow. 333; Robinson v. Campbell, 3 Wheat. 212, 4 L. ed. 373. This seems to have been the rule in Pennsylvania; when the term of the plaintiff expired before the trial, although he could not recover the possession, yet he might proceed for damages for the trespass and for mesne profits. Brown v. Galloway, 1 Pet. C. C. 291, 299. So in South Carolina, in an action of trespass to try titles: Stockdale v. Young, 3 Strobh. 501. In New York the case is now covered by the statutory provision which enacts (Co. Civ. Proc., § 1520): "If the right or title of a plaintiff (in ejectment) expires after the commencement of the action, but before the trial, the verdict must be returned according to the fact, and the plaintiff is entitled to judgment for his damages for the withholding of the property, to the time when his right or title so expired."

that the actual damages should be assessed in the ejectment suit, the division of actions being merely for convenience.[14] The damages can in no case exceed the claim in the petition.[15]

§ 902. Nominal damages in ejectment suit.

But since the ejectment suit was in many jurisdictions not necessarily merged with the action for mesne profits, * it has been decided in New York [16] that a recovery of nominal damages in the action of ejectment is no bar to an action for the mesne profits, and that it is not necessary to enter a *remittitur*. In Pennsylvania, however, it has been decided that the damages in ejectment being merely nominal, a verdict finding for the plaintiff without assessing damages is not thereby vitiated.[17] **

§ 903. Ejectment—Payment for improvements.

* In regard to improvements made on the land while out of the possession of the rightful owner, the general principle of the English law, as well as of our own, is that the owner recovers his land in ejectment without being subjected to the condition of paying for improvements which may have been made upon it by any intruder, or occupant without title. The improvements are considered as annexed to the freehold, and pass with the recovery. Every possessor makes such improvements at his peril, and whether acting on an honest belief in his title or without color of right, the party who is ousted loses all benefit of his expenditures.[18] ** This rule, however, refers only to a simple action of ejectment to recover possession. Where damages are sought, they are often subject to deduction for improvements, as we shall find in considering the determination of mesne profits.[19]

---

[14] Miller v. Melchor, 13 Ired. 439.

[15] Smith v. Royse, 165 Mo. 654, 65 S. W. 994.

[16] Van Alen v. Rogers, 1 Johns. Cas. 281.

[17] Harvey v. Snow, 1 Yeates, 156.

[18] 2 Kent's Com., 335. The same rule holds in an action of trespass by a tenant against his landlord to recover

damages for being ejected before the end of his lease. Schlemmer v. North, 32 Mo. 206.

[19] See *infra*, § 915. One who forcibly disseizes another and improves his land can have no claim for the value of his improvements, because he has no right to improve another's property against the owner's will. But a *bona fide* oc-

The civil law, however, as we shall see, draws a clear line of distinction between the possessor *bonæ fidei* and *malæ fidei* and the latter only loses the benefit of his improvements.[20] This, too, is the case in California [21] and Louisiana.[22]

§ 904. Improvements under the Louisiana Code.

In New Orleans *v.* Gaines,[23] an appeal from a decision under this provision of the Louisiana Code, it was held that, although the defendant could require the plaintiff to elect whether she would have the building demolished or pay the value, the section did not apply where the defendant had not required the plaintiff to make an election. A bill was filed by Mrs. Gaines to compel an account of the rents and profits of land recovered under a former decision of the court in the same litigation, by which the city was held a possessor in bad faith,[24] and liable for rents and profits during its occupation, and to obtain a decree for the amount so ascertained. No rent as such had been derived from the land, but the city had established a draining machine on it, by the use of which a large district belonging to the city, had (as well as the land in question) been drained, and had in consequence become valuable and productive of revenue by taxation. At the beginning of

cupant is entitled to have them taken into account in ascertaining whether the owner of the land has sustained damage or not, both in the case where such improvements were made by the occupant and by one whose title he has purchased. Morrison *v.* Robinson, 31 Pa. 456.

[20] Institutes, § 30, *De Ædificatione ex suâ Materia in Solo Alieno,* and § 35, *De fructibus bonâ fide perceptis.*

[21] Carpenter *v.* Small, 35 Cal. 346.

[22] The Civil Code of Louisiana, Art. 508, provides: "If the works have been made by a third person, evicted but not sentenced to make restitution of the fruits (mesne profits), because such person possessed *bona fide*, the owner shall not have a right to demand the demolition of the works, but he shall have his choice either to reim-

burse the value of the materials and the price of workmanship, or to reimburse a sum equal to the enhanced value of the soil." See Stanbrough *v.* Barnes, 2 La. Ann. 376. This provision of the Louisiana Code (Art. 500, Rev. Code, 1870, 508) is copied from the digest of the civil law of the Territory of Orleans (Dig. Law of Territory of Orleans 1808, book 2, tit. 2, ch. 3, § 1, art. 12) which was itself taken, with very slight verbal alteration, from the Code Napoleon (Code Civil, § 555), and substantially declares the rule of the civil law (Domat, part 1, book 3, tit. 5, § 3; Toullier, liv. 3, tit. 1, §§ 307, 308; and see Pothier, Droit de Propriété, art. 1, ch. 2, § 3, art. 3).

[23] 15 Wall. 624, 21 L. ed. 215.

[24] 6 Wall. 642, 18 L. ed. 950.

the wrongful occupation, which was in September, 1834, the land was worth $2,000. The city had erected on it buildings, which (independent of the drainage machinery) cost $18,000, and the fair rental value of the land and buildings was $2,400 a year. The expense of repairs was $500 a year. The master to whom it was referred to take an account of the rents and profits, made several estimates on different bases. By one of these he charged the defendant with the market value of the premises during the period of wrongful occupation, with interest, and allowed the expense of repairs and interest. The report was excepted to, chiefly on the following grounds: That the defendant's liability should have been limited to the loss of the improvements, and that it should have been protected in the possession of these improvements until the complainant had paid their value or required their removal, and that she should have been compelled to elect which; that the defendant should have been allowed the benefit of the prescription of three years against the claim for rents; [25] that the defendant had received no rent, income, or remuneration, but had expended a large sum for the buildings and draining machine; that it was not liable for any rents, because it had dedicated the property to the use of the public; that other lands of the complainant had been greatly benefited by the drainage effected by the machine; and that the defendant was erroneously treated as a mere trespasser. But the Circuit Court disallowed the exceptions, confirmed the master's report on the above basis, made a decree for the difference between the two sums, amounting to $125,266.79, and this decree was affirmed by the Supreme Court of the United States. [26]

§ 905. Mesne profits and damages.

* As nominal damages only were given in ejectment, it was necessary to provide another remedy for the claimant for the injury sustained by him from the loss of his possession; and this was effected by a new application of the common action

---

[25] La. Code, § 3538.

[26] See also Gaines *v.* New Orleans, 4 Woods, 213; Gibson *v.* Hutchins, 12 La. Ann. 545; Cannon *v.* White, 16 La Ann. 85. Under this statute the oc- cupant in Louisiana may recover for the cost of clearing the land, and for such ameliorations as have added to the permanent value of the land. Sigur *v.* Burguieres, 111 La. 1077, 35 So. 823.

of trespass *vi et armis*, generally termed an action for mesne profits, in which action the plaintiff complained of his ouster and loss of possession, stated the time during which the defendant (the beneficial occupant) had held the lands, and taken the rents and profits, and prayed judgment for the damages which he, as rightful owner, had thereby sustained.[27] **

In most of the States, by statute, these two actions have been blended, and the plaintiff in an action to recover the land is allowed also to recover the mesne profits. The subject of mesne profits, therefore, though it would otherwise properly be considered in connection with actions for injury to real property, will be introduced here, in connection with the action of ejectment. * And the remarks which we shall make, and the authorities cited, will apply to the action for trespass to try titles in those States where by statute this remedy has been made to assume the functions of the former actions of ejectment and trespass for mesne profits, and also to the action of ejectment in those States where the plaintiff is allowed to recover the rents and profits in that proceeding.** But the ejectment and the mesne profits, though they may be combined in one suit, continue to be distinct causes of action; and no recovery can be had on account of mesne profits, unless it is supported by a proper allegation in the complaint or declaration.[28] Nor can recovery be had for mesne profits unless the plaintiff succeeds in the ejectment suit.[29]

---

[27] Adams, Ejectment, by Tillinghast, ch. xiv, 379, 380.

[28] *Alabama:* Cummings v. M'Gehee, 9 Port. 349 (but separate action may be had for damages accruing between entry of judgment and execution of the writ).

California: McKinlay v. Tuttle, 42 Cal. 570.

Colorado: Arnold v. Woodward, 14 Col. 164, 23 Pac. 444.

Minnesota: Qualy v. Johnson, 80 Minn. 408, 83 N. W. 393 (*semble*).

New York: Larned v. Hudson, 57 N. Y. 151; Livingston v. Tanner, 12 Barb. 481.

Pennsylvania: Bayard v. Inglis, 5 W. & S. 465; Cook v. Nicholas, 2 W. & S. 27.

Texas: Parsons v. Hart, 46 S. W. 856.

In *Vermont* where plaintiff was entitled to an undivided portion but sued for a specific part and was defeated, it was held he could not recover the rents and profits of the undivided portion. Smith v. Benson, 9 Vt. 138. In Strong v. Garfield, 10 Vt. 502, it was held that the plaintiff *must* recover mesne profits in the ejectment suit; and a separate suit would not lie.

[29] Cape Girardeau & T. B. T. R. R. v. St. Louis & G. Ry., 222 Mo. 461, 121 S. W. 300.

Whatever the principle of classification adopted by the various courts, it is clear that the rents and profits lost are to be distinguished from the damages suffered by way of actual injury to the premises and consequential or secondary loss. Such damages, as will be seen, are recoverable in the same action in which the profits are claimed, but the mesne profits constitute the subject-matter of a distinct and entire claim, and compensation for their loss is regulated by a specific set of rules.

§ 906. Mesne profits always recoverable.

* The mesne or intermediate profits of lands are those received while the property is withheld from its rightful occupant; and when he recovers possession, the right to the mesne profits follows his recovery.[30] By the Roman law, the *bona fide* possessor of land held without title was not liable to the legitimate owner for the *fructus*, or mesne profits. *Si quis a non domino quem dominum esse crediderit, bonâ fide fundum emerit, vel ex donatione, aliâve quâlibet hustâ causâ, æque bonâ fide acceperit, naturali rationi placuit fructus quos percepit ejus esse pro culturâ et curâ. Et ideo, si postea dominus supervenerit et fundum vindicet, de fructibus ab eo consumtis agere non potest.*[31] This is also the rule of the Scotch [32] and of the French system; [33] and the same principle prevails in Louisiana, the jurisprudence of which State has been largely affected by

[30] "Though a disseizee may have his action of trespass *quare clausum fregit* against the disseizor for the injury done by the disseizin, at which time the plaintiff was seized of the land, he cannot have it for any act done after the disseizin until he hath gained possession by re-entry, and then he may maintain it for the intermediate damage done; for, after his re-entry, the law, by a kind of *jus postliminii*, supposes the freehold to have all along continued in him." 3 Black. Com., 210; 4 Kent's Com., 119; Stevens *v.* Hollister, 18 Vt. 294.

[31] Instit. de Rer. Divisione, lib. ii, tit. i, § 35; Adams, Ejectment, 4th ed., 386, *n.*

[32] Kames' Equity, book iii, ch. i.

[33] Domat, I, 272, book iii, tit. v, § 3. There were, however, before the Revolution, several exceptions to the general principle in France, which will be found noticed by Touillier, in his admirable work, vol. IV, 327, liv. iii, tit. i, ch. iv, § 307, *et seq.* The matter has been put at rest by the Code Napoleon which declares, Art. 549: "The occupant makes the mesne profits his own only in case he is a *bona fide* possessor; if otherwise, he must return the profits with the thing itself to the true owner. The occupant is regarded as a *bona fide* possessor when he holds as proprietor under a derivative title, of the defect of which he is ignorant. The occupant ceases to be so regarded as soon as the defect of title is known to him."

the liberal reasoning and enlightened equity of the civil law.[34] But the common law makes no such distinction, except, as we shall now see, with regard to improvements put on the premises; it looks only to the strict legal title, and the right to recover the mesne profits follows in all cases upon a recovery in ejectment.[35] **

A tenant in common is liable for the mesne profits of land of which he withholds the possession from his co-tenants.[36] Where an action of ejectment is brought against two, and it appears that one of them took possession of the land before the other, mesne profits can be recovered only during the time of their joint possession, in the absence of a statute allowing recovery against them jointly and severally.[37] Where a mortgagee obtains a decree of foreclosure, in which no provision is made as to the disposition of the rents and profits, the mortgagor is entitled to them.[38]

§ 907. Damages given by the early law.

* In an action for mesne profits, the plaintiff, as a general

[34] The Civil Code of Louisiana asserts, Art. 502: "The products of the thing do not belong to the simple possessor, and must be returned with the thing to the owner who claims the same, unless the possessor held it *bona fide*." Art. 503: "He is a *bona fide* possessor who possesses as owner by virtue of an act sufficient in terms to transfer property, the defects of which he was ignorant of; he ceases to be a *bona fide* possessor from the moment these defects are made known to him, or are declared to him by a suit instituted for the recovery of the thing by the owner."

[35] *United States:* Green v. Biddle, 8 Wheat. 1, 80, 5 L. ed. 547.

Alabama: Prestwood v. Watson, 111 Ala. 604, 20 So. 600.

California: Furlong v. Cooney, 72 Cal. 322, 14 Pac. 12.

Colorado: Whitehead v. Callahan, 44 Colo. 396, 99 Pac. 57.

Florida: Norman v. Beekman, 58 Fla. 325, 50 So. 876.

Minnesota: Qualy v. Johnson, 80 Minn. 408, 83 N. W. 393.

New York: Shea v. Campbell, 128 N. Y. Supp. 508.

North Carolina: Camp v. Homesley, 11 Ired. 211.

[36] *Massachusetts:* Backus v. Chapman, 111 Mass. 386.

Missouri: Falconer v. Roberts, 88 Mo. 574.

Pennsylvania: Critchfield v. Humbert, 39 Pa. 427.

See *California:* McGuire v. Lynch, 126 Cal. 576, 59 Pac. 27.

[37] *Florida:* Ashmead v. Wilson, 22 Fla. 255.

Vermont: Edgerton v. Clark, 20 Vt. 264.

The fact that defendant occupied under a joint lease with another party is no ground for reducing the damages. Ryders v. Wheeler, Hill & Den. (N. Y.) 389.

[38] Gilman v. Illinois & M. T. Co., 91 U. S. 603, 23 L. ed. 405.

rule, recovered the annual value of the land from the time of the accruing of his title, or from the time of such title accrued as laid in the declaration in the ejectment suit, if he relied on the record in that suit to establish his recovery. But the jury were not confined in their verdict to the mere rent of the premises, but might give such extra damages as they thought the particular circumstances of the case demanded.[39] ** * What these additional damages should be was not at first clearly laid down. In an early case in England, it was said,[40] "The plaintiff is not confined in this case to the very mesne profits only, but he may recover for his trouble. I have known four times the value of the mesne profits given by a jury in this sort of action of trespass; if it were not to be so sometimes, complete justice could not be done to the party injured." So where [41] an action of trespass for mesne profits was brought, and bankruptcy was pleaded: on demurrer it was admitted that bankruptcy was no bar to demands for torts in general, but it was insisted that the claim here was in substance for the annual value of the land. But judgment was given for the plaintiff, Lord Mansfield saying: "The plaintiff goes for the whole damages occasioned by the tort;" and Mr. J. Buller said: "The damages here are as uncertain as in an action of assault."

"There are certainly some cases," says Mr. Runnington,[42] "in which the jury are not bound by the amount of the rent, but may give extra damages, and after judgment by default the costs in ejectment are recoverable, and are therefore usually declared for as damages in the action for mesne profits." And so the Supreme Court of New York: [43] "The damages in the action for mesne profits are not limited to the rent. Extra damages may be given." "As to the amount of damages," said Washington, J., on the Pennsylvania Circuit,[44] the jury are the only proper judges; there is no general rule, and the quantum depends on the circumstances of the case." And so in Pennsylvania, the jury were told at Nisi Prius, that they might give interest from the time of the commencement of the suit; and on motion for a new trial, the court said: "As to the

[39] Adams, Ejectment, *391.
[40] Goodtitle v. Tombs, 3 Wils. 118.
[41] Goodtitle v. North, 2 Doug. 584.

[42] Ejectment, 439.
[43] Dewey v. Osborn, 4 Cow. 329.
[44] Brown v. Galloway, Pet. C. C. 291.

measure of the damages, the court gave in this respect as favorable a construction as the case could possibly admit of. It would not have been error in the court to have left it to the discretion of the jury to have allowed the plaintiff more than interest upon the amount of the mesne profits. The jury are not confined in their verdict to the mere rent of the premises, although the action is said to be brought to recover the rents and profits of the estate; but may give such extra damages as they may think the particular circumstances of the case demand." [45]

These *dicta* are evidently very loose; ** and * it is plain that the measure of compensation which we are now considering, has been involved in confusion by the technical character of our forms of action. "The *dicta* on the subject," says Gibson, C. J., in Pennsylvania, "seem to have been predicated by judges who had no precise idea of it; for they have not defined it by any landmarks." [46] The action of trespass being one of *tort*, admits of any evidence in aggravation; and therefore, in one sense, it is correct to say, that the damages in this proceeding are entirely at large and under the control of the jury. But, on the other hand, there is nothing necessarily in the action of the nature of a trespass. The property may have been withheld, and the rents received, in entire good faith. In this case, the allegations of force, etc., are purely fictitious, and it certainly never would be tolerated, on such facts, that the jury should give any damages beyond the actual value of the income. **

§ 908. General rule in actions to recover mesne profits.

The general rule settled by modern decisions is that the compensation is to be measured by the annual income of the land, during the time possession is withheld. [47] Thus Ashurst, J.,

---

[45] Drexel v. Man, 2 Pa. St. 271, 44 Am. Dec. 195.

[46] Alexander v. Herr, 11 Pa. 537.

[47] *United States:* Green v. Biddle, 8 Wheat. 1, 5 L. ed. 547; New Orleans v. Gaines, 15 Wall. 624, 21 L. ed. 215; Larwell v. Stevens, 2 McCrary, 311, 12 Fed. 559.

Arizona: Davis v. Simmons, 1 Ariz. 240, 25 Pac. 535.

Florida: Apalachicola v. Apalachicola Land Co., 9 Fla. 340, 79 Am. Dec. 284.

Georgia: Averett v. Brady, 20 Ga. 523.

Illinois: Western B. & S. Co. v. Jevne, 179 Ill. 71, 53 N. E. 565.

in Utterson *v.* Vernon,[48] said: "The action for mesne profits, though in form it is an action of trespass, in effect is to recover the rent." So where the land recovered is uncultivated prairie land, from which no profit ever accrued, nothing can be recovered on account of mesne profits.[49]

It is to be observed that the plaintiff recovers the value of the use of the premises, and not merely what the defendant actually received from his lessee;[50] the defendant's relations with *his* lessee are irrelevant.[51] And conversely, recovery cannot be had for the value of some special use to which the plaintiff might have put the property, but only the market value of the use.[52] The damages should be, not the actual yield or income of the property, but the fair annual value.[53]

Indiana: Grimes *v.* Wilson, 4 Blackf. 331.

Kentucky: Searcy *v.* Reardon, 1 A. K. Marsh. 1.

Maryland: Drury *v.* Connor, 1 H. & G. 220.

New York: Taylor *v.* Taylor, 43 N. Y. 578, 584.

Oregon: Hill *v.* Cooper, 8 Ore. 254.

Pennsylvania: Carman *v.* Beam, 88 Pa. 319; Hanna *v.* Phillips, 1 Grant, 253.

Tennessee: Bains *v.* Perry, 1 Lea, 37.

Virginia: Bolling *v.* Lersner, 26 Gratt. 36.

Washington: Columbia & P. S. R. R. *v.* Histogenetic Medicine Co., 14 Wash. 475, 45 Pac. 29.

England: Dormer *v.* Fortescue, 3 Atk. 124.

Compensation is the purpose of the action. Morrison *v.* Robinson, 31 Pa. 456.

[48] 3 T. R. 539, 547.

[49] Griffey *v.* Kennard, 24 Neb. 174, 38 N. W. 791. Where the *locus* was a highway, since it could not legally be used except for highway purposes, the value for which was not shown, the plaintiff city could recover only a nominal amount by way of mesne profits. Uniontown *v.* Berry, 72 S. W. 295, 24 Ky. L. Rep. 1692.

But in *South Carolina*, where defend-

ant takes possession in good faith, he is liable only for rents and profits actually received, and not for rental value. Rabb *v.* Patterson, 42 S. C. 528, 20 S. E. 540.

[50] *United States:* Lawrence *v.* Rector, 137 U. S. 139, 34 L. ed. 600, 11 Sup. Ct. 33.

Iowa: Bradley *v.* Brown, 86 Ia. 359, 53 N. W. 268.

Missouri: Roberts *v.* St. Louis M. L. I. Co., 126 Mo. 460, 29 S. W. 584.

North Carolina: Credle *v.* Ayres, 126 N. C. 11, 35 S. E. 128, 48 L. R. A. 751.

Pennsylvania: Kille *v.* Ege, 82 Pa. 102.

West Virginia: Bodkin *v.* Arnold, 48 W. Va. 108, 35 S. E. 980.

[51] *United States:* Campbell *v.* Brown, 2 Woods, 349.

Virginia: Bolling *v.* Lersner, 26 Gratt. 36.

[52] McMahan *v.* Bowe, 114 Mass. 140, 19 Am. Rep. 321.

[53] *United States:* New Orleans *v.* Gaines, 15 Wall. 624, 21 L. ed. 215; Larwell *v.* Stevens, 12 Fed. 559, 2 McCr. 311.

Alabama: Scott *v.* Colson, 156 Ala. 450, 47 So. 60.

California: Johnston *v.* Fish, 105 Cal. 420, 38 Pac. 979, 45 Am. St. Rep. 53.

Where the defendant occupied a mill-site having upon it a steam sawmill, the rent of the mill and site was the measure; [54] and where the defendant was in possession of a ferry, the profits of the ferry.[55]

In Starr v. Stark,[56] a suit in equity, the rents and profits consisted of mesne profits which the defendant, in an action of ejectment, had previously recovered from the plaintiff and was thus compelled to restore. Where the wall of a storeroom and a narrow strip of floor along it belonged to the plaintiff, the yearly rental value of the entire room was allowed to go to the jury as an element to be considered.[57] In Woodhull v. Rosenthal,[58] where the plaintiff owned a leasehold interest in the rear part of a city lot, and the defendant in the front part, it was held not error to admit evidence that the rental value of the front part was greater, per square foot, than that of the rear part. The inadequate price paid by the plaintiff for the land cannot, of course, be used to reduce the amount of his recovery.[59] The annual income under prudent management is sometimes stated as the measure.[60]

Not merely the actual receipts, then, are to be recovered, but the income which the land ought to bring.[61] In Massachusetts, where a messuage recovered on a writ of entry was, at

Indian Territory: Case v. Hall, 2 Ind. Ty. 8, 46 S. W. 180.

Indiana: Millington v. O'Dell, 35 Ind. App. 225, 73 N. E. 949.

Minnesota: Nash v. Sullivan, 32 Minn. 189, 20 N. W. 144; Noyes v. French Lumbering Co., 80 Minn. 397, 83 N. W. 385; Curry v Sandusky Fish Co., 88 Minn. 485, 93 N. W. 896 (value for any proper purpose).

Missouri: Phillips v. Stewart, 87 Mo. App. 486.

South Dakota: Baldwin v. Bohl, 23 S. D. 395, 122 N. W. 247.

Texas: McRae v. White (Tex. Civ. App.), 42 S. W. 793.

Virginia: Early v. Friend, 16 Gratt. 21, 78 Am. Dec. 649.

Washington: Columbia & P. S. R. R. v. Histogenetic Medicine Co., 14 Wash. 475, 45 Pac. 29.

England: McArthur v. Cornwall, [1892] A. C. 75, 61 L. J. P. C. 1, 65 L. T. 718.

[54] Morris v. Tinker, 60 Ga. 466.

[55] *Georgia:* Averett v. Brady, 20 Ga. 523.

Texas: Dunlap v. Yoakum, 18 Tex. 582.

[56] 7 Ore. 500.

[57] Jenkins v. Means, 59 Ga. 55.

[58] 61 N. Y. 382.

[59] Love v. Powell, 5 Ala. 58.

[60] *United States:* Campbell v. Brown, 2 Woods, 349.

Virginia: Bolling v. Lersner, 26 Gratt. 36.

[61] *United States:* Campbell v. Brown, 2 Woods, 349.

Pennsylvania: Kille v. Ege, 82 Pa. 102, 112.

In ejectment by a landlord for non-

and after the time when the defendant's title accrued, subject to a right of homestead in the defendant's grantor and his family, and the house was occupied as a homestead by the grantor's wife, who claimed under that right, although without having had her homestead set off to her, it was held that the rentable value of the part occupied by her should not be included in estimating the clear annual value of the premises for which the defendant was liable.[62]

§ 909. Recovery measured by the net profits.

The defendant need of course return only profits in the ordinary sense—that is, the gross receipts, less expenses. Thus, where a ferry was occupied, the defendant was required to return the gross receipts less the expenses of operation.[63] Taxes and expenses of collecting rents may be deducted.[64]

§ 909a. Use of improvements made by defendant.

The expenses incurred by the defendant may amount not merely to those necessary to collect or preserve the ordinary profits of the premises, but may be so important and extensive that they become themselves the real source of the profits, and the question then is practically whether a plaintiff can recover the income arising from improvements made by the defendant. It has been held (and very properly) that the value of the use of improvements made by the defendant cannot be recovered.[65] The case is stronger where there would

payment of rent it was said the jury might award such sum as they thought the landlord entitled to, and as a criterion they might consider the stipulated rent. Cong. Soc. in Newport v. Walker, 18 Vt. 600.

[62] Marsh v. Hammond, 103 Mass. 146.

[63] *Georgia:* Averett v. Brady, 20 Ga. 523.

Texas: Dunlap v. Yoakum, 18 Tex. 582.

[64] *Arkansas:* McCloy v. Arnett, 47 Ark. 445, 2 S. W. 71.

Massachusetts: Raymond v. Andrews,

6 Cush. 265; Hodgkins v. Price, 141 Mass. 162, 5 N. E. 502.

But an occupant without color of title was allowed nothing for taxes paid by him in Napton v. Leaton, 71 Mo. 358.

[65] *Arkansas:* McCloy v. Arnett, 47 Ark. 445, 2 S. W. 71; Reynolds v. Reynolds, 55 Ark. 369, 18 S. W. 377.

Georgia: Averett v. Brady, 20 Ga. 523; Lee v. Humphries, 124 Ga. 539, 52 S. E. 1007.

Iowa: Dungan v. Von Puhl, 8 Iowa, 263.

Kansas: Deitzler v. Wilhite, 55 Kan.

have been no rents at all from the land but for the improvements,[66] or where the improvements have been destroyed by casualty and have imparted permanent value to the land,[67] or where, for other reasons, the defendant cannot claim to set off his expenditures in making the improvements.[68]   In Iowa it has been declared that while the rent recovered should not include the use of improvements (buildings, fixtures, etc.), it should be based upon the value of the land as brought into cultivation by the defendant's efforts and made suitable for

200, 40 Pac. 272; Hentig v. Redden, 1 Kan. App. 163, 41 Pac. 1054.

Maryland: Worthington v. Hiss, 70 Md. 172, 16 Atl. 534, 17 Atl. 1026.

Massachusetts: Hodgkins v. Price, 141 Mass. 162, 5 N. E. 502.

Minnesota: Nash v. Sullivan, 32 Minn. 189, 20 N. W. 144.

New York: Jackson v. Loomis, 4 Cow. 168.

Oregon: Rafferty v. Davis, 52 Ore. 77, 102 Pac. 305.

Texas: Black v. Garner (Tex. Civ. App.), 63 S. W. 918 (see Evetts v. Tendick, 44 Tex. 570).

Virginia: Early v. Friend, 16 Gratt. 21, 78 Am. Dec. 649.

Wisconsin: Blodgett v. Hitt, 29 Wis. 169; Davis v. Louk, 30 Wis. 308.

But see *California:* Carpenter v. Mitchell, 29 Cal. 330.

In Teaver v. Akin, 47 Ark. 528, 1 S. W. 772, it was held that rent on improvements can be withheld only for a period long enough for the rent so withheld to pay for the improvements.

In Gilley v. Williams (Tex. Civ. App.), 43 S. W. 1094, where the improvements were not made in good faith, the plaintiff was allowed to recover the rental value of the land inclusive of the improvements.

In *Alabama* where there has been three years adverse possession, the value of permanent improvements may be recouped by the defendant; or if he has been in possession under color of title, in good faith, the responsibility

for rent or damages is restricted to one year before the commencement of the suit. These defences, however, are not cumulative and he can only set up one of them. Where he restricts the recovery for rent to one year, the rent is to be based on the value of the land at the time he went into occupation and is not increased by improvements made by him; but if he is allowed compensation for the improvements the full rental value is awarded. Southern Cotton Oil Co. v. Henshaw, 89 Ala. 448, 7 So. 760.

The same thing is true in *Mississippi:* Miller v. Ingram, 56 Miss. 510; Phillips v. Chamberlain, 6 Miss. 740.

Where the occupant continues to hold possession after judgment in ejectment, he is liable for the rental value of the entire premises, including improvements. Hardeman v. Turner, 112 Fed. 41, 50 C. C. A. 110.

[66] *Indiana:* Adkins v. Hudson, 19 Ind. 392.

Kansas: Deitzler v. Wilhite, 55 Kan. 200, 40 Pac. 272.

Maryland: Neale v. Hagthrop, 3 Bland, 551, 591.

Texas: Cahill v. Benson, 19 Tex. Civ. App. 30, 46 S. W. 888.

See Ewing v. Handley, 4 Litt. (Ky.) 347, 371, 14 Am. Dec. 140; Hawkins v. King, 1 T. B. Mon. 161; Moore v. Cable, 1 Johns. Ch. 385.

[67] Nixon v. Porter, 38 Miss. 401.

[68] Tatum v. McLellan, 56 Miss. 352.

new purposes.[69] This seems, however, to be a departure from
principle. For the expenditure of labor on the land is as much
a permanent expenditure as is that of money; and if no allowance is made to the defendant for the value of his services, the
error is committed of refusing payment for the expenditure
which has gone into the land and produced the increased permanent value, and at the same time charging for the use of the
land as thereby increased in value. This injustice has never
been committed. In the cases where, contrary to the general
rule, the use of improvements has been included in the rent
recovered,[70] the fact that the defendant was allowed for his
improvements was the ground of recovery. It may be added,
that where this exception is adopted and the defendant pays
rent for improvements, while receiving allowance for their
cost, he should receive interest on his expenditures up to the
time of trial.[71]

§ 910. Waste or injury to the freehold.

Compensation for waste or dilapidation may be recovered
in an action for mesne profits,[72] as well as compensation for
injury to the premises:[73] thus for trespass, such as cutting

[69] *Iowa:* Dungan v. Von Puhl, 8 Ia.
263; see Wolcott v. Townsend, 49 Ia.
456.
[70] *Kentucky:* Bell v. Barnet, 2 J. J.
Marsh. 516.
Mississippi: Miller v. Ingram, 56
Miss. 510; Phillips v. Chamberlain, 61
Miss. 740.
[71] See Evetts v. Tendick, 44 Tex. 570;
Sedgwick & Wait, Trial of Title, etc.,
2d ed., § 678.
[72] *United States:* Field v. Columbet, 4
Sawy. 523.
California: Furlong v. Cooney, 72
Cal. 322, 14 Pac. 12 (not damages to
other land of plaintiff).
Connecticut: Alsop v. Peck, 2 Root,
224.
Florida: Ashmead v. Wilson, 22 Fla.
255, 1 Am. St. Rep. 191; Norman v.
Beekman, 58 Fla. 325, 50 So. 876.
Massachusetts: Raymond v. Andrews,
6 Cush. 265.

Mississippi: Emrich v. Ireland, 55
Miss. 390.
Missouri: Lee v. Bowman, 55 Mo.
400; Sieferer v. St. Louis, 141 Mo. 586,
43 S. W. 163.
Pennsylvania: Morrison v. Robinson,
31 Pa. 456.
West Virginia: Bodkin v. Arnold, 48
W. Va. 108, 35 S. E. 980.
Contra, Alabama: Prestwood v. Wat-
son, 111 Ala. 604, 20 So. 600.
Vermont: Walker v. Hitchcock, 19
Vt. 634.
[73] *Delaware:* Cooch v. Geery, 3 Harr.
423.
Mississippi: Johnson v. Futch, 57
Miss. 73.
New York: Gas Light Co. v. Rome,
W. & O. R. R., 51 Hun, 119.
Pennsylvania: Huston v. Wickersham,
2 W. & S. 308.
Vermont: Lippett v. Kelly, 46 Vt. 516.
Washington: Columbia & P. S. R. R.

timber, pulling down fences and injuring crops,[74] removing a building,[75] or for building a road across the premises.[76] But no recovery can be had on account of a diminution in the value of the property for which the defendant is not chargeable.[77] Thus, where a house on the premises was burned without fault of the defendant during the period of dispossession, the value of the house cannot be recovered.[78]

It has sometimes been held that for damage in the nature of waste and trespass a separate action must be brought;[79] but these cases are exceptional, and have nothing on principle to commend them. No doubt such damages must be specially alleged.

§ 911. Period during which compensation may be recovered.

* As to the time for which the defendant is liable, each occupant is answerable for the time he has been in possession.[80] ** And a defendant cannot be charged in damages for a period when he was not in possession in fact or in judgment of law, either personally or by agent or tenant,[81] and, therefore, a de-

v. Histogenetic Medicine Co., 14 Wash. 475, 45 Pac. 29.

In *Oregon* it has been held that consequential damages for the loss may be recovered. Trotter v. Stayton, 45 Ore. 301, 77 Pac. 395.

[74] *Florida:* Norman v. Beekman, 58 Fla. 325, 50 So. 876.

South Carolina: Lassiter v. Okeetee Club, 70 S. C. 102, 49 S. E. 224.

Texas: Hillman v. Baumbach, 21 Tex. 203; Bonner v. Wiggins, 52 Tex. 125.

[75] Uhl v. Small, 54 Kan. 651, 39 Pac. 178.

[76] Lippett v. Kelley, 46 Vt. 516, 523.

[77] Marvin v. Prentice, 94 N. Y. 295, 301 (*semble*).

[78] Willis v. Morris, 66 Tex. 628, 59 Am. Rep. 634. Nor can the owner recover from the defendant the amount received on a policy of insurance placed by him upon the burned building.

[79] *Alabama:* Prestwood v. Watson, 111 Ala. 604, 20 So. 600.

Indiana: Woodruff v. Garner, 27 Ind. 4, 8, 89 Am. Dec. 477; Bottorff v. Wise, 53 Ind. 32.

Wisconsin: Pacquette v. Pickness, 19 Wis. 219.

[80] *New York:* Morgan v. Varick, 8 Wend. 587, 24 Am. Dec. 105.

Pennsylvania: Zimmerman v. Eschbach, 13 Pa. 417.

England: Holcomb v. Rawlyns, Cro. Eliz. 540.

[81] *United States:* Chirac v. Reinicker, 11 Wheat. 280, 6 L. ed. 474; Gaines v. New Orleans, 17 Fed. 29.

California: Ellis v. Jeans, 26 Cal. 272.

Missouri: Gutzweiler v. Lachman, 28 Mo. 434.

New York: Ryers v. Wheeler, Hill & D. 389; Gilman v. Gilman, 111 N. Y. 265.

England: Doe v. Harlow, 12 A. & E. 40, 42, *n.*; Hunter v. Britts, 3 Camp. 455; Burne v. Richardson, 4 Taunt. 720; Girdlestone v. Porter (K. B. M. T. 39 Geo. 3), Woodf. L. & T. 511.

fendant who interferes in the ejectment merely to maintain the title, not being a trespasser, is not liable for mesne profits.[82] A defendant is, therefore, not liable for profits taken. prior to his entry, by those under whom he claims title.[83]

In Tennessee, where land is sold at execution sale, and the purchaser takes possession, and the land is redeemed, the owner is not entitled to rent or damages for waste before the redemption, but he is entitled to rent for the time he was wrongfully kept out of possession after redemption.[84] The judgment in ejectment is not conclusive as to the length of time the defendant has been in possession.[85] A tenant in common cannot recover for a period during which the defendant's occupancy was not adverse,[86] or during which no ouster has been proved.[87]

§ 912. Time from which compensation may be recovered.

Mesne profits are to be computed only from the time when the plaintiff's title accrued.[88] Thus, an execution purchaser recovers only from the date of the sheriff's deed.[89] Heirs or devisees recover only from the time of the ancestor's or testa-

---

[82] Eastwick v. Saylor, 85 Pa. 15.

[83] *Georgia:* Gardner v. Granniss, 57 Ga. 539.

Illinois: Scheppel v. Weiler, 41 Ill. App. 85.

[84] Kannon v. Pillow, 7 Humph. 281.

[85] *Indiana:* Vance v. Congressional Township, 7 Blackf. 241.

Pennsylvania: Bailey v. Fairplay, 6 Binn. 450, 6 Am. Dec. 486; Sopp v. Winpenny, 68 Pa. 78; Miller v. Henry, 84 Pa. 33.

Vermont: Lippett v. Kelley, 46 Vt. 516.

England: Aslin v. Parkin, 2 Burr. 665, 668; Dodwell v. Gibbs, 2 C. & P. 615.

Contra: Shotwell v. Boehm, 1 Dall. 172.

But if the plaintiff goes back of the time laid in the ejectment suit, the defendant as to that time is not concluded from proving himself rightfully in possession. Huston v. Wickersham, 2 W. & S. 308, 37 Am. Dec. 509; Kille v. Ege, 82 Pa. 102.

[86] Carpentier v. Mendenhall, 28 Cal. 484, 87 Am. Dec. 135.

[87] Miller v. Myers, 46 Cal. 535.

[88] *Georgia:* Mills v. Geer, 111 Ga. 275, 36 S. E. 673 (purchaser; but where credit is claimed by the defendant for improvements made by his grantor, mesne profits as against the grantor may be set up against him).

Missouri: Smith v. White, 165 Mo. 590, 65 S. W. 1013 (widow, as to her own land).

New York: Danziger v. Boyd, 54 N. Y. Super. Ct. 365; Welch v. Winterburn, 25 Hun, 437.

Adams, Ejectment, 4th ed., 389; Sedgwick & Wait, Trial of Title to Land, 2d ed., § 663.

[89] Clark v. Boyreau, 14 Cal. 634, 76 Am. Dec. 449.

tor's death.[90] If no ouster is shown, recovery should date from the institution of the suit.[91] A mortgagee recovers rents and profits from the mortgagor's assignee from the time of notice to quit, or in the absence of notice from the date of the writ.[92] So a vendor who has delivered possession to the vendee recovers from the date of the demand and refusal of the vendee to pay the purchase money.[93]

§ 913. Time to which compensation may be recovered.

An executor recovers, if at all, to the date of the testator's death.[94] A tenant in common recovers from his co-tenant only to the time reasonably necessary for taking possession.[95] A defendant who abandons the premises is not liable, unless the abandonment was secret, for profits subsequently accruing.[96] If the defendant remains in possession, damages should be awarded to the date of the verdict or award.[97]

[90] *Alabama:* Brewster *v.* Buckholz, 3 Ala. 20.

Iowa: Cavender *v.* Smith, 8 Ia. 360.

Minnesota: Watson *v.* Chicago, N. & S. P. Ry., 46 Minn. 321, 48 N. W. 1129.

New York: Hotchkiss *v.* Auburn & R. R. R., 36 Barb. 600.

North Carolina: King *v.* Little, 77 N. C. 138.

[91] Miller *v.* Myers, 46 Cal. 535.

[92] Lyman *v.* Mower, 6 Vt. 345.

In Sanderson *v.* Price, 1 N. J. 637, it was held that the tenant of a mortgagor under a lease made subsequent to the mortgage was liable to the mortgagee only from the latter's actual entry and not from service of the declaration in ejectment.

[93] Fears *v.* Merrill, 9 Ark. 559.

[94] *New York:* Hotchkiss *v.* Auburn R. R., 36 Barb. 600.

North Carolina: King *v.* Little, 77 N. C. 138.

But where the executor is empowered to sell the land, he may recover mesne profits both before and after the death of the testator. Blight *v.* Ewing, 26 Pa. 135.

[95] Hare *v.* Fury, 3 Yeates, 13, where one month was deemed a reasonable time.

[96] *Alabama:* Bumpass *v.* Webb, 3 Ala. 109.

Kansas: Haish *v.* Pollock, 79 Kan. 624, 101 Pac. 3.

New York: Gilman *v.* Gilman, 111 N. Y. 265, 18 N. E. 849.

Pennsylvania: Mitchell *v.* Freedley, 10 Pa. 198.

England: Pilfold's Case, 10 Rep. 115b, 117a.

[97] *Indiana:* Pendergast *v.* McCaslin, 2 Ind. 87.

Mississippi: Bell *v.* Medford, 57 Miss. 31.

Missouri: Stump *v.* Hornback, 109 Mo. 272, 18 S. W. 37.

New York: Danziger *v.* Boyd, 120 N. Y. 628, 24 N. E. 482; Clason *v.* Baldwin, 129 N. Y. 183, 29 N. E. 226.

North Carolina: Whissenhunt *v.* Jones, 78 N. C. 361; Pearson *v.* Carr, 97 N. C. 194, 1 S. E. 916.

Pennsylvania: Dawson *v.* McGill, 4 Whart. 230.

Wisconsin: McCrubb *v.* Bray, 36 Wis. 333.

§ 914. Statute of limitations.

The right to recover mesne profits extends back for six years only, or such other period as is named in the statute of limitations, if the statute be pleaded.[98] But if no statute of limitations is applicable they can be recovered for the whole period of occupation.[99] When the mesne profits are recovered in the same proceeding in which the right to the land is established, mesne profits may be recovered for the time limited before the suit is commenced.[100]

A plaintiff has been allowed to show that a deficiency of profits in one or more of the six years was made up by an ex-

---

In case of appeal, to the time of trial in the higher court. Dunn v. Patrick (N. C.), 72 S. E. 220.

[98] *Arkansas:* Shirey v. Clark, 72 Ark. 539, 81 S. W. 1057.

Connecticut: Bull v. Pratt, 2 Root, 440.

Georgia: Taylor v. James, 109 Ga. 327, 34 S. E. 674.

Illinois: Ringhouse v. Keener, 63 Ill. 230.

Kansas: Gatton v. Tolley, 22 Kan. 678.

Louisiana: Gillaspie v. Citizens' Bank, 35 La. Ann. 779.

Maryland: West v. Hughes, 1 H. & J. 574.

Minnesota: Nash v. Sullivan, 32 Minn. 189, 20 N. W. 144.

New York: Morgan v. Varick, 8 Wend. 587; Jackson v. Wood, 24 Wend. 443; Syracuse G. L. Co. v. Rome, W. & O. R. R., 51 Hun, 119, 5 N. Y. Supp. 459.

North Carolina: Jones v. Coffey, 109 N. C. 515, 14 S. E. 84.

Pennsylvania: Lynch v. Cox, 23 Pa. 265; Hill v. Meyers, 46 Pa. 15.

Rhode Island: Herreshof v. Tripp, 15 R. I. 92, 23 Atl. 104, 2 Am. St. Rep. 879.

Vermont: McFarland v. Stone, 17 Vt. 165, 44 Am. Dec. 325.

Wisconsin: Blodgett v. Hitt, 29 Wis. 169.

[99] New Orleans v. Gaines, 15 Wall. 624, 21 L. ed. 215.

In *New York*, by statute, the recovery is limited to six years, whether the statute of limitations be pleaded or not. Jackson v. Wood, 24 Wend. 443; Grout v. Cooper, 9 Hun, 326.

In Hare v. Fury, 3 Yeates (Pa.), 13, it was held that one who delayed taking possession for an unreasonable time could not recover mesne profits after the expiration of such time.

In Avent v. Hurd, 3 Head (Tenn.), 459, it was held that trespass for mesne profits was dependent upon the action of ejectment and the statute of limitations did not begin to run until entry of judgment in ejectment—that the recovery is not confined to the period of limitation from the institution of the suit but runs back to the date of the demise laid in the declaration.

[100] *New York:* Willis v. McKinnon, 178 N. Y. 451, 70 N. E. 962 (overruling Budd v. Walker, 9 Barb. 493; Gas-Light Co. v. Rome, W. & O. R. R., 51 Hun, 119, 5 N. Y. Supp. 459, and distinguishing Clason v. Baldwin, 129 N. Y. 183, 29 N. E. 226; and see Chace v. Lamphere, 67 Hun, 599, 22 N. Y. Supp. 404).

Rhode Island: Herreshoff v. Tripp, 15 R. I. 92, 23 Atl. 104, 2 Am. St. Rep. 879.

cess of profits in excluded years. But a defendant is not allowed to increase his claim for expenses by proving expenditures during years for which, by availing himself of the statute of limitations, he is not obliged to restore profits.[101]

§ 915. Allowance for improvements.

* The action for mesne profits is everywhere held to be a liberal and equitable action, and one which will allow of every equitable kind of defence.[102] Among the most important considerations that a defendant can urge, in answer to the claim for the rents and profits received by him, is that which the common law has, to a certain extent, adopted from the civil law, and which grows out of permanent improvements made by him upon the premises during his occupancy. The civil law treated the occupant in good faith with lenity.[103] The reasoning of the civilians has so far obtained in many of our tribunals, that a *bona fide* occupant of lands is allowed to mitigate the damages in the action brought by the rightful owner, by offsetting the value of his permanent improvements made in good faith, to the extent of the rent and profits claimed;[104] **

[101] Ewalt *v.* Gray, 6 Watts (Pa.), 427.

If, however, the occupant sets up a claim (under a statute) to compensation for improvements, mesne profits may be set off against the claim, although recovery for them would be barred by lapse of time.

Alabama: Turnipseed *v.* Fitzpatrick, 75 Ala. 297.

Maryland: Tongue *v.* Nutwell, 31 Md. 302.

Wisconsin: Davis *v.* Louk, 30 Wis. 308.

[102] Murray *v.* Gouverneur, 2 Johns. Cas. 438.

[103] Lord Kaims says, book iii, ch. i, 276: "It is a maxim suggested by nature, that reparations and meliorations bestowed upon a house or upon land, ought to be defrayed out of the rents;" and so says the Roman law. *Sumptus in prædium quod alienum esse apparuit, a bona fide possessore facti, neque ab eo qui prædium donavit, neque a domino peti possunt, verum exceptione doli posita, per officium judicis æquitatis ratione servantur, scilicet si fructuum ante litem contestatum perceptorum summam excedunt. Etenim, admissa compensatione, superfluum sumptum meliore prædio facto dominus restituere cogitur.* L. 48, de Rei Vindicatione.

[104] *United States:* Hylton *v.* Brown, 2 Wash. C. C. 165.

Georgia: Averett *v.* Brady, 20 Ga. 523; Dean *v.* Feely, 69 Ga. 804; Dudley *v.* Johnson, 102 Ga. 1, 29 S. E. 50.

Maryland: Tongue *v.* Nutwell, 31 Md. 302.

Missouri: Stump *v.* Hornback, 109 Mo. 272, 18 S. W. 37.

New York: Jackson *v.* Loomis, 4 Cow. 168, 15 Am. Dec. 347.

North Carolina: Merritt *v.* Scott, 81 N. C. 385.

Pennsylvania: Marie *v.* Semple, Addison, 215; Morrison *v.* Robinson, 31 Pa. 456.

and in our own ancient real actions, the improvements of the tenant appear always to have been the subject of set-off or recoupment.[105] The set-off cannot, however, go beyond the value of the rent and profits; the defendant is never allowed to recover a balance, unless (as is the case in some jurisdictions) the recovery of a *balance* for improvements is allowed by statute.[106] This principle, however, properly applies only to the case of a *bona fide* possessor, or one without notice, and does not touch that of a person who, being apprised of a claim of better title and with full notice, and even after suit brought goes on to apply the mesne profits to permanent improvements. It seems very dangerous to make a compulsory allowance for

Virginia: Hollingsworth *v.* Funkhouser, 85 Va. 448, 8 S. E. 592.

West Virginia: Bodkin *v.* Arnold, 48 W. Va. 108, 35 S. E. 980.

Wisconsin: Huebschmann *v.* Von Cotzhausen, 107 Wis. 64, 82 N. W. 720.

Contra, Arkansas: Jacks *v.* Dyer, 31 Ark. 334.

In Cawdor *v.* Lewis, 1 Y. & C. 427, where the defendant had expended money on the premises, an injunction was granted to restrain the suit at law, on the ground that no right of set-off existed in the action for mesne profits.

Under the statute in New Hampshire a claim for improvements made prior to the writ of entry must be made in that action and cannot be proved as a set-off in the action of trespass for mesne profits. Bailey *v.* Hastings, 15 N. H. 525.

[105] "Damage of 40s. and no more was found by the assize, because the land sown and the house well amended and so recouped the damage." Viner's Abr. tit. Discount, where see many other cases in the same connection. See also, Coulter's Case, 5 Co. 30, and Bro. tit. Damages.

[106] *Georgia:* Mills *v.* Geer, 111 Ga. 275, 36 S. E. 673, 52 L. R. A. 934.

Indian Territory: Turner *v.* Gonzales, 3 Ind. Terr. 649, 64 S. W. 565.

Iowa: Parsons *v.* Moses, 16 Ia. 440.

Kansas: Deitzler *v.* Wilhite, 55 Kan. 200, 40 Pac. 272; Hentig *v.* Reddin, 1 Kan. App. 163, 41 Pac. 1054.

Virginia: Hollingsworth *v.* Funkhouser, 85 Va. 448, 8 S. E. 592.

It is commonly provided that compensation for improvements may be allowed if the defendant has been in adverse possession of the land for a certain time.

Alabama: Barrett *v.* Kelly, 131 Ala. 378, 30 So. 824 (three years).

Michigan: Jones *v.* Merrill, 113 Mich. 433, 71 N. W. 838; Boucher *v.* Trembley, 140 Mich. 352, 103 N. W. 819 (six years).

Texas: Black *v.* Garner (Tex. Civ. App.), 63 S. W. 918; Rowan *v.* Rainey (Tex. Civ. App.), 63 S. W. 1031; Overton *v.* Meggs (Tex. Civ. App.), 105 S. W. 208; Haney *v.* Garton, 51 Tex. Civ. App. 577, 113 S. W. 166 (one year).

In *Michigan* the owner may elect to pay the value of the improvements or to abandon the land to the occupant upon being paid the value of the land without improvements. McKenzie *v.* A. P. Cook Co., 113 Mich. 452, 71 N. W. 868.

such an application of funds to property which the defendant is fully apprised will be claimed by another. Such expenditure should be made, it would seem, at the occupant's peril. But this distinction is by many courts not adverted to, and the decisions must, therefore, be distinguished accordingly.

§ 916. Good faith required.

It is usually held that allowance for improvements will be granted only to a defendant who acted in good faith,[107] supposing himself to be the true proprietor of the land, and ignorant that his title is contested by any one claiming a better right to it.[108] Where the defendant was a *bona fide* holder under a void assessment, he was allowed to show the value of improvements made by him, though it was said that profits received before the demise laid in the complaint should first be deducted from the improvements.[109]

[107] *United States:* Green v. Biddle, 8 Wheat. 1, 5 L. ed. 547; Bright v. Boyd, 1 Story, 478; Campbell v. Brown, 2 Woods, 349.

California: White v. Moses, 21 Cal. 34; Love v. Shartzer, 31 Cal. 487; Carpenter v. Small, 35 Cal. 346; Malone v. Roy, 107 Cal. 518, 40 Pac. 1040.

District of Columbia: Gill v. Patten, 1 D. C. (1 Cr. C. C.) 465.

Georgia: Davis v. Smith, 5 Ga. 274, 48 Am. Dec. 279; Beverly v. Burke, 9 Ga. 440; Dean v. Feely, 69 Ga. 804.

Iowa: Parsons v. Moses, 16 Ia. 440, 445.

Kentucky: Whitledge v. Wait, Sneed, 335.

Louisiana: McDade v. Bossier Levee Board, 109 La. 625, 33 So. 628.

Missouri: Dothage v. Stuart, 35 Mo. 251.

New York: Murray v. Gouverneur, 2 Johns. Cas. 438; Putnam v. Ritchie, 6 Paige, 390, 404; Bedell v. Shaw, 59 N. Y. 46; Wood v. Wood, 83 N. Y. 575 (*semble*); Willis v. McKinnon, 79 App. Div. 249, 79 N. Y. Supp. 936.

North Carolina: Finch v. Strickland, 132 N. C. 103, 43 S. E. 552.

South Dakota: Meadows v. Osterkamp, 13 S. D. 571, 83 N. W. 624; Pendo v. Beakey, 15 S. D. 344, 89 N. W. 655 (good faith found); Coleman v. Stalnacke, 15 S. D. 242, 88 N. W. 107.

In the following cases the requirement of good faith was not expressly made, but the facts showed a claim by the defendant in good faith. Turnipseed v. Fitzpatrick, 75 Ala. 297; Oldham v. Woods, 3 T. B. Mon. 47; Worthington v. Young, 8 Oh. 401.

See Story, Equity, § 799a.

[108] *United States:* Green v. Biddle, 8 Wheat. 1, 5 L. ed. 547.

Illinois: Van Tassell v. Wakefield, 214 Ill. 205, 73 N. E. 340 (knowledge of violation of condition).

Oregon: Schettler v. Southern Oregon Co., 19 Ore. 192, 24 Pac. 25 (entry under mere agreement to convey).

An occupant under a tax title may hold in good faith. Franklin v. Campbell (Tex. Civ. App.), 23 S. W. 1003.

[109] Bedell v. Shaw, 59 N. Y. 46.

In Petit v. Flint & P. M. R. R., 114 Mich. 362, 72 N. W. 554, 75 Am. St. Rep. 417, it was said that good faith meant an honest belief of the occupant

In Jackson v. Loomis,[110] the Supreme Court of New York *allowed improvements made after suit brought by the legal owner, and during its pendency, to be given in evidence for the purpose of mitigating damages. The distinction between improvements made before and after notice of suit brought does not, however, appear to have been clearly taken; and the court relied on the case above cited in the Supreme Court of the United States,[111] where the point was not raised.[112] **

§ 917. For what improvements allowance is made.

The improvements must be of a lasting and valuable nature, increasing the value of the land,[113] and no allowance is made for improvements which were not necessary for the profitable enjoyment of the land.[114] The allowance for improvements is measured by the benefit the plaintiff would receive from them, and not by their cost.[115]

in his title and the fact that diligence might have shown error did not necessarily negative good faith.

A defendant may be a *bona fide* holder who knows of an adverse claim but has strong reason to believe it invalid. Cahill v. Bensen, 19 Tex. Civ. App. 30, 46 S. W. 888.

[110] 4 Cow. 168. In Averett v. Brady, 20 Ga. 523, a mere trespasser was allowed to deduct improvements. At the present day this discussion has not a very practical bearing, as the statutes of the different States generally provide for an assessment for betterments. Wherever there is no special provision, and such improvements are allowed, it would seem that the proper rule is the increased market value of the premises on account of the improvements.

[111] Green v. Biddle, 8 Wheat. 1, 5 L. ed. 547.

[112] Dorer v. Hood, 113 Wis. 607, 88 N. W. 1009.

[113] *United States:* Stark v. Starr, 1 Sawy. 15.
Illinois: Ringhouse v. Keener, 63 Ill. 230.
Kentucky: Whitledge v. Wait, Sneed,

335; Oldham v. Woods, 3 T. B. Mon. 47.
Nebraska: Fletcher v. Brown, 35 Neb. 660, 53 N. W. 577.
Ohio: Worthington v. Young, 8 Oh. 401.
Pennsylvania: Noble v. Biddle, 81 Pa. 430.
Utah: Bacon v. Thornton, 16 Utah, 138, 51 Pac. 153.
So no recovery can be had for repairs which merely preserve the property, without increasing its value in the owner's hands. Bank v. Miller, 44 La. Ann. 199, 10 So. 779.

[114] Wykoff v. Wykoff, 3 W. & S. 481; and see Gordon v. Hall, 29 Tex. Civ. App. 230, 69 S. W. 219.

[115] *United States:* Young v. Mahoning County, 53 Fed. 895.
Arkansas: Greer v. Fontaine, 71 Ark. 605, 77 S. W. 56.
Georgia: Thomas v. Thallon, 39 Ga. 328.
Iowa: Childs v. Shower, 18 Ia. 261; McMurray v. Day, 70 Ia. 671, 28 N. W. 476.
Mississippi: Hicks v. Blakeman, 74 Miss. 459, 21 So. 7, 400.

The expenditure must have been made by the defendant himself, and not by a predecessor in title.[116] For this reason the defendant cannot recover, as for improvements placed there by him, on account of a church placed on the land by popular subscription.[117]

§ 918. Payment of necessary expenses by the defendant.

The payment of taxes by the defendant presents itself in several aspects. Such payments cannot be recovered as expenditures for the improvement of the property. It is generally agreed that such payments are properly included in those expenses which the defendant may deduct from the gross profits of the land.[118]

A third question, however, involving a different principle, often arises. When there are no mesne profits, may the defendant set up a counter-claim for taxes paid by him? It is really a question of whether the defendant could in an independent action recover for the money thus paid for the benefit of the plaintiff's land. Under ordinary circumstances, such payments by one occupying the position of a disseizor are not to be protected by the law, and cannot be recovered or set off.[119]

Nebraska: Fletcher v. Brown, 35 Neb. 660, 53 N. W. 577; Lathrop v. Michaelson, 44 Neb. 633, 63 N. W. 28.

North Carolina: Carolina Cent. R. R. v. McCaskill, 98 N. C. 526, 4 S. E. 468.

South Carolina: Harman v. Harman, 54 S. C. 100, 31 S. E. 881.

Tennessee: Fisher v. Edington, 85 Tenn. 23, 1 S. W. 499.

Virginia: Hollingsworth v. Funkhouser, 85 Va. 448, 8 S. E. 592.

So no recovery can be had for the expense of fertilizing the land. Crummey v. Bentley, 114 Ga. 746, 40 S. E. 765.

The value of the improvements when they were made is also immaterial. Taylor v. James, 109 Ga. 327, 34 S. E. 674.

In Petit v. Flint & P. M. R. R., 119 Mich. 492, 78 N. W. 554, 75 Am. St. Rep. 417, it was said that the test must be whether the land would sell for more with the improvements although they might not be adapted to the use to which plaintiff intended to put it.

[116] Schettler v. Southern Oregon Co., 19 Ore. 192, 24 Pac. 25 (*semble*).

See, however, Mills v. Geer, 111 Ga. 275, 36 S. E. 673.

[117] Crummey v. Bentley, 114 Ga. 746, 40 S. E. 765.

[118] *United States:* Semple v. Bank of British Columbia, 5 Sawy. 394, 403; Stark v. Starr, 1 Sawy. 15.

Illinois: Ringhouse v. Keener, 63 Ill. 230.

[119] *United States:* Homestead Co. v. Valley R. R., 17 Wall. 153, 21 L. ed. 622.

Missouri: Napton v. Leaton, 71 Mo. 358.

New York: Marvin v. Lewis, 61 Barb. 49.

But where the defendant was a transferee from a vendor whose vendee brought suit and recovered the land, the defendant being declared trustee, the defendant was held to be entitled, under the circumstances, to reimbursement for taxes, paid to protect the title.[120] A payment of ground rent by the defendant was allowed to be deducted from the sum of damages, as a payment which the plaintiff would himself have had to pay;[121] and so for the same reason was the expense of improvements ordered by a board of health.[122]

§ 919. Interest on mesne profits.

Interest is allowed on mesne profits as damages for delay in paying them.[123] Interest on loss by depreciation caused by waste should run from the time when the plaintiff was let into possession to the date of the assessment or report.[124] And where repairs were made, not only the expense of the repairs, but also interest on such expense is to be deducted from the gross profits.[125] * It seems a general principle that a mortgagee in possession is not to pay interest on rents unless there are special circumstances rendering it equitable that he should do so.[126] **

§ 920. Costs and counsel fees.

* The legal costs of the ejectment suit are also recoverable in this action.[127] Where the ejectment suit has been defended, and the plaintiff's costs taxed, he cannot recover beyond those

In Minnesota, a statute allowing recovery has been held constitutional. Madland v. Beuland, 24 Minn. 372; see Flint v. Douglass, 28 Kan. 414.

[120] United States: Sherman v. Savery, 2 McCrary, 107.

New York: Duffy v. Donovan, 52 N. Y. 634.

[121] Doe v. Hare, 4 Tyr. 29.

[122] Ringhouse v. Keener, 63 Ill. 230.

[123] United States: New Orleans v. Gaines, 15 Wall. 624, 21 L. ed. 215.

Michigan: Lane v. Ruhl, 103 Mich. 38, 61 N. W. 347.

New York: Jackson v. Wood, 24 Wend. 443; Vandevoort v. Gould, 36 N. Y. 639; Low v. Purdy, 2 Lans. 422.

Pennsylvania: Drexel v. Man, 2 Pa. St. 271, 44 Am. Dec. 195; Sopp v. Winpenny, 68 Pa. 78.

Virginia: Bolling v. Lersner, 26 Gratt. 36.

Interest may be allowed, in the discretion of the jury: Heger v. De Groat, 3 N. D. 354, 56 N. W. 150.

[124] Worrall v. Munn, 38 N. Y. 137.

[125] New Orleans v. Gaines, 15 Wall. 624, 21 L. ed. 215.

[126] United States: Story v. Livingston, 13 Pet. 359, 10 L. ed. 200.

Kentucky: Breckenridge v. Brooks, 2 A. K. Marsh, 335.

[127] Aslin v. Parkin, 2 Burr. 665; Sayer 88.

taxed costs; [128] ** but where judgment in ejectment was obtained by default, reasonable counsel fees were allowed.[129] * So in the King's Bench,[130] the plaintiff was allowed to recover, by way of damages, the costs incurred by him in a court of error in reversing a judgment in ejectment obtained in the first place by the defendant; and Lord Tenterden said: "There can be no doubt that the court of error could not award costs to the plaintiff. But the expenses incurred in the court of error were part of the damages sustained by the plaintiff; and I think that the jury might reasonably consider the costs between attorney and client, as the measure of the damages which he had sustained." [131] **

The same rule as to allowing the costs of the ejectment which was laid down by Lord Mansfield, has been declared in some States in this country; [132] in others, counsel fees in the ejectment suit are not allowed.[133]   Where the two actions are combined in one there can of course be no recovery of counsel fees.

§ 921. Dower.

* Where the husband of a woman is seized of an estate of inheritance and dies, the wife is entitled to the third part of all

[128] Doe v. Davis, 1 Esp. 358; Brooke v. Bridges, 7 Moore, 471; Doe v. Filliter, 13 M. & W. 47.

[129] Doe v. Huddart, 4 Dowl. Pr. 437; s. c. 5 Tyr. 846.

[130] Nowell v. Roake, 7 B. & C. 404.

[131] See, also, Symonds v. Page, 1 Cr. & J. 29, and Doe v. Hare, 2 Dowl. P. C. 245. But in a case where the costs were not included in the verdict, the Court of King's Bench refused to assist the plaintiff. Gulliver v. Drinkwater, 2 T. R. 261.

[132] *Arkansas:* Brooke v. Bridges, 7 Moore, 471.

New Hampshire: Fowler v. Owen, 68 N. H. 270, 39 Atl. 329.

New York: Baron v. Abeel, 3 Johns. 481, 3 Am. Dec. 515.

Texas: McRae v. White (Tex. Civ. App.), 42 S. W. 793.

Canada: Patterson v. Reardon, 7 Up. Can. Q. B. 326.

The plaintiff should be compensated for whatever expense he incurred in good faith in regaining the land by legal means: Doe v. Perkins, 8 B. Mon. 198.

[133] *New Jersey:* Pike v. Daly, 54 N. J. L. 4, 23 Atl. 7 (overruling Denn v. Chubb, 1 N. J. L. 466).

North Dakota: Heger v. De Groat, 3 N. D. 354, 56 N. W. 150.

Pennsylvania: Alexander v. Herr, 11 Pa. 537.

Rhode Island: Herreshoff v. Tripp, 15 R. I. 92, 23 Atl. 104, 2 Am. St. Rep. 879.

Tennessee: White v. Clack, 2 Swan, 230.

In Hunt v. O'Neill, 44 N. J. L. 564, costs are allowed in the ejectment suit, though judgment is given by default, if it appears that the defendant was in possession; if it does not appear, costs must be obtained in an action for mesne profits.

the lands and tenements whereof he was seized at any time during the coverture, to hold for the term of her natural life.[134] "A dowress," says Mr. Park,[135] "having no right of entry till her dower is assigned, cannot, if an assignment is refused, maintain a possessory action."[136] In England the legal remedy to enforce an assignment of dower is by a writ of dower, *unde nihil habet*, or by a writ of right of dower, upon which, if she obtains judgment, dower is assigned, and ejectment may then be brought. In consequence, however, of the jurisdiction assumed by courts of equity in regard to setting out dower, the prosecution of a writ of dower has become very unusual, except where it is ordered by Chancery to try a disputed title.[137]

"Dower being a real action," says Mr. Park,[138] "no damages were at the common law recoverable for its detention." "No damages," says Mr. Sayer,[139] "are recoverable, either at the common law or under any statute, in an action of right of dower." But in the action of dower *unde nihil habet*, damages were given by the statute of Merton. This act gave damages to widows who *could not have their dower without plea*. A previous demand was, therefore, necessary, and in an action[140] under this statute, where the jury upon a writ of inquiry assessed damages to the amount of the third part of the value of the land, from the death of the husband to the day of the inquisition, without making deductions for land-tax, repairs or chief-rents, the inquisition was set aside on the two grounds, that these deductions should have been made, and that the damages should have been assessed to the day of awarding the writ of inquiry only; but on this latter point there are conflicting decisions, and the contrary rule seems now to be established.[141]

---

[134] 2 Black. Com. 129.

[135] A Treatise on the Law of Dower, by John James Park, London, 283.

[136] On a plea of *tout temps prist* to a declaration in dower under the statute of Merton, replication of a demand and refusal to render dower before the writ, rejoinder traversing the demand, and issue thereon found for the demandant, the demandant is entitled to damages from the death of her husband, and not

from the date of the demand only. Watson *v.* Watson, 10 C. B. 3.

[137] The writ of right of dower is of rare occurrence if not entirely unknown in this country. 4 Kent's Com. 63.

[138] Park on Dower, 301.

[139] Ch. 6, p. 23.

[140] Penrice *v.* Penrice, Barnes' Notes, 3d ed., 234.

[141] Pilford's case, 10 Co. 115; Walker

It appears that by damages under this statute are to be understood the net profits of the third part of the land subsequent to the death of the husband, or the teste of the original writ, after deducting outgoings.[142] So, if the lands are leased for years before marriage, the wife will recover dower not according to the value of the land, but according to the rents; and it follows that if the rent reserved was nominal, no damages, or none but nominal damages can be recovered.[143] **

* Many other cases have been decided on the statute of Merton, which will be found in Mr. Park's valuable treatise above cited; but equity having, as already said, obtained a very extensive control over the subject of dower, it does not appear necessary to do more than to refer to a repository of the authorities which appertain to this branch of the law.[144] **

In New York, the action of ejectment was early substituted for the former legal remedies for the recovery of dower, writs of dower being formally abolished;[145] and, in this action, it is provided, by statute, that "where a widow recovers dower in property of which her husband died seized, she may also recover, in the same action, damages for withholding her dower to the amount of one-third part of the annual value of the mesne profits of the property, with interest, to be computed, where the action is against the heir, from her husband's death, or where it is against any other person, from the time when she demanded her dower of the defendant; and in each case to the time of the trial, or application for judgment, as the case may be, but not exceeding six years in the whole." Such damages are not to be estimated, however, for the use of any permanent improvements made after the death of the husband, by his heirs or by other persons claiming title.[146]

* It is further enacted that where dower is recovered in

and Nevil's case, 1 Leon. 56; Park on Dower, 308, and cases there cited.

[142] The rule is the same under the American statutes: O'Ferrall v. Simplot, 4 Ia. 381; Rea v. Rea, 63 Mich. 257.

[143] Hitchens v. Hitchens, 2 Vern. 403.

[144] In South Carolina and Ohio, no damages are allowed in a judgment of dower, and the rule prescribed in the statute of Merton is not adopted nor followed. Heyward v. Cuthbert, 1 McCord, 386; Bank of U. S. v. Dunseth, 10 Ohio, 18.

[145] 2 R. S. 343, § 24; 2 R. S. 304, § 2.

[146] Co. Civ. Proc., § 1600.

lands that have been aliened by the heir, the wife shall be entitled, in an action on the case against the heir, to recover her damages for withholding the dower from the time of the husband's death to the time of the alienation, not exceeding six years in all; and any damages so recovered against the heir, or in the dower suit against the heir's grantee, are to be respectively deducted from each other.[147] The provision which gives damages from the time of the husband's death, is an affirmance of the doctrine laid down by the Supreme Court of New York in an early case.[148] The construction of this statute has been settled;[149] and it has been held that where lands were aliened by the husband, the value was to be computed as at the time of the alienation, and no more; and it was further held, that when the widow brings ejectment for dower, although before admeasurement, she is entitled to costs.[150] **

According to the modern practice, the widow is entitled to her share of the rents and profits from the time she demands her dower;[151] and if there is no formal demand, then from the time she brings suit.[152] As in the ordinary case of ejectment, the actual profits received by the defendant do not fix his

[147] Co. Civ. Proc., § 1603. In Virginia, the widow recovers damages against an alienee so far forth as profits are concerned, only from the date of the subpœna. Tod v. Baylor, 4 Leigh, 498. In Maryland, from the time of the demand and refusal to assign; Steiger v. Hillen, 5 G. & J. 121, 25 Am. Dec. 276. In New Jersey, see Woodruff v. Brown, 17 N. J. L. 246.

[148] Hitchcock v. Harrington, 6 Johns. 290. See, also, Jackson v. O'Donaghy, 7 Johns. 247; Humphrey v. Phinney, 2 Johns. 484; Dorchester v. Coventry, 11 Johns. 510; Dolf v. Basset, 15 Johns. 21; Shaw v. White, 13 Johns. 179; Coates v. Cheever, 1 Cow. 460.

[149] Walker v. Schuyler, 10 Wend. 480, 25 Am. Dec. 574.

[150] In Massachusetts, see on this subject Leonard v. Leonard, 4 Mass. 533; Miller v. Miller, 12 Mass. 454; Conner

v. Shepherd, 15 Mass. 164, 167; Ayer v. Spring, 10 Mass. 80; Perry v. Goodwin, 6 Mass. 498, 499; Leavitt v. Lamprey, 13 Pick. 382, 23 Am. Dec. 685; Stearns v. Swift, 8 Pick. 532.

[151] *Illinois:* Bedford v. Bedford, 136 Ill. 354, 26 N. E. 662.
Florida: Roan v. Holmes, 32 Fla. 295, 13 So. 339, 21 L. R. A. 180.
Maine: McAllister v. Dexter & P. R. R., 106 Me. 371, 76 Atl. 891, 29 L. R. A. (N. S.) 726.
If the land is subject to a mortgage, the widow would be charged with her share of the interest. See Hodges v. Phinney, 106 Mich. 537, 64 N. W. 477.

[152] *Illinois:* Bonner v. Peterson, 44 Ill. 253; Marsh v. Irwin, 168 Ill. 50, 47 N. E. 768.
Massachusetts: Whitaker v. Greer, 129 Mass. 417.

liability, but the fair rental value of the land.[153]   The present productive value of the land is the basis, not its value at the time the defendant acquired it, so that the widow obtains the benefit of a general rise in value.[154]   The recovery of mesne profits by the widow is merely incidental to her recovery of the land itself; consequently if she dies before judgment her executor cannot maintain the suit even for the mesne profits.[155]

Where the land cannot be divided the widow may in some jurisdictions be given a money judgment in lieu of dower.   In such a case she is entitled to interest on this gross amount from the time it should have been paid her.[156]

§ 922. Dower in improvements.

Mr. Justice Story, on the Massachusetts circuit;[157] held that when the heir builds on or otherwise improves the estate, the widow shall have her dower of the improvements, otherwise as against a purchaser; but that as against the latter the dowress is to have the benefit of any enhanced value of the land between the alienation and the assignment of dower, arising from the general progress and population of the country; and, if the land has depreciated, she sustains the loss.[158] On the other hand, Chancellor Kent, who critically examined the subject in his Commentaries, declared it to be the ancient and settled rule of the common law, that the widow takes her

[153] *Florida:* Henderson v. Chaires, 35 Fla. 423, 17 So. 574.

Maine: McAllister v. Dexter & P. R. R., 106 Me. 371, 76 Atl. 891, 29 L. R. A. (N. S.) 726.

[154] *District of Columbia:* Baden v. Mc-Kenney, 18 D. C. 268.

Missouri: Young v. Thrasher, 115 Mo. 222, 21 S. W. 1104.

[155] Roan v. Holmes, 32 Fla. 295, 13 So. 339, 21 L. R. A. 180.

[156] *Alabama:* Ware v. Owens, 42 Ala. 212, 94 Am. Dec. 672 (from death of husband).

Kentucky: Hogg v. Hensley, 100 Ky. 719, 39 S. W. 247 (from demand).

South Carolina: Jefferies v. Allen, 34 S. C. 189, 13 S. E. 365 (from death of husband)

[157] Powell v. Monson & B. M. Co., 3 Mason, 347.

[158] Legett v. Steele, 4 Wash. C. C. 305; Coke's Littleton, 32a; Perkins, Dower, §§ 328, 329; Bacon's Abr. Dower, B. 5; Gilbert's Tenures; Gore v. Braizer, 3 Mass. 523, 534; Catlin v. Ware, 9 Mass. 218.   But in New York the point seems doubtful.   Humphrey v. Phinney, 2 Johns. 484; Dorchester v. Coventry, 11 Johns. 510; Shaw v. White, 13 Johns. 179; Hale v. James, 6 Johns. Ch. 258; Roper, Husband and Wife, ch. 9, § 2, 346, 347.   In Pennsylvania and Ohio, Mr. Justice Story's doctrine is upheld.   Dunseth v. Bank of the U. S., 6 Ohio, 76; Thompson v. Morrow, 5 S. & R. 289.

dower according to the value of the land at the time of the alienation, and not according to its value as increased by subsequent improvements; though he assented as to the right of the dowress to be allowed for increased value arising from extrinsic or general causes.[159]

The modern authorities appear to exclude from the computation of net value all improvements placed upon the land since its alienation by the husband or since his death.[160]

---

[159] 4 Kent Com. 65. See Tod v. Baylor, 4 Leigh, 498, in Virginia, which excludes improvements. Wilson v. Oatman, 2 Blackf. 223; Mahoney v. Young, 3 Dana, 588; Wall v. Hill, 7 Dana, 172; Wooldridge v. Wilkins, 3 Howard (Miss.), 360. In Virginia, the act, 1 Rev. Code, ch. 118, § 1, 468, which authorizes the recovery of damages in writs of right, intends such damages as may be recovered in actions of trespass for mesne profits. Purcell v. Wilson, 4 Gratt. 16. See Garrard v. Tuck, 8 C. B. 231 (dower *unde nihil habet*), where it was held that the exact number of acres of land in respect of which dower is demanded is not material in a writ and count in dower. And see the same case as to the effect of outstanding terms, and setting aside and quashing writs of error.

[160] *District of Columbia:* Baden v. McKenney, 18 D. C. 268.

Indiana: Davis v. Hutton, 127 Ind. 481, 26 N. E. 187, 1006.

Missouri: Thomas v. Mallinckrodt, 43 Mo. 58; O'Flaherty v. Sutton, 49 Mo. 583; Griffin v. Regan, 79 Mo. 73; Rannels v. Washington Univ., 96 Mo. 226, 9 Am. St. Rep. 344, 9 S. W. 569; Young v. Thrasher, 115 Mo. 222, 21 S. W. 1104.

CHAPTER XLI

WRONGFUL INTERFERENCE WITH REAL PROPERTY

I.—GENERAL PRINCIPLES

§ 923. Injuries to real property, how compensated.
924. Single or continuing tort.
924a. Permanent tort.
925. Loss of support of land.
926. Recovery by owner of limited interest.

§ 927. Consequential damages.
928. Inevitable loss through other causes.
929. Aggravation.
929a. Reduction and mitigation.
930. Exemplary damages.
930a. Treble damages.

II.—TRESPASS

§ 931. Right of action.
932. General rule.
933. Destruction of trees.
934. Value enhanced by defendant's labor.
934a. The rule in Wisconsin.
935. Removal of minerals.
935a. Removal or destruction of buildings.
935b. Other severance from the realty.
936. Accounts between owners.
937. Destruction of annual crops.

§ 937a. Destruction of permanent crops.
938. Destruction of fences.
939. Removal of soil.
940. Mills and flowage.
941. Diversion or obstruction of water — Avoidable consequences.
942. Flooding land.
943. Removal of chattels.
944. Other injuries to real property.
945. Cattle damage feasant.

III.—NUISANCE

§ 946. Special damage necessary.
947. General rule.

§ 948. Removable nuisance—Elements of loss.
949. Liability and right of recovery.

IV.—WASTE

§ 950. Action of waste.

I.—GENERAL PRINCIPLES

§ 923. Injuries to real property, how compensated.

* We have already seen,[1] when treating of the subject of nominal damages, that every unauthorized entry on the real

---

[1] See ch. vi.

estate of another, whether actual injury be or be not thereby inflicted, lays the foundation for a claim to at least nominal damages. So, says the Supreme Court of Connecticut,[2] "An injury, legally speaking, consists of a wrong done to a person, or, in other words, a violation of his right. For the vindication of every right there is a remedy. Where, therefore, there has been a violation of a right, the person injured is entitled to an action. If he is entitled to an action he is entitled to at least nominal damages, or else he would not be entitled to a recovery. Such damages are given in order to vindicate the right which has been invaded; and such further damages are awarded as are proper to remunerate him for any specific damage which he has sustained. It is upon this principle that a person may sustain an action of trespass for an unauthorized entry on his land, although he shows no actual specific damage to have thereby accrued to him; or even although the defendant may prove that such act was beneficial to the plaintiff." And we have also considered the rules of compensation where the possession of real property has been wrongfully withheld. The present division of our subject is consequently reduced to narrow limits.

As a general rule, the remedy for illegal entries upon real estate, or interference with its enjoyment, is either by an action of trespass, or trespass on the case, or proceedings as for nuisance; in all these proceedings the rules are analogous, and the measure of damages is the amount of injury directly resulting from the wrong complained of.**

§ 924. Single or continuing tort.

We have already examined [3] the distinction between a continuing and a permanent tort. The general rule has been seen to be that where the result of a single wrongful act is an

---

[2] Parker v. Griswold, 17 Conn. 288, 302, 42 Am. Dec. 739.

See to the same effect the following cases:

Alabama: C. W. Zimmerman Mfg. Co. v. Daffin, 147 Ala. 275, 42 So. 858.

New York: New York Rubber Co. v. Rothery, 132 N. Y. 293, 30 N. E. 841.

North Carolina: Sanderlin v. Shaw, 6 Jones, 225.

Texas: Carter v. Wallace, 2 Tex. 206.

Wisconsin: Murphy v. Fond du Lac, 23 Wis. 365; Drummond v. Eau Claire, 85 Wis. 556, 55 N. W. 1028.

[3] §§ 91–95.

injury the effects of which will continue indefinitely, all damages, both past and prospective, may be recovered; but when the wrongful act produces a state of affairs, every moment's continuance of which is a new tort, recovery can be had only for damages caused by the continuance of the tort *to the date of the writ*.

"Every continuance of a nuisance is held to be a fresh one, and therefore a fresh action will lie." [4]   Blackstone,[5] speaking of the same subject, says: "Very exemplary damages will probably be given, if, after one verdict against him, the defendant has the hardiness to continue it." [6]   It follows, therefore, that where the wrong is regarded as completed and not as continuing, damages can be recovered only for the wrong as so defined and limited.   For example, a trespass which results in an ouster is but a single trespass; and until another entry has been made by the plaintiff, he can recover for the single trespass only.[7]   On the other hand, a nuisance continues momentarily, and a separable wrong occurs each moment; so that damages may be recovered up to the time of bringing action.[8]   And for a continuing trespass, or one repeated from

[4] 3 Black. Com. 220; Vedder v. Vedder, 1 Denio, 257. So, also, in New Jersey. Delaware & Raritan Canal Co. v. Wright, 21 N. J. L. 469.

[5] 3 Bl. Com., ch. xiii.

[6] "If the party, against whom a verdict in an action of this kind has been recovered, does not abate the nuisance, another action may be brought for continuing the nuisance, in which the jury will be directed to give large damages." 2 Selw. N. P. 1130.

[7] *Kentucky:* Shields v. Henderson, 1 Lit. 239.

New York: Case v. Shepherd, 2 Johns. Cas. 27; Holmes v. Seely, 19 Wend. 507.

Ohio: Rowland v. Rowland, 8 Ohio, 40.

England: Holcomb v. Rawlyns, Cro. Eliz. 540; Monckton v. Pashley, 2 Ld. Raym. 974, s. c. 2 Salk. 638; 3 Bl. Com. 210.

[8] *Alabama:* Hughes v. Anderson, 68 Ala. 280, 44 Am. Rep. 138.

Arkansas: St. Louis S. W. Ry. v. Mackey, 95 Ark. 297, 129 S. W. 78.

California: Ford v. Santa Cruz R. R., 59 Cal. 290.

Georgia: Langley v. Augusta, 118 Ga. 590, 45 S. E. 486.

Illinois: Chicago, B. & Q. R. R. v. Schaffer, 26 Ill. App. 280; Canteen, H. & F. Assoc. v. Schwartz, 128 Ill. App. 224.

Iowa: Shirely v. Cedar Rapids I. F. & N. Ry., 74 Ia. 169, 37 N. W. 133; Vogt v. Grinnell, 123 Ia. 332, 98 N. W. 782.

Kansas: Kansas City v. Frohwerk, 10 Kan. App. 120, 62 Pac. 432.

Maine: Cole v. Sprowl, 35 Me. 161, 56 Am. Dec. 696.

Maryland: Aberdeen v. Bradford, 94 Md. 670, 51 Atl. 614.

Minnesota: Carli v. Union Depot Co., 32 Minn. 101, 20 N. W. 89.

Missouri: Benson v. Chicago & A. R. R., 78 Mo. 504.

time to time, or for an act which may result in harm but is not in itself necessarily injurious, or one the continuance of which is contingent, the plaintiff can recover damages to the date of his writ only.[9] The continuance of the trespass after the plaintiff brings his suit is a new cause of action for which a new action will lie;[10] and the action will lie though the statutory

New Jersey: Freeman v. Sayre, 48 N. J. L. 37, 2 Atl. 650.

New York: Blunt v. McCormick, 3 Den. 283; Fettretch v. Leamy, 9 Bosw. 510; Van Veghten v. Hudson R. P. T. Co., 103 App. Div. 130, 92 N. Y. Supp. 956.

Pennsylvania: Keppel v. Lehigh C. & N. Co., 200 Pa. 469, 50 Atl. 302.

South Carolina: Duncan v. Markley, 1 Harp. 276.

West Virginia: McHenry v. Parkersburg, 66 W. Va. 533, 66 S. E. 750, 29 L. R. A. (N. S.) 860.

[9] United States: Smith v. Gale, 137 U. S. 577, 34 L. ed. 792, 11 Sup. Ct. 185.

Alabama: Tennessee, C. I. & R. Co. v. Hamilton, 100 Ala. 252, 14 So. 167; Central of G. Ry. v. Windham, 126 Ala. 552, 28 So. 392.

Illinois: Chicago & A. R. R. v. Robbins, 159 Ill. 598, 43 N. E. 332; N. K. Fairbank Co. v. Bahre, 213 Ill. 636, 73 N. E. 322.

Iowa: Close v. Samm, 27 Ia. 503.

Maine: Attwood v. Bangor, 83 Me. 582, 22 Atl. 466.

Michigan: Addison F. M. Co. v. Lake S. & M. S. Ry., 160 Mich. 330, 125 N. W. 347.

Nebraska: Beatrice Gas Co. v. Thomas, 41 Neb. 662, 59 N. W. 925.

New Hampshire: Troy v. Cheshire R. R., 23 N. H. 83, 55 Am. Dec. 177.

New York: Matthews v. Delaware & H. C. Co., 20 Hun, 427; Hartman v. Tully P. L. Co., 71 Hun, 367, 25 N. Y. Supp. 24; Kenyon v. New York C. R. R., 29 App. Div. 80, 51 N. Y. Supp. 386.

North Carolina: Jones v. Kramer & Bros. Co., 133 N. C. 446, 45 S. E. 827.

Texas: Missouri, K. & T. Ry. v. Hopson, 39 S. W. 384.

Vermont: Whipple v. Fair Haven, 63 Vt. 221, 21 Atl. 533.

Wisconsin: Sherman v. Milwaukee R. R., 40 Wis. 645; Carl v. Sheboygan & F. du L. R. R., 46 Wis. 625, 1 N. W. 295; Winchester v. Stevens Point, 58 Wis. 350, 17 N. W. 547.

Contra, Michigan: Cubitt v. O'Dett, 51 Mich. 347, 16 N. W. 679.

In an action for injury to property caused by a mill which was erected near by, throwing dust, etc., on the premises, evidence of dust thrown subsequently to the commencement of the action was excluded, the court saying that if the injury done had been permanent and not connected with the subsequent acts, all damage, both before and after suit, could have been recovered; but that when the subsequent damages were produced by subsequent acts, those acts were not proper criteria of damage done before suit, which could alone be recovered in such an action. Cooper v. Randall, 59 Ill. 317.

[10] United States: Lindquest v. Union Pac. Ry., 33 Fed. 372.

Alabama: Louisville & N. R. R. v. Higginbotham, 153 Ala. 334, 44 So. 872.

Georgia: Savannah & O. C. Co. v. Bourquin, 51 Ga. 378.

Indiana: Valparaiso v. Moffit, 12 Ind. App. 250, 39 N. E. 909.

Iowa: Hunt v. Iowa Cent. R. R., 86 Ia. 15, 52 N. W. 668.

Minnesota: Hartz v. St. Paul R. R., 21 Minn. 358.

period has elapsed since the original act,[11] the statutory time
running from each new cause of action for that particular
action.[12]

Where an action is brought for an injunction against the
continuance of a nuisance, or for abatement by some other
method, in order not to make another action necessary, damages are recovered to the time the nuisance is abated, or to the
time of trial, not merely to the beginning of the action; [13] and
by statute in some jurisdictions damages for a continuing trespass may be recovered to the time of trial.[14]

§ 924a. Permanent tort.

On the other hand, if the injury is of a nature to be permanent, entire damages may be recovered.[15] So where the
defendant made unauthorized use of the plaintiff's party wall
by inserting in it girders and beams, which formed part of a
building erected by the defendant, it was held that the plaintiff
could recover entire damages, as for permanent use of the
wall.[16] So where the defendant maintained a brothel next
the plaintiff's dwelling-house, damages were awarded for the
permanent depreciation in value of the plaintiff's property.[17]
The question whether a tort is or is not permanent is one of
fact, to be decided by the circumstances of each case. The

Nebraska: Omaha & R. V. R. R. *v.* Standen, 22 Neb. 343, 35 N. W. 183.

Wisconsin: Carl *v.* Sheboygan R. R., 46 Wis. 625, 1 N. W. 295.

[11] *Florida:* Savannah, F. & W. Ry. *v.* Davis, 25 Fla. 917, 7 So. 29.

Michigan: Phelps *v.* Detroit, 120 Mich. 447, 79 N. W. 640.

Texas: Tietze *v.* International & G. N. R. R., 35 Tex. Civ. App. 136, 80 S. W. 124.

[12] Missouri Pac. Ry. *v.* Houseman, 41 Kan. 300, 21 Pac. 284.

[13] *New York:* Burditt *v.* New York C. & H. R. R. R., 24 N. Y. Supp. 1137; Beir *v.* Cooke, 37 Hun, 38.

Texas: Comminge *v.* Stevenson, 76 Tex. 642.

England: Fritz *v.* Hobson, 14 Ch. D. 542.

This rule is also applied where plaintiff after filing a bill in equity has sold the land, and is therefore no longer entitled to equitable relief. Cameron *v.* New York El. R. R., 23 Misc. 590, 52 N. Y. Supp. 1036.

[14] *North Carolina:* Dale *v.* Southern Ry., 132 N. C. 705, 44 S. E. 399.

Pennsylvania: Pantall *v.* Rochester & P. C. & I. Co., 204 Pa. 158, 53 Atl. 751; Tustin *v.* Sammons, 23 Pa. Super. Ct. 175.

Canada: Grant *v.* Wolf, 32 N. Sc. 46.

[15] §§ 91–95.

[16] Ritter *v.* Sieger, 105 Pa. 400.

[17] Givens *v.* Van Studdiford, 72 Mo. 129, affirming 4 Mo. App. 498.

presumption is, however, that a wrong will not continue, and therefore that a tort will not be a permanent one.[18] When the defendant trespasses on the plaintiff's land and injures the land by digging or by throwing dirt or erecting a structure upon it, the injury will ordinarily be regarded as permanent, because he can put an end to it only by another trespass.[19] Where, however, the trespass is upon a highway, though the title to the soil is in the plaintiff, the defendant may remove the cause of injury and the damage is therefore not permanent.[20] Where the defendant has the right by proper proceedings to condemn the land for the purpose for which he is using it the injury will also be deemed permanent.[21]

---

[18] Savannah & O. C. Co. v. Bourquin, 51 Ga. 378.

[19] *Illinois:* Chicago & A. R. R. v. Robbins, 159 Ill. 598, 43 N. E. 332.

Minnesota: Ziebarth v. Nye, 42 Minn. 541, 44 N. W. 1027.

Missouri: Walker v. Davis, 83 Mo. App. 374; Tegeler v. Kansas City, 95 Mo. App. 162, 68 S. W. 953.

New York: Vedder v. Vedder, 1 Den. 257.

North Carolina: Cherry v. Lake Drummond Co., 140 N. C. 422, 53 S. E. 138.

Pennsylvania: Ritter v. Sieger, 105 Pa. 400; Barley v. Mill Creek C. Co., 20 Pa. Super. Ct. 186; Hoffman v. Mill Creek C. Co., 16 Pa. Super. Ct. 631.

In the case of Vedder v. Vedder, 1 Den. 257, the plaintiff had a right of action against the defendant for a tortious entry by the latter on his land and committing a nuisance thereon, from which damages ensued. A release was given, and it was held that this discharge extinguished all right of action not only for the original injury and damages up to the time the release was given, but for all future damages; but that if the defendant had placed the nuisance on his own land, and the plaintiff's demand was for consequential damage only, a discharge of the plaintiff would not have extinguished

the right of action for future damages.

In a few cases where defendant's wall encroached on plaintiff's land it has been held that damages cannot be recovered as for a permanent injury.

Connecticut: McGann v. Hamilton, 58 Conn. 69, 19 Atl. 376.

New York: Stowers v. Gilbert, 156 N. Y. 600, 51 N. E. 282 (reversing 85 Hun, 468, 33 N. Y. Supp. 101).

And in one case permanent damages were refused for stringing telephone wires through plaintiff's land. Morrison v. American T. & T. Co., 115 App. Div. 744, 101 N. Y. Supp. 140.

[20] *Minnesota:* Hartz v. St. Paul & S. C. R. R., 21 Minn. 358.

New York: Hartman v. Tully P. L. Co., 71 Hun, 367, 25 N. Y. Supp. 24.

Wisconsin: Ford v. Chicago & N. W. R. R., 14 Wis. 609; Sherman v. Milwaukee L. S. R. R., 40 Wis. 645; Blesch v. Chicago & N. W. Ry., 43 Wis. 183; Carl v. Sheboygan & F. du L. R. R., 46 Wis. 625, 1 N. W. 295.

[21] *United States:* Lindquist v. Union Pac. Ry., 33 Fed. 372.

Florida: Jacksonville, T. & K. W. Ry. v. Lockwood, 33 Fla. 573, 15 So. 327.

Georgia: Cobb v. Wrightsville & T. R. R., 129 Ga. 377, 58 S. E. 862.

Illinois: Galt v. Chicago & N. W. Ry., 157 Ill. 125, 41 N. E. 643.

§ 925. Loss of support of land.

The question of the permanence of injury has been much discussed in actions brought for the loss of support of land. Where the defendant by digging in his own land causes the plaintiff's land to fall, the wrongful act is not the excavation, but the act of allowing the plaintiff's land to fall.[22] Consequently, whenever there is a fall of the land there is a new tort. The case is the same where the plaintiff has an easement of support for a structure, which the defendant fails to support.

It is clear that a claim for damages caused by a new fall of the land is not barred by a recovery of damages for a previous fall. The injury is not a permanent one, in the sense that entire damages should be recovered for all falls likely to be caused by a single excavation. Recovery can be had only for damages caused by such falls of the land as occurred previously to bringing the action.[23]   In Mitchell v. Darley Main Colliery

Indiana: Porter v. Midland Ry., 125 Ind. 476, 25 N. E. 556; Pittsburgh, C. C. & S. L. Ry. v. Noftsker, 26 Ind. App. 614, 60 N. E. 372; Cincinnati R. & M. R. R. v. Miller, 36 Ind. App. 26, 72 N. E. 827.

Iowa: Donald v. St. Louis, K. C. & N. R. R., 52 Ia. 411.

Kentucky: Illinois Cent. R. R. v. Smith, 110 Ky. 203, 61 S. W. 2; Louisville v. Donahue, 131 S. W. 285.

Minnesota: Weaver v. Mississippi & R. R. B. Co., 28 Minn. 534, 11 N. W. 114; Byrne v. Minneapolis & S. L. Ry., 38 Minn. 212, 36 N. W. 339; Fossum v. Chicago, M. & S. P. Ry., 80 Minn. 9, 82 N. W. 979.

Missouri: Mueller v. St. Louis & I. M. R. R., 31 Mo. 262; Soulard v. St. Louis, 36 Mo. 553.

New Jersey: Central R. R. v. Hetfield 29 N. J. Law (5 Dutch.), 206.

New York: Cooper v. New York, L. & W. Ry., 122 App. Div. 128, 106 N. Y. Supp. 611.

Oklahoma: Norman v. Ince, 8 Okla. 412, 58 Pac. 632.

Pennsylvania: Truby v. American N. G. Co., 38 Pa. Super. Ct. 166.

Texas: Owens v. Missouri Pac. Ry., 67 Tex. 679, 4 S. W. 593; McFadden v. Schill, 84 Tex. 77, 19 S. W. 368; Heilbron v. St. Louis S. W. Ry. (Tex. Civ. App.), 113 S. W. 979.

Wisconsin: Davis v. La Crosse & M. R. R., 12 Wis. 16.

In Louisville v. Coleburne, 22 Ky. L. R. 64, 56 S. W. 681, damages for the permanent injury were refused in an action for changing the grade of a street.

In Hunt v. Johnson (Tex. Civ. App.), 129 S. W. 879, permanent damages were allowed for a nuisance caused by operating a gin, though it would seem that no right to operate it could have been obtained by eminent domain.

[22] Schultz v. Bower, 64 Minn. 123, 66 N. W. 139.

[23] *New Jersey:* McGuire v. Grant, 25 N. J. L. 356, 67 Am. Dec. 49.

Pennsylvania: McGettigan v. Potts, 149 Pa. 155, 24 Atl. 198.

Texas: Nading v. Denison & P. S. Ry. (Tex. Civ. App.), 62 S. W. 97.

England: Darley Main Colliery Co. v. Mitchell, 11 App. Cas, 127, affirming Mitchell v. Darley Main Colliery Co.,

Co.,[24] in the Court of Appeal, Brett, M. R., in reply to the argument that the cause of the new fall being the same as that of the previous fall, the action was barred, said: "It may be argued that the causa causans is not the same. The causa causans of the first is the excavation; the causa causans of the second is, as a matter of fact, the excavation unremedied, or the combination of the excavation and of its remaining unremedied." And to the same effect Lord Fitzgerald in the House of Lords said: [25] "There was a complete cause of action in 1868, in respect of which compensation was given, but there was a liability to further disturbance. The defendants permitted the state of things to continue without taking any steps to prevent the occurrence of any future injury. A fresh subsidence took place, causing a new and further disturbance of the plaintiff's enjoyment, which gave him a new and distinct cause of action." But though each new fall gives rise to a new action, and in that sense therefore the injury is a continuing one, yet recovery must be had in a single action for the entire damage, past and prospective, caused by the fall for which action is brought;[26] the measure of damages being ordinarily the diminution of value of the land caused by the fall,[27] but may include consequential damages, as for loss of business.[28]

14 Q. B. D. 125, and overruling Lamb v. Walker, 3 Q. B. D. 389.

Canada: Snarr v. Granite Curling & Skating Co., 1 Ont. 102.

See § 91.

[24] 14 Q. B. Div. 125, 134.

[25] 11 App. Cas. 127, 151.

[26] *Kentucky:* Maysville v. Stanton, 12 Ky. L. Rep. 586, 14 S. W. 675.

Maine: Rockland Water Co. v. Tillson, 69 Me. 255.

Michigan: Conlon v. McGraw, 66 Mich. 194.

Missouri: Williams v. Missouri Furnace Co., 13 Mo. App. 70.

[27] *Illinois:* Barry v. Chicago I. & S. L. S. L. Ry., 149 Ill. App. 626.

Indiana: Moellering v. Evans, 121 Ind. 195, 22 N. E. 989, 61 L. R. A. 449; Orr v. Dayton & M. T. Co., 96 N. E. 462.

Maine: Rockland Water Co. v. Tillson, 69 Me. 255.

Minnesota: Schultz v. Bower, 57 Minn. 493, 59 N. W. 631, 47 Am. St. Rep. 630, 64 Minn. 123, 66 N. W. 139.

Pennsylvania: Rabe v. Schoenberger Coal Co., 213 Pa. 252, 62 Atl. 854.

South Dakota: Ulrick v. Dakota L. & T. Co., 2 S. D. 285, 49 N. W. 1054, 3 S. D. 44, 51 N. W. 1023.

[28] *Maryland:* Shafer v. Wilson, 44 Md. 278.

New York: Schile v. Brokhalus, 80 N. Y. 614.

In White v. Dresser, 135 Mass. 150, 46 Am. Rep. 454, where defendant caused to fall land designed, though not to defendant's knowledge, for a burial place, it was held that plaintiff could not recover for injury to his feelings.

§ 926. Recovery by owner of limited interest.

We have seen [29] that the owner of a limited interest in land recovers such damages as have been caused to his own interest in the land. Thus a mere possessor recovers compensation merely for the injury to his possession; [30] while a person whose interest is a beneficial one, or who legally represents one beneficially interested, recovers the entire amount by which his interest is injured. [31] As between landlord and tenant any arrangement may be made as to repairs, or the recovery of damages for injury, and such an agreement would affect the amount of recovery by the tenant; [32] but in the absence of such arrangement each party is entitled to compensation for that portion of the damage which is to be felt during his period of enjoyment of the land. Thus a lessee recovers the whole amount of the injury, if it was in the nature of a temporary injury the effect of which must pass away before the end of the lease; [33] while if the effect of the injury would be felt after the termination of the lease, the lessee should recover the diminished value of the lease, leaving the reversioner to recover the injury to the re-

[29] §§ 69–75.

[30] Farnsworth v. Western U. T. Co., 6 N. Y. Supp. 735 (receiver).

[31] *Trustee:* De Camp v. Wallace, 45 Misc. 436, 92 N. Y. Supp. 746.

Owner of timber:

Georgia: Atlantic C. L. R. R. v. Davis, 5 Ga. App. 214, 62 S. E. 1022.

New York: De Camp v. Wallace, 45 Misc. 436, 92 N. Y. Supp. 746.

Rhode Island: Clarke v. New York, N. H. & H. R. R., 26 R. I. 59, 58 Atl. 245.

[32] Kernochan v. New York El. R. R., 128 N. Y. 565, 29 N. E. 65; Bly v. Edison Elec. Illuminating Co., 54 App. Div. 427, 66 N. Y. Supp. 737.

In McPhillips v. Fitzgerald, 76 App. Div. 15, 78 N. Y. Supp. 631, affirmed, 177 N. Y. 543, 69 N. E. 1126, it appeared that, while there was no agreement to that effect, the landlord, a religious corporation, was in the habit of renewing its leases. It was held that this fact might be shown as bearing upon the damage to a tenant caused by the destruction of a building on the premises belonging to him and removable by him before the end of the term.

[33] *Alabama:* Seaboard A. L. Ry. v. Brown, 158 Ala. 630, 48 So. 48.

Delaware: Nivin v. Stevens, 5 Harr. 272.

New Hampshire: George v. Fisk, 32 N. H. 32.

New York: Matter of Water Commissioners, 4 Edw. Ch. 545; Buddin v. Fortunato, 10 N. Y. Supp. 115; Dumois v. Mayor of New York, 37 Misc. 614, 76 N. Y. Supp. 161.

Pennsylvania: Duffield v. Rosenzweig, 144 Pa. 520, 23 Atl. 4.

Texas: Holland v. San Antonio, 23 S. W. 756.

Wyoming: Painter v. Stahley, 15 Wyo. 510, 90 Pac. 375.

The injury done to a tenant at will must be determined by the jury. Daniel v. Perkins Logging Co. (Ga. App.), 72 S. E. 438.

reversion.[34] Where the injury renders immediate repairs necessary the tenant may recover the cost of such repairs, in the absence of evidence of a contract by the landlord to repair,[35] and of course if the tenant were under contract with the landlord to repair.[36] So in an action for diverting water from a leased mill, the tenant recovers the diminution in the value of use of the water during the term, the landlord the injury to the reversion.[37]

A mortgagee recovers the diminution in value of his security;[38] and each mortgagee, where there are more than one, may sue and recover the damages he has sustained.[39] A mortgagor, on the other hand, may recover the entire damage[40] except what the mortgagee may have previously recovered:[41] and the same is true of a vendee in possession.[42]

§ 927. Consequential damages.

Recovery may be had for consequential damages on the principles already considered.[43] So where a trespass or other tort to the plaintiff's real estate proximately causes the loss of his property he may recover the value of it.[44] Thus in

[34] *Illinois:* Kankakee & S. R. R. *v.* Horan, 131 Ill. 288, 23 N. E. 621 (lessor gets depreciation in value though tenant at will in possession).

Iowa: Cotes *v.* Davenport, 9 Ia. 227.

Maine: Monroe *v.* Gates, 48 Me. 463 (temporary injury not affecting rent does not damage reversioner).

Massachusetts: Rockwood *v.* Robinsin, 159 Mass. 406, 34 N. E. 521 (tenant for life with power of sale may recover value of gravel taken).

New Hampshire: George *v.* Fisk, 32 N. H. 32.

New York: Conkling *v.* Manhattan Ry., 12 N. Y. Supp. 846.

See §§ 71, 74.

[35] *Missouri:* Burt *v.* Warne, 31 Mo. 296.

New York: Buddin *v.* Fortunato, 10 N. Y. Supp. 115.

Vermont: Weston *v.* Gravlin, 49 Vt. 507.

[36] Walter *v.* Post, 6 Duer, 363.

[37] Halsey *v.* Lehigh V. R. R., 45 N. J. L. 26, 46 Am. Rep. 750.

[38] § 73.

[39] Schalk *v.* Kingsley, 42 N. J. L. 32.

[40] Schuylkill Co. *v.* Thoburn, 7 S. & R. 411.

[41] Delaware & A. T. & T. Co. *v.* Elvins, 63 N. J. L. 243, 43 Atl. 903.

[42] Hueston *v.* Mississippi & R. R. B. Co., 76 Minn. 251, 79 N. W. 92.

[43] *Ante,* ch. vii.

[44] *Illinois:* Gray *v.* Waterman, 40 Ill. 522.

Iowa: Brown *v.* Webster City, 115 Ia. 511, 88 N. W. 1070 (excavation causing injury to trees and crops).

Michigan: Saginaw U. S. Ry. *v.* Michigan Cent. R. R., 91 Mich. 657, 52 N. W. 49 (destruction of armature by cutting wires).

North Carolina: Welch *v.* Pierce, 7 Ire. 365 (loss of hogs by breaking of fence).

Pennsylvania: Kissecker *v.* Monn, 36

trespass *quare clausum*, the plaintiff has been allowed to give
evidence of damage to his crop, occasioned by reason of the
defendant driving away his negroes.[45] Where a plaintiff's
business was broken up or injured through injury to his business
premises he may recover for the injury to the business.[46]
So where plaintiff was tenant of a house which was available
for letting windows to view public processions, and had let a
balcony on the first floor to view the funeral procession of
Edward VII, and the defendant illegally built a stand across
the end of the road which cut off the view from her window,
it was held that she could recover compensation for loss of
rentals.[47] So where a trespass is alleged to have been committed by the entry of diseased cattle, damage from infection
may be stated in aggravation; and so in Connecticut, in an action of trespass *quare clausum fregit*, where the defendant's
sheep, while trespassing on the plaintiff's land, mingled with
his sheep and communicated to them a dangerous disease
of which many died, it was held that the plaintiff might recover for the loss of his sheep as well as the breach of his close,

Pa. 313 (injury to land by trespassing
of cattle through gate opened by defendant).

Tennessee: Damron *v.* Roach, 4
Humph. 134 (loss of cattle by pulling
down fence).

Wisconsin: Weller *v.* Heimbruck, 145
Wis. 217, 129 N. W. 1067 (loss of crops
and pasturage by obstruction of right
of way).

Wyoming: Henderson *v.* Coleman,
115 Pac. 439 (loss of weight of cattle
by exclusion from pasture).

[45] Johnson *v.* Courts, 3 H. & McH.
(Md.) 510. So where defendant ob-
structed the right of way to farm land.
Weller *v.* Heimbruck, 145 Wis. 217, 129
N. W. 1067.

[46] *United States:* Day *v.* Woodworth,
13 How. 370, 14 L. ed. 181.

California: Hawthorne *v.* Siegel, 88
Cal. 159, 25 Pac. 1114.

Indiana: Simplex R. A. Co. *v.* Western R. & B. Co. (Ind. App.), 88 N. E.
682.

Maine: Hammat *v.* Russ, 16 Me. 171.

Maryland: Shafer *v.* Wilson, 44 Md.
268; see Scott *v.* Bay, 3 Md. 431.

Massachusetts: Pye *v.* Faxon, 156
Mass. 471, 31 N. E. 640.

Minnesota: Todd *v.* Minneapolis &
S. L. Ry., 39 Minn. 86, 39 N. W.
318.

New Mexico: De Palma *v.* Weinman,
103 Pac. 782.

New York: Marquart *v.* LaFarge, 5
Duer, 559; Colrick *v.* Swinburne, 105
N. Y. 503, 12 N. E. 427.

Ohio: Dayton *v.* Pease, 4 Oh. St. 80.

Oklahoma: Oklahoma City *v.* Hill, 4
Okla. 521, 50 Pac. 242; Choctaw O. &
G. R. R. *v.* Alexander, 7 Okla. 579, 52
Pac. 944.

Texas: De la Zerda *v.* Korn, 25 Tex.
Supp. 188.

Such damages must be specially alleged. Fleming *v.* Baltimore & O. R.
R., 51 W. Va. 54, 41 S. E. 168.

[47] Campbell *v.* Paddington, [1911] 1
K. B. 869.

and that the defendant's knowledge of the existence of the disease might properly be considered by the jury in estimating damages.[48] Where the injury results proximately in personal suffering by the plaintiff he may recover compensation for it.[49] Compensation is of course refused for consequences which were reasonably avoidable;[50] and the reasonable expense of avoiding consequences may therefore be recovered[51] But an uncertain or purely speculative loss cannot form the basis of recovery.[52] So a plaintiff whose docks are obstructed cannot show that certain individuals would otherwise have made purchases.[53]

In an action for depriving the plaintiff's cattle of pasturage, either by driving them out of their pasture or by destroying the pasturage with other cattle, plaintiff may recover compensation for loss of weight of his cattle,[54] and for the expense of feeding them otherwise.[55]

§ 928. Inevitable loss through other causes.

In an action in the nature of trespass *q. c. f.* to recover dam-

---

[48] Barnum v. Vandusen, 16 Conn. 200; *acc.*, Lee v. Burk, 15 Ill. App. 651.

[49] *Loss of an eye:* Hatchell v. Kimbrough, 4 Jones L. (N. C.) 163.

Mental suffering:

Rhode Island: Vogel v. McAuliffe, 18 R. I. 791, 31 Atl. 1 (anxiety because of illness caused to child).

Vermont: Moore v. Duke, 80 Atl. 194 (embarrassment of town clerk at inability to permit examination of public records taken by trespasser).

See, however, *Alabama:* Woodstock Iron Works v. Stockdale, 143 Ala. 550, 39 So. 335 (recovery refused for sympathetic suffering on account of illness caused to wife).

Where by reason of illness caused by a nuisance plaintiff was unable to plant seed, and it spoiled, the loss of the seed was held too remote. Smith v. San Antonio (Tex. Civ. App.), 57 S. W. 881.

[50] *Alabama:* Louisville & N. R. R. v. Sullivan Timber Co., 138 Ala. 379, 35 So. 327.

Georgia: Daniel v. Perkins Logging Co. (Ga. App.), 72 S. E. 438.

Maine: Fitzpatrick v. Boston & M. R. R., 84 Me. 33, 24 Atl. 432.

Michigan: Talley v. Courter, 93 Mich. 473, 53 N. W. 621.

And see ch. x, *passim.*

[51] *California:* Hawthorne v. Siegel, 88 Cal. 159, 25 Pac. 1114.

Michigan: Breen v. Hyde, 130 Mich. 1, 89 N. W. 732.

Mississippi: Silver Creek N. & I. Co. v. Mangum, 64 Miss. 682, 2 So. 11.

In *Wyoming:* Henderson v. Coleman, 115 Pac. 439, it was held that such expense could not be recovered without a special allegation.

[52] *Ante*, ch. ix.

[53] Garitee v. Baltimore, 53 Md. 422.

[54] *Michigan:* Gilbert v. Kennedy, 22 Mich. 117.

Wyoming: Henderson v. Coleman, 115 Pac. 439.

[55] Cosgriff v. Miller, 10 Wyo. 190, 68 Pac. 206.

ages for the plaintiff's house and furniture which were destroyed by a fire-warden for the purpose of staying a conflagration, it was said that the jury should estimate the value of the property with reference to the peril to which it was exposed, and give nominal damages only for that which could not have been saved.[56] In Maine there is a statute which gives the owner of property destroyed by a mob, a claim against the town for the injury. The value is taken at the time of the destruction. The fact that a destroyed building might have been indicted as a nuisance, cannot be shown in mitigation of damages.[57] Where a right to support exists, a party defendant, whose excavations have caused the plaintiff's building to fall, can show the defective construction of the building in reduction of damages, but such defective construction will not be a bar to the action.[58]

§ 929. Aggravation.

* If the defendant, while a trespasser on the plaintiff's land, commits any other distinct trespass for which a separate action would lie, yet such acts of trespass and their consequences may be alleged and proved in aggravation of damages.[59] Thus in an action for breaking and entering the plaintiff's house, the debauching of his daughter and servant, and the consequential damages to the plaintiff, may be laid in aggravation.[60] ** So spoliation or asportation of trees may be laid as aggravation

[56] Parsons v. Pettingell, 11 All. (Mass.) 507.

[57] Brightman v. Bristol, 65 Me. 426, 20 Am. Rep. 711.

[58] Stevenson v. Wallace, 27 Gratt. (Va.) 77.

[59] *District of Columbia:* Gorman v. Marsteller, 2 Cr. C. C. 311, Fed. Cas. No. 5,629 (trespass q. c. f. in the District of Columbia; may prove in aggravation that the trespass extended to lands outside the District).

Michigan: Fisher v. Dowling, 66 Mich. 370, 33 N. W. 521.

Minnesota: Spencer v. St. Paul & S. C. R. R., 22 Minn. 29.

A new act of aggravation after suit brought cannot be shown. Salmon v.

M. E. Blasier Mfg. Co., 123 App. Div. 171, 108 N. Y. Supp. 448.

[60] Starkie on Evidence, * 1451; Bennett v. Allcott, 2 T. R. 166; Wright v. Chandler, 4 Bibb (Ky.), 422. Sometimes the expression "aggravation of damages" is used where the act is really part of the trespass. So in Keenan v. Cavanaugh, 44 Vt. 268, where, through the defendant's failure to keep fences in repair, his cattle strayed into plaintiff's grounds, the court said that the plaintiff could recover for the entry, and that the plaintiff could show "in aggravation" of damages that the calf bit off some limbs of one of the plaintiff's trees, and broke another tree. Wheeler, J.: "The injury done

in this form of proceeding.[61] So it has been held that a plaintiff can recover in aggravation of damages for the carrying off of personal property, and the damages for the carrying off should be such as would be given in trover.[62] But where trespass was brought for breaking and entering the plaintiff's dwelling-house, and taking and carrying away certain goods and chattels, and converting and disposing of the same to the defendant's use, it not being averred that the chattels belonged to the plaintiff, the judge who tried the cause directed a verdict for the trespass only; and on a motion to increase the damages, this was held right.[63] If a plaintiff in trespass introduces evidence of matters which could be shown in aggravation, he can, of course, only recover in this action provided he first proves an entry.[64]

Damages may also be aggravated by compensation for humiliation and insult, invasion of privacy, interference with comfort, and other non-pecuniary injuries,[65] for slander,[66] and for assault upon persons on the land and exposing them to the weather;[67] and for the purpose of enabling the jury to

by the calf to the trees was an aggravation of the trespass committed by the entry, and although that injury may not be such as cattle are by nature wont to commit, nor of itself alone a trespass of the defendant, the damage done by it can be recovered with the damage done by the trespass it was a part of."

[61] Anderson v. Buckton, 1 Str. 192; Ridgely v. Bond, 18 Md. 433.

[62] *Massachusetts:* Warner v. Abbey, 112 Mass. 355.

Michigan: Wyant v. Crouse, 127 Mich. 158, 86 N. W. 527, 53 L. R. A. 626.

New York: Gaus v. Hughes, 16 N. Y. Supp. 615.

Such damages to be recovered must be specially alleged. Freelove v. Gould, 45 Pac. 454.

[63] Pritchard v. Long, 9 M. & W. 666. Where the owner of land had sold the defendant trees which he did not carry off in a reasonable time, but subsequently entered and carried them off,

the defendant was held liable for the trespass, but not for the value of the trees, for they had become the property of the defendant. Hoit v. Stratton Mills, 54 N. H. 109, 20 Am. Rep. 119.

[64] Brown v. Lake, 29 Oh. St. 64, 23 Am. Rep. 727.

[65] *Alabama:* Snedecor v. Pope, 143 Ala. 275, 39 So. 318; Bessemer L. & I. Co. v. Jenkins, 111 Ala. 135, 18 So. 565 (removal of body of plaintiff's child).

Connecticut: Davenport v. Russell, 5 Day, 145.

New Jersey: Ogden v. Gibbons, 2 South. (5 N. J. L.) 518, 853.

New York: Reed v. New York & R. G. Co., 93 App. Div. 453, 87 N. Y. Supp. 810.

[66] *Michigan:* Wyant v. Crouse, 127 Mich. 158, 86 N. W. 527, 53 L. R. A. 626.

England: Bracegirdle v. Orford, 2 M. & S. 77.

[67] *Alabama:* Snedecor v. Pope, 143 Ala. 275, 39 So. 318.

estimate such injuries the circumstances of the trespass and the malice and bad motives of the defendant may be shown.[68]

§ 929a. Reduction and mitigation.

As the circumstances of the trespass and malice on the part of the defendant may be shown to aggravate damages, so the good faith and circumstances that lack any aggravation may be shown in mitigation of non-pecuniary damages,[69] but not to mitigate pecuniary damages.[70] So circumstances which indicate that the property injured threatened the common weal may be shown to mitigate the damages.[71] In an action for wrongful use of land, damages will not be reduced by showing

Kansas: Mecartney v. Smith, 62 Pac. 540.

Michigan: Wyant v. Crouse, 127 Mich. 158, 86 N. W. 527, 53 L. R. A. 626.

[68] *Colorado:* Omaha & G. S. & R. Co. v. Tabor, 13 Colo. 41, 21 Pac. 925.

Connecticut: Treat v. Barber, 7 Conn. 274.

Georgia: Stevens v. Stevens, 96 Ga. 374, 23 S. E. 312.

Michigan: Druse v. Wheeler, 22 Mich. 439.

South Carolina: Johnson v. Hannahan, 3 Strob. 425.

Texas: Fort Worth & N. O. Ry. v. Smith (Tex. Civ. App.), 25 S. W. 1032.

Canada: Housberger v. Housberger, 5 U. C. Q. B. (O. S.) 479.

It has, however, been held error to instruct the jury that they have the right to consider the "moods" of defendant while upon the premises, in aggravation of the damages. Santford v. Dobyns, 17 Ky. L. Rep. 283, 30 S. W. 996.

[69] *Illinois:* Farwell v. Warren, 51 Ill. 467 (supposed permission).

Kansas: Mecartney v. Smith, 62 Pac. 540.

New Hampshire: Wallace v. Goodall, 18 N. H. 439 (ownership of trees on the land).

New York: Bohun v. Taylor, 6 Cow. 313 (search for missing property); Machin v. Geortner, 14 Wend. 239 (apparent right).

Ohio: Allen v. Champion, Wright, 672 (right to possession); Simpson v. M'Caffrey, 13 Ohio, 508 (suspicion of crime).

South Carolina: Caston v. Perry, 2 Bail. 104 (apparent title).

Wisconsin: Hazleton v. Week, 49 Wis. 661, 6 N. W. 309, 35 Am. Rep. 796.

In *Indiana* it was said that such evidence could be given in mitigation only of exemplary, not of "actual" damages. Moyer v. Gordon, 113 Ind. 282, 14 N. E. 476.

[70] *Connecticut:* Sutton v. Lockwood, 40 Conn. 318.

Maryland: Franklin Coal Co. v. McMillan, 49 Md. 549, 33 Am. Rep. 280.

New Hampshire: Howe v. Batchelder, 49 N. H. 209.

Pennsylvania: Huling v. Henderson, 161 Pa. 553, 29 Atl. 276.

Texas: Hillman v. Baumbach, 21 Tex. 203.

[71] *Iowa:* Abrams v. Ervin, 9 Ia. 87 (building destroyed was house of ill fame).

Pennsylvania: Reed v. Bias, 8 W. & S. 189 (building peaceably torn down under direction of public authorities in time of public disorder, to save neighborhood from threatened violence).

But see *Massachusetts:* Bliss v. Ball, 99 Mass. 597 (cannot show in mitigation of damages for cutting trees that

that the trespass benefited other property of the plaintiff.[72]
A reduction is occasionally provided by statute.[73]

§ 930. Exemplary damages.

The plaintiff is not restrained to the amount of the mere pecuniary loss sustained; he is always at liberty to give in evidence the circumstances which accompany and give character to the trespass. If the act be malicious or oppressive, exemplary damages may therefore be recovered;[74] but if there are no circumstances justifying the award the plaintiff is confined to compensatory damages.[75] So in Pennsylvania, where a party proceeded in the Common Pleas, under the act of that State, to obtain the right to enter on land of a third party to make a railroad, and after the value of the land of the plaintiff was fixed upon, but before judgment was given, proceeded to

the trees rendered defendant's house damp and unhealthy).

[72] *Connecticut:* Pinney v. Winsted, 83 Conn. 411, 76 Atl. 994.

Indiana: Turner v. Rising S. & L. T. Co., 71 Ind. 547.

Michigan: Fisher v. Naysmith, 106 Mich. 71, 64 N. W. 19.

Compare the allowance of benefits in eminent domain proceedings; *post,* ch. xlviii.

[73] Lyons v. Boston & L. R. R., 181 Mass. 551, 64 N. E. 404 (railroad company entitled to benefit of insurance upon property destroyed).

[74] *United States:* Day v. Woodworth, 13 How. 370, 14 L. ed. 181.

Alabama: Mitchell v. Billingsley, 17 Ala. 391; Goodson v. Stewart, 53 So. 239; Hicks v. Swift C. M. Co., 133 Ala. 411, 31 So. 947.

Delaware: Bonsall v. McKay, 1 Houst. 520; Jordan v. Delaware & A. T. Co., 75 Atl. 1014.

Illinois: Best v. Allen, 30 Ill. 30.

New York: Althouse v. Rice, 4 E. D. Sm. 347.

Tennessee: Wilkins v. Gilmore, 2 Humph. 140.

Wyoming: Henderson v. Coleman, 115 Pac. 439.

See *Indiana:* McCormack v. Showalter, 11 Ind. App. 98, 38 N. E. 875.

Ante, §§ 363a et seq.

No exemplary damages can be recovered against a municipal corporation. Ostrom v. San Antonio, 33 Tex. Civ. App. 683, 77 S. W. 829; *ante,* § 380b.

Ratification of a trespass committed by an agent is not a ground for exemplary damages. Leiter v. Day, 35 Ill. App. 248.

[75] *Illinois:* Waldron v. Marcier, 82 Ill. 550.

Indiana: Morford v. Woodworth, 7 Ind. 83.

Maryland: Strasburger v. Barber, 38 Md. 103.

Michigan: Baumier v. Antiau, 65 Mich. 31, 31 N. W. 888.

Mississippi: Illinois C. R. R. v. Hoskins, 80 Miss. 730, 32 So. 150.

Missouri: Ross v. New Home S. M. Co., 24 Mo. App. 353.

New York: Price v. Murray, 10 Bosw. 243.

Wisconsin: Scheer v. Kneisel, 109 Wis. 125, 85 N. W. 138.

Wyoming: Ladd v. Redle, 12 Wyo. 362, 75 Pac. 691.

enter, it was held that though this did not excuse the trespass, it took away all pretext for vindictive damages.[76]

930a. Treble damages.

Sometimes treble damages in the nature of exemplary damages are given by statute. They are not to be recovered unless the trespass was committed wilfully or maliciously.[77] The amount recovered is three times the actual injury at the time of injury, without regard to anything added by way of punishment, or forfeiture of labor expended on articles severed by the trespass.[78]

II.—TRESPASS

§ 931. Right of action.

* It is well settled in England, and generally in the United States, that to entitle the plaintiff to bring an action of trespass

[76] Harvey v. Thomas, 10 Watts, 63.

[77] *California:* Barnes v. Jones, 51 Cal. 303; Galvin v. Gualala M. Co., 98 Cal. 268, 33 Pac. 94 (jury may find actual damages, which the court may treble or the jury itself may find the treble damages).

Connecticut: Hart v. Brown, 2 Root, 301; Bateman v. Goodyear, 12 Conn. 575.

Kansas: Chicago K. & W. R. R. v. Watkins, 43 Kan. 50, 22 Pac. 985 (must be assessed by jury).

Massachusetts: Reed v. Davis, 8 Pick. 514.

Michigan: Wallace v. Finch, 24 Mich. 255; Michigan L. & I. Co. v. Deer Lake Co., 60 Mich. 143, 1 Am. St. Rep. 491, 27 N. W. 10; Longyear v. Gregory, 110 Mich. 277, 68 N. W. 116.

Montana: McDonald v. Montana Wood Co., 14 Mont. 88, 35 Pac. 668, 43 Am. St. Rep. 616.

New York: Robinson v. Kime, 70 N. Y. 147; O'Shaughnessy v. O'Rourke, 73 N. Y. Supp. 1070.

Oregon: Lowenburg v. Rosenthal, 18 Ore. 178, 22 Pac. 601.

Pennsylvania: Kramer v. Goodlander, 98 Pa. 353 (see O'Reilly v. Shadle, 33 Pa. 489).

Vermont: Brown v. Mead, 68 Vt. 215, 34 Atl. 950; Guild v. Prentis, 74 Atl. 1115 (must be trebled by court).

Washington: Gardner v. Lovegren, 27 Wash. 356, 67 Pac. 615.

Wisconsin: Cohn v. Neeves, 40 Wis. 393.

Interest cannot be allowed, as the damages are given as a penalty. McCloskey v. Ryder, 138 Pa. 383, 21 Atl. 150. But when the verdict itself includes interest, that also is to be trebled. Gates v. Comstock, 113 Mich. 127, 71 N. W. 515.

In *California* the allowance of treble damages is said to be discretionary with the court. Isom v. Rex C. O. Co., 140 Cal. 678, 74 Pac. 294; Isom v. Book, 142 Cal. 666, 76 Pac. 506.

Like exemplary damages, treble damages cannot be awarded against a municipal corporation. Hunt v. Boonville, 65 Mo. 620, 27 Am. Rep. 299.

[78] *Kentucky:* Stovall v. Smith, 4 B. Mon. 378.

Oregon: Oregon & C. R. R. v. Jackson, 21 Ore. 360, 28 Pac. 74.

See Newhouse M. & L. Co. v. Avery (Ark.), 140 S. W. 985.

quare clausum fregit, possession, in fact, is indispensable.[79] And as against a wrongdoer bare possession is sufficient.[80] And it results from the same rule, that if the trespass amount to an ouster of the plaintiff, he can recover damages only for the trespass itself, or first entry; for though every subsequent wrongful act is a continuance of the trespass, yet to enable the plaintiff to recover damages for these acts there must be a re-entry.[81] ** Nominal damages at least may be recovered; a mere technical trespass in the eye of the law, imports some damage.[8]

[79] 3 Wooddeson, 193, 194; Bedingfield *v.* Onslow, 3 Lev. 209. The general doctrine that trespass *quare clausum fregit* will not lie by lessor out of possession against a stranger for an injury to real property, is well settled in New York. Campbell *v.* Arnold, 1 Johns. 511; Wickham *v.* Freeman, 12 Johns. 183; unless where the plaintiff shows title to lands not in the actual possession of anyone; in which case the possession follows the title. Van Rensselaer *v.* Radcliffe, 10 Wend. 639, 25 Am. Dec. 582; Holmes *v.* Seely, 19 Wend. 507; and so in Massachusetts, Lienow *v.* Ritchie, 8 Pick. 235; French *v.* Fuller, 23 Pick. 104. And it is equally well settled in Ohio: Miller *v.* Fulton, 4 Oh. 433. And in Kentucky: Foster *v.* Fletcher, 7 T. B. Mon. 534; Owings *v.* Gibson, 2 A. K. Marsh. 515; Carrine *v.* Westerfield, 3 A. K. Marsh. 331. In Texas, also, a lessor cannot maintain an action for a trespass committed on the leased premises while in possession of the tenant: the lessee alone can sue. Reynolds *v.* Williams, 1 Tex. 311. In the ordinary case of carrying on a farm "at the halves," the owner is not so far divested of the possession, but that he may maintain trespass for injury to the inheritance. Cutting *v.* Cox, 19 Vt. 517. And if the plaintiff have the right of property, and of immediate possession, he may maintain trespass though not in actual possession. Mason *v.* Lewis, 1 Greene (Ia.)

494; Poole *v.* Mitchell, 1 Hill (S. C.), 404. In Connecticut, it has been decided that a plaintiff in trespass, having the sole and exclusive possession, may recover against a wrongdoer the whole damage done by him, though the conveyance from some of those under whom he claims was defective. Curtiss *v.* Hoyt, 19 Conn. 154, 48 Am. Dec. 149. So in *Illinois:* Smith *v.* Wunderlich, 70 Ill. 426. But see, as to the rules when an actual and when a constructive possession have been interrupted: McWilliams *v.* Morgan, 75 Ill. 473.

[80] *Connecticut:* Branch *v.* Doane, 18 Conn. 233, 44 Am. Dec. 586.

Massachusetts: First Parish in Shrewsbury *v.* Smith, 14 Pick. 297.

England: Chambers *v.* Donaldson, 11 East, 65; Graham *v.* Peat, 1 East, 244.

[81] *Kentucky:* Shields *v.* Henderson, 1 Litt. 239.

New York: Case *v.* Shepherd, 2 Johns. Cas. 27; Holmes *v.* Seely, 19 Wend. 507.

Ohio: Rowland *v.* Rowland, 8 Oh. 40.

England: Holcomb *v.* Rawlyns, Cro. Eliz. 540; Monckton *v.* Pashley, 2 Ld. Raym. 974, s. c. 2 Salk. 638; 3 Bl. Com. 210.

[82] *Maine:* Tuttle *v.* Walker, 46 Me. 280; Fitzpatrick *v.* Boston & M. R. R., 84 Me. 33, 24 Atl. 432.

Maryland: Baltimore & O. R. R. *v.* Boyd, 67 Md. 32, 10 Atl. 315, 1 Am. St. Rep. 362.

§ 932. General rule.

The general principle upon which compensation for injuries to real property is given, is that the plaintiff should be reimbursed to the extent of the injury to the property.[83] The injury caused by the defendant may be of a permanent nature; in such a case the measure of damages is the diminution in the market value of the property.[84] If the injury caused a total

Texas: Moore v. Smith, 19 S. W. 781.

West Virginia: Glen Jean R. R. v. Kanawha R. R., 47 W. Va. 725, 35 S. E. 978.

Ante, § 98.

[83] *Louisiana:* Redon v. Caffin, 11 La. Ann. 695.

New York: Smiles v. Hastings, 24 Barb. 44.

South Carolina: Jefcoat v. Knotts, 13 Rich. L. 50.

Texas: Ostrom v. San Antonio, 33 Tex. Civ. App. 683, 77 S. W. 829.

Canada: Caverhill v. Robillard, 2 Can. 575.

Nominal damages are to be given if no actual damages are proved.

California: Attwood v. Fricot, 17 Cal. 37.

New York: Fortescue v. Kings County Lighting Co., 128 App. Div. 826, 112 N. Y. Supp. 1010.

Ante, § 107.

No damages can be given on account of litigation expenses. Bendich v. Scobel, 107 La. 242, 31 So. 703.

[84] *United States:* Franklin v. Jackson, 30 Fed. 398 (laying tracks in street).

Alabama: Studenmire v. De Bardelaben, 85 Ala. 85; Gosdin v. Williams, 151 Ala. 592, 44 So. 611 (driving over land and cutting it up); Smith v. New Decatur, 166 Ala. 334, 51 So. 984 (changing grade of street); Buck v. Louisville & N. R. R., 159 Ala. 305, 48 So. 699 (laying tracks on land).

Colorado: Denver, T. & F. W. R. R. v. Dotson, 20 Colo. 304, 38 Pac. 322; Consolidated H. D. & R. Co. v. Hamlin, 6 Colo. App. 341, 40 Pac. 582 (leakage from ditch)

Georgia: Langley v. Augusta, 118 Ga. 590, 45 S. E. 486 (negligent construction of sewer).

Illinois: Donk Bros. C. & C. Co. v. Novero, 135 Ill. App. 633 (causing land to fall); Mohhard v. St. Louis, I. M. & S. Ry., 147 Ill. App. 81 (building embankment).

Indiana: Fort Wayne v. Hamilton, 132 Ind. 487, 32 N. E. 324; Baltimore & O. S. W. R. R. v. Quillen, 34 Ind. App. 330, 72 N. E. 661 (depositing earth).

Iowa: Harrison v. Adamson, 86 Ia. 693, 53 N. W. 334 (grazing land with cattle); Richardson v. Webster City, 111 Ia. 427, 82 N. W. 920 (changing grade of street); Cadle v. Muscatine W. R. R., 44 Ia. 11 (improper construction of street).

Kansas: Chicago, K. & W. R. R. v. Willits, 45 Kan. 110, 25 Pac. 576 (excavations on land); Fort Scott W. & W. Ry. v. Tubbs, 47 Kan. 630, 28 Pac. 612 (destruction of grass by fire); Atchison, T. & S. F. R. R. v. Briggs, 2 Kan. App. 154, 43 Pac. 289 (destruction of crop by fire); Missouri, K. & T. Ry. v. McDowell, 78 Kan. 686, 98 Pac. 201 (destruction of manure by fire).

Kentucky: Louisville v. Bohlsen, 61 S. W. 1014, 22 Ky. L. Rep. 1864 (changing grade of street); Louisville H. & S. L. Ry. v. Roberts, 139 S. W. 1073 (diverting water; question of permanence left to jury).

Maryland: Baltimore Belt R. R. v. McColgan, 83 Md. 650, 35 Atl. 59.

Massachusetts: Hopkins v. American P. S. Co., 194 Mass. 582, 80 N. E. 624 (causing land to fall).

or partial loss of the land for a limited time, the diminution in rental value is the measure.[85] One of these two measures

Michigan: Conlon *v.* McGraw, 66 Mich. 194, 33 N. W. 388 (destruction of building adjoining one in which plaintiff had leasehold interest; recover damages to end of plaintiff's term).

Minnesota: Karst *v.* St. Paul, S. & T. F. R. R., 22 Minn. 118; Baldwin *v.* Chicago, M. & S. P. Ry., 35 Minn. 354, 29 N. W. 5; Ziebarth *v.* Nye, 42 Minn. 541, 44 N. W. 1027 (digging ditches); Nelson *v.* West Duluth, 55 Minn. 497, 57 N. W. 149 (raising embankment); Schultz *v.* Bower, 57 Minn. 493, 59 N. W. 631 (causing land to fall).

Missouri: Williams *v.* Missouri Furnace Co., 13 Mo. App. 70 (causing land to fall); Autenrieth *v.* St. Louis & S. F. R. R., 36 Mo. App. 254 (obstruction of access to land); Faust *v.* Pope, 132 Mo. App. 287, 111 S. W. 878 (change of grade of street, and injury to house from blasting).

New Jersey: Freeman *v.* Sayre, 48 N. J. L. 37, 2 Atl. 650; W. A. Manda *v.* Orange, 77 N. J. L. 285, 72 Atl. 42 (laying pipe in land).

New York: Pappenheim *v.* Metropolitan El. Ry., 128 N. Y. 436, 28 N. E. 518; Rumsey *v.* New York & N. E. R. R., 133 N. Y. 79, 30 N. E. 654, 28 Am. St. Rep. 600, 15 L. R. A. 618 (obstruction of access); Honsee *v.* Hammond, 39 Barb. 89; Agate *v.* Lowenbein, 6 Daly, 291; Goldschmid *v.* New York, 14 App. Div. 135, 43 N. Y. Supp. 447.

North Carolina: Carson *v.* Norfolk & C. R. R., 128 N. C. 95, 38 S. E. 287 (construction of railroad).

Ohio: Upson C. & M. Co. *v.* Williams, 75 Oh. St. 644, 80 N. E. 1134, affirming 28 Oh. C. Ct. 388 (flooding land).

Pennsylvania: Shenongo & A. R. R. *v.* Braham, 79 Pa. 447 (diminution of value for any purpose, not merely as farm); Riddle *v.* Delaware County, 156 Pa. 643, 27 Atl. 569; Elder *v.* Lykens V. C. Co., 157 Pa. 490, 27 Atl. 545, 37 Am. St. Rep. 742 (deposit of earth); Lucot *v.* Rodgers, 159 Pa. 58, 28 Atl. 242; Neff *v.* Pennsylvania R. R., 202 Pa. 371, 51 Atl. 1038 (removal of bridge).

South Carolina: Dent *v.* South-Bound R. R., 61 S. C. 329, 39 S. E. 527 (burning trees).

South Dakota: Ulrick *v.* Dakota L. & T. Co., 2 S. D. 285, 49 N. W. 1054, 3 S. D. 44, 51 N. W. 1023 (causing land to fall).

Tennessee: Tyrus *v.* Kansas City, F. S. & M. R. R., 114 Tenn. 579, 86 S. W. 1074 (flooding by embankment).

Texas: San Antonio *v.* Mullaly, 33 S. W. 256 (excavations in land); Texarkana & F. S. Ry. *v.* Spencer, 28 Tex. Civ. App. 251, 67 S. W. 196 (flooding land); Texas C. R. R. *v.* Brown (Tex. Civ. App.), 86 S. W. 659 (flooding by embankment); St. Louis S. W. Ry. *v.* Clayton (Tex. Civ. App.), 118 S. W. 249 (deposit of dirt); Missouri, K. & T. Ry. *v.* Tolbert (Tex. Civ. App.), 134 S. W. 280 (carrying seeds of weeds on land).

West Virginia: Rowe *v.* Shenandoah Pulp Co., 42 W. Va. 551, 26 S. E. 320.

England: Hosking *v.* Phillips, 3 Ex. 168; Lukin *v.* Goodsall, Pea. Add. Cas. 15.

The recovery is for the effect of the trespass on the market value of the entire tract, not of the portion of it on

[85] *California:* Linforth *v.* San Francisco G. & E. Co., 156 Cal. 58, 103 Pac. 320.
Colorado: Jackson *v.* Kiel, 13 Colo. 378, 22 Pac. 504, 16 Am. St. Rep. 207, 6 L. R. A. 254.
Illinois: McWilliams *v.* Morgan, 75 Ill. 473; Western B. & S. Co. *v.* Jeone,

is always applicable. If the injury is easily reparable, the cost of repairing may be recovered.[86] But it must be shown

which the trespass was committed. Chicago, K. & W. R. R. v. Willits, 45 Kan. 110, 25 Pac. 576. Elements of value may be shown; as that a certain amount of manure had been brought on the land before the surface was destroyed by fire. Champlin v. Baltimore & O. S. W. R. R., 140 Ill. App. 94. But no damages can be recovered for depreciation in market value, not by the trespass itself,but by the apprehension of renewed injury. West Leigh Colliery Co. v. Tunnicliffe, [1908] A. C. 27.

The difference in valuation is between the value directly before and that directly after the trespass; the value at a later time is immaterial.

179 Ill. 71, 53 N. E. 565, affirming 78 Ill. App. 668.

Indiana: Louisville N. A. & C. R. R. v. Marlott (Ind.), 37 N. E. 709; Perry-Matthews-Buskirk Stone Co. v. Smith, 42 Ind. App. 413, 85 N. E. 784.

Iowa: Freeland v. Muscatine, 9 Ia. 461; Graessle v. Carpenter, 70 Ia. 166, 30 N. W. 392; Shirely v. Cedar Rapids I. F. & N. Ry., 74 Ia. 169, 37 N. W. 133.

Kentucky: Bannon v. Rohmeiser, 17 Ky. L. Rep. 1378, 35 S. W. 280; Louisville & N. R. R. v. Carter, 86 S. W. 685, 27 Ky. L. Rep. 748; Long v. Louisville & N. R. R., 128 Ky. 26, 107 S. W. 203, 13 L. R. A. (N. S.) 1063; Rodgers v. Flick, 139 S. W. 1098.

Maryland: Baltimore & O. R. R. v. Boyd, 67 Md. 32, 10 Atl. 315, 1 Am. St. Rep. 362; Chesapeake & P. T. Co. v. Mackenzie, 74 Md. 36, 21 Atl. 690.

Massachusetts: Howes v. Grush, 131 Mass. 207; Cavanagh v. Durgin, 156 Mass. 466, 31 N. E. 643.

Michigan: Walters v. Chamberlain, 65 Mich. 333, 32 N. W. 440.

Florida: Florida Southern Ry. v. Parsons, 33 Fla. 631, 15 So. 338.

Texas: Missouri, K. & T. R. R. v. Graham, 12 Tex. Civ. App. 54, 33 S. W. 576.

And the fact that even after the trespass the land was worth all that the plaintiff paid for it is immaterial. Penn v. Taylor, 24 Ill. App. 292.

The value to be taken is that for the most beneficial use, irrespective of any particular use to which the plaintiff intended to put it.

Iowa: Keirnan v. Heaton, 69 Ia. 136, 28 N. W. 478.

Kansas: Chicago, K. & W. R. R. v. Willets, 45 Kan. 110, 25 Pac. 576.

Minnesota: Carli v. Union D. S. R. & T. Co., 32 Minn. 101, 20 N. W. 89.

New York: Williams v. Brooklyn El. R. R., 126 N. Y. 96, 26 N. E. 1048; Honsee v. Hammond, 39 Barb. 89; Goldschmid v. Mayor of New York, 14 App. Div. 135, 43 N. Y. Supp. 447; Eno v. Christ, 25 Misc. 24, 54 N. Y. Supp. 400; Van Veghten v. Hudson R. P. T. Co., 103 App. Div. 130, 92 N. Y. Supp. 956.

North Carolina: Adams v. Dunham & N. R. R., 110 N. C. 325, 14 S. E. 857.

Ohio: Cincinnati v. Evans, 5 Oh. St. 594.

Oklahoma: Oklahoma City v. Hill, 4 Okla. 52, 50 Pac. 242; Enid & A. Ry. v. Wiley, 14 Okla. 310, 78 Pac. 96.

Pennsylvania: Wall v. Pittsburgh Harbor Co., 152 Pa. 427, 25 Atl. 647, 34 Am. St. Rep. 667; Herbert v. Rainey, 162 Pa. 525, 29 Atl. 725; Irwin v. Nolde, 176 Pa. 594, 35 Atl. 217, 35 L. R. A. 415; Hoffman v. Mill Creek Coal Co., 16 Pa. Super. Ct. 631; Herron v. Jones & Laughlin Co., 23 Pa. Super. Ct. 226;

[86] *United States:* Day v. Woodworth, 13 How. 370, 14 L. ed. 181.

California: Colton v. Onderdonk, 69 Cal. 155; Linforth v. San Francisco

that the repairs were reasonable; and if the cost of repairing the injury is greater than the diminution in market value of

Bricker v. Conemaugh Stone Co., 32 Pa. Super. Ct. 283.

Rhode Island: Whipple v. Wanskuck Co., 12 R. I. 321, 23 Am. Rep. 460.

South Carolina: Mason v. Postal T. C. Co., 74 S. C. 557, 54 S. E. 763.

Texas: Houston, E. & W. T. Ry. v. Adams, 63 Tex. 200.

West Virginia: McHenry v. Parkersburg, 66 W. Va. 533, 66 S. E. 750, 29 L. R. A. (N. S.) 860.

Wisconsin: Carl v. Sheboygan & F. du L. R. R., 46 Wis. 625, 1 N. W. 295.

England: Whitwham v. Westminster B. C. & C. Co., [1896] 2 Ch. 538, 65 L. J. Ch. 741, 74 L. T. Rep. 804, 44 W. R. 698.

The rental value is the value for any ordinary profitable use; the use to which the defendant put it may be less valuable.

Maryland: Jacob Tome Inst. v. Crothers, 87 Md. 569, 40 Atl. 261.

New York: Rumsey v. New York & N. E. R. R., 133 N. Y. 79, 30 N. E. 654, 136 N. Y. 543, 32 N. E. 979; Henry Hall Sons Co. v. Sundstrom & Stratton Co., 123 N. Y. Supp. 390.

But if the defendant put it to a more valuable use than the ordinary one, its value for that use may be recovered. Bunke v. New York Telephone Co., 188 N. Y. 600, 81 N. E. 1161, affirming 110 App. Div. 241, 97 N. Y. Supp. 66, 91 N. Y. Supp. 390 (attaching tele-

phone wires to roof). See Baltimore & O. R. R. v. Boyd (Md.), 20 Atl. 902.

In Higgins v. Los Angeles G. & E. Co., 158 Cal. 355, 115 Pac. 313, an action for injury to a building by explosion, the plaintiff was held to be entitled to recover compensation for loss of rents up to the time when by reasonable diligence he could have restored the building; and even though in fact he did not rebuild two stories, but only one story, he was nevertheless deprived of the rental of the second story up to the time when he could have repaired, and could therefore recover the rental value of a two-story building during that time.

In Negley v. Cowell, 91 Ia. 256, 59 N. W. 48, 51 Am. St. Rep. 344, where the trespasser raised crops on the land, the plaintiff was held entitled to recover the value of the crops, and was not restricted to the rental value.

Though the trespass may be upon part of a tract only, the plaintiff may recover the diminution in rental value of the entire tract.

New York: Kenyon v. New York C. & H. R. R. R., 29 App. Div. 80, 51 N. Y. Supp. 386.

North Carolina: Leigh v. Garysburg Mfg. Co., 132 N. C. 167, 43 S. E. 632.

Pennsylvania: Irwin v. Nolde, 176 Pa. 594, 35 Atl. 217, 35 L. R. A. 415.

G. & E. Co., 156 Cal. 58, 103 Pac. 320.

Delaware: Stimmel v. Brown, 7 Houst. 219, 30 Atl. 996.

Georgia: Harrison v. Kiser, 79 Ga. 588, 595.

Illinois: Donk Bros. C & C. Co. v. Novero, 135 Ill. App. 633.

Iowa: Freeland v. Muscatine, 9 Ia. 461; Graessle v. Carpenter, 70 Ia. 166.

Kansas: Chicago, K. & W. R. R.

v. Watkins, 43 Kan. 50, 22 Pac. 985.

Kentucky: McGuire v. Lovelace, 128 S. W. 309 (see Louisville & N. R. R. v. Hart County, 50 S. W. 60).

Maryland: Hauralian v. Mayor of Baltimore, 114 Md. 517, 80 Atl. 312.

Massachusetts: Shaw v. Cummiskey, 7 Pick. 76; Cavanagh v. Durgin, 156 Mass. 466, 31 N. E. 643.

Michigan: Walters v. Chamberlain,

the land, the latter is always the true measure of damages.[87]
Strictly speaking, therefore, the cost of repairs is not the meas-

65 Mich. 333, 32 N. W. 440 (see Burtraw *v.* Clark, 103 Mich. 383, 61 N. W. 552).

Minnesota: Kopp *v.* Northern Pac. R. R., 41 Minn. 310, 43 N. W. 73; Ziebarth *v.* Nye, 42 Minn. 541, 44 N. W. 1027.

Nebraska: Shiverick *v.* R. J. Gunning Co., 58 Neb. 29, 78 N. W. 460.

New Jersey: W. A. Manda *v.* Orange, 77 N. J. L. 285, 72 Atl. 42.

New York: Slavin *v.* State, 152 N. Y. 45, 46 N. E. 321; Walter *v.* Post, 6 Duer, 363, 4 Abb. Pr. 382; Denken *v.* Canavan, 39 N. Y. Supp. 1078; Berg *v.* Parsons, 90 Hun, 267, 35 N. Y. Supp. 780; Fort Covington *v.* United States & C. R. R., 8 App. Div. 223, 40 N. Y. Supp. 313.

Ohio: Upson C. & M. Co. *v.* Williams, 75 Oh. St. 644, 80 N. E. 1134, affirming 28 Oh. C. Ct. 388.

Oklahoma: Enid & A. Ry. *v.* Wiley, 14 Okla. 310, 78 Pac. 96.

Pennsylvania: Lentz *v.* Carnegie, 145 Pa. 612, 23 Atl. 219, 27 Am. St. Rep. 717; Eshleman *v.* Martic, 152 Pa. 68, 25 Atl. 178; James McNeil & Bro. Co. *v.* Crucible Steel Co., 207 Pa. 493, 56 Atl. 1067; Hoffman *v.* Mill Creek Coal Co., 16 Pa. Super. Ct. 631; Welliver *v.* Pennsylvania Canal Co., 23 Pa. Super. Ct. 79; Herron *v.* Jones & Laughlin Co., 23 Pa. Super. Ct. 226; Bricker *v.* Conemaugh Stone Co., 32 Pa. Super. Ct. 283.

Rhode Island: Whipple *v.* Wanskuck Co., 12 R. I. 321, 23 Am. Rep. 460.

Tennessee: Doss *v.* Billington, 98 Tenn. 375, 39 S. W. 717.

Texas: Hooper *v.* Smith, 53 S. W. 65.

Washington: Kock *v.* Sackman-Phillips Inv. Co., 9 Wash. 405, 37 Pac. 703.

West Virginia: McHenry *v.* Parkersburg, 66 W. Va. 533, 66 S. E. 750, 29 L. R. A. (N. S.) 860.

Wisconsin: Barden *v.* Portage, 79 Wis. 126, 48 N. W. 210.

England: Mayfair Property Co. *v.* Johnston, [1894] 1 Ch. 508, 63 L. J. Ch. 399, 70 L. T. Rep. 485; Bideford Urban Council *v.* Bideford Ry., 68 J. P. 123.

It must appear that the plaintiff has a right to make the repairs. Karst *v.* St. Paul S. & T. P. R. R., 22 Minn. 118. And if the repairs would greatly enhance the value of the property, the entire cost of them cannot be recovered as the damages.

New Jersey: Bates *v.* Warrick, 76 N. J. L. 108, 71 Atl. 1116.

Washington: Kock *v.* Sackman-Phillips Inv. Co., 9 Wash. 405, 37 Pac. 703.

[87] *Illinois:* Swanson *v.* Nelson, 127 Ill. App. 144.

Iowa: Hamilton *v.* Des Moines & K. C. Ry., 84 Ia. 131, 50 N. W. 567.

Massachusetts: Gilmore *v.* Driscoll, 122 Mass. 199.

Michigan: Burtraw *v.* Clark, 103 Mich. 383, 61 N. W. 552.

Minnesota: Nelson *v.* West Duluth, 55 Minn. 497, 57 N. W. 149.

Nevada: Harvey *v.* Sides, 1 Nev. 539.

New York: Hartshorn *v.* Chaddock, 135 N. Y. 116, 31 N. E. 997.

Ohio: Upson C. & M. Co. *v.* Williams, 75 Oh. St. 644, 80 N. E. 1134, 28 Oh. C. Ct. 388.

Oklahoma: Enid & A. Ry. *v.* Wiley, 14 Okla. 310, 78 Pac. 96.

Pennsylvania: Seely *v.* Alden, 61 Pa. 302; Lentz *v.* Carnegie, 145 Pa. 612, 23 Atl. 219, 27 Am. St. Rep. 717; McGowan *v.* Bailey, 155 Pa. 256, 25 Atl. 648; Elder *v.* Lykens V. C. Co., 157 Pa. 490, 27 Atl. 545; Thompson *v.* Citizens' T. Co., 181 Pa. 131, 37 Atl. 205; Eshleman *v.* Martic, 152 Pa. 68, 25 Atl. 178; Hoffman *v.* Mill Creek Coal Co., 16 Pa. Super. Ct. 631; Welliver *v.*

ure of damages, but only evidence of the amount of damages.[88] Thus, in a case where the defendant so felled trees on his own land that the brush was cast on the plaintiff's land, the court said: "The expense (of removing the brush) is not the measure of damages. It is a fact to be considered in connection with other evidence, such as the value of the land before and since the cutting, the uses to which it was adapted, and the extent to which the plaintiff had been deprived of the use. The damages may be more and they may be less than the cost of removing the brush."[89]

Both cost of repairs and permanent depreciation cannot be recovered in the same case. So in a case in New York, where the defendant injured the plaintiff's house by storing ice so near it that the ice melted and water soaked through, and the jury were instructed to give, first, the rental value to the time of trial, and the cost of putting the plaintiff's premises in condition to be unaffected by the proximity of ice, and second, the

Pennsylvania Canal Co., 23 Pa. Super. Ct. 79; Herron v. Jones & Laughlin Co., 23 Pa. Super. Ct. 226; Bricker v. Conemaugh Stone Co., 32 Pa. Super. Ct. 283.

Rhode Island: Whipple v. Wanskuck Co., 12 R. I. 321, 23 Am. Rep. 460.

Tennessee: Hord v. Holston R. R. R., 122 Tenn. 399, 123 S. W. 637.

Texas: Galveston H. & S. A. R. R. v. Becht, 21 S. W. 971.

England: Riley v. Halifax Corporation, 97 L. T. 278, 71 J. P. 428, 23 T. L. R. 613.

So where instead of restoring the property injured an equally good substitute could be procured at much less expense, the expense of procuring the substitute is the measure. Lodge Holes Colliery Co. v. Wednesbury, [1908] A. C. 323.

In a few questionable cases, where property on the land has been destroyed, it is held that the value of the property only, without the added cost of replacing it, may be recovered.

Louisiana: Stoner v. Texas & P. Ry., 45 La. Ann. 115, 11 So. 875 (fruit trees).

Washington: Fidelity & C. Co. v. Seattle, 50 Wash. 391, 97 Pac. 973 (glass in window).

[88] *Iowa:* McMahon v. Dubuque, 107 Ia. 62, 77 N. W. 517.

Kansas: Atchison, T. & S. F. R. R. v. Huitt, 41 Pac. 1051.

Kentucky: Maysville v. Stanton, 12 Ky. L. Rep. 586, 14 S. W. 675.

Massachusetts: Holt v. Sargent, 15 Gray, 97.

[89] Smith, J., in Hutchinson v. Parker, 64 N. H. 89, 90, 5 Atl. 659. *Acc.,* Nelson v. Blackfoot Milling Co., 44 Pac. 81. In an action for failure to keep a drain in repair by which land was overflowed, the court said that whether damages should be measured by the rent of the land, the probable value of the crops that might have been grown, or the permanent deterioration of the land, *one or all,* was to be determined by the jury on the evidence. Hammond v. Port Royal & A. Ry., 15 S. C. 10, 31. This was going too far. The jury should have been given the option between the first and third measures, but no more.

permanent depreciation in value, this was held error.[90]   Finch, J., said: "The cost of prevention and the result of continuance cannot both be given. The award of the one must necessarily exclude the other."

Whatever the nature of the injury, the damages cannot equal the entire value of the land. The rule that prevails in trover, that the wrongdoer cannot, against the will of the owner, return the property and reduce the damages thereby, does not prevail in the case of land.[91]

§ 933. Destruction of trees.

When by an injury to real property trees standing upon the property are destroyed, the value of the trees can be recovered.[92]

[90] Barrick v. Schifferdecker, 123 N. Y. 52, 25 N. E. 365; acc., Maysville v. Stanton, 12 Ky. L. Rep. 586, 14 S. W. 675; Cooper v. New York, L. & W. Ry., 122 App. Div. 128, 106 N. Y. Supp. 611.

[91] Georgia: Allen v. Macon D. & S. R. R., 107 Ga. 838, 33 S. E. 696.

New York: Sprague N. B. v. Erie R. R., 22 App. Div. 526, 48 N. Y. Supp. 65.

Canada: Burland v. Montreal, 33 Can. 373.

[92] United States: E. E. Bolles W. W. Co. v. U. S., 106 U. S. 432, 1 Sup. Ct. 398, 27 L. ed. 230.

Alabama: Ivey v. McQueen, 17 Ala. 408.

Connecticut: Eldridge v. Gorman, 77 Conn. 699, 60 Atl. 643.

Georgia: Smith v. Gonder, 22 Ga. 353.

Indiana: Halstead v. Sigler, 35 Ind. App. 419, 74 N. E. 257.

Iowa: Striegel v. Moore, 55 Ia. 88; Graessle v. Carpenter, 70 Ia. 166.

Kansas: Arn v. Mathews, 39 Kan. 272, 18 Pac. 65.

Kentucky: Meehan v. Edwards, 92 Ky. 574, 18 S. W. 519; Lindsay v. Latham, 107 S. W. 267, 32 Ky. L. Rep. 867.

Louisiana: Watterson v. Jetche, 7 Rob. 20; Shepherd v. Young, 2 La. Ann. 238; Yarborough v. Nettles, 7 La.

Ann. 116; Gardere v. Blanton, 35 La. Ann. 811; Guarantee T. & S. D. Co. v. Holsell, 107 La. 745, 31 So. 999.

Massachusetts: Cutts v. Spring, 15 Mass. 135.

Michigan: Michigan L. & I. Co. v. Deer Lake Co., 60 Mich. 143, 27 N. W. 10, 1 Am. St. Rep. 491; Miller v. Wellman, 75 Mich. 353, 42 N. W. 843; Bockes v. A. Mafee & Son Co., 130 N. W. 313.

Minnesota: Carner v. Chicago, S. P. M. & O. Ry., 43 Minn. 375, 45 N. W. 713.

Montana: Nelson v. Big B. M. Co., 17 Mont. 553, 44 Pac. 81.

Nevada: Ward v. Carson R. W. Co., 13 Nev. 44.

New Hampshire: Foote v. Merrill, 54 N. H. 490, 20 Am. Rep. 151.

New York: Whitbeck v. New York C. R. R., 36 Barb. 644.

North Carolina: Bennett v. Thompson, 13 Ired. 146.

Pennsylvania: Coxe v. England, 65 Pa. 212; Chase v. Clearfield L. Co., 209 Pa. 422, 58 Atl. 813.

Rhode Island: Spink v. New York, N. H. & H. R. R., 26 R. I. 115, 58 Atl. 499.

Tennessee: Ross v. Scott, 15 Lea, 479.

Vermont: Tilden v. Johnson, 52 Vt. 628, 36 Am. Rep. 769; Kilby v. Erwin,

If the trees are full-grown timber-trees, or trees ripe for cutting for cord-wood, this is usually all that can be recovered; though it is often said that the diminution in value of the land may be recovered,[93] a form of statement which in the case of matured timber-trees cannot really result in a different measure of recovery. It is sometimes said that the value of the trees (as timber) and the injury to the realty by their destruction may be recovered.[94] This is practically the same rule, and is

84 Vt. 270, 78 Atl. 1021; Chase v. Hoosac T. & W. R. R., 81 Atl. 236.

Virginia: Virginian Ry. v. Hurt, 72 S. E. 110 (if the burned trees had a value still for timber, this must be considered).

Washington: Park v. Northport S. & R. Co., 47 Wash. 579, 92 Pac. 442.

Wisconsin: Webster v. Moe, 35 Wis. 75; Tuttle v. Wilson, 52 Wis. 643; Cotter v. Plumer, 72 Wis. 476 (except where the statute applies).

So where grass was cut and made into hay by the defendant, the value of the standing grass was given. Lewis v. Courtwright, 77 Ia. 190. Where the trees are not destroyed but merely made more difficult to cut, only the increased cost of cutting is recovered. Gordon v. Grand Rapids & I. R. R., 103 Mich. 379, 61 N. W. 549.

[93] *Alabama:* Davis v. Miller B. L. Co., 151 Ala. 580, 44 So. 639.

California: Chipman v. Hibberd, 6 Cal. 162.

Delaware: Bullock v. Porter, 77 Atl. 943.

Indiana: Knissly v. Hire, 2 Ind. App. 86, 28 N. E. 195.

Iowa: Striegel v. Moore, 55 Iowa, 88, 7 N. W. 413.

Michigan: Achey v. Hall, 7 Mich. 423; Gates v. Comstock, 113 Mich. 127, 71 N. W. 515.

Minnesota: Carner v. Chicago, S. P., M. & O. Ry., 43 Minn. 375, 45 N. W. 713.

New Hampshire: Wallace v. Goodall, 18 N. H. 439.

New York: Edsall v. Howell, 86 Hun, 424, 33 N. Y. Supp. 892; Carter v. Pitcher, 87 Hun, 580, 34 N. Y. Supp. 549; Morrison v. American T. & T. Co., 115 App. Div. 744, 101 N. Y. Supp. 140; Parker v. Sherwood, 125 N. Y. Supp. 297.

North Carolina: Brickell v. Camp Mfg. Co., 147 N. C. 118, 60 S. E. 905; Jenkins v. Montgomery L. Co., 70 S. E. 633; Wall v. Holloman, 72 S. E. 369.

Wisconsin: Nelson v. Churchill, 117 Wis. 10, 93 N. W. 799.

Contra, Georgia: Coody v. Gress Lumber Co., 82 Ga. 793, 10 S. E. 218.

In Argotsinger v. Vines, 82 N. Y. 308, where trees were cut in a farm wood lot, it was held that the diminution in value of the whole farm, rather than the value of the wood cut, was the proper measure of damages, since the cutting of timber on a wood lot which supplies a farm with fuel and fencing may be a serious injury to the farm.

[94] *Maine:* Longfellow v. Quimby, 33 Me. 457.

Michigan: Miller v. Wellman, 75 Mich. 353, 42 N. W. 843.

New York: Dwight v. Elmira C. & N. R. R., 132 N. Y. 199, 30 N. E. 398; McCruden v. Rochester Ry., 5 Misc. 59, 25 N. Y. Supp. 114.

North Carolina: Whitfield v. Rowland Lumber Co., 152 N. C. 211, 67 S. E. 512.

Oregon: Oregon & C. R. R. v. Jackson, 21 Ore. 360, 28 Pac. 74.

unobjectionable. It has been said that where trees were cut and made into lumber by the defendant, and sold in a distant market, the measure of damages is the price obtained less the expenses.[95] This, however, is not strictly correct,[96] though in the absence of more definite evidence as to the value of the trees standing, the price obtained might be shown as evidence of such value.

If, however, the trees are fruit or ornamental trees, or immature trees, they are of more value standing than felled, and the injury therefore goes beyond the mere destruction of the trees; it is an injury to the realty, since the value of that is diminished by more than the value of the trees as timber, because their chief value is for productive or ornamental purposes. The measure of damages when ornamental or fruit-bearing trees or growing timber-trees are cut is therefore the difference in the value of the realty before and after the trespass; [97] and that

Pennsylvania: Krider *v.* Lafferty, 1 Whart. 303.

Tennessee: Ensley *v.* Nashville, 2 Baxt. 144.

Contra, Washington: Gustin *v.* Jose, 11 Wash. 348, 39 Pac. 687.

[95] *Michigan:* Winchester *v.* Craig, 33 Mich. 205.

Pennsylvania: Herdic *v.* Young, 55 Pa. 176, 93 Am. Dec. 739.

South Carolina: Lewis *v.* Virginia-Carolina Co., 69 S. C. 364, 48 S. E. 280.

Wisconsin: Nelson *v.* Churchill, 117 Wis. 10, 93 N. W. 799.

[96] Coxe *v.* England, 65 Pa. 212.

[97] *California:* Chipman *v.* Hibberd, 6 Cal. 162.

Colorado: Manitou & P. P. Ry. *v.* Harris, 45 Colo. 185, 101 Pac. 61.

Connecticut: Hoyt *v.* Southern N. E. T. Co., 60 Conn. 385, 22 Atl. 957; Eldridge *v.* Gorman, 77 Conn. 699, 60 Atl. 643.

Delaware: Jordan *v.* Delaware & A. T. Co., 75 Atl. 1014.

Illinois: Louisville, E. & S. L. C. R. R. *v.* Spencer, 149 Ill. 97, 36 N. E. 91.

Indiana: Knisely *v.* Hire, 2 Ind. App. 86, 28 N. E. 195; Delaware & M.

C. T. Co. *v.* Fisk, 40 Ind. App. 348, 81 N. E. 1100.

Iowa: Hamilton *v.* Des Moines & K. C. Ry., 84 Ia. 131, 50 N. W. 567; Greenfield *v.* Chicago, M. & S. P. Ry., 83 Ia. 270, 49 N. W. 95; Burdick *v.* Chicago, M. & S. P. Ry., 87 Ia. 384, 54 N. W. 439.

Kansas: St. Louis & S. F. Ry. *v.* Hoover, 3 Kan. App. 577, 43 Pac. 854; Kansas Z. M. & S. Co. *v.* Brown, 8 Kan. App. 802, 57 Pac. 304; Wichita G., E. L. & P. Co. *v.* Wright, 9 Kan. App. 730, 59 Pac. 1085; Atchison, T. & S. F. Ry. *v.* Geiser, 68 Kan. 281, 75 Pac. 68.

Kentucky: Lindsay *v.* Latham, 107 S. W. 267, 32 Ky. L. Rep. 867; Kentucky Stave Co. *v.* Page, 125 S. W. 170.

Louisiana: Tissot *v.* Great S. T. & T. Co., 39 La. Ann. 996, 3 So. 261.

Michigan: Bockes *v.* A. Mafee & Son Co., 165 Mich. 7, 130 N. W. 313.

Minnesota: Hoye *v.* Chicago, M. & S. P. Ry., 46 Minn. 269, 48 N. W. 1117.

Missouri: Doty *v.* Quincy, O. & K. C. R. R., 136 Mo. App. 254, 116 S. W. 1126.

was therefore the rule adopted where trees were cut in a pasture, where they had been used as a shade and wind-break for cattle.[98] But the trees of an orchard or an ornamental grove have an actual value *in situ*, apart from any value they may add to the land; and in that case the plaintiff may at his option recover the value of the trees, without regard to the diminished value of the land.[99] So where the trees destroyed were in a

Nebraska: Alberts *v.* Husenetter, 77 Neb. 699, 110 N. W. 657.

New Hampshire: Wallace *v.* Goodall, 18 N. H. 439; Foote *v.* Merrill, 54 N. H. 490, 20 Am. Rep. 151.

New York: Argotsinger *v.* Vines, 82 N. Y. 308; Dwight *v.* Elmira C. & N. R. R., 132 N. Y. 399, 30 N. E. 398; Evans *v.* Keystone Gas Co., 148 N. Y. 112, 42 N. E. 513; Disbrow *v.* Westchester Hardwood Co., 164 N. Y. 415, 58 N. E. 519; Van Deusen *v.* Young, 29 N. Y. 9; Humes *v.* Proctor, 73 Hun, 265, 26 N. Y. Supp. 315, affirmed, 151 N. Y. 520, 45 N. E. 948; Gorham *v.* Eastchester El. Co., 80 Hun, 290, 30 N. Y. Supp. 125; Edsall *v.* Howell, 86 Hun, 424, 33 N. Y. Supp. 892; Carter *v.* Pitcher, 87 Hun, 580, 34 N. Y. Supp. 549.

North Carolina: Bennett *v.* Thompson, 35 N. C. (13 Ired.) 146; Williams *v.* Elm City Lumber Co., 70 S. E. 631; Jenkins *v.* Montgomery Lumber Co., 70 S. E. 633.

North Dakota: Cleveland School Dist. *v.* Northern Ry., 20 N. Dak. 124, 126 N. W. 995.

Texas: Galveston H. & S. A. Ry. *v.* Warnecke, 43 Tex. Civ. App. 83, 95 S. W. 600.

Vermont: Kilby *v.* Erwin, 78 Atl. 1021.

Washington: Park *v.* Northport Co., 47 Wash. 597, 92 Pac. 442.

Wisconsin: Gilman *v.* Brown, 115 Wis. 1, 91 N. W. 227; Miller *v.* Neale, 137 Wis. 426, 119 N. W. 94.

See Central R. R. & B. Co. *v.* Murray, 93 Ga. 256, 20 S. E. 129; Ferguson

v. Buckell, 101 App. Div. 213, 91 N. Y. Supp. 724.

Where defendant had a right to cut, but cut more than he should, the measure of damages is the difference between the value the land would have had after legal cutting and its value after the actual cutting. Meyer *v.* Standard Tel. Co., 122 Ia. 514, 98 N. W. 300.

In Pinkerton *v.* Randolph, 200 Mass. 24, 85 N. E. 892, where the trees cut were shade trees in a highway, and if the abuttors had so requested they must have been removed, this fact was to be considered in estimating the difference in value.

[98] Nixon *v.* Stilwell, 52 Hun, 353, 5 N. Y. Supp. 248.

[99] *Alabama:* Mitchell *v.* Billingsley, 17 Ala. 391.

California: Montgomery *v.* Locke, 72 Cal. 75.

Georgia: Western & A. R. R. *v.* Tate, 129 Ga. 526, 59 S. E. 266.

Indiana: Knisely *v.* Hire, 2 Ind. App. 86, 28 N. E. 195.

Iowa: Burdick *v.* Chicago, M. & S. P. Ry., 87 Ia. 384, 54 N. W. 439.

Kansas: Missouri, K. & T. Ry. *v.* Lycan, 57 Kan. 635, 47 Pac. 526; Atchison, T. & S. F. R. R. *v.* Hamilton, 6 Kan. App. 447, 50 Pac. 102; Missouri, K. & T. Ry. *v.* Steinberger, 6 Kan. App. 585, 51 Pac. 623.

Kentucky: Louisville & N. R. R. *v.* Beeler, 126 Ky. 328, 103 S. W. 300, 11 L. R. A. (N. S.) 930.

Louisiana: Stoner *v.* Texas & P. Ry., 45 La. Ann. 115, 11 So. 875.

Nebraska: Kansas City & O. R. R. *v.*

nursery, the measure of damages for their destruction was held to be their market value.[100] It is no defense nor matter of mitigation in an action for cutting down the plaintiff's shade-trees, that they made the defendant's house damp and unhealthy.[101]

In addition to compensation for the trees destroyed, the plaintiff may recover damages for any other injury to other timber or to the land committed at the same time.[102]

§ 934. Value enhanced by defendant's labor.

In this case, as in others where labor has been expended upon chattels obtained by a trespass on real property, attempts have been made to recover the value of the chattels after the labor has been expended upon them, on the ground that the chattels still remain the plaintiff's property, and he has a right to take them where he finds them, or at his option to recover compensation for the loss of them at that time. It has accordingly been held in many cases that the measure of damages is the value of logs immediately after cutting,[103] or even of

Rogers, 48 Neb. 653, 67 N. W. 602; Hart v. Chicago & N. W. Ry., 83 Neb. 652, 120 N. W. 933.

New York: Evans v. Keystone Gas Co., 148 N. Y. 112, 42 N. E. 513; Whitbeck v. New York C. R. R., 36 Barb. 644.

South Dakota: Bailey v. Chicago, M. & S. P. Ry., 3 S. D. 531, 54 N. W. 596.

Texas: Hooper v. Smith, 53 S. W. 65.

As affecting the value of the trees it may be shown that it would be difficult, on account of the shade of other trees, to grow trees to take the place of those destroyed. Leiber v. Chicago, M. & S. P. Ry., 84 Ia. 97, 50 N. W. 547.

[100] Birket v. Williams, 30 Ill. App. 451.

[101] Bliss v. Ball, 99 Mass. 597, 97 Am. Dec. 58.

[102] *New York:* Disbrow v. Westchester Hardwood Co., 164 N. Y. 415.

Rhode Island: Spink v. New York, N. H. & H. R. R., 26 R. I. 115, 58 Atl. 499.

Canada: Union Bank v. Rideau Lumber Co., 4 Ont. L. R. 721.

See, however, *Washington:* Gustin v. Jose, 11 Wash. 348, 39 Pac. 687.

So it has been held that compensation may be had for leaving the brush on the land.

Indiana: Halstead v. Sigler, 35 Ind. App. 419, 74 N. E. 257.

Pennsylvania: Chase v. Clearfield Lumber Co., 209 Pa. 422, 58 Atl. 813.

But in *Montana* it was held that no damages could be recovered in such a case, where the plaintiff had made a homestead filing for the purpose of clearing the land for cultivation, since he would under any circumstances have been at the expense of removing the brush. Nelson v. Big Blackfoot Mining Co., 17 Mont. 553, 44 Pac. 81.

[103] *Connecticut:* Eldridge v. Gorman, 77 Conn. 699, 60 Atl. 643.

Georgia: Smith v. Gonder, 22 Ga. 353.

Louisiana: Gardere v. Blanton, 35 La. Ann. 811.

timber made from the trees cut.[104] This, however, loses sight of the fact that the action is for a trespass upon real property. Where the trespass was wilful, the defendant having knowingly expended his labor on the plaintiff's property has no legal or equitable claim to the results of his labor; and in such a case it is everywhere held that even in an action for trespass upon the land the value of the chattel after severance may be recovered.[105] But where the defendant acted in good faith, the plaintiff, according to the doctrine now prevailing, is entitled to recover only the value of the trees *in situ*, that is, the stumpage, together with compensation for any injury to the land.[106]

Maryland: Peters *v.* Tilghman, 111 Md. 227, 73 Atl. 726.

New York: Firmin *v.* Firmin, 9 Hun, 571.

North Carolina: Bennett *v.* Thompson, 13 Ired. 146; Gaskin *v.* Davis, 115 N. C. 85, 20 S. E. 188.

Texas: Brown *v.* Pope, 27 Tex. Civ. App. 225, 65 S. W. 42; Galveston, H. & S. A. Ry. *v.* Warnecke, 43 Tex. Civ. App. 83, 95 S. W. 600.

Canada: Union Bank *v.* Rideau Lumber Co., 4 Ont. L. Rep. 721.

[104] *Iowa:* Stuart *v.* Phelps, 39 Ia. 14, 18 Am. Rep. 39.

Michigan: Corning *v.* Woodin, 46 Mich. 44.

Minnesota: Nesbitt *v.* St. Paul L. Co., 21 Minn. 491.

Baker *v.* Wheeler, 8 Wend. 505, 24 Am. Dec. 66; Rice *v.* Hollenbeck, 19 Barb. 664, often cited on this point, are not cases of trespass on real property, but of conversion of felled timber.

[105] *United States:* E. E. Bolles Woodenware Co. *v.* U. S., 106 U. S. 432, 27 L. ed. 230, 1 Sup. Ct. 398; U. S. *v.* Homestake Min. Co., 117 Fed. 481, 54 C. C. A. 303.

Arkansas: Nicklase *v.* Morrison, 56 Ark. 553, 20 S. W. 414.

Kentucky: Jones Lumber Co. *v.* Gatliff, 82 S. W. 295, 26 Ky. L. Rep. 616.

Louisiana: Guarantee T. & S. D. Co. *v.* E. C. Drew Inv. Co., 107 La. 251, 31 So. 736.

Minnesota: King *v.* Merriman, 38 Minn. 47, 35 N. W. 570; Shepard *v.* Pettit, 30 Minn. 481; Hinman *v.* Heyderstadt, 32 Minn. 250; Mississippi R. L. Co. *v.* Page, 68 Minn. 269, 71 N. W. 4.

Missouri: Sligo Furnace Co. *v.* Holart-Lee Tie Co. (Mo. App.), 134 S. W. 585.

New York: Stanton *v.* Pritchard, 4 Hun, 266.

Texas: C. R. Cummings & Co. *v.* Masterton, 42 Tex. Civ. App. 549, 93 S. W. 500; Emporia Lumber Co. *v.* League (Tex. Civ. App.), 105 S. W. 1167; Ripy *v.* Less, 55 Tex. Civ. App. 492, 118 S. W. 1084; Bayle *v.* Norris (Tex. Civ. App.), 134 S. W. 767.

Vermont: Whitney *v.* Adams, 66 Vt. 679, 30 Atl. 32, 44 Am. St. Rep. 875, 25 L. R. A. 598.

Canada: Union Bank *v.* Rideau Lumber Co., 3 Ont. L. Rep. 269.

In *Louisiana* this rule was applied where the taking was under an error of law. Guarantee T. & S. D. Co. *v.* Holsell, 107 La. 745, 31 So. 999; St. Paul *v.* Louisiana C. L. Co., 116 La. 585, 40 So. 906.

[106] *United States:* United States *v.* Eccles, 111 Fed. 490; United States *v.*

The Supreme Court of New Hampshire, in an action of trespass *quare clausum* for cutting and removing the plaintiff's trees, used this unanswerable argument: "Had the defendant set fire to the plaintiff's trees and destroyed them, the measure of damages would have been their value as they stood on the land; and we cannot say that he justly ought to pay any more for cutting and removing than destroying them, nor that the plaintiff justly ought to receive any more in one case than in the other." [107] And though the court was constrained by the authorities to say that the rule might be different in trover, they allowed in the case at bar a recovery for the value of the

Gentry, 119 Fed. 70, 55 C. C. A. 658; Morgan v. United States, 169 Fed. 242, 94 C. C. A. 518.

Alabama: Warrior Coal & C. Co. v. Mabel Min. Co., 112 Ala. 624, 20 So. 918.

Arkansas: Central C. & C. Co. v. John Henry Shoe Co., 69 Ark. 302, 63 S. W. 49.

Louisiana: Gardere v. Blanton, 35 La. Ann. 811; J. F. Ball & Bro. L. Co. v. Simms L. Co., 121 La. 627, 46 So. 674, 18 L. R. A. (N. S.) 244.

Maine: Cushing v. Longfellow, 26 Me. 306.

Michigan: Ayres v. Hubbard, 57 Mich. 322, 23 N. W. 829, 58 Am. Rep. 361, 71 Mich. 594, 40 N. W. 10 (see Gates v. Rifle Boom Co., 70 Mich. 309, 38 N. W. 245).

Minnesota: Whitney v. Huntington, 37 Minn. 197, 33 N. W. 561; King v. Merriman, 38 Minn. 47, 35 N. W. 370; Mississippi R. L. Co. v. Page, 68 Minn. 269, 71 N. W. 4; State v. Clarke, 109 Minn. 123, 123 N. W. 54.

Mississippi: Bond v. Griffin, 74 Miss. 599, 22 So. 187.

Missouri: Sligo Furnace Co. v. Holart-Lee Tie Co. (Mo. App.), 134 S. W. 585.

New Hampshire: Hitchcock v. Libby, 70 N. H. 399, 47 Atl. 269.

New Jersey: Dawson v. Amey (N. J. L.), 13 Atl. 667.

New York: Disbrow v. Westchester Hardwood Co., 164 N. Y. 415, 58 N. E. 519; Clark v. Holdridge, 12 App. Div. 613, 43 N. Y. Supp. 115.

North Carolina: Gaskins v. Davis, 115 N. C. 85, 20 S. E. 188, 44 Am. St. Rep. 439, 25 L. R. A. 813.

Ohio: Hulett v. Fairbanks, 1 Oh. C. Ct. 155, 1 Oh. C. Dec. 89.

Oregon: Oregon & C. R. R. v. Jackson, 21 Ore. 360, 28 Pac. 74.

Pennsylvania: Coxe v. England, 65 Pa. 212.

South Carolina: Lewis v. Virginia-Carolina Chem. Co., 69 S. C. 364, 48 S. E. 280.

Tennessee: Dougherty v. Chestnutt, 86 Tenn. 1, 5 S. W. 444.

Texas: Pettit v. Frothingham, 48 Tex. Civ. App. 105, 106 S. W. 907; Louis Werner Stave Co. v. Pickering (Tex. Civ. App.), 119 S.W. 333; Callen v. Collins (Tex. Civ. App.), 120 S. W. 546.

Vermont: Tilden v. Johnson, 52 Vt. 628, 36 Am. Rep. 769 (see Hassam v. Safford, 82 Vt. 444, 74 Atl. 197).

West Virginia: Darnell v. Wilmoth, 72 S. E. 1023.

Wisconsin: Single v. Schneider, 24 Wis. 299; Hungerford v. Redford, 29 Wis. 345; Tuttle v. Wilson, 52 Wis. 643, 9 N. W. 822; Fleming v. Sherry, 72 Wis. 503, 40 N. W. 375.

[107] Hibbard, J., in Foote v. Merrill, 54 N. H. 490, 491.

trees standing. And the opinion affords strong ground for supposing that upon the case being again presented the same rule would be adopted in trover.

In Adams v. Blodgett [108] the defendant stripped bark from the trees of the plaintiff, and the measure of damages was held to be the market value of the *bark* at the place where it grew. This seems to involve a slight error, for the value of the bark severed would include the cost of stripping, and would in the ordinary case exceed by that amount the injury to the realty.

In some cases it is said that the rule is different in trover and in trespass *quare clausum*, an allowance being made for the defendant's labor in the latter form of action, though not in the former.[109] This question has already been considered.[110]

Where trees cut by a wilful trespasser are improved by the trespasser and then sold to a purchaser who cannot show that he acted in good faith, the purchaser is responsible for the value of the timber or article manufactured from it at the time he bought it.[111] If the defendant acquired the property in good faith, authorities are in conflict. In some jurisdictions the courts applying the doctrine of *caveat emptor*, hold that the purchaser, being guilty of a conversion in buying from one who had no title, is responsible for the entire value of the property bought;[112] while in other jurisdictions, there being no fraud

[108] 47 N. H. 219.

[109] *Alabama:* Brooks v. Rodgers, 101 Ala. 111, 13 So. 386; Davis v. Miller B. L. Co., 151 Ala. 580, 44 So. 639.

Colorado: Omaha & G. S. & R. Co. v. Tabor, 13 Colo. 41.

Florida: Skinner v. Pinney, 19 Fla. 42, 45 Am. Rep. 1.

Kentucky: Kentucky Stave Co. v. Page, 125 S. W. 170.

New Hampshire: Foote v. Merrill, 54 N. H. 490, 20 Am. Rep. 151.

Texas: Brown v. Pope, 27 Tex. Civ. App. 225, 65 S. W. 42; Galveston H. & S. A. Ry. v. Warnecke, 43 Tex. Civ. App. 83, 95 S. W. 600.

[110] §§ 500 et seq.

[111] *United States:* Cunningham v. Metropolitan L. Co., 110 Fed. 332, 49 C. C. A. 72.

Minnesota: Hastay v. Bonness, 84 Minn. 120, 86 N. W. 896.

Tennessee: Holt v. Hayes, 110 Tenn. 42, 73 S. W. 111.

Canada: Smith v. Baechler, 18 Ont. 293.

[112] *United States:* E. E. Bolles Woodenware Co. v. United States, 106 U. S. 432, 27 L. ed. 230, 1 Sup. Ct. 398; United States v. Hielner, 11 Sawy. 406.

Alabama: Birmingham M. R. R. v. Tennessee C. I. & R. R., 127 Ala. 137, 28 So. 679.

Georgia: Parker v. Waycross & F. R. R., 81 Ga. 387, 8 S. E. 871.

Maine: Wing v. Milliken, 91 Me. 387, 40 Atl. 138, 64 Am. St. Rep. 238.

Michigan: Tuttle v. White, 46 Mich. 485, 9 N. W. 528, 41 Am. Rep. 175;

or wrong on the part of the defendant to justify any sort of punishment, it is held that the plaintiff is entitled to mere compensation, which is the value on the stump.[113]   The subject has been considered in an earlier chapter.[114]

§ 934a. The rule in Wisconsin.

In Wisconsin, by statute, where a defendant wrongfully cuts plaintiff's trees, plaintiff may recover the highest value of the timber in any form into which the defendant has changed it between the cutting and the trial,[115] unless the cutting falls within one of the express provisos of the statute, limiting the liability if the cutting was done by mistake, and the defendant files an affidavit to that effect,[116] or was done in good faith under claim of title.[117]   The statute does not apply to an inno-

Saltmarsh v. Chicago & G. T. Ry., 122 Mich. 103, 80 N. W. 981.

Wisconsin: Tuttle v. Wilson, 52 Wis. 643, 9 N. W. 822.

[113] *Arkansas:* Central Coal & C. Co. v. John Henry Shoe Co., 69 Ark. 302, 63 S. W. 49 (*semble*).

Colorado: Omaha & G. S. & R. R. Co. v. Tabor, 13 Colo. 41, 56, 21 Pac. 925, 16 Am. St. Rep. 185, 5 L. R. A. 236.

Minnesota: Hastay v. Bonness, 84 Minn. 120, 86 N. W. 896 (*semble*).

Ohio: Railway Co. v. Hutchins, 32 Oh. St. 571, 30 Am. Rep. 629.

Tennessee: Holt v. Hayes, 110 Tenn. 42, 73 S. W. 111.

Canada: Smith v. Baechler, 18 Ont. 293 (*semble*).

[114] *Ante,* § 504.

[115] Smith v. Morgan, 73 Wis. 375, 41 N. W. 532; Schweitzer v. Connor, 57 Wis. 177, 14 N. W. 922; St. Croix L. & L. Co. v. Ritchie, 78 Wis. 492, 47 N. W. 657.

When defendant transports the logs to his own mill, and there saws them into lumber, the plaintiff recovers the value of the lumber, not of the logs at the mill. Hazeltine v. Mosher, 51 Wis. 443, 8 N. W. 273; McNaughton v. Borth, 136 Wis. 543, 117 N. W. 1031.

The statute applies to a cutting on the public domain. Smith v. Morgan, 68 Wis. 358, 32 N. W. 135. But not to an equitable action for setting aside a deed and recovering damages for cutting. Warren v. Putnam, 63 Wis. 410, 24 N. W. 58. It was applied in a suit begun before its passage. Webster v. Moe, 35 Wis. 75.

[116] Smith v. Morgan, 68 Wis. 358, 32 N. W. 135; Webber v. Quaw, 46 Wis. 118, 49 N. W. 830.

The affidavit must be filed; it is not enough to show at the trial that the cutting was by mistake. Everett v. Gores, 89 Wis. 421, 62 N. W. 82.

An affidavit by one of several joint defendants is sufficient if made on behalf of all. Brown v. Bosworth, 58 Wis. 379, 17 N. W. 241.

Filing the affidavit is no defence where the act was done negligently. Brown v. Bosworth, 58 Wis. 379, 17 N. W. 241. Or under mistake of law, the facts being known. Schweitzer v. Connor, 57 Wis. 177, 14 N. W. 922.

The statute applies if the cutting is by an agent, but defendant on discovery of the facts ratifies the agent's acts, as by refusing to give up the logs to the plaintiff. Lee v. Lord, 76 Wis. 582, 45 N. W. 601.

[117] Fleming v. Sherry, 72 Wis. 503, 40

cent purchaser; [118] nor does it repeal or alter an earlier statute fixing the liability of the personal representative of a trespasser. [119] No interest can be added to the amount recoverable. [120]

§ 935. Removal of minerals.

Where coal, ore, or other valuable mineral is wrongfully but in good faith mined from the plaintiff's land, the measure of damages is generally and properly held to be the value of the coal or ore taken as it lay in the mine; [121] often estimated

N. W. 375 (good faith need not be reasonable); Befoy v. Wilson, 84 Wis. 135, 53 N. W. 1121.

Mere notice of plaintiff's claim is not enough to negative good faith. Warren v. Putnam, 68 Wis. 481, 32 N. W. 533; Fleming v. Sherry, 72 Wis. 503, 40 N. W. 375. But the cutting is not in good faith if the defendant, knowing all the facts as to the plaintiff's claim, believed himself to have a paramount title. Warren v. Putman, 68 Wis. 481, 32 N. W. 533. Nor is it in good faith if he learned the facts before cutting, though after his purchase of the land. Warren v. Putnam, 68 Wis. 481, 32 N. W. 533; or even if he learned them after the cutting, but thereafter removed the logs. Cook L. C. & P. Co. v. Oconto Co., 134 Wis. 426, 114 N. W. 823.

Nor is the cutting in good faith if the defendant's right was of so limited a nature as not to give the right to cut. Smith v. Morgan, 68 Wis. 358, 32 N. W. 135 (school lands certificate).

The owner whose title has been divested by a tax sale is liable under the statute if he knows that fact. Fleming v. Sherry, 72 Wis. 503, 40 N. W. 375. So is his grantee with knowledge. St. Croix L. & L. Co. v. Ritchie, 78 Wis. 492, 47 N. W. 657. See Smith v. Sherry, 54 Wis. 114, 11 N. W. 465.

[118] Wright v. E. E. Bolles Woodenware Co., 50 Wis. 167, 6 N. W. 508. The burden of proof of bad faith or

knowledge in the purchaser is on the plaintiff. Tucker v. Cole, 54 Wis. 539, 11 N. W. 703.

[119] Cotter v. Plumer, 72 Wis. 476, 40 N. W. 379.

[120] Everett v. Gores, 92 Wis. 527, 66 N. W. 616; Smith v. Morgan, 73 Wis. 375, 41 N. W. 532.

[121] *United States:* United States v. Magoon, 3 McLean, 171; Colorado Central Consolidated Mining Co. v. Turck, 70 Fed. 294, 17 C. C. A. 128 (ore); United States v. Homestake Min. Co., 117 Fed. 481, 54 C. C. A. 303 (ore).

Alabama: Warrior C. & C. Co. v. Mabel Min. Co., 112 Ala. 624, 20 So. 918 (coal); Brinkmeyer v. Bethea, 139 Ala. 376, 35 So. 996 (clay).

California: Maye v. Yappen, 23 Cal. 306 (gold).

Colorado: St. Clair v. Cash G. M. & M. Co., 9 Colo. App. 235, 47 Pac. 466 (ore).

Indiana: Sunnyside C. & C. Co. v. Reitz, 14 Ind. App. 478, 39 N. E. 541, 43 N. E. 46 (coal); Kentucky & I. C. Co. v. Morgan, 28 Ind. App. 89, 62 N. E. 68 (cement rock).

Iowa: Stewart v. Colfax C. C. Co., 147 Ia. 548, 126 N. W. 449.

Kentucky: Gerkins v. Kentucky Salt Co., 67 S. W. 821, 23 Ky. L. Rep. 2415 (natural gas).

Massachusetts: Stockbridge Iron Co. v. Cone Iron Works, 102 Mass. 80 (ore).

Minnesota: Viliski v. Minneapolis, 40 Minn. 304.

by taking the value at the mouth of the mine or elsewhere after severance and subtracting the expense of raising it to that point, or if the mineral is there reduced or dressed its value in that state less the expense reasonably incurred.[122] Some cases hold the measure of damages to be the value of the coal or ore directly after it is severed, without allowance for the expense of severing, on the ground that the coal or ore is at that moment converted.[123] But as the injury is really to the

Mississippi: Illinois Cent. R. R. v. Le Blanc, 74 Miss. 626, 21 So. 748 (gravel).

Missouri: Austin v. Huntsville C. & M. Co., 72 Mo. 535 (coal).

Nebraska: Baker v. Meisch, 29 Neb. 227, 45 N. W. 685 (clay).

New York: Dyke v. National Transit Co., 22 App. Div. 360, 49 N. Y. Supp. 180 (oil).

Pennsylvania: Blair Coal Co. v. Lloyd, 1 Walk. 158 (coal); Coleman's Appeal, 62 Pa. 252; Oak Ridge Coal Co. v. Rogers, 108 Pa. 147.

South Carolina: State v. Pacific Guano Co., 22 S. C. 50, 24 S. C. 598 (phosphate).

Tennessee: Ross v. Scott, 15 Lea, 479 (coal: in equity); Coal Creek M. & M. Co. v. Moses, 15 Lea, 300.

England: Livingstone v. Rawyard's C. Co., 5 App. Cas. 25, 42 L. T. 334, 28 W. R. 357, 44 J. P. 392, modifying Wild v. Holt, 9 M. & W. 672; Morgan v. Powell, 3 Q. B. 278; Jegon v. Vivian, L. R. 6 Ch. 742; Hilton v. Woods, L. R. 4 Eq. 432.

Canada: Kirkpatrick v. McNamee, 36 Can. 152.

The difference in value of the land before and after the trespass is not the proper measure. Sunnyside C. & C. Co. v. Reitz, 14 Ind. App. 478, 39 N. E. 541, 43 N. E. 46. See, however, Brinkmeyer v. Bethea, 139 Ala. 376, 35 So. 996.

Where the defendant makes it difficult to estimate the amount of ore taken, the burden is on him to show the amount to be less than that claimed.

California: Antoine Co. v. Ridge Co., 23 Cal. 219.

Colorado: St. Clair v. Cash G. & M. Co., 9 Colo. App. 235, 47 Pac. 466.

[122] *United States:* Aurora Hill C. M. Co. v. 85 M. Co., 12 Sawy. 355; Colorado C. C. M. Co. v. Turck, 70 Fed. 294.

California: Maye v. Tappan, 23 Cal. 306; Goller v. Fett, 30 Cal. 481; Hendricks v. Spring Valley M. & I. Co., 58 Cal. 190, 41 Am. Rep. 257.

Iowa: Chamberlain v. Collinson, 45 Ia. 429.

Michigan: Hartford I. M. Co. v. Cambria Min. Co., 93 Mich. 90, 53 N. W. 4.

Missouri: Austin v. Huntsville C. & M. Co., 72 Mo. 535, 37 Am. Rep. 446.

Montana: Fitzgerald v. Clark, 17 Mont. 100, 42 Pac. 273.

Nevada: Waters v. Stevenson, 13 Nev. 157, 29 Am. Rep. 293.

Pennsylvania: Crawford v. Forest Oil Co., 208 Pa. 5, 57 Atl. 47 (oil).

Tennessee: Dougherty v. Chesnutt, 86 Tenn. 1, 5 S. W. 444.

Texas: Bender v. Brooks, 127 S. W. 168 (oil); Gladys City O. G. & M. Co. v. Right of Way Oil Co. (Tex. Civ. App.), 137 S. W. 171 (oil).

England: In re United M. C. Co., L. R. 15 Eq. 46; Wood v. Morewood, 3 Q. B. 440.

The expense of running levels, drifts, etc., to find the ore cannot be deducted. St. Clair v. Cash G. M. & M. Co., 9 Colo. App. 235, 47 Pac. 466.

[123] *Illinois:* Robertson v. Jones, 71 Ill. 405; McLean C. C. Co. v. Long, 81

realty, the value of which is diminished by the value of the mineral *in situ*, the rule first stated gives compensation, and is the true rule. If the trespass was in bad faith, or with knowledge of the plaintiff's right, the plaintiff may recover the entire value of the chattel in the condition into which the defendant has put it, without any allowance for the labor expended upon it.[124] If injury is done to the land beyond the value of the mineral extracted, it is of course to be compensated.[125]

§ 935a. Removal or destruction of buildings.

The measure of damages for the removal or destruction of a building is sometimes held to be the difference in value of the land with and without the building at the moment of destruction.[126] It is, however, more commonly held to be the actual

Ill. 359; Illinois & S. L. R. R. & C. Co. v. Ogle, 82 Ill. 627, 25 Am. Rep. 342, 92 Ill. 353; Donovan v. Consolidated Coal Co., 187 Ill. 28, 58 N. E. 290, 88 Ill. App. 589.

Maryland: Barton Coal Co. v. Cox, 39 Md. 1, 17 Am. Rep. 525; Franklin C. Co. v. McMillan, 49 Md. 549, 33 Am. Rep. 280; Blaen Avon C. Co. v. Mc-Culloh, 59 Md. 403; Parker v. Wallis, 60 Md. 15; Atlantic & G. C. C. C. Co. v. Maryland Coal Co., 62 Md. 135.

See also the following cases:

Alabama: Nashville, C. & S. L. Ry. v. Karthaus, 150 Ala. 633, 43 So. 791 (in trover).

Indiana: Sunnyside C. & C. Co. v. Reitz, 14 Ind. App. 478, 39 N. E. 541, 43 N. E. 46.

New York: Baker v. Hart, 52 Hun, 363, 5 N. Y. Supp. 345.

Texas: Texas & N. O. R. R. v. White, 25 Tex. Civ. App. 278, 62 S. W. 133.

[124] *United States:* Benson Mining & S. Co. v. Alta Mining & S. Co., 145 U. S. 428, 12 Sup. Ct. 877, 36 L. ed. 762; Cheeney v. Nebraska & C. S. Co., 41 Fed. 740; Durant Mining Co. v. Percy Consolidated Mining Co., 93 Fed. 166, 35 C. C. A. 252; United States v. Ute C. & C. Co., 158 Fed. 20, 85 C. C. A. 302.

Colorado: United Coal Co. v. Canon City Coal Co., 24 Colo. 116, 48 Pac. 1045; St. Clair v. Cash G. M. & M. Co., 9 Colo. App. 235, 47 Pac. 466.

Indiana: Sunnyside C. & C. Co. v. Reitz, 14 Ind. App. 478, 39 N. E. 541, 43 N. E. 46.

Iowa: College v. Western Union Fuel Co., 90 Ia. 380, 54 N. W. 152, 57 N. W. 903.

Nevada: Patchen v. Keeley, 19 Nev. 404, 14 Pac. 347.

[125] *Alabama:* Warrior C. & C. Co. v. Mabel Min. Co., 112 Ala. 624, 20 So. 918.

Kentucky: Patterson v. Waldman, 20 Ky. L. Rep. 514, 46 S. W. 17.

Maryland: Barton Coal Co. v. Cox, 39 Md. 1; Blaen Avon Coal Co. v. Mc-Culloh, 59 Md. 403.

Massachusetts: Stockbridge Iron Co. v. Cone Iron Works, 102 Mass. 80.

Pennsylvania: Forsyth v. Wells, 41 Pa. 291.

England: Livingstone v. Rawyards Coal Co., 5 App. Cas. 25, 42 L. T. 334, 28 W. R. 357, 44 J. P. 392.

[126] *Ohio:* Cincinnati, C. C. & S. L. R. v. McKelvy, 12 Ohio C. Ct. 422.

Texas: Pacific Express Co. v. Lasker R. E. Assoc., 81 Tex. 81, 16 S. W. 792; Pacific Express Co. v. Smith, 16 S. W.

value of the building, as such, *in situ*,[127] which is not the cost of replacement, though such cost may be shown as evidence of the value.[128]   The difference between these rules appears where by reason of change of character or general depreciation of land values in a neighborhood the building was not suited to its location, so that the value of the land with the building upon it was less than the combined values of the land and of the building; [129] and in such a case it would seem that the owner having a right to the building as it stood, should recover the value of the building rather than the depreciation in the land.[130] In a few cases the plaintiff is allowed the cost of replacement,[131] or even the value of the building detached.[132]

For the destruction of part of a building like the roof which must be replaced in order to use the building, the measure of damages is the cost of replacing less an allowance for depreciation.[133]

Where plaintiff's house was wrongfully removed from his land and placed on the land of the defendant, who refused to

998; Wetzel *v.* Satterwhite, 125 S. W. 93.

[127] *Indiana:* Pittsburg, C., C. & S. L. Ry. *v.* Indiana H. Co., 154 Ind. 322, 56 N. E. 766.

Kentucky: Cincinnati, N. O. & T. P. Ry. *v.* Falconer, 97 S. W. 727, 30 Ky. L. Rep. 152.

Massachusetts: Wall *v.* Platt, 169 Mass. 398, 48 N. E. 270.

Michigan: Kent County Agricultural Society *v.* Ide, 128 Mich. 423, 87 N. W. 369.

Missouri: Tighe *v.* Atchison, T. & S. F. Ry., 107 S. W. 1034.

Texas: Sinclair *v.* Stanley, 64 Tex. 67.

Virginia: Norfolk & W. Ry. *v.* Thomas, 110 Va. 622, 66 S. E. 817.

For the value of an unfinished building see Bennett *v.* Clemence, 6 All. (Mass.) 10.

[128] *United States:* Patterson *v.* Kingsland, 8 Blatch. 278.

Massachusetts: Wall *v.* Platt, 169 Mass. 398, 48 N. E. 270.

[129] Cincinnati, C. C. & S. L. R. R. *v.* McKelvy, 12 Ohio C. C. 422.

[130] Cincinnati, N. O. & T. P. Ry. *v.* Falconer, 97 S. W. 727, 30 Ky. L. Rep. 152.

In Wall *v.* Platt, 169 Mass. 398, 48 N. E. 270, the court said: "Ordinarily, in determining the market value of buildings, they are valued either for the purpose of removal, or, as was the case here, in connection with the land on which they stand. The first manifestly would not afford just compensation in the present instance. In the second case, the value depends on the location and other considerations entering into the value of the land, and therefore would not necessarily constitute a just criterion of the loss actually sustained by the destruction of the buildings."

[131] Marks *v.* Culmer, 6 Utah, 419, 24 Pac. 528.

[132] Chicago & N. W. Ry. *v.* Kendall, 186 Fed. 139; 108 C. C. A. 251.

[133] Hearn *v.* McDonald (W. Va.), 71 S. E. 568.

allow the plaintiff to take it, the measure of damages was held to be the value of the house.[134]

§ 935b. Other severance from the realty.

Where a wilful trespasser severs other things from the realty the rule is the same; the value of the chattel after severance is recoverable, without allowance for the labor expended in severing the chattel. So where grass is cut and cured the owner may recover the value of the hay; [135] where wheat is harvested the plaintiff may recover the value of the wheat without allowance for the cost of harvesting; [136] and where ice is cut, the value of the ice as it lies in the water after cutting may be recovered.[137] Where the ice was carried to a distant market, the wilful trespasser has been held for its value there, without deduction for the cost of transportation.[138] And where the defendant wilfully occupied the land of another and raised and harvested a crop, he was held responsible for the entire value of the crop, without deduction for the expense of raising and harvesting it.[139]

On the other hand, where the crop is negligently destroyed, the rule is otherwise. So where a steamboat negligently destroyed plaintiff's ice as it lay on the water the plaintiff was allowed only the value of the ice as it lay on the water, just before cutting.[140]

§ 936. Accounts between owners.

The milder rule has been adopted in adjusting accounts

[134] Jonsson v. Lindstrom, 114 Ind. 152, 16 N. E. 400.

[135] *Connecticut:* Benjamin v. Benjamin, 15 Conn. 347.

Iowa: Acrea v. Brayton, 75 Ia. 719, 38 N. W. 171.

Nebraska: Carpenter v. Lingenfelter, 42 Neb. 728, 60 N. W. 1022.

[136] *Illinois:* Bull v. Griswold, 19 Ill. 631.

Indiana: Ellis v. Wire, 33 Ind. 127.

[137] Washington Ice Co. v. Shortall, 101 Ill. 46, 40 Am. Rep. 196; Piper v. Connelly, 108 Ill. 646.

Where the ice was destroyed before harvesting, the plaintiff may recover

its value when harvested, less expense and shrinkage.

Massachusetts: Handforth v. Maynard, 154 Mass. 414, 28 N. E. 348.

Pennsylvania: Stauffer v. Miller Soap Co., 151 Pa. 330, 25 Atl. 95.

See *New York:* Van Rensselaer v. Mould, 48 Hun, 396, 1 N. Y. Supp. 28.

[138] E. G. Beechwood Ice Co. v. American Ice Co., 176 Fed. 435.

[139] Negley v. Cowell, 91 Ia. 256, 59 N. W. 48.

See, however, McClure v. Thorpe, 68 Mich. 33, 35 N. W. 829.

[140] People's Ice Co. v. The Excelsior,

between owners of particular interests in the same property; so in an action by a mortgagee against a mortgagor for injury to the security.[141] Where, in an action by the landlord against his tenant for digging clay on the demised premises, one count of the plaintiff's complaint was for injury to the reversion, and the other in trover for the value of the clay, and the jury found, that the removal of the clay had diminished the value of the land, by £156, and that the value of the clay as dug was £150, and as a verdict was entered for the larger sum, a motion to increase the verdict by adding to it the sum of £150 was denied by the Irish Court of Queen's Bench.[142] So in an accounting between tenants in common, the value of ore taken from the land by one tenant is to be estimated according to its value *in place.*[143] In Curtis v. Baugh, [144] it was held that a defendant, who had agreed to indemnify the plaintiff against loss by a sale of timber which was on the land, would be liable for what he had obtained for the timber on a sale, *i. e.*, its value as a chattel.

§ 937. Destruction of annual crops.

In the case of the destruction or removal of crops, the plaintiff recovers not the diminution of the market value of the land, but the value of the crops destroyed.[145] In estimating the

44 Mich. 229, 6 N. W. 636, 38 Am. Rep. 246.

[141] Whorton v. Webster, 56 Wis. 356.

[142] Templemore v. Moore, 15 Ir. C. L. 14.

[143] *United States:* Clowser v. Joplin Mining Co., 4 Dill. 469, n.

Pennsylvania: McGowan v. Bailey, 179 Pa. 470, 36 Atl. 325.

[144] 79 Ill. 242.

[145] *Alabama:* Atlanta & B. A. L. Ry. v. Brown, 158 Ala. 607, 48 So. 73.

California: Salstrom v. Orleans B. G. M. Co., 153 Cal. 551, 96 Pac. 292.

Colorado: Colorado C. L. & W. Co. v. Hartman, 5 Colo. App. 150, 38 Pac. 62.

Indiana: Young v. Gentis, 7 Ind. App. 199, 32 N. E. 796.

Iowa: Cole v. Thompson, 134 Ia. 685, 112 N. W. 178 (see Drake v. Chicago, R. I. & P. Ry., 63 Ia. 302, 50 Am. Rep. 746).

Minnesota: Byrne v. Minneapolis & S. L. Ry., 38 Minn. 212, 36 N. W. 339; Ward v. Chicago, M. & St. P. Ry., 61 Minn. 449, 63 N. W. 1104; Burnett v. Great N. Ry., 76 Minn. 461, 79 N. W. 523.

Missouri: Carter v. Wabash R. R., 128 Mo. App. 57, 106 S. W. 611; Deal v. St. Louis, I. M. & S. Ry., 144 Mo. App. 684, 129 S. W. 50.

Nebraska: Fremont, E. & M. V. R. R. v. Marley, 25 Neb. 138, 39 N. W. 948· Chicago, B. & Q. R. R. v. Emmert, 53 Neb. 237, 73 N. W. 540, 68 Am. St. Rep. 602; Morse v. Chicago, B. & Q. Ry., 81 Neb. 745, 116 N. W. 859; Boyd v. Lincoln & N. W. R. R., 132 N. W. 529.

New York: Hatch v. Luckman, 64 Misc. 508, 118 N. Y. Supp. 689.

Pennsylvania: Robb v. Carnegie, 145 Pa. 324, 22 Atl. 649, 14 L. R. A. 329, 27

value of the crop, the prevailing rule seems to be to take its actual value at the time of trespass, not its probable value, assuming that it would have matured.[146] On the other hand, in Smith v. Chicago, C. & D. Railroad [147] the measure of damages was stated to be the difference between the market value of the crops when ripe, and their value in an injured state, less the costs of growing them. This rule, however, assumes without proof that the crops would have come to maturity. In Gulf, Colorado & Santa Fe Railroad v. McGowan,[148] the Supreme Court of Texas said that one way to get at the value of the crops when destroyed was to take the value when ripe less the costs of maturing them, and also allow for the contingencies of loss before maturity. An allowance for the contingencies of loss before maturity would, if not otherwise objectionable,

Am. St. Rep. 694; Vautier v. Atlantic Refining Co., 79 Atl. 814.

Tennessee: Ducktown S. C. & I. Co. v. Barnes, 60 S. W. 593.

Texas: Texas & P. Ry. v. Bayliss, 62 Tex. 570; Sabine & E. T. Ry. v. Johnson, 65 Tex. 389; Missouri, K. & T. Ry. v. Couch (Tex. Civ. App.), 122 S. W. 67; Gulf Pipe Line Co. v. Brymer, (Tex. Civ. App.), 124 S. W. 1007; International & G. N. R. R. v. Foster, 45 Tex. Civ. App. 334, 100 S. W. 1017; Moore v. Graham, 29 Tex. Civ. App. 235, 69 S. W. 200.

Utah: Lester v. Highland B. G. Min. Co., 27 Utah, 470, 76 Pac. 341, 101 Am. St. Rep. 988.

Wisconsin: Folsom v. Apple R. L. D. Co., 41 Wis. 602.

In Brown v. Leath, 17 Tex. Civ. App. 262, 24 S. W. 655, it was held that plaintiff might recover not merely the value of the crop, but also for loss of services of his minor children who would have picked the crop; but this is of questionable correctness.

The fact that in the same year there is subsequently grown and gathered a crop does not relieve the defendant from responsibility. Galveston, H. & S. A. Ry. v. Parr, 8 Tex. Civ. App. 280, 28 S. W. 264. But evidence that an-

other crop of some character may still be raised in the same season is admissible to show the extent of the injury. Ward v. Chicago, M. & S. P. Ry., 61 Minn. 449, 63 N. W. 1104.

[146] *Alabama:* Gresham v. Taylor, 51 Ala. 505.

Arkansas: St. Louis, I. M. & S. Ry. v. Lyman, 57 Ark. 512, 22 S. W. 170.

Massachusetts: King v. Fowler, 14 Pick. 238.

Minnesota: Hinman v. Heyderstadt, 32 Minn. 250, 20 N. W. 155; Lommeland v. St. Paul, M. & M. Ry., 35 Minn. 412, 29 N. W. 119; Byrne v. Minneapolis & S. L. Ry., 38 Minn. 212, 8 Am. St. Rep. 668, 36 N. W. 339.

New York: Richardson v. Northrup, 66 Barb. 85.

Texas: Sabine & E. T. Ry. v. Joachimi, 58 Tex. 456; International & G. N. Ry. v. Benitos, 59 Tex. 326; Texas & S. L. R. R. v. Young, 60 Tex. 201; Gulf, C. & S. F. Ry. v. Pool, 70 Tex. 713; Trinity & S. Ry. v. Schofield, 72 Tex. 496; Sabine & E. T. Ry. v. Smith, 73 Tex. 1.

[147] 38 Ia. 518; *acc.,* Throop v. Fowler, 15 Up. Can. Q. B. 365.

[148] 73 Tex. 355; *acc.,* International & G. N. R. R. v. Pape, 73 Tex. 501.

make this rule result in perfect compensation; but any estimate of the kind must contain elements of uncertainty.

Since a growing crop probably has no market value, the actual value must be shown in some other way; and since some loss has admittedly happened, mere uncertainty in the estimate of damage should not prevent recovery, provided the amount is made as certain as the nature of the case permits If the crop was mature when destroyed, an allowance of its value when marketed less the cost of marketing seems sufficiently certain.[149] If it was immature, but a portion is left to come to maturity, it is a sufficiently certain rule to allow compensation for the portion destroyed on the basis of the value of the portion which matured.[150] If the crop is entirely destroyed before it matures, it would seem to be allowable, in case there is nothing especially uncertain or speculative about the crop, to find its value at the time of destruction, having in consideration what it would have cost to mature and harvest the crop, and what it would have been worth when harvested,[151] bearing also in mind the

[149] *California:* Quint v. Dimond, 147 Cal. 707, 82 Pac. 310.

Iowa: Blunck v. Chicago & N. W. Ry., 142 Ia. 146, 115 N. W. 1013 (hay).

Missouri: Mattis v. St. Louis & S. F. Ry., 138 Mo. App. 61, 119 S. W. 998 (hay); Adam v. Chicago, B. & Q. Ry., 139 Mo. App. 204, 122 S. W. 1136 (alfalfa).

[150] *Arkansas:* Jonesboro L. C. & E. Ry. v. Cable, 89 Ark. 518, 117 S. W. 550.

Missouri: Hunt v. St. Louis, I. M. & S. R. R., 126 Mo. App. 261, 103 S. W. 133.

Texas: Texas & N. O. R. R. v. Ochiltree (Tex. Civ. App.), 127 S. W. 584.

[151] *Arkansas:* St. Louis, I. M. & S. Ry. v. Yarbrough, 56 Ark. 612, 20 S. W. 515.

California: Teller v. Bay & River Dredging Co., 151 Cal. 209, 90 Pac. 942, 12 L. R. A. (N. S.) 267.

Colorado: Colorado C. L. & W. Co. v. Hartman, 5 Colo. App. 150, 38 Pac. 62; Catlin C. C. Co. v. Euster, 19 Colo. App. 117, 73 Pac. 846.

Illinois: St. Louis M. B. T. R. Ass'n v. Schultz, 226 Ill. 409, 80 N. E. 879; Economy L. & P. Co. v. Cutting, 49 Ill. App. 422; Scanland v. Musgrove, 91 Ill. App. 184.

Iowa: Smith v. Chicago C. & D. R. R., 38 Ia. 518; Tretter v. Chicago G. W. Ry., 147 Ia. 375, 126 N. W. 339.

Minnesota: Ward v. Chicago, M. & S. P. Ry., 61 Minn. 449, 63 N. W. 1104.

Montana: Hopkins v. Butte & M. C. Co., 16 Mont. 356, 40 Pac. 865.

Nevada: Malmstrom v. People's D. D. Co., 32 Nev. 246, 107 Pac. 98; Candler v. Washoe L. R. & G. C. D. Co., 28 Nev. 151, 80 Pac. 751.

New Mexico: Smith v. Hicks, 14 N. M. 560, 98 Pac. 138.

Oklahoma: Chicago, R. I. & P. Ry. v. Johnson, 25 Okla. 760, 107 Pac. 662.

Texas: San Antonio & A. P. R. R. v. Kiersey (Tex. Civ. App.), 81 S. W. 1045; Suderman-Dolson Co. v. Rogers, 47 Tex. Civ. App. 67, 104 S. W. 193; Kansas City, M. & O. Ry. v. Mayfield (Tex. Civ. App.), 107 S. W. 940; Missouri, K. & T. Ry. v. Riverhead Farm, 53 Tex. Civ. App. 643, 117

ordinary hazards of agriculture.[152] If nothing is proved with sufficient certainty in this way, it would seem to be permissible, at the option of the plaintiff, in analogy to the rule in actions for breach of contract,[153] to prove the actual expenditures already made upon the land in order to raise the crop, together with the rental value of the land; [154] since the farmer must on the average at the least cover his expenses from his crops, and a crop must therefore in all probability be worth at least what it has cost to produce it.

§ 937a. Destruction of permanent crops.

If, however, the destruction is not of an annual crop, but of a more or less permanent one, as of the turf of a pasture or meadow, the injury becomes an injury to the land itself, and the measure of damages is the diminished value of the land,[155] or,

S. W. 1049; Texas Co. *v.* Lacour (Tex. Civ. App.), 122 S. W. 424; Missouri, K. & T. Ry. *v.* Gilbert (Tex. Civ. App.), 124 S. W. 434; Freeman *v.* Field (Tex. Civ. App.), 135 S. W. 1073.

Washington: Shotwell *v.* Dodge, 8 Wash. 337, 36 Pac. 254.

West Virginia: Kyle *v.* Ohio R. R. R., 49 W. Va. 296, 38 S. E. 489.

Canada: Throop *v.* Fowler, 15 U. C. Q. B. 365.

Contra, Indiana: Chicago & E. R. R. *v.* Barnes, 10 Ind. App. 460, 38 N. E. 428.

Kansas: Hays *v.* Crist, 4 Kan. 350.

[152] Galveston H. & S. A. Ry. *v.* Borsky, 2 Tex. Civ. App. 545, 21 S. W. 1011; Gulf, C. & S. F. Ry. *v.* Haskell, 4 Tex. Civ. App. 550, 23 S. W. 546; Gulf, C. & S. F. Ry. *v.* Nicholson, 25 S. W. 54; Gulf, C. & S. F. Ry. *v.* Carter, 25 S. W. 1023.

[153] *Ante,* § 616.

[154] *Missouri:* Standley *v.* Railway, 121 Mo. App. 537, 97 S. W. 244; Jones *v.* Cooley Lake Club, 122 Mo. App. 113, 98 S. W. 82 (cost of reseeding and rental value of land).

South Carolina: Horres *v.* Chemical Co., 57 S. C. 189, 35 S. E. 500, 52 L. R.

A. 36; Lampley *v.* Atlantic C. L. R. R., 63 S. C. 462, 41 S. E. 517.

The rule laid down in the South Carolina case is discredited in a number of cases, *e. g.,* in Teller Bay & River Dredging Co., 151 Cal. 209, 90 Pac. 942, 12 L. R. A. (N. S.) 267; and see Chicago & E. R. R. *v.* Barnes, 10 Ind. App. 460, 38 N. E. 428; Ducktown S. C. & I. Co. *v.* Barnes (Tenn.), 60 S. W. 593. But as an alternative method of proving the value of the crop it would seem permissible, as has been explained in the text.

[155] *Indiana:* Terre Haute & L. R. R. *v.* Walsh, 11 Ind. App. 13, 38 N. E. 534; Chicago & E. R. R. *v.* Smith, 6 Ind. App. 262, 33 N. E. 241.

Iowa: Swanson *v.* Keokuk & W. R. R., 116 Ia. 304, 89 N. W. 1088.

Minnesota: Ward *v.* Chicago, M. & St. P. Ry., 61 Minn. 449, 63 N. W. 1104.

Missouri: Gates *v.* Chicago & A. Ry., 44 Mo. App. 488; Wiggins *v.* St. Louis & S. F. R. R., 119 Mo. App. 492, 95 S. W. 311, 129 Mo. App. 369, 108 S. W. 574; Adam *v.* Chicago, B. & Q. Ry., 139 Mo. App. 204, 122 S. W. 1136.

Nebraska: Morse *v.* Chicago, B. & Q.

if the meadow can be restored at a reasonable expense, the cost of such restoration, with compensation for the temporary loss of use.[156]

§ 938. Destruction of fences.

In estimating the injury to fences, also, the value of the fence, not the diminished value of the land, should be the measure of damages.[157] The value of the fences is measured by the sum which "will, properly expended, restore the premises to their condition before the interference therewith by the defendant." [158]

Ry., 81 Neb. 745, 116 N. W. 859; Thompson v. Chicago, B. & Q. R. R., 84 Neb. 482, 121 N. W. 447.

New York: Black v. Highland S. S. Co., 98 App. Div. 409, 90 N. Y. Supp. 338.

Texas: Fort Worth & D. C. Ry. v. Hogsett, 67 Tex. 685; Fort Worth & N. O. Ry. v. Wallace, 74 Tex. 581, 12 S. W. 227; Gulf, C. & S. F. Ry. v. Matthews, 3 Tex. Civ. App. 493, 23 S. W. 90; Gulf, C. & S. F. Ry. v. Cusenberry, 5 Tex. Civ. App. 114, 23 S. W. 851; Missouri, K. & T. R. R. v. Pfluger, 25 S. W. 792; Missouri, K. & T. Ry. v. Goode, 7 Tex. Civ. App. 245, 26 S. W. 441; Gulf, C. & S. F. Ry. v. Jagoe, 32 S. W. 717; Gulf, C. & S. F. Ry. v. Reggan, 32 S. W. 846; Baker v. Mims, 14 Tex. Civ. App. 413, 37 S. W. 190; Texas & P. Ry. v. Rice, 24 Tex. Civ. App. 374, 59 S. W. 833; Texas & P. Ry. v. Graffeo (Tex. Civ. App.), 118 S. W. 873; Gulf P. L. Co. v. Brymer (Tex. Civ. App.), 124 S. W. 1007.

See also *Indiana:* Terre Haute & L. R. R. v. Walsh, 11 Ind. App. 13, 38 N. E. 534.

Kansas: Atchison, T. & S. F. Ry. v. Arthurs, 63 Kan. 404, 65 Pac. 651.

[156] *Arkansas:* St. Louis & S. F. Ry. v. Jones, 59 Ark. 105, 26 S. W. 595.

Indiana: Pittsburgh, C. & S. L. Ry. v. Hixon, 110 Ind. 225, 11 N. E. 285.

Iowa: Vermilya v. Chicago, M. & S. P. Ry., 66 Ia. 606, 24 N. W. 234, 55 Am. Rep. 279; Black v. Minneapolis & S. L. R. R., 122 Ia. 32, 96 N. W. 984.

Missouri: Mattis v. St. Louis & S. F. Ry., 138 Mo. App. 61, 119 S. W. 998; Crouch v. Kansas City So. Ry., 141 Mo. App. 256, 124 S. W. 1077.

[157] *Iowa:* Graessle v. Carpenter, 70 Ia. 166, 30 N. W. 392.

Missouri: Waters v. Brown, 44 Mo. 302.

Washington: Koch v. Phillips Inv. Co., 9 Wash. 405, 37 Pac. 703.

See *Texas:* Baker v. Mims, 14 Tex. Civ. App. 413, 37 S. W. 190.

Avary v. Searcy, 50 Ala. 54, a case of this sort, was treated by the court as an action of trover, and evidence offered in mitigation that the plaintiff's land was of little value was excluded.

[158] *New York:* Marvin v. Pardee, 64 Barb. 353, 361.

Texas: Jackel v. Reiman, 14 S. W. 1001; Gulf, C. & S. F. Ry. v. McMurrough, 41 Tex. Civ. App. 216, 91 S. W. 320.

It is the value of the fence which was there and not the value of a fence of another kind though equally effective. Ohio & M. Ry. v. Trapp, 4 Ind. App. 69, 30 N. E. 812.

In Pennybecker v. McDougal, 48 Cal. 160, the plaintiff recovered only the value of the materials after removal, because it was an action of replevin, and not an action complaining of an injury to the inheritance. In

§ 939. Removal of soil.

* In an action of trespass for entering upon the plaintiff's close, and carrying away the soil, the proper measure of damages has been held to be the value of the land removed, and not the expense of restoring the premises to their original condition; [159] ** but if the soil removed were in itself valueless, the diminution in value of the land may be recovered. [160] In an action to recover for injuries to the plaintiff's land, occasioned by its falling in, in consequence of excavations made by the defendant in his own land adjoining, the measure of damages is not what it will cost to restore the lot to its former condition, or to build a wall to support it, but the amount by which the lot is diminished in value by reason of the acts of the defendant; [161] but in an action of trespass for digging a ditch on the plaintiff's land, the measure of damages is the cost of restoring the land to its former condition, with compensation for loss of the use of it, if this altogether is less than the diminu-

Logansport, C. & S. Ry. v. Wray, 52 Ind. 578, it was held that the measure of damages for *failure to perform a contract to erect fences* was the cost of constructing them.

[159] *California:* De Costa v. Massachusetts F. W. & M. Co., 17 Cal. 613.

Illinois: Chicago Dock Co. v. Dunlap, 32 Ill. 207.

Missouri: Mueller v. St. Louis & I. M. R. R., 31 Mo. 262.

New York: Hartshorn v. Chaddock, 135 N. Y. 116, 31 N. E. 997.

Rhode Island: Williams v. Hathaway, 21 R. I. 566, 45 Atl. 578.

England: Jones v. Gooday, 8 M. & W. 146, 10 L. J. Ex. 275.

[160] *United States:* Murray v. Pannaci, 130 Fed. 529, 65 C. C. A. 153 (*semble*).

Alabama: Brinkmeyer v. Bethea, 139 Ala. 376, 35 So. 996.

Iowa: Parrott v. Chicago & G. W. Ry., 127 Ia. 419, 103 N. W. 352.

Minnesota: Karst v. St. Paul, S. & T. P. R. R., 22 Minn. 118, 23 Minn. 401.

New York: Higgins v. New York, L. E. & W. R. R., 78 Hun, 567, 29 N. Y. Supp. 563.

[161] *Indiana:* Moellering v. Evans, 121 Ind. 195.

Massachusetts: Gilmore v. Driscoll, 122 Mass. 199, 23 Am. Rep. 312.

Minnesota: Kopp v. Northern P. R. R., 41 Minn. 310.

New Jersey: McGuire v. Grant, 25 N. J. L. 356, 67 Am. Dec. 49.

Ohio: Keating v. Cincinnati, 38 Oh. St. 141, 43 Am. Rep. 421.

South Dakota: Ulrick v. Dakota Loan & T. Co., 2 S. D. 285, 49 N. W. 1054, 51 N. W. 1023.

In Gilmore v. Driscoll, *supra*, it was held that the defendant was not liable for injuries to the buildings or improvements thereon; that he was liable for damages occasioned by the loss and injury to the soil alone; that he was not liable for the cost of putting the plaintiff's land into and maintaining it in its former condition, and that the plaintiff could not recover the diminished market value of the land, for the diminution in market value was not shown to be due entirely to loss of land. *Acc.*, McGettigan v. Potts, 149 Pa. 155, 24 Atl. 198.

tion in value of the land with the ditch open.[162]   This is on the principle already stated, that if the cost of repairing the injury is greater than the diminution in market value of the land, the latter is always the true measure of damages, the rule of avoidable consequences requiring that in such a case the plaintiff shall diminish the loss as far as possible.

§ 940. Mills and flowage.

* We have already seen that where the injury consists in improperly flooding the land of another, the law presumes nominal damages, even if no actual damage be proved; [163] and so if water be wrongfully diverted from a mill, or a watercourse be obstructed, nominal damages will, at all events, be awarded.[164] So it is not necessary for the plaintiff, in an action for the diversion of a watercourse, to show that he has sustained specific damage thereby; he may recover, notwithstanding he has sustained no actual or perceptible injury.[165]   In Massachusetts, however, where an action was brought for an injury to the plaintiff's mill, by causing the water to flow back on it, the judge instructed the jury, that, if the plaintiff proved his mill to have sustained any actual perceptible damage in consequence of the defendant's act, he was entitled to recover, but that for a theoretic injury or damage to be inferred from the obstruction of the water by the defendant's dam, he was not

[162] *Arkansas:* St. Louis M. Co. *v.* Miller, 11 S. W. 958.

Michigan: Walters *v.* Chamberlin, 65 Mich. 333.

. The plaintiff cannot recover the rental value of the land while he is engaged in bringing suit against the wrong person. Cavanagh *v.* Durgin, 156 Mass. 466, 31 N. E. 643.

[163] *Maine:* Munroe *v.* Stickney, 48 Me. 462.

North Carolina: Wright *v.* Stowe, 4 Jones, L. 516; Little *v.* Stanback, 63 N. C. 285.

Pennsylvania: Miller *v.* Laubach, 47 Pa. 154, 86 Am. Dec. 521.

[164] *Connecticut:* Parker *v.* Griswold, 17 Conn. 288, 42 Am. Dec. 739; Branch

v. Doane, 18 Conn. 233, 44 Am. Dec. 586.

Maine: Butman *v.* Hussey, 12 Me. 407, 28 Am. Dec. 188.

Missouri: Jones *v.* Hannovan, 55 Mo. 462.

Ohio: Tootle *v.* Clifton, 22 Oh. St. 247, 10 Am. Rep. 732.

See *Vermont:* Chatfield *v.* Wilson, 27 Vt. 670.

It is no answer to this action that the defendant first appropriated the water to his own use. Mason *v.* Hill, 3 B. & A. 304.

[165] *Connecticut:* Parker *v.* Griswold, 17 Conn. 288, 42 Am. Dec. 739.

England: Bower *v.* Hill, 1 Bing. N. C. 549.

answerable; and on motion for a new trial this was held right.[166]

The principle of the common law in cases of this kind, as we have seen, is that successive actions can be brought as long as the obstruction exists; and in some of the States of the Union an attempt has therefore been made to regulate the subject by statute. So, in North Carolina, an act was passed, of which the leading feature is to prevent any action being brought against the owner of a mill, unless it be first ascertained on petition, by the verdict of a jury, that the annual damage during the time for which the action is to be brought, amounts to the sum of twenty dollars at least.[167]　Where two or more mills are entitled to a common use of water, the owner of the upper mill must afford the lower mill a fair and reasonable participation in its use. If the injury is trivial the law will not afford redress, but it will interpose to prevent the lower mill being rendered useless or unproductive.[168] **

* In a case in the Queen's Bench, where in an action of trespass for entering the plaintiff's close and destroying a milldam, the defendant justified the trespass on the ground that he was possessed of a mill, and that a stream of water of right flowed thereto, and that the plaintiff's dam obstructed the flow of water to defendant's mill, it was asked whether the plaintiff sought to recover substantial damages; and his counsel not declaring such to be the case, the Lord Chief-Justice said that the action was brought more to try a right than to recover damages, and directed the defendant to begin; and on motion for a new trial this was held right.[169] **

The measure of damages is the diminution in value of the whole tract of land, part of which is overflowed.[170]

[166] Thompson v. Crocker, 9 Pick. 59.
See to the same effect:
Alabama: Burden v. Mobile, 21 Ala. 309.
Massachusetts: Elliott v. Fitchburg R. R., 10 Cush. 191, 57 Am. Dec. 85.
Ohio: McElroy v. Goble, 6 Oh. St. 187.
Pennsylvania: Bell v. McClintock, 9 Watts, 119.
The damage from the stoppage of the plaintiff's mill is an injurious consequence which he may recover in an action of trespass for the destruction of his milldam without specially averring it in the declaration. Spigelmoyer v. Walter, 3 W. & S. 540.
[167] Gilliam v. Canaday, 11 Ired. 106.
[168] Sackrider v. Beers, 10 Johns. 241.
[169] Chapman v. Rawson, 8 Q. B. 673.
[170] *Massachusetts:* Monson & B. M. Co. v. Fuller, 15 Pick. 554.

§ 941. Diversion or obstruction of water—Avoidable consequences.

In this instance, the injury may or may not be permanent; moreover, it may or may not be easily remediable, and the measure of damages will vary accordingly. The value of the use of the water during the time the plaintiff was wrongfully deprived of it will usually be the true measure of damages.[171] Thus, in an early New York case, the damages were arrived at by a comparison of the tolls upon the number of barrels of flour actually ground by the plaintiff's mill, with the number that he might have ground if he had had the use of the water to which he was entitled.[172]   In a less direct way, the loss may be determined by the decrease in the annual value of the property during the continuance of the injury.[173]   But where the in-

Pennsylvania: Schuylkill Nav. Co. *v.* Farr, 4 W. & S. 362.

See *Wisconsin:* Lockhart *v.* Geir, 54 Wis. 133, 11 N. W. 245.

[171] *New York:* Pollitt *v.* Long, 58 Barb. 20.

Utah: Whitmore *v.* Utah Fuel Co., 26 Utah, 488, 73 Pac. 764.

[172] Merritt *v.* Brinckerhoff, 17 Johns. 306, 8 Am. Dec. 404.

See, also, Platt *v.* Root, 15 Johns. 213, 8 Am. Dec. 233.

[173] *Indiana:* Valparaiso C. W. W. *v.* Dickover, 17 Ind. App. 233, 46 N. E. 591.

New York: Honsee *v.* Hammond, 39 Barb. 89; Covert *v.* Valentine, 66 Hun, 632, 21 N. Y. Supp. 219.

For the purpose of establishing this decrease, the effect of the diversion on crops raised on plaintiff's land may be shown.

California: Razzo *v.* Varni, 81 Cal. 289, 22 Pac. 848.

New York: Soper *v.* New York, 71 App. Div. 618, 75 N. Y. Supp. 969.

Washington: Shotwell *v.* Dodge, 8 Wash. 337, 36 Pac. 254.

So, where the defendants cut off the water which worked the plaintiff's mill, the plaintiff was allowed to recover profits he would otherwise have made, which would be the market value less the value of raw material and of labor; or if he engaged his labor by the year, he should deduct the value of the raw material only. Holden *v.* Lake Co., 53 N. H. 552.

It has been said that the effect on the rental value must be determined by the uses to which the property had actually been put in the past, not by a possible use to which it might have been put, as for instance, for building a mill.

Georgia: Southern Marble Co. *v.* Darnell, 94 Ga. 231, 21 S. E. 531.

New York: •Gallagher *v.* Kingston Water Co., 25 App. Div. 82, 49 N. Y. Supp. 250.

Pennsylvania: Clark *v.* Pennsylvania R. R., 145 Pa. 438, 22 Atl. 989, 27 Am. St. Rep. 710.

This, however, is because such alleged loss of value cannot be proved with sufficient certainty; and if it can be certainly proved it should be allowed. So where defendant diverted water and sold it for water power it was held that plaintiff was entitled to recover the value of the water power diverted, without regard to whether he would have made use of it. Green Bay & M. C. Co. *v.* Kaukauna W. P. Co., 112 Wis. 323, 87 N. W. 864.

jury is of a permanent character, the damages should be assessed on that basis.[174]   So it has been held that the measure of damages sustained by a riparian owner, by the unlawful filling of a pond, is the depreciation in the value of the property occasioned thereby, not merely the depreciated value of its use whenever used.[175]   The diminution in market value of the property affected of course becomes the measure of damages.[176]

In either case the question of the cost of obviating the loss may arise.   For example, in an action for injury to a mill-pond by throwing refuse into the stream above, it may be that the cost of removing the deposit would be less than the difference in the value of the land occasioned by it, and the cost of removal would then be the proper measure; or it may be that the cost of removal would be much greater than the injury by the deposit, and the true measure would then be the difference in value; and it will frequently be impossible, until evidence is put in, to determine which rule is applicable.[177] Whenever it appears that to obviate the injury by removal or repairs is the proper course, the plaintiff is allowed whatever sum is reasonably necessary for the purpose, even though this exceed the original cost of the part repaired.[178]   So where

[174] *Iowa:* Mulverhill v. Thompson, 122 Ia. 229, 97 N. W. 1077.

Kentucky: King v. Board of Council of City of Danville, 128 Ky. 321, 107 S. W. 1189.

Massachusetts: Howe v. Weymouth, 155 Mass. 439, 29 N. E. 646.

Montana: Sweeney v. Montana Ry., 25 Mont. 543, 65 Pac. 912.

New York: Spencer v. Kilmer, 151 N. Y. 390, 45 N. E. 865.

Texas: Galveston & S. A. Ry. v. Haas, 37 S. W. 167.

[175] Finley v. Hershey, 41 Ia. 389.

[176] It has been held in Pennsylvania that the general market value for any purpose should be taken, and not merely the market value for the specific uses (farming, mining, etc.) to which the plaintiff may be putting the property. Shenango & Allegheny R. R. v. Braham, 79 Pa. 447, and cases cited.

[177] Agnew, J., Seely v. Alden, 61 Pa.

302.   So where the defendant had merely connected the stream with a pipe of his, the court refused prospective damage, saying that a severance of the connection would cause the water to flow in its accustomed channel, and that there was no permanent injury, for there was no severance of any part of the plaintiff's freehold, nor was there any depositing of a permanent nuisance on the land. Bare v. Hoffman, 79 Pa. 71.

[178] *California:* De Costa v. Massachusetts F. W. & M. Co., 17 Cal. 613.

Maine: Topsham v. Lisbon, 65 Me. 449.

Montana: Sweeney v, Montana Ry., 25 Mont. 543, 65 Pac. 912.

In Hostele v. Farmers' Protective Assn., 53 Pac. 327, plaintiff was allowed to recover the cost of using steam instead of the water power diverted.

the defendant wrongfully cut a pipe used to convey water to the plaintiff's land, the measure of damages is the cost of reconstructing the pipe line and the value of the use of the water while the plaintiff was deprived of it.[179] Where the defendant threw flax shives into the stream below the plaintiff's gristmill, and the shives settled in the plaintiff's pond, forming a bar which caused an obstruction and filled the dam belonging to the mill, it was held that the plaintiff, without having removed the deposit, could recover as damages the amount necessary to restore the mill-pond to the condition it was in before the damage occurred.[180]

§ 942. Flooding land.

In this instance, also, so far as the injury is partial or temporary only, the measure of damages is the actual loss sustained during the continuance of the injury,[181] measured in the ordinary case by the rental value of the land.[182]

[179] Reynolds v. Braithwaite, 131 Pa. 416, 18 Atl. 1110.

[180] O'Riley v. McChesney, 3 Lans. 278; s. c. 49 N. Y. 672.

[181] *Missouri:* Pinney v. Berry, 61 Mo. 359.

Texas: Texas Cent. R. R. v. Wilks, 41 S. W. 848; Gulf, C. & S. F. Ry. v. Haskell, 4 Tex. Civ. App. 550, 23 S. W. 546.

In a proper case this will be the amount of profits lost. Simmons v. Brown, 5 R. I. 299: see § 184. So in an action for overflowing his land by the defendant's milldam, the plaintiff is not confined to the net gain to be derived from the land in its actual condition. The jury should consider the capabilities of the land for more profitable use in a changed condition. Ellington v. Bennett, 59 Ga. 286.

[182] *Arkansas:* Kansas City, F. S. & M. R. R. v. Cook, 57 Ark. 387, 21 S. W. 1066.

Georgia: Georgia R. R. & B. Co. v. Berry, 78 Ga. 744, 4 S. E. 10.

Illinois: Comerford v. Morrison, 145 Ill. App. 615.

Iowa: Sullens v. Chicago, R. I. & P. Ry., 74 Ia. 659, 38 N. W. 545, 7 Am. St. Rep. 501; Willitts v. Chicago, B. & K. C. Ry., 88 Ia. 281, 55 N. W. 313.

Kentucky: Hutchison v. City of Maysville, 100 S. W. 331, 30 Ky. Law Rep. 1173; Pickerill v. City of Louisville, 125 Ky. 213, 100 S. W. 873, 30 Ky. Law Rep. 1239.

Michigan: Witheral v. Muskegon Booming Co., 68 Mich. 48, 35 N. W. 758.

Minnesota: Barrows v. Fox, 39 Minn. 61, 38 N. W. 777; Jungblum v. Minneapolis N. W. & S. W. R. R., 70 Minn. 153, 72 N. W. 971.

Missouri: Jones v. Cooley Lake Club, 122 Mo. App. 113, 98 S. W. 82.

New York: Reichert v. Backenstross, 71 Hun, 367, 24 N. Y. Supp. 1009; Gillett v. Kinderhook, 77 Hun, 604, 28 N. Y. Supp. 1044.

Pennsylvania: Weir v. Plymouth, 148 Pa. 566, 24 Atl. 94.

Texas: Gulf, C. & S. F. Ry. v. Helsley, 62 Tex. 593; Texas & P. Ry. v. Ford (Tex. Civ. App.), 117 S. W. 201.

If the injury is permanent, the diminished market value of the property (comparing the value before and immediately after the completion of the wrongful act) must be taken,[183] not the loss of profits, custom, etc., though these may serve as the basis of a witness' opinion as to the general market value.[184] But if the flowing water separates one part of the complainant's land from another, so as to render bridges or new causeways necessary, it is a direct injury for which damages are to be awarded, and the cost of a new structure would, in some cases, be a proper measure of the injury. Where the value of the land so separated is not enough to justify the outlay, the damages under this rule must be limited to the loss of productive value.[185] If the injury consists in a permanent liability to successive losses, then their amount must be estimated.[186]

Vermont: Willey v. Hunter, 57 Vt. 479.

West Virginia: Pickens v. Coal R. B. & T. Co., 58 W. Va. 11, 50 S. E. 872. But see *Georgia:* Georgia R. R. & B. Co. v. Berry, 78 Ga. 744, 4 S. E. 10. If the flooding of part of a tract causes damage to the whole tract, such damage may be recovered. Hastings v. Chicago, R. I. & P. Ry., 148 Ia. 390, 126 N. W. 786.

[183] *Illinois:* Suehr v. Sanitary Dist. of Chicago, 242 Ill. 496, 90 N. E. 197.

Iowa: Steber v. Chicago & G. W. Ry., 139 Ia. 153, 117 N. W. 304; Kopecky v. Benish, 138 Ia. 362, 116 N. W. 118.

Kentucky: Hutchison v. Maysville, 100 S. W. 331, 30 Ky. L. Rep. 1173; Pickerill v. Louisville, 125 Ky. 213, 100 S. W. 873, 30 Ky. L. Rep. 1239; Illinois Cent. R. R. v. Haynes, 122 S. W. 210, Illinois Cent. R. R. v. Nelson, 127 S. W. 520.

Minnesota: Hueston v. Mississippi & R. R. B. Co., 76 Minn. 251, 79 N. W. 92; Osborn v. Mississippi & R. R. B. Co., 95 Minn. 149, 103 N. W. 879.

Missouri: South Side Realty Co. v. St. Louis & S. F. R. R., 154 Mo. App. 364, 134 S. W. 1034.

Montana: Sweeney v. Montana Cent. Ry., 19 Mont. 163, 47 Pac. 791.

Nebraska: McClure v. Broken Bow., 81 Neb. 385, 115 N. W. 1081.

New York: Gillett v. Kinderhook, 77 Hun, 604, 28 N. Y. Supp. 1044.

Pennsylvania: Schuylkill Nav. Co. v. Farr, 4 W. & S. 362.

Texas: International & G. N. Ry. v. Davis, 29 S. W. 483; San Antonio & A. P. Ry. v. Horkan, 45 S. W. 391; Missouri, K. & T. Ry. v. Chilton, 52 Tex. Civ. App. 516, 118 S. W. 779; Missouri, K. & T. Ry. v. Malone (Tex. Civ. App.), 126 S. W. 936; Missouri, K. & T. Ry. v. Tolbert (Tex. Civ. App.), 134 S. W. 280.

Washington: Ingram v. Wishka Boom Co., 35 Wash. 191, 77 Pac. 34.

West Virginia: Rowe v. Shenandoah Pulp Co., 42 W. Va. 551, 26 S. E. 320.

[184] *Illinois:* Carter v. Cairo V. & C. Ry., 240 Ill. 152, 88 N. E. 493, affirming 145 Ill. App. 653.

Indiana: Terre Haute v. Hudnut, 112 Ind. 542, 13 N. E. 686.

Michigan: Witheral v. Muskegon Booming Co., 68 Mich. 48, 35 N. W. 758. But see *Missouri:* Grant v. St. Louis, I. M. & S. Ry., 149 Mo. App. 306, 130 S. W. 80.

[185] Bates v. Ray, 102 Mass. 458.

[186] Van Pelt v. Davenport, 42 Ia. 308, 20 Am. Rep. 622.

If the injury consists in a past loss for a definite period, together with a partial permanent diminution in value, then both must be covered by the damages.[187] Where it was shown that the land would have been flooded by natural causes, but the defendant's act increased the loss, the measure of damages was the increase of loss.[188]

On the same principle, followed where compensation is sought for the destruction of crops, it is held in an action for overflowing land, whereby it could not be planted, that the measure of damages is the rental value, not the probable value of crops, less cost of cultivation.[189] The plaintiff's right to a recovery is not affected by the fact that another dam besides defendant's contributes to the flowage.[190]

Consequential damages may be recovered, such as physical inconvenience[191] or illness[192] resulting from the flooding; and the cost of restoration or repair can always be recovered, if it was a reasonable expense.[193]

[187] *Indiana:* South Bend v. Paxon, 67 Ind. 228.

Nebraska: Fremont, E. & M. V. R. R. v. Harlin, 50 Neb. 698, 70 N. W. 263.

New York: Walrath v. Redfield, 11 Barb. 368, 18 N. Y. 457.

Texas: Sabine & E. T. Ry. v. Johnson, 65 Tex. 389; Fort Worth & D. C. Ry. v. Flynt (Tex. Civ. App.), 125 S. W. 347.

[188] *Arkansas:* St. Louis, I. M. & S. Ry. v. Morris, 35 Ark. 622.

Nebraska: Stewart v. Schneider, 22 Neb. 286.

England: Workman v. Great N. R. R., 32 L. J. Q. B. 279.

[189] *Arkansas:* St. Louis, I. M. & S. Ry. v. Hardie, 87 Ark. 475, 113 S. W. 31.

Georgia: Gentry v. Richmond & D. R. R., 16 S. E. 893.

Idaho: Young v. Extension Ditch Co., 13 Ida. 174, 89 Pac. 296.

Illinois: Chicago v. Huenerbein, 85 Ill. 594, 28 Am. Rep. 626 (distinguishing Chicago & R. I. R. R. v. Ward, 16 Ill. 522, and apparently overruling it, also saying that the rule laid down in it

has not been followed in subsequent cases).

South Dakota: Quinn v. Chicago, M. & St. P. Ry., 23 S. D. 126, 120 N. W. 884.

See *South Carolina:* Devereux v. Cotton Press Co., 77 S. C. 66.

[190] Jones v. United States, 48 Wis. 385.

[191] *Iowa:* Willits v. Chicago, B. & K. C. Ry., 88 Ia. 281, 55 N. W. 313, 21 L. R. A. 608.

Texas: Houston E. & W. T. Ry. v. Charwaine, 30 Tex. Civ. App. 633, 71 S. W. 401; International & G. N. R. R. v. Stewart (Tex. Civ. App.), 101 S. W. 282.

[192] Texas & P. Ry. v. Maddox, 26 Tex. Civ. App. 297, 63 S. W. 134.

[193] *Connecticut:* Watson v. New Milford, 72 Conn. 561, 45 Atl. 167.

Idaho: Young v. Extension Ditch Co., 13 Ida. 174, 89 Pac. 296.

Illinois: Chicago, R. I. & P. R. R. v. Carey, 90 Ill. 514; Carter v. Cairo V. & C. Ry., 240 Ill. 152, 88 N. E. 493, affirming 145 Ill. App. 653.

Kentucky: Hutchison v. Maysville, 100 S. W. 331, 30 Ky. L. Rep. 1173;

§ 943. Removal of chattels.

Where a trespasser comes upon land and does damage in carrying away property of the owner, the value of such property is the measure of damages.[194] So where a landlord illegally entered the tenant's premises to distrain for rent, and took away property of the tenant, the value of the goods taken may be recovered in an action of trespass *q. c. f.;*[195] or if the goods are sold and applied on the rent, the value less the amount so applied.[196] If the plaintiff paid a judgment obtained in the illegal distress proceedings in order to get back his goods, the judgment and costs so paid may be recovered.[197]

Where, however, the removal of the goods does not injure the plaintiff no damages can be recovered on account of the removal. This may happen where the goods belong to the defendant,[198] or to a stranger,[199] or cannot be valued because the

Illinois Cent. R. R. *v.* Haynes, 122 S. W. 210.

Maryland: New York, P. & N. R. R. *v.* Jones, 94 Md. 24, 50 Atl. 423.

Minnesota: Osborn *v.* Mississippi & R. R. B. Co., 95 Minn. 149, 103 N. W. 879.

Missouri: South Side Realty Co. *v.* St. Louis & S. F. R. R., 154 Mo. App. 364, 134 S. W. 1034.

Montana: Kelly *v.* Butte, 119 Pac. 171.

Pennsylvania: Weir *v.* Plymouth, 148 Pa. 566, 24 Atl. 94; Lynch *v.* Troxell, 207 Pa. 162, 56 Atl. 413; Helbling *v.* Allegheny Cemetery Co., 201 Pa. 171, 50 Atl. 970.

Wisconsin: Davelaar *v.* Milwaukee, 123 Wis. 413, 101 N. W. 361.

See *Indiana:* Robinson *v.* Shanks, 118 Ind. 125, 20 N. E. 713.

[194] *Iowa:* Acrea *v.* Brayton, 75 Ia. 719, 38 N. W. 171.

Maryland: Cate *v.* Schaum, 51 Md. 299.

Massachusetts: Barker *v.* Bates, 13 Pick. 255, 23 Am. Dec. 678.

Missouri: Doty *v.* Quincy, O. & K. C. R. R., 136 Mo. App. 254, 116 S. W. 1126.

New Hampshire: Adams *v.* Blodgett, 47 N. H. 219.

New York: Moore *v.* Baylies, 56 Hun, 647, 10 N. Y. Supp. 62.

South Carolina: Porteous *v.* Hazel, Harp. 332.

England: Attack *v.* Bramwell, 3 B. & S. 520.

[195] Cate *v.* Schaum, 51 Md. 299, 34 Am. Rep. 311.

[196] Cahill *v.* Lee, 55 Md. 319.

[197] Presstman *v.* Silljacks, 52 Md. 647.

[198] *Missouri:* Ross *v.* New H. S. M. Co., 24 Mo. App. 353 (defendant held a chattel mortgage on the goods which by its terms gave him a right to take).

New Hampshire: Plumer *v.* Prescott, 43 N. H. 277 (wrongful entry to remove timber cut under a license); Hoyt *v.* Stratton Mills, 54 N. H. 452 (cutting and removing purchased timber after the specified time; owner recovers only the increased growth of the timber since the agreed time for cutting).

[199] *Arkansas:* Brock *v.* Smith, 14 Ark. 431.

Maine: Whittier *v.* Sanborn, 38 Me. 32 (barn).

plaintiff was using them for an illegal purpose; [200] or where the goods upon removal were left where the plaintiff might easily get them. [201]

§ 944. Other injuries to real property.

In an action for maliciously ousting the plaintiffs of their possession of a mine which they held under a lease, it was held proper to instruct the jury that the measure of damages was what the use of the premises was reasonably worth under the lease during the time the plaintiffs were wrongfully kept out of possession, and also the permanent damage to the leasehold interest, if any, by reason of the mine caving in or getting out of repair, if this resulted from the failure of the defendant to use ordinary care during the time he held possession. [202]   In measuring the damages to premises by an interruption of the easement of light, a jury should not estimate the amount on the assumption that they will continue always to be used for the same purpose for which they are used at the time of the injury. The jury can take into consideration the character of the neighborhood, the use to which the plaintiff's buildings were then applied, and also the use to which they might be applied. MELLOR, J., said: "In estimating the damages you ought not, in my opinion, to stereotype the existing condition of the premises, but to calculate the reasonable probabilities of a different application of them." [203]   If the building can be so altered at reasonable expense as to get as good a light as before the obstruction, the cost of such alterations is the measure of damages. [204]   For removal of fixtures the measure of damages is the value of the fixtures as part of the realty, before removal, not their market value after severance. [205]   Where the defendant's well fell and injured the plaintiff's mill, it was held that the rent recovered should be for such time only as was necessary

---

[200] Plummer v. Harbut, 5 Ia. 308 (liquor).

[201] *Kansas:* Freelove v. Gould, 3 Kan. App. 750, 3 Pac. 750.

New York: Hammond v. Sullivan, 112 App. Div. 788, 99 N. Y. Supp. 472; see De Camp v. Wallace, 45 Misc. 436, 92 N. Y. Supp. 746.

[202] Moffat v. Fisher, 47 Ia. 473.

[203] Moore v. Hall, 3 Q. B. D. 178, 181.

[204] Ring v. Pugsley, 2 P. & B. (N. B.) 303.

[205] *California:* Rhoda v. Alameda County, 58 Cal. 357.

England: Thompson v. Pettitt, 10 Q. B. 101.

to repair the premises.[206] This is an obvious deduction from the rule of avoidable consequences. The damages for an overhanging wall are the diminution in the rental value.[207] Where the house is forcibly detained from the plaintiff, the measure of damages is the value to him of its use.[208] The defendant removed from the plaintiff's land a plank sidewalk belonging to the plaintiff. The measure of damages was held to be the diminished value of the land, not exceeding the value of the sidewalk.[209] For wrongfully shutting off gas from premises, the measure of damages has been held to be the depreciation in value;[210] and for infringement of a ferry franchise the owner may recover for the loss of tolls.[211] Where a judgment creditor, after the debt has been paid, sells the debtor's land the debtor may recover the value of the land.[212]

§ 945. Cattle damage feasant.

* It would be improper, while speaking of trespasses to real property, to omit mention of the right given by the English law to distrain beasts doing damage, or in the old Norman French, "damage feasant." The right is strictly limited to the time when the beasts are actually committing the trespass: "The beasts must be damage-feasant at the time of the distress; and if they were damage-feasant yesterday, and again to-day, they can only be distrained for the damage they are doing when they are distrained. And if many cattle are doing damage, a man cannot take one of them as a distress for the whole damage; but he may distrain one of them for its own damage, and bring an action of trespass for the damage done by the rest." [213] ** If suit is brought for the damages, the owner may recover for the injury to the land,[214] but not

[206] Ludlow v. Yonkers, 43 Barb. 493.

[207] Langfeldt v. McGrath, 33 Ill. App. 158.

[208] Tracy v. Butters, 40 Mich. 406.

[209] Rogers v. Randall, 29 Mich. 41.

[210] Gas Light Co. v. Colliday, 25 Md. 1. Query: for such an injury is merely temporary since the company could be compelled to furnish the gas.

[211] Blackwood v. Tanner, 112 Ky. 672, 66 S. W. 500.

[212] Pope v. Benster, 42 Neb. 304, 60 N. W. 561.

[213] Hoskins v. Robins, 2 Saund. 324, 327; Vaspor v. Edwards, 12 Mod. 658; Clement v. Milner, 3 Esp. 95; Wormer v. Biggs, 2 C. & K. 31.

[214] Warrick v. Reinhardt, 136 Ia. 27, 111 N. W. 983.

for other charges,[215] such as the expense of keeping the animals.[216]

III.—NUISANCE

§ 946. Special damage necessary.

* We next come to the subject of nuisances. A great deal of learning will be found in the books as to the precise nature of a nuisance, and as to what can be so considered and treated. That examination, however, falls beyond the limits of this treatise. "Whatsoever," says BLACKSTONE,[217] "unlawfully annoys or doth damage to another, is a nuisance;" and the remedies for private nuisances he declares [218] to be: an action on the case for damages, in which damages only are recoverable; and an assize of nuisance, by which not only are damages recovered, but the nuisance is itself abated.[219]

The ancient real action which abated the nuisance is, as will be readily seen, one peculiar in its character; but the action on the case, which simply gives damages for the infringement of the plaintiff's right, falls strictly within the class which we are now considering, of disturbances of the enjoyment of real estate (otherwise vindicated in the ordinary actions of trespass or case),[220] and the measure of compensation is to be regulated by the same general principles.

We have already seen,[221] that if the nuisance is so general as to be a common or public nuisance, the remedy is by in-

---

[215] Fleetham v. Therres, 92 Minn. 500, 100 N. W. 377.

[216] North v. McDonald, 47 Barb. (N. Y.) 528.

[217] 3 Bl. Com. 5.

[218] 3 Bl. Com. 220.

[219] This latter remedy has been in New York retained and simplified (4 Kent, 70, note) by the provisions of the Revised Statutes (2 R. S. 256) which prescribe the form of the writ, directing the jury that inquires of the nuisance, if they find for the plaintiff, to assess the damages; and which also declare that the judgment, in case the plaintiff prevails, shall be as heretofore accustomed, that the nuisance be re-

moved, and that the plaintiff recover the damages occasioned thereby. (Still further simplified, Code Civ. Proc., §§ 1660–1663).

[220] To bring an assize of nuisance, it was necessary that the plaintiff should show a freehold estate in the premises; but in the action on the case it is only necessary to prove that he is in possession. Cornes v. Harris, 1 N. Y. 223. The remedy by assize of nuisance has long been obsolete in England, and there is said to have been but one such writ prosecuted in New York. Kintz v. McNeal, 1 Denio, 436.

[221] §§ 34, 35.

dictment, not by private suit. But every individual who suffers actual damage from a common nuisance may maintain an action for his own particular injury, though there may be others equally damnified. It is essential, however, to allege and prove special damage.[222] So it was very early held in England. Thus, in an action for stopping up a highway: "All the court agreed that when an action arises from a public nuisance, there must be a special damage; for he that did the nuisance is punishable at the suit of the public, and to allow all private persons their actions, without special damage, would create an infinite and endless multiplicity of suits." [223]

So, too, in this country: "If a person," said the learned Chancellor Walworth,[224] "sustains no damage (by the erection of a nuisance) but that which the law presumes every citizen to sustain, because it is a common nuisance, no action will lie; but every individual who receives actual damage from a nuisance may maintain a private suit for his own injury, although there may be many others in the same situation." [225] It has been questioned whether the injury from a nuisance, to authorize a private suit, must be direct, or whether a consequential injury would suffice; but it seems now settled that it is sufficient

[222] Allen v. Ormond, 8 East, 4; Winterbottom v. Derby, L. R. 2 Ex. 316.

[223] Iveson v. Moore, 1 Salk. 15.

[224] Lansing v. Smith, 4 Wend. 9, 25, 21 Am. Dec. 89. See also, to S. P. Lansing v. Wiswall, 5 Denio, 213; Dougherty v. Bunting, 1 Sandf. 1; and see also First Baptist Church v. Sch'y & T. R. R., 5 Barb. 79; Irwin v. Dixion, 9 How. 10. See the subject considered in Dobson v. Blackmore, 9 Q. B. 991, where it is held that the obstruction of a public navigable river is not a damage to a reversioner out of possession of premises abutting thereon. So in regard to mandamus, if a nuisance is not more injurious to the relators than to the inhabitants at large, the remedy is only by indictment. Councils of Reading v. Commonwealth, 11 Pa. 196, 51 Am. Dec. 534.

[225] People v. Corporation of Albany, 11 Wend. 539, 27 Am. Dec. 95.
See to the same effect the following cases:
United States: Georgetown v. Alexandria Canal Co., 12 Pet. 91, 9 L. ed. 1012.
Indiana: O'Brien v. Central I. & S. Co., 158 Ind. 218, 63 N. E. 302.
Maine: Simpson v. Seavey, 8 Me. 138, 22 Am. Dec. 228.
Minnesota: Aldrich v. Wetmore, 52 Minn. 164, 53 N. W. 1072.
Nebraska: George v. Peckham, 73 Neb. 794, 103 N. W. 664.
New York: Smith v. Lockwood, 13 Barb. 209.
Ohio: Story v. Hammond, 4 Ohio, 376.
South Carolina: Carey v. Brooks, 1 Hill, 365.
Wisconsin: Tilly v. Mitchell & Lewis Co., 121 Wis. 1, 98 N. W. 969.

if *peculiar* or *special* damage result therefrom, though it be consequential and not direct. So where, in consequence of the defendant's mooring a barge across a canal, the plaintiffs were obliged to carry their goods overland.[226] But a claim for damages against a turnpike company, arising from the plaintiff's *not attempting* at certain times to travel a public highway because of its general badness, is hypothetical, and does not constitute such peculiar damage as to give a private action for a public nuisance.[227] Where the grievance complained of consisted in the erection by the defendant of a dam in a public navigable creek, by means of which the plaintiff was prevented from passing along such creek from his residence above to the land below, and the converse, it was held that such obstruction was not the subject of a private action.[228] **

§ 947. General rule.

If a nuisance results in a permanent injury to the realty,[229] the measure of damages is the diminution in market value of the land,[230] unless it is possible to repair the injury at an ex-

[226] Rose v. Miles, 4 M. & S. 101.

[227] Baxter v. Winooski Turnpike Co., 22 Vt. 114, 58 Am. Dec. 150.

[228] Seeley v. Bishop, 19 Conn. 128.

[229] For the distinction between a permanent and a temporary injury, see §§ 91–95.

[230] *Alabama:* Highland A. & B. R. R. v. Matthews, 99 Ala. 24, 10 So. 67; Alabama C. C. & I. Co. v. Vines, 151 Ala. 398, 44 So. 377; Atlanta & B. A. L. Ry. v. Wood, 160 Ala. 657, 49 So. 426.

Colorado: Denver & R. G. Ry. v. Bourne, 11 Colo. 59.

Georgia: Farley v. Gate City G. L. Co., 105 Ga. 323, 31 S. E. 193; Hodges v. Pine Product Co., 68 S. E. 1107.

Illinois: Chicago & I. R. R. v. Baker, 73 Ill. 316.

Indiana: South Bend v. Paxon, 67 Ind. 228.

Iowa: Finley v. Hershey, 41 Ia. 389; Cadle v. Muscatine W. R. R., 44 Ia. 11; O'Connor v. St. Louis, K. C. & N. Ry.,

56 Ia. 735; Drake v. Chicago, R. I. & P. Ry., 63 Ia. 302, 50 Am. Rep. 746; Chicago, B. & Q. R. R. v. O'Connor, (Ia.), 60 N. W. 326.

Kansas: Central B. U. P. R. R. v. Andrews, 41 Kan. 370, 21 Pac. 276, 13 Am. St. Rep. 292.

Kentucky: Paducah v. Allen, 23 Ky. L. Rep. 701, 63 S. W. 981.

Maryland: Baltimore Belt R. R. v. Sattler, 100 Md. 306, 59 Atl. 654.

Missouri: Givens v. Van Studdiford, 86 Mo. 149, 56 Am. Rep. 421; Stevenson v. Missouri Pac. Ry. (Mo.), 31 S. W. 793; Byers v. Jacobs (Mo. App.), 64 S. W. 156; Morris v. Missouri Pac. Ry., 136 Mo. App. 393, 117 S. W. 687.

New York: Easterbrook v. Erie R. R., 51 Barb. 94; Senglaup v. Acker Process Co., 121 App. Div. 49, 105 N. Y. Supp. 470; Ackerman v. True, 120 App. Div. 172, 105 N. Y. Supp. 12.

North Carolina: Parker v. Norfolk & C. R. R., 119 N. C. 677, 25 S. E. 722.

pense less than such diminution.[231] If the injury is not permanent, the plaintiff may recover the various items of his loss, but not the diminished value of the land.[232] Here as elsewhere, where the plaintiff has it in his power to put an end to the wrong he cannot claim compensation for a permanent injury. In Hatfield v. Central Railroad,[233] where the defendant wrongfully put down its track on the plaintiff's land, and the plaintiff could have had it removed at any time, it was held immaterial

---

Pennsylvania: McKnight v. Ratcliff, 44 Pa. 156; Hanover W. Co. v. Ashland I. Co., 84 Pa. 279; Vanderslice v. Philadelphia, 103 Pa. 102.

Texas: Rosenthal v. Taylor B. & H. Ry., 79 Tex. 325, 15 S. W. 268; San Antonio & A. P. Ry. v. Mohe, 37 S. W. 22; Paris v. Allred, 43 S. W. 62; Denison & P. S. Ry. v. O'Maley, 18 Tex. Civ. App. 200, 45 S. W. 227; Sherman G. & E. Co. v. Belden, 123 S. W. 119, modifying 115 S. W. 897; Hunt v. Johnson (Tex. Civ. App.), 129 S. W. 879; Houston L. & L. Co. v. Texas Co. (Tex. Civ. App.), 140 S. W. 818.

[231] Senglaup v. Acker Process Co., 121 App. Div. 49, 105 N. Y. Supp. 470.

[232] *Connecticut:* Lawton v. Herrick, 83 Conn. 417, 76 Atl. 986.

Georgia: Savannah & O. C. Co. v. Bourquin, 51 Ga. 378; Jones v. F. S. Rayster Guano Co., 6 Ga. App. 506, 65 S. E. 361.

Illinois: N. K. Fairbank Co. v. Nicolai, 167 Ill. 242, 47 N. E. 360.

Iowa: Holbrook v. Griffis, 127 Ia. 505, 103 N. W. 479.

Kansas: Chicago, K. & W. R. R. v. Union Inv. Co., 51 Kan. 600, 33 Pac. 378.

Kentucky: Louisville v. O'Malley, 53 S. W. 287, 21 Ky. L. Rep. 873.

Maine: Cumberland & O. C. Co. v. Hitchings, 65 Me. 140.

Massachusetts: O'Brien v. Worcester, 172 Mass. 348, 52 N. E. 385.

Minnesota: Hartz v. St. Paul & S. C. R. R., 21 Minn. 358.

Mississippi: Mississippi Mills Co. v.

Smith, 69 Miss. 299, 11 So. 26; Tennessee C. I. & R. Co. v. Hamilton (Miss.), 14 So. 167.

New Jersey: Doremus v. Paterson, 73 N. J. Eq. 474, 69 Atl. 225.

New York: Syracuse S. S. Co. v. Rome W. & O. R. R., 11 App. Div. 557, 42 N. Y. Supp. 590.

Pennsylvania: Robb v. Carnegie Bros. & Co., 145 Pa. 324, 22 Atl. 649; Eshleman v. Martic, 152 Pa. 68, 25 Atl. 178.

South Carolina: Threatt v. Brewer Mining Co., 49 S. C. 95, 26 S. E. 970.

Texas: Gulf, C. & S. F. Ry. v. Helsley, 62 Tex. 593; San Antonio v. Mackey, 36 S. W. 760.

[233] 33 N. J. L. 251. The same point was decided in Hopkins v. Western P. R. R., 50 Cal. 190. The court here laid stress on the fact that the nuisance could be abated under the California Practice Act. In Cumberland & Oxford C. Co. v. Hitchings, 65 Me. 140, an action for filling up the plaintiff's canal in the construction of a street, it was held error to instruct the jury that the diminution of the value of the property was an element of damage, the court saying that the plaintiff could only recover for damage to the date of the writ, and for injury thereafter he had a fresh action, this being the rule in all actions where something has been lawfully placed on the land of another, which can and ought to be removed. To the same effect see Savannah & Ogeechee Canal Co. v. Bourquin, 51 Ga. 378.

to show the decreased value of the land, for that could be
avoided by removing the track, and the plaintiff was confined
to the loss he had so far sustained.

§ 948. Removable nuisance—Elements of loss.

1. *Loss of rent.* Compensation is recoverable for the diminution in value of use of premises, measured usually by the
diminution in rental value.[234]

2. *Loss of custom or profits.* In an action for damages for
obstructions which hindered the plaintiff in his business, as the
keeper of a refectory and lodging-house, and diminished his
custom, loss of custom and of profits was held to be the measure
of damages; damages were computed by comparing the actual
receipts of the plaintiff's hotel for a sufficient period previous

[234] *Arkansas:* Czarnecki *v.* Bolen-Darnell Coal Co., 91 Ark. 58, 120 S. W. 376; Junction Lumber Co. *v.* Sharp, 92 Ark. 538, 123 S. W. 370.

Colorado: Jackson *v.* Kiel, 13 Colo. 378, 22 Pac. 504, 16 Am. St. Rep. 207.

Illinois: Chicago *v.* Huenerbein, 85 Ill. 594, 28 Am. Rep. 626.

Indiana: South Bend *v.* Paxon, 67 Ind. 228; Muncie Pulp Co. *v.* Martin, 164 Ind. 30, 72 N. E. 882; Merchant's M. T. Co. *v.* Hirschman, 43 Ind. App. 283, 87 N. E. 238.

Iowa: Park *v.* Chicago & S. W. Ry., 43 Ia. 636; Loughran *v.* Des Moines, 72 Ia. 382, 34 N. W. 172; Shirely *v.* Cedar Rapids, I. F. & N. Ry., 74 Ia. 169, 37 N. W. 133; Randolf *v.* Bloomfield, 77 Ia. 50, 41 N. W. 562, 14 Am. St. Rep. 268; Ferguson *v.* Firmenich Mfg. Co., 77 Ia. 576, 42 N. W. 448; McGill *v.* Pintsch Compressing Co., 140 Ia. 429, 118 N. W. 786.

Kentucky: Crabtree C. Min. Co. *v.* Hamby, 28 Ky. L. Rep. 687, 90 S. W. 226; Long *v.* Louisville & N. R. R., 128 Ky. 26, 107 S. W. 203; Kentucky D. W. Co. *v.* Barrett, 112 S. W. 643; Georgetown *v.* Kelly, 123 S. W. 251.

Massachusetts: O'Brien *v.* Worcester, 172 Mass. 348, 52 N. E. 385.

Minnesota: Carli *v.* Union D. S. R. & T. Co., 32 Minn. 101.

Missouri: Givens *v.* Van Studdiford, 86 Mo. 149, 56 Am. Rep. 421; Krebs *v.* Bambrick Bros. Const. Co., 144 Mo. App. 649, 129 S. W. 425.

Montana: Watson *v.* Colusa-Parrot M. & S. Co., 31 Mont. 513, 79 Pac. 14.

New York: Francis *v.* Schoellkopf, 53 N. Y. 152; Jutte *v.* Hughes, 67 N. Y. 267; Pritchard *v.* Edison E. I. Co., 179 N. Y. 364, 72 N. E. 243; Schwab *v.* Cleveland, 28 Hun, 458; Michel *v.* Monroe Co., 39 Hun, 47; McKeon *v.* See, 4 Rob. 449; Garrett *v.* Wood, 55 App. Div. 281, 67 N. Y. Supp. 122; Miller *v.* Edison E. I. Co., 33 Misc. 664, 68 N. Y. Supp. 900; Reisert *v.* New York, 35 Misc. 413, 71 N. Y. Supp. 965 (no rental value, diminution in actual value); Gerow *v.* Liberty, 106 App. Div. 357, 94 N. Y. Supp. 949; Hey *v.* Collman, 78 App. Div. 584, 79 N. Y. Supp. 778.

North Carolina: Thomason *v.* Seaboard A. L. Ry., 142 N. C. 318, 55 S. E. 198.

Texas: Besso *v.* Southworth, 71 Tex. 765, 10 S. W. 523, 10 Am. St. Rep. 814; Comminge *v.* Stevenson, 76 Tex. 642, 13 S. W. 556; Paris *v.* Jenkins (Tex. Civ. App.), 122 S. W. 411.

to the obstructions, the actual receipts during the continuance of the obstructions and the receipts after they were removed.[235]

3. *Unwholesome and offensive results.* In an action for negligently obstructing a drain, which caused water and filth to flow back into the plaintiff's cellar, the plaintiff could, it was said, recover for any injury which diminished the value of his use and occupation of the house, either by reason of the inconvenience and annoyance of the flowing of the cellar, or of unwholesome or disagreeable smells, or of insects thereby generated or attracted to the house.[236] Where, by a defendant's acts, the carcass of a horse was left near the plaintiff's house, he was allowed to recover damages for illness of his family.[237] And so generally if a nuisance causes illness, the actual expenses incurred by reason of the illness may be recovered.[238] If the nuisance destroys the plaintiff's animals, he may recover compensation for the loss.[239]

4. *Annoyance and inconvenience.* In an action by the owner of land bordering on a public street against a railway company

[235] St. John v. New York, 13 How. Pr. 527, 6 Duer, 315; *acc.*, Cunningham v. Stein, 109 Ill. 375; Terre Haute v. Hudnut (Ind.), 13 N. E. 686; Park v. Chicago & S. W. Ry., 43 Ia. 636; Willis v. Perry, 92 Ia. 297, 60 N. W. 727; French v. Connecticut R. L. Co., 145 Mass. 261, 14 N. E. 113. For a case in which it was held improper to estimate the probable loss of purchasers of building lots, see Jacksonville v. Lambert, 62 Ill. 519.

[236] Emery v. Lowell, 109 Mass. 197; *accord,* Jutte v. Hughes, 67 N. Y. 267.

[237] *Alabama:* Eufaula v. Simmons, 86 Ala. 515, 6 So. 47.

Iowa: Ferguson v. Firmenich Mfg. Co., 77 Ia. 576, 42 N. W. 448.

Massachusetts: Allen v. Boston, 159 Mass. 324, 34 N. E. 519.

Missouri: Ellis v. Kansas City, S. J. & C. B. R. R., 63 Mo. 131, 21 Am. Rep. 436.

Texas: Gulf, C. & S. F. Ry. v. Richards, 32 S. W. 96 (but see Gulf, C. & S. F. Ry. v. Reed, 22 S. W. 283; Texas &

P. Ry. v. O'Mahoney (Tex. Civ. App.), 60 S. W. 902; A. Cohen & Co. v. Rittiman (Tex. Civ. App.), 139 S. W. 59.

[238] *Delaware:* Benson v. Wilmington, 9 Houst. 359, 32 Atl. 1047.

Iowa: Loughran v. Des Moines, 72 Ia. 382, 34 N. W. 172.

Massachusetts: Allen v. Boston, 159 Mass. 324, 34 N. E. 519.

Minnesota: Pierce v. Wagner, 29 Minn. 355, 13 N. W. 170, 43 Am. Rep. 216.

Texas: San Antonio & A. Ry. v. Gwynn, 15 S. W. 509; Paris v. Allred, 43 S. W. 62.

One suing as trustee and not as occupant can only recover for illness in so far as the unhealthy condition of the property injures its value. Cohen v. Bellenot (Va.), 32 S. E. 455.

[239] *Indiana:* West Muncie S. B. Co. v. Slack, 164 Ind. 21, 72 N. E. 879 (fish).

Texas: Benjamin v. Gulf, C. & S. F. Ry., 49 Tex. Civ. App. 473, 108 S. W. 408 (cattle).

for building their railway, without right, along such street, the measure of his damages is the loss and inconvenience he has sustained, in view of the use to which his land has been put during the continuance of the nuisance.[240] So in case of a nuisance to the plaintiff's home, he is not restricted to the diminution in rental value, but may recover compensation for deprivation of the comforts of home.[241]

5. *Expenses of abating the nuisance.* A plaintiff may recover his reasonable expenses in preventing or removing the nuisance, and the expenses of changes and repairs rendered necessary, so far as they are required by reasonable care and diligence.[242]

[240] *New Jersey:* Hatfield *v.* Central R. R., 33 N. J. L. 251.

North Carolina: Thomason *v.* Seaboard A. L. Ry., 142 N. C. 318, 55 S. E. 198.

Ohio: Ohio & W. N. Ry. *v.* Gardner, 45 Oh. St. 309.

An owner of land abutting on a street has no inalienable right to have drays stand at right angles across the street, and cannot include the deprivation of such rights among the items of damage against a street railroad which has illegally placed its track in the street. Taylor *v.* Bay City St. Ry., 101 Mich. 140, 59 N. W. 447.

[241] *Iowa:* Randolf *v.* Bloomfield, .77 Ia. 50, 41 N. W. 562, 14 Am. St. Rep. 268; Churchill *v.* Burlington Water Co., 94 Ia. 89, 62 N. W. 646.

Texas: Sherman G. & E. Co. *v.* Belden, 123 S. W. 119.

See *Kentucky:* Bannon *v.* Murphy, 18 Ky. L. Rep. 989, 38 S. W. 889; Louisville *v.* O'Malley, 53 S. W. 287, 21 Ky. L. Rep. 873.

See *ante,* § 42.

[242] *Kentucky:* Chesapeake & O. Ry. *v.* Gross, 19 Ky. L. Rep. 1926, 43 S. W. 203.

Maine: Plummer *v.* Penobscot L. A., 67 Me. 363.

Massachusetts: Emery *v.* Lowell, 109 Mass. 197.

Missouri: Krebs *v.* Bambrick Bros. Const. Co., 144 Mo. App. 649, 129 S. W. 425.

Nebraska: Beatrice Gas Co. *v.* Thomas, 41 Neb. 662, 59 N. W. 925.

New York: Jutte *v.* Hughes, 67 N. Y. 267.

Pennsylvania: Stevenson *v.* Ebervale Coal Co., 201 Pa. 112, 50 Atl. 818; Bachert *v.* Lehigh C. & N. Co., 208 Pa. 362, 57 Atl. 765.

Texas: Benjamin *v.* Gulf, C. & S. F. Ry., 49 Tex. Civ. App. 473, 108 S. W. 408; Orange Lumber Co. *v.* Thompson, (Tex. Civ. App.), 113 S. W. 563, 126 S. W. 604.

Where a nuisance upon the plaintiff's land was occasioned by the discharge of impure water from the defendant's brewery into the plaintiff's clay pits, through a drain which the defendant dug from his premises to those of the plaintiff, it appeared that the water had become so stagnant and offensive as to be complained of as a nuisance, and that the Boston Board of Health had ordered one of the clay pits to be filled up by the plaintiff; and it was held that the expense of filling up the pit should be included in the assessment of damages. Shaw *v.* Cummiskey, 7 Pick. 76.

6. *Consequential injuries.* Consequential injuries to property to which a private alley was not appurtenant, were held inadmissible in evidence in an action for a nuisance destroying the use of the alley.[243]   In Plummer *v.* Penobscot Lumber Ass'n,[244] the defendant put a boom across a stream which prevented the plaintiff's logs from floating down till it was opened. When it was opened they were carried a great distance, and many of them were lost. It was held that the plaintiff could recover for depreciation in the market value of the logs while they were detained, for loss of the logs carried away, and for the expense of searching for the others. Where defendant built a bridge across a navigable stream without a draw so that plaintiff's boat could not pass, it was held that he could recover the rental value of his boat for the time it was delayed, but not the damage to the cargo which was unloaded and left exposed.[245]

§ 949. Liability and right of recovery.

* It has been questioned how far the defendant is liable after he has parted with the possession of or the title to the premises. As a general rule, the erector of the nuisance is answerable for the continuance of it, not only where he has demised the property with a nuisance on it, reserving rent, but where the erection was made on the land of another, and though he has no right to enter for the purpose of removing it.[246]   On this

---

[243] Commrs. of Kensington *v.* Wood, 10 Pa. 93, 49 Am. Dec. 582.

[244] 67 Me. 363; *acc.,* Ireland *v.* Bowman (Ky.), 114 S. W. 338.

[245] Farmers' C. M. Co. *v.* Albemarle & R. R. R., 117 N. C. 579, 23 S. E. 43.

[246] *Massachusetts:* Staple *v.* Spring, 10 Mass. 72.

New York: Fish *v.* Dodge, 4 Den. 311.

England: Rosewell *v.* Prior, 12 Mod. 635, 1 Lord Raym. 713, 2 Salk. 460; Thompson *v.* Gibson, 7 M. & W. 456; Holmes *v.* Wilson, 10 A. & E. 503.

But, though there is a legal obligation to discontinue a trespass or remove a nuisance, no such obligation lies on a trespasser to replace what he had pulled down or destroyed upon the land of another, though he is liable in trespass to compensate in damages for the loss sustained. Therefore, where the owner of a coal mine excavated as far as the boundary, and continued the excavation wrongfully into the neighboring mine, leaving an aperture in the coal of that mine, through which water passed and did damage, held that, though the party excavating was liable in trespass for breaking into the neighboring mine, he was not liable in case for omitting to close up the aperture on his neighbor's soil, though continuing damage resulted. Clegg *v.* Dearden, 12 Q. B. 576.

point it has been held in New York, that where the defendant has conveyed the lands on which the nuisance had been placed by him, and surrendered the possession to his grantor, before the time when the plaintiff acquired title or possession of the lands which were subsequently injured, and without any covenant of warranty, or agreement to uphold the grantee in the occupancy of the premises, no action will lie against such former owner and erector of the nuisance. But though the defendant is out of possession at the time the injury was committed, and another person has the entire possession, still, if the defendant was the erector of the nuisance, and owner of the premises, and under any agreement to uphold the occupant in possession, or if he have conveyed the premises with warranty,—the action will lie against him on the ground that, by such relation with the occupant, he has affirmed the continuance of the nuisance, and that it may be said to be a continuance by himself; and in such case he is liable, of course, for damages subsequent to the conveyance and down to the commencement of the suit.[247] ** A subsequent purchaser of premises injured by a nuisance erected previous to his purchase, has a remedy for the injury occasioned by the continuance of the nuisance.[248]

IV.—WASTE

§ 950. Action of waste.

* "Waste, *vastum*," says Mr. Justice Blackstone,[249] "is a spoil or destruction in houses, gardens, trees, or other corporeal hereditaments, to the disherison of him that hath the remainder

[247] *Massachusetts:* Staple *v.* Spring, 10 Mass. 72.

New Jersey: East Jersey Water Co. *v.* Bigelow, 60 N. J. L. 201, 38 Atl. 631.

New York: Blunt *v.* Aikin, 15 Wend. 522; Waggoner *v.* Jermaine, 3 Denio, 306.

See Angell on Watercourses, § 402, and cases there cited.

[248] Brady *v.* Weeks, 3 Barb. 157.

[249] 2 Com. 281. See, also, the common law with regard to waste very learnedly expounded by Lord Chief Justice Eyre, in Jefferson *v.* Bishop of Durham, 1 B. & P. 105, 120; Story's Equity Juris., § 909. Waste is well known by the name of *degradations* in the French Law, and it will be found treated of in the Civil Code under the proper head. This subject might, perhaps, be classed among actions for the recovery of real estate; but as the proceeding does not always result in a change of the property, it is more properly classified among suits brought for interferences with its enjoyment.

or reversion in fee simple or fee tail." The punishment for waste was by common law and by the statute of Marlbridge [250] single damages only; but by the statute of Gloucester [251] it was provided that the tenants therein mentioned should forfeit the place wasted, and treble damages to him that had the inheritance.

At common law the action of waste lay against tenants in dower and guardians; and the better opinion seems to be that it also lay against a tenant by the courtesy; [252] but by the statute of Marlbridge and the statute of Gloucester, above referred to, it was given against every person holding a lease for life or lives, or for years; and by the latter act, the damages which before were single, were in the cases specified in that statute trebled. [253] Damages were not, however, recoverable for waste committed pending the suit; and these were given in an action of estrepement. [254] **

* In the action of waste it was originally necessary, in order to entitle the plaintiff to judgment, that the damages found should be something more than nominal; and the sum of three shillings and fourpence appears to have been arbitrarily fixed on as the minimum of damage which would authorize a party to bring such action. [255] This doctrine has been in England extended to the action on the case for injury to the reversion, though not in reason applicable. [256] The commutation was

[250] 52 Hen. III, ch. xxiii.

[251] 6 Edw. I, ch. v.

[252] Sayer on Damages, ch. vii, 29; 2 Inst. 145, 299, 300, 305; 2 Bl. Com. 282.

[253] *Statutum de Malberge.* Statutes made at Marlbridge, 52 Hen, III, A. D. 1267, ch. xxiii. "Also, Fermors during their terms shall not make waste, etc., etc., . . . which thing if they do, and thereof be convicted, they shall yield *full damage*, and shall be punished by amerciament grievously."

Statuta Gloucestr'. Statutes made at Gloucester, 6 Edw. I, A. D. 1278. "It is provided, also, that a man from henceforth shall have a writ of waste, etc., against him that holdeth, by the law of England or otherwise, for term of

life or for term of years, or a woman in dower. And he which shall be attainted of waste, shall leese (*perde*) the thing that he hath wasted, *and moreover shall recompense thrice so much as waste shall be taxed at.*"

[254] Sayer on Damages, ch. vii, 34. "It is common learning," said Heath, J., in Attersoll v. Stevens, 1 Taunt. 183, 198, "that every lessee of land, whether for life or years, is liable in an action of waste to his lessor for all waste done on the land in lease, by whomsoever it may be committed." And this has been recognized in New York, in Cook v. Champlain T. Co., 1 Denio, 91.

[255] Harrow School v. Alderton, 2 B. & P. 86.

[256] Rigg v. Parsons, cited 2 East, 156.

originally introduced on the ground that in an action of waste
the place wasted was forfeited, and it was thought not just
that the tenant should forfeit his estate for every trifling act
of waste; but in actions for injuries to the reversionary interest,
the injury complained of may be merely that the act in question
will perhaps be afterwards relied on as evidence of the tenant's
absolute property in the tenement; here the object of the action
is simply to assert the reversioner's right of property, and not
to recover damages.[257] **

[257] Pindar v. Wadsworth, 2 East, 154;
Redfern v. Smith, 1 Bing. 382; 2 Bing.
262; Gibbons on the Law of Dilapidation and Nuisances, 78.

The following is the report of a case
decided by the Hon. E. Fitch Smith,
First Judge of the Ontario Common
Pleas: Nottingham v. Osgood.

I. In an action on the case in nature
of waste, where the court on the trial
instructed the jury on the subject of
damages, to "inquire whether, by reason of the additions and alterations
made by the defendant, the premises
were rendered less or more valuable;
if less valuable by reason thereof, then
the plaintiff would be entitled to recover the actual damage he had sustained, to be ascertained by the jury
from the evidence in the cause; but if,
from the evidence, the jury should be
satisfied that the premises, by reason
of such alterations and erections, were
in point of fact more valuable,—that
then, although the act of the defendant
was a technical wrong, yet that the
plaintiff, under such circumstances,
would only be entitled to nominal damages." Held erroneous, and for that
reason a new trial ordered.

II. Where a tenant, during the continuance of his term, made material
and essential alteration of the buildings, and erected additions without the
consent of his landlord—held, that he
was not entitled to any remuneration
for the materials and erections, even although the general value of the prem-

ises were thereby enhanced; upon the
principle that, the act being tortious,
he could not claim any benefit or remuneration for his own wrong.

III. In an action on the case in the
nature of waste, the jury, in estimating
the damages, are not to take into consideration whether the general value of
the premises has been enhanced or
depreciated by reason of the act of
the defendant, but simply whether they
are depreciated as to the plaintiff. In
such action, on estimating the plaintiff's damages, where the alterations and
changes made by the tenant are of
such a nature as to admit of the premises being restored to their condition
at the time of the demise, the jury
may take into consideration what sum
would be equivalent to the costs and
expenses incident to the restoration of
the demised premises to their original
state at the time of the demise. Under
a declaration properly framed for that
purpose, if the premises are, at the time
of their surrender, by the act of the
defendant, rendered untenantable, the
jury may also take into consideration
the value of the rent, or the use of the
premises, for such period of time as
would be requisite to put them in a
tenantable condition.

IV. If the changes amount to a total
destruction of any part of the demised
property, such as shade trees and ornamental shrubbery, the jury may also
take into consideration the actual value
of the property totally destroyed, with

*In New York, an action for waste is given by statute against guardians, tenants by the courtesy, tenants in dower, for life or years, or their assigns. If the action be brought by any other than a tenant in common or joint tenant, the plaintiff recovers the place wasted, and treble the damages assessed by the jury.[258] If it be brought by a tenant in common, or joint tenant, against his co-tenant, the plaintiff may elect to take treble damages or to have partition of the premises; and in case he elects the latter, the object is to be effected by actual partition or sale, and in either case the single damages found by the jury are to be deducted from the defendant's share.[259] Damages are not recoverable at common law, as we have said, for waste committed pending the action of waste; and this is provided for by the same statute, which declares, that after the commencement of any action for the recovery of land or for its possession, the court may, by order, restrain the defendant from committing waste; but in the action of waste itself, the positive language of the above provision probably goes far enough to give damages for waste committed pending the suit. The effect of this statute has been said [260] to be to give the Supreme Court the same power to restrain and prevent waste, which is exercised by the Court of Chancery; and in this case, and in another,[261] it was held that the order might be made *ex parte*. And in a later case it has been said [262] to be a copy of the statute of Marlbridge.[263] Independent of the statute, however, there is no doubt that an action on the case can always be maintained, in which the party injured will recover the damages which he has actually sustained.[264] In such a proceeding, however, the forfeiture of the place wasted is waived, at least as far as the proceeding itself is concerned.** In an action in the nature of waste for cutting down trees on an estate,

reference to their original state and condition at the time of the demise, and their value to the owner of the reversion.

[258] Code Civ. Proc., §§ 1651–1655. In an action brought by a remainder-man in fee for injury to the inheritance, the inquiry should not embrace the present damage to the property. Van Deusen *v.* Young, 29 N. Y. 9.

[259] Co. Civ. Proc., §§ 1656, 1658.

[260] Savage, J., in The People *v.* Alberty, 11 Wend. 160, 162.

[261] Bush *v.* Phillips, 3 Wend. 428.

[262] By Nelson, J., in Carris *v.* Ingalls, 12 Wend. 70.

[263] As to estrepement of waste in Pennsylvania, see Dickinson *v.* Nicholson, 2 Yeates, 281.

[264] Winship *v.* Pitts, 3 Paige, 259.

the damages are not necessarily confined to the value of the timber removed, but may include also the permanent injury to the inheritance; [265] the measure of damages being the diminution in value of the inheritance by reason of the waste. [266]

* The statute of Gloucester, in regard to waste, has been declared to be a part of the law of Massachusetts, except in regard to tenants in dower. [267] **

[265] Harder v. Harder, 26 Barb. 499.

[266] *Alabama:* Stoudenmire v. De Bardelaben, 85 Ala. 85, 4 So. 723; Perdue v. Brooks, 85 Ala. 459, 5 So. 126.

New York: McCartney v. Titsworth, 119 App. Div. 547, 104 N. Y. Supp. 45.

[267] Sackett v. Sackett, 8 Pick. 309. See Padelford v. Padelford, 7 Pick. 152, and particularly as to what is waste. In Pennsylvania, as to what is waste, see Hastings v. Crunckleton, 3 Yeates, 261, and Shult v. Barker, 12 S. & R. 272.

CHAPTER XLII

ACTIONS UPON REAL COVENANTS

I.—INTRODUCTORY

§ 951. Real covenants—Restricted recovery.

952. The ancient warranty.

§ 953. Personal covenants in deeds.

954. Civil law analogies.

955. French Code.

II.—COVENANTS OF WARRANTY AND FOR QUIET ENJOYMENT

§ 956. What constitutes a breach.

957. Recovery of consideration on total breach—New York rule.

958. Improvements excluded by New York Rule.

959. The New York rule followed in most states.

960. Good faith required.

§ 961. Assignee's damages.

962. Recovery of value at time of eviction—Improvements included—New England rule.

963. General discussion of the rules.

964. Proof of consideration.

965. Where the consideration is not pecuniary.

III.—COVENANTS OF SEISIN AND RIGHT TO CONVEY

§ 966. Consideration with interest and expenses recoverable.

IV.—COVENANTS AGAINST INCUMBRANCES

§ 967. General principles.

968. Incumbrance removable.

969. Total eviction.

970. Permanent incumbrance on the land.

§ 971. Improvements.

972. Covenant to remove incumbrances.

V.—GENERAL PRINCIPLES

§ 973. Nominal damages.

974. Mortgages.

975. Eviction from part of land.

976. Partial failure of title.

977. After acquired title—American doctrine of estoppel by deed.

978. Reduction of damages.

979. Title perfected by grantee—Expenses recoverable.

§ 980. Expenses must be reasonable.

980a. Consequential damages not recoverable.

981. Interest.

982. Expense of defending or of obtaining possession.

983. Counsel fees.

I.—INTRODUCTORY

§ 951. Real covenants—Restricted recovery.

There would seem at first sight no reason why the measure of

1965

damages in an action on a covenant inserted in a conveyance of real property should differ in principle from that upon a similar covenant relating to personal property. The intention of the covenants being to assure the title of the grantee, he would seem, in case of failure, to be entitled to recover the whole value of what he lost at the time of the loss. Such, however, cannot be said to be the rule with regard to real covenants, except in a few jurisdictions. We find the measure generally to be the consideration or price paid for the land, and recited in the deed. That is, the damages, may be equal to this, or less than this (*e. g.* in case of partial eviction), but not greater, no matter what the value of the land of which the grantee has been deprived. The reason to be assigned for this remarkable difference is to be looked for in the peculiar origin of our system, and the view of landed property taken in a condition of society very different from our own. We are so accustomed to look upon land as something to be bought and sold in the market, and having for the most part an easily ascertainable market value measured in money, that it is not easy to picture to ourselves a state of society in which there was absolutely no market price for land, and when its value depended not upon a pecuniary rental but upon the personal services which its holding entailed. Nevertheless it was in such a state of society that covenants in deeds were first introduced, and as we shall presently see, at the time of their introduction, the idea of a pecuniary standard of compensation for their breach was wholly absent. The design of the ancient warranty was that in case of disseisin, the grantee should be able to compel his grantor to put him in possession of lands as good as those which he had lost—a kind of specific performance. The idea of the loss of a good pecuniary bargain was foreign to the existing legal and social order. As the value of land was not measured in money, so there was no fluctuation in the market, and purchasers did not acquire title with the intention of subsequently conveying to a new purchaser at a profit. Even when the next step was taken and the ordinary purchase and sale of lands began to become common, the idea of fluctuation in value was not thought of, and the consideration named in the deed began to be regarded as a pecuniary equivalent for the old agreement to enfeoff of lands of equal value. Instead of getting land of equal value the plaintiff was to get what both parties had by consent substituted for it—the consideration. So strongly fixed was the old idea, that it was not perceived until at a comparatively recent date that to take the consideration as an arbitrary limit violates all the general rules governing the measure of damages upon breaches of contract applicable in such a case. Thus it violates the rule that the plaintiff should recover the *value* of what he has lost; that this value is measured at the time of the breach and not at the time of the contract; that the recital of a price does not measure it; while it introduces a new rule wholly at variance with the ordinary rules of interpretation, that makes the mere consideration of a contract a sort of liquidated damages for its breach. Moreover, it introduces a rule which cannot be always applied, but must give place to some other whenever the consideration is not mentioned in the deed and cannot be proved. These are certainly formidable objections to the rule, which nevertheless in most jurisdictions still preserves its vitality, and makes the compensation in actions upon covenants in deeds in a great measure arbitrary.

§ 952. The ancient warranty.

* The warranty of the ancient English law was in substance a covenant, whereby the grantor of an estate of freehold and his heirs were bound to warrant the title, and either upon voucher or judgment in a writ of *warrantia chartæ*, to yield other lands to the value of those from which there had been an eviction by a paramount title.[1] Upon eviction of the freehold, no personal action lay at common law upon the warranty. The party had only a writ of *warrantia chartæ* upon his warranty to recover a recompense in value to the extent of his freehold.[2] For reasons assigned by Blackstone,[3] in modern practice the covenant has totally superseded the warranty; and to this end various statutes have contributed. Such is the statute [4] making void all warranties by tenant for

---

[1] Co. Litt. 365*a*, and Reeves' Eng. Law, 448.

[2] 4 Kent's Com. 469.

[3] 2 Bl. Com. 300; and see, also, Co.

Litt. 384*a*, for "divers other diversities between warranties and covenants, which yield but damages."

[4] 4 and 5 Anne, ch. 16, § 21.

life, as against any reversioner or remainder-man; and as against the heir, all collateral warranties by any ancestor who had no estate of inheritance in possession; and these statutes have been generally re-enacted in this country.[5]

§ 953. Personal covenants in deeds.

The usual personal covenants contained in a deed, the rule of damages in relation to which we shall now proceed to examine, are: *First*, that of seizin, or that the grantor is lawfully seized; *Second*, that he has good right to convey, which has been called synonymous with the covenant of seizin; [6] *Third*, that the premises are free from incumbrances; *Fourth*, for quiet enjoyment, or that the grantee shall quietly enjoy; *Fifth*, of warranty, or that the grantor shall warrant and defend the title against all lawful claims; and, *Sixth*, the covenant for further assurance,[7] or that the grantor will execute any further conveyances, to perfect the title, which the grantee can legally require.

In regard to all these covenants the rule is general, that no substantial belief will be given till the party complaining has actually suffered injury. It is not sufficient that he is menaced by an outstanding title or incumbrance. The covenantee cannot have anything more than nominal damages until he has been damnified in consequence of a breach of the covenant.[8] But it often becomes a question what constitutes a breach, and what a damage, sufficient to found a claim for remuneration.

In regard to the first three, if the title is defective, or incum-

---

[5] It is certainly so, at least in New York. The statute of 4 and 5 Anne, ch. 16, was re-enacted in New York in 1788; and finally the Revised Statutes of the same State (vol. i, p. 739, § 141) have abolished both lineal and collateral warranties with all their incidents, and have made heirs and devisees answerable upon the covenant or agreement of the ancestor or testator, to the extent of the lands descended or devised. And it has been further declared (sec. 140), that no covenant shall be implied in any conveyance of real estate, whether such conveyance contain special covenants or not.

[6] Rickert *v.* Snyder, 9 Wend. 416. But it is conceivable that one not seized may have a right to convey, *e. g.*, one having a general power of appointment.

[7] Dimmick *v.* Lockwood, 10 Wend. 142.

[8] Nyce *v.* Obertz, 17 Ohio, 71, 49 Am. Dec. 444.

brances exist at the time of the conveyance, there is a breach
as soon as the deed is executed. But those of a warranty
and quiet enjoyment are prospective, and an actual ouster
or eviction is, in general, necessary to constitute a breach.[9]
It is of the rule of damages for eviction, in a suit brought to
enforce these covenants, that we shall first speak.

It is apparent that the real covenants are, to some extent,
cumulative; thus a covenant for quiet enjoyment is broken
by an eviction under a prior mortgage, which would equally
be a breach of that against incumbrances. The rules of damages on the various covenants consequently run into each
other; but the most intelligible mode of treating the subject
will be, as far as possible, to consider them separately.

§ 954. Civil law analogies.

First, however, we will examine the analogies of the civil
law. The *stipulatio duplex* was the remedy provided by the
Roman law for cases of eviction,[10] and for the breach of warranties that were sometimes required on the sale of property
under the *Edictum Ædilium*.[11] And by the *stipulatio*, the rule

[9] 4 Kent's Com. 471.

[10] Pothier, Pandectes, par Brèard
Neuville, vol. VIII, p. 97.

[11] The *Edictum Ædilium* was applied
more particularly to sales of chattels
than to real estate; but it will not be
considered out of place here.

*Aiunt œdiles, "Qui mancipia ven-
dunt, certiores faciant emptores quid
morbi vitiive cuique sit; quis fugitivus,
errove sit; noxave solutus non sit; eadem-
que omnia cum ea mancipia venibunt,
palam ac recte pronuncianto. Quod si
mancipium adversus ea venisset, sive
adversus quod dictum promissumve
fuerit quum veniret, fuisset, quod ejus
(nomine) prœstari oportere dicetur, emp-
tori, omnibusque ad quos ea res per-
tinet, judicium dabimus ut id mancipium redhibeatur. Si quid autem post
venditionem traditionemque deterius emptoris opera, familiæ procuratorisve ejus
factum erit; sive quid ex eo post venditionem natum, acquisitum fuerit, et si*

*quid aliud in venditione ei accesserit sive
quid ex ea re fructus pervenerit ad emp-
torem; ut ea omnia restituat. Item si
quas accessiones ipse prœstiterit, ut
recipiat.*

*"Item si quod mancipium capitalem
fraudem admiserit, mortis consciscendœ
sibi causâ quid fecerit, inve arenam de-
pugnandi causâ ad bestias intromissus
fuerit, ea omnia in venditione pronuncianto; ex his enim causis judicium dabimus. Hoc amplius, si quis adversus ea,
sciens, dolo malo vendidisse dicetur,
judicium dabimus."* Dig. lib. xxi, tit. 1,
first part, § 1, Ulp. ad Ed. Ædil.

This edict gave three species of actions: (1) the *actio redhibitoria*, which
was similar to our action founded on
the right to return the chattel and demand the price paid; (2) the *actio esti-
matoria*, or *actio quanti minoris*, analogous to our action for the difference
between the actual value and the value
that the article would have had if with-

124

of damage was in most cases fixed at double the price of the article in question. *Quod autem diximus, duplam promitti oportere, sic erit accipiendum, at non ex omni re id accipiamus; sed de his rebus quæ pretiosores essent, si margarita forte, aut ornamenta pretiosa vel vestis serica, vel quid aliud non contemptibile veneat.*[12]

Under the system of the civil law, as introduced into modern Europe, as no distinction was made on this subject between real and personal property, or *mobiles* and *immobiles*, so the remuneration was the same whether the claim was founded on the non-delivery of the article, or an eviction after possession.[13] And in all these cases the price of the article seems to have been the basis of the measure of damages; but as with chattels, so with land, the increased value of the property was

out blemish, or according to the warranty or representation; and (3) the action grounded on the vendor's fraud, given by the last section. And the edict applied to all sorts of animals as well as to slaves. Pothier, Pandectes, ed. de Brèard Neuville, vol. VIII, pp. 8 and 10. And in certain cases to real estate, p. 55.

As to the rule of damages in the actions *redhibitoria et quanti minoris* various cases are stated in the Digest.

Labeo scribit, "Si uno pretio plures servos emisti, et de uno agere velis, (inter) æstimationem servorum proinde fieri debere, atque ut fieret in æstimationem bonitatis agri, quum ob evictam partem fundi agâtur." Dig. lib. xxi, tit. 1, § 72, Pomp. lib. 17.

"Si plura mancipia uno pretio venierint, et de uno eorum ædilitia actione utamur, ita demum pro bonitate ejus æstimatio fiat, si confuse universis mancipiis constitutum, pretium fuerit. Quod si singulorum mancipiorum constituto pretio, universa tanti venierunt, quantum ex consummatione singulorum fiebat, tunc cujusque mancipii pretium, seu pluris, seu minoris id esset, sequi debemus." Dig. lib. xxi, § 36.

So interest was to be paid to the buyer on the price given; and if the slave had made anything while in the buyer's possession, but without his means or assistance, such acquisitions were to be returned with the slave to the purchaser. Poth. Pan. vol. VIII, p. 75.

And in certain cases both the vendor and purchaser were held to give each other guarantees, to which the rule of the *stipulatio duplex* applied. Poth. Pan., vol. VIII, p. 99. The rule of damages in the *actio redhibitoria* was not, however, always the double value.

Redhibitoria actio duplicem habet condemnationem modo enim in duplicem, modo in simplum condemnatur venditor. Nam si neque pretium, neque accessionem solvat, neque eum qui eo nomine obligatus erit, liberet, dupli pretii et accessionis condemnari jubetur; si vero reddat pretium et accessionem, vel eum qui eo nomine obligatus est, liberet, simpli videtur condemnari. Dig. lib. xxi, tit. 1, § 82.

[12] Dig. lib. xxi, tit. 2, 1, 37, § 1, Pothier, Pan. ed. Brèard Neuville, vol. VIII, p. 102.

[13] Pothier, Contrat de Vente, part II, ch. i, § 1; art. 5, § 69.

taken into account, and for this the party evicted had a right to claim. A distinction was, however, made between the seller in good faith and the party who knew he had no title to convey. Thus, if by reason of circumstances which could not have been foreseen at the time of the contract, the value should be very greatly augmented, the seller in good faith would be liable only for the highest sum to which the parties might have reasonably supposed that the value would rise; [14] in many cases, certainly, a difficult inquiry.

So, again, the seller in good faith was only liable for direct damages; while more remote loss would be charged upon the seller in bad faith. Thus, if after the purchaser entered into possession, he should establish an inn on the premises and be subsequently evicted, the seller in good faith was not chargeable for the injury done to the business of the inn. But the seller in bad faith would in such a case be held liable.[15] And even the seller in good faith would be held answerable under similar circumstances, if, at the time of the bargain, the property was intended to be used as an inn. In all these cases much was left to the discretion of the judge.[16]

It was held by the masters of the civil law, that the fortuitous depreciation of the property did not alter the rule; as if, after the contract, buildings were to burn down, and eviction subsequently take place, the measure of damages would still be the price paid,[17] and so it would probably be held with us.

§ 955. French Code.

In the French Code the subject of evictions is treated with the usual brevity, order, and precision of that great work. The clauses which relate to the subject are as follows:

Where a warranty has been given, or where no stipulation

[14] Pothier, Contrat de Vente, part II, ch. i, § 2; art. 5, § 130.

[15] Pothier, Vente, part II, ch. i, § 1; art. 5, § 136.

[16] *Observez*, says Pothier, § 138, *que par la liquidation et estimation de ces dommages, on doit user de beaucoup plus de modération à l'égard d'un vendeur de bonne foi qu'à l'égard d'un vendeur de mauvaise foi.*

This distinction between the vendor acting in bad faith and *bona fide*, will be found clearly illustrated in Lord Kaimes' Equity, 270; Erskine's Inst. 125; and see, also, Green *v.* Biddle, 8 Wheat. 1, 5 L. ed. 547.

[17] Pothier, Vente, art. 69.

has been made on this subject, in such case, if the purchaser
is evicted, he is entitled to demand from the seller:

I. The restitution of the purchase-money.

II. The restitution of any mesne profits which he may be
obliged to pay over to the proprietor who evicts him.

III. The expenses incurred on the demand under the warranty of the buyer, and those incurred by the person originally
making the demand.

IV. The damages and interest as well as the expenses and
legal costs of the contract.

If, at the time of the eviction, the thing sold proves to be
lessened in value or considerably injured, whether by the negligence of the buyer or owing to accidents resulting from superior force, the seller is in either case, liable for the entire purchase-money.

But if the diminution in the value of the article has produced
any profit to the buyer, the seller has a right to deduct from the
purchase-money a sum equal to this profit.

In case the thing sold is increased in value at the time of the
eviction, and even if such increase be independent of any acts
of the purchaser, yet he is entitled to receive from the seller
its actual value over and above the purchase-money.

The seller is bound to reimburse the purchaser, or to cause
him to be reimbursed by the party evicting him, for all actual
improvements and beneficial repairs that he shall have made
to the property

If the seller has sold the lands of a third person in bad faith,
he will be compelled to reimburse the purchaser for all sums
which he may have expended upon them, although such expenses be merely pleasurable or fanciful.[18] **

II.—Covenants of Warranty and for Quiet Enjoyment

§ 956. What constitutes a breach.

It has long been settled that covenants of warranty and for
quiet enjoyment relate to the possession of the subject-matter
of the conveyance rather than to the state of the title. Accordingly it is clear than an actual loss of the land is essential

[18] Code Civ., §§ 1630–1635.

to the plaintiff's claim for substantial damages.[19] And since a covenant of warranty is one of compensation rather than of exoneration, the grantee of land with warranty, who has conveyed all his interest therein with warranty, cannot maintain an action against his grantor for a breach of the warranty subsequently occurring, unless he is compelled to pay damage on his own covenant of warranty,[20] in which event he may recover only what was recovered from himself, and by the usual rule not more than the purchase price paid by himself to the warrantor.[21] So it has been held that a grantee under a warranty deed who immediately mortgages back to the grantor, becoming the latter's tenant, cannot maintain an action on the covenant on account of an entry and ouster by a paramount title, because such entry is not against his own possession

[19] Marston v. Hobbs, 2 Mass. 433, 3 Am. Dec. 61. In this case, Parsons, C. J., defines the effect of the various covenants with great clearness.

See, also, the following cases:
Alabama: Oliver v. Bush, 125 Ala. 534, 27 So. 923.
Indiana: Mauzy v. Flint, 42 Ind. App. 386, 83 N. E. 757.
Iowa: Brandt v. Foster, 5 Ia. 287.
Massachusetts: Twambly v. Henley, 4 Mass. 441; Bearce v. Jackson, 4 Mass. 408; Chapel v. Bull, 17 Mass. 213.
New York: Waldron v. McCarty, 3 Johns. 471; St. John v. Palmer, 5 Hill, 599, and cases there cited.
Ohio: Hill v. Butler, 6 Oh. St. 207.
South Carolina: Singleton v. Allen, 2 Strobh. Eq. 166.
Texas: Huff v. Reilly, 64 S. W. 387, 26 Tex. Civ. App. 101.
Canada: Graham v. Baker, 10 Up. Can. C. P. 426; Snider v. Snider, 13 Up. Can. C. P. 157; Bannon v. Frank, 14 Up. Can. C. P. 295.
In Colburn v. Northern Pac. R. R., 13 Mont. 476, 34 Pac. 1017, it was held that a vendee who has accepted a warranty deed from a vendor who had no title, is not compelled to await eviction and then sue on the covenants of

the deed, but may sue on the contract to convey and recover the money paid on the contract for the purchase of the land.
[20] Wheeler v. Sohier, 3 Cush. 219; the court said: "The plaintiff has not suffered any damage, and he never may sustain any. He is liable on his warranty, it is true; but before he has suffered he cannot sue for indemnity, there being no certainty that he ever will be damnified."
Acc., Connecticut: Booth v. Starr, 1 Conn. 244, 6 Am. Dec. 233.
Kansas: Hammerslough v. Hackett, 48 Kan. 700, 29 Pac. 1079.
Kentucky: Lot v. Parish, 1 Litt. 393.
New York: Withy v. Mumford, 5 Cow. 137; Baxter v. Ryerss, 13 Barb. 267; Sweet v. Bradley, 24 Barb. 549; Burt v. Dewey, 40 N. Y. 283, 100 Am. Dec. 482.
Canada: Scriver v. Myers, 9 Up. Can. C. P. 255.
[21] *North Carolina:* Markland v. Crump, 1 Dev. & B. 94, 27 Am. Dec. 230.
Virginia: Conrad v. Effinger, 87 Va. 59, 12 S. E. 2, 24 Am. St. Rep. 646.

but against that of his mortgagee.[22] But where A conveys to B with covenants, and B conveys to C with covenants, C giving a mortgage back, and C is ejected by paramount title, B may recover of A according to usual rule without having paid C, because the eviction of C prevents recovery by B against C on the mortgage debt.[23]

Upon the plaintiff's eviction the right of action is immediate and complete and the whole damages for a single breach are recoverable in one action.[24] The covenant is not, however, exhausted by a single breach and recovery therefor, damages being recoverable as often as there is an eviction from any part of the land warranted.

As to what will constitute an eviction, the authorities seem in conflict. In North Carolina, where it appeared that at the time of the execution of the deed to the plaintiff, and previous thereto, a third person was in possession of the premises under a paramount title, it was held that this was sufficient to constitute a breach of the covenant for quiet enjoyment; [25] and in another case,[26] the Supreme Court of the United States said: "If the grantee be unable to obtain possession in consequence of an existing possession or seizin by a person claiming and holding under an elder title, this would certainly be equivalent to an eviction and a breach." Such seems to be the generally accepted rule.[27] The earlier New York cases,[28] however, held rigidly to the doctrine that the covenant of quiet enjoyment goes to the *possession* and not to the *title*, and that a disturbance of the possession is indispensable. In St. John v. Palmer,[29] Bronson, J., said: "If the covenantee *never had the possession*, or if he had the possession and retains it still, it is impossible that there should have been an eviction, and no action will lie however hard the case may seem to be. The grantee should

[22] Gilman v. Haven, 11 Cush. 330.

[23] Kane v. Sanger, 14 Johns. 89.

[24] Van Zandt v. The Mayor, 8 Bosw. 375 (*semble*).

[25] Grist v. Hodges, 3 Dev. 198.

[26] Duvall v. Craig, 2 Wheat. 45, 61, 4 L. ed. 181.

[27] *Illinois:* Moore v. Vail, 17 Ill. 185.
Mississippi: Witty v. Hightower, 12 Sm. & M. 478.

Missouri: Murphy v. Price, 48 Mo. 247.

[28] Waldron v. McCarty, 3 Johns. 471; Kortz v. Carpenter, 5 Johns. 120; Kerr v. Shaw, 13 Johns. 236; Webb v. Alexander, 7 Wend. 281; St. John v. Palmer, 5 Hill, 599; Rindskopf v. Farmers' Loan & Trust Co., 58 Barb. 36.

[29] 5 Hill, 599.

have protected himself by other covenants." But the law of New York as later settled is in accordance with the general view.[30]

In Wisconsin it has been held, still further, that if the land is unoccupied land to which the grantor had no title, there is a constructive eviction at once, and the grantee may recover full damages on his covenant;[31] but if the grantor afterwards obtains good title, and the grantee is not actually kept out of possession, he can recover compensation only for such damage as may have been done to the land by the true owner since the date of the conveyance.[32] But as has been stated above it is well established that the mere existence of a paramount legal title is not sufficient to constitute a breach of these covenants, but that the plaintiff must allege and prove an ouster or eviction by a paramount title.[33] Such eviction however, need not be by process of law; the grantee may surrender possession, but, in such case, he assumes the whole burden of proving that the title to which he surrenders without contest, is actually paramount to that derived from his grantor.[34]

The only subject, however, with which we are here concerned is the measure of damages in the case of a covenant which has been broken. Two leading rules have been laid down. These we will now examine, noting their various modifications, the States in which they have respectively found favor, and the comparative merits of each.

§ 957. Recovery of consideration on total breach—New York rule.

* The question as to the measure of compensation came up at an early day in the State of New York.[35] The defendant's testator, Ten Eyck, had conveyed certain lots in Albany to one Walsh, for £300. Walsh had conveyed to Staats, and Staats to Chinn, who had been evicted, and had recovered

[30] Shattuck v. Lamb, 65 N. Y. 499, 22 Am. Rep. 656.
[31] McLennan v. Prentice, 85 Wis. 427, 55 N. W. 764.
[32] McInnis v. Lyman, 62 Wis. 191.
[33] See 4 Kent's Com. 460; 2 Saunders, 181 b., n. 10; Foster v. Pierson, 4 T. R. 617, 621.

[34] St. John v. Palmer, 5 Hill, 599. And the rule is the same in Massachusetts. Hamilton v. Cutts, 4 Mass. 349, 3 Am. Dec. 222; Sprague v. Baker, 17 Mass. 586.
See also: Drew v. Towle, 10 Foster (N. H.), 531.
[35] Staats v. Ten Eyck, 3 Caines, 111.

against the plaintiff Staats. The covenants in Ten Eyck's deed were of seizin and for quiet enjoyment; and the two points were, first, whether the plaintiff was entitled to recover the value at the time of eviction, or only at that of the purchase, and to be ascertained by the consideration given; and, secondly, if the latter, whether the plaintiff was entitled to interest on the purchase-money and the costs of the eviction. The court, in the course of a very able opinion, said, that the rule at common law on a warranty on a writ of *warrantia chartæ*, was that the demandant recovered in compensation only for the land at the time of the warranty made,[36] and that he did not find that the law had been altered since the introduction of personal covenants.

§ 958. Improvements excluded by New York rule.

In a subsequent case,[37] where land had been conveyed with covenants of seizin and quiet enjoyment, and both broken, the questions were raised whether the plaintiff was entitled to recover damages for the improvements made by him, and for the increased value of the land itself. As to the latter point, all the court appear to have concurred with the case last cited; but as to the question of improvements, there was a disagreement. Spencer, J., was disposed to allow for beneficial improvements.

The other members of the court were, however, of a different opinion.

§ 959. The New York rule followed in most States.

These conclusions as to improvements necessarily lead to the

[36] The language of one of the year books, as to the rule on warranties, may be worthy of notice. 6 Ed. II, 187:

En un breve de dower le tenant vouch a'gar' et le gar' fist defaute, le grant cape retorne ove la extent, . . . que la terre est extend trop haut qe chescun acr' de terre est extendu a xvd, ou ele ne voleit al houre qe ele passa hors de nostre seisine qe iiiid qe ele est bien compote marle et ovesque ceo bien edifie et ne fut pas en le temps de alienation per qi nous prioins aver extente autr' qe n'est fait issi qe nous puis-

soins faire a la value soloin ceo que ele passa hors de nostre seisine. . . . Et nota qe Ber' dit qe si le Vic' fist estendre la terre plus haut qe ele ne volust en temps de alienation qant breve de seisine luy voudra qe le tennant puet avoir bon remidie vers luy apres ceo per breve, &c.

Et sic nota la terre le tennant q'est garr' doit estre estendu solom ceo qe ele valust en temps de alienation et non pas en temps de recoveryr.

[37] Pitcher v. Livingston, 4 Johns. 1, 4 Am. Dec. 229.

general rule adopted in New York and other States, that the measure of damages is limited to the consideration, together with interest, and the expenses of defending possession. The rule has been confirmed in New York by repeated decisions.[38]

Pennsylvania.—The general rule, as settled in New York, was adopted at an early day in Pennsylvania, and the price of the land at the date of the deed was taken as the measure of damages.[39]

South Carolina.—* In South Carolina, the rule was not at first adopted. It was held, by Pendleton, J., at *nisi prius* in an action of covenant brought for a breach of warranty in a release of a lot of land in Charleston, that there could be no doubt but that the measure of estimating damages in a case like the present was the value of the land at the time of the eviction; but only a part of the lot being taken, it was left to the jury to apportion the damages according to the amount of injury sustained, or give the full amount of the value of the lot; which latter was done.[40] In a subsequent action on covenant of warranty,[41] there was a difference of opinion on this point, Grimke, J., thinking the purchase-money and interest was the true rule. But Waties and Bay, JJ., thought the value of the lands at the time of the eviction was the best general rule; and on this principle the verdict was given. In an action of warranty of negroes,[42] an attempt was made to apply the same principle to chattels; but while the general rule was acknowledged, the particular case was considered an exception, and the court left it to the jury to give what they thought reasonable. Finally, in a subsequent case, the prior

---

[38] Albee *v.* Harris, 9 Johns. 324; Bennett *v.* Jenkins, 13 Johns. 50; Kane *v.* Sanger, 14 Johns. 89; Baldwin *v.* Munn, 2 Wend. 399, 20 Am. Dec. 627; Dimmick *v.* Lockwood, 10 Wend. 142; Kinney *v.* Watts, 14 Wend. 38; Moak *v.* Johnson, 1 Hill, 99; Kelly *v.* Dutch Church of Schenectady, 2 Hill, 105; Baxter *v.* Ryerss, 13 Barb. 267; Hunt *v.* Raplee, 44 Hun, 149.

[39] Bender *v.* Fromberger, 4 Dall. 436, 441; Brown *v.* Dickerson, 12 Pa. 372;

McClure *v.* Gamble, 27 Pa. 288; Cox *v.* Henly, 32 Pa. 18; Hertzog *v.* Hertzog, 34 Pa. 418; McNair *v.* Crompton, 35 Pa. 23; Dumars *v.* Miller, 34 Pa. 319; McCafferty *v.* Griswold, 99 Pa. 270; Allison *v.* Montgomery, 107 Pa. 455. So in case of a lease: McClowry *v.* Corghan, 31 Pa. 22.

[40] Liber *v.* Parsons, 1 Bay, 19.
[41] Guerard *v.* Rivers, 1 Bay, 265.
[42] Eveleigh *v.* Stitt, 1 Bay, 92.

decisions as to real covenants were distinctly overruled, and the New York rule was adopted.[43]

Virginia.—* In Virginia it was very early said,[44] that if a conveyance had been made with warranty, the value of the land at the time of eviction would fix the damages. This, however, was in equity; and the rule in that State seems to have been long involved in doubt. In a later case,[45] while the rule as just stated was again recognized, it was held not to apply to a conveyance of land with a general warranty of a specific quantity when the quantity fell short, and the value of the deficiency was fixed at the time of the contract. In another case,[46] the doctrine of the last decision was followed. But the rule we are considering does not appear to have controlled either of these cases; and more recently,[47] the whole subject was carefully examined by Green and Coalter, JJ., in able and conflicting opinions; but the case went off on another ground, Brooke, J., reserving his opinion. And the final decision seems to be that the purchase-money, interest and costs of eviction fix the measure of compensation.[48]

Tennessee.—In Tennessee, the purchase-money, with interest, makes the measure of remuneration.[49]

Kentucky.—So, too, in Kentucky, where it was held by the Court of Appeals, that in case of a covenant of warranty and eviction, "the value of the land at the time of sale to be ascertained by the purchase-money, if expressed in the deed or known, together with interest thereon, and the costs, extraordinary as well as legal, expended in defense of the title, is the measure of damages to be recovered; but if the purchase-money be not expressed in the deed, other means may be used

[43] Henning v. Withers, 3 Brev. 458; Ware v. Weathnall, 2 McCord, 413; Bond v. Quattlebaum, 1 McCord, 584; Furman v. Elmore, 2 N. & M'C. 189; Wilson v. Forbes, 2 Dev. 30; Lawrance v. Robertson, 10 S. C. 8.

[44] Mills v. Bell, 3 Call, 320.

[45] Nelson v. Matthews, 2 Hen. & Mun. 164.

[46] Humphrey v. McClenachan, 1 Mun. 493.

[47] Stout v. Jackson, 2 Randolph, 132.

[48] Threlkeld v. Fitzhugh, 2 Leigh, 451; Conrad v. Effinger, 87 Va. 59, 12 S. E. 2, 24 Am. St. Rep. 646.

[49] Talbott v. Bedford, 5 Hall's Am. Law J. 330, cited in notes to Duvall v. Craig, 2 Wheat. 45, 64; Shaw v. Wilkins, 8 Humphreys, 647. See also in Sumner v. Williams, 4 Hall's Am. Law J. 129, 147, the opinion of Luther Martin. Mette v. Dow, 9 Lea, 93; McGuffey v. Humes, 85 Tenn. 26.

to ascertain the value." The case was in chancery.[50] Later Kentucky cases profess to award as damages for breach of warranty the value of the land at the time of conveyance with necessary costs of defending the title. The consideration *per se* is not the measure of recovery being however the best evidence of the value.[51] Upon a covenant by a vendor to render other lands equal in value in case those conveyed should be taken by a better claim the value of the land sold at the date of the covenant and not at the date of eviction was held to be the proper measure of damages.[52]

New Hampshire.—Though the courts of New Hampshire have generally followed the New York rule denying recovery for improvements, a modification of the·rule has been suggested in the intimation that the plaintiff might be allowed compensation for expensive improvements, if he had not been in possession long enough to be allowed the value of them as against the owner in the eviction suit under the statute of betterments.[53]

Michigan.—In Michigan an early case allowed recovery of the value of the land at the time of eviction,[54] but a more recent decision limits the damages on the covenant of warranty to the consideration paid with interest and costs.[55]

The New York rule has been adopted by the Federal courts [56] and prevails in almost every State outside of New England.[57]

[50] Cox v. Strode, 2 Bibb, 273, 280.

[51] Combs v. Tarlton, 2 Dana, 464; Seamore v. Harlan, 3 Dana, 410; Marshall v. McConnell, 1 Litt. 419; Cummins v. Kennedy, 2 Litt. 118, 14 Am. Dec. 45; Robertson v. Lemon, 2 Bush, 301; McMillan v. Ritchie, 3 T. B. Mon. 348, 16 Am. Dec. 107; Pence v. Duvall, 9 B. Mon. 48; Blackwell v. McBride, 14 Ky. L. Rep. 760.

[52] Davis v. Hall, 2 Bibb (Ky.), 590.

[53] Ela v. Card, 2 N. H. 175, 9 Am. Dec. 46.

[54] Eaton v. Knowles, 61 Mich. 625, 28 N. W. 740.

[55] Webb v. Holt, 113 Mich. 338, 71 N. W. 637.

[56] Hopkins v. Lee, 6 Wheat. 118, 5 L. ed. 218; Patrick v. Leach, 1 Mc Cr. 250. So in a Pennsylvania case: American Ice Co. v. Pocono S. W. I. Co., 183 Fed. 193, 105 C. C. A. 625.

[57] *Alabama:* Kingsbury v. Milner, 69 Ala. 502; Allinder v. Bessemer C. I. & L. Co., 164 Ala. 275, 51 So. 234; Prestwood v. McGowin, 128 Ala. 267, 274, 29 So. 386, 80 Am. St. Rep. 136 (evidence of value of land at time of conveyance held not admissible); Copeland v. McAdory, 100 Ala. 553, 13 So. 545.

Arkansas: Logan v. Moulder, 1 Ark. 313, 33 Am. Dec. 338; Carvill v. Jacks, 43 Ark. 439 (*semble*).

California: McGary v. Hastings, 39 Cal. 360, 2 Am. Rep. 456.

§ 960. Good faith required.

It is to be noticed that the circumstances expressly reserved by the court (bad faith or fraud), in Staats *v.* Ten Eyck (*supra*),

Georgia: Davis *v.* Smith, 5 Ga. 274, 48 Am. Dec. 279; Martin *v.* Atkinson, 7 Ga. 228, 50 Am. Dec. 403; Fernander *v.* Dunn, 19 Ga. 497, 65 Am. Dec. 607; Martin *v.* Wright, 21 Ga. 504; Martin *v.* Gordon, 24 Ga. 533.

Illinois: Buckmaster *v.* Grundy, 2 Ill. 310; McKee *v.* Brandon, 3 Ill. 339; Harding *v.* Larkin, 41 Ill. 413; Wood *v.* Kingston Coal Co., 48 Ill. 356, 95 Am. Dec. 554.

Indiana: Blackwell *v.* Lawrence Co., 2 Blackf. 143; Sheets *v.* Andrews, 2 Blackf. 274; Reese *v.* McQuilkin, 7 Ind. 450; Burton *v.* Reeds, 20 Ind. 87; Cincinnati, etc., R. R. *v.* Pearce, 28 Ind. 502; Wood *v.* Bibbins, 58 Ind. 392; Thomas *v.* Hamilton, 71 Ind. 277; Rhea *v.* Swain, 122 Ind. 272.

Iowa: Swafford *v.* Whipple, 3 Green, 261, 54 Am. Dec. 498; Brandt *v.* Foster, 5 Ia. 287; Fawcett *v.* Woods, 5 Ia. 400; Bellows *v.* Litchfield, 83 Ia. 36, 48 N. W. 1062.

Kansas: Stebbins *v.* Wolf, 33 Kan. 765, 7 Pac. 542; Pearson *v.* Ford, 42 Pac. 257, 1 Kan. App. 580; Looney *v.* Reeves, 5 Kan. App. 279, 48 Pac. 606; Craven *v.* Clary, 55 Pac. 679, 8 Kan. App. 295.

Louisiana: Boyer *v.* Amet, 41 La. Ann. 721, 6 So. 734.

Maryland: Crisfield *v.* Storr, 36 Md. 129, 150, 11 Am. Rep. 480.

Minnesota: Moore *v.* Frankenfield, 25 Minn. 540; Devine *v.* Lewis, 38 Minn. 24; Donlan *v.* Evans, 40 Minn. 501, 42 N. W. 472; Wagner *v.* Finnegan, 54 Minn. 251, 55 N. W. 1129 .

Mississippi: Phipps *v.* Tarpley, 31 Miss. 433 (evidence of value excluded); Allen *v.* Miller, 54 So. 731.

Missouri: Coffman *v.* Huck, 19 Mo. 435; Dickson *v.* Desire, 23 Mo. 151, 66 Am. Dec. 661; Tong *v.* Matthews, 23 Mo. 437; Murphy *v.* Price, 48 Mo.

247; Lambert *v.* Estes, 13 S. W. 284; Coleman *v.* Lucksinger, 224 Mo. 1, 123 S. W. 441, 26 L. R. A. (N. S.) 934; Dryden *v.* Kellogg, 2 Mo. App. 87; Matheny *v.* Stewart, 17 S. W. 1014, 108 Mo. 73.

Montana: Taylor *v.* Holter, 1 Mont. 688.

Nebraska: Holmes *v.* Seaman, 72 Neb. 300, 100 N. W. 417.

Nevada: Dalton *v.* Bowker, 8 Nev. 190; Hoffman *v.* Bosch, 18 Nev. 360.

New Hampshire: Ela *v.* Card, 2 N. H. 175, 9 Am. Dec. 46; Willson *v.* Willson, 25 N. H. 229, 57 Am. Dec. 320; Foster *v.* Thompson, 41 N. H. 373; Winnepiseogee P. Co. *v.* Eaton, 65 N. H. 13, 18 Atl. 171; Drew *v.* Towle, 10 Foster, 531.

New Jersey: Stewart *v.* Drake, 9 N. J. L. 139; Miller *v.* Halsey, 14 N. J. L. 48; Morris *v.* Rowan, 17 N. J. L. 304.

North Carolina: Wilson *v.* Forbes, 2 Dev. 30; West *v.* West, 76 N. C. 45; Ramsey *v.* Wallace, 100 N. C. 75, 83 (*semble*).

Ohio: Backus *v.* M'Coy, 3 Oh. 211, 17 Am. Dec. 585; Lloyd *v.* Quimby, 5 Oh. St. 262; Dustin *v.* Newcomer, 8 Oh. 49; Foote *v.* Burnet, 10 Oh. 317, 36 Am. Dec. 90; Clark *v.* Parr, 14 Oh. 118, 45 Am. Dec. 529; Wade *v.* Comstock, 11 Oh. St. 71; Vail *v.* Junction R. R., 1 Cin. Sup. Ct. 571.

Oregon: Stark *v.* Olney, 3 Ore. 88; Rash *v.* Jenne, 26 Ore. 169, 37 Pac. 538.

Tennessee: Talbott *v.* Bedford, 5 Hall's Am. Law J. 330; Hopkins *v.* Yowell, 5 Yerger, 305; McGuffey *v.* Humes, 85 Tenn. 26. ·

Texas: Sutton *v.* Page, 4 Tex. 142; Simpson *v.* Belvin, 37 Tex. 674; Turner *v.* Miller, 42 Tex. 418, 19 Am. Rep. 47; Glenn *v.* Mathews, 44 Tex. 400; Brown *v.* Hearon, 66 Tex. 63, 17 S. W. 395; Kemner *v.* Beaumont Lumber Co., 20 Tex. Civ. App. 307, 49 S. W. 412 (actual value less than purchase price).

as those under which the New York rule would not be applicable, have been again referred to as perhaps necessitating a modification of the rule. Thus, in Taylor v. Barnes,[58] Allen, J., said, "Whether it should be applied when the title fails by the fraud or fault of the grantor and covenantor is, at least, doubtful." There have been intimations of a like modification of the rule in other jurisdictions; the rule adopted in contracts for the sale of real estate being adopted,[59] so that if the breach is due to the defendant's own fraud or wilful default the plaintiff may recover compensation for loss of his bargain.[60]

§ 961.[a] Assignee's damages.

The jurisdictions which follow the New York rule in actions between the immediate parties to a deed, apply it also in an action by the assignee. It has been said that in an action upon the warranty by an assignee, the measure of damages is the sum which the assignor might have recovered had the action been brought in his name.[61] The warrantor must

Virginia: Stout v. Jackson, 2 Rand. 132 (value at time of conveyance the measure of recovery: price paid is best evidence of such value); Threlkeld v. Fitzhugh, 2 Leigh, 451; Lowther v. Com., 1 H. & M. 202; Crenshaw v. Smith, 5 Munf. 415; Wilson v. Spencer, 11 Leigh, 261; Click v. Green, 77 Va. 827; Sheffey v. Gardiner, 79 Va. 313; Conrad v. Effinger, 87 Va. 59, 12 S. E. 2, 24 Am. St. Rep. 646.

West Virginia: Butcher v. Peterson, 26 W. Va. 447, 53 Am. Rep. 89.

Wisconsin: Hall v. Delaplaine, 5 Wis. 206, 68 Am. Dec. 57; Conrad v. Grand G. U. O. Druids, 64 Wis. 258.

Hawaii: Mooris v. Petero, 4 Hawaii, 23.

So also in *Ontario:* Brennan v. Servis, 8 Up. Can. Q. B. 191; Graham v. Leslie, 4 Up. Can. C. P. 176. But in a later case, where the plaintiff was evicted by a dowress, and brought suit on the covenant for quiet enjoyment, it was held that the actual loss could be recovered in an action upon that covenant, though the consideration was

natural love and affection only; for that covenant was not broken until loss happened. Hodgins v. Hodgins, 13 Up. Can. C. P. 146.

In some States this rule is laid down by statute.

South Carolina: Rev. Stat. '82, § 1832.

California: Code, § 3304.

[a] For § 961 of the eighth edition see § 959.

[58] 69 N. Y. 430, 434; *acc.,* Brisbane v. Pomeroy, 13 Daly, 358.

[59] *Post,* § 1010.

[60] *Idaho:* Madden v. Caldwell Land Co., 16 Ida. 59, 100 Pac. 358, 21 L. R. A. (N. S.) 332.

Indiana: Blackwell v. Justices, 2 Blackf. 274; Reese v. McQuilkin, 7 Ind. 450.

Missouri: Coffman v. Huck, 19 Mo. 435.

Pennsylvania: Bender v. Fromberger, 4 Dall. 436; King v. Pyle, 8 S. & R. 166.

[61] Dougherty v. Duvall, 9 B. Mon. (Ky.) 57.

make good his warranty,[62] but nothing more. In other words the maximum recovery is the original consideration received by the warrantor.[63] But where the remote grantee has paid a lesser sum for his own conveyance or where the land at the time of eviction is of less value than the original consideration, the authorities are in conflict as to the proper measure of recovery. In Jenks v. Quinn [64] it was said that if the value of the premises at the time of eviction is less than the consideration moving between the original covenantor and covenantee, the remote grantee can recover no more than the value at the time of eviction. The prevailing view seems to be that the assignee shall recover no more than he himself paid for his conveyance.[65] But in Brooks v. Black [66] it was held that a remote vendee might recover against the original vendor the full price received by the latter although it exceeded the amount paid by the plaintiff for the land.[67] The original consideration being deemed to have been fixed upon as liquidated damages for a breach of the warranty. And in Beasley v. Phillips [68] one who paid nothing for the land recovered against a remote grantor the amount paid to buy in an outstanding title.

[62] *New York:* Sweet v. Bradley, 24 Barb. 549.

Texas: Rogers v. Golson, 31 S. W. 200 (Tex. Civ. App.)

[63] *Georgia:* Martin v. Gordon, 24 Ga. 533.

Missouri: Dickson v. Desire, 23 Mo. 166, 66 Am. Dec. 661; Staed v. Rossier, 137 S. W. 901.

Nebraska: Walton v. Campbell, 51 Neb. 788, 71 N. W. 737.

New York: Jenks v. Quinn, 61 Hun, 427, 16 N. Y. Supp. 240.

Ohio: King v. Kerr, 5 Ohio, 154, 22 Am. Dec. 777.

[64] 61 Hun, 427, 16 N. Y. Supp. 240. *Cf.* Dickson v. Desire, 23 Mo. 166.

[65] *Colorado:* Taylor v. Wallace, 20 Colo. 211, 37 Pac. 963, 46 Am. St. Rep. 285.

Maryland: Crisfield v. Storr, 36 Md. 129, 11 Am. Rep. 480.

Minnesota: Moore v. Frankenfield, 25 Minn. 540.

Missouri: Lee v. Gratz, 92 Mo. App. 422.

North Carolina: Williams v. Beeman, 2 Dev. 483.

Tennessee: Mette v. Dow, 9 Lea, 93; Whitzman v. Hersh, 87 Tenn. 513.

Wisconsin: Eaton v. Lyman, 26 Wis. 61, 7 Am. Rep. 39.

[66] 68 Miss. 161, 8 So. 32, 11 L. R. A. 176, 24 Am. St. Rep. 259.

[67] See to the same effect the following cases:

Iowa: Mischke v. Baughn, 52 Iowa, 528, 3 N. W. 543.

Kentucky: Dougherty v. Duvall, 9 B. Mon. 57.

South Carolina: Lowrance v. Robertson, 10 S. C. 8.

Texas: Hollingworth v. Mexia, 14 Tex. Civ. App. 363, 37 S. W. 455; Lewis v. Ross, 95 Tex. 358, 67 S. W. 405.

[68] 50 N. E. 488, 20 Ind. App. 182.

In some cases a third party, having a bond for a deed, sells to the plaintiff and receives from him the consideration, while he pays a smaller amount to the defendant, his vendor; but for convenience the deed is made directly from defendant to plaintiff. In Massachusetts, in an action on the covenant of seizin, it has been held in such a case that the plaintiff might recover the value of the land at the time of the conveyance,[69] or at his option the consideration actually received by the defendant.[70] In Ontario, on the other hand, it has been held that the plaintiff may recover the consideration he actually paid.[71] It would seem that this case should be treated as if a deed with covenants had been given by the defendant to the third party, and another by the third party to the plaintiff. Hence in Bowne v. Wolcott [72] the plaintiff was awarded only the amount actually received by the grantor although the deed recited the consideration paid by the plaintiff to the intermediate third party.

Obviously one who is a grantee of but a part of the premises originally conveyed by the warrantor is limited to the portion of the land in which he has an interest.[73]

In Shorthill v. Ferguson [74] an assignee of the covenant was allowed to recover, though he only offered evidence to show that the title was doubtful. The action was said to be for breach of warranty, but it seems to have been for rescission, since the plaintiff was required to give up his deed.

§ 962.ᵃ Recovery of value at time of eviction—Improvements included—New England rule.

Though the New York rule has been generally followed and recovery for improvements denied in actions for breach of covenants of warranty and for quiet enjoyment, England and the New England States (except New Hampshire) have adopted a different rule, allowing the plaintiff the *value* of the land at

---

ᵃ For § 962 of the eighth edition see § 961.

[69] Byrnes v. Rich, 5 Gray, 518.

[70] Staples v. Dean, 114 Mass. 125. This was held to be the true measure in Cook v. Curtis, 68 Mich. 611.

[71] Graham v. Leslie, 4 Up. Can. C. P. 176.

[72] 1 N. D. 497, 48 N. W. 426.

[73] Schofield v. Iowa Homestead Co., 32 Iowa, 317, 7 Am. Rep. 197.

[74] 44 Iowa, 249.

the time of eviction, including the value of improvements, without regard to the consideration.

England.—By the latest English decision [75] this has been recognized as the English rule. Thus, in Bunny *v.* Hopkinson,[76] an action for breach of a covenant for quiet enjoyment, the Master of the Rolls allowed the full amount of the vendee's expenditures in converting the land to the purpose for which it was bought, by erecting buildings on it. It does not appear from the report that the purpose was known to the vendor, except as might be inferred from the lots being building land. The value of the improvements and the actual expense of making them seem to have been considered as identical.[77]

Massachusetts.—In Massachusetts, in a case [78] in which the action was brought on the covenant of warranty, Parsons, C, J., delivering the judgment of the Supreme Court of that State, said: "The court are of opinion, conformably to the principles of law applied to personal actions of covenant broken, to the ancient usages of the State, and to the decisions of our predecessors, supported by the practice of the legislature, that the plaintiff in this action ought to recover in damages the value of the estate at the time of the eviction." The land in this case had risen from $9,000 to $15,000, but whether by reason of actual improvements is not stated.[79]

In a later case, [80] it was held by the same court, that, as there was a covenant of warranty in the deed, if the plaintiff had been evicted, the jury should consider the value of the land at the time of the eviction as the proper measure of damages; but there being no eviction, it was held that the measure of damages on the covenant of seizin was the price paid and interest.[81]

[75] Jenkins *v.* Jones, 9 Q. B. Div. 128.

[76] 27 Beav. 565.

[77] *Acc.*, Coleman *v.* Ballard, 13 La. Ann. 512.

[78] Gore *v.* Brazier, 3 Mass. 523, 546, 3 Am. Dec. 182 (decided in 1807). See also Sumner *v.* Williams, 8 Mass. 162, 222, 5 Am. Dec. 83.

[79] And compensation can be recovered for improvements made in good faith after notice of the paramount claim, since the plaintiff had a right to rely on the warranty. Cecconi *v.* Rodden, 147 Mass. 164, 16 N. E. 749.

[80] Caswell *v.* Wendell, 4 Mass. 108.

[81] In 1807 (ch. 75, § 3), an act was passed in Massachusetts, allowing the tenant in real actions, in certain cases, compensation for his improvements, and giving the demandant the increased value of the premises, less the improvements, the provisions of which are in-

But the same court decided [82] that where administrators had conveyed a defective title with this covenant, it was broken at the moment of execution, and that the measure of damages was the consideration in the deed and interest; "or, at most, that amount together with the plaintiff's expenses of defending the possession."

The rule as above established in Massachusetts, that where the covenant is in the future, and the estate in the meantime passes by force of the conveyance, and the grantee becomes seized, and is afterwards evicted by a paramount title, the value of the estate at the time of the eviction is the measure of the plaintiff's damages,—has been repeatedly since held in that State.[83] But it was said in a later case,[84] that this rule may be modified by special circumstances, as, for instance, "cases may be supposed where the outstanding mortgage, though assuming the form of a paramount title, which, if not redeemed, would take the whole estate and evict the covenantee; yet, being very small in amount in comparison with the value of the estate, it would be plainly for the interest of the owner and holder of the equity of redemption to redeem. In such case it would be quite unreasonable to hold that the covenantee on such an eviction should recover damages to the full value of the estate." And this doctrine has been reaffirmed.[85] It is to be borne in mind, that in Massachusetts the mortgagee obtains a conditional judgment, and is put in possession, after which the plaintiff may discharge the incumbrance, and restore himself to possession by paying the debt, with interest and costs of suit; and in such a case, the proper rule of damages was held to be the amount due on the mortgage, with the costs of the mortgage suit against the plaintiff.[86]

corporated in the R. L., ch. 179. Harris *v.* Newell, 8 Mass. 262; Knox *v.* Hook, 12 Mass. 329; see also Bacon *v.* Callender, 6 Mass. 303; Runey *v.* Edmands, 15 Mass. 291; Shaw *v.* Bradstreet, 13 Mass. 241, 7 Am. Dec. 134; Chapel *v.* Bull, 17 Mass. 213; Heath *v.* Wells, 5 Pick. 140; The Society for Prop. of Gospel *v.* Wheeler, 2 Gall. 105.

[82] Sumner *v.* Williams, 8 Mass. 162, 221, 5 Am. Dec. 83.

[83] Norton *v.* Babcock, 2 Met. 510, 518; Bigelow *v.* Jones, 4 Mass. 512; Boyle *v.* Edwards, 114 Mass. 373; Furnas *v.* Durgin, 119 Mass. 500, 20 Am. Rep. 341.

[84] White *v.* Whitney, 3 Met. 81, 89, 37 Am. Dec. 117.

[85] Donahoe *v.* Emery, 9 Met. 63.

[86] Tufts *v.* Adams, 8 Pick. 547.

Maine.—The State of Maine has adhered to the rule of her parent, Massachusetts, that the value of the premises at the time of the eviction forms the necessary damages; and to this have there been added the expenses reasonably and actually incurred in the defense of the suit in which the grantee was evicted.[87] In a case in Maine the plaintiff was an assignee of a mortgage; the defendant, the assignor, had released part of the land covered by the mortgage, but assigned the whole mortgage in good faith. The land actually covered by the mortgage at the time of the assignment was then worth more than enough to satisfy the debt, but it afterwards became less valuable. In an action on the covenant of warranty in the assignment it was held that no more than nominal damages could be recovered.[88] Special circumstances were relied upon by the court to sustain them in their opinion; but on the facts stated the decision was no doubt correct. No possession of the released premises was ever given to the plaintiff; the covenant was therefore broken when the deed was delivered, and at that time the value of the security was greater than the debt.

Connecticut.—In Connecticut, as early as 1786, the same rule was declared.[89] The Superior Court said that in suits on the covenant of warranty the constant rule of the court had been to ascertain damages by the value of the land at the time of eviction. But the action being on a covenant of seizin, this rule was held not to apply. It was said that the purchaser might bring his action immediately upon discovering that his title was defective; and the jury, having computed the damages according to the consideration of the deed, the verdict was accepted by the court.

In the same State it was said: "We consider the rule to have been long since settled in this State, that upon the covenant of seizin the plaintiff has a right to recover the consideration money and interest, and on the covenant of warranty, the

[87] Cushman v. Blanchard, 2 Me. 266, 11 Am. Dec. 76; Swett v. Patrick, 12 Me. 9; Hardy v. Nelson, 27 Me. 525, 46 Am. Dec. 619; Elder v. True, 32 Me. 104, 52 Am. Dec. 642; Ryerson v. Chapman, 66 Me. 557; Williamson v. Williamson, 71 Me. 442; Harrington v. Bean, 89 Me. 470, 36 Atl. 986.

[88] People's Savings Bank v. Hill, 81 Me. 71, 16 Atl. 337.

[89] Hosford v. Wright, Kirby, 3.

value of the land at the time of eviction. . . . We think, too, that when the warrantor has been vouched in to defend his title, the costs which the plaintiff has actually been put to is also a fair ground of damages." [90]

Vermont.—Vermont likewise has adopted the value at the time of eviction as the measure of damages for covenants as to future possession.[91]

Nebraska.—In Nebraska also the rule by which the value at the time of eviction is allowed is the rule adopted by the court.[92]

Civil Law jurisdictions: The same prevails in Quebec.[93] In Louisiana however, there can be recovery only for such improvements and increase in the value of the property as was in the contemplation of the parties at the time of the sale.[94]

§ 963.[a] General discussion of the rules.

* The cases upholding the New York rule seem to have been decided mainly upon the analogy to the ancient real warranty,[95] and the assumed impropriety of applying a different rule to the covenant of quiet enjoyment from that which governs the covenant of seizin. But the rule adopted in regard to the real warranty was established when improvements were much more rare and far less rapid than at the present day; and there seems no reason which forbids a grantor from giving a more effectual remedy against a prospective than an immediate

---

[a] For § 963 of the eighth edition see § 962.

[90] Sterling *v.* Peet, 14 Conn. 245, 254; *acc.*, Butler *v.* Barnes, 61 Conn. 399, 24 Atl. 328.

[91] Drury *v.* Shumway, 1 D. Chip. (Vt.) 110, 1 Am. Dec. 704; Park *v.* Bates, 12 Vt. 381, 36 Am. Dec. 347; Pitkin *v.* Leavitt, 13 Vt. 379; Keith *v.* Day, 15 Vt. 660; Keeler *v.* Wood, 30 Vt. 242; Tillotson *v.* Prichard, 60 Vt. 94, 14 Atl. 302, 6 Am. St. Rep. 95; Farwell *v.* Bean, 82 Vt. 172, 72 Atl. 731.

[92] Beck *v.* Staats, 80 Neb. 482, 114 N. W. 633; Webb *v.* Wheeler, 80 Neb. 438, 114 N. W. 636, 17 L. R. A. (N. S.)

[93] Dupuy *v.* Ducondu, 6 Can. 425.

[94] Lamerlec *v.* Barthelmy, 2 McGloin (La.), 106; Weber *v.* Coussy, 12 La. Ann. 534; Bissell *v.* Erwin, 13 La. 143; Hale *v.* New Orleans, 13 La. Ann. 499 (code); Coleman *v.* Ballard, 13 La. Ann. 512.

[95] Where the value of the land to which title failed was assessed as of the time of the original conveyance. Beauchamp *v.* Damory, 29 Edw. 3, 3*a;* 19 Hen. 6, 46*a* (pl. 95); 19 Hen. 6, 61*a* (pl. 26); Bro. Abr. *Recouverie in Value,* pl. 59; Ballet *v.* Ballet, Godbolt, 151; Humphrys *v.* Knight, Cro. Car. 455.

failure of title; nor is it easy to say why the price should be arbitrarily fixed on as the absolute measure of value in regard to lands, when in regard to chattels it is only *prima facie* evidence of that value. There seems great doubt, too, whether sufficient attention has been paid to the words of the covenant. What is the meaning of the phrase "*quiet enjoyment*," in regard to a city lot, for instance, which is of no use but for buildings, on which erections must be contemplated at the time of purchase by both parties, and of which, without such erections, no *enjoyment* can be had? May not a distinction be well taken between this covenant applied to such property and to farming land? **

The rule generally adopted * destroys the value of all the usual covenants in leases, and is against the general principle in regard to chattels, by which we have seen that if a warranty in regard to them fails, the plaintiff is entitled to recover the difference between their actual value and that which they would have had if the warranty had been complied with. It is very frequently the case, that the rent in leases, especially where ground-rent for a long term is reserved, does not represent their real value to the lessee; that the lease or its good-will, as it is sometimes erroneously termed, is of great actual value; and that on an eviction the tenant must suffer positive loss. Why should a covenant, using the expressive phrase *quiet enjoyment*, be frittered away by an arbitrary assumption that the price paid was the real value? [96] If we apply the ordinary common-law rule of compensation, the grantor, on breach of this covenant, should put the grantee in the same position as if the covenant had been compiled with. The covenant is broken when the vendee is ousted from possession. Compensatory damages, then, should equal the value of the land at the time

---

[96] It may be noticed here that the revisers of the Statutes of New York proposed to fix the measure of damages for eviction, at the value of the premises at the time *of eviction*, with interest and costs, and reasonable expenses of defending the title. But if the consideration were paid in money, it was to be taken as the value of the premises; and in case of partial eviction, the value of a part was to be estimated in proportion to the price paid for the whole. But this provision was not finally adopted. See the chapter on Alienation by Deed (part II, ch. i, art. iv, R. S.), which suffered sadly in the hands of the Legislature.

of the eviction, for if the covenant had not been broken, that is what he would have had. The objection urged against this result, on the ground of hardship, seems of no great force, for there is nothing which requires the grantor to make such a covenant. He could refuse to give any covenant, or any but a covenant of seizin. If he chooses to make such a covenant, and the grantee relies on it, it seems a great hardship on the grantee that he should suffer the loss and have no remedy. In this country especially, where the rise in real property is often extremely rapid, and the expectation of it not infrequently forms to a purchaser the inducement to the investment, there seems no intrinsic equity in giving to a vendee as the sole compensation for his eviction from valuable real estate through the vendor's breach of covenant, even if an innocent one, the original purchase-money and interest, which often together amount only to a small proportion of the actual value of the property. The rule must find its defense in considerations of public policy, since the amount of damages necessary to compensate the vendee might in some cases ruin an innocent vendor.[97]

§ 964.[a] Proof of consideration.

* Assuming it to be settled that the consideration paid furnishes the rule of damages, it still remains to be seen how far the price named as paid and received in the deed, is conclusive proof of that consideration. In England the cases are conflicting, and the rule appears to be against the admission of parol proof to contradict the deed.[98] In a case in the King's Bench [99] the court said: "The deed states the whole purchase-

---

[a] For § 964 of the eighth edition see § 963.

[97] The Supreme Court of Ohio, while recognizing the rule as settled in that State, said "that it will scarcely ever do exact justice to both parties, being either more or less than a fair compensation." Wade v. Comstock, 11 Oh. St. 71. Rawle (Covenants for Title, §§ 165, 166) offers the strongest arguments in support of the New York rule. He points out, however, that it should

not apply in case of improvements which were in the contemplation of both parties at the time of the sale.

[98] King v. Inhabitants of Scammonden, 3 T. R. 474; Rowntree v. Jacob, 2 Taunt. 141; Villers v. Beamont, 2 Dy. 146a; Mildmay's Case, 1 Co. 175; Vernon's Case, 4 Co. 1; Peacock v. Monk, 1 Ves. sen. 127; Craythorne v. Swinburne, 14 Ves. 160; Lampon v. Corke, 5 B. & Ald. 606.

[99] Baker v. Dewey, 1 B. & C. 704.

money to be well and truly paid. The parol evidence is that it never was paid, but a great part of it kept back; and that fact is wholly inconsistent with the statements in the deed, and therefore ought not to have been received in evidence." ** In New York a very accomplished judge has held this language: "When the deed contains no covenant but that of seizin or general warranty, the consideration is not inserted as a mere matter of form, nor for the sole purpose of giving effect and operation to the deed; but it is inserted for the further purpose of fixing the amount of damages to which the grantee will be entitled, in case he is evicted. At least, such are my present impressions, though my brethren are inclined to a different conclusion. But it is not now necessary to decide the question." [100] * But we submit, with deference, that any distinction as to the purpose for which parol proof is admitted, cannot be maintained. If good for one end, it must be good as to all. It would be a solecism for the tribunal to admit evidence to influence their minds as to one result, and to exclude it as to another. If a fact be established, all its legitimate results must follow, whether as to rights or remedies; and so it seems to be now at length definitely settled in New York. Jewett, J., delivering the opinion of the Court of Appeals, said: "It is well settled that for the purpose of ascertaining the damages to which a plaintiff may be entitled in an action at law for the breach of the covenant of seizin in a deed, the true consideration, and that all or any part remains unpaid, may be shown, notwithstanding a different consideration is expressed in the deed, and although it contains an acknowledgment, on the part of the grantors, that it has been paid at the time of or before the execution of the deed." [101] ** Accordingly, though the recital in the deed is *prima facie* evidence of the actual consideration,[102] it seems to be well settled in this country, that, as between the original parties to the transfer, the consideration

[100] Greenvault v. Davis, 4 Hill, 643, 647, per Bronson, J.

[101] Bingham v. Weiderwax, 1 N. Y. 509, 514.

[102] *Connecticut:* Meeker v. Meeker, 16 Conn. 383.

New York: Jenks v. Quinn, 61 Hun, 427, 16 N. Y. Supp. 240.

Pennsylvania: Doyle v. Brundred, 189 Pa. 113, 41 Atl. 1107.

Texas: White v. Street, 67 Tex. 177, 2 S. W. 529.

clause is open to parol proof, as for instance in the common case where a dollar is named as the consideration.[103] But, though parol proof may be admitted as between the original parties, it is generally held that if the grantee has transferred the land, the consideration named is conclusive as between his assigns and the original grantor, at least as against the latter.[104] In a case already cited,[105] Bronson, J.,

[103] *United States:* Patrick v. Leach, 1 McCr. 250.

Arkansas: Barnett v. Hughey, 54 Ark. 195, 15 S. W. 464.

Connecticut: Belden v. Seymour, 8 Conn. 304, 21 Am. Dec. 661; Meeker v. Meeker, 16 Conn. 383.

Georgia: Martin v. Gordon, 24 Ga. 533.

Hawaii: Mooris v. Petero, 4 Haw. 23.

Illinois: Illinois L. & L. Co. v. Bonner, 91 Ill. 114; Lloyd v. Sandusky, 95 Ill. App. 593; Drury v. Holden, 121 Ill. 130, 13 N. E. 547; Howell v. Moores, 127 Ill. 67, 19 N. E. 863.

Iowa: Swafford v. Whipple, 3 Greene, 261, 54 Am. Dec. 498; Williamson v. Test, 24 Ia. 138.

Massachusetts: Bullard v. Briggs, 7 Pick. 533, 19 Am. Dec. 292; Smith v. Strong, 14 Pick. 128; Byrnes v. Rich, 5 Gray, 518.

Michigan: Cook v. Curtis, 68 Mich. 611.

Minnesota: Devine v. Lewis, 38 Minn. 24, 35 N. W. 711; Burns v. Schreiber, 43 Minn. 468, 45 N. W. 861.

Mississippi: Moore v. McKie, 5 Sm. & M. 238 (warranty of slaves).

Missouri: Lambert v. Estes, 99 Mo. 604, 13 S. W. 284.

New Hampshire: Morse v. Shattuck, 4 N. H. 229, 17 Am. Dec. 419.

New York: Bingham v. Weiderwax, 1 N. Y. 509.

Ohio: Vail v. Junction R. R., 1 Cin. Sup. Ct. 571; Lloyd v. Quinby, 5 Oh. St. 262.

Oregon: Stark v. Olney, 3 Ore. 88.

Pennsylvania: Cox v. Henry, 32 Pa. 18; Doyle v. Brundred, 189 Pa. 113, 41 Atl. 1107.

Tennessee: Park v. Cheek, 4 Cold. 20.

Texas: Allison v. Pilkins, 11 Tex. Civ. App. 655, 33 S. W. 293; Larkin v. Trammel, 47 Tex. Civ. App. 548, 105 S. W. 552.

In an early case in Kentucky it was held that the consideration could not be disputed in an action at law, but that it could be inquired into in equity. Yelton v. Hawkins, 2 J. J. Marsh. 1. *Cf.* Garret v. Stuart, 1 McCord (S. C.), 514.

See the English and American cases elaborately reviewed in the court of Errors in New York, in McCrea v. Purmort, 16 Wend. 460. See also Grout v. Townsend, 2 Hill, 554. In New Jersey, see the subject examined in Boiles v. Beach, 22 N. J. L. 680, 692, 53 Am. Dec. 203, where it is said: "When the deed acknowledges the payment of the consideration, it cannot be denied by the grantor, for the purpose of destroying the effect and operation of the deed; though it may be denied for the purpose of recovering the consideration money. This doctrine is now, in this country, supported by such a weight of authority as not readily to be disturbed."

[104] *Illinois:* Illinois Land & Loan Co. v. Bonner, 91 Ill. 114.

Kentucky: Blackwell v. McBride, 14 Ky. L. Rep. 760.

New York: Greenvault v. Davis, 4 Hill, 643.

[105] Greenvault v. Davis, 4 Hill, 643, 649.

said: "It would work the grossest injustice to allow the covenantor to go into the question of how much was actually paid for the land, when the title has failed in the hands of an assignee." In this case it was held the *grantor* could not be allowed as against the assignee, to show that the price paid was less than that named in the deed; but perhaps the same reasons do not apply against the *assignee*, if desirous to prove the price greater.[106] In Georgia and Indiana,[107] however, it has been held that neither the immediate grantee nor an assignee can recover more than the actual consideration received by the original warrantor and that the latter may show that the true consideration was less than that expressed in the deed even as against a remote grantee who had no notice of the actual consideration. And in a case where it was assumed that a remote grantee was limited in his recovery to the consideration paid by himself to his immediate grantor, the recital of the consideration in the deed to the plaintiff was held not even to constitute *prima facie* evidence against the defendant of the sum paid by the plaintiff for the land.[108]

And it is held, still further, that if it can be shown that a fixed part of the purchase-money was given for a specific parcel of land to which the title failed, that fixed sum is the measure of damages.[109] But in a Minnesota case where the deed conveyed lands for one entire pecuniary consideration it was held that evidence was not admissible to prove a prior parol agreement to the effect that the consideration was not applicable to that part of the land from which the plaintiff was evicted by the foreclosure of a mortgage but that the conveyance was gratuitous as to such part.[110] On the other hand it has been

---

In Allison *v.* Pilkins, 11 Tex. Civ. App. 655, 33 S. W. 293, the court said: "This rule we think just and equitable. Parties purchasing land have the right to rely on the covenants of warranty of remote as well as immediate vendors, and when recitals are made in the deed, the parties making them should be estopped from contradicting them as against parties purchasing without notice of secret equities that may exist between the original parties."

[106] Martin *v.* Gordon, 24 Ga. 533.
[107] Gavin *v.* Buckles, 41 Ind. 528.
[108] Allen *v.* Kennedy, 91 Mo. 324, 2 S. W. 142.
[109] *Maine:* Blanchard *v.* Hoxie, 34 Me. 376 (on the covenant of seizin).
Missouri: Guinotte *v.* Chouteau, 34 Mo. 154.
[110] Bruns *v.* Schreiber, 43 Minn. 468, 45 N. W. 861.

held that when such a parcel of land to which title failed was included by mistake, both parties having known it to be owned and possessed by another, that fact may be shown, not of course to contradict the boundaries of the deed, but to show that no consideration was paid for that parcel; and that the plaintiff's damages will therefore be nominal.[111] So, too, parol evidence had been admitted to show that a covenant of warranty did not extend to an incumbrance which the vendee orally assumed to pay as part of the consideration.[112]

Where a third party having a bond for a deed sells to the plaintiff, receiving from him the consideration, and paying a smaller amount to his vendor, the defendant who conveys directly to the plaintiff, the case should be treated as if a deed with covenants had been given by the defendant to the third party and another by the latter to the plaintiff.[113] But where land is conveyed with warranty to a trustee who pays nothing and takes no beneficial interest, conveying immediately by warranty deed to one to whom his grantor has sold it, the consideration of his deed which fixes the limit of his liability on his covenants is the price paid by the third person to his grantor.[114]

§ 965.[a] Where the consideration is not pecuniary.

A logical following out of the New York rule as to recovery for breach of warranty in a deed would require that when the land to which title has failed has been conveyed in exchange for personalty or other land the recovery should be the value of the property given in exchange rather than the value of the land warranted. So upon an exchange of land for a watch the plaintiff was allowed to recover the value of the watch as fixed upon by the parties.[115] But where two pieces of land are exchanged there seems to be a conflict of authority as to the

---

[a] For § 965 of the eighth edition see § 964.

[111] *Illinois:* Lloyd v. Sandusky, 95 Ill. App. 593.
Massachusetts: Leland v. Stone, 10 Mass. 459.
New Hampshire: Barns v. Learned, 5 N. H. 264; Nutting v. Herbert, 35 N. H. 120, 37 N. H. 346.

[112] Pitman v. Connor, 27 Ind. 337.
Contra: Drury v. Holden, 121 Ill. 130.
[113] See § 961 *supra.*
[114] Barnett v. Hughey, 54 Ark. 195, 15 S. W. 464.
[115] Williamson v. Test, 24 Ia. 138.

proper measure of damages.[116]   Where the land was paid for in stock of a corporation at a fictitious valuation it was held that the true value of the stock was the measure of damages,[117] and where bonds were given which were worth less than par the plaintiff was allowed to recover only the value of the bonds.[118]   Where the consideration for the conveyance is a debt, as where land is conveyed by way of mortgage, the measure of damages upon eviction is the amount of the debt,[119] and where the consideration is the compromise of a claim the plaintiff should not be limited to nominal damages.[120]   In a peculiar case in Massachusetts where land of an insolvent debtor was sold at execution sale to a creditor who bid an amount far in excess of its value, the surplus above the execution debt being applied to another execution by the purchaser himself, the measure of damages for breach of the selling officer's covenant that he had obeyed all the directions of the law relative to such sales, was held to be the real value of the property and not the sum bid, as that was merely nominal, the purchaser taking the land for his debt.[121]

Whether or not there can be a recovery by an immediate grantee of a warranty deed, the only consideration for which was love and affection, is in dispute.   In a Kentucky case it

---

[116] Value of the land conveyed by the plaintiff was awarded in the following cases:

Kansas: Looney v. Reeves, 5 Kan. App. 279, 48 Pac. 606.

Michigan: Cook v. Curtis, 68 Mich. 611, 36 N. W. 692.

Minnesota: Burke v. Beveridge, 15 Minn. 205.

Missouri: Evans v. Fulton, 134 Mo. 653, 36 S. W. 230; Howard v. Hurst, 156 Mo. App. 205, 137 S. W. 1.

Texas: Mayer v. Wooten, 46 Tex. Civ. App. 327, 102 S. W. 423.

In Evans v. Fulton, 134 Mo. 653, 36 S. W. 230, 56 Am. St. Rep. 543, damages for breach of a covenant of seisin were held to be the value of the land conveyed by the plaintiff less the amount of an incumbrance thereon.

Where an agreed value was placed

on each parcel of land, the agreed value of the land conveyed by the plaintiff is the amount recoverable.   Howard v. Hurst, 156 Mo. App. 205, 137 S. W. 1.

The value of the land to which title failed was awarded in the following cases:

Minnesota: Donlan v. Evans, 40 Minn. 501, 42 N. W. 472.

Nebraska: Holmes v. Seaman, 72 Neb. 300, 100 N. W. 417.

Texas: White v. Street, 67 Tex. 177, 2 S. W. 529.

[117] McGuffey v. Humes, 85 Tenn. 26, 1 S. W. 506.

[118] Montgomery v. Northern Pac. R. R., 67 Fed. 445.

[119] Lloyd v. Quinby, 5 Oh. St. 262.

[120] Comstock v. Son, 154 Mass. 389, 28 N. E. 296.

[121] Wade v. Merwin, 11 Pick. 280.

was held that such a consideration is sufficient to support a warranty; though where a money consideration is recited in the deed the latter shall be taken as the grantor's valuation and fix the sum to be recovered as though it were the actual consideration.[122] But in Tennessee it was held that though the deed recited that it was given in consideration of services rendered, parol evidence was admissible to determine whether or not the services were actually given and if so whether with intent that they should be paid for. If rendered gratuitously it was said that there could be no recovery on the warranty.[123]

III.—COVENANTS OF SEIZIN AND RIGHT TO CONVEY

§ 966. Consideration with interest and expenses recoverable.

The covenants of seizin and of right to convey are, so far as the question of damages is involved, practically equivalent. In actions upon them it is not necessary, as in the case of the covenants of warranty and of quiet enjoyment, * to allege by way of breach an ouster or eviction. All that is requisite is to negative the words of the covenant.[124] If, at the time of the execution of the deed, the grantor does not own the land, the covenant is broken immediately.[125] If the covenant of seizin were treated as an ordinary contract, by analogy with the general principles of law, the value of the premises, at the time of the breach, would be the proper compensation, for, if the covenant were true, the vendee would have the premises. But though the covenant is broken at the time of the conveyance, here too, as in covenants of warranty, an arbitrary rule of compensation prevails. If the plaintiff is not ousted from possession by an adverse title his discovery, upon a doctrine

---

[122] Hanson v. Buckner, 4 Dana, 251, 29 Am. Dec. 401.

[123] Calcote v. Elkin, 3 Tenn. Cas. 319.

[124] *Missouri:* Adkins v. Tomlison, 121 Mo. 487, 26 S. W. 573; Coleman v. Clark, 80 Mo. App. 339.

New Hampshire: Parker v. Brown, 15 N. H. 176.

New York: Rickert v. Snyder, 9 Wend. 416.

Tennessee: Kincaid v. Brittain, 5 Sneed, 119.

[125] Bull v. Beiseker, 16 N. D. 290, 113 N. W. 870.

But in Watts v. Parker, 27 Ill. 224, it was held that the covenant was satisfied by seizin in fact through entry and claim of fee.

to be discussed later,[126] is limited to nominal damages.[127] And as the parties at the time of the deed agreed upon a fair value for the land, that value, which is the consideration actually paid, is arbitrarily adopted as the measure of damages when there has been an eviction.[128]

[126] See § 973, *infra.*

[127] *Indiana:* Reed v. Hamilton, 18 Ind. 476.

Iowa: Nosler v. Hunt, 18 Iowa, 212, 87 Am. Dec. 382.

Minnesota: Ogden v. Ball, 38 Minn. 237; Sable v. Brockmeier, 54 Minn. 248, 47 N. W. 794.

Missouri: Collier v. Gamble, 10 Mo. 467; Cockrell v. Proctor, 65 Mo. 44.

New Hampshire: Morrison v. Underwood, 20 N. H. 369.

North Dakota: Bowne v. Wolcott, 1 N. Dak. 415, 48 N. W. 336.

Wisconsin: Noonan v. Isley, 22 Wis. 27, 94 Am. Dec. 581; Mecklem v. Blake, 22 Wis. 495; Smith v. Hughes, 50 Wis. 620; McLennan v. Prentice, 85 Wis. 427, 55 N. W. 764.

Contra: Parkinson v. Woulds, 125 Mich. 325, 84 N. W. 292; Kincaid v. Brittain, 5 Sneed (Tenn.), 119 (*semble*).

[128] *Alabama:* Bibb v. Freeman, 59 Ala. 612.

Arkansas: Logan v. Moulder, 1 Ark. 313, 323, 33 Am. Dec. 338.

Colorado: Seyfried v. Knoblauch, 44 Colo. 86, 96 Pac. 993.

Connecticut: Castle v. Peirce, 2 Root, 294; Mitchell v. Hazen, 4 Conn. 495, 10 Am. Dec. 169; Lockwood v. Sturdevant, 6 Conn. 373; Sterling v. Peet, 14 Conn. 245; Hartford & S. O. Co. v. Miller, 41 Conn. 112.

Illinois: King v. Gilson, 32 Ill. 348; Weber v. Anderson, 73 Ill. 439.

Indiana: Phillips v. Reichert, 17 Ind. 120, 79 Am. Dec. 463; Wilson v. Peelle, 78 Ind. 384.

Iowa: Zent v. Picken, 54 Ia. 535.

Kentucky: Cox v. Strode, 2 Bibb, 273, 5 Am. Dec. 603; Triplett v. Gill, 7

J. J. Marsh. 38; Campbell v. Johnston, 4 Dana, 182.

Maine: Stubbs v. Page, 2 Me. 378; Montgomery v. Reed, 69 Me. 510.

Massachusetts: Marston v. Hobbs, 2 Mass. 433, 3 Am. Dec. 61; Caswell v. Wendell, 4 Mass. 108; Nichols v. Walter, 8 Mass. 243; Jenkins v. Hopkins, 8 Pick. 346.

Minnesota: Kimball v. Bryant, 25 Minn. 496.

Mississippi: Herndon v. Harrisson, 34 Miss. 486, 69 Am. Dec. 399.

Missouri: Tapley v. Lebeaume, 1 Mo. 550; Martin v. Long, 3 Mo. 391.

New Hampshire: Parker v. Brown, 15 N. H. 176; Kennison v. Taylor, 18 N. H. 220; Willson v. Willson, 25 N. H. 229, 57 Am. Dec. 320; Nutting v. Herbert, 37 N. H. 346.

New York: Pitcher v. Livingston, 4 Johns. 1, 4 Am. Dec. 229.

North Carolina: Wilson v. Forbes, 2 Dev. 30.

North Dakota: Bowne v. Wolcott, 1 N. Dak. 497, 48 N. W. 426.

Ohio: Backus v. McCoy, 3 Oh. 211, 17 Am. Dec. 585; Clark v. Parr, 14 Oh. 118.

Oregon: Stark v. Olney, 3 Ore. 88.

Pennsylvania: Weiting v. Nissley, 13 Pa. 650.

South Carolina: Witherspoon v. McCalla, 3 Desaus. 245, 4 Am. Dec. 613 (disapproving of earlier South Carolina decisions awarding the actual value of the land. *Semble* that if grantor were guilty of fraud, *i. e.*, had knowledge of defect of title and concealed it from purchaser, there might be recovery of the increased value of the land including improvements at time of eviction.)

Tennessee: Kincaid v. Brittain, 5

Where the price paid cannot be discovered, the value of the land at the time of the sale must be proved, and may then be recovered.[129] When lands are exchanged, and the defendant has no title to the land he conveys, the value of the land conveyed by the plaintiff at the time of its conveyance is the measure, that having been agreed by the parties to be the value of the land conveyed by the defendant;[130] and if the land conveyed by the plaintiff is subject to a mortgage, the amount of the incumbrance must be deducted.[131] In Hodges v. Thayer,[132] which was an action on the covenant of seizin and right to convey, the consideration was the conveyance to a third party of real property belonging to the grantee and personal property belonging to the grantee's wife, and it was held that the measure of damages was the value of this real property and personal property. The court said that the measure of damages was the consideration paid, and that Byrnes v. Rich,[133] rested on the ground that there the consideration could not be proved. The opinion continues: "It does not modify the rule, if the actual consideration was paid in other commodities than money or even in other real estate. It only requires that the value of such other property be ascertained. Nor does it matter that the consideration is, in fact, paid or delivered to another person than the grantor; or that it is itself, before delivery, the property of another than the grantee, provided it is agreed upon between the grantor and the grantee as the consideration upon which the deed is given."

Sneed, 119; Curtis v. Brannon, 98 Tenn. 153, 38 S. W. 1073.

Vermont: Blake v. Burnham, 29 Vt. 437; Flint v. Steadman, 36 Vt. 210.

Virginia: Building L. & W. Co. v. Fray, 96 Va. 565, 32 S. E. 58; Norfolk & W. Ry. v. Mundy, 110 Va. 422, 66 S. E. 61.

Wisconsin: Rich v. Johnson, 2 Pin. 88, 1 Chand. 19, 52 Am. Dec. 144; Blossom v. Knox, 3 Chand. 295; Daggett v. Reas, 79 Wis. 60, 48 N. W. 127.

In Bickford v. Page, 2 Mass. 455, 461, 23 Am. Dec. 66, the court said: "The rule for assessing the damages arising from this breach is very clear. No land passing by the defendant's deed to the plaintiff, he has lost no land by the breach of this covenant; he has lost only the consideration which he paid for it. This he is entitled to recover back, with interest to this time."

[129] Smith v. Strong, 14 Pick. 128.

[130] *Indiana:* Lacey v. Marnan, 37 Ind. 168.

Kansas: Looney v. Reeves, 5 Kan. App. 279, 48 Pac. 606.

[131] Evans v. Fulton, 134 Mo. 653, 36 S. W. 230, 56 Am. St. Rep. 543.

[132] 110 Mass. 286.

[133] 5 Gray, 518.

In Massachusetts this rule is said to be founded on the fact that the money paid for the conveyance was paid upon a consideration failed. "As no estate passed by the conveyance, the plaintiff could lose no estate by the breach of these covenants, and hath lost nothing, but the consideration which he paid for the intended purchase."[134] This explanation of the rule is no more satisfactory than the ordinary one—that the parties have agreed upon the consideration as a limit. It is true that no estate passed if the covenant of seizin is broken, and the plaintiff in one sense might be said to have lost no estate. So in the case of a failure to deliver a specific chattel, he might be said not to have lost the chattel. But his cause of action is the breach of the covenant, and the real measure of his loss is the value of the thing (the estate) which this was designed to assure him.

In Michigan it is said that where the grantee has been in possession, under the deed, the damages should be less than the consideration.[135] In Illinois the recovery rests on a peculiar principle. The purchaser of land can, on discovering that the vendor has not a good right to convey (as that he has an estate *pour autre vie*), and *on tendering a reconveyance*, recover the purchase-money and interest, together with the amount of taxes paid, with deductions for all rents and profits which have been or could have been received, that is, the parties are put in the same position as if no sale had been made.[136] Here again all the ordinary rules are violated. The object of compensation is not to put the parties in the same position as if no contract had been made, but to put them as nearly as possible in the situation they would have occupied had it been performed. An analogous decision is that of Park *v.* Cheek [137] where the defect in title consisted of an outstanding remainder. It was held that upon reconveying to the vendor the vendee might recover in an action on the covenant, the consideration actually paid.

In a Massachusetts case [138] the plaintiff had agreed to pur-

[134] Parsons, C. J., in Marston *v.* Hobbs, 2 Mass. 433, 439, 3 Am. Dec. 61.

[135] Hunt *v.* Middlesworth, 44 Mich. 448.

[136] Frazer *v.* Supervisors of Peoria, 74 Ill. 282.

[137] 4 Cold. (Tenn.) 20.

[138] Staples *v.* Dean, 114 Mass. 125.

chase from a third party certain land, for which he was to give a policy of insurance and his note for $450. The third party not having the title, agreed with the defendant to purchase from him for $475. The defendant made out a deed to the plaintiff, with covenants of seizin and right to convey, receiving the plaintiff's note for $450 and $25 from the third party. It was held that the plaintiff could, at his option, recover either the fair market value of the land at the time of the sale, or the consideration actually received by the grantee. The plaintiff accepted his note, and $25 (the fair market value being about $575), Wells, J., saying: "To the extent of what he (the defendant) actually received, the plaintiff doubtless might hold him liable upon his covenant of seizin and title. But otherwise, the measure of his liability would be the actual value of the land at the time of the conveyance."

The rule that damages for breach of a covenant of seizin are the consideration with interest was departed from in Gilbert v. Bulkley [139] where it was held that if the breach arises solely from the existence of a prior mortgage, damages are the amount due on such mortgage and if before action that has been paid, damages are only nominal.

Taxes paid by the grantee while in possession are not recoverable in an action on a covenant of seizin.[140]

IV.—COVENANTS AGAINST INCUMBRANCES

§ 967. General principles.

* We proceed now to consider the rule in regard to the covenant against incumbrances. And on this subject the Supreme Court of Massachusetts has used this general language, that the defendant is to make good his warranty; that is, he is to pay a sum of money which will put the plaintiff in as good a state as if he had kept his covenant.[141] The cases arising under the covenant against incumbrances resolve themselves into three general heads: First, where the incumbrance con-

[139] 5 Conn. 262.
[140] Vermont: Blake v. Burnham, 29 Vt. 437.
Wisconsin: Daggett v. Reas, 79 Wis. 60, 48 N. W. 127.
[141] Thayer v. Clemence, 22 Pick. 490.

sists of a mortgage or other debt which is already due and which the plaintiff has paid off. *Second*, where the plaintiff has not discharged the incumbrance, though it might have been done. *Third*, where the incumbrance consists of a mortgage or lease not expired, or servitude of any description, which the plaintiff cannot discharge. In Massachusetts, the general rule has been laid down as follows: "If the covenantee has fairly extinguished the incumbrances, he ought to recover the expenses necessarily incurred in doing it. If they remain and consist of mortgages, attachments, and such liens on the estate conveyed as do not interfere with the enjoyment of it by the covenantee, he can recover only nominal damages. But if they are of a permanent nature, such as the covenantee cannot remove, he should recover a just compensation, for the real injury resulting from their continuance." [142] And this seems the law as generally received. So in New York [143] it was held, that if the plaintiff had actually extinguished the incumbrance, he was entitled to recover the amount so paid; but if not extinguished, that then he could only recover nominal damages; and the doctrine has been uniformly adhered to in that State.[144] And, on the same principle, in regard to the mode in which the breach of this covenant must be set out, it is held in New York [145] not to be sufficient to aver that the premises are not unincumbered, but that the plaintiff must allege the extinguishment of the incumbrance.

So in Massachusetts, in an early case, Parsons, C. J., said: "A purchaser from one seized is not obliged to wait in painful suspense until he be evicted, before he can obtain an adequate remedy; but as soon as he can extinguish the incumbrance, he may call on his grantor for an indemnity." So held again in the same State, that the damages in a suit on the covenant against incumbrances are merely nominal, if the plaintiff has paid nothing for their discharge.[146] **

---

[142] Harlow *v.* Thomas, 15 Pick. 66, 69; Batchelder *v.* Sturgis, 3 Cush. 201.

[143] Delavergne *v.* Norris, 7 Johns. 358, 5 Am. Dec. 281.

[144] Hall *v.* Dean, 13 Johns. 105; Stan-ard *v.* Eldridge, 16 Johns. 254, 8 Am. Dec. 313.

[145] Deforest *v.* Leete, 16 Johns. 122.

[146] Prescott *v.* Truman, 4 Mass. 627, 3 Am. Dec. 246; Wyman *v.* Ballard, 12 Mass. 303, 7 Am. Dec. 74; Tufts *v.* Adams, 8 Pick. 547.

§ 968. Incumbrance removable.

The covenant against incumbrances like those of seizin and right to convey is broken when the deed is delivered, if at that time there are any incumbrances.[147] But in accordance with the decisions above stated it is generally held, that if the incumbrance is one which may be removed by the owner of the land there can be no recovery save of nominal damages until the incumbrance has been extinguished or the covenantee suffered eviction.[148] So where A conveyed to B with covenant against incumbrances, who later mortgaged to C without covenants and the premises were sold on foreclosure sale before it was discovered that there had been a prior mortgage at the time of A's conveyance, it was held that B could recover against A only nominal damages as it was not shown that the price obtained at the foreclosure sale was in any way lessened by the existence of the incumbrance.[149]

However, it is just as well settled that without hostile action by the incumbrancer, the covenantee may remove the incumbrance, and within certain limits to be discussed later,[150] may recover the amount reasonably expended in so doing.[151] And

---

[147] *Massachusetts:* Harrington v. Murphy, 109 Mass. 299.
Michigan: Smith v. Lloyd, 29 Mich. 382; Post v. Campau, 42 Mich. 90, 3 N. W. 272.
Ohio: Stambaugh v. Smith, 23 Oh. St. 584.

[148] *Indiana:* Hollman v. Creagmiles, 14 Ind. 177; Black v. Coan, 48 Ind. 385.
Iowa: Harwood v. Lee, 85 Ia. 622, 52 N. W. 521.
Maine: Copeland v. Copeland, 30 Me. 446.
Missouri: Moseley v. Hunter, 15 Mo. 322.
New Hampshire: Andrews v. Davison, 17 N. H. 413, 43 Am. Dec. 584; Willson v. Willson, 25 N. H. 229, 57 Am. Dec. 320.
New York: Taylor v. Eldridge, 16 Johns. 254, 8 Am. Dec. 313; Bldg. Co. v. Jencks, 19 App. Div. 314, 45 N. Y. Supp. 2; General Underwriting Co. v.

Stilwell, 137 App. Div. 890, 123 N. Y. Supp. 653.
Washington: International Development Co. v. Clemans, 59 Wash. 398, 109 Pac. 1034.
Wisconsin: Noonan v. Ilsley, 21 Wis. 138.

[149] McGuckin v. Milbank, 152 N. Y. 297, 46 N. E. 490.

[150] See §§ 979, 980.

[151] *Arkansas:* Farrell Lumber Co. v. Deshon, 65 Ark. 103, 44 S. W. 1036.
Illinois: Richard v. Bent, 59 Ill. 38, 14 Am. Rep. 1.
Indiana: Hollman v. Creagmiles, 14 Ind. 177.
Iowa: Duroe v. Stephens, 101 Ia. 358, 70 N. W. 610.
Kansas: Gilbert v. Rushmer, 49 Kan. 632, 31 Pac. 123.
Massachusetts: Farnum v. Peterson, 111 Mass. 148; Richmond v. Ames, 164 Mass. 467, 44 N. E. 671.

such will be the amount assessed though the covenantee failed to remove the incumbrance until after bringing action upon the covenant.[152] Nor is the rule altered by the fact that the precise amount of the incumbrance was unknown at the time of the conveyance, as in the case of improvement assessments.[153]

And so too, where a mortgage has been foreclosed, but the time for redemption has not run out, the cost of redeeming from it is the measure of damages.[154] And where the action was upon a covenant of warranty and quiet enjoyment, where the right of a prior mortgagee in possession existed at the time of the conveyance of the premises to the plaintiff, and the mortgagee could and did, by virtue of that right, resist the grantee's claim to the possession, it was held, by the Supreme Court of New York, at Special Term, that the covenant of warranty was broken, and that the measure of the grantee's damages was the amount due on the mortgage, with interest.[155]

In an action upon this covenant, the defendant may show that at the time of conveyance money was left in the plaintiff's hands to discharge the incumbrance,[156] or that the plaintiff assumed payment of the same.[157] There may be successive actions by the grantee as successive injuries occur as a consequence of the incumbrance.[158]

§ 969. Total eviction.

In the case of total eviction by reason of the incumbrance

Missouri: Eddington v. Nix, 49 Mo. 134.

Nebraska: Mills v. Saunders, 4 Neb. 190.

New Hampshire: Willson v. Willson, 25 N. H. 229, 57 Am. Dec. 320.

New York: Utica, etc., R. R. v. Gates, 8 App. Div. 181, 40 N. Y. Supp. 316.

[152] *Massachusetts:* Johnson v. Collins, 116 Mass. 392.

Missouri: Mosely v. Hunter, 15 Mo. 322.

Vermont: Potter v. Taylor, 6 Vt. 676.

Contra: Turkendall v. Veough, 2 Ill. App. 493.

[153] *Missouri:* Barnhart v. Hughes, 46 Mo. App. 318.

New Jersey: Cadmus v. Fagan, 47 N. J. L. 549, 4 Atl. 323.

Pennsylvania: Lafferty v. Milligan, 165 Pa. 534, 30 Atl. 1030, 44 Am. St. Rep. 674.

[154] Tufts v. Adams, 8 Pick. 547.

[155] Winslow v. McCall, 32 Barb. 241.

[156] Blood v. Wilkins, 43 Ia. 565; Wachendorf v. Lancaster, 66 Ia. 458.

[157] Corbett v. Wrenn, 25 Ore. 305, 35 Pac. 658.

[158] *Michigan:* Post v. Campau, 42 Mich. 90, 3 N. W. 272.

Ohio: Gardner v. Letson, 8 Ohio Dec. 256.

resulting in acquisition of a valid title in fee by the incumbrancer, the plaintiff recovers, in New York,[159] and other jurisdictions making the consideration the limits of recovery for evictions generally the consideration named in his deed, with interest, and also the costs of the proceeding in which he was evicted; [160] or, in Massachusetts,[161] and other jurisdictions allowing the value, the value of the land, with interest from the time of the eviction.[162]   And in an action upon a covenant against incumbrances, the plaintiff may show an eviction occurring after the bringing of the action for the purpose of increasing the damages.[163]

§ 970.[a] Permanent incumbrance on the land.

Where the land is subject to an incumbrance which cannot be removed by the payment of money, but the entire fee subject to it remains in the grantee, the measure of damages is the depreciation in value of the land by reason of the incumbrance. So in the case of an easement,[164] or of a restrictive

[a] For § 970 of the eighth edition see § 975.

[159] Waldo v. Long, 7 Johns. 173.

[160] See to the same effect the following cases:

Illinois: Willets v. Burgess, 34 Ill. 494.

Indiana: Burton v. Reeds, 20 Ind. 87.

Minnesota: Dana v. Goodfellow, 51 Minn. 375, 53 N. W. 656.

New Hampshire: Willson v. Willson, 25 N. H. 229, 235, 57 Am. Dec. 320 (*semble*).

New Jersey: Stewart v. Drake, 9 N. J. L. 139; DeLong v. Spring Lake, etc., Co., 65 N. J. L. 1, 47 Atl. 491.

New York: Dimmick v. Lockwood, 10 Wend. 142; Greene v. Tallman, 20 N. Y. 191.

Pennsylvania: Patterson v. Stewart, 6 W. & S. 527, 40 Am. Dec. 586.

[161] Barrett v. Porter, 14 Mass. 143. But where there has been no eviction, only the consideration and interest: Chapel v. Bull, 17 Mass. 213; Jenkins v. Hopkins, 8 Pick. 346.

[162] *Acc.*, Beecher v. Baldwin, 55 Conn. 419, 12 Atl. 401, 3 Am. St. Rep. 57.

[163] Mosely v. Hunter, 15 Mo. 322.

[164] *Alabama:* Copeland v. McAdory, 110 Ala. 553, 13 So. 545.

Connecticut: Hubbard v. Norton, 10 Conn. 422.

Georgia: Brantley v. Johnson, 102 Ga. 850, 29 S. E. 486.

Illinois: Morgan v. Smith, 11 Ill. 194.

Indiana: Sherwood v. Johnson, 28 Ind. App. 277, 62 N. E. 645.

Iowa: Myers v. Munson, 65 Ia. 423, 21 N. W. 759, 54 Am. Rep. 11.

Kansas: Smith v. Davis, 44 Kan. 362, 24 Pac. 428.

Kentucky: Vonderhite v. Walton, 7 Ky. L. Rep. 766; Helton v. Asher, 135 Ky. 751, 123 S. W. 285.

Maine: Harrington v. Bean, 89 Me. 470, 36 Atl. 986.

Massachusetts: Harlow v. Thomas, 15 Pick. 66; Prescott v. Trueman, 4 Mass. 627, 3 Am. Dec. 246; Bronson v. Coffin, 108 Mass. 175; Richmond v. Ames, 164 Mass. 467, 41 N. E. 671; Bailey *v.*

covenant.[165] And since the covenant against incumbrances
is broken, if at all, when made, it would seem that the damages
should be estimated upon the value of the land at the time
of the deed,[166] but in Massachusetts it has been held that the
difference between the values of the property with and without the incumbrance at the time of the trial is the proper
criterion.[167]

So in Williamson v. Hall,[168] where the incumbrance was a
right of way owned by a railroad, it was held that the measure of damages was the injury resulting from the existence of
the easement, excluding all consideration of the benefits or
damage common to other land in the vicinity not occupied
by the railroad. To the same effect is Kellogg v. Malin,[169]
where, however, it is intimated that, *prima facie*, it would be
that proportion of the value which the land taken bore to the
whole tract. In this case it appeared that the railroad company did not use its way to the extent of its whole width, but
permitted the plaintiff to cultivate the land not actually occupied by it. It was held that this was a matter between the

Agawam Bank, 190 Mass. 20, 76 N. E.
449, 3 L. R. A. (N. S.) 98.

Minnesota: Fritz v. Pusey, 31 Minn.
368; Mackey v. Harmon, 34 Minn. 168,
57 Am. Rep. 43.

Missouri: Whiteside v. Magruder, 75
Mo. App. 364.

New York: Huyck v. Andrews, 113
N. Y. 81, 10 Am. St. Rep. 432, 30 N. E.
581; Mohr v. Parmelee, 43 N. Y. Super.
Ct. 320; Schaeffer v. Miehling, 13 Misc.
520, 34 N. Y. Supp. 693; Rea v. Mink-
ler, 5 Lans. 196.

Wisconsin: Hall v. Gale, 20 Wis.
292.

England: Sutton v. Baillie, 65 L. T.
Rep. 528; Turner v. Moon, [1901] 2 Ch.
825.

[165] *Missouri:* Streeper v. Abeln, 59
Mo. App. 485.

New Hampshire: Foster v. Foster, 62
N. H. 532.

New York: Roberts v. Levy, 3 Abb.
Pr. (N. S.) 311; Charman v. Hibbler,
31 App. Div. 477, 52 N. Y. Supp. 212;

Doctor v. Darling, 68 Hun, 70, 22 N. Y.
Supp. 594.

Washington: Williams v. Hewitt, 57
Wash. 62, 106 Pac. 496.

Where land conveyed with a covenant against incumbrances was bound
by a covenant for furnishing power at
less than cost for a certain number of
years, the plaintiff could recover the
present value of the total losses in furnishing the power, provided that the
total amount should not exceed the
consideration paid. Schimmelpfenning
v. Brunk (Ia.), 132 N. W. 838.

[166] *Indiana:* Sherwood v. Johnson, 28
Ind. App. 277, 62 N. E. 645.

Iowa: Myers v. Munson, 65 Ia. 423,
21 N. W. 759, 54 Am. Rep. 11.

Kentucky: Vonderhite v. Walton, 7
Ky. L. Rep. 766.

Wisconsin: Hall v. Gale, 20 Wis. 292.

[167] Richmond v. Ames, 164 Mass.
467, 41 N. E. 671.

[168] 62 Mo. 405.

[169] 62 Mo. 429.

company and the plaintiffs, and as the privilege might be withdrawn at any time, it did not affect the rule of damages. In an early New York case,[170] where the incumbrance was a party wall the rule of a proportionate part of the consideration was applied, but in the later case of Hymes v. Esty [171] where the plaintiff was evicted from a portion of the land which had been dedicated by a former owner as a public highway, it was held that though the action was upon a covenant of quiet enjoyment, it was error to measure the damages as the fee value of the strip taken, the true rule being the depreciation of the value of the land by reason of the incumbrance. In a Missouri case [172] however, where the incumbrance was a railway right of way, the fee value of the strip taken was awarded, it being held error to allow the lesser amount of a proportionate part of the purchase price. In Mitchell v. Stanley,[173] the defendants had conveyed to the plaintiffs, with a covenant against incumbrances, a tract of land on which there was an incumbrance in the shape of an easement, a third party having a right to pass and repass to make repairs on a canal. It was held that the plaintiff was not confined to the damage actually suffered before trial; that he could recover the diminution in value of the property by reason of the incumbrance.[174] In regard to the claim of the plaintiffs, that the only actual damage was that suffered before trial, the court said: "It is true that this is the only direct damage they have received from the exercise of the right of way. But is this the actual damage? We think not. The incumbrance is permanent and perpetual, and the estate of the plaintiffs forever burdened with this servitude, which they have no power, as a matter of right, to remove, and which diminishes the value of their land to the amount of $750." [175] Where, in the conveyance of a strip of land to a railroad corporation, the grantor covenanted to maintain a fence along that part of the railroad which ran through his farm, this constituted an incumbrance on his land

[170] Giles v. Dugro, 1 Duer, 331.
[171] 133 N. Y. 342, 31 N. E. 105.
[172] Whiteside v. Magruder, 75 Mo. App. 364.
[173] 44 Conn. 312, 317.

[174] Acc., Clark v. Zeigler, 79 Ala. 346, 85 Ala. 154; Copeland v. McAdory, 100 Ala. 553, 13 So. 545.
[175] See Porter v. Bradley, 7 R. I. 538.

adjoining the railroad; and the measure of damages for a breach of a covenant against incumbrances in a subsequent conveyance of such land was the difference in the fair market value of the estate by reason of the incumbrance, taking into consideration the expense of the fencing, so far only as it exceeded the cost of maintaining any fence which would reasonably have been required to prevent the straying of persons or cattle upon or from those lands if no agreement had been made.[176]

In Alabama, where the breach consists of an incumbrance on a portion of the tract, the measure of damages is the diminished value of the entire tract, not exceeding the entire purchase-money paid, with interest.[177] But in North Carolina, the value of that part only of the whole tract upon which the incumbrance rests is the limit of recovery.[178] This would depend, it would seem, upon whether the unincumbered portion of the tract could be enjoyed as well with the incumbrance as without it.

In Wetherbee v. Bennett [179] it was held that where there was an incumbrance in the nature of right of way over granted premises, in an action on covenant against incumbrances, damages are not merely nominal by reason of the fact that the way was extinguished without expense to the grantee, but are the injury to the estate during the existence of the incumbrance.

Evidence is always admissible to show that the incumbrance which constitutes the breach of the covenant is a benefit rather than a burden to the estate, as that rent incident to an unexpired term passed to the grantee [180] or that the existence of a railway across the land enhances rather than diminishes its value.[181] So where an easement—for instance, a party wall—is found not to lessen the value of the land, the damage is

[176] Bronson v. Coffin, 108 Mass. 175, 11 Am. Rep. 335.

[177] Clark v. Zeigler, 79 Ala. 346.

[178] Price v. Deal, 90 N. C. 291; acc., Kostendader v. Pierce, 37 Ia. 645, 20 Am. Rep. 586; Koestendader v. Pierce, 41 Ia. 204.

[179] 2 Allen (Mass.), 428.

[180] Michigan: Edward v. Clark, 83 Mich. 246, 47 N. W. 112, 10 L. R. A. 659.

Minnesota: Fritz v. Pusey, 31 Minn. 368.

New Jersey: Demars v. Koehler, 62 N. J. L. 203, 41 Atl. 720, 72 Am. St. Rep. 642.

South Carolina: Grice v. Scarborough, 2 Speer, 649, 42 Am. Dec. 391.

See Pennsylvania: Cathcart v. Bowman, 5 Pa. 317.

[181] Wadhams v. Swan, 109 Ill. 46.

nominal.[182] It may also be shown as lessening damages that a restrictive covenant will probably not be enforced owing to changes in the character of the neighborhood.[183]

When the incumbrance is an outstanding lease or a right of dower the measure of damages is governed by principles which will be discussed in a later section.[184]

§ 971.[a] Improvements.

* In New York, the following question was raised.[185] Suit was brought on the covenant against incumbrances; the declaration averred that the plaintiff purchased the land in question for two hundred and fifty dollars, and put on improvements to the value of two thousand dollars; that at the time of the deed, the premises were not free from incumbrances, but that they were subject to a judgment for upward of three thousand dollars on an undivided moiety of the lot, under which incumbrance one-half was sold. Plea, that the plaintiff was only entitled to recover one hundred and twenty-five dollars, one-half of the consideration money paid, and tender of that sum; demurrer and joinder.

This plea proceeded on the ground that under the covenant against incumbrances, the plaintiff can only recover the consideration paid, and nothing for his improvements. So the court held and gave judgment for the defendant. It was even intimated that if he had discharged the incumbrance, he could not recover the amount paid. "Suppose the plaintiff," said Savage, C. J., "instead of building a house, had paid the $3,000, and brought his suit to be reimbursed, he would bring himself within the language of some of the judges who say that a purchaser is entitled to recover what he has paid; and yet I apprehend he would not be permitted to recover that amount." The court laid stress on the admitted fact, that under the covenant of quiet enjoyment, only the consideration money and interest could be recovered, and asked why more should be obtained in the action before them.

[a] For § 971 of the eighth edition see § 976.

[182] Mackey v. Harmon, 34 Minn. 168, 24 N. W. 702, 57 Am. Rep. 43.

[183] Doctor v. Darling, 68 Hun, 70, 22 N. Y. Supp. 594.

[184] See § 976, infra.

[185] Dimmick v. Lockwood, 10 Wend. 142, 154.

This case appears open to much observation: it may not be contrary to the spirit of the rule in regard to the covenant for quiet enjoyment; but if generally applied, it appears greatly to diminish the value of the covenant against incumbrances. By surrendering the property to the previous incumbrancer, a valid claim may always be created to the extent of the consideration money, and to this it seems the recovery under this covenant is in every instance to be limited. A case may, however, easily be imagined, where the incumbrance is well known, where the consideration money is a fair representative of the value without the incumbrance, where the grantor agrees to remove it, and the covenant against incumbrances is inserted for the express purpose of making it certain that he will do so. In such a case the application of this principle would be extremely inequitable. For it must not be forgotten that the severity of the arbitrary rule which declares the consideration named in the deed to be the actual price paid, is but little mitigated by the permission given to the parties to contradict it by parol proof. Such evidence, after the lapse of a few years, will generally be difficult of production, in many cases impossible, and the mere burden of proof is always a serious responsibility. In Massachusetts, also, it has been said that the general rule that the covenantor against incumbrances is liable to refund the sum paid by the grantee to extinguish the incumbrance, must be taken subject to the qualification that the amount thus paid does not exceed that which the grantor would be bound to pay in case of eviction. In other words, he cannot be made liable for more than the value of the estate. But it will be observed, that where the value is fixed by the consideration money paid, as in New York, the rule becomes a very different one in its effect from what it is where the actual value at the time of eviction is taken, as in Massachusetts. In this latter case there appears no objection to it.[186] **

§ 972.[a] Covenant to remove incumbrances.

* Instead of the general covenant that the premises conveyed are free from incumbrances, we sometimes find a special

---

[a] For § 972 of the eighth edition see § 970.

[186] Norton v. Babcock, 2 Met. (Mass.) 510, 516.

agreement to remove certain existing incumbrances; and in such a case in England it was early held that the amount of the incumbrance becomes the measure of damages. In an action by the trustees of the defendant's wife on a covenant to pay off certain incumbrances to the amount of £19,000, no special damage was laid in the declaration, nor proved, and judgment having gone by default, the sheriff's jury gave only nominal damages; but, on motion, the inquisition was set aside; Lord Tenterden, C. J., saying, "If the plaintiffs are only to recover a shilling damages, the covenant becomes of no value;" and Parke, J., said, "At law the trustees were entitled to have this estate unincumbered. How could that be enforced unless they could recover the whole amount of the incumbrances, in an action on the covenant?" [187] **

This rule has been generally adopted in this country, the reason of it being that the covenant to remove the incumbrance is assumed to be covered by the consideration paid for the land; or in other words, the value of the land in the plaintiff's hands is diminished by the amount of the incumbrance. Accordingly, where the vendor agrees to pay all claims against the lot sold, it is not necessary for the purchaser to prove that a judgment which is a lien upon the premises has been enforced, or that he has been evicted. The non-payment of the judgment is all that is necessary in order to show a breach; and the rule of damages upon a breach is the amount of the judgment with interest.[188] In an action for damages for breach of a covenant to pay all such taxes and assessments as should be imposed during the term of the lease, it was held by the Superior Court of New York that nominal damages only could be recovered for the non-payment of an assessment, where the plaintiff had not actually paid it. But this judgment was reversed by the Commission of Appeals, which held that the covenant was not one for indemnity merely, and that the plaintiffs were entitled to judgment for the amount due on the assessment.[189] In Indiana, on the breach of a contract to remove incumbrances the measure of the recovery is now held, in reversal of previous

[187] Lethbridge v. Mytton, 2 B. & A. 772.

[188] Cady v. Allen, 22 Barb. 388.

[189] Trinity Church v. Higgins, 4 Rob. 372, 48 N. Y. 532.

decisions in that State,[190] to be the amount due on the incumbrance, notwithstanding the grantee had neither paid it nor been evicted.[191] Such is the general rule.[192] In a case in Ohio, the plaintiff, after exchanging with the principal defendant certain lands in Ohio for lands in Indiana, discovered that the Indiana land was subject to an attachment levied by the creditors of the defendant, who thereupon executed and delivered to the plaintiff a written undertaking to cancel all incumbrances on the Indiana land within six months. The Indiana land having been sold in the attachment suit, the plaintiff was held entitled to recover its value when lost, with interest from that time.[193] In Illinois and in Missouri in such a case the measure of damages was said to be the consideration.[194] But in a Massachusetts case [195] where the defendant conveyed to plaintiff by way of mortgage covenanting to discharge a prior incumbrance, the measure of damages upon eviction of the plaintiff by a prior mortgagee was held to be such sum as would enable the plaintiff to pay off the incumbrance and defeat the adverse title. Where a covenant was given by a grantee to pay, or allow in account, a certain sum, provided certain incumbrances were removed by the grantor by a given day, and they were removed, but not till a year afterwards, it was held that such deduction must be made from the sum to be allowed to the grantor as any change that

[190] Schooley v. Stoops, 4 Ind. 130; Tate v. Booe, 9 Ind. 13.

[191] Johnson v. Britton, 23 Ind. 105. The decision was based in part on the provisions of the Code of Procedure, under which courts of law have equity jurisdiction, the distinction between actions at law and suits in equity is abolished, and all having an interest in a controversy may be made parties to the suit.

[192] *Indiana:* Scobey v. Finton, 39 Ind. 275.

Missouri: Bohlcke v. Buchanan, 94 Mo. App. 320, 68 S. W. 92.

Canada: McGillivray v. Mimico Real Estate Security Co., 28 Ont. 265.

But in *Tennessee*, where the grantor agreed to remove the incumbrance of an undischarged mortgage and failed to do so, but the mortgage was thereafter barred by the statute of limitations, it was held that the plaintiff could recover only nominal damages, and not the amount of depreciation in value of the premises while the mortgage was in force. Egan v. Yeaman (Tenn.), 46 S. W. 1012.

[193] Manhan v. Smith, 19 Oh. St. 384.

[194] *Illinois:* Howell v. Moores, 127 Ill. 67, 19 N. E. 863.

Missouri: Chinn v. Wagoner, 26 Mo. App. 678.

[195] Wetmore v. Greene, 11 Pick. (Mass.) 462.

In *Minnesota* liquidated damages were allowed in such a case. Fasler v. Beard, 39 Minn. 32, 38 N. W. 755.

had in the interim taken place in the value of the property might render just and proper.[196]

When the covenant is by the grantee rather than by the grantor the same principles apply. So where premises are conveyed subject to a mortgage, which the grantee assumes and agrees to pay, the grantor upon non-payment of the mortgage when due may recover the amount of it, though he has been obliged to pay nothing.[197] And if the premises are sold on foreclosure, leaving a balance due, the grantor may recover the amount of the balance though he has been called upon to pay nothing.[198] But if the whole debt has been satisfied out of the land, the grantor can recover only nominal damages.[199]

This follows from the rule established in the case of contracts to pay the debt of another, discussed in a former chapter,[200] namely, that the amount of the debt may be recovered by the original debtor, whether or not he has been called upon to pay it. The result might be that the land would still be subject to the mortgage, though the amount of it had been recovered by the grantor. But this result may always be avoided by the grantee discharging the incumbrance on suit being brought.

When by reason of the grantee's failure to extinguish the incumbrance assumed, the land of the grantor is lost by foreclosure the value of the land is the measure of recovery.[201] In Kansas, however, it was said that a subsequent grantee of the tract not originally conveyed to the covenantor, if allowed to sue at all, could recover only the consideration recited in

[196] Roberts v. Marston, 20 Me. 275, 37 Am. Dec. 52.

[197] *Indiana:* Lowe v. Turpie, 147 Ind. 652, 44 N. E. 25, 47 N. E. 150.

Iowa: Stout v. Folger, 34 Ia. 71, 11 Am. Rep. 138. (But see Linder v. Lake, 6 Ia. 164; Funk v. Creswell, 5 Ia. 62, restricting recovery to nominal damages).

Massachusetts: Locke v. Homer, 131 Mass. 93, 41 Am. Rep. 199; Furnas v. Durgin, 119 Mass. 500, 20 Am. Rep. 341; Reed v. Paul, 131 Mass. 129; Williams v. Fowle, 132 Mass. 385, 42 Am. Rep. 440.

New York: Seligman v. Dudley, 14 Hun, 186.

[198] McAbee v. Cribbs, 194 Pa. 94, 44 Atl. 1066.

[199] Muhlig v. Fiske, 131 Mass. 110.

[200] § 789.

[201] *Iowa:* Blood v. Wilkins, 43 Ia. 565.

New York: Wilcox v. Campbell, 106 N. Y. 325, 12 N. E. 823.

Oregon: Haas v. Dudley, 30 Ore. 355, 48 Pac. 168.

the deed by the original covenantee to himself.[202] That the grantor or his assignor after knowledge of the grantee's failure to pay the incumbrance does not himself remove it in time to prevent the loss of the land should not affect the amount of recovery [203] but in Indiana it has been held that the rule of avoidable consequences applies to such a case.[204] In Pennsylvania it has been held,[205] that if a vendee covenant to pay an incumbrance out of the purchase-money, and fail to do so, by reason of which the land is sold for the payment of the incumbrance before conveyance and sells for a price exceeding the incumbrance, the vendee is liable to the vendor for damages, the measure of which is the difference between the amount for which the land is sold, and the price which he agreed to pay for it. Since the vendor had received the balance upon the sale to satisfy the incumbrance, this was a recovery of the difference between what the defendant was to pay and what the plaintiff actually received; in other words, the value of the bargain. But on failure to take up a lien on a tract of land the measure of damages has been held in Texas to be limited to the amount of the lien.[206]

V.—GENERAL PRINCIPLES

§ 973.[a] Nominal damages.

Having now examined the peculiar rules adopted by the courts in the case of the common covenants for title, we proceed to consider the general principles applicable in all cases of breach of such covenants. It is almost universally laid down that if there has been no eviction, and the plaintiff's possession has not been interfered with, the plaintiff can recover only nominal damages, whatever may be the nature of the covenant relied upon,[207] the principle being that until

---

[a] For § 973 of the eighth edition see § 971.

[202] Pearson v. Ford, 1 Kan. App. 580, 42 Pac. 257.

[203] Wilcox v. Campbell, 106 N. Y. 325, 12 N. E. 823.

[204] Lowe v. Turpie (Ind.), 44 N. E. 25.

[205] Young v. Stone, 4 Watts & Serg. 45.

[206] Thomas v. Hammond, 47 Tex. 42.

[207] *United States:* Montgomery v. Northern Pac. R. R., 67 Fed. 445.

Connecticut: Davis v. Lyman, 6 Conn. 249, 255 (*semble*); Briggs v. Morse, 42 Conn. 258.

interference with possession the existence of the incumbrance is a mere hypothetical injury. Whether or not this is the true rule upon a covenant of seizin is open to question. This covenant relates to title rather than to possession and if broken at all is broken when made. If a recovery before eviction is limited to nominal damages, and if such a recovery is a bar to any subsequent action upon the covenant,[208] a covenant of seizin is deprived of a large measure

Illinois: Brady v. Spurck, 27 Ill. 478; Willets v. Burgess, 34 Ill. 494.

Indiana: Whisler v. Hicks, 5 Blackf. 100, 33 Am. Dec. 454 (*semble*); Smith v. Ackerman, 5 Blackf. 541; Pomeroy v. Burnett, 8 Blackf. 142; Small v. Reeves, 14 Ind. 163; Hacker v. Blake, 17 Ind. 97; Reed v. Hamilton, 18 Ind. 476; Bundy v. Ridenour, 63 Ind. 406; Jones v. Noe, 71 Ind. 368, 36 Am. Rep. 198; Marsh v. Thompson, 102 Ind. 272.

Iowa: Nosler v. Hunt, 18 Ia. 212, 87 Am. Dec. 382; Boon v. McHenry, 55 Ia. 202; Wilson v. Irish, 62 Ia. 260; Hencke v. Johnson, 62 Ia. 555; Norman v. Winch, 65 Ia. 263.

Kansas: Scoffins v. Grandstaff, 12 Kan. 467; O'Meara v. McDaniel, 49 Kan. 685, 31 Pac. 303; Hammerslough v. Hackett, 48 Kan. 700, 29 Pac. 1079.

Maine: Bean v. Mayo, 5 Me. 94; Randell v. Mallett, 14 Me. 51; Stowell v. Bennett, 34 Me. 422; Reed v. Pierce, 36 Me. 455, 58 Am. Dec. 761.

Massachusetts: Prescott v. Trueman, 4 Mass. 627; Wyman v. Ballard, 12 Mass. 304; Leffingwell v. Elliott, 8 Pick. 455, 19 Am. Dec. 343; Tufts v. Adams, 8 Pick. 547; Harrington v. Murphy, 109 Mass. 299.

Michigan: Wilcox v. Musche, 39 Mich. 101; Norton v. Colgrove, 41 Mich. 544.

Minnesota: Ogden v. Ball, 38 Minn. 237; Sable v. Brockmeier, 45 Minn. 248, 47 N. W. 794.

Missouri: Collier v. Gamble, 10 Mo. 467; Mosely v. Hunter, 15 Mo. 322; Dickson v. Desire, 23 Mo. 151, 66 Am. Dec. 661; Kellogg v. Malin, 62 Mo.

429 (*semble*); Cockrell v. Proctor, 65 Mo. 41; Conklin v. Hannibal & S. J. R. R., 65 Mo. 533; Evans v. Fulton, 134 Mo. 653, 662, 36 S. W. 230, 56 Am. St. Rep. 543.

New Hampshire: Willson v. Willson, 25 N. H. 229, 57 Am. Dec. 320.

New Jersey: Stewart v. Drake, 9 N. J. L. 139 (*semble*).

New York: Delavergne v. Norris, 7 Johns. 358, 5 Am. Dec. 281; Hall v. Dean, 13 Johns. 105; Stanard v. Eldridge, 16 Johns. 254, 8 Am. Dec. 313; Greene v. Tallman (indexed Grant v. Tallman), 20 N. Y. 191, 75 Am. Dec. 384; Giles v. Dugro, 1 Duer, 331; Seventy-Third St. Bldg. Co. v. Jencks, 46 N. Y. Supp. 2.

North Carolina: Wilson v. Forbes, 2 Dev. 30; Lane v. Richardson, 104 N. C. 642; Britton v. Ruffin, 120 N. C. 87, 26 S. E. 642.

North Dakota: Bowne v. Wolcott, 1 N. Dak. 415, 48 N. W. 336.

Ohio: Hill v. Butler, 6 Oh. St. 207; Stambaugh v. Smith, 23 Oh. St. 584.

Texas: Denson v. Love, 58 Tex. 468. (But see Groesbeck v. Harris, 82 Tex. 411, 19 S. W. 850.)

Vermont: Richardson v. Dorr, 5 Vt. 9, 20.

Virginia: Rosenberger v. Keller, 33 Gratt. 489.

Wisconsin: Pillsbury v. Mitchell, 5 Wis. 17; Noonan v. Ilsley, 22 Wis. 27, 94 Am. Dec. 581; Mechlem v. Blak, 22 Wis. 495, 99 Am. Dec. 68; Eaton v. Lyman, 30 Wis. 41; Smith v. Hughes, 50 Wis. 620, 7 N. W. 653.

[208] *Iowa:* Nosler v. Hunt, 18 Ia. 217.

of its value and made practically a covenant for quiet enjoyment.[209] A recovery by the covenantee of the purchase-money would amount to an estoppel of record and prevent any claim by him against any title subsequently acquired by the covenantor. The modern doctrine seems to be but one of the errors resulting from the abuse of the doctrine of estoppel by deed which is discussed in another section.[210]

It is equally well settled that when a purchaser is in undisturbed possession of land conveyed with covenants either of seizin, warranty or against incumbrances, lack of title in the vendor or the presence of a removable incumbrance which the vendee has not yet extinguished is no defense either in law or in equity to an action on a purchase-money note or a foreclosure of a purchase-money mortgage.[211] The rule is other-

Maine: Donnell v. Thompson, 1 Fairf. 174.

[209] See Rawle on Covenants for Title (5th ed.), §§ 176–179.

[210] See § 977.

[211] *United States:* Noonan v. Lee, 2 Black, 499, 17 L. ed. 278; Peters v. Bowman, 98 U. S. 56, 25 L. ed. 91.

Alabama: White v. Beard, 5 Port. 94, 30 Am. Dec. 552; Knight v. Turner, 11 Ala. 636; Patton v. England, 15 Ala. 69; McLemore v. Mabson, 20 Ala. 139; Helvenstein v. Higgason, 35 Ala. 259.

Arkansas: McDaniel v. Grace, 15 Ark. 489; Hoppes v. Cheek, 21 Ark. 588; Busby v. Treadwell, 24 Ark. 456.

California: Norton v. Jackson, 5 Cal. 262, 63 Am. Dec. 128.

Georgia: McCauley v. Moses, 43 Ga. 577; Smith v. Hudson, 45 Ga. 208; Booth v. Saffold, 46 Ga. 278.

Illinois: Cheney v. City Natl. Bank, 77 Ill. 562.

Indiana: Small v. Reeves, 14 Ind. 163; Gibson v. Richart, 83 Ind. 313.

Kentucky: English v. Thomason, 82 Ky. 280; Hoertz v. Marrett, 5 Ky. L. Rep. 698; Trumbo v. Lockridge, 4 Bush, 417; Vance v. House, 5 B. Mon. 537.

Maine: Morrison v. Jewell, 34 Me. 146; Bean v. Harrington, 88 Me. 460, 34 Atl. 268.

Maryland: Timms v. Shannon, 19 Md. 296, 81 Am. Dec. 632.

Massachusetts: Bowley v. Holway, 124 Mass. 395.

Michigan: Griggs v. Detroit & M. R. R., 10 Mich. 117; Detroit & M. R. R. v. Griggs, 12 Mich. 45.

Mississippi: Hoy v. Taliaferro, 8 Sm. & M. 727; Glenn v. Thistle, 23 Miss. 42.

Missouri: Cartwright v. Culver, 74 Mo. 179.

New Jersey: Van Waggoner v. McEwen, 2 N. J. Eq. 412; Glenn v. Whipple, 12 N. J. Eq. 50; Hile v. Davison, 20 N. J. Eq. 228; Hulfish v. O'Brien, 20 N. J. Eq. 230.

New York: York v. Allen, 30 N. Y. 104; Ryerson v. Willis, 81 N. Y. 277; Parkinson v. Jacobson, 13 Hun, 317; Leggett v. McCarty, 3 Edw. Ch. 124; Platt v. Gilchrist, 3 Sandf. 118; Abbott v. Allen, 2 Johns. Ch. 519, 7 Am. Dec. 554; Lattin v. Vail, 17 Wend. 188; Tallmadge v. Wallis, 25 Wend. 107.

North Carolina: Wilkins v. Hogue, 2 Jones Eq. 479.

South Carolina: Johnson v. Purvis, 1 Hill, 322; Carter v. Carter, 1 Bailey, 217; Pordeaux v. Cave, 1 Bailey, 250; Westbrook v. McMillan, 1 Bailey, 259; Van Lew v. Parr, 2 Rich. Eq. 347,

wise where the covenantor is insolvent [212] or guilty of fraud in making the conveyance.[213] In Pennsylvania the opposite rule prevails and such set-off is allowed unless it is clear that the purchaser assumed the risk of the defective title.[214] In Texas a set-off or defence to an action for the price is allowed only when at the time of the conveyance the purchaser was ignorant of the defect constituting the breach of the covenant.[215] In New Jersey however the amount of an outstanding mortgage can always be set off when there is a covenant against incumbrances,[216] but in other respects the New Jersey law corresponds with the rule generally adopted.

As has been pointed out elsewhere no intermediate covenantee can sue his covenantor till he himself has been compelled to pay damages upon his own warranty.[217] But a release of land without warranty to a third person has been held, in Massachusetts, not to prevent a grantee from recovering full damages against his grantor for a breach of the covenant of seizin.[218]

It has been held, however, where the incumbrance cannot

Tennessee: Buchanan v. Alwell, 8 Humph. 516.

Virginia: Beale v. Seiveley, 8 Leigh, 658.

Wisconsin: Ludlow v. Gilman, 18 Wis. 552; Falkner v. Woodard, 104 Wis. 608, 80 N. W. 940.

[212] *Alabama:* Andrews v. McCoy, 8 Ala. 920, 42 Am. Dec. 669.

Kentucky: Willy v. Fitzpatrick, 3 J. J. Marsh. 582; Hatcher v. Andrews, 5 Bush, 561.

Massachusetts: Knapp v. Lee, 3 Pick. 459.

Mississippi: Wofford v. Ashcraft, 47 Miss. 641.

New York: Woodruff v. Bunce, 9 Paige, 443, 38 Am. Dec. 559.

Tennessee: Young v. Butler, 1 Head, 640.

[213] Brady v. McGhee, 1 Tenn. Cas. 154; Ingram v. Morgan, 4 Humph. 66, 40 Am. Dec. 626.

[214] Murphy v. Richardson, 28 Pa. 288, 70 Am. Dec. 124; Wilson v. Coch-

ran, 46 Pa. 229; Knepper v. Kurtz, 58 Pa. 480; Rowland v. Miller, 3 W. & S. 390.

[215] Tarpley v. Poage, 2 Tex. 139; Cooper v. Singleton, 19 Tex. 260, 70 Am. Dec. 333; Herron v. De Bard, 24 Tex. 181; Demarett v. Bennett, 29 Tex. 262; Bryan v. Johnson, 39 Tex. 31; Carson v. Kelley, 57 Tex. 379; May v. Ivie, 68 Tex. 379, 4 S. W. 641; Ogburn v. Whitlow, 80 Tex. 239, 15 S. W. 807; Twohig v. Brown, 85 Tex. 51, 19 S. W. 768; Crouch v. Johnson, 7 Tex. Civ. App. 435, 27 S. W. 9.

[216] Van Riper v. Williams, 2 N. J. Eq. 407; White v. Stretch, 22 N. J. Eq. 79; Union Bank v. Pinner, 25 N. J. Eq. 495.

[217] *Kansas:* Hammerslough v. Hacket, 48 Kan. 700, 29 Pac. 1079. See § 956, *supra.*

New York: Burt v. Dewey, 40 N. Y. 283, 100 Am. Dec. 482; Sweet v. Bradley, 24 Barb. 549.

[218] Cornell v. Jackson, 3 Cush. 506.

be removed by paying off the value of it, that the purchaser may be allowed substantial damages although not evicted.[219] * A grantee can recover nothing more than the nominal damages for a breach of covenant by an incumbrance no longer existing, and not removed at his expense.[220] Such nominal damages are recoverable although the incumbrances are removed by the grantor before the suit is brought.[221] In Newcomb v. Wallace [222] the amount of a certain tax had been deducted from the consideration money at the request of the grantee, and one F., for whose benefit the plaintiff brought the action, had agreed to pay the taxes. The court held that the plaintiff could only recover nominal damages.

Nominal damages only can be recovered if there is no proof of the actual amount of damages; as where, upon breach of covenant of seizin, the amount of the consideration is not shown.[223]

When a covenant is technically broken nominal damages at least may be recovered, though no actual damages are shown.[224]

§ 974.ᵃ Mortgages.

An exception has been made in some States in the case of a mortgage on the ground that the mortgage is a lien which may be satisfied out of the land. It has been held that where land is incumbered by an outstanding mortgage the measure of damages is the amount of the mortgage,[225] if that is less than

---

ᵃ For § 974 of the eighth edition see § 980a.

[219] See § 970, supra.

[220] Herrick v. Moore, 19 Me. 313. (But see Wetherbee v. Bennett, 2 Allen (Mass.), 428, where the covenantee in such a case was allowed to recover for the injury to the estate during the existence of the incumbrance).

[221] Smith v. Jefts, 44 N. H. 482.

[222] 112 Mass. 25.

[223] Coleman v. Lucksinger, 224 Mo. 1, 123 S. W. 441, 26 L. R. A. (N. S.) 934; Blevins v. Smith, 104 Mo. 583, 16 S. W. 213.

[224] Alabama: Tuskegee L. & S. Co. v. Birmingham Realty Co., 161 Ala. 542, 49 So. 378.

Arkansas: Seldon v. Dudley E. Jones Co., 89 Ark. 234, 116 S. W. 217.

Missouri: Jones v. Haseltine, 124 Mo. App. 674, 102 S. W. 40.

New Jersey: Hasselbusch v. Mohmking, 76 N. J. L. 691, 73 Atl. 961.

[225] Massachusetts: Tufts v. Adams, 8 Pick. 547; White v. Whitney, 3 Met. 81, 37 Am. Dec. 117.

Pennsylvania: Funk v. Voneida, 11 S. & R. 109.

Canada: Empire G. M. Co. v. Jones, 19 Up. Can. C. P. 245. This is true, though the mortgage includes other lands which are worth more than the amount of the mortgage. Connell v. Boulton, 25 Up. Can. Q. B. 444.

the value of the land [226] or the consideration,[227] according to the rule adopted on covenants of warranty. But in other States no distinction is made between a mortgage and any other incumbrance; and so long as the mortgage is not foreclosed nor the plaintiff's possession disturbed he is allowed only nominal damages.[228]

§ 975.[a] Eviction from part of land.

* Where the eviction complained of is partial, the recovery is proportioned to the value of the part of the premises to which the title has failed. Where action was brought [229] on the covenant of seizin, the title to part of the premises having failed, it was insisted, on the authority of an English case [230] that this partial failure of title gave the plaintiff a right to recover the entire purchase-money. But the court held otherwise: that it was competent for the defendant to show that the part in regard to which the title had failed was of inferior quality to the other portion conveyed, and that the true measure of damage was the value of the part to which the title had failed, taken in proportion to the price of the whole; the whole computation being on the basis of the consideration money. This rule was deduced by Kent, C. J., from the Year-Books,[231] and enforced by the analogies of the civil law. "*Quod enim,*" says Ulpian, "*si quod in agro pretiosissimum, hoc evictum est; aut quod fuit in agro vilissimum? æstimabitur loci qualitas, et sic ecrit regressus.*" [232] The same principle is also recognized by Pothier.[233] In a case in Massachusetts, it was contended

[a] For § 975 of the eighth edition see § 972.

[226] Furnas v. Durgin, 119 Mass. 500, 20 Am. Rep. 341.

[227] Gibson v. Boulton, 3 Up. Can. C. P. 407.

[228] *Indiana:* Bundy v. Ridenour, 63 Ind. 406.

Kansas: Looney v. Reeves, 5 Kan. App. 279, 48 Pac. 606.

Maine: Randell v. Mallett, 14 Me. 51; Copeland v. Copeland, 30 Me. 446.

New Hampshire: Andrews v. Davison, 17 N. H. 413, 43 Am. Dec. 606; Willson v. Willson, 25 N. H. 229, 57 Am. Dec. 320.

New York: Taylor v. Eldridge, 16 Johns. 254, 8 Am. Dec. 313; Seventy-third St. Bldg. Co. v. Jencks, 19 App. Div. 314, 45 N. Y. Supp. 2.

Wisconsin: Noonan v. Ilsley, 21 Wis. 138.

[229] Morris v. Phelps, 5 Johns. 49, 4 Am. Dec. 323, recognized in Guthrie v. Pugsley, 12 Johns. 126.

[230] Farrar v. Nightingal, 2 Esp. 639.

[231] Beauchamp v. Damory, 29 E. III, 3; 13 E. IV, 3. See, also, Gray v. Briscoe, Noy, 142.

[232] Dig. 21, 2 l. 1, l. 13, and l. 64, § 3.

[233] Contrat de Vente, No. 99, 139, 142.

ACTIONS UPON REAL COVENANTS § 975

that the damages should be determined by the proportion in quantity which the part to which the title had failed bore to the residue; but the court said: "This is not a just rule, for the value may be unequal. The true and just rule is, that the proportional *value*, and not the *quantity*, of the several parts of the land should be the measure of damages." [234] **

As the rule is usually stated, the measure of damages is such part of the original price as bears the same ratio to the whole consideration that the value of the land to which the title has failed bears to the value of the whole tract conveyed; or when action is upon a covenant of warranty in States adopting the New England rule, the actual value of the part from which the grantee has been evicted. [235] If, however, the land

[234] Cornell *v.* Jackson, 3 Cush. 506; see, also, in Ohio, Michael *v.* Mills, 17 Oh. 601.

[235] *United States:* Griffin *v.* Reynolds, 17 How. 609, 15 L. ed. 229; Rust L. & L. Co. *v.* Wheeler, 189 Fed. 321.

Arkansas: Walker *v.* Johnson, 13 Ark. 522; Alexander *v.* Bridgford, 59 Ark. 195, 27 S. W. 69.

Colorado: Seyfried *v.* Knoblauch, 44 Colo. 86, 96 Pac. 993.

Connecticut: Hubbard *v.* Norton, 10 Conn. 422.

Georgia: Kerley *v.* Richardson, 17 Ga. 602.

Illinois: Major *v.* Dunnavant, 25 Ill. 262; Tone *v.* Wilson, 81 Ill. 529.

Indiana: Wiley *v.* Howard, 15 Ind. 169; Phillips *v.* Reichert, 17 Ind. 120, 79 Am. Dec. 463; Hoot *v.* Spade, 20 Ind. 326; Wright *v.* Nipple, 92 Ind. 310; American C. C. Co. *v.* Seitz, 101 Ind. 182; McNally *v.* White, 154 Ind. 163, 172, 54 N. E. 794.

Iowa: Brandt *v.* Foster, 5 Ia. 287; McDunn *v.* Des Moines, 39 Ia. 286; Mischke *v.* Baughn, 52 Ia. 528.

Kentucky: Hunt *v.* Orwig, 17 B. Mon. 73, 66 Am. Dec. 144; Heaton *v.* Timmons, 15 Ky. L. Rep. 62.

Louisiana: Southern W. M. C. & C. Co. *v.* Davenport, 50 La. Ann. 505, 23 So. 448.

Massachusetts: Cornell *v.* Jackson, 3 Cush. 506.

Michigan: Dubay *v.* Kelly, 137 Mich. 345, 100 N. W. 677.

Nevada: Dalton *v.* Bowker, 8 Nev. 190.

New Hampshire: Patridge *v.* Hatch, 18 N. H. 494; Winnepiseogee P. Co. *v.* Eaton, 65 N. H. 13, 18 Atl. 171.

New York: Furniss *v.* Ferguson, 15 N. Y. 437; Olmstead *v.* Rawson, 188 N. Y. 517, 81 N. E. 456; Adams *v.* Conover, 22 Hun, 424; Hunt *v.* Raplee, 44 Hun, 149; Grantier *v.* Austin, 66 Hun, 157, 20 N. Y. Supp. 294; Giles *v.* Dugro, 1 Duer, 331.

North Carolina: Dickens *v.* Shepperd, 3 Murph. 526; Price *v.* Deal, 90 N. C. 291; Lemly *v.* Ellis, 146 N. C. 221, 59 S. E. 683.

Ohio: Nyce *v.* Obertz, 17 Oh. 71, 49 Am. Dec. 444.

Oregon: Stark *v.* Olney, 3 Ore. 88.

Pennsylvania: Lee *v.* Dean, 3 Whart. 316; Fulweiler *v.* Baugher, 15 S. & R. 45; Beaupland *v.* McKeen, 28 Pa. 124, 70 Am. Dec. 115; Doyle *v.* Brundred, 189 Pa. 113, 41 Atl. 1107. (But see King *v.* Pyle, 8 S. & R. 166, where it was held that if defendant were guilty of fraud the actual value of the portion of the tract lost would be recoverable in an action upon a covenant of warranty).

was sold at an agreed price per acre, and title fails to part, the measure of damages is the agreed price per acre for the entire number of acres to which title failed.[236] Evidence is admissible to show that the portion lost was especially valuable in comparison with the portion remaining,[237] but where the strip taken ran through the middle of the whole tract no consequential damages for the resulting inconvenience were allowed.[238] But if it can be shown that a fixed part of the purchase-money was given for a specific parcel of land to which title failed that fixed sum is the measure of damages.[239] Where the deed purported to convey a certain lot, a portion of which was the bed of a lake and, under the law of the jurisdiction, the property of the State, it was held that the valuable rights of the remaining tract as riparian land must be considered in measuring the damages.[240]

Frequently the grantor of land purports to grant by the same warranty deed an easement or profit in other land retained by

South Carolina: Pearson v. Davie, 1 McMull. 37; Wallace v. Talbot, 1 McCord, 466; Hunt v. Nolen, 46 S. C. 356, 24 S. E. 310.

South Dakota: Loiseau v. Threlstad, 14 S. D. 257, 85 N. W. 189.

Tennessee: Whitzman v. Hirsh, 87 Tenn. 513.

Texas: Raines v. Calloway, 27 Tex. 678; Mann v. Mathews, 82 Tex. 98, 17 S. W. 927; Weeks v. Barton, 31 S. W. 1072.

Virginia: Clark v. Hardgrove, 7 Gratt. 399; Nelson v. Matthews, 2 H. & M. 164; Humphreys v. McClenachan, 1 Munf. 493.

Washington: West Coast Manuf. Co. v. West Coast Imp. Co., 31 Wash. 610, 72 Pac. 455; Cameron v. Burke, 112 Pac. 252.

West Virginia: Butcher v. Peterson, 26 W. Va. 447, 53 Am. Rep. 89.

Wisconsin: Messer v. Oestreich, 52 Wis. 684; Bartelt v. Braunsdorf, 57 Wis. 1; Semple v. Whorton, 68 Wis. 626; McLennan v. Prentice, 85 Wis. 427, 442, 55 N. W. 764.

[236] *Alabama:* J. M. Ackley & Co. v.

Hunter, Benn & Co. Co., 154 Ala. 416, 45 So. 909.

South Carolina: Folk v. Graham, 82 S. C. 66, 62 S. E. 1106.

[237] Fulweiler v. Baugher, 15 S. & R. (Pa.) 45.

[238] Pearson v. Davis, 1 McMullan (S. C.), 37. But cf. Louisville Public Warehouse Co., 70 S. W. 1046 (Ky.).

[239] *Illinois:* Lloyd v. Sandusky, 95 Ill. App. 593.

Kentucky: Heaton v. Timmons, 15 Ky. L. Rep. 62.

Maine: Blanchard v. Hoxie, 34 Me. 376.

Massachusetts: Leland v. Stone, 10 Mass. 459.

Minnesota: Bruns v. Schreiber, 43 Minn. 468.

Missouri: Gunotte v. Chouteau, 34 Mo. 154; Adkins v. Tomlinson, 121 Mo. 487, 26 S. W. 573.

New Hampshire: Barns v. Learned, 5 N. H. 264; Nutting v. Herbert, 35 N. H. 120, 37 N. H. 346. And see § 964, *supra.*

[240] Huntsman v. Hendricks, 44 Minn. 423, 46 N. W. 910.

himself. Where such a grant fails, the authorities do not appear to be settled as to the true measure of recovery. Thus in New York the rule of a proportionate part of the consideration was applied to a case where the plaintiff had purchased a hotel with a right to take water from a neighboring spring,[241] but in a similar case in California the value of the lost water right was awarded.[242] When a mill is conveyed with covenants of warranty and a grant of an easement to erect and maintain a dam of a certain height, and by reason of rights of upper riparian owners the grantee is unable to raise the water to the stipulated height, the measure of his recovery on the covenants is the difference between the value of the estate as it is and as the deed purported to convey it.[243]

If the grantor under a covenant of seizin has previously given to a tenant the right to remove rails erected into fences upon the land there is a breach of the covenant for which the grantee may recover the value of the rails for which he is made liable to the tenant in an action by the latter for conversion.[244]

When the partial eviction is due to a right of way or similar incumbrance the authorities are not settled as to the rule to be applied. It is said that if the plaintiff's possession has been interfered with on account of the incumbrance, he recovers the amount of his injury, not exceeding the consideration or the value, as the case may be.[245] So in a case in Iowa,[246] where part of the land had been taken for a public use, it was held that the measure of damages was a sum which bore the same ratio to the consideration money that the market value of the land as depreciated by the incumbrance bore to the market value without the incumbrance. In an early New York case [247] the rule of a proportionate part of the consideration was ap-

[241] Sweet v. Howell, 89 N. Y. Supp. 21.

[242] Lyles v. Perrin, 134 Cal. 417, 66 Pac. 472.

[243] *Wisconsin:* Hall v. Gale, 20 Wis. 292.

Canada: Platt v. Grand Trunk R. R., 12 Ont. 119.

[244] Mott v. Palmer, 1 N. Y. 564, 49 Am. Dec. 359.

[245] *Indiana:* Wright v. Nipple, 92 Ind. 310, 47 Am. Rep. 145.

Massachusetts: Harlow v. Thomas, 15 Pick. 66, 69; Batchelder v. Sturgis, 3 Cush. 201.

Rhode Island: Porter v. Bradley, 7 R. I. 538.

[246] Koestenbader v. Pierce, 37 Ia. 645; Koestenbader v. Pierce, 41 Ia. 204, 20 Am. Rep. 586.

[247] Giles v. Dugro, 1 Duer, 331.

plied when the incumbrance was a party wall, but in a later case [248] where the action was upon a covenant of quiet enjoyment and the incumbrance a public highway the depreciation in the estate was held to measure the damages. In a Missouri case [249] where the incumbrance was a railway right of way the damages upon a covenant against incumbrances were held to be the fee value of the strip taken and not the lesser amount of a proportionate part of the consideration.

§ 976.[a] Partial failure of title.

In the cases which we have just been considering there is an eviction from a part of the land. It often happens that, without any eviction, there is a partial failure of title, through an outstanding particular estate.

When the title fails as to an undivided share of the granted land, the plaintiff recovers that proportion of the purchase-money, or, in New England when the action is upon a covenant of warranty, of the value.[250] Such outstanding right of a co-tenant is a breach of the covenant of warranty without actual eviction and if the covenantee purchases the outstanding right he may recover the amount reasonably expended in so doing.[251] In a Missouri case [252] it was held that if the covenantee surrendered possession to the other co-tenant he might recover the entire purchase-money. Such a holding, however, seems erroneous. In Boyle v. Edwards [253] the plaintiff had been evicted from an undivided one-third. There belonged to the premises a right to build upon a division wall. In an action for breach of warranty it was held that the value of that privilege could be taken into account in estimating the damage.

When the premises conveyed are incumbered by an unex-

[a] For § 976 of the eighth edition see § 973.

[248] Hymes v. Esty, 133 N. Y. 342, 346, 31 N. E. 105.

[249] Whiteside v. Magruder, 75 Mo. App. 364.

[250] *California:* Hoffman v. Kirby, 136 Cal. 26, 68 Pac. 321.

Indiana: Wright v. Nipple, 92 Ind. 310, 47 Am. Rep. 145.

Kansas: Bolinger v. Brake, 4 Kan. App. 180, 45 Pac. 950.

Massachusetts: Lucas v. Wilcox, 135 Mass. 77.

New York: Roake v. Sullivan, 69 Misc. 429, 125 N. Y. Supp. 835.

Texas: Hynes v. Packard, 92 Tex. 44, 45 S. W. 562; Chesnutt v. Chism, 20 Tex. Civ. App. 23, 48 S. W. 549.

Vermont: Downer v. Smith, 38 Vt. 464.

[251] Beasley v. Phillips, 20 Ind. App. 182, 50 N. E. 488.

[252] Egan v. Martin, 71 Mo. App. 60.

[253] 114 Mass. 378.

pired lease it is generally held that the measure of damages upon any of the covenants is the value of the use of the premises for the time during which the grantee is deprived of their use.[254] In New York [255] and Massachusetts [256] it has been suggested that interest upon the purchase-money during the same period is an alternative measure of recovery. If the rent under the lease passes to the grantee as an incident of the reversion it would seem that the fact should be taken into consideration as reducing the damages.[257]

When the outstanding incumbrance is a right of dower there appears to be some conflict in the authorities as to the proper measure of compensation. The problem may arise at several different stages in the claim. Where the right is still inchoate it is frequently held that only nominal damages are recoverable,[258] and in Missouri the cases go so far as to

[254] *Colorado:* Tierney v. Whiting, 2 Colo. 620.

Illinois: Christy v. Ogle, 33 Ill. 295.

Iowa: Wragg v. Mead, 120 Ia. 319, 94 N. W. 856.

Kansas: Clark v. Fisher, 54 Kan. 403, 38 Pac. 493.

Massachusetts: Batchelder v. Sturgis, 3 Cush. 201.

Michigan: Edwards v. Clark, 83 Mich. 246, 47 N. W. 112.

Minnesota: Fritz v. Pusey, 31 Minn. 368.

Missouri: Lansgenberg v. Heer Dry Goods Co., 74 Mo. App. 12.

Nebraska: Downie v. Ladd, 22 Neb. 531; Brass v. Vandecar, 70 Neb. 35, 96 N. W. 1035; Melsbary v. Jacobus, 130 N. W. 424.

New York: Rickert v. Snyder, 9 Wend. 416 (covenant of seizin); Guthrie v. Pugsley, 12 Johns. 126.

Pennsylvania: Ferry v. Diabenstadt, 68 Pa. 400. (But see Cross v. Noble, 67 Pa. 74, allowing diminution in value of premises.)

Tennessee: Brown v. Taylor, 115 Tenn. 1, 88 S. W. 933, 4 L. R. A. (N. S.) 309.

Vermont: Mills v. Catlin, 22 Vt. 98.

Washington: O'Connor v. Enos, 56 Wash. 448, 105 Pac. 1039.

So where the growing crops were taken by paramount title, the measure of damages for breach of the covenant of warranty was the value of the crops at the time of the conveyance. Newburn v. Lucas, 126 Ia. 85, 101 N. W. 730.

[255] Rickert v. Snyder, 9 Wend. 416 (covenant of seizin: costs of defending termor's suit were included).

[256] Batchelder v. Sturgis, 3 Cush. (Mass.) 201.

[257] *Michigan:* Edward v. Clark, 83 Mich. 246, 47 N. W. 112, 10 L. R. A. 659.

New Jersey: Demars v. Koehler, 62 N. J. L. 203, 41 Atl. 720, 72 Am. St. Rep. 642.

South Carolina: Grice v. Scarborough, 2 Speer, 649, 42 Am. Dec. 391.

But see *contra*, Fritz v. Pusey, 31 Minn. 368.

[258] *Maine:* Donnell v. Thompson, 10 Me. 170, 26 Am. Dec. 216; Runnells v. Webber, 59 Me. 488.

New Jersey: Carter v. Denman, 23 N. J. L. 273.

hold that the existence of a contingent right of dower is not a breach of a covenant against incumbrances.[259] But it seems clear that such a right, though contingent, is an incumbrance, and since it is not extinguishable at the option of the covenantee, the measure of damages should be that applied to other permanent incumbrances, i. e., the depreciation in the value of the land by reason of the incumbrance.[260] If, however, the covenantee purchases the right of the dowress he should recover the amount so expended,[261] or if the widow recovers a fixed sum in lieu of dower the amount of her recovery with the costs of defending against her claim should fix the damages to be recovered upon the covenants for title.[262] But where the covenant of warranty or against incumbrances is broken by reason of an assignment of dower by metes and bounds, the damages will go, not to the extent of the consideration money, nor of one-third of the consideration money of the deed, but the extent to which the value of the estate is diminished by carving out the life estate, taking one-third of the consideration money to be the value of one-third of the fee simple interest or in other words, that portion of the consideration which the value of a life estate in a third of the premises bears to the value of a fee in the whole.[263] So where the granted estate was a lease for 99 years, reserving rent, and there was a right of dower outstanding, the rent was abated

---

[259] Maguire v. Riggin, 44 Mo. 512; Hunt v. Marsh, 80 Mo. 396. Cf. Bostwick v. Williams, 36 Ill. 65, 85 Am. Dec. 385.

[260] Brisbane v. Pomeroy, 13 Daly (N. Y.), 358.

[261] Illinois: McCord v. Massey, 155 Ill. 123, 39 N. E. 592, 46 Am. St. Rep. 315.

Maine: Donnell v. Thompson, 10 Me. 170, 26 Am. Dec. 216.

Massachusetts: Shearer v. Ranger, 22 Pick. 447.

Missouri: Walker v. Deaver, 79 Mo. 664 (not limited to one-third the consideration).

New Jersey: Carter v. Denman, 23 N. J. L. 273.

But in Blevins v. Smith, 104 Mo. 583, 16 S. W. 213, a covenantee who paid a substantial sum to remove an inchoate right of dower was awarded only nominal damages.

[262] Blackwell v. McBride, 14 Ky. L. Rep. 760.

North Carolina: Jackson v. Hanna, 8 Jones L. 188.

South Carolina: Jeter v. Glenn, 9 Rich. Law, 374; Welsh v. Kibler, 5 S. C. 405.

[263] Kentucky: Davis v. Logan, 5 B. Mon. 341; Hill v. Golden, 16 B. Mon. 551.

Ohio: Johnson v. Nyce, 17 Ohio, 66, 49 Am. Dec. 444.

one-third during the life of the dowress.[264]   But it is sometimes held that the value of the life estate in the fractional
part of the property is the measure of damages.[265]   Where a
covenant was contained in a conveyance of two-thirds of a
piece of real estate made by one who was seized in fee, subject to an outstanding right of dower, held that the covenant
of warranty was broken on the delivery of the deed, and if
the part subsequently set off to the widow for her life exceeded
in value one-third of the whole, the grantee would be entitled
to damages equivalent to the proportionate diminution in
value of the estate conveyed.   If the part set off did not exceed one-third in value, the damages would be nominal only.[266]

When the deed purports to convey a fee but the conveyance
can take effect only to pass a life estate, it would seem that
whenever the recovery for total failure of title would be the
consideration, the measure of damages for such a partial breach
should be a proportionate part thereof.   That is, there should
be deducted from the consideration such portion thereof as
the value of the life estate bears to the value of a fee.[267]   But
in Connecticut the value of the life estate was deducted from
the purchase price, the action being upon a covenant of seizin.[268]
In an early Tennessee case there was given the difference in
value of a life estate and a fee,[269] but later cases in the same
jurisdiction give to the covenantee a right to recover the whole
purchase-money upon tendering a reconveyance, subject only
to an abatement for rents and profits during the time the
covenantee was in possession.[270]

Where the title fails to timber or coal upon the premises
the measure of damages is that proportion of the contract
price which equals the proportion which the value of the timber
or coal lacking bears to the whole value of the land conveyed.[271]

[264] McAlpin v. Woodruff, 11 Ohio St.
120.

[265] Stewart v. Mathieson, 23 Up.
Can. Q. B. 135.

[266] Blanchard v. Blanchard, 48 Me.
174.

[267] Aiken v. McDonald, 43 S. C. 29, 20
S. E. 796, 49 Am. St. Rep. 817.

[268] Lockwood v. Sturdevant, 6 Conn.
373.

[269] Recohs v. Younglove, 8 Baxt. 385.

[270] Park v. Cheek, 4 Cold. 20; Curtis
v. Brannon, 98 Tenn. 153, 38 S. W.
1073.

[271] Pennsylvania: Fuller v. Mulhol-
lan, 40 Pa. Super. Ct. 257.

Texas: Lumpkin v. Blewitt (Tex.
Civ. App.), 111 S. W. 1072.

Wisconsin: Darlington v. J. L. Gates
Land Co., 142 Wis. 198, 125 N. W. 456.

§ 977ᵃ. After acquired title—American doctrine of estoppel by deed.

It is generally laid down as settled law that a title acquired by a grantor subsequently to a conveyance with covenants enures forthwith to the covenantee and reduces damages upon the covenants to the extent of the title so acquired,[272] and it has been held that this is true even though such title is not acquired by the grantor till after suit brought.[273]   In one of such decisions the court said: "The covenant was intended to secure to the plaintiff a legal seizin in the land conveyed. If it is broken, and he fails of that seizin, he has a right to reclaim the purchase-money.   But if, in virtue of another covenant in the same deed, which was also taken to assure to him the subject-matter of the conveyance, he has obtained that seizin, it would be altogether inequitable that he should have the seizin, and be allowed besides to recover back the consideration paid for it,[274] and in another it was said that if the plaintiff "takes anything by his deed, directly or indirectly, by its own force, or by its co-operation with other instruments or other circumstances, whether it be the entire thing purchased or a part of it, its value must be considered in estimating the damages."[275]

---

[a] For § 977 of the eighth edition see § 974.

[272] *Alabama:* Sayre v. Sheffield L. I. & C. Co., 106 Ala. 440, 18 So. 101.

Connecticut: Miller v. Hartford & S. O. Co., 41 Conn. 112.

Indiana: Overhiser v. McCollister, 10 Ind. 41.

Iowa: Gifford v. Ferguson, 19 Ia. 166; Boon v. McHenry, 55 Ia. 202.

Kansas: Looney v. Reeves, 5 Kan. App. 279, 48 Pac. 606.

Massachusetts: Cornell v. Jackson, 3 Cush. 506; Whiting v. Dewey, 15 Pick. 428.

New York: McCarty v. Leggett, 3 Hill, 134.

North Carolina: Farmers' Bank v. Glenn, 68 N. C. 35.

Pennsylvania: Beaupland v. McKeen, 28 Pa. 124, 70 Am. Dec. 115.

Virginia: Building L. & W. Co. v. Fray, 96 Va. 559, 32 S. E. 58.

Wisconsin: McLennan v. Prentice, 85 Wis. 427, 55 N. W. 764.

[273] *Illinois:* King v. Gilson, 32 Ill. 348, 83 Am. Dec. 269.

New Hampshire: Morrison v. Underwood, 20 N. H. 369.

Pennsylvania: Knowles v. Kennedy, 82 Pa. 445.

Virginia: Young v. McClung, 9 Gratt. 336.

Canada: Boulter v. Hamilton, 15 Up. Can. C. P. 125.

[274] Baxter v. Bradbury, 20 Me. 260, 37 Am. Dec. 49.

[275] Carpenter, J., in Hartford & Salisbury Ore Co. v. Miller, 41 Conn. 112, 130, where the deed by its terms conveyed certain mineral rights which the defendant in façt could not convey,

These decisions are the logical results of the American development of the much misunderstood and misapplied doctrine of estoppel by deed, characterized by an eminent authority [276] as "unsound in principle" and "unjust in its practical results." That a vendor who has purported to convey having no title should be able to force upon an unwilling vendee a title purchased after the property has depreciated in value seems to be justified by no legal theory and without equity. Rather should the aggrieved vendee have an equity to compel the conveyance of the after acquired title to himself at his election. Accordingly it is generally agreed that a vendor cannot assert in mitigation of damages a title acquired after the vendee has suffered eviction. [277]

So, too, by the better opinion the covenantor can not force upon the covenantee a title acquired after the bringing of an action upon the covenants. [278]

On the other hand the courts of Missouri have gone to the extreme of holding that even after the covenantee has obtained a judgment for the consideration, the grantor may buy in the outstanding title and in a court of equity enjoin the enforcement of the judgment and compel the vendee to take the after acquired title. [279] But in the case of Noonan v. Ilsley [280] the Wisconsin Supreme court, hesitating to go so far, said: "The appellant contends that the title acquired by Noonan after the filing of the counter-claim setting up a breach of the covenant of seizin, would not enure to his benefit, but that he had a right to recover for breach of the covenant the full consideration money and interest. Before what act a title thus acquired by a grantor will enure, and after which it will not enure to the

not having the consent of his co-tenants. Afterwards, however, they assented, so that the plaintiff acquired the same rights which he should have secured by the original deed. It was held that only nominal damages could be recovered.

[276] See Rawle on Covenants for Title, 5th ed., §§ 179–186, and ch. XI.

[277] *Indiana:* Burton v. Reeds, 20 Ind. 87.

Massachusetts: Blanchard v. Ellis, 1 Gray, 202, 61 Am. Dec. 417.

Wisconsin: Nichol v. Alexander, 28 Wis. 118; McInnis v. Lyman, 62 Wis. 191, 22 N. W. 405.

[278] *Minnesota:* Resser v. Carney, 52 Minn. 397.

New York: Morris v. Phelps, 5 Johns. 49, 4 Am. Dec. 323; Tucker v. Clarke, 2 Sandf. Ch. 96.

[279] Reese v. Smith, 12 Mo. 344.

[280] 21 Wis. 138.

benefit of his grantee, it may be difficult to determine. We are inclined to the opinion that the rendition of judgment, in an action on the covenant of seizin, for the full consideration money and interest, is such an act. We have some doubts, however, whether judgment without satisfaction is sufficient. For if the judgment alone vests in the grantor the immediate right of possession of the premises which he delivered to his grantee, the latter might be deprived of the possession, and yet be unable to collect his judgment. On the other hand, if the grantor gives to his grantee neither possession nor title, should he be permitted after a delay of years to perfect the title, and, after suit brought on his covenant, then to purchase the land and compel his vendee to take it, when it may have greatly depreciated in value? We leave this question undecided."

Of course the grantee may accept a title purchased by the grantor for his benefit and if he so elects he should be confined to a recovery for expenses reasonably incurred in obtaining the title or seeking possession and damages for loss of the use of the land while deprived thereof.[281]

§ 978.ᵃ Reduction of damages.

It is frequently open to the covenantor to show facts reducing the covenantee's recovery. Thus where the estate is incumbered by an outstanding term for years, the rent of which passes to the grantee as an incident of the reversion, the grantor is entitled to a deduction therefor.[282] So, too, where the grantee has received a life estate under a deed purported to convey a fee, the value of the life estate is to be considered.[283] And as stated above, when title to a part of the

---

ᵃ Part of § 978 of the eighth edition is now § 977.

[281] *South Carolina:* Singleton *v.* Allen, 2 Strobh. Eq. 166.

Texas: Huff *v.* Reilly, 64 S. W. 387.

[282] *Michigan:* Edward *v.* Clark, 83 Mich. 246, 47 N. W. 112, 10 L. R. A. 659.

˙ *New Jersey:* Demars *v.* Koehler, 62 N. J. L. 203, 41 Atl. 720, 72 Am. St. Rep. 642.

South Carolina: Grice *v.* Scarborough, 2 Speer, 649, 42 Am. Dec. 391.

[283] *Connecticut:* Lockwood *v.* Sturdevant, 6 Conn. 373.

South Carolina: Aiken *v.* McDonald, 43 S. C. 29, 20 S. E. 796, 49 Am. St. Rep. 817.

Tennessee: Curtis *v.* Brannon, 98 Tenn. 153, 38 S. W. 1073; Park *v.* Cheek, 4 Cold. 20.

land conveyed fails because of its being in the bed of a lake, the valuable rights of the remaining portion as riparian land affect the amount of recovery.[284] Where the plaintiff has made improvements on the land before eviction, but is entitled by law to compensation for the improvements, he cannot charge the covenantor with them.[285] And where the covenantee had received a deed from one who had entered government land, and the government afterward lawfully cancelled the entry, but allowed the covenantee a preference right to file a new entry on the land, the value of this entry was deducted from the consideration.[286]

On the same principle the covenantor is entitled to credit for any improvements erected by himself upon the land and removed by the covenantee before eviction or for which the covenantor has obtained compensation from the evicting owner.[287] And where the vendors held under a tax deed and the vendee recovered of the owner of the paramount title all taxes due with interest up to the time of eviction, the amount so received by the vendee should be allowed to the vendor as reduction of damages.[288] If the title of the covenantee has become indefeasible by an adverse possession during the statutory period, the damages are but nominal.[289]

§ 979. Title perfected by grantee—Expenses recoverable.

Though the grantee is under no duty to avail himself of an opportunity to buy in an outstanding paramount title at a small price,[290] yet when he has perfected the title, either by buying in the paramount title or by securing the release of an

[284] Huntsman v. Hendricks, 44 Minn. 423, 46 N. W. 910.

[285] Webb v. Wheeler, 80 Neb. 438, 114 N. W. 636, 17 L. R. A. (N. S.) 1178.

[286] Efta v. Swanson (Minn.), 132 N. W. 335.

[287] Kentucky: Wickliffe v. Clay, 1 Dana, 585; Booker v. Bell, 3 Bibb, 173, 6 Am..Dec. 641.
Michigan: Mason v. Kellogg, 38 Mich. 132.
Ohio: King v. Kerr, 5 Ohio, 154, 22 Am. Dec. 777.
Tennessee: Park v. Cheek, 4 Cold. 20.

[288] Stebbins v. Wolf, 33 Kan. 765, 7 Pac. 542.

[289] Arkansas: Benton County v. Rutherford, 33 Ark. 640.
South Carolina: Wilson v. Forbes, 2 Dev. 30.
Wisconsin: Noonan v. Ilsley, 21 Wis. 138; Smith v. Hughes, 50 Wis. 620, 7 N. W. 653.

[290] Arkansas: Alexander v. Bridgford, 59 Ark. 195, 27 S. W. 69.
New Jersey: Miller v. Halsey, 14 N. J. L. 48.
But see Alabama: Gunter v. Beard, 93 Ala. 227, 9 So. 389.

incumbrance, he may, on the principles discussed elsewhere, recover the reasonable and necessary expense of so doing.[291]

[291] *Alabama:* Lewis v. Harris, 31 Ala. 689.
Arkansas: Morris v. Ham, 47 Ark. 293, 296, 1 S. W. 519; Alexander v. Bridgford, 59 Ark. 195, 27 S. W. 69; William Farrell Lumber Co. v. Deshon, 65 Ark. 103, 44 S. W. 1036; Collier v. Cowger, 52 Ark. 322, 12 S. W. 702; Dellahunty v. Little Rock, etc., Co., 59 Ark. 699, 27 S. W. 1002, 28 S. W. 657.
California: McGary v. Hastings, 39 Cal. 360, 2 Am. Rep. 456.
Connecticut: Davis v. Lyman, 6 Conn. 249, 254 (*semble*).
Georgia: Amos v. Cosby, 74 Ga. 793.
Illinois: Richard v. Bent, 59 Ill. 38, 14 Am. Rep. 1; Clapp v. Herdman, 25 Ill. App. 509.
Indiana: Hollman v. Creagmiles, 14 Ind. 177; Beasley v. Phillips, 20 Ind. App. 182, 50 N. E. 488; Worley v. Hineman, 6 Ind. App. 240, 33 N. E. 260; Whisler v. Hicks, 5 Blackf. 100, 33 Am. Dec. 454 (*semble*).
Iowa: Brandt v. Foster, 5 Ia. 287; Fawcett v. Woods, 5 Ia. 400, 68 Am. Dec. 708; Baker v. Corbett, 28 Ia. 317; Richards v. Iowa H. Co., 44 Ia. 304, 24 Am. Rep. 745; Snell v. Iowa H. Co., 59 Ia. 701; Royer v. Foster, 62 Ia. 321; Duroe v. Stephens, 101 Ia. 358, 70 N. W. 610.
Kansas: Dale v. Shively, 8 Kan. 276; McKee v. Bain, 11 Kan. 569.
Maine: Donnell v. Thompson, 10 Me. 170; Spring v. Chase, 22 Me. 505, 39 Am. Dec. 595; Reed v. Pierce, 36 Me. 455, 58 Am. Dec. 761.
Massachusetts: Wyman v. Brigden, 4 Mass. 150; Harlow v. Thomas, 15 Pick. 66, 69; Thayer v. Clemence, 22 Pick. 490; Comings v. Little, 24 Pick. 266, 35 Am. Dec. 319; Batchelder v. Sturgis, 3 Cush. 201; Farnum v. Peterson, 111 Mass. 148; Smith v. Carney, 127 Mass. 179.

Michigan: Long v. Sinclair, 40 Mich. 569.
Minnesota: Kimball v. Bryant, 25 Minn. 496; Brooks v. Mohl, 104 Minn. 404, 116 N. W. 931, 17 L. R. A. (N. S.) 1195.
Mississippi: Allen v. Miller, 54 So. 731; Wade v. Barlow, 54 So. 662.
Missouri: Henderson v. Henderson, 13 Mo. 151; Lawless v. Collier, 19 Mo. 480; St. Louis v. Bissell, 46 Mo. 157; Eddington v. Nix, 49 Mo. 134; Ward v. Ashbrook, 78 Mo. 515.
Nebraska: Mills v. Saunders, 4 Neb. 190.
New Hampshire: Morrison v. Underwood, 20 N. H. 369; Willson v. Willson, 25 N. H. 229, 235, 57 Am. Dec. 320 (*semble*).
New Jersey: Stewart v. Drake, 9 N. J. L. 139 (*semble*); Carter v. Denman, 23 N. J. L. 273; Hartshorn v. Cleveland, 52 N. J. L. 473, 19 Atl. 974.
New York: Andrews v. Appel, 22 Hun, 429; Petrie v. Folz, 54 N. Y. Super. Ct. 223.
North Carolina: Price v. Deal, 90 N. C. 290.
Oregon: Arrigoni v. Johnson, 6 Ore. 167; Cobb v. Klosterman, 114 Pac. 96.
Rhode Island: Porter v. Bradley, 7 R. I. 538.
South Carolina: Jeter v. Glenn, 9 Rich. L. 374.
Texas: Denson v. Love, 58 Tex. 468; James v. Lamb, 2 Tex. Civ. App. 185, 21 S. W. 172; Thomas v. Ellison (Tex. Civ. App.), 110 S. W. 934; Hawkins v. Potter (Tex. Civ. App.), 130 S. W. 643.
Vermont: Turner v. Goodrich, 26 Vt. 707; Cole v. Kimball, 52 Vt. 639.
Virginia: Stockton v. Cook, 3 Munf. 68; Building, Light & Water Co. v. Fray, 96 Va. 559, 32 S. E. 58.
Wisconsin: Hurd v. Hall, 12 Wis. 112; Bailey v. Scott, 13 Wis. 618; Eaton v. Tallmadge, 22 Wis. 526.

"If the covenantee·has fairly extinguished the incumbrances, he is entitled to recover the price he has paid for it." [292] So in an action on a promissory note given for the purchase-money, it was held that the defendant could recoup a tax he had paid, the plaintiff being liable on his covenant against incumbrances. [293] In Stambaugh v. Smith, [294] the court said, that where the damages are the expenses incurred in removing the incumbrance, "the covenantee must show that the legal title to the outstanding estate has been extinguished, so that the covenantor may not be again prosecuted on account of some defect in the warranted title in some other covenant of the deed, after the eviction of a subsequent grantee of the estate at the suit of an innocent purchaser of the outstanding title." In an action for breach of a covenant of warranty on eviction under a mortgage, it was held that the plaintiff, having paid the mortgage before judgment, might recover the whole amount of it, although he had previously conveyed the estate to one who assumed, as a part of the consideration of that conveyance, to pay part of the mortgage. [295]

In Mississippi the recovery for the amount paid to extinguish an outstanding paramount title must be in an action of assumpsit and not upon the covenants. [296]

The extinguishment of the incumbrance need not have taken place before bringing the action, [297] * on the correct ground, that since the cause of action accrued before the commencement of the suit, by reason of the existence of the in-

England: Smith v. Compton, 3 B. & A. 407; Cane v. Allen, 2 Dow, 289, 296.

Although the incumbrance bought in was a mortgage not yet due. Snyder v. Lane, 10 Ind. 424; Funk v. Voneida, 11 S. & R. 109. But see Corbett v. Wrenn, 25 Ore. 305, 35 Pac. 658.

[292] Delavergne v. Norris, 7 Johns. 358, 5 Am. Dec. 281.

[293] Davis v. Bean, 114 Mass. 358. In Braman v. Bingham, 26 N. Y. 483, a grantor covenanted that there were incumbrances on the estate to the extent of $12,400 only. They amounted, in fact, to $12,800. The grantee, having paid a portion of them to an amount exceeding $400, was held entitled to recover that sum only.

[294] 23 Oh. St. 584.

[295] Estabrook v. Smith, 6 Gray, 572, 66 Am. Dec. 445.

[296] Green v. Irving, 54 Miss. 462, 28 Am. Rep. 360; Cummings v. Harrison, 57 Miss. 275.

[297] *Maine:* Kelly v. Low, 18 Me. 244.

Massachusetts: Leffingwell v. Elliott, 10 Pick. 204; Brooks v. Moody, 20 Pick. 474; Johnson v. Collins, 116 Mass. 392.

Missouri: Moseley v. Hunter, 15 Mo. 322.

Vermont: Potter v. Taylor, 6 Vt. 676.

cumbrance, and thus a claim for nominal damages was created, the payment of the incumbrance was mere matter of consequence, which the jury should take into consideration.**

It is frequently said that a covenantee cannot buy in an outstanding paramount claim and assert it against the grantor, but that such subsequently acquired title enures to the benefit of the grantor to the extent that the vendee can ask for no more than reimbursement. Accordingly it is the general rule that the recovery can not exceed the amount actually paid by way of extinguishment with interest.[298] But if the plaintiff was actually evicted by the owner of the paramount title, and thereafter purchased the estate from him, the amount then paid will not limit recovery.[299] Nor can the amount of the recovery exceed the purchase-money and interest, or, in New England, the value of the land.[300] But in extinguishing an

---

[298] *Georgia:* Kerley *v.* Richardson, 17 Ga. 602; Hull *v.* Harris, 64 Ga. 309.

Illinois: McDowell *v.* Milroy, 69 Ill. 498.

Iowa: Brandt *v.* Foster, 5 Ia. 287; Knadler *v.* Sharp, 36 Ia. 232; Castor *v.* Dufur, 133 Ia. 535, 111 N. W. 43.

Kansas: Craven *v.* Clary, 8 Kan. App. 295, 55 Pac. 679.

Massachusetts: Shearer *v.* Ranger, 22 Pick. 447.

Mississippi: Holloway *v.* Miller, 84 Miss. 776, 36 So. 531; Allen *v.* Miller, 54 So. 731.

New Hampshire: Loomis *v.* Bedel, 11 N. H. 74.

North Carolina: Farmers' Bank *v.* Glenn, 68 N. C. 35; Eames *v.* Armstrong, 146 N. C. 1, 59 S. E. 165.

Tennessee: Bank *v.* Johnston, 105 Tenn. 521, 59 S. W. 131.

Texas: McClelland *v.* Moore, 48 Tex. 355; (but see Thiele *v* Axell, 5 Tex. Civ. App. 548, 24 S. W. 803); Tatum *v.* Kincannon, 54 Tex. Civ. App. 633, 117 S. W. 113.

Wisconsin: Patterson *v.* Cappon, 125 Wis. 198, 102 N. W. 1083.

[299] *Georgia:* Martin *v.* Atkinson, 7 Ga. 228, 57 Am. Dec. 403.

Louisiana: Boyer *v.* Amet, 41 La. Ann. 721, 6 So. 734.

Michigan: Long *v.* Sinclair, 40 Mich. 569.

But see *New York:* Cowdrey *v.* Coit, 3 Robert. 210, 44 N. Y. 383, 4 Am. Rep. 690.

[300] *Arkansas:* Dillahunty *v.* Railway, 59 Ark. 629, 28 S. W. 657, 43 Am. St. Rep. 63; Alexander *v.* Bridgford, 59 Ark. 195, 27 S. W. 69.

California: McGary *v.* Hastings, 39 Cal. 369, 2 Am. Rep. 456.

Connecticut: Kelsey *v.* Remer, 43 Conn. 129, 21 Am. Rep. 638; Beecher *v.* Baldwin, 55 Conn. 419, 12 Atl. 401, 3 Am. St. Rep. 57.

Illinois: Brady *v.* Spurck, 27 Ill. 478, 482 (*semble*); Willets *v.* Burgess, 34 Ill. 494.

Iowa: Fawcett *v.* Woods, 5 Ia. 400, 68 Am. Dec. 708; Richards *v.* Iowa H. Co., 44 Ia. 304, 24 Am. Rep. 745.

Kentucky: Norton *v.* Babcock, 2 Met. 510, 516; Mercantile Trust Co. *v.* South Park Co., 94 Ky. 271, 22 S. W. 314.

Louisiana: Pharr *v.* Gall, 104 La. 700, 29 So. 306.

Massachusetts: Johnson *v.* Collins, 116 Mass. 392.

incumbrance upon a part of the land it would seem that the plaintiff is not restricted to a proportional part of the purchase-money. Thus, in extinguishing a right of dower the plaintiff may expend more than one-third of the purchase-money and be reimbursed for it.[301] Nor is the recited consideration binding.[302] Thus where the nominal consideration of a conveyance was one dollar but the real consideration was plaintiff's agreement to build its road and locate its depot on the land so as to improve the defendant's other property, the plaintiff was allowed to recover the amount of a mortgage not exceeding the value of the land.[303]

In a peculiar case, where one who held a paramount title to land, having recovered the land against the grantee of another, had sold and conveyed it to the latter for a specified sum of money, in lieu of the payment of which the grantee executed to the other an assignment of his right of action against his grantor on the covenants in the latter's deed to him, this assignment was held equivalent to the payment of the specified sum; and the measure of the damages of the holder of the paramount title, in his action against his assignor's grantor for the breach of these covenants, was the same that the original grantee's would have been, namely, the consideration named in his original grantor's deed and interest, subject to the limitation that the assignee could recover no more than the consideration or price agreed between him and the original grantee.[304]

Minnesota: Brooks *v.* Mohl, 104 Minn. 404, 116 N. W. 931, 17 L. R. A. (N. S.) 1195.

Missouri: Lee *v.* Gratz, 92 Mo. App. 422.

New Hampshire: Willson *v.* Willson, 25 N. H. 229, 57 Am. Dec. 320 (*semble*).

New York: Dimmick *v.* Lockwood, 10 Wend. 149; Greene *v.* Tallman, 20 N. Y. 191, 75 Am. Dec. 384; Andrews *v.* Appel, 22 Hun, 429; Utica, etc., R. R. *v.* Gates, 8 App. Div. 181, 40 N. Y. Supp. 316.

North Carolina: Farmers' Bank *v.* Glenn, 68 N. C. 35.

Pennsylvania: Cox *v.* Henry, 32 Pa. 18.

Rhode Island: Porter *v.* Bradley, 7 R. I. 538.

Virginia: Roller *v.* Effinger, 88 Va. 641, 14 S. E. 337.

[301] Walker *v.* Deaver, 79 Mo. 664.

[302] See § 964, *supra*.

[303] Utica, etc., R. R. *v.* Gates, 21 Misc. 205, 47 N. Y. Supp. 231.

[304] Eaton *v.* Lyman, 24 Wis. 438, 26 Wis. 61, 7 Am. Rep. 39; *acc.*, Hooper *v.* Sac County Bank, 72 Iowa, 280, 33 N. W. 681.

§ 980. Expenses must be reasonable.

The recovery will extend only to the expense of acts reasonably done, and to the amount reasonably paid; and the burden is on the plaintiff to show that the sum paid to remove the incumbrance or to extinguish the paramount title was a reasonable one.[305]   In Kelsey v. Remer [306] there had been an attachment on land.   The attaching creditor secured a judgment, but levied his execution improperly.   The plaintiff paid off the judgment in good faith, believing, and having reason to believe, that otherwise execution would issue.   It was held that he acted with reasonable prudence and care in regard to the interests of the defendant, and that the amount paid should be the measure of damages.   Park, C. J., said: "We think, in cases where judgment has been rendered in the suit in favor of the attaching creditor, and the owner of the land has conducted in good faith toward his covenantor, in paying the amount of the judgment, in order to free his land from the lien created by the attachment, the amount of the judgment should be the measure of damages if the amount is less than the value of the land attached; but if greater than such value, then the value of the land attached should be the measure of damages." So where a sewer assessment or assessment for street improvement is invalid but the lien itself remains valid, the grantee under a covenant against incumbrances can recover the amount paid after a valid reassessment.[307]   There cannot, however, be recovery for a payment to discharge an incumbrance barred by the statute of limitations.[308]   A covenantee can not recover moneys expended to pay off an incumbrance

---

[305] *Alabama:* Anderson v. Knox, 20 Ala. 156.

Arkansas: Pate v. Mitchell, 23 Ark. 590, 79 Am. Dec. 114.

Illinois: McCord v. Massey, 155 Ill. 123, 39 N. E. 592, 46 Am. St. Rep. 315.

Iowa: Brant v. Foster, 5 Ia. 287; Guthrie v. Russell, 46 Ia. 269, 26 Am. Rep. 135.

Kansas: Gilbert v. Rushmer, 49 Kan. 632, 31 Pac. 123.

Missouri: Walker v. Deaver, 5 Mo. App. 139.

[306] 43 Conn. 129, 139, 21 Am. Rep. 638.

[307] *Massachusetts:* Coburn v. Litchfield, 132 Mass. 449, 42 Am. Rep. 446.

New Jersey: Hartshorn v. Cleveland, 52 N. J. L. 473, 19 Atl. 974; Cadmus v. Fagan, 47 N. J. L. 549.

Wisconsin: Peters v. Myers, 22 Wis. 602.

Contra: Barth v. Ward, 71 N. Y. Supp. 340.

[308] Robinson v. Bierce, 102 Tenn. 428, 52 S. W. 992, 47 L. R. A. 275.

over the covenantor's objections, and after the latter has obtained a temporary injunction restraining adverse action by the incumbrancer and has instituted proceedings to have a judgment in favor of the incumbrancer set aside.[309]

§ 980a. Consequential damages not recoverable.

It is generally held that whatever may be the form of the covenant upon which the action is brought, consequential damages are not recoverable.[310] The question arises most frequently under covenants against incumbrances. In New York it has been said that, in the absence of fraud, in an action brought by a grantee of land against his grantor for a breach of covenant against incumbrances, the measure of damages is the actual amount or value of the incumbrance, and where the purchaser has not enjoyed the premises, the interest, no consequential damages being allowed. "The reason given is that when the incumbrance is actually unknown to the vendor, as is generally the case where he covenants against them, the means of discovering them are, or with proper exertions may be, equally accessible to both parties. If the intended purchaser should make proper examination, he would ordinarily discover an incumbrance; which must be in writing, and the evidence on record; and should he neglect to do that, he cannot reasonably claim more than an exemption from positive loss." [311] So, in Massachusetts, it was said in an early case [312] that the effect of an unexpired lease "*on the sale of the estate*, could not be taken as the true rule; that such effect must in its very nature be imaginary, and supported only by speculative opinions and conjectures;" and that "it was quite too loose and uncertain a mode of estimating damages." Nor will, in such a case, the fact that the estate was purchased by the grantee for resale, be allowed to be proved in order to augment the damages, unless this was known to the grantor.[313] But

[309] Tuggle v. Hamilton, 100 Ga. 292, 27 S. E. 987.

[310] Copeland v. McAdory, 100 Ala. 553, 13 So. 545.

[311] Greene v. Tallman, 20 N. Y. 191, 196, 75 Am. Dec. 384, per Strong, J.;

acc., Claycomb v. Munger, 51 Ill. 373; Greene v. Creighton, 7 R. I. 1.

[312] Batchelder v. Sturgis, 3 Cush. (Mass.) 201.

[313] Stearn v. Hesdorfer, 9 N. Y. Misc. 134, 29 N. Y. Supp. 281.

in Noonan *v.* Isley [314] it was said that damages from loss of a contract of resale would be recoverable in an action on a covenant of seizin if at the time of the conveyance the warrantor knew of the purpose of the purchase, and in Doctor *v.* Darling [315] the plaintiff was allowed to show the price at which he had contracted to resell and the price at which he was compelled to sell because of an incumbrance, as bearing upon the value of the property with and without the incumbrance. In Harrington *v.* Murphy [316] the plaintiff discovered an incumbrance in the shape of an inchoate right of dower. He sold the land at auction, but the purchaser refused it on this account. It was held that the plaintiff could not recover the expenses of the auctioneer in that sale, they being "too remote and indirect."

The covenantee is generally not allowed to recover for time lost in perfecting his title.[317]   However,* in Massachusetts, in an action on the covenant against incumbrances, and of warranty,[318] there was proved a deed by defendants, to plaintiffs; that in the conveyance by the defendants, the land was supposed to be embraced, but it was not; that subsequent to the conveyance by defendants to plaintiffs, the original owners entered, and the plaintiff surrendered, and afterwards paid divers sums to extinguish the original title. The plaintiffs claimed the sums paid to extinguish the adverse titles, with charges for their time spent in extinguishing them, incidental expense for horse and carriage hire, and sums paid for advice of counsel after suit brought. The latter item (*counsel fees*) was disallowed; but the other expenses, subsequent to the service of the writ, were allowed.**   In Guntner *v.* Beard [319] damages for giving up a lucrative business and expenses of moving onto the premises and subsequently removing when evicted were held to be too remote, the court also seeming to rely upon the fact that the plaintiff might have bought in the outstanding incumbrance for an amount less than he owed the covenantor upon the purchase price.

[314] 21 Wis. 138.
[315] 68 Hun, 70, 22 N. Y. Supp. 594.
[316] 109 Mass. 299.
[317] Bradshaw *v.* Crosby, 151 Mass. 237, 24 N. E. 47.

[318] Lefingwell *v.* Elliott, 10 Pick. 204.
[319] 93 Ala. 227, 9 So. 389. See Wragg *v.* Mead, 120 Iowa, 319, 94 N. W. 856; Bautel *v.* American Mach. Co. (Ky.), 137 S. W. 799.

In Lamb *v.* Buker,[320] the owner of a farm sold it to the plaintiff subject to a mortgage. By reason of a defect in the record, though the defendant had a good title, the plaintiff was unable to obtain a loan to pay interest and taxes, and the mortgage was foreclosed. In a suit on the covenant of warranty damages for loss of the land were held to be remote.

The damages paid by the covenantee to his own grantee for breach of his own covenant against incumbrances are not recoverable against the immediate grantor, for such damages have been measured by the value of the land at a different time than of the making of the defendant's covenants.[321] If the plaintiff reasonably resists the claim of a third party to an easement, it has been held that he may recover the damages paid to such third party,[322] but where those damages have been augmented by the plaintiff's unreasonable or tortious conduct he can not so recover.[323]

In a peculiar case in Kansas [324] vacant lands were conveyed with covenants against incumbrances, and of right to convey and warranty. The grantee failed to take possession for 21 years, the land remaining vacant and unoccupied all that time, and was defeated in an action brought by him to obtain possession from one claiming under a paramount, adverse and better title than his own. It was held that the grantee could not recover on the covenant of warranty for though the action did not accrue until the assertion of a superior title, the plaintiff's neglect to take possession of the land for so long a period and protect his title precluded recovery. Such a holding seems to be a misapplication of the doctrine of avoidable consequences, for it is generally held that a covenantor is under no duty to perfect his title and prevent an eviction.[325]

§ 981. Interest.

The rules for the allowance of interest rest upon the following considerations. The damages are assessed as of the time of loss, and upon the general principles already discussed, in-

---

[320] 34 Neb. 485, 52 N. W. 285.
[321] Vonderhite *v.* Walton, 7 Ky. L. Rep. 766.
[322] Smith *v.* Sprague, 40 Vt. 43.

[323] Wilcox *v.* Danforth, 5 Ill. App. 378.
[324] Claflin *v.* Case, 53 Kan. 560, 36 Pac. 1062.
[325] See § 979, *supra.*

terest should be added from that time in order to give complete indemnity. If the grantee is accountable for mesne profits from the time he entered upon the land, it is because he is to be treated as a trespasser from that time, and not as having held the land under the conveyance; consequently the loss under the covenant happened at the time of the conveyance, and interest is to be recovered from that time. But if he is accountable for mesne profits only from a later time, or not at all, the conveyance practically secured him the land, and his loss happened only at the time when he became accountable for mesne profits. The damages therefore are assessed as of that time, and interest runs only from that time.

* In Staats v. Ten Eyck [326] it was said that the interest allowed should be commensurate with the legal claim to mesne profits. And in an action [327] brought by executors for a breach of the covenant of seizin, a verdict was taken by consent for the plaintiffs, for the consideration money expressed in the deed, with interest from the date of the time of trial; but it appearing that the premises had been actually enjoyed, and the mesne profits taken by the grantee, they were only allowed six years' interest, and a deduction was accordingly made. The principle of these decisions was affirmed in a subsequent case,[328] where in an action of covenant, an eviction being proved, the plaintiff was only allowed to recover the consideration paid, interest for six years thereon, and the costs of the eviction suit.** So in the same State, in an action for breach of the covenant of seizin,[329] it appeared that there was only a partial failure; the grantors having the fee in two-sixths of the premises conveyed, and a life estate in the remainder. The court said that interest ought not to be allowed during their lives, "for no one, during that time, will have a right to turn the plaintiff out of possession, or call on him for the mesne profits."

So in Ohio, * in an action on a covenant of warranty of title,[330] where the plaintiff had occupied the premises from the date of the conveyance, the enjoyment was declared to be equiva-

---

[326] 3 Caines, 111.
[327] Bennet v. Jenkins, 13 Johns. 50.
[328] Caulkins v. Harris, 9 Johns. 324.
[329] Guthrie v. Pugsley, 12 Johns. 126.
[330] Clark v. Parr, 14 Oh. 118, 45 Am. Dec. 526.

lent to the interest upon the consideration, and no interest as such recoverable. But as the plaintiff might be compelled to account for rents and profits for *four years*, to the true owner, he was held entitled to recover *interest* for four years in the suit on the covenant.** The principles laid down in these cases have been followed. Interest is usually allowed, whether the recovery is for eviction, or for the amount of expenditure in preventing eviction.[331] Where, however, the plaintiff has been in possession, the enjoyment of the land is regarded as equivalent to interest upon the consideration, and no interest is in such case recoverable [332] unless he is accountable for mesne profits. If he is accountable for mesne profits, he is entitled to interest though he has been in possession,[333] but such in-

---

[331] See all the authorities cited as supporting the general rules; and the following:

Colorado: Seyfried v. Knoblauch, 44 Colo. 86, 96 Pac. 993.

Georgia: Martin v. Gordon, 24 Ga. 533.

Indiana: Burk v. Clements, 16 Ind. 132; Wood v. Bibbins, 58 Ind. 392.

Iowa: Shorthill v. Ferguson, 44 Ia. 249.

Kentucky: Graham v. Dyer, 16 Ky. L. Rep. 541, 29 S. W. 346.

Mississippi: Hibernia B. & T. Co. v. Smith, 89 Miss. 298, 42 So. 345.

Missouri: Lawless v. Collier, 19 Mo. 480.

New York: Caulkins v. Harris, 9 Johns. 324; Greene v. Tallman, 20 N. Y. 191, 75 Am. Dec. 384.

Vermont: Flint v. Steadman, 36 Vt. 210.

Virginia: Norfolk & W. Ry. v. Mundy, 110 Va. 422, 66 S. E. 61.

Wisconsin: Messer v. Oestreich, 52 Wis. 684; McLennan v. Prentice, 85 Wis. 427, 55 N. W. 764.

[332] *Alabama:* Gunter v. Beard, 93 Ala. 227, 9 So. 389.

Illinois: Harding v. Larkin, 41 Ill. 413.

Kansas: Stebbins v. Wolf, 33 Kan. 765; Bolinger v. Brake, 4 Kan. App.

180, 45 Pac. 950; Craven v. Clary, 8 Kan. App. 295, 55 Pac. 679.

Kentucky: Thompson v. Jones, 11 B. Mon. 365.

Missouri: Hutchins v. Roundtree, 77 Mo. 500; Pence v. Gubbert, 70 Mo. App. 201; Staed v. Rossier (Mo. App.), 137 S. W. 901.

North Carolina: Williams v. Beeman, 2 Dev. 483.

Ohio: King v. Kerr, 5 Ohio, 154, 22 Am. Dec. 777.

Texas: Brown v. Hearon, 66 Tex. 63, 17 S. W. 395.

Vermont: Flint v. Steadman, 36 Vt. 210.

Virginia: Click v. Green, 77 Va. 827; Sheffey v. Gardiner, 79 Va. 313.

But in Connecticut the rule in the case of covenants of seizin is the same whether the grantee has been in possession or not, on the ground that the money due for rents and profits has no relation to the covenant broken, but constitutes a separate debt. Mitchell v. Hazen, 4 Conn. 495. This is entirely opposed to the current of authority.

[333] *Alabama:* Gunter v. Beard, 93 Ala. 227, 9 So. 389.

Georgia: Fernander v. Dunn, 19 Ga. 497.

Illinois: Wood v. Kingston Coal Co., 48 Ill. 356, 95 Am. Dec. 554.

terest is to be estimated only for such period as he is so accountable. When the plaintiff never obtains possession he is entitled to interest from the delivery of the deed.[334]

In a case in Maine [335] it was urged that the plaintiff derived no rents or profits from the premises; but the court said: "We think that cannot be taken into consideration to affect the rights of the parties. If a person purchases real estate, it is to be presumed that he does so because the rents and profits of it will be equivalent to the interest of the money he may be content to pay for it. Whether the vendee turns his purchase to a profit or not, is no concern of the vendors." [336]

When interest is recoverable it is to be computed at the legal rate and the fact that the covenantee gave securities for the purchase money on which he paid a higher rate does not entitle him to recover more.[337]

§ 982. Expenses of defending or of obtaining possession.

The legal costs [338] and other necessary expenses of defending

Kentucky: Wickliffe v. Clay, 1 Dana, 585.

Missouri: Lawless v. Collier's Ex'rs, 19 Mo. 480.

New Hampshire: Foster v. Thompson, 41 N. H. 373.

New York: Bennett v. Jenkins, 13 Johns. 50.

Ohio: Wade v. Comstock, 11 Oh. St. 71.

Pennsylvania: Patterson v. Stewart, 6 W. & S. 527, 40 Am. Dec. 586; Cox v. Henry, 32 Pa. 18.

Texas: Brown v. Hearon, 66 Tex. 63, 17 S. W. 395; Mann v. Mathews, 82 Tex. 98, 17 S. W. 927; Grosbeck v. Harris, 82 Tex. 411, 19 S. W. 850.

Wisconsin: Rich v. Johnson, 1 Chand. 19, 2 Pin. 88, 52 Am. Dec. 144.

[334] Hunt v. Nolen, 46 S. C. 551, 24 S. E. 543.

[335] Spring v. Chase, 22 Me. 505, 510, 39 Am. Dec. 595.

[336] Thus where the defendant, being tenant for life, with remainder over, conveyed with covenant of seizin in fee, in a suit on this covenant, the plaintiff having been in possession from the time of the conveyance, was allowed to recover the consideration money without interest, deducting therefrom the value of the life estate. Tanner v. Livingston, 12 Wend. 83. In Spring v. Chase, 22 Me. 505, 39 Am. Dec. 595, it is said, speaking of this case, "to have been held," that interest was not recoverable. But there was no discussion or decision as to the matter of interest; it was the ruling at the trial; the tenant for life, however, not having died, and the plaintiff not being evicted, there was evidently no ground for any allowance of interest.

[337] Blake v. Burnham, 29 Vt. 437.

[338] *Alabama:* Kingsbury v. Milner, 69 Ala. 502.

Connecticut: Sterling v. Peet, 14 Conn. 245; Butler v. Barnes, 61 Conn. 399, 24 Atl. 328.

Hawaii: Mooris v. Petero, 4 Haw. 23.

Kentucky: Blackwell v. McBride, 14 Ky. L. Rep. 760.

Louisiana: Pharr v. Gall, 108 La. 307, 29 So. 306.

or of attempting to obtain possession of the property are recoverable by the grantee.[339] In a Michigan case [340] it was held

Maine: Hardy v. Nelson, 27 Me. 525, 46 Am. Dec. 619.

Michigan: Dubay v. Kelly, 137 Mich. 345, 100 N. W. 677.

Minnesota: Wagner v. Finnegan, 54 Minn. 251, 55 N. W. 1129.

Mississippi: Brooks v. Black, 68 Miss. 161, 8 So. 32, 11 L. R. A. 176, 24 Am. St. Rep. 259.

Missouri: Hazelett v. Woodruff, 150 Mo. 534, 51 S. W. 1048.

Nebraska: Walton v. Campbell, 51 Neb. 788, 71 N. W. 737.

New York: Charman v. Hibbler, 31 App. Div. 477, 2 N.Y. Supp. 212; Charman v. Tatum, 54 App. Div. 61, 66 N. Y. Supp. 275; Caulkins v. Harris, 9 Johns. 324; Baxter v. Ryerss, 13 Barb. 267.

South Carolina: Welsh v. Kibber, 5 S. C. 405; Jeter v. Glenn, 9 Rich. L. 374.

Virginia: Threlkeld v. Fitzhugh, 2 Leigh, 451.

England: Sutton v. Baillie, 65 L. T. Rep. 528.

But see *Illinois:* Christy v. Ogle, 33 Ill. 295.

Texas: Clark v. Munford, 62 Tex. 531.

[339] *Arkansas:* Beach v. Nordman, 90 Ark. 59, 117 S. W. 785.

California: McGrary v. Hastings, 39 Cal. 360, 2 Am. Rep. 456.

Georgia: Fernander v. Dunn, 19 Ga. 497, 65 Am. Dec. 607.

Illinois: Harding v. Larkin, 41 Ill. 413.

Indiana: Burk v. Clements, 16 Ind. 132; Adamson v. Rose, 30 Ind. 380.

Iowa: McDunn v. Des Moines, 39 Ia. 286; Meservey v. Snell, 94 Ia. 222, 62 N. W. 767, 58 Am. St. Rep. 391.

Kansas: Stebbins v. Wolf, 33 Kan. 765, 7 Pac. 542.

Kentucky: Cox v. Strode, 2 Bibb, 273; Barnett v. Montgomery, 6 T. B. Mon. 327, 332 (*semble*); Kyle v. Fauntleroy, 9 B. Mon. 620; Robertson v. Lemon, 2 Bush, 301.

Maine: Ryerson v. Chapman, 66 Me. 557.

Massachusetts: Richmond v. Ames, 164 Mass. 467, 41 N. E. 671; Sumner v. Williams, 8 Mass. 162, 5 Am. Dec. 83; Leffingwell v. Elliott, 10 Pick. 204; Reggio v. Braggiotti, 7 Cush. 166.

Minnesota: Allis v. Nininger, 25 Minn. 525; Brooks v. Mohl, 104 Minn. 404, 116 N. W. 931, 17 L. R. A. (N. S.) 1195.

Missouri: Coleman v. Clark, 80 Mo. App. 339.

Montana: Taylor v. Holter, 1 Mont. 688.

New Hampshire: Haynes v. Stevens, 11 N. H. 28; Kennison v. Taylor, 18 N. H. 220; Willson v. Willson, 25 N. H. 229, 57 Am. Dec. 320; Winnepiseogee P. Co. v. Eaton, 65 N. H. 13, 18 Atl. 171.

New Jersey: Stewart v. Drake, 9 N. J. L. 139; Holmes v. Sinnickson, 15 N. J. L. 313; Morris v. Rowan, 17 N. J. L. 304.

New York: Olmstead v. Rawson, 188 N. Y. 517, 81 N. E. 456; Grantier v. Austin, 66 Hun, 157, 20 N. Y. Supp. 294; Pitcher v. Livingston, 4 Johns. 1, 4 Am. Dec. 229; Waldo v. Long, 7 Johns. 173; Caulkins v. Harris, 9 Johns. 324; Bennet v. Jenkins, 13 Johns. 50; House v. House, 10 Paige, 158; Rickert v. Snyder, 9 Wend. 416, 423; Baxter v. Ryerss, 13 Barb. 267.

Ohio: McAlpin v. Woodruff, 11 Oh. St. 120; Lane v. Fury, 31 Oh. St. 574.

---

[340] Webb v. Holt, 113 Mich. 338, 71 N. W. 637. *Cf.* Walton v. Campbell, 51 Neb. 788, 71 N. W. 737.

Contra: Brooks v. Black, 68 Miss. 161, 24 Am. St. Rep. 259, 8 So. 332.

that the taxable costs incurred by the plaintiff in defending an ejectment suit were recoverable though they were not in fact taxed, but this seems erroneous. In case an action was brought or defended, it must appear that this was reasonably done [341] and it seems proper to require that the grantee must first give the covenantor notice of the litigation and request him to take necessary steps to protect the title.[342]

Where the plaintiff had sold the land to a third party, and upon discovery of the paramount title had submitted the claim of his grantee to arbitration, the owner of the paramount title not having resorted to an eviction suit, it was held that the costs of the arbitration proceedings could not be recovered from the defendant.[343] And so it must appear that any expense for which recovery is sought was reasonably incurred, and was sufficiently proximate to the injury.

§ 983. Counsel fees.

It is generally held that counsel fees reasonably incurred in maintaining or defending an action for possession may be recovered.[344] In some States, however, counsel fees cannot be

Pennsylvania: Cox v. Henly, 32 Pa. 18.

Rhode Island: Point St. Iron Works v. Turner, 14 R. I. 122, 51 Am. Rep. 364.

South Carolina: Welsh v. Kibler, 5 S. C. 405.

Tennessee: Williams v. Burg, 9 Lea, 455.

Vermont: Williams v. Wetherbee, 2 Aik. 329; Pitkin v. Leavitt, 13 Vt. 379; Keeler v. Wood, 30 Vt. 242; Smith v. Sprague, 40 Vt. 43.

England: Smith v. Compton, 3 B. & A. 407; Williams v. Burrell, 1 C. B. 402; Rolph v. Crouch, L. R. 3 Ex. 44.

Contra, Texas: Shook v. Laufer, 100 S. W. 1042.

[341] *Maine:* Stubbs v. Page, 2 Me. 378.
Missouri: Matheny v. Stewart, 108 Mo. 73, 17 S. W. 1014.
New Hampshire: Drew v. Towle, 30 N. H. 531, 64 Am. Dec. 309.
Canada: Parker v. McDonald, 11 Up. Can. C. P. 478; Hodgins v. Hodgins, 13 Up. Can. C. P. 146; Hunter v. Johnson, 14 Up. Can. C. P. 123.

[342] *Alabama:* De Jarnette v. Dreyfus, 166 Ala. 138, 51 So. 932.
Indiana: Worley v. Hineman, 6 Ind. App. 240, 33 N. E. 260; Teague v. Whaley, 20 Ind. App. 26, 50 N. E. 41.

Iowa: Yokum v. Thomas, 15 Ia. 67.
New York: Finton v. Eggleston, 16 N. Y. Supp. 721.
So as to counsel fees in *Missouri:* Pineland Mfg. Co. v. Guardian Tr. Co., 139 Mo. App. 209, 122 S. W. 1133.

[343] Forsyth v. McIntosh, 9 Up. Can. C. P. 492.

[344] *United States:* Allen v. Blunt, 2 Wood & M. 121.
California: Levitsky v. Canning, 33 Cal. 299; McGary v. Hastings, 39 Cal. 360, 2 Am. Rep. 456.
Hawaii: Mooris v. Petero, 4 Haw. 23.

recovered.[345] It is believed that the recovery should depend upon whether or not the covenantor was notified of the pending suit.[346] In Pennsylvania it has been held that where the grantor was notified of the suit and refused to defend, it was unreasonable for the plaintiff to defend, and he therefore cannot recover counsel fees.[347] The contrary has, however, with better reason, been held in England.[348]

Illinois: Harding v. Larkin, 41 Ill. 413.

Iowa: Swartz v. Ballou, 47 Ia. 188, 29 Am. Rep. 470; Meservey v. Snell, 94 Ia. 222, 62 N. W. 767, 58 Am. St. Rep. 391; Alexander v. Staley, 110 Ia. 607, 81 N. W. 803.

Kansas: Dale v. Shively, 8 Kan. 276; McKee v. Bain, 11 Kan. 569; Jewett v. Fisher, 9 Kan. App. 630, 58 Pac. 1023.

Kentucky: Robertson v. Lemon, 2 Bush, 301.

Maine: Swett v. Patrick, 12 Me. 9; Ryerson v. Chapman, 66 Me. 557; Williamson v. Williamson, 71 Me. 442.

Missouri: Hazelett v. Woodruff, 150 Mo. 534, 51 S. W. 1048; Coleman v. Clark, 80 Mo. App. 339.

Montana: Taylor v. Holter, 1 Mont. 688.

Nebraska: Walton v. Campbell, 51 Neb. 788, 71 N. W. 737.

Nevada: Hoffman v. Bosch, 18 Nev. 360, 3 Am. St. Rep. 888.

New Hampshire: Haynes v. Stevens, 11 N. H. 28; Kingsbury v. Smith, 13 N. H. 109; Drew v. Towle, 30 N. H. 531, 64 Am. Dec. 309.

New York: Staats v. Ten Eyck, 3 Caines, 111; Rickert v. Snyder, 9 Wend. 416; Charman v. Hibbler, 31 App. Div. 477, 52 N. Y. Supp. 212.

Ohio: McAlpin v. Woodruff, 11 Oh. St. 120; Lane v. Fury, 31 Oh. St. 574.

Vermont: Pitkin v. Leavitt, 13 Vt. 379; Turner v. Goodrich, 26 Vt. 707; Keeler v. Wood, 30 Vt. 242.

England: Beale v. Thompson, 3 B. & P. 405.

Canada: Brennan v. Servis, 8 Up.

Can. Q. B. 191; Clark v. Robertson, 8 Up. Can. Q. B. 370; Stuart v. Mathieson, 23 Up. Can. Q. B. 135; Stubbs v. Martindale, 7 Up. Can. C. P. 52.

[345] *Georgia:* Gragg v. Richardson, 25 Ga. 566, 71 Am. Dec. 190.

Louisiana: Sarpy v. New Orleans, 14 La. Ann. 311; Late v. Armorer, 14 La. Ann. 826; Citizens' Bank v. Jeansonne, 120 La. 393, 45 So. 367; Lamerlec v. Barthelmy, 2 McGloin, 106.

Massachusetts: Leffingwell v. Elliott, 10 Pick. 204.

Mississippi: Brooks v. Black, 68 Miss. 161, 8 So. 332, 24 Am. St. Rep. 259.

New Hampshire: Kennison v. Taylor, 18 N. H. 220.

South Carolina: Jeter v. Glenn, 9 Rich. L. 374, 380.

Tennessee: Williams v. Burg, 9 Lea, 455.

Texas: Turner v. Miller, 42 Tex. 418 (overruling Rowe v. Heath, 23 Tex. 614, 620).

[346] *Iowa:* Yokum v. Thomas, 15 Ia. 67.

Massachusetts: Richmond v. Ames, 164 Mass. 467, 41 N. E. 671.

Missouri: Leet v. Gratz, 137 Mo. App. 208, 117 S. W. 642; Mackenzie v. Clement, 144 Mo. App. 114, 129 S. W. 730.

[347] Terry v. Drabenstadt, 68 Pa. 400; acc., Myers v. Munson, 65 Ia. 423, 21 N. W. 759, 54 Am. Rep. 11.

[348] Rolph v. Crouch, L. R. 3 Ex. 44; acc., Point St. Iron Works v. Turner, 14 R. I. 122, 51 Am. Rep. 364.

When counsel fees are recoverable they should be estimated upon the basis of the amount which would reasonably compensate the attorneys and not the amount actually paid them.[349] Fees paid counsel for negotiating the purchase of an outstanding title cannot be recovered.[350]

Where after an action of trespass brought against the grantee the latter brought suit and had the deed reformed by inserting a covenant of warranty, the grantee could not recover on the covenant the counsel fees paid in the action of trespass, since they were incurred before the covenant was inserted in the deed.[351]

[349] Charman v. Tatum, 54 App. Div. 61, 66 N. Y. Supp. 275.
[350] Mercantile Trust Co. v. South Park Co., 94 Ky. 271, 22 S. W. 314.
[351] Butler v. Barnes, 61 Conn. 399, 24 Atl. 328.

CHAPTER XLIII

ACTIONS BETWEEN LANDLORD AND TENANT

I.—ACTIONS AGAINST LANDLORD

§ 984. Failure to give possession of leased premises.

984a. Consequential damages for failure to obtain possession.

985. Covenant for quiet enjoyment: early rule.

986. Exception to early rule.

987. Present rule.

988. Wrongful eviction by the landlord.

988a. Consequences of eviction.

989. Lease of farm for share of crop.

990. Tort by landlord upon tenant.

990a. Illegal distraint.

990b. Illegal entry on the demised premises.

§ 990c. Fraud in procuring tenant.

991. Covenant to repair.

992. Consequential loss.

993. Covenant to make improvements.

994. Covenant to rebuild.

995. Covenant to furnish heat and power.

996. Covenant to renew.

997. Covenant to pay for improvements.

998. Covenant to allow removal of buildings, fixtures, etc.

999. Other covenants by the lessor.

II.—ACTIONS AGAINST TENANT

§ 999a. Landlord's action to recover rent.

999b. Reduction and recoupment.

999c. Excuse from payment of rent.

999d. Apportionment of rent.

999e. Action for use and occupation.

999f. Abandonment of lease by tenant.

§ 999g. Tort by tenant.

999h. Covenant to repair.

999i. Covenant to insure.

999j. Covenant to give up possession.

999k. Other covenants by the lessee.

1000. Costs as between lessee and sub-lessee.

I.—ACTIONS AGAINST LANDLORD

§ 984. Failure to give possession of leased premises.

The general principle in this case is the same as in cases of refusal to convey,[1] although the courts are more nearly agreed in adopting the principle of complete compensation for the loss of the bargain. The ordinary rule is to allow the difference between the rental value of the premises for the term and the

---

[1] McClowry *v.* Croghan, 1 Grant, 307; *post,* §§ 1001 *et seq.*

rent reserved.[2] In Williams *v.* Oliphant,[3] which was an action of assumpsit by lessee for lessor's refusal to give possession, the defendant on the trial asked the court to instruct the jury that the rule of damages in the case was the difference between the rent which plaintiff was to pay, and the market value of the rent of the premises at the time they were to be delivered to him; and that, if the rent to be paid was the

[2] *Alabama:* Snodgrass *v.* Reynolds, 79 Ala. 452, 58 Am. Rep. 601 (*semble*).

Arkansas: Rose *v.* Wynn, 42 Ark. 257; Andrews *v.* Winter, 75 Ark. 589, 88 S. W. 822.

Connecticut: Cohn *v.* Norton, 57 Conn. 480; Bernhard *v.* Curtis, 75 Conn. 476, 54 Atl. 213.

Florida: Hodges *v.* Fries, 34 Fla. 62, 15 So. 682; Moses *v.* Autuono, 56 Fla. 499, 47 So. 925, 20 L. R. A. (N. S.) 350.

Georgia: Kenny *v.* Collier, 79 Ga. 743, 8 S. E. 58; Palmer *v.* Ingram, 2 Ga. App. 200, 58 S. E. 362.

Illinois: Green *v.* Williams, 45 Ill. 206; Dobbins *v.* Duquid, 65 Ill. 464; Smith *v.* Wunderlich, 70 Ill. 426; North Chicago St. R. R. *v.* La Grand Co., 95 Ill. App. 435; Birch *v.* Wood, 111 Ill. App. 336.

Iowa: Adair *v.* Bogle, 20 Ia. 238; Alexander *v.* Bishop, 59 Ia. 572, 578, 13 N. W. 714; Chambers *v.* Brown, 69 Ia. 213, 28 N. W. 561; Hall *v.* Horton, 79 Ia. 352, 44 N. W. 569; Herpolsheimer *v.* Christopher, 111 N. W. 359, 9 L. R. A. (N. S.) 1127.

Kentucky: Smith *v.* Phillips, 29 S. W. 358, 16 Ky. L. Rep. 615; Devers *v.* May, 99 S. W. 255, 30 Ky. L. Rep. 528.

Michigan: Taylor *v.* Cooper, 104 Mich. 72 62, N. W. 157.

Minnesota: Knowles *v.* Steele, 59 Minn. 452, 61 N. W. 557.

Missouri: Hughes *v.* Hood, 50 Mo. 350; Huiest *v.* Marx, 67 Mo. App. 418; Jenkins *v.* Womach, 143 Mo. App. 410, 128 S. W. 530.

Nebraska: Brass *v.* Vandecar, 70 Neb.

35, 96 N. W. 1035; Sneller *v.* Hall, 132 N. W. 934.

New Jersey: Albey *v.* Weingart, 71 N. J. L. 92, 58 Atl. 87; Drischman *v.* McManemin, 68 N. J. L. 337, 53 Atl. 548.

New York: Trull *v.* Granger, 8 N. Y. 115, 59 Am. Dec. 473; Dodds *v.* Hakes, 114 N. Y. 260, 21 N. E. 398; Giles *v.* O'Toole, 4 Barb. 261; Dean *v.* Roesler, 1 Hilt. 420; Kelly *v.* Miles, 58 N. Y. Super. Ct. 495, 12 N. Y. Supp. 915; Engelsdorff *v.* Sire, 64 Hun, 209, 18 N. Y. Supp. 907; Shultz *v.* Brenner, 53 N. Y. Supp. 972; Price *v.* Eisen, 31 Misc. 457, 64 N. Y. Supp. 405; Williamson *v.* Stevens, 84 App. Div. 518, 82 N. Y. Supp. 1047; Rosenblum *v.* Riley, 84 N. Y. Supp. 884; Bailey *v.* Krupp, 59 Misc. 459, 110 N. Y. Supp. 994.

North Carolina: Sloan *v.* Hart, 150 N. C. 269, 63 S. E. 1037, 21 L. R. A. (N. S.) 239.

Tennessee: Jonas *v.* Noel, 98 Tenn. 440, 39 S. W. 724, 36 L. R. A. 862.

Texas: Scottish-American Mortg. Co. *v.* Taylor (Tex. Civ. App.), 74 S. W. 564; Graves *v.* Brownson (Tex. Civ. App.), 120 S. W. 560.

Virginia: Newbrough *v.* Walker, 8 Gratt. 16, 56 Am. Dec. 127.

Washington: Engstrom *v.* Merriam, 25 Wash. 73, 64 Pac. 914.

Wisconsin: Poposkey *v.* Munkwitz, 68 Wis. 322, 32 N. W. 35, 60 Am. Rep. 858; Serfling *v.* Andrews, 106 Wis. 78, 81 N. W. 991; Gross *v.* Heckert, 120 Wis. 314, 97 N. W. 952.

Canada: Marrin *v.* Graver, 8 Ont. 39.

[3] 3 Ind. 271.

highest in the neighborhood, and no greater rent could be had for the premises by plaintiff, he was only entitled to nominal damages. The court refused to give the instruction; but gave the following: "Remote or special damages, such as expenses for removing to a more remote farm, are not to be allowed; but for all such as legitimately and directly arise from the breach, you are to give the plaintiff the equivalent of performance in money. If the defendant is delinquent, or in fault by breaking his contract. he is bound to repair the loss of the plaintiff thereby." It was held that the refusal was correct and that the instruction given was, so far as it went, substantially correct. On the breach by the lessor of two contracts for the lease for the season of navigation, of the bar-rooms of four steamers, two of which were laid up for a part of the season, and the others not finished till it was far advanced, the measure of the lessee's damages was held to be the amount of rent paid for the saloons while he was deprived of their use, with interest from the close of navigation (i. e., from the time when the owners seized the boats) until the close of the season.[4] Where a lessor only delivered up part of the premises which he had leased to the plaintiff, and the plaintiff had paid rent for the whole term, it was held that the plaintiff could recover the diminished value of his lease in its not giving him all the premises, and it was further held that he could not include expenditures on the building, nor damages for injury to his business on account of the fact that the lease was only of use to him if he had the whole building, though it was said that he could have recovered for such injury to his business if he had given notice of his object in hiring the premises.[5] In Hexter v. Knox,[6] a plaintiff was allowed to recover the rental value of rooms *for hotel purposes* where the defendant delayed giving him possession of a building adjoining his hotel. The defendant had notice of the plaintiff's object in hiring the premises. It was said that the plaintiff could recover the rental value of those rooms "fur-

[4] McCleary v. Edwards, 27 Barb. 239; see Davies v. Hotchkiss, 112 N. Y. Supp. 233.

[5] Townsend v. Nickerson Wharf Co., 117 Mass. 501.

[6] 39 N. Y. Super. Ct. 109, 63 N. Y. 561.

nished," for which he had furniture.[7] And in general the rental value of the premises will be based upon the most valuable practical use,[8] in view of the condition of the property.[9] But the damages cannot be measured by speculative profits anticipated from use of the premises.[10] If rent has been paid in advance, the amount so paid may be recovered.[11]

In a few jurisdictions, however, the rule which there prevails in case of breach of contract for the sale of land is applied, and the lessee is allowed nominal damages only for failure to get possession of the premises.[12]

§ 984a. Consequential damages for failure to obtain possession.

The lessee who fails to obtain possession of the premises may recover such consequential damages as were within the

---

[7] *Cf.* Korf v. Lull, 70 Ill. 420; Ruff v. Rinaldo, 55 N. Y. 664.

[8] *Missouri:* Huiest v. Marx, 67 Mo. App. 418 (advertising).

New York: Williamson v. Stevens, 84 App. Div. 518, 82 N. Y. Supp. 1047 (special value for putting in telephone call booths for stockbrokers).

[9] *Iowa:* Chambers v. Brown, 69 Ia. 213, 28 N. W. 561 (thickness and depth of coal veins).

Tennessee: Jonas v. Noel, 98 Tenn. 440, 39 S. W. 724, 36 L. R. A. 862 (unusual size of building).

[10] *Florida:* Hodges v. Fries, 34 Fla. 63, 15 So. 682.

Illinois: Haven v. Wakefield, 39 Ill. 509; Cilley v. Hawkins, 48 Ill. 308.

Iowa: Alexander v. Bishop, 59 Ia. 572, 13 N. W. 714; Chambers v. Brown, 69 Ia. 213, 28 N. W. 561.

Kentucky: Smith v. Phillips, 16 Ky. L. Rep. 615, 29 S. W. 358.

Michigan: Taylor v. Cooper, 104 Mich. 72, 62 N. W. 157.

New Jersey: Drischman v. McManemin, 68 N. J. L. 337, 53 Atl. 548.

New York: Kelley v. Miles, 58 N. Y. Super. Ct. 495, 12 N. Y. Supp. 915.

North Carolina: Sloan v. Hart, 150 N. C. 269, 63 S. E. 1037.

Texas: Graves v. Brownson (Tex. Civ. App.), 120 S. W. 560.

Virginia: Newbrough v. Walker, 8 Gratt. 16, 56 Am. Dec. 127.

Washington: Engstrom v. Merriam, 25 Wash. 73, 64 Pac. 914.

Wisconsin: Serfling v. Andrews, 106 Wis. 78, 81 N. W. 991; Gross v. Heckert, 120 Wis. 314, 97 N. W. 952.

But see *California:* Rice v. Whitmore, 74 Cal. 619, 16 Pac. 501, 5 Am. St. Rep. 479.

[11] *Connecticut:* Bernhard v. Curtis, 75 Conn. 476, 54 Atl. 213.

Iowa: Hall v. Horton, 79 Ia. 352, 44 N. W. 569.

Wisconsin: Poposkey v. Munkwitz, 68 Wis. 322, 32 N. W. 35, 60 Am. Rep. 858.

[12] *Indiana:* Williams v. Oliphant, 3 Ind. 271.

Ohio: Wetzell v. Richcreek, 53 Oh. St. 62, 40 N. E. 1004.

Pennsylvania: McCafferty v. Griswold, 99 Pa. 270; Bartram v. Hering, 18 Pa. Super. Ct. 395.

See Poposkey v. Munkwitz, 68 Wis. 322, 32 N. W. 35, 60 Am. Rep. 858.

contemplation of the parties and were not avoidable.[13] So the lessee may recover the expenses incurred in the removal to the premises,[14] such as loss by sale of premises formerly occupied or fixtures there used,[15] and other such expenses;[16] and for other loss caused by failure to obtain possession.[17] But nothing can be recovered for loss not proximately caused by the failure to obtain possession.[18]

§ 985. Covenant for quiet enjoyment—Early rule.

The early cases held that the general rule limiting recovery to the consideration money in actions upon the covenant for quiet enjoyment applied also to leases. Thus in an early case,[19] the plaintiff declared on a lease upon an implied covenant for quiet enjoyment. The court held, that no such covenant could be implied; but that, if there were an express one, the tenant, not having paid any purchase-money on obtaining the lease, would be entitled to nominal damages only, and this although he had made valuable improvements on the premises, saying, "A lease where no purchase-money

---

[13] *Florida:* Hodges *v.* Fries, 34 Fla. 63, 15 So. 682.

Kentucky: Devers *v.* May, 99 S. W. 255, 30 Ky. L. Rep. 528.

Pennsylvania: Sausser *v.* Steinmetz, 88 Pa. 324; McCafferty *v.* Griswold, 99 Pa. 270.

[14] *Connecticut:* Bernhard *v.* Curtis, 75 Conn. 476, 54 Atl. 213.

Indiana: Jennings *v.* Bond, 14 Ind. App. 282, 42 N. E. 957.

Iowa: Adair *v.* Bogle, 20 Ia. 238; Hall *v.* Horton, 79 Ia. 352, 44 N. W. 569.

Wisconsin: Poposkey *v.* Munkwitz, 68 Wis. 322, 32 N. W. 35, 60 Am. Rep. 858.

[15] *New York:* Friedland *v.* Myers, 139 N. Y. 432, 34 N. E. 1055.

Pennsylvania: Yeager *v.* Weaver, 64 Pa. 425, 3 Am. Rep. 601.

[16] Andrews *v.* Minter, 75 Ark. 589, 88 S. W. 822 (fertilizer placed on premises).

Wisconsin: Gross *v.* Heckert, 120 Wis. 314, 97 N. W. 952 (loss on fixtures prepared for new premises).

[17] *Illinois:* Haven *v.* Wakefield, 39 Ill. 509 (damage to goods left unprotected).

New Jersey: Albey *v.* Weingart, 71 N. J. 92, 58 Atl. 87 (expense of storing goods).

New York: Lawrence *v.* Wardwell, 6 Barb. 423 (wages of workmen).

[18] *Nebraska:* Sneller *v.* Hall, 132 N. W. 934 (expense of attempt by force to get possession; lessor not being notified).

New York: Lowenstein *v.* Chappell, 30 Barb. 241 (loss to goods on former premises by packing them in order to deliver those premises to another occupant); Engelsdorff *v.* Sire, 64 Hun, 209, 18 N. Y. Supp. 907 (fixtures placed in temporary quarters); Price *v.* Eisen, 31 Misc. 457, 64 N. Y. Supp. 405 (loss on fixtures and stock of goods procured for the premises, the lessor having no notice).

[19] Kinney *v.* Watts, 14 Wend. 38, 41.

is paid by the lessee, does not differ in principle in this respect from an ordinary conveyance in fee for a valuable consideration."

In a subsequent case,[20] it seems to have been thought that under the covenant for quiet enjoyment, the lessee might, on eviction, recover the value of the lease, less the rent reserved; but by a still later decision,[21] the arbitrary rule which in regard to conveyances, as we have seen, takes the price paid to be the value of the land, was laid down in regard to leases; and Mr. Justice Bronson said: "Following that analogy, the rents reserved in a lease where no other consideration is paid, must be regarded as a just equivalent for the use of the demised premises. The parties have agreed so to consider it. In case of eviction the rent ceases, and the lessee is relieved from a burden which must be deemed equal to the benefit which he would have derived from the continued enjoyment of the property. Having lost nothing, he can recover no damages. He is, however, entitled to the costs he has been put to; and as he is answerable to the true owner for the mesne profits of the land for a period not exceeding six years, he may recover back the rent he has paid during that time with the interest thereon. If this rule will not always afford a sufficient indemnity to the lessee, I can only say, as has often been said in relation to a purchaser, he should protect himself by requiring other covenants."

It is still held in Pennsylvania that, in case of eviction from demised premises, where there was no fraud or misrepresentation of the lessor inducing the taking of the lease, the measure of damages, if rent has been paid in advance, is so much of the moneys advanced as would be payable at the stipulated rate on account of the unexpired part of the lease, with interest. If no rent has been paid in advance, no damages can be recovered by the lessee.[22] His liability to pay rent would cease from the time of the eviction.

§ 986. Exception to early rule.

But in the case of a lease where the lessor fails to give pos-

[20] Moak v. Johnson, 1 Hill, 99.
[21] Kelly v. Dutch Church of Schenectady, 2 Hill, 105, 116.
[22] Lanigan v. Kille, 97 Pa. 120, 39 Am. Rep. 797.

session, being able to do so, the rule is everywhere abandoned. Thus in an early case,* where an agreement in the nature of a lease, but without any covenants, was made to commence from a future day, and the owner, before the commencement of the term, leased the premises to another party, it was held, that the original lessee was not limited to his action of ejectment; that he might sue the lessor for the breach of the implied agreement to give him possession; and that in such action the measure of damages would be the difference between the rent reserved in the lease and the value of the premises for the term.[23] ** In a later case, the court, after stating that on general principles the measure of damages upon the breach of covenants for title would be the value of the estate lost at the time of the breach, said that an arbitrary rule had been established, as "calculated to generally subserve the ends of justice," where there has been no fraud; but if the vendor himself refuses to execute his contract, having power to do so, or after conveyance ousts his grantee, he "puts himself without the pale of protection of this arbitrary rule of damages, and becomes liable upon his broken covenant for the value of the estate he was instrumental in taking from his grantee." [24]

"As no consideration is paid in such case," observes Mr. Justice E. D. Smith, stating the general rule in delivering his opinion in the Court of Appeals of New York, in the same case,[25] "the rent reserved has been regarded as a just equivalent for the use of the demised premises, and as in case of eviction, the rent ceases, and the lessee is discharged from its payment, he recovers nominal damages, and for such mesne profits as he is liable to pay the true owner, and any costs he may have been compelled to pay in defense of his title. But this rule has not been very satisfactory to the courts in this country, and it has been relaxed or modified more or less to meet the injustice done by it to lessees in particular cases." And the ruling of the court below, that the measure of damages for the breach of the covenant for *quiet enjoyment* was

[23] Trull v. Granger, 8 N. Y. 115, 59 Am. Dec. 473.

[24] Masten, J., in Mack v. Patchin, 29 How. Pr. 20.

[25] 42 N. Y. 167, 1 Am. Rep. 503.

the value of the lease at the time of the eviction, over and above the rent reserved, was accordingly affirmed. So in Chatterton *v.* Fox [26] it was held, the eviction having been tortious, that the tenant might recover the difference between the value of his lease for the unexpired term, and the rent reserved.

§ 987. Present rule.

In England, however, the true principle has been finally adopted and the actual loss is recovered. So in an action by a sub-lessee against the executors of his lessor for breach of a covenant of quiet enjoyment, it was held that he might recover the value of the term lost and the mesne profits, and also his costs of defending the actions of ejectment brought by the remainderman.[27] In a later case in the same court [28] the landlord had executed to a tenant in occupation of premises a reversionary lease of them for a term of years, for which he had received a premium. He died before the commencement of the intended term. After his death the lease proved void, it appearing that he was only tenant for life, with power to grant leases in possession, but not in reversion. The intended lessee was compelled to accept another lease from another party, for a much shorter term and at a higher rent. It was held, in an action by the lessee against the representatives of the lessor, that the measure of the plaintiff's damages was the premium paid for the void lease, together with the difference in the value of the two leases and the excess of expenses of the new lease over those of the first. The cost of consulting counsel and surveyors was deducted, by consent. Erle, C. J., used the following language: "And though Sedgwick says that in many parts of America the rule as contended for by the defendant prevails, he pretty clearly intimates that upon the whole his own opinion is the other way. There is no judgment which sustains that contention; and there is a distinct judgment of this court which is opposed to it. It is also negatived by the universal rule, that one who breaks his contract must pay the damages proximately resulting from

[26] 5 Duer, 64.
[27] Williams *v.* Burrell, 1 C. B. 402,

[28] Lock *v.* Furze, 19 C. B. (N. S.) 96, 118,

such breach." This decision was affirmed in the Exchequer Chamber,[29] and was followed in a later case.[30]

The older rule is still enforced in New York, and damages when the lessor has acted in good faith [31] are nominal only. But in most American jurisdictions the plaintiff may recover the value of his lease.[32] Where the leased building was burnt, and the lessor rebuilt and refused to give possession to the tenant, in the mistaken belief that the lease was determined by the fire, the measure of damages was held to be the value of the lease according to the state the building was in just before the fire, and not according to its improved value as rebuilt.[33]

If any rent has been paid in advance, that too may be recovered.[34] But conjectural profits expected from the use of the premises cannot be recovered.[35]

[29] L. R. 1 C. P. 441.

[30] Rolph v. Crouch, L. R. 3 Ex. 44.

[31] Thorley v. Pabst Brewing Co., 179 Fed. 338 (New York law). See Depew v. Ketchum, 75 Hun, 227, 27 N. Y. Supp. 8. So also in *California:* Jeffers v. Easton, 113 Cal. 345, 45 Pac. 680 (sale of leasehold interest).

[32] *Alabama:* Elliott v. Bankston (Ala.), 45 So. 173.

Illinois: Griesheimer v. Botham, 105 Ill. App. 585.

Indiana: Sheets v. Joyner, 11 Ind. App. 205, 38 N. E. 830.

Massachusetts: Dexter v. Manley, 4 Cush. 14; Riley v. Hale, 158 Mass. 240, 33 N. E. 491.

Wisconsin: Raynor v. Valentin Blatz Brew. Co., 100 Wis. 414, 76 N. W. 343.

See also *Pennsylvania:* Irwin v. Nolde, 176 Pa. 594, 35 Atl. 217 (tenant had been deprived of use of part of farm leased without wilful negligence or wrong; measure of damages is not rental value of fields taken, but injury to whole. The loss of a single field, by disarranging operations of the farm, may cause an injury greater than the rental value of the areas taken. Real loss is the value of the use of the part taken in connection with that which remains, and is measured by the difference in rental value).

[33] Hodgkins v. Price, 141 Mass. 162, 5 N. E. 502.

[34] *Massachusetts:* Riley v. Hale, 158 Mass. 240, 33 N. E. 491.

New York: Denison v. Ford, 7 Daly, 384.

[35] *Alabama:* Snodgrass v. Reynolds, 49 Ala. 452, 58 Am. Rep. 601.

Iowa: Alexander v. Bishop, 59 Ia. 572.

Kentucky: Smith v. Phillips, 16 Ky. L. Rep. 615, 29 S. W. 358.

New York: Dodds v. Hakes, 114 N. Y. 260, 21 N. E. 398; Kelley v. Miles, 58 N. Y. Super. Ct. 495, 12 N. Y. Supp. 915.

Texas: Wilkinson v. Stanley (Tex. Civ. App.), 43 S. W. 606.

See *Michigan:* Cornelissens v. Driscoll, 89 Mich. 34, 50 N. W. 749 (tenant cannot recover both the value of the premises to him and the value of his labor in plowing and cultivating the land).

§ 988.[a] Wrongful eviction by the landlord.

The damages for wrongful eviction by the landlord are the same, whether the eviction is accomplished by violence or by rendering the premises useless. If the eviction is wrongful the tenant may sue at once, without waiting for the expiration of the term, and may recover entire damages; [36] which is ordinarily the value of the unexpired portion of the term, that is, the rental value less the amount of rent unpaid, reduced to present value.[37] The actual rental value must be found, based on the condition of the premises and the terms of the lease.[38] If a crop has been raised, and the tenant is

---

[a] For § 988 of the eighth edition see § 999a.

[36] *Indiana:* Carter v. Lacy, 3 Ind. App. 54, 29 N. E. 168.
Michigan: Grove v. Yonell, 110 Mich. 285, 68 N. W. 132, 33 L. R. A. 297.
Oregon: Salzgeber v. Mickel, 37 Ore. 216, 60 Pac. 1009.

[37] *Alabama:* Tyson v. Chestnut, 118 Ala. 387, 405, 24 So. 73.
Arkansas: Crane v. Patton, 57 Ark. 340, 21 S. W. 466.
Georgia: Shuman v. Smith, 100 Ga. 415, 28 S. E. 448; Bass v. West, 110 Ga. 698, 36 S. E. 244.
Illinois: Dobbins v. Duquid, 65 Ill. 464.
Indiana: Ricketts v. Lostetter, 19 Ind. 125; Sheets v. Joyner, 11 Ind. App. 205, 38 N. E. 830; Carter v. Lacy, 3 Ind. App. 54, 29 N. E. 168; Jennings v. Bond, 14 Ind. App. 282, 42 N. E. 597.
Massachusetts: Dexter v. Manley, 4 Cush. 14; Jewett v. Brooks, 134 Mass. 505; Riley v. Hale, 158 Mass. 240, 33 N. E. 491.
Michigan: Coulter v. Norton, 100 Mich. 389, 59 N. W. 163, 43 Am. St. Rep. 458; Taylor v. Cooper, 104 Mich. 72, 62 N. W. 157; Grove v. Yonell, 110 Mich. 285, 68 N. W. 132, 33 L. R. A. 297.
Missouri: Schlemmer v. North, 32 Mo. 206.
Nebraska: Cannon v. Wilbur, 30 Neb.

777, 47 N. W. 85; Schneider v. Patterson, 38 Neb. 680, 57 N. W. 398; Shutt v. Lockner, 77 Neb. 397, 109 N. W. 383.
New York: Mack v. Patchin, 42 N. Y. 167, 1 Am. Rep. 506, 29 How. Pr. 20; Clarkson v. Skidmore, 46 N. Y. 297, 7 Am. Rep. 333; Fitzgibbons v. Freisem, 12 Daly, 419; O'Gorman v. Harby, 18 Misc. 228, 41 N. Y. Supp. 521; Hong Sing v. Wolf Fein, 33 Misc. 608, 67 N. Y. Supp. 1109; Goldstein v. Asen, 46 Misc. 251, 91 N. Y. Supp. 783.
Ohio: Rhodes v. Baird, 16 Oh. St. 573.
Oregon: Salzgeber v. Mickel, 37 Ore. 216, 60 Pac. 1009.
Rhode Island: Porter v. Bradley, 7 R. I. 538.
Texas: Buck v. Morrow, 2 Tex. Civ. App. 361, 21 S. W. 398; Loyd v. Capps (Tex. Civ. App.), 29 S. W. 505; Wanhscaffe v. Pontoja (Tex. Civ. App.), 63 S. W. 663; Campbell v. Howerton (Tex. Civ. App.), 87 S. W. 370.
Utah: Utah Optical Co. v. Keith, 18 Utah, 464, 56 Pac. 155.
Vermont: Amsden v. Atwood, 69 Vt. 527, 38 Atl. 263.
Virginia: Bolling v. Lersner, 26 Gratt. 36.
West Virginia: Moreland v. Metz, 24 W. Va. 119, 49 Am. Rep. 246.

[38] *Massachusetts:* Rice v. Baker, 2 All. 411 (lease not assignable).
Michigan: Taylor v. Cooper, 104 Mich. 72, 62 N. W. 157 (profits realized

deprived of it by the eviction, he may recover the value of the crop less the rent.[39] In Pennsylvania, however, as in other similar cases, the tenant cannot recover the value of the lease.[40]

For partial eviction the tenant recovers the difference in rental value caused by the partial eviction.[41]

§ 988a. Consequences of eviction.

Where the tenant was carrying on business on the premises, damages may be recovered for injury to the business and the good-will.[42] Damages to personal property left on the premises may be recovered,[43] and the value of improvements placed on the land by the tenant may be considered as enhancing the damages.[44] Other consequential damages may be recov-

for several years under the lease may be shown as tending to prove value of lease).

Nebraska: Schneider v. Patterson, 38 Neb. 680, 57 N. W. 398 (quality of sand and cost of removing it shown).

See *New York:* Goldstein v. Asen, 46 Misc. 251, 91 N. Y. Supp. 783 (effect of wrongful acts which constituted eviction on rental value immaterial).

[39] *Mississippi:* Jefcoat v. Gunter, 73 Miss. 539, 19 So. 94.

Vermont: Merritt v. Closson, 36 Vt. 172.

[40] American Ice Co. v. Pocono S. W. J. Co., 165 Fed. 714, 179 Fed. 868, 183 Fed. 193 (Pennsylvania Law).

[41] Gallagher v. Burke, 13 Pa. Super. Ct. 244.

[42] *California:* Dwyer v. Carroll, 86 Cal. 298, 24 Pac. 1015.

Colorado: Gray v. Linton, 38 Colo. 175, 88 Pac. 749.

Georgia: Smith v. Eubanks, 72 Ga. 280; Dass v. West, 110 Ga. 698, 36 S. E. 244.

Indiana: Jennings v. Bond, 14 Ind. App. 282, 295, 42 N. E. 597.

Michigan: Coulter v. Norton, 100 Mich. 389, 59 N. W. 163, 43 Am. St. Rep. 458.

Minnesota: Goebel v. Hough, 26 Minn. 252.

Missouri: Murphy v. Century Bldg. Co., 90 Mo. App. 621.

New York: Snow v. Pulitzer, 142 N. Y. 263, 36 N. E. 1059; Menard v. Stevens, 44 N. Y. Super. 515.

Pennsylvania: Seyfert v. Bean, 83 Pa. 450.

Texas: Dickinson Creamery Co. v. Lyle (Tex. Civ. App.), 130 S. W. 904; Kitchen Bros. H. Co. v. Thilburn, 96 N. W. 487.

But see *Nebraska:* Karbach v. Fogel, 63 Neb. 601, 88 N. W. 659.

Profits of a new or speculative business cannot be recovered:

Kentucky: Throop v. Broadus, 15 Ky. L. Rep. 812.

Missouri: Gildersleeve v. Overstolz, 90 Mo. App. 518, 532.

Ohio: Rhodes v. Baird, 16 Oh. St. 573.

[43] *Alabama:* Snedecor v. Pope, 143 Ala. 275, 39 So. 38.

Indiana: Moyer v. Gordon, 113 Ind. 282, 14 N. E. 476.

See *Wisconsin:* Gaertner v. Bues, 109 Wis. 165, 85 N. W. 388.

[44] *Arkansas:* Baxter v. State, 56 Ark. 312, 19 S. W. 923 (void lease).

California: Fox v. Brissac, 15 Cal. 223.

Indiana: Ricketts v. Lostetter, 19 Ind. 125.

ered in a proper case.[45] Damages may also be recovered for inconvenience, physical pain, and mental anguish, sense of shame and humiliation resulting from the eviction,[46] and for illness caused by the exposure.[47]

§ 989.[a] Lease of farm for share of crop.

In case of the common "cropping" agreement, that is, the lease of a farm for a share of the crop, to be given to the lessor by the lessee, the measure of damages for breach of contract by the lessor, either by failure to give possession or by eviction, is in general what the contract is worth; [48] and the value of the crop which is raised or reasonably expected to be raised may be proved to establish the value.[49] In Texas the court has gone so far as to allow the tenant to recover the market value of the crop he would reasonably be expected to raise

---

Kansas: Deisher *v.* Stein, 34 Kan. 39, 7 Pac. 608 (parol lease).

See, however, *Pennsylvania:* Walters *v.* Transue, 6 North. Co. Rep. 406.

The amount allowed should be, it would seem, only the amount by which they enhance the value of the leasehold interest. In Lanigan *v.* Kille, 97 Pa. 120, 39 Am. Rep. 797, where the lessee was required by the lease to make improvements, he was not allowed, upon eviction, to recover the value of them, though the value of them had been set off by the lessor in an ejectment suit brought by the true owner.

[a] For § 989 of the eighth edition see § 999*h.*

[45] *California:* Leostzky *v.* Canning, 33 Cal. 299 (legal expenses in defending ejectment suit brought by defendant).

Minnesota: Scheerschmidt *v.* Smith, 74 Minn. 224, 77 N. W. 34 (loss of option to purchase).

Texas: Buck *v.* Morrow, 2 Tex. Civ. App. 361, 21 S. W. 398 (injury to cattle while plaintiff was trying to find other pasture).

Vermont: Amsden *v.* Atwood, 69 Vt. 527, 38 Atl. 263 (loss by having logs left on hand, on eviction from mill).

But where the lease is wrongfully

terminated by the landlord, the expense of moving cannot be recovered, if the tenant would have been at the same expense at the end of his term. Eddy *v.* Coffin, 149 Mass. 463, 21 N. E. 870, 14 Am. St. Rep. 441.

[46] *Alabama:* Snedecor *v.* Pope, 143 Ala, 275, 39 So. 38.

Indiana: Moyer *v.* Gordon, 113 Ind. 282, 14 N. E. 476.

Georgia: Harris *v.* Cleghorn, 121 Ga. 314, 48 S. E. 959.

Massachusetts: Fillebrown *v.* Hoar, 124 Mass. 580.

[47] Snedecor *v.* Pope, 143 Ala. 275, 39 So. 38. Not for illness from a journey taken several days later to another place. Fillebrown *v.* Hoar, 124 Mass. 580.

[48] *California:* Cull *v.* San Francisco & Fresno Land Co., 124 Cal. 591, 57 Pac. 456.

Indiana: Chew *v.* Lucas, 15 Ind. App. 595, 43 N. E. 235.

Missouri: Shoemaker *v.* Crawford, 82 Mo. App. 487.

New York: Taylor *v.* Bradley, 39 N. Y. 129.

[49] *Indiana:* Chew *v.* Lucas, 15 Ind. App. 595, 43 N. E. 235.

Missouri: Shoemaker *v.* Crawford, 82 Mo. App. 487 (crop in fact raised).

on the premises during his term, less the expenses necessary in planting, cultivating, harvesting, and marketing the crop.[50] If the tenant is dispossessed at a time when the crop is sufficiently matured to have a value, he may recover the value of his share.[51]

It seems clear that the damages cannot be reduced by the fact that the tenant obtained or should have obtained work elsewhere;[52] and there is no analogy whatever with contracts of service, where, as has been seen, the amount that could have been earned elsewhere is to be considered in arriving at the actual value of the contract.[53] In a Texas case[54] it was said that where by the breach the tenant is thrown into enforced idleness he may recover compensation for such loss of his time; but this, it will be seen, is an increase, not a reduction, of the damages ordinarily given, and is an allowance of consequential damages.

§ 990.[a] Tort by landlord against tenant.

For tort committed by the landlord against the tenant the measure of damages is in general the same as in any other case of tort; the relation between the parties not altering the rule. Exemplary damages may be recovered in a proper case.[55] For wrongful attachment, damages may be recovered for deterioration in value and loss of use of the property attached.[56] Where through the negligence of the landlord the tenant's goods are damaged by water, he may recover the amount by which their value has been diminished; as where water is allowed to leak from pipes in the upper portion of the

---

[a] For § 990 of the eighth edition see § 999h.

[50] Rogers v. McGuffey, 96 Tex. 565, 74 S. W. 753; Brincefield v. Allen, 25 Tex. Civ. App. 258, 60 S. W. 1010. The burden of establishing this amount is of course on the tenant. Springer v. Riley (Tex. Civ. App.), 136 S. W. 580.

[51] *Michigan:* McClure v. Thorpe, 68 Mich. 33, 35 N. W. 829.

South Dakota: Bowers v. Graves, 8 S. D. 385, 66 N. W. 931.

Texas: Tignor v. Toney, 13 Tex. Civ. App. 518, 35 S. W. 881.

Wisconsin: Foley v. Southwestern Land Co., 94 Wis. 329, 68 N. W. 994. As to the value of the crop, see *ante*, § 937.

[52] Wolf v. Studebaker, 65 Pa. 459; *ante*, § 208. But see Somers v. Musolf, 86 Ark. 97, 109 S. W. 1173.

[53] *Ante*, § 667.

[54] Crews v. Cortez, 102 Tex. 111, 113 S. W. 523.

[55] Weber v. Vernon, 2 Pennew. (Del.) 359, 45 Atl. 537.

[56] Patton v. Garrett, 37 Ark. 605.

building,[57] or through the roof by reason of a defect in the plan of construction.[58] So where the landlord's servants negligently left wet wool in a loft, which caused water to drip through the ceiling upon machinery and destroy it, the tenant could recover for the destruction and deterioration of his machinery, and the injury to his business.[59]

§ 990a. Illegal distraint.

The tenant whose goods are wrongfully distrained, even though the wrong consists merely in informality of process, may recover the value of the goods,[60] reduced, according to the better view, by the amount of rent actually due,[61] though in a few cases it is held that no reduction for rent due will be allowed.[62] Exemplary damages may be added in a proper case.[63] Where fixtures are distrained, the tenant is entitled

---

[57] K. B. Koosa & Co. v. Warten, 158 Ala. 496, 48 So. 544.

[58] Evans v. Murphy, 87 Md. 498, 40 Atl. 109.

[59] Hysore v. Quigley, 9 Houst. (Del.) 348, 32 Atl. 960.

[60] *Hawaii:* Silva v. Homen, 9 Haw. 14.

Illinois: Tripp v. Grouner, 60 Ill. 474.

Montana: Bohm v. Dunphy, 1 Mont. 333.

Pennsylvania: Fernwood M. H. Assoc. v. Jones, 102 Pa. 307; Easterly Mach. Co. v. Spencer, 28 W. N. C. 287.

England: Attack v. Bramwell, 3 B. & S. 520, 9 Jur. (N. S.) 892, 32 L. J. Q. B. 146, 7 L. T. Rep. (N. S.) 740, 11 Wkly. Rep. 309, 113 E. C. L. 520; Knight v. Egerton, 7 Ex. 407; Biggins v. Goode, 2 Crompt. & J. 364, 1 L. J. Exch. 129, 2 Tyrw. 447; Whitworth v. Maden, 2 C. & K. 517, 61 E. C. L. 517; Clarke v. Holford, 2 C. & K. 540, 61 E. C. L. 540.

Australia: Crowley v. Apted, 14 N. S. W. L. R. 146.

If the property is returned, the measure of damages is the value of use and the deterioration in value of the property. Johnson v. Hulett (Tex. Civ. App.), 120 S. W. 257.

[61] *Illinois:* Tripp v. Grouner, 60 Ill. 474.

New York: Butts v. Edwards, 2 Den. 164.

Pennsylvania: Mickle v. Miles, 1 Grant, 320.

England: Whitworth v. Maden, 2 C. & K. 517; Knight v. Egerton, 7 Ex. 407; Biggins v. Goode, 2 Cr. & J. 364, 1 L. J. Ex. 129, 2 Tyrw. 447; Proudlove v. Twenlow, 1 Cromp. & M. 326, 2 L. J. Exch. 111, 3 Tyrw. 260; Chandler v. Doulton, 3 H. & C. 553, 11 Jur. (N. S.) 286, 3 L. J. Exch. 89, 11 L. T. Rep. (N. S.) 639.

[62] *Hawaii:* Silva v. Homen, 9 Haw. 14.

England: Attack v. Bramwell, 3 B. & S. 520, 9 Jur. (N. S.) 892, 32 L. J. Q. B. 146, 7 L. T. Rep. (N. S.) 740; Moore v. Drinkwater, 1 F. & F. 134.

Australia: Crowley v. Apted, 14 N. S. W. L. R. 146. See *ante*, § 60.

[63] *Illinois:* Clevenger v. Dunaway, 84 Ill. 367.

Montana: Bohm v. Dunphy, 1 Mont. 333.

Texas: Smith v. Jones, 11 Tex. Civ. App. 18, 31 S. W. 306.

to recover the value of the fixtures *in situ*, as part of the realty measured by what an incoming tenant would pay an outgoing tenant for them.[64] Damages may be obtained for injury to business,[65] and for the expense of obtaining a replevin bond,[66] but not for merely speculative loss.[67]

§ 990b. Illegal entry on the demised premises.

When the landlord enters illegally on the premises and injures the tenant or his property, he is responsible for the damage thereby caused. So where the landlord destroys or carries away personal property on the premises, fixtures or growing crops, he is responsible for the value of them,[68] or if they are returned to the tenant then for the injury.[69] If the landlord cut off power from the tenant, the tenant may recover for diminution in value of the lease.[70] If he injures the roof, the tenant may recover for resulting injury to his property,[71] and, if properly proved, for injury to his business.[72] If the landlord illegally enters and makes repairs, the tenant may recover compensation for the interruption to his business by the repairs.[73] And for other similar injuries the tenant may recover his actual damage.[74]

---

[64] Clarke v. Holford, 2 C. & K. 540; Moore v. Drinkwater, 1 F. & F. 134.

[65] Sherman v. Dutch, 16 Ill. 283.

[66] Watson v. Boswell, 25 Tex. Civ. App. 379, 61 S. W. 407. (But see Smith v. Jones, 11 Tex. Civ. App. 18, 31 S. W. 306.)

[67] Burger v. Rhiney (Tex. Civ. App.), 42 S. W. 590.

[68] *Illinois:* Scanlan v. Musgrove, 91 Ill. App. 184 (crops).
North Carolina: Willis v. Branch, 94 N. C. 142 (fixtures).

[69] *New York:* Nowlan v. Trevor, 2 Sween. 67 (maps, books, etc.)
North Carolina: Willis v. Branch, 2 N. C. 142 (furniture damaged).

[70] *California:* Hawthorne v. Siegel, 88 Cal. 159, 25 Pac. 1114, 22 Am. St. Rep. 291.
New York: Egan v. Browne, 128 App. Div. 184, 112 N. Y. Supp. 689.

[71] Wolff v. Hvass, 11 Misc. 561, 32 N. Y. Supp. 798.

[72] Allison v. Chandler, 11 Mich. 542; see Wolff v. Hvass, 11 Misc. 561, 32 N. Y. Supp. 798.

[73] Goebel v. Hough, 26 Minn. 252, 2 N. W. 847.

[74] Marquart v. La Farge, 5 Duer, 559 (closing of doors: tenant recovers for loss of use of goods and for interruption of business); Eten v. Luyster, 60 N. Y. 252 (tenant's building torn down: he recovers value of building and of chattels lost); Woods v. Kernan, 57 Hun, 215, 10 N. Y. Supp. 654 (expulsion of tenant: he recovers value of use of premises, and value of crops harvested by defendant); Burhmaster v. Ainsworth, 90 Hun, 563, 36 N. Y. Supp. 68 (placing chattels on land; tenant recovers cost of removal).

www.ingramcontent.com/pod-product-compliance
Lightning Source LLC
Chambersburg PA
CBHW021541210326
41599CB00010B/274